LONGMAN

Pocket

ENGLISH

DICTIONARY

Longman

Pearson Education Limited
Edinburgh Gate, Harlow, Essex CM20 2JE, England
and associated companies throughout the world

Visit our website: http://www.longman-elt.com/dictionaries

First published 2001

Words that the editors have reason to believe constitute
trademarks have been described as such. However, neither the
presence nor the absence of such a description should be
regarded as affecting the legal status of any trademark.

ISBN 0 582 50645X

Set in 7pt MetaPlus Normal by Peter Wray
Printed in Spain by Cayfosa-Quebecor, Barcelona

ACKNOWLEDGEMENTS

Director	Della Summers
Editorial Director & Publisher	Pierre-Henri Cousin
Editor & Project Manager	Wendy Lee
Pronunciation Editor	Dinah Jackson
Design	Alex Ingr
Cover design	Abbey Design, Harlow, Essex
Proofreader	Lynda Carey

and the Longman Dictionaries team

▶ Using the Dictionary

▶ The *Longman Pocket English Dictionary* is the ideal handy dictionary for intermediate students of English.

▶ The meanings of over 16 000 words and phrases are explained clearly and simply using the Longman Defining Vocabulary of just 2000 English words. Any additional words, that you may not know, are written in SMALL CAPITAL LETTERS. These additional words are explained in their own alphabetical position. Example sentences and phrases, based on real sentences and phrases in books and newspapers, show how the words are used in natural, everyday English.

▶ Special language notes explain how to use some of the most important English words without making mistakes. The *Longman Pocket Dictionary* also helps with grammar points such as irregular verbs and adjectives, and with prepositions – showing which preposition links the word with the following word or words: for example, *Are you afraid **of** the dark?*

▶ Sometimes words with the same spelling are different in meaning, grammar, or pronunciation. These words are explained in separate entries. For example: **love**[1] is a verb and **love**[2] is a noun; **row**[1] means a line, **row**[2] means a quarrel.

▶ You sometimes want to know about other words you could use instead of the one you are looking at, or to find out which words mean the opposite. The *Longman Pocket Dictionary* gives you this information too. Where these words are useful, they are listed at the end of an entry. The dictionary also has 15 pages of colour pictures showing words connected with common, everyday situations.

▶ By giving you the basic building blocks to work with, the *Longman Pocket Dictionary* helps you to build up your word power, so that you can produce English sentences which are not only accurate but also sound natural.

▶ Pronunciation Table

Consonants

Symbol	Keyword
p	pan
b	ban
t	tip
d	dip
k	cap
g	gap
tʃ	church
dʒ	judge
f	few
v	view
θ	throw
ð	though
s	sip
z	zip
ʃ	fresh
ʒ	measure
h	hot
m	sum
n	sun
ŋ	sung
l	lot
r	rot
j	yet
w	wet

Vowels

Symbol	Keyword
iː	beat
ɪ	bit
e	bet
æ	bat
ɑː	bar
ɒ	block
ɔː	bought
ʊ	book
uː	boot
ʌ	but
ɜː	burn
ə	brother
eɪ	bay
əʊ	bone
aɪ	by
aʊ	bound
ɔɪ	boy
ɪə	beer
eə	bare
ʊə	poor
eɪə	player
əʊə	lower
aɪə	tire
aʊə	flower
ɔɪə	employer

/ˈ/ shows main stress

/ˌ/ shows secondary stress

/ʳ/ at the end of a word means that /r/ is usually pronounced when the next word begins with a vowel sound

/ə/ means that /ə/ may or may not be used

▶ Irregular Verbs

verb	present participle	past tense	past participle
arise	arising	arose	arisen
be	being	was	been
bear	bearing	bore	borne
beat	beating	beat	beaten
become	becoming	became	become
begin	beginning	began	begun
bend	bending	bent	bent
beset	besetting	beset	beset
bet	betting	betted or bet	betted or bet
bind	binding	bound	bound
bite	biting	bit	bitten
bleed	bleeding	bled	bled
bless	blessing	blessed or blest	blessed or blest
blow	blowing	blew	blown
break	breaking	broke	broken
breed	breeding	bred	bred
bring	bringing	brought	brought
broadcast	broadcasting	broadcast	broadcast
build	building	built	built
burn	burning	burned or burnt	burned or burnt
bust	busting	busted or bust	busted or bust
buy	buying	bought	bought
cast	casting	cast	cast
catch	catching	caught	caught
choose	choosing	chose	chosen
cling	clinging	clung	clung
come	coming	came	come
cost	costing	cost	cost
creep	creeping	crept	crept
cut	cutting	cut	cut
deal	dealing	dealt	dealt
die	dying	died	died
dig	digging	dug	dug
dive	diving	dived	dived
do	doing	did	done
draw	drawing	drew	drawn
dream	dreaming	dreamed or dreamt	dreamed or dreamt
drink	drinking	drank	drunk
drive	driving	drove	driven
dwell	dwelling	dwelled or dwelt	dwelled or dwelt
eat	eating	ate	eaten
fall	falling	fell	fallen
feed	feeding	fed	fed
feel	feeling	felt	felt
fight	fighting	fought	fought

verb	present participle	past tense	past participle
find	finding	found	found
fly	flying	flew	flown
forbid	forbidding	forbade	forbidden
foresee	foreseeing	foresaw	foreseen
forget	forgetting	forgot	forgotten
freeze	freezing	froze	frozen
get	getting	got	got
give	giving	gave	given
go	going	went	gone
grind	grinding	ground	ground
grow	growing	grew	grown
hang	hanging	hung or hanged	hung or hanged
have	having	had	had
hear	hearing	heard	heard
hide	hiding	hid	hidden
hit	hitting	hit	hit
hold	holding	held	held
hurt	hurting	hurt	hurt
keep	keeping	kept	kept
kneel	kneeling	knelt	knelt
knit	knitting	knitted or knit	knitted or knit
know	knowing	knew	known
lay	laying	laid	laid
lead	leading	led	led
lean	leaning	leaned or leant	leaned or leant
leap	leaping	leaped or leapt	leaped or leapt
learn	learning	learned or learnt	learned or learnt
leave	leaving	left	left
lend	lending	lent	lent
let	letting	let	let
lie[1]	lying	lay	lain
lie[2]	lying	lied	lied
lose	losing	lost	lost
make	making	made	made
mean	meaning	meant	meant
meet	meeting	met	met
mislead	misleading	misled	misled
misspell	misspelling	misspelled or misspelt	misspelled or misspelt
mistake	mistaking	mistook	mistaken
misunderstand	misunderstanding	misunderstood	misunderstood
mow	mowing	mowed or mown	mowed or mown
outdo	outdoing	outdid	outdone
outgrow	outgrowing	outgrew	outgrown
overcome	overcoming	overcame	overcome
overdo	overdoing	overdid	overdone
overhear	overhearing	overheard	overheard

verb	present participle	past tense	past participle
oversleep	oversleeping	overslept	overslept
overtake	overtaking	overtook	overtaken
overthrow	overthrowing	overthrew	overthrown
panic	panicking	panicked	panicked
pay	paying	paid	paid
picnic	picnicking	picknicked	picknicked
put	putting	put	put
quit	quitting	quit	quit
read	reading	read	read
rebuild	rebuilding	rebuilt	rebuilt
redo	redoing	redid	redone
repay	repaying	repaid	repaid
resit	resitting	resat	resat
rewind	rewinding	rewound	rewound
rewrite	rewriting	rewrote	rewritten
ride	riding	rode	ridden
ring	ringing	rang	rung
rise	rising	rose	risen
run	running	ran	run
saw	sawing	sawed	sawn
say	saying	said	said
see	seeing	saw	seen
seek	seeking	sought	sought
sell	selling	sold	sold
send	sending	sent	sent
set	setting	set	set
sew	sewing	sewed	sewn
shake	shaking	shook	shaken
shear	shearing	sheared	shorn
shed	shedding	shed	shed
shine	shining	shone	shone
shoot	shooting	shot	shot
show	showing	showed	shown
shrink	shrinking	shrank	shrunk
shut	shutting	shut	shut
sing	singing	sang	sung
sink	sinking	sank	sunk
sit	sitting	sat	sat
sleep	sleeping	slept	slept
slide	sliding	slid	slid
sling	slinging	slung	slung
slit	slitting	slit	slit
smell	smelling	smelt	smelt
sow	sowing	sowed	sown
speak	speaking	spoke	spoken
speed	speeding	speeded or sped	speeded or sped
spell	spelling	spelled or spelt	spelled or spelt

verb	present participle	past tense	past participle
spend	spending	spent	spent
spill	spilling	spilled *or* spilt	spilled *or* spilt
spin	spinning	spun	spun
spit	spitting	spat	spat
split	splitting	split	split
spoil	spoiling	spoilt	spoilt
spring	springing	sprang	sprung
stand	standing	stood	stood
steal	stealing	stole	stolen
stick	sticking	stuck	stuck
sting	stinging	stung	stung
stink	stinking	stank	stunk
stride	striding	strode	stridden
strike	striking	struck	struck
strive	striving	strove	striven
swear	swearing	swore	sworn
sweep	sweeping	swept	swept
swell	swelling	swelled	swollen
swim	swimming	swam	swum
swing	swinging	swung	swung
take	taking	took	taken
teach	teaching	taught	taught
tear	tearing	tore	torn
tell	telling	told	told
think	thinking	thought	thought
throw	throwing	threw	thrown
thrust	thrusting	thrust	thrust
tie	tying	tied	tied
tread	treading	trod	trodden
undergo	undergoing	underwent	undergone
understand	understanding	understood	understood
undertake	undertaking	undertook	undertaken
undo	undoing	undid	undone
unwind	unwinding	unwound	unwound
uphold	upholding	upheld	upheld
upset	upsetting	upset	upset
wake	waking	waked *or* woke	woken
wear	wearing	wore	worn
weave	weaving	wove	woven
weep	weeping	wept	wept
wet	wetting	wet *or* wetted	wet *or* wetted
win	winning	won	won
wind	winding	wound	wound
withhold	withholding	withheld	withheld
withdraw	withdrawing	withdrew	withdrawn
withstand	withstanding	withstood	withstood
wring	wringing	wrung	wrung
write	writing	wrote	written

Aa

a /ə; *strong* eɪ/ *indefinite article*
1 one; any ▸ *I gave him a pencil.*
▸ *A bird has two legs.*
2 for each; in each ▸ *The sweets cost
10 cents a bag.* ▸ *three times a year*

An is used instead of **a** before a
word that starts with the sound of
a, e, i, o, or **u.**
LOOK AT: **an**

abandon /ə'bændən/ *verb*
to leave someone or something ▸ *The
baby was abandoned by its mother.*
▸ *We abandoned our holiday because
we had no money.*

abbey /'æbɪ/ *noun*
a large church ▸ *Westminster Abbey*

abbreviation /ə,briːvɪ'eɪʃən/ *noun*
a short way of writing or saying a
word or name ▸ *Mr is the
abbreviation for Mister.*

ABC /,eɪ biː 'siː/ *noun*
the English alphabet ▸ *She's learning
her ABC.*

abdomen /'æbdəmən/ *noun*
the front part of your body below
your waist

abduct /əb'dʌkt/ *verb*
to take someone away illegally and
by using force ▸ *Police believe that
the woman has been abducted.*

ability /ə'bɪlətɪ/ *noun (no plural)*
the power or knowledge to do
something ▸ *Doctors now have the
ability to keep people alive for much
longer.*

ablaze /ə'bleɪz/ *adjective*
burning with a lot of flames ▸ *Soon
the whole building was ablaze.*

able /'eɪbəl/ *adjective*
having the power or the knowledge to
do something ▸ *Is he able to swim?*

▸ *I'm afraid I won't be able to come.*
OPPOSITE: **unable**

abnormal /,æb'nɔːməl/ *adjective*
not normal, especially in a way that is
strange or dangerous ▸ *The doctors
found some abnormal cells in her
body.* (*adverb:* **abnormally**)

aboard /ə'bɔːd/ *preposition, adverb*
on or onto a ship or plane ▸ *Are all
the passengers aboard?*

abolish /ə'bɒlɪʃ/ *verb*
to end something or get rid of it by
law ▸ *The new government abolished
the tax on wine.*

abolition /,æbə'lɪʃən/ *noun (no
plural)*
ending or getting rid of something by
law ▸ *the abolition of taxes*

abortion /ə'bɔːʃən/ *noun*
an operation to stop a baby
developing inside its mother, by
removing the baby so that it dies
▸ *She was told about the dangers of
having an abortion.*

about /ə'baʊt/ *preposition, adverb*
1 concerning ▸ *What are you talking
about?* ▸ *a book about birds*
2 a little more or less than ▸ *Come at
about 6 o'clock.*
3 here and there ▸ *The children were
kicking a ball about.* ▸ *They walked
about the town.*
4 be about to do something to be
just going to do something ▸ *I was
about to come and see you.*
5 how about/what about used when
you are suggesting something
▸ *What about some lunch?* ▸ *How
about going to the cinema?*

above /ə'bʌv/ *adverb, preposition*
1 at a higher place; higher than; over
▸ *The picture is on the wall above my
desk.* ▸ *the blue sky above*
2 more than a certain number or
amount ▸ *children above the age of
five*
OPPOSITE (**1** and **2**): **below**

3 above all more than anything else; most important of all ▶ *I want you to remember this above all.*

abroad /əˈbrɔːd/ *adverb*
in or to a foreign country ▶ *My brother is studying abroad.* ▶ *He wants to go abroad.*

abrupt /əˈbrʌpt/ *adjective*
1 sudden ▶ *an abrupt knock at the door*
2 not polite ▶ *an abrupt answer to his question*
(*adverb:* **abruptly**)

absence /ˈæbsəns/ *noun (no plural)*
not being there ▶ *Her absence was noticed by her friends.*
OPPOSITE: **presence**

absent /ˈæbsənt/ *adjective*
not there; not present ▶ *He was absent from work last Tuesday.*

absentee /ˌæbsənˈtiː/ *noun*
a person who is not where they usually are or where they should be ▶ *There were several absentees.*

absenteeism /ˌæbsənˈtiːɪzəm/ *noun (no plural)*
regular absence from work or school without a good reason ▶ *Absenteeism at the factory is becoming a real problem.*

absent-minded /ˌæbsənt ˈmaɪndɪd/ *adjective*
not noticing things that are happening around you, and often forgetting things

absolute /ˈæbsəluːt/ *adjective*
complete ▶ *Are you telling me the absolute truth?*

absolutely /ˌæbsəˈluːtlɪ/ *adverb*
1 very; completely ▶ *It's absolutely beautiful.* ▶ *You must keep it absolutely secret.*
2 used to show that you agree with someone ▶ *"Do you think I'm right?" "Absolutely!"*

absorb /əbˈsɔːb/ *verb*

1 to take in liquid slowly
2 to learn and understand something thoroughly ▶ *I haven't really absorbed all the information yet.*

absorbent /əbˈsɔːbənt/ *adjective*
able to take in liquid ▶ *This material is quite absorbent.*

absorbing /əbˈsɔːbɪŋ/ *adjective*
very interesting ▶ *an absorbing book*

abstain /əbˈsteɪn/ *verb*
1 to not do something even though you want to ▶ *Patients were advised to abstain from drinking alcohol.*
2 to deliberately not vote ▶ *Four members of the committee abstained.*

abstract /ˈæbstrækt/ *adjective*
based on ideas rather than specific examples or real events ▶ *Beauty is an abstract idea.*

absurd /əbˈsɜːd/ *adjective*
very silly ▶ *The story was so absurd that no one believed it.*
(*adverb:* **absurdly**)

abundant /əˈbʌndənt/ *adjective*
existing in large quantities ▶ *an abundant supply of fresh fruit*

abuse¹ /əˈbjuːz/ *verb (present participle* **abusing**, *past* **abused**)
to call someone rude and insulting names, or speak rudely to them

abuse² /əˈbjuːs/ *noun (no plural)*
1 rude and insulting things said to someone ▶ *He shouted abuse at me.*
2 bad treatment or wrong use ▶ *the problem of drug abuse*

abusive /əˈbjuːsɪv/ *adjective*
using words that are rude and insulting ▶ *an abusive letter*

academic /ˌækəˈdemɪk/ *adjective*
concerning the work done in schools, colleges, or universities ▶ *academic subjects*

academy /əˈkædəmɪ/ *noun (plural* **academies**)
a school or college where students

learn a special subject or skill ▶ *a military academy*

accelerate /ək'seləreɪt/ *verb (present participle **accelerating**, past **accelerated**)*
to make a car go faster ▶ *I accelerated and passed the lorry in front.*

accelerator /ək'seləreɪtə^r/ *noun*
the thing that you press with your foot in a car to make it go faster

accent /'æksənt/ *noun*
a way of speaking, that shows that a person comes from a particular place ▶ *Maria speaks English with an Italian accent.*
COMPARE: **dialect**

accept /ək'sept/ *verb*
1 to receive or take something that is offered to you ▶ *Will you accept my offer?* ▶ *I accepted another piece of cake.*
2 to agree to do something ▶ *David asked three friends to his party, and they all accepted.*

acceptable /ək'septəbəl/ *adjective*
of good enough quality ▶ *Your work is not acceptable.*
OPPOSITE: **unacceptable**

acceptance /ək'septəns/ *noun (no plural)*
agreement to receive or take something that is offered to you ▶ *her acceptance of the offer*

accepted /ək'septɪd/ *adjective*
agreed by most people to be right ▶ *the accepted rules of the game*

access /'ækses/ *noun (no plural)*
a way to get to a place, a person, or a thing ▶ *There is no access **to** the street through that door.* ▶ *Students need access to books.*

accessible /ək'sesəbəl/ *adjective*
easy to reach, find, or use ▶ *The national park is not accessible by road.* ▶ *the wide range of information that is accessible on the Internet*

accessory /ək'sesəri/ *noun (plural **accessories**)*
something such as a belt or jewellery that you wear because it looks nice with your clothes ▶ *a dress with matching accessories*

accident /'æksɪdənt/ *noun*
1 something, often bad, that happens by chance ▶ *John's had an accident – he's been hit by a car.* ▶ *I'm sorry I broke the cup. It was an accident.*
2 by accident by chance; not on purpose ▶ *I did it by accident.*

accidental /æksɪ'dentl/ *adjective*
by chance; not on purpose ▶ *an accidental meeting (adverb: **accidentally**)*

accommodate /ə'kɒmədeɪt/ *verb (present participle **accommodating**, past **accommodated**)*
1 to give someone a place to live or stay in
2 to have space for something ▶ *You could accommodate another four children in your class.*

accommodation /ə,kɒmə'deɪʃən/ *noun (no plural)*
somewhere to live or stay ▶ *I must find some accommodation.*

> Remember that the noun **accommodation** has no plural: *Accommodation will be provided for the students.* ▶ *Do you have any accommodation?*

accompany /ə'kʌmpəni/ *verb (past **accompanied**)*
1 to go with someone ▶ *He accompanied me to the doctor's.*
2 to play music while someone else is singing or playing another instrument ▶ *Maria sang, and I accompanied her on the piano.*

accomplish /ə'kʌmplɪʃ/ *verb*
to do or finish something ▶ *We accomplished a lot during the day.*

accomplished /ə'kʌmplɪʃt/ *adjective*

very good at doing something ▶ *an accomplished musician*

accomplishment /əˈkʌmplɪʃmənt/ *noun*
something that you achieve or are able to do well ▶ *Passing the exam was quite an accomplishment.*

accord /əˈkɔːd/ *noun (no plural)*
of your own accord without being asked ▶ *She went of her own accord.*

accordance /əˈkɔːdəns/ *noun (no plural)*
in accordance with something done in a way that follows a particular system or rule ▶ *Safety checks were made in accordance with the rules.*

accordingly /əˈkɔːdɪŋli/ *adverb*
in a way that is suitable for a particular situation ▶ *He broke the law and was punished accordingly.*

according to /əˈkɔːdɪŋ tuː/ *preposition*
from what is said or written ▶ *According to the map, we're very close to the sea.*

account[1] /əˈkaʊnt/ *noun*
1 a story or description ▶ *an exciting account of the match*
2 a list of payments owed to someone
3 an amount of money kept in a bank ▶ *He paid the money into his bank account.*
4 on account of because of ▶ *We stayed at home on account of the bad weather.*
5 take something into account to consider something before making a decision ▶ *You must take the price into account when choosing which one to buy.*
6 accounts *plural noun* lists of money that a person or company spends and earns

account[2] *verb*
account for to give the reason for something ▶ *I can't account for her*

strange behaviour.

accountable /əˈkaʊntəbəl/ *adjective*
responsible for the effects of your actions, and willing to explain or be criticized for them ▶ *At what age is a person legally accountable for their actions?*

accountancy /əˈkaʊntənsi/ *noun (no plural)*
the job of being an accountant

accountant /əˈkaʊntənt/ *noun*
a person whose job is to keep lists of money spent and money earned, for people or companies

accumulate /əˈkjuːmjʊleɪt/ *verb (present participle accumulating, past accumulated)*
1 to gradually get more and more of something ▶ *During his life, he had accumulated a huge collection of paintings.*
2 to gradually increase ▶ *Her problems started to accumulate after the baby was born.*

accuracy /ˈækjʊrəsi/ *noun (no plural)*
the quality of being exactly right or correct

accurate /ˈækjʊrət/ *adjective*
right; correct ▶ *Is this watch accurate? (adverb: accurately)*
OPPOSITE: **inaccurate**

accusation /ˌækjʊˈzeɪʃən/ *noun*
an act of saying that someone has done something wrong ▶ *accusations of cheating*

accuse /əˈkjuːz/ *verb (present participle accusing, past accused)*
to say that someone has done something wrong ▶ *The teacher accused Paul of cheating.*
COMPARE: **blame**

accusing /əˈkjuːzɪŋ/ *adjective*
showing that you think someone has done something wrong ▶ *"Where have you been?" asked Jenny in an accusing voice. (adverb: accusingly)*

accustomed to /əˈkʌstəmd tuː/
adjective
used to something ➤ *I'm not
accustomed to this sort of behaviour.*

ace¹ /eɪs/ *adjective*
excellent ➤ *He's an ace goalkeeper.*

ace² *noun*
one of four playing cards in a pack,
that can have either the highest or
the lowest value in a game of cards
➤ *the ace of diamonds*

ache¹ /eɪk/ *verb (present participle
aching, past ached)*
to be painful; to hurt ➤ *Her head
ached.*

ache² *noun*
a continuing pain ➤ *a stomach ache*

achieve /əˈtʃiːv/ *verb (present
participle achieving, past achieved)*
to succeed in doing something by
working ➤ *He achieved top marks in
the examination.*

achievement /əˈtʃiːvmənt/ *noun*
something that you have worked hard
for and done well

acid /ˈæsɪd/ *noun*
a powerful liquid that can burn things

acid rain /ˌæsɪd ˈreɪn/ *noun (no
plural)*
rain which causes damage to trees
and plants because it contains acid
put into the air by factories

acknowledge /əkˈnɒlɪdʒ/ *verb
(present participle acknowledging,
past acknowledged)*
1 to agree that something is true
➤ *Do you acknowledge that you were
wrong?*
2 to write to someone to say that you
have received something ➤ *Please
acknowledge my letter.*

acknowledgement /əkˈnɒlɪdʒmənt/
noun
1 something that someone says,
writes, or does to thank someone or
to show that they have received

something ➤ *I haven't received an
acknowledgement of my letter yet.*
2 something that shows you admit or
accept that something is true or that
a situation exists ➤ *an
acknowledgement of defeat*

acne /ˈækni/ *noun (no plural)*
a skin problem which is common
among young people and causes
small spots to appear on the face

acorn /ˈeɪkɔːn/ *noun*
a small nut which grows on OAK trees

acquaintance /əˈkweɪntəns/ *noun*
a person you know slightly because
you have met him or her a few times
COMPARE: **friend**

acquainted /əˈkweɪntɪd/ *adjective*
be acquainted with to know someone
➤ *Are you acquainted with Mr
Smith?*

acquire /əˈkwaɪəʳ/ *verb (present
participle acquiring, past acquired)*
to get or buy something ➤ *How did
you acquire this money?*

acre /ˈeɪkəʳ/ *noun*
a measure of land; 4,047 square
metres

acrobat /ˈækrəbæt/ *noun*
a person who performs in a CIRCUS
and does difficult tricks with their
body

acronym /ˈækrənɪm/ *noun*
a word that is made from the first
letters of a group of words. For
example, TEFL is an acronym for
Teaching English as a Foreign
Language

across /əˈkrɒs/ *adverb, preposition*
from one side of a place to the other;
on the other side of something
➤ *They swam across the river.* ➤ *the
house across the street*

act¹ /ækt/ *verb*
1 to do something or behave in a
certain way ➤ *You're acting like a
fool.*

A

2 to pretend to be someone else, in a play or film
3 act as to be in place of someone or something ► *This room acts as her office.*

act² *noun*
1 an action ► *an act of bravery*
2 something pretended ► *She seems happy, but it's just an act.*
3 a part of a play

acting /ˈæktɪŋ/ *noun (no plural)*
the work done by an ACTOR or ACTRESS

action /ˈækʃən/ *noun*
1 something that you do ► *His quick action saved her life.* ► *The government must take action to help the poor.*
2 in action doing something ► *photographs of the players in action during the match*
3 out of action not working ► *My car is out of action.*

action replay /ˌækʃən ˈriːpleɪ/ *noun*
an interesting part of a sports event that is shown again on television immediately after it happens ► *The action replay showed that the ball crossed the line.*

activate /ˈæktɪveɪt/ *verb (present participle activating, past activated)*
to make something start to work ► *Pressing this button will activate the car alarm.*

active /ˈæktɪv/ *adjective*
1 always doing things ► *He is an active member of the club.* ► *an active old lady*
OPPOSITE: **inactive**
2 doing the action. In the sentence "John kicked the ball", "kicked" is an active verb
OPPOSITE (**2**): **passive**

actively /ˈæktɪvlɪ/ *adverb*
in a way that involves doing things to try to make something happen ► *The government has actively encouraged immigration.*

activist /ˈæktɪvɪst/ *noun*
a person who works hard to change society or a political situation they do not agree with ► *a political activist*

activity /ækˈtɪvətɪ/ *noun*
1 *(plural **activities**)* something you do, especially to enjoy yourself ► *Dancing is her favourite activity.*
2 *(no plural)* being active ► *The classroom was full of activity – every child was busy.*

actor /ˈæktər/ *noun*
a man or woman who acts in plays or films

actress /ˈæktrəs/ *noun (plural **actresses**)*
a woman who acts in plays or films

actual /ˈæktʃʊəl/ *adjective*
real and clear ► *We think he stole the money, but we have no actual proof.*

actually /ˈæktʃʊəlɪ/ *adverb*
1 really; in fact ► *Do you actually believe that?* ► *I've spoken to him on the telephone, but I've never actually met him.*
2 used to say in a polite way that someone has a wrong idea ► *Actually, the film starts at 3 o'clock, not 4.*

acute /əˈkjuːt/ *adjective*
1 very serious or bad ► *patients who suffer acute pain*
2 *(used about angles)* less than 90°

ad /æd/ *noun*
an advertisement

AD /ˌeɪ ˈdiː/
after the birth of Christ, used in dates ► *the year AD 700*

adamant /ˈædəmənt/ *adjective*
determined not to change your opinion or decision ► *She was adamant that she would stay.*

adapt /əˈdæpt/ *verb*
1 to change something to make it more suitable ► *a kitchen adapted for blind people*
2 to become used to something

A

➤ *The children have adapted to their new school.*

adaptable /əˈdæptəbəl/ *adjective*
(used about a person) able to become used to new things easily

adaptation /ˌædæpˈteɪʃən/ *noun*
a play or film that is based on a book ➤ *The film is a modern adaptation of "Romeo and Juliet".*

adapter /əˈdæptəʳ/ *noun*
something that you use to connect two pieces of equipment when you cannot connect them together directly ➤ *an electrical adapter*

add /æd/ *verb*
1 to put something together with something else ➤ *If you add 2 and 7, you get 9.* ➤ *To make the cake, mix the butter and sugar, and then add the flour.*
2 add up to put numbers or amounts together to find a total ➤ *Add up these numbers.* ➤ *I can't add up (=I am not good at putting numbers together and finding the total).*
COMPARE (**2**): **subtract**
3 to say something more

adder /ˈædəʳ/ *noun*
a snake with a dangerous bite

addict /ˈædɪkt/ *noun*
someone who is not able to stop taking harmful drugs

addicted /əˈdɪktɪd/ *adjective*
not able to stop doing something, especially taking a harmful drug ➤ *He was addicted to heroin.* ➤ *My children are completely addicted to computer games.*

addictive /əˈdɪktɪv/ *adjective*
making you addicted to something ➤ *a highly addictive drug*

addition /əˈdɪʃən/ *noun*
1 (*no plural*) adding numbers or amounts together
COMPARE: **subtraction**
2 someone or something added ➤ *an*

addition to the family (=a new baby)
3 in addition to as well as ➤ *In addition to English, the children also learn German and Spanish.*

additional /əˈdɪʃənəl/ *adjective*
added to what is already there ➤ *We always need additional staff over the New Year.*

address¹ /əˈdres/ *noun* (*plural* **addresses**)
the name of the place where you live ➤ *Please write your name and address.*

address² *verb*
1 to write an address on something ➤ *She addressed the letter to Mrs Wilson.*
2 to speak to someone ➤ *The captain addressed his team.*

adept /ˈædept/ *adjective*
good at doing something that needs care or skill ➤ *I'm not very adept at typing.*

adequate /ˈædɪkwət/ *adjective*
enough ➤ *an adequate amount of food*
OPPOSITE: **inadequate**

adjacent /əˈdʒeɪsənt/ *adjective*
next to something ➤ *buildings adjacent to the palace*

adjective /ˈædʒɪktɪv/ *noun*
a word that describes someone or something. In the phrase "a beautiful song", "beautiful" is an adjective

adjoining /əˈdʒɔɪnɪŋ/ *adjective*
next to and connected to another building, room, etc. ➤ *She hurried into the adjoining room.*

adjust /əˈdʒʌst/ *verb*
to make a small change in something or to move it slightly to make it better

adjustable /əˈdʒʌstəbəl/ *adjective*
able to be changed or moved slightly to make it better ➤ *adjustable car seats*

A

adjustment /ə'dʒʌstmənt/ *noun*
a small change that you make in
something to make it better ➤ *We had
to make a few adjustments to our
original plan.*

administer /əd'mɪnɪstə^r/ *verb*
1 to organize or manage something
➤ *A special committee will administer
the scheme.*
2 to give someone a drug or medical
treatment ➤ *Only doctors and nurses
can administer drugs.*

administration /əd,mɪnɪ'streɪʃən/
noun (no plural)
looking after or managing a business
or an organization

administrative /əd'mɪnɪstrətɪv/
adjective
connected with organizing or
managing the work in a company or
an organization ➤ *The company has
13 administrative staff.*

administrator /əd'mɪnɪstreɪtə^r/
noun
a person whose job is to help
organize a particular area of work in a
company or an organization

admirable /'ædmərəbəl/ *adjective*
good and deserving your respect
➤ *He had many admirable qualities,
especially honesty. (adverb:
admirably)*

admiral /'ædmərəl/ *noun*
the most important officer in the
navy

admiration /,ædmə'reɪʃən/ *noun (no
plural)*
thinking a person or thing is very
good, nice to look at, etc.

admire /əd'maɪə^r/ *verb (present
participle admiring, past admired)*
1 to respect and approve of someone
or something
2 to think a person or thing is very
nice to look at ➤ *I was just admiring
your new car.*

admission /əd'mɪʃən/ *noun*
1 agreeing that something
unpleasant about yourself is true,
or saying that you have done
something wrong ➤ *an admission of
guilt*
2 (no plural) permission to go into a
place ➤ *Admission was free for
children.*

admit /əd'mɪt/ *verb (present
participle admitting, past admitted)*
1 to agree that something unpleasant
about yourself is true ➤ *She admitted
she was lazy.*
OPPOSITE: **deny**
2 to let someone into a place ➤ *This
ticket admits two people to the
football match.*

adolescence /,ædəˈlesəns/ *noun (no
plural)*
the time when a young person is
developing into an adult, usually
between the ages of 13 and 18
➤ *Adolescence is a difficult time for
young people.*

adolescent /,ædəˈlesənt/ *noun*
a boy or girl between about 13 and 16
years old

adopt /ə'dɒpt/ *verb*
to take a child into your family and
treat him or her as your own

adoption /ə'dɒpʃən/ *noun (no
plural)*
the act of taking a child into your
family and treating him or her as your
own

adorable /ə'dɔːrəbəl/ *adjective*
very attractive ➤ *What an adorable
little girl!*

adore /ə'dɔː^r/ *verb (present participle
adoring, past adored)*
to love someone or something very
much ➤ *She adored her son.* ➤ *I adore
chocolate.*

adrenalin /ə'drenəlɪn/ *noun (no
plural)*

a substance that your body produces when you are frightened, excited, or angry, and which gives you more energy

adult /'ædʌlt, ə'dʌlt/ noun
a grown-up person ▶ *a group of three adults and four children*

adultery /ə'dʌltəri/ noun (no plural)
the act of having sex when you are married, with someone who is not your husband or wife ▶ *She accused her husband of adultery.*

advance¹ /əd'va:ns/ verb (present participle **advancing**, past **advanced**)
to move forward ▶ *The army advanced towards the town.*
COMPARE: **retreat**

advance² noun
in advance before something happens or before you do something ▶ *You must pay in advance.*

advanced /əd'va:nst/ adjective
of a high or difficult level ▶ *advanced English classes*

advantage /əd'va:ntidʒ/ noun
something that helps a person ▶ *It is an advantage to speak several languages.*
OPPOSITE: **disadvantage**

advent /'ædvent/ noun (no plural)
the time when something important first starts to exist ▶ *Since the advent of computers, offices have changed completely.*

adventure /əd'ventʃər/ noun
an exciting thing that happens to someone

adventurous /əd'ventʃərəs/ adjective
liking a life full of adventures

adverb /'ædvɜ:b/ noun
a word which tells us how, when, or where something is done. In the sentence "She spoke loudly", "loudly" is an adverb

adverse /'ædvɜ:s/ adjective
bad and causing problems ▶ *The illness has had an adverse effect on her school work.* ▶ *Adverse weather conditions caused the accident.*

advert /'ædvɜ:t/ noun
an advertisement

advertise /'ædvətaiz/ verb (present participle **advertising**, past **advertised**)
to put notices in a public place to give people information about something ▶ *The company has spent a lot of money advertising its new shampoo.*

advertisement /əd'vɜ:tɪsmənt/ noun
a notice or a short film offering something for sale ▶ *a newspaper advertisement* ▶ *an advertisement for a new soap*

advertising /'ædvətaizɪŋ/ noun (no plural)
the business of advertising things on television, in public places, etc.

advice /əd'vais/ noun (no plural)
a suggestion about what someone should do ▶ *If you take my advice, you'll go home.* ▶ *That's good advice.*

advisable /əd'vaizəbəl/ adjective
that should be done in order to avoid problems ▶ *It's advisable to book your ticket early.*

advise /əd'vaiz/ verb (present participle **advising**, past **advised**)
to tell someone what you think they should do ▶ *She advised me to go home.*

adviser /əd'vaizər/ noun
a person whose job is to give advice to a company, government, etc. ▶ *a financial adviser*

advocate¹ /'ædvəkeit/ verb (present participle **advocating**, past **advocated**)
to say that you support a particular plan or method ▶ *We have never advocated the use of violence.*

A

advocate² /ˈædvəkət/ *noun*
a person who supports a particular plan or method ➤ *He was an advocate of fascism.*

aerial /ˈeərɪəl/ *noun*
a wire, on top of a building or piece of apparatus, which sends out or receives radio or television signals

aerobic /eəˈrəʊbɪk/ *adjective*
(used about exercise) making your heart and lungs stronger ➤ *an aerobic workout*

aerobics /eəˈrəʊbɪks/ *noun (no plural)*
a form of very active exercise done to music

aeroplane /ˈeərəpleɪn/ *noun*
a large flying machine with wings, in which people can travel

aerosol /ˈeərəsɒl/ *noun*
a container from which a liquid can be SPRAYED

affair /əˈfeəʳ/ *noun*
1 a sexual relationship between two people, especially one which is secret because they are married to other people ➤ *Her husband was having an affair.*
2 an event ➤ *The party was a noisy affair.*
3 affairs *plural noun* things connected with a particular subject ➤ *government affairs*

affect /əˈfekt/ *verb*
to make a difference to someone or something ➤ *The hot weather affected his health* (=made him ill).

affection /əˈfekʃən/ *noun (no plural)*
the feeling of liking and caring for another person

affectionate /əˈfekʃənət/ *adjective*
feeling or showing love (*adverb:* **affectionately**)

affinity /əˈfɪnətɪ/ *noun*
a feeling that you like and under-stand a person or animal ➤ *He had a*
remarkable affinity **with** horses. ➤ *She felt a natural affinity for these people.*

affirmative /əˈfɜːmətɪv/ *adjective*
saying or meaning "yes" ➤ *an affirmative reply*
OPPOSITE: **negative**

afflict /əˈflɪkt/ *verb*
be afflicted by something to be badly affected by a serious disease or problem ➤ *a country that is afflicted by disease and famine*

affliction /əˈflɪkʃən/ *noun*
something that makes people suffer ➤ *Bad eyesight is a common affliction.*

affluent /ˈæfluənt/ *adjective*
rich ➤ *an affluent suburb of Paris*

afford /əˈfɔːd/ *verb*
to have enough money to pay for something ➤ *We can't afford a holiday.*

affordable /əˈfɔːdəbəl/ *adjective*
not too expensive, so that most people have enough money to buy it ➤ *It was difficult to find affordable accommodation.*

affront /əˈfrʌnt/ *noun*
something that someone says or does that offends or upsets you ➤ *The people saw the remark as an affront to their religion.*

afraid /əˈfreɪd/ *adjective*
feeling fear ➤ *Are you afraid of the dark?*
SAME MEANING: **scared**

afresh /əˈfreʃ/ *adverb*
start afresh to start again from the beginning ➤ *You'd better start afresh on a clean piece of paper.*

after /ˈɑːftəʳ/ *preposition, conjunction*
1 later than; following ➤ *My birthday is the day after tomorrow.* ➤ *We were very worried after we'd heard the news.*
OPPOSITE: **before**

2 behind; trying to catch ► *The child ran after her dog.*
3 after all in spite of what you did or thought before ► *I thought it was a mistake, but it was right after all.*
4 after that next; then ► *What did she do after that?*
5 be after something to be trying to get something ► *I think he's after more money.*

aftereffects /ˈɑːftərɪˌfekts/ *plural noun*
the unpleasant results that stay after the end of the condition or event that caused them ► *the aftereffects of the war*

afternoon /ˌɑːftəˈnuːn/ *noun*
the time between the middle of the day and evening ► *Good afternoon, Mrs Brown* (=said as a greeting).

aftershave /ˈɑːftəʃeɪv/ *noun*
a liquid with a nice smell that a man puts on his face after he has SHAVED ► *Are you wearing aftershave?*

afterthought /ˈɑːftəθɔːt/ *noun*
something that you do after doing other things, because you forgot to do it earlier ► *She invited me to the party, but only as an afterthought.*

afterwards /ˈɑːftəwədz/ *adverb*
later; after something has happened ► *We saw the film, and afterwards walked home together.*

again /əˈɡen/ *adverb*
1 one more time; once more ► *Come and see us again soon.*
2 again and again many times
3 now and again sometimes, but not very often ► *My aunt visits us now and again.*

against /əˈɡenst, əˈɡeɪnst/ *preposition*
1 not agreeing with someone or something ► *I'm against killing animals for their fur.*
2 on the other side in a game or match ► *We're playing against the village team.*
3 close to; touching ► *Put the ladder against the wall.*
4 in order to stop something happening ► *government action against the job losses*
5 against the law not allowed by the law ► *It's against the law to drive too fast.*

age /eɪdʒ/ *noun*
1 the number of years someone has lived or something has been ► *What age is he?* ► *He is ten years of age.*
2 *(no plural)* one of the periods of a person's life ► *old age* ► *at a young age*
3 *(no plural)* being old ► *The wine improves with age.*
4 a period of time in history
5 ages a long time ► *We talked for ages.*

aged /eɪdʒd/ *adjective*
being of a particular age ► *children aged six and under*
COMPARE: **old**

agency /ˈeɪdʒənsɪ/ *noun (plural agencies)*
a business that arranges services for people ► *We found the flat through an agency.*

agenda /əˈdʒendə/ *noun*
a list of the things that people are going to discuss at a meeting ► *The next item on the agenda is this year's budget.*

agent /ˈeɪdʒənt/ *noun*
a person who looks after business for someone else ► *our company's agent in New York*

aggravate /ˈæɡrəveɪt/ *verb (present participle aggravating, past aggravated)*
to annoy someone ► *He really aggravates me sometimes.*

aggression /əˈɡreʃən/ *noun (no plural)*

A

angry or violent behaviour or feelings ▶ *You need to learn how to control your aggression.*

aggressive /əˈgresɪv/ *adjective*
behaving angrily, as if you want to fight or attack someone ▶ *He is very aggressive when he plays football.* (adverb: **aggressively**)

agile /ˈædʒaɪl/ *adjective*
able to move quickly and easily ▶ *In spite of her size, Sara is very agile.*

agitated /ˈædʒɪteɪtɪd/ *adjective*
very worried or upset ▶ *You really shouldn't get so agitated.*

ago /əˈgəʊ/ *adverb*
in the past ▶ *We came to live here six years ago.* ▶ *a few minutes ago*

> **Ago** is used with the past tense of verbs, but you cannot use it with past tenses which are formed with **have.** Compare these sentences: *He arrived a month ago.* ▶ *He has been here since last month.*
> LOOK AT: **before, since**

agonize /ˈægənaɪz/ *verb (present participle **agonizing**, past **agonized**)*
to think and worry for a long time about something you have to do ▶ *Don't agonize for too long about any of the questions.*

agonizing /ˈægənaɪzɪŋ/ *adjective*
1 very painful ▶ *an agonizing injury*
2 making you feel very worried or nervous ▶ *Waiting for the results was agonizing.*

agony /ˈægəni/ *noun (no plural)*
very bad pain

agree /əˈgriː/ *verb (past **agreed**)*
1 to have the same opinion as someone else ▶ *I agree **with** you.* ▶ *We all agreed.*
OPPOSITE: **disagree**
2 agree to something to say yes to something ▶ *He agreed to the plan.*

3 agree with something to believe that something is right; to approve of something
OPPOSITE ③: **disagree**

agreeable /əˈgriːəbəl/ *adjective*
pleasant or enjoyable ▶ *a very agreeable young man*

agreed /əˈgriːd/ *adjective*
1 accepted by everyone ▶ *The agreed price for the bike was £50.*
2 be agreed on something to accept something ▶ *Are we all agreed on the date for the next meeting?*

agreement /əˈgriːmənt/ *noun*
1 an arrangement or a promise between people or countries ▶ *Britain has trade agreements with many other countries.*
2 (no plural) having the same opinion as someone else ▶ *They finally reached agreement on the price.*
OPPOSITE: **disagreement**
3 in agreement having the same opinion ▶ *We are all in agreement.*

agricultural /ˌægrɪˈkʌltʃərəl/ *adjective*
used in farming or to do with farming

agriculture /ˈægrɪkʌltʃəʳ/ *noun (no plural)*
the science of growing crops and raising animals

ahead /əˈhed/ *adverb*
1 forward ▶ *Walk straight ahead until you reach the river.*
2 at a distance in front of someone or something ▶ *I saw her ahead of me.*

aid¹ /eɪd/ *noun (no plural)*
help ▶ *aid for poor countries*

aid² *verb*
to help someone
SAME MEANING: **assist**

AIDS /eɪdz/ *noun (no plural)*
a very serious disease which destroys the body's ability to fight illnesses

ailment /ˈeɪlmənt/ *noun*
an illness that is not very serious

▶ *He misses too much work because of minor ailments.*

aim¹ /eɪm/ *verb*
1 to point something and get ready to throw it or fire it towards a person or thing ▶ *to aim a gun **at** someone*
2 to want to do something ▶ *We aim to win.*
COMPARE (**2**): **intend**

aim² *noun*
1 an act of pointing something and getting ready to throw it or fire it towards a person or thing
2 something you want to do

ain't /eɪnt/
a short form of "am not", "is not", "are not", "has not", or "have not" that many people think is not correct ▶ *It ain't true!*

air¹ /eə'/ *noun*
1 *(no plural)* the gas surrounding the Earth, which people breathe
2 an appearance ▶ *an air of excitement*
3 by air in an aircraft ▶ *We travelled by air.*
4 the air the space above you ▶ *He threw his hat into the air.*

air² *verb*
to make a room or clothes fresh by letting in air

air-conditioning /'eə kən,dɪʃənɪŋ/ *noun (no plural)*
machines for keeping the air in a building cool

aircraft /'eəkrɑːft/ *noun (plural aircraft)*
a flying machine

airfare /'eəfeə'/ *noun*
the price of a plane trip ▶ *I couldn't afford the airfare to go and see him.*

airfield /'eəfiːld/ *noun*
a place where aircraft land

airforce /'eəfɔːs/ *noun*
soldiers who use aircraft for fighting
COMPARE: **army, navy**

air hostess /'eə ,həʊstɪs/ *noun (plural air hostesses)*
a woman whose job is to look after the passengers on a plane

airless /'eələs/ *adjective*
without any fresh air ▶ *an airless room*
OPPOSITE: **airy**

airline /'eəlaɪn/ *noun*
a company which carries people or goods by plane

airmail /'eəmeɪl/ *noun (no plural)*
letters and parcels sent by aircraft

airport /'eəpɔːt/ *noun*
a place where aircraft are kept and where they arrive and leave

air raid /'eə reɪd/ *noun*
an attack by soldiers in aircraft

airstrip /'eə,strɪp/ *noun*
a long, narrow piece of land that planes can fly to and from

airtight /'eətaɪt/ *adjective*
completely closed so that air cannot get in or out ▶ *an airtight jar*

airy /'eərɪ/ *adjective (airier, airiest)*
having fresh air inside ▶ *an airy room*
OPPOSITE: **airless**

aisle /aɪl/ *noun*
a narrow passage between rows of seats

ajar /ə'dʒɑː'/ *adjective*
(of a door or window) not quite closed

alarm¹ /ə'lɑːm/ *noun*
1 *(no plural)* a feeling of fear or danger
2 something, such as a bell, that warns people of danger ▶ *a fire alarm*

alarm² *verb*
to worry someone or make them afraid

alarm clock /ə'lɑːm ,klɒk/ *noun*
a clock that makes a noise at the time you want to wake up

A

album /'ælbəm/ *noun*
1 a book with empty pages where you can put photographs, stamps, etc.
2 a record with several songs on each side ▶ *a Michael Jackson album*

alcohol /'ælkəhɒl/ *noun (no plural)*
a strong liquid, in beer and other drinks, which makes you feel drunk

alcoholic /,ælkə'hɒlɪk/ *adjective*
containing alcohol ▶ *an alcoholic drink*

alert /ə'lɜ:t/ *adjective*
awake and quick to notice things

A level /'eɪ ,levəl/ *noun*
ADVANCED LEVEL; an examination in a particular subject that students in England, Wales, and Northern Ireland take when they are 18 ▶ *I have A levels in French and English.*

algebra /'ældʒɪbrə/ *noun (no plural)*
a kind of MATHEMATICS in which you use letters to represent numbers

alias¹ /'eɪlɪəs/ *preposition*
used to give another name that someone uses, after giving their real name ▶ *the writer Eric Blair, alias George Orwell*

alias² *noun (plural **aliases**)*
a false name, usually used by a criminal ▶ *Bates sometimes uses the alias John Smith.*

alibi /'ælɪbaɪ/ *noun*
proof that someone was not at the place where a crime happened ▶ *He has an alibi for the night of the murder.*

alien /'eɪlɪən/ *noun*
a creature from another world ▶ *a spaceship full of aliens*

alienate /'eɪlɪəneɪt/ *verb (present participle **alienating**, past **alienated**)*
to make someone feel that they do not belong to your group ▶ *We don't want to alienate young people.*

alight /ə'laɪt/ *adjective*
burning; on fire ▶ *The house was alight.*

alike /ə'laɪk/ *adjective, adverb*
the same in some way ▶ *They were all dressed alike in white dresses.*

alive /ə'laɪv/ *adjective*
living; not dead ▶ *Is his grandfather still alive?*

all /ɔːl/ *adjective, adverb*
1 the whole amount of ▶ *Don't eat all that bread!*
2 every one of ▶ *all the children*
3 completely ▶ *He was dressed all in black.*
4 **all over** everywhere ▶ *I've been looking all over for you.*
5 **not at all** not in any way ▶ *I'm not at all hungry.* ▶ *She didn't understand it at all.*

all clear /,ɔːl 'klɪəʳ/ *noun*
permission to begin doing something ▶ *We have to wait for the all clear from the safety committee before we can start.*

allegation /,ælɪ'geɪʃən/ *noun*
a statement that someone has done something bad or illegal, but for which there is no proof ▶ *allegations that the police had tortured prisoners*

allege /ə'ledʒ/ *verb (present participle **alleging**, past **alleged**)*
to say that something is true without showing proof ▶ *Baldwin is alleged to have killed two people.*

allegiance /ə'li:dʒəns/ *noun*
loyalty or support given to a leader, country, belief, etc. ▶ *allegiance **to** the king*

allergic /ə'lɜ:dʒɪk/ *adjective*
1 caused by an allergy ▶ *an allergic rash*
2 becoming ill when you eat, drink, or touch a particular thing ▶ *I'm allergic **to** cats.*

allergy /'ælədʒɪ/ *noun (plural **allergies**)*

an illness that causes you to become ill every time you eat, drink, or touch a particular thing

alley /'ælɪ/ *noun*
a very narrow road in a town

alliance /ə'laɪəns/ *noun*
an agreement between countries or groups to work together for a purpose

alligator /'ælɪgeɪtə^r/ *noun*
a large animal with a long body and short legs which lives on land and in rivers in some countries

allocate /'æləkeɪt/ *verb (present participle allocating, past allocated)*
to decide to use an amount of money, time, etc. for a particular purpose ➤ *We have been allocated £5,000 for new computers.*

allow /ə'laʊ/ *verb*
to let someone do something ➤ *You're not allowed to go in there.*
OPPOSITE: **forbid**

allowance /ə'laʊəns/ *noun*
1 money that someone gives you regularly or for a special reason ➤ *His father gives him a small monthly allowance.* ➤ *a travel allowance*
2 make allowances for to consider someone's behaviour or work in a sympathetic way because they have a problem or disadvantage ➤ *Her mum died last week – we have to make allowances for her just now.*

all right *(also* **alright***)* /ˌɔːl 'raɪt/ *adjective, adverb*
1 well; not hurt ➤ *Do you feel all right?*
2 good enough; quite good ➤ *The film was all right, but I've seen better ones.*
3 yes; I agree ➤ *"Shall we go to town?" "All right – let's go now."*

all-round /ˌɔːl 'raʊnd/ *adjective*
good at doing many different things, especially in sports ➤ *an all-round athlete*

allude /ə'luːd/ *verb (present participle alluding, past alluded)*
to mention something, without saying it directly or clearly ➤ *I think he was alluding to your problems at work.*

ally /'ælaɪ/ *noun (plural allies)*
someone who helps you work or fight against someone else

almost /'ɔːlməʊst/ *adverb*
nearly ➤ *It's almost 9 o'clock.*

alone /ə'ləʊn/ *adjective, adverb*
1 not with other people ➤ *He lives alone.*
COMPARE: **lonely**
2 only ➤ *She alone knows the truth.*
3 leave someone or something alone to stop touching or disturbing someone or something ➤ *Leave the dog alone!*

along /ə'lɒŋ/ *preposition, adverb*
1 following the length of; from end to end of something long and thin ➤ *We walked along the road.* ➤ *the houses along the street*
2 forward ➤ *Move along, please!*
3 with you ➤ *Can I bring my friend along?*

alongside /əˌlɒŋ'saɪd/ *preposition, adverb*
by the side of something

aloud /ə'laʊd/ *adverb*
in a voice that is easy to hear ➤ *She read the story aloud.*

alphabet /'ælfəbet/ *noun*
the letters of a language in a special order ➤ *The English alphabet begins with A and ends with Z.*

alphabetical /ˌælfə'betɪkəl/ *adjective*
in the same order as the letters of the alphabet ➤ *The words in this dictionary are in alphabetical order.*

already /ɔːl'redɪ/ *adverb*
1 before now ➤ *He has seen that film twice already.*
2 by this or that time ➤ *It was already*

A

raining when we started our journey.
LOOK AT: **just, yet**

alright /ɔːlˈraɪt/ *adjective, adverb*
another word for **all right**

also /ˈɔːlsəʊ/ *adverb*
as well; too

> When there is only one verb, put
> **also** before the verb, unless it is
> the verb **be**, which must have
> **also** after it: *He enjoys football
> and cricket, and he also likes
> tennis.* ➤ *She likes music and she
> is also interested in sport.* When
> there are two verbs, put **also**
> after the first one: *I would also
> like to come.* ➤ *It is an expensive
> sport which can also be
> dangerous.*

altar /ˈɔːltəʳ/ *noun*
a raised table in a religious place,
where things are offered to a god

alter /ˈɔːltəʳ/ *verb*
to change ➤ *She altered her plans.*

alteration /ˌɔːltəˈreɪʃən/ *noun*
a change

alternate /ɔːlˈtɜːnət/ *adjective*
first one, then another ➤ *He works on
alternate Saturdays* (=he works one
Saturday, does not work the next,
and so on).

alternative¹ /ɔːlˈtɜːnətɪv/ *noun*
something you can do or use instead
of something else ➤ *You must go –
there is no alternative.*

alternative² *adjective*
different from something else ➤ *an
alternative plan*

alternatively /ɔːlˈtɜːnətɪvli/ *adverb*
used to suggest something different
from what you have just said
➤ *I could call you, or alternatively
I could come to your house.*

although /ɔːlˈðəʊ/ *conjunction*
even if; in spite of something
➤ *Although they are poor, they are
happy.*

altitude /ˈæltɪtjuːd/ *noun*
the height of something above sea
level ➤ *Breathing is more difficult at
high altitudes.*

alto /ˈæltəʊ/ *noun*
a female singer with a low voice, or a
male singer with a high voice

altogether /ˌɔːltəˈgeðəʳ/ *adverb*
counting everyone or everything;
completely ➤ *Altogether there were
12 people on the bus.* ➤ *He's not
altogether sure what to do.*

aluminium /ˌæljʊˈmɪnɪəm/ *noun (no
plural)*
a silver metal that is light and easy to
bend

always /ˈɔːlweɪz/ *adverb*
1 at all times ➤ *He always arrives
late.*
OPPOSITE: **never**
2 for ever ➤ *I shall always remember
you.*

> When there is only one verb, put
> **always** before the verb, unless it
> is the verb **be**, which must have
> **always** after it: *We always enjoy
> our holidays.* ➤ *It is always nice to
> see you.* When there are two
> verbs, put **always** after the first
> one: *You must always be careful
> when you cross the road.* ➤ *She is
> always complaining.*

am¹ /ˌeɪ ˈem/
in the morning ➤ *I got up at 8 am*

am² /əm; *strong* æm/ *verb*
the part of the verb **be** that we use
with **I** ➤ *I am very sorry.* ➤ *Am I late
for dinner?* ➤ *I'm* (=I am) *very late,
aren't I?*

amateur /ˈæmətəʳ/ *adjective*
doing something for pleasure rather
than for money ➤ *an amateur golfer*
COMPARE: **professional**

amaze /əˈmeɪz/ *verb (present
participle amazing, past amazed)*
to surprise someone very much

amazement /ə'meɪzmənt/ *noun (no plural)*
very great surprise ➤ *His mouth opened in amazement.*

amazing /ə'meɪzɪŋ/ *adjective*
very surprising and exciting ➤ *What amazing news!*
SAME MEANING: **incredible**

ambassador /æm'bæsədər/ *noun*
an important person who represents his or her government in another country

ambiguous /æm'bɪgjuəs/ *adjective*
having more than one possible meaning ➤ *His comment was rather ambiguous.*

ambition /æm'bɪʃən/ *noun*
1 (no plural) a strong wish to be successful
2 something you very much want to do ➤ *Her ambition was to be a famous singer.*

ambitious /æm'bɪʃəs/ *adjective*
wanting very much to be successful

ambivalent /æm'bɪvələnt/ *adjective*
not sure whether you like or want something ➤ *I feel somewhat ambivalent **about** moving abroad.*

ambulance /'æmbjʊləns/ *noun*
a special vehicle for carrying people who are ill or wounded

ambush¹ /'æmbʊʃ/ *noun (plural ambushes)*
a sudden attack by people who have been waiting and hiding ➤ *Two soldiers were killed in an ambush near the border.*

ambush² *verb*
to suddenly attack someone from a place where you have been hiding

amend /ə'mend/ *verb*
to make small changes or improvements to something that has been written ➤ *The law has been amended several times.*

amendment /ə'mendmənt/ *noun*
a change made in a law or document ➤ *We made a few amendments to the contract.*

amends /ə'mendz/ *noun*
make amends to do something to show that you are sorry for hurting or upsetting someone ➤ *I tried to make amends by inviting him to lunch.*

amenity /ə'miːnəti/ *noun (plural amenities)*
something that is available for you to use in a place, which makes visiting or living there enjoyable and pleasant ➤ *The hotel's amenities include a pool and two bars.*

American /ə'merɪkən/ *adjective*
of, about, or from the United States ➤ *American cars*

American football /ə,merɪkən 'futbɔːl/ *noun (no plural)*
a game played in the US, in which two teams, wearing special clothes to protect them, carry, kick, or throw a ball

amicable /'æmɪkəbəl/ *adjective*
done in a friendly way, without arguing ➤ *an amicable divorce (adverb: amicably)*

amiss /ə'mɪs/ *adjective*
be amiss if something is amiss, there is a problem ➤ *I checked the house, but nothing was amiss.*

ammunition /,æmjʊ'nɪʃən/ *noun (no plural)*
something that you can shoot from a weapon

amnesty /'æmnəsti/ *noun (plural amnesties)*
a period of time when a government lets some people leave prison or does not punish people ➤ *The new government announced an amnesty for political prisoners.*

among /ə'mʌŋ/ *(also **amongst** /ə'mʌŋst/) preposition*

A

1 in the middle of a lot of people or things ▶ *houses among the trees*
2 between three or more people ▶ *The money was shared among the children*
LOOK AT (**2**): **between**
3 in a particular group of people ▶ *a common problem among young people*

amount /əˈmaʊnt/ *noun*
a sum of money or a quantity of something ▶ *a large amount of gold*

amp /æmp/ *noun*
a measure of electricity

ample /ˈæmpəl/ *adjective*
as much as you need and more
COMPARE: **enough**

amplifier /ˈæmplɪfaɪəʳ/ *noun*
a piece of electronic equipment that you use to make music louder

amputate /ˈæmpjʊteɪt/ *verb*
(*present participle* **amputating**, *past* **amputated**)
to cut off a part of someone's body for medical reasons ▶ *After the accident, the doctors had to amputate her leg.*

amuse /əˈmjuːz/ *verb* (*present participle* **amusing**, *past* **amused**)
to make someone laugh or smile

amusement /əˈmjuːzmənt/ *noun*
1 (*no plural*) enjoyment
2 an enjoyable thing to do

amusement park /əˈmjuːzmənt ˌpɑːk/ *noun*
a large park where people can enjoy themselves, for example by riding on big machines such as ROLLER COASTERS

amusing /əˈmjuːzɪŋ/ *adjective*
making you laugh or smile ▶ *an amusing story*
SAME MEANING: **funny**

an /ən; *strong* æn/ *indefinite article*
used instead of **a** before a word that starts with the sound of **a, e, i, o,** or **u** ▶ *an apple* ▶ *an orange*

You use **an** instead of **a** before words beginning with a vowel sound: *a dog* ▶ *a girl* ▶ *a house*, but *an umbrella* ▶ *an elephant* ▶ *an object*. Remember that there is sometimes a difference in the way a word is spelt and the way it sounds. Use **an** before words which begin with a vowel sound but are not spelt with **a, e, i, o,** or **u** at the beginning: *An MG* (=/ˌemˈdʒiː/) *is a type of car.* In the same way, use **a**, not **an**, with words which are spelt with a vowel at the beginning but do **not** begin with a vowel sound: *a European* (/ˌjʊərəˈpiːən/) *country* LOOK AT: **a**

anaesthetic /ˌænəsˈθetɪk/ *noun*
something which is given to people by doctors to stop them feeling pain, especially by making them sleep

anaesthetist /əˈniːsθətɪst/ *noun*
a doctor whose job is to give anaesthetics to people in hospitals

anagram /ˈænəgræm/ *noun*
a word or phrase that you make by changing the order of the letters in another word or phrase ▶ *"Dear" is an anagram of "read".*

analogy /əˈnælədʒɪ/ *noun* (*plural* **analogies**)
a way of explaining one thing by showing how it is similar to another thing ▶ *He made an analogy between the brain and a computer.*

analyse /ˈænəlaɪz/ *verb* (*present participle* **analysing**, *past* **analysed**)
to look at something very carefully to find out what it is made of or to understand it ▶ *We need to analyse this problem carefully before deciding what to do.*

analysis /əˈnæləsɪs/ *noun* (*plural* **analyses** /əˈnæləsiːz/)
a careful examination of something

analyst /'ænəlɪst/ noun
a person whose job is to look at a subject very carefully in order to understand it and explain it to other people ▶ *a political analyst*

anarchist /'ænəkɪst/ noun
a person who believes that there should be no government or laws

anarchy /'ænəki/ noun (no plural)
a situation in which people do not obey the rules or laws and no one has control ▶ *efforts to prevent the country from sliding into anarchy*

anatomy /ə'nætəmɪ/ noun (no plural)
the scientific study of the structure of the body

ancestor /'ænsestəʳ/ noun
a person in your family who lived a long time before you were born
COMPARE: **descendant**

ancestry /'ænsəstrɪ/ noun (no plural)
your ancestors, or the place they came from ▶ *He is of Welsh ancestry.*

anchor /'æŋkəʳ/ noun
a heavy weight dropped down from a ship to the bottom of the sea to stop the ship from moving

ancient /'eɪnʃənt/ adjective
very old ▶ *ancient history* ▶ *an ancient building*

and /ən, ənd; strong ænd/ conjunction
a word used to join two words, expressions, or parts of a sentence ▶ *I went to the station and bought my ticket.* ▶ *I had a drink and a piece of cake.*

anecdote /'ænɪkdəʊt/ noun
an interesting or a funny story about something that really happened ▶ *He told a funny anecdote about his work.*

angel /'eɪndʒəl/ noun
a messenger from God, usually shown in pictures as a person with wings

anger /'æŋgəʳ/ noun (no plural)
the feeling of being very annoyed

angle /'æŋgəl/ noun
the shape made when two straight lines meet each other

angler /'æŋgləʳ/ noun
a person who goes fishing using a rod

angling /'æŋglɪŋ/ noun (no plural)
the activity of fishing with a rod

angry /'æŋgrɪ/ adjective (**angrier**, **angriest**)
feeling very annoyed ▶ *I'm very angry with them.* (adverb: **angrily**)
SAME MEANING: **cross**

anguish /'æŋgwɪʃ/ noun (no plural)
great suffering or pain

angular /'æŋgjʊləʳ/ adjective
having sharp corners

animal /'ænɪməl/ noun
something alive that is not a person or a plant ▶ *Dogs, goats, and lions are animals.*

animated /'ænɪmeɪtɪd/ adjective
1 showing a lot of interest and energy ▶ *an animated discussion*
2 (used about films, cartoons, etc.) having drawings of people or things that seem to move and talk

animation /ˌænɪ'meɪʃən/ noun (no plural)
1 the process of making animated films
2 energy and excitement

ankle /'æŋkəl/ noun
the bottom part of your leg just above your foot, which can bend

annexe /'æneks/ noun
a separate building that has been added to a larger one ▶ *a hospital annexe*

annihilate /ə'naɪəleɪt/ verb (present participle **annihilating**, past **annihilated**)
to destroy something or defeat

someone completely ➤ *In 1314, the English army was annihilated by the Scots.*

anniversary /ˌænɪˈvɜːsərɪ/ *noun* (plural **anniversaries**)
the same date each year that something important happened in the past: *We were married on April 7th 1973, so every year we have a party on our anniversary (=April 7th).*

An **anniversary** is a day when you remember something special or important which happened on the same date in an earlier year: *Their wedding anniversary is June 12th (=they got married on June 12th).* ➤ *Today is the 50th anniversary of the end of the war.* A person's **birthday** is the date on which they were born: *My birthday is October 20th (=I was born on October 20th).*

announce /əˈnaʊns/ *verb* (present participle **announcing**, past **announced**)
to say something in public ➤ *The captain announced that the plane was going to land.*

announcement /əˈnaʊnsmənt/ *noun*
something written or spoken to tell people important news ➤ *a wedding announcement in the newspaper*

announcer /əˈnaʊnsəʳ/ *noun*
a person whose job is to broadcast information to people, on radio or television, or at a station, airport, etc.

annoy /əˈnɔɪ/ *verb*
to make someone slightly angry ➤ *It really annoys me when he rings while we're eating.*

annoyance /əˈnɔɪəns/ *noun* (no plural)
the feeling of being slightly angry ➤ *I tried not to show my annoyance.*

annoyed /əˈnɔɪd/ *adjective*
slightly angry ➤ *Are you annoyed with*

me just because I'm a bit late? ➤ *She was really annoyed at the way he just ignored her.*

annual /ˈænjʊəl/ *adjective*
happening every year ➤ *an annual event*

anonymous /əˈnɒnɪməs/ *adjective*
having a name that other people do not know ➤ *The person who complained wishes to remain anonymous.* (adverb: **anonymously**)

anorak /ˈænəræk/ *noun*
a short, warm coat with a cover for your head

anorexia /ˌænəˈreksɪə/ *noun* (no plural)
a mental illness that makes someone stop eating because they think they are fat ➤ *Many teenage girls suffer from anorexia.*

anorexic /ˌænəˈreksɪk/ *adjective*
very thin and ill because of a mental illness that makes someone stop eating because they think they are fat

another /əˈnʌðəʳ/ *adjective, pronoun*
1 one more ➤ *Would you like another cup of tea?*
2 a different one ➤ *This plate is broken – can you get me another one?*

answer¹ /ˈɑːnsəʳ/ *verb*
1 to say or write something after you have been asked a question ➤ *"Did you do it?" "No, I didn't," she answered.*
SAME MEANING: **reply**
2 answer the door to open the door when someone knocks on it
3 answer the telephone to pick up the telephone when it rings

answer² *noun*
1 something that you say or write after you have been asked a question ➤ *My answer is "No".*
2 the correct result of a sum, or the correct name or fact for a question ➤ *Do you know the answer?*

➤ *That's the wrong answer.*

answering machine /'ɑːnsərɪŋ məʃiːn/ *noun*
a machine which answers your telephone and records messages when you are out

ant /ænt/ *noun*
a small insect that lives in a large group

Antarctic /æn'tɑːktɪk/ *noun*
the Antarctic the most southern part of the world, where it is very cold
COMPARE: **Arctic**

antelope /'æntɪləʊp/ *noun (plural antelope or antelopes)*
a wild animal that runs very fast and has horns on its head

antenna /æn'tenə/ *noun (plural antennae /æn'teniː/)*
one of two long, thin parts on an insect's head that it uses to feel things

anthem /'ænθəm/ *noun*
a song that is sung at special religious, sports, or political ceremonies

anthropology /ˌænθrə'pɒlədʒɪ/ *noun (no plural)*
the scientific study of people, their customs, beliefs, etc

antibiotic /ˌæntɪbaɪ'ɒtɪk/ *noun*
a type of drug used to fight illness in a person's body ➤ *The doctor gave me an antibiotic for my sore throat.*

anticipate /æn'tɪsɪpeɪt/ *verb (present participle anticipating, past anticipated)*
to expect something to happen ➤ *We anticipate a few problems.*

anticipation /ænˌtɪsɪ'peɪʃən/ *noun (no plural)*
a hopeful or slightly nervous feeling that you have when something exciting is going to happen ➤ *The audience waited in eager anticipation.*

anticlimax /ˌæntɪ'klaɪmæks/ *noun (plural anticlimaxes)*
something that is not as exciting as you expected ➤ *The end of the exams is always an anticlimax.*

anticlockwise /ˌæntɪ'klɒkwaɪz/ *adjective, adverb*
in the opposite direction to the way the hands of a clock move round
OPPOSITE: **clockwise**

antics /'æntɪks/ *plural noun*
funny, silly, or annoying behaviour ➤ *We laughed at the children's antics.*

antidote /'æntɪdəʊt/ *noun*
1 something that makes a bad situation better ➤ *Laughter can be an antidote to stress.*
2 a substance that stops a poison harming or killing someone ➤ *The snake's bite is deadly, and there is no known antidote.*

antique /æn'tiːk/ *noun*
an object which is old and worth a lot of money ➤ *an antique table*

antiseptic /ˌæntɪ'septɪk/ *noun, adjective*
a chemical substance that kills harmful BACTERIA, especially on wounds or infected parts of the body

antisocial /ˌæntɪ'səʊʃəl/ *adjective*
upsetting or annoying other people ➤ *Kids as young as eight are turning to vandalism, petty crime, and other forms of antisocial behaviour.*

antler /'æntlə/ *noun*
one of the two horns on the head of a male DEER

anxiety /æŋ'zaɪətɪ/ *noun (no plural)*
a feeling of worry

anxious /'æŋkʃəs/ *adjective*
worried

any¹ /'enɪ/ *adjective*
1 it does not matter which one ➤ *You can buy them in any big shop.* ➤ *on any day of the week*
2 used in questions, and sentences

with "not", to mean "some" ▶ *Do you have any bread?* ▶ *There isn't (=is not) any in the cupboard.*

> Use **any**, not **some**, in questions and in NEGATIVE sentences: *I must buy some coffee.* ▶ *Is there any coffee?* ▶ *There isn't any coffee.* But when you are asking for something or offering something, you use **some**: *Would you like some coffee?* ▶ *Can I have some coffee, please?*

any² *adverb*
used in questions, and sentences with "not", to mean "at all" ▶ *Don't (=do not) drive any faster.* ▶ *Are you feeling any better?*

anybody /'enɪˌbɒdɪ/ *(also **anyone** /'enɪwʌn/) pronoun*
any person ▶ *Has anybody seen my pen?* ▶ *She liked John, but she wouldn't talk to anybody else (=any other person or people).*

> Use **anybody** or **anyone**, not **somebody** or **someone**, in questions and in NEGATIVE sentences: *There was somebody waiting outside.* ▶ *Is there anybody there?* ▶ *There wasn't anybody at home.*

anyhow /'enɪhaʊ/ *adverb*
another word for **anyway**

anyone /'enɪwʌn/ *pronoun*
another word for **anybody**

anything /'enɪθɪŋ/ *pronoun*
1 used in questions and sentences with "not" to mean "something" ▶ *Do you want anything?* ▶ *She didn't want anything else (=any other things) to eat.*

> Use **anything**, not **something**, in questions and in NEGATIVE sentences: *I must get something to drink.* ▶ *Have you got anything to drink?* ▶ *I don't want anything to drink.*

2 it does not matter what thing ▶ *Please tell me if there's anything I can do to help.*

anyway /'enɪweɪ/ *(also **anyhow** /'enɪhaʊ/) adverb*
1 in spite of something else ▶ *The dress cost a lot of money, but I bought it anyway.*
2 used when you are saying something which supports what you have just said ▶ *I don't want to go – anyway, I haven't been invited.*
SAME MEANING (**2**): **besides**

anywhere /'enɪweəʳ/ *adverb*
in, at, or to any place ▶ *I can't find my key anywhere.* ▶ *Have you been anywhere else (=to any other places)?*

apart /ə'pɑːt/ *adverb*
1 separately; away from another, or others ▶ *The two villages are 6 miles apart.*
2 apart from except ▶ *All the children like music, apart from Joseph.*

apartment /ə'pɑːtmənt/ *noun*
a part of a building, on one floor, where someone lives
SAME MEANING: **flat**

apathetic /ˌæpə'θetɪk/ *adjective*
not interested in anything and not willing to make any effort ▶ *People here are too apathetic to organize a strike.*

apathy /'æpəθɪ/ *noun (no plural)*
the feeling of not being interested in anything and being unwilling to make any effort to change things ▶ *public apathy about the coming election*

ape /eɪp/ *noun*
a large animal like a monkey, but with a very short tail or no tail at all

apologetic /əˌpɒlə'dʒetɪk/ *adjective*
saying that you are sorry about something you have done ▶ *He was really apologetic about forgetting my birthday. (adverb: **apologetically**)*

apologize /əˈpɒlədʒaɪz/ *verb*
(present participle **apologizing**, past
apologized)
to say that you are sorry about
something you have done ▶ *He
apologized **for** his bad behaviour.*

apology /əˈpɒlədʒɪ/ *noun* (plural
apologies)
something that you say or write to
show that you are sorry about
something you have done

apostrophe /əˈpɒstrəfɪ/ *noun*
the sign (') used in writing, to show
that letters have been left out, e.g.
"don't" instead of "do not", or with
"s" to show that someone owns
something as in *Karen's book* or
ladies' hats

appal /əˈpɔːl/ *verb* (present participle
appalling, past **appalled**)
if something appals you, it shocks
you because it is so unpleasant ▶ *The
idea of killing animals appals me.*

appalling /əˈpɔːlɪŋ/ *adjective*
very bad ▶ *an appalling accident* ▶ *an
appalling film*

apparatus /ˌæpəˈreɪtəs/ *noun* (no
plural)
tools or other things needed for a
special purpose ▶ *There is sports
apparatus in the gym.*

apparent /əˈpærənt/ *adjective*
clearly able to be seen or understood
▶ *It was apparent that he knew
nothing about how to repair cars.*
SAME MEANING: **obvious**

apparently /əˈpærəntlɪ/ *adverb*
used when you are saying that
something seems to be true
▶ *They've been married for 20 years,
and apparently they're very happy.*

appeal[1] /əˈpiːl/ *verb*
1 to ask for something strongly; to
beg for ▶ *She appealed **to** me **for**
help.*
2 appeal to someone to please or

interest someone ▶ *That type of
holiday doesn't appeal to me.*

appeal[2] *noun*
an act of asking for something ▶ *an
appeal **for** money*

appealing /əˈpiːlɪŋ/ *adjective*
attractive or interesting ▶ *That's an
appealing idea.*

appear /əˈpɪə/ *verb*
1 to seem ▶ *She appears to be
unhappy.*
2 to come into sight suddenly ▶ *Her
head appeared round the door.*
OPPOSITE (**2**): **disappear**

appearance /əˈpɪərəns/ *noun*
1 the sudden arrival or coming into
sight of a person or thing
2 the way a person looks to other
people ▶ *his neat appearance*

appendices /əˈpendɪsiːz/
a plural of **appendix**

appendicitis /əˌpendɪˈsaɪtɪs/ *noun*
(no plural)
an illness in which your appendix
hurts a lot

appendix /əˈpendɪks/ *noun* (plural
appendixes or **appendices** /-dɪsiːz/)
1 a small organ inside your body, near
your stomach
2 a part at the end of a book that has
additional information ▶ *There is a
list of dates in the appendix.*

appetite /ˈæpɪtaɪt/ *noun*
the wish for food ▶ *I lost my appetite
when I was ill.*

applaud /əˈplɔːd/ *verb*
to hit your hands together many
times to show that you liked or
enjoyed something ▶ *Everyone
applauded when the music ended.*
SAME MEANING: **clap**

applause /əˈplɔːz/ *noun* (no plural)
hitting your hands together many
times to show that you liked or
enjoyed something ▶ *the sound of
applause*

A

apple /ˈæpəl/ noun
a round, hard, juicy fruit which is usually red or green

apple pie /ˌæpəl ˈpaɪ/ noun
a type of sweet cake with cooked apples in the middle

appliance /əˈplaɪəns/ noun
an instrument or piece of equipment for doing something useful ▶ kitchen appliances such as washing machines

applicable /əˈplɪkəbəl/ adjective
concerning a particular person or situation ▶ Question 8 on the form is only applicable to married people.

applicant /ˈæplɪkənt/ noun
a person who has formally asked for a job, a place at a college, etc. ▶ We have had an increase in the number of applicants this year.

application /ˌæplɪˈkeɪʃən/ noun
a written paper asking for something ▶ an application for a job

application form /ˌæplɪˈkeɪʃən fɔːm/ noun
a printed piece of paper on which you write the answers to questions about yourself, and why you should get a job, a place at a college, etc. ▶ It took hours to fill in the application form.

apply /əˈplaɪ/ verb (past **applied**)
1 to ask for something ▶ I want to apply **for** the job.
2 to be important or useful to a particular person ▶ The rules apply **to** everyone.
3 to put something on a surface ▶ to apply make-up **to** your face

appoint /əˈpɔɪnt/ verb
to give someone a job ▶ I appointed her as my secretary.

appointment /əˈpɔɪntmənt/ noun
1 a time arranged for seeing someone ▶ I made an appointment to see the doctor.
2 a job

appreciate /əˈpriːʃieɪt/ verb (present participle **appreciating**, past **appreciated**)
to be grateful for something ▶ I appreciate your help.

appreciation /əˌpriːʃiˈeɪʃən/ noun (no plural)
the feeling of being grateful to someone because they have helped you ▶ I gave her some flowers to show my appreciation.

appreciative /əˈpriːʃətɪv/ adjective
showing that you have enjoyed something or feel grateful for it ▶ The audience was very appreciative.

apprehensive /ˌæprɪˈhensɪv/ adjective
worried or nervous about something you have to do in the future ▶ I'm apprehensive **about** taking my driving test.

apprentice /əˈprentɪs/ noun
someone who is learning a job, especially a job you do with your hands

approach¹ /əˈprəʊtʃ/ verb
1 to come near ▶ A man approached me and asked the time.
2 to begin to deal with something ▶ Is this the best way to approach the problem?

approach² noun (plural **approaches**)
1 a way of doing something or dealing with a problem ▶ Mr James had an exciting approach to teaching science.
2 when something comes nearer

approachable /əˈprəʊtʃəbəl/ adjective
friendly and easy to talk to ▶ Dr Grieg seems very approachable.
OPPOSITE: **unapproachable**

appropriate /əˈprəʊprɪət/ adjective
right; suitable (adverb: **appropriately**)
OPPOSITE: **inappropriate**

approval /ə'pruːvəl/ *noun (no plural)*
the judgement or opinion that someone or something is good
OPPOSITE: **disapproval**

approve /ə'pruːv/ *verb (present participle **approving**, past **approved**)*
to think that something is good
► *I don't approve of smoking.*
OPPOSITE: **disapprove**

approx. /ə'proks/
a short way of writing and saying the word **approximately**

approximate /ə'proksɪmət/ *adjective*
not exact ► *Our approximate time of arrival is 2 o'clock* (=it might be just before or just after 2).

approximately /ə'proksɪmətlɪ/ *adverb*
a little more or less than an exact amount, number, time, etc.
► *Approximately a quarter of the students are from Japan.*
SAME MEANING: **roughly**

apricot /'eɪprɪkɒt/ *noun*
a round, soft, yellow fruit

April /'eɪprəl/ *noun*
the fourth month of the year

apron /'eɪprən/ *noun*
a large piece of cloth that you put on top of your other clothes, to keep your clothes clean when you are cooking

aptitude /'æptɪtjuːd/ *noun*
a natural ability to do something well
► *They tested our aptitude for computing.*

aquarium /ə'kweərɪəm/ *noun*
a large, glass box in which live fish are kept

Arabic /'ærəbɪk/ *noun (no plural)*
the language of Arab people, or the religious language of ISLAM

arbitrary /'ɑːbɪtrərɪ/ *adjective*
not based on any practical or good reasons ► *Age limits for films are rather arbitrary.*

arc /ɑːk/ *noun*
a part of a circle, or any curved line

arcade /ɑː'keɪd/ *noun*
1 a building where there are many shops ► *a new shopping arcade*
2 a large room or building where people go to play VIDEO GAMES, etc.

arch /ɑːtʃ/ *noun (plural **arches**)*
a curved shape like the curved part of a bridge

archaeological /ˌɑːkɪə'lɒdʒɪkəl/ *adjective*
of or about archaeology ► *an archaeological dig*

archaeologist /ˌɑːkɪ'ɒlədʒɪst/ *noun*
a person who studies very old things made by people who lived a long time ago

archaeology /ˌɑːkɪ'ɒlədʒɪ/ *noun (no plural)*
the study of very old things made by people who lived a long time ago

archaic /ɑː'keɪ-ɪk/ *adjective*
very old-fashioned ► *the archaic language of Shakespeare*

archbishop /ˌɑːtʃ'bɪʃəp/ *noun*
an important Christian leader; a chief BISHOP

archery /'ɑːtʃərɪ/ *noun (no plural)*
the sport of shooting ARROWS from a BOW

architect /'ɑːkɪtekt/ *noun*
a person whose job is planning and drawing buildings
COMPARE: **builder**

architectural /ˌɑːkɪ'tektʃərəl/ *adjective*
of or about architecture

architecture /'ɑːkɪtektʃər/ *noun (no plural)*
1 the shape and style of buildings
► *modern architecture*
2 the job of planning and drawing buildings ► *He studies architecture.*

A

Arctic /'ɑːktɪk/ *noun*
the Arctic the most northern part of
the world, where it is very cold
COMPARE: **Antarctic**

ardent /'ɑːdənt/ *adjective*
admiring or supporting something
very strongly ▶ *an ardent fan of
Manchester United*

arduous /'ɑːdjuəs/ *adjective*
needing a lot of effort and hard work
▶ *an arduous task*

are /əʳ; *strong* ɑːʳ/ *verb*
the part of the verb **be** that is used
with **we, you** and **they** ▶ *Who are
you?* ▶ *We're* (=we are) *Jane's
friends.* ▶ *They aren't very tall, are
they?*

area /'eərɪə/ *noun*
1 a part of a country, region, or city
▶ *He lives in the Glasgow area* (=near
Glasgow).
2 the measure of a surface ▶ *The
square has an area of 9 square
centimetres.*

area code /'eərɪə ˌkəʊd/ *noun*
the part of a telephone number that
you have to add when you are
telephoning a different town or
country
SAME MEANING: **dialling code**

arena /ə'riːnə/ *noun*
a building with a large, flat area
inside with seats all around it, used
for watching something such as a
sports game ▶ *The concert will be at
Wembley arena.*

aren't /ɑːnt/
1 are not ▶ *Bob and Sue aren't
coming to the party.* ▶ *Aren't you a
clever girl?*
2 used in questions instead of **am not**
▶ *I'm your best friend, aren't I?*

argue /'ɑːgjuː/ *verb (present
participle **arguing**, past **argued**)*
to fight or disagree in words ▶ *They
often argued about money.*

argument /'ɑːgjʊmənt/ *noun*
a disagreement; a quarrel ▶ *They had
an argument.*

argumentative /ˌɑːgjʊ'mentətɪv/
adjective
liking to argue ▶ *Don't be so
argumentative.*

arise /ə'raɪz/ *verb (present participle
arising, past tense **arose** /ə'rəʊz/,
past participle **arisen** /ə'rɪzən/)*
to happen or appear ▶ *A problem has
arisen.*

aristocracy /ˌærɪ'stɒkrəsɪ/ *noun*
the people belonging to the highest
social class in some countries, who
usually have a lot of land, money, and
power

aristocrat /'ærɪstəkræt/ *noun*
a person from an important, old
family

arithmetic /ə'rɪθmətɪk/ *noun (no
plural)*
sums done with numbers, including
addition, division, etc.

arm¹ /ɑːm/ *noun*
the part of your body between your
shoulder and your hand

arm² *verb*
to give someone weapons

armchair /'ɑːmtʃeəʳ/ *noun*
a comfortable chair with places to
rest your arms on

armed /ɑːmd/ *adjective*
carrying a weapon, especially a gun
▶ *an armed robber*
OPPOSITE: **unarmed**

armed forces /ˌɑːmd 'fɔːsɪz/ *plural
noun*
all the soldiers of a country who fight
on land, at sea, or in planes

armour /'ɑːməʳ/ *noun (no plural)*
a covering of metal worn as
protection by soldiers in the past

armoured /'ɑːməd/ *adjective*
protected against bullets or other

A

weapons by a strong layer of metal ► *an armoured car*

armpit /ˈɑːmpɪt/ *noun*
the place under your arm where your arm joins your body

arms /ɑːmz/ *plural noun*
weapons such as guns and bombs

army /ˈɑːmɪ/ *noun (plural* **armies***)*
a large number of soldiers fighting together
COMPARE: **airforce, navy**

aroma /əˈrəʊmə/ *noun*
a strong, pleasant smell ► *the aroma of baking bread*

arose /əˈrəʊz/
the PAST TENSE of the verb **arise**

around /əˈraʊnd/ *(also* **round***)*
preposition, adverb
1 with a movement or shape like a circle ► *We sat around the fire.*
2 on all sides of something ► *a wall around the garden*
3 in or to different places ► *They walked around the town.*
4 not exactly; about ► *at around 10 o'clock*
5 to face another way ► *She walked away, and then turned around and came back.*

arrange /əˈreɪndʒ/ *verb (present participle* **arranging***, past* **arranged***)*
1 to put things in a way which makes them look neat or attractive ► *She arranged the flowers in a vase.*
2 to make plans for something ► *I have arranged a meeting for tomorrow.*

arrangement /əˈreɪndʒmənt/ *noun*
a plan or an agreement that something will happen

arrears /əˈrɪəz/ *plural noun*
be in arrears to owe someone money and not make a payment when you should ► *The family are in arrears with the rent.*

arrest¹ /əˈrest/ *verb*

to make someone a prisoner because they are believed to have done something wrong

arrest² *noun*
an act of arresting someone ► *The police made three arrests yesterday.*

arrival /əˈraɪvəl/ *noun (no plural)*
getting to a place ► *We are sorry for the late arrival of your train.*
OPPOSITE: **departure**

arrive /əˈraɪv/ *verb (present participle* **arriving***, past* **arrived***)*
to get to a place ► *She arrived home very late.* ► *We arrived in London on Tuesday.*

arrogant /ˈærəgənt/ *adjective*
too proud

arrow /ˈærəʊ/ *noun*
1 a sharp stick that is used as a weapon and shot from a BOW
2 a sign which points to where something is

arson /ˈɑːsən/ *noun (no plural)*
the crime of deliberately burning something, especially a building ► *He was accused of arson.*

art /ɑːt/ *noun*
1 *(no plural)* the skill of drawing and painting ► *He's very good at art.*
2 something which you need skill to do ► *the art of cooking*
3 the arts music, writing, painting, films, etc.

artery /ˈɑːtərɪ/ *noun (plural* **arteries***)*
one of the tubes in your body that carry blood from your heart around your body

arthritis /ɑːˈθraɪtɪs/ *noun (no plural)*
a disease that makes your hands, arms, legs, etc. painful and difficult to move

artichoke /ˈɑːtɪtʃəʊk/ *noun*
a green vegetable that looks like a flower

article /ˈɑːtɪkəl/ *noun*
1 a thing ► *articles of clothing*

2 a piece of writing in a newspaper ▶ *an article about ships*

3 the words **a** or **an** (=indefinite article), or **the** (=definite article)

articulate¹ /ɑːˈtɪkjʊlət/ *adjective*
able to express your thoughts and feelings clearly ▶ *He's clever, but not very articulate.*

articulate² /ɑːˈtɪkjʊleɪt/ *verb*
(present participle **articulating**, past **articulated**)
to be able to say what you think or feel ▶ *Some people can find it hard to articulate their feelings.*

artificial /ˌɑːtɪˈfɪʃəl/ *adjective*
not real ▶ *artificial flowers*

artist /ˈɑːtɪst/ *noun*
a person whose job is painting pictures
SAME MEANING: **painter**

artistic /ɑːˈtɪstɪk/ *adjective*
able to make attractive, interesting things, for example by drawing or painting

as /əz; strong æz/ *adverb, preposition, conjunction*
1 when; while ▶ *We sang as we worked.*

2 because ▶ *I can't come as I'm busy.*

3 being a particular thing for a time ▶ *She's working as a teacher for a few months.* ▶ *We can use this box as a table.*

4 as … as (used when comparing things) ▶ *I'm not as old as you.* ▶ *It's just as good as the other one.*

5 as well also ▶ *Can I have some as well?*

a.s.a.p. /ˌeɪ es eɪ ˈpiː/ *adverb*
a short way of writing or saying the words **as soon as possible** ▶ *I will let you know a.s.a.p.*

ascend /əˈsend/ *verb*
to move up or towards the top of something ▶ *The plane ascended rapidly.*
OPPOSITE: **descend**

ascent /əˈsent/ *noun*
the activity of moving up or climbing to the top of something ▶ *a successful ascent of Mount Everest*
OPPOSITE: **descent (1)**

ash /æʃ/ *noun (plural **ashes**)*
the grey powder that is left after something has burned

ashamed /əˈʃeɪmd/ *adjective*
feeling bad about something you have done wrong ▶ *She was very ashamed that she had stolen the money.*
LOOK AT: **embarrassed**

ashore /əˈʃɔːʳ/ *adverb*
onto the land ▶ *Pull the boat ashore!*

ashtray /ˈæʃtreɪ/ *noun*
a small dish in which you put the ash from cigarettes

aside /əˈsaɪd/ *adverb*
to or towards one side; away

ask /ɑːsk/ *verb*
1 to say something that is a question ▶ *"Who are you?" she asked.*

2 to try to get something from someone ▶ *They asked me the time.* ▶ *She asked me **for** some money.*

3 ask someone to something to invite someone to a place or an event

asleep /əˈsliːp/ *adjective*
1 sleeping
OPPOSITE: **awake**

2 fast asleep sleeping deeply

asparagus /əˈspærəgəs/ *noun (no plural)*
a long, thin, green plant which is eaten as a vegetable

aspect /ˈæspekt/ *noun*
a particular part of a situation ▶ *One of the most serious aspects of the problem is the lack of money.*

asphyxiate /æsˈfɪksieɪt/ *verb*
(present participle **asphyxiating**, past **asphyxiated**)
to stop someone breathing, often causing them to die ▶ *The thick*

smoke asphyxiated three children in an upstairs bedroom.

aspirin /'æsprɪn/ *noun*
a medicine taken to make a pain in your body go away

ass /æs/ *noun (plural asses)*
an animal like a small horse, with long ears

assailant /ə'seɪlənt/ *noun*
a person who attacks another person ➤ *He did not know his assailant.*

assassin /ə'sæsɪn/ *noun*
someone who kills an important person for political reasons

assassinate /ə'sæsɪneɪt/ *verb (present participle assassinating, past assassinated)*
to kill an important person for political reasons
COMPARE: **murder**

assassination /ə,sæsɪ'neɪʃən/ *noun*
the killing of an important person for political reasons ➤ *the assassination of President Kennedy*

assault¹ /ə'sɔːlt/ *verb*
to attack or hit someone

assault² *noun*
an attack

assemble /ə'sembəl/ *verb (present participle assembling, past assembled)*
to gather together in a group

assembly /ə'semblɪ/ *noun (plural assemblies)*
a group of people gathered together for a special purpose or meeting

assert /ə'sɜːt/ *verb*
1 **assert your rights/authority** to say strongly that you have rights or authority ➤ *My father decided to assert his authority by refusing to let me go out.*
2 **assert yourself** to say what you think, or ask for what you want, in a confident and determined way

assertive /ə'sɜːtɪv/ *adjective*
behaving in a confident and determined way ➤ *You must be more assertive if you want people to listen to you.*

assess /ə'ses/ *verb*
to examine something and make a decision about it ➤ *First we must assess the cost of repairing the damage.*

asset /'æset/ *noun*
a person or thing that helps you to succeed ➤ *Tom is a real asset to the team.*

assignment /ə'saɪnmənt/ *noun*
a piece of work that someone gives you to do ➤ *a homework assignment*

assist /ə'sɪst/ *verb*
to help someone
SAME MEANING: **aid**

assistance /ə'sɪstəns/ *noun (no plural)*
help

assistant /ə'sɪstənt/ *noun*
a person who helps someone in their job

associate /ə'səʊʃɪeɪt/ *verb (present participle associating, past associated)*
1 to connect two things or ideas in your mind
2 to spend time with someone or be connected with them ➤ *I don't wish to associate with him.*

association /ə,səʊsɪ'eɪʃən/ *noun*
a group of people joined together for one purpose

assortment /ə'sɔːtmənt/ *noun*
a mixture of various different types of thing ➤ *an assortment of chocolates*

assume /ə'sjuːm/ *verb (present participle assuming, past assumed)*
to think that something is true even though no one has said so ➤ *I assumed she was his mother, but in fact she's his aunt.*

assumption /əˈsʌmpʃən/ *noun*
something that you think is true although you have no proof ▶ *We made the assumption that people would come by car.* ▶ *We're working on the assumption that prices will continue to rise.*

assurance /əˈʃʊərəns/ *noun*
a definite statement or promise ▶ *Can you give me an assurance that the plane is safe?*

assure /əˈʃɔːʳ/ *verb (present participle assuring, past assured)*
to tell someone that something is true

asterisk /ˈæstərɪsk/ *noun*
the sign *

asthma /ˈæsmə/ *noun (no plural)*
an illness that makes it difficult for you to breathe ▶ *Both sisters suffer from asthma.*

astonish /əˈstɒnɪʃ/ *verb*
to surprise someone very much

astonished /əˈstɒnɪʃt/ *adjective*
very surprised ▶ *I was astonished at how easy it was.*

astonishing /əˈstɒnɪʃɪŋ/ *adjective*
very surprising ▶ *an astonishing £50,000 profit (adverb: astonishingly)*

astonishment /əˈstɒnɪʃmənt/ *noun (no plural)*
great surprise

astound /əˈstaʊnd/ *verb*
to shock and surprise someone very much

astounding /əˈstaʊndɪŋ/ *adjective*
very surprising and shocking ▶ *The news was astounding.*

astray /əˈstreɪ/ *adverb*
1 go astray to become lost ▶ *My letter went astray in the post.*
2 lead someone astray to encourage someone to do bad things ▶ *Don't let the older girls lead you astray.*

astride /əˈstraɪd/ *adverb, preposition*
with one leg on either side of something ▶ *He was sitting astride his horse.*

astrologer /əˈstrɒlədʒəʳ/ *noun*
a person who studies the PLANETS and stars, believing that they can influence people's characters and change what happens in their lives

astrology /əˈstrɒlədʒɪ/ *noun (no plural)*
the study of the PLANETS and stars, in the belief that they can influence people's characters and change what happens in their lives

astronaut /ˈæstrənɔːt/ *noun*
a person who travels in space

astronomer /əˈstrɒnəməʳ/ *noun*
a person who studies the sun, moon, and stars

astronomy /əˈstrɒnəmɪ/ *noun (no plural)*
the study of the sun, moon, and stars

astute /əˈstjuːt/ *adjective*
clever and quick to understand how to gain advantage from a situation ▶ *an astute politician*

at /ət; *strong* æt/ *preposition*
1 in a particular place ▶ *He left his bag at the station.* ▶ *She is at work.*
2 at a particular time ▶ *It gets cold at night.* ▶ *at one o'clock*
3 towards someone or something ▶ *Look at me!*
4 used to show how much, how old, or how fast ▶ *He got married at 21.* ▶ *driving at 90 miles an hour* ▶ *at a cost of £9.50*

ate /et, eɪt/
the PAST TENSE of the verb **eat**

atheist /ˈeɪθɪ-ɪst/ *noun*
a person who does not believe in God

athlete /ˈæθliːt/ *noun*
someone who is good at sports in which they have to run, jump, or throw things

A

athletic /æθ'letɪk/ *adjective*
physically strong and good at sport

athletics /æθ'letɪks/ *noun (no plural)*
a general name for sports in which people run, jump, or throw things to see who is the best

atlas /'ætləs/ *noun (plural atlases)*
a book of maps

ATM /ˌeɪ tiː 'em/ *noun*
an AUTOMATED TELLER MACHINE; a machine in the wall outside a bank where the customers of the bank can get money
SAME MEANING: **cash dispenser, cashpoint**

atmosphere /'ætməsfɪəʳ/ *noun (no plural)*
1 the air surrounding the Earth
2 a feeling that a place or group of people gives you ▶ *the exciting atmosphere of a football match*

atom /'ætəm/ *noun*
the smallest part of a chemical

atomic /ə'tɒmɪk/ *adjective*
1 of or about atoms ▶ *atomic structure*
2 using the power that is produced by splitting atoms ▶ *atomic weapons*

atomic energy /əˌtɒmɪk 'enədʒɪ/ *noun (no plural)*
power from the forces in an atom, used to make electricity

atrocious /ə'trəʊʃəs/ *adjective*
very bad ▶ *Your spelling is atrocious!* (adverb: **atrociously**)

atrocity /ə'trɒsətɪ/ *noun (plural atrocities)*
a very cruel and violent action
▶ *Both sides in the war committed atrocities.*

attach /ə'tætʃ/ *verb*
to fix something to something else

attached /ə'tætʃt/ *adjective*
be attached to to like someone or something very much ▶ *I was quite attached to that old car.*

attachment /ə'tætʃmənt/ *noun*
1 a strong feeling of liking or loving someone or something ▶ *He had a close attachment to his family.*
2 a document or FILE that you send with an E-MAIL

attack¹ /ə'tæk/ *verb*
to fight against someone or harm them ▶ *The newspaper attacked* (=wrote things against) *the new tax.*
COMPARE: **defend**

attack² *noun*
a violent act to try to harm someone
▶ *an attack on the soldiers*

attacker /ə'tækəʳ/ *noun*
a person who physically attacks another person ▶ *Her attacker ran off.*

attempt¹ /ə'tempt/ *verb*
to try to do something

attempt² *noun*
an act of trying ▶ *She made an attempt to speak their language.*

attend /ə'tend/ *verb*
to be present at an event ▶ *to attend a meeting*

attendance /ə'tendəns/ *noun (no plural)*
being present ▶ *His attendance at school is bad* (=he does not go often enough).

attendant /ə'tendənt/ *noun*
a person whose job is to look after a place or person

attention /ə'tenʃən/ *noun (no plural)*
1 looking at and listening to someone or something ▶ *May I have your attention* (=will you listen to me, please)?
2 **attract someone's attention** to make someone notice you
3 **pay attention to someone** to listen to someone very carefully

attentive /ə'tentɪv/ *adjective*
listening or watching carefully
▶ *The students were very attentive.* (adverb: **attentively**)

A

attic /'ætɪk/ *noun*
a room at the top of a house, inside the roof, often used for storing things
SAME MEANING: **loft**

attitude /'ætɪtjuːd/ *noun*
the way you think or feel about something ▶ her attitude **towards** her job

attract /ə'trækt/ *verb*
1 to make someone or something come near ▶ Many people visited the sea, attracted by the fine weather.
2 to cause interest and admiration ▶ It was his sense of humour that first attracted me **to** him.

attraction /ə'trækʃən/ *noun*
1 something that people like to see or do because it is interesting or enjoyable ▶ Buckingham Palace is one of London's most popular tourist attractions.
2 *(no plural)* the feelings you have for someone when you are interested in them in a sexual way ▶ There was a strong physical attraction between us.

attractive /ə'træktɪv/ *adjective*
pleasing, especially to look at
OPPOSITE: **unattractive**

aubergine /'əʊbəʒiːn/ *noun*
a large vegetable with a dark purple skin

auburn /'ɔːbən/ *noun, adjective*
a reddish-brown colour

auction /'ɔːkʃən/ *noun*
a meeting where things are sold to the person who offers the most money

audible /'ɔːdɪbəl/ *adjective*
loud enough to be heard ▶ His words were clearly audible.

audience /'ɔːdɪəns/ *noun*
all the people watching a play, listening to music, etc.

audio /'ɔːdɪəʊ/ *adjective*
for recording and broadcasting sounds ▶ an audio tape ▶ an audio signal

audiovisual /ˌɔːdɪəʊ'vɪʒʊəl/ *adjective*
having recorded pictures and sound
▶ audiovisual equipment for language teaching

audition /ɔː'dɪʃən/ *noun*
a short performance by an actor or a singer to test whether they are good enough to be in a play or concert ▶ I have an audition for a part in "Annie" tomorrow.

auditorium /ˌɔːdɪ'tɔːrɪəm/ *noun*
the part of a theatre where people sit to watch a performance

August /'ɔːgəst/ *noun*
the eighth month of the year

aunt /ɑːnt/ *noun*
the sister of one of your parents, or the wife of your uncle

au pair /əʊ 'peəʳ/ *noun*
a young woman who stays with a family in a foreign country and looks after their children ▶ I worked for a year as an au pair.

aural /'ɔːrəl/ *adjective*
connected with hearing and listening
▶ aural skills

austere /ɔː'stɪəʳ/ *adjective*
plain and simple ▶ The room was very austere.

austerity /ɔː'sterɪtɪ/ *noun (no plural)*
bad economic conditions in which people do not have enough money to live ▶ the austerity of the post-war years

authentic /ɔː'θentɪk/ *adjective*
not copying or pretending to be something else ▶ The restaurant serves authentic Chinese food. ▶ Is it an authentic Van Gogh painting?

author /'ɔːθəʳ/ *noun*
a person who has written a book

authoritarian /ɔːˌθɒrɪ'teərɪən/ *adjective*
forcing people to obey strict rules or laws and not allowing them any freedom ▶ an authoritarian regime

authority /ɔːˈθɒrətɪ/ *noun*
1 *(no plural)* the power to make people do what you want ➤ *The teacher has authority to punish any pupil.*
2 *(plural* **authorities***)* a person or group in control of or governing something

authorize /ˈɔːθəraɪz/ *verb (present participle* **authorizing***, past* **authorized***)*
to give someone official permission to do something ➤ *You can't go in unless I authorize it.*

autobiography /ˌɔːtəbaɪˈɒɡrəfɪ/ *noun (plural* **autobiographies***)*
a book that someone has written telling the story of their own life
COMPARE: **biography**

autograph /ˈɔːtəɡrɑːf/ *noun*
a famous person's name, written by them
COMPARE: **signature**

automatic /ˌɔːtəˈmætɪk/ *adjective*
working by itself ➤ *automatic doors* (=doors which open and close without being touched)

autopsy /ˈɔːtɒpsɪ/ *noun (plural* **autopsies***)*
an official examination of a dead body to discover why the person died ➤ *Doctors performed an autopsy on the body.*

autumn /ˈɔːtəm/ *noun, adjective*
the season before winter in cool countries, when the leaves fall off the trees

auxiliary /ɔːɡˈzɪljərɪ/ *adjective*
giving additional help or support to others ➤ *auxiliary nurses*

auxiliary verb /ɔːɡˌzɪljərɪ ˈvɜːb/ *noun*
a verb used with another verb to make questions, NEGATIVE sentences, and tenses. In English, the auxiliary verbs are "be", "do", and "have".
COMPARE: **modal verb**

availability /əˌveɪləˈbɪlətɪ/ *noun (no plural)*
the possibility of being able to get, buy, or use something ➤ *I rang to ask about the availability of tickets.*

available /əˈveɪləbəl/ *adjective*
able to be seen, used, bought, etc.
➤ *Is the doctor available?*
OPPOSITE: **unavailable**

avalanche /ˈævəlɑːntʃ/ *noun*
a large amount of snow or a lot of rocks falling down a mountain

avenue /ˈævənjuː/ *noun*
a road in a town, especially one with trees on both sides
COMPARE: **street**

average¹ /ˈævərɪdʒ/ *adjective*
1 usual; ordinary ➤ *The average child enjoys listening to stories.*
2 got by adding several amounts together, and then dividing the total by the number of amounts you have added ➤ *The average age of the children is 12.* ➤ *What is the average rainfall in this area?*

average² *noun*
the amount you get by adding several numbers together, and then dividing the total by the number of amounts. For example, the average of 3, 5, and 7 is 5

avert /əˈvɜːt/ *verb*
to stop something unpleasant from happening ➤ *How can we avert the crisis?*

aviation /ˌeɪvɪˈeɪʃən/ *noun (no plural)*
the activity of flying or making planes
➤ *an expert in aviation*

avid /ˈævɪd/ *adjective*
liking and doing something a lot
➤ *Doug's an avid fan of American football.*

avocado /ˌævəˈkɑːdəʊ/ *noun*
a green, PEAR-shaped fruit with a large stone in the middle and a skin which you cannot eat

avoid /əˈvɔɪd/ *verb*
to keep away from a person, place, or thing ▶ *Are you trying to avoid me?*

await /əˈweɪt/ *verb*
to wait for someone or something

awake /əˈweɪk/ *adjective*
not sleeping ▶ *The baby is awake.*
OPPOSITE: **asleep**

award[1] /əˈwɔːd/ *noun*
a prize or an amount of money, given for a special reason ▶ *an award* **for** *bravery*

award[2] *verb*
to give someone a prize or an amount of money for a special reason

aware /əˈweəʳ/ *adjective*
knowing about something ▶ *I was not aware of the problem.*
OPPOSITE: **unaware**

awash /əˈwɒʃ/ *adjective*
covered with water ▶ *The streets were awash* **with** *flood water.*

away /əˈweɪ/ *adverb*
1 to another place ▶ *Go away!* ▶ *He turned round and walked away.*
2 distant from a place ▶ *Do you live far away?* ▶ *The nearest town is 3 miles away.*
3 not at home or at work ▶ *I'll be away for a few days.*
4 put something away to put something in a safe place

awe /ɔː/ *noun (no plural)*
a feeling of great admiration and sometimes fear ▶ *She gazed with awe at the breathtaking landscape.* ▶ *He was slightly in awe of his boss.*

awesome /ˈɔːsəm/ *adjective*
very impressive, often in a way that is frightening ▶ *an awesome task*

awful /ˈɔːfəl/ *adjective*
1 very bad or frightening ▶ *an awful accident*
2 not pleasing; not liked ▶ *That's an awful book.*
SAME MEANING (**1** and **2**): **dreadful, terrible**

awfully /ˈɔːfəli/ *adverb*
very ▶ *She's awfully clever.*
SAME MEANING: **terribly**

awkward /ˈɔːkwəd/ *adjective*
1 not skilful in handling things; not moving in an easy way ▶ *He's very awkward – he keeps dropping things.*
2 not easy to handle ▶ *The cup is an awkward shape.*
3 making you feel uncomfortable ▶ *There was an awkward silence, when no one knew what to say.*

awoke /əˈwəʊk/
the PAST TENSE of the verb **awake**

awoken /əˈwəʊkən/
the PAST PARTICIPLE of the verb **awake**

axe /æks/ *noun*
a tool with a metal blade fixed onto a handle, used for cutting down trees

axis /ˈæksɪs/ *noun (plural axes /ˈæksiːz/)*
a line at the side or bottom of a GRAPH, where you write the measurements

axle /ˈæksəl/ *noun*
the bar that connects two wheels on a vehicle

Bb

BA /ˌbiː ˈeɪ/ *noun*
BACHELOR OF ARTS; a university degree in a subject such as history or literature ▶ *She has a BA in French.*

baby /ˈbeɪbɪ/ *noun (plural babies)*
a very young child

babyish /ˈbeɪbɪ-ɪʃ/ *adjective*
like a baby ▶ *Don't be so babyish!*

babysit /ˈbeɪbɪsɪt/ *verb (present participle babysitting, past babysat /ˈbeɪbɪsæt/)*
to care for a child while his or her parents are away

babysitter /'beɪbɪˌsɪtəʳ/ *noun*
a person who is paid to care for a child when the child's parents are away

bachelor /'bætʃələʳ/ *noun*
a man who is not married and has never been married
COMPARE: **spinster**

back¹ /bæk/ *noun*
1 the part of your body that is behind you and goes from your neck to your legs ▶ *I lay on my back.* ▶ *Her back aches.*
2 the part that is furthest from the front ▶ *Write this exercise at the back of your book.* ▶ *There's a hut at the back of* (=behind) *the house.*
OPPOSITE (**1** and **2**): **front**
3 back to front with the back where the front should be ▶ *You're wearing your hat back to front.*
4 behind someone's back without someone knowing ▶ *You shouldn't talk about people behind their backs.*
5 turn your back on someone to refuse to help or be friendly with someone ▶ *Now that he's famous, he's turned his back on his friends.*

back² *adverb*
1 in the direction that is behind you; away from the front ▶ *Stand back from the fire; it's very hot.*
2 to a place where something or someone was before ▶ *Put the book back on the shelf when you've finished it.* ▶ *When do you come back from your holiday?*
3 in reply ▶ *I wrote to her, and she wrote back to me the next day.*

back³ *adjective*
at the back ▶ *the back seat of a car*
OPPOSITE: **front**

back⁴ *verb*
1 to make a vehicle move in the direction that is behind you ▶ *She backed the car into the street.*
2 back away from someone or

something to move away from someone or something because you are afraid of them
3 back someone up to support someone by agreeing that what they are saying is true

backache /'bækeɪk/ *noun* (no plural)
pain in your back ▶ *I've got terrible backache.*

backbone /'bækbəʊn/ *noun*
the line of bones going from your neck to your bottom
SAME MEANING: **spine**

backfire /ˌbæk'faɪəʳ/ *verb* (present participle **backfiring**, past **backfired**)
to have the opposite result to the one you wanted ▶ *The plan backfired when I realized I didn't have enough money.*

background /'bækgraʊnd/ *noun*
the area that is behind the main objects or people in a picture ▶ *This is a photo of Mary, with our house in the background.*

backing /'bækɪŋ/ *noun* (no plural)
money or support that a person or an organization gives you in order to help you achieve something ▶ *The government gives financial backing to many small businesses.*

backlog /'bæklɒg/ *noun*
work that still needs to be done and should have been done earlier ▶ *a huge backlog of orders*

backpack /'bækpæk/ *noun*
a bag that you carry on your back
SAME MEANING: **rucksack**

backpacking /'bækˌpækɪŋ/ *noun* (no plural)
an occasion when you go walking and camping, carrying a backpack ▶ *We're going backpacking in Nepal.*

backside /'bæksaɪd/ *noun*
the part of your body that you sit on

backstage /ˌbæk'steɪdʒ/ *adverb, adjective*

in the area behind the stage in a theatre ▶ *We're hoping to go backstage and talk to the actors.*

backstroke /ˈbækstrəʊk/ *noun (no plural)*
a way of swimming which you do lying on your back in the water ▶ *Can you do backstroke?*

back-to-back /ˌbæk tə ˈbæk/ *adjective, adverb*
with the backs of two people or things facing each other ▶ *Stand back-to-back and we'll see who's tallest.*

backup /ˈbækʌp/ *noun*
a copy of a document, especially a computer FILE, that you can use if you lose or damage the original one ▶ *Do you have a backup of this file?*

backward /ˈbækwəd/ *adjective*
1 in the direction that is behind you ▶ *a backward movement*
OPPOSITE: **forward**
2 slow to learn things

backwards /ˈbækwədz/ *adverb*
1 in the direction that is behind you ▶ *The train is going backwards.*
2 starting at the end; in the opposite way to the usual way. For example, if you count backwards from 5, you say 5, 4, 3, 2, 1.
OPPOSITE (**1** and **2**): **forwards**
3 backwards and forwards moving many times, first in one direction and then in the opposite direction ▶ *He travels backwards and forwards between London and New York.*

backyard /ˌbækˈjɑːd/ *noun*
a small area of land behind a house and belonging to it

bacon /ˈbeɪkən/ *noun (no plural)*
meat from the back or sides of a pig, that is prepared in salt, cooked, and eaten hot
COMPARE: **ham**

bacteria /bækˈtɪərɪə/ *plural noun*
living things which are so small that you cannot see them, but which live in dirt and old food and can make people ill

bad /bæd/ *adjective* (**worse** /wɜːs/, **worst** /wɜːst/)
1 not good or nice ▶ *bad news* ▶ *bad behaviour* ▶ *a bad smell*
2 not able to do something well ▶ *I'm really bad at maths.* ▶ *a bad doctor*
OPPOSITE (**1** and **2**): **good**
3 serious or severe ▶ *He's got a very bad cold.*
4 very old and no longer good to eat ▶ *That meat is bad, so don't eat it.*
5 go bad to become old and not good to eat ▶ *This meat has gone bad.*
6 be bad for someone to cause harm to someone ▶ *Smoking is bad for you.*
7 not bad quite good

badge /bædʒ/ *noun*
something that you wear on your clothes to show your name, your job, the name of your school, etc.
COMPARE: **brooch**

badger /ˈbædʒəʳ/ *noun*
a wild animal with black and white fur, that lives in a hole and comes out at night

badly /ˈbædlɪ/ *adverb*
1 not well; not nicely ▶ *She sang very badly.*
OPPOSITE: **well**
2 very much ▶ *to want something badly*
3 severely ▶ *badly hurt*

badminton /ˈbædmɪntən/ *noun (no plural)*
a game like tennis, in which you hit a special type of very light ball with feathers on it

bad-tempered /ˌbæd ˈtempəd/ *adjective*
becoming angry very easily
▶ *You're very bad-tempered today.*
▶ *a bad-tempered man*

baffle /'bæfəl/ verb (present participle **baffling**, past **baffled**)
to cause someone to be unable to understand something ▶ I was completely baffled by his explanation.

bag /bæg/ noun
a container made of cloth, paper, plastic, or leather which opens at the top and which you use for carrying things ▶ a bag of shopping

bagel /'beɪgəl/ noun
a type of bread in the shape of a ring

baggage /'bægɪdʒ/ noun (no plural)
all the bags that you take with you when you travel
SAME MEANING: **luggage**

baggy /'bægɪ/ adjective (**baggier**, **baggiest**)
(used about clothes) very loose ▶ baggy trousers

bail¹ /beɪl/ noun (no plural)
money that you pay to a court so that a prisoner does not have to stay in prison before the TRIAL starts ▶ They released him on £10,000 bail this morning.

bail² verb
bail someone out to help someone who is in trouble, especially by giving them money ▶ She asked her dad to bail her out.

bait /beɪt/ noun (no plural)
food that you use to attract fish or animals so that you can catch them

bake /beɪk/ verb (present participle **baking**, past **baked**)
to cook something using dry heat in a closed box called an OVEN ▶ I'm baking a cake.
COMPARE: **roast**

baked beans /ˌbeɪkt 'biːnz/ plural noun
round, white beans cooked with TOMATOES and sold in tins

baker /'beɪkər/ noun
1 a person whose job is making bread and cakes
2 baker's a shop that sells bread and cakes ▶ I'm going to the baker's to get some bread.

bakery /'beɪkəri/ noun (plural **bakeries**)
a building where bread and cakes are baked for selling

balance¹ /'bæləns/ verb (present participle **balancing**, past **balanced**)
to keep yourself or something else steady, especially in a difficult position ▶ to balance a book on your head

balance² noun (no plural)
1 the ability to stay steady without falling to one side or the other ▶ My balance isn't very good so I can't ride a bicycle.
2 keep your balance to stay steady without falling to one side or the other
3 lose your balance to fall when you are trying to remain steady in a difficult position ▶ I lost my balance and fell when I was walking on the ice.

balanced /'bælənst/ adjective
1 giving equal and fair attention to all sides ▶ He has a very balanced attitude to the situation.
2 including a good mixture of all the things that are needed ▶ a balanced diet

balcony /'bælkəni/ noun (plural **balconies**)
1 a place above the ground on the outside of a building, where people can sit ▶ Our flat has a large balcony.
2 the upstairs part of a theatre or cinema where people sit ▶ We had seats in the balcony.

bald /bɔːld/ adjective
with no hair on the head ▶ a bald old man

B

B

bale /beɪl/ *noun*
a large quantity of goods or material tied tightly together ► *a bale of hay*

ball /bɔːl/ *noun*
1 a round object that you use in some games for throwing or kicking
2 a thing with a round shape ► *a ball of wool*
3 a large, important party at which people dance ► *The queen attended a ball.*

ballad /ˈbæləd/ *noun*
a song that tells a story, especially about love

ballerina /ˌbæləˈriːnə/ *noun*
a female ballet dancer

ballet /ˈbæleɪ/ *noun*
a kind of dance in which the dancers sometimes stand on the ends of their toes and move to music in a way that tells a story

balloon /bəˈluːn/ *noun*
a rubber bag that can be filled with air or gas so that it floats in the air

ballot¹ /ˈbælət/ *noun*
a system of voting, especially in secret

ballot² *verb*
to find out what people think by letting them vote, especially in secret ► *All members will be balloted before any action is taken.*

ballpark /ˈbɔːlpɑːk/ *adjective*
(used about numbers, amounts, etc.) not exactly correct but close enough ► *a ballpark figure of, say, £2 million.*

ballpoint /ˈbɔːlpɔɪnt/ *(also **ballpoint pen** /ˌbɔːlpɔɪnt ˈpen/) noun*
a pen full of ink, with a very small, metal ball at the end you write with
SAME MEANING: **Biro**

ballroom /ˈbɔːlrʊm/ *noun*
a large room where formal dances take place

bamboo /bæmˈbuː/ *noun (no plural)*
a tall, hard grass that is like wood

and is sometimes used for making furniture

ban¹ /bæn/ *verb (present participle **banning**, past **banned**)*
to make a rule or law saying that something is not allowed ► *Smoking is banned in school.*
COMPARE: **forbid, prohibit**

ban² *noun*
an order which says you must not do a particular thing ► *There is a ban on smoking.*

banal /bəˈnɑːl/ *adjective*
ordinary and not interesting ► *a banal conversation*

banana /bəˈnɑːnə/ *noun*
a long fruit with a yellow skin

band /bænd/ *noun*
1 a narrow piece of material used for holding things together ► *Put a rubber band around these books.*
2 a group of people who are together for some purpose ► *a band of thieves*
3 a group of people who play music together

bandage¹ /ˈbændɪdʒ/ *noun*
a long piece of cloth that is tied on to your body to cover a wound
COMPARE: **plaster**

bandage² *verb (present participle **bandaging**, past **bandaged**)*
to tie a bandage on a part of someone's body

bandit /ˈbændɪt/ *noun*
a robber with a gun who is part of a group and attacks travellers in quiet country places

bang¹ /bæŋ/ *noun*
1 a loud noise like the noise made by a gun
2 a blow ► *a bang on the head*

bang² *verb*
1 to hit something ► *He fell and banged his head.* ► *to bang a drum*
2 to shut something with a loud noise ► *Don't bang the door!*

bangle /ˈbæŋɡəl/ *noun*
a piece of jewellery worn around a woman's arm or ankle

banish /ˈbænɪʃ/ *verb*
to send someone away from their own country as a punishment

banister /ˈbænɪstəʳ/ *noun*
a type of fence along the outer edge of stairs to prevent people falling

banjo /ˈbændʒəʊ/ *noun*
a musical instrument with four or more strings and a round body

bank¹ /bæŋk/ *noun*
1 an organization which looks after people's money for them by keeping it safe, and which sometimes lends people money
2 the raised land along the side of a lake or river

bank² *verb*
1 to put or keep money in a bank ▶ *to bank your wages*
2 bank on someone or something to depend on someone or something ▶ *You can never bank on her to help you.*

bank account /ˈbæŋk əˌkaʊnt/ *noun*
an arrangement you make to leave your money in a bank until you need it ▶ *How much money do you have in your bank account?* ▶ *to open a bank account*

banker /ˈbæŋkəʳ/ *noun*
a person who owns or controls a bank

bank holiday /ˌbæŋk ˈhɒlɪdeɪ, -dɪ/ *noun*
a special day which is not a Saturday or Sunday, when everyone has a holiday and all the banks and most of the shops are shut

banking /ˈbæŋkɪŋ/ *noun (no plural)*
the business done by a bank

bank note /ˈbæŋk nəʊt/ *noun*
a piece of paper money
COMPARE: **coin**

bankrupt /ˈbæŋkrʌpt/ *adjective*
not able to pay the money owed to people

bankruptcy /ˈbæŋkrʌptsɪ/ *noun (plural **bankruptcies**)*
a situation in which a company or person is not able to pay the money owed to people ▶ *A series of business failures led to bankruptcy.*

banner /ˈbænəʳ/ *noun*
a long piece of cloth with writing on it, that is usually carried by people ▶ *crowds waving banners that read "Welcome Home"*

banquet /ˈbæŋkwɪt/ *noun*
a special, important meal where there are a lot of people

baptism /ˈbæptɪzəm/ *noun*
the ceremony in which someone, usually a baby, becomes a member of the Christian church

baptize /bæpˈtaɪz/ *verb (present participle **baptizing**, past **baptized**)*
to make someone a member of the Christian church by performing a special ceremony

bar¹ /bɑːʳ/ *noun*
1 a place where people go to buy and drink alcohol
2 a solid piece of something, longer than it is wide ▶ *a bar of soap* ▶ *a bar of chocolate*
3 a long piece of wood or metal for keeping a door, etc. shut or for preventing people from entering or leaving a room ▶ *a window with bars across it*
4 behind bars in PRISON

bar² *verb (present participle **barring**, past **barred**)*
1 to close something firmly with a long piece of wood or metal ▶ *She barred the door.*
2 to block something ▶ *The soldiers barred the road to the city.*

B

barbaric /bɑːˈbærɪk/ *adjective*
violent and cruel ▶ *This was a barbaric crime.*

barbecue /ˈbɑːbɪkjuː/ *noun*
1 a meal that is cooked outside on a type of fire and usually eaten outside
COMPARE: **picnic**
2 a type of fire for cooking food outside

barbed wire /ˌbɑːbd ˈwaɪərˈ/ *noun (no plural)*
wire with short, sharp points in it ▶ *a barbed wire fence*

barber /ˈbɑːbərˈ/ *noun*
1 a person whose job is to cut men's hair
COMPARE: **hairdresser**
2 **barber's** a shop where men can go to have their hair cut ▶ *to go to the barber's*

bar code /ˈbɑː kəʊd/ *noun*
a row of black lines printed on products sold in a shop, that a computer reads when you buy the product

bare /beərˈ/ *adjective*
1 not covered by anything ▶ *bare feet* (=without shoes and socks)
2 empty ▶ *a bare room* (=with no furniture)

barefoot /ˌbeəˈfʊt/ *adjective, adverb*
not wearing any shoes or socks ▶ *to walk barefoot*

barely /ˈbeəlɪ/ *adverb*
just; almost not ▶ *He had barely enough money to buy food.*
SAME MEANING: **hardly**

bargain¹ /ˈbɑːgɪn/ *verb*
to talk or argue about the price of something that you are buying or selling

bargain² *noun*
1 something which you can buy for a little money but is worth more ▶ *These shoes are a bargain at only £10.*
2 an agreement in which two people or groups each promise to do something ▶ *to make a bargain with someone*

barge /bɑːdʒ/ *noun*
a large boat with a flat bottom, used for carrying things such as coal on rivers

bark¹ /bɑːk/ *verb*
to make the sound made by a dog

bark² *noun*
1 (no plural) the strong, hard skin that covers the outside of a tree
2 the sound a dog makes

barley /ˈbɑːlɪ/ *noun (no plural)*
a type of grass that is grown on farms and is used for making beer

barmaid /ˈbɑːmeɪd/ *noun*
a woman whose job is to serve drinks in a BAR or PUB

barman /ˈbɑːmən/ *noun (plural barmen /-mən/)*
a man whose job is to serve drinks in a BAR or PUB

barn /bɑːn/ *noun*
a large building on a farm, used as a place for keeping animals and crops

barometer /bəˈrɒmɪtərˈ/ *noun*
an instrument that tells you if the weather is going to change

barracks /ˈbærəks/ *plural noun*
a building that soldiers live in

barrage /ˈbærɑːʒ/ *noun*
a lot of complaints, questions, sounds, etc. that happen very quickly after each other ▶ *We faced a barrage of criticism after announcing the winner.*

barrel /ˈbærəl/ *noun*
1 a large, round container with flat ends, used for keeping liquids such as oil and beer
2 the part of a gun that is like a tube

barren /ˈbærən/ *adjective*
(used about land, earth, etc.) not able to grow plants and seeds very well ▶ *a barren desert*

barricade¹ /ˈbærɪkeɪd/ *noun*
something that is temporarily built across a road, door, etc. to prevent people from going through

barricade² *verb (present participle barricading, past barricaded)*
to put something across a road, door, etc. to prevent people from going through ▸ *The kids had barricaded themselves into their bedroom.*

barrier /ˈbæriəʳ/ *noun*
a fence or wall ▸ *The police put a barrier across the road.*

barrow /ˈbærəʊ/ *noun*
a small cart that you pull or push by hand and use for carrying things

barter /ˈbɑːtəʳ/ *verb*
to pay for goods or services by giving other goods or services instead of using money ▸ *They bartered food for coal.*

base¹ /beɪs/ *noun*
1 the bottom of something; the part something stands on ▸ *Stand the bottle on its base.*
2 the place where something is controlled from ▸ *The company has offices all over the world, but their base is in London.*

base² *verb (present participle basing, past based)*
1 be based somewhere to have your main home, office, etc. in a place ▸ *We're based in the city, but we spend a lot of time in the country.*
2 base something on something to develop something from something that already exists, or from something that has already happened ▸ *a book based on her experiences during the war*

baseball /ˈbeɪsbɔːl/ *noun (no plural)*
a ball game in which two teams in turn try to hit a ball with a round stick and then run round a specially shaped field

basement /ˈbeɪsmənt/ *noun*
a part of a house, shop, or building which is below the level of the street ▸ *They live in the basement.*
COMPARE: **cellar**

bases /ˈbeɪsiːz/
the plural of **basis**

bash /bæʃ/ *verb*
to hit something or someone hard ▸ *I bashed my leg on the table.*

bashful /ˈbæʃfəl/ *adjective*
embarrassed and shy ▸ *Why are you looking so bashful?*

basic /ˈbeɪsɪk/ *adjective*
simple and more important than anything else ▸ *basic skills such as reading and writing*

basically /ˈbeɪsɪkli/ *adverb*
1 used to introduce a simple explanation of something ▸ *Basically, the team didn't play well enough.*
2 in the most important ways ▸ *Norwegian and Danish are basically the same.*

basics /ˈbeɪsɪks/ *plural noun*
the most important skills or facts of something ▸ *I don't even know the basics of first aid.*

basin /ˈbeɪsən/ *noun*
1 a round dish
2 a large bowl fixed to the wall for washing your hands
COMPARE: (**2**): **sink**

basis /ˈbeɪsɪs/ *noun (plural bases /ˈbeɪsiːz/)*
the part of something from which something else develops ▸ *These ideas formed the basis of the plan.*

bask /bɑːsk/ *verb*
to lie somewhere warm and enjoy doing this ▸ *The cat was basking in the sun.*

basket /ˈbɑːskɪt/ *noun*
1 a container made of thin pieces of shaped wood which you use for carrying things

2 when a player gets the ball into the net at BASKETBALL

basketball /ˈbɑːskɪtbɔːl/ *noun (no plural)*
a game in which two teams try to throw a ball through a round net which is high above the ground

bass¹ /beɪs/ *adjective*
playing low musical notes ➤ *He plays the bass guitar.*

bass² /beɪs/ *noun (plural **basses**)*
a singer or an instrument that sings or plays notes that are the lowest in the range

bass³ /bæs/ *noun (plural **bass** or **basses**)*
a fish used for food

bassoon /bəˈsuːn/ *noun*
a long, wooden musical instrument that makes a low sound

bat¹ /bæt/ *noun*
1 a piece of wood used for hitting the ball in some games ➤ *a baseball bat*
2 a small animal with wings that flies at night and hangs upside down when it sleeps

bat² *verb (present participle **batting**, past **batted**)*
to hit a ball with a special piece of wood

batch /bætʃ/ *noun (plural **batches**)*
a number of people or things arriving or being dealt with together ➤ *to cook a batch of cakes* ➤ *a batch of new students*

bath¹ /bɑːθ/ *noun (plural **baths** /bɑːðz, bɑːθs/)*
1 a large container that you fill with water and then sit in to wash your body
2 baths a swimming pool ➤ *Shall we go to the baths?*
3 have a bath to wash yourself in a bath ➤ *I have a bath every day.*

bath² *verb*
1 to wash someone in a bath ➤ *to bath a baby*
2 to wash yourself in a bath ➤ *She baths every morning.*

> Do not confuse the verb **bath** (=to wash in a bath) with the verb **bathe** (=to swim): *to bathe in the sea.* The verb **bath** is not used often. People usually use the expression "have a bath" instead: *He had a bath and washed his hair.* Do not use "have a bath" instead of **bathe**.

bathe /beɪð/ *verb (present participle **bathing** /ˈbeɪðɪŋ/, past **bathed** /beɪðd/)*
to swim for pleasure in a river or the sea
LOOK AT: **bath**

bather /ˈbeɪðəʳ/ *noun*
a person who is swimming for pleasure in a river or the sea

bathing suit /ˈbeɪðɪŋ ˌsuːt/ *noun*
a piece of clothing that you wear when you swim

bathrobe /ˈbɑːθrəʊb/ *noun*
a type of loose coat that you put on after you have had a bath

bathroom /ˈbɑːθrʊm/ *noun*
a room in a house where people wash their bodies or have baths

battalion /bəˈtæljən/ *noun*
a large group of soldiers that consists of several smaller groups

batter /ˈbætəʳ/ *verb*
to hit someone or something hard, again and again

battered /ˈbætəd/ *adjective*
old and damaged ➤ *a battered old book*

battery /ˈbætəri/ *noun (plural **batteries**)*
a box that produces or stores electricity, like the ones used in radios, etc. or the one used in a car

battle /ˈbætl/ *noun*
a fight between soldiers, ships, or

aircraft ➤ *one of the most important battles of the war*
COMPARE: **war**

battlefield /ˈbætlfiːld/ *noun*
a place where a battle has been fought

battleship /ˈbætlʃɪp/ *noun*
a very large ship used in wars

bawl /bɔːl/ *verb*
to shout or cry loudly ➤ *Can't you stop that child bawling!*

bay /beɪ/ *noun*
a part of the sea that curves inwards so that it is enclosed by land

bazaar /bəˈzɑːʳ/ *noun*
1 a market or a group of shops, especially in the Middle East
2 a sale to collect money for an organization such as a church or school ➤ *the annual church bazaar*

BC /ˌbiː ˈsiː/
before the birth of Christ, used in dates ➤ *It was built in the year 2000 BC.*

be /bɪ; *strong* biː/ *verb*

present tense

singular	plural
I **am** (I**'m**)	We **are** (We**'re**)
You **are** (You**'re**)	You **are** (You**'re**)
He/She/It **is**	They **are**
(He**'s**/She**'s**/It**'s**)	(They**'re**)

past tense

singular	plural
I **was**	We **were**
You **were**	You **were**
He/She/It **was**	They **were**

present participle	**being**
past participle	**been**
negative short forms	**aren't, isn't, wasn't, weren't**

(you can find each of these words in its own place in the dictionary)

1 used to describe or give information about people or things ➤ *His name is Peter.* ➤ *My mother is a teacher.* ➤ *The milk is on the table.* ➤ *I'm* (=I am) *very happy.* ➤ *"How old are you?" "I'm 16."* ➤ *"What's* (=what is) *your name?" "It's* (=it is) *Emma."* ➤ *It was my birthday yesterday.*
2 used with other verbs to show that something is happening now ➤ *"What are you doing?" "I am painting a picture."*
3 used with other verbs to show that something happens to a person or thing ➤ *She is paid to clean her house* (=they pay her to clean their house). ➤ *He was attacked by a dog.* ➤ *The house was built 50 years ago.*
4 **there is** (*plural* **there are**) used to say that someone or something is in a place ➤ *Look – there's* (=there is) *Sue!* ➤ *There are too many people at the party.* ➤ *How many children are there in your class?* ➤ *There was a loud noise.*

beach /biːtʃ/ *noun* (*plural* **beaches**)
a shore covered in sand or stones where people go to swim

beacon /ˈbiːkən/ *noun*
a light that flashes to guide boats or planes

bead /biːd/ *noun*
a small ball of glass with a small hole for string or wire to pass through ➤ *She wore a string of beads round her neck.*

beady /ˈbiːdɪ/ *adjective* (**beadier, beadiest**)
(used about eyes) small and dark ➤ *an old woman with beady eyes*

beak /biːk/ *noun*
the hard, pointed mouth of a bird

beam¹ /biːm/ *noun*
1 a large, long, heavy piece of wood used to support the roof of a building
2 a line of light shining from a bright

B

object ▶ *the sun's beams* ▶ *a beam of light*

beam² *verb*
to smile in a very happy way ▶ *She beamed with pleasure.*

bean /biːn/ *noun*
1 a seed or seed container of a plant which is eaten as a vegetable ▶ *green beans*
2 a seed of a plant which is used for making food or drink ▶ *coffee beans*

bear¹ /beəʳ/ *noun*
a large and sometimes fierce wild animal with a thick coat

bear² *verb (past tense bore /bɔːʳ/, past participle borne /bɔːn/)*
1 to carry or support the weight of something ▶ *These pillars bear the weight of the roof.*
2 to accept something bad without complaining ▶ *The pain was too much for me to bear.*
3 can't bear (used to show that you dislike someone or something very much) ▶ *I can't bear loud music.*

bearable /ˈbeərəbəl/ *adjective*
difficult but not too bad to be accepted or dealt with ▶ *His letters made her loneliness bearable.*
OPPOSITE: **unbearable**

beard /bɪəd/ *noun*
hair on a man's face below his mouth
COMPARE: **moustache**

bearing /ˈbeərɪŋ/ *noun*
1 have a bearing on something to affect something ▶ *Recent events have had a bearing on his decision.*
2 lose your bearings to become lost ▶ *The boat lost its bearings in the fog.*

beast /biːst/ *noun*
1 a wild and dangerous animal
2 an unkind or cruel person ▶ *You beast – I hate you!*

beat¹ /biːt/ *verb (past tense beat, past participle beaten /ˈbiːtn/)*

1 to defeat someone; to have a better result than someone ▶ *We beat the other team at football.*
2 to hit someone or something many times ▶ *to beat a drum*
3 to move regularly ▶ *Her heart was beating fast.*
4 to beat someone up to hit someone until they are hurt

beat² *noun*
a single stroke or movement as part of a regular group ▶ *a beat of your heart*

beaten¹ /ˈbiːtn/
the PAST PARTICIPLE of the verb **beat**

beaten² *adjective*
off the beaten track far away from places that people usually visit ▶ *We want to stay somewhere off the beaten track.*

beautician /bjuːˈtɪʃən/ *noun*
a person who gives beauty treatment to your face and body

beautiful /ˈbjuːtɪfəl/ *adjective*
1 very attractive and nice to look at ▶ *a beautiful woman* ▶ *a beautiful view*
2 very pleasing or nice ▶ *What a beautiful day!* ▶ *beautiful music*

> The adjectives **beautiful** and **pretty** can be used to describe women, children, and things, but they are never used to describe men. A man who is nice to look at can be described as **handsome**.

beautifully /ˈbjuːtɪfəli/ *adverb*
very well; in a way which looks or sounds good ▶ *She speaks French beautifully.*

beauty /ˈbjuːtɪ/ *noun*
1 (no plural) being beautiful ▶ *a place of great beauty*
2 (plural **beauties**) something or someone beautiful ▶ *His mother was a great beauty.*

became /bɪˈkeɪm/
the PAST TENSE of the verb **become**

because /bɪˈkɒz/ *conjunction*
1 (used when you are giving a reason for something) ➤ *I missed the train because I was late.*
2 because of for this reason ➤ *We stayed at home because of the rain.*

beckon /ˈbekən/ *verb*
to make a sign with your finger asking someone to come to you

become /bɪˈkʌm/ *verb* (*present participle* **becoming**, *past tense* **became** /bɪˈkeɪm/, *past participle* **become**)
1 to begin to be something ➤ *The prince became king when his father died.* ➤ *The actor became famous in the 1960s.*
2 What has become of ...? a question you ask when you want to know what has happened to a person or thing, or where someone or something is ➤ *What has become of that friend of yours who went to live in Australia?*

bed /bed/ *noun*
1 a piece of furniture you sleep on ➤ *What time did you go to bed last night* (=go to your bed to sleep)*?*
2 the base or bottom of something ➤ *the bed of a river*
3 make a bed to tidy a bed and make it ready for sleeping in
4 go to bed with someone to have sex with someone

bed and breakfast /ˌbed ən ˈbrekfəst/ *noun*
a family house where you can pay to be a guest for the night. You can have breakfast there, but no other meals ➤ *We stayed in a bed and breakfast.*

bedclothes /ˈbedkləʊðz/ *plural noun*
all the covers put on a bed to keep you warm

bedding /ˈbedɪŋ/ *noun (no plural)*
all the covers put on a bed

bedroom /ˈbedrʊm/ *noun*
a room for sleeping in

bedside /ˈbedsaɪd/ *noun*
the area next to a bed ➤ *His mother stayed at his bedside all night.*

bedsit /ˈbedsɪt/ *noun*
a room used for both living and sleeping in ➤ *Many students live in bedsits.*

bedspread /ˈbedspred/ *noun*
a cloth cover for a bed, used to keep you warm or to make the bed look attractive
COMPARE: **duvet**

bedtime /ˈbedtaɪm/ *noun*
the time when you usually go to bed ➤ *It's past my bedtime.*

bee /biː/ *noun*
a stinging, flying insect that makes
HONEY

beef /biːf/ *noun (no plural)*
the meat from cattle

beefburger /ˈbiːfbɜːɡəʳ/ *noun*
meat that has been cut into very small pieces and then made into a round, flat shape before being cooked
SAME MEANING: **hamburger**

beehive /ˈbiːhaɪv/ *noun*
another word for **hive**

been /biːn, bɪn/
1 the PAST PARTICIPLE of the verb **be** ➤ *It has been very cold this week.*
2 have been somewhere to have gone and come back from a place ➤ *She's been away on holiday* (=but now she's back). ➤ *Have you ever been to Scotland?*
LOOK AT: **gone**

beep /biːp/ *verb*
to make a short, high noise ➤ *The computer beeps when you make a mistake.*

beeper /ˈbiːpəʳ/ *noun*
a small machine that you carry with you which makes a sound to tell you to telephone someone
SAME MEANING: **pager**

B

beer /bɪəʳ/ noun
1 (no plural) an alcoholic drink made from grain
2 a glass or bottle of this drink
▶ Can I have two beers, please?

beetle /'biːtl/ noun
an insect whose outside wings make a hard cover for its body

beetroot /'biːtruːt/ noun
a round, red vegetable that grows under the ground

before¹ /bɪ'fɔːʳ/ adverb
at some earlier time ▶ I have never seen you before (=this is the first time I have seen you).

before² preposition, conjunction
1 earlier than ▶ You must leave before 8 o'clock. ▶ Finish your work before you go. ▶ the day before yesterday
OPPOSITE: after
2 before that used when you want to show that something happens or happened earlier than something else ▶ She was a teacher, and before that she worked in an office.

> Before means "earlier than something else": She left before I arrived. ▶ Clean your teeth before you go to bed. Ago means "in the past": We went to Scotland three years ago. ▶ Our second visit to America was in 1993, and our first visit was three years before (=in 1990). ▶ It happened many years ago. ▶ It happened before the war.
> LOOK AT: ago

beforehand /bɪ'fɔːhænd/ adverb
before something else happens
▶ I knew I was coming because I telephoned her beforehand.

beg /beg/ verb (present participle **begging**, past **begged**)
1 to ask people in the street for money or food
2 to ask someone very strongly to do something ▶ I begged her not to go.

3 I beg your pardon a phrase used when you are sorry because you have done something wrong, or when you did not hear what someone said and you want them to say it again ▶ I beg your pardon, but could you repeat that?

began /bɪ'gæn/
the PAST TENSE of the verb **begin**

beggar /'begəʳ/ noun
a person who asks people in the street for money or food

begin /bɪ'gɪn/ verb (present participle **beginning**, past tense **began** /bɪ'gæn/, past participle **begun** /bɪ'gʌn/)
1 to start ▶ The film begins at 2 o'clock.
OPPOSITE: end
2 to start something ▶ When do you begin your new job? ▶ It's beginning to rain.
3 to begin with at first ▶ To begin with, I didn't like school, but now I enjoy it.

> Remember that the PAST TENSE is began, and the PAST PARTICIPLE is begun.

beginner /bɪ'gɪnəʳ/ noun
a person who is starting to do or learn something ▶ a swimming class for beginners

beginning /bɪ'gɪnɪŋ/ noun
the start ▶ the beginning of the year
OPPOSITE: end

begrudge /bɪ'grʌdʒ/ verb (present participle **begrudging**, past **begrudged**)
to feel upset because someone else has something you would like ▶ I don't begrudge him his success.

begun /bɪ'gʌn/
the PAST PARTICIPLE of the verb **begin**

behalf /bɪ'hɑːf/ noun
on behalf of someone instead of someone; for someone ▶ I have come

on behalf of my brother, as he's ill.
► I paid the money on your behalf
(=for you).

behave /bɪˈheɪv/ *verb (present
participle **behaving**, past **behaved**)*
1 to act in a particular way
► *The children behaved very
badly.*
2 behave yourself to act in a way
which will not annoy or offend other
people

behaviour /bɪˈheɪvjəʳ/ *noun (no
plural)*
the way a person acts ► *What bad
behaviour!*

behind /bɪˈhaɪnd/ *preposition,
adverb*
at the back (of) ► *He hung his coat
on the nail behind the door.* ► *My
brother went in front, and I walked
behind.* ► *She hid behind a tree.*

beige /beɪʒ/ *noun, adjective*
a very light brown colour ► *a beige
dress*

being¹ /ˈbiːɪŋ/
the PRESENT PARTICIPLE of the verb **be**

being² *noun*
a person ► *a being from another
world*

belated /bɪˈleɪtɪd/ *adjective*
happening or done late ► *Myra sent
me a belated birthday card.*

belch /beltʃ/ *verb*
to let air come out noisily from your
stomach through your mouth
SAME MEANING: **burp**

belief /bɪˈliːf/ *noun*
1 *(no plural)* the feeling that
something is true or exists ► *a belief
in God*
2 an opinion or idea which you think
is true ► *religious beliefs*

believable /bɪˈliːvəbəl/ *adjective*
easy to believe ► *His story is very
believable.*
OPPOSITE: **unbelievable**

believe /bɪˈliːv/ *verb (present
participle **believing**, past **believed**)*
1 to think that something is true
► *I don't believe the things you say.*
2 to think that someone is telling the
truth ► *Don't you believe me?*
3 to have an opinion ► *I believe we
will be successful.*
4 believe in something to be sure
that something exists ► *Do you
believe in God?*
5 believe in someone to trust
someone and be sure they will
succeed ► *The soldiers all believe in
their leader.*

believer /bɪˈliːvəʳ/ *noun*
someone who believes that a
particular idea or thing is good
► *He's a great believer in eating lots
of fruit and vegetables.*

bell /bel/ *noun*
a round, hollow, metal object that
makes a musical sound when it is hit
► *church bells*

bellow /ˈbeləʊ/ *verb*
to shout something in a loud, deep
voice ► *"Go away!" he bellowed
angrily.*

belly /ˈbelɪ/ *noun (plural **bellies**)*
your stomach ► *I've got a pain in my
belly.*

belly button /ˈbelɪ ˌbʌtn/ *noun*
the small hole in your stomach
SAME MEANING: **navel**

belong /bɪˈlɒŋ/ *verb*
1 belong to someone to be owned by
someone ► *Who does this coat
belong to (=who is the owner)?*
2 belong to something to be a
member of a group or club

belongings /bɪˈlɒŋɪŋz/ *plural noun*
your own property ► *Please take all
your belongings with you when you
leave the plane.*

beloved /bɪˈlʌvɪd/ *adjective*
loved very much ► *She was the
beloved wife of Tom Smith.*

B

B

below /bɪˈləʊ/ *adverb, preposition*
1 at a lower place; lower than; under ➤ *The children threw sticks from the bridge into the river below.* ➤ *My brother is in the class below mine.*
2 less than a particular amount ➤ *children below the age of five.*
OPPOSITE (1 and 2): **above**

belt /belt/ *noun*
a piece of cloth or leather that you wear around the middle of your body

bemused /bɪˈmjuːzd/ *adjective*
slightly confused ➤ *She looked bemused by what he was saying.*

bench /bentʃ/ *noun (plural **benches**)*
a long, wooden seat ➤ *a bench in the park*

bend¹ /bend/ *verb (past **bent** /bent/)*
1 (*also **bend down, bend over**) to move the top part of your body down towards the ground ➤ *She bent down to pick up a book from the floor.*
2 to move something into a curved position ➤ *to bend your knees*

bend² *noun*
a curve ➤ *a bend in the road*

beneath /bɪˈniːθ/ *preposition*
below; under ➤ *Shall we sit beneath these trees?* ➤ *beneath a sunny sky*

beneficial /ˌbenɪˈfɪʃəl/ *adjective*
helpful or useful ➤ *It might be beneficial to talk to someone about your problems.*

benefit¹ /ˈbenɪfɪt/ *verb*
to be useful or helpful to someone ➤ *The plants benefited from (=were helped by) the rain.*

benefit² *noun*
1 an advantage ➤ *the benefits of a good education*
2 for someone's benefit to help someone ➤ *I did it for your benefit.*

benign /bɪˈnaɪn/ *adjective*
not likely to hurt you or to cause CANCER ➤ *a benign tumour*
OPPOSITE: **malignant**

bent /bent/
the PAST TENSE and PAST PARTICIPLE of the verb **bend**

bereaved /bɪˈriːvd/ *adjective*
having a relative or close friend who has recently died ➤ *a support group for bereaved parents*

bereavement /bɪˈriːvmənt/ *noun*
the situation when a relative or close friend has recently died ➤ *He is away from work because of a family bereavement.*

beret /ˈbereɪ/ *noun*
a flat, round hat made of woollen cloth

berry /ˈberi/ *noun (plural **berries**)*
a small, soft fruit that grows on a bush or tree

berserk /bɜːˈsɜːk/ *adjective*
go berserk to become very angry and violent in a crazy way ➤ *He went berserk and started hitting Sue.*

beset /bɪˈset/ *verb (present participle **besetting**, past **beset**)*
be beset by something to have a lot of problems, difficulties, etc. to deal with ➤ *The company has been beset by financial difficulties.*

beside /bɪˈsaɪd/ *preposition*
next to someone or something ➤ *Come and sit beside me.*

besides /bɪˈsaɪdz/ *adverb*
a word used when you are giving another reason or fact to support what you are saying ➤ *I can't go out tonight because I'm too tired – besides, I haven't got any money.*
SAME MEANING: **anyway**

besiege /bɪˈsiːdʒ/ *verb (present participle **besieging**, past **besieged**)*
1 be besieged by people to be surrounded by a lot of people ➤ *a rock star besieged by fans*
2 be besieged with something to receive a lot of something ➤ *The radio station was besieged with letters of complaint.*

B

best¹ /best/ *adjective*
1 the SUPERLATIVE of **good** ▶ *It was the best film I've ever seen.*
OPPOSITE: **worst**
2 best wishes a phrase used at the end of a letter when the person you are writing to is not a close friend ▶ *Have a happy Christmas, with best wishes from Mrs Jones and family.*

best² *adverb*
1 the SUPERLATIVE of **well** ▶ *the best-dressed person in the room*
OPPOSITE: **worst**
2 most ▶ *The blue dress suits you best.* ▶ *Which one do you like best?*
OPPOSITE: **least**

best³ *noun (no plural)*
1 the best the most good person or thing ▶ *You're the best!* ▶ *She wants her children to have the best of everything* (=the best things possible).
2 do your best to try as hard as you can to succeed in something ▶ *It doesn't matter if you didn't win – you did your best.*

best man /,best 'mæn/ *noun (plural best men* /,best 'men/)
a male friend who is chosen to help and support a man who is getting married ▶ *Will you be best man at my wedding?*
COMPARE: **bridesmaid**

best-seller /,best'selə/ *noun*
a book that a lot of people have bought

bet¹ /bet/ *verb (present participle betting, past bet or betted)*
to risk money on the result of a future event ▶ *He bet me £1 that the team would win.* ▶ *to bet money on a horse* (=in a race)
COMPARE: **gamble**

bet² *noun*
an agreement to risk money on the result of a future event ▶ *a bet of £1*

betray /bɪ'treɪ/ *verb*
to harm someone who trusts you by breaking a promise made to them ▶ *I asked you not to tell anyone, but you betrayed me.*

betrayal /bɪ'treɪəl/ *noun*
the act of harming someone who trusts you by breaking a promise made to them

better¹ /'betə/ *adjective*
1 the COMPARATIVE of **good** ▶ *This book is better than the other one.*
2 not as ill as before ▶ *I hope you are feeling better.*
OPPOSITE: (**1** and **2**): **worse**

better² *adverb*
1 the COMPARATIVE of **well** ▶ *He can sing better than me.*
OPPOSITE: **worse**
2 more ▶ *I like him better than his brother.*
3 had better should; ought to ▶ *You'd* (=you had) *better go home.* ▶ *I'd* (=I had) *better not miss my train.*

better off /,betər 'ɒf/ *adjective*
1 more successful, richer, or having more advantages than you did before ▶ *Most businesses in the area are better off than they were ten years ago.*
OPPOSITE: **worse off**
2 be better off doing something used to give advice about what someone should do ▶ *You'd be better off taking a taxi to the airport.*

between /bɪ'twiːn/ *adverb, preposition*
1 (also **in between**) in the space in the middle of two people or things ▶ *There is a fence between his garden and our garden.* ▶ *April comes between March and May.*
2 in the period before one time and after another ▶ *The shop is open between 9 o'clock and 5 o'clock.*
3 more than one number or amount but less than another number or

amount ▶ *children aged between five and ten*

4 joining two places ▶ *the train between Cambridge and London* ▶ *flights between Paris and Geneva*

5 used when saying how things are shared or divided ▶ *You and I can share the cost between us.*

Use **between** when you are talking about something which is done or shared by two people or things. Use **among** when you are talking about something which is done or shared by more than two people or things: *She divided the cake between the two children.* ▶ *The money was divided among his brothers and sisters.*

beverage /'bevərɪdʒ/ *noun*
a drink ▶ *We do not sell alcoholic beverages.*

beware /bɪ'weə^r/ *verb*
used to tell someone to be careful of something because it is dangerous ▶ *Beware **of** the dog!*

bewildered /bɪ'wɪldəd/ *adjective*
confused and not sure what to do or think ▶ *The children looked bewildered and scared.*

beyond /bɪ'jɒnd/ *adverb, preposition*
past; on the other side of something ▶ *beyond the mountains*

bias /'baɪəs/ *noun (plural **biases**)*
an opinion about whether something is good or bad that unfairly influences how you deal with it ▶ *The judge's decision definitely shows a bias against women.*

biased /'baɪəst/ *adjective*
showing that your personal opinions have unfairly affected your judgement ▶ *Some newspapers are biased in favour of the government.*

bib /bɪb/ *noun*
a piece of material that is tied under a child's chin to keep its clothes clean when it is eating

bible /'baɪbəl/ *noun*
1 the Bible the holy book of the Christian religion
2 a useful and important book on a particular subject ▶ *a textbook that is the medical student's bible*

biblical /'bɪblɪkəl/ *adjective*
from or in the Bible

bibliography /ˌbɪblɪ'ɒgrəfɪ/ *noun (plural **bibliographies**)*
a list of books about a particular subject

bicker /'bɪkə^r/ *verb*
to argue about something that is not very important ▶ *The kids were bickering about who was the fastest runner.*

bicycle /'baɪsɪkəl/ *noun*
a machine with two wheels. You sit on it and move your legs to make it go forward ▶ *to travel by bicycle*
SAME MEANING: **bike, cycle**

bid¹ /bɪd/ *verb (present participle **bidding**, past **bid**)*
to make an offer of money in order to buy something ▶ *He bid £10 for the bicycle.*

bid² *noun*
an offer of an amount of money to buy something

big /bɪg/ *adjective (**bigger, biggest**)*
large in size ▶ *They live in a big house.*
OPPOSITE: **little, small**

bigheaded /ˌbɪg'hedɪd/ *adjective*
thinking that you are more successful or intelligent than other people

bigot /'bɪgət/ *noun*
a person who has strong and unreasonable opinions about people who belong to a different race, religion, or political group

bigoted /'bɪgətɪd/ *adjective*
having strong and unreasonable opinions about people who belong to a different race, religion, or political

group ▶ *a bigoted old man*

bike /baɪk/ *noun*
a machine with two wheels. You sit on it and move your legs to make it go forward ▶ *to travel by bike*
SAME MEANING: **bicycle, cycle**

biker /'baɪkəʳ/ *noun*
a person who rides a MOTORCYCLE, especially as part of a group

bikini /bɪ'ki:nɪ/ *noun*
a garment with two pieces, one covering the breasts and one covering the bottom, which women and girls wear when they swim

bilingual /baɪ'lɪŋgwəl/ *adjective*
1 able to speak two languages equally well ▶ *He's bilingual in French and German.*
2 spoken or written in two languages ▶ *a bilingual dictionary*

bill /bɪl/ *noun*
1 a piece of paper showing the amount you must pay for something ▶ *How much was the electricity bill this month?*
2 a plan for a new law ▶ *The government is considering the new education bill.*

billboard /'bɪlbɔːd/ *noun*
a big sign next to a road that is used to advertise things

billiards /'bɪljədz/ *noun (no plural)*
a game in which you hit balls across a table with long sticks

billion /'bɪljən/ *adjective, noun*
the number 1,000,000,000,000 (=a million million), or, especially in America, 1,000,000,000 (=a thousand million)

billow /'bɪləʊ/ *verb*
to rise into the air in large amounts ▶ *Smoke billowed out of the chimneys.*

bin /bɪn/ *noun*
a large container used for holding things that are to be thrown

away or have been thrown away
COMPARE: **dustbin**

bind /baɪnd/ *verb (past bound* /baʊnd/)
to tie something with rope or string

binge¹ /bɪndʒ/ *noun*
a short period of time when you eat too much food or drink too much alcohol ▶ *He's gone out on a binge with his mates.*

binge² *verb (present participle binging, past binged)*
to eat a lot of food or drink a lot of alcohol in a short period of time

bingo /'bɪŋgəʊ/ *noun (no plural)*
a game played with numbers in order to win prizes

binoculars /bɪ'nɒkjʊləz/ *plural noun*
a pair of special glasses which make things in the distance look bigger
COMPARE: **telescope**

biodegradable /,baɪəʊdɪ'greɪdəbəl/ *adjective*
able to be destroyed by natural processes, in a way that does not harm the environment ▶ *Plastic is not biodegradable.*

biographer /baɪ'ɒgrəfəʳ/ *noun*
a person who writes someone's biography

biography /baɪ'ɒgrəfɪ/ *noun (plural biographies)*
the story of a person's life written by someone else
COMPARE: **autobiography**

biological /,baɪə'lɒdʒɪkəl/ *adjective*
of or about BIOLOGY ▶ *The company does biological research.*

biologist /baɪ'ɒlədʒɪst/ *noun*
a person who studies biology

biology /baɪ'ɒlədʒɪ/ *noun (no plural)*
the scientific study of living things

bird /bɜːd/ *noun*
an animal with wings and feathers ▶ *Most birds can fly.*

B

bird of prey /ˌbɜːd əv ˈpreɪ/ *noun*
(plural **birds of prey**)
a bird that kills and eats other birds
and small animals ➤ *The eagle is a
bird of prey.*

Biro /ˈbaɪrəʊ/ *noun* trademark
a pen which has a very small metal
ball at the end you write with
SAME MEANING: **ballpoint**

birth /bɜːθ/ *noun*
1 the act of a baby being born ➤ *the
birth of a baby* ➤ *the number of births
and deaths this year*
2 give birth to have a baby ➤ *She
gave birth to a baby boy last night.*

birth control /ˈbɜːθ kənˌtrəʊl/ *noun*
(no plural)
ways of limiting the number of
children you have

birthday /ˈbɜːθdeɪ/ *noun*
the day of the year on which a person
was born ➤ *My birthday is on January
6th.*
LOOK AT: **anniversary**

birthmark /ˈbɜːθmɑːk/ *noun*
an unusual mark on someone's skin
that is there when they are born

birthplace /ˈbɜːθpleɪs/ *noun*
the place where someone was born
➤ *Stratford-upon-Avon is the
birthplace of William Shakespeare.*

biscuit /ˈbɪskɪt/ *noun*
a dry, thin cake, usually sweet
➤ *a packet of biscuits*

bisexual /baɪˈsekʃʊəl/ *adjective*
sexually attracted to men and women

bishop /ˈbɪʃəp/ *noun*
a Christian priest who looks after the
churches and the people in a large
area
COMPARE: **vicar**

bit¹ /bɪt/
the PAST TENSE of the verb **bite**

bit² *noun*
1 a small piece or amount ➤ *I must do
a bit of work.* ➤ *He ate every bit of*
food (=all the food). ➤ *Would you like
another bit of cake?*
2 a bit slightly ➤ *I'm sorry I'm a bit
late.* ➤ *It's a bit too cold to go outside.*
3 for a bit for a short time ➤ *Why
don't you go and lie down for a bit?*
4 bit by bit slowly, a little at a time
➤ *Bit by bit, they discovered the
truth.*

bite¹ /baɪt/ *verb* (present participle
biting, past tense **bit** /bɪt/, past
participle **bitten** /ˈbɪtn/)
1 to cut or wound something with the
teeth ➤ *That dog bit me.* ➤ *Does your
dog bite?*
2 (used about an insect) to hurt you
by pricking your skin

bite² *noun*
1 an act of biting ➤ *Do you want a
bite of my apple?*
2 a wound made by biting ➤ *She was
covered in insect bites.*

bitten /ˈbɪtn/
the PAST PARTICIPLE of the verb **bite**

bitter /ˈbɪtəʳ/ *adjective*
1 having a sharp, sour taste
➤ *bitter fruit*
2 angry ➤ *a bitter quarrel*
3 very cold ➤ *a bitter wind*

bitterly /ˈbɪtəli/ *adverb*
very ➤ *It's bitterly cold outside.* ➤ *We
were bitterly disappointed to lose.*

bizarre /bɪˈzɑːʳ/ *adjective*
very unusual and strange ➤ *a bizarre
coincidence* (adverb: **bizarrely**)

black¹ /blæk/ *adjective*
1 of the colour of the sky at night
➤ *black shoes*
2 with dark-coloured skin ➤ *a black
family*
3 (used about tea and coffee) without
milk ➤ *I'd like my coffee black.*
4 black and blue having dark marks
on your skin as a result of being hurt
➤ *Her arm was black and blue after
the accident.*
5 black and white containing only the

colours black, white, and grey ▶ *an old black and white film*

black² *noun*
1 *(no plural)* the colour of the sky at night ▶ *He was dressed in black.*
2 a person with dark-coloured skin

blackberry /'blækbərɪ/ *noun (plural blackberries)*
a small, dark fruit that grows on bushes

blackbird /'blækbɜːd/ *noun*
a bird which is very common in Europe. The male is black and has a yellow beak.

blackboard /'blækbɔːd/ *noun*
a dark board on the wall at the front of a class that the teacher writes on

blackcurrant /'blæk-kʌrənt/ *noun*
a small, round, dark fruit that grows on bushes

black eye /ˌblæk 'aɪ/ *noun*
an area of dark skin around someone's eye where they have been hit ▶ *How did you get that black eye?*

black magic /ˌblæk 'mædʒɪk/ *noun (no plural)*
a type of magic used to do bad or evil things

blackmail¹ /'blækmeɪl/ *noun (no plural)*
a situation in which you make someone do what you want by saying that you will tell secrets about them ▶ *"End your relationship with her, and I might be prepared to forget about it." "That's blackmail!"*

blackmail² *verb*
to make someone do what you want by saying that you will tell secrets about them

black market /ˌblæk 'mɑːkɪt/ *noun*
a system of buying and selling things illegally ▶ *They buy drugs on the black market.*

blackout /'blækaʊt/ *noun*
a short period of time when you suddenly cannot see, hear, or feel anything, for example because you are ill or have hit your head ▶ *I had a blackout and couldn't remember anything.*

blacksmith /'blæksmɪθ/ *noun*
a person who works with iron and makes shoes for horses

bladder /'blædəʳ/ *noun*
the part of your body where URINE stays before it leaves your body

blade /bleɪd/ *noun*
1 the flat, sharp part of anything that is used for cutting ▶ *the blade of a knife*
2 a long, flat leaf of grass

blame¹ /bleɪm/ *verb (present participle blaming, past blamed)*
1 blame someone for something to say that someone is the cause of something bad ▶ *The policeman blamed the car driver for causing the accident.*
COMPARE: **accuse**
2 be to blame for something to be responsible for something bad ▶ *He is to blame for the accident.*

blame² *noun (no plural)*
take the blame for something to accept that you are responsible for something bad

bland /blænd/ *adjective*
1 not interesting or exciting ▶ *the usual selection of bland entertainment*
2 having very little taste ▶ *a rather bland white sauce*

blank /blæŋk/ *adjective*
1 without anything on ▶ *a blank piece of paper* (=one without writing on it) ▶ *a blank cassette* (=one without any sounds on it)
2 not showing any expression ▶ *She looked at him with a blank face.*

blanket /'blæŋkɪt/ *noun*
a thick, woollen cloth, used as a cover on a bed to keep you warm

B

blare /bleə^r/ *verb (present participle blaring, past blared)*
to make a loud and unpleasant noise ▶ *The radio was blaring.*

blast¹ /blɑːst/ *noun*
1 a sudden, strong movement of wind or air ▶ *There was a blast of wind as she opened the door.*
2 a loud sound like the sound made by some instruments which you blow ▶ *The driver gave a blast on his horn.*
3 an explosion ▶ *Many people were killed in the blast.*
4 at full blast as loud as possible ▶ *The television was at full blast.*

blast² *verb*
1 to break something by using an explosion ▶ *They blasted away the rock.*
2 blast off to leave the ground at the beginning of a space flight ▶ *The spaceship blasted off.*

blast-off /'blɑːst ɒf/ *noun*
the moment when a spaceship, etc. leaves the ground

blatant /'bleɪtənt/ *adjective*
easy to notice, in a way that is shocking ▶ *a blatant lie* (adverb: **blatantly**)

blaze¹ /bleɪz/ *noun*
1 a very large, strong fire ▶ *The fire burned slowly at first, but soon became a blaze.*
2 brightly shining light or colour ▶ *The flowers were a blaze of colour.*

blaze² *verb (present participle blazing, past blazed)*
to burn strongly ▶ *The fire was blazing.*

blazer /'bleɪzə^r/ *noun*
a short coat that people often wear as part of a uniform ▶ *She was wearing her school blazer.*

bleach¹ /bliːtʃ/ *verb*
1 to make something white ▶ *Did you bleach this tablecloth?*

2 to make something lighter ▶ *Her hair was bleached by the sun.*

bleach² *noun (no plural)*
a liquid or powder used to make things clean or lighter in colour

bleak /bliːk/ *adjective*
unpleasantly cold ▶ *a bleak winter's day*

bleary-eyed /ˌblɪəri ˈaɪd/ *adjective*
looking tired or as if you have been crying ▶ *She came down to breakfast looking bleary-eyed.*

bleat¹ /bliːt/ *verb*
to make the sound made by a sheep or goat

bleat² *noun*
the sound made by a sheep or goat

bleed /bliːd/ *verb (past bled /bled/)*
to lose blood ▶ *His nose was bleeding.*

bleeding /'bliːdɪŋ/ *noun (no plural)*
the flow of blood from a wound ▶ *She pressed on the wound to stop the bleeding.*

bleep /bliːp/ *verb*
to make a high electronic sound ▶ *The alarm clock was bleeping.*

bleeper /'bliːpə^r/ *noun*
a small machine that you carry with you which makes a sound to tell you to telephone someone
SAME MEANING: **pager**

blemish /'blemɪʃ/ *noun (plural blemishes)*
a small mark that spoils something ▶ *My new dress had a small blemish on the collar.*

blend¹ /blend/ *verb*
1 to mix things together ▶ *Blend the sugar and eggs together.*
2 to go well together ▶ *The colours in the room blend nicely.*

blend² *noun*
a mixture produced by blending things together ▶ *my favourite blend of coffee*

blender /'blendə/ *noun*
a small electric machine used for mixing foods or liquids together

bless /bles/ *verb (past **blessed** or **blest** /blest/)*
1 to ask God's favour and protection for something ▶ *The priest blessed the new ship.*
2 Bless you! something you say to someone when they SNEEZE

blew /blu:/
the PAST TENSE of the verb **blow**

blind¹ /blaɪnd/ *adjective*
not able to see because you have something wrong with your eyes
▶ *She was born blind.*

blind² *noun*
a piece of material that you can pull down to cover a window
COMPARE: **curtain**

blindfold¹ /'blaɪndfəʊld/ *verb*
to cover someone's eyes with material so that they cannot see

blindfold² *noun*
a piece of material used to cover someone's eyes so they cannot see

blinding /'blaɪndɪŋ/ *adjective*
very bright ▶ *There was a blinding flash as the car exploded.*

blink /blɪŋk/ *verb*
to shut and open your eyes quickly
COMPARE: **wink**

bliss /blɪs/ *noun (no plural)*
complete happiness ▶ *A hot bath and a glass of wine is my idea of bliss.*

blister /'blɪstə'/ *noun*
a swelling under your skin, filled with liquid, usually caused by rubbing or burning ▶ *My new shoes have given me blisters.*

blitz /blɪts/ *noun (plural **blitzes**)*
a short period when you use a lot of effort to do something ▶ *We had a blitz on cleaning the house.*

blizzard /'blɪzəd/ *noun*
a very bad storm with snow and with very strong winds
COMPARE: **hurricane**

bloated /'bləʊtɪd/ *adjective*
feeling very full and uncomfortable
▶ *I'd eaten so much I felt bloated.*

blob /blɒb/ *noun*
a drop of thick liquid ▶ *a blob of paint*

block¹ /blɒk/ *noun*
1 a solid mass or piece of wood, stone, etc.
2 a large building divided into separate parts ▶ *a block of flats*
▶ *an office block*
3 a large building or group of buildings between two streets
▶ *She lives two blocks away.*

block² *verb*
to stop someone or something from moving beyond a certain point
▶ *A row of police cars was blocking the road.*

blockade /blɒ'keɪd/ *noun*
a situation in which an army or a navy surrounds a place to stop people getting in or out

blockage /'blɒkɪdʒ/ *noun*
something that blocks a tube or pipe

blockbuster /'blɒk,bʌstə'/ *noun*
a book or film that is very successful
▶ *the latest Hollywood blockbuster*

block capitals /,blɒk 'kæpɪtlz/ *plural noun*
letters in their large form, for example A, B, C, instead of a, b, c

bloke /bləʊk/ *noun*
a man

blond /blɒnd/ *adjective*
(used of hair) light yellow in colour

blonde¹ /blɒnd/ *adjective*
(used of a woman) having light-coloured hair

blonde² *noun*
a woman with light-coloured hair
▶ *a beautiful blonde*

blood /blʌd/ *noun (no plural)*
the red liquid that flows through your body

bloodbath /'blʌdbɑːθ/ *noun*
a situation in which a lot of people are killed violently in one place

bloodcurdling /'blʌdˌkɜːdlɪŋ/ *adjective*
very frightening ▶ *a bloodcurdling scream*

bloodshed /'blʌdʃed/ *noun (no plural)*
the killing of people, especially during a war ▶ *The army has surrendered to avoid further bloodshed.*

bloodshot /'blʌdʃɒt/ *adjective*
slightly red

bloodstream /'blʌdstriːm/ *noun*
the blood flowing around your body ▶ *The drugs get into your bloodstream very quickly.*

bloodthirsty /'blʌdˌθɜːstɪ/ *adjective*
enjoying violence

blood vessel /'blʌd ˌvesəl/ *noun*
one of the tubes in your body that blood flows through

bloody /'blʌdɪ/ *adjective (**bloodier, bloodiest**)*
1 covered in blood ▶ *Her hands were all bloody.*
2 involving actions that kill or wound a lot of people ▶ *a bloody battle*

bloom¹ /bluːm/ *noun*
1 a flower
2 **in full bloom** having a lot of open flowers ▶ *The trees are in full bloom.*

bloom² *verb*
to open out into flowers ▶ *These roses bloom in the summer.*

blossom /'blɒsəm/ *noun (no plural)*
the flowers of a fruit tree ▶ *apple blossom*

blot¹ /blɒt/ *noun*
a dirty mark made by a drop of liquid ▶ *an ink blot*

blot² *verb (present participle **blotting**, past **blotted**)*
to dry wet ink with special paper

blotch /blɒtʃ/ *noun (plural **blotches**)*
a mark on something ▶ *There were red blotches on his face.*

blotting paper /'blɒtɪŋ ˌpeɪpəʳ/ *noun (no plural)*
a special, soft paper used to dry wet ink

blouse /blaʊz/ *noun*
a shirt for women or girls

blow¹ /bləʊ/ *verb (past tense **blew** /bluː/, past participle **blown** /bləʊn/)*
1 to send out air through your mouth ▶ *Don't blow too hard or you will break the whistle.*
2 to move something with a current of air ▶ *The wind blew his hat off.*
3 (used of wind) to move and make a noise ▶ *The wind was blowing all night.*
4 to send air into something so that it makes a sound ▶ *The guard blew his whistle to call for help.*
5 **blow something out** to stop something like a candle burning by using a movement of air ▶ *Blow out the candles on your birthday cake!*
6 **blow something up** (a) to fill something with air ▶ *Can you help me blow up the balloons?*
(b) to destroy something by making it explode ▶ *The bridge was blown up in the war.*
7 **blow your nose** to push air out through your nose to clear it

blow² *noun*
1 a hard stroke with your hand or a weapon ▶ *a blow on the head*
2 a shock and disappointment ▶ *The news of her death was a terrible blow to us all.*

blow-dry /'bləʊ draɪ/ *verb (past **blow-dried**)*
to dry your hair using a HAIRDRYER

blown /bləʊn/
the PAST PARTICIPLE of the verb **blow**

blue /bluː/ *adjective, noun*
the colour of the sky when there are no clouds ▶ *a blue dress* ▶ *the blue of her eyes*

blue-collar /ˌbluː ˈkɒləʳ/ *adjective*
doing jobs such as repairing machines and making things in factories ▶ *blue-collar workers*
COMPARE: **white-collar**

blues /bluːz/ *plural noun*
1 a slow, sad style of music that came from the southern US ▶ *a blues singer*
2 the blues sad feelings

bluff /blʌf/ *verb*
to pretend that you know something or can do something, especially when you want someone to believe you

blunder /ˈblʌndəʳ/ *noun*
a careless or stupid mistake that causes serious problems

blunt /blʌnt/ *adjective*
1 (used of a knife) not able to cut very well
2 (used of a pencil) with a rounded end which needs to be sharpened
OPPOSITE (**1** and **2**): **sharp**

blur /blɜːʳ/ *noun*
something that you cannot see or remember clearly ▶ *The crash is all a blur in my mind.*

blurred /blɜːd/ *adjective*
not easy to see or remember ▶ *The photograph was rather blurred.*

blurt /blɜːt/ *verb*
blurt something out to say something suddenly and without thinking, especially something you should have tried to keep quiet or secret ▶ *Peter blurted out the news before we could stop him.*

blush /blʌʃ/ *verb*
to become red in the face, usually from shame or EMBARRASSMENT

blustery /ˈblʌstəri/ *adjective*
very windy ▶ *a blustery winter day*

board¹ /bɔːd/ *noun*
1 a long, thin, flat piece of wood
2 a flat surface used for a special purpose ▶ *a chopping board* ▶ *The teacher wrote the answers on the board.*
3 a group of people who run a company
4 on board on a ship, plane, train, bus, etc. ▶ *Is everyone on board yet?*

board² *verb*
1 to get on a ship, plane, train, bus, etc. ▶ *Passengers should board the train now.*
2 to sleep and eat in someone else's home and pay them money

boarder /ˈbɔːdəʳ/ *noun*
a pupil who lives at school and goes home in the holidays

boarding school /ˈbɔːdɪŋ ˌskuːl/ *noun*
a school, usually private, at which pupils live

boardroom /ˈbɔːdrʊm/ *noun*
a room where the people who run a company have meetings

boast /bəʊst/ *verb*
to talk too proudly about yourself ▶ *He boasted that he could run very fast.*
SAME MEANING: **brag**

boastful /ˈbəʊstfəl/ *adjective*
talking too proudly about yourself ▶ *He's very boastful about the money he earns.*

boat /bəʊt/ *noun*
a small, open ship ▶ *a fishing boat* ▶ *We're going by boat.*

bob /bɒb/ *verb (present participle **bobbing**, past **bobbed**)*
to move quickly up and down ▶ *The small boat bobbed up and down on the lake.*

bobbed /bɒbd/ *adjective*
(used about hair) the same length all the way around your head

bodily /'bɒdɪlɪ/ *adjective*
of the body ▶ He did not suffer any bodily harm.

body /'bɒdɪ/ *noun (plural bodies)*
1 the whole of a person or an animal
2 the central part of a person or an animal, not the head, arms, or legs ▶ He had a cut on his leg and two more on his body.
3 a dead person or animal ▶ Her body was found in the woods.

bodybuilding /'bɒdɪ,bɪldɪŋ/ *noun (no plural)*
the activity of doing physical exercises to make your muscles bigger and stronger

bodyguard /'bɒdɪgɑːd/ *noun*
a person whose job is to protect someone important

bog¹ /bɒg/ *noun*
an area of soft, wet, muddy ground

bog² *verb*
get bogged down to be unable to make any progress because you have become too involved in dealing with a particular problem ▶ Let's not get bogged down with minor details.

bogus /'bəʊgəs/ *adjective*
false, but pretending to be real ▶ a bogus doctor

boil /bɔɪl/ *verb*
1 to make water or another liquid so hot that it starts to steam ▶ Boil some water to make a cup of coffee.
2 to become very hot and start to steam ▶ The water began to boil.
3 to cook food in boiling water ▶ Boil the eggs for five minutes.

boiler /'bɔɪlə^r/ *noun*
a piece of equipment that heats a large amount of water for people to use

boiling /'bɔɪlɪŋ/ *adjective*
very hot ▶ a boiling hot day

boiling point /'bɔɪlɪŋ ,pɔɪnt/ *noun*
the temperature at which a liquid gets so hot that it starts changing into steam ▶ The boiling point of water is 100° centigrade.

boisterous /'bɔɪstərəs/ *adjective*
noisy, cheerful, and full of energy ▶ a boisterous four-year-old

bold /bəʊld/ *adjective*
not afraid to do dangerous things ▶ He was very bold and tried to stop the thief.

bollard /'bɒlɑːd/ *noun*
a short, thick post that is fixed in the ground to stop cars going onto a piece of land or road

bolt¹ /bəʊlt/ *noun*
1 a piece of metal or wood used for keeping a door closed
2 a screw with no point which fastens into a NUT and holds two things together

bolt² *verb*
1 to fasten something with a bolt ▶ Bolt the door, please.
2 to run away suddenly ▶ The horse bolted and threw its rider to the ground.

bomb¹ /bɒm/ *noun*
a container full of a substance that will explode, used as a weapon

bomb² *verb*
to drop bombs on a place ▶ The airforce bombed two towns.

bombard /bɒm'bɑːd/ *verb*
1 to attack a place with guns and bombs ▶ The city was bombarded from all sides.
2 to ask someone too many questions, give them too much information, etc. to deal with ▶ The radio station has been bombarded with enquiries.

bomber /'bɒmə^r/ *noun*
1 a plane that drops bombs
2 a person who puts a bomb somewhere

bond¹ /bɒnd/ *noun*
a shared feeling or interest that makes people feel love and loyalty towards each other ➤ *There's a strong bond between the two brothers.*

bond² *verb*
1 to develop a special loving relationship with someone ➤ *It takes time to bond* **with** *a new baby.*
2 to join or glue things together firmly

bone /bəʊn/ *noun*
one of the hard, white parts in a person's or an animal's body ➤ *He fell and broke a bone in his leg.*

bone-dry /ˌbəʊn 'draɪ/ *adjective*
completely dry ➤ *After the long, hot summer, the ground was bone-dry.*

bonfire /'bɒnfaɪəʳ/ *noun*
a big fire in the open air

bonfire night /'bɒnfaɪə ˌnaɪt/ *noun*
November 5th, when people in Britain light fires in the open air and have FIREWORKS

bonnet /'bɒnɪt/ *noun*
1 a soft hat that you tie under your chin
2 the part of a car's body that covers the engine

bonus /'bəʊnəs/ *noun (plural* **bonuses***)*
1 money that is added to someone's usual pay ➤ *All members of staff get a Christmas bonus.*
2 something good that you did not expect ➤ *Getting a free printer with the computer was a bonus.*

bony /'bəʊnɪ/ *adjective* (**bonier,** **boniest**)
(used of a person's body) so thin that you can see the bones ➤ *bony fingers*

boo¹ /buː/ *verb*
to shout "boo" at someone, especially in a theatre, to show that you did not like their performance

boo² *interjection*
1 something you say loudly when you want to surprise someone who does not know you are there
2 something you shout at someone, especially in a theatre, to show that you do not like their performance

booby prize /'buːbɪ praɪz/ *noun*
a prize given as a joke to the person who finishes last in a competition

booby trap /'buːbɪ træp/ *noun*
a bomb or another dangerous thing that is hidden in something that seems harmless

book¹ /bʊk/ *noun*
1 a set of sheets of paper fastened together and with writing on them, for reading ➤ *What book are you reading?*
2 a set of sheets of paper fastened together for writing on ➤ *Write a poem in your exercise book* (=a book to do your school work in).

book² *verb*
to arrange to have something that you want to use later ➤ *I've booked tickets for tomorrow night's show.*

bookcase /'bʊk-keɪs/ *noun*
a piece of furniture with shelves for books

booking /'bʊkɪŋ/ *noun*
an arrangement that you make to have a hotel room, a seat on a plane, etc. at a particular time in the future ➤ *Can I make a booking for this evening?*

booklet /'bʊklɪt/ *noun*
a small book that contains information ➤ *a booklet that gives advice to patients with the disease*

bookmaker /'bʊkˌmeɪkəʳ/ *noun*
a person whose job is to serve people who want to BET on the result of a game or competition

bookmark /'bʊkmɑːk/ *noun*
a piece of paper that you put in a book so that you can find the page you want

B

bookshop /'bʊkʃɒp/ *noun*
a shop that sells books

book token /'bʊk ˌtəʊkən/ *noun*
a card that is given to you as a gift so that you can buy books with it ▶ *My uncle gave me a £10 book token for my birthday.*

boom /buːm/ *noun*
a loud, deep sound

boost¹ /buːst/ *noun*
something that helps you become more successful or feel more confident and happy ▶ *The queen's visit gave a great boost to local people.*

boost² *verb*
to increase the value or amount of something ▶ *The hot weather boosted sales of ice cream.*

boot /buːt/ *noun*
1 a shoe that covers your foot and ankle
2 the part of a car's body where bags, boxes, etc. can be carried

booth /buːð/ *noun*
a small, enclosed area, often used for doing something privately ▶ *a telephone booth* ▶ *a voting booth*

booze /buːz/ *noun (no plural)*
alcoholic drink

border /'bɔːdəʳ/ *noun*
1 an edge ▶ *white plates with a blue border*
2 the dividing line between two countries
SAME MEANING (2): **frontier**

bore¹ /bɔːʳ/ *verb (present participle boring, past bored)*
1 to make someone feel uninterested ▶ *He bored me with his stamp collection.*
2 to make a deep, round hole in something, especially rock or stone ▶ *This machine can bore through solid rock.*

bore² *noun*

an uninteresting or a dull person or thing

bore³
the PAST TENSE of the verb **bear**

bored /bɔːd/ *adjective*
feeling tired and uninterested ▶ *She was bored with her job.*
COMPARE: **fed up**
LOOK AT: **boring**

boredom /'bɔːdəm/ *noun (no plural)*
the feeling of being bored

boring /'bɔːrɪŋ/ *adjective*
not interesting; dull ▶ *a boring film*

Do not confuse the adjectives **boring** and **bored**. If something is **boring**, it is not interesting: *a boring lesson*. **Bored** is used to describe the way you feel when something is boring: *The children were bored with the game and did not want to play any more.*

born /bɔːn/ *adjective*
be born to come into the world; to be given life ▶ *The baby was born yesterday.*

borne /bɔːn/
the PAST PARTICIPLE of the verb **bear**

borrow /'bɒrəʊ/ *verb*
to use something which belongs to someone else. You usually ask permission and say when you will return the thing ▶ *Can I borrow your bicycle until Saturday?*

Compare the verbs **borrow** and **lend**. If you **lend** something to a person, you let them use it for a while. If you **borrow** something from someone, you take it from them, knowing that you will give it back to them later. The verb **lend** often has two objects (to lend something to somebody), but **borrow** just has one (to borrow something): *Will you lend me some money?* ▶ *Can I borrow some money?*

bosom /ˈbʊzəm/ *noun*
a woman's breast or breasts

boss[1] /bɒs/ *noun (plural **bosses**)*
a person who is in charge and tells other people what work to do

boss[2] *verb*
boss someone about to tell someone what to do, usually by giving them too many orders ▶ *My brother's always bossing me about.*

bossy /ˈbɒsɪ/ *adjective (**bossier**, **bossiest**)*
liking to give orders to other people ▶ *a bossy older sister*

botany /ˈbɒtənɪ/ *noun (no plural)*
the scientific study of plants

both /bəʊθ/ *adjective, pronoun, adverb*
this one and that one; the two ▶ *Hold the dish with both hands.* ▶ *We both like dancing.*

bother[1] /ˈbɒðə/ *verb*
1 to interrupt someone and annoy them ▶ *I'm sorry to bother you, but I need some help.* ▶ *Don't bother your father now – he's very busy.*
2 to worry someone ▶ *I always know when something is bothering him.*
3 can't be bothered to not want to do something because it is too much effort ▶ *I can't be bothered to go out tonight.*
4 not bother not to make the effort to do something ▶ *Don't bother to dry the plates.* ▶ *He didn't even bother to say goodbye.*

bother[2] *noun (no plural)*
something that causes difficulty ▶ *We had a little bother when the policeman stopped us.*

bottle[1] /ˈbɒtl/ *noun*
a tall, round glass or plastic container, with a narrow neck
COMPARE: **jar**

bottle[2] *verb (present participle **bottling**, past **bottled**)*
to put something into bottles ▶ *This is where they bottle the milk.*

bottle bank /ˈbɒtl bæŋk/ *noun*
a place where old glass bottles are taken so that the glass can be used again

bottled /ˈbɒtld/ *adjective*
kept or sold in bottles

bottleneck /ˈbɒtlnek/ *noun*
a place in a road where the traffic cannot pass easily, so that cars are delayed

bottom /ˈbɒtəm/ *noun*
1 the lowest part of something ▶ *at the bottom of the page*
2 the base of something ▶ *The price is on the bottom of the box.*
3 the lowest position in something, e.g. a class ▶ *He's not very good at maths – he's always at the bottom of the class.*
OPPOSITE: (**1**, **2**, and **3**): **top**
4 the part of the body that you sit on ▶ *He fell on his bottom.*

bought /bɔːt/
the PAST TENSE and PAST PARTICIPLE of the verb **buy**

boulder /ˈbəʊldə/ *noun*
a large rock

boulevard /ˈbuːlvɑːd/ *noun*
a wide road in a town or city, usually with trees along the sides

bounce /baʊns/ *verb (present participle **bouncing**, past **bounced**)*
1 to spring back after hitting something or falling on something ▶ *The baby was bouncing on the bed.*
2 to throw something, e.g. a ball, against something, so that it springs back ▶ *He bounced the ball against the wall.*

bouncer /ˈbaʊnsə/ *noun*
a person whose job is to keep people who behave badly out of a club or bar

bouncy /ˈbaʊnsɪ/ *adjective (**bouncier**, **bounciest**)*

B

B

able to spring back easily after hitting something or after being hit by something ▶ *a bouncy ball* ▶ *a bouncy bed*

bound¹ /baʊnd/ *verb*
to jump around ▶ *The young animals were bounding about the field.*

bound² *noun*
a big jump

bound³
the PAST TENSE and PAST PARTICIPLE of the verb **bind**

boundary /'baʊndəri/ *noun (plural boundaries)*
the dividing line between two places ▶ *the boundary between the two gardens*
COMPARE: **border**

bound to /'baʊnd tu:/ *adjective*
be bound to to be certain to do something or be certain to happen ▶ *You're bound to pass the exams – you've worked very hard.*

bouquet /bəʊ'keɪ/ *noun*
a number of flowers fastened together that you give to someone

bout /baʊt/ *noun*
a short period of illness ▶ *a bout of flu*

boutique /bu:'ti:k/ *noun*
a small shop that sells fashionable clothes

bow¹ /baʊ/ *verb*
to bend the top part of your body forward to show respect ▶ *Everyone bowed to the President.*

bow² /baʊ/ *noun*
an act of bending your body or your head forward to show respect

bow³ /bəʊ/ *noun*
1 a piece of wood held in a curve by a string, used for shooting arrows
2 a long, thin piece of wood with tight strings fastened along it, used for playing musical instruments like the VIOLIN
3 a knot used for tying shoes ▶ *She tied the ribbon in a bow.*

bowel /'baʊəl/ *noun*
the part inside your body that carries solid waste food away from the stomach and out of the body

bowl /bəʊl/ *noun*
a deep, round dish or container ▶ *Fill the bowl with water.*
COMPARE: **plate**

bow-legged /,bəʊ 'legɪd/ *adjective*
having legs that curve outwards at the knees

bowling /'bəʊlɪŋ/ *noun (no plural)*
an indoor game in which you roll a heavy ball along a wooden track in order to knock over pieces of wood

bow tie /,bəʊ 'taɪ/ *noun*
a man's tie fastened in the shape of a BOW

box¹ /bɒks/ *noun (plural boxes)*
a container with straight sides, usually made of cardboard or wood ▶ *a box of matches*

box² *verb*
to fight with tightly closed hands, usually for sport

boxer /'bɒksə'/ *noun*
a man who fights with tightly closed hands, for sport

boxer shorts /'bɒksə ʃɔ:ts/ *plural noun*
loose cotton underwear for men

boxing /'bɒksɪŋ/ *noun (no plural)*
the sport of fighting with tightly closed hands

Boxing Day /'bɒksɪŋ ,deɪ/ *noun*
the day after Christmas

box office /'bɒks ,ɒfɪs/ *noun*
a place in a theatre or cinema where you can buy tickets

boy /bɔɪ/ *noun*
a male child ▶ *They have five children: three boys and two girls.*

boycott /'bɔɪkɒt/ *verb*
to refuse to buy or use something, as

a protest ▸ *The US has threatened to boycott French wine.*

boyfriend /'bɔɪfrend/ *noun*
a boy or man you have a romantic relationship with ▸ *Can my boyfriend come to the party?*

boyhood /'bɔɪhʊd/ *noun (no plural)*
the time during a man's life when he is a boy

boyish /'bɔɪ-ɪʃ/ *adjective*
looking or behaving like an attractive young man ▸ *a slim, boyish figure*

bra /brɑː/ *noun*
a piece of clothing that women wear under other clothes to support their breasts

brace /breɪs/ *noun*
a wire which some children wear inside their mouths to make their teeth straight

bracelet /'breɪslɪt/ *noun*
a band or chain that you wear as an ornament round your wrist

braces /'breɪsɪz/ *plural noun*
cloth bands that you wear over your shoulders to hold up your trousers

brackets /'brækɪts/ *plural noun*
the small, curved lines ( ) that you sometimes use in writing to add information ▸ *Put the dates in brackets.*
SAME MEANING: **parentheses**

brag /bræg/ *verb (present participle bragging, past bragged)*
to talk too proudly about things you have done or about your possessions ▸ *He bragged that he had passed the exam easily.* ▸ *He was bragging about his new expensive car.*
SAME MEANING: **boast**

braid /breɪd/ *noun (no plural)*
threads woven together and used to decorate clothes ▸ *gold braid*

braille /breɪl/ *noun (no plural)*
a type of printing that blind people can read by touching the page

brain /breɪn/ *noun*
the part inside your head with which you think

brainwash /'breɪnwɒʃ/ *verb*
to force someone to believe something that is not true by telling them many times that it is true ▸ *People are brainwashed into believing that being fat is some kind of crime.*

brainwave /'breɪnweɪv/ *noun*
a very good idea that you have suddenly

brainy /'breɪnɪ/ *adjective (brainier, brainiest)*
clever and quick at doing school work
SAME MEANING: **bright**

brake¹ /breɪk/ *noun*
the part of a bicycle, car, train, etc. that you use to stop it or make it go more slowly

brake² *verb (present participle braking, past braked)*
to make a bicycle, car, train, etc. stop or go more slowly by using the brake ▸ *The driver braked quickly to avoid an accident.*

bran /bræn/ *noun (no plural)*
the crushed skin of wheat and other grain, often used in bread

branch /brɑːntʃ/ *noun (plural branches)*
1 a part of a tree that grows from a trunk
COMPARE: **twig**
2 one part or one office of a business ▸ *The bank has branches in all the big towns.*

brand /brænd/ *noun*
the name of a particular kind of goods made by one company ▸ *What brand of soap do you like?*

brandish /'brændɪʃ/ *verb*
to wave a weapon around in a dangerous and threatening way ▸ *He ran into the room brandishing a knife.*

B

brand-new /ˌbrænd ˈnjuː/ *adjective*
completely new; never used before
▶ *a brand-new car*

brandy /ˈbrændɪ/ *noun*
1 (*no plural*) a strong alcoholic drink
2 (*plural* **brandies**) a glass of this
drink ▶ *Can I have two brandies,
please?*

brash /bræʃ/ *adjective*
behaving too confidently and
speaking too loudly ▶ *a brash young
salesperson*

brass /brɑːs/ *noun* (*no plural*)
a very hard, yellow metal which
shines brightly, made by mixing
COPPER and ZINC ▶ *ornaments made of
brass*

brat /bræt/ *noun*
a badly behaved child ▶ *a spoilt brat*

bravado /brəˈvɑːdəʊ/ *noun* (*no
plural*)
behaviour that is intended to show
that you are brave and confident,
even when you are not

brave /breɪv/ *adjective*
not afraid or not showing fear
▶ *a brave fireman* (*adverb:* **bravely**)

bravery /ˈbreɪvərɪ/ *noun* (*no plural*)
willingness to do dangerous things
without feeling afraid ▶ *The fireman
was praised for his bravery.*
SAME MEANING: **courage**
OPPOSITE: **cowardice**

bravo /ˈbrɑːvəʊ/ *interjection*
a word you shout to show that you
like or approve of something

brawl /brɔːl/ *noun*
a noisy fight

breach /briːtʃ/ *noun* (*plural* **breaches**)
the act of breaking a law, rule, or
agreement ▶ *If he leaves, he will be
in breach of his contract.*

bread /bred/ *noun* (*no plural*)
a food made by mixing flour, water,
and YEAST and then baking it ▶ *a loaf
of bread*

breadth /bredθ/ *noun* (*no plural*)
the distance from one side of
something to the other ▶ *What's the
breadth of this river?*

breadwinner /ˈbredˌwɪnəʳ/ *noun*
the person in a family who earns
most of the money that the family
needs ▶ *Mum was the breadwinner
after dad became ill.*

break¹ /breɪk/ *verb* (*past tense* **broke**
/brəʊk/, *past participle* **broken**
/ˈbrəʊkən/)
1 to make something separate into
pieces ▶ *He broke the window with
his football.*
2 to separate into pieces ▶ *The plate
fell on the floor and broke.*
3 to make something not work
▶ *Don't play with the radio – you'll
break it!*
4 break down (used about cars or
machines) to stop working ▶ *My car
broke down on the way to work.*
5 break in to get inside a place using
force ▶ *Someone broke in through
the window* (=broke the window to
get inside the building).
6 break into something to get inside
a place, e.g. a building or something
that is locked, by using force ▶ *The
thief broke into my drawer and stole
my money.*
7 break the law to do something that
the law says you must not do
8 break out (used especially about
fighting or fire) to start suddenly
▶ *The fire broke out at 2 o'clock in
the morning.*
9 break a promise not to do
something that you promised you
would do
10 break up (**a**) to finish a
relationship with a boyfriend or
girlfriend ▶ *John and Sarah broke up
last week.*
(**b**) to stop going to school because
the holidays are starting ▶ *We break
up next week.*

break² *noun*
1 an opening in something made by breaking it ➤ *a break in the clouds*
2 a short rest ➤ *Let's have a break.*

breakable /ˈbreɪkəbəl/ *adjective*
likely to break

breakage /ˈbreɪkɪdʒ/ *noun*
something that has been broken ➤ *All breakages must be paid for.*

breakdown /ˈbreɪkdaʊn/ *noun*
when a car or machine stops working

breakfast /ˈbrekfəst/ *noun*
the first meal of the day

break-in /ˈbreɪk ɪn/ *noun*
the act of breaking a door or window in order to enter a building and steal things ➤ *There was a break-in at the hotel over the weekend.*

breakthrough /ˈbreɪkθruː/ *noun*
an important new discovery or development ➤ *a breakthrough in the treatment of cancer*

breakup /ˈbreɪkʌp/ *noun*
1 the process of ending a marriage or romantic relationship
2 the process of separating an organization or a country into smaller parts ➤ *the fighting that followed the breakup of Yugoslavia*

breast /brest/ *noun*
1 one of the two parts on the front of a woman's body that can produce milk
2 the top part of the front of a person's body
SAME MEANING (**2**): **chest**

breaststroke /ˈbrestˌstrəʊk/ *noun (no plural)*
a way of swimming by pulling the water back with your arms

breath /breθ/ *noun*
1 the air that you take in and let out through your nose and mouth ➤ *He took a deep breath and jumped into the water.*

2 a breath of fresh air a bit of clean air outside ➤ *Let's go to the park for a breath of fresh air.*
3 hold your breath to stop breathing for a little while, especially when you want to swim underwater ➤ *How long can you hold your breath?*
4 be out of breath not to be able to breathe easily for a little while, e.g. after running

breathe /briːð/ *verb (present participle **breathing**, past **breathed**)*
to take air into your body and let it out through your nose and mouth

breather /ˈbriːðəʳ/ *noun*
a short rest ➤ *Let's stop for a breather.*

breathless /ˈbreθləs/ *adjective*
having difficulty breathing, especially after exercise

breathtaking /ˈbreθˌteɪkɪŋ/ *adjective*
very beautiful, impressive, exciting, or surprising ➤ *a breathtaking view of the Grand Canyon*

breed¹ /briːd/ *verb (past **bred** /bred/)*
1 (used about animals) to produce young ➤ *Some animals will not breed in cages.*
COMPARE: **mate**
2 to keep animals so that they will produce young ones ➤ *He breeds cattle.*

breed² *noun*
a type of animal ➤ *a breed of cattle*

breeze /briːz/ *noun*
a light wind ➤ *a cool breeze*

breezy /ˈbriːzɪ/ *adjective (**breezier**, **breeziest**)*
with quite a strong wind ➤ *a warm but rather breezy day*

brew /bruː/ *verb*
1 to make tea, leaving it in the pot until the taste develops ➤ *Let the tea brew for a few minutes.*
2 to make beer

B

3 be brewing to be going to happen ▶ *I think a storm is brewing.*

brewery /'bruːəri/ *noun (plural breweries)*
a place where beer is made, or a company that makes beer

bribe¹ /braɪb/ *verb (present participle bribing, past bribed)*
to offer to give someone money or a present if they help you by doing something that is not honest or legal ▶ *He tried to bribe the policeman to let him go.*

bribe² *noun*
money or a present which you give to someone if they help you by doing something that is not honest or legal ▶ *A policeman should never take bribes.*

bribery /'braɪbəri/ *noun (no plural)*
the act of offering money or a present to someone, or accepting money or a present from them if they help you by doing something that is not honest or legal

brick /brɪk/ *noun*
a block of baked clay, used for building

bridal /'braɪdl/ *adjective*
connected with a bride or a wedding ▶ *a bridal shop*

bride /braɪd/ *noun*
a woman who is going to get married, or who has just got married

bridegroom /'braɪdgruːm/ *noun*
a man who is going to get married, or who has just got married
SAME MEANING: **groom**

bridesmaid /'braɪdz,meɪd/ *noun*
a girl or woman who helps a bride at her wedding
COMPARE: **best man**

bridge /brɪdʒ/ *noun*
a road or railway line built over something ▶ *a bridge across the river*

bridle /'braɪdl/ *noun*
leather bands put on a horse's head to control its movement

brief /briːf/ *adjective*
lasting a short time ▶ *a brief meeting* (adverb: **briefly**)

briefcase /'briːfkeɪs/ *noun*
a thin, flat case for carrying papers or books
COMPARE: **suitcase**

briefs /briːfs/ *plural noun*
underwear that you wear between your waist and the top of your legs ▶ *a pair of cotton briefs*

brigade /brɪ'geɪd/ *noun*
a large group of soldiers who are part of an army

bright /braɪt/ *adjective*
1 sending out a strong, shining light ▶ *bright sunlight*
2 having a strong, clear colour ▶ *My favourite colour is bright yellow.*
3 quick at learning things; clever ▶ *a bright child*
SAME MEANING (**3**): **brainy**

brighten /'braɪtn/ *verb*
brighten up (used about the weather) to become more sunny or lighter and better ▶ *It should brighten up later.*

brilliant /'brɪljənt/ *adjective*
1 very clever ▶ *a brilliant idea* ▶ *a brilliant student*
2 Brilliant! something you say when you think something is very good ▶ *"I got the job." "Brilliant!"*
3 (used about colours and light) very bright

brim /brɪm/ *noun*
1 the edge of a cup, glass, or bowl
2 the part of a hat that stands out around the sides

bring /brɪŋ/ *verb (past brought /brɔːt/)*
1 to carry something to someone or towards a place ▶ *Bring me the ball.*

B

▶ *You can take that book home, but bring it back* (=return it) *tomorrow, please.*
COMPARE: **take**
LOOK AT: **fetch**
2 to take someone with you to a place ▶ *Bring your brother to the party.*
3 bring someone up to care for and educate a child

brink /brɪŋk/ *noun*
be on the brink of something if you are on the brink of something exciting or terrible, it will happen soon ▶ *The country is on the brink of war.*

brisk /brɪsk/ *adjective*
quick and active ▶ *a brisk walk*

bristle /'brɪsəl/ *noun*
one of many short, stiff hairs, wires, etc. growing or placed together ▶ *the bristles on a toothbrush*

British /'brɪtɪʃ/ *adjective*
of, about, or from Great Britain

brittle /'brɪtl/ *adjective*
hard, but easily broken ▶ *brittle glass*

broach /brəʊtʃ/ *verb*
to mention a subject that may be embarrassing or unpleasant ▶ *Parents often find it hard to broach the subject of sex.*

broad /brɔːd/ *adjective*
wide ▶ *broad shoulders*
OPPOSITE: **narrow**

broadcast¹ /'brɔːdkɑːst/ *verb (past **broadcast**)*
to send out PROGRAMMES by radio or television to the public ▶ *The new programme will be broadcast at 7 o'clock.*

broadcast² *noun*
a PROGRAMME that is sent out on the radio or television ▶ *a news broadcast*

broaden /'brɔːdn/ *verb*
1 to make something include more kinds of things or people ▶ *The*

course will broaden your knowledge of computers.
2 broaden out to become wider ▶ *The river broadens out here.*

broadly /'brɔːdli/ *adverb*
in a general way ▶ *I broadly agree with what you are saying.*

broadminded /ˌbrɔːd'maɪndɪd/ *adjective*
willing to accept behaviour or ideas that are different from your own

broccoli /'brɒkəli/ *noun (no plural)*
a green vegetable with green or purple flowers that you cook

brochure /'brəʊʃəʳ/ *noun*
a thin book that gives information or advertises something ▶ *a holiday brochure*

broke /brəʊk/
the PAST TENSE of the verb **break**

broken¹ /'brəʊkən/
the PAST PARTICIPLE of the verb **break**

broken² *adjective*
1 in pieces ▶ *a broken window*
2 not working ▶ *a broken clock*

broken-hearted /ˌbrəʊkən 'hɑːtɪd/ *adjective*
very sad, especially because someone you love has died or left you

broker¹ /'brəʊkəʳ/ *noun*
a person whose job is to buy and sell property, insurance, etc. for other people

broker² *verb*
to arrange the details of a deal, plan, etc. so that everyone can agree to it ▶ *an agreement brokered by the UN*

bronze /brɒnz/ *noun (no plural)*
a hard metal, made by mixing COPPER and TIN

brooch /brəʊtʃ/ *noun (plural **brooches**)*
an ornament that women sometimes pin on their clothes
COMPARE: **badge**

B

brood /bruːd/ verb
to think about something angrily or
sadly for a long time ▶ You can't just
sit there brooding over your
problems.

broom /bruːm/ noun
a brush with a long handle

brothel /ˈbrɒθəl/ noun
a house where men pay to have sex
with women

brother /ˈbrʌðəʳ/ noun
a boy or man with the same parents
as another person ▶ Peter is my
brother.
COMPARE: **sister**

brother-in-law /ˈbrʌðər ɪn lɔː/ noun
(plural **brothers-in-law**)
1 the brother of your wife or husband
2 the husband of your sister

brought /brɔːt/
the PAST TENSE and PAST PARTICIPLE of the
verb **bring**

brow /braʊ/ noun
the part of your face between your
eyes and your hair

brown¹ /braʊn/ adjective, noun
a dark colour like coffee or earth
▶ a brown chair ▶ the brown of her
eyes

browse /braʊz/ verb (present
participle **browsing**, past **browsed**)
1 to spend time looking at things in a
shop without buying anything and
without hurrying
2 to look through a book or magazine
without reading it carefully
3 to look for information on the
INTERNET

browser /ˈbraʊzəʳ/ noun
computer SOFTWARE that you use to
look at information on the INTERNET

bruise¹ /bruːz/ noun
a mark left on your skin after a blow
or when you have fallen down

bruise² verb (present participle
bruising, past **bruised**)

to mark someone's skin with a bruise
▶ She fell and bruised her knee

brunette /bruːˈnet/ noun
a woman who has dark brown hair

brunt /brʌnt/ noun
bear the brunt of something to suffer
the worst part of something
unpleasant ▶ The south coast bore
the brunt of the storm.

brush¹ /brʌʃ/ noun (plural **brushes**)
a group of strong hairs on the end of
a handle that can be used for
cleaning, painting, tidying your hair,
etc.

brush² verb
to clean or tidy something with a
brush ▶ Have you brushed your hair?

brussels sprout /ˌbrʌsəlz ˈspraʊt/
noun
a small, round, green vegetable

brutal /ˈbruːtl/ adjective
very cruel and violent ▶ a brutal
murder (adverb: **brutally**)

brute¹ /bruːt/ noun
1 a cruel, violent man
2 a large, strong animal

brute² adjective
brute force, brute strength physical
strength that is used instead of
gentle, clever methods ▶ He uses
brute force to get what he wants.

BSc /ˌbiː es ˈsiː/ noun
BACHELOR OF SCIENCE; a university
degree in a science subject ▶ He has
a BSc in Chemistry.

bubble¹ /ˈbʌbəl/ noun
a hollow ball of liquid containing air
or gas ▶ soap bubbles

bubble² verb (present participle
bubbling, past **bubbled**)
to make balls of air or gas ▶ The
water was bubbling gently in the pan.

bubbly /ˈbʌblɪ/ adjective (**bubblier**,
bubbliest)
1 full of bubbles

2 cheerful and full of energy ▶ *a bubbly personality*

buck /bʌk/ *noun*
a male deer or rabbit

bucket /'bʌkɪt/ *noun*
a container made of metal or plastic, with a handle, for holding or carrying water

buckle /'bʌkəl/ *noun*
a fastener used for joining the ends of a belt

bud /bʌd/ *noun*
a young flower or leaf before it opens

Buddhism /'bʊdɪzəm/ *noun (no plural)*
the religion based on the teachings of Buddha

Buddhist /'bʊdɪst/ *noun*
a person who follows the teachings of Buddha

buddy /'bʌdɪ/ *noun (plural **buddies**)*
a friend

budge /bʌdʒ/ *verb (present participle **budging**, past **budged**)*
to make something heavy move a little ▶ *I can't budge this rock.*

budget¹ /'bʌdʒɪt/ *noun*
a plan of how to spend money ▶ *a government's budget*

budget² *verb*
to plan how much money you have to spend on certain things

budgie /'bʌdʒɪ/ *noun*
a small, brightly coloured bird, usually kept in a cage as a pet

buffet /'bʊfeɪ/ *noun*
a meal in which people serve themselves at a table and then move away to eat

bug /bʌg/ *noun*
1 a small insect
2 a very small living thing that can get into your body and make you feel unwell ▶ *I can't go to school this week because I've got a bug.*

buggy /'bʌgɪ/ *noun (plural **buggies**)*
a small, folding chair on wheels, in which you can push a small child
SAME MEANING: **pushchair**

bugle /'bjuːgəl/ *noun*
a musical instrument that is played by blowing and is used especially by the army

build¹ /bɪld/ *verb (past **built** /bɪlt/)*
to make something by putting pieces together ▶ *The house is built of brick.*

build² *noun (no plural)*
the size and shape of someone's body ▶ *Maggie is tall with a slim build.*

builder /'bɪldəʳ/ *noun*
a person whose job it is to make houses and other buildings
COMPARE: **architect**

building /'bɪldɪŋ/ *noun*
something with a roof and walls, e.g. a house or an office

building society /'bɪldɪŋ səˌsaɪətɪ/ *noun (plural **building societies**)*
a type of bank where you can save money or borrow money to buy a house

built /bɪlt/
the PAST TENSE and PAST PARTICIPLE of the verb **build**

bulb /bʌlb/ *(also **light bulb**) noun*
the glass part of an electric light that shines when it is turned on

bulge¹ /bʌldʒ/ *verb (present participle **bulging**, past **bulged**)*
to swell out ▶ *His pocket was bulging with sweets.*

bulge² *noun*
a swelling shape

bulk /bʌlk/ *noun*
1 the bulk of something the main or largest part of something ▶ *The bulk of the work has already been done.*
2 in bulk in large quantities ▶ *It's cheaper to buy things in bulk.*

B

bulky /'bʌlkɪ/ *adjective (bulkier, bulkiest)*
having a large, difficult shape
▶ *I can't carry that box – it's too bulky.*

bull /bʊl/ *noun*
the male of the cow family

bulldog /'bʊldɒg/ *noun*
a short, strong dog with a thick neck and short legs

bulldozer /'bʊldəʊzəʳ/ *noun*
a powerful machine that moves earth to make land flat

bullet /'bʊlɪt/ *noun*
a piece of metal that is fired from a gun

bulletin /'bʊlətɪn/ *noun*
a short news report ▶ *Our next bulletin is at 6 o'clock.*

bulletin board /'bʊlətɪn ˌbɔːd/ *noun*
a place on a computer system where a group of people can leave and read messages

bullock /'bʊlək/ *noun*
a young male cow which cannot be the father of young ones

bully¹ /'bʊlɪ/ *noun (plural bullies)*
a person who likes to hurt weaker people or make them afraid

bully² *verb (past bullied)*
to hurt people who are not as strong as you, or make them afraid

bum /bʌm/ *noun*
the part of your body that you sit on

bump¹ /bʌmp/ *verb*
1 to knock something by accident
▶ *I bumped my knee on the chair.*
▶ *He bumped into a tree and hit his head.*
2 bump into someone to meet someone by chance ▶ *I bumped into John in town.*

bump² *noun*
a round swelling on your body where you have knocked it ▶ *He had a bump on his head.*

bumper /'bʌmpəʳ/ *noun*
a bar at the front and back of a car to protect it from knocks

bumpy /'bʌmpɪ/ *adjective (bumpier, bumpiest)*
rough; not smooth ▶ *a bumpy road*

bun /bʌn/ *noun*
a small, round, sweet cake

bunch /bʌntʃ/ *noun (plural bunches)*
several things of the same kind fastened together ▶ *a bunch of flowers*

bundle /'bʌndl/ *noun*
a number of things held together so that you can carry them or put them somewhere ▶ *a bundle of clothes*

bung /bʌŋ/ *verb*
to put something somewhere
▶ *Just bung your coat on the chair.*

bungalow /'bʌŋgələʊ/ *noun*
a house that is all on the same level as the ground

bunk /bʌŋk/ *noun*
a narrow bed which is fixed to the wall on a ship or train

bunk bed /'bʌŋk bed/ *noun*
one of two beds that are put one on top of another and used especially for children to sleep in

bunker /'bʌŋkəʳ/ *noun*
a strongly built room or building where people can shelter from bombs

buoy /bɔɪ/ *noun*
a floating object used to show ships where there are rocks

burden /'bɜːdn/ *noun*
something heavy that you have to carry ▶ *The donkey carried its burden up the mountain.*

bureau /'bjʊərəʊ/ *noun (plural bureaux* /'bjʊərəʊz/*)*
1 an office or organization that collects or provides information
▶ *an employment bureau*

2 a government department, or part of one ▶ *the Federal Bureau of Investigation*
3 a piece of furniture with drawers and a sloping lid that you can open and use as a desk

bureaucracy /bjʊəˈrɒkrəsɪ/ *noun (no plural)*
an official system that annoys and confuses people because it has too many rules

bureaucratic /ˌbjʊərəˈkrætɪk/ *adjective*
involving a lot of official rules and processes in a way that annoys people

bureaux /ˈbjʊərəʊz/
the plural of **bureau**

burger /ˈbɜːgəʳ/ *noun*
meat that has been cut into very small pieces and then made into a round, flat shape before being cooked

burglar /ˈbɜːgləʳ/ *noun*
a person who enters buildings, usually by force, to steal things
COMPARE: **robber, thief**

burglary /ˈbɜːglərɪ/ *noun (plural burglaries)*
the crime of entering a building, usually by force, and stealing things

burgle /ˈbɜːgəl/ *verb (present participle burgling, past burgled)*
to enter a building, usually by force, and steal things from it

burial /ˈberɪəl/ *noun*
the ceremony at which a dead person is put into the ground

burn¹ /bɜːn/ *verb (past burned or burnt* /bɜːnt/)
1 to damage or destroy something with fire, or to be damaged or destroyed in this way ▶ *We burned the old furniture.*
2 to hurt yourself or a part of your body with something very hot

▶ *I've burned my fingers.*
3 burn down (used about a building) to be destroyed completely by fire ▶ *The cinema burned down last year.*

burn² *noun*
a wound or mark on your body caused by fire or by touching something very hot ▶ *a burn on his arm*

burnt /bɜːnt/
the PAST TENSE and PAST PARTICIPLE of the verb **burn**

burp /bɜːp/ *verb*
to let air come out noisily from your stomach through your mouth
SAME MEANING: **belch**

burrow /ˈbʌrəʊ/ *noun*
a hole in the ground made as a home by some small animals, e.g. rabbits

burst /bɜːst/ *verb (past burst)*
1 to break apart because of too much pressure inside ▶ *The bag will burst if you put any more things in it.*
2 to make something break apart by putting too much pressure inside it ▶ *Don't put any more air in the tyre or you'll burst it* (=make it explode).
3 burst into tears to start crying suddenly
4 burst out laughing to start laughing loudly and suddenly

bury /ˈberɪ/ *verb (past buried)*
1 to put a dead body into the ground
2 to put or hide something in the ground ▶ *The dog buried the bone.*

bus /bʌs/ *noun (plural buses)*
a large vehicle that takes people from one place to another ▶ *Let's go into town by bus.*

bus driver /ˈbʌs ˌdraɪvəʳ/ *noun*
a person whose job is driving buses

bush /bʊʃ/ *noun (plural bushes)*
a small tree

bushy /ˈbʊʃɪ/ *adjective (bushier, bushiest)*
growing thickly ▶ *a bushy tail*

busily /'bɪzɪli/ *adverb*
done with great activity and interest ► *busily planning the wedding*

business /'bɪznəs/ *noun*
1 (plural **businesses**) a company that provides a service or sells things to earn money ► *He has a furniture business in town.*
2 (no plural) making, buying, and selling things ► *Business is good this year* (=we are earning a lot of money).
3 **mind your own business** a rude way of telling someone that you are not going to answer their questions about a particular matter ► *"Who are you going to the party with?" "Mind your own business."*
4 **none of your business** a rude way of telling someone that something is not their concern ► *It's none of your business how she spends her money.*

businesslike /'bɪznəslaɪk/ *adjective*
sensible and practical in the way you do things ► *a businesslike manner*

businessman /'bɪznəsmæn/ *noun* (plural **businessmen** /-mən/)
a man who works in business, especially one who owns a company or helps to run it

businesswoman /'bɪznəsˌwʊmən/ *noun* (plural **businesswomen** /-ˌwɪmɪn/)
a woman who works in business, especially one who owns a company or helps to run it

bus stop /'bʌs stɒp/ *noun*
a place where buses stop for people to get off and on

bust¹ /bʌst/ *verb* (past **bust** or **busted**)
to break something ► *Someone's bust the photocopier again!*

bust² *noun*
1 a woman's breasts, or the measurement around a woman's breasts and back

2 a MODEL of someone's head, shoulders, and upper chest ► *a bust of Shakespeare*

bust³ *adjective*
1 **go bust** a business that goes bust has to close because it has lost so much money
2 not working ► *This TV is bust.*

bustle¹ /'bʌsəl/ *noun*
busy and noisy activity

bustle² *verb* (present participle **bustling**, past **bustled**)
to move around and do things in a quick, busy way ► *Linda was bustling around in the kitchen.*

busy /'bɪzi/ *adjective* (**busier**, **busiest**)
1 working; not free; having a lot to do ► *He is busy at the moment, I'm afraid.* ► *He's busy writing letters.*
2 full of activity ► *a busy day* ► *a busy street*

but /bət; *strong* bʌt/ *conjunction*
a word you use when you are saying that although one thing is true, another thing which is opposite to it is also true ► *They are poor, but happy.* ► *I'd like to come, but I can't.*

butcher /'bʊtʃər/ *noun*
1 a person who sells meat
2 **butcher's** a shop that sells meat

butt¹ /bʌt/ *noun*
1 the person that other people often make jokes about ► *Why am I always the butt of their jokes?*
2 the end of a cigarette after it has been smoked

butt² *verb*
butt in to interrupt a conversation ► *Sorry, I didn't mean to butt in.*

butter /'bʌtər/ *noun* (no plural)
yellow fat made from milk ► *bread and butter*

butterfly /'bʌtəflaɪ/ *noun* (plural **butterflies**)
an insect that has delicate wings with

bright colours on them
COMPARE: **moth**

buttocks /'bʌtəks/ *plural noun*
the part of your body that you sit on

button /'bʌtn/ *noun*
1 a small, round object that you push through a hole to fasten clothes
➤ *Do your buttons up; it's cold.*
2 a round object that you push to start or stop a machine

buttonhole /'bʌtnhəʊl/ *noun*
the hole that a button goes through

buy /baɪ/ *verb (past bought /bɔːt/)*
to get something by paying money for it ➤ *I bought a new radio.*
COMPARE: **sell**

buyer /'baɪəʳ/ *noun*
a person who is buying something, especially something expensive
➤ *We've found a buyer for our house.*

buzz /bʌz/ *verb*
1 to make a low, steady noise like the sound a bee makes
2 buzz off a rude way of telling someone to go away ➤ *Buzz off and leave me alone!*

buzzer /'bʌzəʳ/ *noun*
a piece of electric equipment that makes a sudden sound to tell you that something has happened

by¹ /baɪ/ *preposition*
1 near; beside ➤ *He was standing by the window.*
2 past ➤ *He walked by me without saying hello.*
3 used to show who or what does something ➤ *The house was damaged by fire.* ➤ *a story by a famous writer*
4 used to show how something is done ➤ *I earned some money by delivering newspapers.*
5 no later than ➤ *Please do it by tomorrow.*
6 used to show what vehicle, etc. you travel on ➤ *Are you going by car or by train?*

by² *adverb*
past ➤ *I sat and watched people go by.* ➤ *Hundreds of cars drove by.*

bye /baɪ/ *(also bye-bye /,baɪ 'baɪ/) interjection*
a word you say when you leave someone, or when they leave you

byte /baɪt/ *noun*
a unit for measuring the amount of information a computer can use
➤ *There are one million bytes in one megabyte.*

Cc

C a short way of writing the words **Celsius** or **centigrade**

cab /kæb/ *noun*
1 the part of a lorry where the driver sits
2 a car with a driver who will take you somewhere if you pay.
SAME MEANING (2): **taxi**

cabbage /'kæbɪdʒ/ *noun*
a large, round vegetable with thick, green leaves

cabin /'kæbɪn/ *noun*
1 a room on a ship or plane
2 a small, wooden house

cabinet /'kæbɪnət/ *noun*
1 a piece of furniture with shelves or drawers ➤ *a medicine cabinet*
2 the small group of people in a government who have the most power

cable /'keɪbəl/ *noun*
1 a thick rope, usually made of metal
2 a wire that carries electricity or telephone calls

cable television /,keɪbəl 'teləvɪʒən/ *(also cable TV /,keɪbəl ti: 'viː/ or cable) noun (no plural)*
a system of broadcasting television

by sending SIGNALS through cables under the ground ▶ *The hotel has cable TV.* ▶ *The game was on cable.*

cactus /'kæktəs/ *noun (plural **cacti** /'kæktaɪ/ or **cactuses**)*
a plant with sharp prickles and a thick stem that grows in hot, dry places

cafe /'kæfeɪ/ *noun*
a place where you can buy drinks and simple meals
COMPARE: **restaurant**

cafeteria /ˌkæfə'tɪərɪə/ *noun*
a restaurant where you collect your own food and take it to a table to eat it ▶ *a self-service cafeteria*

caffeine /'kæfiːn/ *noun (no plural)*
the substance in coffee, tea, and some other drinks that makes people feel more awake

cage /keɪdʒ/ *noun*
a box with metal bars, in which birds or animals can be kept

cake /keɪk/ *noun*
a sweet, cooked food made of flour, fat, sugar, and eggs ▶ *to bake a cake*

calcium /'kælsɪəm/ *noun (no plural)*
a substance that helps bones and teeth to grow strongly ▶ *Milk contains a lot of calcium.*

calculate /'kælkjʊleɪt/ *verb (present participle **calculating**, past **calculated**)*
to use numbers to find the answer to a sum ▶ *Have you calculated the cost of the journey?*

calculation /ˌkælkjʊ'leɪʃən/ *noun*
the result of using numbers to find the answer to a sum

calculator /'kælkjʊleɪtə'/ *noun*
a small machine that you can use to add, subtract, etc.

calendar /'kæləndə'/ *noun*
a list of the days, weeks, and months of the year

calf /kɑːf/ *noun (plural **calves** /kɑːvz/)*
1 a young cow
2 the part of your leg between your knee and your ankle

call¹ /kɔːl/ *verb*
1 to give someone a name ▶ *They called their baby John.*
2 to shout ▶ *to call for help*
3 **call on** to visit someone ▶ *He called on me last Tuesday.*
4 to telephone someone ▶ *I called my sister today.*
5 to ask someone to come to you ▶ *Mother called the doctor.*

call² *noun*
1 a shout ▶ *a call for help*
2 a visit ▶ *a call from the doctor*
3 an act of talking to someone on the telephone ▶ *There's a call for you, Mr Brown.*

call box /'kɔːl bɒks/ *noun (plural **call boxes**)*
a public telephone box

caller /'kɔːlə'/ *noun*
a person who makes a telephone call ▶ *There was one caller, but he didn't give me his name.*

calm /kɑːm/ *adjective*
quiet; peaceful ▶ *The sea was calm after the storm.* ▶ *He was calm when I told him the bad news. (adverb: **calmly**)*

calorie /'kælərɪ/ *noun*
a unit that measures the amount of energy a particular food can produce ▶ *Don't eat high-calorie food if you're trying to lose weight.*

calves /kɑːvz/
the plural of **calf**

camcorder /'kæmˌkɔːdə'/ *noun*
a machine that you use to take VIDEO films

came /keɪm/
the PAST TENSE of the verb **come**

camel /'kæməl/ *noun*
a large animal with one or two HUMPS

on its back, used to carry things and people in deserts

camera /'kæmərə/ *noun*
a machine for taking photographs, or making films or television programmes

cameraman /'kæmərəmæn/ *noun (plural cameramen /-men/)*
a person whose job is to operate the camera when people are making a film or television programme

camouflage /'kæməflɑːʒ/ *noun (no plural)*
clothes or colours that hide people, animals, or things by making them look the same as the things around them ▶ *All the soldiers were in camouflage.*

camp¹ /kæmp/ *noun*
a place with tents or huts where people live for a short time

camp² *verb*
to live in a tent for a short time

campaign /kæm'peɪn/ *noun*
1 a planned set of battles and movements of soldiers in a war
2 a set of planned activities done to get a result ▶ *a campaign to stop people smoking*

camping /'kæmpɪŋ/ *noun (no plural)*
living in a tent for a short time, especially when you are on holiday ▶ *The children liked camping.*

campsite /'kæmpsaɪt/ *noun*
a large field where people can stay in tents to have a holiday

campus /'kæmpəs/ *noun (plural campuses)*
the land belonging to a university, college, or school

can¹ /kən; *strong* kæn/ *verb*
to know how to; to be able to ▶ *"Can she swim?" "No, she can't (=cannot)."*

can² /kæn/ *noun*
a container made of metal ▶ *Have we got any cans of soup?*

SAME MEANING: **tin**
COMPARE: **box**

canal /kə'næl/ *noun*
a man-made river used for taking goods from one town to another

canary /kə'neəri/ *noun (plural canaries)*
a small, yellow bird with a sweet song

cancel /'kænsəl/ *verb (present participle cancelling, past cancelled)*
to stop some planned event ▶ *We had to cancel the match because so many people were ill.*

cancellation /ˌkænsə'leɪʃən/ *noun*
a situation in which someone decides that they will not do something they were going to do, or that a planned event will not happen ▶ *airport delays and flight cancellations*

cancer /'kænsər/ *noun (no plural)*
a serious illness in which a growth spreads in the body

candidate /'kændɪdət/ *noun*
1 a person who hopes to be picked for a job or position
2 a person who takes an examination

candle /'kændl/ *noun*
a piece of wax with a string in the middle which burns to give light

candlestick /'kændlˌstɪk/ *noun*
an object used to hold a candle

cane¹ /keɪn/ *noun*
a hollow stick from some plants, like sugar

cane² *verb (present participle caning, past caned)*
to hit someone with a stick

cannabis /'kænəbɪs/ *noun (no plural)*
an illegal drug that people smoke
SAME MEANING: **marijuana**

canned /kænd/ *adjective*
sold in cans ▶ *canned food*
SAME MEANING: **tinned**

cannon /'kænən/ *noun*
a large gun

cannot /'kænət, 'kænɒt/
can not ▶ *I cannot understand why she is so angry.*

canoe /kə'nu:/ *noun*
a narrow, light boat for one or two people

canoeing /kə'nu:ɪŋ/ *noun (no plural)*
the sport or activity of using a canoe ▶ *We could go canoeing this weekend.*

can opener /'kæn ˌəʊpənə'/ *noun*
a tool for opening cans of food

can't /kɑ:nt/
can not ▶ *I'm sorry I can't come to your house tomorrow.*

canteen /kæn'ti:n/ *noun*
a place where people in a factory, school, or office can eat meals

canvas /'kænvəs/ *noun (no plural)*
strong cloth used to make tents, bags, etc.

canvass /'kænvəs/ *verb*
to try to persuade people to vote for your political party in an election ▶ *Someone came to the house canvassing for the Labour Party.*

canyon /'kænjən/ *noun*
a deep, narrow valley with steep sides ▶ *the Grand Canyon*

cap /kæp/ *noun*
1 a soft hat
2 a covering for the end of a bottle or tube

capable /'keɪpəbəl/ *adjective*
1 good at something ▶ *She's a very capable student*
2 **capable of** able to do something ▶ *I knew he wasn't capable of murder.*
OPPOSITE (2): **incapable**

capacity /kə'pæsəti/ *noun*
1 *(no plural)* the amount that something can contain ▶ *That bowl has a capacity of 2 pints.*
2 *(plural **capacities**)* an ability to do something ▶ *Paul has a great capacity **for** working hard.*

cape /keɪp/ *noun*
a loose piece of clothing that you wrap around your shoulders and arms
COMPARE: **cloak**

capital /'kæpɪtl/ *noun*
1 the chief city of a country, where the government is
2 *(also **capital letter**)* a large letter that you use at the beginning of a sentence ▶ *A, D, P are capital letters; a, d, p are small letters.*

capitalism /'kæpɪtlɪzəm/ *noun (no plural)*
an economic system in which businesses and industry are owned by private owners and not by the government

capital letter /ˌkæpɪtl 'letə'/
another way of saying **capital** (2)

capital punishment /ˌkæpɪtl 'pʌnɪʃmənt/ *noun (no plural)*
the act of killing someone as official punishment for a serious crime

capsize /kæp'saɪz/ *verb (present participle **capsizing**, past **capsized**)*
if a boat capsizes, or if you capsize it, it turns over in the water

captain /'kæptɪn/ *noun*
1 the person who controls a ship or an aircraft
2 an officer in the army or the navy
3 the leader of a team or group

caption /'kæpʃən/ *noun*
a few words that are written under a photograph or drawing to explain what it is

captive /'kæptɪv/ *noun*
a prisoner

captivity /kæp'tɪvəti/ *noun (no plural)*
being a prisoner ▶ *animals kept in captivity*

capture /'kæptʃə'/ *verb (present participle **capturing**, past **captured**)*
to take someone as a prisoner ▶ *They captured four enemy soldiers.*

car /kɑːʳ/ *noun*
a vehicle on wheels that is driven by an engine and that people can travel in

carat /ˈkærət/ *noun*
a unit for measuring how pure gold is, or how heavy jewels are ▶ *an 18-carat gold ring*

caravan /ˈkærəvæn/ *noun*
a little house on wheels that can be pulled by a car

carbohydrate /ˌkɑːbəʊˈhaɪdreɪt/ *noun*
a substance in some foods that gives your body energy ▶ *Bread and rice contain a lot of carbohydrates.*

carbon /ˈkɑːbən/ *noun (no plural)*
a chemical ELEMENT that is found in coal and petrol

carbon dioxide /ˌkɑːbən daɪˈɒksaɪd/ *noun (no plural)*
the gas produced when people and animals breathe out, or when CARBON is burned in air

card /kɑːd/ *noun*
1 a piece of stiff, thick paper with a picture on the front and a message inside ▶ *a birthday card* ▶ *a Christmas card*
2 a small piece of stiff paper with pictures and numbers, used for various games ▶ *It's my turn to deal the cards.*

cardboard /ˈkɑːdbɔːd/ *noun (no plural)*
stiff, thick paper used for making boxes, book covers, etc.

cardigan /ˈkɑːdɪɡən/ *noun*
a piece of clothing like a JUMPER which opens with buttons down the front

care¹ /keəʳ/ *verb (present participle **caring**, past **cared**)*
1 to feel interest or worry ▶ *Does she care **about** her work?* ▶ *I don't care what you do!*
2 care for someone to look after

someone ▶ *Her son cared for him when he was ill.*
3 care for something to like or want something ▶ *Would you care for a cup of tea, Mrs Brown?*

care² *noun*
1 *(no plural)* the act of looking after a person or thing ▶ *a high standard of medical care* ▶ *Take care of your brother while I am away.*
2 take care to be careful ▶ *When you are crossing the road, take care!*
3 something that makes you sad ▶ *The holiday gave her a chance to forget her cares for a while.*

career /kəˈrɪəʳ/ *noun*
a number of jobs one after another, in which you move on to a more important job as you get older and learn more ▶ *a career in banking*

carefree /ˈkeəfriː/ *adjective*
without any problems or worries ▶ *a carefree childhood*

careful /ˈkeəfəl/ *adjective*
thinking seriously as you do something, so that you do not make a mistake ▶ *Be careful with that hot pan!* (adverb: **carefully**)
OPPOSITE: **careless**

careless /ˈkeələs/ *adjective*
not thinking seriously about what you do ▶ *Careless driving causes accidents.* (adverb: **carelessly**)
OPPOSITE: **careful**

caretaker /ˈkeəˌteɪkəʳ/ *noun*
a person whose job is to look after a building, especially a school

cargo /ˈkɑːɡəʊ/ *noun (plural **cargoes**)*
something carried on a ship or plane ▶ *a cargo **of** oil*

caring /ˈkeərɪŋ/ *adjective*
kind and providing care and support for others ▶ *a warm and caring person*

carnival /ˈkɑːnɪvəl/ *noun*
a big, public party in the streets of a

town, with dancing, drinking, and entertainment ▶ *the Venice carnival*

carnivore /ˈkɑːnɪvɔːʳ/ *noun*
an animal that eats meat

carol /ˈkærəl/ *noun*
a Christmas song

car park /ˈkɑː pɑːk/ *noun*
a building or a piece of land where cars can be parked

carpenter /ˈkɑːpɪntəʳ/ *noun*
a person who makes things out of wood as a job

carpentry /ˈkɑːpəntrɪ/ *noun (no plural)*
the art of making things out of wood

carpet /ˈkɑːpɪt/ *noun*
a covering for floors and stairs, usually made of wool
COMPARE: **mat**

carriage /ˈkærɪdʒ/ *noun*
1 one of the parts of a train, in which people sit
2 a vehicle pulled by horses instead of a motor

carrier bag /ˈkærɪə ˌbæg/ *noun*
a bag made of plastic or paper, used for carrying things that you have bought in a shop

carrot /ˈkærət/ *noun*
a long, orange root that is eaten as a vegetable

carry /ˈkærɪ/ *verb (past carried)*
1 to take something somewhere ▶ *He carried the food to the table.*
2 carry on to continue ▶ *Carry on with your homework.* ▶ *They carried on talking.*
3 carry something out to do or finish something ▶ *The soldiers carried out their orders.*

cart /kɑːt/ *noun*
a wooden vehicle pulled by horses and used for carrying things

carton /ˈkɑːtn/ *noun*
a cardboard box for holding food or drink ▶ *a carton of apple juice*

cartoon /kɑːˈtuːn/ *noun*
1 a film that is made with characters that are drawn, rather than real actors ▶ *a Walt Disney cartoon*
2 a drawing, especially in a magazine or newspaper, that makes a joke about someone or tells a story

carve /kɑːv/ *verb (present participle carving, past carved)*
1 to cut wood, stone, etc. into shapes ▶ *He carved the figure of a woman from a piece of wood.*
2 to cut cooked meat into pieces ▶ *She carved the chicken.*

carving /ˈkɑːvɪŋ/ *noun*
an object that has been made by cutting wood, stone, etc. ▶ *a wooden carving*

case /keɪs/ *noun*
1 one example of something ▶ *This is a typical case of lack of proper planning.*
2 a question that is decided in a court of law ▶ *a case of murder*
3 a large bag for carrying clothes in, for example on holiday ▶ *I'll just take my case up to my room.*
4 in case because something might happen ▶ *I'll take some biscuits in case we get hungry.*
5 in that case as this is true ▶ *"It's raining." "In that case, we'll need coats."*

cash¹ /kæʃ/ *noun (no plural)*
coins and paper money ▶ *Have you any cash?*

cash² *verb*
to get cash in return for a cheque ▶ *I cashed a cheque at the bank this morning.*

cash desk /ˈkæʃ desk/ *noun*
the place in a shop where you pay

cash dispenser /ˈkæʃ dɪˌspensəʳ/ *noun*
a machine in the wall outside a bank, where you can get money from your account

SAME MEANING: **ATM, cashpoint**

cashier /kæ'ʃɪər/ *noun*
a person who takes and gives out money in a bank or shop

cashpoint /'kæʃpɔɪnt/ *noun*
a machine in the wall outside a bank, where you can get money from your account
SAME MEANING: **ATM, cash dispenser**

cash register /'kæʃ ˌredʒɪstər/ *noun*
a machine in a shop that shows how much you should pay

casino /kə'siːnəʊ/ *noun*
a place where people try to win money by playing games with numbers, cards, etc.

cassette /kə'set/ *noun*
a small, plastic container holding a TAPE that plays music when fitted into a special machine

cassette recorder /kə'set rɪˌkɔːdər/ (*also* ***cassette player*** /kə'set ˌpleɪər/) *noun*
a machine which plays and records sounds on CASSETTES

cast¹ /kɑːst/ *verb* (*past* **cast**)
to give an actor a particular part in a film or play ➤ *As usual, Hugh Grant was cast as the typical Englishman.*

cast² *noun*
all of the actors in a film or play ➤ *The film has a brilliant cast.*

castle /'kɑːsəl/ *noun*
a large, strong building made so that no one can attack the people inside

casual /'kæʒʊəl/ *adjective*
1 not planned or arranged ➤ *a casual meeting*
2 casual clothes clothes that you wear at home, not at work or school

casualty /'kæʒʊəltɪ/ *noun* (*plural* **casualties**)
1 a person who is hurt in an accident, a war, etc. ➤ *There have been 20 casualties following an accident on the motorway.*
2 (*no plural*) the part of a hospital where people are taken when they need urgent treatment

cat /kæt/ *noun*
a small animal that people often keep as a pet

catalogue /'kætəlɒg/ *noun*
1 a list of things in a special order ➤ *a catalogue of all the books in the library*
2 a book containing details of things you can buy from a shop or business

catapult /'kætəpʌlt/ *verb*
to make someone or something move through the air very quickly ➤ *The car stopped suddenly, catapulting the boy through the window.*

catastrophe /kə'tæstrəfɪ/ *noun*
a terrible event that causes a lot of damage or death ➤ *the danger of a nuclear catastrophe*

catch¹ /kætʃ/ *verb* (*past* **caught** /kɔːt/)
1 to stop something that is moving in the air and hold it ➤ *The dog caught the ball in its mouth.*
2 to run after something and take hold of it ➤ *We ran after the dog and caught it.*
3 to get something ➤ *I caught the train.* ➤ *She caught a cold.*
4 catch up to get to the same place as someone else ➤ *I tried, but I couldn't catch up with you.*

catch² /kætʃ/ *noun*
the act of catching something ➤ *That was a good catch!*

catching /'kætʃɪŋ/ *adjective*
(used about illnesses) easily passed from one person to another

category /'kætɪgərɪ/ *noun* (*plural* **categories**)
a group of people or things that are like one another ➤ *different categories of books*

cater /'keɪtər/ *verb*
cater for to provide a particular group

of people with what they need or want ▶ *We chose the hotel because it caters for small children.*

caterpillar /'kætəpɪlə'/ *noun*
the young form of some insects, that looks like a worm with many legs

cathedral /kə'θi:drəl/ *noun*
an important, large church

Catholic /'kæθəlɪk/ *noun*
a Christian belonging to the church whose leader is the POPE

cattle /'kætl/ *plural noun*
large animals kept for their meat, milk, and skins

caught /kɔ:t/
the PAST TENSE and PAST PARTICIPLE of the verb **catch**

cauliflower /'kɒlɪˌflaʊə'/ *noun*
a vegetable with green leaves around the outside and a hard, white centre

cause¹ /kɔ:z/ *verb (present participle **causing**, past **caused**)*
to make something happen; be the reason for something ▶ *The heavy rain caused the flood.*

cause² *noun*
1 a person or thing that makes something happen; a reason for something ▶ *The heavy rain was the cause **of** the flood.*
2 an idea you believe in or care about very strongly ▶ *They were all fighting for the same cause.*

caution /'kɔ:ʃən/ *noun (no plural)*
great care ▶ *Drive with caution.*

cautious /'kɔ:ʃəs/ *adjective*
taking care to avoid danger (*adverb:* **cautiously**)
OPPOSITE: **reckless**

cavalry /'kævəlrɪ/ *noun (no plural)*
soldiers who fought on horses in the past

cave /keɪv/ *noun*
a hollow place under the ground or in the side of a mountain or rock

caveman /'keɪvmæn/ *noun (plural **cavemen** /-men/)*
a person who lived many thousands of years ago, when people lived in caves

cavity /'kævɪtɪ/ *noun (plural **cavities**)*
a hole in a tooth

CD /ˌsi: 'di:/ *noun*
a COMPACT DISC; a type of record with very high-quality sound, played on a special machine

CD player /ˌsi: 'di: ˌpleɪə'/ *(also **compact disc player**) noun*
a special machine for playing CDs

CD-ROM /ˌsi: di: 'rɒm/ *noun*
COMPACT DISC READ-ONLY MEMORY; a CD with a lot of information stored on it, which you look at using a computer

cease /si:s/ *verb (present participle **ceasing**, past **ceased**)*
to stop ▶ *Her mother never ceases telling you about her troubles.*

ceasefire /'si:sfaɪə'/ *noun*
an agreement for both sides in a war to stop fighting

ceaseless /'si:sləs/ *adjective*
never stopping

ceiling /'si:lɪŋ/ *noun*
the roof of a room

celebrate /'selɪbreɪt/ *verb (present participle **celebrating**, past **celebrated**)*
to show that you are happy about something by having a special meal or party

celebration /ˌselɪ'breɪʃən/ *noun*
a special meal or party that you have because something good has happened ▶ *There was great celebration when the baby was born.*

celebrity /sə'lebrɪtɪ/ *noun (plural **celebrities**)*
a famous person, especially an actor or entertainer ▶ *There were lots of TV celebrities at the party.*

celery /'selərɪ/ noun (no plural)
a vegetable with long, firm, pale green stems that you eat in a SALAD

cell /sel/ noun
1 a small room in which a prisoner is kept
2 a very small part of a living substance

cellar /'selər/ noun
a room under the ground in a house, used especially for storing things in COMPARE: **basement**

cello /'tʃeləʊ/ noun
a musical instrument like a large VIOLIN, which you hold between your knees

Celsius /'selsɪəs/ noun (no plural)
a system for measuring temperature, in which water freezes at 0° and boils at 100°
SAME MEANING: **centigrade**

cement /sɪ'ment/ noun (no plural)
a powder that becomes hard like stone when mixed with water, used in building

cemetery /'semɪtrɪ/ noun (plural **cemeteries**)
an area of land where dead bodies are put into the ground

censor /'sensər/ verb
to look at books, films, etc. and remove anything that might offend or harm people ▶ It was obvious that the television reports were being censored.

censorship /'sensəʃɪp/ noun (no plural)
the practice of looking at books, films, etc. and removing anything that might offend or harm people ▶ She believes that censorship is wrong.

census /'sensəs/ noun (plural **censuses**)
an occasion on which official information is gathered about the number of people in a country, their ages, jobs, etc.

cent /sent/ noun
a small coin used in some countries

centenary /sen'ti:nərɪ/ noun (plural **centenaries**)
the day or year exactly one hundred years after an important event ▶ We celebrated the club's centenary in 1999.

centigrade /'sentɪgreɪd/ noun
a system for measuring temperature, in which water freezes at 0° and boils at 100°
SAME MEANING: **Celsius**

centimetre /'sentɪˌmiːtər/ noun
a measure of length ▶ There are 100 centimetres in a metre.
▶ 3 centimetres (3cm)

central /'sentrəl/ adjective
in the middle of something

central heating /ˌsentrəl 'hiːtɪŋ/ noun (no plural)
a system for heating buildings, in which pipes carry the heat to every part of the building ▶ Most of these houses have central heating.

centre /'sentər/ noun
1 the middle of something
2 a place where a lot of people come with a special purpose ▶ The doctors worked at the Health Centre. ▶ Have you seen the new shopping centre?

century /'sentʃərɪ/ noun (plural **centuries**)
a period of 100 years ▶ This house was built in the 19th century.

ceramics /sə'ræmɪks/ noun
1 (no plural) the art of making pots, bowls, etc. from clay
2 plural noun artistic objects made from clay ▶ an exhibition of ceramics

cereal /'sɪərɪəl/ noun
a crop such as wheat, rice, or maize, used as food

ceremony /'serɪmənɪ/ noun (plural **ceremonies**)
a number of special actions done and

C

special words spoken in a particular order to mark an important public, social, or religious event ▶ *the wedding ceremony*

certain /'sɜːtn/ *adjective*
1 sure ▶ *I am certain he told me to come at 2 o'clock.*
OPPOSITE: **uncertain**
SAME MEANING: **positive**
2 some ▶ *You cannot smoke in certain restaurants.*

certainly /'sɜːtnli/ *adverb*
1 without doubt ▶ *You've certainly got a lot of books.*
2 of course ▶ *"Will you help me, please?" "Certainly."*

certificate /sə'tɪfɪkət/ *noun*
an important written paper ▶ *Your birth certificate tells people when you were born.*

chain¹ /tʃeɪn/ *noun*
a number of metal rings joined together ▶ *She wore a gold chain around her neck.*

chain² *verb*
to tie something with a chain ▶ *Who chained the poor dog to the fence?*

chair /tʃeəʳ/ *noun*
a piece of furniture you sit on, with four legs and a back
COMPARE: **sofa, stool**

chairman /'tʃeəmən/ *noun (plural* **chairmen** /-mən/)
a person who controls a meeting

chairperson /'tʃeə,pɜːsən/ *noun*
a person who controls a meeting ▶ *They elected a new chairperson.*

chairwoman /'tʃeə,wʊmən/ *noun (plural* **chairwomen** /-,wɪmɪn/)
a woman who controls a meeting

chalk /tʃɔːk/ *noun*
1 *(no plural)* a soft, white substance found in the ground
2 a piece of this substance used for writing or drawing

challenge¹ /'tʃælɪndʒ/ *verb*

(present participle **challenging**, *past* **challenged**)
1 to offer to fight or play a game against someone ▶ *Their school challenged ours to a football match.*
2 to test or question someone ▶ *I did not think he was right, so I challenged him.*

challenge² *noun*
1 an offer to fight or play against someone
2 a test of ability ▶ *To build a bridge in a month was a real challenge.*

challenging /'tʃælɪndʒɪŋ/ *adjective*
difficult but interesting or enjoyable ▶ *Teaching is a very challenging job.*

champagne /ʃæm'peɪn/ *noun (no plural)*
an alcoholic drink with BUBBLES in it

champion /'tʃæmpɪən/ *noun*
a person who is the best at something, especially a sport or game

championship /'tʃæmpɪənʃɪp/ *noun*
a competition to find who is the best at something ▶ *Our team won the swimming championships.*

chance /tʃɑːns/ *noun*
1 *(no plural)* something unexpected ▶ *I met him by chance.*
2 something that may happen ▶ *There is a chance that I will be chosen for the team.*
3 a time when something may be done ▶ *I haven't had a chance to read my letter.*
4 a risk ▶ *He is taking a chance by driving without insurance.*

chancellor /'tʃɑːnsələʳ/ *noun*
1 the head of a university or government ▶ *the Chancellor of York University* ▶ *The German Chancellor has arrived in Britain.*
2 *(also* **Chancellor of the Exchequer** /ɪks'tʃekəʳ/) in Britain, the government minister who is in charge of the money the government spends

chandelier /ˌʃændəˈlɪə/ *noun*
a large decoration made of glass, that holds lights or candles and hangs from the ceiling

change¹ /tʃeɪndʒ/ *verb (present participle **changing**, past **changed**)*
1 to make something different or become different ▶ *This town has changed since I was a child.* ▶ *We've changed the house a lot since we moved in.*
2 to take or put something in the place of something else ▶ *She took the dress back to the shop and changed it (for another).*
3 to put on different clothes ▶ *He changed when he arrived home from school.*
4 change your mind to make a new decision which is opposite to the one before ▶ *I was going out this evening, but I've changed my mind. (=I'm going to stay at home instead).*

change² *noun*
1 something that has become different ▶ *You will see many changes in the village since last year.*
2 *(no plural)* money that you get back when you give too much for something ▶ *I gave him £1 and he gave me 20 pence change.*
3 for a change as something different from usual ▶ *Let's go out to a restaurant tonight for a change.*

channel /ˈtʃænl/ *noun*
a narrow piece of flowing water ▶ *The English Channel is between France and England.*

chant¹ /tʃɑːnt/ *noun*
words or phrases that are repeated again and again ▶ *a football chant*

chant² /tʃɑːnt/ *verb*
to repeat a word or phrase again and again ▶ *an angry crowd chanting slogans*

chaos /ˈkeɪɒs/ *noun (no plural)*
absence of order or control ▶ *After the bomb exploded the town was in chaos.*

chaotic /keɪˈɒtɪk/ *adjective*
very disorganized and confusing ▶ *The whole holiday was chaotic.*

chap /tʃæp/ *noun*
a man ▶ *Frank seems a friendly chap.*

chapel /ˈtʃæpəl/ *noun*
a small church, or part of a church

chaperone /ˈʃæpərəʊn/ *noun*
an older person who in the past went to places with a young person, especially an unmarried woman, to protect and take care of them ▶ *Your aunt will go with you as your chaperone.*

chaplain /ˈtʃæplɪn/ *noun*
a priest who works for the army, a hospital, or a college ▶ *the college chaplain*

chapter /ˈtʃæptə/ *noun*
a part of a book ▶ *Open your books at Chapter 3.*

character /ˈkærɪktə/ *noun*
1 what a person or thing is like ▶ *He has a strong but gentle character.* ▶ *The new buildings have changed the character of the village.*
2 a person in a book, film, or play

characteristic¹ /ˌkærɪktəˈrɪstɪk/ *noun*
a quality or feature that someone or something typically has ▶ *the characteristics of a good manager*

characteristic² *adjective*
typical of a particular person or thing ▶ *Mark, with characteristic kindness, offered to help. (adverb: **characteristically**)*

charcoal /ˈtʃɑːkəʊl/ *noun (no plural)*
a black substance made of burned wood, used for burning as FUEL or for drawing

charge¹ /tʃɑːdʒ/ *verb (present participle **charging**, past **charged**)*
1 to ask money for something ▶ *He only charged me £2 for the book.*

2 to say that a person has done something wrong ▶ *He was charged* **with** *stealing a car.*
3 to run or hurry ▶ *The little boy charged into the room.*

charge² *noun*
1 a price asked for something ▶ *a charge* **for** *the use of the telephone*
2 a statement that a person has done wrong ▶ *a charge* **of** *stealing*
3 a hurried attack
4 be in charge/take charge to be in a position of control and responsibility ▶ *I don't know. Ask Mr Davis. He's in charge.*

charisma /kə'rɪzmə/ *noun (no plural)*
a natural ability to make people like you ▶ *He is a man of great charisma.*

charismatic /ˌkærɪz'mætɪk/ *adjective*
having a natural ability to make people like you ▶ *The president is a very charismatic leader.*

charity /'tʃærɪtɪ/ *noun*
1 *(no plural)* goodness and kindness ▶ *She helped him out of charity.*
2 *(plural charities)* a group of people who collect money from the public and then give money, food, etc. to those who need it

charm¹ /tʃɑːm/ *verb*
to please you very much

charm² *noun*
1 *(no plural)* pleasing behaviour ▶ *He had great charm – everyone liked him.*
2 a thing that is said to bring good luck

charming /'tʃɑːmɪŋ/ *adjective*
beautiful; pleasing

chart /tʃɑːt/ *noun*
1 a map, especially of an area of sea
2 a large piece of paper with information on it in pictures and writing

charter /'tʃɑːtər/ *noun*
a statement of the beliefs, duties,

and purposes of an organization ▶ *the charter of the United Nations*

charter flight /'tʃɑːtə ˌflaɪt/ *noun*
a flight that you buy from a travel company, and that is often cheaper than a flight you buy directly from an AIRLINE ▶ *We managed to get a charter flight to Istanbul.*

chase¹ /tʃeɪs/ *verb (present participle chasing, past chased)*
to follow someone or something quickly ▶ *The boy chased the dog.*

chase² *noun*
following someone or something quickly ▶ *He caught it after a long chase.*

chat¹ /tʃæt/ *verb (present participle chatting, past chatted)*
to talk in a friendly way

chat² *noun*
a friendly talk ▶ *to have a chat*

château /'ʃætəʊ/ *noun (plural châteaux* /-təʊz/ *or châteaus)*
a castle or large country house in some countries

chat show /'tʃæt ʃəʊ/ *noun*
a television or radio show on which someone talks to famous or interesting people ▶ *Brosnan appeared as a guest on her chat show.*

chatter /'tʃætər/ *verb*
to talk quickly, especially about unimportant things ▶ *They just sat and chattered.*

chatty /'tʃætɪ/ *adjective (chattier, chattiest)*
friendly and easy to talk to ▶ *She was very chatty on the telephone.*

chauffeur /'ʃəʊfər/ *noun*
a person whose job is to drive another person's car, and take that person to the places they want to go ▶ *My chauffeur drove me to the airport.*

cheap /tʃiːp/ *adjective*

costing only a little money ▶ *A bicycle is much cheaper than a car.*
OPPOSITE: **expensive**

cheat¹ /tʃiːt/ *verb*
to deceive; to do something which is not honest ▶ *He didn't play the game fairly – he cheated.* ▶ *They cheated him out of £500.*

cheat² *noun*
a person who is not fair or honest

check¹ /tʃek/ *verb*
1 to make sure that something has been done well or is in good order ▶ *You should check your bicycle before you ride it.*
2 check in to report your arrival somewhere ▶ *You must check in at the airport an hour before the plane leaves.*

check² *noun*
1 a careful look to make sure that something is correct or as you want it to be ▶ *a police check on cars and lorries*
2 a pattern of different coloured squares ▶ *The material had checks on it.*

checked /tʃekt/ *adjective*
having a regular pattern of different coloured squares ▶ *a checked shirt*

checklist /'tʃeklɪst/ *noun*
a list that helps to remind you of all the things you have to do

checkout /'tʃekaʊt/ *noun*
a desk in a shop, where you pay for goods

checkpoint /'tʃekpɔɪnt/ *noun*
a place where an official person stops people and vehicles to examine them ▶ *There are several checkpoints along the border.*

checkup (also **check-up**) /'tʃek ʌp/ *noun*
an occasion when a doctor or DENTIST examines you to see if you are healthy ▶ *When was the last time you had a checkup?*

cheek /tʃiːk/ *noun*
one of the two parts on each side of your face under your eyes

cheeky /'tʃiːki/ *adjective* (**cheekier, cheekiest**)
not polite or respectful ▶ *Don't be so cheeky.*

cheer¹ /tʃɪəʳ/ *verb*
1 (also **cheer up**) to make someone happy ▶ *The children's laughter cheered the old woman.*
2 to shout because you are pleased ▶ *The crowd cheered when the film stars arrived.*

cheer² *noun*
a shout of happiness or support ▶ *Let's give three cheers for the winning team.*

cheerful /'tʃɪəfəl/ *adjective*
smiling and happy (*adverb:* **cheerfully**)

cheerleader /'tʃɪəˌliːdəʳ/ *noun*
a member of a group of young women that encourages the crowd at a sports event to cheer for a particular team

cheers /tʃɪəz/ *interjection*
used just before you drink a glass of alcohol with someone, to show friendly feelings

cheese /tʃiːz/ *noun*
a solid food made from milk

cheesecake /'tʃiːzkeɪk/ *noun*
a sweet cake made with soft, white cheese and often fruit ▶ *strawberry cheesecake*

chef /ʃef/ *noun*
a person whose job is to cook food in a restaurant, especially the most important cook in a restaurant

chemical¹ /'kemɪkəl/ *noun*
a substance, especially one made by or used in chemistry

chemical² *adjective*
made by chemistry

chemist /'kemɪst/ *noun*
1 a person who makes and sells medicines
COMPARE: **pharmacist**
2 chemist's a shop where medicines, toiletries, and some goods for the house can be bought
COMPARE: **pharmacy**
3 a person who studies chemistry

chemistry /'kemɪstrɪ/ *noun (no plural)*
the science which studies substances like gas, metals, liquids, etc., what they are made of, and how they behave

cheque /tʃek/ *noun*
a printed piece of paper which you write on to pay for things; it can be exchanged for money at the bank

chequebook /'tʃekbʊk/ *noun*
a small book of cheques

cherry /'tʃerɪ/ *noun (plural cherries)*
a small, round fruit with red or black skin, which grows on trees

chess /tʃes/ *noun (no plural)*
a game that you play by moving different shaped pieces on a board of black and white squares

chest /tʃest/ *noun*
1 the front of your body between your shoulders and your stomach
SAME MEANING: **breast (2)**
2 a large box for storing things in

chest of drawers /ˌtʃest əv 'drɔːz/ *noun (plural chests of drawers)*
a large piece of furniture with drawers

chew /tʃuː/ *verb*
to break up food in your mouth with your teeth

chewing gum /'tʃuːɪŋ ɡʌm/ *noun (no plural)*
a type of sweet that you chew but do not swallow

chic /ʃiːk/ *adjective*
fashionable and showing good style
▶ *We had lunch at a chic little cafe.*

chick /tʃɪk/ *noun*
a young bird, especially a young chicken

chicken /'tʃɪkɪn/ *noun*
a bird that people keep for its eggs and meat

chicken pox /'tʃɪkɪn ˌpɒks/ *noun (no plural)*
an illness that causes a fever and red spots on the skin, especially caught by children ▶ *Ruth's got chicken pox.*

chief¹ /tʃiːf/ *adjective*
most important

chief² *noun*
a leader; the head of a group or tribe
▶ *the chief of police*

chiefly /'tʃiːflɪ/ *adverb*
mostly ▶ *He kept animals – chiefly cattle, with some pigs.*

child /tʃaɪld/ *noun (plural children* /'tʃɪldrən/)
1 a young person older than a baby but not yet fully grown
2 a son or daughter ▶ *They have three children.*
LOOK AT: **son**

childbirth /'tʃaɪldbɜːθ/ *noun (no plural)*
the act during which a baby is born
▶ *Childbirth is very painful.*

childcare /'tʃaɪldkeəʳ/ *noun (no plural)*
an arrangement in which someone looks after children when their parents are at work

childhood /'tʃaɪldhʊd/ *noun*
the time when you are a child

childish /'tʃaɪldɪʃ/ *adjective*
silly and suitable only for a child
▶ *a childish game* (adverb: **childishly**)

childless /'tʃaɪldləs/ *adjective*
having no children ▶ *childless couples*

childminder /'tʃaɪldˌmaɪndəʳ/ *noun*
a person who is responsible for

looking after young children when their parents are at work

childminding /ˈtʃaɪldˌmaɪndɪŋ/ *noun (no plural)*
the job of looking after young children when their parents are at work ▶ *I do a little childminding.*

children /ˈtʃɪldrən/
the plural of **child**

chill¹ /tʃɪl/ *verb*
1 to make something cold ▶ *Chill the champagne before you serve it.*
2 (*also* **chill out**) to relax and rest ▶ *We stayed till about 3 am, then went back to our place to chill.*

chill² *noun*
a feeling of coldness ▶ *There was a chill in the air.*

chilli /ˈtʃɪlɪ/ *noun*
1 (*plural* **chillies**) a small, thin, red or green vegetable with a very hot taste
2 (*no plural*) a dish made with beans, meat, and chillies

chilly /ˈtʃɪlɪ/ *adjective* (**chillier, chilliest**)
cold enough to make you feel uncomfortable ▶ *It's a bit chilly today.*

chime /tʃaɪm/ *verb (present participle* **chiming**, *past* **chimed**)
to make a sound like a bell ▶ *The clock chimed 3 o'clock.*

chimney /ˈtʃɪmnɪ/ *noun*
a pipe that allows smoke to go up and out of a building

chimpanzee /ˌtʃɪmpænˈziː/ *noun*
an African animal like a monkey, but without a tail

chin /tʃɪn/ *noun*
the part of your face below your mouth

china /ˈtʃaɪnə/ *noun (no plural)*
1 cups, plates, etc. that are made from fine baked earth
2 the special kind of white earth from which cups, plates, etc. are made

chip¹ /tʃɪp/ *noun*
1 a small piece broken off something ▶ *a cup with a chip out of it*
2 a long, thin piece of potato cooked in oil
SAME MEANING (**2**): **(French) fry**
COMPARE (**2**): **crisp**
3 a very small piece of metal or plastic used in computers to store information and make the computer work

chip² *verb (present participle* **chipping**, *past* **chipped**)
to break a small piece off something hard ▶ *He chipped the cup when he dropped it.*

chirp /tʃɜːp/ *noun*
a short, high sound made by some birds and insects

chirpy /ˈtʃɜːpɪ/ *adjective* (**chirpier, chirpiest**)
cheerful ▶ *You're very chirpy this morning.*

chisel /ˈtʃɪzəl/ *noun*
a metal tool with a sharp end, used for cutting and shaping wood or stone

chocolate /ˈtʃɒklət/ *noun*
1 (*no plural*) a sweet, hard, brown food made from cocoa
2 a small sweet covered in chocolate ▶ *a box of chocolates*

choice /tʃɔɪs/ *noun*
1 a decision about what you want ▶ *I've got to make a choice between the two jobs.*
2 the result of deciding what you want ▶ *Her choice of dress surprised me.*
3 a variety of things from which you can choose ▶ *There's a wide choice of colours.*

choir /ˈkwaɪəʳ/ *noun*
a number of people who sing together ▶ *the school choir*

choke /tʃəʊk/ *verb (present participle* **choking**, *past* **choked**)

C

to be unable to breathe because of something in your throat ▶ *to choke on a piece of meat*

choose /tʃuːz/ *verb (present participle choosing, past tense chose* /tʃəʊz/, *past participle chosen* /'tʃəʊzən/)
to decide from a number of things or people the one you want ▶ *She chose to study chemistry.*

choosy /'tʃuːzɪ/ *adjective (choosier, choosiest)*
liking only certain things ▶ *I'm very choosy about my food.*

chop¹ /tʃɒp/ *verb (present participle chopping, past chopped)*
to cut something with an axe or a sharp knife

chop² *noun*
a piece of meat with a bone, cut from the side of an animal's body

chopper /'tʃɒpəʳ/ *noun*
a HELICOPTER

chopsticks /'tʃɒpstɪks/ *plural noun*
a pair of thin sticks used for eating food in East Asia

chord /kɔːd/ *noun*
two or more musical notes that you play at the same time ▶ *I can play a few chords on the guitar.*

chore /tʃɔːʳ/ *noun*
a job that you have to do, especially a boring one in the house or garden ▶ *household chores*

choreographer /ˌkɒrɪ'ɒgrəfəʳ/ *noun*
a person whose job is to arrange how dancers should move during a performance

choreography /ˌkɒrɪ'ɒgrəfɪ/ *noun (no plural)*
the art of arranging how dancers should move during a performance

chorus /'kɔːrəs/ *noun (plural choruses)*
1 a group of singers
2 a part of a song that is repeated

chose /tʃəʊz/
the PAST TENSE of the verb **choose**

chosen /'tʃəʊzən/
the PAST PARTICIPLE of the verb **choose**

Christ /kraɪst/
Jesus Christ, the man who Christians believe is the son of God

christen /'krɪsən/ *verb*
to put holy water on someone to make them a member of the Christian church, and to give them a name ▶ *They christened the baby John.*

christening /'krɪsənɪŋ/ *noun*
the Christian ceremony at which a baby is given its name

Christian /'krɪstʃən, -tɪən/ *noun*
a person who follows the teachings of Jesus Christ

Christianity /ˌkrɪstɪ'ænɪtɪ/ *noun (no plural)*
the religion based on the teachings of Jesus Christ

Christian name /'krɪstʃən ˌneɪm/ *noun*
a person's first name, not their family name

Christmas /'krɪsməs/ *noun*
December 25th, the day of the year when Christians thank God for the birth of Jesus. People get together with their families and friends and eat and drink special things.

Christmas Eve /ˌkrɪsməs 'iːv/ *noun*
December 24th, the day before Christmas Day

Christmas stocking /ˌkrɪsməs 'stɒkɪŋ/ *noun*
a long sock that children leave out on the night before Christmas to be filled with presents

chrome /krəʊm/ *noun (no plural)*
a hard, shiny, silver metal that is used for covering objects ▶ *The door has chrome handles.*

chronic /'krɒnɪk/ *adjective*
serious and likely to continue for a

long time ➤ *There is a chronic shortage of nurses.*

chronological /ˌkrɒnəˈlɒdʒɪkəl/ *adjective*
arranged in the same order as events happened ➤ *The children had to put the events of the war in chronological order.*

chubby /ˈtʃʌbɪ/ *adjective (**chubbier, chubbiest**)*
slightly fat ➤ *He was a chubby little baby.*

chuck /tʃʌk/ *verb*
to throw something ➤ *I chucked the ball over the fence.*

chuckle /ˈtʃʌkəl/ *verb (present participle **chuckling**, past **chuckled**)*
to laugh quietly ➤ *He chuckled at the funny story.*

chunk /tʃʌŋk/ *noun*
a large piece of something solid ➤ *I cut off a chunk of cheese.*

church /tʃɜːtʃ/ *noun (plural **churches**)*
a building in which Christians meet and pray

churchyard /ˈtʃɜːtʃjɑːd/ *noun*
a piece of land around a church, where dead people are buried

cider /ˈsaɪdə/ *noun*
1 (no plural) a drink containing alcohol that is made from apples
2 a glass of this drink ➤ *Can I have two ciders, please?*

cigar /sɪˈgɑː/ *noun*
a thick, brown stick of tobacco leaves rolled together for smoking

cigarette /ˌsɪgəˈret/ *noun*
a thin stick made of tobacco cut into small pieces and rolled in white paper for smoking

cinema /ˈsɪnəmə/ *noun*
a building in which you can see films

circle¹ /ˈsɜːkəl/ *noun*
1 a round shape; a ring ➤ *They sat in a circle round the fire.*

2 a group of people who like the same things ➤ *a large circle of friends*

circle² *verb (present participle **circling**, past **circled**)*
to draw a circle round something ➤ *Circle the correct answer.*

circuit /ˈsɜːkɪt/ *noun*
1 a track where people race cars, bicycles, etc. ➤ *The racing cars go three times round the circuit.*
2 the complete circle that an electric current flows around ➤ *an electric circuit*

circular /ˈsɜːkjʊlə/ *adjective*
round; moving in a direction that takes you back to where you started ➤ *It's a circular path so we don't have to come back the same way.*

circulate /ˈsɜːkjʊleɪt/ *verb (present participle **circulating**, past **circulated**)*
to go round and round ➤ *Blood circulates round your body.*

circulation /ˌsɜːkjʊˈleɪʃən/ *noun (no plural)*
the movement of blood round your body

circumcise /ˈsɜːkəmsaɪz/ *verb (present participle **circumcising**, past **circumcised**)*
to cut off the skin at the end of a boy's or man's PENIS, or to cut off part of a girl's sex organs

circumcision /ˌsɜːkəmˈsɪʒən/ *noun*
the act of cutting off the skin at the end of a boy's or man's PENIS, or cutting off part of a girl's sex organs

circumference /səˈkʌmfərəns/ *noun*
the length around the outside edge of a round object

circumstances /ˈsɜːkəmstənsɪz/ *plural noun*
1 in/under the circumstances after what has happened ➤ *In the circumstances, I think I should stay at home.*

C

2 in/under no circumstances never ► *Under no circumstances will I vote for him.*

circus /'sɜːkəs/ *noun (plural circuses)*
a show given by people and trained animals, often in a large tent

citizen /'sɪtɪzən/ *noun*
a person who lives in a country or town and has special rights there

citizenship /'sɪtɪzənʃɪp/ *noun (no plural)*
the legal right to belong to a particular country ► *Peter has British citizenship.*

citrus fruit /'sɪtrəs ˌfruːt/ *noun*
a fruit such as an orange or a LEMON

city /'sɪti/ *noun (plural cities)*
a very large town

civil /'sɪvəl/ *adjective*
1 not connected with military or religious organizations ► *The company makes civil aircraft.* ► *We were married in a civil ceremony, not in church.*
2 related to laws that deal with people's rights, not laws that are related to crimes ► *a civil case*

civilian /sɪ'vɪljən/ *noun*
a person who is not in the armed forces

civilization /ˌsɪvɪlaɪ'zeɪʃən/ *noun*
a way of life in which people have laws, government, and education

civilize /'sɪvɪlaɪz/ *verb (present participle civilizing, past civilized)*
to change the way that people live together, by making laws and having government and education

civilized /'sɪvɪlaɪzd/ *adjective*
1 a civilized society is well organized and has laws and customs ► *Care for the elderly is essential in a civilized society.*
2 behaving politely and sensibly ► *Can't we discuss this in a civilized way?*

civil rights /ˌsɪvəl 'raɪts/ *plural noun*
the legal rights that every person has

civil servant /ˌsɪvəl 'sɜːvənt/ *noun*
a person who works for the government in the civil service

civil service /ˌsɪvəl 'sɜːvɪs/ *noun*
all the people who work for a government except the army, navy, and airforce

civil war /ˌsɪvəl 'wɔːʳ/ *noun*
a war between two groups of people who live in the same country

claim¹ /kleɪm/ *verb*
1 to ask for something that you say is yours ► *I claimed the coat that the teacher found.*
2 to say something is true ► *He claimed that he hadn't done it, but I didn't believe him.*

claim² *noun*
1 something that you ask for ► *They made a claim for higher pay.*
2 something that you say is true ► *I don't believe his claim about how rich he is.*

clairvoyant /kleə'vɔɪənt/ *noun*
a person who says they can see what will happen in the future

clamber /'klæmbəʳ/ *verb*
to climb over something with difficulty, using your hands and feet ► *I clambered over the rocks.*

clammy /'klæmɪ/ *adjective (clammier, clammiest)*
wet and sticky in an unpleasant way ► *clammy hands*

clamour /'klæməʳ/ *verb*
to demand something loudly ► *All the reporters were clamouring for his attention.*

clamp /klæmp/ *verb*
1 to hold something tightly in a particular position so that it does not move ► *He clamped his hand over her mouth.*
2 to fasten a piece of equipment onto

the wheel of a car that has been parked illegally, so that it cannot be moved ▶ *Her car has been clamped again.*

3 clamp down on something to become very strict in order to stop people from doing something ▶ *The police are clamping down on drivers who go too fast.*

clang /klæŋ/ *noun*
the sound of one piece of metal hitting another ▶ *There was a clang as he dropped the tools.*

clap /klæp/ *verb (present participle **clapping**, past **clapped**)*
to make a sound by hitting your hands together, usually to show that you like something ▶ *When the singer finished, we clapped.*
COMPARE: **applaud**

clarify /'klærɪfaɪ/ *verb (past **clarified**)*
to make something easier to understand by explaining it in more detail ▶ *Can you clarify exactly what you mean?*

clarinet /ˌklærɪ'net/ *noun*
a wooden musical instrument like a long, black tube, which you play by blowing into it

clash¹ /klæʃ/ *verb*
1 to fight or disagree ▶ *The police clashed with the angry crowd.*
2 (used about colours) to look wrong together ▶ *His shirt clashed with his coat.*
3 to happen at the same time ▶ *I couldn't go to the wedding as it clashed with my holiday.*

clash² *noun (plural **clashes**)*
1 a fight or disagreement ▶ *a clash with the police*
2 a loud noise of metal on metal ▶ *the clash of weapons*

clasp¹ /klɑːsp/ *verb*
to hold something tightly ▶ *He clasped my arm with fear.*
SAME MEANING: **grip**

clasp² *noun*
something that fastens two things together ▶ *He has a gold clasp on his belt.*

class /klɑːs/ *noun (plural **classes**)*
1 a group of people who learn together ▶ *She was in a class of 30 students.*
2 a group of people or things of the same kind ▶ *Cats belong to one class of animals, fish to another.*

classic /'klæsɪk/ *noun*
a book or film which is very good and of lasting importance ▶ *That film's a classic.*

classical /'klæsɪkəl/ *adjective*
(used about music) serious and of lasting importance ▶ *I prefer classical music to modern music.*

classified /'klæsɪfaɪd/ *adjective*
officially secret ▶ *I can't tell you where they live – that's classified information.*

classify /'klæsɪfaɪ/ *verb (past **classified**)*
to put things into groups according to their type, size, age, etc. ▶ *They classified Bill as a problem child.*

classmate /'klɑːsmeɪt/ *noun*
a person who is in the same class as you at school ▶ *His classmates don't like him.*

classroom /'klɑːsrʊm/ *noun*
a room in which a class meets for a lesson ▶ *Which classroom are we in?*

classwork /'klɑːswɜːk/ *noun (no plural)*
school work that you do in class, not at home ▶ *Do exercises 1 to 4 as classwork.*

clatter /'klætər/ *noun*
the loud noise of hard things knocking together ▶ *The pans fell with a clatter.*

clause /klɔːz/ *noun*
a group of words that contains a verb

➤ The sentence "As I was walking home, I met my friend" contains two clauses. "As I was walking home" is one clause, and "I met my friend" is another.

COMPARE: **sentence**

claustrophobia /ˌklɔːstrəˈfəʊbɪə/ noun (no plural)
the fear of being in a small space ➤ People who suffer from claustrophobia hate going in caves.

claustrophobic /ˌklɔːstrəˈfəʊbɪk/ adjective
afraid of being in a small space

claw¹ /klɔː/ noun
1 one of the sharp, hard points on the foot of a bird or animal
2 the hand of a CRAB or LOBSTER

claw² verb
to tear something with the claws ➤ The cat clawed the chair.

clay /kleɪ/ noun (no plural)
soft, sticky earth from which people make pots and bricks

clean¹ /kliːn/ adjective
1 not dirty ➤ Haven't you got a clean shirt?
2 not yet used ➤ a clean piece of paper

clean² verb
to make something clean ➤ Have you cleaned the kitchen?

cleaner /ˈkliːnəʳ/ noun
a person who cleans houses or other buildings as their job

cleanliness /ˈklenlɪnəs/ noun (no plural)
the state of being clean ➤ Cleanliness is very important in the kitchen.

cleanse /klenz/ verb (present participle **cleansing**, past **cleansed**)
to make something such as a wound or your skin completely clean ➤ Cleanse the wound with antiseptic.

clean-shaven /ˌkliːn ˈʃeɪvən/ adjective
not having a BEARD

clear¹ /klɪəʳ/ adjective
1 easy to understand ➤ It was clear that he wanted to be alone.
SAME MEANING: **plain**
2 easy to see or hear ➤ a clear voice
OPPOSITE (**1** and **2**): **unclear**
3 easy to see through ➤ clear water
4 free from anything that blocks or covers ➤ The road's clear.

clear² verb
1 to take away something that is not wanted ➤ to clear plates from a table
2 clear up (a) to tidy or put things in order ➤ Can you clear up before he arrives, please?
(b) to get better ➤ I hope the weather clears up before Sunday.

clear-cut /ˌklɪə ˈkʌt/ adjective
certain or definite ➤ There's no clear-cut answer to your question.

clearing /ˈklɪərɪŋ/ noun
a small area in a forest where there are no trees

clearly /ˈklɪəli/ adverb
1 in a clear way ➤ Please speak more clearly – we can't hear you.
2 without any doubt ➤ Clearly he's very clever!

cleavage /ˈkliːvɪdʒ/ noun
the space between a woman's breasts ➤ She wore a dress that showed her cleavage.

clench /klentʃ/ verb
to close your hands or your mouth tightly, especially because you are angry ➤ He clenched his fists and started banging the door.
➤ Clenching her teeth, she said "Go away!"

clergy /ˈklɜːdʒɪ/ plural noun
priests and other religious leaders ➤ Catholic clergy are not allowed to marry.

clergyman /ˈklɜːdʒɪmən/ noun (plural **clergymen** /-mən/)
a male member of the clergy

clerical /ˈklerɪkəl/ *adjective*
connected with office work ▶ *We need some more clerical staff.*

clerk /klɑːk/ *noun*
a person who works in an office and writes letters

clever /ˈklevəʳ/ *adjective*
quick at learning and understanding things (*adverb:* **cleverly**)

cliché /ˈkliːʃeɪ/ *noun*
an expression that is used too often and no longer has any real meaning ▶ *His speech was full of clichés like "We must take one day at a time".*

click¹ /klɪk/ *noun*
a short, sharp sound ▶ *There was a loud click as she took the photograph.*

click² *verb*
to make a short, sharp sound ▶ *The door clicked shut.*

client /ˈklaɪənt/ *noun*
a person who pays a professional person for help or advice

clientele /ˌkliːənˈtel/ *noun*
the people who regularly go to a shop or restaurant ▶ *The shop's clientele is mainly women.*

cliff /klɪf/ *noun*
an area of high, steep rock, often close to the sea

climate /ˈklaɪmət/ *noun (no plural)*
the weather that a place regularly has

climax /ˈklaɪmæks/ *noun (plural **climaxes**)*
the most important or exciting part of something ▶ *The competition reaches its climax tomorrow.*

climb¹ /klaɪm/ *verb*
to go up ▶ *The two boys climbed the tree.* ▶ *The road climbed steeply up the hill.*

climb² *noun*
an upward journey ▶ *a long climb up the hill*

climber /ˈklaɪməʳ/ *noun*
a person who climbs mountains or rocks as a sport

climbing /ˈklaɪmɪŋ/ *noun (no plural)*
the sport of climbing mountains or rocks ▶ *We go climbing most weekends.*

cling /klɪŋ/ *verb (past* **clung** /klʌŋ/)
to hold on tightly ▶ *The baby monkey clung to its mother.*

clingfilm /ˈklɪŋfɪlm/ *noun (no plural)*
thin, clear plastic that is used for wrapping food

clinic /ˈklɪnɪk/ *noun*
a place where people go to see a doctor

clinical /ˈklɪnɪkəl/ *adjective*
connected with medical treatment and tests ▶ *The drug needs to have clinical trials.*

clip¹ /klɪp/ *noun*
a small metal object used for fastening things ▶ *The letters were held together with a paper clip.*

clip² *verb (present participle **clipping**, past **clipped**)*
1 to clip things with a clip ▶ *Could you clip those letters together, please?*
2 to cut something with a sharp instrument ▶ *He clipped his fingernails.*

clippers /ˈklɪpəz/ *plural noun*
a tool used for cutting small pieces off something ▶ *a pair of nail clippers*

clipping /ˈklɪpɪŋ/ *noun*
a piece of writing that you cut from a newspaper or magazine ▶ *I found a newspaper clipping about Madonna.*

clique /kliːk/ *noun*
a small group of people who know each other well and are not very friendly to other people ▶ *Jane has become part of their clique.*

cloak /kləʊk/ *noun*
a loose piece of clothing that you

C

wrap around your body, on top of other clothes, to keep you warm
COMPARE: **cape**

cloakroom /'kləʊkrʊm/ noun
1 a room where you leave hats, coats, etc.
2 a TOILET

clock /klɒk/ noun
a machine that tells you what the time is
COMPARE: **watch**

clockwise /'klɒkwaɪz/ adverb
in the same direction as the hands of a clock
OPPOSITE: **anticlockwise**

clockwork /'klɒkwɜːk/ noun
like clockwork in exactly the way that you planned ▶ Production at the factory has been going like clockwork.

clog¹ /klɒg/ (also **clog up**) verb (present participle **clogging**, past **clogged**)
to block something ▶ Leaves had clogged the drains.

clog² noun
a shoe made of wood or with a wooden SOLE

clone¹ /kləʊn/ noun
an exact copy of a plant or an animal that a scientist develops from one of its cells

clone² verb (present participle **cloning**, past **cloned**)
to produce an exact copy of a plant or an animal from one of its cells
▶ Scientists have successfully cloned a sheep.

close¹ /kləʊs/ adjective
1 near ▶ I live close to the shops.
▶ They were standing close together (=very near each other).
2 liking or loving someone
▶ Peter and John are close friends.
3 careful ▶ We kept a close watch on the children.

close² /kləʊz/ verb (present participle **closing**, past **closed**)
1 to shut something ▶ Please close the door.
2 (used about a shop, a bank, etc.) to stop being available for business
▶ What time does the bank close?
OPPOSITE: (**1** and **2**): **open**

close³ /kləʊz/ noun
the end of something ▶ at the close of the day

closed /kləʊzd/ adjective
1 shut ▶ Keep your eyes closed.
▶ The window was closed because it was raining.
2 not ready for business ▶ The shops are closed on Sundays.
OPPOSITE (**1** and **2**): **open**

closely /'kləʊsli/ adverb
1 very carefully ▶ The teacher was watching the students closely.
2 people who are closely related are members of the same family, for example brothers or sisters
3 if people work closely together, they work together and help each other a lot ▶ We have worked closely with the police to solve this crime.

close-up /'kləʊs ʌp/ noun
a photograph of a person that you take when you are standing very near to them ▶ a close-up of the actor's face

closing /'kləʊzɪŋ/ adjective
final ▶ In the closing chapter of the book, Max dies.

closure /'kləʊʒəʳ/ noun
the act of closing a factory, company, school, etc. permanently ▶ Workers are angry at the closure of their factory.

clot /klɒt/ noun
a place where blood or another liquid has become almost solid ▶ She has a blood clot in her leg.

cloth /klɒθ/ noun
1 (no plural) a soft substance made of

wool, cotton, etc. ➤ *She bought some cloth to make some new dresses.*
SAME MEANING: **material**
2 a piece of cloth used for a particular purpose ➤ *A red tablecloth covered the table.* ➤ *He dried the dishes with a dishcloth.*
LOOK AT: **clothes**

clothe /kləʊð/ *verb (present participle **clothing**, past **clothed**)*
to provide clothes for someone ➤ *She earns barely enough to feed and clothe her children.*

clothed /kləʊðd/ *adjective*
fully clothed, partly clothed with all your clothes on or with only some of your clothes on ➤ *She got into bed fully clothed.*

clothes /kləʊðz/ *plural noun*
things that you wear on your body ➤ *I need some new clothes.*

> **Cloth** is NOT the singular of **clothes** (look at the entry for **cloth** above). The word **clothes** is always plural and does not have a singular form. People usually use the name of the thing they are talking about when there is only one: *a shirt* ➤ *a dress*

clothesline /'kləʊðzlaɪn/ *noun*
a rope that you hang clothes on outside so that they will dry

clothes peg /'kləʊðz peg/ *noun*
a small object that you use to fasten clothes to a clothesline

clothing /'kləʊðɪŋ/ *noun (no plural)*
things that are used as clothes ➤ *warm winter clothing*

cloud /klaʊd/ *noun*
a mass of very small drops of water floating in the sky

cloudy /'klaʊdɪ/ *adjective (**cloudier, cloudiest**)*
having lots of clouds ➤ *a cloudy day*

clove /kləʊv/ *noun*
1 one of the parts that a GARLIC plant

is made up of ➤ *Chop up two cloves of garlic.*
2 a small, dried, black flower with a strong, sweet smell, used in cooking

clover /'kləʊvə^r/ *noun (no plural)*
a small plant with white or purple flowers and three round leaves on each stem

clown /klaʊn/ *noun*
a person who wears funny clothes and tries to make people laugh

club /klʌb/ *noun*
1 a group of people who have joined together and meet each other because they share an interest ➤ *a gardening club*
2 a large, heavy stick

clubbing /'klʌbɪŋ/ *noun (no plural)*
the activity of going to a club to dance ➤ *When we were in Ibiza, we went out clubbing every night.*

clue /klu:/ *noun*
something that helps you find the answer to a difficult question ➤ *The police have found a clue which will help them to catch the robber.*

clump /klʌmp/ *noun*
a group of trees, bushes, plants, etc. that are close together ➤ *a clump of trees*

clumsy /'klʌmzɪ/ *adjective (**clumsier, clumsiest**)*
likely to move in an awkward way or drop things ➤ *You are clumsy! You've knocked over my cup of coffee!* (adverb: **clumsily**)

clung /klʌŋ/
the PAST TENSE and PAST PARTICIPLE of the verb **cling**

cluster /'klʌstə^r/ *verb*
to form a group ➤ *Everyone clustered around the television.*

clutch /klʌtʃ/ *verb*
to take hold of something tightly ➤ *She clutched her baby in her arms.*

clutter¹ /ˈklʌtəʳ/ *(also **clutter up**)*
verb
to make something untidy by
covering or filling it with things
► *Books and papers cluttered his
desk.*

clutter² *noun (no plural)*
a lot of things scattered in an untidy
way ► *Please tidy up this clutter
before you leave.*

cm
a short way of writing the words
centimetre or **centimetres** ► *10cm*

Co. /kəʊ/
a short way of writing and saying the
word **company** ► *Hilton, Brooks & Co.*

c/o
a short way of writing the words **care
of**; used as part of an address when
you send a letter to someone who
will give it to the person you are
writing to ► *Michael Miles, c/o Mrs
C. Brown, 219 Park Lane, London*

coach¹ /kəʊtʃ/ *noun (plural **coaches**)*
1 a bus, or part of a train, that can
carry many people
2 a covered vehicle with four wheels,
pulled by horses
3 a person who gives special lessons
► *football coach*

coach² *verb*
to give someone special lessons
► *He coached her for the English
examination.*

coal /kəʊl/ *noun (no plural)*
a hard, black material dug out of the
ground and burned to give heat

coarse /kɔːs/ *adjective*
rough; not smooth or fine

coast /kəʊst/ *noun*
the land next to the sea ► *a town on
the coast*

coastal /ˈkəʊstəl/ *adjective*
on the land near the sea, or in the
sea near the land ► *the coastal
regions of Italy* ► *coastal waters*

coastguard /ˈkəʊstˌɡɑːd/ *noun*
a person whose job is to help boats
and swimmers that are in danger

coastline /ˈkəʊstlaɪn/ *noun*
the edge of the land ► *From the ship,
they saw the rocky coastline.*

coat /kəʊt/ *noun*
1 a piece of clothing that you wear
over your other clothes to keep you
warm when you go outside
2 an animal's fur, wool, or hair
3 a covering of something spread
over a surface ► *a coat of paint*

coat hanger /ˈkəʊt ˌhæŋəʳ/ *noun*
a specially shaped piece of wood or
plastic with a hook on top, used for
hanging up clothes

coax /kəʊks/ *verb*
to persuade someone by kindness or
care ► *She coaxed him to take the
medicine.*

cobweb /ˈkɒbweb/ *noun*
the thin net which a SPIDER spins to
catch flies and insects

cocaine /kəʊˈkeɪn/ *noun (no plural)*
a drug that prevents pain, or that is
taken illegally for pleasure

cock /kɒk/ *noun*
a male bird, especially a male chicken

cockerel /ˈkɒkərəl/ *noun*
a young male chicken

cockpit /ˈkɒkˌpɪt/ *noun*
the part of a plane where the pilot sits

cockroach /ˈkɒkˌrəʊtʃ/ *noun (plural
cockroaches)*
a large, black or brown insect that
lives where food is kept

cocktail /ˈkɒkteɪl/ *noun*
an alcoholic drink made from a
mixture of different drinks

cocky /ˈkɒkɪ/ *adjective (**cockier,
cockiest**)*
too confident about yourself, in a way
that annoys other people ► *He's very
talented, but far too cocky.*

cocoa /ˈkəʊkəʊ/ *noun (no plural)*
1 a brown powder made from the seeds of a tree, from which chocolate is made
2 a hot drink made from this powder

coconut /ˈkəʊkənʌt/ *noun*
a large nut with hard, white flesh and a hollow centre filled with milky juice

cod /kɒd/ *noun (plural cod)*
a sea fish used for food

code /kəʊd/ *noun*
a way of using words, letters, numbers, etc. to keep messages secret ▶ *The letter was written in code and I could not understand it.*

co-ed /ˌkəʊ ˈed/ *adjective*
(used about schools and colleges) CO-EDUCATIONAL; having both male and female students

coerce /kəʊˈɜːs/ *verb (present participle coercing, past coerced)*
to force someone to do something by threatening them ▶ *They coerced him into confessing.*

coffee /ˈkɒfɪ/ *noun*
1 (no plural) (a drink made from) a brown powder from the seeds of the coffee tree
2 a cup of this drink ▶ *Two coffees, please!*

coffee table /ˈkɒfɪ ˌteɪbəl/ *noun*
a low table in a LIVING ROOM

coffin /ˈkɒfɪn/ *noun*
a box in which a dead body is put

coil¹ /kɔɪl/ *verb*
1 to twist a rope, wire, or pipe round and round
2 to go round in a circle ▶ *The snake coiled round the tree.*

coil² *noun*
a set of rings joined to each other; a continuous circular shape ▶ *a coil of rope*

coin /kɔɪn/ *noun*
a piece of money made of metal
COMPARE: **bank note**

coincide /ˌkəʊɪnˈsaɪd/ *verb (present participle coinciding, past coincided)*
if one event coincides with another, the two things happen at the same time ▶ *My birthday coincides with her visit.*

coincidence /kəʊˈɪnsɪdəns/ *noun*
a number of events happening together by chance, which are often surprising ▶ *What a coincidence that I was in London at the same time as you!*

cold¹ /kəʊld/ *adjective*
having little heat ▶ *a cold drink*
OPPOSITE: **hot**

cold² *noun*
1 an illness of the nose and throat ▶ *I've got a cold*
2 (no plural) cold weather ▶ *I don't like the cold.*
OPPOSITE (2): **heat**

cold-blooded /ˌkəʊld ˈblʌdɪd/ *adjective*
cruel and showing no feelings ▶ *This was a cold-blooded murder.*

collaborate /kəˈlæbəreɪt/ *verb (present participle collaborating, past collaborated)*
to work together to produce or achieve something ▶ *Two companies collaborated on this project.*

collaboration /kəˌlæbəˈreɪʃən/ *noun (no plural)*
the act of working together to produce or achieve something

collage /ˈkɒlɑːʒ/ *noun*
a picture that you make by sticking pieces of paper and cloth onto a surface ▶ *The children made a collage of their visit to the zoo.*

collapse /kəˈlæps/ *verb (present participle collapsing, past collapsed)*
to break into pieces; to fall down ▶ *The roof of the old house collapsed.* ▶ *The old man collapsed in the street.*

collar /ˈkɒləʳ/ *noun*
1 the part of a shirt or coat that goes round your neck ▶ *The collar of his shirt was dirty.*
2 a leather or metal band put round the neck of an animal

collarbone /ˈkɒləbəʊn/ *noun*
one of two bones that go from the base of your neck to your shoulders
▶ *I broke my collarbone playing rugby.*

colleague /ˈkɒliːg/ *noun*
a person who you work with ▶ *This is Ian, a colleague of mine.*

collect /kəˈlekt/ *verb*
1 to come together or bring things together in the same place ▶ *A crowd had collected to watch the ceremony.*
▶ *I collect stamps.*
2 to come to take someone or something away ▶ *He collected the children from school.*
3 to get money from people ▶ *I'm collecting for the blind.*

collection /kəˈlekʃən/ *noun*
a group of things which have been brought together ▶ *a large collection of stamps*

collective¹ /kəˈlektɪv/ *adjective*
shared or done by all the members of a group together ▶ *It was a collective decision to give you the money.*
(adverb: **collectively**)

collective² *noun*
a business owned and controlled by the people who work in it

college /ˈkɒlɪdʒ/ *noun*
a place where people study after they have left school
COMPARE: **university**

collide /kəˈlaɪd/ *verb (present participle **colliding**, past **collided**)*
to bang together with great force
▶ *The two trains collided.*

collision /kəˈlɪʒən/ *noun*
a violent crash ▶ *a collision between two trains*

colon /ˈkəʊlɒn/ *noun*
the sign (:) which comes before the first example in the text after 'colour' below

colonel /ˈkɜːnl/ *noun*
an officer in the army

colony /ˈkɒləni/ *noun (plural **colonies**)*
a country that is under the control of another country

colossal /kəˈlɒsəl/ *adjective*
very big ▶ *Global warming is a colossal problem.*

colour¹ /ˈkʌləʳ/ *noun*
the quality that makes things look green, red, yellow, etc. ▶ *"What colour is her hair?" "It's black."*

The word **colour** is not usually used in sentences describing the colour of something: *Her dress is red.* ▶ *He has brown hair.*

colour² *verb*
to put colour on to something
▶ *Sarah is colouring the picture in her book.*

colour-blind /ˈkʌlə ˌblaɪnd/ *adjective*
not able to see the difference between particular colours

coloured /ˈkʌləd/ *adjective*
having a colour such as blue, red, or yellow ▶ *A black dress looks good with a coloured scarf.*

colourful /ˈkʌləfəl/ *adjective*
bright; having lots of colours
▶ *colourful clothes*

colouring /ˈkʌlərɪŋ/ *noun (no plural)*
the colour of someone's hair, skin, eyes, etc. ▶ *She has the same pale colouring as her sister.*

colourless /ˈkʌlələs/ *adjective*
not having any colour ▶ *Water is a colourless liquid.*

column /ˈkɒləm/ *noun*
1 a large post used to support a part of a building

2 something long and narrow ▶ *Can you add up this column of figures?*

coma /'kəʊmə/ *noun*
a condition in which someone is not conscious for a long time, usually as the result of an accident or illness ▶ *Ben was in a coma for six days.*

comb¹ /kəʊm/ *noun*
a thin piece of plastic, metal, etc. with teeth, that you use to make your hair tidy

comb² *verb*
to tidy your hair with a comb ▶ *Have you combed your hair?*

combat¹ /'kɒmbæt/ *noun (no plural)*
fighting during a war ▶ *Many soldiers were killed in combat.*

combat² *verb (present participle combating or combatting, past combated or combatted)*
to try to stop something bad from happening or getting worse ▶ *What is the best way to combat crime?*

combination /ˌkɒmbɪ'neɪʃən/ *noun*
a mixture of separate people or things joined together ▶ *His character is a combination of strength and kindness.*

combine /kəm'baɪn/ *verb (present participle combining, past combined)*
to join or mix together ▶ *The two small shops combined to make one large one.*

come /kʌm/ *verb (present participle coming, past tense came /keɪm/, past participle come)*
1 to move towards the person speaking ▶ *Come here, Mary. I want to speak to you!* ▶ *I'm going out. Are you coming with me?*
2 come about to happen ▶ *This situation should never have come about.*
3 come across someone or something to find someone or

something by chance ▶ *I came across an old friend I hadn't seen for years.*
4 come from to have been born or have lived a long time in a place ▶ *I come from Glasgow.*
5 Come on! Hurry up!
6 come off to become unfastened ▶ *My shoe has come off.*

comeback /'kʌmbæk/ *noun*
make a comeback to return after a long time and become popular or successful again ▶ *a fashion that made a brief comeback in the 1980s*

comedian /kə'miːdɪən/ *noun*
a person whose job is to tell jokes and make people laugh

comedy /'kɒmədɪ/ *noun (plural comedies)*
a funny play, film, etc.; something that makes you laugh
COMPARE: **tragedy**

comet /'kɒmɪt/ *noun*
a very bright object in the sky, like a star with a tail ▶ *A comet flew across the sky.*

comfort¹ /'kʌmfət/ *noun (no plural)*
a state in which you are free from pain, trouble, etc. ▶ *He lived in comfort* (=he had enough money to live well).

comfort² *verb*
to give help to someone or show them kindness when they are in pain or trouble ▶ *She comforted the unhappy child.*

comfortable /'kʌmftəbəl/ *adjective*
1 pleasant to wear, sit in, or be in ▶ *This is a very comfortable chair.*
OPPOSITE: **uncomfortable**
2 with no pain or worries ▶ *We're not rich but we are quite comfortable.* (*adverb:* **comfortably**)

comic¹ /'kɒmɪk/ *adjective*
making people laugh; funny

comic² *noun*
a small book for children, with pictures that tell the story

C

comical /ˈkɒmɪkəl/ adjective
funny in a strange or an unexpected
way ▶ He looked comical with his
hands waving in the air.

comic strip /ˈkɒmɪk strɪp/ noun
a set of pictures in a newspaper or
magazine that tell a short, funny
story

coming /ˈkʌmɪŋ/ adjective
happening soon ▶ We will be very
busy over the coming months.

comma /ˈkɒmə/ noun
the sign (,) used in writing to divide
up a sentence

command¹ /kəˈmɑːnd/ verb
1 to order someone to do something
▶ I command you to go!
2 to be in charge of people
▶ A general commands a large
number of soldiers.

command² noun
1 an order
2 (no plural) power ▶ The officer is in
command of his men.

commander /kəˈmɑːndəʳ/ noun
an officer who is in charge of a
military organization or group

commemorate /kəˈmeməreɪt/ verb
(present participle **commemorating**,
past **commemorated**)
to show that an event or a person is
remembered with respect ▶ a
monument commemorating those
who died in the war

commence /kəˈmens/ verb (present
participle **commencing**, past
commenced)
to begin ▶ The evening performance
will commence at 8 o'clock.
SAME MEANING: **start**

commendable /kəˈmendəbəl/
adjective
deserving praise and admiration ▶ It is
commendable that you want to help.

comment¹ /ˈkɒment/ verb
to make a remark about something,

or give an opinion about something
▶ He commented **on** the bad road.

comment² noun
an opinion or a remark about
something ▶ He's always making rude
comments **about** his boss.

commentary /ˈkɒməntəri/ noun
(plural **commentaries**)
a spoken description of something
that is happening

commentate /ˈkɒmənteɪt/ verb
(present participle **commentating**,
past **commentated**)
to describe an event on television or
radio while it is happening ▶ John
McEnroe is here to commentate on
the event for the BBC.

commentator /ˈkɒmənteɪtəʳ/ noun
someone who describes an event
while it is happening ▶ a radio
commentator

commerce /ˈkɒmɜːs/ noun (no plural)
business; buying and selling goods

commercial /kəˈmɜːʃəl/ adjective
related to the buying and selling of
goods

commercialized /kəˈmɜːʃəlaɪzd/
adjective
too concerned with making money
▶ The holiday resort has become too
commercialized.

commission¹ /kəˈmɪʃən/ noun
1 an official group of people whose
job is to find out about something
or control an activity ▶ The
International Whaling Commission
decides the limits on catching
whales.
2 (no plural) money that a person or
an organization is paid when they sell
something ▶ The bank charges
commission for cashing traveller's
cheques.

commission² verb
to ask someone to do a particular
piece of work for you ▶ The

government commissioned the report.

commit /kə'mɪt/ *verb (present participle* **committing,** *past* **committed)**
to do something wrong ▶ *He said he hadn't committed the murder.*

commitment /kə'mɪtmənt/ *noun*
1 a promise to do something ▶ *They made a commitment to work together.*
2 *(no plural)* determination to work hard and continue with something ▶ *You need commitment to succeed in this sport.*

committed /kə'mɪtɪd/ *adjective*
willing to work hard at something ▶ *He seems committed to his work.*

committee /kə'mɪti/ *noun*
a group of people chosen to study something, plan, and make decisions ▶ *The club committee arranges all the football matches.*

common /'kɒmən/ *adjective*
1 found everywhere; usual ▶ *Red buses are quite common in London.*
OPPOSITE: **rare, uncommon**
2 shared by several people; belonging to or used by several people ▶ *The park is common property – everyone can use it.*

commonly /'kɒmənli/ *adverb*
often ▶ *People with this illness commonly complain of headaches.*

commonplace /'kɒmənpleɪs/ *adjective*
not unusual ▶ *Divorce is now commonplace.*

common sense /ˌkɒmən 'sens/ *noun (no plural)*
the ability to behave in a sensible way and make practical decisions ▶ *Just use your common sense.*

Commonwealth /'kɒmənwelθ/ *noun*
a group of independent countries which used to be part of the British

Empire (=under the control of Britain)

commotion /kə'məʊʃən/ *noun (no plural)*
sudden noise or activity

communicate /kə'mju:nɪkeɪt/ *verb (past participle* **communicating,** *past* **communicated)**
to speak or write to someone ▶ *If you know English, you can communicate* **with** *a lot of people.* ▶ *We communicated by letter.*

communication /kəˌmju:nɪ'keɪʃən/ *noun*
1 *(no plural)* the act of speaking or writing to someone and being understood by them ▶ *Communication between people who speak different languages is difficult.*
2 communications *plural noun* roads, railways, radio, telephones, and all other ways of moving or sending information between places

Communism /'kɒmjunɪzəm/ *noun (no plural)*
a political system based on the idea that people are equal and that the state should own companies

Communist /'kɒmjunɪst/ *noun*
a person who believes in Communism

community /kə'mju:nəti/ *noun (plural* **communities)**
all the people living in one place ▶ *All children in our community go to the same school.*

commute /kə'mju:t/ *verb (present participle* **commuting,** *past* **commuted)**
to regularly travel a long distance to work ▶ *My dad commutes from Oxford to London every day.*

commuter /kə'mju:təʳ/ *noun*
a person who travels a long way to work each day

compact /kəm'pækt, 'kɒmpækt/ *adjective*

C

small and taking up very little space
► *the compact design of modern
computers*

compact disc /ˌkɒmpækt 'dɪsk/ *noun*
a type of record with very high-quality
sound, played on a special machine

compact disc player /ˌkɒmpækt
'dɪsk ˌpleɪəʳ/ (*also* **CD player**) *noun*
a special machine for playing COMPACT
DISCS

companion /kəm'pænjən/ *noun*
a person you are with, often a friend
► *He was my travelling companion for
many months.*

companionship /kəm'pænjənʃɪp/
noun (no plural)
friendship from people who you
spend time with ► *I missed the
companionship of work.*

company /'kʌmpənɪ/ *noun*
1 *(no plural)* a person or people you
are with ► *I had no company on the
journey.*
2 *(plural* **companies***)* a group of
people doing business; a firm
► *I work for a mining company.*

comparable /'kɒmpərəbəl/ *adjective*
similar in size or importance ► *He
was offered a comparable job at
another branch of the company.*

comparative /kəm'pærətɪv/ *noun,
adjective*
a word or a form of a word that
shows that something is bigger,
smaller, better, worse, etc. than
something else; for example,
"bigger" is the comparative form of
"big"
COMPARE: **superlative**

comparatively /kəm'pærətɪvlɪ/
adverb
compared with something else
► *Houses in that area are
comparatively cheap.*

compare /kəm'peəʳ/ *verb (present
participle* **comparing***, past* **compared***)*
to decide in what way things are alike
or different ► *People are always
comparing me* **to** *my sister.* ► *We
compared the prices in the shop* **with**
the prices at the market.

comparison /kəm'pærɪsən/ *noun*
an act of judging two things and
saying whether they are alike or
different ► *My shoes are small in
comparison with my sister's.*

compartment /kəm'pɑːtmənt/ *noun*
1 a room in a train
2 a separate part of a container
► *a special compartment* **for** *meat*

compass /'kʌmpəs/ *noun (plural*
compasses*)*
an instrument with a metal needle
that always points north

compassion /kəm'pæʃən/ *noun (no
plural)*
sympathy for people who are
suffering

compassionate /kəm'pæʃənət/
adjective
feeling sympathy for people who are
suffering

compatible /kəm'pætəbəl/ *adjective*
1 having similar ideas or interests,
and able to have a good relationship
2 able to exist or be used together
without problems ► *Is the new
software compatible* **with** *the old
version?*
OPPOSITE (**1** and **2**): **incompatible**

compel /kəm'pel/ *verb (present
participle* **compelling***, past
compelled***)*
to force someone to do something
► *The floods compelled us to turn
back.*

compelling /kəm'pelɪŋ/ *adjective*
very interesting or exciting ► *a
compelling TV drama*

compensate /'kɒmpənseɪt/ *verb
(present participle* **compensating***,
past* **compensated***)*

to do something good so that the bad effects of something else seem less important ▶ *He bought his kids presents to compensate **for** being away so much.*

compensation /ˌkɒmpənˈseɪʃən/ *noun*
1 (no plural) money that someone is given because they have been injured or badly treated, or have lost something ▶ *The holiday company had to pay the Taylors £1,500 compensation.*
2 something that makes a bad situation seem better ▶ *Being unemployed has its compensations, like not having to get up early.*

compete /kəmˈpiːt/ *verb (present participle **competing**, past **competed**)*
to try to win a race, prize, etc.
▶ *Five children competed in the race.*

competence /ˈkɒmpɪtəns/ *noun (no plural)*
the ability to do a job correctly
OPPOSITE: **incompetence**

competent /ˈkɒmpɪtənt/ *adjective*
good at your work or able to do a job well ▶ *a highly competent doctor*
OPPOSITE: **incompetent**

competition /ˌkɒmpəˈtɪʃən/ *noun*
a test of who is best at something
▶ *She came first in a drawing competition.*

competitive /kəmˈpetɪtɪv/ *adjective*
determined to be more successful than other people ▶ *Boys are usually more competitive than girls.*

competitor /kəmˈpetɪtər/ *noun*
a person who tries to win something

compilation /ˌkɒmpɪˈleɪʃən/ *noun*
a collection of songs or pieces of writing that were originally sold as part of different records or books
▶ *The new CD is a compilation of David Bowie's hit singles.*

compile /kəmˈpaɪl/ *verb (present participle **compiling**, past **compiled**)*

to make a book, list, etc., using different pieces of information
▶ *They compiled a list of the most popular activities.*

complacent /kəmˈpleɪsənt/ *adjective*
too pleased with what you have achieved so that you no longer try to improve ▶ *You should do well in your exams, but you mustn't get complacent.*

complain /kəmˈpleɪn/ *verb*
to say that something is not very good, or that you are unhappy or annoyed with something ▶ *We complained **about** the bad food.*

complaint /kəmˈpleɪnt/ *noun*
something said which expresses annoyance or unhappiness about something ▶ *We made a complaint **about** the food.*

complete¹ /kəmˈpliːt/ *adjective*
1 whole; with nothing left out
▶ *a complete set of stamps*
OPPOSITE: **incomplete**
2 total ▶ *a complete waste of time*

complete² *verb (present participle **completing**, past **completed**)*
to finish something ▶ *to complete a piece of work*

completely /kəmˈpliːtli/ *adverb*
totally ▶ *Have you completely finished your work?*

complex¹ /ˈkɒmpleks/ *adjective*
consisting of many connected parts, especially in a way that is difficult to understand or explain ▶ *the complex nature of the human mind* ▶ *a highly complex issue*

complex² *noun (plural **complexes**)*
a group of buildings used for a similar purpose ▶ *a new shopping complex*

complexion /kəmˈplekʃən/ *noun*
the natural colour and appearance of the skin on your face ▶ *a pale complexion*

C

complicate /'kɒmplɪkeɪt/ *verb*
*(present participle **complicating**,
past **complicated**)*
to make something more difficult to
do or understand ▶ *Bad weather
complicated the attempt to rescue
the climbers.*

complicated /'kɒmplɪkeɪtɪd/
adjective
difficult to understand; not simple
▶ *A car engine is a complicated
machine.*

complication /ˌkɒmplɪ'keɪʃən/
noun
a problem that makes something
more difficult to do or understand
▶ *We don't expect any further
complications in the travel
arrangements.*

compliment[1] /'kɒmplɪmənt/ *noun*
something nice said about someone
OPPOSITE: **insult**

compliment[2] /'kɒmplɪmənt/ *verb*
to say something nice to someone
because they have done something
you think is clever or good ▶ *She
complimented Mary **on** her excellent
Spanish.*

comply /kəm'plaɪ/ *verb (past
complied)*
to obey an order or a request
▶ *Anyone who fails to comply **with**
the law will have to pay a £100 fine.*

component /kəm'pəʊnənt/ *noun*
one of the different parts of a
machine

compose /kəm'pəʊz/ *verb (present
participle **composing**, past
composed)*
1 to write or make up a song, poem,
or a piece of music
2 be composed of to be formed from
different parts ▶ *The course will be
composed of three parts ...*

composer /kəm'pəʊzə[r]/ *noun*
a person who writes music

composition /ˌkɒmpə'zɪʃən/ *noun*
a story, poem, piece of music, etc.
that you have written

compound /'kɒmpaʊnd/ *noun*
a group of buildings and the land
around them

comprehension /ˌkɒmprɪ'henʃən/
noun
1 a test of how well students
understand written or spoken
language
2 *(no plural)* the ability to understand
something ▶ *The students want to
improve their reading comprehension
skills.*

comprehensive /ˌkɒmprɪ'hensɪv/
adjective
including everything that is needed
▶ *a comprehensive range of books*

comprehensive school
/ˌkɒmprɪ'hensɪv ˌskuːl/ *noun*
a SECONDARY school which teaches
pupils of all abilities
COMPARE: **grammar school**

comprise /kəm'praɪz/ *verb (present
participle **comprising**, past
comprised)*
1 be comprised of to consist of
particular parts, groups, or people
▶ *The committee is comprised of
eight members.*
2 to form part of a larger group
▶ *Women comprise over 75% of our
staff.*

compromise[1] /'kɒmprəmaɪz/ *noun*
a situation in which people or groups
accept less than they really want,
especially in order to end an
argument ▶ *Talks will continue until a
compromise is reached.*

compromise[2] *verb (present
participle **compromising**, past
compromised)*
to accept less than you really want,
especially in order to end an
argument ▶ *President Chirac has said*

that he would be ready to compromise.

compulsory /kəmˈpʌlsəri/ *adjective*
that must be done because of a rule or law ▸ *Science is compulsory at our school.*

computer /kəmˈpjuːtə/ *noun*
a machine that stores information and can work out answers to sums very quickly ▸ *a personal computer*

computer game /kəmˈpjuːtə ˌɡeɪm/ *noun*
a game played on a computer

computer programmer /kəmˌpjuːtə ˈprəʊɡræmə/ *noun*
a person who prepares lists of rules that are put into a computer to make the computer give the right information or do the right job

con /kɒn/ *verb (present participle **conning**, past **conned**)*
to trick someone in order to get something you want ▸ *They conned me **into** paying for all the tickets.*

conceal /kənˈsiːl/ *verb*
to hide something ▸ *He tried to conceal the book under his jacket.* ▸ *Sue tried hard to conceal her disappointment from the others.*

concede /kənˈsiːd/ *verb (present participle **conceding**, past **conceded**)*
1 concede defeat to admit that you are not going to win a game, an argument, etc.
2 to admit that something is true, although you do not want to ▸ *She reluctantly conceded that I was right.*

conceited /kənˈsiːtɪd/ *adjective*
too proud of how good, clever, or attractive you are ▸ *He's so conceited about his looks.*

conceivable /kənˈsiːvəbəl/ *adjective*
possible ▸ *It is conceivable that the experts are wrong.*

conceive /kənˈsiːv/ *verb (present participle **conceiving**, past **conceived**)*
to become PREGNANT

concentrate /ˈkɒnsəntreɪt/ *verb (present participle **concentrating**, past **concentrated**)*
to keep your thoughts or attention on one thing ▸ *Are you concentrating **on** your work?*

concentrated /ˈkɒnsəntreɪtɪd/ *adjective*
(used about liquids) thick and strong because most of the water has been removed

concentration /ˌkɒnsənˈtreɪʃən/ *noun*
1 *(no plural)* the ability to think very carefully about something for a long time ▸ *The work requires a lot of concentration.* ▸ *The moment they lose concentration, they forget everything I have told them to do.*
2 a large amount of something in the same place ▸ *The area has a high concentration of wildlife.*

concept /ˈkɒnsept/ *noun*
a general idea ▸ *Many films have been based on the concept of time travel.*

conception /kənˈsepʃən/ *noun (no plural)*
the act of becoming PREGNANT

concern¹ /kənˈsɜːn/ *noun*
worry ▸ *He shows no concern for his children.*

concern² *verb*
1 to be about something ▸ *The story concerns a man who lived in Russia a long time ago.*
2 to be of importance or interest to someone ▸ *This letter concerns you.*
3 to worry someone ▸ *Her refusal to eat concerns us.*

concerned /kənˈsɜːnd/ *adjective*
1 anxious or worried ▸ *I'm very concerned **about** my mother's illness.*

➤ She was concerned for their safety.
2 as far as I'm concerned in my opinion

concerning /kən'sɜːnɪŋ/ *preposition*
about ➤ *Concerning your letter, I am pleased to inform you that ....*
SAME MEANING: **regarding**

concert /'kɒnsət/ *noun*
an occasion when music is played in public for a lot of people

concession /kən'seʃən/ *noun*
something that you agree to in order to end an argument ➤ *She wasn't prepared to make any concessions.*

concise /kən'saɪs/ *adjective*
short and clear, without using too many words ➤ *He gave a concise explanation of the problem.*

conclude /kən'kluːd/ *verb*
(present participle **concluding**, past **concluded**)
1 to finish something ➤ *She concluded her speech with a joke.*
2 to decide that something is true from what you have learned ➤ *When I had heard the story, I concluded that he had told me the truth.*

conclusion /kən'kluːʒən/ *noun*
a judgement or decision that you reach after some thought ➤ *My conclusion was that the boy had told me the truth.*

conclusive /kən'kluːsɪv/ *adjective*
proving that something is definitely true ➤ *There is now conclusive evidence that smoking causes cancer.*
(adverb: **conclusively**)
OPPOSITE: **inconclusive**

concrete /'kɒŋkriːt/ *noun (no plural)*
a grey powder mixed with sand and water, which becomes very hard and is used for building

concussion /kən'kʌʃən/ *noun (no plural)*
slight damage to your brain caused when you hit your head on something

condemn /kən'dem/ *verb*
to send someone to prison for a crime

condemnation /ˌkɒndem'neɪʃən/ *noun*
a statement of very strong disapproval ➤ *There has been widespread condemnation of the bombing.*

condensation /ˌkɒnden'seɪʃən/ *noun (no plural)*
small drops of water that appear on a cold surface when steam or hot air touches it

condescending /ˌkɒndɪ'sendɪŋ/ *adjective*
showing that you think you are better or more important than other people ➤ *He was laughing at her in that condescending way he has.*

condition /kən'dɪʃən/ *noun*
1 the state of someone or something ➤ *The car is in very good condition.*
➤ *Weather conditions are bad today.*
2 something that must happen before something else happens ➤ *One of the conditions of being given the job was that I had to learn English.* ➤ *I was given the job on condition that I learned English.*

conditional /kən'dɪʃənəl/ *adjective*
a conditional part of a sentence begins with "if" or "unless"

conditioner /kən'dɪʃənəʳ/ *noun*
a liquid that you put on your hair after you have washed it to keep it in good condition

condom /'kɒndəm/ *noun*
a thin piece of rubber that a man wears over his PENIS during sex

condone /kən'dəʊn/ *verb*
(present participle **condoning**, past **condoned**)
to approve of or allow behaviour that most people think is wrong ➤ *I cannot condone the use of violence.*

conduct¹ /kən'dʌkt/ *verb*
to lead or guide someone ➤ *He conducted us on a tour of the castle.*

conduct² /'kɒndʌkt/ *noun (no plural)*
the way you behave
SAME MEANING: **behaviour**

conductor /kən'dʌktə'/ *noun*
1 a person who controls a group of people playing music
2 a person who sells tickets on a bus or train

cone /kəʊn/ *noun*
1 a round shape that is pointed at one end, like the end of a sharp pencil
2 a thing that grows on the branches of CONIFER trees, which contains seeds

confederation /kən,fedə'reɪʃən/ *(also confederacy* /kən'fedərəsɪ/*) noun*
an official group of people, organizations, or states that have joined together to achieve an aim

confer /kən'fɜ:'/ *verb (present participle **conferring**, past **conferred**)*
to discuss something with other people so that everyone can express their opinion ➤ *I will have to confer with my colleagues about this.*

conference /'kɒnfərəns/ *noun*
a meeting of people to find out what they think about a subject ➤ *a doctors' conference*

confess /kən'fes/ *verb*
to tell someone about things you have done wrong ➤ *When the police questioned the man, he confessed.*

confession /kən'feʃən/ *noun*
a speech or piece of writing saying what you have done wrong ➤ *He made a confession.*

confetti /kən'fetɪ/ *noun (no plural)*
small pieces of paper that you throw over a man and woman who have just got married

confide /kən'faɪd/ *verb (present participle **confiding**, past **confided**)*
to tell a secret to someone you trust ➤ *She chose to confide in her sister.*

confidence /'kɒnfɪdəns/ *noun (no plural)*
a calm, unworried feeling that you are sure that you can do something ➤ *She plays the piano well, but doesn't have the confidence to play to others.*

confident /'kɒnfɪdənt/ *adjective*
feeling sure or safe ➤ *I was confident that I had passed the examination.*

confidential /,kɒnfɪ'denʃəl/ *adjective*
intended to be kept secret ➤ *confidential information*

confine /kən'faɪn/ *verb*
be confined to to happen in only one place, or to affect only one group of people ➤ *This illness is not confined to older people.*

confirm /kən'fɜ:m/ *verb*
to say for certain that something is true or will happen ➤ *Please confirm your telephone message by writing to me.*

confirmation /,kɒnfə'meɪʃən/ *noun (no plural)*
something that shows other things to be true

confiscate /'kɒnfɪskeɪt/ *verb (present participle **confiscating**, past **confiscated**)*
to take something away from someone, either because they are not allowed to have it or as a punishment ➤ *The police confiscated his gun.*

conflict¹ /'kɒnflɪkt/ *noun*
a fight or an argument ➤ *a conflict between two countries*

conflict² /kən'flɪkt/ *verb*
to disagree ➤ *The two stories conflicted, so I did not know what to believe.*

conform /kən'fɔ:m/ *verb*
1 to behave in the way that most other people behave ➤ *There's always*

C

pressure on kids to conform.
2 to obey or follow an established rule, pattern, etc. ► *Seatbelts must conform to official safety standards.*

confront /kən'frʌnt/ *verb*
1 to deal with a problem or difficult situation rather than ignore it ► *We want to help you to confront your problems.*
2 to try to make someone admit they have done something wrong ► *Richard confronted his sister about her lies.*

confrontation /ˌkɒnfrən'teɪʃən/ *noun*
a situation in which there is a lot of angry disagreement ► *I try to avoid confrontations.*

confuse /kən'fjuːz/ *verb (present participle **confusing**, past **confused**)*
to mix ideas in your mind so that you feel unsure about something ► *I confused the two boys, because they look so alike.*

confused /kən'fjuːzd/ *adjective*
unable to understand something clearly ► *I'm totally confused.* ► *If you're confused **about** anything, call me.*

confusing /kən'fjuːzɪŋ/ *adjective*
difficult to understand ► *This map is really confusing.*

confusion /kən'fjuːʒən/ *noun (no plural)*
a state of mind in which you are uncertain what to think or do ► *The room was **in** complete confusion.*

congestion /kən'dʒestʃən/ *noun (no plural)*
a situation in which there are too many vehicles on a road ► *There is a lot of congestion on the roads today.*

congratulate /kən'grætʃʊleɪt/ *verb (present participle **congratulating**, past **congratulated**)*

to say you are pleased about a happy event ► *I congratulated them **on** the birth of their baby.*

congratulations /kənˌgrætʃʊ'leɪʃənz/ *interjection*
an expression of happiness or admiration for something someone has done ► *Congratulations **on** the birth of your baby!*

congregation /ˌkɒŋgrɪ'geɪʃən/ *noun*
the people who are in a church for a religious ceremony

conifer /'kəʊnɪfə'/ *noun*
a tree that keeps its leaves in winter and has CONES containing its seeds

conjunction /kən'dʒʌŋkʃən/ *noun*
a word such as "and" or "but" that joins two parts of a sentence

conjure /'kʌndʒə'/ *verb (present participle **conjuring**, past **conjured**)*
to make something appear as if by magic ► *The magician conjured the rabbit out of the hat.*

conjurer (also **conjuror**) /'kʌndʒərə'/ *noun*
a person whose job is to do magic tricks

conman /'kɒnmæn/ *noun (plural **conmen** /-men/)*
a person who tries to get money by tricking people

connect /kə'nekt/ *verb*
to join two or more places or things ► *Will you connect this wire **to** the television?*

connected /kə'nektɪd/ *adjective*
1 related ► *Police think the killings may be connected **with** each other in some way.* ► *The two ideas are closely connected.*
2 joined together ► *The computer is connected **to** a laser printer.*

connection /kə'nekʃən/ *noun*
the joining of two or more things; something that joins two or more

things ▶ *The television is not working; is there a loose connection?*

conquer /'kɒŋkəʳ/ *verb*
to defeat someone in war ▶ *to conquer the enemy*

conquest /'kɒŋkwest/ *noun*
the defeat or control of a group of people ▶ *the conquest of the British army*

conscience /'kɒnʃəns/ *noun*
the feeling inside you that tells you whether something is right or wrong ▶ *His conscience troubled him after he took the money.*

conscientious /ˌkɒnʃi'enʃəs/ *adjective*
showing a lot of care and attention in the way you do things ▶ *a conscientious worker*

conscious /'kɒnʃəs/ *adjective*
awake and knowing what is happening around you ▶ *He is badly hurt but still conscious.*
OPPOSITE: **unconscious**

consciousness /'kɒnʃəsnəs/ *noun* (no plural)
the condition of being awake and understanding what is happening ▶ *She lost consciousness at 6 o'clock and died two hours later.* ▶ *Will he ever regain consciousness?*

consecutive /kən'sekjʊtɪv/ *adjective*
happening one after the other ▶ *It rained for three consecutive days.*

consensus /kən'sensəs/ *noun* (no plural)
general agreement between everyone in a group ▶ *The consensus of opinion is that Miller should resign.*

consent¹ /kən'sent/ *verb*
to agree to something ▶ *With great sadness, her father consented **to** her marriage.*

consent² *noun* (no plural)
agreement ▶ *We need your parents' written consent.*

consequence /'kɒnsɪkwəns/ *noun*
something that happens as a result of something else ▶ *As a consequence of being in hospital, Jane decided that she wanted to become a nurse.*

consequently /'kɒnsɪkwəntlɪ/ *adverb*
happening as a result of something else

conservation /ˌkɒnsə'veɪʃən/ *noun* (no plural)
the saving and protecting of animals or plants ▶ *There is a need for the conservation **of** trees, or there will soon be no forests left.*

conservationist /ˌkɒnsə'veɪʃənɪst/ *noun*
a person who works to protect the environment

conservative /kən'sɜːvətɪv/ *adjective*
preferring to do things in the way they are already done, rather than make changes ▶ *a very conservative attitude to education*

conservatory /kən'sɜːvətrɪ/ *noun* (plural **conservatories**)
a room with glass walls and a glass roof, joined to the side of a house

consider /kən'sɪdəʳ/ *verb*
to think about something ▶ *I'm considering changing my job.*

considerable /kən'sɪdərəbəl/ *adjective*
great or large in amount ▶ *I spent a considerable amount of time trying to persuade him to come.* (adverb: **considerably**)

considerate /kən'sɪdərət/ *adjective*
thinking about other people's feelings and needs
OPPOSITE: **inconsiderate**

consideration /kənˌsɪdə'reɪʃən/ *noun* (no plural)
1 thought and attention ▶ *They gave the plan careful consideration.*
2 thought for other people's feelings

C

➤ *You show no consideration for anyone but yourself!*

considering /kənˈsɪdərɪŋ/ *preposition, conjunction*
used before a fact that you know has had an effect on a particular situation ➤ *Considering (that) we missed the bus, we're actually not too late.* ➤ *Considering the strength of the opposition, we did very well.*

consist /kənˈsɪst/ *verb*
consist of to be made up of ➤ *The course consists of some classwork and some practice in the factory.*

consistency /kənˈsɪstənsi/ *noun*
1 (no plural) the fact of always happening or behaving in the same way ➤ *There's no consistency in the way they apply the rules.*
OPPOSITE: **inconsistency**
2 the thickness of a mixture ➤ *a dessert with a nice, creamy consistency*

consistent /kənˈsɪstənt/ *adjective*
1 always happening or behaving in the same way ➤ *Joe's work has shown consistent improvement this term.*
2 be consistent with something to say the same thing or follow the same principles as something else ➤ *His story is not consistent with the facts.*
(adverb: **consistently**)
OPPOSITE (**1** and **2**): **inconsistent**

consolation /ˌkɒnsəˈleɪʃən/ *noun*
something that makes you feel better when you are sad or disappointed ➤ *My only consolation is that everyone else finds the work hard too.*

console[1] /kənˈsəʊl/ *verb* (present participle **consoling**, past **consoled**)
to help to make someone who is sad or disappointed feel better ➤ *No one could console her when her son died.*

console[2] /ˈkɒnsəʊl/ *noun*
a piece of equipment with buttons on it that you connect to a computer and use when you play a game on the computer ➤ *a games console*

consonant /ˈkɒnsənənt/ *noun*
a written letter, or the sound of a letter, which is not **a**, **e**, **i**, **o**, or **u**.
COMPARE: **vowel**

conspicuous /kənˈspɪkjuəs/ *adjective*
very easy to notice because of being different from other people or things ➤ *Being so tall makes him very conspicuous.*

conspiracy /kənˈspɪrəsi/ *noun* (plural **conspiracies**)
a secret plan made by two or more people to do something harmful or illegal ➤ *a conspiracy to overthrow the king*

constable /ˈkʌnstəbəl/ *noun*
a police officer of the lowest rank

constant /ˈkɒnstənt/ *adjective*
happening all the time ➤ *constant rain* (adverb: **constantly**)

consternation /ˌkɒnstəˈneɪʃən/ *noun* (no plural)
a feeling of shock or worry

constipated /ˈkɒnstɪpeɪtɪd/ *adjective*
unable to empty your BOWELS

constipation /ˌkɒnstɪˈpeɪʃən/ *noun* (no plural)
the condition of being unable to empty your BOWELS

constituency /kənˈstɪtʃuənsi/ *noun* (plural **constituencies**)
an area of the country that chooses one member of parliament

constituent /kənˈstɪtʃuənt/ *noun*
a person who votes and lives in a particular constituency

constitute /ˈkɒnstɪtjuːt/ *verb* (present participle **constituting**, past **constituted**)
to be or form something ➤ *His action constitutes a criminal offence.* ➤ *the people that constitute the committee*

constitution /ˌkɒnstɪˈtjuːʃən/ *noun*
a set of laws governing a country, club, etc.

constitutional /ˌkɒnstɪˈtjuːʃənəl/ *adjective*
written in or concerning the set of laws governing a country, club, etc.

constraint /kənˈstreɪnt/ *noun*
something that stops you doing the things you want to do ▶ *the constraints that were placed on Victorian women*

construct /kənˈstrʌkt/ *verb*
to build or make something ▶ *to construct a bridge*

construction /kənˈstrʌkʃən/ *noun*
1 (no plural) building ▶ *a construction company*
2 something that is built

constructive /kənˈstrʌktɪv/ *adjective*
intended to be helpful, or likely to produce good results ▶ *constructive criticism*

consul /ˈkɒnsəl/ *noun*
a person who lives in a foreign city and whose job is to help people from his or her own country

consult /kənˈsʌlt/ *verb*
to talk to someone or look at a book in order to get information ▶ *I consulted George about buying a car.*

consultant /kənˈsʌltənt/ *noun*
1 a person with a lot of experience in a particular subject whose job is to give advice about it ▶ *a marketing consultant*
2 a SENIOR hospital doctor who knows a lot about a particular area of medicine

consultation /ˌkɒnsəlˈteɪʃən/ *noun*
1 a discussion in which people who are affected by a decision can say what they think should be done ▶ *It was all done without any consultation.* ▶ *The plan was drawn up in consultation with the mayor.*

2 a meeting in which you get advice from someone such as a doctor

consume /kənˈsjuːm/ *verb (present participle consuming, past consumed)*
to eat or use something ▶ *The country consumes much more than it produces.*

consumer /kənˈsjuːmər/ *noun*
a person who buys things or uses a service that a company provides ▶ *Consumers are now more aware of their rights.*

consumption /kənˈsʌmpʃən/ *noun (no plural)*
the eating or using of something ▶ *The car's petrol consumption was very high.*

contact¹ /ˈkɒntækt/ *verb*
to talk or write to someone ▶ *She contacted me as soon as she arrived.*

contact² *noun (no plural)*
the touching or coming together of two things or people ▶ *The fire started when two wires came into contact.* ▶ *They have little contact with other people.*

contact lens /ˈkɒntækt ˌlenz/ *noun (plural contact lenses)*
a very small, plastic LENS that you put in your eye instead of wearing glasses

contagious /kənˈteɪdʒəs/ *adjective*
(used about diseases and illnesses) able to be passed from one person to another

contain /kənˈteɪn/ *verb*
to have something inside ▶ *I found a book containing all the information I needed.*

container /kənˈteɪnər/ *noun*
something you can put things into, for example a box, bottle, etc.

contaminate /kənˈtæmɪneɪt/ *verb (present participle contaminating, past contaminated)*

C

to add a substance to something that makes it dirty or dangerous ▶ *The water was contaminated with chemicals.*

contamination /kən,tæmɪˈneɪʃən/ noun (no plural)
the act of adding a substance to something, that makes it dirty or dangerous

contemplate /ˈkɒntəmpleɪt/ verb (present participle **contemplating**, past **contemplated**)
to think about something, especially in a serious way or for a long time ▶ *She even contemplated killing herself.*

contemporary¹ /kənˈtempərərɪ/ adjective
1 modern and belonging to the present time ▶ *She is one of this country's best contemporary artists.*
2 happening or existing in the same period of time ▶ *This information comes from a contemporary record of those events.*

contemporary² noun (plural **contemporaries**)
a person living at the same time as someone else ▶ *Many of Darwin's contemporaries did not agree with his theories.*

contempt /kənˈtempt/ noun (no plural)
a feeling that someone or something does not deserve any respect ▶ *He showed complete contempt **for** the people who worked for him.*

contend /kənˈtend/ verb
contend with something to deal with something that is causing problems and making it difficult to do something else ▶ *The players had to contend with very windy conditions.*

contender /kənˈtendəʳ/ noun
a person who is competing for a title, prize, job, etc.

content /kənˈtent/ adjective
satisfied and happy ▶ *She's not very content at work.*

contented /kənˈtentɪd/ adjective
satisfied and happy ▶ *My father seems more contented in his new job.*
OPPOSITE: **discontented**

contents /ˈkɒntents/ plural noun
the things that are inside something ▶ *The contents of the box fell onto the floor.*

contest /ˈkɒntest/ noun
a fight or competition

contestant /kənˈtestənt/ noun
a person who enters a competition

context /ˈkɒntekst/ noun
1 the situation within which something happens ▶ *You need to consider these events in their historical context.*
2 the words that come before and after a word or phrase, that help you understand its meaning ▶ *Can you guess the meaning of this word from its context?*

continent /ˈkɒntɪnənt/ noun
one of the large areas of land on Earth, such as Africa, Europe, Australia, etc.

continental /,kɒntɪˈnentl/ adjective
of or from all of Europe except Britain ▶ *Continental breakfasts are very different from British breakfasts.*

continual /kənˈtɪnjʊəl/ adjective
happening often or all the time ▶ *continual arguments*

continue /kənˈtɪnjuː/ verb (present participle **continuing**, past **continued**)
1 to go on ▶ *She continued to look at them in silence.*
2 to start again after stopping ▶ *The play will continue in 15 minutes.*
3 to go further in the same direction ▶ *The road continues on down the valley.*

continuity /ˌkɒntɪˈnjuːɪtɪ/ *noun (no plural)*
the state of continuing for a long period of time without change

continuous /kənˈtɪnjʊəs/ *adjective*
never stopping ➤ *a continuous noise*
(*adverb:* **continuously**)

contraception /ˌkɒntrəˈsepʃən/ *noun (no plural)*
methods of stopping a woman becoming PREGNANT

contraceptive /ˌkɒntrəˈseptɪv/ *noun*
a device or drug that stops a woman becoming PREGNANT

contract /ˈkɒntrækt/ *noun*
a written agreement to do work or sell goods at an agreed price

contractor /kənˈtræktər/ *noun*
a person or company that does work for another company ➤ *a building contractor*

contradict /ˌkɒntrəˈdɪkt/ *verb*
1 if one statement contradicts another, the two are different and cannot both be true ➤ *Their stories contradicted each other.*
2 to say that something that someone has just said is not true ➤ *Don't contradict your mother!*

contradiction /ˌkɒntrəˈdɪkʃən/ *noun*
a difference between two statements or facts, that shows they cannot both be true ➤ *There were some obvious contradictions in what he said.*

contradictory /ˌkɒntrəˈdɪktərɪ/ *adjective*
if two statements are contradictory, they are different and cannot both be true

contrary¹ /ˈkɒntrərɪ/ *noun (no plural)*
the opposite ➤ *"You must be tired." "On the contrary – I feel wide awake."*

contrary² *adjective*
not agreeing with something ➤ *He passed the examination, contrary to what I expected.*

contrast¹ /kənˈtrɑːst/ *verb*
to compare two things and find the differences between them ➤ *In the book, the writer contrasts two different ways of planning a garden.*

contrast² /ˈkɒntrɑːst/ *noun*
a difference ➤ *I've never seen such a contrast **between** two brothers.*

contribute /kənˈtrɪbjuːt/ *verb (present participle* **contributing**, *past* **contributed**)
to give money or help ➤ *We all contributed money to buy Richard's present.*

contribution /ˌkɒntrɪˈbjuːʃən/ *noun*
money or help that is offered or given ➤ *Peter collected all the contributions to the school magazine.*

control¹ /kənˈtrəʊl/ *verb (present participle* **controlling**, *past* **controlled**)
to have power over someone or something; to decide or guide the way something or someone works ➤ *He wasn't a bad teacher, but he couldn't control the class.*

control² *noun (no plural)*
1 the state of having the power to decide or guide the way something or someone works ➤ *He wasn't in control of the car.* ➤ *The horse got out of control and the rider fell to the ground.*
2 lose control of something to stop being able to make something do what you want ➤ *He lost control of the car and it crashed.*

control tower /kənˈtrəʊl ˌtaʊər/ *noun*
a high building from which people direct aircraft landing at and taking off from an airport

controversial /ˌkɒntrəˈvɜːʃəl/ *adjective*
causing a lot of disagreement and arguments ➤ *the controversial subject of abortion*

controversy /'kɒntrəvɜːsɪ, kən'trɒvəsɪ/ noun (plural **controversies**)
disagreement and arguments about something ► The controversy **over** the nuclear energy programme is likely to continue.

convenience /kən'viːnɪəns/ noun
usefulness; helpfulness; easiness ► My mother likes the convenience of living close to the shops.

convenient /kən'viːnɪənt/ adjective
suited to your needs; local to where you are ► The school is in a convenient place, near my home.
OPPOSITE: **inconvenient**

convent /'kɒnvənt/ noun
a place where women who lead a religious life (NUNS) live; a school or college run by these women
COMPARE: **monastery**

conventional /kən'venʃənəl/ adjective
of the usual type that has existed or has been used for a long time ► Conventional medicine could not help her, so she tried homeopathy. ► My parents have very conventional views on sex.

conversation /ˌkɒnvə'seɪʃən/ noun
a talk between two or more people ► I had a long conversation **with** your teacher.

conversion /kən'vɜːʃən/ noun
a change from one use to another, or from one religion to another

convert /kən'vɜːt/ verb
to change something into something else ► That building has been converted **into** a school.

convey /kən'veɪ/ verb
to express your feelings, ideas, or thoughts to other people ► Mark's eyes clearly conveyed his disappointment.

convict¹ /kən'vɪkt/ verb
to decide in a law court that someone is guilty of something ► He was convicted of murder.

convict² /'kɒnvɪkt/ noun
a person who has been sent to prison for doing something wrong

conviction /kən'vɪkʃən/ noun
1 the official decision that someone is guilty of a crime ► Bradley had two previous convictions **for** drug offences.
2 a very strong belief or opinion ► religious convictions

convince /kən'vɪns/ verb (present participle **convincing**, past **convinced**)
1 to make a person believe something ► He convinced me that I should study law.
2 be convinced that to be completely certain about something ► I was convinced that he was telling the truth.

convincing /kən'vɪnsɪŋ/ adjective
making you believe that something is true ► a convincing argument

convoy /'kɒnvɔɪ/ noun
a group of vehicles or ships travelling together

cook¹ /kʊk/ verb
to make food ready to eat by heating it ► He's cooking dinner for me tonight.

cook² noun
a person who prepares food for eating ► Sarah is a very good cook.

cooker /'kʊkəʳ/ noun
a machine for cooking food ► a gas cooker

cookery /'kʊkərɪ/ noun (no plural)
the study or activity of preparing food for eating ► cookery lessons

cooking /'kʊkɪŋ/ noun (no plural)
1 the activity of preparing food ► Cooking is fun.
2 food made in a particular way or by a particular person ► Sue's cooking is always good.

cool¹ /kuːl/ *adjective*
1 a little cold ▶ *The room was cool after the sun had gone down.*
2 calm ▶ *Don't get excited about the examination – keep cool.*

cool² *verb*
1 to make or become a little colder ▶ *Leave the cake to cool.*
2 **cool down** (a) to become a little colder (b) to become calmer ▶ *I'll discuss it with her again when she's cooled down a bit.*

cooped up /ˌkuːpt ˈʌp/ *adjective*
kept for too long in a place that is too small ▶ *He kept his dogs cooped up in a kennel.*

cooperate /kəʊˈɒpəreɪt/ *verb* (*present participle* **cooperating**, *past* **cooperated**)
to work together with someone else to get something done ▶ *If we all cooperate, we'll finish this by 5 o'clock.*

cooperation /kəʊˌɒpəˈreɪʃən/ *noun* (no plural)
willingness to work together ▶ *Thank you for your cooperation.*

cooperative /kəʊˈɒpərətɪv/ *adjective*
willing to help other people
OPPOSITE: **uncooperative**

coordinate /kəʊˈɔːdɪneɪt/ *verb* (*present participle* **coordinating**, *past* **coordinated**)
to organize all the different things and people involved in an activity ▶ *I'm responsible for coordinating training courses.*

cop /kɒp/ *noun*
a police officer

cope /kəʊp/ *verb* (*present participle* **coping**, *past* **coped**)
to deal with something successfully ▶ *How do you cope **with** all this work?*

copper /ˈkɒpəʳ/ *noun* (no plural)
a red gold metal

copy¹ /ˈkɒpi/ *verb* (*past* **copied**)
1 to make or do something exactly the same as something else ▶ *Could you copy this down in your books, please?*
2 to cheat by writing exactly the same thing as someone else ▶ *The teacher saw him copying in the history test.*

copy² *noun* (*plural* **copies**)
1 something that is made to look the same as something else ▶ *Please send a copy **of** this letter to Mr Brown.*
2 one magazine, book, or newspaper from the many that have been produced ▶ *Have you got another copy **of** this book?*

coral /ˈkɒrəl/ *noun* (no plural)
a hard pink, white, or red substance that is formed from the bones of very small sea animals

cord /kɔːd/ *noun*
a thin rope

core /kɔːʳ/ *noun*
the hard, central part of certain fruits, which contains the seeds ▶ *an apple core*

coriander /ˌkɒriˈændəʳ/ *noun* (no plural)
a plant with leaves and seeds that you add to food to give it a pleasant, fresh taste

cork /kɔːk/ *noun*
1 (no plural) a light substance that comes from the outside part of the stem of a tree
2 a piece of this, used to fill the holes in the tops of bottles

corkscrew /ˈkɔːkskruː/ *noun*
a tool you use to pull a cork out of a bottle

corn /kɔːn/ *noun* (no plural)
the seed of grain plants, including wheat and maize

corner /ˈkɔːnəʳ/ *noun*
the place where two lines, walls, streets, etc. meet each other ▶ *The*

C

C

table stood in the corner **of** the room.
▶ *His house is on the corner of
School Road and Green Street.*

cornflakes /'kɔːnfleɪks/ *plural noun*
a breakfast food made from crushed
corn and usually eaten with milk and
sugar

coronation /ˌkɒrə'neɪʃən/ *noun*
a ceremony in which someone
officially becomes a king or queen

corporal /'kɔːpərəl/ *noun*
a soldier who has a low rank in the
army

corporation /ˌkɔːpə'reɪʃən/ *noun*
a group of people who run a town,
business, etc.

corpse /kɔːps/ *noun*
the dead body of a person

correct¹ /kə'rekt/ *adjective*
right; with no mistakes ▶ *a correct
answer* (adverb: **correctly**)
OPPOSITE: **incorrect**

correct² *verb*
1 to make something right ▶ *Please
correct this mistake.*
2 to show the mistakes in something
▶ *I've corrected your homework.*

correction /kə'rekʃən/ *noun*
a change that makes something right
or better ▶ *He made several
corrections to the letter.*

correspond /ˌkɒrɪ'spɒnd/ *verb*
to write to someone and receive
letters from them ▶ *to correspond
with a friend*

correspondence /ˌkɒrɪ'spɒndəns/
noun (no plural)
letters

correspondent /ˌkɒrɪ'spɒndənt/
noun
1 someone who writes and receives
letters
2 someone who works for a
newspaper or television company
and reports news from another
country

corridor /'kɒrɪdɔːʳ/ *noun*
a long, narrow part of a building, with
doors into rooms on each side of it
▶ *Go down the corridor to the third
room on the left.*
SAME MEANING: **passage**

corrupt¹ /kə'rʌpt/ *adjective*
dishonest ▶ *a corrupt judge*
▶ *a corrupt political system*

corrupt² *verb*
to encourage someone to behave in a
way that is not honest or moral
▶ *I think that television corrupts the
young.*

corruption /kə'rʌpʃən/ *noun (no
plural)*
dishonest behaviour by politicians or
people who work for the government
▶ *The police are being investigated
for corruption.*

cosmetic /kɒz'metɪk/ *adjective*
intended to make your skin or body
more beautiful ▶ *He had cosmetic
surgery to make his nose smaller.*

cosmetics /kɒz'metɪks/ *plural noun*
substances that you put on the skin
of your face to make you look prettier

cost¹ /kɒst/ *noun*
1 the money that you have to pay
when you buy something ▶ *We gave
her some money to cover the cost **of**
the books she had to buy.*
2 something needed, given, or lost in
order to get something else ▶ *War is
never worth the terrible cost **in**
human life.*
3 at all costs no matter what has to
be given or lost ▶ *We must avoid war
at all costs.*

cost² *verb (past cost)*
1 to have a particular amount as a
price ▶ *"How much did that bag
cost?" "It cost £5!"*
2 cost an arm and a leg to be very
expensive
3 cost a bomb to be very expensive

co-star¹ /'kəʊ stɑːʳ/ *noun*

one of two or more famous actors that work together in a film or play

co-star[2] verb (present participle **co-starring**, past **co-starred**)
to be working in a film or play with other famous actors ➤ *Meryl Streep co-stars with Clint Eastwood in "The Bridges of Madison County".*

costly /ˈkɒstlɪ/ adjective (**costlier**, **costliest**)
costing a lot of money ➤ *The ring was very costly.*
SAME MEANING: **dear, expensive**

costume /ˈkɒstjuːm/ noun
clothes worn for a special reason, or to represent a country or time in history ➤ *They all wore national costume.*

cosy /ˈkəʊzɪ/ adjective (**cosier**, **cosiest**)
warm and comfortable ➤ *a cosy little house*

cot /kɒt/ noun
a bed with high sides, for a baby
COMPARE: **cradle**

cottage /ˈkɒtɪdʒ/ noun
a small, attractive house in the country

cotton /ˈkɒtn/ noun (no plural)
1 a plant grown in hot countries for the fine, white threads that cover its seeds
2 thread or cloth made from the cotton plant ➤ *a cotton dress*

cotton wool /ˌkɒtn ˈwʊl/ noun (no plural)
a soft mass of white material, used especially for cleaning your skin

couch /kaʊtʃ/ noun (plural **couches**)
a long seat on which you can sit or lie
SAME MEANING: **settee, sofa**

cough[1] /kɒf/ noun
a sudden, rough sound made when you send air out of your throat and mouth suddenly ➤ *The child had a bad cough.*

cough[2] verb
to push air out from your throat and mouth with a sudden, rough sound ➤ *The child was coughing all night.*

could /kəd; strong kʊd/ verb
1 the word for **can** in the past ➤ *Before I had a bicycle, I couldn't (=could not) visit my friend.*
2 used in sentences like these ➤ *She would help us if she could, but she can't.*
3 used as a polite way of asking someone something ➤ *Could you help me, please?*

couldn't /ˈkʊdnt/
could not ➤ *I couldn't see because it was dark.*

could've /ˈkʊdəv/
could have ➤ *I could've killed him!*

council /ˈkaʊnsəl/ noun
a group of people who are chosen to make decisions and laws in a town or city ➤ *The town council will decide where to plant the trees.*

councillor /ˈkaʊnsələʳ/ noun
someone chosen to advise people and make decisions and laws in a town or city

counselling /ˈkaʊnsəlɪŋ/ noun (no plural)
the act of giving people PROFESSIONAL advice about their problems ➤ *a counselling service for drug users*

counsellor /ˈkaʊnsələʳ/ noun
a person whose job is to give people advice about their problems ➤ *a marriage counsellor*

count[1] /kaʊnt/ verb
1 to say numbers in the right order ➤ *to count from 1 to 100*
2 to find out how many there are ➤ *She counted the books – there were 14 of them.*
3 to have value or importance ➤ *He said that I had no experience, so my opinion doesn't count.*
4 **count against someone** to help

someone lose or fail in something ▶ *My lack of experience may count against me.*

count² *noun*
1 the total reached by adding everything together ▶ *At the last count, I'd visited 15 countries.*
2 **lose count** to stop remembering how many ▶ *I've lost count of how many times he's said he's leaving her.*

countable /ˈkaʊntəbəl/ *adjective*
in grammar, a countable noun has a singular and a plural form. "Table" (plural "tables") and "man" (plural "men") are examples of countable nouns
OPPOSITE: **uncountable**

countdown /ˈkaʊntdaʊn/ *noun*
the act of counting numbers backwards to zero before something happens ▶ *They began the countdown to take-off.*

counter /ˈkaʊntər/ *noun*
1 a long table where you go and buy things in a shop
2 a small, round piece of plastic or wood, used in playing games

countless /ˈkaʊntləs/ *adjective*
very many ▶ *She's had countless boyfriends.*

country /ˈkʌntrɪ/ *noun*
1 (*plural* **countries**) an area ruled by one government ▶ *France and Germany are European countries.*
2 (*no plural*) the land that is not a town ▶ *He lives in the country.*

country music /ˈkʌntrɪ ˌmjuːzɪk/ (*also* **country and western** /ˌkʌntrɪ ən ˈwestən/) *noun (no plural)*
a type of popular music from the southern and western US

countryside /ˈkʌntrɪsaɪd/ *noun (no plural)*
land outside towns and cities

county /ˈkaʊntɪ/ *noun (plural counties)*

a part of a country ▶ *Devon is a county in the southwest of England.*

coup /kuː/ *noun*
1 a situation in which a group of people suddenly take control of a country, especially by using force
2 an impressive achievement ▶ *Winning that contract was a real coup.*

couple /ˈkʌpəl/ *noun*
1 two things usually thought of together ▶ *I waited for a couple of hours.*
2 two people, usually a man and a woman, who are married, live together, or have a close relationship ▶ *We've invited three other couples to dinner.*

coupon /ˈkuːpɒn/ *noun*
a piece of paper that can be exchanged for goods or money ▶ *Collect three coupons for a free pen.*

courage /ˈkʌrɪdʒ/ *noun (no plural)*
willingness to do dangerous things without feeling afraid ▶ *The soldier showed great courage in the battle.*
SAME MEANING: **bravery**

courageous /kəˈreɪdʒəs/ *adjective*
brave ▶ *a courageous person*

courgette /kʊəˈʒet/ *noun*
a long vegetable with a dark green skin

courier /ˈkʊrɪər/ *noun*
1 a person whose job is to deliver letters and packages
2 a person whose job is to help people who are on holiday with a travel company

course /kɔːs/ *noun*
1 the way that something happens, or the time when something is happening ▶ *During the course of the journey, we saw a lot of new places.*
2 the path or direction that something takes ▶ *The course of the river was marked on the map.* ▶ *The*

plane had to change course and go another way.

3 one part of a meal ➤ *We have three courses: soup, meat and vegetables, and fruit.*

4 a set of lessons ➤ *What course are you taking at college?*

5 of course certainly ➤ *Of course I'll still love you when you're old.*

coursebook /'kɔːsbʊk/ *noun*
a book written to be used by students as part of a particular course of study

court /kɔːt/ *noun*
1 a place where a person is questioned about a crime, and where other people decide whether the person is guilty or not
2 an open space where games are played ➤ *a tennis court*
3 a king or queen and all the people who live with them

courteous /'kɜːtɪəs/ *adjective*
polite (adverb: **courteously**)

courtesy /'kɜːtəsɪ/ *noun (no plural)*
polite behaviour

courtroom /'kɔːtrʊm/ *noun*
the room where someone is judged in a law court

courtyard /'kɔːtjɑːd/ *noun*
an open space inside or in front of a large building

cousin /'kʌzən/ *noun*
the child of your aunt or uncle

cover¹ /'kʌvəʳ/ *verb*
1 to put something over something else ➤ *She covered the table with a cloth.*
2 to be over a particular area or surface ➤ *The town covers 5 square miles.*
3 to include or deal with something ➤ *His talk covered British history between the wars.*
4 cover something up (a) to place something over something else to protect or hide it ➤ *Cover the*

furniture up before you start painting.
(b) to hide something ➤ *She tried to cover up her fear.*

cover² *noun*
1 something that you put over something else ➤ *a cushion cover.*
2 the outside of a book
3 take cover to shelter or hide from something

coverage /'kʌvərɪdʒ/ *noun (no plural)*
the amount of attention given to a news story by television, radio, or the newspapers ➤ *Her death attracted widespread media coverage.*

covering /'kʌvərɪŋ/ *noun*
something that covers something else ➤ *a light covering of snow*

cover-up /'kʌvər ʌp/ *noun*
an attempt to stop people finding out the truth ➤ *The government says there has not been a cover-up.*

cow /kaʊ/ *noun*
a large female animal that farmers keep for milk

coward /'kaʊəd/ *noun*
someone who avoids pain or danger because they are not brave

cowardice /'kaʊədɪs/ *noun (no plural)*
behaviour that shows you are not brave ➤ *She accused him of cowardice.*
OPPOSITE: **bravery**

cowardly /'kaʊədlɪ/ *adjective*
showing too much fear; unwilling to do dangerous things ➤ *cowardly behaviour*
OPPOSITE: **brave**

cowboy /'kaʊbɔɪ/ *noun*
a man who rides a horse and looks after cattle in America

crab /kræb/ *noun*
a sea animal with ten legs and a hard shell

crack¹ /kræk/ *verb*
1 to break so that lines appear on the

surface ▶ *That glass will crack if you pour boiling water into it.*
2 to make a sharp noise, like thunder or a gun

crack² *noun*
1 a thin line on the surface of something ▶ *There's a crack in this cup!*
2 a sharp noise ▶ *a crack of thunder*
3 a sudden, hard hit ▶ *a crack on the head*

crackdown /'krækdaʊn/ *noun*
an official attempt to stop a particular crime or bad behaviour from happening ▶ *The government announced a crackdown on drugs.*

cracked /krækt/ *adjective*
damaged with thin lines on the surface ▶ *a cracked mirror*

crackle /'krækəl/ *verb (present participle crackling, past crackled)*
to make a lot of short noises that sound like wood burning on a fire ▶ *This radio's crackling.*

cradle /'kreɪdl/ *noun*
a bed for a baby, which can be moved from side to side
COMPARE: **cot**

craft /krɑːft/ *noun*
1 a job or trade needing skill, especially skill with your hands ▶ *He knew the craft of making furniture.*
2 (*plural craft*) a boat or plane

craftsman /'krɑːftsmən/ *noun (plural craftsmen /-mən/)*
someone whose job needs a lot of skill, especially skill with their hands

crafty /'krɑːftɪ/ *adjective (craftier, craftiest)*
clever at making other people believe things that are not true

cram /kræm/ *verb (present participle cramming, past crammed)*
to force people or things into a small space ▶ *Lots of people were crammed into the bus.*

cramp /kræmp/ *noun (no plural)*
a bad pain in your muscles

cramped /kræmpt/ *adjective*
not big enough for everyone or everything ▶ *Six of us lived in a tiny, cramped apartment.*

crane /kreɪn/ *noun*
a tall machine for lifting heavy things

crash¹ /kræʃ/ *noun (plural crashes)*
1 a loud noise, like something large falling over ▶ *The car hit the tree with a crash.*
2 an accident in which vehicles hit each other ▶ *a car crash*

crash² *verb*
1 to move noisily ▶ *The injured elephant crashed through the forest.*
2 to make a sudden, loud noise ▶ *The thunder crashed and the rain poured down.*
3 (of a car) to have an accident ▶ *The car crashed into the tree.*

crash course /'kræʃ kɔːs/ *noun*
a short course in which you study the most important things about a subject very quickly ▶ *I had a crash course in French before I went to live in Paris.*

crash helmet /'kræʃ ˌhelmɪt/ *noun*
a hard hat that you wear to protect your head when you ride a MOTORBIKE

crash-land /'kræʃ lænd/ *verb*
to land a plane when it is in trouble

crass /kræs/ *adjective*
stupid and rude in a way that upsets or offends people ▶ *crass remarks*

crate /kreɪt/ *noun*
a big, wooden box ▶ *a crate of fruit*

crater /'kreɪtəʳ/ *noun*
a large hole in the ground or at the top of a VOLCANO ▶ *Hot lava flowed from the crater.*

crawl /krɔːl/ *verb*
to move along the floor on your hands and knees ▶ *The baby crawled towards his father.*

crayon /'kreɪən/ noun
a soft, coloured pencil

craze /kreɪz/ noun
something that is very popular for a short time ▶ the latest fashion craze

crazy /'kreɪzi/ adjective (**crazier, craziest**)
1 mad; foolish ▶ He's crazy to drive his car so fast.
2 be crazy about to like someone or something very much ▶ He's crazy about her.

creak /kriːk/ verb
to make the sound that a door makes when it has not been oiled ▶ The door creaked as she opened it.

cream¹ /kriːm/ noun (no plural)
1 the fatty part of milk that you can eat with other foods
2 a thick liquid that you put on your skin ▶ face cream

cream² adjective, noun
a yellowish-white colour

creamy /'kriːmi/ adjective (**creamier, creamiest**)
containing or looking like cream ▶ creamy soup

crease¹ /kriːs/ noun
a line on cloth, paper, etc. where it has been folded

crease² verb (present participle **creasing**, past **creased**)
to put a crease or creases in a piece of cloth, paper, etc. ▶ Try not to crease your jacket.

create /kriˈeɪt/ verb (present participle **creating**, past **created**)
to make something new ▶ Work on the new road will create a lot of difficulties for traffic.

creation /kriˈeɪʃən/ noun
something that is made

creative /kriˈeɪtɪv/ adjective
good at thinking of new ideas or ways of doing things ▶ one of Japan's most talented and creative film directors

creativity /ˌkriːeɪˈtɪvəti/ noun (no plural)
the ability to use your imagination or skill to produce new ideas or things

creator /kriˈeɪtəʳ/ noun
a person who makes or invents something ▶ Walt Disney, the creator of Mickey Mouse

creature /'kriːtʃəʳ/ noun
an animal or insect

crèche /kreʃ/ noun
a place where babies are looked after while their parents are at work

credibility /ˌkredəˈbɪləti/ noun (no plural)
the quality of being believed and trusted by other people ▶ The scandal has damaged the government's credibility.

credit¹ /'kredɪt/ noun (no plural)
1 attention and approval for something good that has been done ▶ We both made the machine, but James was given the credit for it.
2 a way of buying things in which you pay for them later ▶ We bought the furniture on credit.
3 in credit (used about a bank account) containing money

credit² verb
to add money to a bank account OPPOSITE: **debit**

credit card /'kredɪt ˌkɑːd/ noun
a small, plastic card that allows you to buy things without using coins and notes. You pay for the goods later.

creep /kriːp/ verb (past **crept** /krept/)
to move slowly and quietly

creeps /kriːps/ plural noun
give someone the creeps to make someone feel nervous or frightened ▶ That man gives me the creeps!

creepy /'kriːpi/ adjective (**creepier, creepiest**)
slightly frightening ▶ a creepy ghost story

C

cremate /krɪ'meɪt/ verb (present participle **cremating**, past **cremated**)
to burn the body of a dead person

cremation /krɪ'meɪʃən/ noun
the act of burning the body of a dead person ► a cremation service

crept /krept/
the PAST TENSE and PAST PARTICIPLE of the verb **creep**

crescent /'kresənt/ noun
a curved shape that is wider in the middle and pointed at the ends ► a crescent moon

crest /krest/ noun
1 a group of feathers that stick up on the top of a bird's head
2 the top of something ► the crest of a hill

crevice /'krevɪs/ noun
a narrow crack, especially in rock

crew /kru:/ noun
the people who work on a ship or plane

cricket /'krɪkɪt/ noun
1 (no plural) a ball game played by two teams of 11 players each
2 a small, brown insect that jumps and makes a loud noise

cried /kraɪd/
the PAST TENSE and PAST PARTICIPLE of the verb **cry**

cries /kraɪz/
the plural of **cry**

crime /kraɪm/ noun
1 an action that is wrong and can be punished by the law ► Killing people is a serious crime.
COMPARE: **sin**
2 commit a crime to do something wrong that can be punished by the law

criminal /'krɪmɪnəl/ noun
someone who has done something very wrong and against the law ► The prison contains 325 criminals.

crimson /'krɪmzən/ adjective, noun
a deep red colour, like the colour of blood

cringe /krɪndʒ/ verb (present participle **cringing**, past **cringed**)
to feel embarrassed by something ► I just cringe at the thought of some of the things we used to wear.

cripple /'krɪpəl/ verb (present participle **crippling**, past **crippled**)
to hurt someone so that they cannot use their arms or legs ► She was crippled in the car accident.

crisis /'kraɪsɪs/ noun (plural **crises** /'kraɪsi:z/)
a time when something serious, very worrying, or dangerous happens

crisp¹ /krɪsp/ adjective
1 (used about food) firm and dry; easily broken ► Keep the biscuits in a tin so that they stay crisp.
2 (used about food) firm and fresh ► crisp apples

crisp² noun
a very thin, round piece of potato which you buy in a packet and eat cold ► a packet of crisps
COMPARE: **chip**

crispy /'krɪspi/ adjective (**crispier, crispiest**)
(used about food) pleasantly hard ► crispy bacon

criteria /kraɪ'tɪərɪə/ plural noun
facts or standards used to help you decide something ► What are the criteria for selecting the winner?

critic /'krɪtɪk/ noun
a person whose job is to write about art, music, films, etc. and say whether they are good or bad

critical /'krɪtɪkəl/ adjective
looking for faults ► She was very critical of my work.

criticism /'krɪtɪsɪzəm/ noun
a reason for not liking something or not feeling happy about something ► I listened to all her criticisms in silence.

criticize /'krɪtɪsaɪz/ verb (present

participle **criticizing**, past **criticized**)
to say what is wrong with something;
to find faults in something ▶ *She's
always criticizing me.*

croak /krəʊk/ *verb*
to make a deep, low sound in your
throat ▶ *"Where are you?" she
croaked.*

crockery /'krɒkəri/ *noun
(no plural)*
plates, cups, and dishes that we eat
and drink from

crocodile /'krɒkədaɪl/ *noun*
a large animal with a long body, a
hard skin, and sharp teeth, which
lives in or near rivers in hot countries

crook /krʊk/ *noun*
a dishonest person

crooked /'krʊkɪd/ *adjective*
1 bent or curved ▶ *a crooked road*
2 dishonest

crop /krɒp/ *noun*
1 a plant such as wheat, fruit, or
vegetables that a farmer grows
2 an amount of vegetables, wheat,
etc. that is cut or gathered at one
time ▶ *a crop of apples*

cross¹ /krɒs/ *noun (plural **crosses**)*
a shape (X) with four arms that meet
in the centre

cross² *verb*
to go over from one side of
something to the other ▶ *They
crossed the road.*

cross³ *adjective*
angry ▶ *Why are you cross **with** me?*

cross-country /ˌkrɒs 'kʌntri/
adjective
across fields and not along roads
▶ *cross-country running*

cross-examine /ˌkrɒs ɪg'zæmɪn/ *verb
(present participle **cross-examining**,
past **cross-examined**)*
to ask someone questions about
something they have just said to see
if they are telling the truth, especially

in a law court ▶ *The lawyer cross-
examined the witness for an hour.*

cross-eyed /ˌkrɒs 'aɪd/ *adjective*
having eyes that look in towards your
nose

crossing /'krɒsɪŋ/ *noun*
a special place where you may cross
the road

cross-legged /ˌkrɒs 'legɪd/ *adverb,
adjective*
sitting with your knees wide apart
and your feet crossed ▶ *We sat cross-
legged on the floor.*

cross-reference /ˌkrɒs 'refərəns/ *noun*
a note in a book that tells you where
to look in the same book for more
information

crossroads /'krɒsrəʊdz/ *noun (plural
crossroads)*
a place where several roads meet
each other

cross-section /'krɒs ˌsekʃən/ *noun*
1 a drawing of what something looks
like inside by showing it as if it has
been cut into two pieces ▶ *a cross-
section of the ship, showing all the
levels*
2 a group of people or things that is
typical of a larger group ▶ *The
students here are a cross-section of
the local community.*

crossword /'krɒswɜːd/ *noun*
a game in which you have to guess
words, the letters of which fit into a
pattern of squares down and across
the page

crouch /kraʊtʃ/ *verb*
to make your body come close to the
ground by bending your knees ▶ *She
crouched by the fire to get warm.*

crow /krəʊ/ *noun*
a large, black bird with a low, hard cry

crowd¹ /kraʊd/ *noun*
a large number of people ▶ *There was
a crowd **of** people waiting at the
station.*

C

crowd[2] *verb*
to come together in a large group
▶ *They all crowded round the teacher.*

crowded /'kraʊdɪd/ *adjective*
full of people ▶ *I don't like the market; it is too crowded.*

crown /kraʊn/ *noun*
a special hat made of gold, beautiful stones, etc., worn by a king or queen

crucial /'kruːʃəl/ *adjective*
very important ▶ *It is crucial that we act quickly. (adverb: crucially)*

crucifix /'kruːsɪfɪks/ *noun (plural crucifixes)*
a cross with a figure of Jesus on it

crude /kruːd/ *adjective*
1 raw; in the state in which something is usually found or exists ▶ *Crude oil has to be made pure before it can be used by man.*
2 rude ▶ *a crude joke*

cruel /'kruːəl/ *adjective*
liking to hurt other people or animals
▶ *He is cruel to animals (adverb: cruelly)*
OPPOSITE: **kind**

cruelty /'kruːəltɪ/ *noun (no plural)*
actions that cause pain to a person or an animal ▶ *cruelty to animals*

cruise[1] /kruːz/ *noun*
a sea journey for pleasure

cruise[2] *verb (present participle cruising, past cruised)*
(used about a boat or vehicle) to move in an unhurried way

crumb /krʌm/ *noun*
a little piece of something such as bread or cake

crumble /'krʌmbəl/ *verb (present participle crumbling, past crumbled)*
to break up into little pieces ▶ *The walls of that old house are crumbling.*

crumple /'krʌmpəl/ *verb (present participle crumpling, past crumpled)*
to make paper or clothing full of

irregular folds by pressing or crushing it ▶ *Don't sit on that shirt or you'll crumple it.*

crunch /krʌntʃ/ *verb*
1 to crush food noisily with your teeth
2 to make a noise that sounds like something being crushed ▶ *The stones crunched under the car tyres.*

crunchy /'krʌntʃɪ/ *adjective (crunchier, crunchiest)*
(used about food) pleasantly hard
▶ *a crunchy biscuit*

crush /krʌʃ/ *verb*
to hurt or damage something by pressing it heavily

crust /krʌst/ *noun*
the hard part on the outside of bread

crutch /krʌtʃ/ *noun (plural crutches)*
a piece of wood or metal that supports a person who cannot walk well ▶ *to walk on crutches*

cry[1] /kraɪ/ *verb (past cried)*
1 to shout ▶ *The boy cried for help.*
2 to produce tears from your eyes usually because you are sad ▶ *She began to cry when she heard of her friend's death.*

cry[2] *noun (plural cries)*
a loud shout; a call ▶ *They heard a cry for help.*

cryptic /'krɪptɪk/ *adjective*
having a meaning that is not clear ▶ *a cryptic message*

crystal /'krɪstl/ *noun*
1 a type of rock that is transparent
2 *(no plural)* high-quality glass
▶ *crystal wine glasses*
3 a regular shape that forms naturally when some MINERAL substances become solid ▶ *crystals of ice*
▶ *salt crystals*

cub /kʌb/ *noun*
a young bear, lion, tiger, or fox

cube /kjuːb/ *noun*
a solid shape with six equal square sides

cubicle /ˈkjuːbɪkəl/ *noun*
a small room for one person, especially for changing their clothes in ➤ *the changing cubicles at the swimming pool*

cuckoo /ˈkʊkuː/ *noun*
a bird that has a call which sounds like its name

cucumber /ˈkjuːkʌmbər/ *noun*
a long, thin, green vegetable which is usually eaten without being cooked

cuddle /ˈkʌdl/ *verb (present participle **cuddling**, past **cuddled**)*
to put your arms around someone ➤ *She cuddled her little boy.*
SAME MEANING: **hug**

cue /kjuː/ *noun*
1 a long, thin stick used for hitting the ball in games such as SNOOKER
2 an action or event that is a sign for something else to happen ➤ *His girlfriend's arrival was our cue to leave.*

cuff /kʌf/ *noun*
the end of an arm of a shirt, dress, etc.

cul-de-sac /ˈkʌl də ˌsæk/ *noun*
a street which is closed at one end

culminate /ˈkʌlmɪneɪt/ *verb (present participle **culminating**, past **culminated**)*
culminate in something to have something as an important final result ➤ *a series of arguments that culminated in a divorce*

culprit /ˈkʌlprɪt/ *noun*
a person who has done something wrong or who is guilty of a crime ➤ *The man whose car was damaged was determined to find the culprits.*

cult /kʌlt/ *noun*
a small religion whose members have unusual views ➤ *a member of an extreme religious cult*

cultivate /ˈkʌltɪveɪt/ *verb (present participle **cultivating**, past **cultivated**)*
to grow plants on land that has been specially prepared

cultivation /ˌkʌltɪˈveɪʃən/ *noun (no plural)*
the growing of plants or crops

cultural /ˈkʌltʃərəl/ *adjective*
1 connected with a particular society and its beliefs, customs, and way of life ➤ *the cultural differences between England and Pakistan*
2 related to art, literature, music, etc. ➤ *There aren't many cultural events in this town.*

culture /ˈkʌltʃər/ *noun*
1 the beliefs, customs, and way of life of a particular society
2 *(no plural)* art, literature, music, etc. ➤ *Paris is full of culture.*

cultured /ˈkʌltʃəd/ *adjective*
knowing a lot about art, literature, music, etc.

cumbersome /ˈkʌmbəsəm/ *adjective*
heavy and difficult to move or use ➤ *a large, cumbersome bag*

cunning /ˈkʌnɪŋ/ *adjective*
clever at making people believe things that are not true

cup /kʌp/ *noun*
1 a container, usually with a handle, that you can drink from
2 the drink inside the cup ➤ *a cup of tea*
3 a prize, shaped like a bowl, usually made of silver or gold

cupboard /ˈkʌbəd/ *noun*
a piece of furniture with shelves and a door, in which you keep clothes, plates, food, etc.

curb /kɜːb/ *verb*
to control or limit something ➤ *You must curb your spending.*

cure¹ /kjʊər/ *verb (present participle **curing**, past **cured**)*
to make someone better when they have been ill ➤ *I hope the doctor can cure the pain in my shoulder.*

cure² *noun*
a way of making someone better when they have been ill ➤ *a cure for an illness*

curiosity /ˌkjʊərɪˈɒsɪtɪ/ *noun (no plural)*
the desire to know something or learn about something ➤ *He is full of curiosity.*

curious /ˈkjʊərɪəs/ *adjective*
1 wanting to know about things or people ➤ *I'm very curious about our new neighbours.*
2 odd or strange ➤ *We heard a curious noise upstairs.*

curiously /ˈkjʊərɪəslɪ/ *adverb*
in a way that seems odd or strange

curl¹ /kɜːl/ *verb*
1 to roll or bend in a round or curved shape ➤ *The snake curled round the branch.* ➤ *She curled her hair.*
2 curl up to lie comfortably with your arms and legs drawn close to your body ➤ *She curled up in front of the fire.*

curl² *noun*
a piece of hair that curves around

curly /ˈkɜːlɪ/ *adjective (curlier, curliest)*
(used about hair) bending round and round

currant /ˈkʌrənt/ *noun*
1 a small, dried fruit
2 a small black, red, or white fruit that grows on bushes

currency /ˈkʌrənsɪ/ *noun (plural currencies)*
the money used in a country ➤ *Can I pay in British currency on the boat?*

current¹ /ˈkʌrənt/ *adjective*
happening or being used right now ➤ *Why does he want to change his current job?*

current² *noun*
a flow of water, electricity, etc. ➤ *Don't swim in the river; the current is very fast.*

curriculum /kəˈrɪkjʊləm/ *noun (plural curricula /-lə/ or curriculums)*
all of the subjects that are taught at a school, college, etc.

curried /ˈkʌrɪd/ *adjective*
(used about food) cooked in a hot-tasting liquid

curry /ˈkʌrɪ/ *noun (plural curries)*
an Indian food of meat, vegetables, or fish, cooked in a thick, hot-tasting liquid and usually eaten with rice ➤ *I'll have a chicken curry, please.*

curse¹ /kɜːs/ *verb (present participle cursing, past cursed)*
1 to wish that something unpleasant will happen to someone ➤ *He cursed the person who had stolen his money.*
2 to speak angry words ➤ *He cursed when he hit his head on the shelf.*

curse² *noun*
1 something that you say which expresses anger or hate, or which uses swearwords
2 put a curse on someone to make a wish that, with the help of God or some magical power, something unpleasant will happen to someone ➤ *In the story, the old woman put a curse on the beautiful princess.*

cursor /ˈkɜːsəʳ/ *noun*
a small mark on a computer screen that moves to show where you are writing

curtain /ˈkɜːtn/ *noun*
a piece of hanging cloth that can be pulled across to cover a window or door
COMPARE: **blind**

curve¹ /kɜːv/ *noun*
a line of which no part is straight; a bend ➤ *a curve in the road*

curve² *verb (present participle curving, past curved)*
to make a line which is not straight ➤ *The river curved round the hill.*

curved /kɜːvd/ *adjective*
having the shape of a curve ➤ *a Japanese sword with a curved blade*

cushion /'kuʃən/ *noun*
a bag filled with soft material to sit on or rest against
COMPARE: **pillow**

cushy /'kuʃɪ/ *adjective* (**cushier, cushiest**)
very easy ➤ *Teaching is not a cushy job.*

custard /'kʌstəd/ *noun (no plural)*
a thick, sweet, yellow liquid that you pour over some fruit and sweet foods

custody /'kʌstədɪ/ *noun (no plural)*
the right to take care of a child, given by a law court when the child's parents are legally separated ➤ *My ex-wife has custody of the kids.*

custom /'kʌstəm/ *noun*
a special way of doing something that a person or group of people has

customary /'kʌstəmərɪ/ *adjective*
usual or normal ➤ *It is customary to cover your head in the temple.*

customer /'kʌstəmər/ *noun*
a person who buys things from a shop

customs /'kʌstəmz/ *plural noun*
a place where your cases can be searched when you leave or enter a country, and where you have to pay tax on certain goods

cut¹ /kʌt/ *verb (present participle cutting, past cut)*
1 to break or damage something with a knife or something sharp ➤ *He cut the apple in half.* ➤ *He has cut his leg, and it's bleeding.*
2 to make something shorter ➤ *Could you cut my hair for me?*
3 to remove one part from something bigger ➤ *She cut a piece of cake.*
4 **cut down** to make something fall to the ground by cutting it ➤ *We'll have to cut down that tree.*
5 **cut off** (a) to stop or disconnect something ➤ *They've cut the gas off!* (b) to separate a person or place from the other people or places near them ➤ *Snow has cut off many villages.*
6 **cut something up** to cut something into pieces ➤ *Could you cut up the chicken?*
7 **cut something out** to remove something by cutting it ➤ *She cut a picture out of the newspaper.*

cut² *noun*
an opening or wound made by something sharp ➤ *a cut on the leg*

cute /kjuːt/ *adjective*
pretty or attractive ➤ *her cute little nose*

cutlery /'kʌtlərɪ/ *noun (no plural)*
knives, forks, and spoons used for eating

cut-price /ˌkʌt 'praɪs/ *adjective*
cheaper than normal ➤ *a shop selling cut-price books*

cutting¹ /'kʌtɪŋ/ *noun*
1 a stem or leaf that is cut from a plant to be grown into a new plant
2 a piece of writing that is cut from a newspaper or magazine

cutting² *adjective*
unkind and intended to upset someone ➤ *a cutting remark*

cutting edge /ˌkʌtɪŋ 'edʒ/ *noun*
be at/on the cutting edge to be involved in the most recent and most exciting part of the development of something

CV /ˌsiː 'viː/ *noun*
CURRICULUM VITAE; a document that describes your education and the jobs that you have done, used when you are trying to get a new job

cyberspace /'saɪbəspeɪs/ *noun (no plural)*
a place that is not real, used for describing where electronic messages go when they travel from

one computer to another ▶ *The e-mail was lost somewhere in cyberspace.*

cycle¹ /'saɪkəl/ *noun*
a bicycle
SAME MEANING: **bicycle, bike**

cycle² *verb (present participle **cycling**, past **cycled**)*
to ride a bicycle ▶ *He cycles to school every day.*

cycling /'saɪklɪŋ/ *noun (no plural)*
the sport of riding a bicycle

cyclist /'saɪklɪst/ *noun*
a person who rides a bicycle

cyclone /'saɪkləʊn/ *noun*
a very strong wind that moves in a circle

cylinder /'sɪlɪndəʳ/ *noun*
a long, round shape like a tube or a pencil

cymbal /'sɪmbəl/ *noun*
a round, metal plate that you hit with another metal plate or a stick to make a musical sound

cynic /'sɪnɪk/ *noun*
a person who believes that no one does things for good or honest reasons ▶ *Don't be such a cynic!*

cynical /'sɪnɪkəl/ *adjective*
believing that no one does things for good or honest reasons ▶ *I'm rather cynical about journalists who claim to be helping the public.*

Dd

'd /d/
1 had ▶ *He'd (=he had) eaten all the cake.*
2 would ▶ *I'd (=I would) buy a new car if I had enough money.*

dab¹ /dæb/ *verb (present participle **dabbing**, past **dabbed**)*

to lightly touch something several times in order to dry it or put something on it ▶ *He dabbed at the mark on his trousers.*

dab² *noun*
a small amount of a liquid, cream, etc. ▶ *a dab of paint*

dad /dæd/ *noun*
father

daddy /'dædɪ/ *noun (plural **daddies**)*
(used by and to small children) father

daffodil /'dæfədɪl/ *noun*
a yellow flower which appears in the spring

daft /dɑːft/ *adjective*
foolish or silly ▶ *a daft idea*

dagger /'dægəʳ/ *noun*
a short knife used as a weapon
COMPARE: **sword**

daily /'deɪlɪ/ *adjective, adverb*
happening every day ▶ *Take the medicine twice daily.*

dairy /'deərɪ/ *noun (plural **dairies**)*
a place where milk is kept and foods are made from milk

daisy /'deɪzɪ/ *noun (plural **daisies**)*
a small wild flower that is white with a yellow centre

dalmatian /dæl'meɪʃən/ *noun*
a white dog with black spots

dam¹ /dæm/ *noun*
a wall built to hold back water

dam² *verb (present participle **damming**, past **dammed**)*
to put a dam across something ▶ *to dam a river*

damage¹ /'dæmɪdʒ/ *noun (no plural)*
harm done to something

damage² *verb (present participle **damaging**, past **damaged**)*
to harm something ▶ *The cars were badly damaged in the accident.*

damn¹ /dæm/ *(also **damned** /dæmd/) adverb, adjective*
used to emphasize something in a

rude way, especially when you are
annoyed ▶ *Don't be so damn stupid!*
▶ *The damned thing's broken again.*

damn² *interjection*
used when you are annoyed or
disappointed ▶ *Damn! I forgot to
bring my wallet!*

damp /dæmp/ *adjective*
rather wet ▶ *damp clothes*

dance¹ /dɑːns/ *verb (present
participle* **dancing**, *past* **danced**)
to move to music

dance² *noun*
1 a set of movements you do to music
▶ *to learn a new dance*
2 a party where there is dancing
▶ *Are you going to the dance?*

dancer /ˈdɑːnsər/ *noun*
a person who is dancing, or someone
who dances as their job

dancing /ˈdɑːnsɪŋ/ *noun (no plural)*
moving to music

dandelion /ˈdændɪlaɪən/ *noun*
a yellow flower which grows wild

dandruff /ˈdændrʌf/ *noun
(no plural)*
very small, white pieces of loose skin
in a person's hair

danger /ˈdeɪndʒər/ *noun*
1 (no plural) the possibility of harm
▶ *Danger! Do not enter* (=written on
a notice). ▶ *You are not* **in** *any danger
here* (=there is no danger here).
2 something that can cause harm
▶ *the dangers of smoking*

dangerous /ˈdeɪndʒərəs/ *adjective*
likely to harm people ▶ *a dangerous
driver* ▶ *dangerous drugs*

dangle /ˈdæŋɡəl/ *verb (present
participle* **dangling**, *past* **dangled**)
to hang or swing from something
▶ *The keys were dangling from his
belt.*

dare /deər/ *verb (present participle
daring, *past* **dared**)

1 to be brave enough to do
something ▶ *I daren't refuse.*
2 dare someone to do something to
try to make someone do something
to prove they are not afraid
3 don't you dare a phrase used when
you are angry with someone and are
telling them not to do something
▶ *Don't you dare touch that!*
4 how dare you a phrase used when
you are angry with someone because
they have done something ▶ *How
dare you speak to me like that!*

daren't /deənt/
dare not ▶ *I daren't talk to him.*

daring /ˈdeərɪŋ/ *adjective*
1 willing to do dangerous things ▶ *a
daring rescue attempt*
2 new or unusual in a slightly shocking
way ▶ *a daring evening dress*

dark¹ /dɑːk/ *adjective*
1 like night; not light or bright
▶ *It was getting dark, so we hurried
home.*
2 of a deep colour, nearer black than
white ▶ *She has dark hair.* ▶ *He wore
a dark suit.*

dark² *noun (no plural)*
the lack of light ▶ *We could not see in
the dark.* ▶ *Make sure you are home
before dark* (=before it is night).

darken /ˈdɑːkən/ *verb*
to become darker, or to make
something darker ▶ *The sky darkened
very quickly.*

darkness /ˈdɑːknəs/ *noun (no plural)*
lack of light ▶ *The room was in
darkness* (=was dark).

darling /ˈdɑːlɪŋ/ *noun, adjective*
a name you call someone you love
▶ *Come on darling, or we'll be late.*

dart /dɑːt/ *verb*
to move suddenly and quickly ▶ *A
mouse darted across the floor.*

darts /dɑːts/ *noun (no plural)*
a game in which you throw small

objects with sharp points at a board with numbers on it

dash¹ /dæʃ/ *verb*
to move quickly ▶ *She dashed out of the room.*

dash² *noun (plural **dashes**)*
the sign (–) used in writing, to show a short space, or to separate two parts of a sentence

dashboard /'dæʃbɔːd/ *noun*
the part at the front of a car that has the controls on it

data /'deɪtə, 'dɑːtə/ *noun (no plural)*
facts and information

database /'deɪtəˌbeɪs/ *noun*
a large amount of information stored in a computer system

date /deɪt/ *noun*
1 the day of the month, or the year ▶ *"What date is your birthday?" "It's April 2nd." ▶ The date was 1857. ▶ Please write today's date.*
2 an arrangement to meet a boyfriend or girlfriend ▶ *I've got a date tonight.*
3 a small, sweet, brown fruit
4 out of date not fashionable any more
5 up to date modern

dated /'deɪtɪd/ *adjective*
no longer fashionable or modern ▶ *dated ideas*

daughter /'dɔːtəʳ/ *noun*
your female child ▶ *They have three daughters and one son.*

daughter-in-law /'dɔːtər ɪn lɔː/ *noun (plural **daughters-in-law**)*
the wife of your son

daunted /'dɔːntɪd/ *adjective*
afraid or worried about something you have to do ▶ *He felt daunted by the size of the job.*

daunting /'dɔːntɪŋ/ *adjective*
frightening or worrying ▶ *Being captain of the team is a daunting responsibility.*

dawn /dɔːn/ *noun*
the start of the day when the sun rises
SAME MEANING: **daybreak**

day /deɪ/ *noun*
1 *(no plural)* the time when it is light
OPPOSITE: **night**
2 24 hours ▶ *It hasn't stopped raining for days. ▶ "What day is it today?" "It's Tuesday."*
3 one day, some day at some time in the future ▶ *Some day I'll be rich.*
4 the other day a few days ago ▶ *I went there the other day.*
5 these days at the present time ▶ *Everyone seems so busy these days.*

daybreak /'deɪbreɪk/ *noun (no plural)*
the start of the day when the light first appears
SAME MEANING: **dawn**

daydream /'deɪdriːm/ *verb*
to imagine nice things, especially things you would like to happen in the future

daylight /'deɪlaɪt/ *noun (no plural)*
the light of the day ▶ *We want to travel in daylight (=before it gets dark).*

day off /ˌdeɪ 'ɒf/ *noun (plural **days off**)*
a day when you do not have to go to work or school ▶ *She's having a day off.*

daytime /'deɪtaɪm/ *noun (no plural)*
the time when it is light
OPPOSITE: **nighttime**

day-to-day /ˌdeɪ tə 'deɪ/ *adjective*
happening every day as a regular part of your life ▶ *the day-to-day running of the office*

daze /deɪz/ *noun*
in a daze unable to think clearly ▶ *He wandered around in a daze.*

dazed /deɪzd/ *adjective*
unable to think clearly, usually

because you are shocked or have been in an accident ➤ *The news left him feeling dazed.*

dazzle /'dæzəl/ *verb (present participle* **dazzling**, *past* **dazzled**)
if a light dazzles you, it is so bright that you cannot see clearly for a short time

dead¹ /ded/ *adjective*
not living ➤ *My grandfather has been dead for ten years.*
OPPOSITE: **alive, living**

dead² *plural noun*
the dead dead people ➤ *After the battle, they counted the dead.*
OPPOSITE: **the living**

dead end /,ded 'end/ *noun*
a street with no way out at one end

dead heat /,ded 'hi:t/ *noun*
the result of a race in which two people finish at exactly the same time ➤ *The race ended in a dead heat.*

deadline /'dedlaɪn/ *noun*
a date or time by which you must finish something ➤ *Do you think we'll be able to meet the deadline?*

deadlock /'dedlɒk/ *noun (no plural)*
a situation in which groups or countries cannot agree ➤ *The talks ended in deadlock.*

deadly /'dedlɪ/ *adjective (**deadlier**, **deadliest**)*
likely to cause death ➤ *a deadly poison*
COMPARE: **fatal**

deaf /def/ *adjective*
not able to hear because you have something wrong with your ears

deafen /'defən/ *verb*
if a noise deafens you, it is so loud that it is difficult for you to hear anything ➤ *The music deafened us.*

deal¹ /di:l/ *noun*
1 a business arrangement ➤ *Let's make a deal.* ➤ *a deal between the two governments*

2 a good deal, a great deal a lot ➤ *There's a good deal of work to do.*

deal² *verb (past* **dealt** /delt/)
1 deal with someone to do business with someone
2 deal with something to do what is necessary for something ➤ *I will deal with your questions now* (=answer them).

dealer /'di:lə^r/ *noun*
a person whose job is to buy and sell a certain thing ➤ *a dealer in old cars*

dealt /delt/
the PAST TENSE and PAST PARTICIPLE of the verb **deal**

dear¹ /dɪə^r/ *adjective*
1 loved ➤ *a dear friend*
2 used at the start of a letter to someone ➤ *Dear Sue* ➤ *Dear Sir*
3 costing a lot of money
SAME MEANING (**3**): **costly, expensive**

dear² *interjection*
oh dear an expression you use when you are surprised, annoyed, or disappointed ➤ *Oh dear! I've forgotten my purse.*

death /deθ/ *noun*
the state of being dead, or the act of dying ➤ *the death of his father*

death penalty /'deθ ˌpenltɪ/ *noun (plural* **death penalties**)
the death penalty the legal punishment of killing someone who is guilty of a crime ➤ *He was convicted of the murder and given the death penalty.*

debatable /dɪ'beɪtəbəl/ *adjective*
(used about facts, decisions, etc.) not certain ➤ *It is debatable whether the peace will last.*

debate¹ /dɪ'beɪt/ *noun*
a public talk at which people give opinions about a subject

debate² *verb (present participle* **debating**, *past* **debated**)
to talk about something important

➤ *The government is debating the education laws.*

debit¹ /'debɪt/ *noun*
an amount of money that you take out of your bank account ➤ *Your bank statement shows all your debits and credits.*

debit² *verb*
to take money out of a bank account ➤ *The sum of £50 has been debited from your account.*
OPPOSITE: **credit**

debris /'debri:/ *noun (no plural)*
pieces of material that are left after something has been destroyed ➤ *The road was covered with debris from the crash.*

debt /det/ *noun*
1 money owed ➤ *a debt of £500*
2 be in debt to owe money to someone

debut /'deɪbju:/ *noun*
the first time that an actor, sports player, etc. performs in public ➤ *the band's debut album*

decade /'dekeɪd/ *noun*
a period of ten years

decaffeinated /di:'kæfɪneɪtɪd/ *adjective*
(used about drinks) not containing CAFFEINE (=a substance that makes you feel more awake) ➤ *a cup of decaffeinated coffee*

decay¹ /dɪ'keɪ/ *verb*
to be destroyed slowly; to go bad
SAME MEANING: **rot**

decay² *noun (no plural)*
the state of being bad ➤ *tooth decay*

deceit /dɪ'si:t/ *noun (no plural)*
making someone believe something that is not true

deceive /dɪ'si:v/ *verb (present participle **deceiving**, past **deceived**)*
to make someone believe something that is not true ➤ *He had managed to deceive us all.*

December /dɪ'sembər/ *noun*
the 12th month of the year

decent /'di:sənt/ *adjective*
good ➤ *Make sure you eat a decent breakfast.* ➤ *a decent job*

deceptive /dɪ'septɪv/ *adjective*
something that is deceptive seems very different from how it really is ➤ *She seems very calm, but appearances can be deceptive.* *(adverb: **deceptively**)*

decide /dɪ'saɪd/ *verb (present participle **deciding**, past **decided**)*
to think that you will do something; to choose what to do ➤ *I decided to go home.* ➤ *She could not decide which dress to buy.*

decidedly /dɪ'saɪdɪdli/ *adverb*
very, in a way that is easy to notice ➤ *Her boss was decidedly unsympathetic.*

decimal /'desɪməl/ *noun*
a number less than one, that is shown by a point (.) followed by numbers. For example, a quarter is shown by the decimal 0.25.

decision /dɪ'sɪʒən/ *noun*
a choice ➤ *They couldn't make a decision about where to go on holiday.*

decisive /dɪ'saɪsɪv/ *adjective*
1 having an important effect on the result of something ➤ *a decisive moment in his career*
2 good at making decisions quickly and firmly ➤ *a strong, decisive leader*
OPPOSITE (**2**): **indecisive**
*(adverb: **decisively**)*

deck /dek/ *noun*
a part of a ship, bus, etc. where passengers sit or stand ➤ *the top deck of a bus*

deckchair /'dektʃeər/ *noun*
a type of chair that you can fold until it is flat, and that people sit on outside, especially by the sea

declaration /ˌdeklə'reɪʃən/ *noun*
an official statement ▶ *a declaration of* war

declare /dɪ'kleər/ *verb (present participle **declaring**, past **declared**)*
to say in public what you think or decide ▶ *to declare war on a country* (=to say that your country will fight another country)

decline¹ /dɪ'klaɪn/ *verb (present participle **declining**, past **declined**)*
1 to become less in number or quality ▶ *The number of teachers has declined in recent years.*
2 to refuse to do something ▶ *He declined to answer*

decline² *noun*
a decrease in the number or quality of something

décor /'deɪkɔːr/ *noun (no plural)*
the way that a room looks, and the colours, kind of furniture, etc. in it ▶ *The restaurant had changed its décor.*

decorate /'dekəreɪt/ *verb (present participle **decorating**, past **decorated**)*
1 to put paint or paper on the walls of a house ▶ *We're decorating the bathroom.*
2 to make something look more attractive by adding things to it ▶ *to decorate a cake*

decoration /ˌdekə'reɪʃən/ *noun*
an attractive thing that is added to something to improve its appearance

decorative /'dekərətɪv/ *adjective*
pretty and used to decorate something ▶ *a decorative vase*

decorator /'dekəreɪtər/ *noun*
a person whose job is to put paint or paper on the inside of houses

decrease¹ /dɪ'kriːs/ *verb (present participle **decreasing**, past **decreased**)*
to get less or fewer ▶ *The number of*

children in the school has decreased this year.
OPPOSITE: **increase**

decrease² /'diːkriːs/ *noun (no plural)*
getting less or fewer ▶ *a decrease in the number of pupils*
OPPOSITE: **increase**

decree /dɪ'kriː/ *noun*
an official order that a ruler or government makes

decrepit /dɪ'krepɪt/ *adjective*
old and in bad condition ▶ *a decrepit old car*

dedicate /'dedɪkeɪt/ *verb (present participle **dedicating**, past **dedicated**)*
to say that a book, film, song, etc. has been written or made for someone, to show that you respect or love them ▶ *The book is dedicated to his mother.*

dedicated /'dedɪkeɪtɪd/ *adjective*
working very hard at doing something because you think it is important ▶ *The nurses are all very dedicated.*

dedication /ˌdedɪ'keɪʃən/ *noun (no plural)*
the act of working very hard because you believe that what you are doing is important ▶ *I was impressed by the dedication of the school staff.*

deduce /dɪ'djuːs/ *verb (present participle **deducing**, past **deduced**)*
to decide that something is true, using the information that you have ▶ *From his accent, I deduced that he was not English.*

deduct /dɪ'dʌkt/ *verb*
to take one amount away from another larger amount ▶ *The tax is deducted from your salary each month.*

deed /diːd/ *noun*
an action ▶ *to do a good deed* (=to do something to help someone)

D

deep /diːp/ *adjective*
1 going down a long way ▶ *a deep river* ▶ *How deep is the river?*
OPPOSITE: **shallow**
2 having a low sound ▶ *a deep voice*
3 strong or dark in colour ▶ *deep brown eyes*
4 felt strongly ▶ *a deep love*

deepen /'diːpən/ *verb*
to become worse, or make something become worse ▶ *The crisis deepened.*

deep freeze /ˌdiːp 'friːz/ *noun*
a large container in which you can freeze food and keep it for a long time

deeply /'diːplɪ/ *adverb*
very strongly ▶ *I care deeply about this problem.* ▶ *deeply in love*

deer /dɪər/ *noun (plural **deer**)*
an animal that can run fast. The male usually has horns.

defeat¹ /dɪ'fiːt/ *verb*
to beat an opponent in a war, game, etc.

defeat² *noun*
an experience or event in which you are beaten by an opponent ▶ *The football team suffered a defeat.*
OPPOSITE: **victory**

defect /dɪ'fekt/ *noun*
a fault in something that stops it working properly ▶ *a defect in the plane engine* ▶ *He's had a hearing defect since he was a child.*

defence /dɪ'fens/ *noun (no plural)*
1 protecting someone or something from an attack ▶ *the defence of your country*
2 the defence the lawyers who are trying to prove that someone is not guilty of a crime in a law court ▶ *Is the defence ready to call the first witness?*
OPPOSITE: **prosecution**

defenceless /dɪ'fensləs/ *adjective*
unable to protect yourself ▶ *a defenceless old woman*

defend /dɪ'fend/ *verb*
to fight in order to protect someone or something
COMPARE: **attack**

defendant /dɪ'fendənt/ *noun*
the person in a law court who the police say is guilty of a crime

defensive /dɪ'fensɪv/ *adjective*
1 used for protection against an attack ▶ *defensive weapons*
2 behaving in a way that shows you think someone is criticizing you ▶ *She got really defensive when I asked her why she hadn't finished.*

defiant /dɪ'faɪənt/ *adjective*
bold and not obedient ▶ *defiant behaviour*

deficiency /dɪ'fɪʃənsɪ/ *noun (plural **deficiencies**)*
1 a lack of something ▶ *a vitamin deficiency*
2 a fault that makes something not good enough ▶ *the deficiencies of the public transport system*

define /dɪ'faɪn/ *verb (present participle **defining**, past **defined**)*
to say exactly what a word means or what something is

definite /'defɪnət/ *adjective*
clear; sure ▶ *Let's fix a definite date for the next meeting.*

definite article /ˌdefɪnət 'ɑːtɪkəl/ *noun*
in English, the word **the**
COMPARE: **indefinite article**

definitely /'defɪnətlɪ/ *adverb*
certainly; without any doubt ▶ *I'm definitely going to come.*

definition /ˌdefɪ'nɪʃən/ *noun*
an explanation of what a word means, which you find in a dictionary

deflect /dɪ'flekt/ *verb*
to make something move in a different direction, or to change directions in this way ▶ *The ball hit the post and was deflected for a corner.*

deforestation /diːfɒrəˈsteɪʃən/ noun (no plural)
cutting down or destroying all the trees in an area

deformed /dɪˈfɔːmd/ adjective
not having a normal shape ➤ Mothers who took the drug gave birth to deformed babies.

defrost /diːˈfrɒst/ verb
if frozen food defrosts, or if you defrost it, it slowly stops being frozen until you can cook or eat it ➤ Defrost the chicken thoroughly before cooking.

deft /deft/ adjective
quick and skilful ➤ Katherine drew a picture with a few deft strokes of her pen.

defy /dɪˈfaɪ/ verb (past defied)
to refuse to obey someone and show no respect for them ➤ to defy your parents

degrading /dɪˈɡreɪdɪŋ/ adjective
making you lose respect for yourself ➤ A lot of people say housework is degrading.

degree /dɪˈɡriː/ noun
1 a measurement used for temperatures or angles ➤ an angle of 45 degrees (45°) ➤ a temperature of 80 degrees (80°)
2 a QUALIFICATION that a person gets after studying and taking examinations, usually at university or college ➤ a history degree

dehydrated /diːhaɪˈdreɪtɪd/ adjective
ill or weak because you do not have enough water in your body

delay¹ /dɪˈleɪ/ noun
a time of waiting before something can happen ➤ We are sorry about the delay.

delay² verb
to make something late ➤ The train has been delayed.

delegate¹ /ˈdelɪɡət/ noun
a person that a country or an organization chooses to do something for it, such as speak or vote at a meeting ➤ UN delegates

delegate² /ˈdelɪɡeɪt/ verb (present participle delegating, past delegated)
to give part of your work to someone in a lower position than you ➤ You must learn to delegate more.

delegation /ˌdelɪˈɡeɪʃən/ noun
a small group of people that a country or an organization sends to do something for it, such as vote or find out about something

delete /dɪˈliːt/ verb (present participle deleting, past deleted)
to remove a piece of information from a computer ➤ Are you sure you want to delete this file?

deliberate /dɪˈlɪbərət/ adjective
planned or done on purpose

deliberately /dɪˈlɪbərətli/ adverb
on purpose ➤ I didn't do it deliberately – it was an accident.

delicacy /ˈdelɪkəsi/ noun (plural delicacies)
a rare or an expensive food that is especially nice to eat

delicate /ˈdelɪkət/ adjective
easily harmed, damaged, or broken ➤ a delicate glass ➤ a delicate child who is often ill

delicatessen /ˌdelɪkəˈtesən/ noun
a shop that sells special or unusual food, especially food from foreign countries

delicious /dɪˈlɪʃəs/ adjective
good to eat ➤ a delicious meal

delight¹ /dɪˈlaɪt/ noun (no plural)
great happiness ➤ to laugh with delight

delight² verb
to give great happiness to someone

D

delighted /dɪˈlaɪtɪd/ *adjective*
very pleased ► *We are delighted with the news.*

delightful /dɪˈlaɪtfəl/ *adjective*
very nice or attractive ► *What a delightful idea!* ► *a delightful child*

delirious /dɪˈlɪrɪəs/ *adjective*
unable to think clearly because you are ill

deliver /dɪˈlɪvəʳ/ *verb*
1 to take something to the place where it should go ► *to deliver a letter*
2 to help a baby come out of its mother's body ► *to deliver a baby*

delivery /dɪˈlɪvəri/ *noun (plural deliveries)*
the taking of something to the place where it should go

delta /ˈdeltə/ *noun*
a low area of land where a river separates into many smaller rivers flowing towards the sea ► *the Mississippi Delta*

deluge /ˈdeljuːdʒ/ *noun*
1 a large flood, or a period of time when it rains continuously
2 a large amount of something such as letters, questions, etc. that someone receives all at the same time

de luxe /dɪˈlʌks/ *adjective*
(used about a hotel, car, etc.) costing more money than others of the same kind because it is better ► *We had a de luxe room with a balcony.*

delve /delv/ *verb (present participle delving, past delved)*
to put your hand deep inside a bag, box, etc. in order to find something ► *He delved into his pockets to find his key.*

demand¹ /dɪˈmɑːnd/ *verb*
to say in a very strong and firm way that you want something ► *"Give me my book at once!" she demanded.*

demand² *noun*
1 a very strong request ► *a demand for more money*
2 **in demand** wanted by a lot of people

demanding /dɪˈmɑːndɪŋ/ *adjective*
needing a lot of your time, effort, skill, etc. ► *a very demanding job*

democracy /dɪˈmɒkrəsi/ *noun (plural democracies)*
a government or country where everyone has an equal right to choose their leaders, by voting

democrat /ˈdeməkræt/ *noun*
a person who believes in or supports democracy

democratic /ˌdeməˈkrætɪk/ *adjective*
(used about a country, company, etc.) letting everyone have the right to choose their government by voting

demolish /dɪˈmɒlɪʃ/ *verb*
to destroy a building on purpose, in a controlled way

demolition /ˌdeməˈlɪʃən/ *noun (no plural)*
the destroying of a building on purpose, in a controlled way

demon /ˈdiːmən/ *noun*
an evil spirit

demonstrate /ˈdemənstreɪt/ *verb (present participle demonstrating, past demonstrated)*
1 to show something clearly ► *He demonstrated how to use the new machine.*
2 to walk through the streets in a group to show that you are angry about something or do not agree with something

demonstration /ˌdemənˈstreɪʃən/ *noun*
1 showing how to do something ► *a cookery demonstration*
2 a group of people walking through the streets to show that they are angry about something or do not agree with something

demonstrator /ˈdemənstreɪtəʳ/
noun
a person who takes part in a
demonstration

demoralized /dɪˈmɒrəlaɪzd/
adjective
feeling less confident and hopeful
than before because of bad things
that have happened ▶ *After a year in
the job, I felt totally demoralized.*

demoralizing /dɪˈmɒrəlaɪzɪŋ/
adjective
making you feel less confident and
hopeful than before ▶ *The
announcement had a demoralizing
effect on the staff.*

den /den/ *noun*
a place in which a wild animal lives

denial /dɪˈnaɪəl/ *noun*
a statement that something is not
true ▶ *his denial of guilt*

denim /ˈdenɪm/ *noun (no plural)*
a strong cloth, usually blue in colour,
which is used to make JEANS

dense /dens/ *adjective*
thick ▶ *a dense forest*

dent¹ /dent/ *noun*
a hollow place in the surface of
something where it has been hit or
pressed ▶ *a big dent in the car*

dent² *verb*
to hit or press something, making a
hollow place in its surface

dental /ˈdentl/ *adjective*
of or about teeth ▶ *dental problems*

dentist /ˈdentɪst/ *noun*
a doctor who looks after people's
teeth

dentures /ˈdentʃəz/ *plural noun*
false teeth worn by people who have
lost their real teeth

deny /dɪˈnaɪ/ *verb (past denied)*
to say that something someone has
said about you is not true
OPPOSITE: **admit**

deodorant /diːˈəʊdərənt/ *noun (no
plural)*
a substance that people put under
their arms, to stop their body
smelling bad

depart /dɪˈpɑːt/ *verb*
to leave; to go away ▶ *The York train
will depart from platform 2.*
OPPOSITE: **arrive**

department /dɪˈpɑːtmənt/ *noun*
a part of a business, company,
government, etc.

department store /dɪˈpɑːtmənt
ˌstɔːʳ/ *noun*
a type of shop that is divided into
several parts, each of which sells a
different kind of goods

departure /dɪˈpɑːtʃəʳ/ *noun*
an act of leaving a place ▶ *the day of
his departure*
OPPOSITE: **arrival**

depend /dɪˈpend/ *verb*
1 it depends a phrase used when you
are not sure about something ▶ *"How
long will the journey take?" "I don't
know; it depends."*
2 depend on someone to need
someone very much

dependable /dɪˈpendəbəl/ *adjective*
able to be trusted ▶ *a dependable
employee*

dependant /dɪˈpendənt/ *noun*
a person who depends on someone
for money, e.g. children who depend
on their parents

dependent /dɪˈpendənt/ *adjective*
needing someone or something to
support you
OPPOSITE: **independent**

deport /dɪˈpɔːt/ *verb*
to force someone to leave a country
and return to the country they came
from

depose /dɪˈpəʊz/ *verb (present
participle deposing, past deposed)*
to remove a leader from their position

D

of power ▶ *an attempt to depose the king*

deposit¹ /dɪˈpɒzɪt/ *verb*
1 to put something down and leave it
2 to put money, etc. into a bank

deposit² *noun*
1 part of the cost of something that you pay at once so that the thing will not be sold to anyone else before you pay the rest of the money
2 money that you pay when you rent something and which is returned to you if you do not cause any damage

depot /ˈdepəʊ/ *noun*
a place where goods or vehicles are stored

depress /dɪˈpres/ *verb*
to make someone feel very sad

depressed /dɪˈprest/ *adjective*
very sad ▶ *She's depressed.*

depressing /dɪˈpresɪŋ/ *adjective*
causing you to feel very sad
▶ *depressing news*

depression /dɪˈpreʃən/ *noun (no plural)*
a feeling of great sadness

deprive /dɪˈpraɪv/ *verb (present participle **depriving**, past **deprived**)*
to stop someone having something that they need or that they normally have ▶ *They deprived the prisoners of food.*

deprived /dɪˈpraɪvd/ *adjective*
not having enough of the things that are necessary for a normal, happy life
▶ *a deprived childhood*

depth /depθ/ *noun*
the distance to the bottom of something ▶ *the depth of the river*

deputy /ˈdepjʊtɪ/ *noun (plural **deputies**)*
a person who is second in importance to the head of a business, a school, etc.

derelict /ˈderɪlɪkt/ *adjective*
(used about buildings or land) in bad condition because no one has used it for a long time ▶ *derelict factories*

descend /dɪˈsend/ *verb*
to go down ▶ *to descend the stairs*
OPPOSITE: **ascend**

descendant /dɪˈsendənt/ *noun*
a person in your family who is born a long time after you are dead
COMPARE: **ancestor**

descent /dɪˈsent/ *noun*
1 the act of going down to a lower place ▶ *The plane began its descent.*
OPPOSITE: **ascent**
2 *(no plural)* your family origins, especially the country that they came from ▶ *Tara's family is of Irish descent.*

describe /dɪˈskraɪb/ *verb (present participle **describing**, past **described**)*
to say what someone or something is like

description /dɪˈskrɪpʃən/ *noun*
an account of what someone or something is like

desert /ˈdezət/ *noun*
a large, empty, usually very dry, place where almost nothing grows

deserted /dɪˈzɜːtɪd/ *adjective*
empty of people ▶ *a deserted street*

desert island /ˌdezət ˈaɪlənd/ *noun*
an island with no people living on it

deserve /dɪˈzɜːv/ *verb (present participle **deserving**, past **deserved**)*
to be worthy of something ▶ *You deserve a holiday after all your hard work.*

design¹ /dɪˈzaɪn/ *noun*
1 a pattern ▶ *a design of blue flowers*
2 a drawing of how to make something ▶ *designs for a new house*

design² *verb*
to make a drawing as a plan for something ▶ *to design a building*

designer /dɪˈzaɪnər/ noun
a person whose job is to think of ideas for making things and then draw them

desirable /dɪˈzaɪərəbəl/ adjective
good or useful, and wanted by many people ▶ a desirable apartment in the centre of the city

desire¹ /dɪˈzaɪər/ noun
a strong wish ▶ a desire for power

desire² verb (present participle **desiring**, past **desired**)
to want something very much

desk /desk/ noun
a table for writing on, often with space inside it for keeping books, pens, etc.

despair¹ /dɪˈspeər/ noun (no plural)
a feeling of great sadness and loss of hope

despair² verb
to have no hope

despatch /dɪˈspætʃ/ verb
another word for **dispatch**

desperate /ˈdespərət/ adjective
wanting or needing something very much ▶ to be desperate for money

despise /dɪˈspaɪz/ verb
(present participle **despising**, past **despised**)
to hate a person or thing because you think they are not worth anything

despite /dɪˈspaɪt/ preposition
although something is true ▶ Despite the bad weather, we enjoyed our holiday.

dessert /dɪˈzɜːt/ noun
a sweet dish that you eat at the end of a meal
SAME MEANING: **pudding, sweet**

destination /ˌdestɪˈneɪʃən/ noun
the place you are travelling to ▶ What is your destination?

destined /ˈdestɪnd/ adjective
certain to do or become something in the future ▶ She was destined to become her country's first woman Prime Minister.

destiny /ˈdestɪnɪ/ noun (plural **destinies**)
the things that will happen to someone in the future ▶ Do you think we can control our own destinies?

destroy /dɪˈstrɔɪ/ verb
to break or ruin something completely ▶ The building was destroyed by fire.

destruction /dɪˈstrʌkʃən/ noun (no plural)
the breaking of something completely

detach /dɪˈtætʃ/ verb
to remove a part of something, especially a part that is designed to be removed ▶ Detach the bottom half of the page by tearing along the dotted line.

detached /dɪˈtætʃt/ adjective
(used about houses) not joined to another house

detail /ˈdiːteɪl/ noun
1 one of the small points that makes up the whole of something ▶ Please could you send me details of the conference?
2 **in detail** thoroughly; paying attention to all the facts ▶ We must talk about it in detail.

detailed /ˈdiːteɪld/ adjective
including a lot of information or facts ▶ a detailed analysis of the text

detain /dɪˈteɪn/ verb
(used about the police) to keep someone somewhere and not allow them to leave

detect /dɪˈtekt/ verb
to discover or notice something

detective /dɪˈtektɪv/ noun
a special police officer who tries to discover who has carried out a crime

detector /dɪˈtektər/ noun
a piece of equipment that tells you if

there is a particular substance somewhere ▶ *a smoke detector*

detention /dɪˈtenʃən/ *noun (no plural)*
1 the act of keeping someone in prison because the police think that they have done something illegal
2 a punishment in which pupils have to stay at school after the other pupils have left

deter /dɪˈtɜːʳ/ *verb (present participle **deterring**, past **deterred**)*
to make someone less likely to do something by making it difficult for them to do it ▶ *security measures aimed at deterring shoplifters*

detergent /dɪˈtɜːdʒənt/ *noun*
soap in the form of powder or liquid for washing clothes, dishes, etc.

deteriorate /dɪˈtɪəriəreɪt/ *verb (present participle **deteriorating**, past **deteriorated**)*
to get worse ▶ *Her health has deteriorated.*

determination /dɪˌtɜːmɪˈneɪʃən/ *noun (no plural)*
a strong wish to succeed in doing something ▶ *her determination to win*

determined /dɪˈtɜːmɪnd/ *adjective*
wanting to do something very much so that nothing can stop you ▶ *I'm determined to win.*

determiner /dɪˈtɜːmɪnəʳ/ *noun*
in grammar, a word used before a noun or an adjective to show which thing you mean. In the phrases "the car" and "some new cars", "the" and "some" are determiners.

detest /dɪˈtest/ *verb*
to hate someone or something

detonate /ˈdetəneɪt/ *verb (present participle **detonating**, past **detonated**)*
to explode, or to make a bomb explode ▶ *Nuclear bombs were detonated in tests in the desert.*

detour /ˈdiːtʊəʳ/ *noun*
a way of going from one place to another that is longer than the usual way

devastate /ˈdevəsteɪt/ *verb (present participle **devastating**, past **devastated**)*
to damage a place very badly ▶ *Bombing raids devastated the city of Dresden.*

devastated /ˈdevəsteɪtɪd/ *adjective*
very sad and shocked ▶ *Ellen was devastated **by** the news.*

devastating /ˈdevəsteɪtɪŋ/ *adjective*
1 causing a lot of damage ▶ *Chemical pollution has had a devastating effect on the environment.*
2 making you feel extremely sad and shocked ▶ *Losing your job can be a devastating experience.*

develop /dɪˈveləp/ *verb*
1 to grow ▶ *The fighting could develop into a war.* ▶ *an insect which develops wings*
2 to make something grow or improve ▶ *plans to develop industry in the area*
3 to treat the film from a camera with special chemicals so that you can see the picture ▶ *to develop a photograph*

developing country /dɪˌveləpɪŋ ˈkʌntri/ *noun (plural **developing countries**)*
a country which is just starting to have modern industries

development /dɪˈveləpmənt/ *noun*
1 the latest in a number of real or imaginary events
2 *(no plural)* growth ▶ *a child's development* ▶ *the development of industry in the area*

device /dɪˈvaɪs/ *noun*
a thing that you use for a particular purpose ▶ *a device for opening bottles*

Devil /'devəl/ *noun*
the Devil an evil spirit that is God's powerful enemy in some religions

devious /'di:vɪəs/ *adjective*
dishonest in a clever way ▶ *a devious scheme for making money*

devise /dɪ'vaɪz/ *verb (present participle **devising**, past **devised**)*
to plan or think of a new way of doing something ▶ *software that allows you to devise your own computer games*

devote /dɪ'vəʊt/ *verb (present participle **devoting**, past **devoted**)*
devote yourself to something to give all your time or thoughts to something ▶ *She devoted herself to her work.*

devoted /dɪ'vəʊtɪd/ *adjective*
caring about or loving someone or something a lot ▶ *He is devoted to his family.*

devotion /dɪ'vəʊʃən/ *noun (no plural)*
the state of caring about or loving someone or something a lot ▶ *her devotion to her job*

devour /dɪ'vaʊər/ *verb*
to eat something quickly ▶ *Tony had already devoured half a pizza.*

devout /dɪ'vaʊt/ *adjective*
very religious ▶ *a devout Catholic*

dew /dju:/ *noun (no plural)*
small drops of water that form on the ground or on plants during the night

diabetes /ˌdaɪə'bi:ti:z/ *noun (no plural)*
a disease in which there is too much sugar in your blood

diabetic /ˌdaɪə'betɪk/ *noun*
a person who has diabetes ▶ *Diabetics cannot eat a lot of sweet food.*

diabolical /ˌdaɪə'bɒlɪkəl/ *adjective*
very bad ▶ *This film is diabolical.*

diagnose /'daɪəgnəʊz/ *verb (present participle **diagnosing**, past **diagnosed**)*
to find out what illness someone has ▶ *His doctor diagnosed cancer.*

diagnosis /ˌdaɪəg'nəʊsɪs/ *noun (plural **diagnoses** /-si:z/)*
a statement about what illness someone has ▶ *The doctor's diagnosis was wrong.*

diagonal /daɪ'ægənəl/ *noun*
a straight line that goes between the opposite corners of a square or other shape, dividing it into two parts

diagram /'daɪəgræm/ *noun*
a plan or picture drawn to explain an idea, or to show how something works

dial¹ /'daɪəl/ *noun*
a round part of a machine or an instrument, often with numbers on it ▶ *a telephone dial* ▶ *the dial of a clock*

dial² *verb (present participle **dialling**, past **dialled**)*
to make a telephone call by moving the DIAL to get the right numbers ▶ *to dial a number*

dialect /'daɪəlekt/ *noun*
a form of a particular language that has different words and different sounds and is spoken in only a small area
COMPARE: **accent**

dialling code /'daɪəlɪŋ ˌkəʊd/ *noun*
the part of a telephone number that you have to add when you are telephoning a different town or country
SAME MEANING: **area code**

dialogue /'daɪəlɒg/ *noun*
a conversation between people in a book, film, or play

diameter /daɪ'æmɪtər/ *noun*
a straight line that divides a circle in half

D

diamond /'daɪəmənd/ *noun*
a very hard, bright, clear stone that is worth a lot of money and is set in jewellery

diarrhoea /ˌdaɪə'riːə/ *noun (no plural)*
an illness in which waste from your body is not solid and comes out often ▶ *Too much fruit can give you diarrhoea.*

diary /'daɪərɪ/ *noun (plural diaries)*
a book in which you write about the things that happen or will happen to you each day

dice /daɪs/ *noun (plural dice)*
a small, square block with a different number of spots on each side (from 1 to 6) which is used in games

dictate /dɪk'teɪt/ *verb (present participle dictating, past dictated)*
to say something for someone else to write down ▶ *I dictated a letter to my secretary.*

dictation /dɪk'teɪʃən/ *noun*
a language test in which you must write the words someone says without making mistakes

dictator /dɪk'teɪtə'/ *noun*
a very strong ruler, especially one who is not fair and who uses soldiers to control people

dictatorship /dɪk'teɪtəʃɪp/ *noun*
a political system in which a dictator controls a country

dictionary /'dɪkʃənərɪ/ *noun (plural dictionaries)*
a book that tells you what words mean and how to spell them

did /dɪd/ *verb*
the PAST TENSE of the verb **do** ▶ *"Did you go out today?" "Yes, I did."*

didn't /'dɪdnt/
did not ▶ *I didn't enjoy the film; did you?*

die /daɪ/ *verb (present participle dying, past died)*
1 to stop living ▶ *She died last year.* ▶ *to die of an illness*
2 be dying for something to want something very much ▶ *I'm dying for a cup of tea.*

diesel /'diːzəl/ *noun (no plural)*
a type of FUEL used in some engines

diet /'daɪət/ *noun*
1 the food that you eat ▶ *She has a healthy diet* (=she usually eats healthy food).
2 the things you eat when you are controlling the type of food you have, e.g. because you are too fat or because you are ill ▶ *You are not allowed to eat sugar on this diet.*
3 go on a diet to eat less food than usual, or different types of food, because you are too fat and want to become thinner

differ /'dɪfə'/ *verb*
1 to be different ▶ *This book differs from his other novels.*
2 to have different opinions ▶ *My father and I differ on many subjects.*

difference /'dɪfrəns/ *noun*
1 a way in which things are not the same ▶ *a difference in size* ▶ *a difference in price* ▶ *There isn't much difference between them.*
OPPOSITE: **similarity**
2 make no difference to have no importance or effect ▶ *It makes no difference to me what you say; I've already decided.*

different /'dɪfrənt/ *adjective*
not the same ▶ *I don't like that dress. Do you have any different ones?* ▶ *My ideas are different from yours.*
OPPOSITE: **same**

difficult /'dɪfɪkəlt/ *adjective*
hard to do or understand ▶ *a difficult question* ▶ *a difficult test*
OPPOSITE: **easy, simple**

difficulty /'dɪfɪkəltɪ/ *noun (plural difficulties)*
a problem

dig /dɪg/ *verb (present participle **digging**, past **dug** /dʌg/)*
to make a hole in the ground by moving earth ▶ *He is digging the garden.* ▶ *to dig a hole*

digest /daɪ'dʒest/ *verb*
to break down food in your stomach so that your body can use it

digestion /daɪ'dʒestʃən/ *noun (no plural)*
the process of digesting food ▶ *He has problems with his digestion.*

digit /'dɪdʒɪt/ *noun*
a single number ▶ *a seven-digit phone number*

digital /'dɪdʒɪtl/ *adjective*
1 using a system in which information is shown in the form of changing electrical signals ▶ *a digital recording*
2 giving information in the form of numbers ▶ *a digital watch*

dignified /'dɪgnɪfaɪd/ *adjective*
proud and calm

dignity /'dɪgnɪtɪ/ *noun (no plural)*
a person's feeling that they are worth as much as other people ▶ *Although she is very poor, she has not lost her dignity.*

dilapidated /dɪ'læpɪdeɪtɪd/ *adjective*
(used about buildings and vehicles) old and in bad condition

dilemma /dɪ'lemə/ *noun*
a situation in which you find it difficult to choose between two possible actions ▶ *He's in a dilemma about whether to go to college or not.*

diligent /'dɪlɪdʒənt/ *adjective*
working very hard ▶ *Mary is a very diligent student.*

dilute /daɪ'luːt/ *verb (present participle **diluting**, past **diluted**)*
to make a liquid weaker or thinner by mixing another liquid with it ▶ *Dilute the orange juice with water.*

dim /dɪm/ *adjective (**dimmer**, **dimmest**)*
not very bright ▶ *a dim light* (adverb: **dimly**)

dimensions /daɪ'menʃənz/ *plural noun*
the size of something, including its length, width, and height ▶ *Prices vary according to the dimensions of the room.*

diminish /dɪ'mɪnɪʃ/ *verb*
to become smaller or less important ▶ *The problem diminished as time passed.*

dimple /'dɪmpəl/ *noun*
a small, hollow place on your cheek or chin ▶ *She gets two little dimples when she smiles.*

din /dɪn/ *noun (no plural)*
loud noise ▶ *What a din the children are making!*

dingy /'dɪndʒɪ/ *adjective (**dingier**, **dingiest**)*
dirty, dark, and unpleasant ▶ *The room was small and dingy.*

dining room /'daɪnɪŋ rʊm/ *noun*
a room with a table where you can eat meals

dinner /'dɪnər/ *noun*
the largest meal of the day, eaten in the evening or in the middle of the day
COMPARE: **lunch, supper, tea**

dinner jacket /'dɪnə ˌdʒækɪt/ *noun*
a jacket that men wear on formal occasions

dinosaur /'daɪnəsɔː/ *noun*
a large REPTILE that lived in very ancient times and no longer exists

dip /dɪp/ *verb (present participle **dipping**, past **dipped**)*
to put something into a liquid and then take it out again ▶ *She dipped her hand in the water.*

diploma /dɪ'pləʊmə/ *noun*
a piece of paper given to someone to

D

prove that they have passed an examination

diplomat /'dɪpləmæt/ *noun*
a person employed by a government to live in another country and make sure that their own country is listened to, its citizens are treated correctly, etc.

diplomatic /,dɪplə'mætɪk/ *adjective*
1 of or about political relations between countries ► *Feingold plans to join the diplomatic service.*
2 good at dealing with people in a way that does not offend them
► *He won't give you a thing unless you're very diplomatic.*
(*adverb:* **diplomatically**)

dire /daɪə'/ *adjective*
very serious or terrible ► *They were in dire trouble.*

direct¹ /daɪ'rekt, dɪ-/ *adjective*
going straight towards a person, place, etc. ► *Which is the most direct way to the station?* ► *a direct flight to Paris*
OPPOSITE: **indirect**

direct² *verb*
to tell someone the way to go or what to do ► *Can you direct me to the station?*

direction /dɪ'rekʃən, daɪ-/ *noun*
the way that someone or something is going or pointing

directly /dɪ'rektlɪ, daɪ-/ *adverb*
1 straight towards a person, place, etc.
2 very soon ► *I'll be there directly.*

direct object /,daɪrekt 'ɒbdʒɪkt/ *noun*
the person or thing that is directly affected by the verb in a sentence. In the sentence "Joe ate a sandwich", the direct object is "sandwich"
COMPARE: **indirect object**

director /dɪ'rektə', daɪ-/ *noun*
a person who controls a business
► *He is one of the directors of the company.*

directory /dɪ'rektərɪ, daɪ-/ *noun*
(*plural* **directories**)
a book that tells you where people live or what their telephone numbers are ► *a telephone directory*

direct speech /,daɪrekt 'spi:tʃ/ *noun*
the style used in writing to report what someone said, by repeating the actual words. The sentence *"I don't want to go," said Julia* is an example of direct speech
COMPARE: **reported speech**

dirt /dɜːt/ *noun (no plural)*
anything that stops something being clean ► *He had dirt all over his face.*

dirty /'dɜːtɪ/ *adjective* (**dirtier, dirtiest**)
having dirt on ► *My shoes were dirty.*
OPPOSITE: **clean**

disability /,dɪsə'bɪlətɪ/ *noun* (*plural* **disabilities**)
a physical or mental condition that makes it difficult for someone to do things that most people do easily, such as walk or see ► *children with learning disabilities*

disabled /dɪs'eɪbəld/ *adjective*
not being able to move or use a part of your body properly because of some illness or wound

disadvantage /,dɪsəd'vɑːntɪdʒ/ *noun*
something that makes things more difficult for you ► *the disadvantages of not having a car*
OPPOSITE: **advantage**

disagree /,dɪsə'griː/ *verb (past* **disagreed**)
not to agree with someone; to have different opinions ► *I'm afraid I disagree with you.*
OPPOSITE: **agree**

disagreement /,dɪsə'griːmənt/ *noun*
an argument or a lack of agreement
► *a disagreement over money*
OPPOSITE: **agreement**

disappear /,dɪsə'pɪə'/ *verb*

to go away or go out of sight suddenly ▶ *The boy disappeared round the corner.*
OPPOSITE: **appear**

disappoint /ˌdɪsəˈpɔɪnt/ *verb*
to be less good or less nice than you expected, and so make you sad

disappointed /ˌdɪsəˈpɔɪntɪd/ *adjective*
sad because something is not as good or as nice as you expected ▶ *We were disappointed by the result.*

disappointing /ˌdɪsəˈpɔɪntɪŋ/ *adjective*
not as good or as nice as you expected ▶ *a disappointing film*

disappointment /ˌdɪsəˈpɔɪntmənt/ *noun*
the sad feeling of being disappointed

disapproval /ˌdɪsəˈpruːvəl/ *noun (no plural)*
the judgement or opinion that someone or something is bad or wrong
OPPOSITE: **approval**

disapprove /ˌdɪsəˈpruːv/ *verb (present participle **disapproving**, past **disapproved**)*
not to like someone or something because you think they are bad or wrong ▶ *My mother disapproves **of** my friends.*
OPPOSITE: **approve**

disarmament /dɪsˈɑːməmənt/ *noun (no plural)*
the reduction of the number of soldiers and weapons that a country has ▶ *nuclear disarmament*

disarray /ˌdɪsəˈreɪ/ *noun*
be in disarray to be very untidy or not organized ▶ *After the party, the room was in total disarray.*

disaster /dɪˈzɑːstəʳ/ *noun*
something very bad, especially something that happens to a lot of people and causes damage or harm

disastrous /dɪˈzɑːstrəs/ *adjective*
very bad, or ending in complete failure ▶ *It will be disastrous if we lose.*

disbelief /ˌdɪsbɪˈliːf/ *noun (no plural)*
a feeling that something is not true or does not exist ▶ *He stared at the broken window in disbelief.*

disc /dɪsk/ *noun*
1 any round, flat thing
2 a record (for playing music)

discard /dɪˈskɑːd/ *verb*
to throw something away because you no longer need it ▶ *They were collecting the boxes that others had discarded.*

discharge /dɪsˈtʃɑːdʒ/ *verb (present participle **discharging**, past **discharged**)*
to officially allow someone to leave a place or an organization ▶ *They discharged him **from** hospital yesterday.*

discipline /ˈdɪsɪplɪn/ *noun (no plural)*
the training of people so that they will obey orders and control their own feelings and behaviour ▶ *Soldiers have to learn discipline in the army.*

disc jockey /ˈdɪsk ˌdʒɒkɪ/ *noun*
a person whose job is to play records on the radio, or at parties, etc.

disco /ˈdɪskəʊ/ *(also **discotheque**) noun*
a place where people, especially young people, go to dance in the evenings

discomfort /dɪsˈkʌmfət/ *noun (no plural)*
slight pain, or a feeling of being physically uncomfortable ▶ *Your injury isn't serious, but it may cause some discomfort.*

disconcerting /ˌdɪskənˈsɜːtɪŋ/ *adjective*
making you feel slightly embarrassed, confused, or worried

D

D

▶ *It's disconcerting when someone keeps staring at you.*

disconnect /ˌdɪskə'nekt/ *verb*
to take out the wire, pipe, etc. that connects a machine or piece of equipment to something ▶ *Have you disconnected the phone?*
OPPOSITE: **connect**

discontented /ˌdɪskən'tentɪd/ *adjective*
unhappy or not satisfied
OPPOSITE: **contented**

discotheque /'dɪskətek/ *noun*
another word for **disco**

discount /'dɪskaʊnt/ *noun*
an amount of money taken away from the price of something ▶ *a discount of £5 for students*

discourage /dɪs'kʌrɪdʒ/ *verb (present participle **discouraging**, past **discouraged**)*
to try to stop someone doing something ▶ *We discourage smoking in our offices.*
OPPOSITE: **encourage**

discouraged /dɪs'kʌrɪdʒd/ *adjective*
no longer having the confidence to continue doing something ▶ *She gets discouraged when she doesn't win.*

discover /dɪs'kʌvəʳ/ *verb*
to find something, or to learn about something for the first time
▶ *Columbus discovered America.* ▶ *to discover the truth about something*

discovery /dɪs'kʌvərɪ/ *noun (plural **discoveries**)*
something discovered ▶ *a new discovery in medical science*

discreet /dɪ'skriːt/ *adjective*
careful about what you say or do, so that you do not embarrass or upset people ▶ *It wasn't very discreet of you to call me at the office. (adverb: **discreetly**)*

discrepancy /dɪ'skrepənsɪ/ *noun (plural **discrepancies**)*

a difference between two things that should be the same ▶ *There were discrepancies **between** the two sets of results.*

discretion /dɪ'skreʃən/ *noun (no plural)*
1 the freedom to decide what is the right thing to do in a situation
▶ *Promotions are left to the discretion of the manager.* ▶ *Tipping is entirely at the customer's discretion.*
2 the act of being careful about what you say or do, so that you do not upset or embarrass people ▶ *This situation must be handled with discretion.*

discriminate /dɪ'skrɪmɪneɪt/ *verb (present participle **discriminating**, past **discriminated**)*
to treat one person or group differently from another in a way that is unfair ▶ *It is illegal to discriminate **against** people because of their sex.*

discrimination /dɪˌskrɪmɪ'neɪʃən/ *noun (no plural)*
unfair treatment of people because of the colour of their skin, where they come from, their sex, age, etc.

discus /'dɪskəs/ *noun (plural **discuses**)*
a flat, heavy, circular object that you throw as a sport

discuss /dɪ'skʌs/ *verb*
to talk about something ▶ *I want to discuss your work with you.*

discussion /dɪ'skʌʃən/ *noun*
a talk about something ▶ *a discussion about work*

disease /dɪ'ziːz/ *noun*
an illness, especially a serious one that lasts a long time

disenchanted /ˌdɪsɪn'tʃɑːntɪd/ *adjective*
no longer believing that something is good or important ▶ *She has become very disenchanted **with** her job.*

disfigure /dɪsˈfɪgəʳ/ *verb (present participle* **disfiguring***, past* **disfigured***)*
to damage someone's appearance ▶ *His face was disfigured in the fire.*

disgrace /dɪsˈgreɪs/ *noun (no plural)*
the loss of other people's good opinion of you

disgraceful /dɪsˈgreɪsfəl/ *adjective*
very bad and wrong ▶ *disgraceful behaviour*

disguise¹ /dɪsˈgaɪz/ *verb (present participle* **disguising***, past* **disguised***)*
to make yourself look like someone else so that people do not know who you are

disguise² *noun*
something that you wear to make you look like someone else so that people do not know who you are ▶ *wearing glasses as a disguise*

disgust¹ /dɪsˈgʌst/ *verb*
to make you feel that something is very bad or unpleasant ▶ *Your behaviour disgusts me.*

disgust² *noun (no plural)*
a strong feeling of not liking something or finding it unpleasant

disgusted /dɪsˈgʌstɪd/ *adjective*
feeling strong dislike or disapproval ▶ *I'm disgusted at the way we were treated.*

disgusting /dɪsˈgʌstɪŋ/ *adjective*
very bad and unpleasant ▶ *a disgusting smell*
SAME MEANING: **revolting**

dish /dɪʃ/ *noun (plural* **dishes***)*
1 a container like a large bowl, used for cooking or serving food
2 do the dishes to wash the dirty plates, etc. after a meal

dishcloth /ˈdɪʃklɒθ/ *noun*
a cloth that you use for washing dirty plates, etc.

disheartened /dɪsˈhɑːtnd/ *adjective*
unhappy because you do not think you will achieve something you have been hoping for ▶ *Don't get disheartened if they don't accept your first offer.*

dishevelled /dɪˈʃevəld/ *adjective*
(used about clothes, hair, etc.) untidy ▶ *She looked tired and dishevelled.*

dishonest /dɪsˈɒnɪst/ *adjective*
not honest
OPPOSITE: **honest**

dishonesty /dɪsˈɒnɪstɪ/ *noun (no plural)*
behaviour in which someone tells lies, steals, or cheats ▶ *They accused me of dishonesty.*
OPPOSITE: **honesty**

dishonour /dɪsˈɒnəʳ/ *noun (no plural)*
a lack of respect for someone because of something bad they have done ▶ *You have brought dishonour on your family.*
OPPOSITE: **honour**

dishwasher /ˈdɪʃˌwɒʃəʳ/ *noun*
a machine that washes dirty plates, etc.

disillusioned /ˌdɪsɪˈluːʒənd/ *adjective*
unhappy because you have lost your belief that someone or something is good or right ▶ *He became disillusioned with religion.*

disinfect /ˌdɪsɪnˈfekt/ *verb*
to clean something with a chemical that destroys BACTERIA (=small creatures that spread disease) ▶ *They disinfected all the surfaces.*

disinfectant /ˌdɪsɪnˈfektənt/ *noun (no plural)*
a chemical used to clean things thoroughly, which destroys BACTERIA (=small creatures that spread disease)

disintegrate /dɪsˈɪntɪgreɪt/ *verb (present participle* **disintegrating***, past* **disintegrated***)*

D

to break up into small pieces ► *The plane just disintegrated in midair.*

disk /dɪsk/ *noun*
a small, flat piece of plastic which is round or square and is used in a computer for keeping information

disk drive /'dɪsk draɪv/ *noun*
a piece of equipment in a computer that is used to pass information to or from a disk

dislike[1] /dɪs'laɪk/ *verb (present participle **disliking**, past **disliked**)*
not to like someone or something
OPPOSITE: **like**

> The verb **dislike** is not often used in ordinary conversation because it is rather formal. People usually say that they **don't like** something, rather than they **dislike** it: *I don't like her.* ► *He doesn't like swimming.*

dislike[2] *noun*
a feeling of not liking someone or something

dislocate /'dɪsləkeɪt/ *verb (present participle **dislocating**, past **dislocated**)*
to put a bone in your body out of its normal place because of an accident ► *He's dislocated his shoulder.*

disloyal /dɪs'lɔɪəl/ *adjective*
not faithful or true to someone
OPPOSITE: **loyal**

disloyalty /dɪs'lɔɪəlti/ *noun (no plural)*
behaviour in which you do not support your friends, family, country, etc., or you do things that may harm them ► *He was accused of disloyalty to his country.*
OPPOSITE: **loyalty**

dismal /'dɪzməl/ *adjective*
dull or sad; not bright or happy ► *dismal weather*

dismay /dɪs'meɪ/ *noun (no plural)*
a feeling of surprise and disappointment

dismiss /dɪs'mɪs/ *verb*
1 to send someone away
2 to tell someone they must leave their job because they have done something wrong

disobedience /,dɪsə'biːdiəns/ *noun (no plural)*
the act of refusing to obey someone
OPPOSITE: **obedience**

disobedient /,dɪsə'biːdiənt/ *adjective*
not willing to obey ► *a disobedient child*
OPPOSITE: **obedient**

disobey /,dɪsə'beɪ/ *verb*
not to do what someone tells you to do ► *to disobey your parents*
OPPOSITE: **obey**

disorder /dɪs'ɔːdəʳ/ *noun*
1 *(no plural)* the state of being very untidy ► *The classroom was in a state of disorder.*
OPPOSITE: **order**
2 an illness that stops part of your body working properly ► *She has a rare blood disorder.*

disorderly /dɪs'ɔːdəli/ *adjective*
untidy or uncontrolled ► *The papers were in a disorderly mess.*
OPPOSITE: **orderly**

disorganized /dɪs'ɔːgənaɪzd/ *adjective*
1 not tidy
2 not able to plan or arrange things well
OPPOSITE (**1** and **2**): **organized**

disoriented /dɪs'ɔːriəntɪd/ *(also **disorientated** /dɪs'ɔːriənteɪtɪd/) adjective*
confused and not knowing what is happening or where you are ► *She felt disoriented after the accident.*

dispatch *(also **despatch**)* /dɪ'spætʃ/ *verb*
1 to send someone to a place as part of their job ► *UN troops are being dispatched to protect the airport.*

2 to send a letter, package, etc. to someone ▶ *Father dispatched an angry letter immediately.*

dispense /dɪ'spens/ *verb (present participle **dispensing**, past **dispensed**)*
1 dispense with something to not use or do something because it is no longer necessary ▶ *Your new computer dispenses with the need for a secretary.*
2 to give or provide people with something ▶ *The machines in the hall dispense drinks.*

dispenser /dɪ'spensəʳ/ *noun*
a machine that you can get things such as drinks or money from ▶ *I got a coffee from the drinks dispenser.* ▶ *a cash dispenser*

disperse /dɪ'spɜːs/ *verb (present participle **dispersing**, past **dispersed**)*
to go in different directions, or to make things or people go in different directions ▶ *The police finally managed to disperse the crowd.*

dispirited /dɪ'spɪrɪtɪd/ *adjective*
sad and without hope ▶ *After their defeat, the team felt dispirited.*

display¹ /dɪ'spleɪ/ *verb*
to show something so that many people can see it ▶ *The children's pictures were displayed on the wall.*

display² *noun*
1 a show of something ▶ *a display of the children's work* ▶ *a dancing display*
2 on display being shown for many people to see

disposable /dɪ'spəʊzəbəl/ *adjective*
intended to be used once or for a short time and then thrown away ▶ *a disposable toothbrush*

disposal /dɪ'spəʊzəl/ *noun (no plural)*
the act of getting rid of something

dispose /dɪ'spəʊz/ *verb (present participle **disposing**, past **disposed**)*
dispose of something to get rid of something

disposition /ˌdɪspə'zɪʃən/ *noun*
a person's usual character ▶ *a warm and friendly disposition*

disprove /dɪs'pruːv/ *verb (present participle **disproving**, past **disproved**)*
to show that something is false ▶ *He set out to disprove my theory.*
OPPOSITE: **prove**

dispute /dɪ'spjuːt/ *noun*
a quarrel ▶ *a pay dispute (=a quarrel about pay)*

disqualify /dɪs'kwɒlɪfaɪ/ *verb (past **disqualified**)*
to stop someone taking part in an activity or a competition because they have done something wrong ▶ *The judges disqualified him for taking drugs.*

disregard /ˌdɪsrɪ'gɑːd/ *verb*
to ignore something, especially because you do not think it is important ▶ *The judge ordered us to disregard the witness's last statement.*

disrupt /dɪs'rʌpt/ *verb*
to stop a situation or an event from continuing normally ▶ *Traffic will be severely disrupted by road works.*

disruption /dɪs'rʌpʃən/ *noun*
a situation in which someone or something stops a situation or an event from continuing normally ▶ *After the brief disruption, the game continued.*

dissatisfied /dɪs'sætɪsfaɪd/ *adjective*
not content or pleased enough with something ▶ *We were very dissatisfied **with** the food at the restaurant.*
OPPOSITE: **satisfied**

dissect /dɪ'sekt/ *verb*
to cut up a plant or an animal in order

D

to study it ▶ *In biology, we dissected a rat.*

dissertation /ˌdɪsəˈteɪʃən/ *noun*
a long piece of writing about a subject, especially one that you write as part of a university degree ▶ *She wrote her dissertation on the Romantic poets.*

dissident /ˈdɪsɪdənt/ *noun*
a person who publicly criticizes their government

dissolve /dɪˈzɒlv/ *verb (present participle **dissolving**, past **dissolved**)*
to mix completely with a liquid ▶ *Sugar dissolves **in** water.* ▶ *Dissolve the powder in water.*

distance /ˈdɪstəns/ *noun*
1 the amount of space between two places ▶ *What's the distance between London and Paris?* ▶ *a long distance*
2 in the distance far away

distant /ˈdɪstənt/ *adjective*
far away ▶ *a distant country* ▶ *the distant past*

distaste /dɪsˈteɪst/ *noun (no plural)*
a strong dislike of something ▶ *He has a great distaste for foreign films.*

distil /dɪˈstɪl/ *verb (present participle **distilling**, past **distilled**)*
to turn a liquid into gas and then turn the gas into liquid again, in order to make it purer or stronger ▶ *distilled water*

distinct /dɪˈstɪŋkt/ *adjective*
1 clear; easily seen or heard ▶ *the distinct sound of fighting*
2 separate; different ▶ *There are several distinct languages in every African country.*

distinction /dɪˈstɪŋkʃən/ *noun*
1 a clear difference between things ▶ *The author draws a distinction **between** "crime" and "sin".*
2 a special honour given to someone ▶ *Sol had the distinction of leading the delegation.*

distinctive /dɪˈstɪŋktɪv/ *adjective*
different from others and easy to recognize ▶ *She has a distinctive style of writing.*

distinctly /dɪˈstɪŋktlɪ/ *adverb*
very clearly ▶ *I distinctly remember telling you.*

distinguish /dɪˈstɪŋgwɪʃ/ *verb*
1 to see the difference between things ▶ *to distinguish good **from** bad* ▶ *to distinguish **between** good and bad*
2 to be able to see, hear, or taste something even though it is difficult to do this ▶ *It was dark and I could just distinguish their faces.*

distinguished /dɪˈstɪŋgwɪʃt/ *adjective*
famous and respected by many people ▶ *a distinguished scientist*

distort /dɪˈstɔːt/ *verb*
1 to change the shape or sound of something so that it is strange or unclear ▶ *The heat had distorted the doll's face.*
2 to tell people about a fact, statement, etc. in a way that changes its meaning ▶ *Journalists distorted what he actually said.*

distract /dɪˈstrækt/ *verb*
to take someone's attention away from what they are doing ▶ *Don't distract me while I'm driving!* ▶ *Charles is easily distracted **from** his studies.*

distracted /dɪˈstræktɪd/ *adjective*
anxious and not able to think clearly about what is happening around you ▶ *You seem a little distracted.*

distraction /dɪˈstrækʃən/ *noun*
something that takes your attention away from what you are doing ▶ *I can't work at home – there are too many distractions.*

distraught /dɪ'strɔːt/ *adjective*
very anxious or upset ▶ *She looked distraught.*

distress¹ /dɪ'stres/ *noun (no plural)*
a feeling of sadness, pain, or trouble

distress² *verb*
to make someone sad or upset

distressing /dɪ'stresɪŋ/ *adjective*
making you feel sad or upset
▶ *distressing news*

distribute /dɪ'strɪbjuːt/ *verb (present participle **distributing**, past **distributed**)*
to give or send something to different people or places ▶ *The teacher distributed the books to the children.*

district /'dɪstrɪkt/ *noun*
a part of a country, city, etc.

distrust /dɪs'trʌst/ *noun (no plural)*
a feeling that you cannot trust someone ▶ *There's a certain distrust of technology among older people.*

disturb /dɪ'stɜːb/ *verb*
1 to interrupt someone and stop them working, thinking, sleeping, etc.
▶ *Please don't disturb me while I'm working.*
2 to make someone feel worried or upset ▶ *We were very disturbed by these events.*
3 to change or move something ▶ *Someone had disturbed the papers on his desk.*

disturbance /dɪ'stɜːbəns/ *noun*
a noisy event in which people fight or cause trouble ▶ *There has been a disturbance in the street.*

disturbing /dɪ'stɜːbɪŋ/ *adjective*
making you feel worried or upset
▶ *disturbing news*

disused /ˌdɪs'juːzd/ *adjective*
(used about a place) not used any more ▶ *a disused factory*

ditch /dɪtʃ/ *noun (plural **ditches**)*
a deep, narrow place for water to go along, especially by the side of a road or field

ditto /'dɪtəʊ/ *noun*
two small marks (″)that you write under a word in a list so that you do not have to write the same word again

dive /daɪv/ *verb (present participle **diving**, past **dived**)*
to jump into water with your head and arms first ▶ *He dived into the lake.* ▶ *She dived to the bottom of the river.*

diver /'daɪvə'/ *noun*
a person who works underwater and wears special equipment to help them breathe

diverse /daɪ'vɜːs/ *adjective*
very different from each other
▶ *London is home to people of many diverse cultures.*

diversion /daɪ'vɜːʃən/ *noun*
1 something that takes your attention away from something else ▶ *The prisoners created a diversion so the others could escape.*
2 a situation in which traffic has to use a different road because the usual way is blocked

divert /daɪ'vɜːt/ *verb*
1 to change the direction of something ▶ *Traffic is being diverted to avoid the scene of the accident.*
2 divert attention from something to stop people giving their attention to something ▶ *The government is trying to divert attention from its mistakes.*

divide /dɪ'vaɪd/ *verb (present participle **dividing**, past **divided**)*
1 to split into pieces or parts ▶ *The road divided into three.*
2 to share something ▶ *We divided the money between us.*
3 to find how many times a number will go into a bigger number ▶ *If you*

divide 39 by 3, the answer is 13.
COMPARE: **multiply**

divine /dɪˈvaɪn/ *adjective*
from a god or like a god

diving /ˈdaɪvɪŋ/ *noun (no plural)*
1 the activity of swimming
underwater, using special equipment
to help you breathe
2 the activity or sport of jumping into
water with your head and arms first

diving board /ˈdaɪvɪŋ bɔːd/ *noun*
a special board, often high above the
ground, that you stand on before
jumping or diving (DIVE) into water

divisible /dɪˈvɪzəbl/ *adjective*
able to be divided by another number
exactly ▶ *15 is divisible by 3 and 5.*

division /dɪˈvɪʒən/ *noun*
1 *(no plural)* sums in which you find
how many times a number will go
into a bigger number
2 a part of something ▶ *Which
division of the company do you work
in?*

divorce¹ /dɪˈvɔːs/ *verb (present
participle* **divorcing***, past* **divorced***)*
to arrange by law for a marriage to
end ▶ *They're getting divorced.*

divorce² *noun*
the ending of a marriage according to
the law

DIY /ˌdiː aɪ ˈwaɪ/ *noun (no plural)*
DO-IT-YOURSELF; painting or building
things in your house yourself instead
of paying a painter, builder, etc. to do
it for you

dizzy /ˈdɪzi/ *adjective (***dizzier,
dizziest***)*
feeling as if you are going to fall and
as if things are moving when they are
not ▶ *I feel dizzy when I look out of a
high window.*

DJ /ˌdiː ˈdʒeɪ/ *noun*
DISC JOCKEY; a person whose job it is to
play records on the radio or at
parties, etc.

do¹ /duː/ *verb*

present tense

singular	plural
I **do**	We **do**
You **do**	You **do**
He/She/It	They **do**
does	

past tense

singular	plural
I **did**	We **did**
You **did**	You **did**
He/She/It **did**	They **did**

present participle	**doing**
past participle	**done**
negative short forms	**don't, doesn't, didn't**

(you can find each of these words in
its own place in the dictionary)

1 to carry out an action ▶ *I must do
some work.* ▶ *What are you doing?*
▶ *We're doing* (=learning) *French at
school.*
2 do as you are told to do what
someone, e.g. a parent, tells you to
do
3 do someone good to make
someone feel better or more healthy
▶ *A holiday will do you good.*
4 do something up to fasten
something ▶ *Do up your coat.*
5 do well to be a success
6 could do with to want or need
something ▶ *I could do with some
sleep.*
7 to do with about or concerning
someone or something ▶ *Her job's to
do with looking after old people.*
8 do without something to live or
continue without a particular thing
▶ *I couldn't do without your help.*
9 How do you do? something you say
as a polite greeting when you meet

someone for the first time. The reply
is also "How do you do?" ► *Mother,
this is Doctor Jones." "How do you
do, Doctor Jones?" "How do you do?"*
10 What do you do? What is your job?
11 What have you done with ...?
Where is .../Where have you put ...?
► *What have you done with my book?*

Compare the verbs **do** and **make**.
Use **do** when you are talking
about an action or activity: *to do
some work ► to do the shopping.*
Use **make** when you are talking
about producing something or
producing a result: *to make a
cake ► to make a noise.* You also
use **make** when you are talking
about plans or decisions: *to make
a plan ► to make a choice ► to
make an appointment.*

do² verb
1 used with **not** before another verb,
to say that something is not so ► *I
don't* (=do not) *agree.* ► *He doesn't*
(=does not) *have a car.*
2 used with another verb, to ask a
question ► *Do you like dancing?*
► *Did you find the answer?*
3 used with **not**, to tell someone not
to do something ► *Do not lean out of
the window.* ► *Don't* (=do not) *do
that!*
4 used to make the meaning of
another verb stronger ► *You do talk a
lot!* ► *You do believe me, don't you?*

docile /'dəusaɪl/ *adjective*
quiet and easy to control ► *The horse
was very docile.*

dock¹ /dɒk/ *noun*
a place where goods are taken on
and off ships

dock² *verb*
(used about a ship) to come into a
dock

doctor /'dɒktər/ *noun*
a person who looks after people's
health

document /'dɒkjumənt/ *noun*
a piece of paper with something
official written on it

documentary /ˌdɒkju'mentri/ *noun*
(plural **documentaries**)
a film giving information and facts
about something

documentation /ˌdɒkjumən'teɪʃən/
noun (no plural)
documents that provide a record of
something or show that something is
true ► *Have you got any
documentation to prove who you are?*

dodge /dɒdʒ/ *verb (present
participle* **dodging***, past* **dodged***)*
1 to move quickly to one side to avoid
something
2 to avoid something you should not
avoid ► *to dodge payment of tax*

dodgy /'dɒdʒi/ *adjective*
(**dodgier, dodgiest**)
dishonest or unable to be trusted
► *His friend looked a bit dodgy to me.*

does /dəz; *strong* dʌz/ *verb*
the part of the verb **do** that is used
with **he, she** and **it** ► *Does she have a
job?*

doesn't /'dʌznt/
does not ► *She doesn't like school.*

dog /dɒg/ *noun*
an animal with four legs and a tail,
that eats meat and is sometimes
used to protect buildings. Many
people keep dogs as pets.

dogmatic /dɒg'mætɪk/ *adjective*
having strong beliefs which you are
not willing to change ► *He is very
dogmatic about how languages
should be taught.*

doing¹ /'duːɪŋ/ *noun (no plural)*
1 be sb's (own) doing to be
someone's fault ► *His bad luck was
all his own doing.*
2 take some doing to be hard work
► *Getting the place clean is going to
take some doing.*

D

doing²
the PRESENT PARTICIPLE of the verb **do**

do-it-yourself /ˌduː ɪt jɔːˈself/ *(also DIY)* noun *(no plural)*
painting or building things in your house yourself instead of paying a painter, builder, etc. to do it for you

dole /dəʊl/ noun *(no plural)*
be on the dole to have no job and receive money from the government to help you buy food, clothes, etc. ▶ *He left school at 16, and now he's on the dole.*

doll /dɒl/ noun
a toy made to look like a person, especially a baby, woman, or girl

dollar /ˈdɒlə/ noun
the money used in America and some other countries

dolphin /ˈdɒlfɪn/ noun
a large sea animal that swims about in a group

dome /dəʊm/ noun
a high, round roof

domestic /dəˈmestɪk/ adjective
1 in the home or about the home ▶ *domestic jobs like cleaning and cooking*
2 not wild ▶ *Cattle are domestic animals.*

dominant /ˈdɒmɪnənt/ adjective
strongest, most important, or most noticeable ▶ *TV news is the dominant source of information in our society.*

dominate /ˈdɒmɪneɪt/ verb *(present participle **dominating**, past **dominated**)*
to have power and control over someone or something

domineering /ˌdɒmɪˈnɪərɪŋ/ adjective
trying to control other people without considering their feelings ▶ *a domineering father*

domino /ˈdɒmɪnəʊ/ noun *(plural **dominoes**)*
1 one of a set of small pieces of wood or plastic, with spots on, used for playing a game
2 dominoes *(no plural)* the game played using dominoes

donate /dəʊˈneɪt/ verb *(present participle **donating**, past **donated**)*
to give something to an organization that helps people, such as a hospital ▶ *to donate money*

donation /dəʊˈneɪʃən/ noun
a gift made to an organization that helps people ▶ *a donation of money to the hospital*

done¹ /dʌn/
the PAST PARTICIPLE of the verb **do**

done² adjective
finished ▶ *The work is nearly done.*

donkey /ˈdɒŋki/ noun
an animal like a small horse with long ears

donor /ˈdəʊnə/ noun
someone who gives something ▶ *She is a blood donor (=she gives her blood to be used in the hospital).*

don't /dəʊnt/
do not ▶ *I don't want to go.* ▶ *Don't touch that!*

doom /duːm/ noun *(no plural)*
something bad in the future that you cannot avoid ▶ *I had an awful sense of doom before the exam.*

doomed /duːmd/ adjective
certain to fail ▶ *Our relationship was doomed from the beginning.*

door /dɔːʳ/ noun
1 the flat piece of wood, metal, etc. that shuts the entrance to a building or room ▶ *Please open the door for me.*
2 the entrance to a building or room ▶ *Will you wait at the door?*
3 answer the door to open the door when someone knocks
4 door to door going from one house or building to another ▶ *to sell things door to door*

5 next door to in the building or room next to a place ➤ *He lives next door to my parents* (=in the house next to theirs).

6 out of doors outside ➤ *to work out of doors*

doorbell /'dɔːbel/ *noun*
a bell that you ring when you want someone to open a door, especially at the entrance to a house or building ➤ *to ring a doorbell*

doorknob /'dɔːnɒb/ *noun*
a round handle on a door that you use when you open and close it

doormat /'dɔːmæt/ *noun*
a small mat at the door of a house which you walk on to clean your shoes after you have been outside

doorstep /'dɔːstep/ *noun*
1 a step in front of the door of a house
2 on your doorstep very close to where you live

doorway /'dɔːweɪ/ *noun*
an opening where there is a door ➤ *He stood in the doorway.*

dormice /'dɔːmaɪs/
the plural of **dormouse**

dormitory /'dɔːmɪtrɪ/ *noun (plural dormitories)*
a large room with beds for people to sleep in ➤ *the school dormitory*

dormouse /'dɔːmaʊs/ *noun (plural dormice /'dɔːmaɪs/)*
a small mouse that lives in fields and sleeps in the winter

dose /dəʊs/ *noun*
the amount of a medicine that you should take at one time ➤ *The dose is two spoonfuls every four hours.*

dot /dɒt/ *noun*
a small, round mark ➤ *On the map, towns were marked by a red dot.* ➤ *A small "i" has a dot on it.*

doting /'dəʊtɪŋ/ *adjective*
loving someone very much, in a way

that seems silly to other people ➤ *His doting parents let him do whatever he likes.*

double¹ /'dʌbəl/ *adjective, adverb, noun*
1 twice as much ➤ *I'll pay you double if you finish the work quickly.*
2 (used before a number or letter) happening twice ➤ *My telephone number is 65588 (six, double five, double eight).*
3 with two parts ➤ *a double door*
4 made for two people ➤ *a double bed*
COMPARE: **single**

double² *verb (present participle doubling, past doubled)*
1 to become twice as big or twice as much as before ➤ *Sales of our new car have doubled.*
2 to make something twice as big or twice as much as before ➤ *We have doubled sales of our new car.*

double bass /ˌdʌbəl 'beɪs/ *noun (plural double basses)*
a very large musical instrument, shaped like a VIOLIN, that you play standing up

double-check /ˌdʌbəl 'tʃek/ *verb*
to check something again so that you are completely sure about it ➤ *Could you just double-check that the door is locked?*

double-decker /ˌdʌbəl 'dekər/ *noun*
a bus with two levels

doubles /'dʌbəlz/ *noun*
a game of tennis played by two teams of two people ➤ *I prefer playing doubles.*

doubly /'dʌblɪ/ *adverb*
twice as much ➤ *The job was doubly difficult because of the rain.*

doubt¹ /daʊt/ *verb*
to be not sure whether something is true or will happen ➤ *I doubt if he will pass the examinations.* ➤ *I doubt that they will come.*

D

doubt² *noun*
1 a reason for not being sure about something ► *I have doubts about whether he is the best man for the job.* ► *There is no doubt he is guilty* (=he certainly is guilty).
2 no doubt almost certainly ► *No doubt we'll see you again soon.*

doubtful /'daʊtfəl/ *adjective*
not likely ► *It's doubtful whether she'll succeed.*

doubtless /'daʊtləs/ *adverb*
certainly; without a doubt ► *He will doubtless arrive on the next train.*

dough /dəʊ/ *noun (no plural)*
a soft mixture of flour, water, and YEAST that is cooked to make bread

doughnut /'dəʊnʌt/ *noun*
a small, round, sweet cake that is cooked in oil

dove /dʌv/ *noun*
a white bird that people think of as a sign of peace

dowdy /'daʊdɪ/ *adjective (dowdier, dowdiest)*
(used about people or clothes) dull and not interesting

down¹ /daʊn/ *adverb, preposition*
1 in or to a lower place ► *Sit down, please.* ► *The children ran down the hill.* ► *I must put these bags down.*
2 showing a decrease ► *Our sales have gone down this year.*
OPPOSITE (**1** and **2**): **up**
3 written on paper ► *to put something down in writing* ► *to write something down*
4 down the road, down the street along the road, along the street

down² *adjective*
1 sad ► *Andrew was feeling down.*
2 behind in a game by a particular number of points ► *We were down by six points halfway through the game.*
3 (used about a computer) not working

downfall /'daʊnfɔːl/ *noun*
a situation in which you suddenly stop being successful, rich, or important ► *Greed will be his downfall.*

downhill /ˌdaʊn'hɪl/ *adjective, adverb*
to or towards the bottom of a hill ► *to walk downhill*
OPPOSITE: **uphill**

download /ˌdaʊn'ləʊd/ *verb*
to move information from one part of a computer system to another, especially from the INTERNET to a computer ► *I downloaded the anti-virus update from their website this morning.*

downpour /'daʊnpɔːʳ/ *noun*
a lot of rain falling in a short time

downright /'daʊnraɪt/ *adverb*
completely ► *It was downright stupid to go there on your own.*

downside /'daʊnsaɪd/ *noun*
the downside a bad feature of something that is good in other ways ► *The downside of the job is you have to work at weekends.*

downstairs /ˌdaʊn'steəz/ *adjective, adverb*
in or towards the part of a house which is on the same level as the ground ► *The bathroom is downstairs.* ► *a downstairs bathroom* ► *to walk downstairs*
OPPOSITE: **upstairs**

downstream /ˌdaʊn'striːm/ *adverb*
in the same direction that a river or stream is flowing ► *The boat floated downstream.*

down-to-earth /ˌdaʊn tʊ 'ɜːθ/ *adjective*
sensible and practical ► *For a famous pop star, she's very down-to-earth.*

downwards /'daʊnwədz/ *adverb*
from a higher to a lower place; towards the ground or floor
OPPOSITE: **upwards**

doze¹ /dəʊz/ *verb (present participle* ***dozing****, past* ***dozed****)*
1 to sleep lightly for some time
SAME MEANING: **snooze**
2 doze off to go to sleep without meaning to ▶ *I dozed off watching television.*

doze² *noun*
a short sleep ▶ *to have a doze*
SAME MEANING: **nap**

dozen /'dʌzən/ *noun*
1 twelve ▶ *a dozen eggs*
2 dozens very many ▶ *There were dozens of people there.*

Dr
a short way of writing the word **doctor** when you are writing someone's name ▶ *Dr Brown*

drab /dræb/ *adjective (****drabber****, ****drabbest****)*
not bright or interesting ▶ *The room was painted a drab brown.*

draft¹ /drɑːft/ *noun*
a drawing, plan, or piece of writing that you have not finished yet ▶ *This is just a first draft of my essay.*

draft² *verb*
to write a plan, letter, report, etc. that you will need to change before it is finished ▶ *She drafted a letter of complaint.*

drag /dræg/ *verb (present participle* ***dragging****, past* ***dragged****)*
to pull something heavy along behind you

dragon /'drægən/ *noun*
a fierce animal in stories that has fire coming out of its mouth

drain¹ /dreɪn/ *noun*
a pipe that takes dirty water away

drain² *verb*
to flow away; to make water flow away ▶ *The water drained away slowly.*

drained /dreɪnd/ *adjective*
very tired ▶ *I felt completely drained*

after they had all gone home.

draining board /'dreɪnɪŋ bɔːd/ *noun*
the place next to the SINK in a kitchen, where plates, etc. are left to dry after they have been washed

drainpipe /'dreɪnpaɪp/ *noun*
a pipe on the outside of a building that takes away dirty water or water from the roof

drama /'drɑːmə/ *noun (no plural)*
1 acting and plays ▶ *She's studying drama.*
2 excitement ▶ *I like the drama of a big storm.*

dramatic /drə'mætɪk/ *adjective*
exciting ▶ *a dramatic event*

dramatist /'dræmətɪst/ *noun*
a person who writes plays

dramatize /'dræmətaɪz/ *verb (present participle* ***dramatizing****, past* ***dramatized****)*
1 to use a real event or a story from a book to write a play ▶ *They are dramatizing her life story for TV.*
2 to make an event seem more exciting than it really is ▶ *She tends to dramatize things.*

drank /dræŋk/
the PAST TENSE of the verb **drink**

drastic /'dræstɪk/ *adjective*
sudden, and having a big effect ▶ *The new school principal is planning to make drastic changes. (adverb:* ***drastically****)*

draught /drɑːft/ *noun*
cold air blowing into a room ▶ *a cold draught under the door*

draughts /drɑːfts/ *noun (no plural)*
a game played by two people using 24 round pieces on a board of black and white squares

draughty /'drɑːftɪ/ *adjective (****draughtier****, ****draughtiest****)*
(used about rooms, buildings, etc.) having cold air blowing through

D

D

draw¹ /drɔː/ *verb (past tense **drew***
/druː/, *past participle **drawn*** /drɔːn/)*
1 to make a picture, especially with a
pencil or pen ► *I like drawing.*
► *to draw a picture*
2 to take something out of a place
► *He drew a gun from his pocket.*
► *to draw money out of a bank*
3 to end a game or match with an
equal result so that nobody wins
► *We drew with the London team.*
► *to draw a match*
4 draw back to move away from
someone or something
5 draw near to move towards
someone or something
6 draw the curtains to pull curtains
across so that they cover a window
7 draw up (used about a car) to stop

draw² *noun*
a game or a result where nobody
wins because both sides are equal
► *The match was a draw.* ► *The game
ended in a draw.*

drawback /ˈdrɔːbæk/ *noun*
something that might be a problem
or disadvantage ► *The only drawback
to living in London is the cost.*

drawer /drɔːʳ/ *noun*
a part of a piece of furniture, used for
keeping things in, which has handles
so that it can be pulled out and
pushed in

drawing /ˈdrɔːɪŋ/ *noun*
1 *(no plural)* the making of pictures
with pencils or pens ► *I like to do
some drawing in my spare time.*
2 a picture done by pen or pencil
► *She had done a drawing **of** her
mother.*

drawing pin /ˈdrɔːɪŋ pɪn/ *noun*
a small pin with a round, flat top
which is used for fixing things to a
wall

drawl /drɔːl/ *verb*
to speak slowly with long vowel
sounds ► *"Hi there," he drawled.*

drawn /drɔːn/
the PAST PARTICIPLE of the verb **draw**

dread /dred/ *verb*
to feel very worried about something
that is going to happen ► *I'm really
dreading the interview tomorrow.*
► *I always used to dread going to the
dentist's.*

dreadful /ˈdredfəl/ *adjective*
very bad or unpleasant ► *There's
been a dreadful accident.* ► *I've had a
dreadful day – everything seems to
have gone wrong.*
SAME MEANING: **awful, dreadful,
horrible**

dreadfully /ˈdredfəlɪ/ *adverb*
1 very badly ► *The children behaved
dreadfully.*
2 very ► *She was dreadfully upset.*

dream¹ /driːm/ *verb (past **dreamt***
/dremt/ *or **dreamed***)*
1 to imagine things while you are
asleep ► *I dreamt about you last
night.*
2 to imagine something nice ► *He
dreamt of becoming famous.*

dream² *noun*
1 something that you imagine while
you are asleep
2 something nice that you imagine or
that you want to do ► *It is their
dream to visit Australia.*

dreamt /dremt/
the PAST TENSE and PAST PARTICIPLE of the
verb **dream**

dreary /ˈdrɪərɪ/ *adjective (**drearier,
dreariest**)*
very dull, and making you feel sad
► *a dreary afternoon*

drench /drentʃ/ *verb*
to make someone or something
completely wet ► *I was drenched in
the storm.*

dress¹ /dres/ *verb*
1 to put on and wear clothes ► *She
washed and dressed, and ate her*

breakfast. ▶ *He dresses well (=he wears nice clothes).*
2 to put clothes on someone ▶ *to dress oneself*
OPPOSITE (**1** and **2**): **undress**
3 be dressed to be wearing clothes
▶ *They arrived before I was dressed.*
▶ *She was dressed in red (=wearing red clothes).*
4 get dressed to put on clothes
▶ *It will only take a minute to get dressed.*
5 dress up (a) to put on special clothes for an important occasion **(b)** (used about children) to wear someone else's clothes or to wear a DISGUISE as a game

dress² *noun*
1 *(plural dresses)* a piece of clothing covering the body and legs that is worn by women and girls
2 *(no plural)* clothes of a certain type or for a particular purpose
▶ *evening dress*

dresser /'dresə^r/ *noun*
a piece of furniture with shelves for showing plates

dressing /'dresɪŋ/ *noun (no plural)*
a cold liquid made with oil and put on
SALADS

dressing gown /'dresɪŋ ˌgaʊn/ *noun*
a piece of clothing like a coat that you wear only in the house, often on top of the clothes you wear to sleep in

dressing room /'dresɪŋ rʊm/ *noun*
a room where an actor gets ready before going on stage or on television

dressing table /'dresɪŋ ˌteɪbəl/ *noun*
a table with a mirror on top, used for sitting at while you brush your hair, etc.

dressmaker /'dres,meɪkə^r/ *noun*
a woman whose job is to sew clothes for other women
COMPARE: **tailor**

drew /druː/
the PAST TENSE of the verb **draw**

dribble /'drɪbəl/ *verb (present participle dribbling, past dribbled)*
1 if you dribble, liquid in your mouth comes out onto your chin ▶ *The baby's dribbling on your jacket.*
2 to move a ball forward by kicking or BOUNCING it several times in football or BASKETBALL

dried /draɪd/
the PAST TENSE and PAST PARTICIPLE of the verb **dry**

drier /'draɪə^r/ *noun*
another word for **dryer**

drift /drɪft/ *verb*
to float along or be moved by water or wind ▶ *leaves drifting in the wind*

drill¹ /drɪl/ *verb*
to make a hole in something with a special machine ▶ *to drill a hole in the wall*

drill² *noun*
a machine for making holes

drink¹ /drɪŋk/ *verb (past tense drank* /dræŋk/, *past participle drunk* /drʌŋk/)
to take liquid into your mouth and swallow it ▶ *Would you like something to drink?* ▶ *He drank some coffee.*

drink² *noun*
a liquid which you can swallow ▶ *Can I have a drink?* ▶ *a drink of water*

drip /drɪp/ *verb (present participle dripping, past dripped)*
1 (used about a liquid) to fall in drops
2 to have a liquid dripping from it
▶ *The tap was dripping.*

drive¹ /draɪv/ *verb (present participle driving, past tense drove* /drəʊv/, *past participle driven* /'drɪvən/)
to make a vehicle move in the direction you want ▶ *Can you drive?*
▶ *I drove to town yesterday.* ▶ *to drive a car*

drive² *noun*
1 a journey in a road vehicle ▶ *It is a short drive to the village.*

D

D

2 a short road that goes to one house only ➤ *He left his car in the drive.*
3 a system in a computer that can read or store information ➤ *disk drive* ➤ *hard drive*

drive-in /'draɪv ɪn/ *adjective*
(used about restaurants, cinemas, etc.) that you can use without getting out of your car

drivel /'drɪvəl/ *noun (no plural)*
nonsense ➤ *Don't talk drivel!*

driven /'drɪvən/
the PAST PARTICIPLE of the verb **drive**

driver /'draɪvəʳ/ *noun*
a person whose job is to drive a bus, train, etc. ➤ *a train driver*

drive-through /'draɪv θruː/ *adjective*
(used about restaurants, banks, etc.) that you can use without getting out of your car

driveway /'draɪvweɪ/ *noun*
a short road that goes to one house only ➤ *There is room to park two cars in his driveway.*

driving¹ /'draɪvɪŋ/ *noun (no plural)*
the activity or skill of driving a car ➤ *I love driving.* ➤ *His driving is terrible sometimes.*

driving² *adjective*
(used about rain or snow) falling very heavily and at an angle

driving licence /'draɪvɪŋ ˌlaɪsəns/ *noun*
an official piece of paper that shows you are allowed to drive a car

driving test /'draɪvɪŋ ˌtest/ *noun*
an examination that you must pass before you are allowed to drive a car

drizzle /'drɪzəl/ *verb*
be drizzling to be raining very lightly ➤ *It was only drizzling, so I didn't take an umbrella.*

drool /druːl/ *verb*
1 if you drool, the liquid in your mouth comes out onto your chin ➤ *At the sight of food, the dog began to drool.*
2 to show in a silly way that you like someone or something a lot ➤ *Sarah was drooling over the lead singer through the whole concert!*

droop /druːp/ *verb*
to hang down ➤ *The flowers drooped because they had no water.*

drop¹ /drɒp/ *verb (present participle dropping, past dropped)*
1 to fall or let something fall ➤ *The plate dropped from her hands.* ➤ *She dropped the plate.*
2 drop in on someone to visit someone when they are not expecting you

drop² *noun*
a small amount of liquid ➤ *drops of rain*

dropout /'drɒpaʊt/ *noun*
1 a person who does not want a job or possessions because they do not want to work or live in the usual way
2 a person who leaves school or college without completing their course

drought /draʊt/ *noun*
a time when no rain falls and the land becomes very dry

drove /drəʊv/
the PAST TENSE of the verb **drive**

drown /draʊn/ *verb*
to die underwater because you cannot breathe

drowsy /'draʊzɪ/ *adjective (drowsier, drowsiest)*
wanting to sleep ➤ *to feel drowsy*

drug /drʌg/ *noun*
1 a medicine
2 something that people take to change the way they feel or behave. Many drugs are not allowed by law.

drum¹ /drʌm/ *noun*
1 a musical instrument made of a round, hollow box with skin stretched

tightly over it, which you hit to make a sound

2 a metal container for oil, water, etc.

drum[2] *verb (present participle* **drumming***, past* **drummed***)*
to make music on a drum by hitting it

drummer /'drʌməʳ/ *noun*
a person who plays the drums ➤ *The band has a great new drummer.*

drunk[1] /drʌŋk/ *adjective*
having had too much alcohol and so not able to behave properly ➤ *You're drunk! You can't even walk in a straight line!*
OPPOSITE: **sober**

drunk[2]
the PAST PARTICIPLE of the verb **drink**

drunken /'drʌŋkən/ *adjective*
caused by too much alcohol
➤ *drunken behaviour*

dry[1] /draɪ/ *adjective (***drier, driest***)*
1 not containing water or not covered in water ➤ *This coat will keep you dry in the rain.*
2 without any rain ➤ *a dry day*
OPPOSITE (**1** and **2**): **wet**

dry[2] *verb (past* **dried***)*
1 to become dry ➤ *The clothes dried quickly outside.*
2 to make something dry ➤ *to dry your hair*
OPPOSITE (**2**): **wet**

dry-clean /,draɪ 'kli:n/ *verb*
to clean clothes with chemicals instead of water

dry-cleaner's /,draɪ 'kli:nəz/ *noun*
a shop that cleans clothes in a special way using chemicals not water

dryer (also **drier**) /'draɪəʳ/ *noun*
a machine that dries things, especially clothes or hair ➤ *Put the washing in the dryer.*

dual /'dju:əl/ *adjective*
having two of something ➤ *The car has dual controls.*

dual carriageway /,dju:əl 'kærɪdʒweɪ/ *noun*
a wide road on which cars travelling in opposite directions are kept apart by a narrow piece of land

dubious /'dju:biəs/ *adjective*
1 be dubious about something to have doubts about whether something is good or true ➤ *I'm very dubious about the quality of food in this restaurant.*
2 not seeming honest, safe, or true
➤ *a dubious character*

duchess /'dʌtʃəs/ *noun (plural* **duchesses***)*
the title of a woman from a very important family in Britain ➤ *the Duchess of York*
COMPARE: **duke**

duck[1] /dʌk/ *noun*
a bird that swims on water and can be kept by people for its eggs and meat

duck[2] *verb*
to suddenly move your head or body down because you want to avoid being hit by something or seen by someone

duckling /'dʌklɪŋ/ *noun*
a young duck

due /dju:/ *adjective*
1 expected ➤ *The train is due at 5 o'clock.* ➤ *When is the baby due (=expected to be born)?*
2 needing to be paid ➤ *The rent is due at the end of the month.*
3 owing to someone ➤ *Our thanks are due to you for all your help.*
4 due to because of ➤ *This shop is closed due to illness.*
5 be due for something to be expecting to have something soon
➤ *I'm due for a holiday.*
6 be due to do something to be going to do something ➤ *We're due to leave on the 17th.*

duet /dju:'et/ *noun*
a song or piece of music for two people

dug /dʌɡ/
the PAST TENSE and PAST PARTICIPLE of the verb **dig**

duke /djuːk/ *noun*
the title of a man from a very important family in Britain ▶ *the Duke of York*
COMPARE: **duchess**

dull /dʌl/ *adjective*
1 not bright or light ▶ *a dull, cloudy day* ▶ *a dull brown colour*
2 not interesting or clever ▶ *a dull speech* ▶ *a dull man*
SAME MEANING (**2**): **boring**

dumb /dʌm/ *adjective*
not able to speak because you have a problem with your voice

dummy /'dʌmɪ/ *noun (plural dummies)*
a small, rubber object that you put in a baby's mouth to stop it crying

dump¹ /dʌmp/ *verb*
1 to drop something and leave it ▶ *We dumped our bags on the floor.*
2 to throw something away or get rid of it

dump² *noun*
a place where things can be left when people do not want them any more

dune /djuːn/ *noun*
a hill of sand

dung /dʌŋ/ *noun (no plural)*
solid waste from animals, especially large animals ▶ *cow dung*

dungarees /ˌdʌŋɡə'riːz/ *plural noun*
trousers with a piece of material at the top which covers your chest

dungeon /'dʌndʒən/ *noun*
a dark PRISON underneath a castle

dunk /dʌŋk/ *verb*
to quickly put food into a liquid and then take it out again ▶ *He dunked his biscuit in his coffee.*

dunno /'dʌnəʊ/
an informal way of saying "I don't know" ▶ *"Where's Lucy?" "Dunno."*

dupe /djuːp/ *verb (present participle duping, past duped)*
to tell lies in order to make someone believe or do something ▶ *She was duped into giving the robbers her car keys.*

duplicate¹ /'djuːplɪkət/ *adjective*
made to be exactly the same as something else ▶ *a duplicate key*

duplicate² /'djuːplɪkeɪt/ *verb (present participle duplicating, past duplicated)*
to copy or repeat something exactly ▶ *Scientists were unable to duplicate the results in a laboratory.*

duration /djʊ'reɪʃən/ *noun (no plural)*
the length of time that something continues ▶ *They moved to America for the duration of the war.*

during /'djʊərɪŋ/ *preposition*
1 all the time that something is going on ▶ *They swim every day during the holidays.*
2 at some time while something else is happening ▶ *He fell asleep during the lesson.*

dusk /dʌsk/ *noun (no plural)*
the time in the evening when the sun has just gone down

dust¹ /dʌst/ *noun (no plural)*
fine powder or dirt, carried in the air

dust² *verb*
to clean dust from something ▶ *I dust in the living room every morning.* ▶ *She dusted the table.*

dustbin /'dʌstbɪn/ *noun*
a large metal or plastic container that people keep outside their houses and in which they put things they want to get rid of
COMPARE: **bin**

duster /'dʌstər/ *noun*
a cloth you use to clean DUST from furniture

dust jacket /'dʌst ˌdʒækɪt/ *noun*
the loose cover of a book

dustman /'dʌstmən/ *noun (plural dustmen /-mən/)*
a person whose job is to take away the things inside DUSTBINS

dustpan /'dʌstpæn/ *noun*
a flat container that you use to carry away dust after you have swept the floor

dusty /'dʌsti/ *adjective (dustier, dustiest)*
covered in dust

duty /'dju:ti/ *noun (plural duties)*
1 something you must do because it is right ➤ *You have a duty to look after your family.* ➤ *Everyone has a duty to pay taxes.*
2 off duty (used about people with certain jobs, such as doctors, policemen, or soldiers) not at work or working ➤ *She's off duty tomorrow.*
3 on duty (used about people with certain jobs, such as doctors, policemen, or soldiers) at work or working

duvet /'dju:veɪ/ *noun*
a thick, warm cover with feathers inside it, that you put on a bed
COMPARE: **bedspread**

DVD /ˌdi: vi: 'di:/ *noun*
DIGITAL VIDEO DISC; a small, round piece of hard plastic that pictures and sounds are recorded on like a CD

dwarf /dwɔ:f/ *noun*
a person, a plant, or an animal that is much smaller than usual

dwell /dwel/ *verb (past dwelt /dwelt/ or dwelled)*
dwell on something to think or talk for too long about something unpleasant ➤ *I don't want to dwell on all the details of the accident.*

dye¹ /daɪ/ *verb (present participle dyeing, past dyed)*
to give a different colour to something ➤ *She dyed her hair black.*

dye² *noun*
a liquid or powder that is used to change the colour of things

dying /'daɪ-ɪŋ/
the PRESENT PARTICIPLE of the verb **die**

dynamic /daɪ'næmɪk/ *adjective*
full of energy and ideas ➤ *The new teacher is very dynamic.*

dynamite /'daɪnəmaɪt/ *noun (no plural)*
a substance used to make explosions

dynasty /'dɪnəsti/ *noun (plural dynasties)*
in the past, a family of rulers who controlled a country for a long time ➤ *The Ming dynasty ruled China for 300 years.*

Ee

E
a short way of writing the words **east** or **eastern**

each /i:tʃ/ *adjective, pronoun*
1 every one separately ➤ *Each child has an exercise book to work in.* ➤ *Father Christmas gave a present to each of the children.*
2 each other used to show that two people do the same thing one to the other ➤ *The two brothers help each other* (=each brother helps the other).

eager /'i:gə/ *adjective*
very keen to do something ➤ *The girl was eager to show me her photographs.* (adverb: **eagerly**)

eagle /'i:gəl/ *noun*
a large bird that lives in mountain areas and kills small animals for food

ear /ɪə/ *noun*
1 one of the parts of your body with which you hear

2 the part of a plant where the seed is ➤ *an ear of corn*

earache /'ɪəreɪk/ *noun*
a pain inside your ear

early /'ɜːlɪ/ *adjective, adverb (earlier, earliest)*
1 before the usual or agreed time ➤ *We agreed to meet at 7 o'clock, but I was early; I arrived at 6.30.* ➤ *The bus arrived early.*
2 near the beginning of the day or a period of time ➤ *It often rains in the early morning.* ➤ *Do you get up early?*
OPPOSITE (**1** and **2**): **late**
LOOK AT: **soon**

earn /ɜːn/ *verb*
1 to get money for work you do ➤ *She earns a lot of money.*
2 to get something that you deserve because you have worked hard ➤ *You've earned a good rest.*

earnings /'ɜːnɪŋz/ *plural noun*
money that you get when you work ➤ *Average earnings in Europe have risen by 3%.*

earplug /'ɪəplʌg/ *noun*
one of two small pieces of rubber, WAX, etc. that you put into your ears to keep out noise

earring /'ɪərɪŋ/ *noun*
a piece of jewellery you wear on your ear

earshot /'ɪəʃɒt/ *noun*
within earshot, out of earshot near enough or not near enough to hear what someone is saying ➤ *Make sure the kids are out of earshot before you tell her.*

earth /ɜːθ/ *noun (no plural)*
1 (*also* **Earth**) the world in which we live ➤ *The Earth goes round the sun once a year.* ➤ *the longest river on earth*
2 the substance on the ground in which plants can grow ➤ *She planted the seeds in the wet earth.*

earthquake /'ɜːθkweɪk/ *noun*
a strong and sudden shaking of the ground

ease¹ /iːz/ *noun (no plural)*
1 lack of difficulty ➤ *He passed the examination with ease.*
2 **at ease** feeling comfortable and sure of yourself ➤ *She felt at ease in her new school.*

ease² *verb (present participle easing, past eased)*
to make something better ➤ *The medicine eased the pain.*

easel /'iːzəl/ *noun*
a wooden frame to hold a BLACKBOARD or a picture that is being painted

easily /'iːzɪlɪ/ *adverb*
1 without difficulty ➤ *This recipe can be made quickly and easily.*
2 **easily the best, biggest, most stupid, etc.** definitely the best, biggest, most stupid, etc. ➤ *She is easily the most intelligent girl in the class.*

east /iːst/ *noun, adjective, adverb*
1 the direction from which the sun comes up ➤ *Our house faces east.* ➤ *Norwich is in the east of England.* ➤ *the east coast* ➤ *living east of London*
2 **an east wind** a wind that comes from the east

eastbound /'iːstbaʊnd/ *adjective*
travelling or leading towards the east ➤ *An accident on the eastbound section of the motorway is blocking traffic.*

Easter /'iːstəʳ/ *noun*
a special Sunday in March or April when Christians remember Christ's death and His return to life

Easter egg /'iːstər eg/ *noun*
a chocolate egg eaten at Easter

easterly /'iːstəlɪ/ *adjective*
1 towards the east ➤ *The plane was heading in an easterly direction.*

2 (used about wind) blowing from the east

eastern /'iːstən/ *adjective*
in or of the east

eastward /'iːstwəd/ *adjective*
towards the east ▶ *We drove in an eastward direction.*

eastwards /'iːstwədz/ *adverb*
towards the east ▶ *to travel eastwards*

easy /'iːzɪ/ *adjective* (**easier, easiest**)
not difficult; done with no trouble ▶ *It was an easy job and we did it quickly.*
OPPOSITE: **difficult, hard**

easygoing /ˌiːzɪ'gəʊɪŋ/ *adjective*
relaxed and calm, and not often angry or upset ▶ *The boss is very easygoing.*

eat /iːt/ *verb* (*past tense* **ate** /et, eɪt/, *past participle* **eaten** /'iːtn/)
1 to put food into your mouth and swallow it ▶ *Have you eaten your breakfast yet?*
2 to have a meal ▶ *What time did you eat?*

eccentric /ɪk'sentrɪk/ *adjective*
behaving in a way that is unusual but amusing ▶ *an eccentric old woman* (*adverb:* **eccentrically**)

echo¹ /'ekəʊ/ *verb*
(used about a sound) to come back again ▶ *Our voices echoed in the empty room.*

echo² *noun* (*plural* **echoes**)
a sound that comes back to you and that you can hear again ▶ *the echo of our voices in the cave*

eclipse /ɪ'klɪps/ *noun*
a time when the light from the sun or moon is blocked by the moon or Earth

ecological /ˌiːkə'lɒdʒɪkəl/ *adjective*
relating to the way that plants, animals, and people affect their environment ▶ *ecological problems caused by the huge oil spill ▶ an*

ecological study (*adverb:* **ecologically**)

ecologist /ɪ'kɒlədʒɪst/ *noun*
a person who studies ecology

ecology /ɪ'kɒlədʒɪ/ *noun* (*no plural*)
the relationship between plants, animals, people, and the environment, or the study of this relationship ▶ *The ecology of the forest has been damaged by farming.*

economic /ˌiːkə'nɒmɪk, ˌekə-/ *adjective*
connected with industry and trade ▶ *the country's economic problems*

economical /ˌiːkə'nɒmɪkəl, ˌekə-/ *adjective*
cheap ▶ *Going by train is more economical than going by plane.*

economics /ˌiːkə'nɒmɪks, ˌekə-/ *noun* (*no plural*)
the study of the way in which money, goods, and services are produced and used

economist /ɪ'kɒnəmɪst/ *noun*
a person who studies economics

economize /ɪ'kɒnəmaɪz/ *verb* (*present participle* **economizing**, *past* **economized**)
to try to spend less money, or to use a smaller amount of something ▶ *Try to economize on water during this dry period.*

economy /ɪ'kɒnəmɪ/ *noun* (*plural* **economies**)
the system by which a country's industry and trade are controlled ▶ *The country's economy depends on the amount of goods it sells abroad.*

economy class /ɪ'kɒnəmɪ ˌklɑːs/ *noun* (*no plural*)
the cheaper seats on a plane or the cheaper rooms on a ship ▶ *They travelled to America in economy class.* ▶ *an economy class ticket*

ecstasy /'ekstəsɪ/ *noun* (*no plural*)
a feeling of great happiness ▶ *He had a look of ecstasy on his face.*

E

ecstatic /ɪkˈstætɪk/ *adjective*
feeling very happy and excited ▶ *an ecstatic welcome from thousands of people* (adverb: **ecstatically**)

edge /edʒ/ *noun*
1 the outside end of something; the part which is furthest from the middle ▶ *the edge of a plate* ▶ *the water's edge*
2 the sharp, cutting part of a knife or tool
3 on edge nervous and worried

edible /ˈedɪbəl/ *adjective*
able to be eaten, or safe to eat ▶ *edible mushrooms*

edit /ˈedɪt/ *verb*
to prepare a book, film, etc. by correcting mistakes and deciding which parts to keep

edition /ɪˈdɪʃən/ *noun*
a book or newspaper brought out at a particular time

editor /ˈedɪtər/ *noun*
a person who prepares books or newspapers before they are printed

educate /ˈedjʊkeɪt/ *verb (present participle educating, past educated)*
to teach someone, especially in a school or a college ▶ *He was educated in Scotland.* ▶ *Children should be educated about the dangers of smoking.*

educated /ˈedjʊkeɪtɪd/ *adjective*
having a high standard of knowledge and education ▶ *She is a highly educated woman.*

education /ˌedjʊˈkeɪʃən/ *noun (no plural)*
teaching and learning ▶ *The government believes in the importance of education.*

educational /ˌedjʊˈkeɪʃənəl/ *adjective*
helping you to learn ▶ *an educational toy*

eel /iːl/ *noun*
a long fish shaped like a snake

effect /ɪˈfekt/ *noun*
a result ▶ *Eating too many sweets can have a bad effect on your teeth.*

effective /ɪˈfektɪv/ *adjective*
getting the result you want ▶ *These pills are an effective cure for a headache.*
OPPOSITE: **ineffective**

effectively /ɪˈfektɪvlɪ/ *adverb*
in a way that gets the results that you want ▶ *She controlled the class very effectively.*

efficient /ɪˈfɪʃənt/ *adjective*
working well, quickly, and without waste ▶ *an efficient secretary* ▶ *an efficient central heating system* (adverb: **efficiently**)
OPPOSITE: **inefficient**

effluent /ˈefluənt/ *noun (no plural)*
liquid waste that flows out from a factory, etc., usually into the sea or a river

effort /ˈefət/ *noun*
the use of strength or determination in trying to do something ▶ *With a great effort, he pushed open the door.* ▶ *Please put more effort into your school work.*

effortless /ˈefətləs/ *adjective*
done skilfully in a way that seems easy ▶ *She swam with smooth, effortless strokes. (adverb: effortlessly)*

EFL /ˌiː ef ˈel/ *noun (no plural)*
ENGLISH AS A FOREIGN LANGUAGE; the teaching of English to people who speak a different language

e.g. /ˌiː ˈdʒiː/
a short way of writing or saying the words **for example** ▶ *You can try many different sports on this holiday, e.g. sailing, tennis and swimming.*

egg /eg/ *noun*
a round object with a hard shell, from which baby birds, snakes, fish, or insects come; eggs are often eaten as food ▶ *We had eggs for breakfast.*

ego /'iːgəʊ/ noun
the opinion that you have about yourself ▶ Her remarks were not very good for my ego.

eh /eɪ/ interjection
used to ask someone in an informal way to say something again ▶ "You need a modem." "Eh?"

eight /eɪt/ adjective, noun
the number 8

eighteen /eɪ'tiːn/ adjective, noun
the number 18

eighteenth /eɪ'tiːnθ/ adjective
18th

eighth /eɪtθ/ adjective, noun
1 8th
2 one of eight equal parts

eightieth /'eɪtɪ-əθ/ adjective
80th

eighty /'eɪtɪ/ adjective, noun
the number 80

either /'aɪðəʳ, 'iːðəʳ/ conjunction, adverb
1 one or the other of two people or things ▶ Either the father or one of his sons drives the truck.
2 used in sentences with not, when you add another idea ▶ I haven't been to America, or to England either.

eject /ɪ'dʒekt/ verb
1 to make something come out of a machine by pressing a button ▶ Eject the tape and turn it over.
2 to make someone leave a place, using force ▶ A few people were ejected from the club for fighting.

elaborate /ɪ'læbərət/ adjective
full of detail, with a large number of parts

elastic¹ /ɪ'læstɪk/ adjective
able to go back into shape after being stretched or pulled ▶ Rubber is an elastic substance.

elastic² noun
a material which is elastic ▶ a belt made of elastic

elastic band /ɪˌlæstɪk 'bænd/ noun
a thin piece of elastic that is used to hold things together

elbow /'elbəʊ/ noun
the part of your arm which bends it in the middle

elder /'eldəʳ/ adjective
older of two people ▶ Which brother did you see – the elder one or the younger one?

elderly /'eldəlɪ/ adjective
old ▶ My aunt is rather elderly and needs a lot of care.

eldest /'eldɪst/ adjective
oldest of three or more people ▶ his eldest sister

elect /ɪ'lekt/ verb
to choose someone for an official position, usually by voting ▶ She was elected as chairman of the committee.

election /ɪ'lekʃən/ noun
a time when people are chosen for official positions by voting ▶ His party won the last election. ▶ She's standing for election.

electric /ɪ'lektrɪk/ adjective
working by electricity
▶ an electric cooker

electrical /ɪ'lektrɪkəl/ adjective
concerning or using electricity
▶ The cooker isn't working because of an electrical fault.

electrician /ɪˌlek'trɪʃən, ˌelɪk-/ noun
a person whose job is to fit and repair electrical machinery

electricity /ɪˌlek'trɪsətɪ, ˌelɪk-/ noun (no plural)
power that is sent through wires and is used for lighting, heating, and making machines work

electric shock /ɪˌlektrɪk 'ʃɒk/ noun
a sudden, painful feeling you get if you accidentally touch electricity ▶ I got an electric shock from my hairdryer.

E

electrocute /ɪ'lektrəkjuːt/ *verb*
(present participle **electrocuting**,
past **electrocuted**)
to kill someone by passing electricity
through their body ▶ *He accidentally
electrocuted himself when he
touched the damaged wiring.*
▶ *He was electrocuted for the murder
of two children.*

electronic /ɪˌlek'trɒnɪk, ˌelɪk-/
adjective
using electricity and MICROCHIPS
▶ *"E-mail" stands for "electronic
mail".* ▶ *He likes electronic music.*
(adverb: **electronically**)

electronics /ɪˌlek'trɒnɪks, ˌelɪk-/ *noun*
(no plural)
the study of making machinery such
as radios, televisions, and computers

elegant /'elɪgənt/ *adjective*
pleasing and graceful ▶ *elegant
clothes* (adverb: **elegantly**)

element /'elɪmənt/ *noun*
1 one of the very simple substances
from which everything is made ▶ *Gold
and iron are elements.*
2 a part of a whole ▶ *an important
element of the job*

elementary /ˌelɪ'mentri/ *adjective*
simple and easy ▶ *elementary
exercises for the piano*

elephant /'elɪfənt/ *noun*
a very large, grey animal with a long
nose, which lives in hot countries

eleven /ɪ'levən/ *adjective, noun*
the number 11

eleventh /ɪ'levənθ/ *adjective*
11th

elf /elf/ *noun (plural* **elves** /elvz/)
a small fairy with pointed ears

eligible /'elɪdʒəbəl/ *adjective*
1 having the right to do or receive
something ▶ *Students are eligible for
financial support.* ▶ *Are you eligible
to vote?*
2 (used about men) rich, attractive,

and not yet married, and therefore
desirable as a husband ▶ *an eligible
bachelor*

eliminate /ɪ'lɪmɪneɪt/ *verb*
(present participle **eliminating**,
past **eliminated**)
1 to completely destroy or get rid of
something so that it no longer exists
▶ *We can never eliminate crime from
our society.*
2 **be eliminated** to be defeated in a
sports competition, so that you can
no longer take part in it ▶ *We were
eliminated in the very first game.*

else /els/ *adverb*
1 other; different; instead ▶ *If you
don't like eggs, I can cook something
else.*
2 more; as well ▶ *Would you like
something else to eat?*
3 used in some questions and
phrases ▶ *It's not here; where else
can we look?* ▶ *If the train has gone,
how else can we get home?* ▶ *Hold
the bottle in both hands, or else* (=if
not) *you'll drop it.*

elsewhere /els'weə/ *adverb*
in or to some other place ▶ *They left
the village and went elsewhere.*

ELT /ˌiː el 'tiː/ *noun (no plural)*
ENGLISH LANGUAGE TEACHING; the
teaching of English to people whose
first language is not English

elves /elvz/
the plural of **elf**

e-mail¹ (also **email**) /'iː meɪl/ *noun*
1 (no plural) ELECTRONIC MAIL; a system
for sending messages by computer
▶ *Send the file by e-mail.*
2 a message sent by computer
▶ *I got an e-mail from Josie.*

e-mail² (also **email**) *verb*
to send a message to someone using
e-mail ▶ *He e-mailed me about his
visit yesterday.*

embark /ɪm'bɑːk/ *verb*
1 to get on a ship

2 embark on something to start something new or difficult ▶ *She left school to embark on a career as a model.*

embarrass /ɪmˈbærəs/ *verb*
to make someone feel uncomfortable, nervous, or silly in front of other people

embarrassed /ɪmˈbærəst/ *adjective*
nervous or uncomfortable in front of other people ▶ *I feel so embarrassed when I think of how I behaved.*

1 People feel **embarrassed** about small things that they have done which make them appear silly to other people, such as forgetting someone's name or going to a party in the wrong type of clothes. If someone is sorry because they have done something very bad and important, they feel **ashamed**, not **embarrassed**.

2 Do not confuse **embarrassed** (=feeling uncomfortable and nervous) and **embarrassing** (=making someone feel like this): *It was an embarrassing mistake.* ▶ *We all felt very embarrassed.*

embarrassing /ɪmˈbærəsɪŋ/ *adjective*
making you feel nervous or uncomfortable ▶ *an embarrassing moment*
LOOK AT: **embarrassed**

embarrassment /ɪmˈbærəsmənt/ *noun (no plural)*
the feeling of being nervous or uncomfortable in front of other people

embassy /ˈembəsi/ *noun (plural embassies)*
a place where people work for their government, to represent their own country in another country

embrace¹ /ɪmˈbreɪs/ *verb (present participle embracing, past embraced)*
to hold someone in your arms to show that you love them ▶ *The child embraced his parents.* ▶ *The couple embraced.*

embrace² *noun*
holding someone in your arms as a sign of love

embroider /ɪmˈbrɔɪdəʳ/ *verb*
to sew beautiful patterns with a needle on cloth ▶ *to embroider a dress*

embroidery /ɪmˈbrɔɪdəri/ *noun (no plural)*
beautiful patterns sewn with a needle on cloth ▶ *a dress covered with embroidery*

embryo /ˈembriəʊ/ *noun*
an animal or a human that has just begun to develop inside its mother's body

emerald¹ /ˈemərəld/ *adjective, noun*
a bright green colour

emerald² *noun*
a bright green stone which is very valuable

emerge /ɪˈmɜːdʒ/ *verb (present participle emerging, past emerged)*
to come or appear from somewhere hidden ▶ *The baby birds emerged from their eggs.*

emergency /ɪˈmɜːdʒənsi/ *noun (plural emergencies)*
a sudden dangerous event that needs to be dealt with very quickly ▶ *The hospital has to treat emergencies such as car accidents.* ▶ *In an emergency, phone the police.*

emergency services /ɪˈmɜːdʒənsi ˌsɜːvɪsɪz/ *plural noun*
the emergency services official organizations, such as the police, that deal with crimes, fires, or helping people who are badly hurt or very ill

emigrant /ˈemɪgrənt/ *noun*
a person who leaves their own country in order to live in another country
COMPARE: **immigrant**

E

emigrate /ˈemɪgreɪt/ *verb (present participle* **emigrating**, *past* **emigrated**)
to leave your own country to go and live in another country ▶ *Her family emigrated to Australia.*

emigration /ˌemɪˈgreɪʃən/ *noun (no plural)*
the act of leaving your own country to go and live in another country
COMPARE: **immigration**

eminent /ˈemɪnənt/ *adjective*
famous and respected ▶ *an eminent professor*

eminently /ˈemɪnəntlɪ/ *adverb*
very ▶ *He is eminently qualified to do the job.*

emotion /ɪˈməʊʃən/ *noun*
a strong feeling ▶ *Anger and love are very powerful emotions.*

emotional /ɪˈməʊʃənəl/ *adjective*
having strong feelings that you show, sometimes by crying

emotive /ɪˈməʊtɪv/ *adjective*
making people have strong feelings ▶ *Abortion is an emotive issue.*

emperor /ˈempərə^r/ *noun*
a ruler of a big country or several countries

emphasis /ˈemfəsɪs/ *noun (plural* **emphases** /-siːz/)
the special importance that you give to something ▶ *Most schools do not place enough emphasis on health education.*

emphasize /ˈemfəsaɪz/ *verb (present participle* **emphasizing**, *past* **emphasized**)
to show that something is important ▶ *He emphasized the need for hard work.*
SAME MEANING: **stress**

emphatic /ɪmˈfætɪk/ *adjective*
said in a strong way that shows you are certain about something ▶ *His answer was an emphatic "No."*
(adverb: **emphatically**)

empire /ˈempaɪə^r/ *noun*
a group of countries ruled by one government ▶ *the British Empire*

employ /ɪmˈplɔɪ/ *verb*
to give someone a job ▶ *She is employed as a teacher.* ▶ *The hospital employs hundreds of people.*

employee /ɪmˈplɔɪ-iː/ *noun*
a person who works for someone else ▶ *There are ten employees in his firm.*

employer /ɪmˈplɔɪə^r/ *noun*
a person or group that pays people to work for them

employment /ɪmˈplɔɪmənt/ *noun (no plural)*
the state of having paid work ▶ *She's looking for employment.*
OPPOSITE: **unemployment**

empress /ˈemprəs/ *noun (plural* **empresses**)
a female ruler of a country or several countries; the wife of an EMPEROR

empty¹ /ˈemptɪ/ *adjective (* **emptier**, **emptiest**)
having nothing inside ▶ *The house is empty; no one is living there.*
OPPOSITE: **full**

empty² *verb (past* **emptied**)
to take everything out of something ▶ *He emptied the bottle.*
OPPOSITE: **fill**

empty-handed /ˌemptɪ ˈhændɪd/ *adjective*
without getting anything ▶ *The thieves fled the building empty-handed.*

enable /ɪˈneɪbl/ *verb (present participle* **enabling**, *past* **enabled**)
to make someone able to do something ▶ *The new machines enable us to cut and tie up our wheat quickly.*

enchanting /ɪnˈtʃɑːntɪŋ/ *adjective*
very beautiful ▶ *She looked enchanting.*

E

enclose /ɪnˈkləʊz/ *verb (present participle **enclosing**, past **enclosed**)*
1 to surround something completely ► *The football field is enclosed by a wall.*
2 to put something in an envelope with a letter ► *I enclose a copy of my CV for your attention.*

enclosure /ɪnˈkləʊʒəʳ/ *noun*
an area that has a wall or fence all the way around it ► *The animals are kept in a large enclosure.*

encore /ˈɒŋkɔːʳ/ *noun*
a piece of music that performers add at the end of a performance because people ask for more ► *The band played one of their old hits as an encore.*

encounter¹ /ɪnˈkaʊntəʳ/ *verb*
1 to experience something that causes difficulty ► *The engineers encountered more problems when the rainy season began.*
2 to meet someone or something, especially when you are not expecting to meet them ► *I was just 12 years old when I first encountered him.*

encounter² *noun*
a meeting, especially one that is dangerous or not expected ► *a chance encounter with the famous actor, Wilfred Lawson*

encourage /ɪnˈkʌrɪdʒ/ *verb (present participle **encouraging**, past **encouraged**)*
to give praise and support to someone so that they will do something ► *I encouraged her to start playing tennis.*
OPPOSITE: **discourage**

encouragement /ɪnˈkʌrɪdʒmənt/ *noun (no plural)*
praise and support given to someone so that they will do something ► *Her parents gave her lots of encouragement.*

encouraging /ɪnˈkʌrɪdʒɪŋ/ *adjective*
making you feel hopeful and sure of yourself ► *encouraging news*

encyclopaedia /ɪnˌsaɪkləˈpiːdɪə/ *noun*
a book that gives you knowledge about a lot of things and is usually arranged in alphabetical order

end¹ /end/ *noun*
1 the point where something finishes ► *When you get to the end of this road, turn right.* ► *At the end of the lesson, we went home.* ► *at the end of August*
OPPOSITE: **beginning**
2 in the end at last ► *We walked for hours, but we found the house in the end.*

end² *verb*
1 to finish ► *The party ended at midnight.*
OPPOSITE: **begin**
2 end up to finish in a particular way or place although you did not want to ► *We ended up going by bus.*

endanger /ɪnˈdeɪndʒəʳ/ *verb*
to put someone or something in a dangerous or harmful situation ► *Pollution is endangering our planet.*

ending /ˈendɪŋ/ *noun*
the point where a story, film, or play finishes ► *a happy ending*

endless /ˈendləs/ *adjective*
not pleasant and seeming never to end ► *There is endless work to do when you have children in the house.*

endure /ɪnˈdjʊəʳ/ *verb (present participle **enduring**, past **endured**)*
to patiently suffer pain or deal with a difficult situation for a long time ► *The prisoners had to endure months of hunger.*

enemy /ˈenəmɪ/ *noun (plural **enemies**)*
a person or country that is not friendly to you or wants to harm you ► *He's made a lot of enemies at school.*

E

energetic /ˌenəˈdʒetɪk/ *adjective*
very active ▶ *an energetic tennis player*

energy /ˈenədʒi/ *noun (no plural)*
1 the ability to be active and do a lot without feeling tired ▶ *I have no energy left after playing football.*
2 the power that makes machines work or gives heat ▶ *Coal provides energy for lighting the factory.*

enforce /ɪnˈfɔːs/ *verb (present participle* **enforcing***, past* **enforced***)*
to make people obey a rule or law ▶ *We are finding it difficult to enforce the "no smoking" rule.*

engaged /ɪnˈɡeɪdʒd/ *adjective*
1 busy or being used ▶ *The telephone number you want is engaged; try again in a few minutes.*
2 having promised to marry someone ▶ *My brother is engaged to Anne, and they are getting married next year.*

engagement /ɪnˈɡeɪdʒmənt/ *noun*
1 a promise to marry someone ▶ *My brother has just told me about his engagement to Anne.*
2 an arrangement to go somewhere or meet someone ▶ *I'm unable to come because I have another engagement.*

engine /ˈendʒɪn/ *noun*
a machine that uses petrol, oil, gas, electricity, or steam and makes things work or move ▶ *a car engine*

engine driver /ˈendʒɪn ˌdraɪvəʳ/ *noun*
a person who drives a train

engineer /ˌendʒɪˈnɪəʳ/ *noun*
a person who is trained to plan and build machines, roads, bridges, etc.

engineering /ˌendʒɪˈnɪərɪŋ/ *noun (no plural)*
the science or job of an engineer ▶ *He is studying engineering at college.*

English¹ /ˈɪŋɡlɪʃ/ *noun (no plural)*
the language that is spoken in Great Britain, the United States, Canada, Australia, etc.

English² *adjective*
1 connected with the English language ▶ *an English course*
2 of, about, or from England ▶ *the English countryside*

engrave /ɪnˈɡreɪv/ *verb (present participle* **engraving***, past* **engraved***)*
to cut words or pictures into metal, stone, or glass ▶ *a silver mug engraved with his name*

engrossed /ɪnˈɡrəʊst/ *adjective*
so interested in something that you do not think of anything else ▶ *He was so engrossed in his work that he forgot about lunch.*

enjoy /ɪnˈdʒɔɪ/ *verb*
1 to get pleasure and happiness from something ▶ *She enjoys listening to music.*
2 enjoy yourself to have a good time ▶ *Did you enjoy yourself at the wedding?*

enjoyable /ɪnˈdʒɔɪəbəl/ *adjective*
giving pleasure or happiness ▶ *an enjoyable weekend*

enjoyment /ɪnˈdʒɔɪmənt/ *noun (no plural)*
pleasure ▶ *I get a lot of enjoyment from my job.*

enlarge /ɪnˈlɑːdʒ/ *verb (present participle* **enlarging***, past* **enlarged***)*
to make something bigger ▶ *to enlarge a photograph*

enormous /ɪˈnɔːməs/ *adjective*
very large ▶ *an enormous plate of food*
SAME MEANING: **gigantic, huge, vast**

enormously /ɪˈnɔːməsli/ *adverb*
very much ▶ *I like Jane enormously.*

enough /ɪˈnʌf/ *adjective, adverb, noun*
as much as is needed ▶ *There isn't enough paper to finish my letter.*

E

▶ *I've used six eggs, but are you sure that's enough?* ▶ *The water isn't warm enough to swim in.*
COMPARE: **ample**

enquire /ɪn'kwaɪəʳ/ *verb (present participle enquiring, past enquired)*
another word for **inquire**

enquiring /ɪn'kwaɪərɪŋ/ *adjective*
another word for **inquiring**

enquiry /ɪn'kwaɪərɪ/ *noun (plural enquiries)*
another word for **inquiry**

enrol /ɪn'rəʊl/ *verb (present participle enrolling, past enrolled)*
to become a member of a particular school, college, class, etc. ▶ *I decided to enrol on the chemistry course.*

enrolment /ɪn'rəʊlmənt/ *noun*
the process of becoming a member of a particular school, college, class, etc.

en route /ˌɒn 'ruːt/ *adverb*
on the way to somewhere ▶ *We bought a bottle of wine en route to the party.*

ensure /ɪn'ʃʊəʳ/ *verb (present participle ensuring, past ensured)*
to make certain that something happens ▶ *Please ensure that you sign the form.*

enter /'entəʳ/ *verb*
1 to go or come into a particular place ▶ *He entered the room quietly.*
2 to become part of a profession or an organization ▶ *He decided to enter the law.*
3 to say that you want to take part in something ▶ *She entered the race and won.*
4 to write down information or include it on a computer ▶ *Please enter your name on this list.*

enterprise /'entəpraɪz/ *noun*
1 *(no plural)* the ability to think of and try new things, especially in business

▶ *He showed a lot of enterprise in the way he solved the problem.*
2 a company or business ▶ *She got a loan to set up her new enterprise.*

enterprising /'entəpraɪzɪŋ/ *adjective*
able and willing to do things that are new or difficult ▶ *One enterprising young man started his own radio station.*

entertain /ˌentə'teɪn/ *verb*
1 to do something to amuse or interest people ▶ *He entertained us with stories about life abroad.*
2 to give food and drink to guests ▶ *We entertain a lot at weekends.*

entertainer /ˌentə'teɪnəʳ/ *noun*
a person whose job is to amuse others, for example by telling jokes

entertaining /ˌentə'teɪnɪŋ/ *adjective*
amusing and interesting

entertainment /ˌentə'teɪnmənt/ *noun (no plural)*
activities which amuse or interest people ▶ *For entertainment, we watch television.*

enthral /ɪn'θrɔːl/ *verb (present participle enthralling, past enthralled)*
to keep someone's attention and interest completely ▶ *The kids were absolutely enthralled by the stories.*

enthusiasm /ɪn'θjuːzɪæzəm/ *noun (no plural)*
a strong feeling of being interested in something or wanting to do something ▶ *He is full of enthusiasm for his job.*

enthusiast /ɪn'θjuːzɪæst/ *noun*
a person who is very interested in a particular subject or activity ▶ *My brother is a motorbike enthusiast.*

enthusiastic /ɪnˌθjuːzɪ'æstɪk/ *adjective*
very keen on something or interested in it

E

entice /ɪnˈtaɪs/ verb (present participle **enticing**, past **enticed**)
to persuade someone to do something by offering them something nice ▶ The shops are already enticing customers **with** low prices.

entire /ɪnˈtaɪəʳ/ adjective
whole; complete ▶ The entire class will be there. (adverb: **entirely**)

entitle /ɪnˈtaɪtl/ verb
be entitled to something to have the right to do or have something ▶ You are entitled to have your money back if you are not satisfied.

entrance /ˈentrəns/ noun
1 a place where you go into a building ▶ Where's the entrance **to** the hospital?
2 the arrival or coming in of a person ▶ She made a dramatic entrance down the grand staircase.

entranced /ɪnˈtrɑːnst/ adjective
feeling great pleasure because of something very beautiful which has taken all your attention ▶ We were entranced by her singing.

entrance examination /ˈentrəns ɪgzæmɪˌneɪʃən/ noun
an examination you have to pass before you can go to a particular school or college

entrant /ˈentrənt/ noun
a person who enters a competition, university, or profession

entrepreneur /ˌɒntrəprəˈnɜːʳ/ noun
a person who starts a company

entrust /ɪnˈtrʌst/ verb
to make someone responsible for something ▶ I was entrusted **with** the task of looking after the money.

entry /ˈentrɪ/ noun
1 (no plural) the right to enter a building or country ▶ The sign says "No Entry".
2 (plural **entries**) a person or thing entered for a race or competition

▶ The winning entry was a beautiful photo.

envelope /ˈenvələʊp, ˈɒn-/ noun
a folded paper cover for a letter

envious /ˈenvɪəs/ adjective
wishing you had something that belongs to someone else ▶ He was envious **of** my new car.
SAME MEANING: **jealous**

environment /ɪnˈvaɪərənmənt/ noun
1 the conditions in which you live and work, that affect your life ▶ Children need a happy home environment.
2 the world of land, sea, and air that you live in ▶ Cutting down too many trees destroys the environment.

environmental /ɪnˌvaɪərənˈmentl/ adjective
relating to the world of land, sea, and air that you live in ▶ environmental pollution

environmentalist /ɪnˌvaɪərənˈmentəlɪst/ noun
a person who tries to protect the environment

environmentally friendly /ɪnˌvaɪərənmentəlɪ ˈfrendlɪ/ adjective
(used about products) not containing things that will harm the environment

envisage /ɪnˈvɪzɪdʒ/ verb (present participle **envisaging**, past **envisaged**)
to think that something is likely to happen in the future ▶ I don't envisage any major problems.

envy¹ /ˈenvɪ/ noun (no plural)
a feeling of anger or bitterness because you want something that someone else has got ▶ He was filled with envy because Richard passed the examination and he did not.
SAME MEANING: **jealousy**

envy² verb (past **envied**)
to wish that you had what someone else has got ▶ I envied his success.

E

epic¹ /'epɪk/ *adjective*
very long, exciting, or impressive ➤ *an epic journey in the Himalayas* ➤ *an epic novel*

epic² *noun*
a long book, poem, or film containing exciting adventures ➤ *Homer's epic, "The Odyssey"*

epidemic /ˌepɪ'demɪk/ *noun*
an illness that spreads quickly to a lot of people

episode /'epɪsəʊd/ *noun*
one of the parts of a television or radio story that is broadcast separately ➤ *Tonight's episode of Star Trek starts at 6.30.*

epitaph /'epɪtɑːf/ *noun*
something written about a dead person, often on the stone over their GRAVE ➤ *"He did his best" would be my epitaph.*

equal¹ /'iːkwəl/ *adjective*
the same in size, number, or value ➤ *Divide the cake into four equal parts.* ➤ *Women want equal pay to men.*

equal² *noun*
a person who has the same ability and rights as someone else ➤ *All people should be treated as equals by the law.*

equal³ *verb (present participle equalling, past equalled)*
1 to be the same as something else in number or amount ➤ *Three plus five equals eight (3 + 5 = 8).*
2 to be as good as someone or something else ➤ *None of us can equal Sarah – she's always top of the class.*

equality /ɪ'kwɒlətɪ/ *noun (no plural)*
having the same ability and rights ➤ *Women want equality with men.*

equalize /'iːkwəlaɪz/ *verb (present participle equalizing, past equalized)*
to get a point or goal in a game so

that you have the same number of points or goals as your opponents ➤ *Spain equalized in the 75th minute.*

equally /'iːkwəlɪ/ *adverb*
1 just as much ➤ *Both teams are equally capable of winning.*
2 in equal parts or amounts ➤ *We'll divide the work equally.*
3 in a way that is fair ➤ *We have to try to treat everyone equally.*

equation /ɪ'kweɪʒən/ *noun*
a statement in mathematics showing that two quantities are equal, for example $2y + 4 = 10$

equator /ɪ'kweɪtəʳ/ *noun*
an imaginary line that runs round the middle of the Earth and divides it into north and south

equip /ɪ'kwɪp/ *verb (present participle equipping, past equipped)*
to give someone things that are useful for doing something ➤ *Our school is equipped with a radio.*

equipment /ɪ'kwɪpmənt/ *noun (no plural)*
the things which are used for a particular activity ➤ *office equipment*

equivalent¹ /ɪ'kwɪvələnt/ *adjective*
equal in amount, value, or rank to something or someone else ➤ *The workers received a bonus equivalent to two months' pay.*

equivalent² *noun*
something that has the same value, size, meaning, etc. as something else ➤ *Some French words have no equivalent in English.*

era /'ɪərə/ *noun*
a period of time in history that is different from other periods ➤ *the post-war era*

eradicate /ɪ'rædɪkeɪt/ *verb (present participle eradicating, past eradicated)*
to completely get rid of something such as an illness or a social problem

➤ *We want to eradicate nuclear weapons by 2030.*

erase /ɪˈreɪz/ *verb (present participle* **erasing,** *past* **erased)**
to completely remove written or recorded information ➤ *I erased the file from the computer.*

erect¹ /ɪˈrekt/ *adjective*
upright; standing straight ➤ *He stood erect and saluted the general.*

erect² *verb*
to fit something together and make it stand up ➤ *They erected the tent.*

erode /ɪˈrəʊd/ *verb (present participle* **eroding,** *past* **eroded)**
(used about land) to wear, or be gradually worn away, due to water or the weather ➤ *The coastline is being eroded by the sea.*

erosion /ɪˈrəʊʒən/ *noun (no plural)*
the gradual destruction of land by the weather or by water ➤ *Planting trees will help prevent soil erosion.*

erotic /ɪˈrɒtɪk/ *adjective*
involving or causing feelings of sexual desire ➤ *an erotic dream*
(adverb: **erotically)**

errand /ˈerənd/ *noun*
a short journey made to do something useful or to buy something

erratic /ɪˈrætɪk/ *adjective*
changing often without any reason, or moving in an irregular way
➤ *the England team's rather erratic performance in the World Cup*
(adverb: **erratically)**

error /ˈerəʳ/ *noun*
a mistake ➤ *The doctor's error was very serious.*

erupt /ɪˈrʌpt/ *verb*
(used about a VOLCANO) to explode and throw out fire, ash, and smoke

eruption /ɪˈrʌpʃən/ *noun*
a situation in which a VOLCANO explodes and throws out fire, ash, and smoke

escalator /ˈeskəleɪtəʳ/ *noun*
a set of moving stairs that can take you up or down without you having to walk

escape¹ /ɪˈskeɪp/ *verb (present participle* **escaping,** *past* **escaped)**
1 to get free from a place where you are kept by force ➤ *He escaped from prison.*
2 to get out of a hole or crack in a container ➤ *Gas escaped from the pipes.*

escape² *noun*
the act of escaping ➤ *The prisoner made his escape at night.*

escort¹ /ɪˈskɔːt/ *verb*
to go with someone in order to protect them ➤ *A group of soldiers escorted the President.*

escort² /ˈeskɔːt/ *noun*
people, cars, planes, etc. that travel with someone to protect them
➤ *an escort of soldiers*

ESL /ˌiː es ˈel/ *noun (no plural)*
ENGLISH AS A SECOND LANGUAGE; the teaching of English to students whose first language is not English, but who live in an English-speaking country

especially /ɪˈspeʃəli/ *adverb*
1 very; more than usual ➤ *She is especially good at science*
2 most of all ➤ *I would like a bicycle, especially a blue one.*

essay /ˈeseɪ/ *noun*
a piece of writing on a subject ➤ *She wrote an essay on "My Family".*

essential /ɪˈsenʃəl/ *adjective*
necessary; very important ➤ *If you travel abroad, it is essential that you have the right papers.*

essentials /ɪˈsenʃəlz/ *plural noun*
things that are important or necessary ➤ *We only have enough money for essentials like food and clothing.*

E

establish /ɪˈstæblɪʃ/ *verb*
1 to start a company, an organization, etc., especially one that will exist for a long time ▶ *He established the business in 1999.*
2 to find out facts or prove that something is true ▶ *We have been unable to establish the cause of the accident.*

establishment /ɪˈstæblɪʃmənt/ *noun*
a place for education, training, or RESEARCH ▶ *an educational establishment*

estate /ɪˈsteɪt/ *noun*
a large piece of land, usually with a house or group of buildings on it

estate agent /ɪˈsteɪt ˌeɪdʒənt/ *noun*
a person whose job is to arrange the buying and selling of houses and land

estate car /ɪˈsteɪt ˌkɑːʳ/ *noun*
a large car with a door at the back

estimate¹ /ˈestɪmeɪt/ *verb* (present participle **estimating**, past **estimated**)
to make a reasonable guess about the size or amount of something ▶ *They estimated that the house cost £95,000.*

estimate² /ˈestɪmət/ *noun*
a guess about the size or amount of something

etc. /etˈsetərə/ *adverb*
a short way of writing **etcetera**; and so on ▶ *There are lots of things to buy – tea, sugar, bread, etc.*

eternal /ɪˈtɜːnəl/ *adjective*
continuing for ever ▶ *eternal love* (adverb: **eternally**)

eternity /ɪˈtɜːnɪti/ *noun*
1 (no plural) time that does not end, especially the time after you die
2 an eternity a very long time ▶ *It was an eternity before the phone rung.*

ethical /ˈeθɪkəl/ *adjective*
connected with principles of what is right and wrong ▶ *Research on animals raises difficult ethical questions.* (adverb: **ethically**)

ethics /ˈeθɪks/ *plural noun*
rules of behaviour used to decide what is right and wrong ▶ *the ethics of scientific research*

ethnic /ˈeθnɪk/ *adjective*
relating to a particular race of people ▶ *an ethnic minority*

etiquette /ˈetɪket/ *noun (no plural)*
the rules of polite behaviour

EU /ˌiː ˈjuː/ *noun*
the EU the EUROPEAN UNION

euphemism /ˈjuːfəmɪzəm/ *noun*
a polite word or phrase that you use to avoid saying something that might offend people ▶ *"Passed away" is often used as a euphemism for "died".*

euro /ˈjʊərəʊ/ *noun*
a unit of money intended to be used by all the European Union countries

European¹ /ˌjʊərəˈpiːən/ *adjective*
from or connected with a country in Europe

European² *noun*
a person from a country in Europe

European Union /ˌjʊərəpiːən ˈjuːnjən/ *noun*
the European Union a political and economic organization of European countries

euthanasia /ˌjuːθəˈneɪzɪə/ *noun (no plural)*
the practice of killing very old or ill people in a painless way, so that they will not suffer any more ▶ *Euthanasia is illegal in most countries.*

evacuate /ɪˈvækjʊeɪt/ *verb (present participle **evacuating**, past **evacuated**)*
to move people from a dangerous place to a safer place

evacuation /ɪˌvækjʊˈeɪʃən/ noun
the act of moving people from a dangerous place to a safer place
▶ the evacuation of children from the war zone

evaluate /ɪˈvæljʊeɪt/ verb
(present participle **evaluating**, past **evaluated**)
to carefully consider something or someone in order to decide how good or bad they are ▶ Teachers meet regularly to evaluate the progress of each student.

evaporate /ɪˈvæpəreɪt/ verb
(present participle **evaporating**, past **evaporated**)
if a liquid evaporates, or if something evaporates it, it changes into steam
▶ Salt is produced by evaporating sea water.

evaporation /ɪˌvæpəˈreɪʃən/ noun
(no plural)
the process of removing water from something, usually by heating it

eve /iːv/ noun
the night or day before a religious holiday or important event
▶ Christmas Eve ▶ There were demonstrations on the eve of the election.

even¹ /ˈiːvən/ adjective
1 flat and smooth ▶ an even surface
OPPOSITE: **uneven**
2 equal ▶ He won the first game and I won the second, so we're even.
3 even number a number that can be divided exactly by two – for example, 2, 4, and 6

even² adverb
1 used to show when something is surprising or unusual ▶ Even Peter helped us, and he's usually very busy.
2 used when you are comparing two things to make the second seem stronger ▶ Yesterday it rained hard, and today it's raining even harder.

evening /ˈiːvnɪŋ/ noun
the end of the afternoon and the early part of night

evenly /ˈiːvnli/ adverb
equally ▶ Divide the sweets evenly among the three boys (=give the same number to each boy).

event /ɪˈvent/ noun
something that happens, often something important or unusual
▶ What events do you remember from your schooldays?

eventful /ɪˈventfəl/ adjective
full of interesting or important events
▶ an eventful holiday

eventually /ɪˈventʃəli/ adverb
at last; in the end ▶ I looked everywhere for my glasses, and eventually found them under my chair.

ever /ˈevər/ adverb
1 at any time ▶ Have you ever been abroad? ▶ She used to sing well, but now she sings better than ever.
2 ever since since a particular time long ago ▶ I have lived here ever since I was a child.

every /ˈevri/ adjective
each one; not missing out one ▶ I have read every book on the shelf.

everybody /ˈevribɒdi/ (also **everyone**) pronoun
every person ▶ Everybody wants to watch the match.

Remember that **everybody** and **everyone** are singular words, like **he** or **she**, so you must use them with a singular verb ending:
Everyone knows that sugar is bad for your teeth.

everyday /ˌevriˈdeɪ/ adjective
usual or ordinary ▶ Worries are just part of everyday life.

everyone /ˈevriwʌn/ (also **everybody**) pronoun
every person ▶ She likes everyone in her class. ▶ Everyone agreed that

the concert was a success.
LOOK AT: **everybody**

everything /'evrɪθɪŋ/ pronoun
all things ► *I got everything I needed
at the market.*

everywhere /'evrɪweəʳ/ adverb
in or to every place ► *I looked
everywhere for my watch, but I
couldn't find it.*

evidence /'evɪdəns/ noun (no plural)
words or things that prove something
► *What evidence do you have to
support your theory?*

evident /'evɪdənt/ adjective
plain or clear ► *Her love of animals is
evident.* (adverb: **evidently**)
SAME MEANING: **obvious**

evil /'iːvəl/ adjective
wicked and causing harm ► *In the
film, the good queen saves her from
an evil enemy.*

evolution /ˌiːvəˈluːʃən/ noun (no
plural)
the gradual development of
something over a long period of time,
especially types of plant and animal
► *the evolution of man*

evolve /ɪˈvɒlv/ verb (present
participle **evolving**, past **evolved**)
to develop gradually over a long
period of time ► *a political system
that has evolved over several
centuries*

exact /ɪgˈzækt/ adjective
completely correct ► *Can you tell me
the exact time?*

exactly /ɪgˈzæktlɪ/ adverb
1 with complete correctness ► *Where
exactly do you live?*
2 used to agree with someone ► *"So
you think the school will have to
close?" "Exactly."*
SAME MEANING (**1** and **2**): **precisely**

exaggerate /ɪgˈzædʒəreɪt/ verb
(present participle **exaggerating**,
past **exaggerated**)

to make something seem bigger,
better, worse, etc. than it really is
► *He exaggerated when he said the
dog was the size of a horse.*

exaggeration /ɪgˌzædʒəˈreɪʃən/
noun
a statement saying that something is
bigger, better, worse, etc. than it
really is ► *It would be an
exaggeration to call it a disaster.*

exam /ɪgˈzæm/ noun
an examination ► *Well done for
passing your science exam!*

examination /ɪgˌzæmɪˈneɪʃən/ noun
1 an official test of knowledge in a
subject ► *Please arrive on time for all
examinations.*
2 a careful look at someone or
something ► *a medical examination*

examine /ɪgˈzæmɪn/ verb (present
participle **examining**, past **examined**)
1 to look at someone or something
closely and carefully ► *The doctor
examined my ears.*
2 to ask someone questions to be
sure that they know something ► *The
teacher will examine the students on
everything they have studied this
year.*

example /ɪgˈzɑːmpəl/ noun
1 one thing taken from a number of
things of the same kind to show what
the other things are like ► *I showed
my new employer some examples of
my work.*
2 for example used to give an
example of something which makes
your meaning clearer ► *Heavy rains
cause many problems – for example,
flooding the roads.*

exasperate /ɪgˈzɑːspəreɪt/ verb
(present participle **exasperating**,
past **exasperated**)
to annoy someone or make them
angry

exasperation /ɪgˌzɑːspəˈreɪʃən/ noun
(no plural)

E

a feeling of great annoyance or anger ▶ *She hit the computer in exasperation.*

excavate /'ekskəveɪt/ *verb (present participle **excavating**, past **excavated**)*
to dig up the ground, especially in order to find things from the past ▶ *archaeologists excavating an ancient city*

excavation /,ekskə'veɪʃən/ *noun*
the activity of digging up the ground, especially in order to find things from the past ▶ *the archaeological excavation of an ancient city*

exceed /ɪk'siːd/ *verb*
to be more than a particular amount ▶ *Lorries which exceed this weight cannot cross the bridge.*

excel /ɪk'sel/ *verb (present participle **excelling**, past **excelled**)*
1 to do something very well, or much better than most people ▶ *I never excelled **at** sport.*
2 excel yourself to do something even better than usual

excellence /'eksələns/ *noun (no plural)*
the quality of being very good at doing something ▶ *She won a prize for sporting excellence.*

excellent /'eksələnt/ *adjective*
very good ▶ *This is excellent work, Peter. (adverb: **excellently**)*
SAME MEANING: **outstanding**

except /ɪk'sept/ *preposition*
apart from; not including ▶ *I washed all your clothes except your new shirt.*

exception /ɪk'sepʃən/ *noun*
1 something that is different from what is usually expected ▶ *Most children like sweets, but she is the exception – she hates them!*
2 with the exception of apart from ▶ *They'd all been there before, with the exception of Jim.*

exceptional /ɪk'sepʃənəl/ *adjective*
of unusually high ability ▶ *an exceptional pupil*

exceptionally /ɪk'sepʃənəlɪ/ *adverb*
unusually or especially ▶ *an exceptionally cold winter*

excess /'ekses/ *noun, adjective (plural **excesses**)*
more than is usual or allowed ▶ *You have to pay for excess luggage on a plane.*

excessive /ɪk'sesɪv/ *adjective*
too much or too great ▶ *Excessive dieting can be very harmful. (adverb: **excessively**)*

exchange¹ /ɪks'tʃeɪndʒ/ *verb (present participle **exchanging**, past **exchanged**)*
to give something to someone in return for something else ▶ *This skirt is too small. Maybe the shop will exchange it.*

exchange² *noun*
1 the giving of something in return for something else ▶ *an exchange of prisoners between two countries*
2 in exchange for in place of something that you give to someone ▶ *I gave him the book in exchange for a record.*

exchange rate /ɪks'tʃeɪndʒ ,reɪt/ *noun*
the value of the money of one country compared to that of another country

excite /ɪk'saɪt/ *verb (present participle **exciting**, past **excited**)*
to make someone feel strong feelings of enjoyment or pleasure ▶ *The games excited the children and they all started to shout.*

excited /ɪk'saɪtɪd/ *adjective*
having strong feelings of enjoyment or pleasure; not calm

excitement /ɪk'saɪtmənt/ *noun (no plural)*

the condition of being excited ➤ *The crowd's excitement grew as the match drew to a close* (=got near the end).

exciting /ɪkˈsaɪtɪŋ/ *adjective*
able to make someone excited ➤ *exciting news*

exclaim /ɪkˈskleɪm/ *verb*
to speak loudly and suddenly in surprise ➤ *"Look – there's James on the television!" exclaimed Peter.*

exclamation /ˌekskləˈmeɪʃən/ *noun*
words showing a sudden, strong feeling

exclamation mark /ˌekskləˈmeɪʃən mɑːk/ *noun*
the sign (!) used in writing to show a strong feeling like surprise, or when calling someone ➤ *Come here!* ➤ *I don't believe it!*

exclude /ɪkˈskluːd/ *verb* (present participle **excluding**, past **excluded**)
to stop someone or something from doing something or joining something ➤ *We had to exclude John from the team because he hurt his leg.*
OPPOSITE: **include**

excluding /ɪkˈskluːdɪŋ/ *preposition*
not including ➤ *The shop is open every day, excluding Sundays.*
OPPOSITE: **including**

exclusive¹ /ɪkˈskluːsɪv/ *adjective*
1 expensive and only available to certain people ➤ *an exclusive London club*
2 used or done by only one person or group, and not shared ➤ *an exclusive interview with President Mandela*

exclusive² *noun*
a news story that is only in one newspaper, magazine, etc.

exclusively /ɪkˈskluːsɪvli/ *adverb*
only ➤ *This offer is exclusively available to club members.*

excursion /ɪkˈskɜːʃən/ *noun*
a short journey made for pleasure ➤ *We went on an excursion to the sea.*

excuse¹ /ɪkˈskjuːz/ *verb* (present participle **excusing**, past **excused**)
1 to forgive ➤ *Please excuse this untidy room.*
2 to give someone permission not to do something, or permission to leave ➤ *The teacher excused her from going to the school's sports day.*
3 **Excuse me** used to get someone's attention, leave a group of people, or say sorry for doing something slightly rude ➤ *Excuse me, but have you got the time, please?* ➤ *Excuse me, I didn't mean to step on your foot!*

excuse² /ɪkˈskjuːs/ *noun*
a reason given when you ask someone to forgive you for a mistake or bad behaviour ➤ *Have you any excuse for not finishing the work on time?*

execute /ˈeksɪkjuːt/ *verb* (present participle **executing**, past **executed**)
to kill someone as a punishment decided by law

execution /ˌeksɪˈkjuːʃən/ *noun*
a killing which is a punishment decided by law

executive /ɪgˈzekjʊtɪv/ *noun*
an important manager in a company ➤ *a sales executive*

exercise¹ /ˈeksəsaɪz/ *noun*
1 (no plural) the use of your body to make it stronger or more healthy ➤ *Running is good exercise.*
2 a movement of your body which you do again and again in order to get fit or practise a skill ➤ *Have you done your exercises yet?*
3 a set of questions given in school to help students practise something ➤ *Please do Exercise 3 on page 4.*

exercise² *verb* (present participle **exercising**, past **exercised**)

to use your body or part of it in order
to be healthy ► *The doctor told him
to exercise more.*

exercise book /'eksəsaɪz ˌbʊk/ *noun*
a book with empty pages in which
pupils do their work for school

exhaust¹ /ɪɡ'zɔːst/ *verb*
to make someone very tired ► *The
long journey exhausted her.*

exhaust² *noun*
1 (*no plural*) burnt gas that comes
out from the back of a car
2 a pipe that lets burnt gas out of the
back of a car

exhausted /ɪɡ'zɔːstɪd/ *adjective*
very tired ► *I'm exhausted after that
walk.*

exhausting /ɪɡ'zɔːstɪŋ/ *adjective*
making you very tired ► *Looking after
babies is exhausting.*

exhibit /ɪɡ'zɪbɪt/ *verb*
to show objects, e.g. paintings, in
public ► *She exhibited her paintings
at our school.*

exhibition /ˌeksɪ'bɪʃən/ *noun*
a public show of objects, e.g.
paintings ► *an art exhibition*

exhilarated /ɪɡ'zɪləreɪtɪd/ *adjective*
feeling very happy and excited ► *The
team were exhilarated at their
success.*

exhilarating /ɪɡ'zɪləreɪtɪŋ/ *adjective*
making you feel very happy and
excited ► *an exhilarating helicopter
ride*

exile¹ /'eksaɪl/ *noun*
a person who, as a punishment, often
for political reasons, is not allowed to
live in their own country

exile² *verb* (*present participle* **exiling**,
past **exiled**)
to send a person away from their own
country as a punishment

exist /ɪɡ'zɪst/ *verb*
to be ► *The house where I was born
no longer exists.*

existence /ɪɡ'zɪstəns/ *noun* (*no
plural*)
the state of being ► *The elephant is
the largest land animal in existence.*

existing /ɪɡ'zɪstɪŋ/ *adjective*
being used now ► *The existing
computer network is out of date.*

exit /'eksɪt/ *noun*
a door through which you can leave a
place ► *Where is the exit?*
SAME MEANING: **way out**

exotic /ɪɡ'zɒtɪk/ *adjective*
unusual and exciting, especially
because of a connection with a
distant country ► *an exotic flower
from Africa*

expand /ɪk'spænd/ *verb*
to become larger or make something
larger ► *The business has expanded
from having one office to having ten.*

expansion /ɪk'spænʃən/ *noun*
an increase in size

expect /ɪk'spekt/ *verb*
1 to think that something will happen
► *"Do you expect to win the race?"
"Yes, I expect I will win."*
**2 be expecting someone or
something** to feel sure that someone
or something will arrive, often
because you have arranged it ► *We're
expecting them for lunch.*
3 be expecting (a baby) to be going
to have a baby
4 to ask strongly for certain
behaviour ► *Visitors to the hospital
are expected not to smoke.*

expectant /ɪk'spektənt/ *adjective*
hoping that something good will
happen ► *Hundreds of expectant fans
waited for him to appear.* (*adverb:*
expectantly)

expectation /ˌekspek'teɪʃən/ *noun*
a strong belief or hope that
something will happen ► *He had no
expectation of passing the exam.
► Many refugees arrive in the country
with high expectations.*

expedition /ˌekspəˈdɪʃən/ *noun*
a long, difficult journey, usually to find out something ➤ *an expedition to find where the River Nile starts*

expel /ɪkˈspel/ *verb (present participle* **expelling***, past* **expelled***)*
to force someone to leave a place, especially a school ➤ *The pupils were expelled for stealing.*

expense /ɪkˈspens/ *noun*
money spent on something ➤ *travelling expenses* ➤ *Having a car is a big expense.*

expensive /ɪkˈspensɪv/ *adjective*
costing a lot of money ➤ *It is expensive to travel by plane.*
OPPOSITE: **cheap, inexpensive**
SAME MEANING: **costly, dear**

experience¹ /ɪkˈspɪərɪəns/ *noun*
1 something that happens to you ➤ *The accident was an experience she will never forget.*
2 *(no plural)* work you have done before of the same sort ➤ *a teacher with five years' experience*

experience² *verb (present participle* **experiencing***, past* **experienced***)*
to have something happen to you ➤ *to experience fear*

experienced /ɪkˈspɪərɪənst/ *adjective*
good at something because you have done it before ➤ *an experienced doctor*
OPPOSITE: **inexperienced**

experiment¹ /ɪkˈsperɪmənt/ *noun*
a careful test done to see whether something is true ➤ *a scientific experiment*

experiment² /ɪkˈsperɪment/ *verb*
to do a careful test to see if something is true ➤ *We experimented by putting oil and water together, and we saw that they did not mix.*

expert¹ /ˈekspɜːt/ *noun*
a person who has special skill in something or knowledge of

something ➤ *an expert on Stone Age pottery* ➤ *a cookery expert*

expert² *adjective*
having special skill in something or knowledge of something ➤ *expert advice* ➤ *an expert cook*

expertise /ˌekspɜːˈtiːz/ *noun (no plural)*
special skills or knowledge ➤ *legal expertise*

expire /ɪkˈspaɪə/ *verb (present participle* **expiring***, past* **expired***)*
(used about something which lasts for a period of time) to be unable to be used any longer ➤ *My passport expires in two weeks.*

explain /ɪkˈspleɪn/ *verb*
to make something clear or give the reason for something ➤ *Can you explain what this word means?* ➤ *I explained to him that I'd missed the bus.*

explanation /ˌekspləˈneɪʃən/ *noun*
something that makes something clear or gives the reason for it ➤ *What is your explanation for being late?*

explicit /ɪkˈsplɪsɪt/ *adjective*
1 very clear and easy to understand ➤ *Could you be more explicit?*
2 showing or describing all the details of sex or violence ➤ *explicit love scenes*
(adverb: **explicitly**)

explode /ɪkˈspləʊd/ *verb (present participle* **exploding***, past* **exploded***)*
to burst with a loud noise and force ➤ *A bomb exploded there last night.*

exploit /ɪkˈsplɔɪt/ *verb*
to unfairly use someone's ideas, time, work, etc. without rewarding them for it ➤ *The company was accused of exploiting workers.*

exploits /ˈeksplɔɪts/ *plural noun*
brave or interesting things that someone has done ➤ *My father loved telling us about his exploits in the army.*

E

exploration /ˌeksplə'reɪʃən/ *noun*
a journey through a place to learn about it

explore /ɪk'splɔː^r/ *verb (present participle* **exploring***, past* **explored***)*
to find out about a place by travelling through it ➤ *Have you really explored your nearest town?*

explorer /ɪk'splɔːrə^r/ *noun*
a person who travels into an unknown area to find out about it

explosion /ɪk'spləʊʒən/ *noun*
a sudden, loud noise caused, for example, by a bomb ➤ *The explosion was caused by a burst gas pipe.*

explosive¹ /ɪk'spləʊsɪv/ *adjective*
1 likely to cause an explosion ➤ *an explosive mixture of gases*
2 likely to make people become violent or angry ➤ *an explosive situation*

explosive² *noun*
a substance that can cause an explosion

export¹ /ɪk'spɔːt/ *verb*
to send things out of the country to be sold abroad ➤ *India exports cloth.*
COMPARE: **import**

export² /'ekspɔːt/ *noun*
something that is sent to another country to be sold ➤ *Fruit is one of South Africa's exports.*
COMPARE: **import**

exporter /ɪk'spɔːtə^r/ *noun*
a person or company that sells things to other countries
COMPARE: **importer**

expose /ɪk'spəʊz/ *verb (present participle* **exposing***, past* **exposed***)*
to uncover something ➤ *You shouldn't expose your skin to the sun.*

exposure /ɪk'spəʊʒə^r/ *noun*
1 (*no plural*) the act of putting someone into a harmful situation without any protection ➤ *Exposure to*

tobacco smoke can harm children.
2 (*no plural*) the harmful effects of staying outside for a long time when the weather is extremely cold ➤ *Three climbers died of exposure.*
3 the amount of film that is used each time you take a photograph ➤ *This roll has 36 exposures.*

express¹ /ɪk'spres/ *verb*
to show a feeling or thought by saying or doing something ➤ *He wanted to express his thanks, but he could not think of the best words.*

express² *noun (plural* **expresses***)*
a fast train that makes only a few stops on its journey

express³ *adjective*
going or sent quickly ➤ *express mail*

expression /ɪk'spreʃən/ *noun*
1 a word or group of words with a particular meaning ➤ *You shouldn't use that expression – it's not polite.*
2 the look on someone's face ➤ *a sad expression*

expressive /ɪk'spresɪv/ *adjective*
showing what someone thinks or feels ➤ *She had expressive brown eyes.*

exquisite /ɪk'skwɪzɪt/ *adjective*
very beautiful or delicate ➤ *an exquisite piece of jewellery*

extend /ɪk'stend/ *verb*
1 to make something larger or longer ➤ *The headmaster extended our holiday by four days.*
2 to reach or stretch over an area ➤ *The garden extends all the way to the river.*

extension /ɪk'stenʃən/ *noun*
a part added to make something longer or bigger ➤ *We built an extension onto the school, so now we have two more classrooms.*

extensive /ɪk'stensɪv/ *adjective*
spreading over a large area ➤ *The school has extensive playing fields.*

extent /ɪkˈstent/ *noun*
the size or limit of something ▶ *The extent of the North Pole is not fully known.*

exterior¹ /ɪkˈstɪərɪə'/ *adjective*
on the outside of something ▶ *the exterior walls of the house*
OPPOSITE: **interior**

exterior² *noun*
the outside part of something ▶ *the exterior of the building*
OPPOSITE: **interior**

external /ɪkˈstɜ:nl/ *adjective*
1 outside a place, person, or thing ▶ *external walls*
OPPOSITE: **internal**
2 **for external use only** not to be eaten or drunk

extinct /ɪkˈstɪŋkt/ *adjective*
1 (used about animals or plants) no longer existing
2 (used about VOLCANOES) no longer active

extinction /ɪkˈstɪŋkʃən/ *noun (no plural)*
a situation in which a type of animal or plant no longer exists ▶ *The white tiger is facing extinction.*

extinguish /ɪkˈstɪŋgwɪʃ/ *verb*
to put out a light or fire

extinguisher /ɪkˈstɪŋgwɪʃə'/ *noun*
a container of chemicals that will put out a fire quickly

extra /ˈekstrə/ *adjective, adverb, noun*
more than usual, necessary, or expected ▶ *Can I have extra time to finish my work?* ▶ *This hotel charges extra for a room with a view.*

extract¹ /ɪkˈstrækt/ *verb*
1 to make someone give you information, money, etc. that they do not want to give ▶ *The police failed to extract any information from him.*
2 to remove something ▶ *gaps in her mouth where teeth had been extracted*

extract² /ˈekstrækt/ *noun*
a small part of a story, poem, song, etc. ▶ *an extract from "A Midsummer Night's Dream"*

extracurricular /ˌekstrəkəˈrɪkjʊlə'/ *adjective*
not part of the lessons or work that students have to do in school or college ▶ *extracurricular activities*

extraordinary /ɪkˈstrɔːdənəri/ *adjective*
very unusual or strange ▶ *I heard an extraordinary story the other day.*

extravagance /ɪkˈstrævəgəns/ *noun*
the spending of too much money

extravagant /ɪkˈstrævəgənt/ *adjective*
spending too much money ▶ *She's very extravagant – she spends all her money on clothes. (adverb: extravagantly)*

extreme /ɪkˈstriːm/ *adjective*
1 at the furthest end or edge of something ▶ *the extreme south*
2 very great ▶ *extreme danger*

extremely /ɪkˈstriːmli/ *adverb*
very ▶ *I'm extremely grateful for your help.*

extrovert /ˈekstrəvɜːt/ *noun*
a person who is confident and enjoys being with other people
OPPOSITE: **introvert**

eye /aɪ/ *noun*
1 the part of your head with which you see
2 a small hole at one end of a needle
3 **in someone's eyes** in someone's opinion ▶ *In her eyes, he's perfect.*
4 **keep an eye on** to watch people or things to make sure that they are safe ▶ *Will you keep an eye on my house while I'm away?*
5 **see eye to eye** to agree with someone completely ▶ *My father and I have never seen eye to eye.*

E

eyebrow /'aɪbraʊ/ *noun*
the hairy line above your eye

eyelash /'aɪlæʃ/ *noun (plural eyelashes)*
one of the hairs growing on the part of your eye which shuts

eyelid /'aɪlɪd/ *noun*
either of the pieces of skin which shut over your eye

eye-shadow /'aɪ ˌʃædəʊ/ *noun (no plural)*
a coloured substance that women put on their eyelids

eyesight /'aɪsaɪt/ *noun (no plural)*
your ability to see ► *If your eyesight is very bad, you won't get a driving licence.*

eyesore /'aɪsɔːʳ/ *noun*
a building or an area that is very ugly ► *The glass factory is a real eyesore.*

Ff

F
a short way of writing the word **Fahrenheit** ► 32°F (=32 degrees FAHRENHEIT)

fable /'feɪbəl/ *noun*
a story that teaches people a lesson about how to behave

fabric /'fæbrɪk/ *noun*
material made by weaving; cloth ► *a metre of fabric* ► *a woollen fabric*

fabulous /'fæbjʊləs/ *adjective*
very good or nice ► *a fabulous holiday* ► *a fabulous meal*
SAME MEANING: **wonderful**

face¹ /feɪs/ *noun*
1 the front part of your head, with your eyes, nose, and mouth
2 the part of a clock or watch that has numbers on it

face² *verb (present participle facing, past faced)*
1 to have the front towards something; to look towards something ► *Our house faces the park.*
2 to deal with someone or something you are afraid of or do not like ► *I knew he was angry, and could not face him.* ► *You must face the fact that you are ill.*

facecloth /'feɪsklɒθ/ *noun*
a cloth that you use to wash yourself with

facelift /'feɪslɪft/ *noun*
a medical operation to make your face look younger by removing loose skin

face value /ˌfeɪs 'væljuː/ *noun*
take something at face value to accept something without thinking that it might not be as good or true as it seems

facilities /fə'sɪlətɪz/ *plural noun*
things for you to use, especially in a public place ► *sports facilities* (=places and equipment for playing sport)

fact /fækt/ *noun*
1 something that you know is true; something that you know has happened ► *It is a fact that plants need water.* ► *historical facts*
2 **in fact** something you say when you are telling someone that something is true even if it does not seem likely ► *I don't know him very well – in fact, I've only met him once.*

factor /'fæktəʳ/ *noun*
one of several things that affect or cause a situation ► *The bad weather was an important factor in the crash.*

factory /'fæktərɪ/ *noun (plural factories)*
a place where things are made by machines ► *a car factory* (=a place where cars are made)

factual /ˈfæktʃʊəl/ *adjective*
based on facts ➤ *He gave us a factual account of what happened.*

faculty /ˈfækəltɪ/ *noun (plural faculties)*
a group of university departments ➤ *the Faculty of Engineering*

fad /fæd/ *noun*
something that you are interested in or that is popular for only a short time ➤ *Most of her special diets are just fads.*

fade /feɪd/ *verb (present participle fading, past faded)*
(used about a colour) to become less bright ➤ *If you leave that photograph in the sun, it will fade.*

Fahrenheit /ˈfærənhaɪt/ *noun*
a system for measuring temperature, in which water freezes at 32° and boils at 212°

fail /feɪl/ *verb*
1 not to succeed ➤ *Their attempt to cross the desert failed.* ➤ *The crops have failed because of lack of rain.*
2 not to pass an examination ➤ *He failed his English test.*
3 fail to do something not to do something that people expect ➤ *Our train failed to arrive* (=did not arrive).

failing¹ /ˈfeɪlɪŋ/ *noun*
a fault or weakness ➤ *He loved her in spite of her failings.*

failing² *preposition*
failing that used to say that if one thing is not possible or available there is another one you could try ➤ *You could try phoning but, failing that, a letter only takes a few days.*

failure /ˈfeɪljə^r/ *noun*
someone or something that does not succeed ➤ *The plan was a failure.*
OPPOSITE: **success**

faint¹ /feɪnt/ *adjective*
not strong or clear ➤ *a faint sound* ➤ *a faint light* ➤ *a faint hope*

faint² *verb*
to suddenly become unconscious for a short time

fair¹ /feə^r/ *adjective*
1 equally good to everyone ➤ *I try to be fair to all my children.* ➤ *It's not fair – I want one too!*
OPPOSITE: **unfair**
2 quite good, but not very good ➤ *His writing is good, but his reading is only fair.*
3 pale ➤ *Danish people usually have fair skin and fair hair.*
OPPOSITE (**3**): **dark**

fair² *noun*
a place where people, especially children, go and pay money to ride on special machines and play games in order to win prizes

fairly /ˈfeəlɪ/ *adverb*
a little bit, but not very ➤ *I'm fairly happy with the result.*
SAME MEANING: **quite**

fairy /ˈfeərɪ/ *noun (plural fairies)*
(in stories) a very small person with wings who can do magic things

fairy tale /ˈfeərɪ teɪl/ *noun*
a story for children about magic people or events

faith /feɪθ/ *noun*
1 (no plural) belief in something or someone ➤ *I have faith in you; I am sure you will do well.*
2 a religion

faithful /ˈfeɪθfəl/ *adjective*
able to be trusted ➤ *a faithful friend*

faithfully /ˈfeɪθfəlɪ/ *adverb*
Yours faithfully something you put at the end of a business letter, or a letter to someone you do not know, before you write your name ➤ *Dear Sir … Yours faithfully, B. Wilson*

fake¹ /feɪk/ *noun*
a copy of something valuable that is intended to deceive people ➤ *We thought it was a Picasso, but it was a fake.*

F

fake² *adjective*
made to look like a real object or real material in order to deceive people ➤ *fake fur*

fake³ *verb (present participle* **faking,** *past* **faked)**
1 to pretend to be ill, interested, pleased, etc. when you are not ➤ *I thought he was really hurt, but he was just faking it.*
2 to make an exact copy of something in order to deceive people ➤ *He faked his uncle's signature on the note.*

fall¹ /fɔːl/ *verb (past tense* **fell** /fel/, *past participle* **fallen** /ˈfɔːlən/)
1 to drop to a lower place ➤ *The leaves are falling off the trees.* ➤ *Rain was falling.* ➤ *She fell down the stairs.* ➤ *I fell off my bicycle.* ➤ *Be careful or you'll fall!*
2 to become less in amount; to decrease ➤ *House prices are falling.*
3 fall apart to break into pieces ➤ *These old shoes are falling apart.*
4 fall asleep to start to sleep ➤ *I fell asleep in front of the fire.*
5 fall for someone to start to feel love for someone ➤ *She's fallen for a boy in her class.*
6 fall in love with someone to start to feel love for someone
7 fall out with someone to quarrel with someone ➤ *They're always falling out with each other.*
8 fall over to fall to the ground ➤ *I fell over on the ice.*
9 fall to pieces to break into pieces ➤ *When I sat down, the old chair fell to pieces.*

fall² *noun*
1 an act of falling to the ground ➤ *He had a bad fall and hurt himself.*
2 a decrease ➤ *a fall in prices*

fallen /ˈfɔːlən/
the PAST PARTICIPLE of the verb **fall**

false /fɔːls/ *adjective*
1 not true ➤ *Is this statement true or false?*

2 not real ➤ *false teeth*

fame /feɪm/ *noun (no plural)*
the state of being known and admired by a lot of people

familiar /fəˈmɪliər/ *adjective*
1 well known to you ➤ *This song sounds familiar.*
OPPOSITE: **unfamiliar**
2 be familiar with something to know something ➤ *Are you familiar with that story?*

familiarity /fəˌmɪliˈærəti/ *noun (no plural)*
a good knowledge of something ➤ *a familiarity with Russian poetry*

family /ˈfæməli/ *noun (plural* **families)**
a group of relatives including parents and their children, and sometimes also aunts, uncles, grandmothers, grandfathers and COUSINS ➤ *a family of four* (=with four people in it)

family tree /ˌfæməli ˈtriː/ *noun*
a drawing that shows how all the people in a family are related to each other

famine /ˈfæmɪn/ *noun*
a time when there is not enough food for people to eat

famous /ˈfeɪməs/ *adjective*
well-known and admired ➤ *This town is famous for its beautiful buildings.* ➤ *a famous singer*

fan¹ /fæn/ *noun*
1 an instrument for moving the air around you to make you cooler
2 someone who likes a particular person or thing very much ➤ *I'm a fan of his music.* ➤ *a football fan*

fan² *verb (present participle* **fanning,** *past* **fanned)**
to make the air around you move ➤ *She fanned herself with the newspaper* (=to cool her face).

fanatic /fəˈnætɪk/ *noun*
1 a person who has very strong and

unreasonable beliefs about religion or politics

2 a person who likes something very much ▶ *a football fanatic*

fancy¹ /'fænsɪ/ *adjective* (**fancier, fanciest**)

not ordinary or plain ▶ *fancy clothes*

fancy² *verb* (*past* **fancied**)

1 to want something ▶ *Do you fancy fish for dinner?* ▶ *I fancy a walk.*

2 to be attracted to someone in a sexual way ▶ *I've always fancied his brother.*

fancy dress /ˌfænsɪ 'dres/ *noun* (no plural)

strange clothes that you wear for fun at a party ▶ *a fancy dress party* (= a party where people wear fancy dress)

fanfare /'fænfeəʳ/ *noun*

a short piece of music played loudly on a TRUMPET to introduce an important person or event

fang /fæŋ/ *noun*

a long, sharp tooth of an animal such as a dog or snake

fantasize /'fæntəsaɪz/ *verb* (*present participle* **fantasizing**, *past* **fantasized**)

to imagine that something pleasant is happening to you ▶ *We all fantasize **about** winning the lottery.*

fantastic /fæn'tæstɪk/ *adjective*

very good ▶ *You look fantastic in that dress.* ▶ *a fantastic idea*

SAME MEANING: **great**

fantasy /'fæntəsɪ/ *noun* (plural **fantasies**)

something that you think about that is pleasant but unlikely to happen ▶ *I had fantasies **about** becoming a famous actress.*

far¹ /fɑːʳ/ *adverb* (**farther** /'fɑːðəʳ/ or **further** /'fɜːðəʳ/, **farthest** /'fɑːðɪst/ or **furthest** /'fɜːðɪst/)

1 distant from a place ▶ *How far is it to London?* ▶ *We didn't walk very far.*

OPPOSITE: **near**

Use **far** in questions, in NEGATIVE sentences, and after **too, as**, and **so**: *How far is it to your house?* ▶ *It isn't far.* ▶ *It's too far to walk.* ▶ *We drove as far as the next town.* ▶ *We didn't mean to walk so far.* In other types of sentences, use **a long way**: *We walked a long way.* ▶ *It's a long way from the school to my house.*

2 very much ▶ *I'm far too tired to go out.* ▶ *a far better idea*

3 as far as to a place ▶ *He only drove as far as the end of the road.*

4 far away distant from a place

5 so far until now

far² *adjective*

not near; distant ▶ *the far side of town*

OPPOSITE: **near**

farce /fɑːs/ *noun*

1 an event or a situation that is very badly organized

2 a funny play in which a lot of silly things happen

fare /feəʳ/ *noun*

the amount of money that you have to pay to travel on a bus, train, plane, etc. ▶ *a taxi fare*

farewell /feə'wel/ *noun*

goodbye

far-fetched /ˌfɑː 'fetʃt/ *adjective*

very strange and not likely to be true ▶ *I thought her story was pretty far-fetched.*

farm /fɑːm/ *noun*

land on which people grow food or keep animals

farmer /'fɑːməʳ/ *noun*

a person who owns or works on a farm

farmhouse /'fɑːmhaʊs/ *noun* (plural **farmhouses** /-haʊzɪz/)

the house on a farm where the farmer lives

farming /'fɑːmɪŋ/ *noun* (no plural)

the job of growing food or keeping animals

F

farmyard /'fɑːmjɑːd/ *noun*
the piece of ground next to a farmhouse

farther /'fɑːðəʳ/
the COMPARATIVE of **far**

farthest /'fɑːðɪst/
the SUPERLATIVE of **far**

fascinate /'fæsɪneɪt/ *verb (present participle* **fascinating**, *past* **fascinated**)
to interest someone very much

fascinating /'fæsɪneɪtɪŋ/ *adjective*
extremely interesting, especially because you are learning something new ▶ *a fascinating subject*

fascination /ˌfæsɪ'neɪʃən/ *noun (no plural)*
very strong interest in something

fascism /'fæʃɪzəm/ *noun (no plural)*
an extreme political system in which the state has complete power and controls everything

fascist /'fæʃɪst/ *noun*
a person who supports fascism

fashion /'fæʃən/ *noun*
1 the way of dressing or doing something that is liked by many people at a particular time ▶ *the fashion for short skirts*
2 in fashion liked by many people now ▶ *These ideas are in fashion.*
3 out of fashion no longer liked by many people

fashionable /'fæʃənəbəl/ *adjective*
liked by many people at a particular time ▶ *fashionable clothes*
OPPOSITE: **unfashionable**

fast¹ /fɑːst/ *adjective*
1 quick; not slow ▶ *He is a fast runner.*
2 (used about a clock or watch) showing a time that is later than the real time
OPPOSITE (**1** and **2**): **slow**
3 firmly fixed

fast² *adverb*
1 quickly ▶ *to run fast*
OPPOSITE: **slowly**

2 firmly; tightly ▶ *The boat stuck fast in the mud.*
3 fast asleep sleeping very well

fast³ *verb*
to eat no food, usually for religious reasons
COMPARE: **starve**

fasten /'fɑːsən/ *verb*
to fix something firmly; to join or tie together ▶ *She fastened her coat.*
OPPOSITE: **unfasten**

fastener /'fɑːsənəʳ/ *noun*
something used to join or tie things together

fastening /'fɑːsənɪŋ/ *noun*
something that you use to hold another thing closed

fast food /'fɑːst fuːd/ *noun (no plural)*
cooked food, e.g. HAMBURGERS and CHIPS, that you buy from special shops to eat there or to take away with you

fast-forward /ˌfɑːst 'fɔːwəd/ *verb*
to wind a TAPE forward quickly without playing it

fat¹ /fæt/ *adjective (***fatter, fattest***)*
having a wide, round body ▶ *I think he's too fat.*
OPPOSITE: **thin**

fat² *noun*
an oily substance, especially the oil that comes from meat when it is cooked

fatal /'feɪtl/ *adjective*
causing someone to die ▶ *a fatal car accident* (*adverb:* **fatally**)
COMPARE: **deadly**

fate /feɪt/ *noun (no plural)*
a power which some people believe causes things to happen to you during your life

father /'fɑːðəʳ/ *noun*
your male parent ▶ *my mother and father*

Father Christmas /ˌfɑːðə 'krɪsməs/ *noun*

an old man who children think brings them presents at Christmas, and who wears red clothes and has a long, white beard
SAME MEANING: **Santa Claus**

father-in-law /ˈfɑːðər ɪn lɔː/ noun (plural **fathers-in-law**)
the father of your wife or husband

fatigue /fəˈtiːg/ noun (no plural)
extreme tiredness

fattening /ˈfætn-ɪŋ/ adjective
(used about food) likely to make you fat ▶ Those cakes look fattening.

fatty /ˈfætɪ/ adjective (**fattier, fattiest**)
(used about food) containing a lot of fat

fault /fɔːlt/ noun
1 something that is wrong; a mistake or problem ▶ a fault in the engine
2 the fact of being responsible for something bad ▶ I'm sorry – it's all my fault.

faultless /ˈfɔːltləs/ adjective
having no faults; perfect ▶ faultless work

faulty /ˈfɔːltɪ/ adjective
having a mistake or something wrong ▶ a faulty machine

favour /ˈfeɪvər/ noun
1 something kind done for someone ▶ May I ask you a favour? ▶ Will you do me a favour (=do something for me) and lend me some money?
2 **be in favour of something** to think something is a good idea; to support something ▶ I'm not in favour of the plan. ▶ Are you in favour of changing the law?

favourable /ˈfeɪvərəbəl/ adjective
good and suitable ▶ favourable weather for working outside
OPPOSITE: **unfavourable**

favourite /ˈfeɪvərɪt/ adjective
liked best of all ▶ Orange is my favourite colour.

favouritism /ˈfeɪvərɪtɪzəm/ noun (no plural)
the act of unfairly treating one person or group better than others because you like them more

fax /fæks/ noun (plural **faxes**)
a machine, joined to a telephone, which you use for sending copies of letters or pictures to another place

fear¹ /fɪər/ verb
1 to be afraid of someone or something
2 to worry because you think that something bad has happened or is going to happen ▶ We feared an accident.

fear² noun
1 the feeling of being afraid ▶ a fear of dogs ▶ He was shaking with fear.
2 a feeling of being worried in case something bad has happened or is going to happen ▶ fears of an accident

fearful /ˈfɪəfəl/ adjective
causing fear; very bad ▶ a fearful sound

fearless /ˈfɪələs/ adjective
never showing fear; never afraid ▶ a fearless soldier
SAME MEANING: **brave**

feasible /ˈfiːzəbəl/ adjective
possible, and likely to work or be true ▶ Her story sounds quite feasible.

feast¹ /fiːst/ noun
a large meal of good food for a special reason

feast² verb
to eat a large meal of good food

feat /fiːt/ noun
something that someone does that shows a lot of strength or skill ▶ an amazing feat **of** engineering

feather /ˈfeðər/ noun
one of the things that covers a bird, like a thin stick with soft hairs

F

feature /ˈfiːtʃəʳ/ *noun*
1 a part of your face, especially your eyes, nose, or mouth
2 one part of something that you notice especially, or that is typical of it

February /ˈfebruəri/ *noun*
the second month of the year

fed /fed/
the PAST TENSE and PAST PARTICIPLE of the verb **feed**

federal /ˈfedərəl/ *adjective*
having several states or countries that are joined under one government, but which also decide certain things on their own ▶ *a federal system*

fed up /ˌfed ˈʌp/ *adjective*
not happy because you have had too much of something or because you are annoyed with someone ▶ *I'm fed up with staying at home all day.*
COMPARE: **bored**

fee /fiː/ *noun*
money that you pay to a doctor, lawyer, school, etc.

feeble /ˈfiːbəl/ *adjective*
very weak

feed /fiːd/ *verb* (past **fed** /fed/)
to give food to a person or an animal ▶ *Have you fed the cat?*

feedback /ˈfiːdbæk/ *noun* (no plural)
advice or criticism about how well or badly you have done something ▶ *We are still waiting for feedback on the report.*

feel /fiːl/ *verb* (past **felt** /felt/)
1 to be ▶ *to feel happy* ▶ *to feel ill*
2 to touch something with your fingers to see what it is like
3 to experience something touching you ▶ *to feel the wind in your hair*
4 to think or believe something ▶ *I feel sure she will agree.*
5 feel like something to want something ▶ *I feel like something to eat.* ▶ *I feel like staying in tonight.*

feeling /ˈfiːlɪŋ/ *noun*
1 something that you experience in your body or your mind ▶ *feelings of love* ▶ *a feeling of pain*
2 hurt someone's feelings to upset someone

feet /fiːt/
1 the plural of **foot**
2 on your feet standing up ▶ *I've been on my feet all day.*
3 put your feet up to rest

fell /fel/
the PAST TENSE of the verb **fall**

fellow¹ /ˈfeləʊ/ *noun*
a man

fellow² *adjective*
very like you or from the same place as you ▶ *your fellow students*

felt /felt/
the PAST TENSE and PAST PARTICIPLE of the verb **feel**

felt tip /ˈfelt tɪp/ *noun*
a type of thick, coloured pen, used especially by children

female¹ /ˈfiːmeɪl/ *adjective*
belonging to the sex that gives birth to young ones
OPPOSITE: **male**

female² *noun*
a girl or woman; an animal of the sex that gives birth to young ones
OPPOSITE: **male**

feminine /ˈfemɪnɪn/ *adjective*
like a woman or typical of a woman
OPPOSITE: **masculine**

feminism /ˈfemɪnɪzəm/ *noun* (no plural)
the belief that women should have the same rights and opportunities as men

feminist /ˈfemɪnɪst/ *noun*
a person who believes that women should have the same rights and opportunities as men

fence¹ /fens/ *noun*
a wooden or wire wall round something

fence² *verb (present participle* ***fencing,*** *past* ***fenced****)*
fence something off to put a wooden or wire wall around something ▶ *to fence off some land*

fencing /ˈfensɪŋ/ *noun (no plural)*
a sport in which people fight with long, thin swords

fend /fend/ *verb*
fend for yourself to look after yourself without help from other people ▶ *The children had to fend for themselves while their parents were at work.*

fern /fɜːn/ *noun*
a green plant that has no flowers and grows in places that are wet and dark

ferocious /fəˈrəʊʃəs/ *adjective*
very fierce ▶ *a ferocious animal*

ferry /ˈferi/ *noun (plural* ***ferries****)*
a boat that takes people or things across a stretch of water ▶ *A ferry crosses the river every hour.*

fertile /ˈfɜːtaɪl/ *adjective*
(used about land, earth, etc.) able to grow plants and seeds very well ▶ *His farm is on fertile land.*
OPPOSITE: **infertile**

fertilize /ˈfɜːtɪlaɪz/ *verb (present participle* ***fertilizing****, past* ***fertilized****)*
(used about an egg) to become joined with a SPERM so that a new animal or baby can start to develop

fertilizer /ˈfɜːtɪlaɪzəʳ/ *noun (no plural)*
something that you put on the land to make your crops grow better

festival /ˈfestɪvəl/ *noun*
1 a period of time when there are many special events of a particular type ▶ *a film festival* ▶ *a festival of music*
2 a time when everyone has a holiday from work to enjoy something such as a religious event

festive /ˈfestɪv/ *adjective*
happy or cheerful because people are celebrating something ▶ *a festive occasion*

festivities /feˈstɪvətiz/ *plural noun*
an occasion when people eat, drink, or dance to celebrate something

fetch /fetʃ/ *verb*
to go somewhere and bring someone or something back with you ▶ *Will you fetch some water?*

> Compare the verbs **fetch** and **bring**. If you **bring** something to a place, you have it with you when you go there. If you **fetch** something, you go and get it from somewhere else and then have it with you when you come back: *Please bring a bottle of wine to the party* (=come to the party with a bottle of wine). ▶ *Can you fetch me some milk when you go to the shop* (=go and get it and come back with it)?

fete /feɪt/ *noun*
a special market with games, competitions, and things for sale, arranged by people who want to get money to help a church, a school, or some other organization

feud /fjuːd/ *noun*
an angry argument between two people or groups that continues for a long time ▶ *There has been a feud between the two families for many years.*

fever /ˈfiːvəʳ/ *noun*
an increase of heat in your body, caused by illness ▶ *to have a fever*

feverish /ˈfiːvərɪʃ/ *adjective*
feeling hot because of a fever ▶ *He was pale and feverish.*

few /fjuː/ *adjective, pronoun*
1 not many ▶ *He has few friends.* ▶ *Few people would agree with you.*
OPPOSITE: **many**

F

2 a few a small number of ► *Can I ask you a few questions?* ► *a few days*
3 quite a few quite a lot ► *There were quite a few people at the party.*

fiancé /fɪˈɒnseɪ/ *noun*
a man who has promised to marry a particular woman ► *Her fiancé is called George.*

fiancée /fɪˈɒnseɪ/ *noun*
a woman who has promised to marry a particular man ► *His fiancée is called Susan.*

fiasco /fiˈæskəʊ/ *noun*
an event that is so unsuccessful that people feel embarrassed about it ► *The evening was a total fiasco from start to finish.*

fib /fɪb/ *noun*
a lie; not the truth ► *to tell a fib*

fibre /ˈfaɪbəʳ/ *noun*
a thin thread of a plant or animal substance

fiction /ˈfɪkʃən/ *noun (no plural)*
books and stories about people and events that are not real ► *Most children enjoy reading fiction.*
OPPOSITE: **nonfiction**

fictional /ˈfɪkʃənəl/ *adjective*
(used about people or events) from a book or story that is not real

fiddle[1] /ˈfɪdl/ *verb (present participle fiddling, past fiddled)*
1 to dishonestly take money out of an organization by cheating it in small ways ► *His boss found out that he'd been fiddling his expenses.*
2 fiddle (around) with something to keep moving something around with your hands, especially because you are bored or nervous ► *I wish he'd stop fiddling with his keys.*

fiddle[2] *noun*
1 a VIOLIN
2 a dishonest way of getting money ► *an insurance fiddle*

fiddly /ˈfɪdlɪ/ *adjective*

difficult to use or do because you have to move very small objects ► *a very fiddly job*

fidget /ˈfɪdʒɪt/ *verb*
to keep moving your hands or feet, because you are bored, uncomfortable, or nervous ► *The audience were starting to fidget.*

field /fiːld/ *noun*
a piece of ground, usually with a fence or wall round it, used for growing crops or keeping animals ► *a field of wheat*

fielder /ˈfiːldəʳ/ *noun*
one of the players who tries to catch the ball in BASEBALL or CRICKET

field trip /ˈfiːld trɪp/ *noun*
a trip in which students go somewhere to learn about a subject ► *a geography field trip*

fierce /fɪəs/ *adjective*
violent and angry ► *a fierce dog* ► *a fierce storm*

fiery /ˈfaɪərɪ/ *adjective*
full of strong or angry emotion ► *John has a fiery temper.*

fifteen /fɪfˈtiːn/ *adjective, noun*
the number 15

fifteenth /fɪfˈtiːnθ/ *adjective*
15th

fifth /fɪfθ/ *adjective, noun*
1 5th
2 one of five equal parts

fiftieth /ˈfɪftɪ-əθ/ *adjective*
50th

fifty /ˈfɪftɪ/ *adjective, noun*
the number 50

fifty-fifty /ˌfɪftɪ ˈfɪftɪ/ *adjective, adverb*
1 divided or shared equally between two people ► *I think we should divide the profits fifty-fifty.*
2 a fifty-fifty chance an equal chance that something will happen or will not happen ► *The operation has a fifty-fifty chance of success.*

fig /fɪg/ *noun*
a sweet fruit which is full of small seeds

fight¹ /faɪt/ *verb (past **fought** /fɔːt/)*
1 to use your body or weapons to try and hurt or kill someone ▶ *He fought in the war.* ▶ *to fight an enemy* ▶ *to fight a battle*
2 to quarrel with someone

fight² *noun*
an act of fighting ▶ *The two boys had a fight.*

figure /'fɪgəʳ/ *noun*
1 a written number such as 3 or 8
2 a shape, especially the shape of a human body ▶ *I could see a tall figure near the door.* ▶ *She has a good figure (=her body is an attractive shape).*

file¹ /faɪl/ *noun*
1 a cardboard cover or container for papers
2 a tool with a rough edge that you use for making things smooth ▶ *a nail file*
3 in single file walking one behind the other in a line ▶ *Please walk in single file.*

file² *verb (present participle **filing**, past **filed**)*
1 to put papers into a file ▶ *to file letters*
2 to make something smooth using a file ▶ *to file your nails*
3 to walk in a line one behind the other ▶ *The children filed into the classroom.*

filing cabinet /'faɪlɪŋ ˌkæbɪnət/ *noun*
a tall, narrow piece of furniture with drawers, where important papers are kept

fill /fɪl/ *verb*
1 to put something into something until no more will fit in ▶ *to fill a glass with water*
2 to become full ▶ *The streets filled with people.*
OPPOSITE (**1** and **2**): **empty**

3 fill something in to give the written information you are asked for on an official piece of paper ▶ *Fill in the answers to these questions.*
4 fill something up to fill something completely ▶ *to fill up a car with petrol*

fillet¹ /'fɪlɪt/ *noun*
a piece of meat or fish without any bones

fillet² *verb*
to remove the bones from a piece of meat or fish

filling /'fɪlɪŋ/ *noun*
a substance that a DENTIST puts in a hole in your tooth

filling station /'fɪlɪŋ ˌsteɪʃən/ *noun*
a place where you go to buy petrol for your car

film¹ /fɪlm/ *noun*
1 a story shown in a cinema or on television ▶ *a Charlie Chaplin film*
2 the thing you put into a camera, on which photographs are made

film² *verb*
to make a film of something ▶ *He filmed the football match.*

film star /'fɪlm stɑːʳ/ *noun*
a famous actor or actress who acts in films

filter¹ /'fɪltəʳ/ *noun*
a thing that removes substances that you do not want from a liquid or gas as the liquid or gas flows through it ▶ *the oil filter in a car*

filter² *verb*
to clean a liquid or gas using a filter ▶ *I filter all my drinking water.*

filth /fɪlθ/ *noun (no plural)*
unpleasant dirt ▶ *The old bicycle was completely covered in filth.*

filthy /'fɪlθɪ/ *adjective (**filthier**, **filthiest**)*
very dirty ▶ *filthy clothes*

fin /fɪn/ *noun*
a part on the side of a fish that helps it to swim

F

final¹ /ˈfaɪnl/ *adjective*
coming at the end; last ▶ *the final part of the story*

final² *noun*
the last and most important game in a competition, to decide who will win

finalist /ˈfaɪnəlɪst/ *noun*
one of the people or teams that reach the last part of a competition

finalize /ˈfaɪnəl-aɪz/ *verb (present participle **finalizing**, past **finalized**)*
to finish the last part of a plan, business agreement, etc. ▶ *Can we finalize the details of the deal tomorrow?*

finally /ˈfaɪnəli/ *adverb*
1 after a long delay ▶ *When she finally arrived, it was too late.*
2 a word you use when you come to the last thing you want to say about a subject you have been speaking or writing about ▶ *Finally, let me thank you all for your help in this matter.*
3 a word you use when you are giving the last of a number of instructions ▶ *Finally, bake the cake for 30 minutes.*

finance¹ /ˈfaɪnæns, fɪˈnæns/ *noun (no plural)*
the controlling of large sums of money, e.g. by a bank, a company, or a government

finance² *verb (present participle **financing**, past **financed**)*
to give someone the money for something ▶ *The government will finance the building of the new roads.*

financial /faɪˈnænʃəl/ *adjective*
connected with money ▶ *financial advice*

find /faɪnd/ *verb (past **found** /faʊnd/)*
1 to see or get something after you have been looking for it ▶ *I can't find my keys.* ▶ *to find a job*
OPPOSITE: **lose**

2 to learn or discover something
▶ *to find the answer to a question*
3 find someone guilty to say that someone is guilty of a crime ▶ *The court found him guilty of murder.*
4 find something out to discover the facts about something ▶ *to find out the truth about something*

findings /ˈfaɪndɪŋz/ *plural noun*
the things that people have learned as the result of an official study
▶ *They reported their findings to the Health Minister.*

fine¹ /faɪn/ *adjective*
1 very nice or good ▶ *a fine building*
2 good enough ▶ *"How is your meal?" "Fine, thanks."*
3 very well or happy ▶ *"How are you?" "Fine, thank you."*
4 sunny and without rain ▶ *a fine day* ▶ *fine weather*
5 very thin ▶ *fine lines*

fine² *noun*
money that you pay as a punishment after doing something wrong

fine³ *verb (present participle **fining**, past **fined**)*
to make someone pay money as a punishment after they have done something wrong ▶ *The man was fined £100 by the court.*

finely /ˈfaɪnli/ *adverb*
into very small pieces ▶ *Chop the onion finely.*

finger /ˈfɪŋɡəʳ/ *noun*
one of the five long parts on your hand

fingernail /ˈfɪŋɡəneɪl/ *noun*
one of the hard, flat things that grow at the end of your fingers

fingerprint /ˈfɪŋɡəprɪnt/ *noun*
a mark made by the lines on the end of your fingers, used by the police to IDENTIFY people

fingertip /ˈfɪŋɡətɪp/ *noun*
the end of one of your fingers

finish¹ /'fɪnɪʃ/ *noun*
the end of something
OPPOSITE: **start**

finish² *verb*
1 to end ▶ *the game finished at 4 o'clock*
2 to complete something or to stop doing something ▶ *I finish work at 5 o'clock.* ▶ *I've finished reading the newspaper.*
OPPOSITE (**1** and **2**): **start**
3 finish something off to complete something ▶ *I'm just finishing off a letter.*
4 finish with something to stop using something because you no longer need it ▶ *Have you finished with that pen?*

finished /'fɪnɪʃt/ *adjective*
1 completed ▶ *The finished building will be 200 feet high.*
OPPOSITE: **unfinished**
2 no longer able to be successful ▶ *Most top footballers are finished by the time they are 30.*

fir /fɜːʳ/ *noun*
a tree that grows especially in cold countries and keeps its leaves in winter

fire¹ /faɪəʳ/ *noun*
1 heat and flames which burn and destroy things ▶ *a forest fire* (=a fire which destroys a forest) ▶ *a building destroyed by fire*
2 a mass of burning coal or wood, or a piece of apparatus heated by gas or electricity, used to make a room warm ▶ *to sit in front of the fire* ▶ *a gas fire*
3 catch fire to begin to burn
4 on fire burning ▶ *The house is on fire.*
5 set fire to something to make something burn

fire² *verb (present participle **firing**, past **fired**)*
to shoot with a gun

fire alarm /'faɪər ə,lɑːm/ *noun*
a bell that rings to warn you when a building starts to burn

firearm /'faɪərɑːm/ *noun*
a gun

fire brigade /'faɪə brɪ,geɪd/ *noun*
a group of people whose job is to stop dangerous fires

fire engine /'faɪər ,endʒɪn/ *noun*
a vehicle used by the FIRE BRIGADE, which has water and special apparatus for stopping fires

fire escape /'faɪər ɪ,skeɪp/ *noun*
a set of stairs on the outside of a building that you use to escape when there is a fire

fire extinguisher /'faɪər ɪk,stɪŋgwɪʃəʳ/ *noun*
a metal container with water or chemicals inside for putting on a fire to stop it burning

firefighter /'faɪə,faɪtəʳ/ *noun*
a person whose job is to stop dangerous fires

fireman /'faɪəmən/ *noun (plural **firemen** /-mən/)*
a man whose job is to stop dangerous fires

fireplace /'faɪəpleɪs/ *noun*
the part of the wall of a room where you have a fire

fire station /'faɪə ,steɪʃən/ *noun*
the building where firemen (FIREMAN) are and where the FIRE ENGINE is kept

firewood /'faɪəwʊd/ *noun (no plural)*
wood for burning on a fire

firework /'faɪəwɜːk/ *noun*
a cardboard tube filled with special chemicals, which burns with a loud noise and makes bright lights in the air

firm¹ /fɜːm/ *adjective*
1 not soft ▶ *firm ground*
2 having strong control; not weak ▶ *The teacher was firm with the children.*

F

firm² *noun*
a group of people who work together in a business; a company

firmly /'fɜːmlɪ/ *adverb*
in a way that shows strong control ► She told him firmly that he must wait.

first /fɜːst/ *adjective, adverb*
1 coming before all the others; earliest ► It's his first year at school. ► She came first in the competition. ► We can talk later, but first (=before that) we must finish our work. ► the first day of the month
2 for the first time; before all the other times ► I first visited America two years ago.
OPPOSITE (**1** and **2**): **last**
3 first of all (a) before doing anything else ► First of all, can you tell me your name, sir?
(b) used when you are talking about something which happened before a lot of other things ► First of all we had dinner, then we went to the cinema, and then we went home.
4 at first at the start of something ► At first I didn't enjoy my job, but now I like it.
LOOK AT: **firstly**

first aid /ˌfɜːst 'eɪd/ *noun (no plural)*
simple help that you give to an ill or a wounded person before the doctor comes

first aid box /ˌfɜːst 'eɪd bɒks/ *noun (plural first aid boxes)*
a box containing medicines, etc. to give to someone who is ill or has an accident

first-class /ˌfɜːst 'klɑːs/ *adjective*
of the best or most expensive type ► a first-class train ticket

first floor /ˌfɜːst 'flɔːʳ/ *noun*
the floor of a building on top of the one which is level with the ground

firsthand /ˌfɜːst'hænd/ *adjective, adverb*

learned, discovered, etc. directly, not from being told by other people ► officers with firsthand experience of war ► He saw firsthand the conditions the poorest people were living in.

firstly /'fɜːstlɪ/ *adverb*
a word you use when you are making the first of several points ► Firstly, let me thank everyone for coming here this evening.
OPPOSITE: **lastly**

> **Firstly** does NOT mean "in the beginning". Use **at first** instead: At first I didn't like my new job, but then I started to enjoy it.

first name /'fɜːst neɪm/ *noun*
the name that comes before your family name ► "What is your first name, Mrs Jones?" "It's Anne; I'm Mrs Anne Jones."
COMPARE: **surname**

first person /ˌfɜːst 'pɜːsən/ *noun*
the first person the form of a verb that you use with "I" and "we"

fish¹ /fɪʃ/ *noun (plural fish or fishes)*
a creature that lives in water and can swim, and which people eat as food

fish² *verb*
1 to try to catch fish
2 go fishing to go to a place to try and catch fish

fisherman /'fɪʃəmən/ *noun (plural fishermen /-mən/)*
a person who catches fish for sport or as a job

fishing /'fɪʃɪŋ/ *noun (no plural)*
the sport or job of catching fish ► Fishing is important source of income in this area.

fishing rod /'fɪʃɪŋ rɒd/ *noun*
a long stick with string at the end, used for catching fish

fishmonger /'fɪʃmʌŋgəʳ/ *noun*
1 a person who owns or works in a shop that sells fish
2 fishmonger's a shop that sells fish

fishy /ˈfɪʃɪ/ adjective (**fishier, fishiest**)
seeming bad or dishonest ▶ The deal sounds a bit fishy to me.

fist /fɪst/ noun
a hand with the fingers closed tightly together ▶ She shook her fist angrily.

fit¹ /fɪt/ adjective
1 not ill; well and able to be active as a result of doing sport
2 good enough ▶ This food is not fit for your visitors
OPPOSITE (**1** and **2**): **unfit**

fit² verb (present participle **fitting**, past **fitted**)
1 to be the right size for someone or something ▶ The trousers don't fit him; they are too small.
2 to find space to put someone or something ▶ We can't fit any more people in here.
3 to fix something in place ▶ He fitted a new lock on the door.

Do not confuse the verbs **fit** (=to be the right size for someone or something) and **suit** (=to be right or suitable for someone or something). Compare That dress doesn't fit you (=it's too big/too small) and That dress doesn't suit you (=it doesn't look nice).

fitness /ˈfɪtnəs/ noun (no plural)
the condition of being healthy and able to run or do physical work for a long time ▶ He started to go running to improve his fitness.

five /faɪv/ adjective, noun
the number 5

fix /fɪks/ verb
1 to put something in place firmly ▶ He fixed a picture to the wall.
2 to mend something ▶ Can you fix my bicycle?
3 to arrange something ▶ We have fixed a date for the meeting. ▶ to fix a price (=to agree what it should be)

fixture /ˈfɪkstʃəʳ/ noun
1 a piece of furniture or equipment that is fastened inside a house and is sold as part of the house ▶ bathroom fixtures
2 a sports event that has been arranged

fizz /fɪz/ verb
to make the sound of bubbles of gas bursting ▶ She uncorked the champagne and it came fizzing out of the bottle.

fizzle /ˈfɪzəl/ verb (present participle **fizzling**, past **fizzled**)
fizzle out to gradually end in a weak or disappointing way ▶ Their relationship just fizzled out.

fizzy /ˈfɪzɪ/ adjective (**fizzier, fizziest**)
(used about a drink) containing gas ▶ fizzy water

flabbergasted /ˈflæbə,gɑːstɪd/ adjective
extremely surprised or shocked

flabby /ˈflæbɪ/ adjective (**flabbier, flabbiest**)
having too much soft, loose fat ▶ I've been getting all flabby since I stopped swimming.

flag /flæg/ noun
a piece of cloth with a special pattern on it, used as the sign of a country, club, etc.

flagpole /ˈflægpəʊl/ noun
a tall pole at the top of which you hang a flag

flair /fleəʳ/ noun (no plural)
1 a natural ability to do something very well ▶ Carla's always had a flair for languages.
2 the exciting quality that someone has who does things in an interesting way ▶ Bates' advertising campaigns showed flair and imagination.

flak /flæk/ noun (no plural)
criticism ▶ She got a lot of flak for her decision to move abroad.

F

flake /fleɪk/ *noun*
a small, thin piece of something that has broken off a larger piece

flame /fleɪm/ *noun*
1 a bright piece of burning gas that you see in a fire
2 in flames burning ▶ *The house was in flames.*

flan /flæn/ *noun*
a PIE with no lid that is filled with fruit, cheese, etc.

flannel /ˈflænl/ *noun*
1 a piece of cloth that you use to wash yourself
2 *(no plural)* a type of soft cloth that is warm ▶ *flannel sheets*

flap¹ /flæp/ *verb (present participle* **flapping**, *past* **flapped**)
to move up and down ▶ *The bird flapped its wings.*

flap² *noun*
a piece of something that hangs down over an opening ▶ *a flap on a pocket*

flare¹ /fleəʳ/ *(also* **flare up**) *verb (present participle* **flaring**, *past* **flared**)
to suddenly start, or become more violent ▶ *Fighting has flared up again in the city.*

flare² *noun*
a thing that produces a bright light, used as a sign that someone needs help

flared /fleəd/ *adjective*
(used about trousers or skirts) becoming wider towards the bottom

flash¹ /flæʃ/ *noun (plural* **flashes**)
1 a sudden bright light ▶ *a flash of lightning*
2 a light on a camera that you use when you take a photograph inside a building
3 in a flash very quickly ▶ *The ambulance arrived in a flash.*

flash² *verb*
(used about a light) to shine for a moment

flashback /ˈflæʃbæk/ *noun*
a part of a film, play, book, etc. that shows something that happened earlier in the story

flashy /ˈflæʃɪ/ *adjective (***flashier, flashiest***)*
too big, bright, or expensive, in a way that you disapprove of ▶ *She was showing off her flashy engagement ring.*

flask /flɑːsk/ *(also* **vacuum flask**) *noun*
a special type of bottle for keeping hot drinks hot, or cold drinks cold ▶ *a flask of coffee*

flat¹ /flæt/ *adjective (***flatter, flattest***)*
1 without hills; not sloping ▶ *flat land* ▶ *a flat roof*
2 (used about tyres) having no air inside

flat² *noun*
a number of rooms on one floor of a building, used as a home
SAME MEANING: **apartment**

flat³ *adverb*
in a straight position along a flat surface ▶ *I have to lie flat on my back to sleep.*

flatly /ˈflætlɪ/ *adverb*
flatly refuse, flatly deny to refuse or deny something in a very firm, strong way ▶ *She flatly refused to let me borrow her car.*

flatmate /ˈflætmeɪt/ *noun*
a person who shares a flat with another person but is not a member of their family

flatten /ˈflætn/ *verb*
to make something flat ▶ *The rain flattened the corn.*

flatter /ˈflætəʳ/ *verb*
to say that someone is better, nicer, etc. than they really are because you are trying to please them

flattering /ˈflætərɪŋ/ *adjective*
making you look more attractive ▶ *a flattering dress*

flattery /ˈflætəri/ *noun (no plural)*
nice things that you say to someone because you are trying to please them

flaunt /flɔːnt/ *verb*
to show your wealth, success, beauty, etc. in order to make other people notice it and admire you for it ▶ *I don't like the way he flaunts his money.*

flavour /ˈfleɪvəʳ/ *noun*
a taste ▶ *coffee with a strong flavour*

flavouring /ˈfleɪvərɪŋ/ *noun*
something used to give food or drink a particular taste ▶ *This drink contains artificial flavourings.*

flaw /flɔː/ *noun*
a mistake, mark, or weakness that stops something from being perfect ▶ *She took the material back to the shop because there was a flaw in it.*

flawed /flɔːd/ *adjective*
not perfect because of mistakes, marks, or weaknesses ▶ *a flawed experiment*

flea /fliː/ *noun*
a very small, jumping insect that drinks blood from animals and people

flee /fliː/ *verb (past fled /fled/)*
to run away; to escape

fleece /fliːs/ *noun*
the wool of a sheep

fleet /fliːt/ *noun*
a lot of ships or boats together ▶ *a fleet of fishing boats*

flesh /fleʃ/ *noun (no plural)*
the soft part of your body that covers your bones
COMPARE: **skin**

flew /fluː/
the PAST TENSE of the verb **fly**

flexible /ˈfleksəbəl/ *adjective*
1 able to change or be changed easily ▶ *One good thing about the job is the flexible working hours.*
2 easy to bend
▶ *a flexible plastic tube*
OPPOSITE (**1** and **2**): **inflexible**

flick /flɪk/ *verb*
1 to make something small and light go through the air with a quick movement of your finger or hand ▶ *He flicked the fly off his sleeve.*
2 flick something on/off to press a SWITCH in order to start or stop electrical equipment ▶ *I flicked on the TV.*
3 flick through something to look at a book, magazine, etc. quickly ▶ *She was flicking through a magazine.*

flicker /ˈflɪkəʳ/ *verb*
to burn or shine with an unsteady light ▶ *flickering candles*

flight /flaɪt/ *noun*
1 a journey on a plane ▶ *a flight from New York to Paris*
2 a flight of stairs a set of stairs

flight attendant /ˈflaɪt əˌtendənt/ *noun*
a person whose job is to look after passengers on a plane

flimsy /ˈflɪmzi/ *adjective (flimsier, flimsiest)*
1 not strong, and easily damaged ▶ *Their flimsy boats were destroyed in the storm.*
2 (used about arguments, excuses, etc.) not good or strong enough for you to believe ▶ *The evidence against him is very flimsy.*

flinch /flɪntʃ/ *verb*
to make a sudden, small, backward movement because you are afraid, hurt, or shocked ▶ *The boy flinched when she tried to clean his cuts.*

fling /flɪŋ/ *verb (past flung /flʌŋ/)*
to throw something with force

F

flip /flɪp/ *verb (present participle*
flipping, *past* **flipped**)
1 flip over to turn over quickly ► *The
boat went too fast and flipped over.*
2 (*also* **flip out**) to suddenly become
very angry ► *I just suggested a few
changes, and he flipped.*
3 flip something on/off to press a
SWITCH in order to start or stop
electrical equipment ► *He flipped on
the light.*
4 flip through something to look at a
book, magazine, etc. quickly ► *He
flipped through his diary to find a
free day.*

flip chart /'flɪp tʃɑːt/ *noun*
large sheets of paper on a board,
used to write things on in a meeting
or class

flip-flop /'flɪp flɒp/ *noun*
a light, open shoe with a V-shaped
band to hold your foot

flippant /'flɪpənt/ *adjective*
not serious enough about something,
in a way that shows a lack of respect
► *He was rather flippant **about** her
problems.* ► *Don't get flippant with
me, young man!*
(*adverb:* **flippantly**)

flipper /'flɪpər/ *noun*
1 a broad, flat part of the body which
some sea animals have and which
helps them to swim
2 a kind of broad, flat, plastic shoe
that you wear to help you swim fast
underwater

flirt /flɜːt/ *verb*
to behave in a way that is intended to
attract sexual attention ► *He flirts
with all the women.*

float /fləʊt/ *verb*
to stay on the surface of a liquid
► *The branch of a tree floated by.*
OPPOSITE: **sink**

flock /flɒk/ *noun*
a group of sheep, goats, or birds
COMPARE: **herd**

flog /flɒg/ *verb (present participle*
flogging, *past* **flogged**)
to beat someone with a whip or stick
as a punishment

flood[1] /flʌd/ *noun*
a great quantity of water covering a
place that is usually dry ► *The floods
destroyed many homes.*

flood[2] *verb*
to cover a place with water ► *The
river flooded the fields.*

flooding /'flʌdɪŋ/ *noun (no plural)*
a situation in which an area that is
usually dry becomes covered with
water ► *The heavy rain has caused
more flooding.*

floodlight /'flʌdlaɪt/ *noun*
a very strong light used at night to
show the outside of buildings, or at
sports events

floodlit /'flʌdlɪt/ *adjective*
lit by floodlights ► *floodlit tennis
courts*

floor /flɔːr/ *noun*
1 the part of a room that you walk on
► *a wooden floor*
2 all the rooms on the same level of a
building ► *We live on the third floor*
(=three floors above the ground).

floorboard /'flɔːbɔːd/ *noun*
a long, narrow piece of wood used to
make floors

flooring /'flɔːrɪŋ/ *noun (no plural)*
a material used to make or cover
floors ► *They chose wooden flooring
for the kitchen.*

flop[1] /flɒp/ *verb (present participle*
flopping, *past* **flopped**)
1 to sit or fall down quickly, especially
because you are tired ► *Sarah
flopped down into an armchair.*
2 (used about films, plays, plans,
etc.) to be unsuccessful ► *The
musical flopped on Broadway.*
3 to hang down loosely ► *Her hair
flopped across her face.*

flop² *noun*
something that is unsuccessful ➤ *The show's first series was a complete flop.*

floppy /'flɒpɪ/ *adjective* (**floppier, floppiest**)
soft and hanging loosely down ➤ *a dog with long, floppy ears*

floppy disk /ˌflɒpɪ 'dɪsk/ *noun*
a piece of plastic that you can put into a computer and on which information can be stored
COMPARE: **hard disk**

floral /'flɔːrəl/ *adjective*
made of flowers, or decorated with flowers ➤ *floral wallpaper*

florist /'flɒrɪst/ *noun*
1 a person who sells flowers
2 florist's a shop that sells flowers

flounder /'flaʊndər/ *verb*
to have great difficulty doing something, especially because you do not know what to do ➤ *Some of the younger students seemed to be floundering a bit.*

flour /flaʊər/ *noun* (no plural)
fine powder made from wheat, used for making bread, etc.

flourish /'flʌrɪʃ/ *verb*
to grow well ➤ *The garden is flourishing.*

flow¹ /fləʊ/ *verb*
(used about liquids) to move along ➤ *The river flows through York before it reaches the sea.*

flow² *noun* (no plural)
a smooth movement ➤ *a flow of air*

flower /'flaʊər/ *noun*
the part of a plant which holds the seeds and which is usually pretty and brightly coloured ➤ *a vase of flowers*

flowerbed /'flaʊəbed/ *noun*
an area of earth with flowers planted in it

flowerpot /'flaʊəpɒt/ *noun*
a container in which you grow plants

flowery /'flaʊərɪ/ *adjective*
decorated with pictures of flowers ➤ *a flowery pattern*

flown /fləʊn/
the PAST PARTICIPLE of the verb **fly**

flu /fluː/ (also **influenza**) *noun* (no plural)
a common illness of the nose and throat which is like a bad cold but is more serious ➤ *The whole team has got flu.*

fluctuate /'flʌktʃʊeɪt/ *verb* (present participle **fluctuating**, past **fluctuated**)
to change very often, especially from a high level to a low level and back again ➤ *The price of copper fluctuated wildly.*

fluency /'fluːənsɪ/ *noun* (no plural)
the ability to speak a language very well

fluent /'fluːənt/ *adjective*
speaking a language very well ➤ *He is fluent in English.* (adverb: **fluently**)

fluff /flʌf/ *noun* (no plural)
soft, fine bits that come off animals, wool, etc.

fluffy /'flʌfɪ/ *adjective* (**fluffier, fluffiest**)
made of or covered with something soft such as fur ➤ *a fluffy toy*

fluid¹ /'fluːɪd/ *noun*
a liquid

fluid² *adjective*
liquid; not solid; able to flow

fluke /fluːk/ *noun*
something that only happens because of luck ➤ *The goal was a complete fluke.*

flung /flʌŋ/
the PAST TENSE and PAST PARTICIPLE of the verb **fling**

fluorescent /flʊə'resənt/ *adjective*
1 fluorescent light a light that consists of a long, glass tube containing a special gas

2 (used about colours) very bright

fluoride /ˈflʊəraɪd/ noun (no plural)
a chemical that is added to water and TOOTHPASTE to help protect people's teeth

flush /flʌʃ/ verb
1 to clean a TOILET by making water go down it ▶ to flush a toilet
2 to become red in the face because you are ashamed, angry, etc. ▶ He flushed at her suggestion.

flushed /flʌʃt/ adjective
having a red face ▶ She looked hot and flushed.

flustered /ˈflʌstəd/ adjective
confused because you are nervous or trying to do things too quickly ▶ She got flustered and dropped her papers.

flute /fluːt/ noun
a musical instrument like a pipe, that you hold to one side of your mouth and blow

flutter /ˈflʌtər/ verb
to move in the air quickly and in different directions ▶ dead leaves fluttering to the ground ▶ a flag fluttering in the wind

fly¹ /flaɪ/ verb (past tense **flew** /fluː/, past participle **flown** /fləʊn/)
1 to move through the air ▶ Birds were flying above the houses. ▶ The plane flew from Paris to Rome.
2 to go quickly ▶ She flew (=ran) out of the house.

fly² noun (plural **flies**)
a small, flying insect

flying /ˈflaɪ-ɪŋ/ noun (no plural)
the activity of travelling by plane or being a pilot ▶ fear of flying

flying saucer /ˌflaɪ-ɪŋ ˈsɔːsər/ noun
a SPACESHIP which is round and flat and is shown in pictures and stories

flyover /ˈflaɪəʊvər/ noun
a part of a road that goes up and crosses over another road

FM /ˌef ˈem/ noun (no plural)
FREQUENCY MODULATION; a system used for broadcasting radio programmes

foal /fəʊl/ noun
a baby horse

foam /fəʊm/ noun (no plural)
the white substance that you sometimes see on top of water

focus¹ /ˈfəʊkəs/ verb (present participle **focusing** or **focussing**, past **focused** or **focussed**)
1 to give all your attention to a particular thing ▶ In his speech he focused on the economy.
2 to turn the LENS on a camera, TELESCOPE, etc. so that you can see something clearly

focus² noun
1 (no plural) the person or subject that gets most attention ▶ traditional education, with its focus on basic reading and writing skills ▶ She loves being the focus of attention.
2 in focus (used about photographs) clear
3 out of focus (used about photographs) not clear

foetus /ˈfiːtəs/ noun (plural **foetuses**)
a human or an animal that is growing inside its mother

fog /fɒg/ noun (no plural)
thick cloud close to the ground that makes it difficult to see
COMPARE: **mist**

foggy /ˈfɒgɪ/ adjective (**foggier**, **foggiest**)
having a lot of thick cloud close to the ground so that you cannot see very well ▶ a foggy day
COMPARE: **misty**

foil /fɔɪl/ noun (no plural)
very thin metal used for covering and wrapping food

fold¹ /fəʊld/ verb
1 to turn part of something over another part ▶ She folded the letter

so that it would fit into her bag.
OPPOSITE: **unfold**
2 fold your arms to cross your arms over your chest so that one hand rests on top of one arm and the other hand rests underneath the other arm
3 fold something up to fold something several times so that it becomes smaller ▶ *She folded up the sheets.*

fold² noun
a part of something that has been folded over another part

folder /ˈfəʊldər/ *noun*
a cardboard cover, like the cover of a book, for holding papers, etc.

foliage /ˈfəʊlɪdʒ/ *noun (no plural)*
the leaves of a plant ▶ *She arranged the flowers and foliage in a vase.*

folk¹ /fəʊk/ *plural noun*
people ▶ *The old folk sat and talked.*

folk² adjective
typical of the ordinary people of a particular country or area ▶ *folk music* ▶ *a folk song*

folks /fəʊks/ *plural noun*
1 your parents or family ▶ *My girlfriend has never met my folks.*
2 used to talk to a group of people in an informal and friendly way ▶ *Hi, folks – it's good to see you all.*

follow /ˈfɒləʊ/ *verb*
1 to come or go after someone or something ▶ *He left the room, and I followed.* ▶ *Follow me.* ▶ *Their success follows years of hard work.*
2 to go in the same direction as a road, river, etc. ▶ *Follow the road as far as the church.*
3 to understand something ▶ *I didn't follow what you were saying.*
4 to do what someone tells you to do ▶ *to follow instructions*
5 follow in someone's footsteps to do the same as someone else did in the past ▶ *He's following in his father's footsteps and training to be a doctor.*

follower /ˈfɒləʊər/ *noun*
a person who supports someone or believes in something ▶ *a follower of Karl Marx*

following /ˈfɒləʊɪŋ/ *adjective*
the following day, week, year, etc. the next day, week, year, etc. ▶ *We leave on Friday and return the following Monday.*

fond of /ˈfɒnd ɒv/ *adjective*
liking someone or something ▶ *I'm very fond of you* (=I like you very much).

food /fuːd/ *noun (no plural)*
things that you eat ▶ *He had had no food for two days.*

food poisoning /ˈfuːd ˌpɔɪzənɪŋ/ *noun (no plural)*
an illness that is caused by eating food containing harmful BACTERIA (=small creatures that spread disease) ▶ *I got food poisoning from eating a beefburger.*

fool¹ /fuːl/ *noun*
1 a silly or stupid person
SAME MEANING: **idiot**
2 make a fool of yourself to behave in a way which makes other people think you are silly

fool² verb
1 to trick or deceive someone ▶ *He fooled me into giving him money.*
2 fool about to behave in a silly way ▶ *Stop fooling about!*

foolish /ˈfuːlɪʃ/ *adjective*
not reasonable; silly ▶ *foolish behaviour*

foolproof /ˈfuːlpruːf/ *adjective*
certain to be successful ▶ *a foolproof plan*

foot /fʊt/ *noun (plural feet /fiːt/)*
1 the part of your body that you stand on
2 the bottom of something ▶ *the foot of a hill*
3 a measure of length equal to 12 inches ▶ *The man was 6 feet tall.*

F

4 on foot walking ▶ *They made the journey on foot.*

football /ˈfʊtbɔːl/ *noun*
1 (*no plural*) a game played by two teams who each try to kick a ball into a net
2 a ball filled with air, used for playing the game of football

footballer /ˈfʊtbɔːləʳ/ *noun*
a person whose job is to play football

football pitch /ˈfʊtbɔːl ˌpɪtʃ/ *noun*
(*plural* **football pitches**)
a piece of land where people play the game of football

footnote /ˈfʊtnəʊt/ *noun*
a note at the bottom of a page in a book, that gives more information about something on that page

footpath /ˈfʊtpɑːθ/ *noun* (*plural* **footpaths** /ˈfʊtpɑːðz/)
a narrow path for people to walk on, especially in the country

footprint /ˈfʊtprɪnt/ *noun*
the mark left by a person's foot
▶ *footprints in the snow*

footstep /ˈfʊtstep/ *noun*
the sound of someone walking ▶ *I heard footsteps behind me.*

footwear /ˈfʊtweəʳ/ *noun* (*no plural*)
things that you wear on your feet, such as shoes or boots ▶ *The store has a big footwear department.*

for /fəʳ; *strong* fɔːʳ/ *preposition*
1 meant to be used in this way ▶ *a knife for cutting bread*
2 meant to be given to or used by someone or something ▶ *Here's a letter for you.* ▶ *I'm making some curtains for the bedroom.* ▶ *a school for girls*
3 showing how far or how long ▶ *She has lived in this town for many years.* ▶ *I waited for three hours.*
LOOK AT: **since**
4 towards a place ▶ *the train for London*

5 at a price of ▶ *She bought the dress for £5.*
6 with the meaning of ▶ *What is the word for "tree" in your language?*
7 in favour of someone or something ▶ *The government is for the plan.*
8 at or at a particular time ▶ *We'll be home for Christmas.*
9 used to show the reason for something ▶ *He won a prize for singing.* ▶ *The government is working for peace.* ▶ *They were punished for their bad behaviour.*
10 used to show who is helped by someone or something ▶ *She did some work for her father.*
11 used to show who a feeling is about ▶ *I'm very pleased for you.*

forbid /fəˈbɪd/ *verb* (*present participle* **forbidding**, *past tense* **forbade** /fəˈbæd/, *past participle* **forbidden** /fəˈbɪdn/)
to tell someone they must not do something ▶ *You are forbidden to smoke in school.*
OPPOSITE: **allow**
COMPARE: **ban**

force¹ /fɔːs/ *verb* (*present participle* **forcing**, *past* **forced**)
1 to make someone do something they do not want to do ▶ *He forced me to see a doctor.*
2 to use your strength to make something move ▶ *to force a door open* (=make it open by pushing or pulling)

force² *noun*
1 (*no plural*) power or strength ▶ *to use force to make someone do something* ▶ *the force of an explosion*
2 a group of people like the army, etc. who are trained to fight or work together ▶ *enemy forces* ▶ *the police force*
3 by force using violence, power, or strength

forced /fɔːst/ *adjective*
1 (used about a smile or laugh) given because you feel it is necessary, and not because you really mean it
2 done suddenly because a situation makes it necessary ➤ *The plane had to make a forced landing in a field.*

forceful /'fɔːsfəl/ *adjective*
powerful and strong ➤ *a forceful personality* ➤ *forceful arguments* (adverb: **forcefully**)

forearm /'fɔːrɑːm/ *noun*
the part of your arm between your hand and your elbow ➤ *She has a cut on her left forearm.*

forecast /'fɔːkɑːst/ *noun*
something that says what you think will happen in future ➤ *a weather forecast*

forefather /'fɔːˌfɑːðəʳ/ *noun*
a person in your family who lived a long time before you were born ➤ *the time when our forefathers arrived in America*

forefront /'fɔːfrʌnt/ *noun*
be at the forefront of something to do more than other people in developing something new ➤ *a British company that was at the forefront of computer design*

foregone conclusion /ˌfɔːɡɒn kənˈkluːʒən/ *noun*
a situation where the result is certain ➤ *The election result was a foregone conclusion.*

foreground /'fɔːɡraʊnd/ *noun*
the foreground the part of a picture, photograph, etc. nearest to you

forehead /'fɔːhed, 'fɒrəd/ *noun*
the top part of your face, above your eyes but below your hair

foreign /'fɒrɪn/ *adjective*
of or from a country that is not your country ➤ *a foreign language*

foreigner /'fɒrɪnəʳ/ *noun*
a person who comes from a country that is not your country

foreman /'fɔːmən/ *noun* (plural **foremen** /-mən/)
a man whose job is to tell a group of workers what to do

foremost /'fɔːməust/ *adjective*
the most famous or important ➤ *the foremost scientist of his generation*

forensic /fəˈrensɪk/ *adjective*
connected with the use of scientific methods to solve crimes ➤ *forensic evidence*

foresee /fɔːˈsiː/ *verb* (past tense **foresaw** /-ˈsɔː/, past participle **foreseen** /-ˈsiːn/)
to expect that something will happen in the future ➤ *I don't foresee any problems with the new system.*

foresight /'fɔːsaɪt/ *noun* (no plural)
the ability to imagine what might happen in the future, and consider this in your plans ➤ *Lucy was glad she had had the foresight to keep her money separate from her passport.*

forest /'fɒrɪst/ *noun*
an area where a lot of trees grow together

forever /fərˈevəʳ/ *adverb*
always; for all time in the future ➤ *I shall love you forever.*

foreword /'fɔːwɜːd/ *noun*
a short piece of writing, at the beginning of a book, about the book or its writer

forgave /fəˈɡeɪv/
the PAST TENSE of the verb **forgive**

forge /fɔːdʒ/ *verb* (present participle **forging**, past **forged**)
to make a copy of something in order to deceive people ➤ *He was sent to prison for forging money.*

forgery /'fɔːdʒərɪ/ *noun*
1 (no plural) the crime of making a copy of something in order to deceive people ➤ *to go to prison for forgery*
2 (plural **forgeries**) a copy which is intended to deceive people

F

forget /fəˈget/ *verb (present participle **forgetting**, past tense **forgot** /fəˈgɒt/, past participle **forgotten** /fəˈgɒtn/)*
not to remember something ▶ *"Did you post the letter?" "No, I forgot."* ▶ *She forgot to post the letter.*
OPPOSITE: **remember**

If you want to say **where** you have left something, always use **leave**, not **forget**: *Oh no! I've forgotten my bag!* ▶ *I've left my bag on the bus.*

forgetful /fəˈgetfəl/ *adjective*
often forgetting things

forgive /fəˈgɪv/ *verb (present participle **forgiving**, past tense **forgave** /fəˈgeɪv/, past participle **forgiven** /fəˈgɪvən/)*
to stop being angry with someone ▶ *Please forgive me – I didn't mean to be rude.*

forgot /fəˈgɒt/
the PAST TENSE of the verb **forget**

forgotten /fəˈgɒtn/
the PAST PARTICIPLE of the verb **forget**

fork¹ /fɔːk/ *noun*
1 an instrument with a handle and two or more points at the end, which you use to eat food
2 a place where a road or a river divides into two ▶ *a fork **in** the road*

fork² *verb*
(used about a road or river) to divide into two

forlorn /fəˈlɔːn/ *adjective*
sad and lonely ▶ *a forlorn figure sitting on a park bench*

form¹ /fɔːm/ *noun*
1 a school class ▶ *Which form are you in?* ▶ *the sixth form*
2 a shape ▶ *a birthday cake in the form of the number 18*
3 a type of something ▶ *a new form of government*
4 a piece of printed paper on which

you have to write things or answer questions about yourself

form² *verb*
1 to start to appear or exist ▶ *These rocks were formed 4000 million years ago.*
2 to make or produce something ▶ *to form a plan*
3 to make a particular shape ▶ *The children formed a circle (=stood together in the shape of a circle).*
4 to start an organization or group ▶ *to form a club*

formal /ˈfɔːməl/ *adjective*
suitable for an official or important occasion ▶ *a formal letter* ▶ *formal clothes*
OPPOSITE: **informal**

formality /fɔːˈmælɪti/ *noun (plural **formalities**)*
an official part of a process ▶ *After going through the usual formalities, we got on the plane.*

format¹ /ˈfɔːmæt/ *noun*
the way that something is organized or designed ▶ *This week the show has a new format.*

format² *verb (present participle **formatting**, past **formatted**)*
to organize the space on a computer DISK so that you can store information on it

formation /fɔːˈmeɪʃən/ *noun (no plural)*
the process during which something starts to exist or develop ▶ *the formation of ice crystals*

former¹ /ˈfɔːməʳ/ *noun*
the former the first of two people or things which have just been mentioned ▶ *Britain has agreements with both Germany and Italy, but its agreement with the former (=Germany) will soon change.*
OPPOSITE: **the latter**

former² *adjective*
at an earlier time but not any more

➤ *the former president of the United States* ➤ *her former husband* (adverb: **formerly**)

formidable /'fɔːmɪdəbəl/ *adjective*
powerful and slightly frightening ➤ *a formidable opponent*

formula /'fɔːmjʊlə/ *noun* (plural **formulas** or **formulae** /'fɔːmjʊliː/)
a list of the substances used to make something ➤ *the secret formula for the new drug*

formulate /'fɔːmjʊleɪt/ *verb* (present participle **formulating**, past **formulated**)
to develop a plan and decide all the details ➤ *He soon formulated a plan of escape.*

fort /fɔːt/ *noun*
a strong building where soldiers lived in the past and where people could go to be safe from attack

forthcoming /ˌfɔːθˈkʌmɪŋ/ *adjective*
1 happening soon ➤ *the forthcoming election*
2 given or offered to someone ➤ *If more money is not forthcoming, we'll have to close the theatre.*
3 willing to give information ➤ *Michael wasn't very forthcoming about his plans.*

forthright /'fɔːθraɪt/ *adjective*
saying what you think honestly and directly ➤ *Bill answered in his usual forthright manner.*

fortieth /'fɔːtɪ-əθ/ *adjective*
40th

fortnight /'fɔːtnaɪt/ *noun*
two weeks ➤ *We're going on holiday for a fortnight* (=we will be away for two weeks). ➤ *We're going on holiday in a fortnight* (=we leave two weeks after today).
LOOK AT: **time**

fortnightly /'fɔːtnaɪtlɪ/ *adverb*
happening once every two weeks

fortress /'fɔːtrəs/ *noun* (plural **fortresses**)
a big, strong building that people use for defending a place

fortunate /'fɔːtʃənət/ *adjective*
lucky (adverb: **fortunately**)
OPPOSITE: **unfortunate**

fortune /'fɔːtʃən/ *noun*
1 (no plural) luck or chance ➤ *to have good fortune* (=to be lucky)
2 a very large amount of money ➤ *He made a fortune by selling houses.*
3 tell someone's fortune to tell someone what is going to happen to them in the future

forty /'fɔːtɪ/ *adjective, noun*
the number 40

forward /'fɔːwəd/ *adjective*
1 in the direction that is in front of you ➤ *a forward movement*
OPPOSITE: **backward**
2 look forward to something to think about something that is going to happen and feel pleased about it ➤ *I'm looking forward to meeting you.*

forwards /'fɔːwədz/ *adverb*
in the direction that is in front of you ➤ *to move forwards*
OPPOSITE: **backwards**

fossil /'fɒsəl/ *noun*
a part of an animal or a plant that lived thousands of years ago and that has turned hard like rock

foster[1] /'fɒstə/ *verb*
1 to encourage a feeling or skill to develop ➤ *We want to foster a friendly atmosphere in the office.*
2 to take care of someone else's child for a period of time, without becoming the child's legal parent ➤ *They fostered two children for nearly a year.*

foster[2] *adjective*
1 foster parents people who foster someone else's child
2 foster children children who are fostered

F

fought /fɔːt/
the PAST TENSE and PAST PARTICIPLE of the verb **fight**

foul /faʊl/ *adjective*
unpleasant and dirty ▶ *a foul smell*

found¹ /faʊnd/
the PAST TENSE and PAST PARTICIPLE of the verb **find**

found² *verb*
to start ▶ *He founded the school in 1954.*

foundation /faʊnˈdeɪʃən/ *noun*
1 something basic or important on which something else is based ▶ *Reading and writing are the foundations of learning.*
2 an organization that gives money for special purposes ▶ *The kit was paid for by the AIDS Foundation.*

foundations /faʊnˈdeɪʃənz/ *plural noun*
the parts of the walls of a building that are under the ground

founder /ˈfaʊndəʳ/ *noun*
a person who starts an organization ▶ *one of the original founders of the company*

fountain /ˈfaʊntən/ *noun*
water thrown high into the air from a pipe, e.g. in a garden or park

fountain pen /ˈfaʊntən pen/ *noun*
a pen that is filled with ink

four /fɔːʳ/ *adjective, noun*
the number 4

fourteen /fɔːˈtiːn/ *adjective, noun*
the number 14

fourteenth /fɔːˈtiːnθ/ *adjective*
14th

fourth /fɔːθ/ *adjective*
4th

fowl /faʊl/ *noun*
a bird, usually one that is kept for food

fox /fɒks/ *noun (plural **foxes**)*
a wild animal like a dog, with a thick tail

foyer /ˈfɔɪeɪ/ *noun*
a room at the entrance to a hotel, a theatre, or some other large building ▶ *I'll meet you in the foyer of the nightclub.*

fraction /ˈfrækʃən/ *noun*
a division or part of a number, e.g. $^1/_4$, $^1/_2$

fracture¹ /ˈfræktʃəʳ/ *verb (present participle **fracturing**, past **fractured**)*
to crack or break ▶ *to fracture your skull*

fracture² *noun*
a crack or break

fragile /ˈfrædʒaɪl/ *adjective*
able to be broken easily

fragment /ˈfrægmənt/ *noun*
a small piece broken off something ▶ *a fragment of glass*

fragrance /ˈfreɪgrəns/ *noun*
a sweet or pleasant smell ▶ *the fragrance of flowers*
SAME MEANING: **perfume**

fragrant /ˈfreɪgrənt/ *adjective*
having a sweet or pleasant smell
COMPARE: **smelly**

frail /freɪl/ *adjective*
weak and not healthy

frame¹ /freɪm/ *noun*
1 the bars around which a building, car, etc. is made ▶ *a building with a steel frame* (=with steel supports inside it) ▶ *a tent frame*
2 a piece of wood or metal round the edges of a picture, window, mirror, etc.

frame² *verb (present participle **framing**, past **framed**)*
to put a wooden or metal frame around the edges of a picture

frames /freɪmz/ *plural noun*
the part of a pair of glasses that holds the two pieces of glass ▶ *He sat on my glasses and broke the frames.*

F

framework /ˈfreɪmwɜːk/ *noun*
1 a set of rules, facts, or beliefs that people use to make plans or decisions ➤ *We must work within the framework of the existing budget.*
2 the bars around which a building, car, etc. is made

frank /fræŋk/ *adjective*
honest and not afraid to say what is true ➤ *a frank talk*

frankly /ˈfræŋkli/ *adverb*
1 used when you want to show that you are giving your true opinion about something, even if you know other people will think you are wrong ➤ *Frankly, I think you are wasting your time.*
2 in an honest way ➤ *They talked very frankly.*

frantic /ˈfræntɪk/ *adjective*
1 hurrying in a way that is not organized ➤ *There was a frantic rush for tickets.*
2 very anxious or upset ➤ *We've been frantic with worry – where have you been?*
(adverb: **frantically**)

fraud /frɔːd/ *noun (no plural)*
the crime of deceiving people, especially in order to get money

fraught /frɔːt/ *adjective*
1 fraught with problems/difficulty/danger full of problems, difficulty, or danger
2 very anxious or worried ➤ *The survivors were met at the airport by fraught relatives.*

frayed /freɪd/ *adjective*
(used about clothes or material) having loose threads at the edges ➤ *a frayed dress*

freak /friːk/ *noun*
a person or an animal that is very strange

freckle /ˈfrekəl/ *noun*
a very small, brown spot on a person's skin

free¹ /friː/ *adjective*
1 able to do what you like ➤ *You are free to leave at any time.*
2 not in prison
3 not working or busy ➤ *Are you free this evening?*
4 not costing any money ➤ *a free ticket*
5 free of charge not costing any money ➤ *Our help is free of charge.*
6 free time time when you are not busy or working and can do what you want
7 set someone free to allow someone to leave a prison

free² *verb (past* **freed***)*
to let a person or an animal leave a place where they have been kept as a prisoner ➤ *They freed the birds from the cages.*

free³ *adverb*
1 without having to pay any money ➤ *Children under 12 travel free.*
2 not controlled by someone or held in a particular position ➤ *He held my arm, but I pulled it free.*

freedom /ˈfriːdəm/ *noun (no plural)*
being able to do what you want without being a prisoner and without being under another person's control

freelance /ˈfriːlɑːns/ *adjective, adverb*
working independently for several different organizations ➤ *a freelance journalist* ➤ *How long have you been working freelance?*

freely /ˈfriːli/ *adverb*
1 without anyone trying to control you or prevent you from doing something ➤ *We encourage our students to speak freely.* ➤ *People can now travel freely across the border.*
2 freely admit/acknowledge to agree that something is true ➤ *I freely admit I made a bad choice.*

free speech /ˌfriː ˈspiːtʃ/ *noun (no plural)*

the right to express your opinions ► *If the government believes in free speech, why does it try to stop us protesting?*

freeze /friːz/ *verb (present participle* **freezing**, *past tense* **froze** /frəʊz/, *past participle* **frozen** /'frəʊzən/)
to become very cold and change from a liquid into a solid ► *When water freezes, it becomes ice.*

freezer /'friːzə^r/ *noun*
a machine that keeps food very cold, so that it stays fresh for a long time

freezing /'friːzɪŋ/ *adjective*
very cold ► *I'm freezing!* ► *It's freezing outside.*

freezing point /'friːzɪŋ ˌpɔɪnt/ *noun (no plural)*
the temperature at which water changes to become ice

freight /freɪt/ *noun (no plural)*
goods that are being taken from one place to another by train, road, plane, or ship ► *a freight train*

French fry /ˌfrentʃ 'fraɪ/ *noun (plural* **French fries)**
a long, thin piece of potato cooked in oil
SAME MEANING: **chip**

frenzy /'frenzi/ *noun (no plural)*
a situation in which you are so anxious, excited, etc. that you are unable to control your behaviour ► *In a frenzy, Brady began kicking and punching the police officers.*

frequency /'friːkwənsi/ *noun*
1 *(no plural)* the number of times that something happens, or the fact that it happens a lot ► *Her headaches have increased in frequency.*
2 *(plural* **frequencies)** the rate at which a sound or light wave is repeated ► *The human ear cannot hear sounds of very high frequency.*

frequent /'friːkwənt/ *adjective*
happening often ► *They make*

frequent trips abroad. *(adverb:* **frequently)**
OPPOSITE: **infrequent**

fresh /freʃ/ *adjective*
1 (used about food) in good condition because of being picked, killed, etc. a short time ago ► *fresh fish* ► *fresh vegetables*
2 new and different ► *Write your answer on a fresh sheet of paper.*
3 fresh air pleasant, cool air outside, not in a building ► *I'm going for a walk to get some fresh air.*

freshly /'freʃli/ *adverb*
very recently ► *the smell of freshly baked bread*

friction /'frɪkʃən/ *noun (no plural)*
1 a situation in which people disagree with each other and argue in an unfriendly way ► *There seemed to be some friction between Joe and Pete.*
2 the action of one surface rubbing against another ► *Friction produces heat.*

Friday /'fraɪdeɪ, -di/ *noun*
the sixth day of the week

fridge /frɪdʒ/ *(also* **refrigerator)** *noun*
a type of electric cupboard that you keep in your kitchen and use for keeping food cool and fresh

fried¹ /fraɪd/
the PAST TENSE of the verb **fry**

fried² *adjective*
cooked in hot oil ► *fried eggs*

friend /frend/ *noun*
1 a person who you know well and who you like and trust ► *He is my friend.* ► *He is a friend of mine.* ► *We are friends.*
COMPARE: **acquaintance**
2 make friends with someone to start to know someone and be their friend

friendly /'frendli/ *adjective* **(friendlier, friendliest)**
behaving in a nice, kind way like a friend
OPPOSITE: **unfriendly**

friendship /'frendʃɪp/ *noun*
the state of being friends ➤ *The boys have had a long friendship.*

fries /fraɪz/ *plural noun*
French fries ➤ *I'll have a cheeseburger and fries.*
SAME MEANING: **chips**

fright /fraɪt/ *noun (no plural)*
1 a feeling of fear
2 give someone a fright to make someone feel afraid suddenly

frighten /'fraɪtn/ *verb*
to make someone afraid ➤ *The noise frightened me.*
SAME MEANING: **scare**

frightened /'fraɪtnd/ *adjective*
afraid ➤ *He's frightened of dogs.*
SAME MEANING: **scared**

frightening /'fraɪtnɪŋ/ *adjective*
making you afraid ➤ *a frightening film*

frill /frɪl/ *noun*
a decoration on the edge of a piece of cloth, made from another piece of cloth with many small folds in it

frilly /'frɪlɪ/ *adjective (**frillier, frilliest**)*
decorated with many folds of cloth around the edges ➤ *a frilly blouse*

fringe /frɪndʒ/ *noun*
1 hair that goes in a line across the top of your face, above your eyes
2 threads that hang in a straight line around the edge of something

frivolity /frɪ'vɒlətɪ/ *noun (plural **frivolities**)*
behaviour that is not serious or sensible ➤ *My father disapproves of frivolity.*

frivolous /'frɪvələs/ *adjective*
behaving in a silly way when you should be serious or sensible ➤ *She kept making frivolous comments.*

frizzy /'frɪzɪ/ *adjective (**frizzier, frizziest**)*
(used about hair) curled very tightly ➤ *My hair's gone all frizzy.*

fro /frəʊ/ *adverb*

to and fro first in one direction and then in the opposite direction ➤ *He was walking to and fro in front of the house.*

frock /frɒk/ *noun*
a dress for a girl or woman

frog /frɒg/ *noun*
a small brown or green jumping animal that lives in water and on land

frogman /'frɒgmən/ *noun (plural **frogmen** /-mən/)*
a person whose job is to work underwater wearing a rubber suit and special equipment for breathing ➤ *Frogmen are searching for the body in the river.*

from /frəm; *strong* frɒm/ *preposition*
1 starting at or coming from a place; starting at a time ➤ *The train goes from Paris to Rome.* ➤ *He's from Spain.* ➤ *from Monday to Friday*
2 given or sent by someone ➤ *This letter is from my uncle.*
3 used to show how far away something is ➤ *a town 10 miles from here*
4 out of a place ➤ *books from the cupboard*
5 away ➤ *Her children were taken from her.*
6 using something ➤ *Bread is made from flour.*
7 because of something ➤ *She was crying from the pain.*

front¹ /frʌnt/ *noun*
1 the side opposite the back ➤ *sitting at the front of the class*
OPPOSITE: **back, rear**
2 in front of at the front of someone or something ➤ *I'll meet you in front of the cinema.*

front² *adjective*
at the front of something ➤ *the front seat of a car*
OPPOSITE: **back**

front door /ˌfrʌnt 'dɔː/ *noun*
the door at the front of the house, that you use when you go in

F

frontier /ˈfrʌntɪəʳ/ *noun*
the dividing line between two
countries
SAME MEANING: **border**

frost /frɒst/ *noun (no plural)*
frozen water that stays on every
outdoor surface in cold weather
➤ *The trees were white with frost.*

frostbite /ˈfrɒstbaɪt/ *noun (no plural)*
a medical condition in which your
fingers or toes become frozen and
badly damaged

frosty /ˈfrɒstɪ/ *adjective (**frostier, frostiest**)*
very cold or covered with FROST ➤ *It
was a frosty morning.*

froth /frɒθ/ *noun (no plural)*
a lot of small BUBBLES on top of a
liquid ➤ *He blew the froth off his
coffee.*

frown /fraʊn/ *verb*
to look as if you are angry or thinking
very hard by bringing your EYEBROWS
together so that lines appear at the
top of your face

froze /frəʊz/
the PAST TENSE of the verb **freeze**

frozen[1] /ˈfrəʊzən/
the PAST PARTICIPLE of the verb **freeze**

frozen[2] *adjective*
preserved by being kept very cold ➤ *I
bought a bag of frozen peas.*

frozen food /ˌfrəʊzən ˈfuːd/ *noun (no plural)*
food that you buy after it has been
frozen, and which you keep in a
FREEZER

fruit /fruːt/ *noun (no plural)*
the part of a plant that carries the
seeds; it is often sweet and good to
eat ➤ *Would you like some fruit – an
apple or an orange?* ➤ *a bowl of fruit*

fruitful /ˈfruːtfəl/ *adjective*
producing good results ➤ *Was it a
fruitful meeting?*

fruit juice /ˈfruːt dʒuːs/ *noun (no plural)*
a drink made by pressing fruit and
getting liquid from it

fruitless /ˈfruːtləs/ *adjective*
failing to produce good results,
especially after much effort ➤ *They
spent three fruitless weeks looking
for the body.*

fruity /ˈfruːtɪ/ *adjective (**fruitier, fruitiest**)*
tasting or smelling strongly of fruit
➤ *This wine has a fruity smell.*

frustrate /frʌˈstreɪt/ *verb
(present participle **frustrating**,
past **frustrated**)*
to make you feel impatient or angry
because you are unable to do what
you want to do ➤ *It frustrates me
when she doesn't listen.*

frustrating /frʌˈstreɪtɪŋ/ *adjective*
making you feel impatient or angry
because you are unable to do what
you want to do ➤ *They keep sending
me the wrong forms – it's very
frustrating.*

frustration /frʌˈstreɪʃən/ *noun*
the feeling of being impatient or
angry because you want to do
what you want to do ➤ *She threw her
pen on the floor in frustration.*

fry /fraɪ/ *verb (past **fried**)*
to cook something in hot oil ➤ *to fry
an egg*

frying pan /ˈfraɪ-ɪŋ ˌpæn/ *noun*
a wide, flat pan used for cooking food
in hot oil

ft
a short way of writing the words **foot**
or **feet** when they are used for
measuring things ➤ *He's 6ft (=6 feet)
tall.*

fuel /ˈfjuːəl/ *noun*
a substance that burns to give heat,
light, or power ➤ *Gas and coal are
fuels.*

fugitive /'fjuːdʒɪtɪv/ noun
a person who has escaped and is trying to avoid being caught, especially by the police ▶ a fugitive from justice

fulfil /fʊlˈfɪl/ verb (present participle **fulfilling**, past **fulfilled**)
to do what you have promised or are expected to do ▶ to fulfil a promise ▶ to fulfil an ambition

fulfilled /fʊlˈfɪld/ adjective
completely satisfied with your life or your job ▶ It is important to feel fulfilled in your work.

fulfilling /fʊlˈfɪlɪŋ/ adjective
making you feel satisfied ▶ Is your relationship a fulfilling one?

full /fʊl/ adjective
1 containing as much as possible ▶ My cup is full.
OPPOSITE: **empty**
2 having had as much as you want to eat ▶ I couldn't eat any more – I'm full.
3 complete or whole ▶ What's your full address?
4 **be full of something** to contain a lot of something ▶ The streets were full of people.
5 **full up** (used about a place or thing) containing as much of something, or as many people, as possible ▶ The restaurant is full up.

full-blown /ˌfʊl ˈbləʊn/ adjective
fully developed ▶ full-blown AIDS

full-grown /ˌfʊl ˈgrəʊn/ (also **fully-grown**) adjective
(used about an animal, a plant, or a person) having developed completely, or grown to its full size ▶ A full-grown blue whale can weigh 30 tons.

full-length /ˌfʊl ˈleŋθ/ adjective
not shorter than the normal length ▶ I've seen the full-length version of the film.

full moon /ˌfʊl ˈmuːn/ noun
the moon when it looks completely round ▶ There's going to be a full moon tonight.

full-scale /ˌfʊl ˈskeɪl/ adjective
1 using all possible powers or forces ▶ a full-scale nuclear war ▶ a full-scale inquiry into the disaster
2 (used about a model, copy, picture, etc.) that is the same size as the thing it represents

full stop /ˌfʊl ˈstɒp/ noun
the sign (.) used in writing, to show the end of a sentence, or after a short form of a word such as **Mr.** or **ft.**

full-time /ˌfʊl ˈtaɪm/ adverb, adjective
working or studying, or giving work or study, all day during the whole working week ▶ I'm looking for a full-time job.
COMPARE: **part-time**

fully /'fʊlɪ/ adverb
completely ▶ I am fully aware of the situation.

fully-grown /ˌfʊlɪ ˈgrəʊn/ adjective
another word for **full-grown**

fumble /'fʌmbəl/ verb (present participle **fumbling**, past **fumbled**)
to try with difficulty to find, move, or hold something, using your hands in an awkward way ▶ She fumbled in her bag for her keys.

fume /fjuːm/ verb
be fuming to be very angry ▶ I was an hour late coming home, and my mother was fuming.

fumes /fjuːmz/ plural noun
gas or smoke that has a strong smell and is unpleasant to breathe ▶ They had breathed in poisonous fumes.

fun /fʌn/ noun (no plural)
1 amusement, enjoyment, or pleasure ▶ That was really good fun.
2 **have fun** to enjoy yourself ▶ The children all had a lot of fun.

F

3 make fun of someone to laugh at someone in a cruel way or to make other people laugh at them ▶ *You shouldn't make fun of him just because he's fat.*

function[1] /ˈfʌŋkʃən/ *noun*
the purpose of someone or something, or the job that they do

function[2] *verb*
to work ▶ *He functions as her deputy when she's away.*

fund /fʌnd/ *noun*
an amount of money collected for a particular reason ▶ *a fund to build a new church*

fundamental /ˌfʌndəˈmentl/ *adjective*
relating to the most basic and important parts of something ▶ *fundamental changes to the education system* (adverb: **fundamentally**)

fund-raising /ˈfʌnd ˌreɪzɪŋ/ *noun (no plural)*
the activity of collecting money for a particular purpose ▶ *concerts and other fund-raising activities*

funeral /ˈfjuːnərəl/ *noun*
a ceremony in which the body of a dead person is burned or put into the ground

funfair /ˈfʌnfeəʳ/ *noun*
a place where people go to enjoy themselves by paying to ride on special machines and by playing games for small prizes

fungus /ˈfʌŋɡəs/ *noun (plural fungi* /ˈfʌŋɡaɪ, -dʒaɪ/)
a plant such as a MUSHROOM which has no leaves or flowers

funky /ˈfʌŋkɪ/ *adjective (funkier, funkiest)*
(used about music) having a strong beat and enjoyable to listen to

funnel /ˈfʌnl/ *noun*
1 a tube which is wide at the top and narrow at the bottom, used for pouring things into a narrow opening
2 a pipe through which smoke leaves a ship or an engine

funny /ˈfʌnɪ/ *adjective (funnier, funniest)*
1 making you laugh; amusing ▶ *a funny joke*
2 strange; unusual ▶ *What's that funny smell?*

fur /fɜːʳ/ *noun (no plural)*
the soft hair on some animals such as cats and rabbits ▶ *a fur coat* (=a coat made of animal fur)

furious /ˈfjʊərɪəs/ *adjective*
very angry

furnace /ˈfɜːnɪs/ *noun*
a large, covered fire for heating metals

furnish /ˈfɜːnɪʃ/ *verb*
to put furniture in a place ▶ *to furnish a house*

furnished /ˈfɜːnɪʃt/ *adjective*
having furniture in ▶ *a furnished room*

furniture /ˈfɜːnɪtʃəʳ/ *noun (no plural)*
things used in a house, like beds, tables, and chairs

furry /ˈfɜːrɪ/ *adjective (furrier, furriest)*
covered in soft hairs ▶ *a furry animal*
COMPARE: **hairy**

further /ˈfɜːðəʳ/
the COMPARATIVE of **far**

further education /ˌfɜːðər edjʊˈkeɪʃən/ *noun (no plural)*
study that you do after leaving school, but not at a university ▶ *a college of further education*
COMPARE: **higher education**

furthest /ˈfɜːðɪst/
the SUPERLATIVE of **far**

furtive /ˈfɜːtɪv/ *adjective*
behaving as if you want to keep something secret ▶ *She gave him a furtive smile.* (adverb: **furtively**)

fury /ˈfjʊərɪ/ noun (no plural)
very great anger
SAME MEANING: **rage**

fuse¹ /fjuːz/ noun
a short wire inside a piece of electrical equipment that melts if too much electricity passes through it ➤ This plug needs a new fuse.

fuse² verb (present participle **fusing**, past **fused**)
1 to join together and become one thing, or to join two things together ➤ The bones of the spine had become fused together.
2 if an electrical system fuses, or if you fuse it, it stops working because the fuse has melted ➤ The lights had fused.

fuss¹ /fʌs/ noun (no plural)
1 worry or excitement about something which is not important ➤ What's all the fuss about?
2 **make a fuss** to cause trouble, especially by complaining ➤ He was making a fuss because the waitress had forgotten him.
3 **make a fuss of someone** to be very kind to someone and give them a lot of attention ➤ My grandparents always make a fuss of me when I visit.

fuss² verb
to worry too much about things that are not important, or to give too much attention to them

fussy /ˈfʌsɪ/ adjective (**fussier**, **fussiest**)
thinking too much about small things that are not important

futile /ˈfjuːtaɪl/ adjective
certain not to be effective or successful ➤ The police made a futile attempt to rescue him.

future /ˈfjuːtʃər/ noun (no plural)
1 **the future** time that will come; things that have not happened yet ➤ Do you have any plans for the future?
COMPARE: **past**

2 **in future** after now ➤ In future, please be more careful (=in the past, you were not careful enough).

future tense /ˌfjuːtʃə ˈtens/ noun
the form of a verb that you use when you are talking about the future, e.g. in English, "I will go" is in a future tense

fuzzy /ˈfʌzɪ/ adjective (**fuzzier**, **fuzziest**)
unclear ➤ The TV picture's gone fuzzy.

Gg

g
a short way of writing the words **gram** or **grams** ➤ 500g

gabble /ˈgæbəl/ verb (present participle **gabbling**, past **gabbled**)
to speak so quickly that people cannot understand you

gadget /ˈgædʒɪt/ noun
a machine or tool that is small but useful ➤ a clever little gadget for cutting bread

gag¹ /gæg/ verb (present participle **gagging**, past **gagged**)
to cover someone's mouth with a piece of cloth so that they cannot make any noise ➤ The robbers tied him up and gagged him.

gag² noun
a piece of cloth used to cover someone's mouth so that they cannot make any noise

gain /geɪn/ verb
1 to increase in something ➤ The baby's gaining weight.
2 to get something useful ➤ What will you gain from doing the course? ➤ She's gaining good experience in the job.

G

gala /'gɑːlə/ noun
a special public performance of
sports, etc. ➤ *a swimming gala*

galaxy /'gæləksɪ/ noun (plural
galaxies)
a very big group of stars in space
➤ *One day, people might be able to
travel to other galaxies.*

gale /geɪl/ noun
a very strong wind

gall /gɔːl/ noun
have the gall to do something to do
something that is rude without caring
what other people think ➤ *She had
the gall to say I was being childish!*

gallery /'gælərɪ/ noun (plural
galleries)
a building or a large, long room where
paintings, photographs, etc. are
shown to the public ➤ *an art gallery*

gallon /'gælən/ noun
a measure of liquid equal to 8 pints

gallop¹ /'gæləp/ verb
(used about a horse) to run very fast

gallop² noun
the very fast run of a horse

gamble¹ /'gæmbəl/ noun
something you do in which you take a
risk because you hope to get
something ➤ *The doctors say the
operation is a bit of a gamble which
may not succeed.*

gamble² verb (present participle
gambling, past **gambled**)
1 to try to win money on card games,
horse races, etc. ➤ *He lost a lot of
money by gambling.*
COMPARE: **bet**
2 to take a risk because you hope to
get something

gambler /'gæmblər/ noun
a person who tries to win money on
card games, horse races, etc.

gambling /'gæmblɪŋ/ noun (no
plural)
the activity of trying to win money by

guessing the result of card games,
horse races, etc. ➤ *Many more people
are now using the Internet for
gambling.*

game¹ /geɪm/ noun
1 an activity in which you follow
certain rules in order to get points
and defeat another person or team
➤ *Football is a team game.* ➤ *a game
of cards*
2 a secret plan that is usually not
honest ➤ *I don't know what his game
is, but he's up to something.*
3 **give the game away** to tell people
something that should be a secret
4 **games** plural noun sports in which
people compete ➤ *The winter games
were very exciting.*

game² noun (no plural)
wild animals or birds that people
hunt for food or sport

Gameboy /'geɪmbɔɪ/ noun
trademark
a small computer on which you play
games

game show /'geɪm ʃəʊ/ noun
a television programme in which
people play games to win money or
prizes

gang¹ /gæŋ/ noun
1 a group of people working together,
e.g. building workers or criminals
2 a group of young people who cause
trouble

gang² verb
gang up to get together in a group
and behave badly to someone ➤ *The
older children ganged up against the
younger ones.*

gangster /'gæŋstər/ noun
a member of a group of violent
criminals

gaol /dʒeɪl/ noun
another word for **jail**

gap /gæp/ noun
1 a space between two things or
between two parts of something ➤ *He*

G

has a gap **between** his two front teeth.
▶ *There was a small gap in the fence.*
2 a difference between two groups, amounts, or situations ▶ *the gap between rich and poor*
3 something that is missing in a situation, so that the situation is not complete ▶ *There's been a gap in my life since my father died.*
4 a period of time when nothing happens or is said ▶ *a gap in the conversation*

gape /geɪp/ *verb (present participle gaping, past gaped)*
to look at something or someone in surprise, with your mouth open ▶ *He just stood there gaping at the mess.*

gaping /'geɪpɪŋ/ *adjective*
open very wide ▶ *The crash left a gaping hole in the wall.* ▶ *a gaping wound*

garage /'gæraːʒ/ *noun*
1 a place where cars, buses, etc. are kept
2 a place where you can buy petrol or have your car repaired

garbled /'gaːbəld/ *adjective*
mixed up and difficult to understand ▶ *She left a garbled message about being late.*

garden /'gaːdn/ *noun*
a piece of land where trees, flowers, or vegetables are grown, round a house or in a public place

gardener /'gaːdnər/ *noun*
a person who works in a garden, for pleasure or as a job

gardening /'gaːdnɪŋ/ *noun (no plural)*
work in a garden ▶ *He enjoys gardening.*

gargle /'gaːgəl/ *verb (present participle gargling, past gargled)*
to clean your throat with water or a special liquid that you do not swallow ▶ *If you have a sore throat, try gargling with salt water.*

garish /'geərɪʃ/ *adjective*
very brightly coloured and unpleasant to look at ▶ *The curtains are very garish.*

garland /'gaːlənd/ *noun*
a ring of flowers or leaves, worn for decoration

garlic /'gaːlɪk/ *noun (no plural)*
a plant used in cooking to give a strong taste

garment /'gaːmənt/ *noun*
a piece of clothing ▶ *This garment should be washed by hand.*

garnish /'gaːnɪʃ/ *verb*
to decorate food with small pieces of fruit or vegetables ▶ *I garnished the meat with some herbs.*

gas /gæs/ *noun*
1 *(plural gases)* any substance like air that is not liquid or solid
2 *(no plural)* a substance like air, that is used in the home to give heat and light ▶ *She cooks with gas.*

gash /gæʃ/ *noun (plural gashes)*
a deep cut in something ▶ *She had a deep gash in her leg.*

gasp¹ /gaːsp/ *verb*
to take a quick, short breath ▶ *I gasped as I jumped into the cold river.*

gasp² *noun*
the sound of a quick, short breath ▶ *a gasp of surprise*

gate /geɪt/ *noun*
1 a door which closes an opening in a wall or fence
2 an entrance or way out at an airport

gâteau /'gætəʊ/ *noun (plural gâteaux /-təʊz/)*
a large cake, often filled and decorated with cream and fruit ▶ *a piece of chocolate gâteau*

gatecrash /'geɪtkræʃ/ *verb*
to go to a party or an event that you have not been invited to ▶ *People always gatecrash my parties.*

G

gateway /'geɪtweɪ/ *noun*
an opening in a fence or in an outside wall that can be closed with a gate

gather /'gæðə/ *verb*
1 to come together in a group ▶ *A crowd soon gathered to see what had happened.*
2 to collect flowers or crops ▶ *In the summer, the farmers gather the fruit.*
SAME MEANING (**2**): **pick**

gathering /'gæðərɪŋ/ *noun*
a meeting or coming together of a lot of people in one place

gaudy /'gɔːdɪ/ *adjective* (**gaudier, gaudiest**)
very bright, in a way that is unpleasant ▶ *He was wearing a gaudy tie.*

gauge /geɪdʒ/ *noun*
an instrument that measures the amount of something ▶ *A petrol gauge shows the amount of petrol left in a car.*

gaunt /gɔːnt/ *adjective*
very thin and pale, especially because of illness ▶ *He was looking sick and gaunt.*

gave /geɪv/
the PAST TENSE of the verb **give**

gay /geɪ/ *adjective*
1 sexually attracted to people of the same sex; HOMOSEXUAL
2 bright and attractive ▶ *gay colours*

gaze /geɪz/ *verb* (present participle **gazing**, past **gazed**)
to look steadily at something for a long time ▶ *The child gazed at the toys in the shop window.*

GCSE /ˌdʒiː siː es ˈiː/ *noun*
GENERAL CERTIFICATE OF SECONDARY EDUCATION; an examination in a choice of subjects taken in British schools by pupils who are 15 or 16 years old

gear /gɪəʳ/ *noun*
1 a set of wheels with teeth in an engine, which work together to make the wheels of a car go faster or more slowly ▶ *The lorry driver changed gear to go up the hill.*
2 (no plural) the special clothes or things you need for a particular sport ▶ *tennis gear*

geese /giːs/
the plural of **goose**

gel /dʒel/ *noun (no plural)*
a thick liquid that you put on your hair to make it stay in the right position

gem /dʒem/ *noun*
any sort of stone which is worth a lot of money and is used as jewellery

gender /'dʒendəʳ/ *noun*
(used about a person) the state of being male or female

gene /dʒiːn/ *noun*
the part of a cell of a living thing that controls its development, and which is passed from the parent to the young child, animal, or plant ▶ *Brothers and sisters share some of the same genes.*

general¹ /'dʒenərəl/ *adjective*
1 concerning most people or places ▶ *How soon will the drug be available for general use?*
2 concerning the whole of something, rather than its parts ▶ *The house's general condition is good, although it needs painting.*
3 in general in most cases ▶ *In general, I like the people I work with.*

general² *noun*
a very important officer in the army

general election /ˌdʒenərəl ɪ'lekʃən/ *noun*
a time when the people of a country vote to choose their government

generalization /ˌdʒenərəlaɪ'zeɪʃən/ *noun*
a statement about all people or things of a particular kind, which may not be true about every one ▶ *It is*

G

silly to make generalizations about all students.

general knowledge /ˌdʒenərəl ˈnɒlɪdʒ/ *noun (no plural)*
knowledge about many different subjects

generally /ˈdʒenərəlɪ/ *adverb*
usually ► *Children in England generally start school when they are five.*

generate /ˈdʒenəreɪt/ *verb (present participle **generating**, past **generated**)*
to make heat or power ► *We use coal to generate electricity.*

generation /ˌdʒenəˈreɪʃən/ *noun*
the people born at a certain time ► *My parents and I belong to different generations.*

generator /ˈdʒenəreɪtər/ *noun*
a machine that makes electricity

generosity /ˌdʒenəˈrɒsətɪ/ *noun (no plural)*
the willingness to give money, help, or presents ► *a card thanking him for his generosity*

generous /ˈdʒenərəs/ *adjective*
willing to give money, help, or presents ► *How generous of you to lend us your car!*
OPPOSITE: **mean**

genetic /dʒɪˈnetɪk/ *adjective*
relating to or caused by GENES ► *genetic diseases*

genetically modified /dʒɪˌnetɪklɪ ˈmɒdɪfaɪd/ *adjective*
(used about plants) having received GENES from another plant in a scientific process ► *These burgers contain genetically modified soya.*

genetics /dʒɪˈnetɪks/ *noun (no plural)*
the study of how the development and form of living things are affected by their GENES

genitals /ˈdʒenɪtlz/ *plural noun*
the parts on the outside of your body that are used for having sex and producing babies

genius /ˈdʒiːnɪəs/ *noun (plural **geniuses**)*
a person who is very, very clever

gentle /ˈdʒentl/ *adjective*
kind and calm; not rough or violent ► *Be gentle with the baby.* ► *a gentle voice (adverb: **gently**)*

gentleman /ˈdʒentlmən/ *noun (plural **gentlemen** /-mən/)*
1 a kind man who behaves well towards other people
2 a polite word for a man ► *This gentleman has been waiting for an hour.*

Gents /dʒents/ *noun*
the Gents the men's TOILET ► *He's gone to the Gents.*
COMPARE: **Ladies**

genuine /ˈdʒenjuɪn/ *adjective*
real and true ► *This ring is genuine gold. (adverb: **genuinely**)*

geography /dʒɪˈɒgrəfɪ/ *noun (no plural)*
the study of the countries of the world and things like seas, mountains, and weather

geology /dʒɪˈɒlədʒɪ/ *noun (no plural)*
the study of rocks, and how they were made

geometric /ˌdʒiːəˈmetrɪk/ *(also **geometrical** /ˌdʒiːəˈmetrɪkəl/) adjective*
1 having regular shapes and lines ► *The rugs have geometric designs.*
2 of or about geometry

geometry /dʒɪˈɒmətrɪ/ *noun (no plural)*
the study of measuring shapes, lines, etc.

germ /dʒɜːm/ *noun*
a very small, living thing that grows in dirty places and makes people ill

G

German measles /ˌdʒɜːmən ˈmiːzəlz/ *noun (no plural)*
a disease that causes red spots on your body ▶ *Sam's got German measles.*

germinate /ˈdʒɜːmɪneɪt/ *verb (present participle germinating, past germinated)*
(used about seeds) to begin to grow

gerund /ˈdʒerənd/ *noun*
a noun with the same form as the PRESENT PARTICIPLE of a verb – for example, "reading" in the sentence "He enjoys reading."

gesture¹ /ˈdʒestʃər/ *noun*
a movement of your hands, head, etc. done to express something

gesture² *verb (present participle gesturing, past gestured)*
to move your head, hands, etc. in order to express something ▶ *He gestured angrily at me.*

get /get/ *verb (present participle getting, past got /gɒt/)*
1 to obtain something ▶ *I must get a birthday present for my mother.* ▶ *Can I get you a drink?*
2 to have or receive something ▶ *I got a real shock when I heard the news.* ▶ *The boy got a bicycle from his aunt.* ▶ *I don't get much time for reading.*
3 to become ▶ *She got very cross with me.* ▶ *The weather is getting colder.*
4 to bring or fetch something ▶ *Could you get me a glass of water, please?* ▶ *She went to get the children from school.*
5 get away to escape from a place ▶ *Four prisoners got away.*
6 get back to return, usually to your home ▶ *When did you get back from your holiday?*
7 get off to climb down from something such as a bus, train, or horse ▶ *The train stopped and he got off.* ▶ *She got off her bicycle.*

8 get on to climb onto something such as a bus, train, or horse ▶ *I got on at the library.* ▶ *She got on her bike and rode home.*
9 get on with someone to be friendly with someone ▶ *Do you get on well with your neighbours?*
10 get up to rise from a lying or sitting position, especially from your bed after sleeping ▶ *What time do you usually get up on Sundays?*

getaway /ˈgetəweɪ/ *noun*
make a getaway to escape quickly from a place, especially after doing something illegal ▶ *The robbers made a quick getaway after stealing the money.*

get-together /ˈget təˌgeðər/ *noun*
a friendly, informal meeting or party ▶ *We're having a family get-together tomorrow.*

ghastly /ˈgɑːstli/ *adjective*
very bad ▶ *ghastly news* ▶ *ghastly food*
SAME MEANING: **awful**

ghetto /ˈgetəʊ/ *noun (plural ghettoes)*
a part of a city where a lot of very poor people live

ghost /gəʊst/ *noun*
the form of a dead person that some people believe can be seen

ghostly /ˈgəʊstli/ *adjective (ghostlier, ghostliest)*
making people afraid, as if there were ghosts ▶ *a ghostly light.*

giant¹ /ˈdʒaɪənt/ *noun*
a very large, strong man in children's stories

giant² *adjective*
very large

gibberish /ˈdʒɪbərɪʃ/ *noun (no plural)*
things someone says or writes that have no meaning or are difficult to understand ▶ *I tried to read the*

instruction book, but it was all gibberish.

gibe /dʒaɪb/ noun
another word for **jibe**

giddy /'gɪdɪ/ adjective (**giddier**, **giddiest**)
having a sick feeling that everything is moving around you ➤ She felt giddy when she looked down from the high bridge.

gift /gɪft/ noun
1 a present ➤ a gift shop
2 a special ability to do something ➤ a gift for languages

gifted /'gɪftɪd/ adjective
very intelligent or having a natural ability to do something very well ➤ a school for gifted children ➤ Paul's a very gifted artist.

gig /gɪg/ noun
a popular music or JAZZ concert

gigantic /dʒaɪ'gæntɪk/ adjective
very big
SAME MEANING: **enormous**

giggle /'gɪgəl/ verb (present participle **giggling**, past **giggled**)
to laugh in a silly way ➤ The girls were giggling in class.

gills /gɪlz/ plural noun
the part of a fish, near its head, through which it breathes

gimmick /'gɪmɪk/ noun
something unusual that is used to make people interested in something ➤ The news story was just a gimmick to sell more tickets.

gin /dʒɪn/ noun
1 (no plural) a strong alcoholic drink that has no colour ➤ Her favourite drink is gin and tonic.
2 a glass of this drink ➤ Can I have two gins, please?

ginger¹ /'dʒɪndʒə/ noun (no plural)
1 a plant with a root which can be used to give food a strong taste
2 a colour between orange and brown

ginger² adjective
with a colour between orange and brown ➤ ginger hair ➤ a ginger cat ➤ a man with a ginger beard

gingerly /'dʒɪndʒəlɪ/ adverb
slowly, carefully, and gently ➤ She crept gingerly into the room.

gipsy (also **gypsy**) /'dʒɪpsɪ/ noun (plural **gipsies**)
one of a race of people who travel around in CARAVANS, earning money by selling flowers, etc.

giraffe /dʒɪ'rɑːf/ noun
a tall African animal with a very long neck, very long legs, and large, brown spots on its coat

girder /'gɜːdə/ noun
a long, thick piece of iron or steel, used to build bridges or buildings ➤ Huge iron girders held up the roof.

girl /gɜːl/ noun
a female child ➤ She has two children: a girl and a boy. ➤ There are four girls in our class.

girlfriend /'gɜːlfrend/ noun
a girl or woman you have a romantic relationship with

Girl Guide /gɜːl 'gaɪd/ noun
a member of a special club for girls

gist /dʒɪst/ noun
the main points or general meaning of what someone says or writes ➤ I understood the gist of what he was saying.

give /gɪv/ verb (present participle **giving**, past tense **gave** /geɪv/, past participle **given** /'gɪvən/)
1 to hand or pass something to someone for them to use, or as a present ➤ Please give that back to me when you've finished. ➤ His uncle gave him a toy train for his birthday.
2 to let or make someone have something ➤ That child has given us a lot of trouble. ➤ Can I give you some advice?

G

3 to perform an action ▸ *She gave a cry of anger when she heard the news.* ▸ *He gave us a talk about the history of the city.*

4 give way to allow other cars, etc. to go before you when you are driving ▸ *You have to give way to traffic coming from the left.*

5 give something away (**a**) to make known something that is secret ▸ *She begged him not to give away her secret to anyone.* (**b**) to let someone keep something of yours, usually because you do not want it any more ▸ *I'm giving away all the clothes that are too small for the children.*

6 give something back to return something to its owner ▸ *I'll give you back your CDs next week.*

7 give something in to hand something to the person in charge ▸ *Give your exam papers in as you leave the room.*

8 give something out to give something to each of several other people ▸ *The teacher gave out the books.*

9 give something up to stop having or doing something ▸ *She's trying to give up smoking.*

giveaway /'gɪvəweɪ/ *noun*
be a (dead) giveaway to make it very easy for someone to guess something ▸ *Vince was lying. His red face was a dead giveaway.*

given¹ /'gɪvn/
the PAST PARTICIPLE of the verb **give**

given² *adjective*
1 (used about times, dates, etc.) previously arranged ▸ *All claims have to be made by a given date.*
2 any given …, a given … a particular time or thing that can be used as an example of what you are talking about ▸ *There are thousands of homeless people in London at any given time.*

given³ *preposition*
if you consider ▸ *Given the circumstances, you've coped well.*

glacier /'glæsɪər/ *noun*
a very large mass of ice in the mountains that moves very slowly along the ground

glad /glæd/ *adjective* (**gladder, gladdest**)
pleased and happy ▸ *I am glad to see you. (adverb: **gladly**)*

glamorous /'glæmərəs/ *adjective*
attractive and exciting, especially because of being connected with wealth or success

glamour /'glæmər/ *noun* (no plural)
the quality of being attractive and exciting, and connected with wealth or success ▸ *I love the glamour of Hollywood.*

glance¹ /glɑːns/ *verb* (present participle **glancing**, past **glanced**)
to look quickly at someone or something ▸ *She glanced **at** her watch.*

glance² *noun*
a quick, short look

gland /glænd/ *noun*
a small organ in the body that produces a liquid, such as SWEAT or SALIVA ▸ *The glands in her neck are swollen.*

glare¹ /gleər/ *verb* (present participle **glaring**, past **glared**)
1 to shine with an unpleasantly bright light ▸ *The sun glared down.*
2 to look at someone angrily ▸ *She glared **at** me and then walked away.*

glare² *noun*
1 an angry look
2 unpleasant brightness ▸ *The glare of the sun made her eyes hurt.*

glaring /'gleərɪŋ/ *adjective*
1 (used about lights) very bright, making your eyes hurt if you look at them ▸ *the car's glaring headlights*

2 (used about a mistake) very bad and very noticeable

glass /glɑːs/ *noun*
1 (*no plural*) a clear, hard substance used for windows and bottles
2 (*plural glasses*) a cup made of glass, without a handle
3 glasses *plural noun* specially shaped pieces of glass or plastic that you wear in front of your eyes to help you see better

glaze /gleɪz/ (*also glaze over*) *verb* (*present participle glazing, past glazed*)
(used about eyes) to show no expression because you are bored or tired ► *As soon as he mentioned football, her eyes started to glaze over.*

gleam /gliːm/ *verb*
to shine ► *The river gleamed in the moonlight.*

glean /gliːn/ *verb*
to find out information slowly and with difficulty ► *It's difficult to glean any information from Dan.*

glide /glaɪd/ *verb* (*present participle gliding, past glided*)
to move forward smoothly

glider /ˈglaɪdə^r/ *noun*
an aircraft without an engine

glimmer[1] /ˈglɪmə^r/ *verb*
to give a faint light ► *lights glimmering in the distance*

glimmer[2] *noun*
a faint light

glimpse[1] /glɪmps/ *noun*
a very quick look ► *I only caught a glimpse of the thief's face, so I can't describe it.*

glimpse[2] *verb* (*present participle glimpsing, past glimpsed*)
to see something very quickly and usually by chance

glint /glɪnt/ *verb*
to give out small flashes of light ► *His glasses glinted in the sun.*

glisten /ˈglɪsən/ *verb*
to shine as if wet ► *eyes glistening with tears*

glitter[1] /ˈglɪtə^r/ *verb*
to shine brightly with flashes of light ► *The sea glittered in the sun.*

glitter[2] *noun*
a bright light that seems to flash

gloat /gləʊt/ *verb*
to show in an annoying way that you are happy about your success or about someone else's failure ► *Dick was still gloating over his team's win.*

global /ˈgləʊbəl/ *adjective*
affecting or including the whole world ► *global environmental issues* (*adverb: globally*)

global warming /ˌgləʊbəl ˈwɔːmɪŋ/ *noun* (*no plural*)
an increase in temperatures around the world, because gases caused by POLLUTION trap the sun's heat

globe /gləʊb/ *noun*
1 a ball with a map of the world on it
2 the Earth ► *She's travelled all over the globe.*

gloom /gluːm/ *noun* (*no plural*)
1 almost complete darkness ► *He could just make out a distant figure in the gloom.*
2 a strong feeling of sadness and having no hope ► *News of her arrest filled them with gloom.*

gloomy /ˈgluːmɪ/ *adjective* (*gloomier, gloomiest*)
1 rather dark ► *a gloomy day*
2 sad and having little hope ► *a gloomy expression on his face* (*adverb: gloomily*)

glorious /ˈglɔːrɪəs/ *adjective*
1 having great honour ► *the country's glorious history*
2 very pleasant ► *a glorious holiday*

glory /ˈglɔːrɪ/ *noun* (*no plural*)
fame and respect that is given to someone who has done something great

G

glossary /ˈglɒsəri/ noun (plural **glossaries**)
a list of technical or unusual words and what they mean, printed at the end of a book ▶ a glossary of technical terms

glossy /ˈglɒsi/ adjective (**glossier**, **glossiest**)
1 shiny and smooth ▶ a small dog with glossy, black fur
2 (used about magazines, photographs, etc.) printed on good-quality paper that is shiny

glove /glʌv/ noun
a piece of clothing that you wear on your hand, with separate parts for all your fingers

glow¹ /gləʊ/ verb
to shine with a dull light ▶ The fire glowed in the dark.

glow² noun
a soft, warm light ▶ the glow of a sunset

glower /ˈglaʊəʳ/ verb
to look at someone in an angry way ▶ I started to speak, but Chris glowered at me so I stopped.

glowing /ˈgləʊɪŋ/ adjective
praising someone or something a lot ▶ The play got a glowing review.

glue¹ /gluː/ noun (no plural)
a substance used for sticking things together ▶ She stuck the handle onto the cup with glue.

glue² verb (present participle **glueing** or **gluing**, past **glued**)
to stick something with glue ▶ She glued the pieces together.

glum /glʌm/ adjective (**glummer**, **glummest**)
sad (adverb: **glumly**)

glut /glʌt/ noun
too many things of the same kind that exist or are available at the same time ▶ There's a glut of violent American films around at the moment.

gm
a short way of writing the words **gram** or **grams**

GM /ˌdʒiː ˈem/ adjective
GENETICALLY MODIFIED; used to describe foods which contain GENES that have been artificially changed

GMT /ˌdʒiː em ˈtiː/ noun (no plural)
GREENWICH MEAN TIME; the time in London, used as an international measure

gnaw /nɔː/ verb
to bite on something for a long time ▶ The rat gnawed a hole in the wooden box.

go¹ /gəʊ/ verb (past tense **went** /went/, past participle **gone** /gɒn/)
1 to move towards a place ▶ She went into the kitchen. ▶ This car is going too fast.
2 to leave a place ▶ The train goes in five minutes.
LOOK AT: **gone**
3 to travel somewhere, usually in order to do something ▶ They've gone shopping.
4 to become ▶ His hair is going grey.
5 (used about a machine) to work properly ▶ My watch won't go since it fell in the bath.
6 be going to used to say that something will happen in the future ▶ I think it's going to snow. ▶ I'm going to buy that bicycle.
7 go well to be successful ▶ The game went very well for my team.
8 go away to leave ▶ She's gone away for a few months.
9 go out to leave a building ▶ She took her bag and went out.
10 go up to increase ▶ Prices have really gone up this year.

go² noun (plural **goes**)
a try ▶ Can I have a go at mending the bicycle?

go-ahead /ˈgəʊ əˌhed/ noun
give someone the go-ahead to give someone official permission to start

doing something ▶ *The council gave them the go-ahead to build the new stadium.*

goal /gəʊl/ *noun*
1 the space between two posts, into which you try to hit or kick the ball in games like football
2 a point that you win when the ball goes into the goal ▶ *Our team won by three goals to one.*
3 an aim ▶ *My goal is to go to college.*

goalie /ˈgəʊli/ *noun*
a GOALKEEPER

goalkeeper /ˈgəʊkliːpəʳ/ *noun*
the player in games like football who tries to stop the ball before it goes into the GOAL

goalpost /ˈgəʊlpəʊst/ *noun*
one of the two posts on each side of the GOAL in games such as football

goat /gəʊt/ *noun*
an animal like a sheep that is kept for milk and for its hairy coat

gobble /ˈgɒbəl/ *(also* **gobble up***)* *verb (present participle* **gobbling***, past* **gobbled***)*
to eat something very quickly ▶ *Matt gobbled up his dinner and ran back outside.*

goblin /ˈgɒblɪn/ *noun*
a small, ugly creature in children's stories, who often does bad things

god /gɒd/ *noun*
any being to whom people pray, and who is believed to control the world

God /gɒd/ *noun*
the being who, especially in the Christian, Muslim, and Jewish religions, is believed to be the maker and ruler of the world ▶ *to pray to God*

godchild /ˈgɒdtʃaɪld/ *noun (plural* **godchildren** /-ˌtʃɪldrən/*)*
in the Christian religion, a person's godchild is a child whose religious

education that person has promised at a religious ceremony to be responsible for

goddess /ˈgɒdes/ *noun (plural* **goddesses***)*
a female god

godfather /ˈgɒdˌfɑːðəʳ/ *noun*
in the Christian religion, a man who promises at a religious ceremony to be responsible for a child's religious education

godmother /ˈgɒdˌmʌðəʳ/ *noun*
in the Christian religion, a woman who promises at a religious ceremony to be responsible for a child's religious education

godparent /ˈgɒdˌpeərənt/ *noun*
in the Christian religion, a person who promises at a religious ceremony to be responsible for a child's religious education

goes /gəʊz/
the THIRD PERSON SINGULAR of the PRESENT TENSE of the verb **go**

goggles /ˈgɒgəlz/ *plural noun*
large, round glasses that you wear to keep your eyes safe, e.g. when swimming or working with dangerous chemicals, fire, etc.

going[1] /ˈgəʊɪŋ/ *noun (no plural)*
the speed at which you travel or work ▶ *We got there in four hours, which wasn't bad going.*

going[2] *adjective*
the going rate the usual amount that you have to pay for a service or that you get for doing a job ▶ *What's the going rate for private lessons at the moment?*

goings-on /ˌgəʊɪŋz ˈɒn/ *plural noun*
things that happen which are strange or interesting ▶ *There have been some interesting goings-on at the house next door.*

go-kart /ˈgəʊ kɑːt/ *noun*
a low vehicle with no roof and a small

engine that people drive in races for pleasure

gold /gəʊld/ *noun (no plural)*
1 a yellow metal that costs a lot of money ▶ *a ring made of gold*
2 the colour of this metal

golden /'gəʊldən/ *adjective*
like gold or made of gold ▶ *a golden sky* ▶ *a golden plate*

goldfish /'gəʊldfɪʃ/ *noun (plural goldfish)*
a small, orange fish, usually kept as a pet

golf /gɒlf/ *noun (no plural)*
a game in which a small, hard ball is hit into a number of holes in the ground using special sticks

golf course /'gɒlf kɔːs/ *noun*
an area of land where people play golf

gone /gɒn/
the PAST PARTICIPLE of the verb **go**

> Look at the difference between **been** and **gone**. If you have **been** to a place, you have travelled there and returned. If you have **gone** to a place, you have travelled there and have not yet returned: *Liz has gone to Spain* (=she is in Spain now). ▶ *Liz has been to Spain* (=she went there and now she has returned).

gong /gɒŋ/ *noun*
a flat piece of metal that is hung up and hit with a stick to make a noise

gonna /'gɒnə/
an informal way of saying "going to"
▶ *We're gonna spend the evening in Bar Rita.*

good¹ /gʊd/ *adjective* (**better** /'betə'/, **best** /best/)
1 of a high standard or quality
▶ *a good school* ▶ *a very good memory*
2 pleasant or favourable ▶ *Have a good time.* ▶ *a good party*

3 skilful or successful at something
▶ *She's good at languages.* ▶ *He's good with babies.*
4 right for a particular purpose ▶ *This music is good for dancing.*
5 (used about children) well-behaved
▶ *She's got very good children.*
6 kind ▶ *He's been very good to me.*
7 healthy and strong ▶ *good teeth*
OPPOSITE (**1** to **7**): **bad**
8 Good for you! used to show you approve of what someone has done
▶ *"I've passed all my exams." "Good for you!"*

good² *noun (no plural)*
1 advantage ▶ *What's the good of having a car if you can't drive?*
2 for good for ever ▶ *She's left her job for good.*
3 do someone good to do something that will make someone feel well ▶ *A walk will do you good.*

good afternoon /gʊd ˌɑːftə'nuːn/ *interjection*
an expression you use to greet someone in the afternoon

goodbye /gʊd'baɪ/ *interjection*
a word you use when you leave someone or someone leaves you
COMPARE: **hello**

good evening /gʊd 'iːvnɪŋ/ *interjection*
an expression you use to greet someone in the evening

Good Friday /gʊd 'fraɪdeɪ, -dɪ/ *noun*
the Friday before EASTER, a Christian religious holiday

good-looking /gʊd 'lʊkɪŋ/ *adjective*
(used about a person) attractive
▶ *He's very good-looking.*

good morning /gʊd 'mɔːnɪŋ/ *interjection*
an expression you use to greet someone in the morning

goodness¹ /'gʊdnəs/ *noun (no plural)*
kindness

goodness² *interjection*
a word used in expressions which
show you are surprised or annoyed
➤ *Goodness me!*

goodnight /gʊd'naɪt/ *interjection*
an expression you use when you are
going home at night or before you go
to bed

goods /gʊdz/ *plural noun*
things like food or clothes that are
bought and sold

gooey /'guːɪ/ *adjective* (**gooier,
gooiest**)
sticky, soft, and usually sweet ➤ *a
gooey chocolate cake*

goose /guːs/ *noun* (*plural* **geese** /giːs/)
a white bird that looks like a large duck

gorge /gɔːdʒ/ *noun*
a very narrow valley with steep sides
➤ *The railway runs through a
beautiful gorge.*

gorgeous /'gɔːdʒəs/ *adjective*
very nice or beautiful ➤ *a gorgeous
dress*
SAME MEANING: **lovely**

gorilla /gə'rɪlə/ *noun*
a very large, strong animal that looks
like a very large monkey

gory /'gɔːrɪ/ *adjective* (**gorier,
goriest**)
(used about films, stories, etc.)
involving a lot of violence and blood
➤ *The ending was too gory for me.*

gosh /gɒʃ/ *interjection*
something you say when you are
surprised ➤ *Gosh! What are you doing
here?*

gossip¹ /'gɒsɪp/ *noun*
1 (*no plural*) unkind talk about
people's private lives ➤ *You shouldn't
listen to gossip.*
2 a person who talks unkindly about
other people's private lives

gossip² *verb*
to talk unkindly about other people's
private lives

got /gɒt/
the PAST TENSE and PAST PARTICIPLE of the
verb **get**
LOOK AT: **have**

gourmet¹ /'gʊəmeɪ/ *adjective*
relating to good food and drink ➤ *a
gourmet restaurant*

gourmet² *noun*
a person who enjoys and knows a lot
about good food and drink

govern /'gʌvən/ *verb*
to control and rule a country and its
people ➤ *a country governed by the
army*

government /'gʌvəmənt/ *noun*
the people who control what happens
in a country

governor /'gʌvənəʳ/ *noun*
a person who controls a state or
prison

gown /gaʊn/ *noun*
a long dress for a woman ➤ *a
beautiful evening gown*

GP /,dʒiː 'piː/ *noun*
a GENERAL PRACTITIONER; a doctor who
treats people for ordinary health
problems

grab /græb/ *verb* (*present participle*
grabbing, *past* **grabbed**)
to take hold of something quickly and
roughly ➤ *The thief grabbed my bag.*
SAME MEANING: **snatch**

grace /greɪs/ *noun* (*no plural*)
1 an attractive way of moving ➤ *She
dances with such grace.*
2 a short prayer before or after a
meal ➤ *Who is going to say grace?*

graceful /'greɪsfəl/ *adjective*
attractive and smooth in movement
(*adverb:* **gracefully**)

gracious /'greɪʃəs/ *adjective*
1 kind, polite, and pleasant ➤ *a
gracious smile*
2 Gracious!, Good Gracious! a phrase
used when you are surprised
➤ *Gracious! What are you doing here?*

G

grade¹ /greɪd/ *noun*
1 a level, size, or quality ▸ *We sell three grades of egg.*
2 a mark you get for an examination or piece of work at school

grade² *verb (present participle* **grading**, *past* **graded)**
to put things into groups according to size, quality, etc. ▸ *The farmers graded the apples into several sizes.*

gradient /'greɪdɪənt/ *noun*
a measurement of how steep a slope is, especially on a road or railway ▸ *Ringstead Road was on a steep gradient.*

gradual /'grædʒʊəl/ *adjective*
happening slowly ▸ *a gradual improvement in his work (adverb:* **gradually)**

graduate¹ /'grædʒʊeɪt/ *verb (present participle* **graduating**, *past* **graduated)**
to take and pass the last examination at a university ▸ *She graduated from a French university.* ▸ *She graduated in history.*

graduate² /'grædʒʊət/ *noun*
a person who has passed the last examination at a university

graduation /ˌgrædʒʊˈeɪʃən/ *noun*
the act of completing a university degree, or the ceremony at which you receive your degree ▸ *After graduation, Sally trained as a teacher.*

graffiti /græˈfiːtɪ/ *noun (no plural)*
writing and pictures that people draw illegally in public places ▸ *The school walls were covered with graffiti.*

grain /greɪn/ *noun*
1 *(no plural)* a crop like wheat, maize, or rice that has seeds which we eat ▸ *Grain is used for making flour.*
2 a seed, or small, hard piece of something ▸ *a few grains of salt*

gram *(also* **gramme)** /græm/ *noun*
a measure of weight. There are 1,000 grams in a kilogram ▸ *500 grams* (=500g)

grammar /'græmə'/ *noun (no plural)*
the rules of a language ▸ *English grammar*

grammar school /'græmə skuːl/ *noun*
a school in Britain, especially in the past, for clever children between the ages of 11 and 18
COMPARE: **comprehensive school**

grammatical /grəˈmætɪkəl/ *adjective*
correct according to the rules of language ▸ *"I aren't" is not grammatical.*

gramme /græm/ *noun*
another word for **gram**

gramophone /'græməfəʊn/ *noun*
a machine on which records can be played, so that you can hear the music or words

gran /græn/ *noun*
a grandmother

grand /grænd/ *adjective*
very large and fine ▸ *He lives in a rather grand house.*

grandchild /'græntʃaɪld/ *noun (plural* **grandchildren** /-ˌtʃɪldrən/)
the child of your son or daughter

granddad /'grændæd/ *noun*
a grandfather

granddaughter /'grændɔːtə'/ *noun*
the daughter of your son or daughter

grandfather /'grænfɑːðə'/ *noun*
the father of one of your parents

grandma /'grænmɑː/ *noun*
a grandmother

grandmother /'grænmʌðə'/ *noun*
the mother of one of your parents

grandpa /'grænpɑː/ *noun*
a grandfather

grandparent /'grænpeərənt/ *noun*
the parent of your mother or father

grandson /'grænsʌn/ *noun*
the son of your son or daughter

G

granny /'grænɪ/ *noun (plural grannies)*
(used by children) a grandmother

grant¹ /grɑːnt/ *verb*
to give or allow someone something, often officially ▶ *The children were granted a holiday from school.*

grant² *noun*
an allowed sum of money ▶ *The government gave us a grant to build another classroom.*

granule /'grænjuːl/ *noun*
a very small, hard piece of something, especially dried coffee ▶ *instant coffee granules*

grape /greɪp/ *noun*
a small, round, juicy fruit that grows in bunches and is used to make wine

grapefruit /'greɪpfruːt/ *noun*
a large, round, yellow fruit that is like an orange but not as sweet

graph /grɑːf/ *noun*
a drawing that shows how two or more sets of measurements are related to each other ▶ *They made a graph of how hot the weather was every day for a month.*

graphic /'græfɪk/ *adjective*
very clear and giving a lot of details ▶ *She gave a graphic description of the accident.*

graphic design /ˌgræfɪk dɪ'zaɪn/ *noun (no plural)*
the job or art of combining pictures with the writing in books, magazines, etc.

graphics /'græfɪks/ *plural noun*
drawings or pictures, especially the ones that a computer produces ▶ *The new version of the software has brilliant graphics.*

graph paper /'grɑːf peɪpəʳ/ *noun (no plural)*
paper with squares on it for making GRAPHS

grasp /grɑːsp/ *verb*
1 to take hold of something firmly ▶ *He grasped the rope and pulled himself up.*
2 to understand something ▶ *I could not grasp what the teacher said.*

grass /grɑːs/ *noun (no plural)*
a common plant with thin leaves that covers fields and gardens ▶ *We sat on the grass to have our picnic.*

grasshopper /'grɑːsˌhɒpəʳ/ *noun*
an insect with strong back legs for jumping

grassy /'grɑːsɪ/ *adjective (grassier, grassiest)*
covered with grass

grate¹ /greɪt/ *noun*
a metal frame put in front of a fire

grate² *verb (present participle grating, past grated)*
to cut food into small, thin pieces by rubbing it against an instrument with a rough surface ▶ *to grate cheese*

grateful /'greɪtfəl/ *adjective*
feeling that you want to thank someone ▶ *I am grateful to you for helping me.* (adverb: **gratefully**)
OPPOSITE: **ungrateful**

grater /'greɪtəʳ/ *noun*
a kitchen tool used for grating food

gratitude /'grætɪtjuːd/ *noun (no plural)*
the feeling of wanting to thank someone ▶ *He expressed his gratitude to everyone involved.*
OPPOSITE: **ingratitude**

gratuitous /grə'tjuːɪtəs/ *adjective*
done without a good reason, in a way that offends people ▶ *There is too much gratuitous violence on television.*

grave¹ /greɪv/ *noun*
a hole in the ground where a dead body is buried

G

grave² *adjective*
serious ➤ *a grave accident* (adverb: **gravely**)

gravel /'grævəl/ *noun (no plural)*
a mixture of small stones and sand, used on the surfaces of roads and paths

gravestone /'greɪvstəʊn/ *noun*
a stone put up over a grave, with the name of the dead person on it

graveyard /'greɪvjɑːd/ *noun*
a piece of ground where people are buried

gravity /'grævəti/ *noun (no plural)*
the force that makes things fall to the ground when they are dropped

gravy /'greɪvi/ *noun (no plural)*
a liquid that is made with meat juices and poured over meat and other food

graze¹ /greɪz/ *verb (present participle **grazing**, past **grazed**)*
1 to eat grass ➤ *Cattle were grazing in the field.*
2 to cut the surface of your skin by rubbing it against something ➤ *He grazed his knee when he fell.*

graze² *noun*
a small wound on the surface of your skin

grease¹ /griːs/ *noun (no plural)*
oil or fat ➤ *You put grease on a wheel to make it turn more easily.*

grease² *verb (present participle **greasing**, past **greased**)*
to put oil or fat on something

greasy /'griːsi/ *adjective (**greasier**, **greasiest**)*
covered with oil or fat

great /greɪt/ *adjective*
1 large in size or amount ➤ *She had great difficulty in doing her homework.* ➤ *a great big dog*
2 important or famous ➤ *one of our greatest poets*

3 very good ➤ *It was a great party.* ➤ *I feel great.*
SAME MEANING (**3**): **fantastic, marvellous**

great-grandchild /,greɪt 'græntʃaɪld/ *noun (plural **great-grandchildren** /-,tʃɪldrən/)*
the son or daughter of your GRANDCHILD

great-granddaughter /,greɪt 'grændɔːtəʳ/ *noun*
the daughter of your GRANDCHILD

great-grandfather /,greɪt 'grænfɑːðəʳ/ *noun*
the father of your grandmother or grandfather

great-grandmother /,greɪt 'grænmʌðəʳ/ *noun*
the mother of your grandmother or grandfather

great-grandson /,greɪt 'grænsʌn/ *noun*
the son of your GRANDCHILD

greatly /'greɪtli/ *adverb*
very much ➤ *She greatly admired his poems.*

greed /griːd/ *noun (no plural)*
the feeling that you want more than enough food, money, or power

greedy /'griːdi/ *adjective (**greedier**, **greediest**)*
wanting too much of something ➤ *He's so greedy he ate all our sweets.*

green¹ /griːn/ *adjective*
1 the colour of growing leaves and grass ➤ *She wore a green dress.*
2 covered with grass and trees ➤ *Cities need more green areas.*

green² *noun*
1 the colour of leaves and grass ➤ *She was dressed in green.*
2 an area of grass in the middle of an English village

green card /'griːn kɑːd/ *noun*
an official piece of paper that allows you to live and work in America, although you are not American

G

greengrocer /'griːnˌɡrəʊsəʳ/ *noun*
1 a person who has a shop selling fruit and vegetables
2 greengrocer's a shop selling fruit and vegetables

greenhouse /'griːnhaʊs/ *noun*
(plural **greenhouses** /-haʊzɪz/)
a glass building in which you grow plants

greenhouse effect /'griːnhaʊs ˌfekt/ *noun*
the greenhouse effect a problem caused by POLLUTION, which stops the sun's heat from escaping and causes the air around the Earth to become warmer

greenhouse gas /'griːnhaʊs ɡæs/ *noun* (plural **greenhouse gases**)
gases, caused by POLLUTION, which trap the sun's heat and make the Earth's temperature rise

greet /griːt/ *verb*
to welcome someone with words or actions ► *He greeted her with a smile.*

greeting /'griːtɪŋ/ *noun*
words you say or write when you meet someone or send them good wishes ► *a friendly greeting* ► *Christmas greetings*

grenade /ɡrɪ'neɪd/ *noun*
a small bomb that can be thrown or fired from a gun

grew /ɡruː/
the PAST TENSE of the verb **grow**

grey /ɡreɪ/ *adjective, noun*
the colour of rain clouds; a mixture of black and white ► *She wore a grey dress.* ► *She was dressed in grey.*

grid /ɡrɪd/ *noun*
a pattern of straight lines that cross each other and form squares

gridlock /'ɡrɪdlɒk/ *noun* (no plural)
a situation when the roads are so full of traffic that nothing can move

grief /ɡriːf/ *noun* (no plural)
great sadness, usually because

someone you love has died ► *She did not show her grief when her son died.*

grievance /'ɡriːvəns/ *noun*
something that you think is unfair and that you complain about, especially to someone in authority ► *The manager called a meeting to try and deal with our grievances.*

grieve /ɡriːv/ *verb* (present participle **grieving**, past **grieved**)
to feel very sad, usually because someone you love has died

grill¹ /ɡrɪl/ *verb*
to cook meat, fish, etc. under direct heat

grill² *noun*
a metal frame under direct heat, on which you can cook things

grim /ɡrɪm/ *adjective* (**grimmer, grimmest**)
1 serious and worrying ► *grim news*
2 (used about a place) not pleasant or attractive

grimace /ɡrɪ'meɪs/ *verb* (present participle **grimacing**, past **grimaced**)
to twist your face in an ugly way because something is hurting you or because you do not like something ► *Trevor was grimacing with pain.*

grime /ɡraɪm/ *noun* (no plural)
thick, black dirt ► *The factory walls were covered in grime.*

grimy /'ɡraɪmɪ/ *adjective* (**grimier, grimiest**)
covered in thick, black dirt ► *a row of grimy houses near the railway*

grin¹ /ɡrɪn/ *verb* (present participle **grinning**, past **grinned**)
to smile widely, showing your teeth ► *He grinned with pleasure when we gave him the money.*

grin² *noun*
a wide smile ► *She had a big grin on her face.*

grind /ɡraɪnd/ *verb* (past **ground** /ɡraʊnd/)

G

to crush something so that it becomes powder ▶ *We grind grain to make flour.*

grip[1] /grɪp/ *verb (past participle **gripping**, past **gripped**)*
to hold something very tightly ▶ *She gripped his hand in fear.*
SAME MEANING: **clasp**

grip[2] *noun*
a tight hold ▶ *She kept a firm grip **on** the bag.*

grisly /'grɪzlɪ/ *adjective (**grislier**, **grisliest**)*
extremely unpleasant and connected with violence or death ▶ *the grisly discovery of a body in the cellar*

grit[1] /grɪt/ *noun (no plural)*
very small pieces of stone ▶ *I had a piece of grit stuck in my shoe.*

grit[2] *verb (present participle **gritting**, past **gritted**)*
grit your teeth to use all your determination to continue doing something in a difficult or painful situation ▶ *He gritted his teeth against the pain.*

groan[1] /grəʊn/ *noun*
a low sound of pain or unhappiness ▶ *There was a groan from the class when the teacher gave them the test.*
SAME MEANING: **moan**

groan[2] *verb*
to make a low noise of pain or unhappiness ▶ *He groaned with pain.*
SAME MEANING: **moan**

grocer /'grəʊsəʳ/ *noun*
1 a person who sells foods like sugar, tea, and rice
2 grocer's a shop selling foods like sugar, tea, and rice

groceries /'grəʊsərɪz/ *plural noun*
foods like sugar, tea, and rice which you can buy in a grocery

grocery /'grəʊsərɪ/ *noun (plural **groceries**)*
a shop where you can buy foods like sugar, tea, and rice

groggy /'grɒgɪ/ *adjective (**groggier**, **groggiest**)*
feeling weak and ill or tired ▶ *The injection made him feel groggy.*

groin /grɔɪn/ *noun*
the place where your legs join at the front of your body ▶ *a groin injury*

groom /gruːm/ *noun*
a man who is getting married ▶ *The groom wore a dark blue suit.*
SAME MEANING: **bridegroom**

groove /gruːv/ *noun*
a line cut into the surface of something ▶ *a pattern of deep grooves*

grope /grəʊp/ *verb (present participle **groping**, past **groped**)*
to use your hands to look for something that you cannot see ▶ *He groped **for** his matches in the dark.*

gross /grəʊs/ *adjective*
1 very unpleasant to look at or think about ▶ *His jokes are really gross.*
2 gross amount the total amount of money before taxes or costs have been taken away ▶ *Our gross profit was £50,000.*
3 very serious ▶ *children suffering from gross neglect*

grossly /'grəʊslɪ/ *adverb*
very much ▶ *He is grossly overweight.*

grotesque /grəʊ'tesk/ *adjective*
ugly or strange in a way that is unpleasant or frightening

grouchy /'graʊtʃɪ/ *adjective (**grouchier**, **grouchiest**)*
feeling annoyed and complaining a lot ▶ *Dad's always grouchy in the morning.*

ground[1] /graʊnd/ *noun*
1 *(no plural)* the surface of the earth ▶ *an apple fell to the ground.*
2 *(no plural)* soil or land ▶ *The ground was too hard to plant seeds in.*
3 a piece of land used for a particular purpose ▶ *a football ground*
4 grounds *plural noun* the land around a large building

G

ground²
the PAST TENSE and PAST PARTICIPLE of the verb **grind**

ground floor /,graʊnd ˈflɔːʳ/ noun
the floor of a building on the same level as the ground

groundnut /ˈgraʊndnʌt/ noun
a nut that grows in a soft shell under the ground ▶ *groundnut oil*
SAME MEANING: **peanut**

group /gruːp/ noun
1 a number of people or things together ▶ *A group **of** girls was waiting by the school*
2 a small number of people who sing and play popular music together

grovel /ˈgrɒvəl/ verb (present participle **grovelling**, past **grovelled**)
to try very hard to please someone, because you are frightened of them or you have upset them ▶ *I don't care how important she is; I'm not going to grovel to her.*

grow /grəʊ/ verb (past tense **grew** /gruː/, past participle **grown** /grəʊn/)
1 to get bigger, taller, etc. ▶ *Some plants grow very quickly.*
2 to care for plants and help them to grow ▶ *The farmer is growing potatoes.*
3 to let your hair get longer ▶ *Jack is growing a beard.*
4 to become ▶ *My uncle is growing old.*
5 grow out of something to become too big or too old for something ▶ *My daughter's grown out of all her dresses.*
6 grow up to change from being a child to a man or a woman ▶ *He grew up on a farm.*

growl¹ /graʊl/ verb
(used about a dog) to make a low, angry noise in the throat ▶ *The dog growled at the visitors.*

growl² noun
the low, angry noise made by a dog

grown /grəʊn/
the PAST PARTICIPLE of the verb **grow**

grown-up¹ /,grəʊn ˈʌp/ adjective
old enough to be a man or woman, not a child ▶ *Her children are all grown-up now.*

grown-up² noun
a man or woman, not a child ▶ *"Be quiet – the grown-ups are coming," said the little girl.*
SAME MEANING: **adult**

growth /grəʊθ/ noun (no plural)
the act of getting bigger or developing ▶ *the growth of the company* ▶ *a tree's growth*

grub /grʌb/ noun
the young form of an insect, without wings

grubby /ˈgrʌbɪ/ adjective (**grubbier, grubbiest**)
rather dirty ▶ *Those shorts look a bit grubby.*

grudge /grʌdʒ/ noun
an unfriendly or angry feeling that you have towards someone because of something they said or did in the past ▶ *He always had a grudge **against** me after I beat him in the race.*

gruelling /ˈgruːəlɪŋ/ adjective
very difficult and tiring ▶ *a gruelling 10-mile run*

gruesome /ˈgruːsəm/ adjective
very unpleasant and connected with violence or death ▶ *This castle has a gruesome history.*

grumble¹ /ˈgrʌmbəl/ verb (past participle **grumbling**, past **grumbled**)
to complain in a quiet but cross way ▶ *She was grumbling about the cost of the food.*

grumble² noun
a complaint ▶ *You're full of grumbles today!*

grumpy /ˈgrʌmpɪ/ adjective (**grumpier, grumpiest**)

G

bad-tempered ► *a tired and grumpy child*

grunt¹ /grʌnt/ *verb*
to make a short, low noise like a pig

grunt² *noun*
a short, low noise like the noise made by a pig

guarantee¹ /ˌɡærənˈtiː/ *noun*
1 a promise ► *There's no guarantee that they will repair the car today.*
2 a written promise by the maker of an article to repair it or give you another one if it goes wrong within a certain time ► *a watch with a two-year guarantee*

guarantee² *verb (past* **guaranteed***)*
1 to promise ► *He guaranteed that he would do it today.*
2 to promise to repair an article if it goes wrong within a certain time ► *This radio is guaranteed for three years.*

guard¹ /ɡɑːd/ *verb*
1 to keep something safe from danger by watching it carefully ► *The dog guards the house when we go out.*
2 to watch a prisoner so that they do not escape

guard² *noun*
1 a person who watches over someone or something to prevent danger or escape ► *a prison guard*
2 **be on guard, stand guard** to stand near a building ready to protect it ► *There was a policeman on guard outside.*

guardian /ˈɡɑːdɪən/ *noun*
a person who looks after a child because the child's parents are dead or away

guava /ˈɡwɑːvə/ *noun*
a pink, round fruit with a yellow skin

guerrilla /ɡəˈrɪlə/ *noun*
a member of an unofficial military group that is fighting for political reasons ► *guerrilla warfare*

guess¹ /ɡes/ *verb*
to give an answer that you feel may be right although you are not sure ► *I didn't know where she was from, but I could guess.* ► *Can you guess my age?*

guess² *noun (plural* **guesses***)*
an answer that you think is right, although you do not know for sure ► *If you don't know the answer, make a guess.*

guest /ɡest/ *noun*
1 a visitor to someone's house ► *We have three guests for dinner tonight.*
2 a person who is staying in a hotel

guidance /ˈɡaɪdns/ *noun (no plural)*
help and advice ► *With my teacher's guidance, I finished the work.*

guide¹ /ɡaɪd/ *verb (present participle* **guiding***, past* **guided***)*
to lead or show the way to someone ► *He guided the old woman across the busy street.*

guide² *noun*
1 a person who shows you round a place of interest or helps you to travel in a dangerous area ► *They had a guide to show them the city.* ► *a mountain guide*
2 a book that teaches you about something ► *a guide for parents*

guide book /ˈɡaɪd bʊk/ *noun*
a book that gives tourists information about a place

guide dog /ˈɡaɪd dɒɡ/ *noun*
a dog that is specially trained to guide a blind person

guidelines /ˈɡaɪdlaɪnz/ *plural noun*
official advice about how to do something ► *guidelines on health and safety at work*

guilt /ɡɪlt/ *noun (no plural)*
1 the unhappy feeling you have when you know you have done something wrong ► *She doesn't seem to feel any guilt for her bad behaviour.*

G

2 the fact of having broken the law ▶ *The court was sure of his guilt.*
OPPOSITE (**1** and **2**): **innocence**

guilty /'ɡɪltɪ/ *adjective* (**guiltier, guiltiest**)
1 showing or feeling unhappiness because you have done something wrong ▶ *a guilty look*
2 having broken a law ▶ *He was guilty of stealing the money.*
OPPOSITE (**1** and **2**): **innocent**

guinea pig /'ɡɪnɪ pɪɡ/ *noun*
a small, furry animal that looks like a rat without a tail and is sometimes kept as a pet

guitar /ɡɪ'tɑːr/ *noun*
a musical instrument with six strings, a long neck, and a wooden or plastic body

guitarist /ɡɪ'tɑːrɪst/ *noun*
a person who plays the guitar ▶ *the guitarist, Jimi Hendrix*

gulf /ɡʌlf/ *noun*
a narrow piece of sea with land on three sides of it ▶ *the Persian Gulf*

gull /ɡʌl/ *noun*
a seagull

gullible /'ɡʌlɪbəl/ *adjective*
easily tricked as a result of always trusting other people ▶ *I was angry with myself for being so gullible.*

gulp¹ /ɡʌlp/ *verb*
to swallow food or drink quickly ▶ *He gulped down the water.*

gulp² *noun*
a swallow ▶ *He drank it in one gulp.*

gum /ɡʌm/ *noun*
1 (no plural) a sticky substance used for joining things together
2 **gums** plural noun the pink part of your mouth in which your teeth grow
3 CHEWING GUM

gun /ɡʌn/ *noun*
a weapon that sends out bullets and is used for hurting or killing animals or people

gunfire /'ɡʌnfaɪər/ *noun* (no plural)
the repeated firing of guns ▶ *The sound of gunfire shattered the peace of this normally quiet town.*

gunman /'ɡʌnmæn/ *noun* (plural **gunmen** /-men/)
a person who shoots another person

gunpoint /'ɡʌnpɔɪnt/ *noun*
at gunpoint under the threat of being shot, or while threatening to shoot you ▶ *The victims were held at gunpoint while the thief stole their car.* ▶ *The man kidnapped her at gunpoint.*

gunpowder /'ɡʌnpaʊdər/ *noun* (no plural)
a substance that explodes easily and is used in guns

gunshot /'ɡʌnʃɒt/ *noun*
1 the sound made when a gun is fired ▶ *We heard three gunshots.*
2 (no plural) the bullets fired from a gun ▶ *a gunshot wound*

gurgle /'ɡɜːɡəl/ *verb* (present participle **gurgling**, past **gurgled**)
to make a sound like flowing water ▶ *The baby gurgled with pleasure.*

guru /'ɡuːruː/ *noun*
1 a person that people respect because they are very wise or skilful in a particular subject ▶ *a top management guru*
2 a Hindu religious teacher

gush /ɡʌʃ/ *verb*
to flow quickly in large quantities ▶ *Blood gushed from the cut in his leg.*

gust /ɡʌst/ *noun*
a sudden, strong wind ▶ *A gust of wind blew the leaves along.*

gut¹ /ɡʌt/ *adjective*
gut feeling, gut reaction a feeling that something is right, although you cannot say why you are sure ▶ *My gut reaction was to refuse.*

G

gut² *noun*
1 *(also* **guts***)* the tube in your body that food passes through after it leaves your stomach ➤ *I had a pain in my gut.*
2 guts *plural noun* courage and determination to do something difficult ➤ *Have you got the guts to ask for a pay rise?*

gut³ *verb (present participle* **gutting***, past* **gutted***)*
1 to destroy the inside of a building completely ➤ *The school was completely gutted by fire.*
2 to remove the organs from inside a fish or an animal in order to prepare it for cooking

gutted /ˈɡʌtɪd/ *adjective*
very disappointed ➤ *The team were gutted when they lost.*

gutter /ˈɡʌtəʳ/ *noun*
an open pipe along the edge of a roof, or a narrow ditch on the side of the road, which carries away rain water

guy /ɡaɪ/ *noun*
a man ➤ *What a nice guy!*

guzzle /ˈɡʌzəl/ *verb (present participle* **guzzling***, past* **guzzled***)*
to drink or eat a lot very quickly ➤ *The children were guzzling lemonade.*

gym /dʒɪm/ *noun*
1 a large room that is used for doing exercises or training
2 *(also* **gymnastics***) (no plural)* exercises for your body that make you strong and able to move easily ➤ *a gym class*

gymnasium /dʒɪmˈneɪzɪəm/ *noun*
a GYM

gymnast /ˈdʒɪmnæst/ *noun*
a person who is trained in gymnastics

gymnastics /dʒɪmˈnæstɪks/ *noun (no plural)*
another word for **gym (2)**

gypsy /ˈdʒɪpsɪ/ *noun (plural* **gypsies***)*
another word for **gipsy**

Hh

habit /ˈhæbɪt/ *noun*
something that you always do, often without thinking about it ➤ *She has a habit of biting her fingernails.*

habitat /ˈhæbɪtæt/ *noun*
the natural environment in which a plant grows or an animal lives ➤ *Pollution is damaging many wildlife habitats.*

habitual /həˈbɪtʃʊəl/ *adjective*
1 typical or happening often ➤ *Jane was in her habitual bad temper this morning.*
2 doing something often because it is a habit ➤ *a habitual smoker (adverb:* **habitually***)*

hack /hæk/ *verb*
hack into to use a computer to enter someone else's computer system ➤ *John managed to hack into the company's computer network.*

had /d, əd, həd; *strong* hæd/
the PAST TENSE and PAST PARTICIPLE of the verb **have**

haddock /ˈhædək/ *noun (plural* **haddock***)*
a sea fish used for food

hadn't /ˈhædnt/
had not ➤ *I hadn't finished making dinner when everyone arrived.*

hag /hæg/ *noun*
an ugly or unpleasant old woman

haggard /ˈhægəd/ *adjective*
looking tired, thin, and ill ➤ *His face looked haggard and pale.*

haggle /ˈhægəl/ *verb (present participle* **haggling***, past* **haggled***)* to argue about the amount that you will pay for something ▶ *We were haggling **over** the price for an hour.*

hail[1] /heɪl/ *noun (no plural)*
drops of hard, icy rain ▶ *We had a hail storm yesterday.*

hail[2] *verb*
to rain with hard, icy drops ▶ *It's halling.*

hailstone /'heɪlstəʊn/ *noun*
a hard, icy drop of rain

hair /heə[r]/ *noun*
1 one of the fine threads that grow on the head and skin of people and animals ▶ *There's a hair in my soup!*
2 *(no plural)* a lot of these threads together, for example on your head ▶ *I must get my hair cut.*
3 make your hair stand on end to make you feel very afraid

hairbrush /'heəbrʌʃ/ *noun (plural hairbrushes)*
a brush for keeping your hair tidy

haircut /'heəkʌt/ *noun*
1 the style in which your hair is cut ▶ *I like your new haircut.*
2 have a haircut to have your hair cut ▶ *I must have a haircut.*

hairdresser /'heə,dresə[r]/ *noun*
1 a person whose job is to wash, cut, and shape your hair
COMPARE: **barber**
2 hairdresser's a shop where you go to get your hair cut

hairdryer /'heə,draɪə[r]/ *noun*
a machine that you use to dry your hair after washing it

hairgrip /'heəgrɪp/ *noun*
a thin piece of metal, used to hold hair in place

hair-raising /'heə ,reɪzɪŋ/ *adjective*
frightening but exciting ▶ *a hair-raising fairground ride*

hairstyle /'heəstaɪl/ *noun*
the style in which your hair is cut or arranged ▶ *I like your new hairstyle.*

hairy /'heərɪ/ *adjective (hairier, hairiest)*
(used about a part of your body) covered with a lot of hairs ▶ *a man with a hairy chest*
COMPARE: **furry**

half /hɑːf/ *noun (plural halves /hɑːvz/)*
1 one of the two parts of something ▶ *I gave half the apple to my brother.* ▶ *We had half each.*
2 in half into two equal pieces ▶ *I cut the apple in half.*
3 half past 30 minutes after an hour ▶ *It's half past ten (=30 minutes after 10 o'clock).*

half-brother /'hɑːf ,brʌðə[r]/ *noun*
a brother who has either the same mother or father as you, but not both

half-hearted /,hɑːf 'hɑːtɪd/ *adjective*
done without any real effort or interest ▶ *He made a half-hearted attempt to talk to me.*

half-price /,hɑːf 'praɪs/ *adjective*
costing half the usual amount ▶ *half-price tickets*

half-sister /'hɑːf ,sɪstə[r]/ *noun*
a sister who has either the same mother or father as you, but not both

half term /,hɑːf 'tɜːm/ *noun (no plural)*
a short holiday in the middle of a school term

half time /,hɑːf 'taɪm/ *noun (no plural)*
the middle point in a game or match when the players stop to rest

halfway /,hɑːf'weɪ/ *adverb*
in the middle between two places or things ▶ *I live halfway **between** London and Guildford.*

hall /hɔːl/ *noun*
1 a large room or building ▶ *The children were in the school hall.*
2 the room just inside the front door of a house ▶ *Hang your coat in the hall.*

H

hallo (also **hello, hullo**) /həˈləʊ/
interjection
the usual word that you say when you
meet someone or talk on the telephone
▶ *Hallo John.* ▶ *Hallo. My name's Anne.*

hall of residence /ˌhɔːl əv ˈrezɪdəns/
noun (plural **halls of residence**)
a college or university building where
students live

Hallowe'en /ˌhæləʊˈiːn/ *noun*
the last night in October, when
children dress in strange clothes, and
visit people's houses to ask for
sweets or to play tricks on them

hallucinate /həˈluːsɪneɪt/ *verb*
(*present participle* **hallucinating**,
past **hallucinated**)
to see, feel, or hear something that is
not really there ▶ *Jim started
hallucinating after he took the drugs.*

hallucination /həˌluːsɪˈneɪʃən/ *noun*
something you see, feel, or hear that
is not really there ▶ *They suffered
from strange hallucinations.*

hallway /ˈhɔːlweɪ/ *noun*
a HALL in a house

halo /ˈheɪləʊ/ *noun*
in paintings, a golden circle above the
head of a holy person ▶ *The angel
had wings and a halo.*

halt¹ /hɔːlt/ *verb*
to stop ▶ *The policemen halted all the
traffic.* ▶ *The car halted by the house.*

halt² *noun* (no plural)
a stop ▶ *The car came to a halt.*

halve /hɑːv/ *verb* (*present participle*
halving, *past* **halved**)
to divide something into two pieces
▶ *James and I halved the apple* (=we
each had half of it).

halves /hɑːvz/
the plural of **half**

ham /hæm/ *noun* (no plural)
meat from a pig's leg that has had
salt added to stop it going bad
COMPARE: **bacon**

hamburger /ˈhæmbɜːgəʳ/ *noun*
meat that has been cut into very
small pieces and then made into a
round, flat shape before being
cooked
SAME MEANING: **beefburger**

hammer¹ /ˈhæməʳ/ *noun*
a tool with a metal head and a
wooden handle, used for knocking
nails into things or for breaking
things

hammer² *verb*
to hit something with a hammer

hammock /ˈhæmək/ *noun*
a large net or piece of material that
hangs between two trees or poles,
used for sleeping on

hamper¹ /ˈhæmpəʳ/ *verb*
to make it difficult for someone to do
something ▶ *Storms hampered our
attempts to reach the crash victims.*
▶ *Shearer was hampered by a leg
injury.*

hamper² *noun*
a large basket with a lid, used for
carrying food somewhere ▶ *a picnic
hamper*

hamster /ˈhæmstəʳ/ *noun*
a small animal like a mouse, which
keeps its food in its cheeks and which
children sometimes keep as a pet

hand¹ /hænd/ *noun*
1 the part of your body at the end of
your arm, with which you hold things
2 by hand not by machine ▶ *This toy
was made by hand.*
3 give someone a hand to help
someone ▶ *Will you give me a hand
with the cleaning?*
4 hand in hand holding each other by
the hand ▶ *They were walking hand
in hand.*
5 hold hands (with somebody) if two
people hold hands, they hold each
other by the hand ▶ *They sat there,
holding hands throughout the entire
film.*

H

6 the part of a clock that moves to show the time ▶ *When the minute hand points to 12 and the hour hand points to 3, it's 3 o'clock.*

hand² *verb*
1 to give something to someone using your hands ▶ *Hand me that plate, please.* ▶ *She handed the letter to John.*
2 hand something in to give something to someone, usually to a teacher ▶ *Please hand in your books at the end of the lesson.*
3 hand things out to give one thing to each person ▶ *Could you hand out the forms, please?*

handbag /'hændbæg/ *noun*
a woman's bag for keeping money and small things in, carried in her hand or over her shoulder

handbook /'hændbʊk/ *noun*
a small book with instructions and information about a particular subject ▶ *an employee handbook*

handbrake /'hændbreɪk/ *noun*
the part of a car that you pull up with your hand to stop the car from moving

handcuffs /'hændkʌfs/ *plural noun*
two metal rings joined together and put round a prisoner's wrists

handful /'hændfʊl/ *noun*
1 a small number or amount ▶ *a handful of people*
2 the amount that you can hold in your hand ▶ *a handful of rice*

handicap¹ /'hændɪkæp/ *noun*
something that makes it difficult for you to do something ▶ *His sore leg will be a handicap in the race.*

handicap² *verb (present participle handicapping, past handicapped)*
to make it difficult for someone to do something ▶ *She has been handicapped by her illness.*

handicapped /'hændɪkæpt/ *adjective*
not able to use a part of your body or

mind normally because it has been damaged ▶ *schools for mentally handicapped children*

handkerchief /'hæŋkətʃɪf/ *noun*
a square piece of cloth for cleaning your nose

handle¹ /'hændl/ *noun*
the part of a tool or an instrument that you hold in your hand

handle² *verb (present participle handling, past handled)*
1 to hold or touch something ▶ *Please don't handle the fruit.*
2 to control someone or something ▶ *He doesn't handle the children very well.*

handlebars /'hændl,bɑːz/ *plural noun*
the parts of a bicycle that you hold when you ride it

handler /'hændlə^r/ *noun*
used in job titles to show what someone works with ▶ *airport baggage handlers* ▶ *a police dog handler*

handmade /ˌhænd'meɪd/ *adjective*
made by a person, not a machine ▶ *handmade furniture*

handout /'hændaʊt/ *noun*
1 money or food that is given to someone, usually because they are poor
2 a piece of paper with information on it that a speaker gives to the people in a class or a meeting

handshake /'hændʃeɪk/ *noun*
an action in which two people hold each other's right hand and move it up and down when they meet or leave each other ▶ *a firm handshake*

handsome /'hænsəm/ *adjective*
(used about men) attractive to look at
SAME MEANING: **good-looking**
LOOK AT: **beautiful**

hands-on /ˌhændz ɒn/ *adjective*
(used about experience or training) obtained from doing something rather than studying it

H

handwriting /'hænd,raɪtɪŋ/ *noun (no plural)*
1 writing done by hand with a pen or pencil
2 the style of someone's writing

handy /'hændɪ/ *adjective (handier, handiest)*
1 near ► *This house is handy for the market.*
2 useful ► *It's very handy having a car.*

hang /hæŋ/ *verb*
1 *(past hung* /hʌŋ/) to fix something at the top so that the lower part is free ► *I hung my coat up on a hook.*
2 *(past hanged)* to kill someone, usually as a punishment, by holding them above the ground with a rope around their neck
3 hang about to stand and do nothing or to wait around without any reason ► *He was hanging about outside my house.*
4 hang on to wait ► *Hang on – I want to talk to you.*
5 hang on to something to hold something tightly ► *Hang on everybody! The road's very bumpy.*

hangar /'hæŋəʳ/ *noun*
a large building where aircraft are kept

hanger /'hæŋəʳ/ *noun*
a specially shaped piece of wire or wood for hanging clothes on

hangover /'hæŋəʊvəʳ/ *noun*
have a hangover to feel sick because you have drunk too much alcohol the evening before

hankie *(also hanky)* /'hæŋkɪ/ *noun (plural hankies)*
a handkerchief

haphazard /hæp'hæzəd/ *adjective*
not planned or organized ► *We work in a very haphazard way. (adverb: haphazardly)*

happen /'hæpən/ *verb*
1 to take place ► *The accident happened outside my house.*

If an event **occurs** or **happens**, it is not planned: *The explosion happened on Friday evening.* If an event **takes place**, it is the result of a plan or an arrangement: *The wedding will take place on June 6th.*

2 happen to do something to do something by chance ► *If you happen to see her, will you give her a message?*

happening /'hæpənɪŋ/ *noun*
an event ► *a strange happening*

happily /'hæpɪlɪ/ *adverb*
in a pleased or cheerful way ► *They were laughing happily.*
OPPOSITE: **unhappily**

happiness /'hæpɪnəs/ *noun (no plural)*
pleasure ► *They've had years of happiness together.*

happy /'hæpɪ/ *adjective (happier, happiest)*
very pleased ► *I am happy to see you again.* ► *Happy Birthday* ► *Happy New Year (=said or written to someone to wish them happiness on those occasions)*
OPPOSITE: **unhappy**

harass /'hærəs/ *verb*
to deliberately annoy or threaten someone, often over a long period of time ► *They claim that they are being harassed by the police.*

harassment /'hærəsmənt/ *noun (no plural)*
behaviour that threatens or offends someone ► *racial harassment*

harbour /'hɑːbəʳ/ *noun*
a place on the shore where ships can shelter safely

hard¹ /hɑːd/ *adjective*
1 not moving or soft when touched; firm like rock or metal ► *This ground is too hard to dig.*
OPPOSITE: **soft**

H

2 difficult to do or understand ➤ *a hard exam*
OPPOSITE (**2**): **easy**

hard² *adverb*
a lot; very much ➤ *It's raining hard.* ➤ *Are you working hard?*

hard-and-fast /ˌhɑːd ən ˈfɑːst/ *adjective*
hard-and-fast rules rules that cannot be changed ➤ *There are no hard-and-fast rules for success.*

hardback /ˈhɑːdbæk/ *noun*
a book that has a strong, stiff cover
COMPARE: **paperback**

hard-boiled /ˌhɑːd ˈbɔɪld/ *adjective*
(used about eggs) boiled until the yellow part becomes solid

hard disk /ˌhɑːd ˈdɪsk/ *noun*
a part fixed inside a computer on which you can store information
COMPARE: **floppy disk**

harden /ˈhɑːdn/ *verb*
to become firm

hard-headed /ˌhɑːd ˈhedɪd/ *adjective*
able to make difficult decisions without being influenced by your emotions

hard-hearted /ˌhɑːd ˈhɑːtɪd/ *adjective*
not kind to other people ➤ *She's a very hard-hearted woman.*
OPPOSITE: **kind-hearted**

hardly /ˈhɑːdli/ *adverb*
almost not at all; only just ➤ *It was so dark that I could hardly see.* ➤ *He hardly ever* (=almost never) *eats meat.*
SAME MEANING: **barely**

hard-nosed /ˌhɑːd ˈnəʊzd/ *adjective*
not affected by your emotions, and determined to get what you want ➤ *a hard-nosed negotiator*

hardship /ˈhɑːdʃɪp/ *noun*
something that makes your life unpleasant, especially not having enough money ➤ *The family suffered years of poverty and hardship.* ➤ *the hardships of war*

hard shoulder /ˌhɑːd ˈʃəʊldəʳ/ *noun*
the area at the side of a big road where you are allowed to stop if you have a problem with your car

hard-up /ˌhɑːd ˈʌp/ *adjective*
not having enough money ➤ *We were very hard-up when I was young.*

hardware /ˈhɑːdweəʳ/ *noun (no plural)*
1 computer machinery and equipment
COMPARE: **software**
2 equipment and tools you use in your home and garden ➤ *a hardware store*

hard-working /ˌhɑːd ˈwɜːkɪŋ/ *adjective*
working with a lot of effort ➤ *a hard-working student*

hardy /ˈhɑːdi/ *adjective* (**hardier, hardiest**)
strong and able to exist in difficult conditions ➤ *hardy plants*

hare /heəʳ/ *noun*
an animal like a large rabbit that has long ears and long back legs

harm¹ /hɑːm/ *noun (no plural)*
1 hurt ➤ *Modern farming methods do a lot of harm to the environment.*
2 come to no harm to not be hurt or damaged ➤ *We left the dog outside last night, but she came to no harm.*
3 there's no harm in ... there is nothing bad in ... ➤ *There's no harm in asking him for a job.*

harm² *verb*
to hurt someone or something ➤ *Our dog won't harm you.*

harmful /ˈhɑːmfl/ *adjective*
dangerous ➤ *Smoking is harmful to your health.*

harmless /ˈhɑːmləs/ *adjective*
not dangerous ➤ *a harmless snake*

H

harmonica /haːˈmɒnɪkə/ *noun*
a small musical instrument with holes along the side that you blow into and move from side to side

harmony /ˈhaːmənɪ/ *noun*
1 *(no plural)* the state of not arguing or fighting ▶ *Why can't people live in harmony?*
2 *(plural harmonies)* musical notes that sound good together

harness¹ /ˈhaːnɪs/ *noun (plural harnesses)*
1 a set of bands that you put round a horse so that you can control it or it can pull a vehicle
2 a set of bands that hold someone or stop them from falling ▶ *The climbers used safety harnesses.*

harness² *verb*
to use the energy from something ▶ *ways of harnessing the sun's energy*

harp¹ /haːp/ *noun*
a large musical instrument with strings stretched on a frame with three corners

harp² *verb*
harp on about something to talk about something all the time, in a way that is annoying or boring ▶ *I wish he'd stop harping on about his bad back.*

harsh /haːʃ/ *adjective*
very unpleasant; cruel ▶ *a harsh punishment* (adverb: **harshly**)

harvest¹ /ˈhaːvɪst/ *noun*
1 the time when the crops are gathered ▶ *I hope it doesn't rain much during the harvest.*
2 the amount of food collected during the harvest ▶ *The harvest was good this year.*

harvest² *verb*
to gather a crop

has /z, əz, s, həz; *strong* hæz/
the part of the verb **have** that we use with **he, she,** and **it** ▶ *She has three children.*

has-been /ˈhæz biːn/ *noun*
a person who is no longer important or popular

hash /hæʃ/ *noun*
make a hash of something to do something very badly

hasn't /ˈhæzənt/
has not ▶ *Hasn't he finished yet?*

hassle¹ /ˈhæsəl/ *noun*
something that is annoying because it takes a lot of time or effort ▶ *I didn't want the hassle of moving house again.*

hassle² *verb (present participle hassling, past hassled)*
to continuously ask someone to do something, in a way that is annoying ▶ *He keeps hassling me about the money I owe him.*

haste /heɪst/ *noun (no plural)*
quick movement or action often done without care ▶ *In my haste I forgot my coat.*

hasten /ˈheɪsən/ *verb*
1 to make something happen sooner ▶ *The accident hastened his death.*
2 **hasten to do something** to do or say something quickly ▶ *Gina hastened to assure him that everything was fine.*

hasty /ˈheɪstɪ/ *adjective (hastier, hastiest)*
done in a hurry ▶ *He ate a hasty lunch.* (adverb: **hastily**)

hat /hæt/ *noun*
a piece of clothing that you wear on your head

hatch /hætʃ/ *verb*
to come out of an egg ▶ *The chickens hatched this morning.*

hatchet /ˈhætʃɪt/ *noun*
a small tool like an AXE that you use to cut wood into small pieces

hate /heɪt/ *verb (present participle hating, past hated)*

not to like someone or something at all ► *I hate snakes.*
OPPOSITE: **love**

hatred /'heɪtrɪd/ (also **hate**) noun (no plural)
a very strong feeling of not liking someone or something ► *She looked at me with an expression of hatred.*
OPPOSITE: **love**

hat trick /'hæt trɪk/ noun
three GOALS that are SCORED by the same player in one game of football or HOCKEY

haul /hɔːl/ verb
to lift or pull something with difficulty ► *They hauled the boat up onto the shore.*
SAME MEANING: **heave**

haunt /hɔːnt/ verb
(used about the spirits of dead people) to visit or be in a place ► *People say that the spirit of his dead wife haunts the house.*

haunted /'hɔːntɪd/ adjective
visited by the spirits of dead people ► *The old church is haunted.*

haunting /'hɔːntɪŋ/ adjective
beautiful, sad, and staying in your thoughts for a long time ► *haunting landscapes*

have /v, əv, həv; *strong* hæv/ verb

present tense

singular
I **have** (I**'ve**)
You **have** (You**'ve**)
He/She/It **has** (He**'s**/She**'s**/It**'s**)

plural
We **have** (We**'ve**)
You **have** (You**'ve**)
They **have** (They**'ve**)

past tense

singular
I **had** (I**'d**)
You **had** (You**'d**)
He/She/It **had** (He**'d**/She**'d**/It**'d**)

plural
We **had** (We**'d**)
You **had** (You**'d**)
They **had** (They**'d**)

present participle   **having**
past participle   **had**
negative short   **haven't, hasn't,**
forms   **hadn't**

(you can find each of these words in its own place in the dictionary)

1 a word that helps another word to say that something happened in the past: *We have been to the shops.* ► *When I arrived, she had already gone away.*
2 to own; to hold; to keep: *Do you have a car?* ► *She has blue eyes.* ► *I haven't any money.* ► *He has two sisters.* ► *I have a good job.* You can use **have got** instead of **have** with this meaning of the verb: *Have you got a car?* ► *I haven't got any money.* ► *She's got blue eyes.* ► *He's got two sisters.* ► *I've got a good job.*
3 to feel or experience something (especially a pain): *She has a headache.* You can use **have got** instead of **have** with this meaning of the verb: *She's got a headache.*
4 to do something: *I usually have my breakfast at 8 o'clock.* ► *I think I'll have a swim.*

haven't /'hævənt/
have not ► *I haven't seen that film.*

have to /'hæv tuː/ (also **have got to** /həv 'gɒt tuː/) verb
must ► *We have to leave now, if we want to catch the bus.* ► *We've got to be there by 6 o'clock.*

havoc /'hævək/ noun (no plural)
a situation in which there is a lot of confusion ► *The failure of the airport's computer system caused havoc.*

hawk /hɔːk/ noun
a large bird that kills small animals and birds for food

hay /heɪ/ noun (no plural)
dry grass fed to cattle

H

hay fever /'heɪ ˌfiːvəʳ/ *noun (no plural)*
a medical condition like a bad COLD, caused by breathing in dust from plants

hazard /'hæzəd/ *noun*
a danger ➤ *There are many hazards in a journey across Africa.*

hazardous /'hæzədəs/ *adjective*
dangerous ➤ *hazardous chemicals*

haze /heɪz/ *noun (no plural)*
fine clouds which stop you seeing clearly

hazy /'heɪzɪ/ *adjective (hazier, haziest)*
not clear ➤ *Since it was hazy, we couldn't see the mountains.*

he /ɪ, hɪ; *strong* hiː/ *pronoun (plural they* /ðeɪ/)
the male person or animal that the sentence is about ➤ *He is my brother.* ➤ *Be careful of that dog – he bites.*

head¹ /hed/ *noun*
1 the top part of your body, where your brain, eyes, ears, and mouth are
2 your brain ➤ *His head's full of ideas.*
3 the most important position of something ➤ *She sat at the head of the table.*
4 someone who is in charge of a group of people ➤ *the head of a large firm*
5 the front ➤ *At the head of the queue of cars was a bus.*
6 the teacher in charge of a school
7 keep your head to stay calm
8 lose your head to do things without thinking because you are too afraid or angry

head² *verb*
1 to be at the front or the top of something ➤ *The list was headed "Things to do".*
2 to hit a ball with your head
3 head for something to go towards something ➤ *I'm heading for home.*

headache /'hedeɪk/ *noun*
a pain in your head ➤ *I've got a headache.*

headfirst /ˌhed'fɜːst/ *adverb*
with your head in front and the rest of your body following ➤ *He fell headfirst into the lake.*

heading /'hedɪŋ/ *noun*
something written at the top of a piece of writing

headlight /'hedlaɪt/ *(also headlamp* /'hedlæmp/) *noun*
one of the big lights at the front of a car

headline /'hedlaɪn/ *noun*
words printed in large letters at the top of a newspaper story

headlong /'hedlɒŋ/ *adverb*
1 rush headlong into something to do something important without thinking carefully about it first ➤ *Fran isn't the type to rush headlong into marriage.*
2 with your head going first ➤ *Ben went tumbling headlong down the hill.*

headmaster /hed'mɑːstəʳ/ *noun*
the man who is in charge of a school

headmistress /hed'mɪstrəs/ *noun (plural headmistresses)*
the woman who is in charge of a school

head-on /ˌhed 'ɒn/ *adverb, adjective*
(used about two vehicles) with the front part of one vehicle hitting the front part of the other ➤ *A car and a truck had collided head-on.* ➤ *a head-on crash*

headphones /'hedfəʊnz/ *plural noun*
things that fit over your head and ears and are used for listening to music

headquarters /hed'kwɔːtəz/ *plural noun*
the main office of a business or of some other group

H

head start /ˌhed ˈstɑːt/ *noun*
an advantage that helps you to be successful ➤ *His education gave him a head start.*

headteacher /hedˈtiːtʃəʳ/ *noun*
the teacher in charge of a school

headway /ˈhedweɪ/ *noun*
make headway to make progress ➤ *We have made little headway towards a solution.*

heal /hiːl/ *verb*
to make something healthy again or become healthy again ➤ *The wound on my arm has healed.*

health /helθ/ *noun (no plural)*
how well your body is ➤ *His health is not good (=he is often ill).*

health club /ˈhelθ klʌb/ *noun*
a place where you pay to use equipment to do physical exercises

health food /ˈhelθ fuːd/ *noun (no plural)*
food that contains only natural substances ➤ *a health food shop*

healthy /ˈhelθɪ/ *adjective (healthier, healthiest)*
1 strong and well in your body ➤ *healthy children* ➤ *a healthy plant*
2 good for your body ➤ *It is healthy to eat fruit.*
OPPOSITE **(1 and 2): unhealthy**

heap¹ /hiːp/ *noun*
a number of things put untidily on top of each other ➤ *A heap of old clothes was lying in the corner.*
SAME MEANING: **pile**

heap² *verb*
to put a lot of things on top of each other ➤ *He heaped his plate with food.*
SAME MEANING: **pile**

hear /hɪəʳ/ *verb (past heard* /hɜːd/*)*
1 to notice sounds through your ears ➤ *I heard the rain on the roof.*
2 to be given information about something ➤ *I heard that he was ill.*

3 hear from someone to get news of someone ➤ *Have you heard from John recently?*
4 have heard of someone or something to know about someone or something ➤ *I've never heard of her.*

hearing /ˈhɪərɪŋ/ *noun (no plural)*
your ability to hear ➤ *My hearing is getting worse.*

hearing aid /ˈhɪərɪŋ ˌeɪd/ *noun*
a small object that makes sounds louder and is put in your ear so that you can hear better

hearse /hɜːs/ *noun*
a large car for carrying a dead body in a COFFIN at a funeral

heart /hɑːt/ *noun*
1 the part of your body in your chest that pumps the blood round your body
2 your feelings ➤ *He has a kind heart.*
3 the middle ➤ *in the heart of the forest*
4 a shape like the shape of a heart
5 break someone's heart to make someone very unhappy
6 by heart so that you can remember something perfectly
7 lose heart to have less courage and hope ➤ *We had hoped they were still alive, but we're losing heart now.*
8 take heart to be encouraged and more hopeful about something
9 with a heavy heart sadly
10 with all your heart with deep feeling ➤ *I love you with all my heart.*

heart attack /ˈhɑːt əˌtæk/ *noun*
a serious medical condition in which a person's heart suddenly stops beating normally or regularly, sometimes causing death

heartbeat /ˈhɑːtbiːt/ *noun*
the movement or sound of someone's heart

heartbreaking /ˈhɑːtˌbreɪkɪŋ/ *adjective*

H

making you feel very sad
▶ *heartbreaking pictures of starving children*

heartbroken /ˈhɑːˌbrəʊkən/ *adjective*
very unhappy

heartfelt /ˈhɑːtfelt/ *adjective*
honest and sincere ▶ *a heartfelt apology*

hearth /hɑːθ/ *noun*
the part of the floor around a FIREPLACE

heartily /ˈhɑːtɪli/ *adverb*
1 loudly and cheerfully ▶ *He laughed heartily.*
2 very much or completely ▶ *I heartily agree.*

heartless /ˈhɑːtləs/ *adjective*
not kind; cruel

heartwarming /ˈhɑːtˌwɔːmɪŋ/ *adjective*
making you feel happy and hopeful
▶ *a heartwarming story*

hearty /ˈhɑːti/ *adjective* (**heartier, heartiest**)
1 very cheerful and friendly ▶ *We were given a hearty welcome.*
2 (used about meals) very large

heat[1] /hiːt/ *noun*
1 (no plural) the feeling of something hot ▶ *The heat of the sun made her feel ill.*
2 a race run earlier than the main race, to decide who will run in the main race
3 (no plural) hot weather ▶ *I hate the heat.*
OPPOSITE (**3**): **cold**

heat[2] *verb*
to make something hot ▶ *It's expensive to heat big rooms.*

heated /ˈhiːtɪd/ *adjective*
1 kept warm by using a heater
▶ *a heated swimming pool*
2 (used about arguments, discussions, etc.) causing people to become very angry and excited

heater /ˈhiːtəʳ/ *noun*
a machine that makes things hot

heather /ˈheðəʳ/ *noun*
a small bush with purple or white flowers that grows on hills

heating /ˈhiːtɪŋ/ *noun* (no plural)
a system for keeping rooms warm

heatwave /ˈhiːtweɪv/ *noun*
a period of unusually hot weather

heave /hiːv/ *verb* (present participle **heaving**, past **heaved**)
to lift or pull something with difficulty
▶ *I heaved the heavy box up the steps.*
SAME MEANING: **haul**

heaven /ˈhevən/ *noun* (no plural)
a place where people think God or the gods live, and good people will go after they die
COMPARE: **hell**

heavily /ˈhevɪli/ *adverb*
very much or a lot ▶ *It was still raining heavily.* ▶ *They rely heavily on government aid.*

heavy /ˈhevi/ *adjective* (**heavier, heaviest**)
1 weighing a lot ▶ *This bag is too heavy to carry.*
2 great in amount ▶ *heavy rain*
▶ *heavy traffic*
OPPOSITE (**1** and **2**): **light**
3 a heavy sleeper someone who sleeps deeply
4 a heavy smoker someone who smokes a lot

heavy-handed /ˌhevi ˈhændɪd/ *adjective*
1 not considering people's feelings
▶ *He dealt with the problem in a heavy-handed way.*
2 using too much force ▶ *They were criticized for their heavy-handed treatment of the crowds.*

heavy metal /ˌhevi ˈmetl/ *noun* (no plural)
a type of rock music played on electric instruments and drums

H

heavyweight /ˈhevɪweɪt/ *noun*
1 a person who has a lot of power and importance ➤ *one of the heavyweights of the film industry*
2 a BOXER from the heaviest weight group

heck /hek/ *noun*
used when you are annoyed, surprised, etc. ➤ *Where the heck have you been?* ➤ *Moving all that furniture will be a heck of a job.*

hectare /ˈhektɑːʳ, ˈhekteəʳ/ *noun*
a measure of land, equal to 10,000 square metres

hectic /ˈhektɪk/ *adjective*
very busy or full of activity ➤ *It's been a really hectic week.*

he'd /hiːd/
1 he had ➤ *He'd met her before.*
2 he would ➤ *He said he'd tell me tomorrow.*

hedge /hedʒ/ *noun*
a row of small trees planted between fields or along roads to make a wall

hedgehog /ˈhedʒhɒg/ *noun*
a small animal whose body is covered in sharp points

heel /hiːl/ *noun*
1 the back part of your foot below your ankle
2 the part of a shoe or sock under your heel

hefty /ˈheftɪ/ *adjective* (**heftier, heftiest**)
1 large ➤ *She had to pay a hefty fine.*
2 heavy and slightly fat ➤ *He used to be quite hefty before he started jogging.*

height /haɪt/ *noun*
how tall or far from the ground something is ➤ *He measured the height of the bridge.*

heighten /ˈhaɪtn/ *verb*
to increase, or make something increase ➤ *The film has heightened public awareness of AIDS.*

heir /eəʳ/ *noun*
a person who gets money or goods when someone dies

heiress /ˈeərəs/ *noun (plural heiresses)*
a woman who gets money or goods when someone dies

heirloom /ˈeəluːm/ *noun*
a valuable object that the same family has owned for many years ➤ *Carrie's ring is a family heirloom.*

held /held/
the PAST TENSE and PAST PARTICIPLE of the verb **hold**

helicopter /ˈhelɪkɒptəʳ/ *noun*
a flying machine with blades which go round on its top

helium /ˈhiːlɪəm/ *noun (no plural)*
a gas that is lighter than air

hell /hel/ *noun (no plural)*
a place where people think that the Devil lives and where bad people will go after they die
COMPARE: **heaven**

he'll /hiːl/
he will ➤ *He'll be here soon.*

hello (*also* **hallo, hullo**) /həˈləʊ/ *interjection*
the usual word that you say when you meet someone or talk on the telephone ➤ *Hello, June!*
COMPARE: **goodbye**

helmet /ˈhelmɪt/ *noun*
a hard hat that you wear to stop your head being hurt

help¹ /help/ *verb*
1 to do something for someone ➤ *Could you help me move this box?*
2 cannot help something cannot stop or control something ➤ *I couldn't help laughing when I saw his funny hat.*
3 help yourself to take what you want ➤ *Help yourself to a drink.*

help² *noun*
someone or something that makes things easier or better for someone

H

else ➤ *If you want any help, just ask me.*

helpful /'helpfəl/ *adjective*
doing something to help someone else ➤ *She's so kind and helpful.*
OPPOSITE: **unhelpful**

helping /'helpɪŋ/ *noun*
the amount of food on a plate ➤ *Would you like another helping of soup?*

helpless /'helpləs/ *adjective*
not able to do things for yourself ➤ *a helpless child*

hem /hem/ *noun*
the bottom edge of a skirt, shirt, etc. when turned under ➤ *I'll let down the hem of that dress for you.*

hemisphere /'hemɪsfɪəʳ/ *noun*
one of the two halves of the Earth ➤ *the northern hemisphere*

hen /hen/ *noun*
a female chicken

hence /hens/ *adverb*
for this reason ➤ *The department is short of money: hence the need to reduce spending.*

her /əʳ, həʳ; *strong* hɜːʳ/ *pronoun, adjective*
1 a woman or girl (used in sentences like this) ➤ *I saw her last week.* ➤ *Give her the book.* ➤ *I had a letter from her.*
2 belonging to a woman or girl ➤ *Her baby is two months old now.*

herb /hɜːb/ *noun*
a plant used for medicine or for giving a special taste to food

herbal /'hɜːbəl/ *adjective*
made from herbs ➤ *herbal medicine*

herd¹ /hɜːd/ *noun*
a group of animals of the same kind ➤ *a herd of cattle*
COMPARE: **flock**

herd² *verb*
to make a group of people or animals move in a certain direction

here /hɪəʳ/ *adverb*
1 at or to this place ➤ *Come here and sit beside me.*
COMPARE: **there**
2 **here and there** in different places ➤ *There were a few colourful boats here and there on the water.*
3 **Here you are** a phrase used when you are giving someone something that they want

hereditary /hə'redɪtəri/ *adjective*
(used about qualities or diseases) passed to a child by its parents

heresy /'herəsi/ *noun (plural heresies)*
a belief that a religious or political group thinks is wrong

heritage /'herɪtɪdʒ/ *noun (no plural)*
things that have been in a society for a long time, especially things that people think are valuable ➤ *We must protect our musical heritage.*

hero /'hɪərəʊ/ *noun (plural heroes)*
1 a man who does something great or brave
2 a person you admire very much ➤ *Robbie Williams is my hero.*

heroic /hɪ'rəʊɪk/ *adjective*
very brave

heroin /'herəʊɪn/ *noun (no plural)*
a very strong, illegal drug

heroine /'herəʊɪn/ *noun*
a woman who does something great or brave

heroism /'herəʊɪzəm/ *noun (no plural)*
great courage

hers /hɜːz/ *pronoun*
something belonging to a woman or girl ➤ *My hand touched hers.*

herself /ə'self; *strong* hə'self/ *pronoun (plural themselves /ðəm'selvz/)*
1 the same girl or woman as the subject of the sentence ➤ *The woman dressed herself in her best clothes.*

H

2 used to give the word "she" a stronger meaning ► *She gave me some money, although she didn't have much herself.*
3 by herself alone; without help ► *She went for a walk by herself.* ► *She prepared that wonderful meal all by herself.*

he's /hi:z/
he is ► *He's a doctor.*

hesitant /'hezɪtənt/ *adjective*
slow to do something because you are nervous or uncertain ► *a hesitant smile* (adverb: **hesitantly**)

hesitate /'hezɪteɪt/ *verb (present participle* **hesitating***, past* **hesitated***)*
to stop what you are doing for a short time ► *He hesitated before he answered because he didn't know what to say.*

hesitation /ˌhezɪ'teɪʃən/ *noun*
a short stop or wait before you do something, because you feel uncertain

heterosexual /ˌhetərə'sekʃuəl/ *adjective*
sexually attracted to people of the opposite sex

hexagon /'heksəgən/ *noun*
a flat shape with six sides

hey /heɪ/ *interjection*
used to get someone's attention, or to show someone you are surprised or annoyed ► *Hey! Look who's here!*

hi /haɪ/ *interjection*
a friendly word that you use when you meet other people

hibernate /'haɪbəneɪt/ *verb (present participle* **hibernating***, past* **hibernated***)*
(used about animals) to sleep all the time during winter

hiccup¹ /'hɪkʌp/ *noun*
1 hiccups *plural noun* sudden, loud sounds in your throat that you sometimes make after eating or drinking too quickly

2 a small problem ► *There were a few small hiccups before the concert began.*

hiccup² *verb*
to make sudden, loud sounds in your throat after eating or drinking too quickly

hid /hɪd/
the PAST TENSE of the verb **hide**

hidden¹ /'hɪdn/
the PAST PARTICIPLE of the verb **hide**

hidden² *adjective*
difficult to see, find, or notice ► *They were filmed with hidden cameras.*

hide¹ /haɪd/ *verb (present participle* **hiding***, past tense* **hid** /hɪd/, *past participle* **hidden** /'hɪdn/)
1 to put something in a place where no one can see it or find it ► *Where did you hide the money?*
2 to go to a place where no one can see or find you ► *I hid behind the door, so that no one would see me.*
3 to not tell people about something ► *She hid her feelings.*
4 hide and seek a children's game in which one child hides and the others have to find him or her

hide² *noun*
the skin of an animal

hideous /'hɪdɪəs/ *adjective*
very ugly or unpleasant ► *a hideous yellow and purple dress*

hiding /'haɪdɪŋ/ *noun*
be in hiding to be hiding somewhere because you are in danger or you have done something wrong ► *The couple have been in hiding since the allegations were made public.*

hi-fi /ˌhaɪ 'faɪ/ *noun*
a machine that plays records or CDs and TAPES

high /haɪ/ *adjective*
1 tall, or far from the ground ► *The highest mountain in Africa is Mount Kilimanjaro.* ► *It is nearly 20,000 feet high.*

H

2 stronger, greater, or larger than usual ➤ *a high wind* ➤ *travelling at high speed* ➤ *high prices*
3 near the top of a set of sounds that the ear can hear ➤ *a high voice*
OPPOSITE (**1**, **2** and **3**): **low**

high-class /ˌhaɪ ˈklɑːs/ *adjective*
of good quality and style, and usually expensive ➤ *a high-class restaurant*

higher education /ˌhaɪər edjʊˈkeɪʃən/ *noun (no plural)*
study after you have left school, for example at university or college
COMPARE: **further education**

high jump /ˈhaɪ dʒʌmp/ *noun*
the high jump a sport in which you run and jump over a bar that is raised higher after each successful jump

highlands /ˈhaɪləndz/ *plural noun*
land which has a lot of hills, or is high up in the hills

highlight[1] /ˈhaɪlaɪt/ *verb*
1 to make something the main subject or problem that people pay attention to ➤ *In his speech, the President highlighted the issue of crime.*
2 to cover written words with a line or block of colour, so that you can see them more easily

highlight[2] *noun*
the most important, interesting, or enjoyable part of something ➤ *You can see highlights of today's game after the news.*

highly /ˈhaɪlɪ/ *adverb*
1 very ➤ *a highly intelligent girl*
2 think highly of someone to respect and admire someone a lot ➤ *His employees think very highly of him.*

Highness /ˈhaɪnəs/ *noun (plural Highnesses)*
a way of talking to or about certain royal people ➤ *His Royal Highness the Prince of Wales*

high-pitched /ˌhaɪ ˈpɪtʃt/ *adjective*
high and sharp, and unpleasant to hear ➤ *a high-pitched scream*

high-powered /ˌhaɪ ˈpaʊəd/ *adjective*
1 (used about machines) very powerful ➤ *a high-powered speedboat*
2 having an important job with a lot of responsibility ➤ *a high-powered executive*

high-rise /ˈhaɪ raɪz/ *adjective*
(used about buildings) very tall and modern ➤ *high-rise apartment blocks*

high school /ˈhaɪ skuːl/ *noun*
a school for children between 11 and 18 years old

high street /ˈhaɪ striːt/ *noun*
the main road in a town, where all the shops are

high-tech (*also* **hi-tech**) /ˌhaɪ ˈtek/ *adjective*
using the most modern and advanced ways of doing things in business and industry ➤ *a new, high-tech camera*

high tide /ˌhaɪ ˈtaɪd/ *noun*
the time when the sea is very high up the shore
OPPOSITE: **low tide**

highway /ˈhaɪweɪ/ *noun*
a main road

hijack /ˈhaɪdʒæk/ *verb*
to force the driver of a plane, lorry, etc. to take you somewhere

hijacker /ˈhaɪdʒækə/ *noun*
a person who forces the driver of a plane, lorry, etc. to take them somewhere

hike[1] /haɪk/ *verb (present participle hiking, past hiked)*
to take a long walk in the countryside or mountains for pleasure ➤ *The Lake District is a great place to go hiking.*

hike[2] *noun*
a long walk in the countryside or mountains for pleasure ➤ *The*

weather was too bad for us to go for a hike.

hilarious /hɪˈleərɪəs/ *adjective*
very funny ➤ *a hilarious film*

hill /hɪl/ *noun*
a piece of ground higher than usual; a small mountain

hillside /ˈhɪlsaɪd/ *noun*
the sloping side of a hill ➤ *a hotel built high on the hillside*

hilly /ˈhɪlɪ/ *adjective* (**hillier, hilliest**)
with a lot of hills ➤ *The surrounding countryside was very hilly.*

him /ɪm; *strong* hɪm/ *pronoun*
a man or boy (used in sentences like this) ➤ *I saw him last week.* ➤ *Give him the book.* ➤ *I had a letter from him.*

himself /ɪmˈself; *strong* hɪmˈself/ *pronoun* (*plural* **themselves** /ðəmˈselvz/)
1 the same man or boy as the subject of the sentence ➤ *Peter bought himself some new clothes.*
2 used to give the word "he" a stronger meaning ➤ *He told me so himself.*
3 by himself alone; without help ➤ *He stayed at home by himself.* ➤ *He repaired the roof all by himself.*

hinder /ˈhɪndə/ *verb*
to make it more difficult for someone to do something

hindsight /ˈhaɪndsaɪt/ *noun* (no plural)
the ability to understand or judge an event only after it has happened ➤ *With hindsight, I should never have let her use my car.*

Hindu /ˈhɪnduː/ *noun*
a person who follows the main religion of India

Hinduism /ˈhɪnduːɪzəm/ *noun* (no plural)
the main religion of India

hinge /hɪndʒ/ *noun*
a piece of metal that joins two things

together so that one of them can swing freely ➤ *We need a new hinge on that door.*

hint¹ /hɪnt/ *verb*
to say something in a way that is not direct ➤ *He hinted that he was looking for another job.*

hint² *noun*
1 something said in a way that is not direct ➤ *When she said she was tired, it was a hint that she wanted us to go.*
2 a piece of useful advice ➤ *helpful hints for cleaning children's clothes*

hip /hɪp/ *noun*
the part of your body where your legs join your bottom

hippie (also **hippy**) /ˈhɪpɪ/ *noun*
a person who deliberately does not live or dress like ordinary people and who believes in love and peace. People first started becoming hippies in the 1960s

hippopotamus /ˌhɪpəˈpɒtəməs/ *noun* (*plural* **hippopotamuses**)
a large, African animal with short legs and thick, hairless skin, that lives near rivers

hippy /ˈhɪpɪ/ *noun* (*plural* **hippies**)
another word for **hippie**

hire¹ /haɪə/ *verb* (*present participle* **hiring**, *past* **hired**)
to pay for the use of something or for someone's help ➤ *He hired a car for two days.*

> Use **hire** only when you are talking about paying to use something for a short time: *We hired a car for a few days.* Compare **rent**, which is used when talking about longer periods of time, e.g. you rent a house to live in; you do not hire it.

hire² *noun* (no plural)
the use of something for a certain amount of money ➤ *Boats for hire.*

his /ɪz; *strong* hɪz/ *adjective, pronoun*
1 belonging to a man or boy ▶ *He sat drinking his coffee.*
2 something belonging to a man or boy ▶ *My hand touched his.*

Hispanic /hɪˈspænɪk/ *adjective*
of or from a country where Spanish or Portuguese is spoken

hiss¹ /hɪs/ *verb*
to make a sound like a continuous "s" by forcing air out through your teeth or mouth ▶ *The snake hissed angrily.*

hiss² *noun (plural* **hisses**)
a sound like a continuous "s"

historian /hɪˈstɔːriən/ *noun*
a person who studies or writes about history

historic /hɪˈstɒrɪk/ *adjective*
important in the past ▶ *a historic meeting between the two leaders*

historical /hɪˈstɒrɪkəl/ *adjective*
in or about the past ▶ *historical facts*

history /ˈhɪstəri/ *noun (no plural)*
1 things that happened in the past
2 the study of things that happened in the past ▶ *a history lesson*

hit¹ /hɪt/ *verb (present participle* **hitting**, *past* **hit**)
to touch something suddenly and with a lot of force ▶ *He hit me in the stomach.* ▶ *She hit her head on the low roof.*

hit² *noun*
1 an act of touching something suddenly and forcefully ▶ *I got a direct hit with my first shot.*
2 a song or film that is popular and successful ▶ *That song was a hit last year.*

hit-and-run /ˌhɪt ən ˈrʌn/ *adjective*
hit-and-run accident an accident in which a car driver hits someone and then drives away without stopping to help

hitch¹ /hɪtʃ/ *verb*
1 to stand beside a road and ask for free rides in other people's cars ▶ *We tried to hitch a ride into Manchester.*
2 to fasten one thing to another ▶ *Dad hitched the boat to the back of the car.*

hitch² *noun (plural* **hitches**)
a small problem that causes a delay ▶ *The presentation went off without a hitch.*

hitchhike /ˈhɪtʃhaɪk/ *verb (present participle* **hitchhiking**, *past* **hitchhiked**)
to stand beside a road and ask for free rides in other people's cars

hitchhiker /ˈhɪtʃˌhaɪkəʳ/ *noun*
a person who stands beside a road and asks for free rides in other people's cars

hi-tech /ˌhaɪ ˈtek/ *adjective*
another word for **high-tech**

HIV /ˌeɪtʃ aɪ ˈviː/ *noun (no plural)*
1 HUMAN IMMUNODEFICIENCY VIRUS; a type of infection that enters the body through the blood or sexual activity, and can cause AIDS
2 **be HIV positive** to have the HIV infection in your blood

hive /haɪv/ *(also* **beehive**) *noun*
a wooden box made for bees to live in

h'm *(also* **hmm**) /m, hm/ *interjection*
a sound that you make when you are thinking what to say or do

hoard¹ /hɔːd/ *verb*
to collect and store things but not use them ▶ *squirrels hoarding nuts for the winter*

hoard² *noun*
a large amount of something that has been stored ▶ *a hoard of gold coins*

hoarse /hɔːs/ *adjective*
(used about a person's voice) rough, as when your throat is sore and dry ▶ *His voice was hoarse after speaking for an hour.*

hoax /həʊks/ *noun (plural **hoaxes**)*
an attempt to make people believe something that is not true ➤ *The bomb threat turned out to be a hoax.*

hob /hɒb/ *noun*
the surface on the top of a COOKER where you cook food in pans

hobble /ˈhɒbl/ *verb (present participle **hobbling**, past **hobbled**)*
to walk slowly and with difficulty ➤ *I had to hobble after I hurt my leg.*

hobby /ˈhɒbi/ *noun (plural **hobbies**)*
an activity that you enjoy doing in your free time ➤ *He works in a bank, but his hobby is building model boats.*

hockey /ˈhɒki/ *noun (no plural)*
a game played by two teams who use curved sticks to hit a ball into a net

hoe /həʊ/ *noun*
a tool used to loosen the ground in your garden

hog¹ /hɒg/ *noun*
go the whole hog to do something thoroughly or completely ➤ *Why don't we go the whole hog and get champagne?*

hog² *verb (present participle **hogging**, past **hogged**)*
to keep or use all of something for yourself ➤ *Katie always hogs the duvet.*

hoist /hɔɪst/ *verb*
to pull something up or raise it to a high place, often using ropes

hold¹ /həʊld/ *verb (past **held** /held/)*
1 to have something in your hand or arms ➤ *The little girl held the toy tightly in her arms.*
2 to keep something in a particular position ➤ *Can you hold the picture up for a minute, please?*
3 to have something inside ➤ *This bottle holds one litre.*
4 to arrange and make something happen ➤ *The meeting will be held next week.*

5 to have something ➤ *He holds an important position at the bank.*
6 hold someone back to stop someone from moving forwards ➤ *The police tried to hold the crowd back.*
7 hold a conversation to talk to someone
8 hold your breath to stop breathing for a short time ➤ *You have to hold your breath underwater.*
9 hold the line to wait for a short time when you are talking on the telephone ➤ *Hold the line. I'll see if I can find the manager.*
10 hold on to wait for a short time ➤ *Could you hold on, please? I'll see if he's in.*

hold² *noun*
1 the place on a ship where goods are stored
2 get hold of, take hold of to take something in your hand and keep it there ➤ *He took hold of the rope and pulled.*

holdall /ˈhəʊldɔːl/ *noun*
a bag used for carrying clothes, tools, etc.

holder /ˈhəʊldəʳ/ *noun*
1 used to show that someone has a particular position, place, or thing ➤ *the Olympic record holder* ➤ *UK passport holders*
2 something that holds or contains something else ➤ *a leather chequebook holder*

hold-up /ˈhəʊld ʌp/ *noun*
1 a delay ➤ *I'm sorry I'm late, but there was a hold-up near the bridge.*
2 an occasion when robbers use guns to persuade other people to give them money ➤ *a hold-up in a bank*

hole /həʊl/ *noun*
an empty space or opening in something ➤ *a hole in the road*

holiday /ˈhɒlɪdeɪ, -di/ *noun*
1 a time when you do not work or go to school ➤ *Next Friday is a holiday.*

2 on holiday not at school or work ► *I'm on holiday next week.*

3 go on holiday to go to another place for a short time to have a rest from school or work

hollow /ˈhɒləʊ/ *adjective*
having an empty space inside ► *a hollow tree*
OPPOSITE: **solid**

holly /ˈhɒlɪ/ *noun (no plural)*
a small tree with dark green, prickly leaves and red berries

hologram /ˈhɒləgræm/ *noun*
a picture made in a special way so that the image looks as if it is real, because you can see the sides as well as the front of it

holy /ˈhəʊlɪ/ *adjective (holier, holiest)*
1 concerning God or religion ► *the holy city of Mecca*
2 very good and pure; religious ► *a holy man*

home¹ /həʊm/ *noun*
1 the place where someone lives ► *Her home is in Wales.*
2 a place where a particular group of people or animals are cared for ► *a children's home*
3 at home in your own house ► *I stayed at home to read.*

home² *adjective*
1 of or being the place where someone or something lives or is based ► *my home town*
2 playing on your own sports field and not that of the other team ► *the home team*

home³ *adverb*
to or at your own home ► *Let's go home.*

homeland /ˈhəʊmlænd/ *noun*
the country where you were born ► *She returned to her homeland, Somalia.*

homeless /ˈhəʊmləs/ *adjective*
having nowhere to live

homely /ˈhəʊmlɪ/ *adjective (homelier, homeliest)*
ordinary and comfortable in a way that makes you feel relaxed ► *a small, family hotel with a homely atmosphere*

homemade /ˌhəʊmˈmeɪd/ *adjective*
made at home and not bought from a shop ► *homemade jam*

homeopathy /ˌhəʊmɪˈɒpəθɪ/ *noun (no plural)*
a method of treating illness that involves using very small amounts of natural substances

home page /ˈhəʊm peɪdʒ/ *noun*
a place on the INTERNET where you can find information about a person, company, etc. ► *Visit our home page for more information and links to other sites.*

homesick /ˈhəʊmsɪk/ *adjective*
sad because you are away from home ► *I felt homesick living in Paris by myself.*

homeward /ˈhəʊmwəd/ *adjective*
going towards home ► *my homeward journey*

homework /ˈhəʊmwɜːk/ *noun (no plural)*
work that a teacher gives you to do at home

homicide /ˈhɒmɪsaɪd/ *noun*
the crime of murder

homosexual /ˌhəʊməˈsekʃʊəl/ *adjective*
sexually attracted to people of the same sex

honest /ˈɒnɪst/ *adjective*
not likely to lie, steal, or cheat; truthful ► *an honest face*
OPPOSITE: **dishonest**

honestly /ˈɒnɪstlɪ/ *adverb*
1 without lying, stealing, or cheating ► *If I can't get the money honestly, I'll have to think of something else.*

H

2 speaking truthfully ▶ *I honestly don't mind working late tonight.*
3 Honestly! a word used to express annoyance ▶ *Honestly! What a stupid thing to do.*

honesty /ˈɒnɪstɪ/ *noun (no plural)*
behaviour in which you tell the truth, and do not lie, steal, or cheat ▶ *He was praised for his honesty when he returned the money.*
OPPOSITE: **dishonesty**

honey /ˈhʌnɪ/ *noun (no plural)*
a sweet, sticky liquid that is made by bees and that people can eat

honeymoon /ˈhʌnɪmuːn/ *noun*
a holiday taken by a man and a woman who have just got married

honk /hɒŋk/ *verb*
to make a loud noise using a car HORN ▶ *A taxi driver honked his horn behind her.*

honour /ˈɒnəʳ/ *noun (no plural)*
1 great respect ▶ *The things that he has done have brought honour to our country.*
OPPOSITE: **dishonour**
2 in honour of someone, in someone's honour done to show respect for someone ▶ *a ceremony in honour of the soldiers who died*

honourable /ˈɒnərəbəl/ *adjective*
behaving in a way that people think is morally right, which makes them respect you ▶ *an honourable man* (*adverb:* **honourably**)

hood /hʊd/ *noun*
1 a piece of cloth on a coat or other piece of clothing that you can pull up to cover your head and neck
2 the covering of an open car ▶ *It's raining. Put the hood up.*

hoof /huːf/ *noun (plural **hooves** /huːvz/)*
the foot of a horse, cow, sheep, or goat

hook /hʊk/ *noun*
1 a bent piece of metal or hard plastic for hanging something on or for catching something ▶ *He hung his coat on the hook behind the door.*
▶ *a fish hook*
2 off the hook having the telephone receiver lifted so that the telephone will not ring

hooked /hʊkt/ *adjective*
1 be hooked on something to like something a lot and not want to stop doing it or using it ▶ *Thousands of children are hooked on computer games.*
2 shaped like a hook ▶ *a hooked nose*

hooligan /ˈhuːlɪgən/ *noun*
a noisy, violent young person who causes trouble by fighting and breaking things

hoop /huːp/ *noun*
a round band of wood, plastic, or metal

hooray /hʊˈreɪ/ *interjection*
another word for **hurray**

hoot¹ /huːt/ *verb*
to make a loud noise like the noise of a car's horn ▶ *The bus driver hooted at the man who stepped onto the road.*

hoot² *noun*
1 the sound made by a car's horn
2 the sound made by an OWL
3 a shout of laughter

hoover /ˈhuːvəʳ/ *verb*
to clean the floor using a machine that sucks up dirt ▶ *Most days I hoover the floor after breakfast.*
SAME MEANING: **vacuum**

Hoover /ˈhuːvəʳ/ *noun trademark*
a VACUUM CLEANER
SAME MEANING: **vacuum**

hooves /huːvz/
the plural of **hoof**

hop¹ /hɒp/ *verb (present participle **hopping**, past **hopped**)*
1 (used about people) to jump on one foot

H

2 (used about small birds and animals) to jump with both legs together

hop² noun
1 a small jump
2 a short aircraft flight ▶ We'll do the final hop from Cairo to Luxor tomorrow.

hope¹ /həʊp/ verb (present participle **hoping**, past **hoped**)
to want something to happen and to think it probably will happen ▶ I hope to go to college. ▶ Is she coming? I hope so. ▶ I hope not.

hope² noun
1 an idea that something will happen as you want it to ▶ Hopes of reaching an agreement are fading.
2 someone or something that could make everything happen as you want it to ▶ You're my last hope.
3 **give up hope, lose hope** to stop thinking that everything will happen as you want it to ▶ Don't lose hope.
4 **hope for the best** to hope that everything will be all right in the end

hopeful /'həʊpfəl/ adjective
feeling quite sure about something ▶ I am hopeful that she will come tomorrow.

hopefully /'həʊpfəli/ adverb
1 in a hopeful way ▶ The dog waited hopefully beside the table for some food.
2 if everything goes well ▶ Hopefully, we'll be there by dinner time.

hopeless /'həʊpləs/ adjective
1 with no sign of something getting better ▶ a hopeless situation
2 very bad or lacking in skill ▶ I am hopeless at science.
(adverb: **hopelessly**)

horde /hɔːd/ noun
a very large crowd ▶ Hordes of reporters were waiting at the airport.

horizon /hə'raɪzən/ noun
the line between the land or sea and the sky ▶ I could see a ship on the horizon.

horizontal /ˌhɒrɪ'zɒntl/ adjective
in a flat position, along or parallel to the ground ▶ a horizontal surface
COMPARE: **vertical**

hormone /'hɔːməʊn/ noun
a substance produced by your body, which helps it to grow or causes it to change in some other way

horn /hɔːn/ noun
1 one of the two hard pieces sticking out from the heads of some animals
2 an instrument on a car, bus, etc. that gives a short, loud sound as a warning ▶ He sounded his horn at the car in front.
3 a musical instrument that you blow into

horoscope /'hɒrəskəʊp/ noun
a description of your character and things that will happen to you in the future, based on the position of the stars and PLANETS when you were born

horrendous /hɒ'rendəs/ adjective
very bad or unpleasant ▶ The traffic was horrendous.
(adverb: **horrendously**)

horrible /'hɒrəbl/ adjective
very unpleasant ▶ There was a horrible accident here yesterday.
SAME MEANING: **terrible, dreadful**

horrid /'hɒrɪd/ adjective
unpleasant ▶ horrid food

horrific /hɒ'rɪfɪk/ adjective
very shocking and unpleasant ▶ That was a horrific accident.

horrify /'hɒrɪfaɪ/ verb (past **horrified**)
to shock someone or make them feel fear ▶ I was horrified by the news.

horror /'hɒrəʳ/ noun (no plural)
great fear and shock ▶ I watched in horror as the cars crashed into each other.

horse /hɔːs/ noun
a large animal that people ride on and use for pulling heavy things

H

horseback /'hɔːsbæk/ *noun*
on horseback riding on a horse

horse-riding /'hɔːsˌraɪdɪŋ/ *noun (no plural)*
the sport of riding horses

horseshoe /'hɔːsʃuː/ *noun*
a piece of iron shaped like a half-circle, which is nailed to a horse's foot to protect it

hose /həʊz/ *noun*
a long piece of tube that bends easily, used for getting water from one place to another

hospitable /'hɒspɪtəbəl/ *adjective*
friendly and generous to someone who is visiting you ▶ *Greek people are very hospitable.*

hospital /'hɒspɪtl/ *noun*
a building where doctors and nurses care for people who are ill

hospitality /ˌhɒspɪ'tæləti/ *noun (no plural)*
kind attention given to visitors ▶ *The people of your village showed me great hospitality.*

host /həʊst/ *noun*
a person who has invited other people to their house for a social event

hostage /'hɒstɪdʒ/ *noun*
a person taken and kept as a prisoner by someone to force other people to do something, e.g. pay money

hostel /'hɒstl/ *noun*
a building where students, or other people living away from home, can eat and sleep cheaply

hostess /'həʊstɪs/ *noun (plural hostesses)*
a woman who has invited people to her house for a social event

hostile /'hɒstaɪl/ *adjective*
not friendly ▶ *a hostile crowd*

hostility /hɒ'stɪləti/ *noun (no plural)*
unfriendly and angry feelings or behaviour ▶ *There has always been hostility between the two countries.*

hot /hɒt/ *adjective (hotter, hottest)*
1 having a lot of heat ▶ *the hottest day of the year* ▶ *The soup's really hot.*
OPPOSITE: **cold**
2 having a strong, burning taste ▶ *a hot curry*
OPPOSITE: **mild**

hot dog /ˌhɒt 'dɒg/ *noun*
a special sort of long, red SAUSAGE eaten in a long piece of bread

hotel /həʊ'tel/ *noun*
a building where people can pay for a room to sleep in and for meals

hotline /'hɒtlaɪn/ *noun*
a special telephone number that people can call for information or advice

hound /haʊnd/ *noun*
a dog used for hunting or racing

hour /aʊəʳ/ *noun*
1 a measure of time; 60 minutes ▶ *There are 24 hours in a day.*
2 a particular time of day or night ▶ *There won't be any trains at this hour.*
3 a time when you usually do a particular thing ▶ *Our business hours are 9.30 to 5.30.* ▶ *my lunch hour*
4 for hours for a long time ▶ *I've been waiting here for hours.*
5 in an hour after one hour has passed ▶ *I'll meet you in an hour.*
6 on the hour at 1 o'clock, 2 o'clock, etc. ▶ *The trains leave on the hour.*

hourly /'aʊəli/ *adjective*
happening every hour ▶ *There are hourly trains to London.*

house /haʊs/ *noun (plural houses* /'haʊzɪz/)
a building that people live in

housebound /'haʊsbaʊnd/ *adjective*
unable to leave your house, because you are ill or cannot walk far

household /'haʊsˌhəʊld/ *noun*
all the people who live in a house together

H

housekeeper /'haʊsˌkiːpə^r/ *noun*
someone who is paid to clean, cook, and look after your house for you

houseproud /'haʊspraʊd/ *adjective*
spending a lot of time cleaning and taking care of your home

house-to-house /ˌhaʊs tə 'haʊs/ *adjective*
visiting every house in an area ▶ *The police are making house-to-house enquiries.*

housewarming /'haʊsˌwɔːmɪŋ/ *noun*
a party to celebrate moving into a new house

housewife /'haʊswaɪf/ *noun (plural **housewives** /-waɪvz/)*
a married woman who works in the house for her family

housework /'haʊswɜːk/ *noun (no plural)*
work that you do at home, such as cleaning, washing, etc. ▶ *I usually do the housework at weekends.*

housing /'haʊzɪŋ/ *noun (no plural)*
houses for people to live in ▶ *More money is needed for housing, education, and health.*

hover /'hɒvə^r/ *verb*
to stay in the air in one place ▶ *The great bird hovered above the field, looking for a mouse.*

hovercraft /'hɒvəkrɑːft/ *noun*
a sort of boat that travels over land and water by floating on air that is pushed out by its engines

how /haʊ/ *adverb*
1 in what way ▶ *How do you open this box?*
2 used in questions about time, amount, or size ▶ *How much did you pay?* ▶ *How many children do you have?* ▶ *How old are you?*
3 How is ...?, How are ...? used to ask about someone's health ▶ *How is your mother?* ▶ *How are you?*

4 How do you do? an expression used as a greeting when you first meet someone
5 used to make something you say stronger ▶ *How nice of you to remember my birthday!*

however /haʊ'evə^r/ *adverb*
1 in whatever way; it does not matter how ▶ *She goes swimming every day, however cold it is.*
2 but ▶ *I don't think we can do it – however, we'll try.*

howl[1] /haʊl/ *verb*
to make a long, loud crying sound ▶ *The dog howled when it was shut in the house.* ▶ *Wind howled round the house.*

howl[2] *noun*
a long, loud cry

HQ /ˌeɪtʃ 'kjuː/ *noun*
the HEADQUARTERS of a business or of some other group

hr
a short way of writing the word **hour**

huddle /'hʌdl/ *verb (present participle **huddling**, past **huddled**)*
to move close to the other people in a small group ▶ *We huddled round the fire to keep warm.*

huff[1] /hʌf/ *noun*
in a huff angry because someone has offended you ▶ *Ray walked out in a huff.*

huff[2] *verb*
huff and puff to breathe in a noisy way, especially because you are doing something tiring ▶ *When we got to the top of the hill, we were all huffing and puffing.*

hug[1] /hʌg/ *verb (present participle **hugging**, past **hugged**)*
to put your arms round someone and hold them because you love them ▶ *He hugged his daughter and tried to comfort her.*
SAME MEANING: **cuddle**

hug² *noun*
an act of holding someone close to you in your arms ➤ *He gave her a hug.*
SAME MEANING: **cuddle**

huge /hjuːdʒ/ *adjective*
very large ➤ *a huge amount of food* (adverb: **hugely**)
SAME MEANING: **enormous, massive, vast**

hull /hʌl/ *noun*
the main part of a ship

hullo (also **hallo, hello**) /həˈləʊ/ *interjection*
the usual word you say when you meet someone or talk on the telephone

hum /hʌm/ *verb (present participle* **humming**, *past* **hummed**)
1 to make a low, steady noise like a bee
2 to sing with your lips closed

human /ˈhjuːmən/ *adjective*
of or like a person ➤ *the human voice*

human being /ˌhjuːmən ˈbiːɪŋ/ *noun*
a man, woman, or child, not an animal

humane /hjuːˈmeɪn/ *adjective*
kind; not cruel ➤ *the humane treatment of animals* (adverb: **humanely**)
OPPOSITE: **inhumane**

humanitarian /hjuːˌmænɪˈteərɪən/ *adjective*
concerned with trying to help people who are ill, hungry, etc. ➤ *The UN has sent humanitarian aid to help the refugees.*

humanity /hjuːˈmænətɪ/ *noun (no plural)*
1 kindness, respect, and sympathy towards other people ➤ *a man of great humanity*
2 people in general ➤ *the danger to humanity caused by pollution*

human race /ˌhjuːmən ˈreɪs/ *noun*
the human race all people, rather than animals or other types of life

➤ *There are many things that threaten the survival of the human race.*

human rights /ˌhjuːmən ˈraɪts/ *plural noun*
the basic rights that everyone has to be free and to be treated fairly, especially by their government

humble /ˈhʌmbəl/ *adjective*
1 thinking that you are not better or more important than other people; not proud ➤ *She was always humble about her work, although she helped many people.*
2 simple or poor ➤ *a humble home*

humid /ˈhjuːmɪd/ *adjective*
very warm and wet in an unpleasant way ➤ *Florida is extremely humid in the summer.*

humiliate /hjuːˈmɪlɪeɪt/ *verb (present participle* **humiliating**, *past* **humiliated**)
to make someone feel stupid or weak ➤ *He often humiliated other people in meetings.*

humorous /ˈhuːmərəs/ *adjective*
funny; making you laugh ➤ *a humorous book*

humour /ˈhjuːməʳ/ *noun (no plural)*
the ability to laugh at things or to make others laugh ➤ *He doesn't have a sense of humour.*

hump /hʌmp/ *noun*
1 a large lump, for example on a camel's back
2 a small hill or raised part in a road

hunch /hʌntʃ/ *noun*
have a hunch to have a feeling that something is true or will happen, even though you have no definite information about it ➤ *I had a hunch that something would go wrong.*

hunched /hʌntʃt/ *adjective*
sitting or standing with your back and shoulders bent forwards ➤ *He was sitting in his study, hunched over his books.*

H

hundred /'hʌndrəd/ *adjective, noun*
1 *(plural **hundred**)* the number 100 ► *a hundred years ago* ► *three hundred people*
2 hundreds a very large number of people or things ► *We received hundreds of letters after mum died.*

hundredth /'hʌndrədθ/ *adjective*
100th

hung /hʌŋ/
the PAST TENSE and PAST PARTICIPLE of the verb **hang**

hunger /'hʌŋgə*r*/ *noun (no plural)*
the feeling of wanting or needing to eat
COMPARE: **thirst**

hungry /'hʌŋgrɪ/ *adjective (**hungrier, hungriest**)*
wanting or needing food ► *Can I have an apple? I'm hungry.*
COMPARE: **thirsty**

hunk /hʌŋk/ *noun*
1 an attractive man who has a strong body
2 a thick piece of something, especially food ► *a hunk of bread*

hunt /hʌnt/ *verb*
1 to chase and kill wild animals or birds for food or sport
2 hunt for something to try to find something ► *I hunted everywhere for that book.*

hunter /'hʌntə*r*/ *noun*
a person who chases and kills wild animals or birds, usually for food

hunting /'hʌntɪŋ/ *noun (no plural)*
the activity of chasing wild animals or birds in order to catch and kill them
► *Is fox-hunting cruel?*

hurdle /'hɜːdl/ *noun*
1 a small fence that a person or horse jumps over during a race ► *the 100-metre hurdles*
2 a problem or difficulty that you have to deal with ► *Exams are a hurdle that everyone has to face.*

hurl /hɜːl/ *verb*
to throw something with force ► *He hurled the brick through the window.*

hurray *(also **hooray**)* /hʊ'reɪ/ *interjection*
a shout of joy or approval ► *We've won! Hurray!*

hurricane /'hʌrɪkən/ *noun*
a bad storm with a very strong wind
COMPARE: **blizzard**

hurried /'hʌrɪd/ *adjective*
done more quickly than usual, especially because there is not much time ► *He said a hurried goodbye and ran for the bus. (adverb: **hurriedly**)*

hurry¹ /'hʌrɪ/ *verb (past **hurried**)*
1 to move quickly or do something quickly ► *You'll catch the train if you hurry.*
2 hurry up to do something more quickly ► *I wish you'd hurry up!*

hurry² *noun*
be in a hurry to try to do things quickly because you do not have much time ► *You always seem to be in a hurry.*

hurt¹ /hɜːt/ *verb (past **hurt**)*
1 to damage part of a person's body or bring pain to them ► *I fell over and hurt myself.* ► *Sorry – did I hurt you?*
2 to cause you pain ► *My feet hurt.*
3 to make someone unhappy ► *I tried not to hurt her feelings.*

hurt² *adjective*
1 damaged or feeling pain ► *He was badly hurt.*
2 unhappy ► *She's hurt because you haven't visited her.*

hurtful /'hɜːtfəl/ *adjective*
making you feel upset or unhappy
► *a hurtful remark*

hurtle /'hɜːtl/ *verb (present participle **hurtling**, past **hurtled**)*
to move very fast ► *We hurtled down the road at 100km an hour.*

H

husband /ˈhʌzbənd/ *noun*
the man to whom a woman is married
COMPARE: **wife**

hush /hʌʃ/ *noun (no plural)*
a peaceful silence

husky /ˈhʌskɪ/ *adjective (**huskier, huskiest**)*
(used about voices) deep and sounding rough but attractive

hustle¹ /ˈhʌsəl/ *verb (present participle **hustling**, past **hustled**)*
to make someone move somewhere quickly, often by pushing them
▶ *Steve hustled his son into the house and shut the door.*

hustle² *noun (no plural)*
hustle and bustle busy and noisy activity

hut /hʌt/ *noun*
a small building often made of wood

hutch /hʌtʃ/ *noun (plural **hutches**)*
a wooden box that people keep rabbits in

hydraulic /haɪˈdrɒlɪk/ *adjective*
moved or operated by the pressure of water or another liquid ▶ *a hydraulic pump*

hydroelectric /ˌhaɪdrəʊ-ɪˈlektrɪk/ *adjective*
using water power to produce electricity ▶ *The hydroelectric plant provides the town with energy.*

hydrogen /ˈhaɪdrədʒən/ *noun (no plural)*
a very light, colourless gas

hyena /haɪˈiːnə/ *noun*
a wild animal like a large dog

hygiene /ˈhaɪdʒiːn/ *noun (no plural)*
the practice of keeping yourself and the things around you clean in order to prevent diseases ▶ *The children are taught the importance of personal hygiene.*

hygienic /haɪˈdʒiːnɪk/ *adjective*
clean and likely to stop diseases from spreading

hymn /hɪm/ *noun*
a religious song

hype /haɪp/ *noun (no plural)*
talking about something on television, in newspapers, etc. to make it sound good or important
▶ *The media hype surrounding the event is incredible.*

hypermarket /ˈhaɪpəˌmɑːkɪt/ *noun*
a very large shop outside a town, that sells many different kinds of food and other things

hyphen /ˈhaɪfən/ *noun*
the sign (-) used to join two words or parts of words ▶ *half-price*

hypnosis /hɪpˈnəʊsɪs/ *noun (no plural)*
a method of putting someone into a state like a deep sleep, so that you can influence what they think or do
▶ *Under hypnosis, Jean was able to remember exactly what had happened that day.*

hypnotize /ˈhɪpnətaɪz/ *verb (present participle **hypnotizing**, past **hypnotized**)*
to make someone go into a state like a deep sleep, so that you can influence what they think or do

hypocrisy /hɪˈpɒkrəsɪ/ *noun (no plural)*
the practice of pretending to have particular feelings or opinions, but then behaving in a way that shows that you do not really have them
▶ *The government was accused of hypocrisy.*

hypocrite /ˈhɪpəkrɪt/ *noun*
a person who says that they have particular feelings or opinions, but then behaves in a way that shows that they do not really have them
▶ *He's such a hypocrite!*

hysterical /hɪˈsterɪkəl/ *adjective*
1 very upset, afraid, or excited, and not able to control yourself ▶ *She was so hysterical that no one could stop her screaming*

H

2 very funny ▶ *The play was hysterical!* (adverb: **hysterically**)

Ii

I /aɪ/ *pronoun (plural **we** /wɪ; strong wiː/)*
the person who is speaking ▶ *I want to go home.* ▶ *My friend and I went to the cinema.* ▶ ***I'm** (=I am) very glad to see you.* ▶ ***I've** (=I have) been waiting a long time.* ▶ ***I'll** (=I will or I shall) wait a little longer.* ▶ *When **I'd** (=I had) written the story, I read it to my friend.* ▶ *I thought that **I'd** (=I would) miss the bus, but I didn't.*

ice /aɪs/ *noun (no plural)*
water which is so cold that it has become hard ▶ *He put some ice in his drink.* ▶ *There was ice on the roads this morning.*

iceberg /ˈaɪsbɜːg/ *noun*
a very large piece of ice floating in the sea

ice-cold /ˌaɪs ˈkəʊld/ *adjective*
very cold ▶ *an ice-cold drink*

ice cream /ˌaɪs ˈkriːm/ *noun (no plural)*
a sweet food made from milk which has been frozen ▶ *a bowl of chocolate ice cream*

ice cube /ˈaɪs kjuːb/ *noun*
a small, square piece of ice that you put in a drink to make it cold

ice hockey /ˈaɪs ˌhɒki/ *noun (no plural)*
a game played on ice, in which two teams of players use long, curved sticks to hit a hard, flat object into a GOAL

ice skate[1] /ˈaɪs skeɪt/ *noun*
a special shoe that you wear for moving or dancing on ice

ice-skate[2] *verb (present participle **ice-skating**, past **ice-skated**)*
to move or dance on ice wearing special shoes ▶ *to go ice-skating*

ice-skating /ˈaɪs skeɪtɪŋ/ *noun (no plural)*
the sport of moving or dancing on ice wearing special shoes

icicle /ˈaɪsɪkəl/ *noun*
a long, thin piece of ice that hangs down from something ▶ *There were icicles hanging from the edge of the roof.*

icing /ˈaɪsɪŋ/ *noun (no plural)*
a mixture of sugar and water, or sugar and butter, put on top of cakes

icon /ˈaɪkɒn/ *noun*
1 a small picture on a computer SCREEN that you choose in order to make the computer do something ▶ *Select the print icon, using the right-hand mouse button.*
2 a person or thing that many people admire and connect with an important idea ▶ *a feminist icon*

icy /ˈaɪsi/ *adjective (**icier, iciest**)*
1 very cold ▶ *an icy wind*
2 covered with ice ▶ *icy roads*

ID /ˌaɪ ˈdiː/ *noun (no plural)*
a document that shows your name, address, etc., usually with a photograph ▶ *Do you have any ID?*

I'd /aɪd/
1 I had ▶ *I'd already left by the time she arrived.*
2 I would ▶ *I'd like a cup of coffee, please.*

idea /aɪˈdɪə/ *noun*
1 a thought or plan that you form in your mind ▶ *I've got an idea – why don't we have a party?* ▶ *What a good idea!*
2 **have no idea** not to know something ▶ *"What time is it?" "I've no idea."* ▶ *I had no idea that you had a brother.*

ideal /aɪ'dɪəl/ *adjective*
the best possible ➤ *This book is an ideal Christmas present.*

idealistic /ˌaɪdɪə'lɪstɪk/ *adjective*
believing in principles and high standards, even if they cannot be achieved in real life

ideally /aɪ'dɪəlɪ/ *adverb*
1 used to say how you would like things to be, even if it is not possible ➤ *Ideally, we would like an extra month to finish this project.*
2 very well ➤ *The hotel is ideally located.*

identical /aɪ'dentɪkəl/ *adjective*
exactly the same ➤ *identical twins* (=looking the same)

identification /aɪˌdentɪfɪ'keɪʃən/ *noun (no plural)*
something which shows who someone is or what something is ➤ *Have you any identification with you?*

identify /aɪ'dentɪfaɪ/ *verb (past identified)*
to say who someone is or what something is ➤ *Can you identify the man in the picture?*

identity /aɪ'dentətɪ/ *noun (plural identities)*
who someone is or what something is ➤ *The police do not know the identity of the dead man* (=do not know his name).

ideology /ˌaɪdɪ'ɒlədʒɪ/ *noun (plural ideologies)*
a set of beliefs or ideas, especially political beliefs ➤ *socialist ideology*

idiom /'ɪdɪəm/ *noun*
a group of words which have a special meaning when they are used together ➤ *To have cold feet about something is an English idiom which means to be worried or nervous about doing something.*

idiomatic /ˌɪdɪə'mætɪk/ *adjective*

(used about language) containing idioms, and typical of the way people usually talk and write

idiot /'ɪdɪət/ *noun*
a silly or stupid person
SAME MEANING: **fool**

idiotic /ˌɪdɪ'ɒtɪk/ *adjective*
very stupid ➤ *Don't ask idiotic questions.*

idle /'aɪdl/ *adjective*
1 (used about a machine) doing no work ➤ *idle machines in a factory*
2 (used about a person) lazy

idol /'aɪdl/ *noun*
1 a famous person who is loved and admired by many people
2 something such as a STATUE which people worship as a god

idolize /'aɪdəl-aɪz/ *verb (present participle idolizing, past idolized)*
to admire someone so much that you think they are perfect ➤ *Herman idolized his father.*

i.e. /ˌaɪ 'iː/
a short way of writing or saying **that is**, used when you want to give more information to show what you mean by something ➤ *The total cost of the holiday, i.e. including hotel, food, and travel, is £500.*

if /ɪf/ *conjunction*
1 on condition that ➤ *You can catch the bus if you go now.*
2 whether ➤ *I don't know if he will come or not.*
3 whenever ➤ *I always visit them if I go to the city.*
4 as if like; used when you are describing something ➤ *It looks as if it is going to rain.* ➤ *He talks to me as if I'm stupid.*
5 if I were you ... a phrase used when you are giving advice to someone ➤ *If I were you, I'd buy a cheaper car.*
6 Do you mind if ...? a polite way of asking someone if you can do something ➤ *Do you mind if I smoke?*

I

ignite /ɪg'naɪt/ verb (present participle **igniting**, past **ignited**)
to start burning, or to make something start burning

ignition /ɪg'nɪʃən/ noun
the electrical part of a car engine that starts the engine ➤ He put the key in the ignition.

ignorance /'ɪgnərəns/ noun (no plural)
the state of being without knowledge or education

ignorant /'ɪgnərənt/ adjective
not knowing very much; not educated ➤ She is very ignorant **about** her own country.

ignore /ɪg'nɔːʳ/ verb (present participle **ignoring**, past **ignored**)
to take no notice of someone or something; to pretend that someone or something is not there ➤ I tried to tell her, but she ignored me.

ill /ɪl/ adjective
1 not feeling healthy; unwell ➤ She can't go to work because she is ill.
2 be taken ill to become ill suddenly ➤ He was taken ill last night.

I'll /aɪl/
I will; I shall ➤ I'll come with you.

illegal /ɪ'liːgəl/ adjective
not allowed by law ➤ It is illegal to park here. (adverb: **illegally**)
OPPOSITE: **legal**

illegible /ɪ'ledʒəbəl/ adjective
not able to be read ➤ illegible writing
OPPOSITE: **legible**

illegitimate /ˌɪlɪ'dʒɪtɪmət/ adjective
having parents who are not married ➤ an illegitimate child

illiterate /ɪ'lɪtərət/ adjective
(used especially about men or women, not children) not able to read or write

illness /'ɪlnəs/ noun
1 (plural **illnesses**) a disease ➤ to have an illness

2 (no plural) a time of being not healthy or well ➤ She has suffered years of illness.

illogical /ɪ'lɒdʒɪkəl/ adjective
not reasonable ➤ I have an illogical fear of the dark.
OPPOSITE: **logical**

illuminate /ɪ'luːmɪneɪt/ verb (present participle **illuminating**, past **illuminated**)
to light something ➤ The room was illuminated by a single lamp.

illusion /ɪ'luːʒən/ noun
something that seems to be true or real but is not ➤ In expensive cars, you get the illusion that you are floating on air. ➤ Terry is under the illusion that we are paying for him.

illustrate /'ɪləstreɪt/ verb (present participle **illustrating**, past **illustrated**)
to add pictures to a book or magazine ➤ The book was illustrated with colour photographs.

illustration /ˌɪlə'streɪʃən/ noun
a picture in a book or magazine

I'm /aɪm/
I am ➤ I'm very pleased to meet you.

image /'ɪmɪdʒ/ noun
1 a picture of someone or something which you have in your mind
2 the way a person or an organization appears to other people ➤ You need to have a more modern image (=wear more modern clothes, etc.)
3 be the image of someone to look exactly like someone ➤ He's the image of his father.

imaginary /ɪ'mædʒɪnərɪ/ adjective
not real; existing only in your mind ➤ a story about an imaginary king

imagination /ɪˌmædʒɪ'neɪʃən/ noun (no plural)
the ability that you have to form pictures or ideas in your mind ➤ You didn't really see it – it was just your imagination.

imaginative /ɪˈmædʒɪnətɪv/ *adjective*
1 able to think of new and interesting ideas ➤ *an imaginative writer*
2 containing new and interesting ideas ➤ *an imaginative story*
(adverb: **imaginatively**)

imagine /ɪˈmædʒɪn/ *verb (present participle **imagining**, past **imagined**)*
1 to make a picture in your mind of someone or something ➤ *I tried to imagine what life was like a hundred years ago.*
2 to think or believe something ➤ *John imagines that we don't like him, but it isn't true.*

imitate /ˈɪmɪteɪt/ *verb (present participle **imitating**, past **imitated**)*
to copy someone ➤ *She imitated the way her teacher talked.*

imitation /ˌɪmɪˈteɪʃən/ *noun*
a copy ➤ *This isn't a real gun; it's only an imitation.*

immature /ˌɪməˈtjʊəʳ/ *adjective*
(used about a man or woman) rather silly and behaving in a way which is only suitable for someone much younger
OPPOSITE: **mature**

immediate /ɪˈmiːdɪət/ *adjective*
happening at once ➤ *I need an immediate answer.*

immediately /ɪˈmiːdɪətlɪ/ *adverb*
1 without any delay ➤ *Open this door immediately!*
2 next to something in position, or just before or after something in time ➤ *They live immediately above us.*

immense /ɪˈmens/ *adjective*
very large ➤ *He made an immense amount of money in business.*
SAME MEANING: **enormous**

immensely /ɪˈmenslɪ/ *adverb*
very much ➤ *I enjoyed the concert immensely.*

immerse /ɪˈmɜːs/ *verb (present participle **immersing**, past **immersed**)*

1 be **immersed in something**, **immerse yourself in something** to be completely involved in something ➤ *Grant is completely immersed in his work.*
2 to put something in a liquid so that the liquid covers it completely ➤ *Immerse the fabric in the dye and leave for two hours.*

immigrant /ˈɪmɪɡrənt/ *noun*
a person from another country who comes to your country to live
COMPARE: **emigrant**

immigration /ˌɪmɪˈɡreɪʃən/ *noun (no plural)*
coming to live in a foreign country ➤ *The government wants to control immigration.*
COMPARE: **emigration**

immoral /ɪˈmɒrəl/ *adjective*
bad or wicked ➤ *immoral behaviour*
OPPOSITE: **moral**

immortal /ɪˈmɔːtl/ *adjective*
living or continuing for ever ➤ *man's immortal soul* ➤ *Nobody is immortal.*

immune /ɪˈmjuːn/ *adjective*
1 not affected by a disease ➤ *Only a few people are immune **to** tuberculosis.*
2 not affected by problems, criticisms, etc. that affect other people ➤ *Their business seems to be immune **to** economic pressures.*

immunization /ˌɪmjʊnaɪˈzeɪʃən/ *noun*
the act of immunizing someone ➤ *immunization **against** polio*

immunize /ˈɪmjʊnaɪz/ *verb (present participle **immunizing**, past **immunized**)*
to put an amount of a substance that causes an illness into a person's body, usually by using a special needle, so that the person will not catch that illness in the future

impact¹ /ˈɪmpækt/ *noun*
1 the effect something or someone has ➤ *Paul has had a positive impact **on** my life.*

2 (no plural) the force of one object hitting another ▶ *The impact of the crash made her car turn over.* ▶ *missiles that explode on impact*

impact² /ɪmˈpækt/ *verb*
impact on something to have a noticeable effect on something ▶ *The closure of the airport will seriously impact on the city's economy.*

impaired /ɪmˈpeəd/ *adjective*
1 damaged or made weaker ▶ *Radio reception had been impaired by the storm.*
2 visually impaired, hearing impaired unable to see or hear very well

impartial /ɪmˈpɑːʃəl/ *adjective*
not supporting or preferring one person, group, or opinion rather than another ▶ *We offer impartial help and advice.*

impassive /ɪmˈpæsɪv/ *adjective*
not showing any emotions ▶ *His face was impassive as the judge spoke.*

impatience /ɪmˈpeɪʃəns/ *noun (no plural)*
feelings of anger because you have to wait for something
OPPOSITE: **patience**

impatient /ɪmˈpeɪʃənt/ *adjective*
not being able to wait calmly for something to happen because you want it to happen now ▶ *After an hour's delay, the passengers were starting to get impatient. (adverb: **impatiently**)*
OPPOSITE: **patient**

impeccable /ɪmˈpekəbəl/ *adjective*
perfect and without any mistakes ▶ *Her English is impeccable. (adverb: **impeccably**)*

impediment /ɪmˈpedɪmənt/ *noun*
speech impediment, hearing impediment a problem that makes speaking or hearing difficult

impending /ɪmˈpendɪŋ/ *adjective*
going to happen very soon ▶ *He sensed the impending danger.*

imperative /ɪmˈperətɪv/ *noun, adjective*
the form of a verb that you use when you are telling someone to do something ▶ *In the sentence "Come here!", "come" is in the imperative.*

imperfect¹ /ɪmˈpɜːfɪkt/ *adjective*
not completely perfect ▶ *It's an imperfect world.*

imperfect² *noun*
the form of a verb that shows an incomplete action in the past. In "We were walking down the road", the verb "were walking" is in the imperfect.

impersonal /ɪmˈpɜːsənəl/ *adjective*
not showing any feelings of kindness, friendliness, etc. ▶ *Sue complained about the doctor's impersonal manner.*

impersonate /ɪmˈpɜːsəneɪt/ *verb (present participle **impersonating**, past **impersonated**)*
to copy the way someone talks, behaves, etc., in order to trick people or make them laugh ▶ *They were arrested for impersonating police officers.*

impertinent /ɪmˈpɜːtɪnənt/ *adjective*
rude, especially to older people or people you should respect ▶ *She scolded her son for being impertinent.* ▶ *an impertinent remark*

impetuous /ɪmˈpetʃʊəs/ *adjective*
doing things quickly, without thinking ▶ *They are young and impetuous.*

implausible /ɪmˈplɔːzəbəl/ *adjective*
not likely to be true ▶ *His excuse is totally implausible.*
OPPOSITE: **plausible**

implement¹ /ˈɪmplɪment/ *verb*
to begin to use a plan or system ▶ *The company has until next year to implement the new safety recommendations.*

implement² /ˈɪmplɪmənt/ *noun*
a tool ▶ *farming implements*

implicate /'ɪmplɪkeɪt/ *verb*
(*present participle* **implicating**,
past **implicated**)
to show or suggest that someone is
involved in something bad or illegal
▶ *Howard was implicated in the
crime.*

implication /ˌɪmplɪ'keɪʃən/ *noun*
a possible result of a plan, an action,
etc. ▶ *This research has many
important implications.*

imply /ɪm'plaɪ/ *verb* (*past* **implied**)
to suggest that something is true
without saying or showing it directly
▶ *He implied that the money had
been stolen rather than lost.*

impolite /ˌɪmpə'laɪt/ *adjective*
rather rude in the way you speak or
behave towards other people
OPPOSITE: **polite**

import¹ /ɪm'pɔːt/ *verb*
to bring goods into a country for use
there ▶ *We import machinery that we
cannot make in our country.*
COMPARE: **export**

import² /'ɪmpɔːt/ *noun*
something that is imported
▶ *Machinery is one of our biggest
imports.*
COMPARE: **export**

importance /ɪm'pɔːtəns/ *noun* (*no
plural*)
great value or power ▶ *the
importance of a good education*

important /ɪm'pɔːtənt/ *adjective*
1 very useful or valuable ▶ *an
important meeting*
2 having power ▶ *an important
person*
OPPOSITE: **unimportant**

importer /ɪm'pɔːtər/ *noun*
a person or an organization whose
business is to bring goods into a
country for use there ▶ *a wine
importer*
COMPARE: **exporter**

impose /ɪm'pəʊz/ *verb* (*present
participle* **imposing**, *past* **imposed**)
to force people to accept a rule, a tax,
beliefs, etc. ▶ *The king imposed his
authority on the whole country.*

imposing /ɪm'pəʊzɪŋ/ *adjective*
large and impressive ▶ *an imposing
building*

impossible /ɪm'pɒsəbəl/ *adjective*
not possible; not able to happen
▶ *I can't come today; it's impossible.*
OPPOSITE: **possible**

impostor (*also* **imposter**) /ɪm'pɒstər/
noun
a person who pretends to be
someone else in order to trick people

impractical /ɪm'præktɪkəl/ *adjective*
not sensible ▶ *an impractical
suggestion*
OPPOSITE: **practical**

imprecise /ˌɪmprɪ'saɪs/ *adjective*
not exact ▶ *Our measurements were
imprecise.*
OPPOSITE: **precise**

impress /ɪm'pres/ *verb*
to make someone feel admiration
▶ *He was trying to impress me.*

impressed /ɪm'prest/ *adjective*
feeling admiration for someone or
something ▶ *I was really impressed
by how well the team played in its
first game.*

impression /ɪm'preʃən/ *noun*
1 the way something seems to you
▶ *My impression is that she is not
telling the truth.*
2 make an impression on someone
to make someone remember you,
usually with admiration

impressionable /ɪm'preʃənəbəl/
adjective
easy to influence ▶ *The children are
at an impressionable age.*

impressive /ɪm'presɪv/ *adjective*
very good and so causing admiration
▶ *His work was very impressive.*

imprint¹ /'ɪmprɪnt/ *noun*
the mark left by an object that has been pressed onto something ▶ *Fossils are rocks that have imprints of animals on them.*

imprint² /ɪm'prɪnt/ *verb*
be imprinted on your mind/memory to make you unable to forget something ▶ *The whole conversation is imprinted on my memory.*

imprison /ɪm'prɪzən/ *verb*
to put someone in prison ▶ *He was imprisoned for two years.*

imprisonment /ɪm'prɪzənmənt/ *noun (no plural)*
the state of being in prison ▶ *He was given two years' imprisonment.*

improper /ɪm'prɒpə/ *adjective*
not correct according to moral, social, or professional rules *(adverb:* **improperly)**

improve /ɪm'pruːv/ *verb*
(present participle **improving**, *past* **improved)**
1 to become better ▶ *My tennis is improving.*
2 to make something better ▶ *I want to improve my tennis.*

improvement /ɪm'pruːvmənt/ *noun*
1 a change which makes something better ▶ *to make improvements to your house*
2 a change which shows that something is becoming better ▶ *There has been an improvement in trade.* ▶ *Her health is showing signs of improvement.*

improvise /'ɪmprəvaɪz/ *verb*
(present participle **improvising**, *past* **improvised)**
to do or make something without preparing first, using whatever you have got ▶ *If you do not have a screwdriver, you will have to improvise and use the end of a knife.*

impulse /'ɪmpʌls/ *noun*
a sudden wish to do something ▶ *She*

had an impulse to buy a new dress.
▶ *She bought the dress on impulse.*

impulsive /ɪm'pʌlsɪv/ *adjective*
doing things without thinking about them carefully first ▶ *an impulsive decision*

in /ɪn/ *preposition, adverb*
1 inside a place or thing ▶ *They were sitting in the kitchen.* ▶ *She opened the washing machine and put the clothes in.*
2 at a place ▶ *We live in the country.* ▶ *We stayed at a hotel in London.*
3 surrounded by something ▶ *to walk in the rain*
4 during a period of time ▶ *The house was built in 1950.* ▶ *It's his birthday in June.*
5 after a period of time ▶ *I'll be ready in a few minutes.*
6 at home or in the place where you work ▶ *I'm afraid Mrs Jones is not in at the moment.*
OPPOSITE (**6**): **out**
7 using ▶ *She spoke in a quiet voice.* ▶ *The words were written in pencil.* ▶ *They were talking in French.*
8 wearing ▶ *Who's the woman in the black dress?*
9 in all in total ▶ *It will cost you £50 in all.*

inability /ˌɪnə'bɪlətɪ/ *noun (no plural)*
the state of not being able to do something ▶ *They were worried about their son's inability to make friends.*
OPPOSITE: **ability**

inaccurate /ɪn'ækjʊrət/ *adjective*
not correct; having mistakes in it ▶ *an inaccurate news report*
OPPOSITE: **accurate**

inactive /ɪn'æktɪv/ *adjective*
not doing anything or not working ▶ *An inactive lifestyle can lead to health problems.*
OPPOSITE: **active**

inadequate /ɪnˈædɪkwət/ *adjective*
not enough or not good enough
▶ *inadequate health care services*
OPPOSITE: **adequate**

inadvertently /ˌɪnədˈvɜːtəntlɪ/ *adverb*
without intending to do something
▶ *She inadvertently knocked his arm.*

inanimate /ɪnˈænɪmət/ *adjective*
not living ▶ *an inanimate object such as a stone*

inappropriate /ˌɪnəˈprəʊprɪət/ *adjective*
not suitable or right ▶ *Those clothes are inappropriate **for** work. (adverb: **inappropriately**)*
OPPOSITE: **appropriate**

inaugurate /ɪˈnɔːgjʊreɪt/ *verb (present participle **inaugurating**, past **inaugurated**)*
to have a formal ceremony in order to show that someone new has an important job, or that a new building is open ▶ *The President was inaugurated in January.*

incapable /ɪnˈkeɪpəbəl/ *adjective*
not able to do something ▶ *Since her accident, she has been incapable **of** working.*
OPPOSITE: **capable**

incarcerate /ɪnˈkɑːsəreɪt/ *verb (present participle **incarcerating**, past **incarcerated**)*
to put someone in prison

incense /ˈɪnsens/ *noun (no plural)*
a substance that has a pleasant smell when you burn it

incentive /ɪnˈsentɪv/ *noun*
something that encourages you to work harder, or to start something new ▶ *Money is a good incentive for hard work.*

incessant /ɪnˈsesənt/ *adjective*
never stopping ▶ *Incessant rain caused floods and mudslides. (adverb: **incessantly**)*

inch /ɪntʃ/ *noun (plural **inches**)*
a measure of length, equal to 2.5 CENTIMETRES ▶ *There are 12 inches (=12 ins) in a foot.*

incident /ˈɪnsɪdənt/ *noun*
an event or something that happens

incidentally /ˌɪnsɪˈdentlɪ/ *adverb*
a word which you use when you are adding more information to something you have just said, or when you have just remembered an interesting fact ▶ *I saw Peter the other day. Incidentally, he's invited us to lunch next week.*

incite /ɪnˈsaɪt/ *verb (present participle **inciting**, past **incited**)*
to deliberately make someone feel so angry or excited that they do something bad ▶ *One man was jailed for inciting a riot.*

inclination /ˌɪŋklɪˈneɪʃən/ *noun*
the desire to do something ▶ *His first inclination was to laugh at Jean's mistake.*

incline /ɪnˈklaɪn/ *verb*
be inclined to do something to be likely to do something, or to tend to do something ▶ *I am inclined to be lazy sometimes.*

include /ɪnˈkluːd/ *verb (present participle **including**, past **included**)*
1 to have something as part of a whole ▶ *The price of the holiday includes meals.* ▶ *The group included several women.*
OPPOSITE: **exclude**
2 to count someone or something as part of a whole ▶ *I included my uncle in my list of people to invite.*

including /ɪnˈkluːdɪŋ/ *preposition*
a word used to show that some people or things are part of a larger group ▶ *All the family is going, including the children (=they are going too).*
OPPOSITE: **excluding**

inclusion /ɪnˈkluːʒən/ *noun (no plural)*
the act of including someone or something in a larger group ▶ *There were never any doubts about her inclusion in the team.*

inclusive /ɪnˈkluːsɪv/ *adjective*
1 including a particular thing, especially the price of something ▶ *The cost is £600, inclusive of insurance.*
2 including the first and last number, letter, etc. you say, plus all those in between ▶ *He will be on holiday from March 22nd to 24th inclusive.*

income /ˈɪŋkʌm, -kəm/ *noun*
all the money you receive ▶ *What is your annual income?*

income tax /ˈɪŋkəm ˌtæks/ *noun (no plural)*
money taken by the government from what people earn

incompatible /ˌɪnkəmˈpætəbəl/ *adjective*
1 having different ideas or interests, and not able to have a good relationship
2 not able to exist or be used together without problems ▶ *Some software may be incompatible with your computer.*
OPPOSITE: (**1** and **2**): **compatible**

incompetence /ɪnˈkɒmpɪtəns/ *noun (no plural)*
the lack of ability or skill to do a job correctly
OPPOSITE: **competence**

incompetent /ɪnˈkɒmpɪtənt/ *adjective*
lacking the ability or skill to do a job correctly ▶ *Airlines need to get rid of incompetent pilots.*
OPPOSITE: **competent**

incomplete /ˌɪnkəmˈpliːt/ *adjective*
not finished ▶ *The work is incomplete.*
OPPOSITE: **complete**

incomprehensible /ɪnˌkɒmprɪˈhensəbl/ *adjective*
impossible to understand ▶ *The instructions were incomprehensible.*

inconclusive /ˌɪnkənˈkluːsɪv/ *adjective*
not leading to any decision or result ▶ *The medical tests were inconclusive.*
OPPOSITE: **conclusive**

inconsiderate /ˌɪnkənˈsɪdərət/ *adjective*
not thinking about other people's feelings or needs ▶ *Inconsiderate drivers can cause accidents.*
OPPOSITE: **considerate**

inconsistency /ˌɪnkənˈsɪstənsɪ/ *noun*
1 (*plural* **inconsistencies**) something in a report, an argument, etc. that cannot be true if something else in the report or argument is also true ▶ *the inconsistencies in her statement*
2 (*no plural*) the act of changing your ideas too often or of doing something differently each time, so that people do not know what you think or want ▶ *There's too much inconsistency in the way the rules are applied.*
OPPOSITE: (**1** and **2**): **consistency**

inconsistent /ˌɪnkənˈsɪstənt/ *adjective*
1 not doing things in the same way each time, or not following an expected principle ▶ *Children get confused if parents are inconsistent.*
2 be inconsistent with something to say different things or follow different principles ▶ *His story was inconsistent with the evidence.*
OPPOSITE: (**1** and **2**): **consistent**

inconvenience¹ /ˌɪnkənˈviːnɪəns/ *noun*
difficulty ▶ *I hope that the delay won't cause you any inconvenience.*

inconvenience² *verb (present participle* **inconveniencing**, *past* **inconvenienced**) to make things difficult for someone ► *I hope I'm not inconveniencing you by staying here.*

inconvenient /ˌɪnkən'viːnɪənt/ *adjective*
not suitable; causing difficulty ► *I hope this isn't an inconvenient time for me to visit you.*
OPPOSITE: **convenient**

incorporate /ɪn'kɔːpəreɪt/ *verb (present participle **incorporating**, past **incorporated**)*
to include something as part of a group, system, etc. ► *This style of karate incorporates kicks and punches.*

incorrect /ˌɪnkə'rekt/ *adjective*
not right; wrong ► *incorrect spelling (adverb: **incorrectly**)*
OPPOSITE: **correct**

increase¹ /ɪn'kriːs/ *verb (present participle **increasing**, past **increased**)*
1 to become more in amount or number ► *My wages have increased this year.* ► *The noise suddenly increased.*
2 to make something more in amount or number ► *My employer has increased my wages.*
OPPOSITE (1 and 2): **decrease**

increase² /'ɪnkriːs/ *noun*
a rise in amount ► *an increase **in** your wages* ► *a price increase **of** 10%*
OPPOSITE: **decrease**

increasingly /ɪn'kriːsɪŋlɪ/ *adverb*
more and more ► *It's becoming increasingly difficult to find work.*

incredible /ɪn'kredəbəl/ *adjective*
1 very good ► *What incredible luck!*
2 very large in amount ► *an incredible sum of money*
3 very strange or unusual ► *an incredible story*
SAME MEANING (1, 2, and 3): **amazing**

incredibly /ɪn'kredəblɪ/ *adverb*
1 very ► *The show is incredibly popular among teenagers.*

2 in a way that is difficult to believe ► *Incredibly, no one was hurt in the crash.*

incubator /'ɪŋkjubeɪtəʳ/ *noun*
a machine used in hospitals to keep weak babies alive

incur /ɪn'kɜːʳ/ *verb (present participle **incurring**, past **incurred**)*
to have to deal with something unpleasant because of something you have done ► *If the amount is not paid within seven days, you will incur a charge of £15.*

incurable /ɪn'kjʊərəbəl/ *adjective*
impossible to cure ► *an incurable disease*

indecent /ɪn'diːsənt/ *adjective*
likely to offend or shock people because of being related to sex ► *indecent photographs*

indecisive /ˌɪndɪ'saɪsɪv/ *adjective*
not able to make decisions ► *a weak, indecisive leader*
OPPOSITE: **decisive**

indeed /ɪn'diːd/ *adverb*
1 used in answers to questions when you want to say **yes** or **no** very strongly ► *"Did he really say that?" "He did indeed."*
2 used when you want to make the meaning of **very** even stronger ► *He runs very fast indeed.*

indefinite /ɪn'defɪnət/ *adjective*
not clear or fixed ► *I am staying for an indefinite length of time (=I'm not sure how long I will stay). (adverb: **indefinitely**)*

indefinite article /ɪnˌdefɪnət 'ɑːtɪkəl/ *noun*
in English, the word **a** or **an**
COMPARE: **definite article**

independence /ˌɪndɪ'pendəns/ *noun (no plural)*
1 the quality of being able to look after yourself ► *Old people want to keep their independence.*

2 the state of being free from the control of another country ▶ *the American War of Independence* ▶ *India gained its independence in 1947.*

independent /ˌɪndɪˈpendənt/ *adjective*

1 able to look after yourself; not needing help and support from other people ▶ *Although she is young, she is very independent.*
OPPOSITE: **dependent**

2 free; not controlled or governed by another country ▶ *India became independent from Britain in 1947.*

in-depth /ˈɪn depθ/ *adjective*
considering all the details ▶ *an in-depth interview with the prime minister*

index /ˈɪndeks/ *noun (plural **indexes** or **indices** /ˈɪndɪsiːz/)*
a list in a book which tells you what can be found in the book, and on what page

index finger /ˈɪndeks ˌfɪŋɡəʳ/ *noun*
the finger which is next to your thumb

Indian /ˈɪndiən/ *adjective*
of or from India ▶ *Do you like Indian food?*

Indian summer /ˌɪndiən ˈsʌməʳ/ *noun*
a period of warm weather in the autumn

indicate /ˈɪndɪkeɪt/ *verb (present participle **indicating**, past **indicated**)*
to show someone something ▶ *Please indicate your choice on the form provided.*

indication /ˌɪndɪˈkeɪʃən/ *noun*
a sign that tells you that something may be true or may happen ▶ *Did he give you any indication of when the work will be finished?*

indicative /ɪnˈdɪkətɪv/ *adjective*
1 be indicative of something to show that something exists or is likely to

be true ▶ *They've lost a few games, but this is not really indicative of the team's ability.*

2 indicative verb a verb that expresses a fact or an action

indicator /ˈɪndɪkeɪtəʳ/ *noun*
one of the two lights on a car that are used to show that the car is going to turn left or right

indices /ˈɪndɪsiːz/
a plural of **index**

indifference /ɪnˈdɪfərəns/ *noun (no plural)*
the state of not being interested in or not caring about something or someone ▶ *The factory's indifference to safety rules led to several injuries.*

indifferent /ɪnˈdɪfərənt/ *adjective*
not interested in or not caring about something or someone ▶ *How could a father be so indifferent to his own children?*

indigestion /ˌɪndɪˈdʒestʃən/ *noun (no plural)*
an uncomfortable pain in your stomach that you get when you eat too much or too fast

indignant /ɪnˈdɪɡnənt/ *adjective*
angry and surprised because of something that appears wrong *(adverb: **indignantly**)*

indignity /ɪnˈdɪɡnəti/ *noun (plural **indignities**)*
a situation that makes you feel very ashamed, unimportant, and not respected ▶ *I suffered the final indignity of being taken to the police station.*

indirect /ˌɪndɪˈrekt/ *adjective*
not going straight towards a person, place, etc. ▶ *an indirect route (adverb: **indirectly**)*
OPPOSITE: **direct**

indirect object /ˌɪndɪrekt ˈɒbdʒɪkt/ *noun*
the person or thing that receives something as a result of the action of

the verb. In the sentence "Joe gave her a sandwich", "her" is the indirect object

COMPARE: **direct object**

indirect speech /ˌɪndɪrekt 'spiːtʃ/ noun (no plural)
REPORTED SPEECH
COMPARE: **direct speech**

indiscriminate /ˌɪndɪ'skrɪmɪnət/ adjective
done without considering who will be affected or harmed ▶ indiscriminate killings by teenage gangs

indispensable /ˌɪndɪ'spensəbəl/ adjective
too important or useful to manage without ▶ The information he provided was indispensable to our research.

indistinguishable /ˌɪndɪ-'stɪŋgwɪʃəbəl/ adjective
so similar that you cannot see any difference ▶ The copy was almost indistinguishable from the original.

individual¹ /ˌɪndɪ'vɪdʒʊəl/ noun
a person, not a group ▶ something which happens in the life of each individual

individual² adjective
single; for one person only ▶ The children had individual desks.

individuality /ˌɪndɪvɪdʒʊ'ælətɪ/ noun (no plural)
the quality that makes someone different from everyone else ▶ work that allows children to express their individuality

individually /ˌɪndɪ'vɪdʒʊəlɪ/ adverb
separately, not together in a group ▶ The children were taught individually.

indoor /'ɪndɔːʳ/ adjective
inside a building ▶ If it rains, we play indoor games.
OPPOSITE: **outdoor**

indoors /ɪn'dɔːz/ adverb
inside a building ▶ Let's stay indoors out of the rain.
OPPOSITE: **outdoors**

induce /ɪn'djuːs/ verb (present participle **inducing**, past **induced**)
to cause someone to do something, or cause something to happen ▶ Can too much exercise induce illness?

indulge /ɪn'dʌldʒ/ verb (present participle **indulging**, past **indulged**)
to let yourself do something that you enjoy, especially something that you should not do ▶ I often indulge myself with chocolates.

indulgent /ɪn'dʌldʒənt/ adjective
willing to let someone have whatever they want, even if it is bad for them ▶ an indulgent grandparent

industrial /ɪn'dʌstrɪəl/ adjective
having a lot of factories ▶ an industrial town

industrialized /ɪn'dʌstrɪəlaɪzd/ adjective
with a lot of industry ▶ industrialized nations

industry /'ɪndəstrɪ/ noun (plural **industries**)
the making of things in factories ▶ What are the important industries in the town? ▶ Our town has a lot of heavy industry.

ineffective /ˌɪnɪ'fektɪv/ adjective
not getting the result you want ▶ The drug has been ineffective against this disease.
OPPOSITE: **effective**

inefficient /ˌɪnɪ'fɪʃənt/ adjective
not working well, and wasting time, money, or energy ▶ We have an inefficient railway system. (adverb: **inefficiently**)
OPPOSITE: **efficient**

inequality /ˌɪnɪ'kwɒlətɪ/ noun (plural **inequalities**)
an unfair situation in which some

groups in society have less money, fewer opportunities, etc. than others ► *the many inequalities in our legal system*

inevitable /ɪˈnevɪtəbəl/ *adjective*
definitely going to happen ► *Getting older is inevitable.*

inexcusable /ˌɪnɪkˈskjuːzəbəl/ *adjective*
(used about behaviour) too bad or too rude to be forgiven

inexpensive /ˌɪnɪkˈspensɪv/ *adjective*
not costing a lot of money, but good ► *an inexpensive holiday*
OPPOSITE: **expensive**

inexperienced /ˌɪnɪkˈspɪəriənst/ *adjective*
not having much experience of something ► *The team had a number of young, inexperienced players.*
OPPOSITE: **experienced**

inexplicable /ˌɪnɪkˈsplɪkəbəl/ *adjective*
very strange, and impossible to explain or understand ► *For some inexplicable reason, he started to laugh.*

infallible /ɪnˈfæləbəl/ *adjective*
never wrong ► *Scientists are not infallible.*

infancy /ˈɪnfənsɪ/ *noun (no plural)*
the period when you are a baby or young child

infant /ˈɪnfənt/ *noun*
a baby or young child

infantry /ˈɪnfəntrɪ/ *noun (no plural)*
soldiers who fight on foot, not on horses or in vehicles

infatuated /ɪnˈfætʃʊeɪtɪd/ *adjective*
having unreasonably strong feelings of romantic or sexual love for someone ► *He's been infatuated with Clare for a couple of years.*

infect /ɪnˈfekt/ *verb*
to give an illness to someone ► *One of the women at work had a cold and infected everyone else.*

infected /ɪnˈfektɪd/ *adjective*
containing harmful BACTERIA ► *This cut has become infected.*

infection /ɪnˈfekʃən/ *noun*
an illness ► *a throat infection*

infectious /ɪnˈfekʃəs/ *adjective*
(used about an illness) able to be given to other people ► *an infectious disease*

inferior /ɪnˈfɪəriə/ *adjective*
not as good as someone or something else ► *Luke had a way of looking at me that always made me feel inferior.* ► *Larry's work is inferior to Ben's.*
OPPOSITE: **superior**

infertile /ɪnˈfɜːtaɪl/ *adjective*
(used about land, earth, etc.) not able to grow plants and seeds very well ► *infertile, stony soil*
OPPOSITE: **fertile**

infidelity /ˌɪnfɪˈdelətɪ/ *noun*
the act of having sex with someone when you are already having a serious relationship with someone else

infiltrate /ˈɪnfɪltreɪt/ *verb*
*(present participle **infiltrating**, past **infiltrated**)*
to become part of a group, an organization, etc., especially a criminal one, in order to get information about it ► *Trent was ordered to try and infiltrate the terrorists' group.*

infinite /ˈɪnfɪnət/ *adjective*
very large or great and seeming to have no limit ► *a teacher with infinite patience*

infinitely /ˈɪnfɪnətlɪ/ *adverb*
very much ► *I feel infinitely better after my holiday.*

infinitive /ɪnˈfɪnɪtɪv/ *noun*
the part of a verb which is used with the word **to** ► *In the sentence "I want to go", "to go" is an infinitive.*

infinity /ɪnˈfɪnətɪ/ *noun* (no plural)
space or time that has no end or limit
▶ *It's difficult to understand the idea of infinity.*

inflamed /ɪnˈfleɪmd/ *adjective*
red, painful, and SWOLLEN ▶ *an inflamed throat*

inflammable /ɪnˈflæməbəl/ *adjective*
that will burn very easily
▶ *inflammable gases*
OPPOSITE: **nonflammable**

inflammation /ˌɪnfləˈmeɪʃən/ *noun*
redness, pain, and swelling on or in a part of the body ▶ *inflammation of the knee*

inflatable /ɪnˈfleɪtəbəl/ *adjective*
needing to be filled with air before being used ▶ *an inflatable boat*

inflate /ɪnˈfleɪt/ *verb* (present participle **inflating**, past **inflated**)
to fill something with air ▶ *to inflate a tyre*

inflated /ɪnˈfleɪtɪd/ *adjective*
1 (used about prices, figures, etc.) higher than is reasonable or usual ▶ *Fans are prepared to pay hugely inflated prices for the tickets.*
2 filled with air or gas ▶ *an inflated life jacket*

inflation /ɪnˈfleɪʃən/ *noun* (no plural)
the continuing increase in prices, or the rate at which prices increase
▶ *the Mexican government's efforts to control inflation*

inflection (also **inflexion**) /ɪnˈflekʃən/ *noun*
the way the ending of a word changes to show that it is plural, in the past tense, etc.

inflexible /ɪnˈfleksəbəl/ *adjective*
1 not able to change or be changed easily ▶ *As we get older, our attitudes become more inflexible.*
2 not easy to bend
OPPOSITE (**1** and **2**): **flexible**

inflexion /ɪnˈflekʃən/ *noun*
another word for **inflection**

inflict /ɪnˈflɪkt/ *verb*
to make a person, place, etc. suffer something unpleasant ▶ *The earthquake inflicted an enormous amount of damage **on** the whole area.*

influence[1] /ˈɪnfluəns/ *noun*
1 have an influence on someone to have the power to change what a person thinks or does ▶ *Her parents have a strong influence on her.*
2 be a bad influence on someone to make someone behave badly because you yourself behave badly
3 be a good influence on someone to make someone behave in a better way than usual because you yourself behave well

influence[2] *verb* (present participle **influencing**, past **influenced**)
to change what happens ▶ *My teacher influenced my decision to study science* (=made me decide to do it).

influential /ˌɪnfluˈenʃəl/ *adjective*
important and having the power to change people or things ▶ *an influential politician* ▶ *an influential speech*

influenza /ˌɪnfluˈenzə/ *noun* (no plural)
another word for **flu**

info /ˈɪnfəʊ/ *noun* (no plural)
information

inform /ɪnˈfɔːm/ *verb*
to tell someone something ▶ *The teacher informed us that the school would be closed for one day next week.* ▶ *I will inform you **of** my decision.*

informal /ɪnˈfɔːməl/ *adjective*
happening or done in an easy, friendly way and not according to rules ▶ *an informal meeting* ▶ *an informal party*
OPPOSITE: **formal**

information /ˌɪnfəˈmeɪʃən/ *noun (no plural)*
facts; knowledge ▶ *Could you give me some information **about** the times of the buses?* ▶ *I need to find information **on** the car industry.* ▶ *a tourist information office (=a place where tourists go to ask about things they want to know)*

information superhighway /ˌɪnfəməʃən ˌsuːpəˈhaɪweɪ/ *noun*
the information superhighway the INTERNET

information technology /ˌɪnfəˈmeɪʃən tekˌnɒlədʒi/ *noun (no plural)*
the use of computers to store and manage information

informative /ɪnˈfɔːmətɪv/ *adjective*
providing useful information or ideas ▶ *a very informative book*

informed /ɪnˈfɔːmd/ *adjective*
having plenty of knowledge and information about something ▶ *It is important for everyone to keep well informed about what's going on in the world.*

informer /ɪnˈfɔːməʳ/ *noun*
a person who helps the police by secretly giving them information about crimes and criminals

infrequent /ɪnˈfriːkwənt/ *adjective*
not happening often ▶ *one of our infrequent visits to Uncle Edwin's house (adverb: **infrequently**)*
OPPOSITE: **frequent**

infuriate /ɪnˈfjʊərieɪt/ *verb (present participle **infuriating**, past **infuriated**)*
to make someone very angry ▶ *It infuriates me when she behaves so badly.*

infuriating /ɪnˈfjʊərieɪtɪŋ/ *adjective*
making someone very angry ▶ *He can be infuriating at times.*

ingenious /ɪnˈdʒiːniəs/ *adjective*
very clever ▶ *What an ingenious idea!*

ingratitude /ɪnˈɡrætɪtjuːd/ *noun (no plural)*
the state of not being grateful for something when you should be
OPPOSITE: **gratitude**

ingredient /ɪnˈɡriːdiənt/ *noun*
something that you add when you are making something, especially in cooking ▶ *Flour, butter, eggs, and sugar are the main ingredients.*

inhabit /ɪnˈhæbɪt/ *verb*
1 to live in a place ▶ *a country inhabited by 20 million people*
2 be inhabited to have people living there ▶ *The island is not inhabited.*

inhabitant /ɪnˈhæbɪtənt/ *noun*
a person who lives in a place ▶ *the inhabitants of the village*

inhale /ɪnˈheɪl/ *verb (present participle **inhaling**, past **inhaled**)*
to breathe air, smoke, or gas into your lungs ▶ *Percy lit a cigarette and inhaled deeply.*

inherit /ɪnˈherɪt/ *verb*
to get something from someone when they die ▶ *He inherited the farm from his parents.*

inheritance /ɪnˈherɪtəns/ *noun*
money or other things that you receive from a person after they have died

inhospitable /ˌɪnhɒˈspɪtəbəl/ *adjective*
1 (used about places) difficult to live in because of the heat, cold, etc. ▶ *an inhospitable climate*
2 unfriendly to people who are visiting you ▶ *There was no need to be quite so inhospitable.*

inhuman /ɪnˈhjuːmən/ *adjective*
very cruel ▶ *inhuman acts of violence and terrorism*

inhumane /ˌɪnhjuːˈmeɪn/ *adjective*
treating people or animals in a cruel and unacceptable way ▶ *inhumane living conditions*
OPPOSITE: **humane**

initial¹ /ɪˈnɪʃəl/ noun
the first letter of a name, used to represent the name ▶ *His name is John Smith, so his initials are J. S.*

initial² adjective
first; at the beginning ▶ *The initial plan was to build a new hospital, but now the council has decided to repair the old hospital instead.* (adverb: **initially**)

initiative /ɪˈnɪʃətɪv/ noun (no plural)
the ability to make decisions and take action without waiting for someone to tell you what to do ▶ *I was impressed by the initiative she showed.*

inject /ɪnˈdʒekt/ verb
to give someone medicine by using a special needle to go through their skin

injection /ɪnˈdʒekʃən/ noun
an act of giving someone medicine by using a special needle to go through their skin ▶ *to have an injection* ▶ *an injection against a disease*

injure /ˈɪndʒər/ verb (present participle **injuring**, past **injured**)
to harm or wound a person or an animal ▶ *Two people were injured in the accident.* ▶ *I injured myself playing football.*
SAME MEANING: **hurt**

injury /ˈɪndʒərɪ/ noun (plural **injuries**)
a wound ▶ *The people in the accident had serious injuries.*

injustice /ɪnˈdʒʌstɪs/ noun
1 (no plural) the fact of being unfair ▶ *the injustice of the situation*
OPPOSITE: **justice**
2 something unfair ▶ *a great injustice*
3 do someone an injustice to judge someone in an unfair way by thinking something bad about them which is not true

ink /ɪŋk/ noun (no plural)
a coloured liquid used for writing or printing

inland¹ /ˈɪnlənd/ adjective
not near the sea ▶ *an inland town*

inland² /ɪnˈlænd/ adverb
away from the sea ▶ *We travelled 20 kilometres inland.*

in-laws /ˈɪn lɔːz/ plural noun
the parents of your husband or wife, or other members of their family ▶ *We're spending Christmas with my in-laws this year.*

inn /ɪn/ noun
a place that sells drinks and food, and is sometimes a hotel as well ▶ *The travellers stopped to eat at a small inn.*

inner /ˈɪnər/ adjective
further in, or in the middle ▶ *the inner ear* (=the part inside your head)

inner city /ˌɪnə ˈsɪtɪ/ noun (plural **inner cities**)
the part of a city that is near the centre, especially the part where the buildings are in a bad condition and the people are poor ▶ *the problem of crime in our inner cities*

inning /ˈɪnɪŋ/ noun
one of the nine periods of play in a game of BASEBALL

innings /ˈɪnɪŋz/ noun (plural **innings**)
one of the periods of play in a game of CRICKET

innocence /ˈɪnəsəns/ noun (no plural)
the fact of having done nothing bad or wrong
OPPOSITE: **guilt**

innocent /ˈɪnəsənt/ adjective
having done nothing bad or wrong ▶ *to be innocent of a crime*
OPPOSITE: **guilty**

innocuous /ɪˈnɒkjuəs/ adjective
not likely to harm anyone or cause trouble ▶ *It seemed like a fairly innocuous thing to say.*

innovation /ˌɪnəˈveɪʃən/ noun
an exciting new idea or method that people are using for the first time

➤ *scientific and technological innovations*

input /'ɪnpʊt/ *noun* (no plural)
ideas, advice, money, or effort that you put into a job, meeting, etc. in order to help it succeed ➤ *At the start of a project, everyone's input is very welcome.* ➤ *Thanks for coming to the meeting, Julie – we value your input.*

inquest /'ɪŋkwest/ *noun*
an official process to try and discover why someone has died suddenly

inquire (also **enquire**) /ɪn'kwaɪə'/ *verb* (present participle **inquiring**, past **inquired**)
to ask for information about something ➤ *He inquired **about** the times of trains to London.*

inquiring (also **enquiring**) /ɪn'kwaɪərɪŋ/ *adjective*
always wanting to find out new things ➤ *a lively boy with a very inquiring mind*

inquiry (also **enquiry**) /ɪn'kwaɪəri/ *noun* (plural **inquiries**)
1 a question asking for information about something ➤ *an inquiry **about** a job*
2 **make inquiries** to ask for information ➤ *to make inquiries **about** someone*

inquisitive /ɪn'kwɪzɪtɪv/ *adjective*
wanting to know too many things, especially about other people

ins
a short way of writing the words **inch** or **inches** ➤ *6ins*

insane /ɪn'seɪn/ *adjective*
mad ➤ *He must be insane to go out with her!*
OPPOSITE: **sane**

insect /'ɪnsekt/ *noun*
a very small creature that has six legs ➤ *Bees and ants are insects.*

insecure /ˌɪnsɪ'kjʊə'/ *adjective*
not feeling confident about yourself,

your abilities, your relationships, etc. ➤ *I was young, very shy, and insecure.*

insensitive /ɪn'sensɪtɪv/ *adjective*
not noticing other people's feelings and often doing or saying things that will make them unhappy ➤ *He can be rude and insensitive.* ➤ *insensitive remarks about religion*

inseparable /ɪn'sepərəbəl/ *adjective*
always together and very friendly ➤ *As children, my brother and I were inseparable.*

insert /ɪn'sɜːt/ *verb*
to put something into something else ➤ *to insert a key in a lock*

inside¹ /ɪn'saɪd/ *noun*
the part that is in the middle of something or contained by something ➤ *Have you seen the inside of the house?*
OPPOSITE: **outside**

inside² /ɪn'saɪd/ *preposition, adverb*
in or onto something ➤ *She put the money inside her bag.* ➤ *Don't stand out there in the sun; come inside (=into the house).*
OPPOSITE: **outside**

inside³ /'ɪnsaɪd/ *adjective*
in the middle of something or contained by something ➤ *the inside walls of a house*
OPPOSITE: **outside**

inside out /ˌɪnsaɪd 'aʊt/ *adverb*
with the parts that are usually inside on the outside ➤ *You're wearing your socks inside out.*

insight /'ɪnsaɪt/ *noun*
the ability to understand something clearly because you have done it, studied it, etc. ➤ *The museum gave us a real insight **into** how people used to live.*

insignificant /ˌɪnsɪg'nɪfɪkənt/ *adjective*
too small or unimportant to think or worry about ➤ *I felt small and*

insignificant beside all those important people.
OPPOSITE: **significant**

insincere /ˌɪnsɪnˈsɪəʳ/ *adjective*
pretending to be pleased, sympathetic, etc., but not really meaning what you say or do ▶ *an insincere smile* (adverb: **insincerely**)
OPPOSITE: **sincere**

insist /ɪnˈsɪst/ *verb*
to say that something must happen or be done ▶ *I insist that you stop doing that.* ▶ *She insisted on seeing the manager.*

insistence /ɪnˈsɪstəns/ *noun* (no plural)
the act of demanding that something must happen or be done ▶ *My parents' insistence on good manners was a very good thing.*

insistent /ɪnˈsɪstənt/ *adjective*
saying very firmly that something must happen or be done ▶ *He was insistent that you call him back.*

insolent /ˈɪnsələnt/ *adjective*
rude and not showing someone respect ▶ *an insolent smile*

insoluble /ɪnˈsɒljʊbəl/ *adjective*
not disappearing when mixed with water ▶ *Sand is insoluble.*

insomnia /ɪnˈsɒmnɪə/ *noun* (no plural)
the problem you have when you regularly cannot sleep ▶ *Dad's suffered from insomnia for years.*

inspect /ɪnˈspekt/ *verb*
to look at something carefully, to see if there is anything wrong ▶ *He inspected the car carefully before he bought it.*

inspection /ɪnˈspekʃən/ *noun*
a careful look to see if there is anything wrong with something

inspector /ɪnˈspektəʳ/ *noun*
1 an official whose job is to visit places and see if there is anything

wrong with them ▶ *a school inspector*
2 a police officer

inspiration /ˌɪnspɪˈreɪʃən/ *noun*
new ideas about what to do, or the feeling that you can do something ▶ *These gardening programmes give people inspiration for their own homes.*

inspire /ɪnˈspaɪəʳ/ *verb* (present participle **inspiring**, past **inspired**)
to make someone want to do something, especially by giving them new ideas ▶ *He inspired me to write a poem.*

inspired /ɪnˈspaɪəd/ *adjective*
very skilful ▶ *It was an inspired piece of football.*

install /ɪnˈstɔːl/ *verb*
to put in new machinery, etc. ▶ *We have installed a new computer system at work.*

instalment /ɪnˈstɔːlmənt/ *noun*
1 one of several payments that you make over a period of time in order to buy something ▶ *She paid for her car in instalments.*
2 one part of a long story which is told in several parts on television, in a magazine, etc.

instance /ˈɪnstəns/ *noun*
for instance for example ▶ *She's totally unreliable – for instance, she often leaves the children alone.*

instant[1] /ˈɪnstənt/ *adjective*
1 happening or working at once ▶ *The new shop was an instant success.*
2 very quick to prepare ▶ *instant coffee*

instant[2] *noun*
a moment ▶ *He waited for an instant before answering the question.*

instantaneous /ˌɪnstənˈteɪnɪəs/ *adjective*
happening immediately ▶ *The effect of the drug was instantaneous.* (adverb: **instantaneously**)

instantly /ˈɪnstəntlɪ/ *adverb*
at once

instead /ɪnˈsted/ *adverb*
in place of someone or something
else ▶ *I didn't have a pen, so I used a
pencil instead.*

instead of /ɪnˈsted ɒv/ *preposition*
in place of someone or something
else ▶ *Can you come on Saturday
instead of Sunday?* ▶ *Instead of
going shopping, why don't we go for
a walk?*

instil /ɪnˈstɪl/ *verb (present participle
instilling, past instilled)*
to make someone think, feel, or
behave in a particular way ▶ *It's my
job to instil confidence into the team.*

instinct /ˈɪnstɪŋkt/ *noun*
a force or ability that makes you do
things without thinking about them
or learning them ▶ *Cats kill birds by
instinct.*

institute /ˈɪnstɪtjuːt/ *noun*
a group of people who study a special
thing, or the building used by such a
group

institution /ˌɪnstɪˈtjuːʃən/ *noun*
a large organization such as a school,
a hospital, or a bank

instruct /ɪnˈstrʌkt/ *verb*
1 to teach someone something
2 **instruct someone to do something**
to tell someone that they must do
something ▶ *I've been instructed to
wait here.*

instruction /ɪnˈstrʌkʃən/ *noun*
a piece of information that tells you
how to do something ▶ *Read the
instructions before you use the
machine.*

instructor /ɪnˈstrʌktəʳ/ *noun*
a person who teaches a skill or an
activity ▶ *a sports instructor*

instrument /ˈɪnstrʊmənt/ *noun*
1 a tool used for doing a particular
thing ▶ *medieval writing instruments*
2 an object used for making music
▶ *A piano is a musical instrument.*

instrumental /ˌɪnstrʊˈmentl/
adjective
1 **be instrumental in doing something** to be the thing or person that
makes something happen ▶ *a clue
that was instrumental in solving the
mystery*
2 (used about music) played on
instruments, not sung by people

insufficient /ˌɪnsəˈfɪʃənt/ *adjective*
not enough ▶ *The people here have
insufficient food and water.*
OPPOSITE: **sufficient**

insulate /ˈɪnsjʊleɪt/ *verb (present
participle insulating, past insulated)*
to cover something with a material
that stops electricity, sound, heat,
etc. getting in or out ▶ *Make sure you
insulate your pipes before winter.*

insulin /ˈɪnsjʊlɪn/ *noun (no plural)*
a substance that your body produces
so that it can use sugar for energy

insult¹ /ɪnˈsʌlt/ *verb*
to be rude to someone and offend
them

insult² /ˈɪnsʌlt/ *noun*
something rude said to offend someone ▶ *He shouted insults at the boys.*

insurance /ɪnˈʃʊərəns/ *noun (no
plural)*
money you pay to a company which
then agrees to pay an amount of
money if something bad happens to
you or your property

insure /ɪnˈʃʊəʳ/ *verb (present
participle insuring, past insured)*
to pay money regularly to a company
so that it will give you an amount of
money if something bad happens to
you or your property ▶ *to insure your
house against fire*

intact /ɪnˈtækt/ *adjective*
not broken or damaged
▶ *The package arrived intact.*

intake /'ɪnteɪk/ *noun*
1 the amount of food, liquid, etc. that you eat or drink ▶ *If you're on a diet, you should reduce your sugar intake.*
2 the number of people that join a school, profession, etc. at a particular time ▶ *The school has an intake of about 100 children each year.*

integral /'ɪntɪgrəl/ *adjective*
forming a necessary part of something ▶ *Training is an integral part of any team's preparation.*

integrate /'ɪntɪgreɪt/ *verb (present participle* **integrating**, *past* **integrated**)
to become part of a group or a society, or to help someone do this ▶ *Our neighbours have never really integrated* **into** *the local community.*

integrity /ɪn'tegrəti/ *noun (no plural)*
the quality of being honest and having high moral standards ▶ *a man of integrity*

intellect /'ɪntɪlekt/ *noun*
the ability to understand things and think in an intelligent way ▶ *a woman of superior intellect*

intellectual /ˌɪntɪ'lektʃʊəl/ *adjective*
related to the ability to think and understand ideas and information ▶ *the intellectual development of children*

intelligence /ɪn'telɪdʒəns/ *noun (no plural)*
the ability to learn and understand things ▶ *a creature of low intelligence*

intelligent /ɪn'telɪdʒənt/ *adjective*
quick to learn and understand things; clever

intelligible /ɪn'telɪdʒəbəl/ *adjective*
easy to understand

intend /ɪn'tend/ *verb*
to plan to do something ▶ *What do you intend to do today?*
COMPARE: **aim**

intense /ɪn'tens/ *adjective*
very strong ▶ *He had an intense love of music.* ▶ *The pain in my leg was intense.*

intensify /ɪn'tensɪfaɪ/ *verb (past* **intensified**)
to increase in strength, size, or amount, or to make something do this ▶ *The pressure at work had slowly intensified.*

intensive /ɪn'tensɪv/ *adjective*
involving a lot of work or effort in a short time ▶ *an intensive advertising campaign*

intent /ɪn'tent/ *adjective*
be intent on doing something to be determined to do something ▶ *She was intent on making a good impression.*

intention /ɪn'tenʃən/ *noun*
a plan ▶ *What are your intentions?* ▶ *I have no intention of going there.*

intentional /ɪn'tenʃənəl/ *adjective*
done deliberately ▶ *I'm sorry if I upset you – it wasn't intentional.* (*adverb:* **intentionally**)

interact /ˌɪntər'ækt/ *verb*
to talk to people and make friends with them ▶ *Children need to learn to interact* **with** *each other at an early age.*

interactive /ˌɪntər'æktɪv/ *adjective*
involving communication between a computer, television, etc. and the person who is using it ▶ *interactive CD-ROMs* ▶ *interactive video materials*

intercept /ˌɪntə'sept/ *verb*
to stop someone or something that is moving from one place to another ▶ *The aircraft was intercepted and shot down.*

intercom /'ɪntəkɒm/ *noun*
a system that people in a large building use to speak to other people in different parts of the building

➤ *They made the announcement over the intercom.*

interest¹ /ˈɪntrəst/ *noun*
1 a wish to know more about something ➤ *to take an interest **in** something*
2 something you do or study because you enjoy it; a HOBBY ➤ *Her interests are music and sport.*

interest² *verb*
to make someone want to know more about something ➤ *Her story interested me.*

interested /ˈɪntrəstɪd/ *adjective*
wanting to do something or know more about something ➤ *He's very interested **in** history.* ➤ *Are you interested in coming with us?*

interesting /ˈɪntrəstɪŋ/ *adjective*
making you want to pay attention ➤ *an interesting story* ➤ *an interesting idea*
OPPOSITE: **boring, uninteresting**

interfere /ˌɪntəˈfɪərˈ/ *verb*
(*present participle* **interfering**, *past* **interfered**)
1 to annoy another person by giving your opinions about things which have nothing to do with you, or by trying to take part in things where you are not wanted ➤ *Just go away and stop interfering!*
2 to prevent something or to make something different ➤ *The rain interfered **with** our plans to go out.*

interference /ˌɪntəˈfɪərəns/ *noun* (*no plural*)
1 the act of interfering in something ➤ *I resented his interference in my personal life.*
2 noise caused by bad weather or an electrical problem that makes it difficult to hear a radio signal or see a television programme

interior¹ /ɪnˈtɪərɪəˈ/ *noun*
the inside ➤ *the interior **of** a house*
OPPOSITE: **exterior**

interior² *adjective*
on the inside of something ➤ *the interior walls of a house*
OPPOSITE: **exterior**

interjection /ˌɪntəˈdʒekʃən/ *noun*
a word or phrase that is used to express surprise, shock, pain, etc. In the sentence "Ouch! That hurts!", "Ouch!" is an interjection

intermediate /ˌɪntəˈmiːdɪət/ *adjective*
(used about a student or a class) of the middle level

intermission /ˌɪntəˈmɪʃən/ *noun*
a period of time when a play, film, game, etc. stops for a short time before starting again ➤ *We had an ice cream during the intermission.*
SAME MEANING: **interval**

internal /ɪnˈtɜːnl/ *adjective*
of or on the inside ➤ *an internal injury*
OPPOSITE: **external**

international /ˌɪntəˈnæʃənəl/ *adjective*
for or by many countries ➤ *an international agreement* ➤ *an international airport*

Internet /ˈɪntənet/ *noun*
the Internet a system that allows people using computers around the world to send and receive information ➤ *You can find all the latest information **on** the Internet.*

interpret /ɪnˈtɜːprɪt/ *verb*
1 to put the words of one language into the words of another language by talking ➤ *to interpret from French into English*
COMPARE: **translate**
2 to explain or understand information, someone's actions, etc. ➤ *His silence was interpreted as guilt.*

interpretation /ɪnˌtɜːprɪˈteɪʃən/ *noun*
a way of explaining or understanding information, someone's actions, etc. ➤ *Their interpretation **of** the evidence was very different from ours.*

interpreter /ɪnˈtɜːprɪtəʳ/ *noun*
a person whose job is to put the words of one language into the words of another language by talking

interrogate /ɪnˈterəgeɪt/ *verb*
(*present participle* **interrogating**, *past* **interrogated**)
to ask someone a lot of questions, often in an unpleasant way ➤ *Forty people were arrested and interrogated by military police.*

interrogative /ˌɪntəˈrɒgətɪv/ *noun*
a word or sentence that asks a question

interrogator /ɪnˈterəgeɪtəʳ/ *noun*
a person who tries to get information by asking lots of questions, often in an unpleasant way ➤ *She managed to trick her interrogators and escape.*

interrupt /ˌɪntəˈrʌpt/ *verb*
to say something when someone else is already speaking, and cause them to stop ➤ *It is rude to interrupt.* ➤ *Don't interrupt me!*

interruption /ˌɪntəˈrʌpʃən/ *noun*
something which stops you from continuing what you are doing for a while ➤ *I couldn't work because there were so many interruptions.*

intersection /ˈɪntəˌsekʃən/ *noun*
a place where two roads, lines, etc. meet, especially where they cross each other ➤ *Meet me at the intersection of Main Street and Queen Street.*

interval /ˈɪntəvəl/ *noun*
1 a time or space between things ➤ *an interval between the first part and the second part of a film*
2 **at intervals** happening regularly, with a period of time or space between ➤ *There were trees at intervals along the road.*

intervene /ˌɪntəˈviːn/ *verb* (*present participle* **intervening**, *past* **intervened**)
to do something to try to stop an argument, a problem, a war, etc.
➤ *Police eventually had to intervene in the dispute.*

interview¹ /ˈɪntəvjuː/ *noun*
1 a meeting to decide if a person is suitable for a job ➤ *to go for an interview*
2 a meeting at which a person, usually someone famous, is asked about their opinions or their life, e.g. for a newspaper, or on television or radio

interview² *verb*
1 to talk to someone to see if they are suitable for a job
2 to ask someone questions for a newspaper, etc., or on television or radio

interviewer /ˈɪntəvjuːəʳ/ *noun*
a person whose job is to interview people, especially famous people, on television or radio

intestine /ɪnˈtestɪn/ *noun*
the long tube in your body that carries food away from your stomach

intimate /ˈɪntɪmət/ *adjective*
very private or personal ➤ *She wrote all her most intimate thoughts in her diary.*

intimidate /ɪnˈtɪmɪdeɪt/ *verb*
(*present participle* **intimidating**, *past* **intimidated**)
to frighten someone, especially so that they do what you want ➤ *Some of the older boys were trying to intimidate him into giving them money.*

into /ˈɪntə; *strong* ˈɪntuː/ *preposition*
1 so as to be inside or in something ➤ *They went into the house.*
2 used to show how something changes ➤ *She made the material into a dress.* ➤ *He cut the cake into six pieces.*
3 used when dividing one number by another number ➤ *5 into 20 goes 4 times.*

intolerable /ɪnˈtɒlərəbəl/ *adjective*
very unpleasant or painful ▶ *In the middle of the day, the heat was intolerable.*

intolerant /ɪnˈtɒlərənt/ *adjective*
not willing to accept ways of thinking and behaving that are different from your own
OPPOSITE: **tolerant**

intranet /ˈɪntrənet/ *noun*
a system, which is similar to the INTERNET but smaller, for sending computer messages between people who work for the same company or organization

intransitive /ɪnˈtrænsətɪv/ *adjective*
(used about a verb) not taking an object; where the action is not done to a person or thing ▶ *In the sentence "When he had finished, he sat down", "finish" and "sit" are intransitive verbs.*
COMPARE: **transitive**

intricate /ˈɪntrɪkət/ *adjective*
containing a lot of details or different parts ▶ *intricate carved statues*

intrigue /ɪnˈtriːg/ *verb* (present participle **intriguing**, past **intrigued**)
to interest someone a lot, especially by being strange or mysterious ▶ *I was intrigued by the story of the young girl who used to live in the house.*

introduce /ˌɪntrəˈdjuːs/ *verb* (present participle **introducing**, past **introduced**)
1 to cause two people to meet each other for the first time, and tell each person the name of the other person ▶ *He introduced his friend to me.*
2 to bring in a new thing ▶ *to introduce a new subject in a school*

introduction /ˌɪntrəˈdʌkʃən/ *noun*
1 (*no plural*) the bringing in of something new for the first time ▶ *the introduction of a new law*
2 a piece of writing at the beginning

of a book, which tells you what the rest of the book is about

introductory /ˌɪntrəˈdʌktəri/ *adjective*
1 coming at the beginning of something and introducing the subject ▶ *an introductory lesson in Arabic*
2 available for a short time when something new is being sold ▶ *The software is available at an introductory price of £175.*

introvert /ˈɪntrəvɜːt/ *noun*
a person who is quiet and shy and does not like to be with other people
OPPOSITE: **extrovert**

introverted /ˈɪntrəvɜːtɪd/ *adjective*
quiet and shy ▶ *Jake has always been a bit introverted.*

intrude /ɪnˈtruːd/ *verb* (present participle **intruding**, past **intruded**)
to go into a place or become involved in a situation where you are not wanted ▶ *I'm sorry to intrude, but I need to talk to you.*

intruder /ɪnˈtruːdər/ *noun*
a person who enters a building or an area without permission ▶ *The alarm will go off if there's an intruder.*

intuition /ˌɪntjuˈɪʃən/ *noun*
the feeling that you know something is correct or true, although you do not have any definite facts ▶ *My intuition told me not to trust him.*

invade /ɪnˈveɪd/ *verb* (present participle **invading**, past **invaded**)
to attack and enter a country or place with an army ▶ *The army invaded the town.*

invalid /ˈɪnvəlɪd/ *noun*
a person who is weak because they are ill ▶ *He helps to look after his grandfather who is an invalid.*

invaluable /ɪnˈvæljuəbəl/ *adjective*
very useful ▶ *I gained invaluable experience while I was working abroad.*

invariably /ɪnˈveərɪəblɪ/ *adverb*
almost always ➤ *The trains are invariably late in the morning.*

invasion /ɪnˈveɪʒən/ *noun*
the act of an army attacking and entering a country or place in order to control it ➤ *an enemy invasion*

invent /ɪnˈvent/ *verb*
to think of and plan something completely new that did not exist before ➤ *Who invented the telephone?*

invention /ɪnˈvenʃən/ *noun*
1 *(no plural)* the thinking of a new idea and making of something that did not exist before ➤ *the invention of the telephone*
2 something completely new that has just been thought of and made ➤ *This machine is their latest invention.*

inventive /ɪnˈventɪv/ *adjective*
good at thinking of new and interesting ideas ➤ *Ed's a very inventive cook.*

inventor /ɪnˈventər/ *noun*
a person who thinks of and plans something completely new ➤ *the inventor of the telephone*

inverted commas /ɪnˌvɜːtɪd ˈkɒməz/ *plural noun*
the signs (' ') or (" "), used in writing to show what somebody says
SAME MEANING: **speech marks**

invest /ɪnˈvest/ *verb*
to give money to a bank, business, etc. so that you can get a profit later

investigate /ɪnˈvestɪgeɪt/ *verb*
*(present participle **investigating**, past **investigated**)*
to search for information about someone or something by looking, asking questions, etc. ➤ *The police are investigating the crime.*

investigation /ɪnˌvestɪˈgeɪʃən/ *noun*
a search for information about someone or something ➤ *a police investigation into the crime*

investment /ɪnˈvestmənt/ *noun*
1 *(no plural)* the act of putting money in a bank or buying something, in order to get a profit later ➤ *We need more investment in small businesses.*
2 something that you buy because it will be more valuable or useful later ➤ *We bought the house as an investment.*

invisible /ɪnˈvɪzəbl/ *adjective*
not able to be seen ➤ *Air is invisible.*
OPPOSITE: **visible**

invitation /ˌɪnvɪˈteɪʃən/ *noun*
an offer, in words or writing, of a chance to do something or to go somewhere ➤ *a party invitation* ➤ *an invitation **to** a party*

invite /ɪnˈvaɪt/ *verb (present participle **inviting**, past **invited**)*
to ask someone to come to your house, to go out with you, etc. ➤ *She invited us **to** her party.*

> People do not use the verb **invite** when they are asking you if you want to go somewhere or do something. Instead they say things like *Would you like to come to dinner at my house?* or *Do you want to come to a party tonight?* (NOTE **never** say *I invite you …*)

inviting /ɪnˈvaɪtɪŋ/ *adjective*
attractive and making you want to have, enjoy, or use something ➤ *The swimming pool looked very inviting.*

invoice /ˈɪnvɔɪs/ *noun*
a list showing how much money you must pay for things you have received or work that has been done ➤ *You haven't paid these invoices.*

involve /ɪnˈvɒlv/ *verb (present participle **involving**, past **involved**)*
1 to make a person or thing be a part of something ➤ *Don't involve me **in** your argument.*
2 to make something necessary ➤ *The job will involve a lot of hard work.*

I

3 be involved in something, be involved with something to take part in something ▶ *She's involved in politics.*

involvement /ɪnˈvɒlvmənt/ *noun (no plural)*
the act of taking part in something ▶ *They thanked us for our involvement in the project.*

inward /ˈɪnwəd/ *adjective*
1 towards the middle or the inside of something
OPPOSITE: **outward**
2 (used about a thought or feeling) not shown to other people ▶ *an inward feeling of happiness*

inwards /ˈɪnwədz/ *adverb*
towards the middle or the inside of something ▶ *The walls fell inwards.*
OPPOSITE: **outwards**

IPA /ˌaɪ piː ˈeɪ/ *noun (no plural)*
INTERNATIONAL PHONETIC ALPHABET; a system of signs showing the sounds made in speech

irate /ˌaɪˈreɪt/ *adjective*
very angry ▶ *An irate customer complained to the manager.*

irk /ɜːk/ *verb*
to annoy someone ▶ *It irks me how he never helps his mother.*

iron¹ /ˈaɪən/ *noun*
1 (no plural) a hard, grey metal
2 an instrument that is heated and then used to make clothes smooth

iron² *verb*
to press clothes with a hot iron to make them smooth ▶ *to iron a shirt*

iron³ *adjective*
made of the metal iron ▶ *an iron gate*

ironic /aɪˈrɒnɪk/ *adjective*
using words that are different from what you really mean, in order to be amusing or show that you are annoyed ▶ *I think when he said "Thanks a lot" he was being ironic. (adverb: ironically)*

ironing /ˈaɪənɪŋ/ *noun (no plural)*
do the ironing to press clothes with a hot iron to make them smooth

ironing board /ˈaɪənɪŋ ˌbɔːd/ *noun*
a narrow table on which you iron clothes

irony /ˈaɪərəni/ *noun (no plural)*
1 the part of a situation that is strange or amusing because what happens is completely different from what you expected ▶ *The irony was that the more the media criticized the film, the more the audiences liked it.*
2 the use of words that are different from what you really mean, in order to be amusing or show that you are annoyed ▶ *The author uses irony to convey his true feelings about the government.*

irrational /ɪˈræʃənəl/ *adjective*
not sensible or reasonable ▶ *She has an irrational fear of mice.*
OPPOSITE: **rational**

irregular /ɪˈreɡjʊlə/ *adjective*
(used about nouns, verbs, etc.) not following the usual rules of grammar ▶ *"To go" is an irregular verb.*
OPPOSITE: **regular**

irrelevant /ɪˈreləvənt/ *adjective*
not important and having no effect in a particular situation ▶ *She thinks my opinion is irrelevant.*
OPPOSITE: **relevant**

irresistible /ˌɪrɪˈzɪstəbəl/ *adjective*
impossible not to want, like, enjoy, etc. ▶ *The chocolate cake was irresistible.*

irresponsible /ˌɪrɪˈspɒnsəbəl/ *adjective*
behaving in a careless way, without thinking of the bad results you might cause ▶ *It's irresponsible to leave small children alone.*
OPPOSITE: **responsible**

irreversible /ˌɪrɪˈvɜːsəbəl/ *adjective*
impossible to change back to the

previous state ➤ *irreversible brain damage*
OPPOSITE: **reversible**

irrigate /'ɪrɪgeɪt/ *verb (present participle **irrigating**, past **irrigated**)*
to make water flow onto dry land so that crops can grow

irrigation /ˌɪrɪ'geɪʃən/ *noun (no plural)*
the supplying of water to dry land so that crops can grow

irritable /'ɪrɪtəbəl/ *adjective*
easily annoyed ➤ *He's always irritable in the morning.*

irritate /'ɪrɪteɪt/ *verb (present participle **irritating**, past **irritated**)*
1 to annoy someone ➤ *The noise the children were making was irritating me.*
2 to make a part of your body sore ➤ *The sun irritates my eyes.*

is /s, z, əz; *strong* ɪz/ *verb*
the part of the verb **be** that you use with **he, she**, and **it** ➤ *She is Peter's sister.* ➤ *He's (=he is) her brother.* ➤ *That boy's (=boy is) in my class.* ➤ *He's not (=he is not) very clever.* ➤ *She isn't (=she is not) my friend.*

Islam /'ɪzlɑːm/ *noun (no plural)*
the religion of the Muslims

Islamic /ɪz'læmɪk/ *adjective*
of or about Islam ➤ *Islamic traditions* ➤ *the Islamic faith*

island /'aɪlənd/ *noun*
a piece of land surrounded by water

isle /aɪl/ *noun*
used in the names of some islands ➤ *Jersey is one of the Channel Isles.*

isn't /'ɪzənt/
is not ➤ *She isn't coming.* ➤ *It's a lovely day, isn't it?*

isolate /'aɪsəleɪt/ *verb (present participle **isolating**, past **isolated**)*
to keep one person or thing separate from others ➤ *We isolate dangerous prisoners in another part of the prison.*

isolated /'aɪsə,leɪtɪd/ *adjective*
far from other houses, towns, etc. ➤ *an isolated house* ➤ *an isolated village*

isolation /ˌaɪsə'leɪʃən/ *noun (no plural)*
1 a feeling of being lonely ➤ *Moving to a new town can lead to a sense of isolation.*
2 in isolation happening or existing separately from other things ➤ *These events cannot be examined in isolation from one another.*

issue¹ /'ɪʃuː/ *verb (present participle **issuing**, past **issued**)*
to supply someone with something ➤ *The teacher issued paper and pencils to all the children.*

issue² *noun*
1 a subject that many people think is important ➤ *new government policy on the issue **of** health*
2 something that is printed in large numbers and sold at one time ➤ *today's issue of the newspaper*

it /ɪt/ *pronoun (plural **they** /ðeɪ/)*
1 the thing or animal that the sentence is about ➤ *I've lost my book, and I can't find it anywhere.* ➤ *It's (=it is) not in my room.* ➤ *It was an interesting film.*
2 used when you are talking about the weather, time, and date ➤ *It is very hot today.* ➤ *It's nearly 4 o'clock.* ➤ *It is Thursday, September 2nd.*
3 used when you are talking about a happening or a fact ➤ *It's a long way to the town.* ➤ *"What's that noise?" "It's a car."*
4 used when you are asking or saying who is there ➤ *"Who is it?"* ➤ *"It's me – Peter."*

IT /ˌaɪ 'tiː/ *noun (no plural)*
INFORMATION TECHNOLOGY

italics /ɪ'tælɪks/ *plural noun*
a style of printed letters that slope to

the right ► *The examples in this dictionary are written in italics.*

itch¹ /ɪtʃ/ *verb*
(used about your skin) to be sore and making you want to rub it ► *The insect bite itched all night.*

itch² *noun (plural* **itches)**
a sore and annoying feeling on your skin that makes you want to rub it

itchy /ˈɪtʃi/ *adjective (***itchier, itchiest)**
(used about a part of your body) making you want to rub it ► *itchy skin*

it'd /ˈɪtəd/
1 it would ► *It'd be lovely to see you.*
2 it had ► *It'd taken us two hours to get there.*

item /ˈaɪtəm/ *noun*
a thing ► *There was an interesting item in the newspaper today.* ► *On the desk there were two books, a pen, and some other items.*

itinerary /aɪˈtɪnərəri/ *noun (plural* **itineraries)**
a plan or list of the places you will visit on a trip ► *The first stop on our itinerary is Rome.*

it'll /ˈɪtl/
it will ► *It'll soon be the holidays.*

its /ɪts/ *adjective*
of it; belonging to it ► *She gave the cat its food.* ► *The dog hurt its foot.*

> Do not confuse **its** (=belonging to it) with **it's** (=it is or it has) which is spelt with (').

it's /ɪts/
1 it is ► *It's very nice to meet you.*
2 it has ► *It's stopped raining.*
LOOK AT: **its**

itself /ɪtˈself/ *pronoun (plural* **themselves** /ðəmˈselvz/*)*
the same thing or animal as the one that the sentence is about
► *The house stands by itself* (=alone) *outside the village.*

I've /aɪv/
I have ► *I've got two sisters.*

ivory /ˈaɪvəri/ *noun (no plural)*
the hard, yellow substance taken from the TUSKS (=long teeth) of elephants

ivy /ˈaɪvi/ *noun*
a plant with dark green, shiny leaves that grows on the walls of buildings ► *The cottage was covered in ivy.*

Jj

jab¹ /dʒæb/ *verb (present participle* **jabbing***, past* **jabbed)**
to push something long or sharp forward with a lot of force ► *I jabbed the needle into my finger.* ► *He kept jabbing his finger into my back until I turned round.*

jab² *noun*
a quick, sharp push ► *I felt a jab in my back.*

jack¹ /dʒæk/ *noun*
1 a piece of equipment used for lifting something heavy, such as a car
2 a playing card with a picture of a young man on it

jack² *verb*
jack something in to stop doing something, such as your job or a course of study ► *I'd love to jack in my job.*

jackal /ˈdʒækɔːl/ *noun*
a wild animal like a small dog

jacket /ˈdʒækɪt/ *noun*
1 a short coat
2 the loose cover of a book

jackpot /ˈdʒækpɒt/ *noun*
a large amount of money that you can win ► *The lottery jackpot is £3 million.*

jaded /ˈdʒeɪdɪd/ *adjective*
no longer feeling excited about something because you are tired of it

or it no longer interests you ▸ *She felt
jaded after the long journey.*

jagged /'dʒæɡɪd/ *adjective*
having a rough, uneven edge with
many sharp points ▸ *I cut myself on
the jagged edge of the tin.* ▸ *jagged
rocks*

jaguar /'dʒæɡjʊəʳ/ *noun*
a large, wild cat with spots

jail *(also* **gaol***)* /dʒeɪl/ *noun*
a place where criminals are kept
locked up as a punishment ▸ *The
man was sent to jail.*
SAME MEANING: **prison**

jam¹ /dʒæm/ *verb (present participle
jamming, past jammed)*
1 to press things or people tightly
together into a place ▸ *I jammed all
my clothes into a case.*
2 to make something unable to move
▸ *I've jammed the lock and I can't
open the door.*
3 to become stuck and unable to
move ▸ *I can't ride my bicycle
because the brakes have jammed.*

jam² *noun*
1 a lot of people or things pressed so
tightly together that movement is
stopped ▸ *a traffic jam*
2 *(no plural)* a sweet food made of
fruit boiled with sugar, usually eaten
with bread

jangle /'dʒæŋɡəl/ *verb (present
participle jangling, past jangled)*
to make a sharp noise like metal
hitting metal ▸ *She jangled her keys
in her pocket.*

January /'dʒænjʊəri/ *noun*
the first month of the year

jar /dʒɑːʳ/ *noun*
a container like a bottle with a short
neck and a wide opening ▸ *a jam jar*

jargon /'dʒɑːɡən/ *noun (no plural)*
words and phrases that are used by
people doing the same type of work,
and that other people find difficult to
understand ▸ *legal jargon*

javelin /'dʒævəlɪn/ *noun*
a light spear which is thrown as a
sport

jaw /dʒɔː/ *noun*
either of the two bony parts of your
face which hold your teeth

jazz /dʒæz/ *noun (no plural)*
a kind of music with a strong beat
▸ *Do you like listening to jazz?*

jealous /'dʒeləs/ *adjective*
1 unhappy because you want
something that someone else has ▸ *I
was very jealous of Linda's new
bicycle.*
SAME MEANING: **envious**
2 afraid that you will lose someone's
love because they seem to love
another person more ▸ *Her husband
gets jealous if she talks to other men.*
(adverb: **jealously***)*

jealousy /'dʒeləsi/ *noun (no plural)*
1 the unhappiness that you feel when
you want something that someone
else has
SAME MEANING: **envy**
2 the fear that you feel when you
think you will lose someone's love
because you want to love another
person more

jeans /dʒiːnz/ *plural noun*
trousers made of a strong, cotton
cloth, usually blue ▸ *a pair of jeans*

Jeep /dʒiːp/ *noun trademark*
a car that has a strong engine and
can be used on rough roads

jeer /dʒɪəʳ/ *verb*
to laugh rudely at someone or shout
unkind remarks ▸ *The crowd jeered at
the politician.*

jeers /dʒɪəz/ *plural noun*
rude laughter; unkind remarks

jelly /'dʒeli/ *noun*
1 *(plural jellies)* a sweet, soft DESSERT
made with fruit and sugar
2 *(no plural)* any substance that is
between liquid and solid

J

jellyfish /'dʒelɪˌfɪʃ/ *noun (plural **jellyfish** or **jellyfishes**)*
a soft sea creature that is nearly transparent and can sting

jerk¹ /dʒɜːk/ *verb*
1 to pull something suddenly and quickly ► *She jerked the rope, but it wouldn't move.*
2 to move with a sudden movement ► *Her hand jerked as she dropped her drink.*

jerk² *noun*
a short, hard pull or sudden movement ► *The old bus started with a jerk.*

jerky /'dʒɜːkɪ/ *adjective (**jerkier, jerkiest**)*
rough and sudden, not smooth ► *We had a very jerky ride in his car.*

jersey /'dʒɜːzɪ/ *noun*
a piece of clothing, usually made of wool, that covers the top part of your body.
SAME MEANING: **jumper, pullover, sweater**

Jesus /'dʒiːzəs/ *(also **Jesus Christ** /ˌdʒiːzəs 'kraɪst/) noun*
the man on whose life and teaching Christianity is based

jet /dʒet/ *noun*
1 a narrow stream of gas, air, or liquid that comes out of a small hole ► *The fireman sent jets of water into the burning house.*
2 a kind of aircraft that can go very fast ► *a jet engine*

jet lag /'dʒet læg/ *noun (no plural)*
the feeling of being very tired after a long journey on a plane ► *Do you get jet lag after a long flight?*

jetty /'dʒetɪ/ *noun (plural **jetties**)*
a kind of wall built out into water, used for getting on and off boats

Jew /dʒuː/ *noun*
a person who follows the religion of Judaism

jewel /'dʒuːəl/ *noun*
a stone that is worth a lot of money and worn as an ornament ► *She wore beautiful jewels round her neck.*

jeweller /'dʒuːələ'/ *noun*
a person who sells or makes jewellery ► *The jeweller fixed my watch.*

jewellery /'dʒuːəlrɪ/ *noun (no plural)*
things such as rings, etc. that people wear as ornaments

Jewish /'dʒuːɪʃ/ *adjective*
belonging to a group of people whose religion is Judaism

jibe *(also **gibe**)* /dʒaɪb/ *noun*
something that you say that criticizes someone or makes them seem silly ► *She's always making jibes about my weight.*

jigsaw puzzle /'dʒɪgsɔː ˌpʌzəl/ *(also **jigsaw**) noun*
a game in which you must fit together many small pieces to make one big picture ► *Let's do a jigsaw puzzle.*

jilt /dʒɪlt/ *verb*
to suddenly end a romantic relationship with someone ► *She jilted him the day before their wedding.*

jingle /'dʒɪŋgəl/ *verb (present participle **jingling**, past **jingled**)*
to make a ringing noise, like little bells ► *The coins jingled in his pocket.*

jittery /'dʒɪtərɪ/ *adjective*
worried and nervous ► *I get very jittery about going to the dentist.*

job /dʒɒb/ *noun*
1 a piece of work that must be done ► *My mother does all the jobs about the house.*
SAME MEANING: **task**
2 work that you are paid to do ► *"What is your job?" "I'm a teacher."*
LOOK AT: **work**
3 a good job a phrase used when you think it is lucky or a good thing that

something has happened ▶ *It's a good job* (=it's lucky) *you were here to help me.*

jockey /'dʒɒkɪ/ *noun*
a person who rides in horse races

jog¹ /dʒɒg/ *verb (present participle **jogging**, past **jogged**)*
to run slowly, usually for exercise ▶ *She jogs every morning.*

jog² *noun*
a slow, steady run, which you do as exercise ▶ *Let's go for a jog.*

jogger /'dʒɒgəʳ/ *noun*
a person who goes running as a form of exercise

jogging /'dʒɒgɪŋ/ *noun (no plural)*
the activity of running for exercise ▶ *I love jogging.*

join¹ /dʒɔɪn/ *verb*
1 to put or bring two or more things together ▶ *Join the two pieces of rope with a strong knot.* ▶ *This road joins the two villages.*
2 to come together; to meet ▶ *Where do the two roads join?*
3 to go and be with someone, usually so that you can do something together ▶ *Will you join me for a drink* (=will you have a drink with me)? ▶ *I am joining my family for Christmas.*
4 to become a member of something ▶ *He joined the army in 1939.*
5 join hands to hold each other's hands ▶ *We all joined hands and danced round in a circle.*
6 join in to take part in an activity, a game, etc. ▶ *We all joined in the singing.* ▶ *We're going to play football; do you want to join in?*

join² *noun*
a place where two things have been joined together ▶ *There's a join in this piece of material.*

joint¹ /dʒɔɪnt/ *noun*
1 a place where two bones in your body meet

2 a place where two things are joined together
3 a large piece of meat for cooking, usually with a bone in it

joint² *adjective*
shared by two or more people ▶ *We wrote it together; it was a joint effort.* ▶ *His sons are joint owners of the business.* ▶ *We have a joint bank account.* (adverb: **jointly**)

joke¹ /dʒəʊk/ *noun*
1 something that you say or do to make people laugh ▶ *Our teacher told us a funny joke.* ▶ *Do you know any jokes?*
2 play a joke on someone to do something funny to someone to make other people laugh ▶ *Let's play a joke on Michael.*
3 practical joke a trick played on someone to make them look silly and to make other people laugh

joke² *verb (present participle **joking**, past **joked**)*
to say things to make people laugh ▶ *I didn't mean that seriously – I was only joking.*

jolly¹ /'dʒɒlɪ/ *adjective (**jollier**, **jolliest**)*
happy; pleasant ▶ *a jolly person*

jolly² *adverb*
very ▶ *You were jolly lucky!*

jolt¹ /dʒəʊlt/ *noun*
1 a sudden shake or movement ▶ *The lorry started with a jolt.*
2 a shock or surprise ▶ *The telephone rang in the middle of the night and gave me a bit of a jolt.*

jolt² *verb*
to move with sudden, rough shakes ▶ *The bus jolted along the mountain road.*

jostle /'dʒɒsəl/ *verb (present participle **jostling**, past **jostled**)*
to push against other people in a crowd ▶ *Spectators jostled for a better view.*

J

jot /dʒɒt/ verb (present participle **jotting**, past **jotted**)
jot something down to write something down quickly ► I jotted down her address on my newspaper.

journal /'dʒɜːnl/ noun
1 a serious newspaper or magazine for a special subject ► a medical journal
2 a record of the things you do each day

journalism /'dʒɜːnl-ɪzəm/ noun (no plural)
the job of writing for a newspaper or magazine

journalist /'dʒɜːnl-ɪst/ noun
a person who writes for a newspaper or magazine

journey /'dʒɜːnɪ/ noun
a trip, usually a long one ► How long is the journey to the coast?

joy /dʒɔɪ/ noun
1 something that gives great happiness ► Her child was a joy to her.
2 (no plural) great happiness ► She cried with joy when her son was born.

joyful /'dʒɔɪfəl/ adjective
full of great happiness ► a joyful occasion (adverb: **joyfully**)

joyrider /'dʒɔɪ,raɪdəʳ/ noun
a person who steals a car and drives it in a fast and dangerous way

joyriding /'dʒɔɪ,raɪdɪŋ/ noun (no plural)
the activity of stealing a car and driving it in a fast and dangerous way ► He was arrested for joyriding.

joystick /'dʒɔɪ,stɪk/ noun
a handle that you use to control something in a computer game

Judaism /'dʒuː-deɪ-ɪzəm/ noun (no plural)
the religion of the Jews

judge¹ /dʒʌdʒ/ noun
1 a person who can decide questions of law in a court ► The judge decided

to send the man to prison for two years.
2 a person who decides who is the winner of a competition

judge² verb (present participle **judging**, past **judged**)
1 to form an opinion about something or someone, especially after you have thought carefully ► How can you judge which dictionary to buy?
2 to decide who or what is the winner of a competition ► Who is judging the poetry competition?
COMPARE: **decide**

judgement /'dʒʌdʒmənt/ noun
1 the decision made by a judge in a court of law
2 (no plural) what you decide after thinking about something carefully ► I think John is lying, but you will have to make your own judgement.

judo /'dʒuːdəʊ/ noun (no plural)
a fighting sport in which you try to throw the other person to the ground

jug /dʒʌg/ noun
a container with a handle, for holding and pouring liquids ► a jug of water

juggle /'dʒʌgəl/ verb (present participle **juggling**, past **juggled**)
to throw several things into the air and keep them moving by throwing and catching them many times, as a trick

juggler /'dʒʌgləʳ/ noun
a person who does juggling tricks for people to watch

juice /dʒuːs/ noun (no plural)
the liquid that comes out of fruit or vegetables ► a glass of orange juice

juicy /'dʒuːsɪ/ adjective (**juicier**, **juiciest**)
having a lot of juice ► a juicy orange

July /dʒʊ'laɪ/ noun
the seventh month of the year

jumble¹ /'dʒʌmbəl/ noun (no plural)
1 a lot of things which are mixed together in an untidy way

2 a lot of different, old things, usually which you do not want to keep any more

jumble² verb (present participle **jumbling**, past **jumbled**)
to mix things together in an untidy way ▶ The clothes were all jumbled up in the drawer.

jumble sale /'dʒʌmbəl ˌseɪl/ noun
an event where people sell a lot of different, old things, usually to make money to help people

jumbo /'dʒʌmbəʊ/ adjective
larger than other things of the same type ▶ jumbo sausages

jumbo jet /ˌdʒʌmbəʊ ˌdʒet/ noun
a large aircraft that can carry a lot of passengers

jump¹ /dʒʌmp/ verb
1 to push yourself up in the air or over something, using your legs ▶ The children jumped up and down with excitement. ▶ The horse jumped over the fence.
2 to move suddenly because of fear or surprise ▶ That noise made me jump.
3 jump to your feet to get up quickly, especially to go and do something ▶ She jumped to her feet when the post arrived.

jump² noun
the act of pushing yourself up in the air or over something, using your legs ▶ He got over the fence in one jump.

jumper /'dʒʌmpə'/ noun
a piece of clothing, usually made of wool, that covers the top part of your body
SAME MEANING: **jersey, pullover, sweater**

junction /'dʒʌŋkʃən/ noun
a place where two or more things join or meet ▶ Turn left at the junction.

June /dʒuːn/ noun
the sixth month of the year

jungle /'dʒʌŋgəl/ noun
a thick forest in hot countries

junior /'dʒuːnjə'/ adjective
1 younger ▶ a junior school (=a school for young children)
2 low in importance or position ▶ a junior member of the company
OPPOSITE (**1** and **2**): **senior**

junior school /'dʒuːnjə ˌskuːl/ noun
a school for children who are between seven and eleven years old

junk /dʒʌŋk/ noun (no plural)
useless things that you do not want ▶ That room is full of junk.
COMPARE: **rubbish**

junk food /'dʒʌŋk fuːd/ noun (no plural)
food that is not healthy because it contains a lot of fat or sugar ▶ You eat too much junk food.

junk mail /'dʒʌŋk meɪl/ noun (no plural)
letters that companies send to your house to tell you about the things they sell ▶ I get far too much junk mail, and most of it goes in the bin.

juror /'dʒʊərə'/ noun
a member of a jury ▶ The jurors must decide whether or not he is guilty.

jury /'dʒʊərɪ/ noun (plural **juries**)
a group of people who decide if a person is guilty or not in a law court ▶ The jury decided the man was guilty and he was sent to prison.

just¹ /dʒʌst/ adverb
1 a very short time ago ▶ I've just got home.

> **Just** (**1**), **already**, and **yet** usually used with the PRESENT PERFECT TENSE (=the tense formed with **have** + the PAST PARTICIPLE) and not with the simple past tense: He had just heard the news. ▶ I've already seen that film. ▶ Have you finished yet?

2 by a very short time ▶ You just missed the bus.

J

3 at the moment; now ➤ *The telephone rang just as I was leaving.* ➤ *I'm just making some coffee – would you like some?*
4 exactly at a particular time or place ➤ *I'm not hungry just yet* (=right now). ➤ *I live just here.*
5 the exact amount; not more, not less ➤ *I've got just enough money to get home.*
6 only ➤ *I rang just to say hello.*
7 just a minute, just a moment a phrase used when you want to ask someone to wait a little bit until you can help them ➤ *"Can I speak to Mr Jones?" "Just a minute, please. I'll find him for you."*
8 just now at the moment ➤ *I'm busy just now, but I can help you later.*

just² *adjective*
fair and right ➤ *a just punishment*
OPPOSITE: **unjust**

justice /'dʒʌstɪs/ *noun (no plural)*
1 treatment of people which is fair and right ➤ *to fight for justice*
OPPOSITE: **injustice**
2 the system of law in a country

justifiable /'dʒʌstɪfaɪəbəl/ *adjective*
able to be justified ➤ *a justifiable decision*

justification /ˌdʒʌstɪfɪ'keɪʃən/ *noun (no plural)*
a good reason for doing something ➤ *There's no justification for violence.*

justified /'dʒʌstɪfaɪd/ *adjective*
fair and done for good reasons ➤ *Her criticism is justified.*

justify /'dʒʌstɪfaɪ/ *verb (past justified)*
to give a good reason for doing something that other people think is not reasonable ➤ *He keeps trying to justify his bad behaviour.*

juvenile /'dʒuːvənaɪl/ *adjective*
of or about young people ➤ *There has been an increase in juvenile crime.*

Kk

kangaroo /ˌkæŋgə'ruː/ *noun*
an Australian animal that jumps along on its large back legs and keeps its young in a special pocket

karate /kə'rɑːtɪ/ *noun (no plural)*
a Japanese sport in which you fight using your hands and legs

keen /kiːn/ *adjective*
eager to do something; having a strong interest and liking for something ➤ *He was keen to see the new film.* ➤ *Are you keen on swimming? (adverb: keenly)*

keep¹ /kiːp/ *verb (past kept /kept/)*
1 to continue to have something which you do not need to give to anyone ➤ *You can keep it. I don't need it any more.*
2 to store something in a particular place so that you can find it easily ➤ *Where do you keep the tea?*
3 to make someone or something stay in a place or state ➤ *Keep still while I take your photo!* ➤ *They kept her in hospital for a week.*
4 to stay fresh ➤ *Milk only keeps for a few days.*
5 keep doing something to do something again and again ➤ *I kept making the same mistake.*
6 keep a secret not to tell a secret
7 keep off to stay off or away from a place ➤ *Please keep off the grass.*
8 keep someone up to make someone stay awake and out of bed ➤ *I'm sorry I kept you up so late last night.*
9 keep up to move as fast as a person or thing so that you stay the same ➤ *I can't keep up with you when you walk so fast.*

keep² *noun (no plural)*
the cost of someone's food, clothes,

etc. ▶ *He earns his keep by working with his uncle.*

keeper /'ki:pə^r/ *noun*
the person who takes care of the animals in a zoo

kennel /'kenl/ *noun*
a small house for a dog to sleep in

kept /kept/
the PAST TENSE and PAST PARTICIPLE of the verb **keep**

kerb /k3:b/ *noun*
a line of raised stones separating the path at the side of a road from the road itself

ketchup /'ketʃʌp/ *noun (no plural)*
a thick liquid made from TOMATOES, eaten with food to give a pleasant taste

kettle /'ketl/ *noun*
a metal pot with a lid, a handle, and a long, narrow mouth for pouring; it is used for boiling water ▶ *Let's put the kettle on and make some tea.*

key /ki:/ *noun*
1 a shaped piece of metal used for locking and unlocking things ▶ *car keys* ▶ *the keys for the cupboard*
2 a button on a computer or TYPEWRITER that you press when you use it
3 one of the narrow black and white bars that you press to make music on some musical instruments ▶ *the keys of a piano*
4 a set of answers to a test or exercise ▶ *See if your answers are right by looking in the key at the back of the book.*

keyboard /'ki:bɔ:d/ *noun*
a set of keys on a computer or a musical instrument such as a piano, that you press to produce letters or sounds

keyhole /'ki:həʊl/ *noun*
the part of a lock that a key fits into

key ring /'ki: rɪŋ/ *noun*
a ring on which you can keep keys

kg
a short way of writing the words **kilogram** or **kilograms**

khaki /'kɑːkɪ/ *adjective, noun (no plural)*
a yellow-brown colour; a strong, cotton cloth of this colour

kick^1 /kɪk/ *verb*
1 to hit someone or something with your foot ▶ *He kicked the ball over the fence.*
2 to move your legs strongly ▶ *The baby kicked happily.*
3 kick off to start a football match
4 kick someone out to force someone to leave a place

kick^2 *noun*
1 a strong movement of your leg or foot ▶ *If the door won't open, give it a kick.*
2 a feeling of pleasure or excitement ▶ *I get a kick out of driving fast.*

kickoff /'kɪkɒf/ *noun*
the time when a game of football begins ▶ *Kickoff is at 3 o'clock.*

kid /kɪd/ *noun*
1 a child
2 a young goat

kidnap /'kɪdnæp/ *verb (present participle kidnapping, past kidnapped)*
to take someone away and ask for money in return for bringing them back safely

kidnapper /'kɪdnæpə^r/ *noun*
a person who KIDNAPS someone

kidney /'kɪdnɪ/ *noun*
one of the two parts inside your body which remove waste liquid from your blood

kill /kɪl/ *verb*
to make a plant, an animal, or a person die ▶ *Ten people were killed in the train crash.* ▶ *The cat killed the bird.*
COMPARE: **murder**

K

killer /'kɪlə^r/ *noun*
a person, an animal, or a thing that kills ➤ *The police are searching for the killer.*
COMPARE: **murderer**

killing /'kɪlɪŋ/ *noun*
a murder ➤ *The killing took place outside a nightclub.*

kilo /'ki:ləʊ/ *noun*
a kilogram ➤ *a kilo of sugar*

kilobyte /'kɪləbaɪt/ *noun*
a unit for measuring computer information

kilogram (also **kilogramme**) /'kɪləgræm/ *noun*
a measure of weight; 1,000 grams ➤ *3 kilograms* (=3kg)

kilometre /'kɪləmi:tə^r, kɪ'lɒmɪtə^r/ *noun*
a measure of length; 1,000 metres ➤ *500 kilometres* (=500km)

kilt /kɪlt/ *noun*
a skirt traditionally worn by Scottish men

kin /kɪn/ *noun (no plural)*
people in your family ➤ *The dead man's next of kin* (=his closest relative) *was told about his death.*

kind¹ /kaɪnd/ *noun*
a type or group which is different from other groups ➤ *She is the kind of woman who helps people.* ➤ *What kind of car has he got?*
SAME MEANING: **type, sort**

kind² *adjective*
helpful, caring, and wanting to do things that make other people happy ➤ *She was kind to me when I was unhappy.* ➤ *It's very kind of you to help me.*
OPPOSITE: **unkind**

kindergarten /'kɪndəgɑ:tn/ *noun*
a school for children aged between two and five

kind-hearted /,kaɪnd 'hɑ:tɪd/ *adjective*
caring and sympathetic ➤ *a kind-hearted person*
OPPOSITE: **hard-hearted**

kindly /'kaɪndlɪ/ *adverb*
1 used when someone has done something kind or generous ➤ *Mr Thomas has kindly offered to let us use his car.*
2 in a kind way ➤ *Miss Havisham looked kindly at Joe.*

kindness /'kaɪndnəs/ *noun (no plural)*
the quality of being kind ➤ *Thank you very much for your kindness.*

king /kɪŋ/ *noun*
1 a male ruler of a country, especially one who comes from a family of rulers ➤ *the King of Spain*
2 a playing card with a picture of a king on it
COMPARE: **queen**

kingdom /'kɪŋdəm/ *noun*
a country ruled by a king or queen

kiosk /'ki:ɒsk/ *noun*
a small shop where you can buy things such as newspapers or tickets through a window

kipper /'kɪpə^r/ *noun*
a dried fish kept in salt

kiss¹ /kɪs/ *verb*
to touch someone with your lips, as a sign of love or greeting ➤ *He kissed his wife goodbye.*

kiss² *noun (plural **kisses**)*
a touch with your lips ➤ *He gave his daughter a kiss.*

kit /kɪt/ *noun*
1 *(no plural)* all the things that you need for doing a particular sport ➤ *I've forgotten my football kit.*
2 a set of small pieces from which to make something ➤ *We made a model plane out of a kit.*

kitchen /'kɪtʃɪn/ *noun*
a room used for preparing and cooking food

K

kite /kaɪt/ *noun*
a toy with a light frame covered with plastic or cloth, which flies in the air on the end of a long string

kitten /'kɪtn/ *noun*
a young cat

kitty /'kɪti/ *noun*
money that a group of people have collected and saved for something

kiwi fruit /'kiːwi fruːt/ *noun (plural kiwi fruit or kiwi fruits)*
a small, round, green fruit with a rough skin

Kleenex /'kliːneks/ *noun trademark (plural Kleenex or Kleenexes)*
a piece of soft, thin paper used especially for cleaning your nose

km
a short way of writing the words **kilometre** or **kilometres**

knack /næk/ *noun*
the ability to do something well ▶ *She has a real knack for writing memorable songs.*

knead /niːd/ *verb*
to make and press a mixture of flour and water etc. with your hands so that it becomes ready to cook

knee /niː/ *noun*
1 the joint in the middle of your leg where the leg bends
2 **on your knee** on the top part of your leg when you are sitting down ▶ *The baby sat on my knee.*

kneecap /'niːkæp/ *noun*
the bone at the front of your knee

knee-deep /ˌniː 'diːp/ *adjective*
be knee-deep in something to be standing in something that is deep enough to reach your knees ▶ *We were knee-deep in water.*

knee-high /ˌniː 'haɪ/ *adjective*
tall enough to reach your knees ▶ *a pair of knee-high boots*

kneel /niːl/ *verb (past knelt /nelt/)*
to bend your legs and rest on your knees ▶ *She knelt down to pray.*

knew /njuː/
the PAST TENSE of the verb **know**

knickers /'nɪkəz/ *plural noun*
a piece of clothing for women and girls, for the lower part of the body, worn under skirts or trousers, not covering the legs
SAME MEANING: **pants**

knife /naɪf/ *noun (plural knives /naɪvz/)*
a blade with a handle, used for cutting things or as a weapon

knight /naɪt/ *noun*
1 a man who is given a title by the king or queen in Britain, and whose name then has "Sir" in front of it
2 a noble soldier of the Middle Ages, trained to fight on his horse

knighthood /'naɪthʊd/ *noun*
a special title that is given to a man by the king or queen in Britain

knit /nɪt/ *verb (present participle knitting, past knitted or knit)*
to make clothes by joining wool or another thread with long needles or on a special machine ▶ *She's knitting some clothes for her baby.*
COMPARE: **sew**

knitting /'nɪtɪŋ/ *noun (no plural)*
the activity of making things by knitting; a piece of knitted work

knitting needle /'nɪtɪŋ ˌniːdl/ *noun*
a long, thin stick that you use for knitting

knives /naɪvz/
the plural of **knife**

knob /nɒb/ *noun*
1 a round handle on a door or a drawer
2 a round control button on a machine

knobbly /'nɒbli/ *adjective (knobblier, knobbliest)*
not smooth, with hard parts sticking out ▶ *knobbly knees*

K

knock¹ /nɒk/ *verb*
1 to make a noise by hitting something several times ➤ *I knocked on the door.*
2 to hit something hard so that it moves or falls ➤ *He knocked the glass off the table.*
3 knock something down to destroy or remove a building ➤ *They knocked down the houses to build a shopping centre.*
4 knock someone down to hit someone with a car, bus, etc. so that they fall to the ground ➤ *She was knocked down by a bus.*
5 knock someone out to make someone go to sleep or become unconscious ➤ *Those sleeping pills really knocked me out.*

knock² *noun*
the sound made by hitting something ➤ *a knock on the door*

knockout /'nɒk-aʊt/ *noun*
a situation in which a BOXER hits another boxer so that he falls on the ground and cannot get up ➤ *Tyson won in 15 minutes with a knockout.*

knot¹ /nɒt/ *noun*
1 a fastening made by tying two ends of string or rope together ➤ *She tied a knot in her belt.*
2 a measure of the speed of a ship, about 1,853 metres per hour

knot² *verb (present participle knotting, past knotted)*
to tie something with a knot

know /nəʊ/ *verb (past tense knew /njuː/, past participle known /nəʊn/)*
1 to have something in your mind which you are sure is true ➤ *Do you know where they went?* ➤ *They don't know your address.*
2 to have learned and be able to use a language or skill ➤ *Do you know French?* ➤ *She knows how to cook.*
3 to have learned about something from studying or experience ➤ *I don't know anything about history.*

Compare **know**, **learn**, and **teach**. If you **know** something, you already have the facts or information about it: *She knows a lot about computers.* If you **learn** something, you discover facts about it, or discover how to do it, either on your own or with a teacher: *He's learning to drive.* ➤ *The children are learning maths at school.* If you **teach** someone something, you make them learn it by giving them help and information: *He is teaching me to drive.* ➤ *She teaches maths to the first years* (=the children in the first year at school).

4 to be familiar with a person or a place ➤ *I know Mary well.* ➤ *Do you know London?*
5 I know a phrase used to show you agree with someone ➤ *"It's a bad idea." "I know."*
6 you know a phrase used when you want to explain something more clearly ➤ *It's the building on the left. You know – the new one.*

know-all /'nəʊ ɔːl/ *noun*
an annoying person who thinks they know more than everyone else

know-how /'nəʊ haʊ/ *noun (no plural)*
knowledge that you need to do something ➤ *We don't have the know-how to build our own house.*

knowingly /'nəʊɪŋlɪ/ *adverb*
if you knowingly do something wrong, you do it even though you know that it is wrong ➤ *He claimed he'd never knowingly sold alcohol to teenagers.*

knowledge /'nɒlɪdʒ/ *noun (no plural)*
information or understanding that you have in your mind ➤ *His knowledge of languages is excellent.*

knowledgeable /'nɒlɪdʒəbəl/ *adjective*

having a lot of information or understanding about something ➤ *She's very knowledgeable **about** that subject.*

known /nəʊn/
the PAST PARTICIPLE of the verb **know**

knuckle /'nʌkəl/ *noun*
one of the joints in your fingers ➤ *Our fingers bend at the knuckles.*

koala /kəʊ'ɑːlə/ *noun*
an Australian animal like a small bear

Koran /kɔː'rɑːn/ *noun*
the Koran the holy book of the MUSLIMS

kosher /'kəʊʃər/ *adjective*
(used about food) prepared according to JEWISH law

kung fu /ˌkʌŋ 'fuː/ *noun (no plural)*
a Chinese sport in which people fight with their hands and feet

kw
a short way of writing the words **kilowatt** or **kilowatts**

Ll

l
a short way of writing the words **litre** or **litres** ➤ *a 2l bottle of beer*

lab /læb/ *noun*
a LABORATORY

label¹ /'leɪbəl/ *noun*
a piece of paper fixed to something which gives you information about it ➤ *Put a label on the box – then we'll know what's inside.*

label² *verb (present participle* **labelling**, *past* **labelled**)
to put or fix a label on something ➤ *The parcel wasn't labelled, so it got lost.*

laboratory /lə'bɒrətərɪ/ *noun (plural* **laboratories**)
a room or building in which scientific work is done

laborious /lə'bɔːrɪəs/ *adjective*
needing a lot of time and effort to do ➤ *the laborious process of examining all the data*

labour¹ /'leɪbər/ *noun (no plural)*
1 hard work that you do with your hands ➤ *Her beautiful home was the result of many years of labour.*
2 the workers in a country or factory ➤ *There is a shortage of skilled labour in the region.*

labour² *verb*
to work hard ➤ *We laboured all day to finish the job.*

labourer /'leɪbərər/ *noun*
a person who does hard work with their hands ➤ *a farm labourer*
COMPARE: **worker**

lace¹ /leɪs/ *noun*
1 a piece of string for fastening a shoe ➤ *I need some new laces for my shoes.*
2 *(no plural)* ornamental cloth with holes in it, made from fine thread ➤ *My dress has lots of pretty lace around the neck and sleeves.*

lace² *verb (present participle* **lacing**, *past* **laced**)
lace something up to tie something with a lace ➤ *Lace your shoes up.*

lack¹ /læk/ *verb*
to have none or too little of something ➤ *He lacked the strength to lift the box.*

lack² *noun (no plural)*
not having something, or not having enough of it ➤ *The plants died through lack **of** water.*

lad /læd/ *noun*
a boy ➤ *He moved here when he was a young lad.*

ladder /'lædər/ *noun*
two long pieces of wood or metal, joined together by shorter pieces that form steps for climbing ➤ *I need a ladder to reach the roof.*

laden /'leɪdn/ *adjective*
carrying something, especially a large amount ► *The lorry was laden* **with** *boxes of fruit.*

Ladies /'leɪdɪz/
the Ladies the women's TOILET ► *She's gone to the Ladies.*
COMPARE: **Gents**

ladle /'leɪdl/ *noun*
a big, deep spoon with a long handle, used for serving soup

lady /'leɪdɪ/ *noun (plural ladies)*
1 a polite word for a woman ► *the lady in the shop* ► *a lady doctor*
2 a title given to certain women who have done important things in British public life ► *Lady Thatcher*
3 a noble woman or the wife of a lord
4 Ladies and Gentlemen a way to start a formal talk to a group of people

ladybird /'leɪdɪbɜːd/ *noun*
a small, round insect that is red with black spots

lag /læg/ *verb (present participle lagging, past lagged)*
lag behind to move or develop more slowly than other people ► *Gina lagged behind, waiting for Rob.* ► *My daughter is lagging behind in her studies.*

lager /'lɑːgə/ *noun*
1 *(no plural)* a kind of light beer
2 a glass or bottle of light beer ► *Two lagers, please.*

lagoon /lə'guːn/ *noun*
an area of sea water that is separated from the sea by sand

laid /leɪd/
the PAST TENSE and PAST PARTICIPLE of the verb **lay**
LOOK AT: **lay¹**

laid-back /ˌleɪd 'bæk/ *adjective*
relaxed and not worried about anything ► *She seems very laid-back about her exams.*

lain /leɪn/
the PAST PARTICIPLE of the verb **lie**
LOOK AT: **lay¹**

lake /leɪk/ *noun*
a big pool of water with land all round it
COMPARE: **pond**

lamb /læm/ *noun*
a young sheep

lame /leɪm/ *adjective*
not able to walk easily, usually because of a hurt leg or foot
► *My horse is lame – I can't ride her.*

lamp /læmp/ *noun*
a small light which you have on a table, etc. ► *a bedside lamp*

lamppost /'læmp-pəʊst/ *noun*
a tall post in the street with a light at the top

lampshade /'læmpʃeɪd/ *noun*
a cover put over a lamp to soften its light or make it look nice

land¹ /lænd/ *noun*
1 *(no plural)* ground that people own ► *The big farmers own most of the land.*
2 *(no plural)* ground for farming ► *excellent land for wheat*
3 *(no plural)* the dry part of the Earth not covered by the sea ► *They reached land after six weeks at sea.*
4 a country ► *foreign lands*

land² *verb*
to arrive somewhere after a journey by plane ► *We landed in Rome at 6 in the evening.*
OPPOSITE: **take off**

landing /'lændɪŋ/ *noun*
1 the space at the top of a set of stairs in a building ► *The bedroom opens onto the landing.*
2 the action of a plane coming down from the air onto the ground ► *The plane made a safe landing.*

landlady /'lænd,leɪdɪ/ *noun (plural landladies)*

L

a woman who owns a building which she lets other people use or live in, in return for money

landlord /'lændlɔːd/ *noun*
a man who owns a building which he lets other people use or live in, in return for money

landmark /'lændmɑːk/ *noun*
1 something that helps you recognize where you are, such as a famous building ▶ *The Eiffel Tower is a well-known landmark in Paris.*
2 a very important event, change, or discovery in the development of something ▶ *a landmark in the history of aviation*

landowner /'lænd,əʊnəʳ/ *noun*
a person who owns a lot of land

landscape /'lænd,skeɪp/ *noun (no plural)*
the way an area of land looks ▶ *a landscape of mountains and lakes*

landslide /'lændslaɪd/ *noun*
1 soil and rocks falling down the side of a hill or mountain ▶ *The village was destroyed in a landslide.*
2 a situation in which a person or political party wins a lot more votes than the others in an election ▶ *It was a landslide victory for the Labour Party.*

lane /leɪn/ *noun*
a narrow road ▶ *We walked down the lane past the farm*

language /'læŋgwɪdʒ/ *noun*
the words that people use in speaking and writing ▶ *a foreign language* ▶ *the English language* ▶ *business language*

lantern /'læntən/ *noun*
a lamp in a glass case, often with a handle for carrying it

lap¹ /læp/ *noun*
1 the flat surface formed by the upper parts of your legs when you are sitting down ▶ *Her little girl sat on her lap.*

2 the distance once around the track in a race ▶ *a six-lap race*

lap² *verb (present participle **lapping**, past **lapped**)*
to drink liquid with the tongue, like a dog ▶ *The cat lapped its milk.*

lapel /lə'pel/ *noun*
one of the parts at the front of a coat or JACKET that is joined to the collar and folds back on each side

lapse¹ /læps/ *noun*
1 the act of forgetting something or not paying attention to something for a short time ▶ *a lapse of concentration*
2 the act of making a mistake or behaving badly, in a way that does not seem typical ▶ *Apart from the occasional lapse, her work seems quite good.*

lapse² *verb (present participle **lapsing**, past **lapsed**)*
to end, especially because the official period when something is allowed to continue has ended ▶ *Your membership of the tennis club has lapsed.*

laptop /'læptɒp/ *noun*
a small computer that you can carry with you

larder /'lɑːdəʳ/ *noun*
a cupboard or small room in which food is kept

large /lɑːdʒ/ *adjective*
big ▶ *They need a large house because they have nine children.*
OPPOSITE: **small**

largely /'lɑːdʒlɪ/ *adverb*
mostly or mainly ▶ *The delay was largely due to bad weather.*

large-scale /,lɑːdʒ 'skeɪl/ *adjective*
happening over a large area or involving a lot of people ▶ *large-scale unemployment*

laser /'leɪzəʳ/ *noun*
an apparatus with a very strong, very

L

narrow beam of light, used in some machines or in medical operations ▶ *a laser printer*

lash /læʃ/ *noun (plural* **lashes***)*
one of the hairs that grow round your eye

last¹ /lɑːst/ *adjective, adverb*
1 coming after all others ▶ *The last girl who came in was Mary.* ▶ *Who came in last?*
OPPOSITE: **first**
2 happening just before this time; the time before now ▶ *I saw my friend last week, but I haven't seen him since.* ▶ *I haven't seen his sister since last July* (=July of last year). ▶ *When did you last read an exciting book?*
3 at last in the end, when you are getting tired of waiting ▶ *The bus came at last.*

last² *verb*
1 to continue to happen for a period of time ▶ *Our holiday lasted ten days.*
2 to stay in good condition or unchanged ▶ *Good shoes last longer.* ▶ *She was very angry yesterday, but it didn't last.*
3 to be enough for a certain time ▶ *Two loaves of bread will last us for two days.*

lasting /ˈlɑːstɪŋ/ *adjective*
continuing for a long time ▶ *We want to have a lasting relationship.*

lastly /ˈlɑːstlɪ/ *adverb*
a word you use when you are making several points and you come to the last one ▶ *Lastly, I would like to thank everyone who has worked to make the new school such a success.*
OPPOSITE: **firstly**

last-minute /ˌlɑːst ˈmɪnɪt/ *adjective*
happening or done very late within a period of time ▶ *last-minute Christmas shopping*

last name /ˈlɑːst neɪm/ *noun*
your family's name which, in English, comes after your other names

SAME MEANING: **surname**

latch /lætʃ/ *noun (plural* **latches***)*
a fastening for a door, gate, or window

late /leɪt/ *adjective, adverb*
1 after the usual or agreed time ▶ *I missed the meeting because I got up late.*
2 near the end (of a day, year, etc.) ▶ *It's very late – I should be in bed. He began the work in late May.*
OPPOSITE: (**1** and **2**): **early**

lately /ˈleɪtlɪ/ *adverb*
in the recent past ▶ *Have you seen him lately?*

later /ˈleɪtəʳ/ *adverb*
1 after some time ▶ *I can't do it now, but I'll do it later.*
2 later on after some time ▶ *I can't do it now, but I'll do it later on.*

latest /ˈleɪtɪst/ *adjective*
most recent ▶ *Have you heard the latest news?* ▶ *Please arrive by 9 o'clock at the latest* (=and no later).

Latin /ˈlætɪn/ *noun (no plural)*
the language of the ancient Romans ▶ *A few children still study Latin at school.*

latitude /ˈlætɪtjuːd/ *noun (no plural)*
a position on the Earth shown on maps by lines (lines of latitude) that go from east to west
COMPARE: **longitude**

latter /ˈlætəʳ/ *noun*
the latter the second of two people or things which have just been mentioned ▶ *Britain has agreements with both Germany and Italy, but its agreement with the latter* (=Italy) *has been more successful.*
OPPOSITE: **the former**

laugh¹ /lɑːf/ *verb*
1 to make a sound that shows you are pleased, happy, or think something is funny ▶ *It was so funny we couldn't stop laughing.*

L

2 laugh at someone or something to treat a person or thing as very foolish, or make jokes about them ➤ *They'll laugh at you if you wear that awful coat.*

laugh² *noun*
the sound you make when you find something funny ➤ *We had a good laugh at his mistake.*

laughter /'lɑːftə'/ *noun (no plural)*
the act or sound of laughing

launch¹ /lɔːntʃ/ *noun (plural launches)*
a small boat driven by an engine

launch² *verb*
to put a ship into the water or to send a spaceship into space

launderette /ˌlɔːndə'ret/ *noun*
a shop where you pay to wash your clothes and sheets etc. in a machine

laundry /'lɔːndrɪ/ *noun*
1 (plural **laundries**) a place where clothes and sheets etc. are washed
2 (no plural) clothes and sheets etc. that need washing or have just been washed

lava /'lɑːvə/ *noun (no plural)*
very hot, liquid rock that comes out of the top of a VOLCANO

lavatory /'lævətrɪ/ *noun (plural lavatories)*
1 a container joined to a waste pipe, used for taking away body waste
2 a room with this in it ➤ *Where is the ladies' lavatory, please?*
SAME MEANING (**1** and **2**): **toilet, loo**

law /lɔː/ *noun*
1 a rule made by the government that all people must obey ➤ *a law against drinking and driving*
2 the law the whole system of laws in a country
3 against the law not allowed by the law ➤ *Driving without a seat belt is against the law.*

lawful /'lɔːfəl/ *adjective*
allowed by the law
SAME MEANING: **legal**

lawn /lɔːn/ *noun*
an area of short grass outside a house or in a park

lawnmower /'lɔːnˌməʊə'/ *noun*
a machine for cutting the grass in a garden or park

lawyer /'lɔːjə'/ *noun*
a person who advises people about the law, and speaks for them in court

lay¹ /leɪ/ *verb (past laid /leɪd/)*
1 to put something down ➤ *She laid her coat over a chair.*
2 lay the table to arrange knives, forks, plates, and other things on a table ready for a meal
3 to make eggs and send them out of the body ➤ *The hen laid three eggs.*

> Do not confuse the verb **lay** (PAST TENSE and PAST PARTICIPLE **laid**) with the verb **lie** (past tense **lay**, PAST PARTICIPLE **lain**). **Lay¹** means "to put something down" and is **always** used with an object: *She laid the clothes on the bed.* **Lie** means "to have your body flat on something", and is **never** used with an object: *She lay on her bed.* There is another verb **lie** (PAST TENSE and PAST PARTICIPLE **lied**), which means "to say something which is not true" and which is also used without an object.

lay²
the PAST TENSE of the verb **lie**

lay-by /'leɪ baɪ/ *noun*
an area at the side of a road, where vehicles can stop ➤ *We pulled into a lay-by for a rest.*

layer /'leɪə'/ *noun*
a covering that is spread on top of something or in between two things ➤ *This cake has got a layer of chocolate in the middle.*

L

layout /ˈleɪaʊt/ *noun*
the way in which rooms or objects are arranged ➤ *a picture showing the layout of Buckingham Palace*

laze /leɪz/ *(also laze around) verb (present participle lazing, past lazed)*
to relax and not do very much ➤ *two cats lazing in the sun*

lazy /ˈleɪzɪ/ *adjective (lazier, laziest)*
not wanting to work ➤ *He won't work; he's just too lazy.*

lb *(plural lbs)*
a short way of writing the words **pound** or **pounds**, when used about weight ➤ *1lb flour* ➤ *3lbs potatoes*

lead¹ /liːd/ *verb (past led /led/)*
1 to show someone the way, usually by going in front ➤ *You lead and we'll follow.* ➤ *She led us to the town centre.*
2 to go to a place ➤ *This path leads to the church.*
3 to be the chief person doing a thing; to be first or at the front, especially in a race or competition ➤ *He's going to lead the climb up Mount Everest.* ➤ *The English team was leading at half time.*
4 **lead a ... life** to experience a particular kind of life ➤ *She led a very lonely life.*

lead² /liːd/ *noun*
1 a position in front of the others ➤ *The Spanish runner now has a lead of 50 metres.*
2 **be in the lead** to be winning in a game or competition
3 a piece of rope, leather, etc. for holding an animal ➤ *Please keep your dog on a lead.*
SAME MEANING (**3**): **leash**

lead³ /led/ *noun*
1 (no plural) a heavy, soft, grey metal ➤ *as heavy as lead* ➤ *old lead pipes* ➤ *a lead roof*
2 the part inside a pencil that you write with

leader /ˈliːdəʳ/ *noun*
a person who leads other people ➤ *the team leader* ➤ *leaders of the world's richest nations*

leadership /ˈliːdəʃɪp/ *noun (no plural)*
1 the position of leader ➤ *the leadership of the Labour Party*
2 the qualities necessary in a leader

leading /ˈliːdɪŋ/ *adjective*
most important ➤ *the world's leading sports people*
SAME MEANING: **top**

leaf /liːf/ *noun (plural leaves /liːvz/)*
one of the green, flat parts of a plant or tree that grow out of branches or stems ➤ *Some plants have leaves that grow straight out of the ground*

leaflet /ˈliːflɪt/ *noun*
a piece of paper with a notice or an advertisement printed on it

league /liːg/ *noun*
1 a group of people or teams that play against each other in a competition ➤ *the Football League*
2 a group of people or countries who have joined together to work for a special aim

leak¹ /liːk/ *noun*
a hole or crack through which gas or liquid may pass in or out ➤ *There's a leak in the roof.*

leak² *verb*
(used about gas or liquid) to escape through a hole or crack ➤ *The roof leaks and the rain's coming in.*

leaky /ˈliːkɪ/ *adjective (leakier, leakiest)*
having a leak ➤ *The roof is leaky and the rain comes in.*

lean¹ /liːn/ *verb (past leaned or leant /lent/)*
1 to bend forwards, sideways, or backwards ➤ *Don't lean out of the window – you might fall.*
2 to put something against another thing to support it ➤ *She leant her bicycle against the wall.*

3 to rest your body against something to support it

lean² *adjective*
not containing very much fat ➤ *lean meat* ➤ *lean cattle*

leant /lent/
the PAST TENSE and PAST PARTICIPLE of the verb **lean**

leap¹ /liːp/ *verb (past leaped or leapt /lept/)*
1 to jump very high or a long way ➤ *The dog leapt over the fence.*
2 to increase suddenly ➤ *Prices have leapt up recently.*

leap² *noun*
1 a sudden jump which goes very high or a long way ➤ *With a great leap, she crossed the stream.*
2 a sudden, large increase ➤ *a leap in oil prices*

leap year /ˈliːp jɪəʳ/ *noun*
a year, once every four years, in which February has 29 days instead of 28 days ➤ *The years 1996 and 2000 were leap years.*

learn /lɜːn/ *verb (past learned or learnt /lɜːnt/)*
1 to get knowledge of something or the ability to do something ➤ *Have you learnt to swim?* ➤ *I am learning English.*
2 to fix something in the memory ➤ *She learnt the whole poem so that she could repeat it the next day.*
LOOK AT: **know**

learner /ˈlɜːnəʳ/ *noun*
a person who is learning ➤ *She's a slow learner.* ➤ *a learner driver*

learning /ˈlɜːnɪŋ/ *noun (no plural)*
knowledge that you get by reading and studying, or the activity of reading and studying ➤ *Learning should be fun.*

learnt /lɜːnt/
the PAST TENSE and PAST PARTICIPLE of the verb **learn**

leash /liːʃ/ *noun (plural leashes)*
a piece of rope, leather, etc. used for holding an animal ➤ *I have to keep my dog on a leash.*
SAME MEANING: **lead²**

least¹ /liːst/ *adverb*
1 the smallest amount or number ➤ *the least expensive one* (=the cheapest one). ➤ *They arrived when I least expected them* (=when I did not expect them at all).
2 less than all the others ➤ *Of all your friends, I like him the least.*
OPPOSITE (**1** and **2**): **most**
3 at least not less than and probably more than a certain amount ➤ *He's going away for at least a week* (=a week or longer).
4 least of all especially not ➤ *I don't like any of them, least of all Debbie.*
5 not in the least not at all ➤ *I'm not in the least interested in what she says.*

least² *adjective, pronoun*
the smallest amount or number ➤ *Buy the one that costs the least.* ➤ *Do it the way that takes the least time.*
OPPOSITE: **most**

leather /ˈleðəʳ/ *noun (no plural)*
the skin of dead animals used for making things such as shoes and bags ➤ *a leather belt*

leave¹ /liːv/ *verb (present participle leaving, past left /left/)*
1 to go away from a place or person ➤ *The train leaves in five minutes.* ➤ *She left Australia for Britain in 1963.* ➤ *He left his wife.*
2 to let a thing stay in a place ➤ *I left my bag in the office.*
LOOK AT: **forget**
3 to let things stay as they are ➤ *Leave the dishes – I'll wash them later.*
4 to give something to someone after your death ➤ *My aunt left me her house.*

L

5 leave someone or something alone
not to touch, move, worry, or annoy a
person or thing ▶ *Leave the dog
alone.* ▶ *Leave those cakes alone or
there won't be enough for tea.*
6 leave off to stop ▶ *Let's start from
where we left off yesterday.*
7 leave someone or something out to
fail to include a person or thing ▶ *I
left out a really important idea.*
▶ *They left me out of the team.*

leave² *noun (no plural)*
a period of time away from work
▶ *The soldiers had six weeks' leave.*

leaves /liːvz/
the plural of **leaf**

lecture¹ /'lektʃəʳ/ *noun*
a talk given to a group of people
about a particular subject ▶ *The
students have lectures every day.*

lecture² *verb*
to talk to a group of people about a
particular subject ▶ *She lectures on
Shakespeare at Edinburgh University.*

lecturer /'lektʃərəʳ/ *noun*
a person who teaches at a university
or college or who gives talks to a
group of people about a particular
subject ▶ *a chemistry lecturer*

led /led/
the PAST TENSE and PAST PARTICIPLE of the
verb **lead**

ledge /ledʒ/ *noun*
1 a narrow shelf, such as the one at
the bottom of a window
2 a narrow, flat piece on the side of a
rock or cliff

leek /liːk/ *noun*
a long, green and white vegetable
that tastes like onion

left¹ /left/
the PAST TENSE and PAST PARTICIPLE of the
verb **leave**

left² *noun (no plural)*
the opposite side to the hand that
most people write with ▶ *The school
is to the left of the church.*

OPPOSITE: **right**

left³ *adjective, adverb*
on or towards the left ▶ *Turn left at
the corner.*
OPPOSITE: **right**

left-hand /ˌleft 'hænd/ *adjective*
on the left side of something ▶ *The
house is on the left-hand side of the
street.*

left-handed /ˌleft 'hændɪd/ *adjective*
using your left hand more than your
right hand
OPPOSITE: **right-handed**

left luggage office /ˌleft 'lʌɡɪdʒ
ˌɒfɪs/ *noun*
a place at a station or an airport
where you can leave your case for a
period of time

leftover /'leftəʊvəʳ/ *adjective*
remaining after you have used what
you need ▶ *leftover food*

leftovers /'leftəʊvəz/ *plural noun*
food that has not been eaten during a
meal

left-wing /ˌleft 'wɪŋ/ *adjective*
supporting the political ideas of
groups such as Socialists and
Communists ▶ *left-wing voters*

leg /leɡ/ *noun*
1 one of the two parts of your body
that you use for walking ▶ *She broke
her leg skiing last year.*
2 one of the parts on which chairs,
tables, etc. stand ▶ *a chair with a
broken leg*

legal /'liːɡəl/ *adjective*
allowed by the law ▶ *Drinking alcohol
is legal in Britain (adverb: **legally**)*
OPPOSITE: **illegal**
SAME MEANING: **lawful**

legalize /'liːɡəlaɪz/ *verb (present
participle **legalizing**, past **legalized**)*
to change the law so that something
is made legal ▶ *They want the
government to legalize the drug.*

legend /'ledʒənd/ *noun*

1 a story about people who lived in the past, which may not be true
2 a very famous person ➤ *Elvis Presley was a legend in his lifetime.*

legendary /'ledʒəndəri/ *adjective*
very famous and admired ➤ *the legendary singer, Frank Sinatra*

leggings /'legɪŋz/ *plural noun*
a piece of women's clothing that fits closely around the legs ➤ *She wore a pair of red leggings.*

legible /'ledʒəbəl/ *adjective*
clear enough to read ➤ *legible writing*
OPPOSITE: **illegible**

legitimate /lɪ'dʒɪtɪmət/ *adjective*
1 not illegal ➤ *legitimate business activities*
2 fair and reasonable ➤ *a legitimate question*

leisure /'leʒəʳ/ *noun (no plural)*
the time when you are not at work and can do things that you enjoy ➤ *What do you do in your leisure time?*

leisure centre /'leʒə ˌsentəʳ/ *noun*
a place where people can go and do a large number of different sports

leisurely /'leʒəli/ *adjective*
done in a relaxed way because you do not have to hurry ➤ *a leisurely walk around the park*

lemon /'lemən/ *noun*
a yellow fruit with a sour taste, which grows on trees in hot places

lemonade /ˌlemə'neɪd/ *noun (no plural)*
a sweet drink made from lemons

lemon juice /'lemən ˌdʒuːs/ *noun (no plural)*
the liquid from lemons

lend /lend/ *verb (past lent* /lent/*)*
to let someone use or have something for a time, after which they must give it back ➤ *Can you lend me that book for a few days?*
LOOK AT: **borrow**

length /leŋθ/ *noun (no plural)*
the distance from one end of something to the other; how long something is ➤ *The room is 4 metres in length.*

lengthen /'leŋθən/ *verb*
to make something longer ➤ *to lengthen a dress*
OPPOSITE: **shorten**

lengthways /'leŋθweɪz/ *(also lengthwise* /-waɪz/*) adverb*
in the direction of the longest side ➤ *Cut the carrots lengthways.*

lengthy /'leŋθi/ *adjective (lengthier, lengthiest)*
too long ➤ *a lengthy speech*

lens /lenz/ *noun (plural lenses)*
one of the shaped pieces of glass used to bend light in an instrument for seeing things clearly, like a pair of glasses, a camera, or a microscope

lent /lent/
the PAST TENSE and PAST PARTICIPLE of the verb **lend**

Lent /lent/ *noun (no plural)*
the 40 days before Easter, when some Christians stop eating particular foods or doing other things which they enjoy

lentil /'lentəl/ *noun*
a round orange, green, or brown seed that can be cooked and eaten

leopard /'lepəd/ *noun*
a big cat with a spotted coat which lives in Africa or Asia

leotard /'liːətɑːd/ *noun*
a piece of women's clothing like a SWIMSUIT, used for dancing or exercising

lesbian /'lezbiən/ *noun*
a woman who is sexually attracted to other women ➤ *lesbian and gay rights*

less¹ /les/ *adverb*
1 not as; not so much ➤ *This one is less expensive.* ➤ *I definitely walk*

less since I've had the car. ➤ The next train was less crowded **than** the first one.

OPPOSITE: **more**

2 less and less gradually becoming smaller in amount or degree ➤ He comes here less and less. ➤ Our trips became less and less frequent.

OPPOSITE: **more and more**

less² adjective, pronoun
a smaller amount (of something) ➤ You ought to eat less salt. ➤ Most single parents earn £100 a week or less. ➤ She spends less **of** her time abroad now. ➤ I live less **than** a mile from here.

OPPOSITE: **more**

lessen /'lesən/ verb
1 to make something less ➤ The medicine will lessen the pain.
2 to become less ➤ The pain lessened.

lesson /'lesən/ noun
something you must learn; a time when you learn things in school ➤ We have four history lessons a week.

let /let/ verb (present participle **letting**, past **let**)
1 to allow ➤ My mother wouldn't let me go to the film. ➤ They won't let people in without a ticket.
2 to allow someone to use a house or some land in return for money ➤ They let their house to another family when they went away.
3 Let's a word used when you ask someone to do something with you ➤ Let's go down to the river and have a swim.
4 let go to stop holding something ➤ Hold the ladder for me and don't let go.
5 let someone know to tell someone about something ➤ Let me know what time you'll be arriving.
6 let someone down to cause someone to be disappointed when you do not do what you should do

➤ You've let us down by not working for your exam.

letdown /'letdaʊn/ noun
something that disappoints you as it is not as good as you expected ➤ That film was a real letdown.

lethal /'liːθəl/ adjective
able to kill you ➤ a lethal dose of heroin

letter /'letər/ noun
1 one of the signs we use to write words ➤ A, B, C, and D are the first four letters in the alphabet.
2 a written message sent to someone by post ➤ I got a letter from my dad this morning.

LOOK AT: **yours**

letterbox /'letəbɒks/ noun (plural **letterboxes**)
1 a box in the street or post office in which letters are put when you are sending them

SAME MEANING: **postbox**

2 a hole or box in the front of a building, into which letters are delivered

lettuce /'letɪs/ noun
a vegetable with large, soft, green leaves which are eaten without being cooked

level¹ /'levəl/ adjective
1 flat; without higher or lower places ➤ We need a level piece of ground to plant the tree.
2 at the same height or position as something else ➤ He bent down so that his face was level with the little boy's (=the little boy's face).

level² noun
a place or position of a particular height ➤ The house was built on two levels.

level³ verb (present participle **levelling**, past **levelled**)
to make something flat ➤ They levelled the piece of ground so that we could play football on it.

L

level crossing /ˌlevəl ˈkrɒsɪŋ/ *noun*
a place where a railway crosses a road, and traffic has to wait for trains to pass

level-headed /ˌlevəl ˈhedɪd/ *adjective*
calm and sensible ► He's a firm and level-headed leader.

lever¹ /ˈliːvəʳ/ *noun*
1 a long bar for lifting or moving heavy things
2 a handle on a machine, which you push or pull to work the machine

lever² *verb*
to move something with a lever ► I levered the lid off the box with a stick.

liability /ˌlaɪəˈbɪlɪti/ *noun (no plural)*
legal responsibility for something
► We accept no liability for cars that are left here overnight.

liable /ˈlaɪəbəl/ *adjective*
likely ► He's liable to get angry if people keep him waiting.

liar /ˈlaɪəʳ/ *noun*
someone who tells lies

liberal /ˈlɪbərəl/ *adjective*
willing to understand and accept the different behaviour or ideas of other people

liberate /ˈlɪbəreɪt/ *verb (present participle liberating, past liberated)*
to free someone from a situation or place that they could not get out of
► US soldiers liberated the prisoners.

liberation /ˌlɪbəˈreɪʃən/ *noun (no plural)*
the act of freeing people from a situation or place that they could not get out of ► the black liberation movement

liberty /ˈlɪbəti/ *noun (no plural)*
the state in which you are free and do not have to do what other people order ► They fought for their liberty.

librarian /laɪˈbreərɪən/ *noun*
a person who works in a library

library /ˈlaɪbrəri/ *noun (plural libraries)*
a collection of books that people can borrow, or a room or building in which they are kept ► There's a very good library in the next town.

lice /laɪs/
the plural of **louse**

licence /ˈlaɪsəns/ *noun*
a piece of paper showing that the law allows you to do something, like drive a car ► The policeman asked to see my driving licence.

license /ˈlaɪsəns/ *verb (present participle licensing, past licensed)*
to give someone a licence ► a licensed restaurant ► a hall licensed for music

lick /lɪk/ *verb*
to touch something with your tongue
► She licked the stamps and stuck them on the letter.

lid /lɪd/ *noun*
a cover for a box, pan, or other container, which can be taken off
SAME MEANING: **top**

lie¹ /laɪ/ *verb (present participle lying, past tense lay /leɪ/, past participle lain /leɪn/)*
to have your body flat on something or to get into this position ► He was lying in the shade of the tree. ► She lay down on her bed.
LOOK AT: **lay**

lie² *verb (present participle lying, past lied)*
to say things that are not true ► She lied to him **about** her age.
LOOK AT: **lay**

lie³ *noun (plural lies)*
something said which is not true
► Why did he tell her a lie?

lieutenant /lefˈtenənt/ *noun*
an officer of low rank in the army or the navy

L

life /laɪf/ noun
1 (no plural) the ability that we have to grow and feel ➤ a baby's first moments of life
2 (plural **lives** /laɪvz/) the time during which someone is alive ➤ She had lived in the same village all her life.
3 (plural **lives**) the way in which someone lives or spends their time ➤ He leads a happy life in the country.
4 (no plural) activity and cheerfulness ➤ She was four years old and full of life.

lifeboat /'laɪfbəʊt/ noun
a boat used for saving people who are in danger at sea

lifeguard /'laɪfɡɑːd/ noun
a person whose job is to help swimmers who are in danger at the beach or at a swimming pool

life jacket /'laɪf ˌdʒækɪt/ noun
a special piece of clothing that you wear round your chest to make you float in water

lifelike /'laɪflaɪk/ adjective
looking very much like a real person or thing ➤ The statue is quite lifelike.

lifelong /'laɪflɒŋ/ adjective
continuing all through your life ➤ She was my mother's lifelong friend.

life-size /'laɪf saɪz/ adjective
(used about a picture or model) being the same size as the real thing ➤ She painted a life-size picture of her dog.

lifestyle /'laɪfstaɪl/ noun
the way in which you live, including the conditions you live in, the things you own, and the things you do ➤ a healthy lifestyle

lifetime /'laɪftaɪm/ noun
the time for which someone is alive ➤ In my father's lifetime, there have been many changes in the village.

lift¹ /lɪft/ verb
to pick something up ➤ Can you lift the other end of the table? ➤ "Lift me up so I can see over the fence," said the little girl.

lift² noun
1 a machine that carries people or things between the floors of a tall building
2 a free ride in a vehicle ➤ He drives to the station, and he sometimes gives me a lift.

lift-off /'lɪft ɒf/ noun
the moment when a space vehicle rises up into the air at the beginning of its journey

light¹ /laɪt/ noun
1 (no plural) the force from the sun that allows our eyes to see ➤ There's more light near the window.
2 a thing that gives out light ➤ Turn off the lights when you go to bed.

light² adjective
1 not dark in colour; pale ➤ a light blue shirt
OPPOSITE: **dark**
2 easy to lift; not heavy ➤ The basket is very light – I can easily carry it myself.
3 not great in amount ➤ The traffic was very light this evening.
OPPOSITE (**2** and **3**): **heavy**

light³ verb (past **lit** /lɪt/ or **lighted**)
to make a thing like a lamp, fire, or cigarette burn or give out light ➤ Will you light the fire for me?

light bulb /'laɪt bʌlb/ (also **bulb**) noun
the glass part of an electric lamp that gives out light

lighten /'laɪtn/ verb
to make something light or lighter in weight or colour

lighter /'laɪtəʳ/ noun
an instrument for lighting a cigarette

lighthouse /'laɪthaʊs/ noun (plural **lighthouses** /-haʊzɪz/)
a tall building with a powerful flashing light that guides ships or warns them of dangerous rocks

L

Picture Dictionary

first floor

skyscraper

second floor

block of flats

ground floor

balcony

fire escape

terraced houses

roof

bungalow

semi-detached house

satellite dish

wall

chimney

patio

clothesline

phone box

basement

detached house

streetlight

attic

window

window sill

lamp-post

garage

shutter

garden

letter box

drive

gate

fence

pavement

drain

road

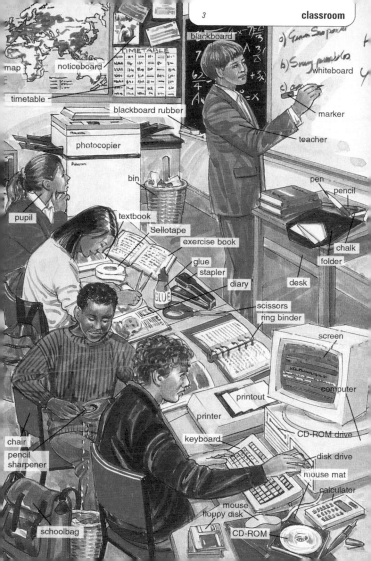

map

noticeboard

timetable

blackboard

whiteboard

blackboard rubber

marker

teacher

photocopier

bin

pen

pencil

pupil

textbook

Sellotape

exercise book

glue

stapler

diary

chalk

folder

desk

scissors

ring binder

screen

computer

printout

printer

CD-ROM drive

chair

pencil sharpener

keyboard

disk drive

mouse mat

calculator

mouse

floppy disk

CD-ROM

schoolbag

yellow

white

mauve

green

navy

red

black

blue

khaki

orange

purple

pink

maroon

tartan

beige

brown

striped

flowery

checked

spotted / spotty

plain

patterned

grey

peak/summit

cloud

mountain

valley

forest

cave

stream

boulder

grass

waterfall

track

island

lake

hill

hedge

bridge

field

cliff

coast

sea

cottage

river

wave

wood

path

beach

sand

pebble

rock

dune

bush

stone

Global warming

Air pollution stops heat leaving the atmosphere. The gradual warming of the Earth is called global warming.

Travel

Cars cause pollution and congestion. Other ways of travelling are less harmful to the environment.

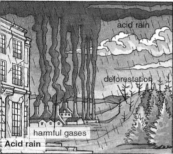

Acid rain

Acid rain is rain that contains acid from industrial pollution. It is harmful to trees and buildings.

Energy

Energy that comes from wind, water or solar power is better for the environment.

Waste

Harmful chemicals from factories and waste from houses pollute fields and rivers.

Recycling

Some things like paper, plastic, cans and glass can be collected and used again. This is called recycling.

HEIGHT

small

short

tall

medium height

BUILD slim   overweight   petite   plump   thin   well-built

long curly hair

ponytail

short curly hair

short hair

stubble

straight dark hair — parting

bobbed hair

fringe

receding hair

spiky hair

plait

white hair

shoulder length wavy hair

moustache

bald

beard

HAIR

sad

happy

surprised

bored

tired

confused/puzzled

embarrassed

shy

worried

angry

furious

scared/frightened

bread

cake

slice

lump

butter

bunch

grapes

bananas

ham

pinch

hunk

meat

cheese

salt

chunk

sliver

orange

segment

biscuits

sugar

bar

cube

square

chocolate

crumb

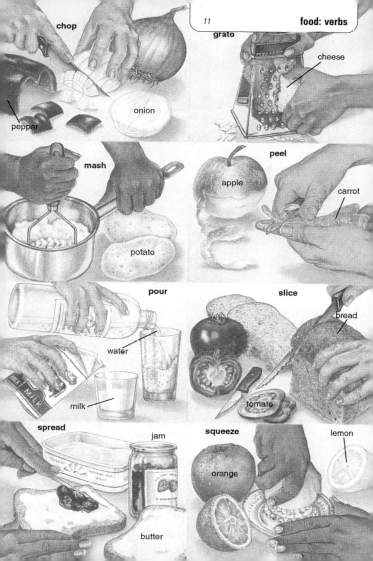

chop

grate

cheese

pepper

onion

mash

peel

apple

carrot

potato

pour

slice

bread

water

milk

tomato

spread

jam

squeeze

lemon

orange

butter

ring

tick

crash

squeak

creak

bang

splash

buzz

rustle

rattle

click

crunch

sizzle

crackle

fizz

hiss

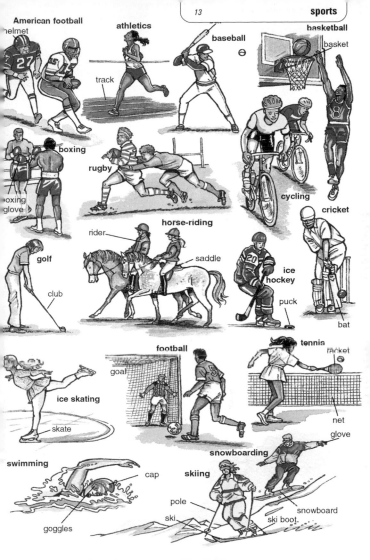

American football
helmet

athletics
track

baseball

basketball
basket

boxing
boxing glove

rugby

cycling

cricket

golf
club

horse-riding
rider
saddle

ice hockey
puck

bat

ice skating
skate

football
goal

tennis
racket
net

glove

swimming
cap
goggles

snowboarding

skiing
pole
ski

snowboard
ski boot

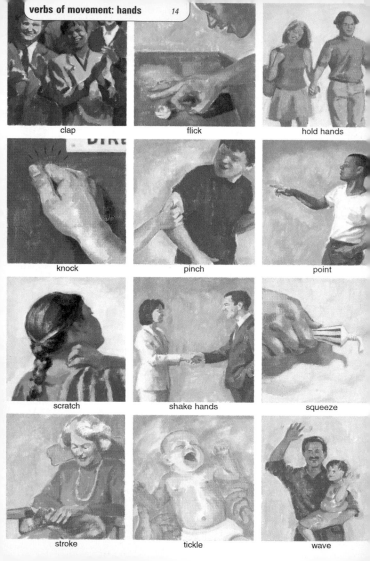

clap

flick

hold hands

knock

pinch

point

scratch

shake hands

squeeze

stroke

tickle

wave

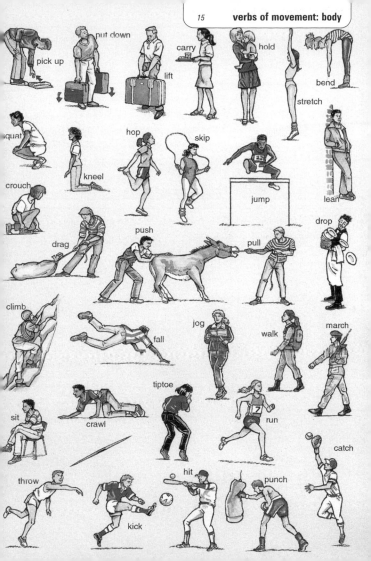

pick up

put down

lift

carry

hold

bend

stretch

squat

kneel

hop

skip

jump

lean

crouch

drag

push

pull

drop

climb

fall

jog

walk

march

sit

crawl

tiptoe

run

catch

throw

kick

hit

punch

AIR

helicopter · control tower · hanga[r] · terminal · airport · runway · wing · plane/aeroplane

LAND

carriage · engine · crossroads · caravan · lorry · train · roundabou[t] · platform · railway station · car · van · bus stop · traffic lights · railway · bicycle · bus · taxi/cab · level crossing · motorbike/motorcycle · moped

SEA

ship · lighthouse · yacht · pier · harbou[r] · ferry · hovercraft · speedboat · rowing boat

lighting /'laɪtɪŋ/ *noun (no plural)*
the system that gives light to a place
▶ *We need better lighting in this office.*

lightly /'laɪtli/ *adverb*
with only a small amount of weight or force ▶ *She touched me lightly on the arm.*

lightning /'laɪtnɪŋ/ *noun (no plural)*
a bright flash of light in the sky, followed by thunder, that happens during a storm

likable *(also likeable)* /'laɪkəbəl/ *adjective*
(used about a person) friendly and easy to like

like¹ /laɪk/ *verb (present participle liking, past liked)*
to find someone or something pleasant ▶ *I like bananas.* ▶ *Do you like dancing?* ▶ *I've never liked her brother.* ▶ *I didn't like the film very much.*
OPPOSITE: **dislike**

like² *preposition*
1 in the same way as ▶ *I wish I could sing like her.*
2 with the same qualities as ▶ *Mary's dress is red, like mine.*
OPPOSITE (**2**): **unlike**

likeable /'laɪkəbəl/ *adjective*
another word for **likable**

likelihood /'laɪklihʊd/ *noun (no plural)*
the chance that something might happen ▶ *What's the likelihood of you passing your exams?*

likely /'laɪkli/ *adjective*
1 expected ▶ *The train is likely to be late.*
2 suitable ▶ *She is the most likely girl to win the prize.*
OPPOSITE (**1** and **2**): **unlikely**

likeness /'laɪknəs/ *noun (plural likenesses)*
a way in which two people look the

same ▶ *There is a family likeness between the two brothers.*

likewise /'laɪkwaɪz/ *adverb*
in the same way; the same; also ▶ *We respect his wishes, and we hope you will do likewise.*

liking /'laɪkɪŋ/ *noun*
a fondness for something ▶ *a liking for fast cars*

lily /'lɪli/ *noun (plural lilies)*
a plant with large white or coloured flowers

limb /lɪm/ *noun*
an arm or a leg

lime /laɪm/ *noun*
1 *(no plural)* a white substance that farmers use to improve the soil
2 a green fruit with a sour taste from a tree of the orange family, and which grows in hot places

limelight /'laɪmlaɪt/ *noun*
be in the limelight to have the attention of a lot of people ▶ *Sanchez loves being in the limelight.*

limit¹ /'lɪmɪt/ *noun*
1 the point or place which is as far as you can go or are allowed to go; a greatest amount or furthest distance ▶ *There is a limit to the amount of money I can afford.* ▶ *a 30 mile an hour speed limit in towns*
2 the edge of an area of ground ▶ *The fence shows the limit of the field.*

limit² *verb*
to stop a thing from going past a point or level ▶ *The government limits the amount of money you can take out of the country.* ▶ *a limited knowledge of science (=not very great)*

limitations /ˌlɪmɪˈteɪʃənz/ *plural noun*
the limits of what someone or something is able to do ▶ *You have to understand the limitations of the software.*

L

limited /'lɪmɪtɪd/ adjective
small in amount or number ➤ There
are only a limited number of tickets.
OPPOSITE: **unlimited**

limousine /'lɪməziːn/ noun
a big, expensive car, usually driven by
a CHAUFFEUR ➤ He arrived at the party
in a black limousine.

limp¹ /lɪmp/ adjective
not firm or stiff ➤ a few limp lettuce
leaves

limp² verb
to walk badly because one leg or foot
has been hurt ➤ He limped off the
football field.

limp³ noun
a way of walking that you have when
one leg or foot is hurt ➤ to walk with
a limp

line¹ /laɪn/ noun
1 a long and very narrow mark ➤ Draw
a straight line from A to B.
2 a group of people or things one
after the other or beside each other;
a row ➤ a line of people outside the
cinema
3 a long piece of string or rope ➤ Can
you fetch the clothes off the washing
line?

line² verb (present participle **lining**,
past **lined**)
1 to stand in a line ➤ People lined the
streets to see the procession go past.
➤ Line up please, children!
2 to cover the inside, sides, or edges
of something ➤ The box was lined
with soft paper to protect the things
inside.

lined /laɪnd/ adjective
1 (used about skirts, coats, etc.)
having a piece of material covering
the inside ➤ a fur-lined coat
2 (used about paper) having straight
lines printed on it

linen /'lɪnɪn/ noun
(no plural)
1 a kind of cloth

2 things like sheets and coverings for
tables ➤ bed linen

linger /'lɪŋgəʳ/ verb
to stay somewhere for a long time
➤ The smell of cigarettes lingered in
the room.

linguistic /lɪŋ'gwɪstɪk/ adjective
relating to language and how well
someone speaks or understands it
➤ The children had different linguistic
abilities.

lining /'laɪnɪŋ/ noun
the cloth covering the inside of a
piece of clothing ➤ The lining of my
coat is torn.

link¹ /lɪŋk/ noun
1 something which connects two
other things or places ➤ There's a
new rail link **between** the two
towns.
2 one ring of a chain

link² verb
to join two things or places together
➤ The two towns are linked by a
railway.

lion /'laɪən/ noun
a dangerous wild animal like a big
cat, which lives in Africa

lioness /'laɪənes/ noun (plural
lionesses)
a female lion

lip /lɪp/ noun
one of the edges of your mouth ➤ He
kissed her on the lips.

lipstick /'lɪpstɪk/ noun (no plural)
colour, often red or pink, that women
sometimes put on their lips ➤ a new
lipstick ➤ Does she use lipstick?

liquid¹ /'lɪkwɪd/ noun
a thing like water or milk that can be
poured

liquid² adjective
in the form of a liquid ➤ liquid oxygen

list¹ /lɪst/ noun
a lot of names, or things you must
do, written down one under another

➤ *I must make a list of things to pack.*
➤ *a shopping list*

list² *verb*
to write or say things as a list ➤ *I listed the things I wanted to buy.*

listen /'lɪsən/ *verb*
to try to hear something; to take notice of what someone is saying ➤ *Listen. What's that noise?* ➤ *Are you listening to what I'm saying?*

> Remember to use **to** after **listen**: *Listen to me!* ➤ *We were listening to the radio.*

listener /'lɪsənəʳ/ *noun*
1 a person who listens to someone or something, especially to the radio ➤ *Most of the radio station's listeners are young people.*
2 a good listener a person who listens in a sympathetic way to other people

lit /lɪt/
the PAST TENSE and PAST PARTICIPLE of the verb **light**

literally /'lɪtərəli/ *adverb*
1 according to the basic or original meaning of a word or expression ➤ *The word "melodrama" literally means "a play with music".*
2 used to emphasize that what you are saying is true, even if it seems unlikely ➤ *I was literally shaking with fear.*

literary /'lɪtərəri/ *adjective*
of or about literature ➤ *She won a literary prize for her first book.*

literature /'lɪtərətʃəʳ/ *noun (no plural)*
good books and writing, including plays and poetry ➤ *She's a specialist in French literature.* ➤ *We're doing Shakespeare in English Literature.*

litre /'liːtəʳ/ *noun*
a measure of liquid ➤ *The bottle holds a litre of beer.* ➤ *A litre is equal to about 1¾ pints.*

litter /'lɪtəʳ/ *noun (no plural)*
waste paper and other things lying on the ground ➤ *There was litter all over the street.*
COMPARE: **rubbish**

litter bin /'lɪtə bɪn/ *noun*
a large container in a public place for people to put their waste paper in

little¹ /'lɪtl/ *adjective*
1 small ➤ *It's only a little house.* ➤ *The girl was carrying a little dog.*
OPPOSITE: **big**
2 (used about time and distance) short ➤ *I'll wait a little while and call again.* ➤ *She walked a little way down the road with me.*

little² *noun, pronoun, adverb* (**less** /les/, **least** /liːst/)
1 a very small amount which is sometimes not enough ➤ *You eat very little, don't you?* ➤ *I go out very little* (=not often).
2 a little some, but not much ➤ *There isn't much milk, but we only need a little for the tea.* ➤ *Add a little salt to the sauce.* ➤ *I feel a little better.*

live¹ /lɪv/ *verb (present participle living, past lived)*
1 to have life; not to be dead
2 to have your home in a place ➤ *I live in a small town by the sea.*
3 live on something to keep alive by eating something or by earning some money ➤ *Cows live on grass.* ➤ *I can live on very little money.*

live² /laɪv/ *adjective*
1 not dead ➤ *a live animal*
2 (used about music) not recorded; performed by musicians who are present ➤ *live music tonight* ➤ *a live performance*

livelihood /'laɪvlɪhʊd/ *noun*
the job that you do to earn money in order to live ➤ *Painting is my livelihood.*

lively /'laɪvli/ *adjective* (**livelier, liveliest**)

L

full of life ► *a lively person* ► *a lively conversation*

liven /'laɪvən/ *verb*
liven something up to make something more interesting or exciting ► *We need some music to liven the party up.*

liver /'lɪvəʳ/ *noun*
a large part inside your body which cleans your blood

lives /laɪvz/
the plural of **life**

livid /'lɪvɪd/ *adjective*
very angry ► *My mother was livid when she saw the mess.*

living¹ /'lɪvɪŋ/ *adjective*
alive ► *She has no living relatives*
OPPOSITE: **dead**

living² *noun*
1 (*no plural*) the way in which you earn money ► *"What does he do for a living?" "He's a builder."*
2 the living *plural noun* people who are alive

living room /'lɪvɪŋ rʊm/ *noun*
the main room in a house, in which people sit and do things together

lizard /'lɪzəd/ *noun*
an animal that has four short legs and a skin like a snake

'll /l/ *verb*
1 will ► *She'll do it tomorrow.*
2 shall ► *We'll see you soon.*

load¹ /ləʊd/ *noun*
things that are carried, especially by a train, lorry, or ship ► *The lorry was carrying a load of bananas.*

load² *verb*
1 to put things onto a lorry, a ship, or some other vehicle ► *We loaded the lorry with bananas.*
2 to put bullets in a gun so that they can be fired out of it
OPPOSITE (**1** and **2**): **unload**

loaded /'ləʊdɪd/ *adjective*
1 containing bullets or film ► *Is the camera loaded?*
2 loaded with something containing a lot of something ► *The shelves were loaded with trophies.*
3 very rich ► *His grandmother's loaded.*

loaf /ləʊf/ *noun (plural loaves /ləʊvz/)*
a large piece of bread that can be cut into smaller pieces

loan¹ /ləʊn/ *noun*
a thing, especially money, lent to another person ► *I asked the bank for a loan.*

loan² *verb*
to lend someone something, especially money

loathe /ləʊð/ *verb (present participle loathing, past loathed)*
to hate ► *I loathe washing dishes.*

loaves /ləʊvz/
the plural of **loaf**

lobby /'lɒbi/ *noun (plural lobbies)*
a large room inside the entrance of a building ► *Wait for me in the hotel lobby.*

lobster /'lɒbstəʳ/ *noun*
a sea animal that people eat, with a shell, a tail, and ten legs

local /'ləʊkəl/ *adjective*
in the area near a place; near where you live ► *My children go to the local school.*

locate /ləʊ'keɪt/ *verb (present participle locating, past located)*
1 to find the exact position of something ► *We need to locate the gas pipe.*
2 be located in/on/at, etc. to be in a particular place or position ► *The engine is located in the front of the car.*

location /ləʊ'keɪʃən/ *noun*
a particular place or position ► *The map shows the location of the church.*

lock¹ /lɒk/ *noun*
an instrument for fastening things like doors, gates, or drawers, that can only be opened or closed with the right key

lock² *verb*
1 to close a lock with a key ▸ *Did you remember to lock the door?* ▸ *My father accidentally locked me out of the house* (=he locked the door so that I could not get back into the house).
2 lock up to make a building safe by closing all the doors with keys ▸ *Don't forget to lock up when you go out.*

locker /'lɒkəʳ/ *noun*
a small cupboard, often with a lock, for keeping things in ▸ *At the station, there were lockers where people could leave suitcases.*

locust /'ləʊkəst/ *noun*
an insect that travels in a large group in hot countries, eating all the plants

lodge /lɒdʒ/ *verb (present participle lodging, past lodged)*
to pay to live in a room in someone else's house

lodger /'lɒdʒəʳ/ *noun*
someone who pays to live in a room in someone else's house

lodgings /'lɒdʒɪŋz/ *plural noun*
a room in someone else's house which you pay to live in

loft /lɒft/ *noun*
a room or space at the top of a house inside the roof, used for storing things
SAME MEANING: **attic**

log¹ /lɒg/ *noun*
a large piece of wood from a tree ▸ *Put another log on the fire.*

log² *verb (present participle logging, past logged)*
1 log on to do the things needed to start using a computer

2 log off to do the things needed to stop using a computer

logic /'lɒdʒɪk/ *noun (no plural)*
a sensible way of thinking ▸ *There does not seem to be any logic in what they are planning to do.*

logical /'lɒdʒɪkəl/ *adjective*
reasonable and sensible ▸ *There's no logical reason for you to be jealous.* (adverb: **logically**)
OPPOSITE: **illogical**

logo /'ləʊgəʊ/ *noun*
a design that is the official sign of a company or an organization and is put on their products, letters, etc.

lollipop /'lɒlɪpɒp/ *noun*
a sweet made from boiled sugar or frozen juice on the end of a stick

lonely /'ləʊnlɪ/ *adjective (lonelier, loneliest)*
unhappy because you are alone ▸ *He was lonely without his wife.*

loner /'ləʊnəʳ/ *noun*
a person who prefers to be alone

long¹ /lɒŋ/ *adjective*
measuring a great distance or time from one end to the other ▸ *Julie has got long hair.* ▸ *It's a long way to school from here.* ▸ *How long does it take you to walk home?*

long² *adverb*
1 for a long time ▸ *Have you been waiting long?*
2 at a distant time ▸ *He died long ago.* ▸ *Not long* (=a short time) *after that, he got married.*
3 as long as, so long as on condition that ▸ *You can go out, as long as you promise to be back before 9 o'clock.*

long³ *verb*
to want something very much ▸ *I longed for a holiday.* ▸ *She longed to go home.*

long-distance /ˌlɒŋ 'dɪstəns/ *adjective*
between places that are a long way from each other ▸ *a long-distance telephone call*

L

longing /ˈlɒŋɪŋ/ *noun*
a strong feeling of wanting something

longitude /ˈlɒndʒɪtjuːd/ *noun (no plural)*
a position on the Earth shown on maps by lines (lines of longitude) that go from north to south
COMPARE: **latitude**

long jump /ˈlɒŋ dʒʌmp/ *noun*
a sport in which you jump as far as possible ▶ *She's quite good at the long jump.*

longsighted /ˌlɒŋˈsaɪtɪd/ *adjective*
able to see or read things clearly only when they are far from your eyes
OPPOSITE: **shortsighted**

long-standing /ˌlɒŋ ˈstændɪŋ/ *adjective*
having continued or existed for a long time ▶ *a long-standing agreement between the two countries*

long-term /ˌlɒŋ ˈtɜːm/ *adjective*
continuing for a long period of time ▶ *the long-term effects of smoking*
OPPOSITE: **short-term**

loo /luː/ *noun*
a TOILET
SAME MEANING: **lavatory**

look¹ /lʊk/ *verb*
1 to turn your eyes towards something so that you can see it ▶ *She looked **at** me angrily.* ▶ *He was sitting looking out of the window.*
LOOK AT: **watch**
2 to seem to be ▶ *That dog looks dangerous.*
3 **Look!** a word you use when you want someone to notice something ▶ *Look! I don't want to argue with you, but I think you've made a mistake.*
4 **look as if, look like** to seem probable ▶ *It looks as if we're going to miss the plane.*
5 **What does ... look like?** a question people use when they are asking someone to describe the appearance of someone or something ▶ *"What does your sister look like?" "She's tall and she's got dark hair."*
6 **look after someone or something** to take care of someone or something ▶ *She looked after my dog while I was on holiday.*
7 **look for someone or something** to try to find someone or something ▶ *I'm looking for my key.*
8 **look forward to something** to feel happy because you are going to do something that you will enjoy ▶ *We're looking forward to the party.* ▶ *I'm looking forward to meeting you.*
9 **look something up** to find a piece of information in a book ▶ *Did you look that word up in the dictionary?*

look² *noun*
1 an act of looking at something ▶ *Have a look **at** this book.*
2 the way something appears ▶ *I don't like the look **of** the weather* (=I think it is bad).
3 the expression on someone's face ▶ *an angry look*
4 **looks** *plural noun* the way a person appears ▶ *He was always afraid of losing his looks.*

lookout /ˈlʊkaʊt/ *noun*
be on the lookout for something to pay attention to things around you because you hope to see or find something ▶ *I'm always on the lookout for good, cheap clothes.*

loom /luːm/ *noun*
a machine for weaving cloth

loop /luːp/ *noun*
a ring made by something like rope or string crossing itself ▶ *Make a loop, then put the end of the rope through it.*

loophole /ˈluːphəʊl/ *noun*
a small mistake in a law that makes it possible to legally avoid doing what the law says ▶ *Because of a loophole in the law, he pays no tax.*

L

loose /luːs/ *adjective*
1 not fitting tightly ▶ *loose trousers*
2 not firmly fixed ▶ *The screw's loose.*
OPPOSITE (**1** and **2**): **tight**
3 free from control ▶ *The dog's loose.*

loosen /ˈluːsən/ *verb*
to make something looser ▶ *I've eaten too much – I shall have to loosen my belt.*
OPPOSITE: **tighten**

loot¹ /luːt/ *verb*
to steal things during a war or RIOT ▶ *Shops were looted and burned down.*

loot² *noun (no plural)*
things that have been stolen

lop-sided /ˌlɒpˈsaɪdɪd/ *adjective*
having one side that is heavier or lower than the other ▶ *a lop-sided grin*

lord /lɔːd/ *noun*
1 a title for a nobleman, used before his name
2 the Lord God or Jesus Christ

lorry /ˈlɒrɪ/ *noun (plural lorries)*
a large vehicle for carrying heavy goods on the road
SAME MEANING: **truck**

lose /luːz/ *verb (present participle losing, past lost /lɒst/)*
1 not to have something any more, and not to know where it is ▶ *I think I've lost my watch.*
OPPOSITE: **find**
2 not to do well; not to win ▶ *Our team lost the football match.*
OPPOSITE: **win**
3 lose your temper to become angry
4 lose your way to go in the wrong direction and not know where you are when you are making a journey

loser /ˈluːzəʳ/ *noun*
someone who loses

loss /lɒs/ *noun (plural losses)*
1 the act of losing something, or something that you have lost ▶ *The*

loss of their home was a great shock. ▶ *the loss of her sight*
2 income which is less than what you have spent ▶ *The company made a big loss this year.*

lost¹ /lɒst/
the PAST TENSE and PAST PARTICIPLE of the verb **lose**

lost² *adjective*
not knowing where you are ▶ *He went for a walk and got lost.*

lost property /ˌlɒst ˈprɒpətɪ/ *noun (no plural)*
things that people have lost ▶ *We went to the lost property office at the station.*

lot /lɒt/ *noun*
a large amount or number ▶ *There was a lot of mud on the ground.* ▶ *I picked a lot of flowers.*
COMPARE: **lots**
LOOK AT: **much**

lotion /ˈləʊʃən/ *noun*
a liquid for putting on your skin or on wounds ▶ *suntan lotion*

lots /lɒts/ *plural noun*
a large amount or number ▶ *There was lots of mud on the ground.* ▶ *I picked lots of flowers.*
COMPARE: **lot**
LOOK AT: **much**

lottery /ˈlɒtərɪ/ *noun (plural lotteries)*
a competition in which you can win a prize if you have a ticket with the right number

lotus /ˈləʊtəs/ *noun (plural lotuses)*
a water plant of Asia with white or pink flowers and round leaves on tall stems

loud /laʊd/ *adjective*
making a lot of noise ▶ *The radio's rather loud – can you turn it down?* ▶ *loud music* ▶ *a loud voice (adverb: loudly)*
OPPOSITE: **quiet**

L

loudspeaker /laʊd'spiːkəʳ/ *noun*
something that makes your voice
sound louder ➤ *The police called to
him through a loudspeaker.*

lounge /laʊndʒ/ *noun*
a room in a house or hotel, with
comfortable chairs

louse /laʊs/ *noun (plural lice /laɪs/)*
a small insect that lives on the skin
and in the hair of people and animals

lousy /'laʊzi/ *adjective (lousier,
lousiest)*
bad ➤ *What a lousy day I've had!*

lovable /'lʌvəbəl/ *adjective*
so nice as to be loved very much
➤ *a lovable child*

love¹ /lʌv/ *verb (present participle
loving, past loved)*
1 to have a very strong, warm feeling
for someone ➤ *the first boy I ever loved*
2 to like something very much
➤ *Maria loves reading.*
OPPOSITE **(1 and 2): hate**

love² *noun (no plural)*
1 a strong, warm feeling of liking
someone or something very much
➤ *her love for her husband* ➤ *a great
love of music*
OPPOSITE: **hatred**
2 Love a word used at the end of a
letter to someone you love, a friend,
or someone in your close family
3 fall in love to begin to love
someone ➤ *He fell in love with a
dancer.*

love affair /'lʌv əˌfeəʳ/ *noun*
an experience of love, often sexual
love, between two people who are
not married to each other

lovely /'lʌvli/ *adjective (lovelier,
loveliest)*
very much liked; very beautiful ➤ *a
lovely, cool drink* ➤ *You look lovely in
that new shirt.*

lover /'lʌvəʳ/ *noun*
1 a person who you have sex with
outside marriage

2 a person who enjoys something
➤ *an art lover*

loving /'lʌvɪŋ/ *adjective*
showing that you love someone ➤ *He
gave her a loving kiss. (adverb:
lovingly)*

low /ləʊ/ *adjective*
1 near the ground; not high ➤ *a low
fence*
2 small; smaller than usual ➤ *low
temperatures* ➤ *low prices*
3 not loud; not high in sound ➤ *a low
voice*
OPPOSITE **(1, 2, and 3): high**

lower /'ləʊəʳ/ *verb*
to make a thing nearer the ground or
less high or loud ➤ *They lowered the
load to the ground.* ➤ *Can you lower
your voice, please?*
OPPOSITE: **raise**

low tide /ˌləʊ ˈtaɪd/ *noun*
the time when the sea is very low and
far from the shore
OPPOSITE: **high tide**

loyal /'lɔɪəl/ *adjective*
faithful ➤ *a loyal supporter of the
local football club* ➤ *loyal to your
country*
OPPOSITE: **disloyal**

loyalty /'lɔɪəlti/ *noun (no plural)*
faithfulness ➤ *his loyalty to his
friends*
OPPOSITE: **disloyalty**

LP /ˌel ˈpiː/ *noun*
a record which plays for about 20
minutes on each side

Ltd
a short way of writing the word
limited; written after a name to tell
you that it is a business company
➤ *F. Jones and Company Ltd*

luck /lʌk/ *noun (no plural)*
the good and bad things that happen
to you by chance ➤ *It was good luck
that I met you here – I didn't expect
to see you.*

luckily /'lʌkɪlɪ/ adverb
used to say that you are glad that
something happened or did not
happen ▶ Luckily, it didn't rain all day.

lucky /'lʌkɪ/ adjective (**luckier,
luckiest**)
having or bringing good luck ▶ It was
lucky that I met you here. ▶ Some
people think that black cats are lucky
(=bring good luck).
OPPOSITE: **unlucky**

ludicrous /'lu:dɪkrəs/ adjective
stupid, wrong, and unreasonable
▶ That's a ludicrous idea.

luggage /'lʌgɪdʒ/ noun (no plural)
the bags, containers, and other
things you take with you when you
travel
SAME MEANING: **baggage**

lukewarm /ˌlu:k'wɔːm/ adjective
not very warm but not cold
▶ lukewarm water

lull /lʌl/ noun
a short period when there is less
activity or noise than usual ▶ a lull in
the conversation

lullaby /'lʌləbaɪ/ noun (plural
lullabies)
a song that you sing to babies to
make them sleep

lumber /'lʌmbəʳ/ verb
to give someone something to do
when they do not want to do it ▶ I got
lumbered **with** the job of cleaning the
floor.

luminous /'lu:mɪnəs/ adjective
able to shine in the dark ▶ The clock
has luminous hands.

lump /lʌmp/ noun
1 a hard piece of something, without
a special shape ▶ a lump **of** rock
2 a swelling on a person's body ▶ I've
got a lump on my head where I hit it
against the door.

lumpy /'lʌmpɪ/ adjective (**lumpier,
lumpiest**)
full of lumps, usually when you do
not want them ▶ a lumpy bed

lunar /'lu:nəʳ/ adjective
of or about the moon ▶ the lunar
surface

lunatic /'lu:nətɪk/ noun
a mad person ▶ She must be a lunatic
to drive her car so fast.

lunch /lʌntʃ/ noun (plural **lunches**)
the meal that you eat in the middle of
the day
COMPARE: **dinner, tea**

lunch hour /'lʌntʃ ˌaʊəʳ/ noun
the break for lunch between the
morning's and the afternoon's work
▶ I do my shopping in my lunch hour.

lunchtime /'lʌntʃtaɪm/ noun (no
plural)
the time at which you have lunch

lung /lʌŋ/ noun
one of the two parts inside your chest
with which you breathe

lurch /lɜːtʃ/ verb
to move in an unsteady or
uncontrolled way ▶ The car lurched
forward.

lure /lʊəʳ/ verb (present participle
luring, past **lured**)
to persuade someone to do
something by making it seem
attractive or exciting ▶ He lured her
into his home by pretending to be an
artist.

lurk /lɜːk/ verb
to wait in hiding, especially for some
bad purpose ▶ There's someone
lurking behind that bush.

lust /lʌst/ noun (no plural)
a very strong sexual feeling towards
someone

luxurious /lʌg'zjʊərɪəs/ adjective
very comfortable and expensive

luxury /'lʌkʃərɪ/ noun
1 (no plural) great comfort ▶ They live
in luxury in a very big house. ▶ a
luxury hotel

L

2 (plural **luxuries**) something that you do not really need, but that is very pleasant ▶ *Foreign holidays are a real luxury.*

lying /ˈlaɪ-ɪŋ/
the PRESENT PARTICIPLE of the verb **lie**

lyrics /ˈlɪrɪks/ *plural noun*
the words of a popular song

Mm

m
a short way of writing the words **metre** or **metres** ▶ *14m*

'm /m/ *verb*
am ▶ *I'm hungry*

MA /ˌem ˈeɪ/ *noun*
MASTER OF ARTS; a higher university degree in a subject such as history or literature ▶ *She is studying for an MA in music.*

mac /mæk/ *noun*
a MACKINTOSH

machine /məˈʃiːn/ *noun*
an instrument made up of many parts, used to do certain work ▶ *a sewing machine*

machine gun /məˈʃiːn gʌn/ *noun*
a gun that fires bullets very quickly one after another

machinery /məˈʃiːnəri/ *noun (no plural)*
the parts of a machine. or a number of machines together

macho /ˈmætʃəʊ/ *adjective*
having male qualities such as strength or courage, but lacking qualities such as sympathy or understanding

mackintosh /ˈmækɪntɒʃ/ *noun (plural **mackintoshes**)*
a light coat which keeps out the rain

mad /mæd/ *adjective (**madder, maddest**)*

1 ill in the mind ▶ *He behaves very strangely – I think he's mad.*
2 very foolish ▶ *You're mad to drive your car so fast.*
3 very angry ▶ *She was mad **with** him for being late.*
4 **mad about** liking someone or something very much ▶ *He's mad about football.*
5 **drive someone mad** to annoy someone very much ▶ *That noise is driving me mad.*
6 **go mad** to become ill in the mind ▶ *He's gone quite mad in his old age.*
7 **like mad** very hard or fast ▶ *If you run like mad, you might catch the train.*

madam /ˈmædəm/ *noun*
a polite way of speaking or writing to a woman whom you do not know ▶ *The letter began "Dear Madam".*
COMPARE: **sir**

maddening /ˈmædənɪŋ/ *adjective*
very annoying ▶ *The most maddening thing is that it's my own fault.*

made /meɪd/
the PAST TENSE and PAST PARTICIPLE of the verb **make**

madly /ˈmædli/ *adverb*
1 in a wild way ▶ *She rushed madly from room to room.*
2 **be madly in love** to love someone very much

madman /ˈmædmən/ *noun (plural **madmen** /-mən/)*
a man who behaves in a very dangerous or stupid way ▶ *He was driving like a madman.*

madness /ˈmædnəs/ *noun (no plural)*
very stupid and often dangerous behaviour ▶ *It would be madness to try to cross the desert on your own.*

magazine /ˌmægəˈziːn/ *noun*
a book with paper covers, containing stories, articles, and pictures, which you buy weekly or monthly

M

magic¹ /'mædʒɪk/ *noun (no plural)*
1 a special power that makes strange or wonderful things happen ► *He turned the thread into gold by magic.*
2 clever or strange tricks done to amuse people

magic² *adjective*
using the special power that makes strange or wonderful things happen ► *a magic trick*

magical /'mædʒɪkəl/ *adjective*
strange and exciting ► *It was a magical evening.* (adverb: **magically**)

magician /mə'dʒɪʃən/ *noun*
a person who can do clever or strange tricks to amuse people

magistrate /'mædʒɪstreɪt/ *noun*
a person who decides if people are guilty in a law court that deals with less serious crimes

magnet /'mægnɪt/ *noun*
a piece of iron that draws other pieces of iron towards it

magnetic /mæg'netɪk/ *adjective*
having the power of a magnet

magnetism /'mægnətɪzəm/ *noun (no plural)*
1 the power that a MAGNET has to attract things
2 a quality that makes other people feel attracted to you

magnification /,mægnɪfɪ'keɪʃən/ *noun*
the act or result of MAGNIFYING something

magnificent /mæg'nɪfɪsənt/ *adjective*
very good or beautiful ► *What a magnificent building!* (adverb: **magnificently**)

magnify /'mægnɪfaɪ/ *verb (past magnified)*
to make things look larger than they really are

magnifying glass /'mægnɪfaɪ-ɪŋ ,glɑːs/ *noun (plural magnifying glasses)*
a curved piece of glass with a handle, which makes things appear larger than they really are

maid /meɪd/ *noun*
a woman servant

maiden /'meɪdn/ *adjective*
maiden flight, maiden voyage the first trip that a plane or ship makes

maiden name /'meɪdn ,neɪm/ *noun*
the family name of a woman before she marries and takes her husband's name

mail /meɪl/ *noun (no plural)*
the letters and parcels that you send by post
SAME MEANING: **post**

mailbox /'meɪlbɒks/ *noun (plural mailboxes)*
1 a box where letters are put when they are delivered to your house or office
2 a FILE on a computer where you store E-MAIL messages

maim /meɪm/ *verb*
to wound or injure someone very seriously and often permanently ► *The accident left him maimed for life.*

main /meɪn/ *adjective*
most important ► *the main meal of the day*

mainland /'meɪnlænd/ *noun*
the mainland the main part of a country, not the islands near it ► *People living on the islands come over to the mainland at least once a month to do shopping.*

mainly /'meɪnlɪ/ *adverb*
mostly ► *That hospital is mainly for older people.*

main road /,meɪn 'rəʊd/ *noun*
a large, important road

maintain /meɪn'teɪn/ *verb*
1 to make something continue in the same way as before ► *We need to maintain good relations with our customers.*

M

2 to keep something in good condition ▶ *The car has always been properly maintained.*

maintenance /'meɪntənəns/ *noun (no plural)*
keeping something in good condition ▶ *He took a course to learn about car maintenance.*

maize /meɪz/ *noun (no plural)*
a tall plant which produces SWEETCORN, a vegetable which can be eaten

majestic /mə'dʒestɪk/ *adjective*
very fine and important-looking ▶ *a majestic figure (adverb: **majestically**)*

Majesty /'mædʒəstɪ/ *noun (plural **Majesties**)*
a word used when you are talking to or about a king or queen ▶ *Her Majesty will arrive at 10 o'clock.*

major¹ /'meɪdʒəʳ/ *adjective*
most important ▶ *a major city*
OPPOSITE: **minor**

major² *noun*
an officer in the army

majority /mə'dʒɒrətɪ/ *noun (no plural)*
the largest part or most things or people in a group ▶ *The majority of children in our class have brown eyes; only two have blue eyes.*
OPPOSITE: **minority**

make /meɪk/ *verb (present participle **making**, past **made** /meɪd/)*
1 to do something ▶ *We need to make a decision.* ▶ *I'll make some coffee.*
2 to produce or build something ▶ *He made a model plane out of wood.*
LOOK AT: **do**
3 to earn ▶ *I don't make enough money to have expensive holidays.*
4 to force someone to do something, or cause something to happen ▶ *I don't like milk, but she made me drink it.* ▶ *That dress makes you look very pretty.*
5 to have something as a result or total ▶ *Two and two make four.*

6 make a bed to tidy a bed by straightening the sheet and covers
7 make it to arrive in time ▶ *Even if we hurry, we won't make it.*
8 What time do you make it? What time does your watch say?
9 make for someone or something to move towards someone or something ▶ *He made for the door.*
10 make something out to see, hear, or understand something with difficulty ▶ *I could just make out the shape of the house in the darkness.*
11 make sure to be certain ▶ *Make sure you lock the door.*
12 make something up to think of and tell other people about a story that is not true ▶ *He made up that story about being a policeman.*
13 make up your mind to decide something ▶ *I've made up my mind to go to Spain this summer.*

maker /'meɪkəʳ/ *noun*
a person or company that makes something ▶ *Honda is a Japanese car maker.* ▶ *a furniture maker*

makeshift /'meɪkʃɪft/ *adjective*
made quickly from things that you have available ▶ *They slept in a makeshift tent made from a sheet.*

make-up /'meɪk ʌp/ *noun (no plural)*
special coloured powder and creams that women sometimes put on their faces to make themselves look pretty

malaria /mə'leərɪə/ *noun (no plural)*
an illness in which the person has very high fevers, caused by the bite of certain MOSQUITOES

male¹ /meɪl/ *adjective*
belonging to the sex that does not give birth to young ▶ *The male bird is brightly coloured.*
OPPOSITE: **female**

male² *noun*
a person or an animal that does not give birth to young, such as a man or boy
OPPOSITE: **female**

M

malice /'mælɪs/ *noun (no plural)*
the feeling of wanting to hurt someone ▶ *Her eyes were full of malice.*

malicious /mə'lɪʃəs/ *adjective*
intended to hurt or upset someone ▶ *a malicious lie*

malignant /mə'lɪgnənt/ *adjective*
containing CANCER cells ▶ *They are doing tests to see if the growth is malignant.*
OPPOSITE: **benign**

mall /mɔːl/ *noun*
a covered area that contains a lot of shops ▶ *a huge shopping mall*

mammal /'mæməl/ *noun*
an animal that is fed on its mother's milk when it is young, for example a cow, a lion, or a human baby

mammoth /'mæməθ/ *adjective*
very big ▶ *We had the mammoth task of organizing the concert.*

man /mæn/ *noun*
1 (*plural* **men** /men/) a fully-grown human male
COMPARE: **woman**
2 (*plural* **men**) a person; a human being ▶ *Men have lived here for thousands of years.*
3 (no plural) all humans ▶ *Man uses animals in many ways.*

manage /'mænɪdʒ/ *verb (present participle* **managing**, *past* **managed**)*
1 to succeed in doing something ▶ *He managed to avoid an accident.*
2 to control something or be in charge of a business or an activity ▶ *The horse was difficult to manage.* ▶ *He managed the supermarket when the owner was away.*

management /'mænɪdʒmənt/ *noun (no plural)*
1 the people who control a business ▶ *We're meeting the management tomorrow.*
2 the control of something such as a business or money

manager /'mænɪdʒər/ *noun*
a person who controls a business, shop, restaurant, or group of workers

manageress /,mænɪdʒə'res/ *noun (plural* **manageresses**)*
a woman who controls a shop or restaurant

mane /meɪn/ *noun*
the long hair on the necks of some animals

mangled /'mæŋgəld/ *adjective*
badly crushed or twisted ▶ *Rescuers managed to reach the mangled car and help the driver.*

mango /'mæŋgəʊ/ *noun (plural* **mangoes**)*
a sweet, juicy, yellow or green fruit with one large seed, from a tree that grows in hot countries

manhandle /'mænhændl/ *verb (present participle* **manhandling**, *past* **manhandled**)*
to move someone roughly, using force ▶ *He claimed the police manhandled him.*

maniac /'meɪniæk/ *noun*
a person who behaves in a stupid or dangerous way ▶ *You drive like a maniac.*

manicure /'mænɪkjʊər/ *noun*
a treatment for the hands and nails that includes cutting and painting the nails

manipulate /mə'nɪpjʊleɪt/ *verb (present participle* **manipulating**, *past* **manipulated**)*
to make someone do what you want without letting them know that you are influencing them, and in a way that other people disapprove of ▶ *He is willing to manipulate his friends if it will help his career.*

mankind /mæn'kaɪnd/ *noun (no plural)*
all human beings

M

man-made /ˌmæn ˈmeɪd/ *adjective*
made by people, not grown or
produced by or in the earth ➤ *a man-
made material*

manner /ˈmænəʳ/ *noun*
1 the way in which someone behaves
with other people ➤ *She has a very
friendly manner.*
2 manners *plural noun* the way you
behave and speak ➤ *It's bad manners
to eat like that.*

manoeuvre¹ /məˈnuːvəʳ/ *verb*
(*present participle* **manoeuvring**,
past **manoeuvred**)
to move something into a different
position ➤ *Small boats are easier to
manoeuvre.*

manoeuvre² *noun*
a skilful or carefully planned
movement ➤ *a complicated
manoeuvre*

mansion /ˈmænʃən/ *noun*
a large house

mantelpiece /ˈmæntlpiːs/ *noun*
a shelf above a fireplace

manual¹ /ˈmænjʊəl/ *adjective*
done with your hands, not by machine
➤ *manual work* (*adverb*: **manually**)

manual² *noun*
a book that tells you how to do
something ➤ *a computer manual*

manufacture¹ /ˌmænjʊˈfæktʃəʳ/ *verb*
(*present participle* **manufacturing**,
past **manufactured**)
to make things in large numbers in a
factory, usually by machinery

manufacture² *noun* (*no plural*)
the making of things in large
numbers in a factory ➤ *the
manufacture of cars*

manufacturer /ˌmænjʊˈfæktʃərəʳ/
noun
a company that makes large numbers
of goods, using machines ➤ *an
aircraft manufacturer*

manuscript /ˈmænjʊskrɪpt/ *noun*

a piece of writing that has been
written, not printed ➤ *a medieval
manuscript*

many /ˈmenɪ/ *adjective, pronoun*
(*more* /mɔːʳ/, *most* /məʊst/)
1 a lot; a large number of ➤ *Not many
of the children can read.*
2 How many a phrase used in
questions asking about the number
of people or things there are ➤ *How
many people were there?*

map /mæp/ *noun*
a flat drawing of a town, a country, or
an area ➤ *Have you got a map of
Scotland?*

marathon¹ /ˈmærəθən/ *noun*
a race in which people run 26 miles
➤ *He's going to run the New York
marathon.*

marathon² *adjective*
continuing for a very long time ➤ *a
marathon session of Parliament*

marble /ˈmɑːbəl/ *noun*
1 (*no plural*) a hard stone that can be
made smooth and shiny and is used
in making buildings
2 a small glass or stone ball used in a
game ➤ *to play marbles*

march¹ /mɑːtʃ/ *verb*
1 to walk with regular steps like a
soldier
2 to make someone walk quickly
➤ *The policeman marched him into
the police station.*

march² *noun* (*plural* **marches**)
the distance of a walk ➤ *They had a
long march ahead of them.*

March /mɑːtʃ/ *noun*
the third month of the year

margarine /ˌmɑːdʒəˈriːn/ *noun* (*no
plural*)
a soft food like butter, made from
animal or vegetable fats

margin /ˈmɑːdʒɪn/ *noun*
the space without writing or printing
at each edge of a page

M

marijuana /ˌmærɪˈwɑːnə/ *noun (no plural)*
an illegal drug that some people smoke
SAME MEANING: **cannabis**

marina /məˈriːnə/ *noun*
a small area of water near the sea where people pay to keep their boats

marine /məˈriːn/ *adjective*
of or about the sea ▸ *marine life*

mark¹ /mɑːk/ *noun*
1 a spot or cut that spoils the appearance of something ▸ *You have a dirty mark on your face.*
2 a spot on the surface of something ▸ *Our dog has a white mark on its ear.*
3 a figure or letter given by a teacher to say how good someone's work is ▸ *The teacher gave me a good mark for my story.*

mark² *verb*
1 to put words or signs on something to give information about it ▸ *The door was marked "private".*
2 to say whether a piece of work is right or wrong, or to show how good it is ▸ *The teacher marked our examination papers.*
3 to put a spot or line on something which spoils it ▸ *She marked her white dress when she sat on the grass.*

marker /ˈmɑːkər/ *noun*
a large pen with a thick point

market /ˈmɑːkɪt/ *noun*
1 a place, often outside, where many people come to buy and sell goods
2 be on the market to be for sale ▸ *Their house has been on the market for six months.*

marketing /ˈmɑːkɪtɪŋ/ *noun (no plural)*
the job of deciding how to advertise and sell a product ▸ *Stella works in marketing.*

marking /ˈmɑːkɪŋ/ *noun*
1 markings *plural noun* coloured shapes or patterns on something ▸ *The road markings aren't very clear.* ▸ *The young birds have paler markings on their wings.*
2 *(no plural)* the work teachers do when they read students' work and give it a mark ▸ *I've got some marking to do tonight.*

marmalade /ˈmɑːməleɪd/ *noun (no plural)*
a kind of orange JAM that British people eat at breakfast

maroon¹ /məˈruːn/ *noun, adjective*
a dark red colour

maroon² *verb*
be marooned to be left in a place that you cannot escape from ▸ *the story of a sailor who was marooned on a desert island*

marquee /mɑːˈkiː/ *noun*
a very big tent used for shows and parties ▸ *We hired a marquee for the wedding.*

marriage /ˈmærɪdʒ/ *noun*
1 the ceremony in which a man and woman get married ▸ *The marriage took place in church.*
SAME MEANING: **wedding**
2 the relationship between a husband and wife ▸ *They have had a long and happy marriage.*

married /ˈmærɪd/ *adjective*
1 having a husband or wife ▸ *a married man*
OPPOSITE: **single, unmarried**
2 get married to become husband and wife ▸ *They've just got married.*

marry /ˈmæri/ *verb (past married)*
1 to take someone as a husband or wife ▸ *I am going to marry John.*
2 to join two people as husband and wife ▸ *They were married by a priest.*

marsh /mɑːʃ/ *noun (plural marshes)*
an area of low, wet, soft ground

M

martial art /ˌmɑːʃəl ˈɑːt/ *noun*
a sport such as KARATE in which you fight using your hands and feet

marvel¹ /ˈmɑːvəl/ *verb (present participle **marvelling**, past **marvelled**)*
to admire something that is very impressive in a surprising way ▶ *I marvel at his ability to learn.*

marvel² *noun*
something or someone that is very impressive and that you admire ▶ *Laser surgery is one of the marvels of modern medicine.*

marvellous /ˈmɑːvələs/ *adjective*
wonderful ▶ *a marvellous film.*
SAME MEANING: **great, fantastic**

mascara /mæˈskɑːrə/ *noun (no plural)*
a dark substance that women use to colour their EYELASHES ▶ *She was wearing mascara.*

mascot /ˈmæskət/ *noun*
an animal, a toy, etc. that a team or an organization thinks will bring them good luck

masculine /ˈmæskjʊlɪn/ *adjective*
like a man, or typical of a man
OPPOSITE: **feminine**

mash /mæʃ/ *verb*
to crush food to make it soft ▶ *Mash the potatoes with a fork.*

mask /mɑːsk/ *noun*
a covering over all or part of someone's face ▶ *We all wore masks at the party and no one knew who we were.*

mass /mæs/ *noun (plural **masses**)*
a large quantity of something with no special shape ▶ *Before the rain, the sky was a mass of clouds.*

Mass /mæs/ *noun*
the main religious ceremony in some Christian churches ▶ *a Roman Catholic Mass*

massacre¹ /ˈmæsəkəʳ/ *verb (present participle **massacring** /ˈmæsəkrɪŋ/, past **massacred**)*
to kill a large number of people in a violent and cruel way

massacre² *noun*
the cruel killing of many people

massage¹ /ˈmæsɑːʒ/ *verb (present participle **massaging**, past **massaged**)*
to press and rub someone's body with your hands to stop their muscles hurting or to help them relax ▶ *He gently massaged my neck.*

massage² *noun*
the action of pressing and rubbing someone's body with your hands to stop their muscles hurting or to help them relax ▶ *He gave me a massage.*

massive /ˈmæsɪv/ *adjective*
very large ▶ *a massive rise in the cost of living.*
SAME MEANING: **huge, enormous**

mass media /ˌmæs ˈmiːdɪə/ *noun*
the newspapers, radio, and television that give news and information to the public

mast /mɑːst/ *noun*
1 a tall length of wood or metal that supports the sails on a ship
2 a metal post that sends out radio or television signals

master¹ /ˈmɑːstəʳ/ *noun*
1 a man in control of people or animals ▶ *The dog obeyed his master.*
2 a male teacher
COMPARE (2): **mistress**
3 a man of great skill or ability ▶ *The painting is the work of a master.*

master² *verb*
to learn how to do something well ▶ *It takes years to master a new language.*

masterpiece /ˈmɑːstəpiːs/ *noun*
a work of art, piece of writing, etc. that is of an excellent standard or is the best someone has produced

mat /mæt/ *noun*
a small piece of rough, strong

M

material used as a floor covering
COMPARE: **carpet, rug**

match¹ /mætʃ/ verb
to be like something else in size,
shape, colour, etc. ➤ *These shoes do
not match my dress.*

match² noun (plural **matches**)
1 a small stick of wood that produces
a flame when you rub the end against
a rough surface ➤ *a box of matches*
2 a game between two people or two
teams ➤ *a football match*

matching /'mætʃɪŋ/ adjective
having the same colour, style,
pattern, etc. as something else ➤ *The
twins wore matching T-shirts.*

mate¹ /meɪt/ noun
1 a friend or a person you work with
➤ *He's a mate of mine.*
2 one of a male and female pair of
animals or birds

mate² verb (present participle
mating, past **mated**)
(used about animals) to have sex in
order to have young ➤ *Birds mate in
the spring.*
COMPARE: **breed**

material /mə'tɪəriəl/ noun
1 anything from which something can
be made ➤ *Building materials are
expensive.*
2 (no plural) cloth ➤ *blue cotton
material*
SAME MEANING (**2**): **fabric**

maternity /mə'tɜːnɪtɪ/ adjective
for a woman who is going to have a
baby or who has recently had a baby
➤ *a maternity dress* ➤ *maternity pay*

mathematical /,mæθə'mætɪkəl/
adjective
concerning the study of numbers,
shapes, etc.

mathematician /,mæθəmə'tɪʃən/
noun
a person who studies or teaches
mathematics

mathematics /,mæθə'mætɪks/ noun
(no plural)
the study or science of numbers,
shapes, etc.

maths /mæθs/ noun (no plural)
mathematics

matinee /'mætɪneɪ/ noun
an afternoon showing of a play or film

matron /'meɪtrən/ noun
1 a woman who looks after the health
of the children in a school ➤ *Go and
see matron if you feel ill.*
2 a chief nurse in a hospital

matter¹ /'mætə'/ noun
1 (no plural) the substance of which
things are made and which we can
see and touch
2 an important event or fact that
people must talk about or think
about ➤ *I have an important matter to
talk to you about.*
3 as a matter of fact in fact ➤ *As a
matter of fact, I'm only 35, so don't
say I'm old.*
4 no matter it is not important
➤ *We'll finish the job, no matter how
long it takes.*
5 What's the matter? What is wrong?
➤ *What's the matter with the radio?*
➤ *What's the matter? Are you ill?*

matter² verb
to be important ➤ *It doesn't matter if
I miss the bus – I can walk.*

mattress /'mætrəs/ noun (plural
mattresses)
a large, flat bag full of soft material or
springs, which fits onto a bed and
which you sleep on

mature¹ /mə'tjʊə'/ adjective
sensible and behaving like a grown-
up person ➤ *She's a very mature girl.*
OPPOSITE: **immature**

mature² verb (present participle
maturing, past **matured**)
1 to become fully grown
2 (used about certain foods and

M

drinks) to become ready to drink or eat ➤ *After six years, the wine will have matured.*

mature student /məˌtjʊə ˈstjuːdənt/ *noun*
a student at college or university who starts studying after they are 25 years old

mauve /məʊv/ *adjective, noun*
a pale purple colour

maximum¹ /ˈmæksɪməm/ *noun*
the largest possible amount, number, or size ➤ *Temperatures will reach a maximum of 30 degrees today.*
OPPOSITE: **minimum**

maximum² *adjective*
biggest; largest ➤ *The car has a maximum speed of 125 miles per hour.*
OPPOSITE: **minimum**

may /meɪ/ *verb*
1 used to show that something is possible but is not sure to happen ➤ *He may come tonight, but I'm not sure.*
2 to be allowed to do something ➤ *Please may I use your phone?*
3 used to show that you hope that something will happen ➤ *May the best team win!*

May /meɪ/ *noun*
the fifth month of the year

maybe /ˈmeɪbi/ *adverb*
perhaps; possibly ➤ *"Are you coming to the party?" "Maybe; I don't know yet."*

mayonnaise /ˌmeɪəˈneɪz/ *noun (no plural)*
a thick white SAUCE that you put on cold food

mayor /meəʳ/ *noun*
a person who is the head of the local government in a town or city

maze /meɪz/ *noun*
a set of small roads or passages that is difficult to find your way through

➤ *I was lost in a maze of long, dark corridors*

me /miː/ *pronoun*
the person who is speaking ➤ *She handed the book to me.* ➤ *Can you see me?*

meadow /ˈmedəʊ/ *noun*
a field with wild grass and flowers

meagre /ˈmiːgəʳ/ *adjective*
very small in amount ➤ *They paid him a meagre salary.*

meal /miːl/ *noun*
the food we eat at one time, usually three times a day ➤ *an evening meal*

mean¹ /miːn/ *adjective*
1 wanting to keep everything for yourself, especially money ➤ *He's so mean he didn't even get his son a birthday present.*
OPPOSITE: **generous**
2 unkind ➤ *Don't be mean to your little sister.*

mean² *verb (past **meant** /ment/)*
1 to represent something ➤ *What does this mean in English?* ➤ *The red light means stop.*
2 to plan or want to do something ➤ *I meant to give you this book today, but I forgot.*
3 **mean everything to someone, mean a lot to someone** to be very important to someone ➤ *His work means a lot to him.*

meaning /ˈmiːnɪŋ/ *noun*
1 the information that is given or represented by someone or something ➤ *If you don't know the meaning of a word, look it up in your dictionary.*
2 **What is the meaning of this?** Why have you done this?

meaningful /ˈmiːnɪŋfəl/ *adjective*
serious and important ➤ *a meaningful discussion about religion*

meaningless /ˈmiːnɪŋləs/ *adjective*
without any purpose or meaning ➤ *Her whole life felt meaningless.*

M

means /miːnz/ *plural noun*
1 the money that someone has and can use ➤ *He wants to go to college, but his family haven't the means to help him.*
2 by all means certainly ➤ *"May I borrow your paper?" "By all means."*
3 by means of by using something ➤ *He climbed the tree by means of a ladder.*
4 by no means not at all ➤ *It is by no means certain that they will come.*

meant /ment/
the PAST TENSE and PAST PARTICIPLE of the verb **mean**

meantime /'miːntaɪm/ *noun*
in the meantime in the time between two things happening or while something is happening ➤ *I'll phone for a taxi, and in the meantime you pack your case.*

meanwhile /'miːnwaɪl/ *adverb*
in the time before something happens or while something else is happening ➤ *They'll arrive in a few minutes – meanwhile, we'll have a cup of tea.*

measles /'miːzəlz/ *noun (no plural)*
an illness which makes you feel very hot and gives you small, red spots on your face and body

measure¹ /'meʒə/ *noun*
an amount of, or a way of measuring size, weight, etc. ➤ *A metre is a measure of length.*

measure² *verb (present participle* **measuring**, *past* **measured**)
to find out the size, weight, or amount of something ➤ *He measured the width of the room.*

measurement /'meʒəmənt/ *noun*
a number showing how long, tall, wide, etc. something is

meat /miːt/ *noun (no plural)*
the parts of an animal's body used as food ➤ *I don't eat much meat.*

mechanic /mɪ'kænɪk/ *noun*

a person who has trained to make or repair machines

mechanical /mɪ'kænɪkəl/ *adjective*
of a machine; done or made by machine (*adverb:* **mechanically**)

mechanism /'mekənɪzəm/ *noun*
the part of a machine that does a particular job ➤ *The door has a special locking mechanism.*

medal /'medl/ *noun*
a piece of metal, usually round or shaped like a cross, given to honour someone who has done something special

medallist /'medl-ɪst/ *noun*
a person who has won a medal in a competition ➤ *She's an Olympic medallist.* ➤ *the silver medallist*

meddle /'medl/ *verb (present participle* **meddling**, *past* **meddled**)
to try to change or influence a situation, even though you should not because it does not involve you ➤ *Stop meddling in my affairs.*

media /'miːdɪə/ *noun*
the media television, radio, and newspapers ➤ *The crime was reported by the media.* ➤ *The President's visit got a lot of media coverage.*

mediaeval /ˌmediˈiːvəl/ *adjective*
another word for **medieval**

medical /'medɪkəl/ *adjective*
concerning medicine and the job of treating people who are ill ➤ *He is a medical student.*

medication /ˌmedɪ'keɪʃən/ *noun (no plural)*
medicine ➤ *Are you taking any medication at present?*

medicine /'medsɪn/ *noun*
1 *(no plural)* the study of treating and understanding illnesses
2 something that you drink or eat when you are ill, to help you to get better

M

medieval (also **mediaeval**)
/ˌmedɪˈiːvəl/ adjective
of or about the MIDDLE AGES, the period
of European history from about 1100
to 1500 AD ➤ a medieval castle

mediocre /ˌmiːdɪˈəʊkəʳ/ adjective
not very good in quality ➤ The food
was mediocre.

meditate /ˈmedɪteɪt/ verb (present
participle **meditating**, past **meditated**)
to stay silent and calm for a period of
time as part of your religion or to
help you relax ➤ Buddhist priests
were meditating in the park.

meditation /ˌmedɪˈteɪʃən/ noun
(no plural)
the activity of staying silent and calm
for a period of time as part of your
religion or to help you relax ➤ We
spent 15 minutes in meditation.

medium /ˈmiːdɪəm/ adjective
not big or small; of middle size or
amount ➤ She is of medium height.

medium-sized /ˈmiːdɪəm ˌsaɪzd/
(also **medium-size** /ˈmiːdɪəm ˌsaɪz/)
adjective
not very small and not very large ➤ a
medium-sized bed

meet /miːt/ verb (past **met** /met/)
1 to be in the same place at the same
time as someone else ➤ I met my
teacher in the street today. ➤ Let's
meet at your house tonight.
2 to get to know someone ➤ I would
like you to meet my father.

meeting /ˈmiːtɪŋ/ noun
a gathering of people to discuss
something ➤ She's in a meeting. Can I
take a message?

megabyte /ˈmegəbaɪt/ noun
a unit for measuring the amount of
information a computer can use. There
are one million megabytes in a BYTE

mellow[1] /ˈmeləʊ/ adjective
1 pleasant and smooth ➤ mellow
music ➤ a mellow wine

2 gentle or calm because of age or
experience ➤ My dad's pretty mellow
these days.

mellow[2] verb
to become more relaxed and calm, or
to make someone more relaxed and
calm ➤ She's mellowed over the
years.

melody /ˈmelədɪ/ noun (plural
melodies)
a song or tune

melon /ˈmelən/ noun
a large, juicy fruit with a thick green
or yellow skin

melt /melt/ verb
to make or become a liquid by
heating ➤ The ice is melting in the
sun.

member /ˈmembəʳ/ noun
a person who belongs to a group, a
club, or an organization ➤ a member
of the football team

Member of Parliament /ˌmembər
əv ˈpɑːləmənt/ noun (plural
Members of Parliament)
a person who has been elected to
speak in Parliament for a particular
area of the country

membership /ˈmembəʃɪp/ noun (no
plural)
the fact of belonging to a group, or
the people who belong to a group
➤ Membership costs £20 a year.

memento /məˈmentəʊ/ noun (plural
mementos or **mementoes**)
a small object that you keep to
remind you of someone or something
➤ The photograph is a memento of
my school days.

memo /ˈmeməʊ/ noun
a short, official note that you write to
another person working in the same
organization

memoirs /ˈmemwɑːz/ plural noun
a book that someone has written
about their life and experiences ➤ The

ex-Prime Minister has published his memoirs.

memorable /ˈmemərəbəl/ *adjective*
very good, and likely to be remembered ➤ *a memorable film*

memorial¹ /məˈmɔːrɪəl/ *adjective*
done to remind people of someone who has died ➤ *a memorial service for people who died in the war*

memorial² *noun*
a building or some other structure that is built to remind people of someone who has died ➤ *a war memorial*

memorize /ˈmeməraɪz/ *verb (present participle **memorizing**, past **memorized**)*
to learn and remember words, music, or other information ➤ *She memorized her speech.*

memory /ˈmeməri/ *noun (plural **memories**)*
1 the ability to remember things ➤ *She has a good memory **for** faces.*
2 a thought about the past; something that you can remember from the past ➤ *I have happy memories **of** my school.*

men /men/
the plural of **man**

menace /ˈmenɪs/ *noun*
a person or thing that causes danger to people ➤ *That man's a menace when he's driving.*

mend /mend/ *verb*
to repair or fix something that is broken or damaged ➤ *Can you mend the hole in my shirt, mum?*

mental /ˈmentl/ *adjective*
1 done with your mind ➤ *This will need a lot of mental effort.*
2 concerning illness of the mind ➤ *a mental hospital*
*(adverb: **mentally**)*
COMPARE (**1** and **2**): **physical**

mention /ˈmenʃən/ *verb*
to speak or write about something in a few words with no details ➤ *He mentioned that he had been ill.*

menu /ˈmenjuː/ *noun*
1 a list of food that you can choose to eat in a restaurant
2 a list of different choices shown on a computer

merchant /ˈmɜːtʃənt/ *noun*
a person who buys and sells goods, often buying them in one country and selling them in another

merciful /ˈmɜːsɪfəl/ *adjective*
willing to be kind to someone instead of punishing them

merciless /ˈmɜːsɪləs/ *adjective*
cruel; without any kindness
*(adverb: **mercilessly**)*

mercury /ˈmɜːkjʊri/ *noun (no plural)*
a liquid, silver metal, used in THERMOMETERS

mercy /ˈmɜːsi/ *noun (no plural)*
kindness shown to other people by a person with power ➤ *The soldier showed mercy to his prisoner and set him free.*

mere /mɪəʳ/ *adjective*
only; not more than ➤ *She can't do that sort of work - she's a mere child.*
*(adverb: **merely**)*

merge /mɜːdʒ/ *verb (present participle **merging**, past **merged**)*
to join together to form one thing ➤ *Havering College is merging **with** the University.*

merit¹ /ˈmerɪt/ *noun (no plural)*
greatness; goodness ➤ *a book of great merit* ➤ *Is there any merit in trying again?*

merit² *verb*
to deserve something ➤ *His work merits a prize.*

mermaid /ˈmɜːmeɪd/ *noun*
a creature in children's stories, with a woman's body and a fish's tail

M

merry /'merɪ/ *adjective (**merrier, merriest**)*
happy; full of laughter ➤ *Have a merry Christmas! (adverb: **merrily**)*

merry-go-round /'merɪ gəʊ ˌraʊnd/ *noun*
a big machine that children can ride on for pleasure while it turns round and round

mesh /meʃ/ *noun (no plural)*
material made of threads or wires that have been fastened together like a net ➤ *The windows were protected by metal mesh.*

mess¹ /mes/ *noun*
1 many things mixed up together in a dirty, untidy way ➤ *Your room is in a dreadful mess. Please tidy it.*
2 a set of conditions or events full of problems and trouble ➤ *My life's a mess.*

mess² *verb*
1 mess something up to make something dirty or untidy; to make something go wrong ➤ *I've just cleaned the floor, and you've instantly messed it up again!*
2 mess about, mess around to play instead of working; to be silly ➤ *Stop messing about – finish your work.*

message /'mesɪdʒ/ *noun*
a piece of information that one person sends to another ➤ *There's a message for you.*

messenger /'mesɪndʒə/ *noun*
a person who brings a message

messy /'mesɪ/ *adjective (**messier, messiest**)*
1 untidy or dirty ➤ *What a messy room!*
2 unpleasant and causing you to get dirty ➤ *That's a messy job!*

met /met/
the PAST TENSE and PAST PARTICIPLE of the verb **meet**

metal¹ /'metl/ *noun*
a substance such as iron, tin, gold, etc.

metal² *adjective*
made of iron, tin, gold, etc. ➤ *a metal box*

metallic /mə'tælɪk/ *adjective*
made of metal, or like metal ➤ *metallic colours*

meteor /'miːtɪə/ *noun*
a small piece of rock or metal that moves through space and can be seen as a bright, burning line in the sky

meteorite /'miːtɪəraɪt/ *noun*
a small meteor that has landed on the Earth's surface

meter /'miːtə/ *noun*
a machine used for measuring the amount of something used ➤ *an electricity meter*

method /'meθəd/ *noun*
a way of doing something ➤ *new methods of teaching languages*

methodical /mə'θɒdɪkəl/ *adjective*
done in a careful and well-organized way, or always doing things this way ➤ *a methodical search* ➤ *a methodical worker (adverb: **methodically**)*

metre /'miːtə/ *noun*
a measure of length equal to 100 CENTIMETRES ➤ *3 metres (=3m)*

metric /'metrɪk/ *adjective*
concerning the system of measuring using metres, grams, and litres

mg
a short way of writing the words **milligram** or **milligrams**

miaow /mɪ'aʊ/ *verb*
to make the sound that a cat makes

mice /maɪs/
the plural of **mouse**

microchip /'maɪkrəʊˌtʃɪp/ *noun*
a small part of a computer or a machine, containing the electronic parts that control what the machine does

microcomputer /'maɪkrəʊkəmˌpjuː-tə/ *noun*

a small computer that you can use at home or at school

microphone /'maɪkrəfəʊn/ *noun*
an instrument for making sounds louder or recording them

microprocessor /'maɪkrəʊˌprəʊsesə'/ *noun*
the main MICROCHIP in a computer

microscope /'maɪkrəˌskəʊp/ *noun*
an instrument that helps you to see very small things by making them look much bigger ➤ *She looked at the insect under a microscope.*

microwave¹ /'maɪkrəˌweɪv/ *(also* **microwave oven** /ˌmaɪkrəweɪv 'ʌvən/*) noun*
a machine that cooks food very quickly, using electric waves instead of heat

microwave² *verb (present participle* **microwaving,** *past* **microwaved)**
to cook food in a microwave oven

mid /mɪd/ *adjective*
in the middle of a time or place ➤ *They went to Boston in mid June.* ➤ *She was born in the mid 1980s.*

midair /ˌmɪd'eə'/ *noun*
in midair in the sky or in the air ➤ *The ball seemed to stop in midair.*

midday /ˌmɪd'deɪ/ *noun (no plural)*
the middle of the day; 12 o'clock ➤ *She arrived just before midday.*
SAME MEANING: **noon**

middle¹ /'mɪdl/ *noun*
the centre of something ➤ *Please stand in the middle **of** the room.* ➤ *I woke in the middle of the night.*

middle² *adjective*
in the centre ➤ *There are three shops at the end of the street – the baker's is the middle one.*

middle-aged /ˌmɪdl 'eɪdʒd/ *adjective*
(used about people) between about 40 and 60 years old

Middle Ages /ˌmɪdl 'eɪdʒɪz/ *plural noun*
the Middle Ages the period in European history between about 1100 and 1500 AD

middle class /ˌmɪdl 'klɑːs/ *noun*
the middle class people such as teachers, doctors, or managers, who are neither very rich nor very poor

middle-class /ˌmɪdl 'klɑːs/ *adjective*
of or about the middle class ➤ *a middle-class family*

middle name /ˌmɪdl 'neɪm/ *noun*
the name that comes between your first name and your family name

middle school /'mɪdl skuːl/ *noun*
a school for children between the ages of 9 and 13

midnight /'mɪdnaɪt/ *noun (no plural)*
12 o'clock at night

midway /ˌmɪd'weɪ/ *adjective, adverb*
at the middle point between two places, or in the middle of a period of time ➤ *He collapsed midway through the performance.* ➤ *The Comoros lie midway between Madagascar and the coast of Tanzania.*

midweek /ˌmɪd'wiːk/ *adjective, adverb*
in the middle of the week ➤ *I never go to parties midweek.* ➤ *a midweek match*

midwife /'mɪdwaɪf/ *noun (plural* **midwives** /-waɪvz/*)*
a nurse who has been trained to help women when they are having a baby

might¹ /maɪt/ *verb*
1 the PAST TENSE of the verb **may** ➤ *I asked if I might borrow the book.*
2 used to show that something is possible, but not certain ➤ *I might come and see you tomorrow.*

might² *noun (no plural)*
strength; power ➤ *He tried with all his might to open the door, but it stayed shut.*

might've /'maɪtəv/ *verb*
might have ➤ *This might've been a bad idea.*

M

mighty /'maɪtɪ/ adjective (**mightier**, **mightiest**)
strong and powerful ▶ He gave it a mighty push and it opened.

migraine /'miːɡreɪn/ noun
a very bad HEADACHE

migrant /'maɪɡrənt/ noun
a person, a bird, or an animal that regularly moves from one place to another ▶ The farm employs a large number of migrant workers.

migrate /maɪ'ɡreɪt/ verb (present participle **migrating**, past **migrated**)
1 to move in large numbers from one place to another ▶ People sometimes have to migrate to find work.
2 (used about birds and fish) to travel at the same time every year from one part of the world to another

migration /maɪ'ɡreɪʃən/ noun
moving to another place ▶ Many people study the migration of birds.

mike /maɪk/ noun
a MICROPHONE

mild /maɪld/ adjective
1 (used about people) gentle ▶ He's got a very mild manner
2 (used about the weather) not hot and not cold ▶ It's mild today.
3 (used about food) not strong in taste ▶ I usually find Indian food too hot, but I like this – it's very mild.
OPPOSITE (3): hot

mile /maɪl/ noun
a measure of length equal to 1,760 yards or 1.6 kilometres

mileage /'maɪlɪdʒ/ noun (no plural)
1 the total number of miles a vehicle has travelled ▶ The mileage is very low for the age of the vehicle.
2 get a lot of mileage out of something to get as much use or advantage from something as you possibly can ▶ The newspapers could get a lot of mileage out of that story.

military /'mɪlɪtərɪ/ adjective
of soldiers ▶ a military hospital.

militia /mɪ'lɪʃə/ noun
the militia an organized group of soldiers who are not members of an official army

milk¹ /mɪlk/ noun (no plural)
the white liquid that comes from female animals as food for their young ▶ cow's milk ▶ goat's milk

milk² verb
to get milk from an animal ▶ The farmer's going to milk the cows.

milkman /'mɪlkmən/ noun (plural **milkmen** /-mən/)
(in Britain) a person who takes milk to people's houses

milk shake /ˌmɪlk 'ʃeɪk/ noun
a cold drink made from milk mixed with fruit or chocolate

mill /mɪl/ noun
1 a place where corn is made into flour
2 a place where things are made by machinery ▶ an old cotton mill

millennium /mɪ'lenɪəm/ noun (plural **millennia** /-nɪə/)
a period of 1,000 years ▶ the start of a new millennium

milligram (also **milligramme**) /'mɪlɪɡræm/ noun
a measure of weight. There are 1,000 milligrams in a gram

millilitre /'mɪlɪˌliːtər/ noun
a measure of liquid. There are 1,000 millilitres in a litre

millimetre /'mɪlɪˌmiːtər/ noun
a measure of length. There are 1,000 millimetres in a metre. ▶ 60 millimetres (=60mm)

million /'mɪljən/ adjective, noun
1 (plural **million**) the number 1,000,000
2 **millions** a very large number ▶ "How many people were there?" "Millions."

millionaire /ˌmɪljə'neər/ noun
a person who is very, very rich

M

mime¹ /maɪm/ *verb (present participle **miming**, past **mimed**)*
to use actions instead of speech to show stories and feelings

mime² *noun (no plural)*
the use of actions instead of speech to show stories and feelings ▶ *a mime artist*

mimic¹ /'mɪmɪk/ *verb (present participle **mimicking**, past **mimicked**)*
to copy someone's speech or actions in order to make other people laugh ▶ *He mimicked the teacher's voice.*

mimic² *noun*
a person who is good at copying someone else's speech or actions, especially to make other people laugh

mince¹ /mɪns/ *verb (present participle **mincing**, past **minced**)*
to cut meat up into very small pieces

mince² *noun (no plural)*
meat that has been cut into very small pieces ▶ *We had mince for dinner.*

mind¹ /maɪnd/ *noun*
1 your thoughts; your way of thinking or feeling ▶ *I have a clear picture of him in my mind.*
2 change your mind to decide to do something different ▶ *I was going to leave tomorrow, but I've changed my mind.*
3 make up your mind to decide ▶ *I can't make up my mind which film to go and see.*
4 out of your mind mad
5 take your mind off something to make you stop thinking about something ▶ *I need a holiday to take my mind off all my problems.*

mind² *verb*
1 to look after a child ▶ *Will you mind the children while I go out?*
2 to be annoyed about something ▶ *Do you mind if I smoke?*
3 to take notice of something that is

in your way or could cause you to fall ▶ *Mind the step!*
4 Do you mind ...?, Would you mind ...? a polite way of asking someone to do something ▶ *Would you mind moving your bag, please?*
5 Mind out! Watch out!; Be careful! ▶ *Mind out! There's a car coming!*
6 I don't mind I would be happy with either thing ▶ *"Would you like orange juice or apple juice?" "I don't mind."*
7 Never mind It doesn't matter ▶ *"I've just broken a glass." "Never mind – they weren't expensive."*

mine¹ /maɪn/ *pronoun*
something that belongs to the person speaking ▶ *"Whose coat is this?" "It's mine."* ▶ *an old friend of mine*

mine² *noun*
1 a deep hole in the ground from which people dig out coal, iron, gold, etc.
2 a kind of bomb that is put just under the ground or in the sea and explodes when it is touched

mine³ *verb (present participle **mining**, past **mined**)*
1 to dig something out of the ground ▶ *They were mining for silver.*
2 to put bombs in the ground or the sea

minefield /'maɪnfiːld/ *noun*
1 an area of land or sea where bombs have been hidden
2 a situation in which there are many hidden difficulties and dangers ▶ *The whole process is a legal minefield.*

miner /'maɪnə^r/ *noun*
a person who works under the ground digging out coal, iron, gold, etc.

mineral /'mɪnərəl/ *noun*
a substance like iron, coal, or oil, that has formed under the ground

mineral water /'mɪnərəl ˌwɔːtə^r/ *noun (no plural)*
a type of water that comes from

M

under the ground, and is sometimes put in bottles and sold to people as a drink

mingle /'mɪŋgəl/ *verb*
(*present participle* **mingling**, *past* **mingled**)
(used about sounds, smells, or feelings) to mix together ➤ *The smells of flowers and spices mingled in the hot air.*

miniature /'mɪnətʃər/ *adjective*
very small ➤ *a miniature railway*

minimal /'mɪnɪməl/ *adjective*
very small, and therefore not something you should worry about ➤ *The accident caused only minimal damage to the car.* (*adverb:* **minimally**)

minimize /'mɪnɪmaɪz/ *verb*
(*present participle* **minimizing**, *past* **minimized**)
to make something as small as possible ➤ *We hope to minimize the effects of pollution.*

minimum¹ /'mɪnɪməm/ *noun*
the smallest possible amount, number, or size ➤ *You must get a minimum of 40 questions right to pass the examination.*
OPPOSITE: **maximum**

minimum² *adjective*
smallest in amount that is possible or needed ➤ *The minimum pass mark in the examination is 40 out of 100.*
OPPOSITE: **maximum**

mining /'maɪnɪŋ/ *noun (no plural)*
the job or process of digging coal, iron, gold, etc. out of the ground

minister /'mɪnɪstər/ *noun*
1 an important person in the government
2 a Christian priest

ministry /'mɪnɪstrɪ/ *noun (plural* **ministries***)*
a part of the government ➤ *the Ministry of Education*

minor /'maɪnər/ *adjective*
smaller; not very important ➤ *a minor illness*
OPPOSITE: **major**

minority /maɪ'nɒrətɪ/ *noun (no plural)*
the smaller part or number of something ➤ *Only a minority of the children wear uniform.*
OPPOSITE: **majority**

mint /mɪnt/ *noun*
1 a type of sweet
2 (*no plural*) a plant with a strong, fresh smell and taste, used in drinks and food

minus /'maɪnəs/ *preposition*
less ➤ *10 minus 2 is 8 (10 − 2 = 8).*
COMPARE: **plus**

minute¹ /'mɪnɪt/ *noun*
1 a measure of time, of which there are 60 in an hour ➤ *The train arrived at four minutes past eight.*
2 **in a minute** very soon ➤ *I'll be ready in a minute*
3 **Just a minute** Wait for a moment, please ➤ *Just a minute – I'll get some money.*
4 **this minute** straight away; now ➤ *Come here this minute.*

minute² /maɪ'njuːt/ *adjective*
very small ➤ *minute writing*
SAME MEANING: **tiny**

miracle /'mɪrəkəl/ *noun*
a wonderful happening that people believe is caused by God

miraculous /mɪ'rækjʊləs/ *adjective*
surprising and wonderful ➤ *a miraculous cure for an illness* (*adverb:* **miraculously**)

mirror /'mɪrər/ *noun*
a flat piece of glass with a shiny back in which you can see yourself ➤ *She looked at herself in the mirror.*

misbehave /ˌmɪsbɪ'heɪv/ *verb*
(*present participle* **misbehaving**, *past* **misbehaved**)

M

to behave badly ▶ *The teacher was angry because the children were misbehaving.*

miscellaneous /ˌmɪsəˈleɪnɪəs/ *adjective*
of many different kinds ▶ *a miscellaneous assortment of books*

mischief /ˈmɪstʃɪf/ *noun (no plural)*
be up to mischief, get into mischief
to behave badly, in a way that is annoying but causes no serious harm ▶ *He was a lively boy, always up to mischief.*

mischievous /ˈmɪstʃɪvəs/ *adjective*
behaving badly, in a way that is annoying but causes no serious harm ▶ *mischievous children*

miserable /ˈmɪzərəbəl/ *adjective*
1 very unhappy ▶ *I'm feeling miserable; I'm tired, cold, and very hungry.*
2 making people unhappy ▶ *What miserable weather!*

misery /ˈmɪzəri/ *noun (no plural)*
great unhappiness ▶ *the misery of the people who had lost their homes in the fire*

misfortune /mɪsˈfɔːtʃən/ *noun*
bad luck; something bad that happens to you ▶ *He had the misfortune to lose his job.*

misjudge /ˌmɪsˈdʒʌdʒ/ *verb (present participle misjudging, past misjudged)*
to make a wrong decision about what someone or something is like ▶ *The President had badly misjudged the mood of the voters.*

mislead /mɪsˈliːd/ *verb (past misled /mɪsˈled/)*
to deliberately give someone incorrect information ▶ *They misled us into believing that the order had already been sent.*

misprint /ˈmɪsˌprɪnt/ *noun*
a mistake in the way a word is spelled in a book, magazine, etc.

miss /mɪs/ *verb*
1 not to hit or catch something ▶ *He threw the ball to me, but I missed it and it landed on the ground.* ▶ *He shot at me but missed.*
2 to not go to something ▶ *I'll have to miss the meeting tomorrow.*
3 to arrive too late to catch a bus, train, etc. ▶ *Hurry up or we'll miss the train.*
4 to feel sad when someone is not there ▶ *We'll all miss you when you go away.*
5 **miss something out** to not include something ▶ *You've missed out your telephone number.*

Miss /mɪs/ *noun (plural Misses)*
the title of a girl or an unmarried woman ▶ *Have you seen Miss Johnson?*
COMPARE: **Mrs, Ms**

missile /ˈmɪsaɪl/ *noun*
something that is thrown or fired to harm or damage something else ▶ *Bottles and other missiles were thrown at the police.*

missing /ˈmɪsɪŋ/ *adjective*
not in the correct place and not able to be found ▶ *A book is missing **from** my desk.*

mission /ˈmɪʃən/ *noun*
an important job that someone has been sent to do ▶ *The men were on an important mission from their government.* ▶ *The soldiers' mission was to destroy the bridge.*

missionary /ˈmɪʃənəri/ *noun (plural missionaries)*
a person who goes to another country to teach others about his or her religion

misspell /ˌmɪsˈspel/ *verb (past misspelled or misspelt /-ˈspelt/)*
to spell a word wrongly

mist /mɪst/ *noun (no plural)*
thin cloud near the ground ▶ *We couldn't see through the mist.*
COMPARE: **fog**

M

mistake¹ /mɪˈsteɪk/ *noun*
1 something which is not correct ▶ *a spelling mistake*
2 by mistake doing something wrong which you did not plan to do ▶ *I took your pen by mistake.*

mistake² *verb (present participle* **mistaking**, *past tense* **mistook** /mɪˈstʊk/, *past participle* **mistaken** /mɪˈsteɪkən/)*
1 be mistaken to think that something is correct when it is not ▶ *I was mistaken when I told you she was a teacher; she's a doctor.*
2 mistake someone for someone else to wrongly think that someone is someone else ▶ *I am sorry; I mistook you for someone I know.*

mistaken /mɪˈsteɪkən/
the PAST PARTICIPLE of the verb **mistake**

Mister /ˈmɪstəʳ/ *noun*
Mʀ

mistook /mɪˈstʊk/
the PAST TENSE of the verb **mistake**

mistress /ˈmɪstrəs/ *noun (plural* **mistresses**)*
a woman teacher
COMPARE: **master**

mistrust¹ /mɪsˈtrʌst/ *noun (no plural)*
the feeling that you cannot trust someone ▶ *Susan has a mistrust of strangers.*

mistrust² *verb*
to not trust someone ▶ *Jenny mistrusts salesmen.*

misty /ˈmɪsti/ *adjective (*mistier, mistiest*)*
having a lot of thin cloud near the ground ▶ *a misty morning.*
COMPARE: **foggy**

misunderstand /ˌmɪsʌndəˈstænd/ *verb (past* **misunderstood** /-ˈstʊd/)*
to not understand something correctly ▶ *He must have misunderstood my instructions.*

misunderstanding /ˌmɪsʌndəˈstændɪŋ/ *noun*
1 (no plural) a failure to understand something correctly ▶ *We need to be clear in order to avoid any misunderstanding.*
2 an argument that is not very serious ▶ *It was just a small misunderstanding.*

misunderstood /ˌmɪsʌndəˈstʊd/
the PAST TENSE of the verb **misunderstand**

mitten /ˈmɪtn/ *noun*
a type of GLOVE that does not have separate parts for each finger

mix /mɪks/ *verb*
1 to put different things together to make something new; to join together ▶ *Mix the butter and flour together.*
2 mix someone up with to think that a person is someone else ▶ *It's easy to mix him up with his brother.*
3 mix things up to put things together so that there is no order ▶ *Someone has mixed up my papers.*

mixed /mɪkst/ *adjective*
1 consisting of a lot of different types of things, people, ideas, etc. ▶ *a packet of mixed nuts* ▶ *Kelly had mixed feelings about going to college.*
2 for both males and females ▶ *Simon goes to a mixed school.*

mixed up /ˌmɪkst ˈʌp/ *adjective*
confused ▶ *Tony got mixed up and went to the wrong house.*

mixer /ˈmɪksəʳ/ *noun*
a piece of kitchen equipment that you use for mixing food

mixture /ˈmɪkstʃəʳ/ *noun*
a number of different things or people put together ▶ *This tea is a mixture of two different types.*

mix-up /ˈmɪks ʌp/ *noun*
a mistake or problem that happens when people get confused or do not

M

understand each other ➤ *There was a mix-up with our bags at the airport.*

ml
a short way of writing the words **millilitre** or **millilitres** ➤ *20ml*

mm
a short way of writing the words **millimetre** or **millimetres** ➤ *60mm*

moan¹ /məʊn/ *verb*
to make a low sound of pain ➤ *The child lay moaning gently.*
SAME MEANING: **groan**

moan² *noun*
a low sound of pain
SAME MEANING: **groan**

mob¹ /mɒb/ *noun*
a large, noisy crowd of angry, violent people ➤ *a mob of demonstrators*

mob² *verb (present participle* **mobbing**, *past* **mobbed**)
(used about an excited group of people) to crowd round someone, to either hurt or admire them ➤ *Gallagher was mobbed by fans at the airport.*

mobile¹ /ˈməʊbaɪl/ *adjective*
1 able to move or be moved quickly and easily ➤ *She's 83 now, and not really very mobile.* ➤ *Professional people have become increasingly mobile in recent years.*
2 mobile library/shop/clinic, etc. a library, shop, clinic, etc. that is in a vehicle and can be driven from one place to another

mobile² *noun*
1 a decoration made of small objects that is hung up and moves when air blows around it
2 a MOBILE PHONE

mobile phone /ˈməʊbaɪl ˈfəʊn/ *noun*
a telephone that you can carry with you wherever you go

mock /mɒk/ *verb*
to laugh unkindly at someone ➤ *You shouldn't mock the way he walks.*

modal verb /ˈməʊdəl ˈvɜːb/ *(also* **modal**) *noun*
a verb such as "can", "might", or "must" that is used with other verbs to show ideas such as possibility, permission, or intention
COMPARE: **auxiliary verb**

model¹ /ˈmɒdl/ *noun*
1 a small copy of something ➤ *a model of an aeroplane*
2 a person who wears new clothes at special shows so that people will see them and want to buy them

model² *verb (present participle* **modelling**, *past* **modelled**)
1 to make a shape of something with a soft substance such as clay
2 to wear new clothes at special shows so that people will see them and want to buy them

model³ *adjective*
a very small copy of something ➤ *a model car*

modelling /ˈmɒdl-ɪŋ/ *noun (no plural)*
the work of wearing new clothes at special shows so that people will see them and want to buy them ➤ *She moved from modelling into acting.*

modem /ˈməʊdəm/ *noun*
a piece of electronic equipment used for sending information from one computer to another down a telephone line

moderate /ˈmɒdərət/ *adjective*
neither high nor low, fast nor slow, large nor small ➤ *a moderate speed* ➤ *a moderate amount (adverb:* **moderately**)

moderation /ˌmɒdəˈreɪʃən/ *noun (no plural)*
in moderation not too much ➤ *He only drinks in moderation.*

modern /ˈmɒdən/ *adjective*
new; and in the style that is popular now ➤ *modern clothes* ➤ *modern music*
OPPOSITE: **old-fashioned**

M

modernize /ˈmɒdənaɪz/ *verb*
(*present participle* **modernizing**,
past **modernized**)
to change something so that it uses
new methods, new equipment, or new
ideas ▶ *The airline has modernized
its planes.* ▶ *The new president
hopes to modernize society.*

modest /ˈmɒdɪst/ *adjective*
not talking too much about the things
that you do well ▶ *She is very modest
about the prizes she has won.*

modesty /ˈmɒdɪsti/ *noun (no plural)*
the quality of not talking too much
about the things that you do well

modify /ˈmɒdɪfaɪ/ *verb (past
modified)*
1 to make small changes to
something in order to improve it
▶ *Safety procedures have been
modified since the fire.*
2 if one word modifies another, it
gives more information about it. In
the sentence "She sings beautifully",
the adverb "beautifully" modifies the
verb.

Mohammed /məʊˈhæmɪd/ *noun*
another word for **Muhammad**

moist /mɔɪst/ *adjective*
a little wet; not dry ▶ *His eyes were
moist with tears.*

moisten /ˈmɔɪsən/ *verb*
to make something slightly wet ▶ *Add
milk to moisten the mixture.*

moisture /ˈmɔɪstʃəʳ/ *noun (no plural)*
small drops of water ▶ *The desert air
contains very little moisture.*

moisturizer /ˈmɔɪstʃəˌraɪzəʳ/ *noun*
a cream you put on your skin to keep
it soft and stop it being too dry

molar /ˈməʊləʳ/ *noun*
one of the large teeth at the back of
your mouth

mole /məʊl/ *noun*
1 a small animal that lives in holes
under the ground

2 a small, round, dark spot on
someone's skin

molecule /ˈmɒlɪkjuːl/ *noun*
the smallest part into which a
substance can be broken up without
changing its form

molehill /ˈməʊlhɪl/ *noun*
a small heap of earth thrown up by a
mole when it is digging

molest /məˈlest/ *verb*
to sexually attack or harm someone,
especially a woman or a child

moment /ˈməʊmənt/ *noun*
1 a very short time
2 at any moment at any time now or
very soon ▶ *He might come back at
any moment.*
3 at the moment now ▶ *At the
moment, I have a very good job.*
4 in a moment very soon ▶ *The
doctor will see you in a moment.*

momentarily /ˈməʊməntərɪli/
adverb
for a very short time ▶ *He paused
momentarily, then began speaking
again.*

momentary /ˈməʊməntəri/
adjective
continuing for a very short time
▶ *There was a momentary silence
before anyone dared to speak.*

momentous /məʊˈmentəs/
adjective
very important ▶ *the momentous
events in Central Europe*

momentum /məʊˈmentəm/ *noun
(no plural)*
1 the force that makes a moving
object continue to move ▶ *The ball
lost momentum and stopped rolling.*
2 the process of continuing to
increase, develop, or become
successful ▶ *We've won three games
in a row now, so we need to keep up
the momentum.*

monarch /ˈmɒnək/ *noun*
a king or queen

monarchy /'mɒnəkɪ/ noun (plural **monarchies**)
a country that is ruled by a king or queen

monastery /'mɒnəstrɪ/ noun (plural **monasteries**)
a place where religious men (MONKS) live
COMPARE: **convent**

Monday /'mʌndeɪ, -dɪ/ noun
the second day of the week

money /'mʌnɪ/ noun (no plural)
1 coins and paper bank notes ▶ I haven't got much money.
2 make money to get or earn money ▶ He makes a lot of money selling cars.

monitor[1] /'mɒnɪtə[r]/ noun
a piece of computer equipment with a screen that shows information or pictures

monitor[2] verb
to watch or measure something carefully for a period of time to see how it changes ▶ The study monitored the health of 87,000 women for 10 years.

monk /mʌŋk/ noun
one of a group of men who live together and have given their lives to a religion
COMPARE: **nun**

monkey /'mʌŋkɪ/ noun
an animal that is like a small person in shape but has a long tail and lives in trees

monopoly /mə'nɒpəlɪ/ noun (plural **monopolies**)
a situation in which one person or organization controls all of a particular business or industry and there is no competition ▶ The group once had a monopoly **on** telephone services in the US.

monotonous /mə'nɒtənəs/ adjective
always the same and never interesting ▶ My job is rather monotonous.

monsoon /mɒn'suːn/ noun
the heavy rain which falls at a particular time of year in parts of Asia

monster /'mɒnstə[r]/ noun
a large animal with a strange or unusual shape, usually fierce

monstrous /'mɒnstrəs/ adjective
big and ugly

month /mʌnθ/ noun
one of the 12 parts into which a year is divided
LOOK AT: **time**

monthly /'mʌnθlɪ/ adjective, adverb
happening every month or once a month ▶ a monthly meeting

monument /'mɒnjʊmənt/ noun
something that is built to help people to remember an important person or event

moo /muː/ verb
to make the noise that a cow makes

mood /muːd/ noun
the way you feel at any one time ▶ The beautiful sunny morning put me in a good mood.

moody /'muːdɪ/ adjective (**moodier, moodiest**)
becoming angry or unhappy quickly and without any warning ▶ a moody teenager

moon /muːn/ noun
the large, round thing that shines in the sky at night
COMPARE: **sun**

moonlight /'muːnlaɪt/ noun (no plural)
the light from the moon

moonlit /'muːn,lɪt/ adjective
made bright by the light from the moon ▶ a beautiful moonlit night

moor[1] /mʊə[r]/ noun
an area of open land covered with rough grass or low bushes

moor[2] verb
to tie up a boat

M

mop¹ /mɒp/ *noun*
a stick with soft material at one end, used for cleaning floors

mop² *verb (present participle* **mopping,** *past* **mopped)**
1 to clean a floor with a mop
2 mop something up to use a piece of soft material to clean liquid from a surface ▶ *Sara used some paper towels to mop up the milk she had spilled.*

mope /məʊp/ *(also* **mope around** /ˌməʊp əˈraʊnd/) *verb (present participle* **moping,** *past* **moped)**
to feel unhappy and not make any effort to become cheerful again

moped /ˈməʊped/ *noun*
a large, strong bicycle with a small engine

moral¹ /ˈmɒrəl/ *adjective*
relating to what is right and wrong ▶ *He believes we have a moral duty to help the homeless.*

moral² *noun*
1 a lesson about what is right and wrong that you learn from a story or an event ▶ *The moral of the story was that we should be kind to other people.*
2 morals *plural noun* the set of ideas about what is right and wrong that you use when deciding how to live your life

morale /məˈrɑːl/ *noun (no plural)*
the confidence and hope that a person or group feels ▶ *The team's morale is low after losing several games.*

morality /məˈrælətɪ/ *noun (no plural)*
ideas about what is right and wrong ▶ *Some religious leaders questioned the morality of the war.*

more¹ /mɔːʳ/ *adverb*
1 to a greater degree ▶ *You'll have to be more careful next time.* ▶ *My meal was more expensive than Dan's.*

2 a greater number of times or for longer than before ▶ *She goes out a lot more now that she has a car.* ▶ *We see our grandchildren more than we used to.*
OPPOSITE (**1** and **2**): **less**
3 more and more continuing to become greater in amount ▶ *He got more and more angry.*
4 not any more no longer ▶ *They don't live here any more.*
5 more or less about ▶ *The holiday will cost £600, more or less.*
6 once more again ▶ *Read that page once more, please.*

more² *adjective, pronoun*
1 a larger amount or number ▶ *There are more people without jobs these days.* ▶ *In some bars, orange juice costs more than beer.*
OPPOSITE: **less**
2 another thing or amount, in addition to what you have already ▶ *Would you like some more tea?* ▶ *I have to make a few more phone calls.*
3 more and more continuing to become greater in amount ▶ *These days, more and more people travel long distances to work.*
4 more or less about; almost ▶ *This article says more or less the same thing as the other one.*

moreover /mɔːˈrəʊvəʳ/ *adverb*
used when you give additional information which supports something that you have just said ▶ *The new design is not acceptable. Moreover, it would delay the project even further.*

morning /ˈmɔːnɪŋ/ *noun*
the time from when the sun rises until midday or until you have your midday meal

Morse code /ˌmɔːs ˈkəʊd/ *noun (no plural)*
a way of sending messages using flashing lights or sounds

M

mortgage /ˈmɔːgɪdʒ/ noun
money you borrow from a bank in order to buy a house

mosaic /məʊˈzeɪɪk/ noun
a pattern or picture made from small pieces of coloured stone, glass, etc.

Moslem /ˈmɒzlɪm/ noun, adjective
another word for **Muslim**

mosque /mɒsk/ noun
a building in which Muslims worship

mosquito /mɒˈskiːtəʊ/ noun (plural **mosquitoes**)
a fly that drinks blood from people or animals and can carry MALARIA from one person to another

moss /mɒs/ noun (no plural)
a bright green plant that grows in a thick mass on wet ground, trees, and stones

most¹ /məʊst/ adverb
more than all the others ➤ Of course, the coat I liked best cost the most. ➤ I forgot to tell you the most important thing!
OPPOSITE: **least**

most² adjective, pronoun
1 almost all of a group of people or things ➤ Most people go on holiday in July and August. ➤ Most of the kids I know love ice cream.

> Use **most** when you are talking about people or things in general: Most children like sweets. ➤ Most people have a television. Use **most of** when you are talking about a particular group of people or things: Most of the people he works with are friendly. ➤ I've read most of her books.

2 more than anyone or anything else ➤ Ricardo's restaurant gives you the most food for your money. ➤ Whoever scored most in the last game goes first.
OPPOSITE (**2**): **least**

3 at most, at the most not more than a particular amount or number ➤ It will take an hour at the most.

4 make the most of something to use something in the best way possible ➤ We've only got two days here, so let's make the most of them.

mostly /ˈməʊstlɪ/ adverb
1 usually ➤ When I go to London, it's mostly on business.
2 almost all ➤ The people at the party were mostly students.

motel /məʊˈtel/ noun
a hotel where people who are travelling by car can stay

moth /mɒθ/ noun
an insect like a BUTTERFLY which flies at night

mother /ˈmʌðəʳ/ noun
a female parent ➤ Her mother is a teacher.

motherhood /ˈmʌðəhʊd/ noun (no plural)
the state of being a mother

mother-in-law /ˈmʌðəʳ ɪn lɔː/ noun (plural **mothers-in-law**)
the mother of your wife or husband

motion /ˈməʊʃən/ noun (no plural)
in motion moving ➤ You must not get off the train when it is in motion.

motionless /ˈməʊʃənləs/ adjective
not moving ➤ The cat sat motionless, waiting for the mouse to move.

motivate /ˈməʊtɪveɪt/ verb (present participle **motivating**, past **motivated**)
1 to make someone want to achieve something, especially by encouraging them to work harder ➤ Part of your job will be to motivate the team.
2 to be the reason why someone does something ➤ The theft was motivated by greed.

motivation /ˌməʊtɪˈveɪʃən/ noun
1 (no plural) the quality of being keen and willing to do something ➤ Jack is smart, but he lacks motivation.

M

2 the reason why you want to do something ▶ *What was your motivation for writing the book?*

motive /ˈməʊtɪv/ *noun*
a reason for doing something ▶ *Police are questioning everyone who had a motive for killing the man.*

motor /ˈməʊtəʳ/ *noun*
an engine that makes things move or work

motorbike /ˈməʊtəbaɪk/ *noun*
a large, heavy bicycle worked by an engine

motorboat /ˈməʊtəbəʊt/ *noun*
a small boat with an engine

motorcar /ˈməʊtəkɑːʳ/ *noun*
a car

motorcycle /ˈməʊtəˌsaɪkəl/ *noun*
a large, heavy bicycle worked by an engine

motorcyclist /ˈməʊtəˌsaɪklɪst/ *noun*
a person who rides a motorcycle

motorist /ˈməʊtərɪst/ *noun*
a person who drives a car

motorway /ˈməʊtəweɪ/ *noun*
a wide road built for vehicles to travel fast for long distances

motto /ˈmɒtəʊ/ *noun (plural **mottoes** or **mottos**)*
a short statement that says what the aims or principles of a person or an organization are

mould¹ /məʊld/ *verb*
to make something into a particular shape

mould² *noun*
1 a hollow container that shapes whatever is poured into it
2 *(no plural)* a greenish-white substance that grows on old food and in cold, wet buildings

mouldy /ˈməʊldɪ/ *adjective (**mouldier**, **mouldiest**)*
covered with MOULD ▶ *mouldy bread*

moult /məʊlt/ *verb*
(used about animals or birds) to lose hair or feathers so that new ones can grow

mound /maʊnd/ *noun*
a small hill ▶ *a mound of earth*

mount¹ /maʊnt/ *verb*
to get onto a horse or bicycle

mount² *noun*
a mountain ▶ *Mount Everest is the highest mountain in the world.*

mountain /ˈmaʊntɪn/ *noun*
a very high hill ▶ *Mount Everest is the highest mountain in the world.*

mountain bike /ˈmaʊntɪn ˌbaɪk/ *noun*
a strong bicycle with wide, thick tyres

mountaineer /ˌmaʊntəˈnɪəʳ/ *noun*
a person who climbs mountains

mountaineering /ˌmaʊntəˈnɪərɪŋ/ *noun (no plural)*
the sport of climbing mountains

mountainous /ˈmaʊntɪnəs/ *adjective*
having a lot of mountains ▶ *a mountainous region*

mourn /mɔːn/ *verb*
to be very sad because someone has died ▶ *She mourned for her dead child.*

mourner /ˈmɔːnəʳ/ *noun*
a person who is at a funeral

mourning /ˈmɔːnɪŋ/ *noun (no plural)*
1 a feeling of great sadness because someone has died
2 in mourning dressed in black clothes or behaving in a way that shows how sad you are at someone's death ▶ *She's in mourning for her father.*

mouse /maʊs/ *noun*
1 *(plural **mice** /maɪs/)* a small animal with a long tail which lives in houses or in fields
COMPARE: **rat**
2 *(plural **mouses**)* a small object connected to a computer, that you move with your hand and press to give commands to the computer

mouse mat /'maʊs mæt/ *noun*
a flat piece of rubber or plastic that you use a computer mouse on

mousse /muːs/ *noun*
1 a substance that you put in your hair to hold it in position
2 a cold, sweet food made from cream, eggs, and fruit or chocolate

moustache /mə'stɑːʃ/ *noun*
the hair that grows above a man's mouth
COMPARE: **beard**

mouth /maʊθ/ *noun (plural mouths* /maʊðz/)
1 the opening in your face through which you speak and take in food
2 the place where a river meets the sea

mouthful /'maʊθfʊl/ *noun*
the amount of food or drink that fills your mouth at one time

mouthwash /'maʊθwɒʃ/ *noun (no plural)*
a liquid that you use to make your mouth clean and your breath smell fresh

move /muːv/ *verb (present participle moving, past moved)*
1 to go from one place to another ▸ *Sit still and don't move.*
2 to change something's position or to take something from one place and put it in another ▸ *I can't move my legs.* ▸ *Could you move your car, please?*
3 to go to a new home ▸ *I moved house last week.*
4 move in to go and live in a new home ▸ *We should be able to move in next week.*
5 move out to leave the place where you have been living ▸ *Mr Smith moved out last week.*

movement /'muːvmənt/ *noun*
a change in position from one place to another ▸ *Suddenly I saw a movement behind the curtain.*

movie /'muːvi/ *noun*
a film

moving /'muːvɪŋ/ *adjective*
making you feel strong emotions, especially sadness or sympathy ▸ *a moving story*

mow /məʊ/ *verb (past tense mowed, past participle mown* /məʊn/)
to cut grass with a machine

MP /,em 'piː/ *noun*
a Member of Parliament

MP3 /,em piː 'θriː/ *noun*
a piece of music on the INTERNET that you can put on your own computer

mph
a short way of writing the words **miles per hour** ▸ *The car was travelling at 85 mph when it crashed.*

Mr /'mɪstə^r/ *noun*
a word put before a man's family name when you are speaking or writing to him ▸ *This is Mr Brown.*

Mrs /'mɪsɪz/ *noun*
a word put before a married woman's family name when you are speaking or writing to her ▸ *This is Mrs Brown.*
COMPARE: **Miss, Ms**

Ms /mɪz, məz/ *noun*
a word put before the family name of a woman who does not wish to call herself "Miss" or "Mrs"

MSc /,em es 'siː/ *noun*
MASTER OF SCIENCE; a higher university degree in a science subject ▸ *She is studying for an MSc in biology.*

Mt
a short way of writing the word **mount**

much¹ /mʌtʃ/ *adverb (more* /mɔː^r/, *most* /məʊst/)
1 a lot ▸ *Dad's feeling much better now.* ▸ *She's much cleverer than I am.*
2 used to show the degree to which someone does something or something happens ▸ *Thank you very much!* ▸ *I know how much he likes*

M

you. ► I feel so much better now.
3 often ► I don't see her much because she lives so far away.

much² adjective, pronoun
1 a lot or a large amount of something ► We haven't got much time. ► Do you get much chance to travel in your job?

> **Much** (1) is used in questions and in NEGATIVE sentences: How much does it cost? ► It doesn't cost much. For other types of sentences, use **a lot of** instead: It cost a lot of money. ► He has a lot of work to do.

2 how much used to ask about the amount or cost of something ► How much milk is left? ► I wonder how much that shirt costs.
3 too much more than you need or want ► I've got far too much work to do.
4 as much as the same amount as someone or something ► We haven't got as much money as the Browns.

muck¹ /mʌk/ noun (no plural)
dirt or mud ► There's some muck on the carpet.

muck² verb
1 muck about, muck around to behave in a silly way and waste time ► Don't muck about while I'm working.
2 muck someone about, muck someone around to cause trouble for someone by changing your mind a lot or by not being honest ► Jim's really mucked me around – first he wants to go, then he doesn't.

mud /mʌd/ noun (no plural)
wet earth

muddle¹ /'mʌdl/ noun
having everything mixed up and in the wrong place ► She was in such a muddle she couldn't even remember what day it was.

muddle² verb (present participle **muddling**, past **muddled**)

1 to put everything in the wrong place ► My papers were all muddled.
2 to confuse someone so that they do not understand ► All these difficult instructions just muddle me.

muddy /'mʌdɪ/ adjective (**muddier, muddiest**)
covered with wet earth ► Take those muddy boots off!

muesli /'mjuːzlɪ/ noun (no plural)
a breakfast food of nuts, grain and fruit, which you eat with milk

muffle /'mʌfəl/ verb (present participle **muffling**, past **muffled**)
to make a sound less loud or clear ► Thick curtains muffled the traffic noise.

mug /mʌg/ noun
a big cup with straight sides

muggy /'mʌgɪ/ adjective (**muggier, muggiest**)
(used about the weather) unpleasantly wet and warm

Muhammad /mʊ'hæmɪd/ (also **Mohammed** /məʊ'hæmɪd/) noun
a PROPHET who taught the ideas that the Islamic religion is based on

mule /mjuːl/ noun
an animal which is half horse and half donkey

mull /mʌl/ verb
mull something over to think about something carefully ► He wanted to be left alone to mull things over.

multicultural /ˌmʌltɪ'kʌltʃərəl/ adjective
involving people and ideas from many different countries, religions, etc. ► America is a multicultural society.

multimedia /ˌmʌltɪ'miːdɪə/ adjective
using a mixture of sounds, pictures, etc. to give information, especially on a computer ► multimedia software

multiple /'mʌltɪpəl/ adjective
involving many parts, people, events,

M

etc. ➤ *The driver died from multiple injuries.*

multiple choice /ˌmʌltɪpəl ˈtʃɔɪs/ *adjective*
having several possible answers from which you must choose the correct one ➤ *a multiple choice question*

multiplication /ˌmʌltɪplɪˈkeɪʃən/ *noun (no plural)*
sums in which you add a number to itself a particular number of times

multiply /ˈmʌltɪplaɪ/ *verb (past multiplied)*
to increase by a number of times ➤ *2 multiplied by 3 is 6 (2 x 3 = 6).*
COMPARE: **divide**

multiracial /ˌmʌltɪ ˈreɪʃəl/ *adjective*
involving people from many different races

multitude /ˈmʌltɪtjuːd/ *noun*
a very large number of things or people ➤ *She left for a multitude of reasons.*

mum /mʌm/ *noun*
mother

mumble /ˈmʌmbəl/ *verb (present participle mumbling, past mumbled)*
to speak in a way that is difficult to hear or understand ➤ *He mumbled something to me, but I could not hear what he said.*

mummy /ˈmʌmɪ/ *noun (plural mummies)*
a word for mother used by children

mumps /mʌmps/ *noun (no plural)*
an illness that causes fever, and swelling in the neck

munch /mʌntʃ/ *verb*
to eat food that is hard and makes a noise as you eat it ➤ *He was munching an apple.*

municipal /mjuˈnɪsɪpəl/ *adjective*
relating to the government of a town or city ➤ *municipal elections*

mural /ˈmjʊərəl/ *noun*
a picture painted on a wall

murder¹ /ˈmɜːdəʳ/ *verb*
to kill a person on purpose when it is against the law
COMPARE: **assassinate**

murder² *noun*
the crime of killing someone on purpose

murderer /ˈmɜːdərəʳ/ *noun*
a person who kills someone on purpose when it is against the law
COMPARE: **killer**

murky /ˈmɜːkɪ/ *adjective (murkier, murkiest)*
dark and difficult to see through ➤ *a murky river*

murmur¹ /ˈmɜːməʳ/ *verb*
to make a soft sound; to speak quietly ➤ *The child murmured in her sleep.*

murmur² *noun*
1 a soft, low sound ➤ *the murmur of voices*
2 without a murmur without complaint ➤ *The children went to bed without a murmur.*

muscle /ˈmʌsəl/ *noun*
one of the parts of your body under your skin which make you strong and help you to move

muscular /ˈmʌskjʊləʳ/ *adjective*
1 having a lot of big muscles ➤ *strong, muscular arms*
2 of or about the muscles ➤ *a muscular disease*

museum /mjuːˈziːəm/ *noun*
a building in which you can see old, interesting, or beautiful things ➤ *the Museum of Modern Art*

mushroom /ˈmʌʃruːm/ *noun*
a brown or white plant with a short stem and round top, which can be eaten

music /ˈmjuːzɪk/ *noun (no plural)*
1 the pleasant sounds made by voices or by instruments ➤ *to listen to music*
2 a written or printed set of musical notes ➤ *a sheet of music*

M

musical /'mjuːzɪkəl/ *adjective*
1 concerning or connected with music ▶ *musical instruments*
2 skilled in music ▶ *She is very musical.*

musician /mjuːˈzɪʃən/ *noun*
a person who plays an instrument or writes music

Muslim /'mʊzlɪm/ *(also **Moslem**) noun*
a follower of the religion that believes in the teachings of Mohammed as written in the Koran

must /məst; *strong* mʌst/ *verb*
1 used with another verb to show what is necessary or what has to be done ▶ *I must go or I'll be late.*
2 used to show that you think something is very likely or certain ▶ *It is very late; it must be nearly 12 o'clock.* ▶ *I can't open the door – somebody must have locked it.*

mustard /'mʌstəd/ *noun (no plural)*
a yellow powder, made from the seeds of a plant, which is mixed with water to give a hot taste to food

mustn't /'mʌsənt/
must not ▶ *You mustn't be late for school.*

must've /'mʌstəv/ *verb*
must have ▶ *Jane doesn't seem to be here; she must've left.*

mutilated /'mjuːtɪleɪtɪd/ *adjective*
very badly cut or damaged, especially having parts missing ▶ *the discovery of several mutilated bodies*

mutter /'mʌtəʳ/ *verb*
to speak in a low voice which is difficult to hear ▶ *He's always muttering to himself.*

mutton /'mʌtn/ *noun (no plural)*
meat from a sheep, eaten as food

mutual /'mjuːtʃʊəl/ *adjective*
1 used to say that people have the same feelings about each other ▶ *a marriage based on mutual love and respect*
2 shared by two or more people ▶ *We have a mutual friend.* (*adverb:* **mutually**)

my /maɪ/ *adjective*
belonging to the person speaking ▶ *I hurt my knee when I fell off my bicycle.*

myself /maɪˈself/ *pronoun*
1 the same person as the one who is speaking ▶ *I looked at myself in the mirror.*
2 used to give the word "I" a stronger meaning ▶ *I made this shirt myself.*

mysterious /mɪˈstɪəriəs/ *adjective*
very strange, and difficult to explain or understand ▶ *He died suddenly of a mysterious illness.* (*adverb:* **mysteriously**)

mystery /'mɪstəri/ *noun (plural **mysteries**)*
a strange thing that is difficult to explain or understand ▶ *"Who had taken the money?" "It was a mystery."*

mystical /'mɪstɪkəl/ *adjective*
connected with religious or magical powers that people cannot understand ▶ *While he was in the desert, he had some kind of mystical experience.*

mystify /'mɪstɪfaɪ/ *verb (past **mystified**)*
to make someone feel confused because they cannot explain or understand something ▶ *a case that mystified the police*

myth /mɪθ/ *noun*
1 something that is not true, although many people believe it ▶ *the myth that America is a free and open society*
2 an old story about gods and people ▶ *Greek myths about the creation of the world*

mythical /'mɪθɪkəl/ *adjective*
1 of or about myths ▶ *mythical creatures such as the Minotaur*

M

2 not real or true, but only imagined ▶ *the mythical Wild West of popular fiction*

Nn

N
a short way of writing the words **north** or **northern**

nag /næg/ *verb (present participle nagging, past nagged)*
to keep complaining to someone because you want them to do something ▶ *Stop nagging me! I'll tidy the room later.*

nagging /'nægɪŋ/ *adjective*
making you worry or feel pain all the time ▶ *a nagging headache*

nail¹ /neɪl/ *noun*
1 a thin, pointed piece of metal with one flat end that you use to join pieces of wood together
COMPARE: **screw**
2 one of the hard, flat parts at the end of your fingers and toes

nail² *verb*
to fasten or fix something with a nail ▶ *The windows were nailed shut.*

nail-biting /'neɪl ˌbaɪtɪŋ/ *adjective*
very exciting because you do not know what will happen next ▶ *a nail-biting finish*

nailbrush /'neɪlbrʌʃ/ *noun (plural nailbrushes)*
a small brush for cleaning your nails

nail varnish /'neɪl ˌvɑːnɪʃ/ *noun (no plural)*
paint for women's nails ▶ *She wore pink nail varnish.*

naive /naɪ'iːv/ *adjective*
lacking experience and always expecting that people will be nice and that things will happen easily ▶ *I was young and naive. (adverb: naively)*

naked /'neɪkɪd/ *adjective*
not wearing any clothes ▶ *a naked body*
SAME MEANING: **nude**

name¹ /neɪm/ *noun*
1 the word that you use when speaking to or about a person or thing ▶ *My name is Jane Smith.* ▶ *What is the name of this town?*
2 make a name for yourself to become well-known ▶ *She's made a name for herself as an artist.*

name² *verb (present participle naming, past named)*
to give a name to someone or something ▶ *They named the baby Ann.*

namely /'neɪmli/ *adverb*
that is ▶ *There is only one problem – namely, how to get more money.*

namesake /'neɪmseɪk/ *noun*
someone's namesake a person who has the same name as someone ▶ *Mr Yeats, like his famous namesake, is also a poet.*

nanny /'næni/ *noun (plural nannies)*
a woman who is paid to live with a family and look after the children

nap /næp/ *noun*
a short sleep during the day ▶ *He always has a nap in the afternoon.*
SAME MEANING: **doze**

napkin /'næpkɪn/ *noun*
a square of cloth or paper used at meals to keep your clothes, hands, and mouth clean
SAME MEANING: **serviette**

nappy /'næpi/ *noun (plural nappies)*
a piece of cloth or paper worn between a baby's legs and round its bottom

narcotic /nɑː'kɒtɪk/ *noun*
a drug, especially one that is illegal ▶ *He was arrested for possession of narcotics.*

N

narrative /'nærətɪv/ noun
the description of events in a story
▶ an exciting narrative

narrator /nə'reɪtəʳ/ noun
a person who tells a story or explains
what is happening in a book or a film
▶ At the start of the film, you hear the
voice of the narrator.

narrow /'nærəʊ/ adjective
small from one side to the other
▶ The gate is too narrow for cars to
go through.
OPPOSITE: **wide**

narrowly /'nærəʊlɪ/ adverb
only by a small amount ▶ They
narrowly avoided being killed.

narrow-minded /,nærəʊ 'maɪndɪd/
adjective
not willing to accept ideas that are
new and different from your own

nasal /'neɪzəl/ adjective
1 (used about sounds or voices)
coming mostly through your nose
▶ She had a high, nasal voice.
2 of or for your nose ▶ a nasal spray

nasty /'nɑːstɪ/ adjective (**nastier,
nastiest**)
1 not pleasant to see, taste, smell,
etc. ▶ nasty medicine
2 not kind in behaviour ▶ Don't be
nasty to your sister.
SAME MEANING (**1** and **2**): **horrible**

nation /'neɪʃən/ noun
all the people belonging to a country
and living under its government
▶ The whole nation supported the
government. ▶ the African nations

national /'næʃənəl/ adjective
of or belonging to a country ▶ a
national holiday

national anthem /,næʃənəl 'ænθəm/
noun
the official song of a country, sung on
special days and occasions

nationalism /'næʃənəlɪzəm/ noun
(no plural)

the feeling of being proud of your
country, especially when you believe
that your country is much better than
other countries ▶ We are worried
about the growth of nationalism.

nationalist /'næʃənəlɪst/ noun
a person who is very proud of their
country and believes that it is better
than other countries

nationality /,næʃə'nælətɪ/ noun
(plural **nationalities**)
the fact of belonging to a particular
country ▶ Richard and John have
different nationalities: Richard is
American and John is British.

nationalize /'næʃənə,laɪz/ verb
(present participle **nationalizing**,
past **nationalized**)
if a government nationalizes an
organization or industry, it takes
control of it ▶ Cardenos was the
president who nationalized Mexico's
oil industry in 1938.
OPPOSITE: **privatize**

nationally /'næʃənəlɪ/ adverb
in all of a country ▶ a TV show that is
broadcast nationally

nationwide /,neɪʃən'waɪd/
adjective, adverb
happening or existing in every part of
a country ▶ There was a nationwide
search for the missing girl. ▶ adverts
that appear nationwide

native¹ /'neɪtɪv/ noun
a person born in a certain place
▶ Mary is a native **of** northern
Australia.

native² adjective
belonging to or being the place where
you were born ▶ Her native language
is Spanish.

Native American /,neɪtɪv
ə'merɪkən/ noun
a member of one of the groups of
people who were living in North
America before the Europeans arrived

native speaker /ˌneɪtɪv ˈspiːkəʳ/
noun
someone who learned to speak a
language when they were a baby, as
their first language ► *Laurence is not
a native speaker of English.*

natter /ˈnætəʳ/ verb
to talk a lot about unimportant things
► *What are you two nattering about?*

natural /ˈnætʃərəl/ adjective
1 not made by people or machines
► *earthquakes and other natural
disasters*
2 usual or expected ► *It's natural to
feel nervous before an exam.*
SAME MEANING **(2): normal**
OPPOSITE **(2): unnatural**

naturalist /ˈnætʃərəlɪst/ noun
a person who studies plants and
animals

naturalize /ˈnætʃərəˌlaɪz/ verb
be naturalized to be given the official
right to live in a country where you
were not born

naturally /ˈnætʃərəlɪ/ adverb
1 not made or caused by anyone
► *Her hair is naturally straight.*
2 without looking or sounding
different from usual ► *She talked
quite naturally, even though she was
frightened.*
3 of course ► *Naturally, you must talk
to your parents before you decide.*

natural resources /ˌnætʃərəl
rɪˈzɔːsɪz/ plural noun
things such as oil, coal, gas, or
metals that exist in a country and can
be used by people ► *Japan has few
natural resources of its own.*

nature /ˈneɪtʃəʳ/ noun
1 (no plural) the world and everything
in it which people have not made –
for example, weather, plants, etc.
► *These mountains are one of
nature's loveliest sights.*
2 the character of a person or thing
► *Peter has a happy nature.*

naughty /ˈnɔːtɪ/ adjective (**naughtier,
naughtiest**)
(used about children) not well-
behaved ► *Don't do that, you
naughty boy!* (adverb: **naughtily**)

nausea /ˈnɔːzɪə/ noun (no plural)
the feeling that you are going to be
sick ► *The medication may cause
feelings of nausea.*

nauseating /ˈnɔːzɪeɪtɪŋ/ adjective
1 very unpleasant, or very annoying
► *What a nauseating little person she
is!*
2 very unpleasant, and making you
feel as if you are going to be sick
► *the nauseating smell of rotting
flesh*

nautical /ˈnɔːtɪkəl/ adjective
relating to ships and sailing
► *England's nautical history*

naval /ˈneɪvəl/ adjective
related to the ships belonging to a
country which are used in war
► *naval battles*

navel /ˈneɪvəl/ noun
the small hole in your stomach
SAME MEANING: **belly button**

navigate /ˈnævɪgeɪt/ verb (present
participle **navigating**, past
navigated)
to decide which direction a ship, plane,
or car should go in, using a map or
other instruments ► *He navigated the
plane through the low cloud.*

navigation /ˌnævɪˈgeɪʃən/ noun (no
plural)
decisions and planning about which
direction a ship, plane, or car should
go in, using a map or other
instruments ► *Navigation is difficult
on the river because of the rocks.*

navigator /ˈnævɪgeɪtəʳ/ noun
the person on a ship or plane who
plans and says where it should go

navy /ˈneɪvɪ/ noun (plural **navies**)
the ships of a country used to

prevent or make war, with the officers and crew of these ships ➤ *My son is in the navy.*
COMPARE: **army, airforce**

navy blue /ˌneɪvɪ ˈbluː/ *(also navy)* noun, adjective
a dark blue colour

nb *(also NB)* /ˌen ˈbiː/
used to tell someone to pay attention to something important you have written

near /nɪəʳ/ *adjective, adverb, preposition*
not far; close; at a short distance ➤ *Our school is very near.* ➤ *My aunt lives quite near.* ➤ *He sat in a chair near the window.*

nearby /nɪəˈbaɪ/ *adjective, adverb*
close to a place ➤ *We went swimming in a nearby river.* ➤ *Is the school nearby?*

nearly /ˈnɪəlɪ/ *adverb*
1 almost ➤ *We have nearly finished.*
2 not nearly not at all ➤ *I haven't got nearly enough money to buy that book.*

nearsighted /ˌnɪəˈsaɪtɪd/ *adjective*
unable to see things clearly unless they are close to you
SAME MEANING: **shortsighted**

neat /niːt/ *adjective*
1 clean and well arranged ➤ *She always kept her room neat and tidy.*
2 careful and tidy ➤ *her neat writing (adverb: neatly)*
OPPOSITE (**1** and **2**): **messy**

neatness /ˈniːtnəs/ *noun (no plural)*
the quality of being neat

necessarily /ˈnesəsərəlɪ/ *adverb*
not necessarily used to say that something may not be true, or may not always happen ➤ *Expensive restaurants do not necessarily have the best food.*

necessary /ˈnesəsərɪ/ *adjective*
which you need or must have ➤ *It*

may be necessary **for** you to have an operation.
OPPOSITE: **unnecessary**

necessity /nəˈsesətɪ/ *noun (plural necessities)*
something that you need or must have – for example, food

neck /nek/ *noun*
1 the part of your body between your head and your shoulders
2 the narrow part at the end of something ➤ *the neck of a bottle*
3 up to your neck in something very concerned with something difficult ➤ *He is up to his neck in debt.*

necklace /ˈnekləs/ *noun*
a string of jewels or BEADS, or a chain of gold or silver that you wear around your neck

need¹ /niːd/ *noun*
1 something that you want or must have ➤ *The needs of a very small baby are simple.*
2 in need without enough food or money ➤ *We're collecting money for children in need.*
3 in need of something wanting or needing something ➤ *After working so hard, I felt in need of a good holiday.*

need² *verb*
1 to want something that is necessary ➤ *I'm working extra hours because I need the money.* ➤ *You need computer experience for this job.*
2 need to do something to have to do something because it is necessary ➤ *You need to see a doctor as soon as you can.* ➤ *Do we need to book?*
3 need not do something, needn't do something used when saying that it is not necessary to do something ➤ *You needn't wait if you're in a hurry.*

needle /ˈniːdl/ *noun*
1 a very thin piece of pointed metal with a hole at one end for thread, used in sewing

2 a long, thin, pointed piece of plastic or metal used to make clothes from wool ▶ *knitting needles*

needless /'niːdləs/ *adjective*
needless to say of course ▶ *Needless to say, it rained the day we wanted to go for a walk.*

needn't /'niːdnt/
need not ▶ *You needn't do It If you don't want to.*

needy /'niːdɪ/ *adjective* (**needier, neediest**)
having very little food or money ▶ *a needy family*

negative¹ /'negətɪv/ *adjective*
saying or meaning "no" ▶ *a negative answer*
OPPOSITE: **affirmative**

negative² *noun*
the piece of film from which a photograph can be made

neglect¹ /nɪ'glekt/ *verb*
to give too little attention or care to someone or something ▶ *The animals were thin and ill because the farmer had neglected them.*

neglect² *noun (no plural)*
failure to look after someone or something well ▶ *children suffering from neglect*

neglected /nɪ'glektɪd/ *adjective*
not well cared for or looked after ▶ *a neglected garden*

negligence /'neglɪdʒəns/ *noun (no plural)*
a situation in which someone who is legally responsible for something does not do it properly with the result that something bad happens ▶ *They have accused the doctor of negligence.*

negligent /'neglɪdʒənt/ *adjective*
not doing something that you are responsible for, causing something bad to happen

negligible /'neglɪdʒəbəl/ *adjective*
very small and unimportant ▶ *The damage was negligible.*

negotiate /nɪ'gəʊʃɪeɪt/ *verb* (*present participle* **negotiating**, *past* **negotiated**)
to discuss a political problem or business arrangement in order to reach an agreement ▶ *The government has failed to negotiate an agreement.*

negotiations /nɪˌgəʊʃɪ'eɪʃənz/ *plural noun*
official discussions between two groups who are trying to reach an agreement ▶ *Israel held secret negotiations with the PLO in Norway.*

neigh /neɪ/ *verb*
to make the long, loud sound that a horse makes

neighbour /'neɪbər/ *noun*
someone who lives near you ▶ *a next-door neighbour*

neighbourhood /'neɪbəhʊd/ *noun*
the small area around a place and the people living there ▶ *You will find several shops in the neighbourhood.*

neighbouring /'neɪbərɪŋ/ *adjective*
near to a place ▶ *a bus going to the town and the neighbouring villages*

neither /'naɪðə[r]/ *adjective, conjunction*
1 not one and not the other of two people or things ▶ *Neither boy could swim, but they both wanted to learn.*
2 used in negative expressions when you are saying that two or more things are not true ▶ *I was neither angry nor upset.*

neon /'niːɒn/ *noun (no plural)*
a gas used in tubes in electric lights and signs ▶ *neon lights*

nephew /'nefjuː/ *noun*
the son of your brother or sister
COMPARE: **niece**

nerve /nɜːv/ *noun*
1 a very small part in your body like a

thread, which carries feelings and messages to and from your brain

2 nerves *plural noun* great excitement and worry ▶ *She's always full of nerves before a race.*

3 get on someone's nerves to make someone annoyed ▶ *That loud music is really getting on my nerves.*

nerve-racking (also **nerve-wracking**) /'nɜːv,rækɪŋ/ *adjective*
very worrying or frightening ▶ *Appearing on TV was a nerve-racking experience.*

nervous /'nɜːvəs/ *adjective*
1 worried or afraid ▶ *She's nervous about travelling alone.*
2 related to the nerves in your body ▶ *the nervous system*

nervous breakdown /,nɜːvəs 'breɪkdaʊn/ *noun*
a mental illness in which someone becomes very worried and unhappy, and cannot live a normal life

nest /nest/ *noun*
the home built by a bird or by some animals and insects

nestle /'nesəl/ *verb* (*present participle* **nestling**, *past* **nestled**)
1 to move into a comfortable position, in which you are gently touching someone or something ▶ *The little cat nestled in his arms.*
2 to be in a position that is protected by a group of hills, trees, buildings, etc. ▶ *The village nestled among the Torridon Hills.*

net /net/ *noun*
1 (*no plural*) material with open spaces between knotted thread, string, or wire ▶ *net curtains*
2 a piece of this material used for a particular purpose ▶ *a football net* ▶ *a fishing net*

Net /net/ *noun*
the Net the INTERNET

netball /'netbɔːl/ *noun* (*no plural*)
a game usually played by seven girls

or women, in which a ball is thrown into two high rings at opposite ends of a court

nettle /'netl/ *noun*
a wild plant with leaves that can hurt you

network /'netwɜːk/ *noun*
a large group of lines, wires, etc. which cross or meet each other ▶ *a railway network*

neurotic /nju'rɒtɪk/ *adjective*
very worried or frightened about something in a way that does not seem normal ▶ *My mother's neurotic about her health.*

neutral¹ /'njuːtrəl/ *adjective*
not supporting any of the countries or people who are in a war or an argument ▶ *Iran remained neutral in the Gulf War.*

neutral² *noun*
the position of the GEARS of a car when the engine does not turn the wheels ▶ *Start the car in neutral.*

never /'nevəʳ/ *adverb*
not at any time; not ever ▶ *I'll never forget her kindness.* ▶ *My brother never lets me ride his bicycle.*
OPPOSITE: **always**

nevertheless /,nevəðə'les/ *adverb*
in spite of what you have just said ▶ *It is safer to wear seat belts when driving. Nevertheless, many people do not wear them.*
SAME MEANING: **nonetheless**

new /njuː/ *adjective*
1 recently made, built, or bought ▶ *We've got a new car.* ▶ *new ideas*
OPPOSITE: **old**
2 not seen, known, or experienced before ▶ *I'm learning a new language – Russian.*
3 new to something not familiar with something ▶ *a young doctor new to the job*

newborn /'njuːbɔːn/ *adjective*
just born ▶ *newborn lambs*

newcomer /ˈnjuːkʌməʳ/ *noun*
a person who has recently come to a place or has recently started an activity ➤ *a newcomer to the city*

newly /ˈnjuːlɪ/ *adverb*
recently ➤ *The house was newly built.*

news /njuːz/ *noun (no plural)*
information about things that have just happened ➤ *We listen to the news on the radio.* ➤ *Have you had any news of your family?*

newsagent /ˈnjuːzˌeɪdʒənt/ *noun*
1 a person who has a shop selling newspapers, magazines, and sometimes sweets
2 newsagent's a shop selling newspapers, magazines, and sometimes sweets

news bulletin /ˈnjuːz ˌbʊlətɪn/ *noun*
a short news programme on the radio or television ➤ *And now we go over to our studio for the 10 o'clock news bulletin.*

newscaster /ˈnjuːzˌkɑːstəʳ/ *noun*
a person whose job is to read the news on television or radio

newsflash /ˈnjuːzflæʃ/ *noun (plural newsflashes)*
a special, short news programme about something important that has just happened ➤ *There was a newsflash about her death.*

newsletter /ˈnjuːzˌletəʳ/ *noun*
a sheet of printed news about an organization that is sent regularly to its members ➤ *The office newsletter comes out each month.*

newspaper /ˈnjuːzˌpeɪpəʳ/ *noun*
a set of sheets of paper containing news and advertisements, which is sold every day or week ➤ *an evening newspaper*

newsreader /ˈnjuːzˌriːdəʳ/ *noun*
a person whose job is to read the news on television or radio

New Year /ˌnjuː ˈjɪəʳ/ *noun (no plural)*
the time when you celebrate the beginning of the year ➤ *Happy New Year!*

New Year's Day /ˌnjuː jɪəz ˈdeɪ/ *noun*
January 1st

New Year's Eve /ˌnjuː jɪəz ˈiːv/ *noun*
December 31st

next¹ /nekst/ *adjective*
1 nearest ➤ *There was music coming from the next room.*
2 coming after the present one ➤ *I'll see you next week.*

next² *adverb*
1 just after something ➤ *What did he do next?*
2 (used when you are talking about the following stage in a story or instructions) ➤ *First, read the instructions. Next, write your name at the top of the page.*
3 next to beside ➤ *Come and sit next to me.*

next door /ˌnekst ˈdɔːʳ/ *adverb*
in the next room or building ➤ *The Simpsons live next door.* ➤ *The baker's is right next door to the school.*

next-door /ˌnekst ˈdɔːʳ/ *adjective*
in the next room or building ➤ *next-door neighbours*

next of kin /ˌnekst əv ˈkɪn/ *noun (plural next of kin)*
your closest relative who is still alive ➤ *His next of kin was informed about the accident.*

nib /nɪb/ *noun*
the pointed part of a pen, out of which the ink comes

nibble /ˈnɪbəl/ *verb (present participle nibbling, past nibbled)*
to take little bites of food ➤ *She was nibbling a piece of bread.*

nice /naɪs/ *adjective*
1 pleasant; good ➤ *Have a nice time at the party.* ➤ *a nice, warm day*

N

2 kind and friendly ▶ *What a nice person!*

nice-looking /ˌnaɪs ˈlʊkɪŋ/ *adjective*
attractive ▶ *Your brother's really nice-looking.*

nicely /ˈnaɪsli/ *adverb*
1 in a pleasant or attractive way ▶ *Belinda is always so nicely dressed.*
2 very well ▶ *His arm is healing nicely.*
3 in a polite or friendly way ▶ *Ask nicely and I'll give you some chocolate.*

nick¹ /nɪk/ *noun*
1 a small cut in the surface of something ▶ *a tiny nick on her hand*
2 in good nick, in bad nick in good condition or in bad condition ▶ *Our car's old but it's in good nick.*

nick² *verb*
1 to accidentally cut the surface of something ▶ *I nicked my chin when I was shaving.*
2 to steal something ▶ *Someone's nicked my purse!*

nickel /ˈnɪkəl/ *noun*
1 *(no plural)* a hard, silver-white metal that is an ELEMENT and is used for making other metals
2 a coin used in the US and Canada worth 5 cents

nickname /ˈnɪkneɪm/ *noun*
a name given informally to someone which is not their real name ▶ *John's nickname is "Tiny", because he is very small.*

nicotine /ˈnɪkəti:n/ *noun (no plural)*
the ADDICTIVE substance in tobacco

niece /ni:s/ *noun*
the daughter of your brother or sister
COMPARE: **nephew**

niggle /ˈnɪgəl/ *verb (present participle* **niggling**, *past* **niggled)**
1 to annoy or worry you slightly ▶ *This pain has been niggling me for days.*

2 to complain about small details that are not important ▶ *She niggled over every detail of the bill.*

night /naɪt/ *noun*
1 the time when it is dark and the sun cannot be seen ▶ *It rained during the night.* ▶ *Nurses sometimes have to work at night.*
OPPOSITE: **day**
2 the evening ▶ *We're going to a play on Saturday night.*
3 by night during the night ▶ *In the desert, they travelled by night.*
4 the other night a few nights ago

nightclub /ˈnaɪtklʌb/ *noun*
a place where people go late in the evening to drink and dance ▶ *London has some great nightclubs.*

nightdress /ˈnaɪtdres/ *(also*
nightgown /ˈnaɪtgaʊn/) *noun (plural* **nightdresses)**
a type of loose dress which women and girls wear in bed

nightie /ˈnaɪti/ *noun*
a type of loose dress which women and girls wear in bed

nightingale /ˈnaɪtɪŋgeɪl/ *noun*
a bird known for its beautiful song, which it sings at night

nightlife /ˈnaɪtlaɪf/ *noun (no plural)*
entertainment that is available in the evening in a town ▶ *The big attraction in Berlin is the nightlife.*

nightly /ˈnaɪtli/ *adjective, adverb*
happening every night ▶ *The bar is open nightly from 9.30.* ▶ *a nightly news broadcast*

nightmare /ˈnaɪtmeəʳ/ *noun*
a dream which makes you very afraid

night school /ˈnaɪt sku:l/ *noun (no plural)*
classes taught in the evening ▶ *I'm studying Spanish at night school.*

nighttime /ˈnaɪttaɪm/ *noun*
the time each day when it is dark
OPPOSITE: **daytime**

N

night watchman /ˌnaɪt ˈwɒtʃmən/ noun (plural **night watchmen** /-mən/)
a person who guards buildings at night

nil /nɪl/ noun
nothing; zero ▶ *Their team won the game four nil (=4–0).*

nimble /ˈnɪmbəl/ adjective
able to move quickly and skilfully ▶ *nimble fingers* ▶ *a nimble climber* (adverb: **nimbly**)

nine /naɪn/ adjective, noun
the number 9

nineteen /ˌnaɪnˈtiːn/ adjective, noun
the number 19

nineteenth /ˌnaɪnˈtiːnθ/ adjective
19th

ninetieth /ˈnaɪntɪəθ/ adjective
90th

nine-to-five /ˌnaɪn tə ˈfaɪv/ adverb
work nine-to-five to work every day from 9 o'clock in the morning until 5 o'clock in the evening

ninety /ˈnaɪntɪ/ adjective, noun
the number 90

ninth /naɪnθ/ adjective, noun
1 9th
2 one of nine equal parts

nip /nɪp/ verb (present participle **nipping**, past **nipped**)
to bite someone ▶ *That dog nipped my leg yesterday.*

nipple /ˈnɪpəl/ noun
one of the two small, dark circles on your chest. Babies suck milk through their mother's nipples

nitrogen /ˈnaɪtrədʒən/ noun (no plural)
a gas that is the main part of the Earth's air

no /nəʊ/ adverb, adjective
1 used to refuse something, to show that something is not true, or to show that you do not agree with something

▶ *"Would you like some tea?" "No, thanks."*
2 not any ▶ *There are no children in the classroom.*

no. (plural **nos.**)
a short way of writing the word **number** ▶ *page nos. 12 to 16*

nobility /nəʊˈbɪlətɪ/ noun
the nobility the group of people in some countries who have the highest social rank

noble /ˈnəʊbəl/ adjective
1 belonging to the highest social rank
2 showing courage to help others ▶ *It was very noble of you to give up your holiday to look after your mum.*

nobody /ˈnəʊbədɪ/ pronoun
another word for **no one**

nod¹ /nɒd/ verb (present participle **nodding**, past **nodded**)
to bend your head forward and then up again to greet someone or show that you agree with someone ▶ *She nodded when I asked if she liked the film.*

nod² noun
a movement of your head which is forward and then up ▶ *He greeted me with a nod.*

noise /nɔɪz/ noun
a sound, often loud and unpleasant ▶ *the noise of the traffic* ▶ *My car's making strange noises.*
LOOK AT: **sound**

noisy /ˈnɔɪzɪ/ adjective (**noisier**, **noisiest**)
making a lot of noise ▶ *"What a noisy class you are!" said the teacher.* (adverb: **noisily**)
OPPOSITE: **quiet**

nomad /ˈnəʊmæd/ noun
a person who travels about with their tribe and who has no fixed home

nomadic /nəʊˈmædɪk/ adjective
not living in one place, but moving from one place to another

N

nominate /'nɒmɪneɪt/ *verb (present participle **nominating**, past **nominated**)*
to officially suggest that someone should be given a job or prize ► *The team nominated Harry **as** captain.*

nomination /ˌnɒmɪ'neɪʃən/ *noun*
an official suggestion that someone should be given a job or prize, or the act of suggesting this ► *the Oscar nominations*

non-alcoholic /ˌnɒn ælkə'hɒlɪk/ *adjective*
(used about drinks) containing no alcohol

none /nʌn/ *pronoun*
not one; not any ► *None of the pupils knew the answer.* ► *"Can I have some more bread?" "Sorry, there's none left."*

nonetheless /ˌnʌnðə'les/ *adverb*
in spite of what you have just said ► *Martin was not well, but he came to school nonetheless.*
SAME MEANING: **nevertheless**

nonexistent /ˌnɒnɪg'zɪstənt/ *adjective*
not existing at all ► *Industry is practically nonexistent in the area.*

nonfiction /ˌnɒn'fɪkʃən/ *noun (no plural)*
books about real facts or events ► *I read a lot of nonfiction.*
OPPOSITE: **fiction**

nonflammable /ˌnɒn'flæməbəl/ *adjective*
difficult or impossible to burn
OPPOSITE: **inflammable**

no-nonsense /ˌnəʊ 'nɒnsəns/ *adjective*
working in a practical way, making decisions quickly, and not spending too much time discussing things ► *a no-nonsense approach to work*

nonsense /'nɒnsəns/ *noun (no plural)*

1 something which has no sense or meaning ► *You're talking nonsense.*
2 a word you use if you strongly believe that something is silly or not true ► *"This book is too difficult for me" "Nonsense!"*
SAME MEANING (**1** and **2**): **rubbish**

nonsmoking /nɒn'sməʊkɪŋ/ *adjective*
(used about buildings or areas) in which people are not allowed to smoke

nonstarter /nɒn'stɑːtəʳ/ *noun*
an idea or a plan that is very unlikely to succeed ► *The whole idea sounds like a nonstarter.*

nonstop /ˌnɒn'stɒp/ *adjective, adverb*
without a pause ► *We caught a nonstop flight from London to Singapore.*

noodles /'nuːdlz/ *plural noun*
long, thin pieces of food made from flour, water, and eggs, which you cook by boiling them in water

noon /nuːn/ *noun (no plural)*
the middle of the day; 12 o'clock ► *At noon, the sun is high in the sky.*
SAME MEANING: **midday**

no one /'nəʊ wʌn/ *(also **nobody**) pronoun*
not anyone; no person ► *I knocked on the door, but no one answered.* ► *No one liked him.*

noose /nuːs/ *noun*
a circle at the end of a rope, that becomes tighter as it is pulled

nor /nɔːʳ/ *conjunction*
a word used between two choices after the words **neither** or **not** ► *Neither Anna nor Maria likes cooking.*

norm /nɔːm/ *noun*
the norm something that is thought to be usual or normal ► *Going to university is becoming the norm.*

normal /'nɔːməl/ *adjective*
usual or expected ➤ *It's normal to feel tired after working so hard.*
SAME MEANING: **natural**

normality /nɔː'mælətɪ/ *noun (no plural)*
a situation in which everything happens in the usual or expected way

normally /'nɔːməlɪ/ *adverb*
usually ➤ *Normally I get up at 7 o'clock, but today I got up late.*

north /nɔːθ/ *noun, adjective, adverb*
the direction that is on the left when you look at the sun at the start of the morning ➤ *Manchester is in the north of England.* ➤ *The north part of the house doesn't get a lot of sun.* ➤ *Birds fly north in summer.* ➤ *living north of Oxford*

northbound /'nɔːθbaʊnd/ *adjective*
travelling or leading towards the north ➤ *northbound traffic*

northeast /ˌnɔːθ'iːst/ *noun, adjective, adverb*
the direction which is in the middle between north and east

northeastern /ˌnɔːθ'iːstən/ *adjective*
in or from the northeast part of something, especially a country

northerly /'nɔːðəlɪ/ *adjective*
1 towards the north ➤ *a northerly direction*
2 (used about the wind) blowing from the north

northern /'nɔːðən/ *adjective*
in or of the north

northerner /'nɔːðənə'/ *noun*
a person who comes from the north of a country

North Pole /ˌnɔːθ 'pəʊl/ *noun*
the most northern point of the Earth

northward /'nɔːθwəd/ *adjective*
towards the north ➤ *They headed in a northward direction.*

northwards /'nɔːθwədz/ *adverb*
towards the north ➤ *We drove northwards.*

northwest /ˌnɔːθ'west/ *noun, adjective, adverb*
the direction which is in the middle between north and west

northwestern /ˌnɔːθ'westən/ *adjective*
in or from the northwest part of something, especially a country

nose /nəʊz/ *noun*
1 the part of your face through which you breathe and with which you smell
2 **turn up your nose at something** to think that something is not good or important enough for you
3 **under someone's nose** right in front of someone ➤ *I looked for my pen everywhere and it was under my nose all the time!*

nosebleed /'nəʊzbliːd/ *noun*
have a nosebleed to have blood coming out of your nose

nosedive /'nəʊzdaɪv/ *noun*
1 a sudden, steep drop by a plane, with its front end pointing towards the ground
2 **take a nosedive** (used about amounts, prices, etc.) to fall suddenly ➤ *Profits took a nosedive last year.*

nosey /'nəʊzɪ/ *adjective*
another word for **nosy**

nostalgia /nɒ'stældʒə/ *noun (no plural)*
the slightly sad feeling you have when you think about nice things that happened in the past ➤ *Dad is full of nostalgia for his college days.*

nostril /'nɒstrɪl/ *noun*
one of the two holes in your nose through which you breathe

nosy (also **nosey**) /'nəʊzɪ/ *adjective* (**nosier, nosiest**)
always trying to find out about things that other people want to keep secret ➤ *Don't be so nosy!*

not /nɒt/ *adverb*
a word that gives the opposite meaning to another word or a sentence ➤ *I'm not going home yet.* ➤ *It's red, not pink.*

notable /'nəʊtəbəl/ *adjective*
important, interesting, or unusual ➤ *This area is notable for its forests.*

notably /'nəʊtəblɪ/ *adverb*
used when you are giving an especially important or interesting example ➤ *Some politicians, most notably the President, refused to comment.*

notch¹ /nɒtʃ/ *noun (plural **notches**)*
a cut in a surface that is in the shape of a V ➤ *The arrow has a notch in the end for the bowstring.*

notch² *verb*
notch something up to achieve a victory or a particular total ➤ *He has notched up four goals in four games.*

note¹ /nəʊt/ *noun*
1 a single sound in music
2 a short written message ➤ *I'll write a note to thank her for the party.*
3 a few words written down to help you remember something ➤ *Please make a note of my new address.*
4 a piece of paper money ➤ *a ten-pound note*

note² *verb (present participle **noting**, past **noted**)*
1 to pay attention to something so that you remember it ➤ *Please note that the shop is closed on Saturdays.*
2 note something down to write something down so that you remember it ➤ *He noted down our new address.*

notebook /'nəʊtbʊk/ *noun*
a book in which you write things that you need to remember

notepaper /'nəʊtˌpeɪpər/ *noun (no plural)*
paper for writing letters on

nothing /'nʌθɪŋ/ *pronoun*
1 not any thing ➤ *There is nothing in this box – it's empty.* ➤ *She said nothing about her holiday.*
2 for nothing for no money ➤ *If you buy the table, you can have the chairs for nothing.*

notice¹ /'nəʊtɪs/ *noun*
a written or printed paper that is put in a public place and gives information to people ➤ *The notice on the door said that the library was closed.*

notice² *verb (present participle **noticing**, past **noticed**)*
to see, hear, or smell something ➤ *I noticed that he was getting nervous.* ➤ *Did you notice the funny smell?*

noticeable /'nəʊtɪsəbəl/ *adjective*
easily recognized or seen ➤ *There has been a noticeable improvement in your work.*

noticeboard /'nəʊtɪsˌbɔːd/ *noun*
a board fixed to a wall, on which you put notices telling people about things

notify /'nəʊtɪfaɪ/ *verb (past **notified**)*
to tell someone something officially ➤ *She immediately notified the police.*

notion /'nəʊʃən/ *noun*
an idea or a belief about something ➤ *I had a notion that you were looking for a new job.*

notorious /nəˈtɔːrɪəs/ *adjective*
famous because of being so bad ➤ *a notorious criminal*

nought /nɔːt/ *noun*
the number o
SAME MEANING: **zero**
LOOK AT: **o**

noun /naʊn/ *noun*
a word that is the name of a person, place, animal, or thing. In the sentence "The boy threw a stone at the dog", "boy", "stone", and "dog" are nouns.

nourish /'nʌrɪʃ/ *verb*
to give a person, an animal, or a plant the food they need in order to live and grow ▶ *The cream contains vitamins A and E to nourish the skin.*

novel /'nɒvəl/ *noun*
a book that tells a story which someone has written

novelist /'nɒvəlɪst/ *noun*
a person who writes novels

novelty /'nɒvəltɪ/ *noun*
1 (plural **novelties**) something that is new and unusual ▶ *at a time when television was still a novelty*
2 (no plural) the quality of being new, different, and unusual ▶ *the novelty of using e-mail*

November /nəʊ'vembə'/ *noun*
the 11th month of the year

novice /'nɒvɪs/ *noun*
a person who has just begun learning how to do something ▶ *I am a novice at chess.*

now /naʊ/ *adverb*
1 at the present time ▶ *We used to live in a village, but now we live in a city.* ▶ *I must go now – I can't wait any longer.*
2 used to get someone's attention or start talking about something else ▶ *Now, children, open your books at page 6.*

nowadays /'naʊədeɪz/ *adverb*
used to talk about what happens now, compared to the past ▶ *People tend to live longer nowadays.*

nowhere /'nəʊ,weə'/ *adverb*
not anywhere ▶ *We looked for the key everywhere, but it was nowhere to be found* (=we couldn't find it anywhere).

nuclear /'nju:klɪə'/ *adjective*
concerned with or using the very great power made by splitting an atom or joining atoms ▶ *nuclear war* ▶ *nuclear power*

nuclear reactor /,nju:klɪə rɪ'æktə'/ *noun*
a large machine that produces nuclear energy

nucleus /'nju:klɪəs/ *noun* (plural **nuclei** /'nju:klɪaɪ/)
the central part of something, round which other parts gather ▶ *A nucleus is the central part of an atom.*

nude /nju:d/ *adjective*
not wearing any clothes
SAME MEANING: **naked**

nudge¹ /nʌdʒ/ *verb*
(present participle **nudging**, past **nudged**)
to push someone lightly, usually with your elbow ▶ *She nudged me when it was time to go.*

nudge² *noun*
a gentle push, usually given with your elbow ▶ *He gave her a nudge.*

nudity /'nju:dətɪ/ *noun* (no plural)
the state of not wearing any clothes ▶ *There's too much nudity on TV.*

nuisance /'nju:səns/ *noun*
someone or something that makes you cross or worried ▶ *What a nuisance! I've missed my train!*

numb /nʌm/ *adjective*
not able to feel anything ▶ *My feet were numb with cold.*

number¹ /'nʌmbə'/ *noun*
1 a figure such as 1, 2, or 3
2 a group of numbers that you use to telephone someone ▶ *Can you give me her number?*
3 more than one person or thing in a group ▶ *Birds gather in large numbers beside the river.*
4 a number of several ▶ *A number of people asked me where I had bought my hat.*

number² *verb*
to give a figure or number to something ▶ *Number the pages from 1 to 100.*

numbered /'nʌmbəd/ *adjective*
with a number ▶ *Seats in a theatre are usually numbered.*

number plate /'nʌmbə ˌpleɪt/ *noun*
a sign at the front and back of a car, lorry, etc., which shows its number ▶ *The number plate was F360 XJB.*

numeral /'njuːmərəl/ *noun*
a sign used to represent a number ▶ *Roman numerals*

numerous /'njuːmərəs/ *adjective*
many ▶ *Your work has numerous mistakes in it.*

nun /nʌn/ *noun*
one of a group of women who live together and have given their lives to a religion
COMPARE: **monk**

nurse¹ /nɜːs/ *noun*
1 a person, often a woman, who is trained to help doctors and look after people who are ill, injured, or very old
2 a woman who is trained to look after young children

nurse² *verb (present participle* **nursing**, *past* **nursed**)
to look after people who are ill, injured, or very old ▶ *She nursed her mother when she was ill.*

nursery /'nɜːsəri/ *noun (plural* **nurseries**)
1 a place where young children are taken care of while their parents are at work
2 the room in a house in which young children play and sleep

nursery rhyme /'nɜːsəri ˌraɪm/ *noun*
a short, well-known song for young children

nursery school /'nɜːsəri ˌskuːl/ *noun*
a school for young children between three and four years old

nursing /'nɜːsɪŋ/ *noun (no plural)*
the job of looking after people who are ill, injured, or very old ▶ *What made you choose nursing as a career?*

nut /nʌt/ *noun*
1 the dried fruit of a tree, with a hard shell
2 a shaped piece of metal with a hole in it which is used with a BOLT to fasten things together

nutrient /'njuːtriənt/ *noun*
a chemical or food that helps plants, animals, or people to live and grow ▶ *Plants absorb nutrients from the soil.*

nutritious /njuː'trɪʃəs/ *adjective*
(used about food) containing the substances that your body needs to be healthy ▶ *nutritious and cheap recipe ideas*

nylon /'naɪlɒn/ *noun (no plural)*
a strong material, made by machines ▶ *nylon stockings*

o /əʊ/ *noun*
used in speech when you are giving a telephone number ▶ *The number is 60275* (=six o two seven five)

> Always use **o** when you are giving a telephone number; do not use **zero** or **nought**.

oak /əʊk/ *noun*
1 a big tree with hard wood
2 *(no plural)* the wood of this tree ▶ *an oak table*

oar /ɔː/ *noun*
a long, wooden pole with a flat blade at the end, used to make a boat move through the water

oasis /əʊ'eɪsɪs/ *noun (plural* **oases** /əʊ'eɪsiːz/)
a place in the desert where there is water and where trees can grow

oath /əʊθ/ *noun (plural* **oaths** /əʊðz/)

a very serious promise ➤ *She swore an oath to tell the truth in court.*

oats /əʊts/ *plural noun*
a grain that is used as food

obedience /əʊˈbiːdɪəns/ *noun (no plural)*
behaviour in which you do what people tell you to do ➤ *Mrs Jones expects obedience from all her pupils.*
OPPOSITE: **disobedience**

obedient /əʊˈbiːdɪənt/ *adjective*
willing to do what people tell you to do ➤ *an obedient child. (adverb: obediently)*
OPPOSITE: **disobedient**

obese /əʊˈbiːs/ *adjective*
much too fat, in a way that is dangerous to your health ➤ *The doctor told her she was obese and had to go on a diet.*

obey /əʊˈbeɪ/ *verb*
to do what someone tells you to do ➤ *You should obey your teacher.*
OPPOSITE: **disobey**

object¹ /ˈɒbdʒɪkt/ *noun*
1 a thing that you can touch ➤ *What is that big, red object over there?*
2 an aim or a purpose ➤ *The object of this exercise is to find out how many people like cats more than dogs.*
3 a word used in grammar to describe the person or thing that is affected by the verb in a sentence. In the sentence "Jane bought some bread", "bread" is the object.
COMPARE (**3**): **subject**

object² /əbˈdʒekt/ *verb*
to say that you do not like or do not agree with something ➤ *She objected to our plan.*

objection /əbˈdʒekʃən/ *noun*
something that you say or feel about something you do not like or do not agree with ➤ *She had strong objections to working on Sundays.*

objective¹ /əbˈdʒektɪv/ *noun*
something that you are trying to achieve ➤ *Our main objective is to raise money.*

objective² *adjective*
not influenced by your own feelings or opinions ➤ *We need an objective approach to the problem. (adverb: objectively)*
COMPARE: **subjective**

obligation /ˌɒblɪˈɡeɪʃən/ *noun*
something that you must do because it is your duty

obligatory /əˈblɪɡətəri/ *adjective*
that must be done because of a law or rule ➤ *Attending school is obligatory.*

oblige /əˈblaɪdʒ/ *verb (present participle obliging, past obliged)*
to make it necessary for someone to do something ➤ *It was raining so hard that I was obliged to stay at home.* ➤ *I felt obliged to tell her the truth.*
SAME MEANING: **force**

obliterate /əˈblɪtəreɪt/ *verb (present participle obliterating, past obliterated)*
to destroy something completely ➤ *The whole city was obliterated by bombing.*

oblivious /əˈblɪvɪəs/ *adjective*
not noticing what is happening around you ➤ *The children were fast asleep, oblivious to the noise.*

oblong /ˈɒblɒŋ/ *noun*
a shape with four straight sides and four equal angles that is longer than it is wide
SAME MEANING: **rectangle**

obnoxious /əbˈnɒkʃəs/ *adjective*
very unpleasant or rude ➤ *What an obnoxious man!*

oboe /ˈəʊbəʊ/ *noun*
a wooden musical instrument shaped like a narrow tube, which you play by blowing into it

obscene /əb'si:n/ *adjective*
showing or talking about sex in an offensive and shocking way ▶ *obscene photographs* ▶ *obscene language*

obscure¹ /əb'skjʊəʳ/ *adjective*
difficult to understand ▶ *Jarrett didn't like the plan, for some obscure reason.*

obscure² *verb (present participle **obscuring**, past **obscured**)*
to prevent something from being seen ▶ *The top of the hill was obscured by clouds.*

observant /əb'zɜ:vənt/ *adjective*
good at noticing things ▶ *It was very observant of you to notice his shoes.*

observation /ˌɒbzə'veɪʃən/ *noun (no plural)*
1 careful watching ▶ *His father is very ill and is going into hospital for observation.*
2 under observation watched carefully, especially by the police or in a hospital ▶ *The police kept him under observation.*

observe /əb'zɜ:v/ *verb (present participle **observing**, past **observed**)*
to watch someone or something carefully ▶ *Children can learn to do things by observing other people.*

obsess /əb'ses/ *verb*
be obsessed with something to think about something all the time, in a way that is not normal ▶ *Julie is obsessed with losing weight.*

obsession /əb'seʃən/ *noun*
something that you think about all the time, in a way that is not normal ▶ *He has an obsession **with** money.*

obsolete /'ɒbsəli:t/ *adjective*
old, and no longer used ▶ *Our computer system will soon be obsolete.*

obstacle /'ɒbstəkəl/ *noun*
something that gets in the way or causes a problem ▶ *Cars were driving slowly because the storm had left many obstacles in the road.*

obstinate /'ɒbstɪnət/ *adjective*
having a strong will and not willing to change your ideas easily ▶ *She is an obstinate child – she won't eat unless she wants to.*
SAME MEANING: **stubborn**

obstruct /əb'strʌkt/ *verb*
to get in the way of something or stop it completely ▶ *Do not obstruct this entrance.*

obstruction /əb'strʌkʃən/ *noun*
something that blocks the way ▶ *The accident caused an obstruction on the road.*

obtain /əb'teɪn/ *verb*
to get something ▶ *Maps can be obtained from the tourist office.*

obtainable /əb'teɪnəbəl/ *adjective*
that you can get ▶ *Fresh fish is easily obtainable.*

obvious /'ɒbvɪəs/ *adjective*
clear and easy to see or understand ▶ *It is obvious that she is lying. (adverb: **obviously**)*
SAME MEANING: **evident**

occasion /ə'keɪʒən/ *noun*
1 a time when something happens ▶ *I've spoken to him on several occasions.*
2 a special event ▶ *I only wear a tie on special occasions.*

occasional /ə'keɪʒənəl/ *adjective*
happening from time to time ▶ *an occasional visit (adverb: **occasionally**)*

occupant /'ɒkjʊpənt/ *noun*
a person who lives in a building or room, or who is using it ▶ *The occupants of the house were away.*

occupation /ˌɒkjʊ'peɪʃən/ *noun*
1 a job ▶ *"What is your occupation?" "I am a doctor."*
2 something that you do in your free time ▶ *Reading is one of her favourite occupations.*

occupied /ˈɒkjupaɪd/ *adjective*
(used about rooms, seats, etc.) being
used by someone ▶ *All the seats in
the row were occupied.*
OPPOSITE: **free, unoccupied**

occupy /ˈɒkjupaɪ/ *verb (past
occupied)*
1 to live in a place ▶ *Three families
occupy that big house.*
2 to fill a certain position or space
▶ *His records occupy a lot of space.*
3 to keep someone busy ▶ *This game
will keep the children occupied all
afternoon.*
4 occupy yourself to use time to do
something ▶ *He occupied himself
with his computer.*

occur /əˈkɜːʳ/ *verb (present participle
occurring, past occurred)*
1 to happen ▶ *The accident occurred
at 5 o'clock.*
LOOK AT: **happen**
2 occur to someone to come into
someone's mind ▶ *That idea has
never occurred to me before.* ▶ *It
occurred to him that he should take
his aunt to the station.*

occurrence /əˈkʌrəns/ *noun*
something that happens ▶ *Stress-
related illness is now a fairly common
occurrence.*

ocean /ˈəʊʃən/ *noun*
a very large sea ▶ *the Atlantic Ocean*

o'clock /əˈklɒk/ *adverb*
a word used to tell what time it is
▶ *"What time is it?" "It's 4 o'clock."*

octagon /ˈɒktəgən/ *noun*
a flat shape with eight sides

October /ɒkˈtəʊbəʳ/ *noun*
the tenth month of the year

octopus /ˈɒktəpəs/ *noun (plural
octopuses)*
a soft sea creature with eight long
limbs

odd /ɒd/ *adjective*
1 strange or unusual ▶ *It's odd that
he hasn't telephoned me.*

SAME MEANING: **peculiar**
2 separated from the pair to which
it belongs ▶ *You've got odd socks
on – one's blue and the other's
green!*
3 odd number a number that cannot
be divided exactly by two ▶ *13 and 15
are odd numbers*

oddly /ˈɒdli/ *adverb*
1 in a strange or an unusual way
▶ *Roger's been behaving very oddly.*
2 oddly enough used when
something seems strange or
surprising ▶ *Oddly enough, she
didn't seem offended.*

odds /ɒdz/ *plural noun*
1 the possibility that something will
or will not happen, often expressed
as a number ▶ *The odds of winning
the lottery are about fourteen million
to one.*
2 against all the odds even though a
good result seemed very unlikely
▶ *He recovered from his injury
against all the odds.*

odds and ends /ˌɒdz ənd ˈendz/
plural noun
various different little things which
are not very important or useful ▶ *a
box full of odds and ends.*

odour /ˈəʊdəʳ/ *noun*
a smell, especially an unpleasant one
▶ *He noticed a strange odour in the
room.*

of /əv; *strong* ɒv/ *preposition*
1 forming part of something;
belonging to something ▶ *the wheels
of a car* ▶ *the streets of London*
2 a word which shows a relationship
between people or things ▶ *a friend
of mine* ▶ *the colour of her hair*
3 containing ▶ *a cup of tea* ▶ *a bag of
sweets* ▶ *a room full of people*
4 a word used in expressions which
show amounts ▶ *Have some of my
sweets.* ▶ *a pound of butter* ▶ *a piece
of cake* ▶ *a group of people.*

O

5 made from ▶ *a bar of steel*
6 about ▶ *I often think of you.*
7 used in dates ▶ *the 12th of June*

off¹ /ɒf/ *adverb, preposition*
1 away from something ▶ *Can you get this lid off?* ▶ *One of my buttons has fallen off.* ▶ *He fell off the chair.*
2 not on ▶ *All the lights were off.* ▶ *Switch the computer off.*
OPPOSITE (**1** and **2**): **on**
3 away to another place ▶ *He drove off.* ▶ *She went off without saying goodbye.*
4 not working ▶ *He's off for three days.*
5 off your food not hungry because you are ill

off² *adjective*
(used about food) old, and no longer good to eat or drink ▶ *This milk is off.*

off-chance /ˈɒf tʃɑːns/ *noun*
on the off-chance hoping that something will happen, although it is unlikely ▶ *He only went to the party on the off-chance that Pippa might be there.*

offence /əˈfens/ *noun*
1 something that is wrong; a crime ▶ *It is an offence to ride a bicycle at night without lights.*
2 take offence to feel unhappy or angry about something someone says to you ▶ *She took offence when I asked her how old she was.*

offend /əˈfend/ *verb*
to make someone feel unhappy or angry ▶ *I offended him by not answering his letter.*
SAME MEANING: **upset**

offender /əˈfendər/ *noun*
a person who is guilty of a crime ▶ *a prison for young offenders*

offensive¹ /əˈfensɪv/ *adjective*
likely to upset or offend people ▶ *She said some very offensive things.*

offensive² *noun*
1 an attack on a place by an army ▶ *a military offensive*

2 go on the offensive to attack or criticize people ▶ *We have to go on the offensive if we are going to win this election.*

offer¹ /ˈɒfər/ *verb*
1 to show someone that you want to give them something ▶ *I offered James some of my chocolates.*
2 to tell or show someone that you are willing to help them ▶ *She offered to help her mother with the shopping.*

offer² *noun*
1 an act of showing that you are happy to help with something ▶ *Thank you for your offer of help.*
2 the amount of money that you say you will pay for something ▶ *They made us a good offer for the house.*

offhand /ˌɒfˈhænd/ *adverb*
immediately, without time to think ▶ *I don't know his address offhand.*

office /ˈɒfɪs/ *noun*
a place where people do written work and do business ▶ *She works in an office.*

officer /ˈɒfɪsər/ *noun*
1 a person in the army, navy, etc., who can give orders to other people
2 a person who has an important job in an organization ▶ *a police officer* ▶ *a prison officer*

official¹ /əˈfɪʃəl/ *adjective*
approved by someone in power ▶ *an official letter*
OPPOSITE: **unofficial**

official² *noun*
a person who has an important job, especially in the government or an organization ▶ *an official in the Department of Health*

officially /əˈfɪʃəli/ *adverb*
1 in an official or formal way ▶ *The new bridge was officially opened this morning.*
2 according to the reason or information that has been given, which may not be true ▶ *The meeting*

was cancelled, officially because of bad weather.

off-licence /'ɒf ˌlaɪsəns/ *noun*
a shop that sells alcoholic drinks

off-peak /ˌɒf 'piːk/ *adjective*
1 (used about hours or periods of time) when fewer people want to do or use something – for example, travel, use their telephones, etc.
2 (used about travel, electricity, etc.) cheaper because it is done or used at these less busy times ► *off-peak rail services*

offside /ˌɒf'saɪd/ *adjective, adverb*
in a position where you are not allowed to receive the ball in games such as football ► *I hadn't noticed I was offside.*

often /'ɒfən/ *adverb*
1 many times ► *I often go to bed early.*
2 How often ...? used to ask how many times something happens ► *How often does it rain here?* ► *How often do you go to the cinema?*

oh /əʊ/ *interjection*
something you say when you feel surprised, happy, annoyed, etc. ► *Oh, no! I've missed the bus!*

oil¹ /ɔɪl/ *noun (no plural)*
thick liquid that comes from under the ground or under the sea, used for cooking, burning, or for making machines work smoothly

oil² *verb*
to put oil on something to make it work more smoothly ► *You should oil that machine more often.*

oil paint /'ɔɪl peɪnt/ *noun*
a special paint with oil in it, used by artists

oil painting /'ɔɪl ˌpeɪntɪŋ/ *noun*
a picture painted with oil paints

oil rig /'ɔɪl rɪg/ *noun*
a special, large piece of machinery used as a base for getting oil from under the ground or under the sea

oil slick /'ɔɪl slɪk/ *noun*
a layer of oil on the sea or a river, which has come out of a ship carrying oil

oil well /'ɔɪl wel/ *noun*
a big hole made in the ground to get oil out

oily /'ɔɪli/ *adjective* (**oilier, oiliest**)
covered with oil, or containing a lot of oil ► *He wiped his oily hands on a rag.*

ointment /'ɔɪntmənt/ *noun (no plural)*
oily cream that you rub on your skin for medical reasons

OK (also **okay**) /əʊ'keɪ/ *adjective, adverb*
1 a word used to say you agree; yes ► *"Shall we go for a walk?" "OK."*
2 all right ► *"How is your mother?" "She's OK."*

old /əʊld/ *adjective*
1 having lived a long time ► *My grandmother is very old.*
OPPOSITE: **young**
2 the word we use to show our age ► *How old are you?* ► *I am 11 years old.*
COMPARE (**2**): **aged**
3 having been used for a long time; having existed for a long time ► *old clothes* ► *an old building*
OPPOSITE (**3**): **new**
4 having lasted for a long time ► *We are very old friends – we've known each other since we were children.*

old age /ˌəʊld 'eɪdʒ/ *noun (no plural)*
the time in your life when you are old ► *You should save some money for your old age.*

old-fashioned /ˌəʊld 'fæʃənd/ *adjective*
not common any more ► *old-fashioned clothes* ► *old-fashioned ideas*
OPPOSITE: **modern**
COMPARE: **out-of-date**

olive /ˈɒlɪv/ *noun*
a small fruit which is green or black, from the olive tree

olive oil /ˌɒlɪv ˈɔɪl/ *noun (no plural)*
oil made from olives and used in cooking

Olympic /əˈlɪmpɪk/ *adjective*
of the Olympic Games ➤ *She won two Olympic gold medals.*

Olympic Games /əˌlɪmpɪk ˈɡeɪmz/ *(also Olympics /əˌlɪmpɪks/) plural noun*
an international sports competition which takes place every four years

omelette /ˈɒmlɪt/ *noun*
a mixture of eggs beaten together and cooked in hot fat in a flat pan

ominous /ˈɒmɪnəs/ *adjective*
making you feel that something bad is going to happen ➤ *ominous black clouds* (adverb: **ominously**)

omit /əˈmɪt/ *verb (present participle omitting, past omitted)*
to leave something out; not to include something ➤ *You have omitted my name from the list.*

omnibus /ˈɒmnɪbəs/ *noun (plural omnibuses)*
a radio or television programme that consists of several previous programmes ➤ *I missed an episode, so I'll have to watch the omnibus at the weekend.*

on /ɒn/ *preposition, adverb*
1 used to show where something is ➤ *I put the glass on the shelf.*
2 in use; working ➤ *Is the kitchen light on?*
OPPOSITE (2): **off**
3 covering a part of your body ➤ *He had a big coat on.* ➤ *She looks very nice with her new dress on.*
4 used with days or dates, to show when something happens ➤ *The party is on March 12th.* ➤ *I'll see you on Monday.*
5 inside a bus, train, or plane, or

travelling by bicycle ➤ *I saw Jane on the bus.* ➤ *We watched that film on a plane.*
6 further; more ➤ *I stopped to look at a map, and then drove on.*
7 used to show that when something happened, something else happened ➤ *On arriving* (=when she arrived), *she telephoned her mother.*
8 being shown ➤ *What's on television tonight* (=what programmes are being shown)?
9 on foot walking ➤ *Let's go on foot.*
10 on the left, on the right at the left or right side of something ➤ *There was a cinema on the left and a church on the right.*

once /wʌns/ *adverb*
1 one time ➤ *I have only been to America once.* ➤ *We go shopping once a week.*
2 some time ago ➤ *My grandmother was a teacher once.*
3 when ➤ *It was easy once I learnt how to do it.*
4 at once (a) now; straight away ➤ *We must leave at once.*
(b) at the same time ➤ *You can't do three different things at once.*
5 once more one more time ➤ *Try ringing the bell once more – perhaps they're in the garden and didn't hear.*
6 once or twice only a few times ➤ *"Have you ever been to a football match?" "Once or twice."*
7 once upon a time (an expression used at the beginning of some children's stories) a long time ago

one /wʌn/ *adjective, noun, pronoun*
1 the number 1
2 a single thing or person ➤ *Do you have you any books on farming? – I'd like to borrow one* (=a book on farming). ➤ *That girl has only got one shoe on.*
3 some; a ➤ *John telephoned me one day last week.* ➤ *Let's go for a drink one evening.*

4 the same ▶ *They all ran off in one direction.*

5 any person ▶ *One should try to help other people.*

6 one another used to show that two people do the same thing one to the other ▶ *The two boys hit one another.* ▶ *Mark and Sarah like one another* (=Mark likes Sue and Sue likes Mark).

one-off /ˌwʌn ˈɒf/ *adjective*
happening only once ▶ *a one-off payment*

oneself /wʌnˈself/ *pronoun*
1 used in sentences with "one", to speak or write about the same person ▶ *One cannot blame oneself all the time.*
2 by oneself alone ▶ *Sometimes it's nice to be by oneself.*

one-to-one /ˌwʌn tə ˈwʌn/ *adjective*
between two people ▶ *tuition on a one-to-one basis*

one-way /ˈwʌn weɪ/ *adjective*
moving only in one direction; allowing movement only in one direction ▶ *one-way traffic* ▶ *a one-way street*

onion /ˈʌnjən/ *noun*
a round, white vegetable with a strong smell, which is made up of one skin inside another and is often used in cooking

online (*also* **on-line**) /ˈɒnlaɪn/ *adjective, adverb*
using a computer, especially one that is connected to the INTERNET ▶ *an online information service* ▶ *We do most of our work online.*

onlooker /ˈɒnˌlʊkəʳ/ *noun*
a person who watches something happening but is not involved in it ▶ *A crowd of onlookers had gathered.*

only¹ /ˈəʊnlɪ/ *adjective, adverb*
1 being the one person or thing of a particular kind ▶ *She is the only girl in her family; all the other children are boys.*

2 and nothing more; and no one else ▶ *You can only have one piece of cake.* ▶ *This room is for teachers only.*
3 just ▶ *We're only trying to help.*
4 an only child a child with no brothers or sisters
5 only just hardly; nearly not ▶ *This box is very heavy; I can only just lift it.*

only² *conjunction*
but; except for ▶ *I'd love to come with you, only I have to stay at home and help my mother.*

onto /ˈɒntə; *strong* ˈɒntuː/ *preposition*
to a place ▶ *He climbed onto a rock.*

onwards /ˈɒnwədz/ *adverb*
forward in time or space ▶ *They hurried onwards.* ▶ *From Monday onwards, I shall be in another class.*

ooze /uːz/ *verb* (*present participle* **oozing**, *past* **oozed**)
to move or flow slowly ▶ *The blood oozed from his knee.*

opal /ˈəʊpəl/ *noun*
a white stone used in jewellery

open¹ /ˈəʊpən/ *adjective*
1 not shut ▶ *She's not asleep; her eyes are open.*
2 ready for business ▶ *Is the bank open yet?*
OPPOSITE (**1** and **2**): **closed**
3 not surrounded by other things ▶ *We drove through open country.*
4 in the open air outside ▶ *We ate our lunch in the open air.*

open² *verb*
1 to make something open ▶ *Open your books at page 3.*
2 to become open ▶ *The door opened and a man came in.*
3 to begin business ▶ *The shop doesn't open until 10 o'clock.*
OPPOSITE (**1**, **2**, and **3**): **close**

open-air /ˌəʊpən ˈeəʳ/ *adjective*
outside, not in a building ▶ *an open-air concert* ▶ *an open-air swimming pool*

O

open day /ˈəʊpən deɪ/ *noun*
a day when people can visit a school or company and see what is done there

opener /ˈəʊpənə/ *noun*
an instrument for opening things ➤ *a tin opener* ➤ *a bottle opener*

opening /ˈəʊpənɪŋ/ *noun*
a hole or space in something ➤ *an opening **in** the fence*

openly /ˈəʊpənlɪ/ *adverb*
honestly and without keeping anything secret ➤ *a chance to talk openly about your problems*

openness /ˈəʊpən-nəs/ *noun (no plural)*
the quality of being honest and not keeping things secret

open-plan /ˌəʊpən ˈplæn/ *adjective*
(used about a building) not having walls to divide it into separate rooms ➤ *an open-plan office*

opera /ˈɒpərə/ *noun*
a type of play that has songs and music instead of spoken words

operate /ˈɒpəreɪt/ *verb (present participle **operating**, past **operated**)*
1 to make something work ➤ *Do you know how to operate this machine?*
2 to work ➤ *How does this machine operate?*
3 to cut open the body of someone who is ill and make the unhealthy part better ➤ *The doctors operated **on** her stomach.*

operation /ˌɒpəˈreɪʃən/ *noun*
the cutting open of a part of the body of someone who is ill to make them better ➤ *She needs an operation **on** her stomach.*

operator /ˈɒpəreɪtə/ *noun*
1 a person who controls telephones and whom you can ring for information
2 a person whose job is to control a machine

opinion /əˈpɪnjən/ *noun*
what someone thinks about something ➤ *He asked his father's opinion about his plans.* ➤ *In my opinion (=I think), you're wrong.*
SAME MEANING: **view**

opinion poll /əˈpɪnjən ˌpəʊl/ *noun*
another way of saying **poll**

opponent /əˈpəʊnənt/ *noun*
someone who is on the opposite side in a game or competition ➤ *We beat our opponents at football.*

opportunity /ˌɒpəˈtjuːnətɪ/ *noun (plural **opportunities**)*
a chance or time to do something ➤ *I have been offered a job; it's a great opportunity.*

oppose /əˈpəʊz/ *verb (present participle **opposing**, past **opposed**)*
to be against something or not agree with something ➤ *She wanted to get married at 16, but her father opposed her wish.*

opposed /əˈpəʊzd/ *adjective*
1 be opposed to something to be against something or not agree with something ➤ *Most people are opposed to the death penalty.*
2 as opposed to used to compare two different things or amounts ➤ *The discount price is £25, as opposed to the usual price of £50.*

opposite¹ /ˈɒpəzɪt/ *noun*
a person or thing that is as different as possible from another ➤ *High is the opposite **of** low.*

opposite² *adjective*
1 as different as possible ➤ *The buses went in opposite directions – one went south and the other went north.*
2 facing ➤ *The library is on the opposite side of the road from the school.*

opposite³ *preposition*
facing ➤ *The library is opposite the school.*

opposition /ˌɒpə'zɪʃən/ *noun*
1 (*no plural*) the act of strongly disagreeing with something ➤ *There was a lot of opposition **to** the plan.*
2 the opposition the person or team that you are trying to defeat in a game or competition
3 the Opposition the second biggest political party in parliament, which is not in the government

oppress /ə'pres/ *verb*
to treat people in an unfair and cruel way

oppression /ə'preʃən/ *noun* (*no plural*)
the act of treating people in an unfair and cruel way ➤ *They suffered years of oppression.*

oppressive /ə'presɪv/ *adjective*
1 unfair and cruel ➤ *an oppressive military government*
2 making you feel uncomfortable ➤ *oppressive heat*

opt /ɒpt/ *verb*
1 to choose something or choose to do something ➤ *I opted **for** the cheaper car.* ➤ *You can opt to pay in instalments.*
2 opt out to choose not to be involved in something ➤ *Several countries may opt out of the agreement.*

optical illusion /ˌɒptɪkəl ɪ'luːʒən/ *noun*
something that you think you are seeing but is not actually there, because your eyes are being tricked

optician /ɒp'tɪʃən/ *noun*
a person who tests your eyesight, and makes and sells glasses

optimism /'ɒptɪmɪzəm/ *noun* (*no plural*)
the belief that good things will happen ➤ *optimism about the country's economic future*
OPPOSITE: **pessimism**

optimist /'ɒptɪmɪst/ *noun*
a person who always believes that good things will happen
OPPOSITE: **pessimist**

optimistic /ˌɒptɪ'mɪstɪk/ *adjective*
full of hope; believing good things will happen ➤ *I'm optimistic that we'll win the game.*
OPPOSITE: **pessimistic**

option /'ɒpʃən/ *noun*
a choice; the power to choose ➤ *The train was late but there was no bus, so I had no option but to wait* (=there was nothing I could do except wait).

optional /'ɒpʃənəl/ *adjective*
not needed according to a rule or law, but able to be chosen or done if you want ➤ *Games are optional* (=you don't have to do them if you don't want to) *at our school.*

or /əʳ; *strong* ɔːʳ/ *conjunction*
used when giving a choice ➤ *Do you want tea or coffee?*

oral /'ɔːrəl/ *adjective*
spoken, not written ➤ *an oral test*

orange¹ /'ɒrɪndʒ/ *noun*
1 a round, sweet, juicy fruit with a thick skin
2 the colour of this fruit, between red and yellow

orange² *adjective*
of the colour of the skin of an orange when it is ripe; a mixture of yellow and red

orbit¹ /'ɔːbɪt/ *noun*
the path of one thing moving around another in space

orbit² *verb*
to move in a circle round something in space ➤ *The spaceship orbited the moon.*

orchard /'ɔːtʃəd/ *noun*
a field in which fruit trees grow

orchestra /'ɔːkɪstrə/ *noun*
a large group of people who play musical instruments together

ordeal /ɔːˈdiːəl/ *noun*
a very difficult and unpleasant experience ➤ *The journey was a real ordeal.*

order¹ /ˈɔːdəʳ/ *noun*
1 a command; something you must do because your parents, or people who control you, tell you to ➤ *The captain gave the order to attack.*
2 *(no plural)* a special way in which things are arranged or placed ➤ *in alphabetical order* (=words and letters arranged in a system which starts at A and finishes at Z) ➤ *in order of importance* (=starting with the most important and finishing with the least important)
3 in order to so that something else can happen ➤ *He stood on a chair in order to* (=so that he could) *reach the top shelf.*
4 keep things in order to keep things neatly arranged ➤ *Try to keep these important papers in order.*
5 out of order not working ➤ *The telephone is out of order.*

order² *verb*
1 to give a command to someone ➤ *The officer ordered the soldiers to attack.*
2 to ask a shop to get something for you ➤ *I've ordered a new table, but it won't arrive until next week.*
3 to ask a waiter to bring you something in a restaurant, etc. ➤ *I've ordered two coffees.*

orderly /ˈɔːdəlɪ/ *adjective*
arranged or organized in a neat way ➤ *Her wardrobe is very neat and orderly.*
OPPOSITE: **disorderly**

ordinarily /ˈɔːdnərɪlɪ/ *adverb*
usually ➤ *Ordinarily, I would drive but I have a headache today.*

ordinary /ˈɔːdnrɪ/ *adjective*
1 usual or common; not special ➤ *It was a very ordinary day today – nothing special happened.*
2 out of the ordinary unusual or strange ➤ *Did you notice anything out of the ordinary at school today?*

ore /ɔːʳ/ *noun*
a type of rock or earth in which metal is found ➤ *iron ore*

organ /ˈɔːgən/ *noun*
1 a part of an animal or a plant that has a special purpose ➤ *the liver and other internal organs*
2 a large musical instrument which has long pipes and is often played in a church

organic /ɔːˈgænɪk/ *adjective*
(used about vegetables, fruit, etc.) grown using natural substances, not chemicals ➤ *organic carrots* (adverb: **organically**)

organism /ˈɔːgənɪzəm/ *noun*
a living thing ➤ *a microscopic organism*

organization /ˌɔːgənaɪˈzeɪʃən/ *noun*
1 a group of people with a special purpose, like a club or a business
2 *(no plural)* the way in which you organize or plan something ➤ *Good organization makes your work easier.*

organize /ˈɔːgənaɪz/ *verb (present participle **organizing**, past **organized**)*
1 to plan and make all the arrangements for an event ➤ *Did you organize the wedding by yourself or did your parents help you?*
2 to put things in order ➤ *I must organize my files – I can never find the one I want.*

organized /ˈɔːgənaɪzd/ *adjective*
1 neat; arranged carefully ➤ *Her desk is always very organized*
2 good at planning and doing things ➤ *John is very organized – he always does his work well and quickly.*
OPPOSITE (**1** and **2**): **disorganized**

organizer /ˈɔːgənaɪzəʳ/ *noun*
someone who plans and makes all the arrangements for an event ➤ *the organizers of the race*

oriental /ˌɔːriˈentl/ *adjective*
of or from Asia ➤ *an oriental rug*

origin /ˈɒrɪdʒɪn/ *noun*
1 the place that someone comes from
2 the beginning or cause of something
➤ *the origin of life on Earth*

original /əˈrɪdʒɪnəl/ *adjective*
1 first; earliest ➤ *Who was the original owner of this house?*
2 new and different ➤ *an original idea for a game*
3 not copied ➤ *This is the original painting, and these others are copies.*

originality /əˌrɪdʒɪˈnæləti/ *noun (no plural)*
the quality of being completely new and different ➤ *The design is good, but lacks originality.*

originally /əˈrɪdʒɪnəli/ *adverb*
in the beginning ➤ *My family is originally from Thailand.*

originate /əˈrɪdʒɪneɪt/ *verb (present participle* **originating**, *past* **originated**)
to start to exist in a particular place or at a particular time ➤ *This type of music originated in the 15th century.*

ornament /ˈɔːnəmənt/ *noun*
something that people have because it is beautiful, not because it is useful ➤ *Their house is full of little ornaments.*

orphan /ˈɔːfən/ *noun*
a child whose mother and father are dead

orphanage /ˈɔːfənɪdʒ/ *noun*
a home for children whose parents are dead

orthodox /ˈɔːθədɒks/ *adjective*
(used about ideas or methods) accepted by most people as being right and normal ➤ *orthodox methods of treating disease*

ostrich /ˈɒstrɪtʃ/ *noun (plural* **ostriches**)
a very large bird with long legs which runs fast but cannot fly

other /ˈʌðər/ *adjective, pronoun*
1 not the same; a different one ➤ *I sleep in this room, and my brother sleeps in the other room.* ➤ *Alice didn't like the dress, so she asked to see some others.*
2 the remaining thing or person ➤ *These two pens are mine, but you can have all the others.* ➤ *I can take Peter and Mary, but all the others will have to go by bus.*
3 **other people** people in general, not including you ➤ *I don't care what other people think.*
4 **the other day** on a recent day; not many days ago ➤ *I saw John the other day.*

otherwise /ˈʌðəwaɪz/ *adverb*
1 if not ➤ *You should go now, otherwise you'll miss the bus.*
2 apart from that ➤ *I've just got to comb my hair, but otherwise I'm ready.*
3 differently ➤ *I was planning to stay with my friends this weekend, but mum has decided otherwise* (=has decided that I can't).

ouch /aʊtʃ/ *interjection*
something you say when something hurts you a little

oughtn't /ˈɔːtnt/
ought not

ought to /ˈɔːt tuː/ *verb*
used to show what you think someone should do ➤ *She ought to look after her children a bit better.*

ounce /aʊns/ *noun*
a measure of weight equal to 28.35 grams ➤ *There are 16 ounces* (=16 oz) *in one pound.*

our /aʊər/ *adjective*
belonging to us ➤ *We put our books in our bags.*

ours /aʊəz/ *pronoun*
something that belongs to us ➤ *They left their books at school, but we took ours home.*

O

O

ourselves /ˌaʊəˈselvz/ *pronoun*
1 the same people as **we** or **us** in a sentence ▶ *We could see ourselves in the mirror.* ▶ *We bought a lot of things for ourselves.*
2 by ourselves (a) without help from anyone ▶ *We painted the bedroom by ourselves.*
(b) alone, without anyone else ▶ *Our mother never lets us go to the cinema by ourselves.*

out /aʊt/ *adverb*
1 not in a place; away from a place ▶ *Shut the gate, or the dog will get out.*
2 not at home or not at work ▶ *My dad's out at the moment.*
OPPOSITE (**1** and **2**): **in**
3 not shining ▶ *The lights were out and the house was dark.*
4 (used with some verbs) loudly ▶ *He called out, but his friend didn't hear him.*
5 out of from; away from something ▶ *She took the keys out of her bag.* ▶ *He walked out of the room.*

outbreak /ˈaʊtbreɪk/ *noun*
the sudden start of something bad ▶ *We were living in Austria at the outbreak of the war.*

outcome /ˈaʊtkʌm/ *noun*
the final result of an event or a situation ▶ *What was the outcome of the meeting?*

outdated /ˌaʊtˈdeɪtɪd/ *adjective*
no longer useful or modern ▶ *factories full of outdated machinery*

outdo /aʊtˈduː/ *verb (past tense **outdid** /aʊtˈdɪd/, past participle **outdone** /aʊtˈdʌn/)*
to be better or more successful than someone else ▶ *The two brothers were always trying to outdo each other.*

outdoor /ˈaʊtdɔːʳ/ *adjective*
happening outside; used outside ▶ *an outdoor job.*
OPPOSITE: **indoor**

outdoors /ˌaʊtˈdɔːz/ *(also **out-of-doors**) adverb*
outside; in the open air ▶ *It's a nice day; let's eat outdoors.*
OPPOSITE: **indoors**

outer /ˈaʊtəʳ/ *adjective*
on the outside or edge of something; far away from the middle ▶ *Pull off the outer leaves and chop the lettuce finely.*
OPPOSITE: **inner**

outer space /ˌaʊtə ˈspeɪs/ *noun (no plural)*
the area outside the Earth's air, where the stars and PLANETS are

outfit /ˈaʊtfɪt/ *noun*
a set of clothes, especially for a special purpose ▶ *I want to buy a new outfit because I've been invited to a wedding.*

outgoing /ˌaʊtˈgəʊɪŋ/ *adjective*
enjoying meeting and talking to people ▶ *a girl with a very outgoing personality*

outgrow /aʊtˈgrəʊ/ *verb (past tense **outgrew** /aʊtˈgruː/, past participle **outgrown** /aʊtˈgrəʊn/)*
to grow too big for your clothes ▶ *Jack has outgrown his coat, so I need to buy him a bigger one.*

outing /ˈaʊtɪŋ/ *noun*
a short trip to enjoy yourself, usually no longer than one day ▶ *We are going on an outing to the zoo tomorrow.*

outlaw¹ /ˈaʊtlɔː/ *verb*
to officially say that something is illegal ▶ *Gambling was outlawed here in 1980.*

outlaw² *noun*
a person who is hiding from the police

outline /ˈaʊtlaɪn/ *noun*
a line showing the shape of something ▶ *He drew the outline of a house.*

outlive /aʊt'lɪv/ *verb (present participle **outliving**, past **outlived**)*
to live longer than someone ➤ *Women usually outlive men.*

outlook /'aʊtlʊk/ *noun*
your attitude to life and the world ➤ *I think I have a positive outlook on life.*

outnumber /aʊt'nʌmbəʳ/ *verb*
to be greater in number than another group ➤ *Women outnumber men in the nursing profession.*

out of bounds /ˌaʊt əv 'baʊndz/ *adjective*
(used about a place) where you are not allowed to go ➤ *The kitchen's out of bounds when I'm cooking.*

out-of-date /ˌaʊt əv 'deɪt/ *adjective*
old; no longer useful ➤ *out-of-date information*
COMPARE: **old-fashioned**

out-of-doors /ˌaʊt əv 'dɔːz/ *adverb*
another word for **outdoors**

out-of-work /ˌaʊt əv 'wɜːk/ *adjective*
having no paid work ➤ *an out-of-work actor*

outpatient /'aʊtˌpeɪʃənt/ *noun*
someone who goes to a hospital for treatment and then goes home on the same day

output /'aʊtpʊt/ *noun*
the amount of goods that a country, company, etc. produces ➤ *Britain's industrial output fell by 2% in May.*

outrageous /aʊt'reɪdʒəs/ *adjective*
making you feel very angry or shocked ➤ *His drunken behaviour was completely outrageous.* ➤ *That's an outrageous price to pay.*

outside¹ /'aʊtsaɪd/ *noun*
the outer part or surface of something ➤ *The outside of the house was painted white.*
OPPOSITE: **inside**

outside² /aʊt'saɪd/ *adverb*
out; out of a building ➤ *He opened the door and went outside.* ➤ *He left his bicycle outside.*
OPPOSITE: **inside**

outside³ /'aʊtsaɪd/ *preposition, adjective*
at the outer part of something ➤ *I'll meet you outside the cinema.* ➤ *an outside toilet*
OPPOSITE: **inside**

outsider /aʊt'saɪdəʳ/ *noun*
a person who does not belong to a group, an organization, etc. ➤ *I felt like an outsider when I first started at the college.*

outskirts /'aʊtskɜːts/ *plural noun*
the parts of a town that are not in the centre ➤ *We live on the outskirts of the city.*

outspoken /aʊt'spəʊkən/ *adjective*
saying what you think, even though it may shock or offend people ➤ *an outspoken critic of the government's economic policy*

outstanding /aʊt'stændɪŋ/ *adjective*
very good ➤ *an outstanding pupil.*
SAME MEANING: **excellent**

outstretched /ˌaʊt'stretʃt/ *adjective*
(used about arms or hands) stretched out as far as possible ➤ *She ran into her father's outstretched arms.*

outward /'aʊtwəd/ *adjective*
towards the edge or the outside of something
OPPOSITE: **inward**

outwards /'aʊtwədz/ *adverb*
towards the outside; away from the middle ➤ *This box opens outwards.*
OPPOSITE: **inwards**

oval /'əʊvəl/ *noun*
a shape like an egg

ovary /'əʊvəri/ *noun (plural **ovaries**)*
the part of a woman or a female animal that produces eggs

oven /'ʌvən/ *noun*
a box that can be made hot to cook food in

over¹ /ˈəʊvəʳ/ adverb, adjective
1 across to the other side ▶ We can cross over when the traffic stops.
2 down to a lying position ▶ He knocked the glass over and it broke. ▶ She fell over.
3 from the start to the finish ▶ Think it over before you decide. ▶ Read this letter over and tell me if there are any mistakes.
4 finished ▶ When we arrived, the film was already over.
5 remaining; not used ▶ Did you spend all the money I gave you, or did you have any over?
6 over and over again many times; again and again ▶ I've told you over and over again that you mustn't play near the road.
7 over there used when you are pointing to a place that is not near you ▶ I'll sit here, and you sit over there.

over² preposition
1 above ▶ The sign over the door said "No Exit".
2 covering; on top of ▶ My father went to sleep with a newspaper over his face.
3 across; from one side to the other ▶ He jumped over the wall.
4 more than ▶ Children over 12 don't come to this school.
5 all over in every part; everywhere ▶ all over the world.

overall /ˈəʊvərɔːl/ noun
1 a garment that you put over other clothes to keep them clean
2 overalls plural noun loose trousers with a top part that you wear over other clothes to keep them clean

overboard /ˈəʊvəbɔːd/ adverb
over the side of a boat into the water ▶ He fell overboard.

overcame /ˌəʊvəˈkeɪm/
the PAST TENSE of the verb **overcome**

overcast /ˌəʊvəˈkɑːst/ adjective
dark and cloudy ▶ an overcast November day

overcoat /ˈəʊvəkəʊt/ noun
a warm coat that you wear outside when it is cold

overcome /ˌəʊvəˈkʌm/ verb
(present participle **overcoming**, past tense **overcame** /ˌəʊvəˈkeɪm/, past participle **overcome**)
1 to succeed in controlling a feeling or problem ▶ I'm trying to overcome my fear of flying.
2 be overcome (by something) to be strongly affected by something that you become weak or unable to control your feelings ▶ I was so overcome that I could hardly speak.

overcrowded /ˌəʊvəˈkraʊdɪd/ adjective
filled with too many people ▶ overcrowded prisons

overdo /ˌəʊvəˈduː/ verb
(past tense **overdid** /ˌəʊvəˈdɪd/, past participle **overdone** /ˌəʊvəˈdʌn/)
to do or use too much of something ▶ It's good to take some exercise, but don't overdo it.

overdraft /ˈəʊvədrɑːft/ noun
an arrangement with your bank that allows you to spend more money than you have in your account ▶ The bank have agreed to give me a £1,000 overdraft.

overdrawn /ˌəʊvəˈdrɔːn/ adjective
be overdrawn, go overdrawn to have spent more money than the amount you have in your bank account ▶ If I go overdrawn again, the bank will charge me twice.

overdue /ˌəʊvəˈdjuː/ adjective
late in arriving or being done ▶ Her baby's ten days overdue. ▶ Salary increases are long overdue.

overestimate /ˌəʊvərˈestɪmeɪt/ verb
(present participle **overestimating**, past **overestimated**)
to think that something is bigger, longer, etc. than it really is ▶ I

overestimated how long the journey would take.

overflow /ˌəʊvəˈfləʊ/ *verb*
to flow over the edge of something ▶ *The bath overflowed because I forgot to turn the water off.*

overhead /ˌəʊvəˈhed/ *adverb*
over your head; in the sky ▶ *The plane flew overhead.*

overheads /ˈəʊvəhedz/ *plural noun*
money that a business has to spend on rent, electricity, etc.

overhear /ˌəʊvəˈhɪəʳ/ *verb (past **overheard** /ˌəʊvəˈhɜːd/)*
to hear something that other people are saying when they do not know you are listening ▶ *I overheard them talking about me.*

overlap /ˌəʊvəˈlæp/ *verb (present participle **overlapping**, past **overlapped**)*
1 if two things overlap, part of one thing covers part of the other ▶ *a pattern of overlapping circles*
2 (used about two subjects, activities, ideas, etc.) to be similar in some ways, but not in others ▶ *Our responsibilities in the office overlap slightly.*

overload /ˌəʊvəˈləʊd/ *verb*
to put too many people or things into a vehicle ▶ *It's dangerous to overload your car.*

overlook /ˌəʊvəˈlʊk/ *verb*
1 to have a view of something from above ▶ *Our house overlooks the sea.*
2 not to see or notice something ▶ *It's easy to overlook mistakes in your own work.*

overnight /ˌəʊvəˈnaɪt/ *adjective, adverb*
for the whole night ▶ *We stayed overnight with my sister.*

overpopulated /ˌəʊvəˈpɒpjʊleɪtɪd/ *adjective*
(used about a place) having too many people living in it

overpowering /ˌəʊvəˈpaʊərɪŋ/ *adjective*
very strong ▶ *Sam woke up with a feeling of overpowering excitement.*

overpriced /ˌəʊvəˈpraɪst/ *adjective*
more expensive than it should be ▶ *It's a nice restaurant, but it's a little overpriced.*

overseas /ˌəʊvəˈsiːz/ *adverb, adjective*
to, in, or of places across the sea from your own country ▶ *My brother lives overseas.* ▶ *overseas students*

oversight /ˈəʊvəsaɪt/ *noun*
a small mistake made because you did not notice something or you forgot to do something

oversleep /ˌəʊvəˈsliːp/ *verb (past **overslept** /ˌəʊvəˈslept/)*
to sleep longer than you had wanted to ▶ *I was late for school this morning because I overslept.*

overtake /ˌəʊvəˈteɪk/ *verb (present participle **overtaking**, past tense **overtook** /ˌəʊvəˈtʊk/, past participle **overtaken** /ˌəʊvəˈteɪkən/)*
to pass another person or vehicle going in the same direction ▶ *The car overtook the lorry.*

overthrow /ˌəʊvəˈθrəʊ/ *verb (past tense **overthrew** /ˌəʊvəˈθruː/, past participle **overthrown** /ˌəʊvəˈθrəʊn/)*
to remove a leader or government from power by using force ▶ *The country's military leaders plan to overthrow the government.*

overtime /ˈəʊvətaɪm/ *noun (no plural)*
time that you work in addition to your usual working hours

overtook /ˌəʊvəˈtʊk/
the PAST TENSE of the verb **overtake**

overturn /ˌəʊvəˈtɜːn/ *verb*
to turn over completely or fall onto its side ▶ *The car overturned on a country road.*

O

P

overweight /ˌəʊvəˈweɪt/ *adjective*
too fat ➤ *The doctor told her she was overweight and should do more exercise.*

overwhelm /ˌəʊvəˈwelm/ *verb*
if a feeling overwhelms you, you feel it very strongly ➤ *Gary was overwhelmed with sadness.*

overwhelming /ˌəʊvəˈwelmɪŋ/ *adjective*
1 (used about feelings) affecting you very strongly ➤ *Shari felt an overwhelming urge to cry.*
2 very big in amount or number ➤ *The Conservative Party won by an overwhelming majority.*

overworked /ˌəʊvəˈwɜːkt/ *adjective*
working too much ➤ *overworked nurses*

owe /əʊ/ *verb (present participle owing, past owed)*
1 to have to give money to someone later because they lent you some ➤ *I owe John £10 because he paid for my ticket.* ➤ *I can pay you £20 now, but I'll have to owe you the other £10.*
2 to feel grateful to someone for something ➤ *He owes his teachers a lot, because he got a very good job when he left school.*

owing to /ˈəʊɪŋ tuː/ *preposition*
because of ➤ *They arrived late, owing to the traffic.*

owl /aʊl/ *noun*
a large bird that flies at night and kills small animals for food

own¹ /əʊn/ *adjective, pronoun*
1 belonging to oneself ➤ *I like writing with my own pen.* ➤ *That bicycle isn't his own; it belongs to his brother.*
2 **on your own** alone, with no one else with you or helping you ➤ *I was on my own all afternoon.* ➤ *Did you write this story on your own?*

own² *verb*
to have something that belongs to you ➤ *Who owns this house?*

owner /ˈəʊnəʳ/ *noun*
a person who owns something ➤ *Who is the owner of this car?*

ox /ɒks/ *noun (plural oxen* /ˈɒksən/)
a BULL that cannot be the father of young ones and is used for work on farms

oxygen /ˈɒksɪdʒən/ *noun (no plural)*
a gas in the air that people must breathe in order to live

oyster /ˈɔɪstəʳ/ *noun*
a small sea animal that has a shell and makes a jewel called a PEARL

oz
a short way of writing the words **ounce** or **ounces**

ozone /ˈəʊzəʊn/ *noun (no plural)*
a gas high above the surface of the Earth

ozone-friendly /ˈəʊzəʊn ˈfrendlɪ/ *adjective*
not harmful to the OZONE LAYER ➤ *ozone-friendly products*

ozone layer /ˈəʊzəʊn ˌleɪəʳ/ *noun (no plural)*
a layer of OZONE which protects the Earth from the bad effects of the sun

Pp

p¹ /piː/ *noun*
a short way of writing or saying the words **penny** or **pence** ➤ *This apple cost 25p* ➤ *a 2p piece*

p² *(plural pp)*
a short way of writing the word **page** ➤ *See the picture on p 3.* ➤ *See pp 15–37.*

PA /ˌpiː ˈeɪ/ *noun*
1 a PERSONAL ASSISTANT; a secretary who works for just one person
2 a PUBLIC ADDRESS system; equipment that makes someone's

voice louder when they are speaking to a crowd of people

pace¹ /peɪs/ *noun*
1 (*no plural*) the speed at which you move forwards, especially when running or walking ▶ *She heard someone behind her and quickened her pace.*
2 a single step or the distance that you move with a single step ▶ *The tree is about ten paces from the wall.*

pace² *verb* (*present participle* **pacing**, *past* **paced**)
to walk slowly backwards and forwards, especially when you are waiting or worried

pacifist /'pæsɪfɪst/ *noun*
a person who believes that all wars are wrong

pack¹ /pæk/ *verb*
1 to put things together in a case or other container ▶ *She packed her bags and left.* ▶ *The eggs are packed and sent to the shops.*
OPPOSITE: **unpack**
2 pack up to finish work ▶ *We were so tired that we just packed up and left.*

pack² *noun*
1 a group of things packed together for sale ▶ *a pack of chocolate bars*
2 a large bag that you carry on your back
3 a set of cards for playing a game
4 a group of animals that hunt together

package /'pækɪdʒ/ *noun*
a parcel ▶ *The postman brought a package for you.*

package holiday /'pækɪdʒ ,hɒlɪdeɪ/ *noun*
a holiday which you buy at a fixed price and which includes the cost of travel, hotel, and meals

packaging /'pækɪdʒɪŋ/ *noun* (*no plural*)
the bag or box that a product is in when you buy it

packed /pækt/ *adjective*
full of people

packet /'pækɪt/ *noun*
a small container or parcel in which goods are packed ▶ *a packet of cigarettes*

packing /'pækɪŋ/ *noun* (*no plural*)
the action of putting things into cases or boxes ▶ *I'll do my packing the night before we leave.*

pact /pækt/ *noun*
an important agreement between two countries

pad¹ /pæd/ *noun*
1 a thick piece of soft material used to protect or clean a part of your body or a wound
2 a number of sheets of paper stuck together at one edge ▶ *a writing pad*

pad² *verb* (*present participle* **padding**, *past* **padded**)
to fill something with soft material in order to protect it or make it more comfortable

padded /'pædɪd/ *adjective*
filled with soft material to be made more comfortable or thicker ▶ *a padded envelope*

paddle¹ /'pædl/ *noun*
a piece of wood with a broad, flat end, used for moving a boat through water

paddle² *verb* (*present participle* **paddling**, *past* **paddled**)
1 to move a boat through water using a paddle
2 to walk about in water which is not very deep ▶ *The children paddled in the sea.*
COMPARE (2): **wade**

paddock /'pædək/ *noun*
a small field in which horses are kept

paddy /'pædɪ/ (*also* **paddy field** /'pædɪ fiːld/) *noun* (*plural* **paddies**)
a field for growing rice

P

padlock /ˈpædlɒk/ *noun*
a movable lock that can be used on doors, boxes, etc.

page /peɪdʒ/ *noun*
1 one of the sheets of paper in a book or newspaper ▶ *The book has 220 pages.*
2 the boy servant of a king or queen in the past

pager /ˈpeɪdʒəʳ/ *noun*
a small machine that you carry with you which makes a sound to tell you to telephone someone
SAME MEANING: **beeper**

paid /peɪd/
the PAST TENSE and PAST PARTICIPLE of the verb **pay**

pail /peɪl/ *noun*
a bucket

pain /peɪn/ *noun*
1 a feeling of hurting in your body or suffering in your mind ▶ *I've got an awful pain in my leg.*
2 a pain, a pain in the neck a very annoying person or thing ▶ *He's a real pain when he's tired.*
3 take (great) pains to make a big effort to do something

painful /ˈpeɪnfəl/ *adjective*
causing pain ▶ *a painful cut on the leg*
OPPOSITE: **painless**

painkiller /ˈpeɪnˌkɪləʳ/ *noun*
a medicine which helps to stop pain

painless /ˈpeɪnləs/ *adjective*
causing no pain
OPPOSITE: **painful**

painstaking /ˈpeɪnzˌteɪkɪŋ/ *adjective*
done very carefully ▶ *the painstaking work of the research team*

paint¹ /peɪnt/ *noun*
a sticky, coloured substance that is used to cover walls, or to make pictures ▶ *She brought a box of paints to school.* ▶ *There's paint on your clothes.*

paint² *verb*
1 to put paint on a surface ▶ *They painted the house green.*
2 to make a picture of someone or something using paint ▶ *She loves painting the sea.*

paintbrush /ˈpeɪntbrʌʃ/ *noun* (plural **paintbrushes**)
a brush that you use for painting

painter /ˈpeɪntəʳ/ *noun*
1 a person who paints buildings as a job
2 a person who paints pictures
SAME MEANING (**2**): **artist**

painting /ˈpeɪntɪŋ/ *noun*
a painted picture ▶ *a painting of a boat*

pair /peəʳ/ *noun*
1 two things of the same kind that are usually used together ▶ *a pair of socks*
2 something with two parts joined and used together ▶ *a pair of trousers* ▶ *a pair of scissors*
3 two people who are closely connected ▶ *Jenny and her husband make a lovely pair.*

pal /pæl/ *noun*
a friend

palace /ˈpælɪs/ *noun*
a large, beautiful building in which a king, a queen, or some other important person lives

pale /peɪl/ *adjective*
1 (used about your skin) having little colour ▶ *She was very pale after her illness.*
2 not light or bright ▶ *pale green*
OPPOSITE (**2**): **dark**

palm /pɑːm/ *noun*
1 a tall, tropical tree with no branches and a group of large leaves at the top ▶ *a coconut palm*
2 the flat part inside your hand ▶ *He put the insect on the palm of his hand.*

pamper /ˈpæmpəʳ/ verb
to give someone a lot of care and
attention ➤ You pamper that boy too
much!

pamphlet /ˈpæmflət/ noun
a thin book with a paper cover, which
gives you information about
something

pan /pæn/ noun
a round, metal pot, usually with a long
handle, for cooking things over heat

pancake /ˈpænkeɪk/ noun
a very thin, flat cake that is cooked in
a round pan

panda /ˈpændə/ noun
a large, black and white bear which
comes from China

pandemonium /ˌpændəˈməʊnɪəm/
noun (no plural)
a lot of noise and activity caused by
people who are angry, excited, etc.
➤ When Brazil scored, pandemonium
broke out.

pander /ˈpændəʳ/ verb
pander to someone to give someone
what they want, even though you
know it is not good for them ➤ You
shouldn't pander to the children
when they ask you for sweets.

pane /peɪn/ noun
a single piece of glass used in
windows ➤ Who broke this pane of
glass?

panel /ˈpænl/ noun
1 a flat piece of wood used in a door
or on a wall
2 a group of speakers who answer
questions on a radio or television
show

pang /pæŋ/ noun
a sudden, strong feeling of pain,
sadness, or hunger ➤ I had a pang of
guilt about leaving Sally alone.

panic¹ /ˈpænɪk/ noun
a sudden feeling of great fear which
makes you lose control of yourself

➤ There was panic when the fire
started.

panic² verb (present participle
panicking, past **panicked**)
to feel a sudden fear which makes
you lose control of yourself ➤ The
crowd panicked at the sound of guns.

panic-stricken /ˈpænɪk ˌstrɪkən/
adjective
very afraid and not able to think
clearly

pant /pænt/ verb
to breathe hard and quickly,
especially because you are doing
something that needs a lot of effort
➤ He was panting when he reached
the top of the hill.

pantomime /ˈpæntəmaɪm/ noun
a funny play produced at Christmas,
usually telling an old story

pantry /ˈpæntrɪ/ noun (plural
pantries)
a small room in which food is kept

pants /pænts/ plural noun
a piece of clothing for women and
girls, for the lower part of the body,
worn under skirts or trousers, not
covering the legs
SAME MEANING: **knickers**

paper /ˈpeɪpəʳ/ noun
1 (no plural) thin material used for
writing on or wrapping parcels ➤ I
haven't got any writing paper. ➤ a
paper bag
2 a newspaper ➤ Here's today's paper.
3 **papers** plural noun official pieces of
paper which give information about
who you are and what you are
allowed to do ➤ At the airport, they
asked for his papers.

paperback /ˈpeɪpəbæk/ noun
a book with a thin, cardboard cover
COMPARE: **hardback**

paper clip /ˈpeɪpə klɪp/ noun
a small, curved piece of wire used to
hold sheets of paper together

P

paperwork /'peɪpəwɜːk/ noun (no plural)
1 work such as writing letters or reports ► I have to do a lot of paperwork in my job.
2 the documents that you need for a business deal, journey, etc. ► I've left all the paperwork in the office.

par /pɑːʳ/ noun
be on a par with something to be of the same standard as something ► Technological developments in the US are now on a par with those in Japan.

parachute /'pærəʃuːt/ noun
a large, round piece of cloth that fills with air, and lets someone or something fall slowly to Earth from an aircraft

parade¹ /pə'reɪd/ noun
a number of people walking or marching in a long line on an important occasion

parade² verb (present participle **parading**, past **paraded**)
to walk or march together, in a long line ► The soldiers paraded through the town.

paradise /'pærədaɪs/ noun
1 heaven
2 a place of complete happiness ► Paradise for me is lying on the beach all day.

paradox /'pærədɒks/ noun (plural **paradoxes**)
something that seems strange because it contains two very different ideas ► It's a paradox that there are so many poor people living in such a rich country.

paraffin /'pærəfɪn/ noun (no plural)
a colourless oil that can be burnt and used for cooking and lighting

paragraph /'pærəɡrɑːf/ noun
one part of a piece of writing that begins on a new line and deals with one particular idea ► Read from your book, starting at the second paragraph.

parallel /'pærəlel/ adjective
running side by side, but always the same distance away from each other ► The railway runs parallel **to** the road. ► parallel lines

paralyse /'pærəlaɪz/ verb (present participle **paralysing**, past **paralysed**)
to prevent someone from being able to move some or all of their body

paralysed /'pærəlaɪzd/ adjective
unable to move your body or part of your body because of an injury or illness ► He was paralysed from the waist down after a motorcycle accident.

paralysis /pə'ræləsɪs/ noun (no plural)
being unable to move

paramedic /ˌpærə'medɪk/ noun
a person who is trained to help people who are ill or injured but is not a doctor or nurse

paramilitary /ˌpærə'mɪlɪtəri/ adjective
organized like an army, but not part of a country's official army ► a paramilitary terrorist group

paramount /'pærəmaʊnt/ adjective
more important than anything else ► The safety of the children is paramount.

paranoid /'pærənɔɪd/ adjective
wrongly thinking that everyone is against you or wants to hurt you ► Stop being so paranoid!

paraphrase /'pærəfreɪz/ verb (present participle **paraphrasing**, past **paraphrased**)
to express what someone says or writes in a shorter and clearer way

parasite /'pærəsaɪt/ noun
a plant or an animal that lives on another plant or animal and gets food from it

P

paratrooper /ˈpærətruːpəʳ/ noun
a soldier who is trained to jump out
of planes using a PARACHUTE

parcel /ˈpɑːsəl/ noun
something wrapped in paper and
tied, for posting or carrying ▶ She
sent a parcel of books to her brother.

pardon¹ /ˈpɑːdn/ noun (no plural)
a word used to ask someone to say
something again, because you did
not hear them the first time
▶ Pardon? How much did you say it
costs?

pardon² verb
Pardon me used to say sorry politely
▶ Pardon me – I hope I didn't hurt you.

parent /ˈpeərənt/ noun
a father or mother ▶ My parents live
in London.

parenthood /ˈpeərənthʊd/ noun
(no plural)
the state of being a parent

parish /ˈpærɪʃ/ noun (plural **parishes**)
an area looked after by one Christian
priest or served by one church

park¹ /pɑːk/ noun
a large piece of ground in a town,
usually covered in grass and used by
the public for pleasure

park² verb
to leave a car, bus, etc. somewhere
for a time ▶ She parked the car near
the bank.

parking /ˈpɑːkɪŋ/ noun (no plural)
1 the leaving of a car, bus, etc. in a
particular place for a time
2 No Parking a phrase used on a sign
to show that you are not allowed to
leave your car somewhere

parking meter /ˈpɑːkɪŋ ˌmiːtəʳ/ noun
a small machine at the side of the
street, into which you put money to
pay for parking a car next to it

parking ticket /ˈpɑːkɪŋ ˌtɪkɪt/ noun
a piece of paper that is put on your
car to tell you that you must pay an
amount of money because you have
parked your car somewhere you
should not

parliament /ˈpɑːləmənt/ noun
a group of people chosen by the
people of a country to make laws

parliamentary /ˌpɑːləˈmentərɪ/
adjective
of or about parliament ▶ a
parliamentary committee

parody¹ /ˈpærədɪ/ noun (plural
parodies)
a piece of writing, music, etc. that
copies someone else's style in an
amusing way ▶ a parody of the
Frankenstein movies

parody² verb (past **parodied**)
to copy someone's style or behaviour
in an amusing way

parrot /ˈpærət/ noun
a brightly coloured tropical bird with
a short, curved beak

parsley /ˈpɑːslɪ/ noun (no plural)
a small plant with strong-tasting
leaves, often used in cooking

parsnip /ˈpɑːsnɪp/ noun
a white or yellow vegetable that is
the root of a plant

part¹ /pɑːt/ noun
1 some, but not all, of a thing or
things ▶ Which part **of** the town do
you live in?
2 any of the pieces into which
something is divided ▶ You can see
the second part **of** the film next week.
3 a character acted by an actor in a
play or film ▶ James played the part
of the soldier.
4 a piece of a machine which you use
in place of a broken one ▶ The car
needs some new parts.
5 take part in to do an activity with
other people ▶ He took part in lots of
sports at school.

part² verb
1 to separate or leave one another

P

➤ *The friends parted: Jane went home and Mary went to the library.*
2 part with something to give away something that you are fond of ➤ *She hates parting with her old toys.*

partial /ˈpɑːʃəl/ *adjective*
not complete ➤ *The meeting was only a partial success.* (*adverb:* **partially**)

participant /pɑːˈtɪsɪpənt/ *noun*
a person who takes part in an activity with other people

participate /pɑːˈtɪsɪpeɪt/ *verb*
(*present participle* **participating**, *past* **participated**)
to take part in an activity with other people

participation /pɑːˌtɪsɪˈpeɪʃən/ *noun*
(*no plural*)
the act of taking part in an activity with other people ➤ *We want to encourage more participation by women in sport.*

participle /ˈpɑːtɪsɪpəl/ *noun*
one of two forms of a verb. The past participle of "sing" is "sung", and the present participle is "singing".

particle /ˈpɑːtɪkəl/ *noun*
a very small piece of something ➤ *particles of dust*

particular /pəˈtɪkjʊləˈ/ *adjective*
1 special ➤ *Did you have a particular reason for choosing this book?*
2 this one and not others ➤ *On that particular day, I wasn't feeling well.*
3 in particular especially ➤ *He likes sports, and football in particular.*

particularly /pəˈtɪkjʊləli/ *adverb*
especially ➤ *It was particularly hot that day.*

parting /ˈpɑːtɪŋ/ *noun*
the line on your head that you make when you separate your hair with a comb ➤ *She has a centre parting.*

partition /pɑːˈtɪʃən/ *noun*
a thin wall that separates one part of a room from another ➤ *There's a*

partition between the two offices.

partly /ˈpɑːtli/ *adverb*
not completely ➤ *The accident was partly my fault.*

partner /ˈpɑːtnəˈ/ *noun*
1 a person who you dance with or make a pair with in a game ➤ *a tennis partner*
2 any of the owners of a business
3 a person to whom you are married or with whom you have a relationship

partnership /ˈpɑːtnəʃɪp/ *noun*
a situation in which two people or organizations work together ➤ *a scheme organized by the business community in partnership with local colleges*

part of speech /ˌpɑːt əv ˈspiːtʃ/ *noun*
(*plural* **parts of speech**)
one of the groups into which words are divided – for example "noun", "verb", or "adjective"

part-time /ˌpɑːt ˈtaɪm/ *adverb, adjective*
working during only a part of the usual working time ➤ *I work part-time now.*
COMPARE: **full-time**

party /ˈpɑːti/ *noun* (*plural* **parties**)
1 a meeting at which people enjoy themselves, eat, drink, etc. ➤ *a birthday party*
2 a group of people who are doing something together ➤ *Our teacher is taking a party of children to the library.*
3 a group of people with the same opinions in politics ➤ *Are you a member of a political party?*

pass¹ /pɑːs/ *verb*
1 to go past a person or a thing ➤ *She waved at me as she passed my house.*
2 to give something to someone ➤ *Pass the salt, please.*
3 (used about time) to go by ➤ *Time passes very slowly when you're waiting.*

4 to kick, throw, or hit a ball to someone in your own team during a game such as football
5 to succeed in a test or an examination ▶ *I'm having a party when I pass my driving test!*
6 pass away to die ▶ *I was sorry to hear that your aunt had passed away.*
7 pass out to faint ▶ *He always passes out at the sight of blood.*

pass² *noun (plural **passes**)*
1 a successful result in an examination ▶ *In this class, there were seven passes.*
2 a high mountain road
3 a paper allowing you to go somewhere or have something ▶ *I showed my pass to the man at the factory gate, and was allowed in.*

passage /ˈpæsɪdʒ/ *noun*
1 a narrow way in a building, which connects different rooms ▶ *The bathroom is at the end of the passage on the left.*
SAME MEANING: **corridor**
2 a short part of a piece of written work ▶ *He read a passage on rice farming from the geography book.*

passenger /ˈpæsɪndʒəʳ/ *noun*
a person who rides in a car, bus, train, etc., but does not drive it ▶ *There were ten passengers on the bus.*

passer-by /ˌpɑːsə ˈbaɪ/ *noun (plural **passers-by**)*
a person who walks past a place in the street ▶ *A passer-by told me the time.*

passing¹ /ˈpɑːsɪŋ/ *noun*
in passing if you say something in passing, you mention it while you are mainly talking or writing about something else ▶ *She mentioned in passing that she knew Dan.*

passing² *adjective*
only continuing for a short period of time, and often not very important ▶ *a passing thought*

passion /ˈpæʃən/ *noun*
a very strong, deep feeling, especially of love or anger ▶ *She spoke with passion about human rights.*

passionate /ˈpæʃənət/ *adjective*
with very strong, deep feelings ▶ *She is passionate about caring for animals.*

passive /ˈpæsɪv/ *adjective*
if a verb or sentence is passive, the subject of the verb or sentence is affected by the action of the verb. In the sentence "The ball was kicked by John", "was kicked" is a passive verb.
OPPOSITE: **active**

passport /ˈpɑːspɔːt/ *noun*
a small book which has in it your photograph and facts about you, and which you must have if you are going to a foreign country

password /ˈpɑːswɜːd/ *noun*
a secret word that allows you to use a computer system or enter a place ▶ *I've forgotten my password.*

past¹ /pɑːst/ *noun (no plural)*
1 all the time that has already gone ▶ *Farming is much easier now than it was in the past.*
2 a person's life until now ▶ *I don't know anything about his past*
3 the past the past tense ▶ *What's the past of "to go"?*
COMPARE (**1, 2,** and **3**): **future**

past² *adjective*
having happened or existed before the present time ▶ *I've been ill for the past two weeks.*
COMPARE: **next**

past³ *preposition, adverb*
1 up to and beyond ▶ *Did he drive past the school?* ▶ *Yes, he drove past, but he didn't stop.*
2 beyond a particular time ▶ *It's just past 4 o'clock.*

pasta /ˈpæstə/ *noun (no plural)*
an Italian food made from flour and water, and often eaten with a SAUCE

P

paste¹ /peɪst/ *noun (no plural)*
1 a wet substance used for sticking things together
2 a soft, wet mixture such as that made from flour and water

paste² *verb (present participle **pasting**, past **pasted**)*
to stick something onto something else with paste

pastel /'pæstəl/ *adjective*
(used about colours) soft, pale, and light ➤ *Her bedroom was painted in pastel pink.*

pastime /'pɑːstaɪm/ *noun*
something that you enjoy doing when you are not working ➤ *His pastimes include watching TV and reading.*

past participle /,pɑːst 'pɑːtɪsɪpəl/ *noun*
the part of a verb which is used to show an action done or happening in the past. "Done" and "walked" are the past participles of the verbs "do" and "walk"

past perfect /,pɑːst 'pɜːfɪkt/ *noun*
the past perfect the tense of a verb that shows that an action was completed before another event or time in the past. In the sentence "I had finished my breakfast before Rick phoned", "had finished" is in the past perfect

pastry /'peɪstrɪ/ *noun*
1 *(plural **pastries**)* a small, sweet cake
2 *(no plural)* a mixture of flour, fat, and water which you fill with some other food and bake

past tense /,pɑːst 'tens/ *noun*
the form of a verb which shows past time. The past tense of the verb "go" is "went"

pasture /'pɑːstʃəʳ/ *noun*
land that is covered with grass which cows and sheep can eat

pat¹ /pæt/ *verb (present participle **patting**, past **patted**)*
to touch something gently several times with your open hand ➤ *She patted the dog on its head.*

pat² *noun*
a light, friendly touch with your open hand ➤ *a pat on the cheek*

patch¹ /pætʃ/ *noun (plural **patches**)*
1 a piece of material used for covering a hole or a worn place in something
2 a small area that looks different from the rest ➤ *wet patches on the wall*

patch² *verb*
to put a piece of material over a hole or a worn place in order to mend it ➤ *You can patch a bicycle tyre with a piece of rubber.*

patchwork /'pætʃwɜːk/ *noun (no plural)*
a type of sewing in which many different-coloured pieces of cloth are sewn together ➤ *a patchwork quilt*

patently /'peɪtntlɪ/ *adverb*
patently obvious, patently false, etc. completely obvious, false, etc., in a way that anyone can notice ➤ *That's patently untrue!*

paternity /pə'tɜːnɪtɪ/ *noun (no plural)*
the state of being a father

path /pɑːθ/ *noun (plural **paths** /pɑːðz/)*
a track for walking on ➤ *There was a narrow path through the forest.*

pathetic /pə'θetɪk/ *adjective*
very bad, useless, or weak ➤ *Stop crying – you're being pathetic!* ➤ *That's a pathetic excuse. (adverb: **pathetically**)*

patience /'peɪʃəns/ *noun (no plural)*
the ability to deal with difficulties or wait for something for a long time without getting cross or upset ➤ *You need a lot of patience to be a teacher.*
OPPOSITE: **impatience**

patient¹ /'peɪʃənt/ *adjective*
able to deal with difficulties or wait

for something calmly and without getting upset or cross ➤ *I know your leg hurts, but just be patient until the doctor arrives.* (adverb: **patiently**)
OPPOSITE: **impatient**

patient² *noun*
a sick person who is being treated by a doctor ➤ *There are 450 patients in this hospital.*

patio /'pætɪəʊ/ *noun*
an outdoor area with a hard surface near a house, where you can sit, eat, relax, etc.

patriot /'pætrɪət/ *noun*
a person who is very proud of their country

patriotic /ˌpætrɪ'ɒtɪk/ *adjective*
very proud of your country ➤ *That's not a very patriotic thing to say!*

patriotism /'pætrɪətɪzəm/ *noun (no plural)*
the state of being very proud of your country

patrol¹ /pə'trəʊl/ *noun*
1 a small group of police officers or soldiers who move round an area or a building in order to protect it
2 **on patrol** (used about soldiers or police officers) keeping watch ➤ *There are four policemen on patrol outside the prison.*

patrol² *verb (present participle **patrolling**, past **patrolled**)*
to go round an area or a building in order to protect it ➤ *Every hour, a policeman patrolled our street.*

patronize /'pætrənaɪz/ *verb (present participle **patronizing**, past **patronized**)*
to speak to someone in a way that shows you think they are less important or intelligent than you ➤ *Don't patronize me.*

patronizing /'pætrənaɪzɪŋ/ *adjective*
talking to someone in a way that shows you think they are less important or intelligent than you ➤ *I*

thought his remarks were very patronizing to women.

patter /'pætər/ *verb*
to make a light knocking noise ➤ *The rain pattered on the roof.*

pattern /'pætən/ *noun*
1 an ornamental arrangement of shapes and colours ➤ *a pattern of flowers on dress material*
2 a shape which you copy if you want to make something, especially a piece of clothing ➤ *a dress pattern*

patterned /'pætənd/ *adjective*
decorated with a pattern ➤ *a patterned skirt*

pause¹ /pɔːz/ *noun*
a short time when you stop what you are doing ➤ *There was a pause in the conversation when Mary came in.*

pause² *verb (present participle **pausing**, past **paused**)*
to stop for a short time ➤ *When he reached the top of the hill, he paused for a minute to rest.*

pave /peɪv/ *verb (present participle **paving**, past **paved**)*
to cover a path or road with a surface of flat stones

pavement /'peɪvmənt/ *noun*
a path made of flat stones at the side of a road for people to walk on

paving stone /'peɪvɪŋ stəʊn/ *noun*
a flat piece of stone used to make a surface for walking on

paw /pɔː/ *noun*
the foot of an animal such as a dog or cat

pawn /pɔːn/ *noun*
a piece in the game of CHESS

pawpaw /'pɔːpɔː/ *noun*
a large, orange fruit grown in hot places

pay¹ /peɪ/ *verb (past **paid** /peɪd/)*
1 to give money to someone for something you have bought from them or work they have done for you

P

➤ *She paid for the coffee and stood up.* ➤ *He paid a lot of money for the suit.* ➤ *They paid him £5 to wash the car.*
2 pay attention to listen or watch carefully ➤ *Pay attention to the story, children.*
3 pay someone back to return the money that you have borrowed from someone ➤ *I'll pay you back your £10 next week.*

pay² *noun (no plural)*
the money that you receive for work that you have done ➤ *You'll get your pay on Friday.*

payable /'peɪəbəl/ *adjective*
1 (used about amounts of money) that must be paid ➤ *A deposit of £50 is payable when you order the goods.*
2 make a cheque payable to someone to write someone's name on a cheque, etc. to show that the money must be paid to them ➤ *Please make the cheque payable to Millennium Editions Ltd.*

payday /'peɪdeɪ/ *noun (no plural)*
the day when your wages are paid

payment /'peɪmənt/ *noun*
1 (no plural) the act of paying ➤ *This money is in payment for your work.*
2 an amount of money that you pay ➤ *monthly payments*

pay phone /'peɪ fəʊn/ *noun*
a public telephone into which you put coins or a card when you use it

payroll /'peɪrəʊl/ *noun*
the payroll a list of the people who work in an organization ➤ *They have over 500 staff on the payroll.*

PC¹ /ˌpiː 'siː/ *noun*
1 a PERSONAL COMPUTER; a small computer that is used by one person at a time
2 a POLICE CONSTABLE; a policeman of the lowest rank

PC² *adjective*
POLITICALLY CORRECT

PE /ˌpiː 'iː/ *noun (no plural)*
physical education; sports and exercises that are taught as a school subject

pea /piː/ *noun*
a very small, round, green vegetable

peace /piːs/ *noun (no plural)*
1 quietness and calm ➤ *I love the peace of this village.* ➤ *Go away and leave me in peace.*
2 a time when there is no war or fighting ➤ *world peace*

peaceful /'piːsfəl/ *adjective*
1 quiet and calm ➤ *I spent a peaceful day at the beach.*
2 not violent ➤ *A peaceful crowd marched to the city centre.*
(*adverb:* **peacefully**)

peacekeeping /'piːsˌkiːpɪŋ/ *adjective*
peacekeeping forces, peacekeeping operations, etc. in a place where there is a war, soldiers or military activities that try to stop the fighting

peacetime /'piːstaɪm/ *noun (no plural)*
a period of time when a country is not fighting a war

peach /piːtʃ/ *noun (plural peaches)*
a juicy fruit with one large seed and a soft yellow or pink skin

peacock /'piːkɒk/ *noun*
a large bird with a long, brightly coloured tail covered with blue-green spots

peak /piːk/ *noun*
1 the pointed top of a hill or mountain
2 the front part of a cap which sticks forward over your eyes

peal /piːl/ *noun*
1 the loud, ringing sound of bells
2 long, loud sounds which follow each other ➤ *a peal of laughter*

peanut /'piːnʌt/ *noun*
a small nut which grows under the ground and which you can eat
SAME MEANING: **groundnut**

peanut butter /ˌpiːnʌt ˈbʌtəʳ/ *noun*
(no plural)
a soft food made from crushed
peanuts that is usually eaten on
bread

pear /peəʳ/ *noun*
a juicy, yellow or green fruit which is
the size of an apple, but is narrow at
one end and wide at the other

pearl /pɜːl/ *noun*
a small, round, white thing, found in
the shells of some sea animals and
used to make expensive jewellery

peasant /ˈpezənt/ *noun*
a person who lives in the country and
works on their own small piece of
land

pebble /ˈpebəl/ *noun*
a small stone

peck /pek/ *verb*
(used about birds) to take a small,
quick bite ➤ *The hens pecked at the
corn.*

peculiar /pɪˈkjuːliəʳ/ *adjective*
strange or unusual, especially in a
way that worries you ➤ *a peculiar
smell*
SAME MEANING: **odd**

peculiarity /pɪˌkjuːliˈærətɪ/ *noun*
(plural **peculiarities**)
an unusual habit that only one
person has ➤ *One of her peculiarities
is sleeping on the floor.*

pedal¹ /ˈpedl/ *noun*
a part of a machine that you move
with your foot ➤ *a bicycle pedal*

pedal² *verb (present participle
pedalling, past **pedalled**)*
to move a pedal with your foot,
especially when riding a bicycle ➤ *We
pedalled slowly up the hill.*

peddle /ˈpedl/ *verb (present
participle **peddling**, past **peddled**)*
to sell something, especially
something illegal ➤ *He was found
guilty of peddling drugs.*

pedestal /ˈpedɪstəl/ *noun*
a base for something such as a
STATUE

pedestrian /pəˈdestriən/ *noun*
a person walking ➤ *This path is only
for pedestrians and not cars.*

pedestrian crossing /pəˌdestriən
ˈkrɒsɪŋ/ *noun*
a special place in the road where
people who are walking can cross
safely

pedigree¹ /ˈpedɪgriː/ *noun*
the parents and other past family
members of an animal, or the written
record of them

pedigree² *adjective*
(used about animals) having parents,
grandparents, etc. from the same
BREED, and therefore of high quality

peek¹ /piːk/ *verb*
to look at something quickly and
secretly ➤ *The door was open, so I
peeked into the room.*

peek² *noun*
a quick look at something ➤ *Take a
peek in the oven and see if the cake's
done.*

peel¹ /piːl/ *noun (no plural)*
the outside part of a fruit or
vegetable ➤ *Apples have red or green
peel.*

peel² *verb*
to take off the outside part of a
vegetable or fruit ➤ *Peel the orange
and cut it into slices.*

peep¹ /piːp/ *verb*
to look at something quickly, and
sometimes secretly ➤ *I peeped through
the window to see if she was there.*

peep² *noun*
a quick, sometimes secret, look ➤ *He
took a peep at the back of the book
to check the answer.*

peer /pɪəʳ/ *verb*
to look very hard or carefully at
something

P

P

peers /pɪəz/ (also **peer group** /'pɪə gruːp/) plural noun
the people who are the same age as you or who have the same type of job or social position ▶ *Teenagers prefer to spend their time with their peers.*

peeved /piːvd/ adjective
annoyed ▶ *Jim was rather peeved that his guest did not thank him for the meal.*

peg /peg/ noun
1 a wooden or metal hook fixed to a wall, on which you can hang clothes, etc.
2 a small, wooden or plastic object that you use to fasten clothes to a washing line

pellet /'pelət/ noun
a small, hard ball made from something such as paper or metal ▶ *a gun that fires plastic pellets*

pelt¹ /pelt/ verb
pelt someone with something to attack someone by throwing a lot of things at them ▶ *Two kids were pelting each other with snowballs.*

pelt² noun
at full pelt as fast as possible ▶ *She came running down the road at full pelt.*

pen /pen/ noun
1 a long, narrow object which is filled with ink, and is used to write or draw with
COMPARE: **pencil**
2 a small piece of land surrounded by a fence, in which cattle are kept

penalize /'piːnəl-aɪz/ verb (present participle **penalizing**, past **penalized**)
1 to treat someone unfairly and make them have a disadvantage ▶ *The current system penalizes people who live alone.*
2 to punish someone, for example a player or sports team, by giving an advantage to the other team ▶ *Our team was penalized for taking too much time.*

penalty /'penltɪ/ noun (plural **penalties**)
1 a punishment for breaking a law or rule ▶ *What is the penalty for dangerous driving?*
2 an advantage given in sports to one team after the other has broken one of the rules of the game

pence /pens/ noun
the plural of **penny**

pencil /'pensəl/ noun
a long, narrow, wooden object filled with a stick of a black or coloured substance with which you draw or write
COMPARE: **pen**

pendant /'pendənt/ noun
a piece of jewellery that hangs from a chain around your neck

pendulum /'pendjʊləm/ noun
a long object with a weight at the bottom that moves from side to side inside a large clock

penetrate /'penɪtreɪt/ verb (present participle **penetrating**, past **penetrated**)
to go into or through something that is difficult to enter ▶ *The sun penetrated through the thick clouds.*

penetrating /'penɪtreɪtɪŋ/ adjective
penetrating look, penetrating stare
a look that makes you feel uncomfortable because the other person seems to know what you are thinking

pen friend /'pen frend/ (also **pen pal**) noun
a person in a foreign country to whom you write and who writes to you, even though you may never meet

penicillin /ˌpenɪ'sɪlɪn/ noun (no plural)
a medicine that destroys BACTERIA that are in your body and making you ill

peninsula /pəˈnɪnsjʊlə/ *noun*
a long, thin piece of land that is almost completely surrounded by water but is joined to a larger area of land

penis /ˈpiːnɪs/ *noun (plural **penises**)*
the male sex organ

penknife /ˈpennaɪf/ *noun (plural **penknives** /-ˌnaɪvz/)*
a small knife with a folding blade that you can carry in your pocket

pen name /ˈpen neɪm/ *noun*
a name used by a writer instead of their real name

penniless /ˈpenɪləs/ *adjective*
having no money ➤ *I'll be penniless if I keep giving you money.*

penny /ˈpenɪ/ *noun (plural **pence** /pens/ or **pennies**)*
a British coin ➤ *There are 100 pence in a pound.*

pen pal /ˈpen pæl/ *noun*
another way of saying **pen friend**

pension /ˈpenʃən/ *noun*
money given to a person regularly by their employer or the government when they are too old to work

pensioner /ˈpenʃənə/ *noun*
a person who has stopped work and is receiving a pension

pensive /ˈpensɪv/ *adjective*
thinking about something a lot and seeming slightly worried or sad ➤ *He sat by the river, looking pensive.* (adverb: **pensively**)

pentagon /ˈpentəgən/ *noun*
a flat shape with five sides

people /ˈpiːpəl/
the plural of **person** ➤ *There were hundreds of people at the dance.*

pepper /ˈpepə/ *noun*
1 *(no plural)* a powder made from the seeds of a particular plant and used to give food a hot taste
2 a hollow red, green, or yellow vegetable, which can be eaten raw or used in cooking

peppermint /ˈpepəmɪnt/ *noun*
1 *(no plural)* oil from a plant with a special, strong taste, used in sweets or TOOTHPASTE
2 a sweet that tastes of this

per /pə; *strong* pɜː/ *preposition*
for each; during each ➤ *How much do you earn per week?* ➤ *The fruit costs £1.50 per kilo.*

perceive /pəˈsiːv/ *verb (present participle **perceiving**, past **perceived**)*
1 to understand or think about something in a particular way ➤ *It is a difficult situation, but we don't perceive it as a major problem.*
2 to notice, hear, or see something that is not easy to notice ➤ *It is difficult to perceive the difference between the two sounds.*

per cent /pəˈsent/ *noun*
out of a hundred ➤ *Sixty per cent of the pupils are boys (=60%; out of every hundred pupils, sixty are boys).*

percentage /pəˈsentɪdʒ/ *noun*
an amount that is part of a larger amount ➤ *A high percentage of Internet users are children.*

perception /pəˈsepʃən/ *noun*
your opinion of what something is like ➤ *You have a strange perception of marriage.*

perceptive /pəˈseptɪv/ *adjective*
good at noticing and understanding things or how someone is feeling ➤ *a funny and perceptive novel about family life*

perch /pɜːtʃ/ *verb*
to sit on something narrow ➤ *birds perched on the branch*

percussion /pəˈkʌʃən/ *noun (no plural)*
drums and other musical instruments that you hit

perfect¹ /ˈpɜːfɪkt/ *adjective*
1 without any faults or bad points ➤ *a perfect day*

2 without any mistakes ➤ *She speaks perfect French.*

perfect² /pə'fekt/ *verb*
to make something very good or perfect ➤ *They worked hard to perfect their dance.*

perfect³ /'pɜːfɪkt/ *noun*
the PRESENT PERFECT form of an English verb

perfection /pə'fekʃən/ *noun (no plural)*
the quality of being perfect

perfectionist /pə'fekʃənɪst/ *noun*
a person who is not satisfied with anything unless it is completely perfect ➤ *Jo is a perfectionist and her work is always beautifully presented.*

perfectly /'pɜːfɪktlɪ/ *adverb*
1 completely ➤ *perfectly happy*
2 very well, without any mistakes or bad points ➤ *The house suits us perfectly.*

perforated /'pɜːfəreɪtɪd/ *adjective*
(used about paper) having a line of small holes in it so that a part of it can be torn off easily

perform /pə'fɔːm/ *verb*
1 to do something to amuse people in a play, concert, etc. ➤ *They're performing a new play tonight.*
2 to work well ➤ *This car performs well in bad weather.*

performance /pə'fɔːməns/ *noun*
1 the act of doing something to amuse people in a play, concert, etc. ➤ *the excellent performance of the lead actor*
2 your ability to do something ➤ *her poor performance in the test*

performer /pə'fɔːməʳ/ *noun*
a person who PERFORMS – for example, an actor or a singer

perfume /'pɜːfjuːm/ *noun (no plural)*
1 a liquid which women put on their skin to make them smell nice
SAME MEANING: **scent**

2 a sweet or pleasant smell
SAME MEANING: **fragrance, scent**

perhaps /pə'hæps/ *adverb*
possibly ➤ *Perhaps our team will win.*

peril /'perɪl/ *noun*
great danger ➤ *fears that our soldiers were in great peril* ➤ *the perils of experimenting with drugs*

perilous /'perɪləs/ *adjective*
very dangerous ➤ *a perilous journey*
(adverb: **perilously**)

period /'pɪərɪəd/ *noun*
1 a length of time ➤ *There were long periods when we didn't hear from him.*
2 a particular time in history or in a person's life ➤ *After she left school, she went through a difficult period.*

periodic /ˌpɪərɪ'ɒdɪk/ (also **periodical** /ˌpɪərɪ'ɒdɪkəl/) *adjective*
regular but not very frequent ➤ *one of her periodic visits to the dentist*
(adverb: **periodically**)

peripheral /pə'rɪfərəl/ *adjective*
a peripheral idea or activity is less important than the main one

perish /'perɪʃ/ *verb*
to die ➤ *The crops all perished because there was no rain.*

perjury /'pɜːdʒərɪ/ *noun (no plural)*
the crime of telling a lie in a law court ➤ *He was found guilty of perjury.*

perk¹ /pɜːk/ *noun*
something such as a car or free meals that you get from your work in addition to your pay ➤ *Free travel is one of the perks of the job.*

perk² *verb*
perk up to become more cheerful and interested in what is happening around you, or to make someone feel this way ➤ *Meg soon perked up when his letter arrived.*

perm¹ /pɜːm/ *noun*
a method of putting curls into straight hair by treating it with chemicals ➤ *I've decided to have a perm.*

perm² *verb*
to put curls into straight hair using chemicals ➤ *Debbie's had her hair permed.*

permanent /'pɜːmənənt/ *adjective*
lasting for a long time or for ever ➤ *a permanent job* (adverb: **permanently**)
COMPARE: **temporary**

permission /pəˈmɪʃən/ *noun (no plural)*
the right to do something ➤ *Did you get permission to use her computer?*

permit¹ /pəˈmɪt/ *verb (present participle **permitting**, past **permitted**)*
to allow someone to do something ➤ *You are not permitted to bring food into the library.*

permit² /'pɜːmɪt/ *noun*
a piece of paper saying that you are allowed to do something ➤ *a fishing permit*

perpetrate /'pɜːpɪtreɪt/ *verb (present participle **perpetrating**, past **perpetrated**)*
to do something that is wrong ➤ *crimes perpetrated by young people*

perplexed /pəˈplekst/ *adjective*
very confused ➤ *He looked totally perplexed.*

persecute /'pɜːsɪkjuːt/ *verb (present participle **persecuting**, past **persecuted**)*
to treat someone cruelly and unfairly, especially because of their beliefs ➤ *a writer persecuted for criticizing the government*

perseverance /ˌpɜːsəˈvɪərəns/ *noun (no plural)*
determination to keep trying to do something difficult ➤ *I admire her perseverance.*

persevere /ˌpɜːsəˈvɪəʳ/ *verb (present participle **persevering**, past **persevered**)*
to keep trying to do something difficult because you want to succeed ➤ *My father wants me to persevere with my studies.*

persist /pəˈsɪst/ *verb*
1 to continue to do something, even though it is difficult or other people do not like it ➤ *At his trial for war crimes, he persisted in denying the charges.*
2 to continue to exist or happen ➤ *Problems with the computer persist.*

persistent /pəˈsɪstənt/ *adjective*
1 continuing for a long time ➤ *the problem of persistent unemployment*
2 continuing to try to do something even though someone is opposing you ➤ *She keeps saying no, but he's very persistent.* (adverb: **persistently**)

person /'pɜːsən/ *noun (plural **people** /'piːpəl/ or **persons**)*
a human being; a man, woman, or child ➤ *She's a lovely person.* ➤ *You're just the person I need.*

1 The usual plural of **person** is **people**. **Persons** is very formal and is used only in official notices and ANNOUNCEMENTS: *Would all persons wishing to buy tickets, please come to the tourist office.*
2 Do **not** say "all people"; use **everyone** or **everybody** instead.

personal /'pɜːsənəl/ *adjective*
concerning or belonging to a particular person ➤ *We work together, but she's also a personal friend.* ➤ *a personal letter*

personal computer /ˌpɜːsənəl kəmˈpjuːtəʳ/ *noun*
a small computer which you can use for business or at home

personality /ˌpɜːsəˈnælətɪ/ *noun (plural **personalities**)*
1 the character of a particular person ➤ *She has a lovable personality.*

P

2 a well-known person ► *a television personality*

personalized /ˈpɜːsənəlaɪzd/ *adjective*
personalized objects have the name OR INITIALS of the owner on them ► *a car with personalized number plates*

personally /ˈpɜːsənəlɪ/ *adverb*
a word you use when you are giving your own opinion about something ► *Personally, I think he is dishonest, but many people trust him.*

personal organizer /ˌpɜːsənəl ˈɔːgənaɪzəʳ/ *noun*
a small book or a very small computer for recording addresses, times of meetings, etc.

personal pronoun /ˌpɜːsənəl ˈprəʊnaʊn/ *noun*
in grammar, a PRONOUN, such as I, you, or they

personal stereo /ˌpɜːsənəl ˈsterɪəʊ/ *noun*
a small machine that plays CASSETTES or CDs. You carry it with you and listen through EARPHONES (=thin wires with a special piece on each end that you put in your ears)

personnel /ˌpɜːsəˈnel/ *plural noun*
the people who work in an organization ► *military personnel*

perspective /pəˈspektɪv/ *noun*
1 a way of thinking about something ► *Foreign travel gives you a whole new perspective on life.*
2 keep/get something in perspective to think sensibly about something and not imagine that it is worse than it is

perspiration /ˌpɜːspəˈreɪʃən/ *noun (no plural)*
SWEAT

persuade /pəˈsweɪd/ *verb (present participle **persuading**, past **persuaded**)*
to talk with someone and give them reasons until they agree with what

you say ► *He persuaded her to go to school, even though she didn't want to.*

persuasion /pəˈsweɪʒən/ *noun (no plural)*
the act of persuading someone ► *After a lot of persuasion, she agreed to go.*

persuasive /pəˈsweɪsɪv/ *adjective*
good at persuading people to do or believe something ► *Salesmen can be very persuasive.*

pervert /ˈpɜːvɜːt/ *noun*
someone whose sexual behaviour is unnatural and unacceptable

pessimism /ˈpesɪmɪzəm/ *noun (no plural)*
the belief that bad things will happen
OPPOSITE: **optimism**

pessimist /ˈpesɪmɪst/ *noun*
a person who always thinks that something bad will happen
OPPOSITE: **optimist**

pessimistic /ˌpesɪˈmɪstɪk/ *adjective*
always believing that something bad will happen
OPPOSITE: **optimistic**

pest /pest/ *noun*
1 an animal that is harmful or annoying
2 a person who annoys or worries you ► *That boy next door is such a pest!*

pester /ˈpestəʳ/ *verb*
to annoy someone by asking them all the time for something ► *Stop pestering me – I'll wash the car tomorrow!*

pesticide /ˈpestɪsaɪd/ *noun*
a chemical substance that you put on plants to kill insects that cause damage to the plants

pet /pet/ *noun*
1 an animal that you look after and keep in your house for company ► *She has two monkeys as pets.*

2 teacher's pet a pupil who the teacher of a class particularly likes

petal /ˈpetl/ *noun*
one of the brightly coloured parts of a flower

peter /ˈpiːtər/ *verb*
peter out to gradually become smaller and then come to an end ▶ *After a few days, our food supplies petered out.*

petite /pəˈtiːt/ *adjective*
small and slim ▶ *a petite woman*

petition /pəˈtɪʃən/ *noun*
a letter signed by a lot of people and sent to a government or some other official group in order to ask for or complain about something ▶ *The villagers all signed a petition asking for a hospital to be built.*

petrified /ˈpetrɪfaɪd/ *adjective*
very frightened ▶ *I'm petrified of spiders.*

petrol /ˈpetrəl/ *noun (no plural)*
a liquid used in cars, etc. to make the engine work

petroleum /pəˈtrəʊliəm/ *noun (no plural)*
oil from under the ground that is used to make petrol and other chemical substances

petrol station /ˈpetrəl ˌsteɪʃən/ *noun*
a place where you can buy petrol for cars, etc.

pet shop /ˈpet ʃɒp/ *noun*
a shop where you can buy animals to keep in your house as pets, as well as food, toys, etc. for them

petticoat /ˈpetɪkəʊt/ *noun*
a piece of clothing that a girl or woman wears under a skirt or dress

petty /ˈpeti/ *adjective (**pettier, pettiest**)*
1 not serious or important ▶ *a petty argument*
2 caring too much about small, unimportant rules or details ▶ *She*

can be very petty about money.
3 petty crime crime that is not very serious

pew /pjuː/ *noun*
a long, wooden seat in a church

phantom /ˈfæntəm/ *noun*
a GHOST

pharaoh /ˈfeərəʊ/ *noun*
a ruler of ancient Egypt

pharmacist /ˈfɑːməsɪst/ *noun*
a person who prepares and sells medicines
COMPARE: **chemist**

pharmacy /ˈfɑːməsi/ *noun (plural **pharmacies**)*
a shop which sells medicines

phase¹ /feɪz/ *noun*
one part of a process ▶ *Phase 1 of the project will start next week.*

phase² *verb (present participle **phasing**, past **phased**)*
1 phase something in to gradually start using something or doing something ▶ *The government is phasing in new smoking laws.*
2 phase something out to gradually stop using something or doing something ▶ *The old car design will be phased out over the next few years.*

PhD *(also **Ph.D.**)* /ˌpiː eɪtʃ ˈdiː/ *noun*
DOCTOR OF PHILOSOPHY; the highest university degree

phenomena /fɪˈnɒmɪnə/
the plural of **phenomenon**

phenomenal /fɪˈnɒmɪnəl/ *adjective*
very unusual and impressive ▶ *a phenomenal achievement (adverb: **phenomenally**)*

phenomenon /fɪˈnɒmɪnən/ *noun (plural **phenomena** /-nə/)*
something that happens or exists, especially something that is unusual or difficult to understand ▶ *natural phenomena like earthquakes and hurricanes*

philosopher /fɪˈlɒsəfəʳ/ *noun*
a person who studies PHILOSOPHY

philosophical /ˌfɪləˈsɒfɪkəl/ *(also*
philosophic /ˌfɪləˈsɒfɪk/) *adjective*
1 of or about philosophy ▸ *a*
philosophical discussion
2 accepting difficult or unpleasant
things calmly ▸ *Anderson is*
philosophical about his defeat.
(adverb: **philosophically**)

philosophy /fɪˈlɒsəfɪ/ *noun (no*
plural)
the study of life and what it means,
how we should live, etc.

phobia /ˈfəʊbɪə/ *noun*
a strong, unreasonable fear of
something ▸ *Holly has a phobia*
about snakes.

phone¹ /fəʊn/ *(also **telephone**) noun*
a machine you use to speak to
someone who is in another place
▸ *Can I use your phone, please?* ▸ *a*
phone call

phone² *(also **telephone**) verb (present*
*participle **phoning**, past **phoned**)*
to speak to someone by phone ▸ *I*
phoned my parents to tell them the
news.

phone book /ˈfəʊn bʊk/ *noun*
a book that contains the names,
addresses, and telephone numbers of
the people in an area

phone box /ˈfəʊn bɒks/ *(also **phone**
booth /ˈfəʊn buːð/) noun (plural*
phone boxes)
a small shelter in the street where
there is a public telephone

phone call /ˈfəʊn kɔːl/ *noun*
when you speak to someone on the
telephone ▸ *I need to make a quick*
phone call.

phone-in /ˈfəʊn ɪn/ *noun*
a radio or television programme in
which ordinary people give their
opinions, ask questions, etc. by
telephone

phone number /ˈfəʊn ˌnʌmbəʳ/
noun
the number that you need to ring
when you want to talk to someone on
the telephone ▸ *What's your phone*
number?

phonetic /fəˈnetɪk/ *adjective*
using special signs to show the
sounds you make when speaking
▸ *This dictionary uses a phonetic*
alphabet to show you how to
pronounce words.

phonetics /fəˈnetɪks/ *noun (no plural)*
the study of the sounds you make
when speaking

phoney /ˈfəʊnɪ/ *adjective (**phonier**,*
phoniest)
false or not real, and intended to
deceive someone ▸ *I gave the police*
a phoney address.

photo /ˈfəʊtəʊ/ *noun*
a photograph ▸ *She took a photo of*
the garden.

photocopier /ˈfəʊtəʊˌkɒpɪəʳ/ *noun*
a machine that makes photocopies of
documents

photocopy¹ /ˈfəʊtəˌkɒpɪ/ *noun*
*(plural **photocopies**)*
a copy of a piece of writing made on
a special machine ▸ *Here's a*
photocopy of the letter.

photocopy² *verb (past **photocopied**)*
to make a copy of a piece of writing
on a special machine

photograph¹ /ˈfəʊtəɡrɑːf/ *verb*
to take a photograph of someone or
something ▸ *He has photographed*
many film stars.

photograph² *noun*
a picture made by a camera

photographer /fəˈtɒɡrəfəʳ/ *noun*
a person who takes photographs,
especially as their job

photographic /ˌfəʊtəˈɡræfɪk/
adjective
connected with photographs and

photography ➤ *expensive photographic equipment*

photography /fə'tɒɡrəfɪ/ *noun (no plural)*
the art or business of producing photographs

phrasal verb /ˌfreɪzəl 'vɜːb/ *noun*
a verb that is used with an adverb or a preposition, which has a different meaning from the verb used alone. "Set off" and "put up with" are examples of phrasal verbs

phrase /freɪz/ *noun*
a group of words that does not make a full sentence ➤ *"Later that day" and "on the way home" are phrases.*

physical /'fɪzɪkəl/ *adjective*
1 concerning the body rather than the mind ➤ *physical exercise*
COMPARE: **mental**
2 concerning things that you can see and touch

physician /fɪ'zɪʃən/ *noun*
a doctor

physicist /'fɪzɪsɪst/ *noun*
a person who studies physics

physics /'fɪzɪks/ *noun (no plural)*
the study of natural forces, such as heat, light, and movement

physiotherapist /ˌfɪzɪəʊ'θerəpɪst/ *noun*
a person whose job is giving other people physiotherapy

physiotherapy /ˌfɪzɪəʊ'θerəpɪ/ *noun (no plural)*
medical treatment for muscles, using exercises, rubbing, heat, etc.

physique /fɪ'ziːk/ *noun*
the shape and size of your body ➤ *a tall man with a powerful physique*

pianist /'piːənɪst/ *noun*
a person who plays a piano

piano /pɪ'ænəʊ/ *noun*
a large musical instrument that you play by pressing small, black and white bars

P

pick¹ /pɪk/ *verb*
1 to choose someone or something ➤ *The child picked the biggest sweet.*
2 to pull a flower or a fruit from a plant or tree ➤ *She picked an apple from the tree.*
3 pick someone's pocket to steal something from someone's pocket
4 pick on someone to treat someone unfairly or unkindly ➤ *He's always picking on the smaller children.*
5 pick something up to take hold of something and lift it up ➤ *Pick up your toys and put them in the box.*
6 pick someone up to collect someone from somewhere ➤ *I'll pick you up at the hotel at 8 o'clock.*

pick² *noun (no plural)*
take your pick to choose something ➤ *You can take your pick of these cakes.*

pickaxe /'pɪkæks/ (*also* **pick**) *noun*
a sharp, metal tool with a long handle, for making holes in rock or hard ground

picket /'pɪkɪt/ *noun*
a person who stands outside a shop or factory during an argument with an employer, to stop people going to work

pickle /'pɪkəl/ *noun*
a cold SAUCE made with vegetables that have been preserved in VINEGAR or salt

pickpocket /'pɪkˌpɒkɪt/ *noun*
a person who steals things from people's pockets, especially in a crowd

picky /'pɪkɪ/ *adjective* (**pickier, pickiest**)
only liking a few things, and difficult to please ➤ *a picky eater* ➤ *Kelly's so picky about her clothes!*

picnic¹ /'pɪknɪk/ *noun*
a meal eaten outside, when you are away from home ➤ *We had a picnic by the sea.*
COMPARE: **barbecue**

picnic² verb (present participle **picknicking**, past **picknicked**)
to have a meal outside, but not at home

picture¹ /ˈpɪktʃəʳ/ noun
1 something represented on paper as a drawing, painting, or photograph ▶ She drew a picture **of** me.
2 **take a picture** to take a photograph of someone or something

picture² verb (present participle **picturing**, past **pictured**)
to imagine something ▶ She pictured herself as a beautiful queen.

picturesque /ˌpɪktʃəˈresk/ adjective
very attractive ▶ the picturesque villages of southern Spain

pie /paɪ/ noun
a cooked dish of meat, fish, or fruit covered with pastry ▶ apple pie
COMPARE: **tart**

piece /piːs/ noun
a part of something which is separated from a larger thing, or which has broken off ▶ He took a piece **of** the cake. ▶ The plate which I had dropped lay in pieces on the floor.

pier /pɪəʳ/ noun
a structure that is built out into the sea so that people can walk along it

pierce /pɪəs/ verb (present participle **piercing**, past **pierced**)
to make a hole in something ▶ The needle pierced the material.

piercing /ˈpɪəsɪŋ/ adjective
(used about sounds) loud and unpleasant ▶ a piercing cry

pig /pɪɡ/ noun
1 a fat, pink, farm animal kept for its meat
2 a person who eats too much or behaves very badly to other people

pigeon /ˈpɪdʒən/ noun
a common, grey bird with short legs that is often seen in towns

pigheaded /ˌpɪɡˈhedɪd/ adjective
determined to do things in a particular way, even when there are good reasons for not doing them in that way ▶ I've never met a woman so obstinate and pigheaded.

piglet /ˈpɪɡlət/ noun
a young pig

pigsty /ˈpɪɡstaɪ/ noun (plural **pigsties**)
a place on a farm where pigs are kept

pigtail /ˈpɪɡteɪl/ noun
hair that has been twisted together and tied ▶ a fat child with hair in pigtails

pile¹ /paɪl/ noun
a number of things put on top of each other ▶ a pile **of** books

pile² verb (present participle **piling**, past **piled**)
to put things in a pile ▶ She piled the boxes on top of each other.

pile-up /ˈpaɪl ʌp/ noun
a road accident involving several vehicles ▶ a 16-car pile-up

pilgrim /ˈpɪlɡrɪm/ noun
a person who goes to pray at a holy place far away from their home

pilgrimage /ˈpɪlɡrɪmɪdʒ/ noun
a journey to a holy place far away from your home

pill /pɪl/ noun
a small, hard ball of medicine that you swallow when you are not well
SAME MEANING: **tablet**

pillar /ˈpɪləʳ/ noun
a strong, round post, usually made of stone ▶ The roof of the church was supported by stone pillars.

pillow /ˈpɪləʊ/ noun
a cloth bag filled with soft material to put your head on when you are in bed
COMPARE: **cushion**

pillowcase /ˈpɪləʊkeɪs/ noun
a cover that you put on a pillow to keep it clean

pilot /'paɪlət/ noun
1 a person who flies an aircraft
2 a person who guides ships into a harbour or along a river

pimple /'pɪmpəl/ noun
a small, rough spot on your skin

pin¹ /pɪn/ noun
a small, pointed bit of metal used for fastening or joining together pieces of paper, cloth, etc.

pin² verb (present participle **pinning**, past **pinned**)
1 to fasten or join things with a pin
2 **pin something up** to put a notice on the wall with a pin so it can be read easily

pinch¹ /pɪntʃ/ verb
1 to take something between your thumb and fingers and press it ➤ She pinched my arm hard, and it still hurts.
2 to steal something ➤ He pinched an apple.

pinch² noun (plural **pinches**)
1 a very small amount ➤ a pinch of salt
2 an act of pressing something tightly between your thumb and fingers

pine /paɪn/ noun
a tree that has thin leaves like needles

pineapple /'paɪnæpəl/ noun
a large, yellow, tropical fruit with a hard skin and stiff leaves on top

ping-pong /'pɪŋ pɒŋ/ noun (no plural)
a game in which two or four players hit a small ball across a net on a table
SAME MEANING: **table tennis**

pink /pɪŋk/ noun, adjective
the colour made by mixing red and white

pins and needles /ˌpɪnz ənd 'niːdlz/ plural noun
the sharp, slightly uncomfortable pain you get in your arms or legs after you have been sitting in an awkward position ➤ I woke up with pins and needles in my foot.

pint /paɪnt/ noun
a measure of liquid, equal to 0.57 litres ➤ There are 8 pints in a gallon.

pinup /'pɪnʌp/ noun
a picture of someone famous or attractive, often wearing very few clothes

pioneer /ˌpaɪə'nɪər/ noun
a person who goes somewhere or does something before other people ➤ His father was one of the pioneers of space travel.

pious /'paɪəs/ adjective
having strong religious beliefs
(adverb: **piously**)

pip /pɪp/ noun
the seed of some fruits

pipe /paɪp/ noun
1 a tube for carrying water or gas ➤ a metal pipe
2 a small tube with a round bowl at one end, used for smoking

pipeline /'paɪp-laɪn/ noun
1 pipes used for carrying a liquid or gas over long distances
2 **in the pipeline** being prepared and going to happen soon ➤ The band's third album is in the pipeline.

piping¹ /'paɪpɪŋ/ noun (no plural)
a system of pipes, used for carrying a liquid or gas ➤ lead piping

piping² adverb
piping hot very hot ➤ piping hot soup

pirate /'paɪərət/ noun
a person who sails on the sea attacking and robbing other ships

pistol /'pɪstl/ noun
a small gun
SAME MEANING: **revolver**

pit /pɪt/ noun
1 a deep hole in the ground
2 a coalmine

pitch¹ /pɪtʃ/ *noun (plural pitches)*
1 a part of a field on which games are played
2 how high or low a sound is

pitch² *verb*
to set up a tent ▶ *We pitched our tent near the river.*

pitch-black /ˌpɪtʃ ˈblæk/ *(also pitch-dark* /ˌpɪtʃ ˈdɑːk/) *adjective*
completely black or dark ▶ *It was pitch-black in the basement.*

pitcher /ˈpɪtʃəʳ/ *noun*
1 a container used for holding and pouring liquids ▶ *a pitcher of beer*
2 the BASEBALL player who throws the ball to the BATTER

pitiful /ˈpɪtɪfəl/ *adjective*
1 making you feel sad and sympathetic ▶ *a pitiful sight*
2 extremely bad ▶ *His performance last night was pitiful.*

pity¹ /ˈpɪtɪ/ *noun (no plural)*
1 the sadness that you feel when someone else is hurt, in trouble, etc. ▶ *I feel great pity for people with nowhere to live.*
2 a pity a sad or unfortunate event or state of affairs ▶ *What a pity you can't come and see us!*

pity² *verb (past pitied)*
to feel sadness for someone else because they are hurt, in trouble, etc. ▶ *I pity anyone who has to work in such bad conditions.*

pivot /ˈpɪvət/ *noun*
a central point that something balances or turns on

pixel /ˈpɪksəl/ *noun*
the smallest unit of an image on a computer screen

pixie /ˈpɪksɪ/ *noun*
a small, imaginary person who has magic powers

pizza /ˈpiːtsə/ *noun*
a round, flat piece of DOUGH covered with cheese and other foods and then baked

placard /ˈplækɑːd/ *noun*
a large sign that is carried by a person ▶ *Protesters were carrying placards.*

place¹ /pleɪs/ *noun*
1 a particular area, building, town, or country ▶ *This is the place where I first saw her.* ▶ *He travelled to places all over the world.*
2 the spot where you usually keep something ▶ *Keep your passport in a safe place.*
3 your house or home ▶ *He's got a lovely place.*
4 a seat ▶ *Is this place taken?*
5 in place of instead of
6 take place to happen ▶ *When will the ceremony take place?*
LOOK AT: **happen**

place² *verb (present participle placing, past placed)*
1 to put something somewhere ▶ *She placed a book on the table.*
2 place an order to ask a shop, factory, etc. for some goods

placid /ˈplæsɪd/ *adjective*
calm and peaceful ▶ *He is a very placid baby.* ▶ *the placid waters of the lake (adverb: placidly)*

plagiarism /ˈpleɪdʒərɪzəm/ *noun*
the act of using another person's words or ideas in something you write, and pretending that they are your own ▶ *She was accused of plagiarism in her thesis.*

plague /pleɪg/ *noun*
a disease that spreads quickly, killing a lot of people

plaice /pleɪs/ *noun (plural plaice)*
a flat, sea fish that people eat

plain¹ /pleɪn/ *adjective*
1 easy to see, hear, or understand ▶ *He made it plain that he did not like me.*
SAME MEANING: **clear**
2 simple ▶ *plain food*
3 without a pattern on ▶ *a plain dress*

plain² *noun*
a large, flat piece of country

plainly /'pleɪnlɪ/ *adverb*
clearly ▸ *It was plainly too hot to be working in the sun.*

plait¹ /plæt/ *verb*
to twist together three or more pieces of rope, hair, etc.

plait² *noun*
three or more lengths of hair that are twisted together into one piece ▸ *She wore her hair in plaits.*

plan¹ /plæn/ *noun*
1 something you have arranged to do in the future ▸ *Have you made any plans for the weekend?*
2 a drawing showing all the parts of a new building, garden, or machine

plan² *verb (present participle **planning**, past **planned**)*
to think about what you are going to do in the future and how to do it ▸ *The government plans to build a bridge over the river.*

plane /pleɪn/ *noun*
a vehicle that flies ▸ *What time does the plane land?*

planet /'plænɪt/ *noun*
one of the large masses in space, like the Earth, that go round the sun or a star

plank /plæŋk/ *noun*
a long, flat, thin piece of wood

plant¹ /plɑːnt/ *noun*
something living that is not an animal ▸ *a tomato plant*

plant² *verb*
to put plants or seeds in the ground to grow ▸ *Spring is the best time to plant flowers.* ▸ *Have you planted any vegetables yet?*

plantation /plɑːn'teɪʃən/ *noun*
a large piece of land on which tea, sugar, cotton, or rubber is grown

plaster¹ /'plɑːstəʳ/ *noun*
1 (*no plural*) a soft, white substance

which becomes hard when dry, and is spread on walls to make them smooth
2 a thin piece of sticky material that you put on your skin to protect a cut
COMPARE (**2**): **bandage**

plaster² *verb*
to cover a wall with plaster

plaster cast /ˌplɑːstə 'kɑːst/ *noun*
a hard cover made from a special type of plaster, used to protect a broken bone

plastic /'plæstɪk/ *adjective, noun*
a strong, man-made substance used to make containers, toys, etc. ▸ *I always give the baby a plastic bowl so she can't break it.*

plastic surgery /ˌplæstɪk 'sɜːdʒərɪ/ *noun (no plural)*
a medical operation or operations to improve the way someone looks ▸ *She needed plastic surgery after she was badly burnt in a fire.*

plate /pleɪt/ *noun*
a flat, usually round, dish for food ▸ *a dinner plate*
COMPARE: **bowl**

platform /'plætfɔːm/ *noun*
1 the part of a station where you get on and off trains ▸ *The train at platform 2 will call at Newcastle and York.*
2 a raised part of a floor on which people may stand ▸ *The headmaster gave his speech from a platform at one end of the hall.*

platinum /'plætɪnəm/ *noun (no plural)*
an expensive, white metal, used for making jewellery

platonic /plə'tɒnɪk/ *adjective*
(used about relationships) friendly but not sexual

plausible /'plɔːzəbəl/ *adjective*
likely to be true ▸ *That's not a plausible excuse for being late.*
OPPOSITE: **implausible**

P

play¹ /pleɪ/ *verb*
1 to spend time with toys or taking part in games ▶ *The little girl was playing in the garden.*
2 to take part in a game or sport ▶ *He plays football every Sunday.*
3 to make sounds on a musical instrument ▶ *She plays the drums.*

play² *noun*
1 (*no plural*) activity done for amusement by children ▶ *Children learn a lot through play.*
2 a story acted in a theatre, on the radio or television, etc. ▶ *She is in a new play about a famous singer.*

player /'pleɪəʳ/ *noun*
a person who plays a game or a sport ▶ *a tennis player*

playful /'pleɪfəl/ *adjective*
full of fun ▶ *a playful little dog*

playground /'pleɪgraʊnd/ *noun*
a special piece of ground for children to play on

playgroup /'pleɪgruːp/ *noun*
an organized group where small children go to play, learn, etc. in the years before they go to school

playing card /'pleɪ ɪŋ ˌkɑːd/ *noun*
one of a set of thin pieces of cardboard that are printed with numbers and pictures and used to play games

playing field /'pleɪ ɪŋ ˌfiːld/ *noun*
a large area of grass where people play sport

playtime /'pleɪtaɪm/ *noun* (*no plural*)
a period of time when children at school can play

playwright /'pleɪraɪt/ *noun*
a person who writes plays

plea /pliː/ *noun*
1 an urgent request for something ▶ *Neighbours ignored her desperate pleas for help.*
2 in a law court, the answer someone gives when they are asked whether they are guilty or not guilty of a crime ▶ *a plea of not guilty*

plead /pliːd/ *verb*
1 to beg ▶ *He pleaded with her to listen to his advice.*
2 to say officially in a court of law whether you are guilty or not guilty of a crime ▶ *The woman pleaded not guilty.*

pleasant /'plezənt/ *adjective*
nice or enjoyable ▶ *We spent a pleasant day in the country.*
(*adverb*: **pleasantly**)
OPPOSITE: **unpleasant**

please¹ /pliːz/ *verb* (*present participle* **pleasing**, *past* **pleased**)
to give happiness or pleasure to someone ▶ *I'm tired of trying to please everyone.*

please² *interjection*
a word added to a question or an order, to make it polite ▶ *Please bring me that book.* ▶ *Could I have a glass of water, please?*

pleased /pliːzd/ *adjective*
happy or satisfied ▶ *I'm so pleased to see you.*

pleasurable /'pleʒərəbəl/ *adjective*
enjoyable ▶ *a pleasurable experience*

pleasure /'pleʒəʳ/ *noun* (*no plural*)
the feeling of happiness or satisfaction that you get from doing something you enjoy ▶ *She looked at the paintings with great pleasure.*

pleat /pliːt/ *noun*
a narrow, flat fold in a piece of clothing

pleated /'pliːtɪd/ *adjective*
(used about clothing) having a lot of pleats

pledge¹ /pledʒ/ *noun*
a formal promise to do something ▶ *Several countries made pledges of aid.*

pledge² *verb* (*present participle* **pledging**, *past* **pledged**) to make a formal promise to do something ▶ *They have pledged to cut inflation.*

plentiful /'plentɪfəl/ *adjective*
existing in large amounts or numbers ▶ *Fruit is plentiful in summer.*

plenty /'plentɪ/ *pronoun*
a lot ▶ *We have plenty of time to catch the train.* ▶ *She thought there wasn't enough bread, but there was plenty.*

pliers /'plaɪəz/ *plural noun*
a tool that looks like a pair of strong scissors and is used for cutting wire or for removing nails

plight /plaɪt/ *noun*
a difficult, dangerous, or sad situation that someone is in ▶ *the plight of the homeless*

plod /plɒd/ *verb (present participle plodding, past plodded)*
to walk slowly and heavily

plot¹ /plɒt/ *noun*
1 a small piece of ground
2 a secret plan by a group of people to do something wrong
3 the story of a book, film, etc. ▶ *The film had an exciting plot.*

plot² *verb (present participle plotting, past plotted)*
to plan secretly to do something wrong ▶ *They were plotting to kill the king.*

plough¹ /plaʊ/ *noun*
a farming tool for cutting up and turning over the earth before seeds are planted

plough² *verb*
to break and cut up the earth with a special tool ▶ *A farmer must plough the land before planting crops.*

ploy /plɔɪ/ *noun*
a dishonest but clever way of getting what you want ▶ *He's not really ill – it's just a ploy to avoid going to school.*

pluck /plʌk/ *verb*
to pull off the feathers of a bird before you cook and eat it

plug¹ /plʌg/ *noun*
1 a piece of rubber, plastic, etc. which stops water running out of a basin
2 a plastic object joined to an electric wire, which you put into special holes in a wall to get electrical power

plug² *verb (present participle plugging, past plugged)*
1 to block or close a hole with something
2 **plug something in** to connect an electrical machine to a supply of electricity ▶ *You need to plug in the lamp before it'll work.*

plughole /'plʌghəʊl/ *noun*
a hole in a bath or SINK, where the water can flow out

plum /plʌm/ *noun*
a sweet, juicy, red or yellow fruit with a smooth skin and one large seed

plumber /'plʌmə'/ *noun*
a person whose job is to fit and repair water pipes

plumbing /'plʌmɪŋ/ *noun (no plural)*
all the water pipes put into a building so that there can be running water

plume /pluːm/ *noun*
1 a small cloud of smoke or dust that is moving upwards ▶ *a plume of smoke*
2 a large feather ▶ *ostrich plumes*

plump /plʌmp/ *adjective*
nicely fat ▶ *the baby's plump arms*

plunder /'plʌndə'/ *verb*
to steal or take large amounts of money or things from somewhere ▶ *Foreign armies plundered and burned the city.*

plunge /plʌndʒ/ *verb (present participle plunging, past plunged)*
to move or jump down suddenly ▶ *He plunged into the river.*

pluperfect /pluː'pɜːfɪkt/ *noun*
the pluperfect the PAST PERFECT

P

plural /'pluǝrǝl/ *adjective, noun*
more than one ▶ *"Dogs" is the plural of "dog".*
OPPOSITE: **singular**

plus /plʌs/ *preposition*
added to; and ▶ *Four plus two is six* (4 + 2 = 6).
COMPARE: **minus**

plutonium /pluːˈtǝʊniǝm/ *noun (no plural)*
a metal used for producing NUCLEAR power

plywood /'plaɪwʊd/ *noun (no plural)*
board made from thin sheets of wood stuck together

pm /piː ˈem/
in the afternoon or evening ▶ *It is 4.30 pm.*

pneumonia /njuːˈmǝʊniǝ/ *noun (no plural)*
a serious disease of the lungs

PO Box /ˌpiː ˈǝʊ bɒks/ *noun (plural PO Boxes)*
post office box; a box with a number in a post office, where you can have mail sent instead of to your home

pocket /'pɒkɪt/ *noun*
a piece of material sewn onto clothes to make a little bag for keeping things in

pocket money /'pɒkɪt ˌmʌni/ *noun (no plural)*
money given to a child every week to spend as he or she wants

pod /pɒd/ *noun*
a long, narrow part of some plants in which seeds grow

podium /'pǝʊdiǝm/ *noun*
a small, raised area on which a performer or speaker stands ▶ *The orchestra's conductor stepped up to the podium.*

poem /'pǝʊɪm/ *noun*
a piece of writing with regular lines and sounds, that expresses

something in powerful or beautiful language ▶ *He wrote a poem about war.*

poet /'pǝʊɪt/ *noun*
a person who writes poems

poetic /pǝʊˈetɪk/ *adjective*
about or typical of poetry ▶ *poetic language*

poetry /'pǝʊɪtri/ *noun (no plural)*
poems in general ▶ *a book of poetry*

poignant /'pɔɪnjǝnt/ *adjective*
making you have strong feelings of sadness ▶ *a poignant farewell*

point¹ /pɔɪnt/ *verb*
to show where something is with your finger stretched out ▶ *He pointed to the building on the corner and said, "That's where I work."*

point² *noun*
1 the sharp end of something ▶ *the point of a nail*
2 *(no plural)* use or purpose ▶ *I don't see the point of repairing a car as old as this one.*
3 a mark that you win in a game or sport ▶ *Our team won by 15 points to 10.*
4 a certain moment in time ▶ *At that point, I began to get seriously worried.*
5 a sign (.) used to separate a whole number from the decimals which follow ▶ *3.8* (=three point eight)
6 the point the most important idea or argument ▶ *Stop talking so much and get to the point!*
7 on the point of doing something just about to do something ▶ *I was on the point of phoning the police when she arrived home.*

point-blank /ˌpɔɪnt ˈblæŋk/ *adjective, adverb*
1 at point-blank range shooting at someone from an extremely close position ▶ *The victim was shot dead at point-blank range.*
2 in a very firm and often rude way,

without any explanation ➤ *She refused point-blank to help them.*

pointed /ˈpɔɪntɪd/ *adjective*
having a sharp end

pointer /ˈpɔɪntəʳ/ *noun*
a helpful piece of advice ➤ *Sharon may be able to give you some pointers about public speaking.*
SAME MEANING: **tip**

pointless /ˈpɔɪntləs/ *adjective*
without purpose; not useful ➤ *a pointless meeting*

point of view /ˌpɔɪnt əv ˈvjuː/ *noun (plural points of view)*
a particular way of thinking about something ➤ *From a purely practical point of view, this is not a good decision.* ➤ *The story is told from a 14-year-old's point of view.*
SAME MEANING: **standpoint**

poised /pɔɪzd/ *adjective*
ready to move or do something ➤ *The army was poised to attack.*

poison¹ /ˈpɔɪzən/ *noun (no plural)*
a substance that kills or harms you if it gets into your body

poison² *verb*
to kill a person or an animal with poison ➤ *The farmer poisoned the rats.*

poisoning /ˈpɔɪzənɪŋ/ *noun (no plural)*
an illness that is caused by swallowing, touching, or breathing a substance that contains poison ➤ *lead poisoning*

poisonous /ˈpɔɪzənəs/ *adjective*
containing poison ➤ *a poisonous plant*

poke /pəʊk/ *verb (present participle **poking**, past **poked**)*
to push a pointed object into someone or something ➤ *He poked the fire with a stick.*

poker /ˈpəʊkəʳ/ *noun*
a card game that you usually play for money

poky /ˈpəʊkɪ/ *adjective (**pokier**, **pokiest**)*
too small and not pleasant or comfortable ➤ *a poky flat*

polar /ˈpəʊləʳ/ *adjective*
of the North or South Pole ➤ *a polar winter*

polar bear /ˌpəʊlə ˈbeəʳ/ *noun*
a large, white bear that lives near the North Pole

pole /pəʊl/ *noun*
1 a long, narrow piece of wood usually used to support something
2 one end of the Earth ➤ *the North Pole*

pole vault /ˈpəʊl vɔːlt/ *noun (no plural)*
a sport in which you jump over a high bar using a special long pole

police /pəˈliːs/ *noun (no plural)*
the group of men and women whose job is to protect people and property and to make sure that everyone obeys the law ➤ *The police are searching for the thief.* ➤ *a police car*

police force /pəˈliːs ˌfɔːs/ *noun*
the official police organization in a country or an area ➤ *The city is proud of its police force.*

policeman /pəˈliːsmən/ *noun (plural **policemen** /-mən/)*
a male member of the police

police officer /pəˈliːs ˌɒfɪsəʳ/ *noun*
a member of the police

police station /pəˈliːs ˌsteɪʃən/ *noun*
an office or a building used by the police

policewoman /pəˈliːsˌwʊmən/ *noun (plural **policewomen** /-ˌwɪmɪn/)*
a female member of the police

policy /ˈpɒləsɪ/ *noun (plural **policies**)*
a general plan agreed by a political party, a government, or a company ➤ *Government policy is to improve standards in education.*

polio /ˈpəʊliəʊ/ *noun (no plural)*
a serious disease that makes you unable to move your muscles

polish¹ /ˈpɒlɪʃ/ *verb*
to rub something so that it shines ▶ *I need to polish my dirty shoes.*

polish² *noun (no plural)*
an oily substance which helps to make things shine

polite /pəˈlaɪt/ *adjective*
having a kind and respectful way of behaving; not rude ▶ *A polite child always says thank you.* (adverb: **politely**)
OPPOSITE: **impolite, rude**

political /pəˈlɪtɪkəl/ *adjective*
of or about the power relationships and government of a country ▶ *a political party* ▶ *political beliefs*

politically correct /pəˌlɪtɪklɪ kəˈrekt/ *adjective*
speaking or behaving in a way that shows you are being careful not to offend women, people of a particular race, DISABLED people, etc. ▶ *It's not politically correct to say "handicapped" any more.*

politician /ˌpɒləˈtɪʃən/ *noun*
a person who takes part, or wants to take part, in the government of a country

politics /ˈpɒlɪtɪks/ *noun*
1 *(no plural)* activities concerned with the power relationships and government of a country ▶ *Are you interested in politics?*
2 *(no plural)* the study of the power relationships and government of a country ▶ *He has a degree in politics.*
3 *plural noun* opinions about the power relationships and government of a country ▶ *I don't agree with his politics.*

poll¹ /pəʊl/ *(also opinion poll) noun*
the process of asking a lot of people a question in order to find out what they think about someone or

something ▶ *Recent polls show that the mayor is still popular.*

poll² *verb*
to try to find out what people think about a subject by asking a lot of people the same question ▶ *We polled 600 teachers, asking their opinion about the changes.*

pollen /ˈpɒlən/ *noun (no plural)*
a powder produced by flowers, which is carried by the wind or insects to make other flowers produce seeds

pollinate /ˈpɒlɪneɪt/ *verb (present participle pollinating, past pollinated)*
to make a flower or plant produce seeds by giving it pollen

polling day /ˈpəʊlɪŋ deɪ/ *noun*
the day when people vote in an election

pollute /pəˈluːt/ *verb (present participle polluting, past polluted)*
to make the air, water, or soil dirty or dangerous by adding harmful substances ▶ *Chemicals from factories have polluted the lake.*

polluted /pəˈluːtɪd/ *adjective*
full of pollution ▶ *The rivers are heavily polluted.*

pollution /pəˈluːʃən/ *noun (no plural)*
the process of making the air, water, or soil dirty and dangerous
▶ *Pollution is doing great harm to the environment.*

polo neck /ˈpəʊləʊ nek/ *noun*
a JUMPER with a high band at the top that covers most of your neck

polystyrene /ˌpɒlɪˈstaɪriːn/ *noun (no plural)*
a very light, plastic substance, used especially to make containers

polytechnic /ˌpɒlɪˈteknɪk/ *noun*
a college where, in the past, you could study TECHNICAL subjects; polytechnics have now become UNIVERSITIES

pompous /ˈpɒmpəs/ *adjective*
trying to make people think you are

important, especially by using a lot of formal words ▶ *a pompous little man*

pond /pɒnd/ *noun*
an area of water, smaller than a lake ▶ *There's a duck pond in the middle of the village.*
COMPARE: **pool, puddle**

ponder /'pɒndəʳ/ *verb*
to think carefully and seriously about something ▶ *He pondered the problem for a long time.*

pony /'pəʊnɪ/ *noun (plural ponies)*
a small horse

ponytail /'pəʊnɪteɪl/ *noun*
hair tied together in a bunch at the back of your head ▶ *to have your hair in a ponytail*

poodle /'puːdl/ *noun*
a type of dog with thick, curly hair

pool /puːl/ *noun*
1 a small area of water, usually formed naturally ▶ *a rock pool on the beach*
COMPARE: **puddle, pond**
2 an area of water built for people to swim in ▶ *I hate swimming in an indoor pool.*

poor /pʊəʳ/ *adjective*
1 not having very much money ▶ *She was too poor to buy clothes for the children.*
OPPOSITE: **rich, wealthy**
2 needing kindness or help ▶ *The poor animal hadn't been fed.*
3 not of a good standard ▶ *Your writing is poor.*

poorly /'pʊəlɪ/ *adverb*
badly ▶ *The work was hard and poorly paid.*

pop¹ /pɒp/ *noun*
1 a sudden noise like the sound of the top being pulled out of a bottle
2 *(no plural)* music or songs with a strong beat that many younger people like and dance to

pop² *verb (present participle popping, past popped)*

1 to burst with a short, loud sound
2 to go somewhere or put something somewhere quickly ▶ *I'm just popping out to buy some milk.* ▶ *Can you pop the letter under her door?*

popcorn /'pɒpkɔːn/ *noun (no plural)*
corn that is heated until it swells and bursts open, and then is eaten

pope /pəʊp/ *noun*
the head of the Roman Catholic church

pop group /'pɒp gruːp/ *noun*
a group of people who play and sing pop music

poppy /'pɒpɪ/ *noun (plural poppies)*
a bright red flower with small, black seeds

pop star /'pɒp stɑːʳ/ *noun*
a person who is famous for singing and playing pop music

popular /'pɒpjʊləʳ/ *adjective*
liked by many people ▶ *She is popular at school.* ▶ *This dance is popular **with** young people.*
OPPOSITE: **unpopular**

popularity /ˌpɒpjʊ'lærətɪ/ *noun (no plural)*
the quality or state of being liked by a lot of people

popularly /'pɒpjʊləlɪ/ *adverb*
popularly believed, popularly known as, etc. believed to be the case, or called a particular name by many people ▶ *Crime in this part of town is much more common than is popularly believed.*

populated /'pɒpjʊleɪtɪd/ *adjective*
used to describe the type or number of people that live in an area ▶ *England is a densely populated country.*

population /ˌpɒpjʊ'leɪʃən/ *noun*
the number of people living in a place ▶ *What is the population **of** this city?*

porcelain /'pɔːsəlɪn/ *noun (no plural)*

P

1 a hard, shiny, white substance that is used to make expensive plates, cups, etc.
2 plates, cups, etc. made of this substance

porch /pɔːtʃ/ *noun (plural **porches**)*
an entrance covered by a roof built onto a house or church

porcupine /'pɔːkjupaɪn/ *noun*
an animal with long needles on its back and sides

pore¹ /pɔːʳ/ *noun*
one of the small holes in your skin that SWEAT can pass through

pore² *verb (present participle **poring**, past **pored**)*
pore over something to read or look at something very carefully for a long time ▶ *He spent hours poring over the photographs.*

pork /pɔːk/ *noun (no plural)*
meat from pigs

pornographic /ˌpɔːnə'græfɪk/ *(also **porn** /pɔːn/) adjective*
(used about magazines, films, etc.) designed to make people feel sexually excited

pornography /pɔː'nɒɡrəfi/ *(also **porn** /pɔːn/) noun (no plural)*
magazines, films, etc. that are meant to make people feel sexually excited

porous /'pɔːrəs/ *adjective*
with small holes that allow liquid, air, etc. to pass through slowly ▶ *It's best to keep your plants in pots made of porous material such as clay.*

porridge /'pɒrɪdʒ/ *noun (no plural)*
a breakfast food made by boiling grain in water until it is very soft

port /pɔːt/ *noun*
a harbour, or a town with a harbour

portable /'pɔːtəbəl/ *adjective*
small and easy to carry ▶ *a portable stereo*

porter /'pɔːtəʳ/ *noun*
a person whose job is to carry things

for people at stations, airports, and hotels

porthole /'pɔːthəʊl/ *noun*
a small, round window in the side of a ship or an aircraft

portion /'pɔːʃən/ *noun*
a part or share of something ▶ *A small portion of ice-cream costs £2.*

portrait /'pɔːtreɪt/ *noun*
a painting, drawing, or photograph of a person ▶ *He painted a portrait of his daughter.*

portray /pɔː'treɪ/ *verb*
to describe or show something or someone in a story, film, etc. ▶ *The film portrayed him as evil.*

pose¹ /pəʊz/ *verb (present participle **posing**, past **posed**)*
1 pose a problem, pose a danger, etc.
to cause a problem or danger ▶ *The chemicals pose a risk to people.*
2 to sit or stand in a particular position in order to be photographed or painted ▶ *In the photograph, a woman poses with her sleeping child.*

pose² *noun*
1 the position that someone stands or sits in while they are being painted or photographed
2 when someone behaves in a way that is different from their real character and pretends to be a different kind of person ▶ *He's not really the macho type – it's all just a pose.*

posh /pɒʃ/ *adjective*
1 expensive and used by rich people ▶ *a posh hotel*
2 typical of people from a high social class ▶ *a posh voice*

position /pə'zɪʃən/ *noun*
1 a place where a person or thing is ▶ *Our seats were in a good position to hear the music.*
2 a job ▶ *He has an important position in the company.*
3 the state or condition that a person

is in ▶ *I am in a difficult position as I have just lost my job.*
4 the way in which someone sits, stands, or lies ▶ *That's an uncomfortable position to sleep in.*

positive /'pɒzətɪv/ *adjective*
sure that something is true ▶ *I am positive that I gave you his address.*
SAME MEANING: **certain**

positively /'pɒzətɪvli/ *adverb*
used to emphasize what you are saying ▶ *This is positively the worst party I've ever been to.*

possess /pə'zes/ *verb*
to have or own something

possession /pə'zeʃən/ *noun*
something that you own ▶ *He lost all his possessions in the fire.*

possessive¹ /pə'zesɪv/ *adjective*
1 not wanting to share someone's love or attention with other people ▶ *He is very possessive about his wife.*
2 not wanting to share the things you own with other people ▶ *My daughter has always been very possessive about her toys.*

possessive² *noun*
a word such as **my, mine, your,** or **their,** used to show who something belongs to

possibility /,pɒsə'bɪləti/ *noun (plural* **possibilities***)*
something that might happen or might be true ▶ *They say there's a possibility of rain at the weekend.*

possible /'pɒsəbəl/ *adjective*
able to happen or exist ▶ *Is it possible to get a direct train all the way?* ▶ *It's possible that she'll still come. (adverb:* **possibly***)*
OPPOSITE: **impossible**

post¹ /pəust/ *noun*
1 a thick bar of wood, metal, or stone fixed in the ground ▶ *The fence was held up by wooden posts.*

2 *(no plural)* the mail ▶ *I sent it by post.*
3 a job ▶ *All new posts will be advertised.*

post² *verb*
to send a letter or parcel

postage /'pəustɪdʒ/ *noun (no plural)*
the amount of money that you pay to post something ▶ *The postage for this parcel is very expensive.*

postage stamp /'pəustɪdʒ ˌstæmp/ *noun*
a small piece of paper that you stick on a letter or parcel to show how much you have paid to send it by post

postal /'pəustl/ *adjective*
relating to sending letters or packages by post ▶ *postal charges*

postbox /'pəustbɒks/ *noun (plural* **postboxes***)*
an official box into which you put letters if you want to send them by post

postcard /'pəustka:d/ *noun*
a small card, often with a picture on one side, which people send by post when they go on holiday

postcode /'pəustkəud/ *noun*
a group of letters and numbers at the end of someone's address

poster /'pəustə'/ *noun*
a large, printed notice or picture advertising something, which is put up in a public place

posterity /pɒ'sterəti/ *noun (no plural)*
the people who will live after you are dead ▶ *I photographed the scene for posterity.*

postgraduate /,pəust'grædʒuət/ *noun*
a person who has done a degree and is now doing advanced studies at a university

postman /'pəustmən/ *noun (plural* **postmen** /-mən/*)*

a man who collects and delivers letters and parcels

postmark /ˈpəʊstmɑːk/ noun
a mark on an envelope that shows the place and time it was sent

postmortem /ˌpəʊstˈmɔːtəm/ noun
an official medical examination of a dead body to discover why the person died

post office /ˈpəʊst ˌɒfɪs/ noun
a place where you can buy stamps, post parcels, etc.

postpone /pəˈspəʊn/ verb (present participle **postponing**, past **postponed**)
to change the time of some event to a later time ➤ We postponed the match from March 5th to March 19th.

posture /ˈpɒstʃər/ noun
the way that you sit or stand ➤ Good posture is important if you want to avoid backache.

pot /pɒt/ noun
a round container, used especially for cooking ➤ I've made a big pot of soup.

potato /pəˈteɪtəʊ/ noun (plural **potatoes**)
a round, white vegetable that grows under the ground and is cooked before eating

potent /ˈpəʊtənt/ adjective
strong or powerful ➤ This homemade wine is very potent. ➤ Advertising has a potent influence on what we buy.

potential¹ /pəˈtenʃəl/ adjective
not existing now but likely to exist in the future ➤ We believe that Rob is a potential tennis champion. ➤ a potential danger (adverb: **potentially**)

potential² noun (no plural)
1 natural abilities or qualities that may possibly develop and make someone or something very successful or useful ➤ She has great potential as a dancer.
2 the possibility that something will

develop or happen in a particular way ➤ There is always the potential for trouble at football games.

potter /ˈpɒtər/ (also **potter around**, **potter about**) verb
to spend time doing unimportant but pleasant things ➤ I like just pottering around at home.

pottery /ˈpɒtəri/ noun (no plural)
1 plates, cups, and other objects made from clay
2 the making of plates, cups, and other objects from clay

potty /ˈpɒti/ noun (plural **potties**)
a plastic pot that a very young child uses as a toilet

pouch /paʊtʃ/ noun (plural **pouches**)
1 a small bag
2 a pocket of skin that animals such as KANGAROOS carry their babies in

poultry /ˈpəʊltri/ noun (no plural)
hens and other birds kept for eggs or meat

pounce /paʊns/ verb (present participle **pouncing**, past **pounced**)
to jump on something suddenly in order to catch it ➤ The cat pounced on the bird.

pound¹ /paʊnd/ noun
1 the money used in Britain and some other places ➤ I bought a car for nine hundred pounds (=£900).
2 a measure of weight equal to 0.454 kilograms ➤ Can I have two pounds (=2lbs) of apples, please?

pound² verb
to crush something by hitting it hard and often ➤ She pounded the corn to a fine powder.

pour /pɔːr/ verb
1 to make a liquid or other substance flow into or out of a container ➤ She poured some sugar into a bowl. ➤ He poured me a cup of tea.
2 to rain hard and steadily ➤ It's pouring outside.

poverty /'pɒvətɪ/ *noun (no plural)*
the state of being poor ➤ *She has lived in poverty all her life.*

POW /ˌpi: əʊ 'dʌbəlju:/ *noun*
A PRISONER OF WAR; a person who is caught by the enemy during a war and is kept as a prisoner until the end of the war ➤ *a POW camp*

powder /'paʊdəʳ/ *noun*
a substance in the form of fine grains, like dust ➤ *They washed the clothes with soap powder.*

power /'paʊəʳ/ *noun*
1 *(no plural)* control over people or a place ➤ *The British queen has no real power.*
2 the right or permission to do something ➤ *the power of the police to stop someone in the street*
3 *(no plural)* the force that is used to make a machine work ➤ NUCLEAR power

powerful /'paʊəfəl/ *adjective*
very strong or having a lot of power ➤ *a powerful nation*

powerless /'paʊələs/ *adjective*
without power or strength ➤ *I felt powerless to help her.*

power station /'paʊə ˌsteɪʃən/ *noun*
a building where electricity is made

pp
a short way of writing the word **pages**
➤ *Read pp 20–35.*

PR /ˌpi: 'ɑ:ʳ/ *noun (no plural)*
PUBLIC RELATIONS; the activity of giving people information about an organization so that they have a good opinion of it

practical /'præktɪkəl/ *adjective*
1 good at doing things with your hands ➤ *He is very practical – he can mend almost anything.*
2 sensible and effective in making decisions and dealing with problems ➤ *We've got to be practical and buy only what we can afford.*
OPPOSITE (**1** and **2**): **impractical**

practical joke /ˌpræktɪkəl 'dʒəʊk/ *noun*
a trick that is intended to surprise someone and make other people laugh at them

practically /'præktɪklɪ/ *adverb*
almost ➤ *I've practically finished – I'll come in a minute.*

practice /'præktɪs/ *noun*
1 *(no plural)* doing something regularly to improve your skill or ability in it ➤ *You need more practice before you can play for our team.*
2 out of practice unable to do something well because you have not done it regularly enough

practise /'præktɪs/ *verb (present participle* **practising***, past* **practised***)*
to do something regularly so as to become better at it ➤ *You'll never be a good singer if you don't practise.*

practising /'præktɪsɪŋ/ *adjective*
practising Catholic, practising Jew, etc. a person who obeys the rules of a particular religion

prairie /'preərɪ/ *noun*
a large area of flat land in North America that is covered in grass

praise[1] /preɪz/ *verb (present participle* **praising***, past* **praised***)*
to say that you admire someone or something ➤ *She praised her daughter's hard work.*

praise[2] *noun (no plural)*
expression of admiration ➤ *Her new album has received a lot of praise.*

pram /præm/ *noun*
a carriage with wheels, for a baby, which is pushed by hand
COMPARE: **pushchair**

prawn /prɔ:n/ *noun*
a small, pink, sea animal that you can eat

pray /preɪ/ *verb*
to talk to God or a god, giving thanks or asking for something

prayer /preə^r/ *noun*
1 *(no plural)* the act of praying
2 a set of words that you say when you are praying

preach /pri:tʃ/ *verb*
to give a religious talk to people about how they should live, usually as part of a religious service

preacher /'pri:tʃə^r/ *noun*
a person who gives a religious talk, usually as part of a religious service

precaution /prɪ'kɔ:ʃən/ *noun*
something that is done to prevent something bad or dangerous from happening ▶ *He took the precaution of locking his door when he went out.*

precede /prɪ'si:d/ *verb (present participle **preceding**, past **preceded**)*
to happen or exist before something else ▶ *Mr Clark preceded Miss Lee as head teacher.*

precedence /'presɪdəns/ *noun*
take precedence over something to be more important than something else ▶ *For me, education takes precedence over everything else.*

precedent /'presɪdənt/ *noun*
an action or official decision that is used as an example for a similar action or decision that is taken in the future ▶ *The trial set a precedent for civil rights legislation.*

precinct /'pri:sɪŋkt/ *noun*
shopping precinct, pedestrian precinct an area with shops in a town, where cars are not allowed

precious /'preʃəs/ *adjective*
1 very valuable or expensive ▶ *Water is precious in the desert.* ▶ *a precious stone*
2 very special to you ▶ *precious memories of our holiday*

precipice /'presəpɪs/ *noun*
a steep side of a high mountain

precise /prɪ'saɪs/ *adjective*
exact and correct ▶ *Your instructions to the students need to be more precise.*
OPPOSITE: **imprecise**

precisely /prɪ'saɪslɪ/ *adverb*
1 exactly ▶ *I don't know precisely why she lost her job.*
2 a word you use to show you agree with someone ▶ *"So you think he was wrong?" "Precisely."*
SAME MEANING (**1** and **2**): **exactly**

precision /prɪ'sɪʒən/ *noun (no plural)*
the state of being measured or described very exactly ▶ *This watch keeps time with incredible precision.*

preconceived /ˌpri:kən'si:vd/ *adjective*
(used about ideas) formed before you know what something is really like ▶ *He has a lot of preconceived ideas about life in America.*

predator /'predətə^r/ *noun*
an animal that kills and eats other animals

predecessor /'pri:dɪsesə^r/ *noun*
the person who had a job before the person who has it now ▶ *My predecessor worked here for ten years.*

predicament /prɪ'dɪkəmənt/ *noun*
a difficult situation when you do not know what is the best thing to do

predict /prɪ'dɪkt/ *verb*
to say what is going to happen before it happens ▶ *The teacher predicted that we would all pass the examination, and we did.*

predictable /prɪ'dɪktəbəl/ *adjective*
behaving or happening in the way that you expect, and not different or interesting ▶ *The ending of the film was so predictable. (adverb: **predictably**)*

prediction /prɪ'dɪkʃən/ *noun*
a statement that something is going to happen before it happens ▶ *It's*

hard to make a prediction about who will win the championship.

predominantly /prɪ'dɒmɪnəntlɪ/ *adverb*
mostly or mainly ➤ *a predominantly working-class area*

preface /'prefəs/ *noun*
an introduction at the beginning of a book

prefect /'priːfekt/ *noun*
an older boy or girl who helps to control the pupils in a school

prefer /prɪ'fɜːʳ/ *verb (present participle preferring, past preferred)*
to like one thing more than another ➤ *Which of these two dresses do you prefer?* ➤ *I prefer swimming to cycling.*

preferable /'prefərəbəl/ *adjective*
more suitable, or better ➤ *We accept credit cards, but cash is preferable.* *(adverb: preferably)*

preference /'prefərəns/ *noun*
a liking for one thing rather than another ➤ *My preference is for the theatre rather than the cinema.*

prefix /'priːfɪks/ *noun (plural prefixes)*
a group of letters that can be added to the beginning of another word to change the meaning ➤ *If we add the prefix "un-" to the word "happy", we make the word "unhappy".*
COMPARE: **suffix**

pregnancy /'pregnənsɪ/ *noun (plural pregnancies)*
the condition of having a baby developing in your body ➤ *a difficult pregnancy*

pregnant /'pregnənt/ *adjective*
having a baby developing in your body ➤ *She is four months pregnant.* ➤ *She's pregnant with her third child.*

prehistoric /ˌpriːhɪ'stɒrɪk/ *adjective*
relating to the time a long way in the past before anything was written down ➤ *prehistoric cave drawings*

prejudice /'predʒʊdɪs/ *noun*
an unfair opinion that is not based on facts or reason ➤ *Why have you got a prejudice against women drivers? They can drive just as well as men.*

prejudiced /'predʒʊdɪst/ *adjective*
having an unfair opinion about something that is not based on facts or reason ➤ *Why are you so prejudiced against people who didn't go to university?*

preliminary /prɪ'lɪmɪnərɪ/ *adjective*
happening or done at the beginning of a process, usually to prepare for what will come later ➤ *European leaders meet tomorrow for preliminary talks.*

premature /'premətʃəʳ/ *adjective*
happening too early ➤ *Smoking causes premature death. (adverb: prematurely)*

premeditated /priː'medɪteɪtɪd/ *adjective*
planned in advance ➤ *a premeditated murder*

premiere /'premɪeəʳ/ *noun*
the first public performance of a film or play ➤ *All the stars were at the premiere.*

premises /'premɪsɪz/ *plural noun*
the buildings and land that a shop or company uses ➤ *No children are allowed on the premises.*

premonition /ˌpremə'nɪʃən/ *noun*
a feeling that something bad is going to happen ➤ *I had a premonition that the plane was going to crash.*

preoccupied /prɪ'ɒkjʊpaɪd/ *adjective*
thinking or worrying about something a lot, so that you do not pay attention to other things ➤ *I was too preoccupied with my own problems to notice.*

preparation /ˌprepə'reɪʃən/ *noun*
1 *(no plural)* the act of getting

something ready ▶ *Teachers have to do a lot of preparation before each lesson.*

2 preparations *plural noun* arrangements for something that will happen in the future ▶ *She's very busy with preparations **for** the wedding.*

prepare /prɪˈpeəʳ/ *verb (present participle **preparing**, past **prepared**)* to make something ready ▶ *I prepared the food for the party myself.* ▶ *We're preparing a room for our guests.*

prepared /prɪˈpeəd/ *adjective* **1** ready to deal with something ▶ *He wasn't really prepared **for** the interviewer's questions.*

2 prepared to do something willing to do something ▶ *Are you prepared to work hard for this promotion?*

preposition /ˌprepəˈzɪʃən/ *noun* a word like **to, for, on, by,** etc.; a word which is put in front of a noun to show where, when, how, etc. In the sentences "She sat by the fire" and "They went to town", "by" and "to" are prepositions

preposterous /prɪˈpɒstərəs/ *adjective* completely unreasonable or silly ▶ *What a preposterous idea!*

prep school /ˈprep skuːl/ *noun* a private school for children aged between 8 and 13

preschool¹ /ˈpriːskuːl/ *adjective* for children who are not old enough to go to school ▶ *a preschool playgroup*

preschool² *noun* a school for children aged between two and five

prescribe /prɪˈskraɪb/ *verb (present participle **prescribing**, past **prescribed**)* to say what medicine someone should take when they are ill

prescription /prɪˈskrɪpʃən/ *noun* a special paper written by a doctor, ordering medicine for someone ▶ *The doctor wrote me a prescription for medicine for my cough.*

presence /ˈprezəns/ *noun* **1** *(no plural)* the state of being present at a particular time ▶ *His presence was not even noticed at work last week.*
OPPOSITE: **absence**

2 in the presence of someone seen or watched by someone ▶ *The results were read out in the presence of all the parents.*

present¹ /ˈprezənt/ *adjective* **1** in a particular place at a particular time ▶ *There are 20 children present today.*

2 existing now ▶ *What is your present job?*

present² *noun* **1** something that you give to someone as a gift ▶ *He gave her a birthday present.*

2 at present at the moment of speaking ▶ *He's on holiday at present.*

present³ /prɪˈzent/ *verb* to give something to someone, often as part of an official ceremony ▶ *Who is going to present the gold cup **to** the winner?*

presentation /ˌprezənˈteɪʃən/ *noun* the act of giving something to someone, often as part of an official ceremony ▶ *The presentation of prizes starts at 3 o'clock.*

present continuous /ˌprezənt kənˈtɪnjʊəs/ *noun* the tense of a verb, formed with *-ing*, which tells you what is true now or at the moment of speaking. In the sentence "I am studying English at the moment", the verb "study" is in the present continuous tense

presenter /prɪˈzentəʳ/ *noun*

a person who introduces a television or radio programme

presently /'prezntlɪ/ *adverb*
soon ▶ *The taxi will arrive presently.*

present participle /ˌprezənt
'pɑːtɪsɪpəl/ *noun*
the form of a verb which ends in -ing and is used in certain tenses. In the sentence "The child is sleeping", "sleeping" is a present participle

present perfect /ˌprezənt 'pɜːfɪkt/
noun
the form of an English verb which uses the verb "have" and the PAST PARTICIPLE of the verb. In the sentence "I have eaten my dinner", "have eaten" is in the present perfect

present tense /ˌprezənt 'tens/ *noun*
the tense of a verb which expresses the time now or at the moment of speaking

preservation /ˌprezə'veɪʃən/ *noun*
(no plural)
the action of keeping something unharmed or unchanged ▶ *We are fighting for the preservation **of** this forest.*

preservative /prɪ'zɜːvətɪv/ *noun*
a chemical substance that is added to food to keep it in good condition

preserve /prɪ'zɜːv/ *verb (present
participle **preserving**, past **preserved**)*
to keep something from being damaged, or from going bad ▶ *You can preserve meat or fish in salt.*

presidency /'prezɪdənsɪ/ *noun
(plural **presidencies**)*
the job of being president, or the period of time that someone is president ▶ *towards the end of his presidency*

president /'prezɪdənt/ *noun*
1 the head of government in many countries that do not have a king or queen ▶ *the President **of** America* ▶ *President Bush*

2 the head of a big company or of an important organization

presidential /ˌprezɪ'denʃəl/ *adjective*
relating to the president of a country ▶ *the presidential election*

press¹ /pres/ *verb*
to push steadily on something ▶ *He pressed the doorbell.*

press² *noun (no plural)*
all newspapers and magazines, and the reporters working for them ▶ *the freedom of the press*

press conference /'pres ˌkɒnfərəns/
noun
a meeting at which an important or famous person answers questions asked by people from newspapers, television, etc.

press release /'pres rɪˌliːs/ *noun*
an official statement giving information to newspapers, radio, and television

press-ups /'pres ʌps/ *noun*
an exercise in which you lie facing the ground and push your body up using your arms
SAME MEANING: **push-up**

pressure /'preʃə/ *noun*
1 the force caused by the weight of one thing pressing on another
2 the demands of your life which can cause you worry ▶ *the pressures of modern life*

pressure group /'preʃə gruːp/ *noun*
a group of people who try to make the government, a company, etc. do a particular thing ▶ *an environmental pressure group*

pressurize /'preʃəraɪz/ *verb (present
participle **pressurizing**, past
pressurized)*
to try to make someone do something by threatening them, arguing with them, etc. ▶ *I was pressurized **into** lending him the money.*

P

prestige /pre'sti:ʒ/ *noun (no plural)*
respect and admiration that you
receive because of what you have
achieved

prestigious /pre'stɪdʒəs/ *adjective*
admired or respected as one of the
best and most important ➤ *a
prestigious award*

presumably /prɪ'zju:məblɪ/ *adverb*
used to say that something is
probably true ➤ *Presumably you've
heard the news by now.*

presume /prɪ'zju:m/ *verb (present
participle **presuming**, past **presumed**)*
to think that something is probably
true ➤ *I presume they'll be finished by
2 o'clock.*

pretence /prɪ'tens/ *noun*
1 the act of pretending that something
is true ➤ *He seemed confident, but I
knew it was just a pretence.*
2 under false pretences dishonestly,
by pretending that something is true
➤ *They were found guilty of obtaining
money under false pretences.*

pretend /prɪ'tend/ *verb*
to do something to make people
believe that something is true or real
when it is not ➤ *He pretended that he
was ill so that he could stay at home.*
➤ *She pretended to be asleep.*

pretentious /prɪ'tenʃəs/ *adjective*
trying to seem more important or
clever than you really are

pretext /'pri:tekst/ *noun*
a false reason that you give for doing
something ➤ *She went to see James
on the pretext of wanting to borrow a
book.*

pretty¹ /'prɪtɪ/ *adjective* (**prettier,
prettiest**)
attractive and nice to look at ➤ *a
pretty girl* ➤ *a pretty little village*
LOOK AT: **beautiful**

pretty² *adverb*
fairly; quite ➤ *It was a pretty serious
accident.*

prevent /prɪ'vent/ *verb*
1 to stop something from happening
➤ *He threw water on the fire to
prevent it from spreading.*
2 to stop someone from doing
something ➤ *I tried to prevent her
from leaving her job.*

preventative /prɪ'ventətɪv/
adjective
another word for **preventive**

prevention /prɪ'venʃən/ *noun (no
plural)*
the action of stopping something
from happening ➤ *the prevention of
crime*

preventive /prɪ'ventɪv/ *(also
preventative) adjective*
intended to prevent something bad
from happening ➤ *preventive
medicine (=medicine that prevents
people from becoming ill)*

preview /'pri:vju:/ *noun*
1 an occasion when you see a film or
show before the rest of the public
2 an advertisement for a film or
television programme, which consists
of short parts from it

previous /'pri:vɪəs/ *adjective*
happening before the present time
➤ *In my previous job, I used to travel
to the city every day.* (adverb:
previously)

prey /preɪ/ *noun (no plural)*
an animal that is hunted and caught
by another animal

price /praɪs/ *noun*
the money that you must pay to buy
something ➤ *House prices are going
up again.*

priceless /'praɪsləs/ *adjective*
very valuable ➤ *a priceless painting*

pricey /'praɪsɪ/ *adjective* (**pricier,
priciest**)
expensive ➤ *a pricey restaurant*

prick /prɪk/ *verb*
to make a small hole in something

with a sharp object ➤ *He pricked his finger on the needle.*

prickly /ˈprɪklɪ/ *adjective (***pricklier, prickliest***)*
covered with sharp points ➤ *a prickly cactus*

pride /praɪd/ *noun (no plural)*
the feeling of pleasure and satisfaction that you have because of something good that you have done or something nice that you own ➤ *She showed us her new home with great pride.*

priest /priːst/ *noun*
a religious person whose job is to lead ceremonies, say prayers, and look after the religious part of people's lives

primarily /ˈpraɪmərəlɪ/ *adverb*
mainly ➤ *a course aimed primarily at adult students*

primary /ˈpraɪmərɪ/ *adjective*
main or most important

primary school /ˈpraɪmərɪ ˌskuːl/ *noun*
a school for children between 5 and 11 years old

prime¹ /praɪm/ *adjective*
1 main or most important ➤ *Smoking is one of the prime causes of heart disease.*
2 of the very best quality or kind ➤ *a house in a prime location*
3 a prime example a very good example of something

prime² *noun*
be in your prime, be in the prime of life to be at the time in your life when you are strongest and most active

prime minister /ˌpraɪm ˈmɪnɪstə^r/ *noun*
the head of government in many countries

primitive /ˈprɪmətɪv/ *adjective*
early in human history ➤ *Primitive people lived in caves.*

prince /prɪns/ *noun*
1 the son of a king or queen
2 the ruler of a country

princess /prɪnˈses/ *noun (plural* **princesses***)*
the daughter of a king or queen, or the wife of a prince

principal¹ /ˈprɪnsɪpəl/ *adjective*
most important ➤ *What is your principal reason for staying here?*

principal² *noun*
the head of a school and some colleges

principally /ˈprɪnsɪplɪ/ *adverb*
mostly ➤ *The school spends money principally on books.*

principle /ˈprɪnsɪpəl/ *noun*
a general rule or idea that you believe is right and that you try to follow in your life ➤ *It is a principle of mine to help people when I can.*

print¹ /prɪnt/ *verb*
1 to press words and pictures onto paper or cloth by machine ➤ *The books are printed in Hong Kong.*
2 to write something without joining the letters together ➤ *Please print your name clearly.*

print² *noun*
1 (no plural) words printed on a page ➤ *The print is too small for me to read.*
2 a mark made on a surface in the shape of the thing pressed into it

printer /ˈprɪntə^r/ *noun*
1 a machine that can copy documents from a computer onto paper
2 a person or company whose job is to print books, magazines, etc.

printout /ˈprɪntˌaʊt/ *noun*
a piece of paper containing information printed from a computer

prior /ˈpraɪə^r/ *adjective*
1 existing or happening before something else ➤ *The bomb exploded without any prior warning.*

P

2 prior to before ➤ *Prior to this, we had never had any trouble.*

priority /praɪˈɒrɪtɪ/ *noun (plural priorities)*
the thing that you think is most important and should be dealt with first ➤ *The government's priority is education.* ➤ *His family took priority over everything else.* ➤ *Hospitals must give priority to people who are seriously ill.*

prise /praɪz/ *verb (present participle prising, past prised)*
to force something open or away from something else ➤ *I tried to prise open the door.*
SAME MEANING: **pry**

prison /ˈprɪzən/ *noun*
a place where criminals are kept locked up as a punishment ➤ *He was in prison for ten years.*
SAME MEANING: **jail**

prisoner /ˈprɪzənəʳ/ *noun*
a person who is kept in a prison

privacy /ˈprɪvəsɪ/ *noun (no plural)*
the state of being alone so that other people cannot see or hear you ➤ *You must respect her privacy.*

private¹ /ˈpraɪvət/ *adjective*
1 belonging to one person or group; not public ➤ *This is private land; you can't walk across it.*
2 not connected with your work or business ➤ *I don't talk about my private life at the office.*

private² *noun*
in private without other people listening or seeing ➤ *Can I speak to you in private?*

privatize /ˈpraɪvətaɪz/ *verb (present participle privatizing, past privatized)*
to sell an organization, industry, etc. that was previously owned by a government ➤ *The railways have been privatized.*
OPPOSITE: **nationalize**

privilege /ˈprɪvɪlɪdʒ/ *noun*
a special right allowed to one person or only a few people ➤ *These prisoners have the privilege of getting letters every day.*

prize /praɪz/ *noun*
something that you win in a game, race, or competition ➤ *I won first prize in the competition.*

probability /ˌprɒbəˈbɪlɪtɪ/ *noun (no plural)*
the chance that something will happen ➤ *What's the probability of the disease coming back?*

probable /ˈprɒbəbəl/ *adjective*
likely to happen or be true ➤ *She might just go tomorrow, but as she's not feeling well it's not very probable.*

probably /ˈprɒbəblɪ/ *adverb*
likely to happen or be true ➤ *We'll probably go to France next year.*

probation /prəˈbeɪʃən/ *noun (no plural)*
a system of keeping an official check on criminals, instead of keeping them in prison ➤ *He has to go to the police station every week while he's on probation.*

probe /prəʊb/ *verb (present participle probing, past probed)*
to ask a lot of questions in order to find out information ➤ *I don't want people probing into my private life!*

problem /ˈprɒbləm/ *noun*
1 a difficult question or state of affairs; a cause of worry ➤ *The problem was how to move the heavy machinery.*
2 no problem a phrase you use to tell someone you can easily do something for them

procedure /prəˈsiːdʒəʳ/ *noun*
the correct or normal way of doing something ➤ *What's the procedure for getting a driver's licence?*

proceed /prəˈsiːd/ *verb*
to go forward in a particular direction

➤ *After stopping to rest, they proceeded up the hill.*

proceedings /prəˈsiːdɪŋz/ *plural noun*
1 an event, or things that happen at an event ➤ *We watched the proceedings from a third floor window.*
2 legal actions taken in a law court ➤ *divorce proceedings*

proceeds /ˈprəʊsiːdz/ *plural noun*
the money that you get from selling something or from holding an event ➤ *The proceeds from the concert will go to charity.*

process /ˈprəʊses/ *noun (plural processes)*
1 a set of actions that you do in order to get a particular result ➤ *Building the boat is not a simple process.*
2 a set of changes that happen naturally ➤ *a chemical process*

procession /prəˈseʃən/ *noun*
a line of people or vehicles following one another as part of a ceremony ➤ *They watched the procession go past.*

proclaim /prəˈkleɪm/ *verb*
to formally tell people something ➤ *The country proclaimed its independence in 1956.*

prod /prɒd/ *verb (present participle **prodding**, past **prodded**)*
to push someone or something with your finger or a long object ➤ *She prodded the girl next to her and asked what was going on.*

prodigy /ˈprɒdɪdʒɪ/ *noun (plural prodigies)*
a young person who is unusually good at doing something ➤ *Mozart was a child prodigy.*

produce¹ /prəˈdjuːs/ *verb (present participle **producing**, past **produced**)*
1 to have something as a result ➤ *This drug has produced some very serious side effects.*

2 to make something, especially in large quantities ➤ *The factory produces 500 cars a week.*
3 to grow something ➤ *The farm produces wheat.*
4 to control the organization of a play or film for the public to see

produce² /ˈprɒdjuːs/ *noun (no plural)*
something produced by growing or farming ➤ *a market full of fresh produce*

producer /prəˈdjuːsəʳ/ *noun*
a person who produces a play or film

product /ˈprɒdʌkt/ *noun*
something that is produced in a factory ➤ *plastic products*

production /prəˈdʌkʃən/ *noun (no plural)*
1 the act of producing something, especially for sale
2 a play or film, or the act of producing it ➤ *I really enjoyed the play – what an excellent production!*

productive /prəˈdʌktɪv/ *adjective*
producing or achieving a lot ➤ *That was a very productive meeting.*

productivity /ˌprɒdʌkˈtɪvətɪ/ *noun (no plural)*
the speed at which goods are produced and the amount that is produced ➤ *Productivity at the factory has increased by 5% over the last year.*

Prof.
a short way of writing the word **professor** when you are writing someone's name ➤ *Prof. Mortimer*

profession /prəˈfeʃən/ *noun*
a job which needs a high standard of education and special training ➤ *Teaching is a satisfying profession, even if it is badly paid.*

professional /prəˈfeʃənəl/ *adjective*
1 working in a job which needs a high standard of education and special training ➤ *You should get some professional advice from your doctor.*

P

2 doing something for money, rather than for pleasure ▶ *a professional football player*
COMPARE (**2**): **amateur**

professor /prəˈfesəʳ/ *noun*
a teacher of the highest rank in a university

proficiency /prəˈfɪʃənsɪ/ *noun (no plural)*
the ability to do something well ▶ *her proficiency in French*

profile /ˈprəʊfaɪl/ *noun*
1 a side view of someone's head ▶ *a drawing of her in profile*
2 a short description that gives important details about someone's character, work, life, etc. ▶ *a profile of Paul McCartney in a Sunday paper*
3 keep a low profile to avoid doing things that will make people notice you

profit /ˈprɒfɪt/ *noun*
money that you gain when you sell something for more than you paid for it ▶ *The fruit seller made 2 pence profit on each orange.*

profitable /ˈprɒfɪtəbəl/ *adjective*
making a lot of profit ▶ *This business is not very profitable.*

profound /prəˈfaʊnd/ *adjective*
1 affecting someone very strongly ▶ *Her death was a profound shock to all of us.*
2 showing a lot of knowledge and understanding of a subject ▶ *a profound remark*
(*adverb:* **profoundly**)

program¹ /ˈprəʊgræm/ *noun*
a set of instructions that a computer follows

program² *verb (present participle* **programming**, *past* **programmed**)
to give a computer the instructions it needs to do something

programme /ˈprəʊgræm/ *noun*
1 printed information about a play,

concert, etc. that you are attending
2 a show broadcast by radio or television ▶ *We watched a programme about travelling through the desert.*

programmer /ˈprəʊgræməʳ/ *noun*
a person whose job is to write sets of instructions for computers ▶ *a computer programmer*

progress¹ /ˈprəʊgres/ *noun (no plural)*
1 movement in a particular direction
2 continuous improvement in something ▶ *You have made good progress with your English.*

progress² /prəˈgres/ *verb*
1 to go on or continue ▶ *I became very tired as the trip progressed.*
2 to improve or become more advanced in something ▶ *We progressed from the beginners' class to intermediate.*

progressive¹ /prəˈgresɪv/ *adjective*
1 supporting or using modern ideas and methods ▶ *progressive teaching methods*
2 happening gradually and continuously over a period of time ▶ *the progressive decline of the coal industry*
(*adverb:* **progressively**)

progressive² *noun*
the progressive the form of a verb that consists of "be" and the PRESENT PARTICIPLE – for example, "she was reading"

prohibit /prəˈhɪbɪt/ *verb*
to not allow something by law ▶ *Smoking is prohibited in this building.*
COMPARE: **ban**

project /ˈprɒdʒekt/ *noun*
1 a plan to do something ▶ *a project to build a new road*
2 an activity in which students collect and present information about something in order to learn about it

projector /prə'dʒektə'/ *noun*
a piece of equipment for showing film or pictures on a screen

prolific /prə'lɪfɪk/ *adjective*
producing a lot of something ➤ *a prolific writer*

prolong /prə'lɒŋ/ *verb*
to make something continue for longer ➤ *Heart transplants have prolonged many people's lives.*

prolonged /prə'lɒŋd/ *adjective*
continuing for a long time ➤ *a prolonged period of silence*

prominent /'prɒmɪnənt/ *adjective*
1 large and easily noticeable ➤ *a prominent nose*
2 important and well-known ➤ *a prominent doctor*

promise¹ /'prɒmɪs/ *verb (present participle* **promising**, *past* **promised***)*
to say that you will certainly do something ➤ *She promised her brother that she would write to him.* ➤ *She promised to write to him.* ➤ *We promised her a mobile phone for her birthday.*

promise² *noun*
something you have said you will certainly do ➤ *She made a promise to her son to buy him a bike.* ➤ *He broke his promise and did not come to see me.*

promising /'prɒmɪsɪŋ/ *adjective*
likely to be successful in the future ➤ *a promising young singer*

promote /prə'məʊt/ *verb (present participle* **promoting**, *past* **promoted***)*
to give someone a higher position at work ➤ *Our teacher has been promoted to headmaster.*

promotion /prə'məʊʃən/ *noun*
a move to a higher position at work

prompt /prɒmpt/ *adjective*
quick; without delay ➤ *a prompt answer to a letter (adverb:* **promptly***)*

prone /prəʊn/ *adjective*
likely to do something bad, or likely to suffer from something ➤ *He was prone* **to** *jealousy.* ➤ *Young drivers are more accident-prone (=have more accidents) than older ones.*

pronoun /'prəʊnaʊn/ *noun*
a word like "he", "she", "it", "they", which is used instead of using a noun again ➤ *Instead of saying "Peter went to school", we can use a pronoun and say "He went to school".*

pronounce /prə'naʊns/ *verb (present participle* **pronouncing**, *past* **pronounced***)*
to make the sounds of a word ➤ *How do you pronounce your name?*

pronunciation /prə,nʌnsɪ'eɪʃən/ *noun (no plural)*
the way in which a word or sound is spoken ➤ *American pronunciation*

proof /pruːf/ *noun (no plural)*
facts which prove that something is true ➤ *Have you any proof that he took the money?*

prop¹ /prɒp/ *verb (present participle* **propping**, *past* **propped***)*
1 to lean or rest something on or against something ➤ *He propped his bike against the fence.*
2 **prop something up** to prevent something from falling by putting something against it or under it ➤ *We propped the fence up with some old bits of wood.*

prop² *noun*
an object that is used in a play or film

propaganda /,prɒpə'gændə/ *noun (no plural)*
false information that a political organization gives to the public to influence them ➤ *This is just government propaganda.*

propeller /prə'pelə'/ *noun*
a wheel of curved blades which turn quickly to make a ship or an aircraft move

proper /'prɒpəʳ/ *adjective*
correct or suitable ▶ *I need some proper summer clothes.*

properly /'prɒpəlɪ/ *adverb*
in a correct or suitable way ▶ *You haven't done the job properly – you'll have to do it again.*

proper noun /ˌprɒpə 'naʊn/ *noun*
a noun such as "Mike" or "Paris" that is the name of a person, place, or thing and is spelled with a capital letter in English

property /'prɒpətɪ/ *noun*
1 *(no plural)* something which belongs to you ▶ *Their job is to protect the property of the company.*
2 *(plural* **properties***)* land or buildings ▶ *Properties in the town are expensive.*

prophecy /'prɒfəsɪ/ *noun (plural* **prophecies***)*
the telling of what will happen in the future

prophet /'prɒfɪt/ *noun*
1 a person who tells people what is going to happen in the future
2 a person who believes that God has told them to teach or lead a special religion

proportion /prə'pɔːʃən/ *noun*
the amount of something compared to something else ▶ *The proportion of girls to boys in the school is about equal.*

proposal /prə'pəʊzəl/ *noun*
1 a formal plan or suggestion ▶ *a proposal to build a new school*
2 an offer of marriage

propose /prə'pəʊz/ *verb (present participle* **proposing***, past* **proposed***)*
1 to suggest something ▶ *He proposed that the company should move to another factory.*
2 to ask someone to marry you ▶ *He proposed to her, and she accepted.*

proposition /ˌprɒpə'zɪʃən/ *noun*
an offer or a suggestion, especially in business or politics ▶ *They came to me with a business proposition.*

pros /prəʊz/ *plural noun*
the pros and cons the good and bad points of something ▶ *I spent some time considering the pros and cons, but eventually decided to accept the job.*

prose /prəʊz/ *noun (no plural)*
ordinary written language, not poetry ▶ *a great prose writer*

prosecute /'prɒsɪkjuːt/ *verb (present participle* **prosecuting***, past* **prosecuted***)*
to say officially that you think someone is guilty of a crime and must be judged in a law court ▶ *The police decided to prosecute him* **for** *dangerous driving.*

prosecution /ˌprɒsɪ'kjuːʃən/ *noun*
the prosecution the lawyers who are trying to prove that someone is guilty of a crime in a law court ▶ *The prosecution have a good case.*
OPPOSITE: **defence**

prospect /'prɒspekt/ *noun*
1 the chance that something will happen soon ▶ *There's little prospect* **of** *ending the war.*
2 something you think will happen in the future and your idea of what it will be like ▶ *The prospect* **of** *making a speech at the wedding fills me with dread.*

prospective /prə'spektɪv/ *adjective*
likely to do or be something in the future ▶ *Find out as much as you can about your prospective employer before the interview.*

prospectus /prə'spektəs/ *noun (plural* **prospectuses***)*
a small book in which a university, school, or company gives information about itself

prosper /'prɒspəʳ/ *verb*
to do well and become rich ▶ *His company is prospering.*

prosperity /prɒˈsperəti/ *noun (no plural)*
success and wealth

prosperous /ˈprɒspərəs/ *adjective*
rich and successful ▶ *a prosperous family*

prostitute /ˈprɒstɪtjuːt/ *noun*
a person who earns money by having sex with people

prostitution /ˌprɒstɪˈtjuːʃən/ *noun (no plural)*
the practice of earning money by having sex with people

protect /prəˈtekt/ *verb*
to prevent someone or something from being harmed or damaged ▶ *The fence is to protect the farmer's cattle.*

protection /prəˈtekʃən/ *noun (no plural)*
the act of keeping a person or thing safe from harm or damage ▶ *Her summer clothes gave her no protection against the cold.*

protective /prəˈtektɪv/ *adjective*
1 intended to protect someone or something from being damaged
▶ *The players wear protective helmets.*
2 wanting to protect someone from being harmed ▶ *She was very protective towards her children*

protein /ˈprəutiːn/ *noun*
a substance in food such as meat and eggs, which helps your body to grow and be healthy

protest¹ /prəˈtest/ *verb*
to say strongly that you do not agree with something ▶ *The children protested that they had been punished unfairly.*

protest² /ˈprəutest/ *noun*
a strong public complaint about something ▶ *Many people joined the protest against government plans.*

Protestant /ˈprɒtɪstənt/ *noun, adjective*
(a person) belonging to a Christian church that is not Roman Catholic

protester /prəˈtestər/ *noun*
one of a group of people who are showing publicly that they do not agree with something ▶ *a demonstration by anti-war protesters*

protractor /prəˈtræktər/ *noun*
a flat object shaped like a half-circle, used for measuring and drawing angles

proud /praud/ *adjective*
1 feeling pleased or satisfied about something you or someone close to you has done ▶ *He is proud of his sons's ability to speak four languages.*
2 feeling that you are better than other people ▶ *She is too proud to admit she was wrong.*
(*adverb:* **proudly**)

prove /pruːv/ *verb (present participle **proving**, past **proved**)*
to show that something is certainly true ▶ *I can prove that you were in town – James saw you there.*
OPPOSITE: **disprove**

proven /ˈpruːvən/ *adjective*
shown to be good, effective, or true
▶ *a proven method of learning*

proverb /ˈprɒvɜːb/ *noun*
a short, well-known saying

provide /prəˈvaɪd/ *verb (present participle **providing**, past **provided**)*
to give something to someone ▶ *We provided food for the hungry children.*

provided /prəˈvaɪdɪd/ *conjunction*
if and only if ▶ *I'll go to see her, provided you come too.*

province /ˈprɒvɪns/ *noun*
an area of a country, often with its own government for education, hospitals, etc.

provincial /prəˈvɪnʃəl/ *adjective*
from a part of a country not near to the main city

P

provision /prə'vɪʒən/ noun
1 provisions plural noun food and drink ▶ Have you got enough provisions for your journey?
2 (no plural) the act of giving something to people who need it

provisional /prə'vɪʒənəl/ adjective
likely to be changed ▶ A provisional date for the meeting had been agreed.

provocation /ˌprɒvə'keɪʃən/ noun (no plural)
something that is likely to make someone angry and want to attack another person ▶ The police acted calmly in the face of great provocation.

provoke /prə'vəʊk/ verb (present participle **provoking**, past **provoked**)
to annoy someone on purpose so that they get very angry

prowl /praʊl/ verb
to move round quietly, especially when hunting

prudent /'pruːdənt/ adjective
sensible and careful ▶ prudent use of resources

prune¹ /pruːn/ verb (present participle **pruning**, past **pruned**)
to cut some of the branches of a tree or bush to make them grow back more strongly or thickly

prune² noun
a dried PLUM

pry /praɪ/ verb (past **pried**)
1 to try to find out about someone's private life, when the person does not want you to ▶ I don't mean to pry, but are you still seeing Tom?
2 to force something open or away from something else ▶ I used a screwdriver to pry off the lid.
SAME MEANING (**2**): **prise**

P.S. /ˌpiː 'es/
POSTSCRIPT; used at the end of a letter when you want to add something

after you have signed your name
▶ P.S. Don't forget Jane's birthday.

psalm /sɑːm/ noun
a religious song or poem

pseudonym /'sjuːdənɪm/ noun
a false name used by a writer ▶ She wrote under a pseudonym.

psychiatric /ˌsaɪkɪ'ætrɪk/ adjective
relating to mental illness ▶ a psychiatric hospital

psychiatrist /saɪ'kaɪətrɪst/ noun
a doctor who treats people who have a mental illness

psychiatry /saɪ'kaɪətri/ noun (no plural)
the study and treatment of mental illness

psychic¹ /'saɪkɪk/ adjective
relating to strange events or things that science cannot explain, for example when people see GHOSTS ▶ a fortune-teller who claimed to have extraordinary psychic powers

psychic² noun
a person who is believed to have strange powers, such as the ability to see into the future

psychological /ˌsaɪkə'lɒdʒɪkəl/ adjective
relating to the way people's minds work and the way this affects their behaviour ▶ psychological problems (adverb: **psychologically**)

psychologist /saɪ'kɒlədʒɪst/ noun
a person who studies the way people's minds work and how mental problems can be treated

psychology /saɪ'kɒlədʒi/ noun (no plural)
the scientific study of the mind and how it works ▶ a professor of psychology

psychopath /'saɪkəpæθ/ noun
a person who is very violent because of mental illness

pub /pʌb/ noun
a building where people go to meet their friends, and to buy and drink alcohol

puberty /'pjuːbətɪ/ noun (no plural)
the time when your body changes from a child's to an adult's ▶ Has she reached puberty yet?

public¹ /'pʌblɪk/ adjective
1 for everyone to use and see ▶ a public library ▶ public phones
2 concerning people in general ▶ Public opinion is now against the government.

public² noun (no plural)
1 people in general ▶ This pool is now open to the public.
2 in public with other people hearing and seeing

publication /ˌpʌblɪ'keɪʃən/ noun
1 (no plural) the act of printing a book and making it available to the public ▶ The date of publication is May 1st.
2 a book or magazine ▶ scientific publications

public holiday /ˌpʌblɪk 'hɒlɪdeɪ/ noun
a day when people in a country do not work and the shops are closed

publicity /pʌ'blɪsətɪ/ noun (no plural)
1 attention that someone or something gets from newspapers, television, etc. ▶ a murder trial that received a lot of publicity
2 the business of making sure that people know about an event or a new film, book, etc.

publicize /'pʌblɪsaɪz/ verb (present participle **publicizing**, past **publicized**)
to tell people about an event or a new film, book, etc., especially in the newspapers and on television ▶ She appeared on TV to publicize her new film.

public relations /ˌpʌblɪk rɪ'leɪʃənz/ noun (no plural)
the work of explaining what a company, an organization, etc. does, and keeping a good relationship between it and the public ▶ the public relations department

public school /ˌpʌblɪk 'skuːl/ noun
a private school in Britain for children from 13 to 18 years old

publish /'pʌblɪʃ/ verb
to print and sell a book, newspaper, or magazine ▶ This company publishes children's books.

publisher /'pʌblɪʃə'/ noun
a person or company that publishes books, newspapers, or magazines

publishing /'pʌblɪʃɪŋ/ noun (no plural)
the business of printing and selling books

puck /pʌk/ noun
a hard, flat circular piece of rubber, used instead of a ball in the game of ICE HOCKEY

pudding /'pʊdɪŋ/ noun
a sweet dish, served at the end of a meal ▶ What's for pudding?
SAME MEANING: **dessert, sweet**

puddle /'pʌdl/ noun
a small amount of rainwater lying on the ground
COMPARE: **pond, pool**

puff¹ /pʌf/ verb
to breathe quickly, usually after doing something tiring ▶ I was puffing after swimming so far.

puff² noun
a short burst of air, smoke, etc. ▶ A puff of wind blew the papers off the table.

pull¹ /pʊl/ verb
1 to move something or someone towards yourself ▶ I managed to pull the drawer open. ▶ Mum, Sara's pulling my hair!
2 to move something along ▶ carts pulled by horses

3 pull down a building to destroy a building ▶ *They pulled down a lot of houses to build the new road.*

pull² *noun*
an act of pulling ▶ *He gave a pull on the rope.*

pulley /ˈpʊlɪ/ *noun*
a piece of equipment that has a wheel and a rope, used for lifting things

pullover /ˈpʊləʊvəʳ/ *noun*
a woollen garment that covers the top part of your body, and is pulled over your head
SAME MEANING: **jersey, jumper, sweater**

pulp /pʌlp/ *noun (no plural)*
1 the soft, inside part of a fruit or vegetable
2 a soft substance made by crushing something ▶ *wood pulp*

pulpit /ˈpʊlpɪt/ *noun*
a place where a priest stands to speak to people in a church

pulse /pʌls/ *noun*
the regular beating of your heart, especially as it can be felt at your wrist

pump¹ /pʌmp/ *noun*
a machine for making liquid or gas go into or out of something ▶ *a bicycle pump*

pump² *verb*
to use a pump to empty or fill something with a liquid or gas ▶ *to pump up a tyre*

pumpkin /ˈpʌmpkɪn/ *noun*
a very large, round, yellow or orange vegetable

pun /pʌn/ *noun*
a joke that is based on two words that sound the same but have different meanings

punch¹ /pʌntʃ/ *verb*
1 to hit a person with your closed hand ▶ *He punched him on the nose.*
COMPARE: **slap**
2 to make a hole in something ▶ *He*

punched two holes in the oilcan, and then poured the oil out.

punch² *noun (plural **punches**)*
a strong blow made with your closed hand

punchline /ˈpʌntʃlaɪn/ *noun*
the last few words of a joke or story, that make it funny or clever ▶ *I've forgotten the punchline.*

punctual /ˈpʌŋktʃuəl/ *adjective*
arriving at exactly the right time; not late ▶ *She is always punctual, but her friend is always late.* (*adverb:* **punctually**)

punctuate /ˈpʌŋktʃueɪt/ *verb*
(*present participle **punctuating**, past **punctuated**)*
to divide up a piece of writing into sentences, etc. by using special signs like (,) (;) (.) and (?)

punctuation /ˌpʌŋktʃuˈeɪʃən/ *noun*
(*no plural*)
signs like (,) (;) (.) and (?) used to divide up a piece of writing into sentences, etc.

puncture¹ /ˈpʌŋktʃəʳ/ *noun*
a hole in something such as a tyre, through which air or liquid can get out

puncture² *verb (present participle **puncturing**, past **punctured**)*
to make a small hole in something so that air or liquid gets out of it

punish /ˈpʌnɪʃ/ *verb*
to make someone suffer because they have done something wrong ▶ *The teacher punished the children by making them stay after school.*

punishment /ˈpʌnɪʃmənt/ *noun*
the act of making someone suffer because they have done something wrong ▶ *They deserved their punishment.*

punk /pʌŋk/ *noun*
1 (*also **punk rock** /ˌpʌŋk ˈrɒk/*) (*no plural*) a type of loud, violent music,

popular in the late 1970s and early
1980s
2 (*also* **punk rocker** /ˌpʌŋk ˈrɒkəʳ/) a
person who likes punk music, and
who typically wears torn clothing,
pins, and chains, and has brightly
coloured hair

puny /ˈpjuːnɪ/ *adjective (**punier,
puniest**)*
small, thin, and weak ▶ *a puny little
kid*

pupil /ˈpjuːpəl/ *noun*
a person being taught, especially at a
school

puppet /ˈpʌpɪt/ *noun*
a small figure of a person or an
animal which you can move by
pulling the strings connected to it, or
by putting your hand inside it

puppy /ˈpʌpɪ/ *noun (plural **puppies**)*
a young dog

purchase¹ /ˈpɜːtʃɪs/ *noun*
1 (*no plural*) the act of buying
something
2 something you have bought ▶ *Let
me see all your purchases.*

purchase² *verb (present participle
purchasing, past **purchased**)*
to buy something

pure /pjʊəʳ/ *adjective*
not mixed with anything, and
therefore very clean ▶ *The water in
mountain rivers is usually pure.*

puree /ˈpjʊəreɪ/ *noun*
food that is boiled or crushed until it
is almost a liquid ▶ *tomato puree*

purely /ˈpjʊəlɪ/ *adverb*
only ▶ *a decision taken for purely
political reasons*

purple /ˈpɜːpəl/ *noun, adjective*
the colour made by mixing red and
blue together

purpose /ˈpɜːpəs/ *noun*
1 a reason for doing something; an
aim ▶ *The purpose of his trip to town
was to buy a new television.*

2 on purpose intentionally ▶ *She
broke the cup on purpose.*

purposely /ˈpɜːpəslɪ/ *adverb*
intentionally ▶ *It wasn't a mistake –
you purposely opened my letter!*

purr /pɜːʳ/ *verb*
to make the soft, low noise that cats
make when they are happy

purse /pɜːs/ *noun*
a small bag for carrying money, used
especially by women

pursue /pəˈsjuː/ *verb (present
participle **pursuing**, past **pursued**)*
to go after someone hoping to catch
them
SAME MEANING: **chase**

pursuit /pəˈsjuːt/ *noun*
1 (*no plural*) the act of chasing
someone in order to try to catch them
▶ *The police followed in hot pursuit*
(=closely behind).
2 pursuits *plural noun* things that
you spend time doing ▶ *outdoor
pursuits such as climbing and sailing*

push¹ /pʊʃ/ *verb*
to press or lean steadily so as to
move someone or something ▶ *They
pushed the door open and rushed in.*
▶ *He pushed me off the chair.*

push² *noun (plural **pushes**)*
an act of pushing ▶ *She gave a hard
push, and the door opened.*

pushchair /ˈpʊʃ-tʃeəʳ/ *noun*
a small, folding chair on wheels, in
which you can push a small child
SAME MEANING: **buggy**
COMPARE: **pram**

push-ups /ˈpʊʃ ʌps/ *noun*
an exercise in which you lie facing the
ground and push your body up using
your arms
SAME MEANING: **press-up**

pushy /ˈpʊʃɪ/ *adjective (**pushier,
pushiest**)*
determined to get what you want, in
a way that seems rude ▶ *a pushy
salesman*

P

put /pʊt/ *verb (present participle **putting**, past **put**)*
1 to place or lay something in a particular position ➤ *Put the books on the shelf, please.* ➤ *Where did I put my keys?*
2 **put something down** to put something onto a surface such as a table or the floor ➤ *She put down her knitting.*
3 **put something off** to delay something till a later date ➤ *The meeting's been put off till next week.*
4 **put something on (a)** to put clothes on your body ➤ *She put on her coat and went out.*
(b) to make a light or machine work by pressing a button
5 **put a fire out** to stop a fire from burning
6 **put a light out** to stop a light from shining

puzzle¹ /ˈpʌzəl/ *noun*
1 a person or thing which you cannot understand or explain ➤ *It's a puzzle where all my money goes each week.*
2 a game or toy which is difficult to do ➤ *Can you do this jigsaw puzzle?*

puzzle² *verb (present participle **puzzling**, past **puzzled**)*
to make you feel that you do not understand something ➤ *The new machine puzzled me until Sarah explained how it worked.*

puzzled /ˈpʌzəld/ *adjective*
unable to understand something ➤ *Don had a puzzled expression on his face.*

puzzling /ˈpʌzlɪŋ/ *adjective*
difficult to understand ➤ *I find his reaction puzzling.*

pyjamas /pəˈdʒɑːməz/ *plural noun*
a loose shirt and trousers that you wear in bed ➤ *a pair of pyjamas*

pyramid /ˈpɪrəmɪd/ *noun*
a solid shape which is square at the base and pointed at the top

python /ˈpaɪθən/ *noun*
a large snake that kills the animals it eats by crushing them

Qq

quack /kwæk/ *verb*
to make the noise that a duck usually makes

quadruple /ˈkwɒdrʊpəl/ *verb (present participle **quadrupling**, past **quadrupled**)*
to become four times as big as before, or make something become four times as big as before ➤ *Sales of digital televisions have quadrupled over the last year.*

quaint /kweɪnt/ *adjective*
attractive in an old-fashioned way ➤ *a quaint little village*

quake /kweɪk/ *verb (present participle **quaking**, past **quaked**)*
to shake because you are afraid ➤ *She was quaking with fear.*

qualification /ˌkwɒlɪfɪˈkeɪʃən/ *noun*
proof that you have passed an examination, done special training, or learnt a special skill ➤ *You need some qualifications to find a job.*

qualified /ˈkwɒlɪfaɪd/ *adjective*
having the right training or skills to do something ➤ *She is very well qualified **for** this job.*

qualifier /ˈkwɒlɪfaɪəʳ/ *noun*
1 a game that you have to win to take part in a sports competition ➤ *a World Cup qualifier*
2 a person or team who achieves the standard that is needed to enter a sports competition ➤ *Johnson was the fastest qualifier.*

qualify /ˈkwɒlɪfaɪ/ *verb (past **qualified**)*

to finish the training to do a particular job ▶ She qualified **as** a doctor last year.

quality /ˈkwɒlətɪ/ noun (plural **qualities**)
1 how good something is ▶ We only sell cloth of the finest quality.
2 a good part of someone's character ▶ Her best qualities are courage and cheerfulness.

quantifier /ˈkwɒntɪfaɪəʳ/ noun
a word or phrase such as "much", "few", or "a lot of", which is used with a noun to show an amount

quantity /ˈkwɒntətɪ/ noun (plural **quantities**)
an amount ▶ Large quantities of drugs were found in their luggage.

quarantine /ˈkwɒrəntiːn/ noun (no plural)
a period of time when a person who, or an animal which may have a disease, is kept apart from other people or animals so that they do not get the disease too ▶ Animals coming to Britain must be kept in quarantine.

quarrel¹ /ˈkwɒrəl/ noun
an angry argument ▶ We had a quarrel **about** money.
SAME MEANING: **row**

quarrel² verb (present participle **quarrelling**, past **quarrelled**)
to have an angry argument ▶ Those children are always quarrelling **over** little things.

quarry /ˈkwɒrɪ/ noun (plural **quarries**)
a large hole in the ground from which stone or sand is dug out

quart /kwɔːt/ noun
a measure of liquid equal to 1.13 litres ▶ There are 2 pints in a quart and 4 quarts in a gallon.

quarter /ˈkwɔːtəʳ/ noun
1 one of four equal parts of something; 1/4 ▶ We divided the orange into quarters and each ate a piece.
2 15 minutes before or after the hour ▶ The meeting started at a quarter to two, not a quarter past two.
3 an area of a town, often where a particular kind of person lives ▶ the student quarter

quarterfinal /ˌkwɔːtəˈfaɪnl/ noun
one of the last four games at the end of a sports competition. The winners play in the two SEMIFINALS

quarterly /ˈkwɔːtəlɪ/ adjective, adverb
every three months ▶ a quarterly bank statement

quartz /kwɔːts/ noun (no plural)
a type of hard rock used for making electronic watches and clocks

quash /kwɒʃ/ verb
1 to officially say that a decision is no longer legal or correct ▶ The Court of Appeal quashed his conviction for murder.
2 to use force to stop fighting or protests ▶ Troops were sent in to quash the rebellion.

quay /kiː/ noun
a place where boats tie up and unload ▶ The quay looked like a long, stone road going into the sea.

queasy /ˈkwiːzɪ/ adjective (**queasier**, **queasiest**)
feeling as if you are going to be sick ▶ The awful smell was making me feel queasy.

queen /kwiːn/ noun
1 the female ruler of a country, especially one who is the daughter of the former ruler
COMPARE: **king**
2 the wife of a king
3 a playing card with a picture of a queen on it

queer /kwɪəʳ/ adjective
odd; strange ▶ He has some queer opinions on education.

Q

quench /kwentʃ/ *verb*
quench your thirst to drink as much as you need to stop being thirsty

query[1] /'kwɪərɪ/ *noun (plural queries)*
a question ► *I have several queries about the work you gave me.*

query[2] *verb (past queried)*
to ask about something, usually because you are not sure that it is right ► *If you think the price is too high, you should query it.*

quest /kwest/ *noun*
a long and difficult search ► *the quest for life on Mars*

question[1] /'kwestʃən/ *noun*
1 something you ask someone ► *You haven't answered my question.*
2 a problem to be talked about and dealt with ► *I want to buy the house, but it's a question of money.*

question[2] *verb*
1 to ask about something ► *A man is being questioned about the murder.*
2 to express doubts about something ► *I do not question his honesty.*

questionable /'kwestʃənəbəl/ *adjective*
not seeming likely to be completely true, correct, or honest ► *It's questionable whether she's telling the truth.*

question mark /'kwestʃən ˌmɑːk/ *noun*
the sign (?), used in writing at the end of a sentence which asks a question ► *Where are you going?*

questionnaire /ˌkwestʃə'neəʳ/ *noun*
a set of written questions that you answer in order to give information about something ► *Could you fill in this questionnaire?*

queue[1] /kjuː/ *noun*
a line of people or vehicles waiting for something ► *There was a long queue outside the theatre.*

queue[2] *verb (present participle queuing, past queued)*
to stand in a line of other people or vehicles to wait for something ► *We queued for the bus.*

quibble /'kwɪbəl/ *verb (present participle quibbling, past quibbled)*
to argue about something that is not very important ► *Let's stop quibbling over small details.*

quick /kwɪk/ *adjective*
doing something or happening in a short time ► *We had a quick meal and then ran to catch the train.* ► *This is the quickest way to get to school.* ► *a quick worker*

quickly /'kwɪklɪ/ *adverb*
fast, or done in a short amount of time ► *I promise I'll do it as quickly as I can.* ► *He quickly put the money back in the box.*
LOOK AT: **soon**

quicksand /'kwɪksænd/ *noun (no plural)*
wet sand that is dangerous to walk on because you sink into it

quid /kwɪd/ *noun (plural quid)*
a pound in British money ► *Can you lend me a quid?*

quiet[1] /'kwaɪət/ *adjective*
1 having or making very little noise ► *The streets were quiet at night.* ► *He has a quiet voice; I can't always catch what he says.*
OPPOSITE: **loud, noisy**
2 without much activity ► *I had a quiet day reading at home.*

quiet[2] *noun (no plural)*
the state of being quiet ► *Your brother needs peace and quiet because he's working.*

quieten /'kwaɪətn/ *(also quieten down) verb*
to become quiet, or to make someone or something become quiet ► *His speech failed to quieten the protestors.*

quietly /'kwaɪətlɪ/ *adverb*
without making much noise ➤ *She quietly turned the key.* ➤ *"I'm sorry," he said quietly.*

quilt /kwɪlt/ *noun*
a soft, thick covering for a bed

quirky /'kwɜːkɪ/ *adjective* (**quirkier, quirkiest**)
slightly strange ➤ *a quirky sense of humour*

quit /kwɪt/ *verb* (present participle **quitting**, past **quit**)
to stop doing something ➤ *I quit drinking coffee at night because it kept me awake.*

quite /kwaɪt/ *adverb*
1 completely ➤ *I quite agree with you.* ➤ *That fruit is not quite ripe.*
SAME MEANING: **absolutely**
2 a little bit, but not very ➤ *I was quite busy last week.*
SAME MEANING (2): **fairly**
COMPARE (2): **very**

quiver /'kwɪvə'/ *verb*
to shake a little ➤ *She quivered with excitement at the news.*

quiz /kwɪz/ *noun* (plural **quizzes**)
a game or competition in which people try to answer questions correctly

quota /'kwəʊtə/ *noun*
an amount of something that someone is allowed to have ➤ *The city has already had its quota of financial help from the government.*

quotation /kwəʊ'teɪʃən/ *noun*
words taken from speech or writing and repeated exactly by someone else

quotation mark /kwəʊ'teɪʃən ˌmɑːk/ *noun*
a sign (" or ") that you write before and after words to show that they are spoken by someone

quote /kwəʊt/ *verb* (present participle **quoting**, past **quoted**)
to say or write something that has been said or written before by someone else, especially a famous person

Qur'an /kɔː'rɑːn/ *noun*
the Qur'an the KORAN

Rr

rabbi /'ræbaɪ/ *noun*
a Jewish religious leader

rabbit /'ræbɪt/ *noun*
a small animal with long ears which lives in holes under the ground

rabble /'ræbəl/ *noun* (no plural)
a noisy crowd of people who are behaving badly ➤ *Get this rabble to be quiet.*

rabies /'reɪbiːz/ *noun* (no plural)
a disease that kills animals and people that are bitten by an infected animal

race¹ /reɪs/ *noun*
1 a competition to see who can run, swim, walk, etc., fastest ➤ *Who won the race?* ➤ *a boat race*
2 a group of humans different from other groups in shape, colour, size, etc.

race² /reɪs/ *verb* (present participle **racing**, past **raced**)
to compete in a race ➤ *Paul raced John to the house.* ➤ *She's racing against Mary in the 100 metres.*

racecourse /'reɪs-kɔːs/ *noun*
a place where horses compete in races

racehorse /'reɪshɔːs/ *noun*
a horse that competes in races

racetrack /'reɪs-træk/ *noun*
a special path on which runners, cars, or horses race

racial /'reɪʃəl/ *adjective*

1 connected with a person's race
2 between different races of people

racing /'reisiŋ/ *noun (no plural)*
a sport in which horses or cars race
▶ *horse racing*

racism /'reisizəm/ *noun (no plural)*
1 the idea that some races of people
are not as good as others
2 the bad treatment of people of
other races

racist /'reisist/ *noun*
1 a person who believes that some
races of people are not as good as
others
2 a person who treats people of other
races badly

rack /ræk/ *noun*
a frame on which things can be kept
▶ *The bottles were stored in a rack.*

racket /'rækit/ *noun*
an instrument used to hit the ball in
games like tennis

radar /'reidɑːʳ/ *noun (no plural)*
a way of finding the position and
speed of ships and planes by using
radio waves

radiant /'reidiənt/ *adjective*
full of happiness or love in a way that
shows in your face ▶ *Mary, you look
radiant.*

radiate /'reidieit/ *verb (present
participle **radiating**, past **radiated**)*
1 to show a feeling very strongly in
your appearance or behaviour ▶ *She
radiated confidence.*
2 to send out light or heat ▶ *A huge
fire radiated warmth around the room.*

radiation /ˌreidi'eiʃən/ *noun (no
plural)*
a form of energy that comes from a
NUCLEAR reaction, that can be
extremely harmful to living things
▶ *The process produces high levels of
radiation.*

radiator /'reidieitəʳ/ *noun*
1 a flat, metal apparatus on a wall,

which hot water passes through,
used to heat a room
2 an instrument for making the water
in the engine of a car cool

radical¹ /'rædikəl/ *adjective*
1 (used about changes) very big and
having important effects ▶ *radical
legal reforms* ▶ *Don't do anything too
radical with my hair.*
2 supporting big political and social
changes ▶ *radical left-wing MPs
(adverb: **radically**)*

radical² *noun*
a person who wants to make big
political and social changes

radii /'reidiai/
the plural of **radius**

radio /'reidiəu/ *noun*
1 (no plural) the sending out or
receiving of sounds by electrical
waves ▶ *Ships send messages to
each other by radio.*
2 a machine which receives messages
or sounds sent by electrical waves,
and plays them to you ▶ *He was
listening to music on the radio.*
3 (no plural) programmes which are
broadcast for people to listen to ▶ *I
prefer television to radio.*

radioactive /ˌreidiəu'æktiv/
adjective
containing or sending out radiation
▶ *Plutonium is highly radioactive.*
▶ *radioactive nuclear waste*

radioactivity /ˌreidiəuæk'tivəti/
noun (no plural)
the process of producing or sending
out radiation ▶ *High levels of
radioactivity have been found in
drinking water.*

radius /'reidiəs/ *noun (plural **radii**
/'reidiai/)*
the distance from the centre of a
circle to the edge

raffle /'ræfəl/ *noun*
a competition in which people buy

tickets with numbers on them and
will a prize if one of their numbers is
chosen ▶ *Would you like to buy some
raffle tickets?*

raft /rɑːft/ *noun*
large pieces of wood joined together
to make a rough, flat boat

rag /ræg/ *noun*
1 an old cloth ▶ *He cleaned the
machine with an oily rag.*
2 rags *plural noun* torn, old clothes

rage /reɪdʒ/ *noun*
very great anger ▶ *My father was
speechless with rage.*
SAME MEANING: **fury**

ragged /'rægɪd/ *adjective*
torn or in bad condition ▶ *a pair of
ragged shorts*

raid¹ /reɪd/ *noun*
a sudden attack ▶ *a bank raid*

raid² *verb*
to attack a place ▶ *They raided the
village at dawn.*

rail /reɪl/ *noun*
1 a fixed metal bar ▶ *a clothes rail*
2 by rail by train

railings /'reɪlɪŋz/ *plural noun*
a fence made of a number of metal
bars ▶ *a little garden with railings
round it*

railway /'reɪlweɪ/ *noun*
1 a track for trains to run on ▶ *They're
building a new railway to the south.*
2 the tracks, stations, etc. used in
carrying people and goods by train
▶ *a book about railways*

railway line /'reɪlweɪ ˌlaɪn/ *noun*
a track for trains to run on ▶ *A tree
has fallen across the railway line.*

railway station /'reɪlweɪ ˌsteɪʃən/
noun
a building near a railway where trains
stop and people can get on and off

rain¹ /reɪn/ *verb*
(used about water) to fall from the
sky ▶ *It rained last night.*

rain² *noun (no plural)*
water falling from the sky ▶ *There
was a lot of rain in the night.*

rainbow /'reɪnbəʊ/ *noun*
an arch of different colours in the sky
that is often seen after rain

raincoat /'reɪnkəʊt/ *noun*
a light coat that keeps out the rain

raindrop /'reɪndrɒp/ *noun*
a single drop of rain

rainfall /'reɪnfɔːl/ *noun*
the total amount of rain that falls on
an area in a particular period of time
▶ *Sri Lanka has an annual rainfall of
200–510cm.*

rain forest /'reɪn ˌfɒrɪst/ *noun*
a wet, tropical area where trees grow
thickly together ▶ *They are working
to save the Brazilian rain forest.*

rainy /'reɪni/ *adjective (**rainier,
rainiest**)*
having a lot of rain ▶ *a rainy day*

raise /reɪz/ *verb (present participle
raising, past raised)*
to lift something up or make
something higher ▶ *He raised his
arms above his head.* ▶ *Her wages
were raised last week.*
OPPOSITE: **lower**

raisin /'reɪzən/ *noun*
a small, dried GRAPE

rake¹ /reɪk/ *noun*
a tool that you pull along the ground
in order to make the ground level and
take leaves and small stones off the
surface

rake² *verb (present participle raking,
past raked)*
to pull a rake over a piece of ground

rally¹ /'ræli/ *noun (plural rallies)*
1 a very large, public meeting that
shows support for a political idea
▶ *30,000 workers attended a rally in
the capital, Buenos Aires.*
2 a race for cars or MOTORCYCLES on
public roads

R

rally² *verb (past* **rallied***)*
1 to come together to support someone or something ▶ *The Prime Minister is trying to rally support in rural areas.*
2 rally around *(also* **rally round***)* to support someone when they are in a difficult situation ▶ *My family always rallied round each other in a crisis.*

ram¹ /ræm/ *verb (present participle* **ramming***, past* **rammed***)*
to crash into something with a lot of force ▶ *The driver lost control and rammed into the back of my car.*

ram² *noun*
a male sheep

RAM /ræm/ *noun (no plural)*
RANDOM-ACCESS MEMORY; the part of a computer that keeps information that you want to use immediately

ramble¹ /'ræmbəl/ *verb (present participle* **rambling***, past* **rambled***)*
to talk in a boring or confused way ▶ *The teacher was rambling on at the front of the class.*

ramble² *noun*
a long walk for pleasure

ramp /ræmp/ *noun*
a slope that has been built to connect two places that are at different levels ▶ *ramps for wheelchair users*

rampage¹ /ræm'peɪdʒ/ *verb (present participle* **rampaging***, past* **rampaged***)*
to rush around in a group behaving in a noisy or violent way ▶ *rioters rampaging through the streets*

rampage² *noun*
on the rampage rushing around in a noisy and violent way ▶ *gangs on the rampage*

rampant /'ræmpənt/ *adjective*
increasing quickly, and difficult to control ▶ *The disease is rampant throughout the population.* ▶ *rampant inflation*

ramshackle /'ræmʃækəl/ *adjective*
(used about a building) in bad condition and looking as if it might fall down ▶ *a ramshackle old shed*

ran /ræn/
the PAST TENSE of the verb **run**

ranch /rɑːntʃ/ *noun (plural* **ranches***)*
a large cattle farm in the US or Canada

rancid /'rænsɪd/ *adjective*
(used about food) no longer fresh, and smelling or tasting unpleasant ▶ *the smell of rancid butter*

random /'rændəm/ *noun*
at random in no particular order ▶ *Ten people were chosen at random from the audience.*

rang /ræŋ/
the PAST TENSE of the verb **ring**

range /reɪndʒ/ *noun*
1 a line of mountains or hills
2 a number of different things ▶ *You can choose from a wide range of goods.*
3 the distance that something can reach or travel ▶ *missiles with a range of 150 kilometres*

ranger /'reɪndʒəʳ/ *noun*
a person whose job is to look after a forest or an area of public land ▶ *a forest ranger*

rank /ræŋk/ *noun*
a group or class which is higher or lower than other groups, especially in the armed forces ▶ *A general is an army officer with a high rank.*

ransack /'rænsæk/ *verb*
to damage a place and make it very untidy, often because you are looking for something ▶ *The thieves ransacked the house and stole jewellery worth £2,000.*

ransom /'rænsəm/ *noun*
money that is asked for by criminals who have taken a person away and are keeping them as a prisoner

➤ *He was asked to pay a million dollar ransom* **for** *his daughter.*

rant /rænt/ *verb*
to talk for a long time in an angry way ➤ *My father was ranting on about me coming home too late.*

rap /ræp/ *noun (no plural)*
a type of popular music in which the words are spoken to a rhythm and not sung

rape¹ /reɪp/ *verb (present participle* **raping**, *past* **raped**)
to force someone to have sex when they do not want to ➤ *She was attacked and raped on her way home from work.*

rape² *noun*
the crime of raping someone

rapid /'ræpɪd/ *adjective*
done or happening very quickly ➤ *rapid political changes (adverb:* **rapidly**)

rapids /'ræpɪdz/ *plural noun*
a part of a river where the water looks white because it is moving very fast over rocks

rapist /'reɪpɪst/ *noun*
a person who forces someone else to have sex when they do not want to

rare /reəʳ/ *adjective*
not happening or seen very often ➤ *That bird is very rare in this country.*
OPPOSITE: **common**

rarely /'reəlɪ/ *adverb*
not very often ➤ *She is old and rarely goes out.*
SAME MEANING: **seldom**

raring /'reərɪŋ/ *adjective*
be raring to go to be eager to start doing something ➤ *Come on! We're all raring to go!*

rascal /'rɑːskəl/ *noun*
a badly behaved person

rash¹ /ræʃ/ *adjective*
acting quickly without thinking enough what might happen ➤ *It was rash to say you'd buy it when you haven't got any money. (adverb:* **rashly**)

rash² *noun (plural* **rashes**)
red spots on your skin ➤ *With some common childhood illnesses, you get a rash.*

raspberry /'rɑːzbərɪ/ *noun (plural* **raspberries**)
a small, soft, sweet, red fruit that grows on bushes

rat /ræt/ *noun*
a small animal like a mouse but larger, which often eats food or grain that is stored

rate /reɪt/ *noun*
1 the money paid for a fixed amount of work; the amount produced, bought, used, etc. in a period of time ➤ *He was paid at the rate of £8 an hour.*
2 the speed of something ➤ *Our money was running out at an alarming rate (=very quickly).*

rate of exchange /,reɪt əv ɪks'tʃeɪndʒ/ *noun (plural* **rates of exchange**)
the value of the money of one country compared to that of another country ➤ *"What's the rate of exchange?" "It's about $1.50 to the pound."*

rather /'rɑːðəʳ/ *adverb*
1 a little ➤ *It's rather cold today.*
2 would rather would prefer ➤ *"Shall we go and see that film?" "I'd (=I would) rather stay in."*

rating /'reɪtɪŋ/ *noun*
1 a measurement of how good or popular something or someone is ➤ *The hotel had a five-star rating, and was very expensive.*
2 the ratings a list that shows which films, television programmes, etc. are the most popular ➤ *Her show is at the top of the ratings.*

ratio /'reɪʃɪəʊ/ *noun*
a relationship between two amounts written as two numbers that show

how much bigger one amount is than the other ▶ *an office where the ratio of men to women is about 5:1*

ration¹ /'ræʃən/ *verb*
to limit the goods that someone can have ▶ *The government had to ration petrol during the war.*

ration² *noun*
a limited quantity of food, petrol, etc., allowed to each person for a period, especially during a war

rational /'ræʃənəl/ *adjective*
1 based on real facts or scientific knowledge, and not influenced by feelings ▶ *There must be a rational explanation for their disappearance.*
2 able to make decisions based on the facts of a situation, and not influenced too much by feelings ▶ *Let's try to discuss this like rational human beings.*
(*adverb:* **rationally**)
OPPOSITE (**1** and **2**): **irrational**

rat race /'ræt reɪs/ *noun*
the rat race the way people live when they are always competing against each other in order to be richer or more successful

rattle¹ /'rætl/ *verb (present participle* **rattling**, *past* **rattled**)
to shake something, making a noise ▶ *She rattled some coins in the box.*

rattle² *noun*
a toy which a baby shakes to make a noise

rattlesnake /'rætl,sneɪk/ *noun*
a poisonous American snake that makes a noise with its tail

ravage /'rævɪdʒ/ *verb (present participle* **ravaging**, *past* **ravaged**)
to destroy or badly damage a town or an area ▶ *The enemy soldiers attacked, ravaging villages and towns.*

rave¹ /reɪv/ *noun*
a large party where young people dance to electronic music

rave² *verb (present participle* **raving**, *past* **raved**)
1 to talk in an excited way about something because you think it is very good ▶ *Sam's always raving about this music, but I don't like it much.*
2 to talk for a long time in an angry way ▶ *She raved on at me about the state of the garden.*

rave³ *adjective*
rave reviews strong praise for a new film, book, or play, especially in newspapers, on the television, etc.

ravenous /'rævənəs/ *adjective*
very hungry ▶ *The kids were ravenous when they came in from football practice.*

ravine /rə'viːn/ *noun*
a deep, narrow valley with steep sides

raving /'reɪvɪŋ/ *adjective*
crazy ▶ *He was acting like a raving lunatic.*

raw /rɔː/ *adjective*
not cooked ▶ *raw meat*

ray /reɪ/ *noun*
a line of light ▶ *the rays of the sun*

razor /'reɪzər/ *noun*
an instrument for removing hair, especially from a man's face

razor blade /'reɪzə ,bleɪd/ *noun*
a thin, very sharp piece of metal that is put inside a razor

Rd
a short way of writing the word **road** in an address ▶ *17 Nelson Rd, Oxford*

're /ər/ *verb*
are ▶ *We're late.*

reach¹ /riːtʃ/ *verb*
1 to get to a place or arrive at a place ▶ *They reached London on Thursday.* ▶ *She's reached the age when she can amuse herself.*
2 to stretch out your hand ▶ *I reached up and took an apple from the tree.*

reach² *noun (no plural)*
1 within reach near enough to touch by stretching out your arm
2 out of reach not near enough to touch by stretching out your arm

react /rɪˈækt/ *verb*
to behave in a particular way because of something that has happened ➤ *How did your mother react to the news?* ➤ *She reacted by getting very angry.*

reaction /rɪˈækʃən/ *noun*
the feeling you have or the way you behave because of something that has happened ➤ *What was his reaction when you told him?*

read /riːd/ *verb (past read* /red/)
1 to look at words and understand them ➤ *She was reading the newspaper.* ➤ *He read the story to his son.* ➤ *He read his son a story.* ➤ *I like reading.*
2 read something out to read something aloud for other people to hear ➤ *Can you read out the list of names?*

reader /ˈriːdər/ *noun*
a person who reads

readership /ˈriːdəʃɪp/ *noun*
the number or type of people who read a newspaper, magazine, etc. ➤ *The newspaper has a readership of 460,000.*

readily /ˈredɪli/ *adverb*
easily ➤ *I can readily believe that she's lazy at home – she does nothing at all at school.*

readiness /ˈredɪnəs/ *noun (no plural)*
willingness to do something ➤ *Small children have a natural readiness to learn.*

reading /ˈriːdɪŋ/ *noun*
1 *(no plural)* the activity of looking at and understanding written words ➤ *I enjoy reading in bed.*
2 a number or an amount shown on a measuring instrument ➤ *a thermometer reading of 40°C*

ready /ˈredi/ *adjective (**readier, readiest**)*
1 prepared ➤ *Is breakfast ready?* ➤ *Come on – aren't you ready yet?* ➤ *Is everything ready for the party?* ➤ *He got his tools ready to start the job.* ➤ *These apples are nearly ready to eat.*
2 willing ➤ *I'm always ready to help.*

ready-made /ˌredi ˈmeɪd/ *adjective*
already made or provided, and ready for you to use ➤ *a ready-made Christmas cake* ➤ *a ready-made excuse*

real /rɪəl/ *adjective*
actually existing; not imagined ➤ *That's a real dog, not a toy.*

realistic /rɪəˈlɪstɪk/ *adjective*
judging and dealing with situations in a sensible, practical way because you realize which things are possible ➤ *Be realistic! We can't possibly afford to buy that car! (adverb: **realistically**)*
OPPOSITE: **unrealistic**

reality /rɪˈæləti/ *noun (no plural)*
the way something really is, not the way you imagine it to be or would like it to be ➤ *He finds it difficult to face up to reality.*

realization /ˌrɪəlaɪˈzeɪʃən/ *noun (no plural)*
the understanding or coming to know something that you did not know before ➤ *the realization that he was guilty*

realize /ˈrɪəlaɪz/ *verb (present participle **realizing**, past **realized**)*
to know or understand something as true, especially suddenly ➤ *When I heard the noise on the roof, I realized that it was raining.*

really /ˈrɪəli/ *adverb*
1 in fact or very much ➤ *I am really worried about my work.* ➤ *He is really nice.*
2 Really? used to show that you are interested in something or surprised

R

by it ► *"Have you heard? Ann's going to have a baby!" "Really?"*

reap /riːp/ *verb*
to cut a crop and gather it

reappear /ˌriːəˈpɪəʳ/ *verb*
to appear again after not being seen for some time ► *At that moment, the door opened and Anna reappeared.*

rear¹ /rɪəʳ/ *adjective*
at the back ► *the rear wheels of a car*
OPPOSITE: **front**

rear² *noun*
the back part ► *We sat at the rear of the bus.*
OPPOSITE: **front**

rear³ *verb*
to care for animals or children while they grow up ► *to rear a family*

rearrange /ˌriːəˈreɪndʒ/ *verb (present participle rearranging, past rearranged)*
1 to change the position or order of things ► *We could rearrange these chairs to make a little more space.*
2 to change the time of a meeting or an event ► *The match has been rearranged for April 28th.*

reason /ˈriːzən/ *noun*
1 why something is done or happens ► *The reason she resigned was that she didn't like her boss.*
2 *(no plural)* the power of thinking and deciding

reasonable /ˈriːzənəbəl/ *adjective*
1 having good sense ► *Be reasonable – we just can't afford it.*
2 fair ► *a reasonable price*
OPPOSITE (**1** and **2**): **unreasonable**

reasonably /ˈriːzənəblɪ/ *adverb*
1 fairly and sensibly ► *You can't reasonably expect people to work for nothing.*
2 quite ► *It was reasonably cheap.*

reasoning /ˈriːzənɪŋ/ *noun (no plural)*
the process of thinking carefully

about something in order to form an opinion or make a decision ► *a decision based on sound reasoning*

reassure /ˌriːəˈʃʊəʳ/ *verb (present participle reassuring, past reassured)*
to comfort someone and stop them feeling anxious ► *His mother reassured him that everything would be all right.*

rebel¹ /rɪˈbel/ *verb (present participle rebelling, past rebelled)*
to fight against a leader or government ► *The students rebelled against the government.*

rebel² /ˈrebəl/ *noun*
a person who fights against a leader or government

rebellion /rɪˈbeljən/ *noun*
opposition to someone in a position of control

rebellious /rɪˈbeljəs/ *adjective*
deliberately disobeying someone in authority ► *At 15, Karl began to get very rebellious.*

rebuild /ˌriːˈbɪld/ *verb (past rebuilt /-ˈbɪlt/)*
to build something again, after it has been damaged or destroyed ► *The cathedral had to be rebuilt after the war.*

rebuke /rɪˈbjuːk/ *verb (present participle rebuking, past rebuked)*
to criticize someone because they have done something wrong ► *My mother rebuked me for being unkind.*

recall /rɪˈkɔːl/ *verb*
to remember something ► *I don't recall meeting him.*

recap /ˈriːkæp/ *noun*
the act of repeating the main points of something you have already said ► *It's time for a quick recap of tonight's main news.*

recede /rɪˈsiːd/ *verb (present participle receding, past receded)*
1 to move further away, or become

less strong or less likely ➤ *The sound receded into the distance.* ➤ *Hopes for a peaceful solution are receding.*
2 be receding to be losing the hair at the front of your head

receipt /rɪˈsiːt/ *noun*
a piece of paper which someone gives you to show that you have paid them money ➤ *Ask him to give you a receipt when you pay the bill.*

receive /rɪˈsiːv/ *verb (present participle **receiving**, past **received**)*
to get something or be given something ➤ *Did you receive my letter?*

receiver /rɪˈsiːvəʳ/ *noun*
the part of a telephone that you hold to your ear ➤ *Lift the receiver and dial the number.*

recent /ˈriːsənt/ *adjective*
happening a short time ago ➤ *a recent visit to the city (adverb:* **recently**)

reception /rɪˈsepʃən/ *noun*
1 *(no plural)* the office or department in a hotel or large organization which helps visitors and gives information ➤ *Leave your key at reception.*
2 a large, formal party ➤ *a wedding reception*

receptionist /rɪˈsepʃənɪst/ *noun*
a person whose job is to welcome and help people at a hotel, an office, etc.

receptive /rɪˈseptɪv/ *adjective*
willing to listen to new ideas or opinions ➤ *The other members of staff were quite receptive **to** my ideas.*

recess /rɪˈses/ *noun (plural **recesses**)*
1 a period of time when a parliament, committee, or law court is not working ➤ *The bill will not be passed before Parliament begins its autumn recess.*
2 a space in the wall of a room for shelves, cupboards, etc.

recession /rɪˈseʃən/ *noun*
a period when there is less business

activity, trade, etc. than usual, and a country's ECONOMY is no longer successful ➤ *The recession hit many small businesses very hard.*

recharge /riːˈtʃɑːdʒ/ *verb (present participle **recharging**, past **recharged**)*
to put more electricity into a BATTERY ➤ *I need to recharge the car's battery.*

recipe /ˈresəpɪ/ *noun*
a piece of writing telling you how to cook something ➤ *In the recipe, it tells you to use two eggs.* ➤ *a recipe for a chocolate cake*

reciprocal /rɪˈsɪprəkəl/ *adjective*
involving two people, groups, or countries who do something for each other ➤ *It's a reciprocal arrangement – our students visit their school, and their students visit ours.*

recite /rɪˈsaɪt/ *verb (present participle **reciting**, past **recited**)*
to repeat the words of something you have learned, such as a poem or list of facts ➤ *Susan recited the whole poem without a single mistake.*

reckless /ˈrekləs/ *adjective*
careless and dangerous ➤ *His reckless driving caused a serious accident. (adverb:* **recklessly**)
OPPOSITE: **careful, cautious**

reckon /ˈrekən/ *verb*
1 to guess because you have thought about something ➤ *I reckon he must have finished eating by now.*
2 reckon something up to add up or count something ➤ *She reckoned up the money we owed her.*

reclaim /rɪˈkleɪm/ *verb*
to ask for something that is yours to be given back to you ➤ *If you pay now, you can reclaim the money later.*

recline /rɪˈklaɪn/ *verb (present participle **reclining**, past **reclined**)*
to lie or sit back in a relaxed way so that part of your body is supported ➤ *Alice was reclining on the sofa, reading a magazine.*

R

reclining /rɪˈklaɪnɪŋ/ *adjective*
a reclining chair has a back that you can move so that it slopes backwards

recognition /ˌrekəɡˈnɪʃən/ *noun (no plural)*
the act of being known by someone when they see you ▶ *She hoped to avoid recognition by wearing dark glasses.*

recognize /ˈrekəɡnaɪz/ *verb (present participle **recognizing**, past **recognized**)*
to know someone or something when you see them ▶ *I recognized Peter although I hadn't seen him for ten years.* ▶ *I don't recognize this word – what does it mean?*

recoil /rɪˈkɔɪl/ *verb*
to move back suddenly, away from something that is unpleasant or that you are afraid of ▶ *Emily recoiled at the sight of the snake.*

recollect /ˌrekəˈlekt/ *verb*
to remember something ▶ *I don't recollect the name of the hotel.*

recollection /ˌrekəˈlekʃən/ *noun*
1 *(no plural)* the ability to remember something ▶ *I woke up in the morning with no recollection of where I was.*
2 something that you remember ▶ *We listened to his recollections of life during the war.*

recommend /ˌrekəˈmend/ *verb*
to tell someone that a person or thing is good for a particular purpose ▶ *If you're going to London, I recommend the County hotel – it's very nice.* ▶ *He recommended the new hotel to me.*

recommendation /ˌrekəmenˈdeɪʃən/ *noun*
the suggestion that someone or something is good for a particular purpose ▶ *I went to the new hotel on your recommendation.*

reconcile /ˈrekənsaɪl/ *verb (present participle **reconciling**, past **reconciled**)*

be reconciled to become friendly with someone again after you have had a serious argument ▶ *They were finally reconciled **with** each other, after two years of not speaking.*

reconsider /ˌriːkənˈsɪdər/ *verb*
to think about something again so that you can decide whether you should change your opinion ▶ *Won't you reconsider our offer?*

reconstruct /ˌriːkənˈstrʌkt/ *verb*
1 to produce a description or picture of something using the information you have ▶ *Police have reconstructed the events leading up to the crime.*
2 to build or make something again after it has been destroyed

record¹ /rɪˈkɔːd/ *verb*
1 to write about something or put it on a computer so that the information is stored for later
2 to copy television programmes on a special machine called a VIDEO so that you can watch them later
3 to store sounds electrically so that they can be listened to later ▶ *He recorded his most popular songs in 1998.*

record² /ˈrekɔːd/ *noun*
1 a round, thin, flat piece of plastic that stores sounds, and which you play on a special machine
2 information that is written down and kept ▶ *medical records*
3 something done better, quicker, etc. than anyone else has done it ▶ *He holds the world record **for** the high jump.*
4 **break a record** to do something better, quicker, etc. than it has ever been done before ▶ *She broke the record for the 100 metres.*

recorder /rɪˈkɔːdər/ *noun*
a musical instrument like a pipe

recording /rɪˈkɔːdɪŋ/ *noun*
a piece of music or speech that has been recorded so that you can listen to it ▶ *the group's latest recording*

record player /'rekɔːd ˌpleɪə'/ *noun*
a machine which is used to play
records

recount¹ /'riːkaʊnt/ *noun*
an act of counting votes again

recount² /rɪ'kaʊnt/ *verb*
to tell a story or describe events ➤ *a
TV film recounting the war years*

recover /rɪ'kʌvə'/ *verb*
to get well again after you have been
ill ➤ *Have you recovered **from** your
cold yet?*

recovery /rɪ'kʌvəri/ *noun (no plural)*
a return to good health after an
illness ➤ *She made a quick recovery
after her accident.*

recreate /ˌriːkri'eɪt/ *verb (present
participle **recreating**, past **recreated**)*
to make something so that it looks
like it did in the past, or like something
in another place ➤ *The zoo aims to
recreate the animals' natural habitats
as closely as possible.*

recreation /ˌrekri'eɪʃən/ *noun*
rest or play after you have been
working ➤ *Football and watching
television are the boys' main
recreations.* ➤ *You can't work all the
time – you must have some time for
recreation.*

recruit¹ /rɪ'kruːt/ *noun*
a new member of an organization,
especially of the armed forces

recruit² *verb*
to get a new member of an
organization ➤ *to recruit new police
officers*

rectangle /'rektæŋɡəl/ *noun*
a flat shape with four straight sides
and four equal angles, that is longer
than it is wide
SAME MEANING: **oblong**

rectangular /rek'tæŋɡjʊlə'/ *adjective*
having a flat shape with four straight
sides and four equal angles, that is
longer than it is wide ➤ *a rectangular
table*

rectify /'rektɪfaɪ/ *verb (past **rectified**)*
to change something that is wrong
and make it right ➤ *The mistake will
be rectified on your next bill.*

recuperate /rɪ'kjuːpəreɪt/ *verb
(present participle **recuperating**,
past **recuperated**)*
to spend time resting after an illness
or an injury until you feel better again
➤ *Atherton spent the summer
recuperating after a back operation.*

recur /rɪ'kɜː/ *verb (present participle
recurring, past **recurred**)*
to happen again ➤ *The doctor told me
to come back if the problem recurred.*

recycle /riː'saɪkəl/ *verb (present
participle **recycling**, past **recycled**)*
to use something again rather than
throw it away ➤ *These bottles can be
recycled.*

red /red/ *adjective, noun (**redder**,
reddest)*
the colour of blood ➤ *a red dress*
➤ *dressed in red*

red-handed /ˌred 'hændɪd/ *adjective*
catch someone red-handed to catch
someone at the moment when they
are doing something wrong ➤ *The
police caught the burglars red-
handed, climbing in the window.*

redhead /'redhed/ *noun*
a person who has red hair, especially
a woman

red-hot /ˌred 'hɒt/ *adjective*
very hot ➤ *red-hot metal*

redo /riː'duː/ *verb (past tense **redid**
/-'dɪd/, past participle **redone** /-'dʌn/)*
to do something again ➤ *I've just
cleaned this room, and I don't want
to have to redo it.*

red tape /ˌred 'teɪp/ *noun (no plural)*
official rules that seem unnecessary
and prevent people from doing things
quickly and easily ➤ *There's so much
red tape – it took me ages to get my
visa.*

R

reduce /rɪ'djuːs/ *verb (present participle **reducing**, past **reduced**)*
to make something smaller or less ▶ *They've reduced the prices in the shop, so it's a good time to buy.*

reduction /rɪ'dʌkʃən/ *noun*
the act of making something smaller or less ▶ *price reductions*

redundant /rɪ'dʌndənt/ *adjective*
make someone redundant to stop employing someone because there is not enough work for them any more ▶ *Part of the factory was closed, and 100 workers were made redundant.*

reed /riːd/ *noun*
a tall plant, like grass, which grows in or near water

reef /riːf/ *noun*
a line of sharp rocks or a raised area near the surface of the sea, often made of CORAL

reek /riːk/ *verb*
to smell strongly of something unpleasant ▶ *He came in reeking of cigarettes and beer.*

reel /riːl/ *noun*
a round thing on which thread, film, etc. can be wound ▶ *a reel of cotton*

refer /rɪ'fɜː/ *verb (present participle **referring**, past **referred**)*
1 refer to something to go to a book to get a piece of knowledge ▶ *Refer to a dictionary if you don't know what a word means.*
2 refer to someone or something to speak about someone or something ▶ *He didn't refer to Jack in his letter.*

referee /ˌrefə'riː/ *noun*
a person who watches a game and decides if it is fair

reference /'refərəns/ *noun*
1 *(no plural)* the act of looking at something for information ▶ *I keep the dictionary on my desk for reference.*
2 a letter written by someone about your character and ability, which is sent to someone who may give you a job

reference book /'refərəns ˌbʊk/ *noun*
a book, for example a dictionary, which you look at to get particular information about a subject

referendum /ˌrefə'rendəm/ *noun*
an occasion when the people of a country vote on one particular political subject, not on who will govern the country ▶ *The government has promised that there will be a referendum to decide whether Britain should remain in the EU.*

refill[1] /ˌriː'fɪl/ *verb*
to fill something again ▶ *Waitresses kept coming round refilling our glasses.*

refill[2] /'riːfɪl/ *noun*
a container filled with a substance that you use to refill something ▶ *refills for a pen*

refine /rɪ'faɪn/ *verb (present participle **refining**, past **refined**)*
1 to use an industrial process to make a natural substance more pure ▶ *The sugar is refined and then shipped abroad.*
2 to improve a method, plan, system, etc. by making small changes to it

refined /rɪ'faɪnd/ *adjective*
1 improved and made more effective
2 made more pure using an industrial process ▶ *refined sugar*
3 polite, educated, and interested in art, music, and literature ▶ *the refined world of 19th-century Paris*

refinery /rɪ'faɪnəri/ *noun (plural **refineries**)*
a factory where something such as oil, sugar, or metal is made pure by using an industrial process ▶ *an oil refinery*

reflect /rɪ'flekt/ *verb*
1 to throw back light, heat, a picture, etc. ▶ *A mirror reflects a picture of*

you when you look in it.
2 to think ▶ *Take some time to reflect on your decision.*

reflection /rɪˈflekʃən/ *noun*
1 (no plural) the throwing back of light, heat, etc.
2 what you see in a mirror or water ▶ *We looked at our reflections in the lake.*
3 (no plural) thinking ▶ *After a minute's reflection, he answered "no".*

reflective /rɪˈflektɪv/ *adjective*
1 made of material that reflects light, so that it looks very bright when light shines on it ▶ *If you're cycling at night, you should wear a reflective belt.*
2 thinking quietly ▶ *in a reflective mood*

reflex /ˈriːfleks/ *noun* (plural **reflexes**)
a quick, physical reaction that your body makes without you thinking about it ▶ *Goalkeepers need to have good reflexes.*

reflexive /rɪˈfleksɪv/ *adjective*
a reflexive verb or PRONOUN shows that an action affects the person or thing that does the action. In the sentence "I enjoyed myself", "myself" is a reflexive pronoun.

reform¹ /rɪˈfɔːm/ *verb*
to improve an organization or a system by making changes to it ▶ *The government is planning to reform the law on drinking and driving.*

reform² *noun*
a change that improves an organization or a system ▶ *the reform of the tax system*

refrain /rɪˈfreɪn/ *verb*
to stop yourself from doing something ▶ *She politely refrained from saying what she really thought.*

refresh /rɪˈfreʃ/ *verb*
to make someone less hot or tired

refreshed /rɪˈfreʃt/ *adjective*
less hot or tired ▶ *I felt refreshed after my bath.*

refreshing /rɪˈfreʃɪŋ/ *adjective*
making you feel less hot or tired ▶ *a refreshing drink*

refreshments /rɪˈfreʃmənts/ *plural noun*
food and drink which you have at an event or on a journey ▶ *They provided refreshments in the middle of the match.*

refrigerate /rɪˈfrɪdʒəreɪt/ *verb*
(present participle **refrigerating**, past **refrigerated**)
to put food or drinks in a refrigerator in order to keep them cold

refrigerator /rɪˈfrɪdʒəreɪtəʳ/ *noun*
another word for **fridge**

refuge /ˈrefjuːdʒ/ *noun*
a safe place

refugee /ˌrefjuˈdʒiː/ *noun*
a person who has to leave their own country because they are in danger

refund¹ /ˈriːfʌnd/ *noun*
money that is given back to you in a shop, restaurant, etc., for example because you are not satisfied with what you have bought ▶ *The shop assistant gave me a refund.*

refund² /rɪˈfʌnd/ *verb*
to give back money that has been paid to you for goods or services ▶ *They agreed to refund the cost of postage.*

refurbish /riːˈfɜːbɪʃ/ *verb*
to improve a building by decorating it and buying new equipment for it ▶ *The old cinema has been completely refurbished.*

refusal /rɪˈfjuːzəl/ *noun*
the act of not accepting an offer, or saying that you will not do something ▶ *her refusal of my help* ▶ *his refusal to help me*

refuse /rɪˈfjuːz/ *verb* (present participle **refusing**, past **refused**)
to say firmly that you are not willing to accept or do something ▶ *She refused to let me help.*

R

regain /rɪˈɡeɪn/ *verb*
to get something back after you have
lost it ▶ *It took me a few minutes to
regain my self-control.*

regal /ˈriːɡəl/ *adjective*
typical of a king or queen, and
therefore very impressive ▶ *a regal
mansion*

regard¹ /rɪˈɡɑːd/ *verb*
to think of someone in a particular
way ▶ *We regard him **as** our cleverest
student.*

regard² *noun (no plural)*
care ▶ *He always says what he thinks,
without regard **for** other people's
feelings.*

regarding /rɪˈɡɑːdɪŋ/ *preposition*
about ▶ *I wrote you a letter regarding
my daughter's school examinations.*
SAME MEANING: **concerning**

regardless /rɪˈɡɑːdləs/ *adverb*
without caring ▶ *He always says what
he thinks, regardless of other
people's feelings.*

regards /rɪˈɡɑːdz/ *plural noun*
best wishes ▶ *Give my regards to
your parents.*

reggae /ˈreɡeɪ/ *noun (no plural)*
a type of popular music from the West
Indies with a strong regular beat

regime /reɪˈʒiːm/ *noun*
a system of government or
management, especially one you
disapprove of ▶ *the Communist
regime*

regiment /ˈredʒɪmənt/ *noun*
a large group of soldiers who are part
of an army

regimented /ˈredʒɪmentɪd/ *adjective*
strictly controlled ▶ *Her lessons are
always highly regimented.*

region /ˈriːdʒən/ *noun*
an area ▶ *This is a farming region.*

regional /ˈriːdʒənəl/ *adjective*
of or about a particular region
▶ *the regional government*

register¹ /ˈredʒɪstəʳ/ *noun*
a list, such as one that has the names
of all the children in a class

register² *verb*
1 to have a name or an event put on a
list ▶ *The car is registered in my
sister's name.*
2 to show something ▶ *The
thermometer registered 25°C.*

registration /ˌredʒɪˈstreɪʃən/ *noun
(no plural)*
the act of having a name or an event
put on a list

registration number /redʒɪˈstreɪʃən
ˌnʌmbəʳ/ *noun*
the numbers and letters on a car's
NUMBER PLATE

regret¹ /rɪˈɡret/ *verb (present
participle **regretting**, past **regretted**)*
to be sorry about something ▶ *I regret
spending so much money on these
shoes.* ▶ *I regret to say that he failed.*

regret² *noun*
a feeling of being sorry

regrettable /rɪˈɡretəbəl/ *adjective*
that you wish had never happened
▶ *a regrettable mistake (adverb:
regrettably)*

regular /ˈreɡjʊləʳ/ *adjective*
1 happening or being at fixed times
▶ *He is a regular visitor – he comes
every Sunday at 2 o'clock.*
2 ordinary; usual ▶ *Is he your regular
doctor?*
3 (used about nouns, verbs, etc.)
following the usual rules of grammar.
The verb "walk", for example, is
regular but "be" is not
OPPOSITE (3): **irregular**

regularity /ˌreɡjʊˈlærəti/ *noun (no
plural)*
the state in which something
happens again and again after the
same period of time has passed
▶ *She asks if she can borrow money
with depressing regularity.*

regularly /ˈregjʊlǝlɪ/ *adverb*
often; after the same period every time has passed ➤ *He visits the old man regularly.*

regulate /ˈregjʊleɪt/ *verb (present participle **regulating**, past **regulated**)*
1 to control an activity or a process with rules ➤ *The Bank of England regulates the printing of bank notes.*
2 to keep something at a particular speed, temperature, etc. ➤ *Special equipment regulates the swimming pool's temperature.*

regulation /ˌregjʊˈleɪʃǝn/ *noun*
an official rule

rehabilitation /ˌriːhǝbɪlɪˈteɪʃǝn/ *noun (no plural)*
treatment to help someone stop taking drugs or drinking alcohol

rehearsal /rɪˈhɜːsǝl/ *noun*
a practice of a performance before it is shown to the public ➤ *All the children in the play must come to the rehearsal.*

rehearse /rɪˈhɜːs/ *verb (present participle **rehearsing**, past **rehearsed**)*
to do or say something again and again, to make it as good as possible ➤ *He rehearsed his speech for hours last night.*

reign[1] /reɪn/ *verb*
to be king or queen

reign[2] *noun*
the time when a king or queen rules a country ➤ *It happened in the reign of George IV.*

rein /reɪn/ *noun*
a long, narrow piece of leather used to control a horse ➤ *The rider pulled on the reins, and the horse stopped.*

reincarnation /ˌriːɪnkɑːˈneɪʃǝn/ *noun (no plural)*
the belief that people are born again in another body after they have died

reinforce /ˌriːɪnˈfɔːs/ *verb (present participle **reinforcing**, past **reinforced**)*
1 to support an opinion, a feeling, a system, etc. and make it stronger ➤ *Parents should try to reinforce the reading skills their children learn at school.*
2 to make something such as a part of a building, a piece of clothing, etc. stronger ➤ *a wall reinforced with concrete*

reinforcements /ˌriːɪnˈfɔːsmǝnts/ *plural noun*
more soldiers or police officers that go to help other soldiers or police officers ➤ *It's time to send in reinforcements.*

reinstate /ˌriːɪnˈsteɪt/ *verb (present participle **reinstating**, past **reinstated**)*
to give a job back to someone ➤ *Two employees who were wrongfully fired will be reinstated.*

reiterate /riːˈɪtǝreɪt/ *verb (present participle **reiterating**, past **reiterated**)*
to say something again so that people take notice of it ➤ *Let me reiterate that smoking is not allowed anywhere on the school premises.*

reject /rɪˈdʒekt/ *verb*
to decide that you do not want something or someone ➤ *We rejected his idea for a music club, and decided to have an art club instead.*

rejection /rɪˈdʒekʃǝn/ *noun*
1 the act of deciding that you do not want something ➤ *He felt disappointed at the publisher's rejection of his first novel.*
2 (no plural) the state of not being given love or attention by someone ➤ *I can't take any more rejection.*

rejoice /rɪˈdʒɔɪs/ *verb (present participle **rejoicing**, past **rejoiced**)*
to be very happy

relapse /rɪˈlæps/ *noun*
a situation in which someone becomes ill again after they were getting better ➤ *Unfortunately, he had a relapse and had to return to the hospital.*

R

relate /rɪ'leɪt/ *verb (present participle* **relating***, past* **related***)*
1 to have a connection with something ➤ *This film relates to what we were learning about metals last week.*
2 to tell a story ➤ *I related my adventure to my family.*

related /rɪ'leɪtɪd/ *adjective*
1 of the same family ➤ *I'm related to him – he's my uncle.*
2 connected ➤ *The book is about electricity and related subjects.*

relation /rɪ'leɪʃən/ *noun*
a member of the same family ➤ *Some of my relations, my mother's aunt and uncle, live in America.*

relationship /rɪ'leɪʃənʃɪp/ *noun*
1 being related ➤ *"Do you know her relationship to that girl?" "She's her sister."*
2 the feelings between two people ➤ *The teacher has a very good relationship with her students.*

relative¹ /'relətɪv/ *noun*
a member of the same family; a relation

relative² *adjective*
measured or judged when compared with something of the same kind ➤ *the relative costs of travelling by train and by coach*

relative clause /,relətɪv 'klɔːz/ *noun*
a part of a sentence that has a verb in it and is joined to the rest of the sentence by a RELATIVE PRONOUN such as "which"

relatively /'relətɪvlɪ/ *adverb*
when compared with something of the same kind ➤ *Travelling by train is relatively expensive.*

relative pronoun /,relətɪv 'prəʊnaʊn/ *noun*
a PRONOUN such as "who", "which", or "that", which connects a RELATIVE CLAUSE to the rest of the sentence

relax /rɪ'læks/ *verb*
to become less worried, angry, tight, etc. ➤ *Don't worry about it – just try to relax.*

relaxation /,riːlæk'seɪʃən/ *noun*
rest and amusement after hard work or worry

relaxed /rɪ'lækst/ *adjective*
calm and not worried
OPPOSITE: tense

relaxing /rɪ'læksɪŋ/ *adjective*
making you calm and less worried ➤ *a relaxing evening listening to music*

relay /'riːleɪ/ *(also* **relay race** /'riːleɪ reɪs/) *noun*
a race in which each member of a team runs or swims part of the distance ➤ *the 100-metre relay*

release¹ /rɪ'liːs/ *verb (present participle* **releasing***, past* **released***)*
to let someone or something go ➤ *I released the horse and it galloped away.* ➤ *Four prisoners were released.*

release² *noun*
the letting go of someone or something ➤ *After their release, the prisoners came home.*

relegate /'relɪgeɪt/ *verb (present participle* **relegating***, past* **relegated***)*
1 to make someone or something less important than before ➤ *He's been relegated to the role of assistant.*
2 if a sports team is relegated, it has to play in a lower group of teams because it has finished in the bottom place of the higher group

relent /rɪ'lent/ *verb*
to let someone do something that you would not let them do before ➤ *Park officials relented, and allowed campers to stay.*

relentless /rɪ'lentləs/ *adjective*
continuing without getting any less severe or determined ➤ *I'm sick of his relentless criticism.* (*adverb:* **relentlessly**)

relevance /'reləvəns/ *noun (no plural)*
the degree to which something is connected with the subject or problem being discussed ➤ *a statement with no relevance to the issue*

relevant /'reləvənt/ *adjective*
directly relating to the subject or problem being discussed ➤ *The question is not relevant to my point.*
OPPOSITE: **irrelevant**

reliable /rɪ'laɪəbəl/ *adjective*
able to be trusted ➤ *He is a very reliable person – if he says he will do something, he will do it.*
OPPOSITE: **unreliable**

reliance /rɪ'laɪəns/ *noun (no plural)*
the state of depending on something or someone ➤ *the country's reliance on imported oil*

reliant /rɪ'laɪənt/ *adjective*
be reliant on to depend on something or someone ➤ *She's still reliant on her parents for money.*

relic /'relɪk/ *noun*
something from the past that still exists ➤ *a relic of ancient times*

relief /rɪ'liːf/ *noun (no plural)*
a feeling of happiness after an unpleasant feeling ➤ *I felt great relief when I heard I had passed the examination.*

relieve /rɪ'liːv/ *verb (present participle **relieving**, past **relieved**)*
to make pain or trouble less ➤ *The medicine relieved his headache.*

relieved /rɪ'liːvd/ *adjective*
happy after a period of anxiety ➤ *Your mother will be very relieved to hear that you are safe.*

religion /rɪ'lɪdʒən/ *noun*
1 *(no plural)* belief in one or more gods ➤ *Almost every country has some form of religion.*
2 a special set of beliefs in one or more gods ➤ *the Hindu religion*

religious /rɪ'lɪdʒəs/ *adjective*
1 connected with religion ➤ *religious belief*
2 showing a strong belief in a religion and obeying its rules ➤ *a very religious man*

religiously /rɪ'lɪdʒəslɪ/ *adverb*
carefully or regularly ➤ *I clean my teeth religiously every night.*

relish /'relɪʃ/ *verb*
relish the thought of something to enjoy the thought that something good is going to happen ➤ *I don't relish the thought of another argument*

relive /,riː'lɪv/ *verb (present participle **reliving**, past **relived**)*
to remember, describe, or show something so clearly that it seems as if it is happening again ➤ *We spent the whole morning reliving our schooldays.*

relocate /,riː'ləʊ'keɪt/ *verb (present participle **relocating**, past **relocated**)*
to move to a new place ➤ *The company is relocating to London.*

reluctant /rɪ'lʌktənt/ *adjective*
not willing ➤ *The child was reluctant to leave her mother.*

rely /rɪ'laɪ/ *verb (past **relied**)*
to trust in someone or something ➤ *You can rely on me to help you.*

remain /rɪ'meɪn/ *verb*
to stay ➤ *I went to town, but my brother remained at home.* ➤ *We remained friends for many years.*

remainder /rɪ'meɪndə'/ *noun*
the rest; what is left ➤ *I'll go ahead with three of you, and the remainder of the group can wait here.*

remaining /rɪ'meɪnɪŋ/ *adjective*
left when other people have gone, or other things have been dealt with or used ➤ *The two remaining children went to live with their grandparents.*

R

R

remains /rɪ'meɪnz/ *plural noun*
parts which are left ➤ *We found the remains of a meal on the table.*

remand¹ /rɪ'mɑ:nd/ *verb*
be remanded in custody to be kept in prison until your TRIAL

remand² *noun*
be on remand to be in prison waiting for your TRIAL

remark¹ /rɪ'mɑ:k/ *noun*
something said ➤ *He made a rude remark about the woman in front.*

remark² *verb*
to say something because you have just thought about it or just noticed it ➤ *"That's where Jane lives," she remarked.*

remarkable /rɪ'mɑ:kəbəl/ *adjective*
unusual, usually in a good way ➤ *a remarkable escape* (adverb: **remarkably**)

remarry /ˌri:'mærɪ/ *verb* (past **remarried**)
to marry again ➤ *He said he would never remarry after his wife died.*

remedy /'remədɪ/ *noun* (plural **remedies**)
1 an answer to a problem
2 something that cures pain or illness ➤ *a remedy for a stiff neck*

remember /rɪ'membə'/ *verb*
to keep something or someone in your mind ➤ *Did you remember to feed the animals?*
OPPOSITE: **forget**

remind /rɪ'maɪnd/ *verb*
1 to make someone remember ➤ *Remind me to write to my uncle.* ➤ *That smell reminds me of the seaside.* ➤ *Remind me about the flowers for Aunt Jane – I mustn't forget them.*
2 **remind you of someone** to be like someone else ➤ *That man reminds me of Charlie Chaplin.*

reminder /rɪ'maɪndə'/ *noun*

something that makes you remember something else ➤ *The photos were a painful reminder of his first wife.*

reminisce /ˌremɪ'nɪs/ *verb* (present participle **reminiscing**, past **reminisced**)
to talk about pleasant events in your past ➤ *They sat reminiscing about the old days.*

reminiscent /ˌremɪ'nɪsənt/ *adjective*
making you think of someone or something similar ➤ *The garden was reminiscent of a jungle.*

remnant /'remnənt/ *noun*
a small part of something that remains after the rest no longer exists ➤ *the remnants of the defeated army*

remorse /rɪ'mɔ:s/ *noun* (no plural)
a feeling that you are sorry for something bad that you have done ➤ *He showed no remorse for his crime.*

remote /rɪ'məʊt/ *adjective*
far from where people live ➤ *They have a remote farm in the hills.*

remote control /rɪˌməʊt kən'trəʊl/ *noun*
a special thing you use to turn a machine on or off without getting out of your chair and going to it

remotely /rɪ'məʊtlɪ/ *adverb*
not in any way ➤ *He is not remotely like me.*

removal /rɪ'mu:vəl/ *noun*
the act of taking something away from a place or moving it ➤ *the removal of the pictures from the walls*

removal van /rɪ'mu:vəl ˌvæn/ *noun*
a large vehicle used to move all the things from one house to another when people go to live in a new house

remove /rɪ'mu:v/ *verb* (present participle **removing**, past **removed**)
to take something away ➤ *Will you remove your books from my desk?*

rename /riːˈneɪm/ *verb (present participle **renaming**, past **renamed**)*
to change the name of something ➤ *St Petersburg was renamed Leningrad.*

rendezvous /ˈrɒndɪvuː/ *noun (plural **rendezvous** /-vuːz/)*
an arrangement to meet someone ➤ *He had arranged a secret rendezvous with his girlfriend.*

renew /rɪˈnjuː/ *verb*
1 to put something new in the place of something of the same kind ➤ *He renewed his driving licence (=paper saying that he was allowed to drive a car).*
2 to start something again ➤ *The soldiers renewed their attack on the town.*

renounce /rɪˈnaʊns/ *verb (present participle **renouncing**, past **renounced**)*
to say publicly that you no longer support or want something ➤ *Why won't you renounce violence?*

renovate /ˈrenəveɪt/ *verb (present participle **renovating**, past **renovated**)*
to repair a building so that it looks new

renowned /rɪˈnaʊnd/ *adjective*
famous for something ➤ *The restaurant is renowned for its excellent food.*

rent¹ /rent/ *noun*
money paid regularly for the use of a house, an office, etc. ➤ *He pays £150 a week rent.*

rent² *verb*
to have the use of a house or car, or let someone use a house or car, in return for money ➤ *My father rents an office in the city.*
LOOK AT: **hire**

rental /ˈrentl/ *noun*
an arrangement to use something that belongs to someone else in return for money ➤ *a car rental*

agreement ➤ *Bike rental is £8.*

reorganize /riːˈɔːɡənaɪz/ *verb (present participle **reorganizing**, past **reorganized**)*
to organize something in a new and better way ➤ *The filing system needs to be reorganized.*

rep /rep/ *noun*
a person whose job is to sell products for a company ➤ *a sales rep*

repaid /rɪˈpeɪd/
the PAST TENSE and PAST PARTICIPLE of the verb **repay**

repair¹ /rɪˈpeəʳ/ *verb*
to make something that is broken or old good again ➤ *Have you repaired the chair yet?*
SAME MEANING: **mend**

repair² *noun*
something done to an old or a broken object to make it good again ➤ *I haven't paid for the repairs to my bicycle.*

repay /rɪˈpeɪ/ *verb (past **repaid** /rɪˈpeɪd/)*
to give money back to someone ➤ *I'll repay you tomorrow.*

repayment /rɪˈpeɪmənt/ *noun*
an amount of money that you give back to someone ➤ *Your first repayment is due next week.*

repeal /rɪˈpiːl/ *verb*
to officially end a law

repeat /rɪˈpiːt/ *verb*
to say something or do something again ➤ *Could you repeat the question?*

repeated /rɪˈpiːtɪd/ *adjective*
done again and again ➤ *She made repeated attempts to escape. (adverb: **repeatedly**)*

repel /rɪˈpel/ *verb (present participle **repelling**, past **repelled**)*
to force someone or something away ➤ *sprays that repel insects*

repellent[1] /rɪˈpelənt/ noun
a substance that keeps insects away
➤ mosquito repellent

repellent[2] adjective
very unpleasant ➤ She'd always found
her cousin quite repellent.

repent /rɪˈpent/ verb
to be sorry for something bad that
you have done ➤ If you repent, you
will be forgiven.

repercussions /ˌriːpəˈkʌʃənz/ plural
noun
bad things that happen as a result of
something that you do ➤ The decision
is likely to have serious repercussions.

repetition /ˌrepɪˈtɪʃən/ noun (no
plural)
the saying or doing of the same thing
again

repetitive /rɪˈpetɪtɪv/ adjective
doing or saying the same thing many
times in a way that seems boring
➤ repetitive exercises

rephrase /ˌriːˈfreɪz/ verb
(present participle **rephrasing**,
past **rephrased**)
to say or write something in different
words so that its meaning is clearer
➤ OK – let me rephrase the question.

replace /rɪˈpleɪs/ verb (present
participle **replacing**, past **replaced**)
1 to put something back in its place
2 to put a new or different thing in
place of something ➤ The man who
sold me the radio said he'd replace it
if it didn't work.

replacement /rɪˈpleɪsmənt/ noun
something new or different in the
place of something old or broken
➤ My new radio doesn't work – I'm
going to get a replacement.

replay[1] /ˈriːpleɪ/ verb
to play a match, such as a football
match, again

replay[2] /ˈriːpleɪ/ noun
a match, such as a football match,
played again because neither team or
person won it last time ➤ the replay
between Liverpool and Arsenal

replica /ˈreplɪkə/ noun
an exact copy of something

reply[1] /rɪˈplaɪ/ verb (past **replied**)
to give an answer ➤ "Did you forget?"
I asked. "Of course not," she replied.
➤ I replied that I would do it later.
➤ Have they replied **to** your letter?

reply[2] noun (plural **replies**)
an answer ➤ Have you had a reply **to**
your letter?

report[1] /rɪˈpɔːt/ verb
1 to tell people about something,
often because it is your job or duty
➤ The accident was reported on the
radio. ➤ He reported that the
company had made a profit.
2 to complain about someone or
something ➤ She was stealing money
and they reported her **to** the police.

report[2] noun
facts told or written ➤ We read a
report **of** the accident. ➤ a newspaper
report

reported speech /rɪˌpɔːtɪd ˈspiːtʃ/
noun (no plural)
the style of writing that is used for
telling people what someone says,
without repeating the actual words.
The sentence "Julia said she didn't
want to go" is an example of reported
speech
SAME MEANING: **indirect speech**
COMPARE: **direct speech**

reporter /rɪˈpɔːtər/ noun
a person who writes reports in
newspapers or tells news stories on
television or radio

represent /ˌreprɪˈzent/ verb
1 to act officially for another person
or group of people ➤ He represented
his company at the meeting.
2 to be a sign of ➤ The sign "&"
represents the word "and".

representative /ˌreprɪˈzentətɪv/ *noun*
a person who acts officially for
another person or group of people
▶ *They sent a representative to the
meeting.*

repress /rɪˈpres/ *verb*
1 to stop yourself from saying or
showing what you really feel ▶ *It's
not good to repress your feelings.*
2 to control people by force ▶ *a brutal
leader who repressed his people*

repressive /rɪˈpresɪv/ *adjective*
cruel and very strict ▶ *a repressive
government*

reprieve /rɪˈpriːv/ *noun*
a period of time when something bad
that was going to happen does not
happen ▶ *I got a last-minute reprieve.*

reprimand /ˈreprɪmɑːnd/ *verb*
to tell someone officially that they
have done something wrong ▶ *His
manager reprimanded him for being
late.*

reprisal /rɪˈpraɪzəl/ *noun*
something that is done to punish an
enemy ▶ *He's afraid to help the police
for fear of reprisals against his family.*

reproach /rɪˈprəʊtʃ/ *verb*
to blame someone in a sad way, not
an angry way

reproduce /ˌriːprəˈdjuːs/ *verb*
*(present participle **reproducing**,
past **reproduced**)*
1 to produce young
2 to make a copy of something ▶ *The
paintings were all reproduced in the
book.*

reproduction /ˌriːprəˈdʌkʃən/ *noun*
1 *(no plural)* producing young ones
▶ *human reproduction*
2 a copy of something ▶ *a
reproduction of a famous picture*

reptile /ˈreptaɪl/ *noun*
an animal such as a snake whose
blood changes temperature according
to the temperature around it

republic /rɪˈpʌblɪk/ *noun*
a country whose head is a president,
not a king

republican /rɪˈpʌblɪkən/ *noun*
a person who believes in having a
republic

repulsive /rɪˈpʌlsɪv/ *adjective*
very unpleasant ▶ *What a repulsive
smell!*

reputable /ˈrepjʊtəbəl/ *adjective*
respected for being honest and doing
good work ▶ *a reputable builder*

reputation /ˌrepjʊˈteɪʃən/ *noun*
the opinion that people have about
someone or something ▶ *The hotel
has an excellent reputation.*

request¹ /rɪˈkwest/ *verb*
to ask politely for something
▶ *Visitors are requested to be quiet in
the hospital.* ▶ *Please request help if
you need it.*

request² *noun*
something that you ask for politely
▶ *She's made a request **for** some new
computers.*

require /rɪˈkwaɪəʳ/ *verb (present
participle **requiring**, past **required**)*
to need something ▶ *These plants
require a lot of light.*

requirement /rɪˈkwaɪəmənt/ *noun*
something that is needed ▶ *This shop
can supply all your requirements.*

resat /ˌriːˈsæt/
the PAST TENSE and PAST PARTICIPLE of the
verb **resit**

rescue¹ /ˈreskjuː/ *verb (present
participle **rescuing**, past **rescued**)*
to save someone from danger ▶ *They
rescued the boy from the river.*

rescue² *noun*
the saving of someone from danger
▶ *a big rescue operation after a ship
sank in the North Sea*

research¹ /rɪˈsɜːtʃ, ˈriːsɜːtʃ/ *noun (no
plural)*

R

careful study, especially to find out
something new ► *scientific research*
► *medical research*

research² /rɪˈsɜːtʃ/ *verb*
to study something to find out new
things

resemblance /rɪˈzembləns/ *noun*
a way in which two people or things
look like each other ► *There is no
resemblance **between** the two
brothers.*

resemble /rɪˈzembəl/ *verb (present
participle **resembling**, past **resembled**)*
to look like another person or thing
► *She resembles her mother in the way
she moves her hands when she talks.*

resent /rɪˈzent/ *verb*
to feel angry about something
because you think you have been
treated unfairly ► *He resents being
treated as a child.*

resentful /rɪˈzentfəl/ *adjective*
angry and upset about something
that someone has done ► *I'm very
resentful about losing my job.*

resentment /rɪˈzentmənt/ *noun (no
plural)*
the feeling of being angry because
you think you have been treated
unfairly

reservation /ˌrezəˈveɪʃən/ *noun*
an arrangement to make sure that
something is kept for your use ► *Have
you made a reservation at the hotel?*

reserve¹ /rɪˈzɜːv/ *verb (present
participle **reserving**, past **reserved**)*
to keep something for someone or
arrange for something to be kept ► *I
have reserved a table for us at the
restaurant.*

reserve² *noun*
1 an amount of something which is
kept for possible future use ► *We
have large reserves **of** oil.*
2 a place where wild animals live and
are protected ► *Africa has many
wildlife reserves.*

reserved /rɪˈzɜːvd/ *adjective*
unwilling to show or talk about your
thoughts and feelings ► *a cool,
reserved young man*

reservoir /ˈrezəvwɑːʳ/ *noun*
a place where a lot of water is stored

residence /ˈrezɪdəns/ *noun*
1 the place where you live ► *the
President's official residence*
2 *(no plural)* the fact of having your
home in a place ► *residence in the
United Kingdom*

resident /ˈrezɪdənt/ *noun*
a person who lives in a place
► *residents **of** Oxford*

residential /ˌrezɪˈdenʃəl/ *adjective*
related to where people live rather than
where they work ► *a residential area*

residue /ˈrezɪdjuː/ *noun*
a substance that remains after
something else has disappeared or
been removed ► *an oily residue*

resign /rɪˈzaɪn/ *verb*
1 to leave your job ► *He resigned
from the government.*
2 resign yourself to something to
accept something unpleasant calmly
► *I resigned myself to a long wait.*

resignation /ˌrezɪgˈneɪʃən/ *noun*
1 a letter saying you are leaving your
job ► *I handed in my resignation last
week.*
2 *(no plural)* calm acceptance of
something unpleasant

resilient /rɪˈzɪliənt/ *adjective*
strong enough to get better quickly
after problems, illness, damage, etc.
► *Small babies can be remarkably
resilient.*

resist /rɪˈzɪst/ *verb*
1 to fight back against attack ► *They
tried to resist the enemy attack.*
2 to fight against something ► *He
resists any kind of change.*
3 to stop yourself doing something
you would like to do ► *I can't resist
teasing him.*

resistance /rɪˈzɪstəns/ *noun (no plural)*
the act of fighting against someone or something

resistant /rɪˈzɪstənt/ *adjective*
1 not easily harmed or damaged by something ▶ *a fire-resistant coat*
2 unwilling to accept new ideas or changes ▶ *people who are resistant to change*

resit /ˌriːˈsɪt/ *verb (present participle **resitting**, past **resat** /-ˈsæt/)*
to take a test or an examination again ▶ *I've got to resit my history exam.*

resolution /ˌrezəˈluːʃən/ *noun*
a decision to do something that you ought to do ▶ *I made a resolution to work hard.*

resolve /rɪˈzɒlv/ *verb (present participle **resolving**, past **resolved**)*
to decide ▶ *I resolved to work hard until the examination.*

resort /rɪˈzɔːt/ *noun*
a town where people go on holiday ▶ *a seaside resort* ▶ *a tourist resort*

resounding /rɪˈzaʊndɪŋ/ *adjective*
1 used for emphasizing that something is very successful ▶ *a resounding victory*
2 very loud ▶ *a resounding crash*

resourceful /rɪˈzɔːsfəl/ *adjective*
good at finding ways to deal with problems

resources /rɪˈzɔːsɪz/ *plural noun*
the things or the money that a country or an organization has that make it possible for them to do things ▶ *natural resources such as oil*

respect¹ /rɪˈspekt/ *noun*
1 *(no plural)* a good opinion of someone ▶ *He has great respect for his parents.*
2 a way ▶ *In some respects, he is like his father.*

respect² *verb*
to feel admiration for someone's

good qualities ▶ *All the children respected their teacher.*

respectable /rɪˈspektəbəl/ *adjective*
with a good, honest character ▶ *a respectable young man*

respectful /rɪˈspektfəl/ *adjective*
showing respect for someone or something ▶ *They maintained a respectful silence while the funeral procession went past.*
OPPOSITE: **disrespectful**

respective /rɪˈspektɪv/ *adjective*
used to talk about each different person or thing in order ▶ *I invited three friends and their respective boyfriends. (adverb: **respectively**)*

respiratory /rɪˈspɪrətəri/ *adjective*
relating to breathing ▶ *Smoking causes respiratory illnesses.*

respite /ˈrespaɪt/ *noun*
a short period when something unpleasant stops happening ▶ *The northwest should have a brief respite from the rain today.*

respond /rɪˈspɒnd/ *verb*
to answer ▶ *How did she respond to your question?* ▶ *She responded by laughing.*

response /rɪˈspɒns/ *noun*
an answer ▶ *I've had no response to my letter.*

responsibility /rɪˌspɒnsəˈbɪləti/ *noun (plural **responsibilities**)*
something which it is your duty to do or look after ▶ *My children are my own responsibility.*

responsible /rɪˈspɒnsəbəl/ *adjective*
taking care of someone or something, and taking the blame if anything goes wrong ▶ *Simon is a responsible boy – we can leave him to look after the smaller children.* ▶ *She's responsible for organizing the whole show.*

responsibly /rɪˈspɒnsəbli/ *adverb*
in a sensible way, so that other

people trust you ▶ *Can I trust you to behave responsibly while I'm gone?*

responsive /rɪˈspɒnsɪv/ *adjective*
paying attention to what people need, and doing something to help them ▶ *The government needs to be responsive to people's needs.*

rest¹ /rest/ *noun*
1 a time of quiet away from work or play ▶ *I had an hour's rest after work.*
2 the rest the remaining part or parts of something ▶ *Have you seen the rest of the children?* ▶ *We'll eat the rest of the cake tomorrow.*

rest² *verb*
1 to have a quiet time away from work or play ▶ *I rested for an hour before I went out.*
2 to put something down somewhere ▶ *I rested my elbows on the table.*

restaurant /ˈrestərɒnt/ *noun*
a place where you can buy and eat food
COMPARE: **cafe**

restful /ˈrestfəl/ *adjective*
pleasantly peaceful ▶ *a restful evening*

restless /ˈrestləs/ *adjective*
not able to keep still ▶ *You were very restless in bed last night.*

restore /rɪˈstɔːʳ/ *verb (present participle **restoring**, past **restored**)*
1 to repair something so that it looks new ▶ *to restore an old building*
2 to give back something that was lost or stolen

restrain /rɪˈstreɪn/ *verb*
to stop or hold back ▶ *She couldn't restrain her tears.*

restraint /rɪˈstreɪnt/ *noun*
1 *(no plural)* the quality of behaving in a calm way, even though a situation is very difficult ▶ *The police showed great restraint.*
2 something that limits what you can do ▶ *The government has introduced new restraints on free speech.*

restrict /rɪˈstrɪkt/ *verb*
to keep something within a limit ▶ *new laws to restrict the sale of guns*

restricted /rɪˈstrɪktɪd/ *adjective*
limited to a small group of people or things ▶ *Cancer is not restricted to old people.*

restriction /rɪˈstrɪkʃən/ *noun*
a limit ▶ *parking restrictions in the city centre*

result¹ /rɪˈzʌlt/ *noun*
something that happens because something else has happened ▶ *When will I have the results of my blood test?* ▶ *We arrived late, with the result that we missed the train.*

result² *verb*
to have something as a result ▶ *The accident resulted in three people being killed.*

resume /rɪˈzjuːm/ *verb (present participle **resuming**, past **resumed**)*
to start again ▶ *We shall resume the meeting in a quarter of an hour.*

resuscitate /rɪˈsʌsɪteɪt/ *verb (present participle **resuscitating**, past **resuscitated**)*
to make someone start breathing again ▶ *Doctors tried to resuscitate her, but it was too late.*

retail¹ /ˈriːteɪl/ *noun (no plural)*
the activity of selling things to people in shops ▶ *Retail figures are rising steadily.*

retail² /rɪˈteɪl/ *verb*
to be sold for a particular price in shops ▶ *The Toshiba KT3301S retails at around £900.*

retailer /ˈriːteɪləʳ/ *noun*
a person or company that sells things to people in shops

retain /rɪˈteɪn/ *verb*
to keep something ▶ *The village has retained its charm.*

retaliate /rɪˈtælieɪt/ *verb (present participle **retaliating**, past **retaliated**)* to do something unpleasant to someone because they have done something unpleasant to you ▶ *The police retaliated by firing tear gas grenades.*

retaliation /rɪˌtælɪˈeɪʃən/ *noun (no plural)*
the act of doing something unpleasant to someone because they have done something unpleasant to you

reticent /ˈretɪsənt/ *adjective*
not wanting to say what you know or think about something ▶ *Bryn is reticent **about** his part in the war.*

retire /rɪˈtaɪə/ *verb (present participle **retiring**, past **retired**)*
to stop work because of old age or illness ▶ *He retired from the business when he was 65.*

retirement /rɪˈtaɪəmənt/ *noun*
the period of a person's life after they have stopped working because they are old or ill ▶ *She plans to spend her retirement travelling.*

retiring /rɪˈtaɪərɪŋ/ *adjective*
shy and nervous with other people ▶ *a shy, retiring type of man*

retreat¹ /rɪˈtriːt/ *verb*
to go back or away from something or someone ▶ *The soldiers had to retreat as the enemy advanced.*
COMPARE: **advance**

retreat² *noun*
a movement back, away from someone or something

retribution /ˌretrɪˈbjuːʃən/ *noun (no plural)*
the act of hurting or punishing someone for something they have done ▶ *They would not give evidence against the men for fear of retribution.*

retrieve /rɪˈtriːv/ *verb (present participle **retrieving**, past **retrieved**)*
to find something and bring it back ▶ *I retrieved my bags from the car.*

retrospect /ˈretrəspekt/ *noun*
in retrospect used when you are thinking about something that happened in the past, and you know more about it now than you knew then ▶ *In retrospect, I shouldn't have sold my computer.*

return¹ /rɪˈtɜːn/ *verb*
1 to come or go back ▶ *He returned to his own country.*
2 to give something back ▶ *Could you return the book I lent you?*

return² *noun*
1 the act of coming or going back ▶ *On my return from work, I saw that the door was open.*
2 a ticket for a journey to a place and back again ▶ *Two returns to Edinburgh, please.* ▶ *a return ticket*
COMPARE (**2**): **single**

reunion /riːˈjuːnjən/ *noun*
a meeting of people who have not met for a long time ▶ *a college reunion*

reunite /ˌriːjuːˈnaɪt/ *verb (present participle **reuniting**, past **reunited**)*
to bring people together again ▶ *He was at last reunited **with** his family.*

rev /rev/ *(also **rev up**) verb (present participle **revving**, past **revved**)*
to make an engine work faster ▶ *Rev the engine by pressing on the accelerator.*

reveal /rɪˈviːl/ *verb*
to say or show something that was covered up or secret before

revealing /rɪˈviːlɪŋ/ *adjective*
1 showing what someone or something is really like, or what someone really feels ▶ *Some of her comments were very revealing.*
2 (used about clothes) showing parts of your body that are usually kept covered ▶ *a revealing blouse*

revel /ˈrevəl/ *verb (present participle **revelling**, past **revelled**)*

revel in something to enjoy something very much ▶ *He was secretly revelling in his new fame.*

revelation /ˌrevəˈleɪʃən/ *noun* a fact that people did not know before ▶ *newspaper revelations about her private life*

revenge /rɪˈvendʒ/ *noun (no plural)* something bad that you do to someone who has done something bad to you ▶ *He broke Mary's pen and in revenge she tore up his school work.*

revenue /ˈrevənjuː/ *noun (no plural)* money that a company or an organization earns ▶ *Most of the theatre's revenue comes from ticket sales.*

Reverend /ˈrevərənd/ *noun* a title for a Christian priest ▶ *Reverend Jones*

reverse /rɪˈvɜːs/ *verb (present participle **reversing**, past **reversed**)*
1 to move backwards ▶ *The driver reversed the lorry into the narrow road.*
2 to change the order of things to the opposite of what it was before

reversible /rɪˈvɜːsəbəl/ *adjective*
1 able to be changed back to how it was before ▶ *Any side effects of the treatment are easily reversible.*
OPPOSITE: **irreversible**
2 (used about clothes) able to be worn with the inside part on the outside

revert /rɪˈvɜːt/ *verb*
revert to something to change back to how something was before ▶ *Leningrad reverted to its former name of St Petersburg.*

review¹ /rɪˈvjuː/ *noun* a piece of writing telling you what the writer thinks about something such as a new book or film

review² *verb* to look at new books, films, etc. and say what you think about them

revise /rɪˈvaɪz/ *verb (present participle **revising**, past **revised**)*
1 to prepare for an examination by studying things again ▶ *I've been revising all week.*
2 to look through something again and change things where needed ▶ *He was revising what he had written.*

revision /rɪˈvɪʒən/ *noun (no plural)* work in which you study things again to prepare for an examination

revival /rɪˈvaɪvəl/ *noun* the process of becoming popular or successful again ▶ *the revival of seventies music*

revive /rɪˈvaɪv/ *verb (present participle **reviving**, past **revived**)* to become conscious again or to make someone conscious again ▶ *She managed to revive the woman she had saved from the river.*

revolt¹ /rɪˈvəʊlt/ *verb* to fight in a mass against leaders or a government ▶ *The soldiers revolted **against** their officers.*

revolt² *noun* an event in which a lot of people fight against their leaders or government ▶ *The army officers led a revolt **against** the king.*

revolting /rɪˈvəʊltɪŋ/ *adjective* making you ill through looking at or thinking about something ▶ *What a revolting smell!*
SAME MEANING: **disgusting**

revolution /ˌrevəˈluːʃən/ *noun* a great change, especially in the government of a country ▶ *the Russian revolution*

revolutionary /ˌrevəˈluːʃənəri/ *adjective*
1 connected with revolution
2 completely new and different ▶ *a revolutionary way of growing rice*

revolutionize /ˌrevə'luːʃənaɪz/ verb (present participle **revolutionizing**, past **revolutionized**)
to completely change the way people do something ▶ E-mail has revolutionized the way we work.

revolve /rɪ'vɒlv/ verb (present participle **revolving**, past **revolved**)
to go round and round ▶ The wheels began to revolve slowly. ▶ The Earth revolves round the sun.

revolver /rɪ'vɒlvə'/ noun
a small gun
SAME MEANING: **pistol**

reward¹ /rɪ'wɔːd/ noun
something given in return for good work, kindness, bravery, etc. ▶ The police are offering a reward **for** information about the robbery.

reward² verb
to give a reward to someone who has done something good ▶ How can I reward you **for** all your help?

rewarding /rɪ'wɔːdɪŋ/ adjective
making you feel happy and satisfied ▶ a rewarding job

rewind /riː'waɪnd/ verb (past **rewound** /riː'waʊnd/)
to make a TAPE go back towards the beginning

rewrite /ˌriː'raɪt/ verb (present participle **rewriting**, past tense **rewrote** /riː'rəʊt/, past participle **rewritten** /riː'rɪtn/)
to write something again in a different way in order to improve it ▶ They rewrote the ending of the film.

rhetorical question /rɪˌtɒrɪkəl 'kwestʃən/ noun
a question that you ask in order to make a statement, without expecting an answer

rheumatism /'ruːmətɪzəm/ noun (no plural)
a disease causing pain or stiffness in the joints or muscles

rhino /'raɪnəʊ/ noun
a RHINOCEROS

rhinoceros /raɪ'nɒsərəs/ noun (plural **rhinoceroses**)
a large, wild animal with a hard skin and two horns on its nose, which lives in Africa or Asia

rhyme¹ /raɪm/ noun
1 a word with the same sound as another word
2 a short thing you say or sing which has rhymes in it

rhyme² verb (present participle **rhyming**, past **rhymed**)
(used about words) to end with the same sound ▶ "Weigh" rhymes **with** "play."

rhythm /'rɪðəm/ noun
a regular sound like a drum in music ▶ I can't dance to music without a good rhythm.

rib /rɪb/ noun
one of the narrow bones which go round your chest

ribbon /'rɪbən/ noun
a long, narrow piece of material used for tying things and making them look pretty ▶ ribbons in her hair

rice /raɪs/ noun (no plural)
a food of white or brown grains grown in wet, tropical places, especially in India and China

rich /rɪtʃ/ adjective
1 having a lot of money
OPPOSITE: **poor**
SAME MEANING: **well-off**
2 cooked with a lot of oil, sugar, etc. ▶ I don't like rich food.

riches /'rɪtʃɪz/ plural noun
money and goods ▶ Success has brought her vast riches.

rickety /'rɪkɪti/ adjective
in bad condition and likely to break ▶ a rickety old chair

ricochet /'rɪkəʃeɪ/ verb (present participle **ricocheting** or **ricochetting**,

R

past **ricocheted** or **ricochetted**)
to hit a surface and move away from
it in a different direction ► *The bullet
ricocheted off the windscreen.*

rid /rɪd/ *verb*
get rid of something to remove
something or someone you do not
want ► *He got rid of his motorbike
and bought a car.*

ridden /'rɪdn/
the PAST PARTICIPLE of the verb **ride**

riddle /'rɪdl/ *noun*
a question which is a trick and which
makes people laugh ► *Here's a riddle
for you: "Why is 'smiles' the longest
word in the world? Because it's made
of two s's with a 'mile' between them."*

riddled /'rɪdld/ *adjective*
riddled with something containing a
lot of something bad ► *His argument
is riddled with contradictions.*

ride¹ /raɪd/ *verb (present participle
riding, past tense **rode** /rəʊd/, past
participle **ridden** /'rɪdn/)*
to go along on or in a vehicle or on an
animal ► *She was riding a bicycle.*
► *Can you ride a horse?*

ride² *noun*
a journey on or in a vehicle or on a
horse, especially for pleasure ► *Can I
have a ride on your bike* (=bicycle)?
► *They've gone out for a ride in the
car.*

rider /'raɪdə'/ *noun*
a person who rides, especially
someone who rides a horse ► *The
rider was thrown off his horse.*

ridge /rɪdʒ/ *noun*
a long, narrow, raised part of
something such as the top of a hill
► *The waves had pushed the sand
into little ridges.*

ridicule¹ /'rɪdɪkjuːl/ *noun (no plural)*
the act of laughing at someone or
something and saying unkind things
about them ► *She became an object
of ridicule.*

ridicule² *verb (present participle
ridiculing, past **ridiculed**)*
to laugh and say unkind things about
someone or something ► *They
ridiculed his appearance.*

ridiculous /rɪ'dɪkjʊləs/ *adjective*
very silly ► *Don't be ridiculous – you
can't play outside in the rain.*

ridiculously /rɪ'dɪkjʊləslɪ/ *adverb*
too much, in a way that seems silly
► *Their clothes are ridiculously
expensive.*

riding /'raɪdɪŋ/ *noun (no plural)*
the sport of riding horses

rife /raɪf/ *adjective*
very common ► *Burglary is rife in
large cities.*

rifle /'raɪfəl/ *noun*
a long gun that you hold up against
your shoulder to fire

rift /rɪft/ *noun*
a serious disagreement between
people ► *The argument created a rift
between them.*

rig¹ /rɪg/ *verb (present participle
rigging, past **rigged**)*
to dishonestly influence the result of
an election, a competition, etc. ► *They
claim the election was rigged.*

rig² *noun*
a large structure that is used for
getting oil or gas from under the
bottom of the sea

right¹ /raɪt/ *adjective*
1 correct; good ► *Do you know the
right time?* ► *I don't think it's right to
let children eat too many sweets.*
► *She was right to tell the doctor.*
► *You were right about Mary – she's
very nice.* ► *"Is this Piccadilly Circus?"
"Yes, that's right."*
OPPOSITE: **wrong**
2 on the side of the hand that most
people write with ► *Take the next
right turn.* ► *He broke his right arm.*
OPPOSITE: **left**

right² *noun*
1 *(no plural)* what is fair and good
▶ *You must learn the difference
between right and wrong.*
OPPOSITE: **wrong**
2 what is or should be allowed by law
▶ *We must work for equal rights for
everyone.*
3 the side on the same side as the
hand most people write with ▶ *The
school is on the left of the road, and
his house is on the right.*
OPPOSITE (**3**): **left**

right³ *adverb*
1 correctly ▶ *I got all my sums right.*
OPPOSITE: **wrong**
2 towards the right side ▶ *Turn right
at the corner.*
OPPOSITE: **left**
3 completely; all the way ▶ *I read
right to the end of the book.*
4 directly; straight ▶ *That's our house
right in front of you.*
5 right away, right now without any
delay

right angle /'raɪt æŋgəl/ *noun*
an angle of 90°; the shape made when
two sides of a square meet at a corner

right-angled /'raɪt æŋgəld/ *adjective*
(used about TRIANGLES) having two
sides that join each other at 90°

rightful /'raɪtfəl/ *adjective*
according to what is legally and
morally right ▶ *He is the rightful
owner of the house.* (adverb:
rightfully)

right-hand /'raɪt hænd/ *adjective*
on or near your right side ▶ *Their
house is on the right-hand side of the
road.*

right-handed /,raɪt 'hændɪd/
adjective
using your right hand for things such
as writing
OPPOSITE: **left-handed**

rightly /'raɪtlɪ/ *adverb*
correctly or for a good reason ▶ *His*

opponents point out, quite rightly,
that government money is taxpayers'
money.

right of way /,raɪt əv 'weɪ/ *noun*
(no plural)
the right to drive into or across a road
before other vehicles

right-wing /,raɪt 'wɪŋ/ *adjective*
not liking changes in society, and
supporting CAPITALISM rather than
SOCIALISM ▶ *a right-wing pressure
group*

rigid /'rɪdʒɪd/ *adjective*
1 stiff and not easy to bend ▶ *rigid
cardboard*
2 not easy to change ▶ *rigid laws*
▶ *rigid ideas*

rigorous /'rɪgərəs/ *adjective*
done in a careful and thorough way
▶ *Some people are demanding more
rigorous safety checks.* (adverb:
rigorously)

rile /raɪl/ *verb (present participle
riling, past riled)*
to make someone very angry ▶ *It riled
her to think that Henry was lying.*

rim /rɪm/ *noun*
the outside edge of something ▶ *a
pattern round the rim of a plate*

rind /raɪnd/ *noun*
the hard, outer skin of fruit, cheese,
etc.

ring¹ /rɪŋ/ *noun*
1 a circle ▶ *The children sat in a ring
under the trees.*
2 a circular, metal band that you wear
on your finger ▶ *a wedding ring*
3 give someone a ring to telephone
someone ▶ *I'll give you a ring some
time tomorrow.*

ring² *verb (past tense **rang** /ræŋ/,
past participle **rung** /rʌŋ/)*
1 to make a sound like a bell ▶ *He
heard the telephone ringing.* ▶ *He
rang the bell, but no one came to the
door.*

R

2 ring off to end a telephone conversation ► *I'd better ring off now – there's someone at the door.*

3 ring someone up to telephone someone ► *She rang me up to say she'd be home late.*

ringleader /'rɪŋˌliːdə/ *noun*
a person who leads a group that is doing something illegal or wrong ► *Police arrested the two ringleaders last night.*

rink /rɪŋk/ *noun*
a specially prepared area where you can ICE-SKATE or ROLLER-SKATE

rinse¹ /rɪns/ *verb (present participle rinsing, past rinsed)*
to wash the soap out of something you have washed ► *I rinsed the jumpers three times.*

riot¹ /'raɪət/ *noun*
a noisy fight by an angry crowd of people ► *There was a riot when the workers were told they had lost their jobs.*

riot² *verb*
to fight in an angry crowd

riotous /'raɪətəs/ *adjective*
noisy and excited ► *riotous New Year's celebrations*

rip /rɪp/ *verb (present participle ripping, past ripped)*
to tear ► *As he climbed over the fence, he ripped his trousers on a nail.*

ripe /raɪp/ *adjective*
full-grown and ready to eat ► *The tomatoes aren't quite ripe yet.*

ripen /'raɪpən/ *verb*
to become ripe ► *As the tomatoes ripen, they change from green to red.*

rip-off /'rɪp ɒf/ *noun*
something that is too expensive, so you feel that you are being cheated ► *Some designer clothes are a rip-off.*

ripple¹ /'rɪpəl/ *noun*
a little wave

ripple² *verb (present participle rippling, past rippled)*
(used about water) to move in little waves

rise¹ /raɪz/ *verb (present participle rising, past tense rose /rəʊz/, past participle risen /'rɪzən/)*
to come or get up ► *Smoke rose from the chimney.* ► *The sun rose at 7 o'clock.* ► *The land rises steeply from the river.* ► *rising prices*

rise² *noun*
an increase ► *a rise in prices*

risen /'rɪzən/
the PAST PARTICIPLE of the verb **rise**

risk¹ /rɪsk/ *verb*
to take a chance of something bad happening or of losing something ► *He risked his life when he saved the child from the fire.* ► *You risk losing all your money.*

risk² *noun*
the chance of being in danger ► *the risks involved in starting up a business*

risky /'rɪski/ *adjective (riskier, riskiest)*
involving a chance that something bad will happen ► *Travelling alone can be risky.*

ritual¹ /'rɪtʃuəl/ *noun*
a ceremony or set of actions that is always done in the same way ► *The priest began the ritual of lighting the candles.*

ritual² *adjective*
done as part of a ritual ► *a ritual sacrifice*

rival /'raɪvəl/ *noun*
a person who tries to do better than another ► *Ann's a good swimmer too – we've always been rivals for the swimming prize.*

rivalry /'raɪvəlri/ *noun (plural rivalries)*
competition between people who want to do better than each other

➤ *There is great rivalry **between** the two sisters.*

river /'rɪvəʳ/ *noun*
a continuous flow of water along a course to the sea ➤ *The longest river in Africa is the Nile.*

rivet /'rɪvɪt/ *verb*
be riveted to be unable to stop looking at or listening to something because it is very interesting ➤ *We sat riveted **to** the TV news.*

road /rəʊd/ *noun*
1 a hard, wide track that people and traffic can use to go from one place to another ➤ *Where's the best place to cross the road?* ➤ *Which road do you live in?* ➤ *the road to Cambridge*
2 by road by car, bus, etc. and not on the train ➤ *transporting goods by road*

roadblock /'rəʊdblɒk/ *noun*
a place where the police or army have blocked the road ➤ *Police have set up roadblocks to stop the terrorists escaping.*

road rage /'rəʊd reɪdʒ/ *noun (no plural)*
sudden feelings of anger that cause drivers to start shouting at or attacking other drivers because of the way they are driving

roadside /'rəʊdsaɪd/ *noun (no plural)*
the land at the edge of a road ➤ *We ate our picnic at the roadside.*

road works /'rəʊd wɜːks/ *plural noun*
work that is being done to repair a road

roam /rəʊm/ *verb*
to wander ➤ *The visitors roamed around the town.*

roar¹ /rɔːʳ/ *verb*
to make a deep, angry noise, like a lion

roar² *noun*
a deep, angry noise such as the noise made by a lion

roaring /'rɔːrɪŋ/ *adjective*
(used about fires) burning with a lot of flames and heat

roast¹ /rəʊst/ *verb*
to cook food such as meat by baking it without water, or over a fire

roast² *adjective*
cooked by baking without water, or over a fire ➤ *It's roast chicken for dinner.*

rob /rɒb/ *verb (present participle **robbing**, past **robbed**)*
to take something from a person, a bank, or a shop when it is not yours ➤ *They planned to rob a bank.* ➤ *They robbed her of everything she possessed.*

Compare **rob** and **steal**. Someone **robs** a person or an organization, but **steals** things such as money: *I've been robbed!* ➤ *He was sent to prison for robbing a bank.* ➤ *Someone has stolen my bag.* ➤ *She stole the money.*

robber /'rɒbəʳ/ *noun*
a person who steals something from a person, a bank, or a shop ➤ *a bank robber*
COMPARE: **burglar, thief**

robbery /'rɒbəri/ *noun (plural **robberies**)*
the crime of stealing something from a person, a bank, or a shop ➤ *He was charged with robbery.* ➤ *a bank robbery*

robe /rəʊb/ *noun*
a long, loose piece of clothing that covers much of your body

robin /'rɒbɪn/ *noun*
a small, brown bird with a red chest

robot /'rəʊbɒt/ *noun*
a machine that does work instead of a person, for example making cars in a car factory

robust /rə'bʌst/ *adjective*
strong and not likely to become ill or

be damaged ▶ *a surprisingly robust 70-year-old*

rock¹ /rɒk/ *noun*
1 (no plural) stone that forms part of the earth
2 a large piece of stone that sticks up out of the ground or the sea ▶ *danger from falling rocks* ▶ *ships driven on to the rocks by a storm*
3 (no plural) popular modern dance music with a strong beat, which is played on electric instruments

rock² *verb*
to move regularly, first one way and then the opposite way ▶ *Waves were making the boat rock.* ▶ *a mother rocking her baby*

rock and roll /ˌrɒk ən ˈrəʊl/ *noun* (no plural)
ROCK 'N' ROLL

rock bottom /ˌrɒk ˈbɒtəm/ *noun*
hit rock bottom, reach rock bottom to become as bad as it is possible to be ▶ *His musical career has now hit rock bottom.*

rocket /ˈrɒkɪt/ *noun*
1 a machine driven into the air by burning gas, used to lift a weapon or a spaceship from the ground
2 a FIREWORK (=container which bursts with a loud noise and pretty lights) which goes up into the air

rocking chair /ˈrɒkɪŋ tʃeəʳ/ *noun*
a chair with two curved pieces of wood on the bottom that allow it to move backwards and forwards when you sit on it

rock 'n' roll /ˌrɒk ən ˈrəʊl/ *noun* (no plural)
a type of music with a strong, loud beat for dancing

rocky /ˈrɒkɪ/ *adjective* (**rockier, rockiest**)
covered with rocks ▶ *a rocky path*

rod /rɒd/ *noun*
a thin bar ▶ *a fishing rod*

rode /rəʊd/
the PAST TENSE of the verb **ride**

rodent /ˈrəʊdənt/ *noun*
an animal such as a rat or a rabbit that has long, sharp front teeth

rogue /rəʊg/ *noun*
a person who is bad or not honest

role /rəʊl/ *noun*
a character in a play or film ▶ *He played the role of the old king in our school play.*

role model /ˈrəʊl ˌmɒdl/ *noun*
a person you admire and try to copy ▶ *A father should be a good role model for his sons.*

roll¹ /rəʊl/ *verb*
1 to move along by turning over and over or on wheels ▶ *The ball rolled under the table.* ▶ *She rolled the bed out from the wall.*
2 to make a rounded shape by turning something over and over ▶ *Roll the carpet up so that it doesn't get damaged.* ▶ *Roll the paper – don't fold it.*

roll² *noun*
1 something rolled up into a long, round shape ▶ *a roll of cloth*
2 a small, round loaf of bread ▶ *a cheese roll* (=with cheese inside)

roll call /ˈrəʊl kɔːl/ *noun*
the act of reading out all the names on a list to check who is there ▶ *We must take a roll call to make sure everyone is here.*

Rollerblade /ˈrəʊləˌbleɪd/ *noun*
trademark
a boot with a single row of wheels fixed under it that you wear for SKATING

rollerblading /ˈrəʊləˌbleɪdɪŋ/ *noun* (no plural)
the sport or activity of SKATING when you are wearing Rollerblades ▶ *We went rollerblading in the park.*

roller coaster /ˈrəʊlə ˌkəʊstəʳ/ *noun*

a small railway which carries people up and down a steep track very fast for fun at FAIRS

roller skate /'rəʊlə skeɪt/ *noun*
a frame with wheels for fitting under a shoe

roller skating /'rəʊlə ˌskeɪtɪŋ/ *noun (no plural)*
the sport or activity of riding on roller skates

rolling /'rəʊlɪŋ/ *adjective*
be rolling in it to be very rich

ROM /rɒm/ *noun (no plural)*
READ-ONLY MEMORY; the part of a computer that stores permanent instructions and information

Roman¹ /'rəʊmən/ *adjective*
of or from ancient Rome ▶ *the Roman Empire*

Roman² *noun*
a citizen of the ancient empire or city of Rome

Roman Catholic /ˌrəʊmən 'kæθəlɪk/ *adjective*
belonging to the church whose head is the Pope

romance /rəʊ'mæns/ *noun*
1 a relationship between two people who are in love ▶ *a romance **between** a king and a poor girl*
2 a story about love

romantic /rəʊ'mæntɪk/ *adjective*
showing strong feelings of love

roof /ruːf/ *noun*
the top covering of a building, car, etc. ▶ *There's a cat on our roof.*

rooftop /'ruːftɒp/ *noun*
the top surface of a roof ▶ *Beyond the rooftops, she could see the bay.*

room /ruːm, rʊm/ *noun*
1 one of the parts of a house separated by walls and doors ▶ *The house had six rooms.*
2 (no plural) space ▶ *There isn't room for anyone else in the car.* ▶ *This desk takes up a lot of room.*

roommate /'ruːmˌmeɪt/ *noun*
a person that you share a room with, especially at college

roomy /'ruːmɪ/ *adjective* **(roomier, roomiest)**
having plenty of space inside ▶ *a roomy car*

rooster /'ruːstəʳ/ *noun*
a male chicken

root /ruːt/ *noun*
the part of a plant which grows down, and is usually below the ground

rope /rəʊp/ *noun*
a strong, thick cord
COMPARE: **string**

rose¹ /rəʊz/
the PAST TENSE of the verb **rise**

rose² *noun*
a beautiful and sweet-smelling flower

rosé /'rəʊzeɪ/ *noun (no plural)*
pink wine

roster /'rɒstəʳ/ *noun*
a list of people's names showing the jobs they must do and when they must do them
SAME MEANING: **rota**

rostrum /'rɒstrəm/ *noun*
a small, raised area that someone stands on, for example to make a speech

rosy /'rəʊzɪ/ *adjective* **(rosier, rosiest)**
pink ▶ *a baby with rosy cheeks*

rot /rɒt/ *verb (present participle **rotting**, past **rotted**)*
to go bad and soft because of being old or wet ▶ *The ripe fruit was left to rot.*
SAME MEANING: **decay**

rota /'rəʊtə/ *noun*
a list of people's names showing the jobs they must do and when they must do them
SAME MEANING: **roster**

rotate /rəʊ'teɪt/ *verb (present participle **rotating**, past **rotated**)*

R

to go round like a wheel ▶ *The Earth rotates round the sun.*

rotation /rəʊˈteɪʃən/ *noun*
a movement round and round like the movement of a wheel ▶ *the rotation of the Earth round the sun*

rote /rəʊt/ *noun*
learn something by rote to learn something by repeating it many times until you remember it

rotten /ˈrɒtn/ *adjective*
1 bad and soft because it is old or wet ▶ *rotten fish*
2 bad ▶ *The way he treated her was really rotten.* ▶ *a rotten cold*

rough /rʌf/ *adjective*
1 not even or smooth ▶ *a rough surface* ▶ *a rough mountain road* ▶ *rough skin*
OPPOSITE: **smooth**
2 rather violent; not gentle ▶ *He's too rough with the baby.* ▶ *a rough sea*

roughly /ˈrʌflɪ/ *adverb*
1 about ▶ *I had roughly 4 kilometres to go.*
SAME MEANING: **approximately**
2 not gently

round¹ /raʊnd/ *adjective*
like a ring or circle ▶ *a large, round plate*

round² (*also **around***) *adverb, preposition*
1 with a movement like a circle ▶ *The wheel is still spinning round.*
2 going in a circle, on all sides of something ▶ *She wore a belt round her dress.* ▶ *The children stood round the teacher.*
3 moving to face the opposite direction ▶ *Turn your chair round to face the front.*
4 to different places ▶ *They walked round the town for an hour.*
5 **round and round** going continuously in a circle ▶ *The dog ran round and round the tree.*

roundabout /ˈraʊndəbaʊt/ *noun*

1 a place where roads cross each other and the traffic goes round in a circle to join each road
2 a round machine on which children can ride sitting on plastic or wooden animals

rounded /ˈraʊndɪd/ *adjective*
curved, not pointed or sharp ▶ *a knife with a rounded end*

round trip /ˌraʊnd ˈtrɪp/ *noun*
a journey to a place and back again

roundup /ˈraʊndʌp/ *noun*
1 the act of bringing together a lot of people or animals, often by force ▶ *a roundup of criminals by the police*
2 a short description of the most important pieces of news ▶ *Here's a roundup of today's news.*

rousing /ˈraʊzɪŋ/ *adjective*
making people feel excited and eager to do something ▶ *The song has a rousing chorus.*

route /ruːt/ *noun*
a way which you plan or follow from one place to another ▶ *What's the shortest route from London to Edinburgh?*

routine /ruːˈtiːn/ *noun*
a set way of doing things ▶ *I arrive at 9 o'clock, teach until 12.30, and then eat. That's my morning routine.*

row¹ /rəʊ/ *noun*
a line ▶ *a row **of** pots on a shelf*

row² /raʊ/ *noun*
a noisy, angry quarrel ▶ *The two men were having a row.*

row³ /rəʊ/ *verb*
to move OARS through water to make a boat move

rowdy /ˈraʊdɪ/ *adjective* (**rowdier, rowdiest**)
behaving in a noisy and uncontrolled way ▶ *a rowdy gang*

rowing boat /ˈrəʊɪŋ bəʊt/ *noun*
a small boat that is moved through the water using OARS

royal /'rɔɪəl/ *adjective*
of, belonging to, or like, a king or
queen ➤ *the royal family*

royalty /'rɔɪəltɪ/ *noun (no plural)*
members of the family of a king or
queen

RSVP /ˌɑːr es viː' piː/
an abbreviation that is written on
invitations to ask someone to reply

rub /rʌb/ *verb (present participle*
rubbing, *past* **rubbed**)
1 to move something back and
forward over something else ➤ *She
rubbed her shoes with a cloth to
make them shine.* ➤ *She rubbed
cream into her hands.*
2 rub something out to remove
something written in pencil or chalk
by rubbing it

rubber /'rʌbəʳ/ *noun*
1 *(no plural)* a soft material that
comes from a tree and can be
stretched. **Rubber** is used for making
things such as car tyres.
2 a small piece of this material used
for getting rid of pencil marks

rubber band /ˌrʌbə 'bænd/ *noun*
a piece of rubber in a ring shape that
is used to fasten things together

rubbish /'rʌbɪʃ/ *noun (no plural)*
1 things that you do not want and will
throw away ➤ *The cupboard was full
of old papers, broken toys, and other
rubbish.*
COMPARE: **junk**
2 anything silly ➤ *I thought that story
was rubbish.*
SAME MEANING **(2)**: **nonsense**

rubble /'rʌbəl/ *noun (no plural)*
broken stones or bricks from a
building that has been destroyed
➤ *After the explosion, the house was
just a pile of rubble.*

ruby /'ruːbɪ/ *noun (plural* **rubies**)
a dark red stone often used in rings
and other jewellery

rucksack /'rʌksæk/ *noun*
a large bag that you carry on your
back
SAME MEANING: **backpack**

rudder /'rʌdəʳ/ *noun*
a flat part at the back of a boat or
plane, that is turned in order to
change direction

rude /ruːd/ *adjective*
saying or doing unpleasant things
that are not polite or kind ➤ *It's rude
to say you don't like the food.*
➤ *Don't be so rude **to** your father.*
➤ *She was rude about my old car.*
OPPOSITE: **polite**

rudimentary /ˌruːdɪ'mentərɪ/
adjective
very simple and basic ➤ *I have only a
rudimentary knowledge of grammar.*

ruffle /'rʌfəl/ *verb (present participle*
ruffling, *past* **ruffled**)
to move something that was smooth
and make it uneven or untidy ➤ *He
gently ruffled my hair.*

rug /rʌg/ *noun*
1 a thick floor mat
COMPARE: **carpet**
2 a large, thick cloth to wrap round
you to keep you warm

rugby /'rʌgbɪ/ *noun (no plural)*
a rough ball game played by two
teams with an egg-shaped ball

rugged /'rʌgɪd/ *adjective*
rough and wild; full of rocks ➤ *rugged
country*

ruin¹ /'ruːɪn/ *verb*
to destroy something ➤ *She poured
water all over my painting and ruined
it.* ➤ *a ruined castle*

ruin² *noun*
1 a building that has been almost
destroyed ➤ *There was a ruin on the
top of the hill.*
2 ruins *plural noun* the remaining
parts of a destroyed building ➤ *We
saw the ruins **of** the church.*

R

rule¹ /ruːl/ *verb (present participle **ruling**, past **ruled**)*
to have power in a country and control it ▶ *The king ruled for 30 years.*

rule² *noun*
1 a law; something that tells you what you must or must not do ▶ *It's against the rules to pick up the ball.*
2 *(no plural)* government or control ▶ *a country under military rule*

ruled /ruːld/ *adjective*
(used about paper) having lines printed across it for you to write on

ruler /ˈruːləʳ/ *noun*
1 a person who governs a country
2 a piece of wood, plastic, or metal with a straight edge used for measuring and for drawing straight lines

ruling¹ /ˈruːlɪŋ/ *noun*
an official decision that is made by a law court ▶ *The company is refusing to accept the court's ruling.*

ruling² *adjective*
having the most power in a country or an organization ▶ *the ruling class*

rum /rʌm/ *noun*
1 *(no plural)* a strong alcoholic drink made from sugar
2 a glass of this drink ▶ *Can I have two rums, please?*

rumble /ˈrʌmbəl/ *verb (present participle **rumbling**, past **rumbled**)*
to make a long, low noise, like thunder in the distance

rumour /ˈruːməʳ/ *noun*
something that people tell each other but that may not be true ▶ *I heard a rumour that the headmaster is leaving.*

rumoured /ˈruːməd/ *adjective*
if something is rumoured to be true, people are saying that it may be true but no one is sure ▶ *The band is rumoured to be splitting up.*

rump /rʌmp/ *noun*
the part of an animal that is at the top of its back legs

run¹ /rʌn/ *verb (present participle **running**, past tense **ran** /ræn/, past participle **run**)*
1 to move on your legs very quickly ▶ *He ran across the road.*
2 to pass or go somewhere ▶ *The road runs along the river bank.*
3 (used about a bus or train) to travel somewhere at an arranged time ▶ *Trains run every hour.*
4 (used about machines) to work ▶ *Don't touch the engine while it's running.*
5 to make something work ▶ *We don't have enough money to run the hospital properly.*
6 run away to go away from a place because you are unhappy ▶ *He ran away **from** home when he was 13.*
7 run someone down to knock someone down with a car and hurt them
8 run into someone or something to hit someone or something with a car or other vehicle that you are driving ▶ *I nearly ran into a lamppost.*
9 run off to run away ▶ *They took her handbag and ran off.*
10 run out of something to no longer have enough of something ▶ *I've run out of petrol.*

run² *noun*
1 an act of running ▶ *I always go for a run before breakfast.*
2 a journey by car or train ▶ *We had quite a good run – it only took us 50 minutes.*
3 a point in the game of cricket

runaway¹ /ˈrʌnəweɪ/ *adjective*
1 moving fast and out of control ▶ *a runaway train*
2 happening quickly and in a way that is difficult to control ▶ *Their first record was a runaway success.*

runaway² *noun*
a young person or child who has left home without telling anyone

rundown /ˈrʌndaʊn/ *noun*
a quick description or explanation ▶ *I gave him a rundown on what had happened.*

run-down /ˌrʌn ˈdaʊn/ *adjective*
1 in very bad condition ▶ *a run-down block of flats*
2 feeling tired and ill ▶ *He's been feeling run-down lately.*

rung¹ /rʌŋ/
the PAST PARTICIPLE of the verb **ring**

rung² *noun*
one of the bars in a ladder

runner /ˈrʌnəʳ/ *noun*
a person who runs, especially for sport or exercise

runner-up /ˌrʌnər ˈʌp/ *noun (plural runners-up)*
the person or team that finishes second in a competition

running /ˈrʌnɪŋ/ *adjective*
(used about water) flowing continuously whenever you need it in your home ▶ *a village house with hot and cold running water*

runny /ˈrʌni/ *adjective (runnier, runniest)*
more liquid than usual ▶ *This paint is too runny to use on the ceiling.*
OPPOSITE: **thick**

runway /ˈrʌnweɪ/ *noun*
a long, wide road that planes use when they are landing or taking off

rural /ˈrʊərəl/ *adjective*
in, of, or belonging to the country, not the town ▶ *Crops are grown in rural areas.*

rush¹ /rʌʃ/ *verb*
to hurry ▶ *She rushed into the room to tell us the news.*

rush² *noun (no plural)*
a hurry ▶ *I can't stop – I'm in a rush.*

rushed /rʌʃt/ *adjective*
1 done too quickly and without enough care ▶ *Your work always looks rushed and badly presented.*

2 rushed off your feet very busy
▶ *I've been rushed off my feet all day.*

rush hour /ˈrʌʃ aʊəʳ/ *noun*
the time of day when there is a lot of traffic because people are going to and from work ▶ *If you leave by 7, you should miss the rush hour.*

rust¹ /rʌst/ *noun (no plural)*
a red-brown substance that forms on iron when it has been wet ▶ *an old car covered in rust*

rust² *verb*
to become covered with rust ▶ *If you leave your metal tools outside in the rain, they will rust.*

rustle¹ /ˈrʌsəl/ *verb (present participle rustling, past rustled)*
to make a light sound like the sound of paper being moved ▶ *The leaves rustled in the wind.*

rustle² *noun (no plural)*
a light sound like the sound of paper being moved ▶ *the rustle of leaves*

rusty /ˈrʌsti/ *adjective (rustier, rustiest)*
covered with rust ▶ *a rusty old car*

rut /rʌt/ *noun*
a deep, narrow track made by a wheel in soft ground

ruthless /ˈruːθləs/ *adjective*
cruel and not caring about other people ▶ *The judge described Marshall as a ruthless killer. (adverb: ruthlessly)*

rye /raɪ/ *noun (no plural)*
a type of grain that is used for making bread and WHISKY

Ss

S
a short way of writing the words
south or **southern**

's /z, s/
1 is ► *What's your name?*
2 has ► *She's gone.*
3 used to show who is the owner of something ► *Those are Tom's books* (=those books belong to Tom).

When there is more than one owner, write **s'**, not **'s**: *the boy's books* (=1 boy) ► *the boys' books* (=several boys).

sabotage /'sæbətɑːʒ/ *verb (present participle **sabotaging**, past **sabotaged**)*
to secretly damage or destroy something ► *He tried to sabotage her plans.*

sachet /'sæʃeɪ/ *noun*
a small packet containing a liquid or powder ► *a sachet of shampoo*

sack¹ /sæk/ *noun*
1 a large bag made of thick, strong material ► *a sack of rice*
2 **get the sack** to be dismissed from your job

sack² *verb*
to dismiss someone from their job

sacred /'seɪkrɪd/ *adjective*
connected with God or religion ► *A church is a sacred building.*

sacrifice¹ /'sækrɪfaɪs/ *noun*
1 an animal or a person that is killed and offered to a god
2 something important to you that you give up for some good purpose ► *Her parents made many sacrifices so that she could study abroad.*

sacrifice² *verb (present participle **sacrificing**, past **sacrificed**)*
1 to kill an animal or a person and offer them to a god
2 to give up something important for a good purpose ► *She sacrificed her job to look after her children.*

sad /sæd/ *adjective (**sadder, saddest**)*
unhappy ► *She felt very sad that the holiday was ending.*

sadden /'sædn/ *verb*
to make someone feel unhappy or disappointed ► *They were shocked and saddened by his death.*

saddle /'sædl/ *noun*
1 a seat which you put on a horse's back
2 the seat on a bicycle or motorcycle

sadly /'sædlɪ/ *adverb*
1 in a sad way ► *She smiled sadly.*
2 a word used to say that you are sorry or disappointed about something ► *Sadly, the museum will have to close next year.*

safari /sə'fɑːrɪ/ *noun*
a journey to look at or hunt wild animals, especially in Africa

safe¹ /seɪf/ *adjective*
1 not dangerous or harmful ► *This town is very safe at night.* ► *Are these toys safe for young children?*
2 not in danger ► *Will you be safe travelling by yourself?*
(adverb: **safely***)*

safe² *noun*
a strong box or cupboard with a lock, for keeping important things safely

safety /'seɪftɪ/ *noun (no plural)*
a safe place ► *They managed to escape the fire and run to safety.*

safety belt /'seɪftɪ ˌbelt/ *noun*
a belt fixed to a seat in a car or an aircraft which helps to protect you in an accident
SAME MEANING: **seat belt**

safety pin /'seɪftɪ pɪn/ *noun*
a bent, metal pin with a cover over the point, used for fastening cloth

sag /sæg/ *verb (present participle **sagging**, past **sagged**)*
to hang down heavily ► *The shelf sagged in the middle because the books on it were too heavy.*

saga /'sɑːgə/ *noun*
a long, complicated story or a description of a long series of events

S

sage /seɪdʒ/ *noun (no plural)*
a plant with grey-green leaves that you use in cooking

said /sed/
the PAST TENSE and PAST PARTICIPLE of the verb **say**

sail¹ /seɪl/ *noun*
a large cloth used to catch the wind and make a boat move

sail² *verb*
1 to travel on water ▸ *His ship sails today.*
2 to direct a boat with sails ▸ *She sailed the boat without any help.*

sailing /'seɪlɪŋ/ *noun (no plural)*
the sport or activity of sailing boats

sailor /'seɪlə^r/ *noun*
a person who works on a ship, especially as a member of a navy

saint /seɪnt/ *noun*
a person who has lived a very good and religious life

sake /seɪk/ *noun*
1 for someone's sake in order to help someone or make them happy ▸ *She only stays with her husband for the sake of her children.*
2 for goodness sake something you say when you are annoyed ▸ *Oh, for goodness sake, hurry up!*

salad /'sæləd/ *noun*
a dish of cold, usually raw, vegetables

salami /sə'lɑːmɪ/ *noun*
a large SAUSAGE with a strong taste that is cut into thin pieces and eaten cold

salary /'sælərɪ/ *noun (plural salaries)*
a fixed amount of money paid to someone every month for the job they do
SAME MEANING: **pay**

sale /seɪl/ *noun*
1 selling ▸ *He got £30 from the sale of his drawing.*

2 a time when shops sell things at lower prices ▸ *The shoe shop is having a sale this week.*

salesman /'seɪlzmən/ *noun (plural salesmen /-mən/)*
a man whose job is to sell things

salesperson /'seɪlz,pɜːsən/ *noun (plural salespeople /-,piːpəl/)*
a person whose job is to sell things

saleswoman /'seɪlz,wʊmən/ *noun (plural saleswomen /-,wɪmɪn/)*
a woman whose job is to sell things

saliva /sə'laɪvə/ *noun (no plural)*
the liquid that you produce naturally in your mouth

salmon /'sæmən/ *noun (plural salmon)*
a large river and sea fish that you can eat

salon /'sælɒn/ *noun*
a place where you can get your hair cut, have BEAUTY TREATMENTS, etc. ▸ *a beauty salon*

saloon /sə'luːn/ *noun*
1 a place where alcoholic drinks were sold and drunk in the US in the 19th century
2 a car that has a separate enclosed space for bags, cases, etc. ▸ *a four-door saloon*

salt /sɔːlt/ *noun (no plural)*
a white chemical found in sea water, rocks, etc., which you can put on food to make it taste better

salty /'sɔːltɪ/ *adjective (saltier, saltiest)*
tasting of salt, or having salt in

salute¹ /sə'luːt/ *verb (present participle saluting, past saluted)*
to hold your hand against the side of your head as a sign of respect ▸ *The soldier saluted his officer.*

salute² *noun*
a sign made by holding your hand against the side of your head, done out of respect to someone, especially in the army, etc.

S

salvage /'sælvɪdʒ/ verb (present participle **salvaging**, past **salvaged**)
to save something from a situation in which other things have been damaged or lost ▶ They managed to salvage a few of their things from the fire.

same /seɪm/ adjective, pronoun
1 the same alike in one or more ways ▶ Your pen is the same as mine. ▶ They all look the same to me.
OPPOSITE: **different**
2 exactly the thing or things spoken or written about; not any other ▶ We go to the same school.

sample /'sɑ:mpəl/ noun
a small part of something which shows what the whole thing is like ▶ a sample of his work ▶ a blood sample

sanction /'sæŋkʃən/ verb
to officially allow something to happen ▶ The UN refused to sanction the use of force.

sanctions /'sæŋkʃənz/ plural noun
laws that stop trade with another country, as a punishment when the country has behaved badly ▶ They agreed to end the sanctions against China.

sanctuary /'sæŋktʃʊərɪ/ noun (plural **sanctuaries**)
a place where people or animals are protected from danger ▶ The refugees sought sanctuary in a nearby church. ▶ a bird sanctuary

sand /sænd/ noun (no plural)
fine, white or yellow grains, made of rock, often found next to the sea and in deserts

sandal /'sændl/ noun
an open shoe that you wear in hot weather

sandcastle /'sænd,kɑ:səl/ noun
a pile of sand in the shape of a castle, that children make on the beach

sandpaper /'sænd,peɪpəʳ/ noun (no plural)
strong, rough paper that you rub on a wooden surface in order to make it smooth

sandwich /'sændwɪtʃ/ noun (plural **sandwiches**)
two pieces of bread put together with something else in between them ▶ I made a chicken sandwich.

sandy /'sændɪ/ adjective (**sandier, sandiest**)
covered with sand ▶ a sandy shore

sane /seɪn/ adjective
having a healthy mind and able to think clearly and make decisions
OPPOSITE: **insane**

sang /sæŋ/
the PAST TENSE of the verb **sing**

sanity /'sænɪtɪ/ noun (no plural)
the ability to think normally and clearly ▶ Kate was having doubts about her own sanity.

sank /sæŋk/
the PAST TENSE of the verb **sink**

Santa Claus /'sæntə klɔːz/ (also **Santa** /'sæntə/) noun
an old man who children think brings them presents at Christmas. He wears red clothes and has a long, white beard.
SAME MEANING: **Father Christmas**

sap /sæp/ noun (no plural)
the liquid inside a plant which feeds it

sapphire /'sæfaɪəʳ/ noun
a blue stone used in making rings, other jewellery, etc.

sarcasm /'sɑːkæzəm/ noun (no plural)
a way of speaking or writing in which you say the opposite of what you mean in order to make an unkind joke or to offend someone ▶ "I'm glad you could make it," said Jim, with heavy sarcasm.

sarcastic /sɑːˈkæstɪk/ *adjective*
unkind and intending to offend
someone ➤ *sarcastic remarks*

sardine /sɑːˈdiːn/ *noun*
a small fish that is often used for food

sari /ˈsɑːrɪ/ *noun*
a type of loose dress worn especially
by Indian women

sash /sæʃ/ *noun (plural sashes)*
a long piece of cloth that you wear
around your waist or across one
shoulder ➤ *a red, satin sash*

sat /sæt/
the PAST TENSE and PAST PARTICIPLE of the
verb **sit**

Satan /ˈseɪtn/ *noun*
the DEVIL

satchel /ˈsætʃəl/ *noun*
a small bag which you can hang over
one shoulder. It is often used by
schoolchildren.

satellite /ˈsætəlaɪt/ *noun*
1 something which moves round the
Earth or another PLANET ➤ *the moon is
a satellite of the Earth.*
2 an object sent into space to receive
signals from one part of the world
and send them to another ➤ *The
television broadcast came from
America by satellite.*

satellite dish /ˈsætəlaɪt ˌdɪʃ/ *noun
(plural satellite dishes)*
a large, circular piece of metal on a
building, that receives television or
radio signals from a satellite

satin /ˈsætɪn/ *noun (no plural)*
a type of smooth, shiny cloth ➤ *a red
satin dress*

satire /ˈsætaɪər/ *noun*
an amusing way of talking or writing
about someone or something,
especially so that people see their
faults ➤ *The play is a satire on
modern American life.*

satirical /səˈtɪrɪkəl/ *adjective*
using satire ➤ *a satirical TV show*

satisfaction /ˌsætɪsˈfækʃən/ *noun (no
plural)*
a feeling of pleasure ➤ *I get great
satisfaction from working with
children.* ➤ *job satisfaction*

satisfactory /ˌsætɪsˈfæktəri/ *adjective*
good enough ➤ *Is your room
satisfactory, sir?*
OPPOSITE: **unsatisfactory**

satisfied /ˈsætɪsfaɪd/ *adjective*
pleased; happy ➤ *My father is never
satisfied with my exam results.* ➤ *a
satisfied customer*
OPPOSITE: **dissatisfied**

satisfy /ˈsætɪsfaɪ/ *verb (past satisfied)*
to be enough for someone; to make
someone pleased and happy

satisfying /ˈsætɪsfaɪɪŋ/ *adjective*
making you feel pleased and happy,
especially because you have got what
you wanted ➤ *a satisfying career*

satsuma /sætˈsuːmə/ *noun*
a sweet, juicy fruit like a small orange

saturate /ˈsætʃəreɪt/ *verb (present
participle saturating, past saturated)*
to make something completely wet
➤ *The back of his shirt was saturated
with sweat.*

Saturday /ˈsætədeɪ, -dɪ/ *noun*
the seventh day of the week

sauce /sɔːs/ *noun*
a liquid that you put on food to
improve its taste ➤ *cheese sauce*

saucepan /ˈsɔːspən/ *noun*
a pan with a handle for cooking
things over heat

saucer /ˈsɔːsər/ *noun*
a small plate that a cup stands on

sauna /ˈsɔːnə/ *noun*
a room that is made very hot with
steam, where people sit because it is
considered healthy

saunter /ˈsɔːntər/ *verb*
to walk in a slow and confident way
➤ *He sauntered up to her and
grinned.*

sausage /'sɒsɪdʒ/ *noun*
a mixture of finely cut meat cooked inside a long, thin skin

savage /'sævɪdʒ/ *adjective*
wild and fierce ➤ *savage fighting*

save /seɪv/ *verb (present participle saving, past saved)*
1 to help someone or something to be safe ➤ *I saved the animals **from** the flood.* ➤ *I was drowning, but Peter saved my life.*
2 to keep something, especially money, so that you can use it some other time ➤ *How much money have you saved this month?* ➤ *We're saving to buy a car.* ➤ *Don't drink all the orange juice; save some **for** tomorrow.*
3 to use less of something; not to waste something ➤ *We'll save time if we go this way.*

savings /'seɪvɪŋz/ *plural noun*
money that you keep without spending ➤ *He used his savings to buy a bicycle.*

saviour /'seɪvjəʳ/ *noun*
a person who saves others from danger or evil

savoury /'seɪvəri/ *adjective*
(used about food) having the taste of meat, cheese, vegetables, etc. rather than something sweet ➤ *a savoury snack*

saw¹ /sɔː/
the PAST TENSE of the verb **see**

saw² *noun*
a tool with a blade with metal teeth, used for cutting through wood or metal

saw³ *verb (past participle sawn /sɔːn/)*
to cut something with a saw ➤ *He sawed the wood into three pieces.*

saxophone /'sæksəfəʊn/ *noun*
a metal musical instrument that you blow into

say /seɪ/ *verb (past said /sed/)*
to speak words ➤ *He said that he wanted to go to town.* ➤ *"I'm going to town," he said.* ➤ *Don't believe anything she says; she's a liar.*

Compare **say** and **tell** in these sentences: *She said something.* ➤ *She told me something.* ➤ *He said he was busy.* ➤ *He told me he was busy.* **Say** never has a person as its object (to say something **to somebody**), but **tell** often has a person as its object (to tell **somebody** something).

saying /'seɪ-ɪŋ/ *noun*
a wise statement that people use often ➤ *"Every dog has his day" is a saying meaning that everyone gets a chance to do well.*

scab /skæb/ *noun*
a hard covering of skin which grows over a wound

scaffolding /'skæfəldɪŋ/ *noun (no plural)*
a framework of metal bars fixed to a building for builders to stand on while they work

scald /skɔːld/ *verb*
to burn something with steam or boiling liquid ➤ *She scalded herself with the hot milk.*

scale /skeɪl/ *noun*
1 a set of marks on a measuring instrument ➤ *I need a ruler with a metric scale.*
2 the way distances or sizes are shown on a map, a model, etc. ➤ *The scale of this map is one centimetre to the kilometre* (=on this map, every centimetre represents one kilometre of country).
3 a set of musical notes going up or down in order
4 one of the small, round pieces of hard, dry skin that cover the body of a fish, snake, etc.

scales /skeɪlz/ *plural noun*
a machine for weighing things or people

scalp /skælp/ *noun*
the skin and hair on top of your head

scaly /ˈskeɪlɪ/ *adjective (scalier, scaliest)*
(used about animals) covered with small, round pieces of hard, dry skin ➤ *Birds have tough, scaly skin on their legs.*

scamper /ˈskæmpəʳ/ *verb*
to run lightly and quickly ➤ *The little dog scampered along the road.*

scan /skæn/ *verb (present participle scanning, past scanned)*
1 to read something very quickly ➤ *She scanned the lists, looking for her name.*
2 to use a special machine called a scanner to copy a picture, printed text, etc. into a computer ➤ *Once the image has been scanned, you can make it bigger or smaller.*

scandal /ˈskændl/ *noun*
something which causes a lot of people to talk and show that they do not approve ➤ *There was a huge scandal when we found out that the local doctor had been arrested.*

scanner /ˈskænəʳ/ *noun*
a piece of equipment that copies a picture, printed text, etc. into a computer

scar¹ /skɑːʳ/ *noun*
a mark left on your skin by an old wound or cut

scar² *verb (present participle scarring, past scarred)*
to leave a mark on your skin ➤ *His face was badly scarred after the car accident.*

scarce /skeəs/ *adjective*
not often seen or found; uncommon ➤ *That bird has become scarce in this country.* ➤ *Food became scarce during the war.*

scarcely /ˈskeəslɪ/ *adverb*
hardly; not very much ➤ *She scarcely said a word all evening.*

scare¹ /skeəʳ/ *verb (present participle scaring, past scared)*
to make someone afraid ➤ *What was that noise? It scared me.*
SAME MEANING: **frighten**

scare² *noun*
something sudden or unexpected that makes you afraid ➤ *You gave me a scare; I didn't know you were in the house.*

scarecrow /ˈskeəkrəʊ/ *noun*
a wooden figure dressed in old clothes and put in a field of crops to make birds go away

scared /skeəd/ *adjective*
afraid ➤ *We were scared that something terrible might happen.* ➤ *She's always been scared of flying.* ➤ *I was scared stiff* (=very scared) *that someone would find us.*
SAME MEANING: **frightened**

scarf /skɑːf/ *noun (plural scarves /skɑːvz/)*
a piece of cloth that you wear round your neck or head to keep warm or to make your clothes look more attractive

scarlet /ˈskɑːlət/ *noun, adjective*
bright red ➤ *scarlet drops of blood*

scarves /skɑːvz/
the plural of **scarf**

scary /ˈskeərɪ/ *adjective (scarier, scariest)*
frightening ➤ *It's a really scary film.*

scatter /ˈskætəʳ/ *verb*
1 to make things or people go in different directions ➤ *The farmer scattered the corn in the yard for the hens.*
2 to go quickly in different directions ➤ *The crowd scattered when it began to rain.*

scene /siːn/ *noun*
1 everything that you can see in a

S

particular place ▶ *He painted a lovely country scene, with trees and a river.*
2 the place where something happens ▶ *a crowd at the scene of the accident*
3 a short part of a play that shows what happens in one place ▶ *This play is divided into three acts, and each act has three scenes.*

scenery /'si:nərɪ/ *noun (no plural)*
1 the things that you see around you in the country ▶ *The scenery in the mountains is very beautiful.*
2 the painted pictures at the back of a stage

scenic /'si:nɪk/ *adjective*
having beautiful views of the countryside ▶ *If you have time, take the scenic coastal route.*

scent /sent/ *noun*
1 a nice smell ▶ *the scent of flowers*
2 (*no plural*) liquid with a nice smell which you put on your skin ▶ *What a lovely smell! Are you wearing scent?*
SAME MEANING (**1** and **2**): **perfume**

scented /'sentɪd/ *adjective*
having a nice smell ▶ *scented bath oil*

sceptical /'skeptɪkəl/ *adjective*
doubting whether something is true or right ▶ *Many doctors are sceptical about this new treatment.*

schedule /'ʃedjuːl/ *noun*
1 a list of times when buses or trains should come
2 a plan of when work is to be done ▶ *The schedule shows the book will take a year to finish.*

scheme¹ /skiːm/ *noun*
a plan ▶ *He thought of a scheme to get some money.*

scheme² *verb (present participle* **scheming,** *past* **schemed)**
to make plans, especially ones which are not honest ▶ *They schemed to steal money from the bank.*

scholar /'skɒləʳ/ *noun*
1 a person who knows a lot because they have studied a lot and read a lot of books
2 a clever student who has been given money so that they can continue to study

scholarship /'skɒləʃɪp/ *noun*
money given to a clever student so that they can continue to study ▶ *She won a scholarship to Cambridge.*

school /skuːl/ *noun*
a place where children go to learn ▶ *I went to school in England.* ▶ *I'm learning to play the piano at school.*

schoolboy /'skuːlbɔɪ/ *noun*
a boy who goes to school

schoolchild /'skuːltʃaɪld/ *noun (plural* **schoolchildren** /-,tʃɪldrən/*)*
a child who goes to school

schooldays /'skuːldeɪz/ *plural noun*
the time during your life when you go to school

schoolgirl /'skuːlgɜːl/ *noun*
a girl who goes to school

schoolteacher /'skuːl,tiːtʃəʳ/ *noun*
a teacher in a school

science /'saɪəns/ *noun (no plural)*
the study of nature and the way things in the world are made or behave

science fiction /,saɪəns 'fɪkʃən/ *noun (no plural)*
books and films about imaginary things that happen in the future or in other parts of the universe

scientific /,saɪən'tɪfɪk/ *adjective*
of or about science ▶ *scientific studies*

scientist /'saɪəntɪst/ *noun*
a person who studies or practises science

sci-fi /'saɪ faɪ/ *noun (no plural)*
SCIENCE FICTION

scissors /'sɪzəz/ *plural noun*
an instrument for cutting with two

blades joined together ▶ *a pair of scissors*

scoff /skɒf/ *verb*
to criticize and make fun of a person or an idea that you think is stupid ▶ *He scoffed at my suggestions for improving the system.*

scold /skəʊld/ *verb*
to tell a child in an angry way that they have done wrong ▶ *My mother scolded me when I dropped the plates.*

scoop /skuːp/ *verb*
to take out something with your hands or with a spoon ▶ *She scooped flour out of the bag.*

scooter /ˈskuːtər/ *noun*
1 a small, light motorcycle
2 a board with two small wheels and a handle, which children ride by having one foot on the board and pushing on the ground with the other one

scope /skəʊp/ *noun*
the range of subjects that a piece of work deals with or discusses ▶ *Looking at the airline's safety records will be within the scope of this inquiry.*

scorch /skɔːtʃ/ *verb*
to burn something lightly, usually so that there is a brown mark ▶ *I scorched my dress with the iron.*

scorching /ˈskɔːtʃɪŋ/ *adjective*
(used about the weather) very hot ▶ *It's been a scorching summer.*

score¹ /skɔːr/ *noun*
1 the marks or points that you get in a game or test ▶ *The score at the end of the football game was 4–1 (=four points for one team, one point for the other team).*
2 **keep the score** to write down or remember how many points each person or team has

score² *verb (present participle scoring, past scored)*

1 to win points in a game or test ▶ *How many points did you score?*
2 to keep a note of the points which each person or team has ▶ *Will you score for us?*

scoreboard /ˈskɔːbɔːd/ *noun*
a large sign showing the score of a game

scorer /ˈskɔːrər/ *noun*
a person who scores a point in a game or competition ▶ *the club's top goal scorer*

scorn¹ /skɔːn/ *verb*
to think that someone or something is worthless; not to respect someone or something

scorn² *noun (no plural)*
lack of respect ▶ *Scientists treated the findings with scorn.*

scorpion /ˈskɔːpɪən/ *noun*
a small creature which stings with its tail

Scotch /skɒtʃ/ *noun (no plural)*
a strong, alcoholic drink made in Scotland ▶ *a bottle of Scotch*
SAME MEANING: **whisky**

scour /skaʊər/ *verb*
to search for something very carefully ▶ *I scoured the library for more information.*

scout /skaʊt/ *(also boy scout) noun*
a boy who belongs to an association which teaches boys to do good and useful things

scowl¹ /skaʊl/ *verb*
to look in an angry way at someone ▶ *The teacher scowled at me because I was late.*

scowl² *noun*
an angry look on someone's face ▶ *Sam had a dreadful scowl on his face.*

scramble /ˈskræmbəl/ *verb (present participle scrambling, past scrambled)*

S

to move over something quickly but with difficulty ▶ *The children scrambled up the hill.*

scrambled eggs /ˌskræmbəld 'egz/ *plural noun*
eggs mixed together with milk and cooked

scrap /skræp/ *noun*
a small piece ▶ *a scrap of paper*

scrapbook /'skræpbʊk/ *noun*
a book of empty pages in which you can keep pictures and pieces of writing that you collect

scrape /skreɪp/ *verb (present participle scraping, past scraped)*
to remove something by rubbing it off with a hard instrument ▶ *Scrape the mud off your shoes with this knife.*

scratch¹ /skrætʃ/ *verb*
1 to make marks with something sharp ▶ *The stick scratched the side of the car.*
2 to rub your nails lightly over a part of your body ▶ *Don't scratch those mosquito bites; they'll feel worse.*

scratch² *noun (plural scratches)*
a mark or small wound made by something sharp ▶ *a scratch on her hand*

scrawl /skrɔːl/ *verb*
to write something in a careless or an untidy way ▶ *She scrawled her phone number on the back of an envelope.*

scream¹ /skriːm/ *verb*
to give a loud, high cry, usually because of fear or excitement ▶ *She screamed with terror.*

scream² *noun*
a loud, high cry of fear or excitement

screech¹ /skriːtʃ/ *verb*
to make a loud, high, unpleasant noise ▶ *The car screeched round the corner at top speed.*

screech² *noun (plural screeches)*
a loud, high, unpleasant noise

screen /skriːn/ *noun*
1 a flat, square surface on which information or pictures can be shown ▶ *a television screen* ▶ *a computer screen*
2 a covered frame used to stop someone or something being seen ▶ *The doctor asked him to undress behind the screen.*

screw¹ /skruː/ *noun*
a thing like a nail which you can fix into something by turning it round and round

screw² *verb*
1 to fasten or fix something to a place with screws ▶ *He screwed the mirror to the wall.*
2 to fasten or tighten something by turning it round and round ▶ *Screw the lid on tightly.*

screwdriver /'skruːˌdraɪvəʳ/ *noun*
a tool with a narrow blade with which you can fix a screw into something

scribble /'skrɪbəl/ *verb (present participle scribbling, past scribbled)*
to write quickly and carelessly ▶ *I'll scribble a note to say what time we'll be home.*

script /skrɪpt/ *noun*
1 the words of a speech, play, film, etc. that have been written down ▶ *He began his career writing scripts for daytime TV shows.*
2 the letters used to write a language ▶ *Arabic script*

scripture /'skrɪptʃəʳ/ *noun*
a piece of old religious writing

scroll /skrəʊl/ *verb*
to move information up or down a computer screen so that you can read it ▶ *Scroll down until you reach the end of the file.*

scrounge /skraʊndʒ/ *verb (present participle scrounging, past scrounged)*
to get something you want by asking someone to give it to you, instead of buying it yourself ▶ *I scrounged a*

S

cigarette **off** the girl sitting next to me.

scrub /skrʌb/ *verb* (*present participle* **scrubbing**, *past* **scrubbed**)
to rub something hard to clean it, especially using a brush

scruffy /'skrʌfi/ *adjective* (**scruffier**, **scruffiest**)
dirty and untidy ▸ *a scruffy old man*

scrupulous /'skru:pjʊləs/ *adjective*
1 done very carefully so that every detail is correct ▸ *scrupulous attention to detail*
2 always careful to be honest and fair ▸ *A less scrupulous person might have been tempted to accept the bribe.* (*adverb:* **scrupulously**)

scrutinize /'skru:tınaız/ *verb* (*present participle* **scrutinizing**, *past* **scrutinized**)
to examine something very carefully and thoroughly ▸ *The customs official scrutinized his passport.*

scrutiny /'skru:tıni/ *noun* (*no plural*)
a careful and thorough examination of something ▸ *Close scrutiny of the document showed it to be a forgery.* ▸ *Famous people have to live their lives under constant public scrutiny.*

scuba diving /'sku:bə ˌdaıvıŋ/ *noun* (*no plural*)
the sport of swimming underwater using a container of air to help you breathe

sculptor /'skʌlptər/ *noun*
an artist who cuts shapes and figures from wood, stone, or metal

sculpture /'skʌlptʃər/ *noun*
1 a figure made from wood, stone, or metal
2 (*no plural*) the art of making figures from wood, stone, or metal

scum /skʌm/ *noun* (*no plural*)
1 an unpleasant, dirty layer that forms on the surface of a liquid ▸ *The pond was covered with scum.*

2 people you hate and have a very low opinion of

scurry /'skʌri/ *verb* (*past* **scurried**)
to move very quickly with small steps ▸ *A couple of chipmunks scurried about, collecting seeds.*

sea /si:/ *noun*
1 (*no plural*) the salt water that covers much of the Earth's surface
2 a large area of salt water ▸ *the Mediterranean Sea*
3 by sea on a ship ▸ *We're sending the goods to America by sea.*

seabed /'si:bed/ *noun*
the land at the bottom of the sea ▸ *a wrecked ship lying on the seabed*

seafood /'si:fu:d/ *noun* (*no plural*)
sea creatures that you eat ▸ *We eat a lot of seafood.*

seagull /'si:gʌl/ *noun*
a bird that lives near the sea and eats fish and sea creatures

seal¹ /si:l/ *noun*
an animal with a thick coat and flat limbs that it uses for swimming. It lives on cold sea coasts

seal² *verb*
to close something firmly so that it cannot open by mistake ▸ *She sealed the envelope and put a stamp on it.*

sea lion /'si: ˌlaıən/ *noun*
a large type of SEAL

seam /si:m/ *noun*
a line of sewing where two pieces of cloth are joined together

search¹ /sɜ:tʃ/ *verb*
to look carefully in a place because you want to find something ▸ *The police searched the house.* ▸ *I've searched everywhere for my keys.*

search² *noun* (*plural* **searches**)
an act of searching ▸ *After a long search, they found the lost child.*

seashell /'si:ʃel/ *noun*
the shell of some types of small sea

S

creature which you often find empty on the shore

seashore /'si:ʃɔːʳ/ *noun*
the land along the edge of the sea

seasick /'si:sɪk/ *adjective*
feeling sick because of the movement of a boat on water ▶ *He felt seasick because the sea was very rough.*

seaside /'si:saɪd/ *noun*
the seaside a place by the sea where people go on holiday

season /'si:zən/ *noun*
1 one of the four parts of the year ▶ *Summer is the hottest season.*
2 a special time of the year during which a sport or an activity takes place ▶ *the football season*

seasoning /'si:zənɪŋ/ *noun (no plural)*
salt, pepper, etc. that you add to food to give it more flavour

season ticket /'si:zən ˌtɪkɪt/ *noun*
a ticket that you can use for a lot of journeys or events during a fixed period of time

seat /si:t/ *noun*
a place to sit, or a thing to sit on ▶ *I could not find a seat on the bus.*
▶ *Please take a seat.* (=sit down).

seat belt /'si:t ˌbelt/ *noun*
a belt fixed to a seat in a car or on an aircraft, which helps to protect you in an accident
SAME MEANING: **safety belt**

seating /'si:tɪŋ/ *noun (no plural)*
the seats in a theatre, restaurant, plane, etc. ▶ *a comfortable, modern ferry with seating for 3,000 passengers*

seaweed /'si:wi:d/ *noun (no plural)*
a plant that grows in the sea and is often found on beaches

secluded /sɪ'klu:dɪd/ *adjective*
very quiet and private ▶ *a secluded beach*

second¹ /'sekənd/ *adjective*

2nd ▶ *This is the second time I have met him.*

second² *noun*
a very short length of time; there are 60 seconds in one minute

secondary school /'sekəndərɪ ˌsku:l/ *noun*
a school for children over 11 years old

second best /ˌsekənd 'best/ *adjective*
not as good as the best thing of the same type ▶ *Hunt has the second best scoring record at the club.*

second-class /ˌsekənd 'klɑ:s/ *adjective*
not the most expensive or best quality ▶ *a second-class stamp* ▶ *a second-class train ticket*

second-hand /ˌsekənd 'hænd/ *adjective, adverb*
previously owned by someone else ▶ *a cheap, second-hand computer* ▶ *I bought the car second-hand.*

second language /ˌsekənd 'læŋgwɪdʒ/ *noun*
a language that you speak in addition to the language that you learned to speak as a child

secondly /'sekəndlɪ/ *adverb*
used to introduce a second fact, reason, etc. ▶ *And secondly, we must consider the cost.*

second nature /ˌsekənd 'neɪtʃəʳ/ *noun (no plural)*
something you have done so often that you do it almost without thinking ▶ *Wearing a seat belt is second nature to most drivers.*

second person /ˌsekənd 'pɜːsən/ *noun*
the second person the form of a verb that you use with "you" in English

secrecy /'si:krəsɪ/ *noun (no plural)*
the state of being secret ▶ *The operation was carried out in total secrecy.*

S

secret¹ /ˈsiːkrət/ *noun*
something that has not been told to
other people ▶ *Don't tell anyone
about our plan – it's a secret.* ▶ *Can
you keep a secret (=can you be sure
you will not tell this to anyone else)?*

secret² *adjective*
not known about by other people ▶ *a
secret plan*

secret agent /ˌsiːkrət ˈeɪdʒənt/ *noun*
a person whose job is to discover
secret information, usually about
another country
SAME MEANING: **spy**

secretary /ˈsekrətəri/ *noun (plural
secretaries)*
1 a person who does office work,
writes letters, etc. for an employer
2 in some countries, a government
officer ▶ *the Secretary of Education*

secretive /ˈsiːkrətɪv/ *adjective*
unwilling to tell people about
something ▶ *John was very secretive
about his new girlfriend.*

sect /sekt/ *noun*
a group of people with its own set of
beliefs or religious practices that
separate it from a larger group

section /ˈsekʃən/ *noun*
a part of something ▶ *One section
of the bookcase contained
photograph albums.* ▶ *A section of
the road was closed because of an
accident.*

sector /ˈsektər/ *noun*
a part of an economic system, such
as business, industry, or trade ▶ *the
nation's manufacturing sector*

secure /sɪˈkjʊər/ *adjective*
1 safe; not likely to be stolen or taken
away ▶ *Keep your money in a secure
place.* ▶ *a secure job*
2 fixed firmly; that will not move or
fall easily ▶ *Is this shelf secure
enough for these heavy books?*

security /sɪˈkjʊərəti/ *noun (no plural)*
being safe and protected ▶ *The
government is responsible for the
security of the country.*

sedate¹ /sɪˈdeɪt/ *adjective*
moving in a slow, formal way ▶ *The
funeral procession moved off at a
sedate pace.*

sedate² *verb (present participle
sedating, past sedated)*
to give someone a drug to make them
feel sleepy or calm ▶ *The patient was
heavily sedated before the operation.*

sedative /ˈsedətɪv/ *noun*
a drug used to make someone feel
sleepy or calm

seductive /sɪˈdʌktɪv/ *adjective*
attractive, especially in a sexual way
▶ *her soft, seductive voice*

see /siː/ *verb (past tense saw /sɔː/,
past participle seen /siːn/)*
1 to use your eyes to notice something
▶ *It's too dark in here; I can't see
anything.* ▶ *I've lost my watch. Have
you seen it?*
2 to watch something, especially on
television or at the cinema ▶ *Did you
see that programme about drugs last
night?* ▶ *What film shall we go and
see?*
LOOK AT (**1** and **2**): **watch**
3 to understand something ▶ *Do you
see what I mean?* ▶ *I can't see why we
have to pay so much.*
4 to meet or visit someone ▶ *I'll see
you outside the theatre.* ▶ *You should
go and see a doctor.*
5 to find out something ▶ *Go and see
how many people have arrived.* ▶ *I'll
see if Mr Jones wants a cup of coffee
while he waits.*
6 I'll see something you say when
you want to think about something
before deciding ▶ *"Can I borrow the
car on Saturday?" "I'll see."*
7 let's see something you say when
you stop for a little while to think
about something ▶ *Who are we going*

S

to invite to the party? Let's see ...
Mark, Julia ...
8 See you a way of saying goodbye
to a friend

seed /siːd/ *noun*
a small grain from which a plant grows

seedy /'siːdɪ/ *adjective* (**seedier,
seediest**)
looking dirty or poor, and often
connected with activities that are
wrong or against the law ► *a seedy
nightclub*

seek /siːk/ *verb* (*past* **sought** /sɔːt/)
to look for something ► *We sought an
answer to the problem, but couldn't
find one.*

seem /siːm/ *verb*
1 to appear to be ► *Your sister seems
very nice.* ► *They seem to have
forgotten that it's my birthday.*
2 It seems that ... It appears to be
true or likely that ... ► *It seems that
we'll never know who the murderer is.*

seemingly /'siːmɪŋlɪ/ *adverb*
used to say how something appears
to be ► *a seemingly endless list of
jobs*

seen /siːn/
the PAST PARTICIPLE of the verb **see**

seep /siːp/ *verb*
(used about a liquid) to flow slowly
from or through something ► *Rain
seeped through the roof.*

seesaw /'siːsɔː/ *noun*
a long piece of wood balanced on
something high in the middle, so that
when a person sits at each end, they
can swing up and down

seethe /siːð/ *verb* (*present participle*
seething, *past* **seethed**)
to be very angry, but not show it ► *By
this time, I was quietly seething.*

segment /'segmənt/ *noun*
one of the parts that something is
divided into ► *a segment of orange*
► *a large segment of the population*

segregate /'segrɪgeɪt/ *verb*
(*present participle* **segregating,**
past **segregated**)
to separate one group of people from
others, especially because of race,
sex, religion, etc. ► *Black and white
people were segregated both at
home and at work.*

seize /siːz/ *verb* (*present participle*
seizing, *past* **seized**)
to take hold of something quickly and
firmly ► *The policeman seized the
robber's arm.*

seldom /'seldəm/ *adverb*
only a few times; not often ► *The
children are seldom ill.*
SAME MEANING: **rarely**

select /sɪ'lekt/ *verb*
to choose something or someone ► *I
was selected for the team.*

selection /sɪ'lekʃən/ *noun*
a group of things that have been
chosen by someone ► *Here is a
selection of our products.*

selective /sɪ'lektɪv/ *adjective*
careful about what you choose to do,
buy, etc. ► *She's very selective about
who she sees.*

self /self/ *noun* (*plural* **selves** /selvz/)
your whole being, especially your
character ► *Caroline has been a bit
unhappy lately, but today she was her
usual friendly self.*

self-centred /ˌself 'sentəd/
adjective
only thinking of yourself and not
other people
SAME MEANING: **selfish**

self-confidence /ˌself 'kɒnfɪdəns/
noun (no plural)
the belief that you can be successful,
look attractive, etc. that means you
are not shy or nervous with other
people ► *He lost his self-confidence
completely when he was made
redundant.*

self-confident /ˌself ˈkɒnfɪdənt/ *adjective*
feeling sure about your ability to be successful, look attractive, etc., and not shy or nervous with other people

self-conscious /ˌself ˈkɒnʃəs/ *adjective*
worried and embarrassed about what you look like or what other people think of you ▶ *He felt self-conscious in his new suit.*

self-defence /ˌself dɪˈfens/ *noun (no plural)*
the use of force to protect yourself when you are attacked ▶ *He said he killed the man in self-defence.*

self-employed /ˌself ɪmˈplɔɪd/ *adjective*
providing services directly for other people rather than being employed by a company

self-esteem /ˌself ɪˈstiːm/ *noun (no plural)*
the way you feel about yourself and whether, for example, you feel that you are a nice or successful person ▶ *Many of our patients suffer from low self-esteem.*

self-indulgent /ˌself ɪnˈdʌldʒənt/ *adjective*
allowing yourself to have or do something that you do not need but which you enjoy having or doing

selfish /ˈselfɪʃ/ *adjective*
only thinking of yourself and not other people ▶ *Let your brother play with your toys. Don't be so selfish!* (*adverb:* **selfishly**)
SAME MEANING: **self-centred**
OPPOSITE: **unselfish**

self-pity /ˌself ˈpɪti/ *noun (no plural)*
a feeling of being too sorry for yourself ▶ *He sank into remorse and self-pity after the accident.*

self-portrait /ˌself ˈpɔːtrɪt/ *noun*
a picture that you paint or draw of yourself

self-respect /ˌself rɪˈspekt/ *noun (no plural)*
a feeling of confidence and pride in your abilities, ideas, and character ▶ *He lost all his self-respect after his wife left him.*

self-service /ˌself ˈsɜːvɪs/ *adjective*
set out so that you can serve yourself ▶ *a self-service restaurant* ▶ *a self-service petrol station*

sell /sel/ *verb (past* **sold** /səʊld/*)*
1 to give something in exchange for money ▶ *She sold her old bicycle to me.* ▶ *What does that shop sell?* ▶ *Do you sell milk?*
COMPARE: **buy**
2 sell out to sell all of a particular thing and so have none left ▶ *We've sold out of newspapers.*

sell-by date /ˈsel baɪ ˌdeɪt/ *noun*
the date printed on a food product after which a shop should not sell it ▶ *This yoghurt's past its sell-by date.*

Sellotape /ˈseləteɪp/ *noun trademark (no plural)*
thin, clear TAPE used for sticking things together

selves /selvz/
the plural of **self**

semicircle /ˈsemɪsɜːkəl/ *noun*
half a circle

semicolon /ˌsemɪˈkəʊlən/ *noun*
the sign (;) used in writing to separate parts of a sentence

semi-detached /ˌsemi dɪˈtætʃt/ *adjective*
(used about houses) joined on one side to another house

semifinal /ˌsemɪˈfaɪnl/ *noun*
one of a pair of matches played in a competition to decide which players or teams will compete in the FINAL

seminar /ˈsemɪnɑːʳ/ *noun*
a class in which a small group of students meet to study or talk about a subject

S

senate /'senət/ *noun*
one of the groups which make up the government in some countries

senator /'senətər/ *noun*
a member of a senate

send /send/ *verb (past* **sent** /sent/)
1 to cause a thing to go somewhere ▶ *She sent me a present.*
2 to make someone go somewhere ▶ *Send him to me when he gets in.*
▶ *They sent their children to school in America.*
3 send for someone to ask someone to come to you ▶ *Alice was very ill, so her mother sent for the doctor.*

sender /'sendər/ *noun*
the person who sends a letter or a parcel

send-off /'send ɒf/ *noun*
an occasion when people gather together to say goodbye to someone who is leaving ▶ *The team got a great send-off at the airport.*

senile /'siːnaɪl/ *adjective*
mentally confused because of old age

senior /'siːnjər/ *adjective*
1 older ▶ *She teaches a senior class.*
2 higher in position or importance ▶ *She started as a secretary, but now she has a senior position in the company.*
OPPOSITE (**1** and **2**): **junior**

senior citizen /ˌsiːnɪə 'sɪtɪzən/ *noun*
a person who is over the age of 65

sensation /sen'seɪʃən/ *noun*
1 a feeling in your body ▶ *She felt a burning sensation on the back of her neck.*
2 *(no plural)* excited interest ▶ *The new show caused a sensation.*

sensational /sen'seɪʃənəl/ *adjective*
very interesting, exciting, or good ▶ *Her performance in that film was sensational.*

sense¹ /sens/ *noun*
1 a natural power that people have;

hearing, seeing, tasting, feeling, and smelling are the five senses ▶ *He has a good sense of smell.*
2 *(no plural)* good understanding and the ability to think clearly and make good decisions ▶ *I think she's got enough sense to ring if she's in trouble.*
3 make sense to have a meaning that you can understand ▶ *Does this sentence make sense to you?*

sense² *verb (present participle* **sensing,** *past* **sensed**)
to know something that is not said or shown openly ▶ *The dog sensed that I was afraid.*

senseless /'sensləs/ *adjective*
1 happening or done for no good reason or with no purpose ▶ *a senseless killing*
2 not conscious ▶ *The ball hit him on the head and knocked him senseless.*

sensible /'sensɪbəl/ *adjective*
having or showing good sense ▶ *Tom's parents trust him because he is very sensible.* ▶ *a sensible decision* (*adverb:* **sensibly**)

sensitive /'sensɪtɪv/ *adjective*
able to understand how other people feel, and careful not to say or do anything that will make them unhappy
OPPOSITE: **insensitive**

sensual /'senʃʊəl/ *adjective*
relating to physical pleasure, especially sexual pleasure ▶ *sensual music*

sensuous /'senʃʊəs/ *adjective*
making you feel physical pleasure ▶ *the sensuous feel of silk*

sent /sent/
the PAST TENSE and PAST PARTICIPLE of the verb **send**

sentence /'sentəns/ *noun*
a group of words which makes a statement or a question. It begins with a capital letter and ends with a

FULL STOP or a question mark
COMPARE: **clause**

sentimental /ˌsentɪˈmentl/ *adjective*
showing emotions such as love, pity,
and sadness too strongly or in a silly
way ▶ *an old-fashioned, sentimental
movie*

sentry /ˈsentrɪ/ *noun (plural
sentries)*
a soldier who stands outside a
building, guarding it

separate¹ /ˈsepərət/ *adjective*
different; apart ▶ *We sleep in
separate rooms.* ▶ *She keeps her
work separate from her home life.*

separate² /ˈsepəreɪt/ *verb (present
participle separating, past separated)*
1 to move people or things apart
▶ *The teacher separated the two boys
who were fighting.*
2 to keep two things apart ▶ *A fence
separated the cows from the pigs.*

separated /ˈsepəreɪtɪd/ *adjective*
not living with your husband, wife, or
partner any more ▶ *My husband and I
are separated.*

separation /ˌsepəˈreɪʃən/ *noun*
1 *(no plural)* the act of separating
people or things, or the state of being
separate ▶ *Separation from their
parents is very hard on children.*
2 a legal agreement between a
husband and wife to live apart from
each other

September /sepˈtembər/ *noun*
the ninth month of the year

septic /ˈseptɪk/ *adjective*
infected by disease ▶ *It looks as if the
wound has gone septic.*

sequel /ˈsiːkwəl/ *noun*
a film, book, etc. that continues the
story of an earlier one

sequence /ˈsiːkwəns/ *noun*
a series of events that are connected
to each other ▶ *A long sequence of
events has led up to this crisis.*

sergeant /ˈsɑːdʒənt/ *noun*
an officer in the army or police force

serial /ˈsɪərɪəl/ *noun*
a story which is told or written in parts

series /ˈsɪəriːz/ *noun (plural series)*
a number of things coming one after
the other ▶ *He saw a series of white
arrows painted on the road.* ▶ *a
series of programmes on dance*

serious /ˈsɪərɪəs/ *adjective*
1 thinking carefully about things
rather than laughing or having fun
▶ *He is a serious boy.*
2 very bad and worrying ▶ *a serious
illness*
3 important and worthy of attention
▶ *a serious article* ▶ *a serious
conversation*

seriously /ˈsɪərɪəslɪ/ *adverb*
1 in a worrying way ▶ *She is seriously
thinking of leaving her husband.*
▶ *seriously ill*
2 take something seriously to treat
something as important ▶ *The police
are taking the threats seriously.* ▶ *I
was only joking – don't take
everything so seriously!*

sermon /ˈsɜːmən/ *noun*
a talk given by a priest in a church

serpent /ˈsɜːpənt/ *noun*
a snake

servant /ˈsɜːvənt/ *noun*
a person who works for someone in
their house

serve /sɜːv/ *verb (present participle
serving, past served)*
1 to do work for a person or an
organization ▶ *He served in the army
for 15 years.*
2 to provide a customer with help in a
shop ▶ *Are you being served,
madam?*
3 to put food on plates ready to eat
▶ *Shall I serve, or do you want to
help yourselves?*
4 It serves you right something you
say when you think someone

S

S

deserves the bad thing that has happened to them ▶ *He's failed his exams – it serves him right for not studying.*

server /'sɜːvəʳ/ *noun*
the main computer in a NETWORK

service /'sɜːvɪs/ *noun*
1 (*no plural*) the work that people do in a public place, especially in a restaurant or a shop ▶ *The service in that new restaurant is very slow.*
2 (*no plural*) the work that you do for someone else ▶ *He was praised for his service **to** the blind.*
3 something useful that the public can use to help them ▶ *a regular bus service* ▶ *a free information service*
4 a church ceremony ▶ *the morning service*
5 services *plural noun* the work that a professional person does for someone ▶ *We need the services of a lawyer.*

service station /'sɜːvɪs ˌsteɪʃən/ *noun*
a place beside a road that sells petrol, food, etc.

serviette /ˌsɜːvɪ'et/ *noun*
a small square of cloth or paper that you use at meals to keep your clothes clean and to clean your mouth and fingers
SAME MEANING: **napkin**

serving /'sɜːvɪŋ/ *noun*
an amount of food that is enough for one person

session /'seʃən/ *noun*
a meeting of people for some purpose ▶ *a training session*

set¹ /set/ *noun*
1 a group of things that belong together ▶ *a set **of** plates*
2 a television ▶ *We can't watch television at the moment – our set's broken.*
3 the scenery for a play or television programme

set² *verb* (*present participle **setting**, past **set***)
1 to put something somewhere carefully ▶ *She set the flowers on the table.*
2 to give work to someone ▶ *The teacher set us a test.*
3 (used about the sun) to go down in the sky ▶ *The sun was setting.*
4 set an example to behave well so that other people will also behave well ▶ *Parents should set a good example **to** their children.*
5 set fire to something to make something burn
6 set someone free to let a prisoner go free
7 set the table to put plates, etc. on a table, ready for a meal
8 set off to start a journey ▶ *What time shall we set off tomorrow?*
9 set out to start a journey ▶ *He set out for the office at 8 this morning.*

setback /'setbæk/ *noun*
a bad event that stops you from being successful for a while ▶ *Today's result was a setback, but we can still win the championship.*

settee /se'tiː/ *noun*
a long, soft chair for two or more people to sit on
SAME MEANING: **couch, sofa**

setting /'setɪŋ/ *noun*
1 the place where something happens ▶ *It was the perfect setting for a romantic meal.*
2 one of the positions that the controls on a machine can be turned to ▶ *Use your hairdryer on its lowest setting.*

settle /'setl/ *verb* (*present participle **settling**, past **settled***)
1 to go and live in a place ▶ *My son has settled happily in America.*
2 to decide something, especially after an argument or a talk ▶ *We finally settled who should pay for the accident.*

3 to rest on something ▶ *The insect settled on a leaf.*

4 settle a bill to pay a bill

5 settle down to become calmer and more comfortable ▶ *He switched on the television and settled down for the evening.* ▶ *Settle down now, children – it's time to go to sleep.*

6 settle in to get used to a new place or job ▶ *How are you settling in?*

settled /'setld/ *adjective*
1 happy in your new house, job, or school ▶ *I'm beginning to feel a bit more settled.*
2 (used about the weather) dry and warm, and not likely to change ▶ *The weather should stay settled for the next few days.*
OPPOSITE (**1** and **2**): **unsettled**

settlement /'setlmənt/ *noun*
a formal decision or agreement at the end of an argument or a talk ▶ *After hours of talks, they finally reached a settlement.*

set-up /'set ʌp/ *noun*
1 the way that something is organized ▶ *I didn't understand the set-up at the college.*
2 a dishonest plan that is intended to trick someone ▶ *I should have realized it was a set-up.*

seven /'sevən/ *adjective, noun*
the number 7

seventeen /ˌsevən'tiːn/ *adjective, noun*
the number 17

seventeenth /ˌsevən'tiːnθ/ *adjective*
17th

seventh /'sevənθ/ *adjective, noun*
1 7th
2 one of seven equal parts

seventieth /'sevəntɪ-ɪθ/ *adjective*
70th

seventy /'sevəntɪ/ *adjective, noun*
the number 70

sever /'sevər/ *verb*
1 to cut through something completely ▶ *His finger was severed in the accident.*
2 to completely end a relationship or an agreement with someone ▶ *The US severed all ties with Iraq.*

several /'sevərəl/ *adjective*
more than two, but not many ▶ *She has several friends in the town.* ▶ *I've been to Pam's several times.*

severe /sə'vɪər/ *adjective*
1 hard; not kind or gentle ▶ *a severe punishment*
2 very bad ▶ *a severe pain* ▶ *a severe winter*

severely /sɪ'vɪəlɪ/ *adverb*
very badly ▶ *Her mother was severely injured in the crash.*

severity /sə'verətɪ/ *noun (no plural)*
the quality of being very bad ▶ *We didn't understand the severity of the problem.*

sew /səʊ/ *verb (past participle **sewn** /səʊn/)*
to make or mend clothes by using a needle and thread ▶ *He sewed a button on his shirt.*
COMPARE: **knit**

sewage /'sjuːɪdʒ/ *noun (no plural)*
waste material that is carried away from homes and factories through pipes

sewer /'sjuːər/ *noun*
a pipe under the ground that carries away sewage

sewing /'səʊɪŋ/ *noun (no plural)*
1 the activity of making or mending things using a needle and thread ▶ *My sister is very good at sewing.*
2 something that you are making or mending with a needle and thread ▶ *Where did I put my sewing?*

sewing machine /'səʊɪŋ məʃiːn/ *noun*
a machine for sewing pieces of material together

S

sewn / səʊn/
the PAST PARTICIPLE of the verb **sew**

sex /seks/ noun (no plural)
1 being male or female ➤ What sex is your cat?
2 the things done between a male and female to make babies

sexism /'seksɪzəm/ noun (no plural)
the practice of treating someone, especially a woman, in an unfair way because of their sex

sexist /'seksɪst/ adjective
treating someone, especially a woman, in an unfair way because of their sex ➤ I get a lot of sexist comments at work.

sexual /'sekʃʊəl/ adjective
1 relating to sex ➤ I'm not ready for a sexual relationship.
2 relating to whether someone is male or female ➤ Sexual discrimination at work is illegal. (adverb: **sexually**)

sexual harassment /ˌsekʃʊəl 'hærəsmənt/ noun (no plural)
a situation in which someone you work with speaks to you or touches you in a sexual way when you do not want them to

sexuality /ˌsekʃʊ'ælətɪ/ noun (no plural)
someone's sexual activities and feelings about sex

sexy /'seksɪ/ adjective (**sexier, sexiest**)
sexually attractive ➤ He had sexy brown eyes.

sh (also **shh**) /ʃ/ interjection
used to tell someone to be quiet

shabby /'ʃæbɪ/ adjective (**shabbier, shabbiest**)
rather old, cheap, and dirty ➤ shabby clothes

shack /ʃæk/ noun
a small building that has not been built very well

shade¹ /ʃeɪd/ noun
1 (no plural) shelter from the sun or light ➤ They sat in the shade because the sun was too hot.
2 a particular type of one colour ➤ I want a darker shade **of** blue. ➤ various shades of green

shade² verb (present participle **shading**, past **shaded**)
to shelter something from the sun or light ➤ I shaded my eyes with my hand.

shadow /'ʃædəʊ/ noun
a dark shape made by something when it blocks the light ➤ The shadows of the trees grew longer as the afternoon went on.

shady /'ʃeɪdɪ/ adjective (**shadier, shadiest**)
sheltered from sunlight ➤ It's cool and shady under this tree.

shaft /ʃɑːft/ noun
a deep, straight hole ➤ a lift shaft

shake /ʃeɪk/ verb (present participle **shaking**, past tense **shook** /ʃʊk/, past participle **shaken** /'ʃeɪkən/)
1 to move quickly from side to side, up and down, etc. ➤ The house shook as the heavy lorry went past. ➤ She shook the box to see if there was any money in it.
2 shake hands to take someone's right hand in yours and move it up and down when you meet them or say goodbye
3 shake your head to move your head from side to side to say no

shake-up /'ʃeɪk ʌp/ noun
big changes that are made to the way that something is organized ➤ There's going to be a big shake-up in the company where she works.

shaky /'ʃeɪkɪ/ adjective (**shakier, shakiest**)
weak and unsteady because you are ill, old, or have had a shock ➤ I was still feeling a bit shaky after the accident.

S

shall /ʃəl; *strong* ʃæl/ *verb*
1 a word used instead of **will** with **I** and **we** to say that something is going to happen ▶ *I shall see you at school tomorrow.* ▶ *I shan't* (=shall not) *tell anyone that you're leaving.*
COMPARE: **will**
2 used with **I** and **we** in questions when asking or offering to do something ▶ *Shall we all go to the film tonight?* ▶ *Shall I help you with that?*

shallow /'ʃæləʊ/ *adjective*
only a short distance from the bottom to the top ▶ *The sea is shallow here.* ▶ *the shallow end of a swimming pool* (=where the water is not very deep)
OPPOSITE: **deep**

shambles /'ʃæmblz/ *noun*
be a shambles to be very untidy or badly organized ▶ *The place was a shambles.*

shame /ʃeɪm/ *noun (no plural)*
1 the feeling you have when you have done something wrong or silly ▶ *He hung his head in shame.*
2 What a shame! something you say to show you think something is sad or disappointing ▶ *"Julie won't be able to come to the cinema." "What a shame!"*

shameful /'ʃeɪmfəl/ *adjective*
so bad that someone should be ashamed ▶ *a shameful waste of money*

shameless /'ʃeɪmləs/ *adjective*
behaving badly and not caring that other people do not approve ▶ *This was a shameless attempt to cheat.*

shampoo /ʃæm'pu:/ *noun*
a special liquid for washing your hair

shan't /ʃɑːnt/
shall not ▶ *I shan't be home until 8.*

shape¹ /ʃeɪp/ *noun*
the form of something ▶ *a card in the shape of a heart*

shape² *verb (present participle **shaping**, past **shaped**)*
to make something into a certain form ▶ *He shaped the clay into a pot.*

share¹ /ʃeəʳ/ *verb (present participle **sharing**, past **shared**)*
1 to divide something so that two or more people can have some ▶ *We shared the sweets between us.*
2 to have or use something together with someone else ▶ *I share a flat **with** two other girls.*

share² *noun*
1 a part of something that has been divided ▶ *We gave each of the five children an equal share.*
2 one of the equal parts into which the OWNERSHIP of a company is divided, which are bought and sold ▶ *Shares in Tait Rubber rose by almost 20%.*

shark /ʃɑːk/ *noun*
a large, fierce fish

sharp /ʃɑːp/ *adjective*
1 having an edge that cuts easily ▶ *a sharp knife*
2 having a fine point ▶ *a sharp needle* ▶ *a sharp pencil*
OPPOSITE: **(1 and 2): blunt**
3 (used about changes) sudden and big ▶ *a sharp increase in petrol prices*
4 able to see or hear things that are far away ▶ *sharp eyes* ▶ *sharp ears*

sharpen /'ʃɑːpən/ *verb*
to make something sharp ▶ *to sharpen a knife* ▶ *to sharpen a pencil*

sharpener /'ʃɑːpnəʳ/ *noun*
a thing that you use to sharpen knives, pencils, etc. ▶ *a pencil sharpener*

sharply /'ʃɑːpli/ *adverb*
changing suddenly and a lot ▶ *Prices have risen sharply.*

shatter /'ʃætəʳ/ *verb*
to break into many pieces ▶ *The glass shattered when I dropped it.*

shattered /ˈʃætəd/ *adjective*
1 very shocked and upset ▶ *They were shattered when they heard the news.*
2 very tired

shave¹ /ʃeɪv/ *verb (present participle **shaving**, past **shaved**)*
to take hair from the face or body by cutting it very close ▶ *My father shaves every morning before breakfast.*

shave² *noun*
an act of shaving ▶ *He had a shave before he went out.*

shaver /ˈʃeɪvəʳ/ *noun*
an electric tool for removing hair from a man's face

shawl /ʃɔːl/ *noun*
a long piece of cloth which women wear round their shoulders and head

she /ʃi; *strong* ʃiː/ *pronoun (plural **they**)*
the female person or animal that the sentence is about ▶ *My sister's name is Mary – she's (=she is) nine and she's (=she has) got long, brown hair.*

shear /ʃɪəʳ/ *verb (past participle **shorn** /ʃɔːn/)*
to cut wool from a sheep or goat

shears /ʃɪəz/ *plural noun*
large scissors for cutting grass, plants, etc.

shed¹ /ʃed/ *noun*
a small, wooden hut used for keeping things in

shed² *verb (present participle **shedding**, past **shed**)*
to let something fall off ▶ *Some trees shed their leaves in the autumn.*

she'd /ʃɪd; *strong* ʃiːd/
1 she would ▶ *She'd like to meet you.*
2 she had ▶ *She'd already left.*

sheep /ʃiːp/ *noun (plural **sheep**)*
an animal that is kept for meat and for the wool from its thick coat

sheepish /ˈʃiːpɪʃ/ *adjective*
embarrassed because you have done something silly or wrong ▶ *She came back looking sheepish.*

sheer /ʃɪəʳ/ *adjective*
straight down; very steep ▶ *There was a sheer drop from where we stood to the sea below us.*

sheet /ʃiːt/ *noun*
1 a large, flat piece of something ▶ *a sheet **of** paper* ▶ *a sheet of glass*
2 a large, thin piece of cloth for putting on a bed

shelf /ʃelf/ *noun (plural **shelves** /ʃelvz/)*
a board fixed to a wall or in a cupboard, for putting things on ▶ *He took the cup off the shelf.*

shell /ʃel/ *noun*
the hard outside covering of some animals, nuts, seeds, or eggs

she'll /ʃɪl; *strong* ʃiːl/
she will ▶ *She'll ring you tomorrow.*

shellfish /ˈʃelfɪʃ/ *noun (plural **shellfish**)*
a small animal that lives in water, has a shell, and is eaten as food

shelter¹ /ˈʃeltəʳ/ *noun*
1 a place where you can be protected from bad weather or danger ▶ *a bus shelter (=a place where you can wait for a bus when it is raining)*
2 *(no plural)* protection from bad weather or danger ▶ *We took shelter under some trees.*

shelter² *verb*
1 to protect someone or something from bad weather or danger ▶ *The wall sheltered the garden **from** the wind.*
2 to stay in a place which can protect you from bad weather or danger ▶ *People sheltered in shop doorways as the rain came down.*

shelve /ʃelv/ *verb (present participle **shelving**, past **shelved**)* to decide not to continue with a plan, although you might continue with it later ▶ *The project has been shelved due to lack of funding.*

shelves /ʃelvz/
the plural of **shelf**

shepherd /ˈʃepəd/ *noun*
a person who looks after sheep

sherry /ˈʃerɪ/ *noun*
1 *(no plural)* a strong, Spanish wine
2 *(plural sherries)* a glass of this drink ▶ *Can I have two sherries, please?*

she's /ʃɪz; *strong* ʃiːz/
1 she is ▶ *She's very tall.*
2 she has ▶ *She's got a new car.*

shh /ʃ/ *interjection*
another word for **sh**

shield¹ /ʃiːld/ *noun*
a piece of wood or metal that, in the past, soldiers used to hold in front of them to protect their bodies in battle

shield² *verb*
to protect something by holding something over or in front of it ▶ *He shielded his eyes from the sun.*

shift¹ /ʃɪft/ *verb*
to move ▶ *I can't shift the bed – it's too heavy.*

shift² *noun*
1 one of the periods of work in a place like a hospital or a factory ▶ *I'm on night shift this week.*
2 the group of people who work together in one of these periods

shimmer /ˈʃɪmə/ *verb*
to shine with a soft light that seems to shake slightly ▶ *a lake shimmering in the moonlight*

shin /ʃɪn/ *noun*
the front part of your leg between your knee and your foot

shine /ʃaɪn/ *verb (present participle shining, past shone /ʃɒn/)*
1 to give out light ▶ *The sun was shining that day.*

2 to look bright, especially when light falls on something ▶ *The lake shone in the sunlight.*

shiny /ˈʃaɪnɪ/ *adjective (shinier, shiniest)*
bright; throwing back the light ▶ *He rubbed his shoes until they were shiny.* ▶ *clean, shiny hair*

ship /ʃɪp/ *noun*
a large boat that sails on the sea

shipping /ˈʃɪpɪŋ/ *noun (no plural)*
ships considered as a group ▶ *The canal has been closed to shipping.*

shipwreck¹ /ˈʃɪp-rek/ *noun*
an accident in which a ship is destroyed at sea ▶ *survivors of a shipwreck*

shipwreck² *verb*
be shipwrecked if people are shipwrecked, the ship they are travelling in is destroyed in an accident at sea, but they manage to reach land

shirk /ʃɜːk/ *verb*
to avoid doing something you should do ▶ *George worked hard and never shirked his responsibilities.*

shirt /ʃɜːt/ *noun*
a piece of clothing with buttons down the front that covers the upper part of your body and your arms

shiver /ˈʃɪvə/ *verb*
to shake with cold or fear ▶ *They were all shivering in the cold.*

shoal /ʃəʊl/ *noun*
a large group of fish that swim together

shock¹ /ʃɒk/ *noun*
1 the feeling caused by an unpleasant surprise; something causing this feeling ▶ *It was a great shock for him when his wife died.* ▶ *You gave me a shock* (=you frightened me).
2 a pain caused by electricity going through you ▶ *An electric shock can kill you.*

shock² /verb/
to give someone an unpleasant surprise ▶ *I was shocked when I heard about your accident.*

shocking /'ʃɒkɪŋ/ *adjective*
very upsetting and wrong ▶ *a shocking crime*

shoddy /'ʃɒdɪ/ *adjective* (**shoddier, shoddiest**)
badly done or made ▶ *markets selling cheap, shoddy goods*

shoe /ʃuː/ *noun*
something you wear on your foot when you go outside ▶ *a pair of shoes*
COMPARE: **sock**

shoelace /'ʃuːleɪs/ *noun*
a string used to fasten a shoe

shone /ʃɒn/
the PAST TENSE and PAST PARTICIPLE of the verb **shine**

shook /ʃʊk/
the PAST TENSE of the verb **shake**

shoot¹ /ʃuːt/ *verb* (past **shot** /ʃɒt/)
1 to fire at something or someone with a gun ▶ *He shot the bird with his gun.*
2 to move quickly ▶ *He shot out of school when the bell rang.* ▶ *The ball shot past my head.*

shoot² *noun*
a part of a plant that is just starting to grow or has just appeared above the ground

shooting /'ʃuːtɪŋ/ *noun*
1 a situation in which someone is killed or injured by a gun ▶ *Two men have died after a shooting at a pub in Liverpool.*
2 (no plural) the sport of killing animals and birds with guns

shop¹ /ʃɒp/ *noun*
a place where you can buy things

shop² *verb* (present participle **shopping,** past **shopped**)
to go to the shops to buy things ▶ *We often shop in Oxford Street.*

shop assistant /'ʃɒp əˌsɪstənt/ *noun*
a person who works in a shop serving customers

shopkeeper /'ʃɒpˌkiːpəʳ/ *noun*
a person who owns or manages a small shop

shoplifting /'ʃɒpˌlɪftɪŋ/ *noun* (no plural)
the crime of taking things from shops without paying for them ▶ *She was arrested for shoplifting.*

shopping /'ʃɒpɪŋ/ *noun* (no plural)
1 the activity of going to the shops to buy things ▶ *I like shopping **for** clothes.* ▶ *I have to go shopping today.*
2 the things you have just bought from the shops ▶ *Put the shopping on the table.* ▶ *a bag of shopping*

shopping centre /'ʃɒpɪŋ ˌsentəʳ/ *noun*
a group of shops that are built together in one area, often inside one large building

shore /ʃɔːʳ/ *noun*
the flat land at the edge of the sea or a large area of water ▶ *We walked along the shore.*

shorn /ʃɔːn/
the PAST PARTICIPLE of the verb **shear**

short /ʃɔːt/ *adjective*
1 not a very big distance from one end to another ▶ *It's a short distance from here to the bank.* ▶ *short hair*
2 not lasting a very long time ▶ *a short holiday* ▶ *a short song*
OPPOSITE (**1** and **2**): **long**
3 not as tall as expected ▶ *She's the shortest girl in the class.*
OPPOSITE: **tall**
4 be short of something not to have enough of something ▶ *I'm a bit short of money this week.*

shortage /'ʃɔːtɪdʒ/ *noun*
a lack of something ▶ *a food shortage* ▶ *a shortage **of** water*

short cut /ˌʃɔːt ˈkʌt/ *noun*
a quicker, more direct way of going somewhere or doing something
► *We took a short cut over the fields to the station.*

shorten /ˈʃɔːtn/ *verb*
to make something shorter ► *to shorten a dress*
OPPOSITE: **lengthen**

shorthand /ˈʃɔːthænd/ *noun (no plural)*
a fast method of writing down what people say using special signs instead of letters, words, and phrases

shortlist /ˈʃɔːtlɪst/ *noun*
a list of the most suitable people for a job or prize, chosen from a larger group ► *Her first novel was on the shortlist for an important literary prize.*

short-list /ˈʃɔːt lɪst/ *verb*
be short-listed to be chosen for a shortlist ► *No women were short-listed for the job.*

shortly /ˈʃɔːtli/ *adverb*
soon ► *Liz left home shortly after 8 am.*

shorts /ʃɔːts/ *plural noun*
trousers which stop above your knee ► *a pair of shorts*

shortsighted (also **short-sighted**) /ˌʃɔːtˈsaɪtɪd/ *adjective*
1 unable to see things clearly unless they are close to you
SAME MEANING: **nearsighted**
OPPOSITE: **longsighted**
2 thinking only about the effect that something will have immediately, rather than thinking about the effect it will have over a longer period of time ► *shortsighted planning*

short-term /ˌʃɔːt ˈtɜːm/ *adjective*
continuing for only a short time ► *We have had some short-term financial problems.*
OPPOSITE: **long-term**

shot¹ /ʃɒt/
the PAST TENSE and PAST PARTICIPLE of the verb **shoot**

shot² *noun*
1 the act of a gun being fired ► *I heard two shots in the street.*
2 the act of hitting or kicking a ball, especially to win a point in a game ► *That was a good shot.*

shotgun /ˈʃɒtɡʌn/ *noun*
a long gun, used especially for shooting animals and birds

should /ʃəd; *strong* ʃʊd/ *verb*
1 used to say what you think would be a good idea ► *You should ring your parents to let them know you will be late.* ► *We should invite Robert and Ann to the party.*
2 used to say what you think will happen or what you think is true ► *They should arrive soon.* ► *It should be a good film.*
3 used with **I** and **we** in sentences when you want to say what would happen or what would be true ► *I should be very happy to accept your invitation.*
4 used in sentences with **if** about things that may happen ► *If David should ring, please ask him to call back tomorrow.*

shoulder /ˈʃəʊldə/ *noun*
the top part of your body between your neck and the top of your arm

shoulder bag /ˈʃəʊldə ˌbæɡ/ *noun*
a small bag that a woman carries over her shoulder

shoulder blade /ˈʃəʊldə ˌbleɪd/ *noun*
one of the two flat bones below your shoulders on your back

shouldn't /ˈʃʊdnt/
should not ► *You shouldn't eat so much chocolate.*

should've /ˈʃʊdəv/
should have ► *You should've told me that you would be late.*

S

shout¹ /ʃaʊt/ *verb*
to speak in a loud voice ➤ *"Help!" he shouted.* ➤ *Don't shout at me.*

shout² *noun*
a loud cry or call ➤ *to give a shout*

shove /ʃʌv/ *verb (present participle shoving, past shoved)*
to push someone or something in a rough or careless way ➤ *People were shoving each other, trying to get on the bus.* ➤ *He shoved the clothes into his bag.*

shovel¹ /ʃʌvəl/ *noun*
a tool made of a wide piece of metal on a handle, used for moving things like earth

shovel² *verb (present participle shovelling, past shovelled)*
to move something with a shovel

show¹ /ʃəʊ/ *verb (past participle shown /ʃəʊn/)*
1 to let someone see something ➤ *He showed me his new camera.* ➤ *This photograph shows me with my family on holiday.* ➤ *He showed the picture to his friends.*
2 to make something clear ➤ *The report shows a rise in unemployment.*
3 to be noticeable ➤ *Don't worry about that hole in your sock – it doesn't show.*
4 show someone how to do something to explain to someone how to do something ➤ *The teacher showed us how to use the computer.*
5 show off to try and get people to notice you because you want them to see how clever, rich, etc. you are ➤ *No one likes him very much because he's always showing off.*
6 show something off to make people notice something you have, especially because it is new and you are proud of it ➤ *He drove to school to show off his new car.*

show² *noun*
1 something that people like to go and watch, especially a play, singing, etc.
2 a lot of things gathered together for people to see ➤ *A lot of people went to see the flower show.*

show business /ʃəʊ ˌbɪznəs/ *(also showbiz* /ʃəʊbɪz/*) noun (no plural)*
the industry that deals with providing entertainment for people ➤ *a career in show business*

shower /ʃaʊəʳ/ *noun*
1 the act of washing yourself by standing under running water ➤ *He's having a shower.*
2 the apparatus you use to wash yourself in this way
3 a short period of light rain ➤ *It's only a shower. Let's wait until it stops.*

showery /ʃaʊəri/ *adjective*
raining frequently for short periods ➤ *a showery day*

shown /ʃəʊn/
the PAST PARTICIPLE of the verb **show**

show-off /ʃəʊ ɒf/ *noun*
a person who tries to show how clever, funny, etc. they are in order to make other people admire them

showroom /ʃəʊrʊm/ *noun*
a large room where you can look at things that are for sale ➤ *a car showroom*

shrank /ʃræŋk/
the PAST TENSE of the verb **shrink**

shred /ʃred/ *noun*
a small piece torn off something ➤ *The cat tore the paper to shreds.*

shrewd /ʃruːd/ *adjective*
clever, and able to act or make decisions in a way that is to your own advantage

shriek¹ /ʃriːk/ *verb*
to make a high, loud cry of fear or laughter ➤ *She shrieked in terror.*

shriek² *noun*
a high, loud cry of fear or laughter

shrill /ʃrɪl/ *adjective*
having an unpleasantly loud, high sound ▶ *a shrill voice*

shrimp /ʃrɪmp/ *noun*
a small, pink, sea animal that has ten legs, a soft shell, and is eaten as food

shrine /ʃraɪn/ *noun*
a holy place

shrink /ʃrɪŋk/ *verb (past tense* **shrank** /ʃræŋk/, *past participle* **shrunk** /ʃrʌŋk/)
to get smaller ▶ *The dress shrank when I washed it.*

shrivel /ʃrɪvəl/ *(also* **shrivel up**) *verb (present participle* **shrivelling**, *past* **shrivelled**)
to dry out and become smaller ▶ *A lot of the plants had shrivelled up in the heat.*

shroud¹ /ʃraʊd/ *noun*
a cloth that is wrapped around a dead person's body before it is buried

shroud² *verb*
be shrouded in something to be covered and hidden by something such as mist or smoke ▶ *It was early morning and the hills were shrouded in mist.*

shrub /ʃrʌb/ *noun*
a small, low tree

shrug /ʃrʌɡ/ *verb (present participle* **shrugging**, *past* **shrugged**)
to lift and drop your shoulders to show that you do not know something or do not care ▶ *I asked her if she liked her new school, but she just shrugged her shoulders.*

shrunk /ʃrʌŋk/
the PAST PARTICIPLE of the verb **shrink**

shudder¹ /ˈʃʌdəʳ/ *verb*
to shake with fear, unpleasant shock, etc. ▶ *He shuddered when he saw the dead animal.*

shudder² *noun*
a sudden feeling of fear or unpleasantness which goes through

your body ▶ *She gave a shudder when she saw the snake.*

shuffle /ˈʃʌfəl/ *verb (present participle* **shuffling**, *past* **shuffled**)
1 to walk in a slow or lazy way without lifting your feet off the ground ▶ *Granddad got up and shuffled across the room.*
2 to mix playing cards into a different order before playing a game ▶ *Shall I shuffle?*

shut /ʃʌt/ *verb (present participle* **shutting**, *past* **shut**)
1 to move something so that it is not open; to close ▶ *Please will you shut the door?* ▶ *He shut his eyes and went to sleep.*
2 (used about a shop or business) to close ▶ *The shops shut at 5.30.*
OPPOSITE (**1** and **2**): **open**
3 **Shut up!** a rude way of telling someone to stop talking

shutter /ˈʃʌtəʳ/ *noun*
a wooden or metal cover that you close in front of a window

shuttle¹ /ˈʃʌtl/ *noun*
1 a plane, bus, or train that makes regular short trips between two places ▶ *I arrived at Heathrow and caught the shuttle to Gatwick.*
2 a vehicle that can travel into space and return to Earth more than once ▶ *They have had to delay the launch of the space shuttle.*

shuttle² *verb (present participle* **shuttling**, *past* **shuttled**)
to move people between one place and another ▶ *Passengers are shuttled to and from the hotel by bus.*

shy /ʃaɪ/ *adjective* (**shier, shiest**)
nervous or afraid to be with other people ▶ *The child was shy and hid behind his mother.*

sibling /ˈsɪblɪŋ/ *noun*
your brother or sister

S

sick /sɪk/ *adjective*
1 ill ▶ *My father's sick – he's got to stay in bed.*
2 be sick to bring food up from your stomach ▶ *She was sick on the bus.*
3 be off sick not to be at work because you are ill ▶ *John's off sick this week.*
4 feel sick to want to bring up food from your stomach ▶ *I felt sick when the ship started to move.*
5 make someone sick to make someone feel very angry and annoyed ▶ *This company wastes such a lot of money. It makes me sick!*

sickly /'sɪklɪ/ *adjective* (**sicklier, sickliest**)
1 weak and often ill ▶ *She was a pale, sickly woman.*
2 (used about smells, tastes, etc.) very unpleasant and making you feel a little sick

sickness /'sɪknəs/ *noun (no plural)*
the condition of being ill ▶ *soldiers suffering from hunger and sickness*

side /saɪd/ *noun*
1 one of the parts of something that is not the top, bottom, back, or front ▶ *He went round to the side of the house.* ▶ *I have a pain in my left side* (=the left part of my body).
2 either of the two surfaces of a flat thing ▶ *Write on both sides of the paper.*
3 a team ▶ *Which side do you want to win?*

sideboard /'saɪdbɔːd/ *noun*
a long, low piece of furniture in which you keep plates and glasses

side-effect /'saɪd ɪˌfekt/ *noun*
a bad effect that a drug has on your body while you are using it to cure an illness ▶ *Antibiotics can have serious side-effects.*

sidetrack /'saɪdtræk/ *verb*
to make someone stop talking about or dealing with the main subject or problem by making them interested

in something else that is less important ▶ *I think we're getting sidetracked from the main issue here.*

sideways /'saɪdweɪz/ *adverb*
1 to one side ▶ *He stepped sideways to let me pass.*
2 turned so that the side is at the front ▶ *We turned the table sideways to get it into the room.*

siege /siːdʒ/ *noun*
a military operation in which an army surrounds a place and stops supplies of food, weapons, etc. from getting to it ▶ *The city was under siege for six months.* ▶ *the siege of Sarajevo*

sieve /sɪv/ *noun*
a piece of kitchen equipment that looks like a net, used for separating solid food from liquid, or small pieces of food from larger pieces ▶ *I put the soup through a sieve.*

sift /sɪft/ *verb*
1 to put flour, sugar, etc. through a sieve in order to remove any large pieces
2 (*also* **sift through**) to examine something very carefully in order to find something ▶ *Police investigators are still sifting through the evidence.*

sigh¹ /saɪ/ *verb*
to breathe deeply once, because you are tired, sad, etc.

sigh² *noun*
an act or sound of sighing ▶ *"I wish I had finished this work," she said with a sigh.*

sight /saɪt/ *noun*
1 (*no plural*) the power to see ▶ *She lost her sight in an accident.*
2 a thing that you see ▶ *The fire was a frightening sight.*
3 catch sight of something to see something suddenly ▶ *I caught sight of the robber running out of the bank.*
4 the sights the places that are interesting to visit in a city, country, etc.

sighting /'saɪtɪŋ/ *noun*
an occasion when something is seen, especially something unusual or rare ➤ *UFO sightings*

sightseeing /'saɪt,siːɪŋ/ *noun (no plural)*
visiting interesting places when you are on holiday ➤ *Shall we go sightseeing today?*

sign¹ /saɪn/ *noun*
a movement, mark, or set of words which carry a message ➤ *He made a sign for me to follow him.* ➤ *The sign by the road said "No Parking"* (=you cannot leave your car here).

sign² *verb*
to write your name, for example at the end of a letter

signal¹ /'sɪgnəl/ *noun*
a movement or thing which tells you what to do ➤ *The railway signal showed that the train could pass.*

signal² *verb (present participle signalling, past signalled)*
to give a signal ➤ *The teacher signalled to the boy to begin.*

signature /'sɪgnətʃə'/ *noun*
a person's name written in their own particular way, especially on a letter, cheque, etc.
COMPARE: **autograph**

significance /sɪg'nɪfɪkəns/ *noun (no plural)*
meaning ➤ *What is the significance of this speech?*

significant /sɪg'nɪfɪkənt/ *adjective*
1 large and important ➤ *a significant increase in crime*
OPPOSITE: **insignificant**
2 having a special meaning ➤ *Do you think it is significant that he didn't bring his wife to the party?*

signify /'sɪgnɪfaɪ/ *verb (past signified)*
to be a sign of something ➤ *Losing weight can signify a variety of health problems.*

sign language /'saɪn ,læŋwɪdʒ/ *noun (no plural)*
a language that uses hand movements, used by people who cannot hear

signpost /'saɪnpəʊst/ *noun*
a road sign which shows people which way to go and tells them how far it is to a place

Sikh /siːk/ *noun*
a member of an Indian religious group that developed from Hinduism

silence /'saɪləns/ *noun (no plural)*
complete quiet ➤ *They worked in silence.*

silent /'saɪlənt/ *adjective*
without any noise; completely quiet (*adverb:* **silently**)

silhouette /,sɪlu'et/ *noun*
a dark shape or shadow on a light background ➤ *The silhouette of a man appeared on the wall.*

silicon /'sɪlɪkən/ *noun (no plural)*
a chemical substance that is used for making glass, bricks, and computer parts ➤ *All computers have silicon chips.*

silk /sɪlk/ *noun (no plural)*
a fine cloth made from smooth threads

silky /'sɪlkɪ/ *adjective (silkier, silkiest)*
soft and smooth ➤ *silky hair*

silly /'sɪlɪ/ *adjective (sillier, silliest)*
not reasonable or clever ➤ *Don't be silly; that insect can't hurt you.* ➤ *a silly little boy*

silver /'sɪlvə'/ *noun (no plural)*
1 a soft, shiny, grey-white metal used for rings, earrings, etc.
2 the colour of this metal

similar /'sɪmɪlə'/ *adjective*
1 alike ➤ *Our dresses are similar.*
2 similar to like; the same as ➤ *My hair is similar to yours.*

S

similarity /ˌsɪmɪˈlærətɪ/ *noun (plural*
similarities)
the quality of being like someone or
something ▶ *Can you see any
similarities **between** the two
brothers?*
OPPOSITE: **difference**

simmer /ˈsɪmərˈ/ *verb*
to cook food in liquid that is boiling
very gently ▶ *Let the soup simmer for
five minutes.*

simple /ˈsɪmpəl/ *adjective*
1 easy to understand ▶ *a simple
question*
OPPOSITE: **difficult**
2 without a lot of unnecessary
decorations or additions; plain
▶ *simple clothes* ▶ *simple food*

simplify /ˈsɪmplɪfaɪ/ *verb (past
simplified)*
to make something easier to
understand or do ▶ *The story has
been simplified so that children can
read it.*

simply /ˈsɪmplɪ/ *adverb*
1 in a simple way ▶ *Let me explain it
simply.*
2 just; only ▶ *I simply wanted to help.*

simultaneous /ˌsɪməlˈteɪnɪəs/
adjective
happening or done at the same time
as something else ▶ *a simultaneous
broadcast on TV and radio (adverb:
simultaneously)*

sin /sɪn/ *noun*
something people think is very bad;
something your religion teaches you
is wrong ▶ *It's a sin to tell lies.*
COMPARE: **crime**

since /sɪns/ *adverb, preposition*
between a time in the past and now
▶ *He came to school last week, but I
haven't seen him since.* ▶ *She has
been ill since Christmas.* ▶ *He has
lived in London since 1990.* ▶ *It has
been a long time since I wrote to her.*
▶ *We have been friends ever since*

then (=from that particular time until
now).
LOOK AT: **ago**

Compare **for** and **since**. Use **for**
when you are talking about a
period of time such as a week, a
month, a year, etc.: *I've been
studying English for three years.*
▶ *I lived there for six months* (but
I don't live there any more). Use
since when you are talking about
the exact moment in the past
when something began: *I've been
studying English since 1992.*
Since always refers to something
which began in the past but
continues until now, so you must
use it with the PRESENT PERFECT
tense, not the past tense: *I've
lived here since October* (=I came
to live here in October and I am
still living here).

sincere /sɪnˈsɪərˈ/ *adjective*
true and honest ▶ *a sincere apology*
OPPOSITE: **insincere**

sincerely /sɪnˈsɪəlɪ/ *adverb*
1 in a sincere way ▶ *I sincerely hope
we meet again.*
2 Yours sincerely something you
write at the end of a letter to
someone whose name you know
LOOK AT: **yours**

sing /sɪŋ/ *verb (past tense **sang**
/sæŋ/, past participle **sung** /sʌŋ/)*
to make music with your voice ▶ *She
sang a song.* ▶ *I can hear the birds
singing.*

singer /ˈsɪŋərˈ/ *noun*
a person who sings

single¹ /ˈsɪŋɡəl/ *adjective*
1 only one ▶ *a single flower*
2 not married ▶ *Are you single or
married?*
SAME MEANING: **unmarried**
3 for a journey to a place but not
back ▶ *a single ticket*
COMPARE: **return**

S

4 for one person only ▶ *a single bed*
COMPARE: **double**

5 in single file in a line, one person behind the other ▶ *Walk in single file, please.*

single² noun
a ticket for a journey to a place but not back ▶ *a single to Heathrow*
COMPARE: **return**

single-handedly /ˌsɪŋɡəl ˈhændɪdlɪ/ *(also single-handed* /ˌsɪŋɡəl ˈhændɪd/*) adverb*
done by one person with no help from anyone else ▶ *She's brought up four kids single-handedly.*

single-minded /ˌsɪŋɡəl ˈmaɪndɪd/ *adjective*
very determined to achieve one particular thing ▶ *Clare has always been very single-minded about her career.*

single parent /ˌsɪŋɡəl ˈpeərənt/ *noun*
a mother or father who looks after their children alone, without the other parent

singly /ˈsɪŋɡlɪ/ *adverb*
separately or one at a time ▶ *You can buy stamps singly or in books of ten.*

singular /ˈsɪŋɡjʊləʳ/ *noun*
only one ▶ *"Dog" is the singular of "dogs".*
OPPOSITE: **plural**

sinister /ˈsɪnɪstəʳ/ *adjective*
unpleasant or frightening in a way that seems bad or evil ▶ *She moved towards me with a sinister laugh.*

sink¹ /sɪŋk/ *noun*
a large basin for washing clothes or dishes in

sink² *verb (past tense sank* /sæŋk/*, past participle sunk* /sʌŋk/*)*
1 to go down below or below something ▶ *The sun sank behind the mountain.*
2 to go down under the water ▶ *The ship is sinking.*
OPPOSITE: **(2): float**

3 to make something go down under the water ▶ *to sink a ship*

sinking /ˈsɪŋkɪŋ/ *adjective*
a sinking feeling a feeling you have when you realize that something bad is going to happen ▶ *I opened the letter with a sinking feeling.*

sip¹ /sɪp/ *verb (present participle sipping, past sipped)*
to drink something by taking very small amounts in your mouth ▶ *She sipped the hot tea.*

sip² noun
a very small amount of a drink ▶ *I had a sip of his beer.*

siphon¹ *(also syphon)* /ˈsaɪfən/ *noun*
a tube that you use to take liquid out of a container

siphon² *(also syphon) verb*
to remove liquid from a container using a siphon ▶ *She caught him siphoning petrol out of her car.*

sir /sɜːʳ/ *noun*
1 a polite way of speaking or writing to a man, especially a man you do not know ▶ *I began my letter "Dear Sir".* ▶ *Can I help you, sir?* (=said by a person who works in a shop to one of their customers)
COMPARE: **madam**
2 the title of a KNIGHT ▶ *Sir Steve Redgrave*

siren /ˈsaɪərən/ *noun*
something which makes a loud, long sound to warn you about a danger ▶ *the siren on a police car*

sister /ˈsɪstəʳ/ *noun*
1 a girl who has the same parents as you ▶ *She is my sister.* ▶ *We are sisters.* ▶ *Have you any brothers or sisters?*
COMPARE: **brother**
2 an important nurse who looks after one part of a hospital
3 a NUN

sister-in-law /ˈsɪstər ɪn ˌlɔː/ *noun (plural sisters-in-law)*

1 the sister of your wife or husband

2 the wife of your brother

sit /sɪt/ *verb (present participle sitting, past sat /sæt/)*

1 to rest your bottom on something such as a chair ▶ *Come and sit here.* ▶ *He was sitting on a chair in front of the fire.*

2 sit down to move your body down, after you have been standing up, so that your bottom rests on something ▶ *Would you like to sit down?*

3 sit up to move your body up, after you have been lying down, so that your weight is on your bottom ▶ *I sat up in bed when I heard the noise.*

sitcom /'sɪtkɒm/ *noun*
a funny television programme that is shown regularly and has the same characters but a different story each time

site /saɪt/ *noun*

1 a place where a building is, was, or will be ▶ *The site of the new hotel is right by the sea.*

2 the place where something happened ▶ *the site of a battle*

sitting room /'sɪtɪŋ rʊm/ *noun*
the room in a house where people sit to rest, watch television, etc.

situated /'sɪtʃʊeɪtɪd/ *adjective*
in or at a particular place ▶ *The hotel is situated ten minutes from the sea.*

situation /ˌsɪtʃʊ'eɪʃən/ *noun*
the things that are happening at a particular time and place ▶ *The political situation is very dangerous.*

sit-ups /'sɪt ʌps/ *plural noun*
an exercise in which you lie down on your back and then lift the top part of your body towards your feet ▶ *He does 100 sit-ups every morning.*

six /sɪks/ *adjective, noun*
the number 6

sixteen /ˌsɪk'stiːn/ *adjective, noun*
the number 16

sixteenth /ˌsɪk'stiːnθ/ *adjective*
16th

sixth /sɪksθ/ *adjective, noun*

1 6th

2 one of six equal parts

sixth form /'sɪksθ fɔːm/ *noun*
the last class in a British school, for pupils between 16 and 18 years old ▶ *to be in the sixth form* ▶ *a sixth form college*

sixtieth /'sɪkstɪ-əθ/ *adjective*
60th

sixty /'sɪkstɪ/ *adjective, noun*
the number 60

size /saɪz/ *noun*
how big something or someone is ▶ *Look at the size of that ship!* ▶ *The two rooms were roughly the same size.* ▶ *These shoes are size 5.*

sizzle /'sɪzəl/ *verb (present participle sizzling, past sizzled)*
to make the sound of food cooking in hot oil ▶ *The sausages were sizzling in the pan.*

skate¹ /skeɪt/ *verb (present participle skating, past skated)*
to move smoothly over ice or over ground wearing special shoes ▶ *She skated over the ice towards us.*

skate² *noun*
a special shoe with wheels or a blade fixed under it ▶ *roller skates* ▶ *ice skates*

skateboard /'skeɪtbɔːd/ *noun*
a short board with wheels under it which you stand on and ride along the ground for fun

skateboarding /'skeɪtˌbɔːdɪŋ/ *noun (no plural)*
the activity of riding on a skateboard

skating /'skeɪtɪŋ/ *noun (no plural)*
the sport of moving or dancing over ice or over the ground wearing special shoes

skeleton /'skelɪtən/ *noun*
the bones of a whole animal or person

sketch¹ /sketʃ/ *noun (plural **sketches**)*
a quick, rough drawing

sketch² *verb*
to draw quickly and roughly

sketchy /'sketʃɪ/ *adjective (**sketchier, sketchiest**)*
including only a few details or pieces of information, and not showing exactly or completely what something is like ▶ *The police could only give us some very sketchy information.*

ski¹ /skiː/ *noun*
one of a pair of long, narrow pieces of wood, plastic, or metal which you wear on your feet to travel on snow

ski² *verb*
to travel on snow wearing long, narrow pieces of wood, plastic, or metal on your feet, as a sport ▶ *to go skiing*

skid /skɪd/ *verb (present participle **skidding**, past **skidded**)*
to slip sideways on a wet surface ▶ *The car skidded on a pool of oil and ran into the fence.*

skiing /'skiːɪŋ/ *noun (no plural)*
the sport of travelling on snow with skis on your feet ▶ *Do you like skiing?*

skilful /'skɪlfəl/ *adjective*
doing something well ▶ *a skilful driver* ▶ *a skilful performance (adverb: **skilfully**)*

skill /skɪl/ *noun*
1 something you learn to do ▶ *skills such as reading and writing*
2 *(no plural)* being able to do something well ▶ *He shows great skill as a footballer.*

skilled /skɪld/ *adjective*
1 having the knowledge or training to do a particular thing well ▶ *skilled workers*
2 needing special knowledge or training ▶ *a skilled job*

skim /skɪm/ *verb (present participle **skimming**, past **skimmed**)*
1 *(also **skim through**)* to read something very quickly and not very carefully ▶ *I only had time to skim through the newspaper.*
2 to remove something that is floating on the surface of a liquid ▶ *Skim the fat off the soup.*

skimmed milk /ˌskɪmd 'mɪlk/ *noun (no plural)*
milk that has had most of the fat removed from it

skin /skɪn/ *noun*
the outside of a person, an animal, a vegetable, or a fruit ▶ *a banana skin* ▶ *She has pale skin.*
COMPARE: **flesh**

skinny /'skɪnɪ/ *adjective (**skinnier, skinniest**)*
(used about people and animals) too thin ▶ *a skinny child*
COMPARE: **slim**

skip /skɪp/ *verb (present participle **skipping**, past **skipped**)*
to jump up and down over a rope (=a skipping rope) which you swing over your head and under your feet

skirt /skɜːt/ *noun*
a piece of women's clothing that hangs from the waist and covers part of the legs

skive /skaɪv/ *(also **skive off**) verb (present participle **skiving**, past **skived**)*
to not go to school or work when you should ▶ *He skived off work and went fishing.*

skull /skʌl/ *noun*
the bone which forms your head

sky /skaɪ/ *noun (plural **skies**)*
the space above the Earth which you can see if you look up ▶ *The sky was blue and cloudless.*

skyscraper /'skaɪˌskreɪpəʳ/ *noun*
a very tall, modern building, usually in a city

slab /slæb/ *noun*
a large, flat block of something ▸ *a slab of stone*

slack /slæk/ *adjective*
1 loose ▸ *a slack rope*
OPPOSITE: **tight**
2 not busy ▸ *Things are very slack at work.*

slam /slæm/ *verb (present participle slamming, past slammed)*
to shut a door or window with a loud noise ▸ *He slammed the door angrily.*

slang /slæŋ/ *noun (no plural)*
language you use when talking to friends, people you work with, etc. which is not always suitable or correct ▸ *army slang*

slant¹ /slɑːnt/ *verb*
to lean or slope to one side

slant² *noun*
a sloping position or angle ▸ *The house is on a slant.*

slap¹ /slæp/ *verb (present participle slapping, past slapped)*
to hit someone or something with the flat, inside part of the hand
SAME MEANING: **smack**
COMPARE: **punch**

slap² *noun*
a hit with the flat, inside part of the hand ▸ *a slap across the face*

slap-up /ˈslæp ʌp/ *adjective*
slap-up meal, slap-up dinner a big and good meal

slash¹ /slæʃ/ *verb*
1 to cut something in a violent way, making a long, deep cut ▸ *A gang of boys slashed our tyres.*
2 to reduce something by a lot ▸ *Many companies are slashing prices.*

slash² *noun (plural slashes)*
1 a long, deep cut
2 (also **slash mark**) a line (/) used in writing to separate words, numbers, etc.

slate /sleɪt/ *noun (no plural)*
a type of dark grey rock, or a thin piece of this rock that is used for covering roofs

slaughter¹ /ˈslɔːtər/ *noun (no plural)*
1 the killing of large numbers of people in a cruel way
2 the killing of animals for food

slaughter² *verb*
1 to kill large numbers of people
2 to kill animals for food

slave¹ /sleɪv/ *noun*
a person who is owned by another person and is not free

slave² *verb (present participle slaving, past slaved)*
to work very hard ▸ *I spend all day slaving in the kitchen.*

slavery /ˈsleɪvəri/ *noun (no plural)*
1 the state of being a slave ▸ *to live in slavery*
2 having slaves ▸ *a law against slavery*

sledge /sledʒ/ *noun*
a specially shaped piece of wood or plastic which you sit on for sliding down slopes covered with snow and ice
COMPARE: **sleigh**

sledgehammer /ˈsledʒˌhæmər/ *noun*
a large, heavy hammer

sleek /sliːk/ *adjective*
(used about hair, fur, etc.) smooth and shiny

sleep¹ /sliːp/ *verb (past slept /slept/)*
to rest with your eyes closed and your mind unconscious, the way people do in their beds at night

sleep² *noun*
1 (no plural) the state of not being awake ▸ *I need to get some sleep.*
2 a time when you are in this state ▸ *He had a long sleep.*
3 go to sleep to begin to sleep ▸ *She went to sleep as soon as she closed her eyes.*

sleeping bag /'sli:pɪŋ ˌbæg/ noun
a large bag which you sleep in to keep warm, usually when you are sleeping outdoors

sleepless /'sli:pləs/ adjective
a sleepless night a night when you cannot sleep, for example because you are worried

sleepy /'sli:pɪ/ adjective (**sleepier, sleepiest**)
wanting to sleep ▶ I felt sleepy all day.

sleet /sli:t/ noun (no plural)
a mixture of rain and snow

sleeve /sli:v/ noun
the part of a piece of clothing which covers your arm ▶ a shirt with short sleeves

sleeveless /'sli:vləs/ adjective
without sleeves ▶ a sleeveless shirt

sleigh /sleɪ/ noun
a vehicle for moving over snow and ice, which is pulled by animals ▶ Father Christmas's sleigh
COMPARE: **sledge**

slender /'slendəʳ/ adjective
thin in an attractive way ▶ a slender figure
SAME MEANING: **slim**

slept /slept/
the PAST TENSE and PAST PARTICIPLE of the verb **sleep**

slice¹ /slaɪs/ noun
a flat piece cut from something ▶ a slice **of** meat ▶ a slice of bread

slice² verb (present participle **slicing**, past **sliced**)
to cut something into thin, flat pieces ▶ I sliced the bread thinly.

slide¹ /slaɪd/ verb (present participle **sliding**, past **slid** /slɪd/)
to move smoothly over a surface ▶ She slid across the ice.

slide² noun
a tall piece of apparatus found in parks, etc., with a slope for children to slide down

slight /slaɪt/ adjective
small; not important ▶ I have a slight headache.

slightly /'slaɪtlɪ/ adverb
a little bit ▶ She's slightly older than me. ▶ I'm slightly worried about the cost.

slim¹ /slɪm/ adjective (**slimmer, slimmest**)
thin in an attractive way ▶ He's tall and slim.
SAME MEANING: **slender**
COMPARE: **skinny**

slim² verb (present participle **slimming**, past **slimmed**)
to try to become thinner by eating less food

slime /slaɪm/ noun (no plural)
a thick, sticky liquid that looks or smells unpleasant ▶ The sink was covered in slime.

slimy /'slaɪmɪ/ adjective (**slimier, slimiest**)
1 covered with slime ▶ slimy rocks
2 friendly in a way that is not sincere

sling¹ /slɪŋ/ noun
a piece of cloth passed round something to support it ▶ He had to keep his broken arm in a sling.

sling² verb (past **slung** /slʌŋ/)
to throw something roughly or carelessly

slip¹ /slɪp/ verb (present participle **slipping**, past **slipped**)
1 to slide on a smooth surface by accident ▶ He slipped on the ice and fell.
2 to move quickly, smoothly, or quietly ▶ She slipped out of the room when nobody was looking.
3 to put something somewhere quickly and without people noticing ▶ He slipped the money into his pocket.

slip² noun
1 a small mistake
2 a small piece of paper

S

slipper /ˈslɪpəʳ/ *noun*
a soft shoe that you wear inside your home ▶ *a pair of slippers*

slippery /ˈslɪpəri/ *adjective*
smooth; causing you to slide ▶ *a slippery floor*

slit¹ /slɪt/ *noun*
a long, narrow cut or opening

slit² *verb* (*present participle* **slitting**, *past* **slit**)
to make a long, narrow cut in something ▶ *I slit open the letter with a knife.*

sliver /ˈslɪvəʳ/ *noun*
a small, thin, often pointed piece that has been cut or broken off something ▶ *a sliver of glass* ▶ *a sliver of cheese*

slob /slɒb/ *noun*
a person who is lazy, dirty, or untidy

slogan /ˈsləʊɡən/ *noun*
a short, clever phrase that people will remember, used in advertising and politics

slope¹ /sləʊp/ *noun*
a surface which is higher on one side than the other ▶ *He ran up the slope to the top of the hill.*

slope² *verb* (*present participle* **sloping**, *past* **sloped**)
to have a slope ▶ *The hill slopes down to the town.*

sloppy /ˈslɒpi/ *adjective* (**sloppier**, **sloppiest**)
1 (used about clothes) very loose and not tidy ▶ *a sloppy T-shirt*
2 not careful enough ▶ *sloppy work*

slot /slɒt/ *noun*
a narrow opening ▶ *Put a coin in the slot and see how much you weigh.*

slot machine /ˈslɒt məʃiːn/ *noun*
a machine which you put money into in order to buy something that is inside it or to play a game on it

slouch /slaʊtʃ/ *verb*
to stand, sit, or walk in a lazy way, with your shoulders bent forward

▶ *My mother's always telling me not to slouch.*

slow¹ /sləʊ/ *adjective*
1 taking a long time; not fast ▶ *a slow journey* ▶ *a slow speed*
2 (used about clocks and watches) showing a time that is earlier than the real time ▶ *My watch is a minute slow.*
OPPOSITE (**1** and **2**): **fast**

slow² *verb*
slow down to go less fast than before
▶ *Slow down – you're driving too fast.*
OPPOSITE: **speed up**

slowly /ˈsləʊli/ *adverb*
in a way that takes a long time ▶ *He speaks very slowly.*
OPPOSITE: **fast**

slow motion /ˌsləʊ ˈməʊʃən/ *noun*
in slow motion (used about parts of films or television programmes) shown at a slower speed than the real speed ▶ *Let's look at the end of the race again in slow motion.*

slug /slʌɡ/ *noun*
a soft creature without bones or legs that lives on land and eats plants

slum /slʌm/ *noun*
a poor part of the city, where all the houses are in very bad condition

slump /slʌmp/ *verb*
to suddenly go down in amount, price, or value ▶ *House prices slumped last year.*

slumped /slʌmpt/ *adjective*
be slumped to be sitting with your body bent forwards as if you were unconscious

slung /slʌŋ/
the PAST TENSE and PAST PARTICIPLE of the verb **sling**

slurp /slɜːp/ *verb*
to drink in a noisy way ▶ *Stop slurping your tea!*

slush /slʌʃ/ *noun* (no plural)
snow that has partly melted and looks wet and dirty

sly /slaɪ/ *adjective* (**slier, sliest**)
clever at deceiving people

smack¹ /smæk/ *verb*
to hit someone with your open hand ▶ *She smacked him hard across the face.*
SAME MEANING: **slap**

smack² *noun*
a hit ▶ *Don't do that or you'll get a smack!*

small /smɔːl/ *adjective*
little ▶ *He has a small farm.* ▶ *small children*
OPPOSITE: **big, large**

smallpox /'smɔːlpɒks/ *noun* (no plural)
a serious disease that killed a lot of people in the past

smart /smɑːt/ *adjective*
1 dressed in good, clean clothes ▶ *My sister always looks smart.* ▶ *She always wears smart clothes.*
2 clever ▶ *a smart politician*

smash¹ /smæʃ/ *verb*
1 to break into pieces ▶ *She dropped the plate and it smashed.*
2 to break something into pieces ▶ *to smash a window*

smash² *noun* (plural **smashes**)
1 the sound of something breaking into pieces
2 a car accident

smashing /'smæʃɪŋ/ *adjective*
very good or nice ▶ *We had a smashing time.*
SAME MEANING: **lovely**

smear¹ /smɪərⁿ/ *verb*
to leave a sticky, dirty, or oily mark on something ▶ *The child's face was smeared with chocolate.*

smear² *noun*
a dirty mark ▶ *a smear of grease*

smell¹ /smel/ *verb* (past **smelt** /smelt/)
1 to use your nose to notice or discover something ▶ *He smelt the*

flowers. ▶ *I can smell gas.*
2 to have a particular effect on your nose ▶ *The flowers smell lovely.* ▶ *This fish smells bad.* ▶ *It smells of cigarettes in here.*

smell² *noun*
something that you can notice or discover only through your nose ▶ *There's a bad smell in here.* ▶ *the smell of cooking*

smelly /'smelɪ/ *adjective* (**smellier, smelliest**)
having a bad, strong smell
COMPARE: **fragrant**

smelt /smelt/
the PAST TENSE and PAST PARTICIPLE of the verb **smell**

smile¹ /smaɪl/ *verb* (present participle **smiling**, past **smiled**)
to turn up the corners of your mouth to show that you are happy or pleased ▶ *to smile at someone*

smile² *noun*
a smiling expression ▶ *He had a big smile on his face.*

smirk /smɜːk/ *verb*
to smile in an unpleasant way, as though you are laughing at someone ▶ *The other girls pointed at her and smirked.*

smog /smɒg/ *noun* (no plural)
unhealthy air in cities that is a mixture of smoke, gases, chemicals, etc.

smoke¹ /sməʊk/ *noun* (no plural)
dark-coloured gas caused by something burning

smoke² *verb* (present participle **smoking**, past **smoked**)
1 to use cigarettes or a pipe ▶ *Do you smoke?* ▶ *to smoke a cigarette*
2 (used about a fire) to make smoke

smoker /'sməʊkərⁿ/ *noun*
a person who uses cigarettes or a pipe ▶ *This part of the restaurant is for smokers.*

smoking /'sməʊkɪŋ/ noun (no plural)
the habit of using cigarettes or a pipe
▶ *Smoking is not allowed in school.*
▶ *No Smoking* (=a sign which means
that you must not smoke)

smoky /'sməʊkɪ/ adjective (**smokier,
smokiest**)
full of smoke ▶ *a smoky room*

smooth /smuːð/ adjective
1 having a flat, even surface without
any lumps ▶ *smooth skin*
OPPOSITE: **rough**
2 without problems or difficulties
▶ *a smooth journey*

smoothly /'smuːðlɪ/ adverb
well and without problems or
difficulties ▶ *Everything went
smoothly at work.*

smother /'smʌðəʳ/ verb
1 to stop air from reaching a person
by putting something on their face
2 to cover something completely ▶ *a
cake smothered with chocolate*

smoulder /'sməʊldəʳ/ verb
to burn slowly without a flame

smudge¹ /smʌdʒ/ noun
a dirty spot or area caused by touching
or rubbing something wet or soft

smudge² verb (present participle
smudging, past **smudged**)
(used about ink, paint, etc.) to
become unclear because someone
has rubbed it, especially accidentally
▶ *Now look! You've smudged my
drawing!*

smug /smʌg/ adjective (**smugger,
smuggest**)
very pleased with yourself, in a way
that is annoying to other people ▶ *"I
told you that would happen," she
said, trying not to sound too smug.*

smuggle /'smʌgəl/ verb (present
participle **smuggling**, past **smuggled**)
to bring people or things secretly into
a country in a way which is against
the law ▶ *to smuggle drugs into a
country*

smuggler /'smʌgləʳ/ noun
a person who breaks the law by
bringing things secretly into a country
▶ *drug smugglers*

snack /snæk/ noun
a small, quick meal

snack bar /'snæk bɑːʳ/ noun
a place where you can buy drinks and
small, quick meals

snag /snæg/ noun
a small difficulty or problem

snail /sneɪl/ noun
a soft creature, without bones or legs
but with a round shell on its back,
which eats plants

snake /sneɪk/ noun
a very long, thin animal without legs.
Some snakes make you ill or kill you
if they bite you

snap¹ /snæp/ verb (present participle
snapping, past **snapped**)
1 to break with a sharp noise ▶ *The
branch snapped under his foot.*
2 to try to bite someone ▶ *Your dog
snapped at me.*
3 to speak quickly in an angry way
▶ *"Leave me alone!" she snapped.*

snap² noun
1 a sharp sound of something breaking
2 a photograph ▶ *holiday snaps*

snarl /snɑːl/ verb
1 (used about animals) to make an
angry noise with the mouth open and
teeth showing ▶ *The two dogs
snarled at each other, and then
started fighting.*
2 to say something in a very fierce
way

snatch /snætʃ/ verb
to take hold of something quickly and
roughly ▶ *She snatched the book
from my hands.*
SAME MEANING: **grab**

sneak /sniːk/ verb
to go quietly because you do not
want people to see or hear you ▶ *The*

children sneaked out of school and went to the park.

sneaking /ˈsniːkɪŋ/ *adjective*
have a sneaking suspicion, have a sneaking feeling to think you know something without being sure ➤ *I have a sneaking suspicion that she's lying.*

sneaky /ˈsniːkɪ/ *adjective* (**sneakier, sneakiest**)
doing things in a secret and clever but unfair way

sneer /snɪəʳ/ *verb*
to smile in a nasty way to show that you have a low opinion of someone or something ➤ *He sneered at the mention of his name.*

sneeze /sniːz/ *verb* (*present participle* **sneezing,** *past* **sneezed**)
to suddenly push air out of your nose and mouth, making a noise, usually because you have a cold

sniff /snɪf/ *verb*
1 to take air into your nose in short breaths, for example when you have a cold or when you are crying ➤ *Stop sniffing – use a handkerchief!*
2 to smell something by taking air into your nose ➤ *The dog sniffed the bone.*

snigger /ˈsnɪɡəʳ/ *verb*
to laugh quietly in an unkind way ➤ *What are you sniggering at?*

snip /snɪp/ *verb* (*present participle* **snipping,** *past* **snipped**)
to cut something with quick, small cuts, using scissors ➤ *Snip the corner off the packet.*

snippet /ˈsnɪpɪt/ *noun*
a small piece of information or news ➤ *I heard snippets of the story from my sister.*

snob /snɒb/ *noun*
a person who admires people who are from rich and important families, and has a low opinion of people who are not

snooker /ˈsnuːkəʳ/ *noun (no plural)*
a game played on a table with a green top in which people try to push balls into holes using long sticks

snoop /snuːp/ *verb*
to try to find out about someone's activities by secretly looking at their things ➤ *I caught her snooping around in my office.*

snooze¹ /snuːz/ *verb* (*present participle* **snoozing,** *past* **snoozed**)
to have a short, light sleep ➤ *She was snoozing in her armchair.*
SAME MEANING: **doze**

snooze² *noun (no plural)*
a short, light sleep ➤ *to have a snooze*

snore /snɔːʳ/ *verb* (*present participle* **snoring,** *past* **snored**)
to make a noise in your nose or throat when you are asleep

snorkel /ˈsnɔːkəl/ *noun*
a tube which lets you breathe when you are swimming underwater

snort /snɔːt/ *verb*
to make a loud noise by forcing air out through your nose because you think something is unpleasant or funny ➤ *He read the letter and snorted in disgust.*

snot /snɒt/ *noun (no plural)*
an impolite word for the thick liquid in your nose

snout /snaʊt/ *noun*
the long nose of some animals, such as pigs

snow¹ /snəʊ/ *noun (no plural)*
soft, white pieces of frozen water which fall from the sky and cover the ground when it is cold

snow² *verb*
when it snows, snow falls down from the sky ➤ *It's snowing!*

snowball /ˈsnəʊbɔːl/ *noun*
a small ball of snow which children make and throw at each other for fun

S

snowboard /'snəʊbɔːd/ *noun*
a long, wide board which you place your feet on and use to move over snow in the sport called snowboarding

snowboarding /'snəʊˌbɔːdɪŋ/ *noun (no plural)*
a sport in which you move over snow on a snowboard

snowflake /'snəʊfleɪk/ *noun*
a soft, white piece of frozen water which falls from the sky

snowman /'snəʊmæn/ *noun (plural* **snowmen** /-men/)
a figure like a man, made with two large lumps of snow

snowplough /'snəʊplaʊ/ *noun*
a vehicle for removing snow from roads

snowy /'snəʊɪ/ *adjective (**snowier**, **snowiest**)*
having a lot of snow or covered in snow ➤ *snowy weather* ➤ *snowy hills*

snub /snʌb/ *verb (present participle* **snubbing**, *past* **snubbed**)
to deliberately not talk to someone or not be friendly towards them ➤ *She always snubs me when she sees me.*

snug /snʌg/ *adjective (**snugger**, **snuggest**)*
warm and comfortable ➤ *a snug little bed*

snuggle /'snʌgəl/ *verb (present participle* **snuggling**, *past* **snuggled**)
to get into a warm, comfortable position ➤ *Ed and Sara snuggled up on the sofa.*

so¹ /səʊ/ *adverb, adjective*
1 in such a way; to such a point ➤ *I was so tired that I fell asleep on the bus.*
2 also ➤ *Ann was there, and so was Mary.*
3 very; very much ➤ *You have been so kind to me.*
4 the same; that same thing ➤ *"Will I need my coat?" "I don't think so."*

➤ *"Is dinner ready?" "I hope so."*
5 used to show agreement ➤ *"Look – it's raining!" "So it is!"*
6 so far up to this time ➤ *I've read 20 pages of the book so far.*
7 or so used when you are not giving the exact number or amount ➤ *The journey takes an hour or so.*

so² *conjunction*
1 therefore ➤ *I promised to send him a letter, so I'll write it now.* ➤ *I was very hungry so I had another sandwich.*
2 in order to do something or make something happen ➤ *We got up early so **that** we could go for a swim.* ➤ *I put your keys in the drawer so they wouldn't get lost.*

soak /səʊk/ *verb*
1 to leave something in a liquid ➤ *She soaked the shirt to get the stain out.*
2 to make something very wet ➤ *The rain soaked us through.*

soaked /səʊkt/ *adjective*
very wet ➤ *I'm absolutely soaked.*

soaking /'səʊkɪŋ/ *adjective*
very wet ➤ *My clothes are soaking wet.*

soap /səʊp/ *noun (no plural)*
a substance that cleans things when it is put with water ➤ *a bar of soap*

soap opera /'səʊp ˌɒpərə/ *noun*
a radio or television story about the lives and problems of a group of imaginary people, which is shown very frequently ➤ *the soap opera "Eastenders"*

soap powder /'səʊp ˌpaʊdəʳ/ *noun (no plural)*
a powder which you put in water for washing clothes

soapy /'səʊpɪ/ *adjective (**soapier**, **soapiest**)*
containing soap ➤ *soapy water*

soar /sɔːʳ/ *verb*
1 to fly high in the air

S

2 to rise or become very high ▶ *Prices are soaring again.*

sob /sɒb/ *verb (present participle **sobbing**, past **sobbed**)*
to cry noisily

sober /ˈsəʊbəʳ/ *adjective*
not having had too much alcoholic drink
OPPOSITE: **drunk**

so-called /ˌsəʊ ˈkɔːld/ *adjective*
used to show that you think the word used to describe something is wrong ▶ *The so-called expert turned out to be a research student.*

soccer /ˈsɒkəʳ/ *noun (no plural)*
football ▶ *a soccer team*

sociable /ˈsəʊʃəbəl/ *adjective*
enjoying the company of other people

social /ˈsəʊʃəl/ *adjective*
1 concerning people and the way they live together ▶ *social problems such as crime* ▶ *social class*
2 concerning activities in which you enjoy the company of other people when you are not working ▶ *He has a lot of friends and a good social life.*

socialism /ˈsəʊʃəl-ɪzəm/ *noun (no plural)*
a political system that tries to give equal opportunities to all people, and in which many industries are owned by the state

socialist /ˈsəʊʃəlɪst/ *noun*
a person who believes in socialism

socialize /ˈsəʊʃəlaɪz/ *verb (present participle **socializing**, past **socialized**)*
to spend time with other people in a friendly way

social security /ˌsəʊʃəl sɪˈkjʊərəti/ *noun (no plural)*
money paid by the government to people without a job or without much money

social work /ˈsəʊʃəl wɜːk/ *noun (no plural)*
the job of helping people with social problems, because, for example, they live in bad conditions, are very ill, or have difficulties with their families

social worker /ˈsəʊʃəl ˌwɜːkəʳ/ *noun*
someone who is trained to help people with social problems, because, for example, they live in bad conditions, are very ill, or have difficulties with their families

society /səˈsaɪəti/ *noun*
1 (no plural) people who live together with shared ideas about how to live ▶ *Society makes laws to protect people.*
2 (plural **societies**) a club; a group of people with shared interests ▶ *a music society*

sociology /ˌsəʊsiˈɒlədʒi/ *noun (no plural)*
the study of the relationships between different groups of people in society

sock /sɒk/ *noun*
a soft piece of clothing you wear on your foot and the bottom part of your leg
COMPARE: **shoe**

socket /ˈsɒkɪt/ *noun*
a hole or set of holes for something to fit into ▶ *an electric socket*

soda /ˈsəʊdə/ (also **soda water** /ˈsəʊdə ˌwɔːtəʳ/) *noun*
water that contains BUBBLES, that you mix with other drinks

sofa /ˈsəʊfə/ *noun*
a long, soft chair for two or more people to sit on ▶ *sitting on the sofa in front of the television*
SAME MEANING: **couch, settee**

soft /sɒft/ *adjective*
1 moving inwards when pressed ▶ *a soft bed*
OPPOSITE: **hard**
2 feeling smooth and pleasant ▶ *soft skin*
3 quiet and pleasant ▶ *soft music*
4 not bright ▶ *soft colours*

soft drink /'sɒft drɪŋk/ noun
a drink with no alcohol in it

soften /'sɒfən/ verb
to become softer, or to make
something become softer ➤ Your
shoes will soften as you wear them.

softly /'sɒftlɪ/ adverb
quietly ➤ to speak softly

software /'sɒftweəʳ/ noun (no plural)
computer PROGRAMS ➤ Which software
can I use with this computer?
COMPARE: **hardware**

soggy /'sɒgɪ/ adjective (**soggier,
soggiest**)
full of water and very wet

soil /sɔɪl/ noun (no plural)
the earth in which plants grow

solar /'səʊləʳ/ adjective
of or using the sun ➤ solar heat

solar panel /'səʊlə ˌpænl/ noun
a piece of equipment that changes
the sun's light into electricity

solar system /'səʊlə ˌsɪstəm/ noun
the solar system the sun and all the
PLANETS that move around it

sold /səʊld/
the PAST TENSE and PAST PARTICIPLE of the
verb **sell**

soldier /'səʊldʒəʳ/ noun
a person in the army

sold-out /ˌsəʊld 'aʊt/ adjective
if a concert or other event is sold out,
all the tickets have been sold

sole /səʊl/ noun
the part of your foot or shoe which is
on the ground when you stand

solely /'səʊl-lɪ/ adverb
only ➤ Grants are awarded solely on
the basis of need.

solemn /'sɒləm/ adjective
serious ➤ a solemn face ➤ a solemn
promise (adverb: **solemnly**)

solicitor /sə'lɪsɪtəʳ/ noun
a type of lawyer

solid¹ /'sɒlɪd/ adjective
1 hard; not liquid or gas ➤ The milk
was frozen solid.
2 made of one material all the way
through ➤ This table is solid wood.

solid² noun
a substance that is hard, not a liquid
or gas

solitary /'sɒlɪtərɪ/ adjective
a solitary person or thing is the only
one in a place ➤ A solitary tree grew
on the hilltop.

solo¹ /'səʊləʊ/ adjective, adverb
done alone, without anyone else
helping you ➤ his first solo flight

solo² noun
a piece of music for one performer

soloist /'səʊləʊɪst/ noun
a musician who performs a solo

solution /sə'luːʃən/ noun
the answer to a problem or question
➤ to find the solution to a problem

solve /sɒlv/ verb (present participle
solving, past **solved**)
to find the answer to something ➤ to
solve a crime (=to discover who did it)

sombre /'sɒmbəʳ/ adjective
sad and serious ➤ He was in a
sombre mood.

some /səm; strong sʌm/ adjective,
pronoun, adverb
1 an amount of; a number of; not all
➤ She had a big piece of cake and
gave me some too. ➤ Would you like
some sweets? ➤ We invited all our
friends, but only some of them came.
➤ Would you like some more coffee?
LOOK AT: **any**
2 used when speaking about people
or things without saying exactly
which ones ➤ Some people just don't
like cats.

somebody /'sʌmbədɪ/ (also
someone) pronoun
1 any person ➤ Can somebody answer
the phone?

2 some unknown person, or a person the speaker does not name ▶ *There is somebody knocking at the door.* ▶ *I know somebody who could help.*
LOOK AT: **anybody**

someday /'sʌmdeɪ/ *adverb*
at an unknown time in the future ▶ *Maybe someday I'll get married!*

somehow /'sʌmhaʊ/ *adverb*
in some way that is not known ▶ *We will get the money somehow.*

someone /'sʌmwʌn/ *pronoun*
another word for **somebody**
LOOK AT: **anybody**

somersault /'sʌməsɔːlt/ *noun*
an action in which you jump and turn upside down at the same time ▶ *to do a somersault*

something /'sʌmθɪŋ/ *pronoun*
a thing that is not known or not described ▶ *I want to tell you something.* ▶ *She bought something to eat.* ▶ *She said something about it, but I can't remember what it was.*
LOOK AT: **anything**

sometime /'sʌmtaɪm/ *adverb*
at some time in the past or in the future ▶ *I hope I'll see you again sometime.*

sometimes /'sʌmtaɪmz/ *adverb*
at times; now and then ▶ *Sometimes I help my mother in the house.* ▶ *We sometimes go to the cinema, but not very often.*

somewhat /'sʌwɒt/ *adverb*
more than a little, but not very ▶ *I was somewhat annoyed.*

somewhere /'sʌmweəʳ/ *adverb*
in, to, or at some place ▶ *At last he found somewhere to park the car.* ▶ *She's looking for somewhere to live.*

son /sʌn/ *noun*
your male child ▶ *I have a son and a daughter.*

The word **son** is used when you are talking about a male child only. Compare the questions: *Do you have any sons* (=do you have any male children)*?* and *Do you have any children* (=do you have any sons or daughters)*?*

song /sɒŋ/ *noun*
a piece of music with words that are sung
COMPARE: **tune**

son-in-law /'sʌn ɪn lɔː/ *noun (plural sons-in-law)*
the husband of your daughter

soon /suːn/ *adverb*
1 in a short time ▶ *Dinner will be ready soon.* ▶ *Come and see me again soon.*

Compare these sentences: *I must go to bed soon* (=in a short time from now). ▶ *I must go to bed early* (=before the usual time). Compare also **soon** and **quickly**: *Do it soon* (=do it in a short time from now). ▶ *Do it quickly* (=do it fast).

2 soon after a short time after ▶ *He arrived soon after 8 o'clock.*

3 as soon as when; at the earliest possible moment ▶ *I'll do it as soon as I can.* ▶ *She came as soon as she had finished work.*

4 too soon too early ▶ *It's too soon to know the results of the test.*

soot /sʊt/ *noun (no plural)*
the black powder left by smoke inside a chimney

soothe /suːð/ *verb (present participle soothing, past soothed)*
1 to make someone calm when they are angry or afraid
2 to make something less painful ▶ *medicine to soothe a sore throat*

sophisticated /sə'fɪstɪkeɪtɪd/ *adjective*
1 (used about people) having a lot of experience of modern, fashionable life ▶ *a sophisticated city girl*

S

2 (used about machines) designed in a very clever way ▶ *a sophisticated computer*

soppy /ˈsɒpi/ *adjective* (**soppier, soppiest**)
expressing sadness or love in a way that seems silly ▶ *a soppy film*

soprano /səˈprɑːnəʊ/ *noun*
a woman, girl, or young boy singer with a very high voice

sordid /ˈsɔːdɪd/ *adjective*
unpleasant and dishonest ▶ *He told me all the sordid details of his love affair.*

sore¹ /sɔːʳ/ *adjective*
painful ▶ *a sore throat*

sore² *noun*
a painful place on your skin, especially one caused by a disease

sorrow /ˈsɒrəʊ/ *noun*
a feeling of great sadness

sorry /ˈsɒri/ *adjective* (**sorrier, sorriest**)
1 sad ▶ *I was sorry to hear your bad news.* ▶ *I'm sorry, but I can't come to your party.*
2 sad about something you have done ▶ *I'm sorry about the trouble I've caused.*
3 used when you want someone to repeat something they have said because you did not hear it ▶ *I'm sorry – what did you say your name was?* ▶ *Sorry? Can you repeat that?*

sort¹ /sɔːt/ *noun*
kind; type ▶ *A hammer is a sort of tool.*
LOOK AT: **kind**

sort² *verb*
1 to put together things that are alike ▶ *The post office sorts letters according to which town they are going to.*
2 sort something out to find an answer to a problem ▶ *We have a few problems to sort out.*

SOS /ˌes əʊ ˈes/ *noun*
"save our souls"; used as a SIGNAL to call for help when a ship, plane, or person is in danger

so-so /ˈsəʊ səʊ/ *adjective, adverb*
not very good ▶ *"How was the film?" "So-so."*

sought /sɔːt/
the PAST TENSE and PAST PARTICIPLE of the verb **seek**

soul /səʊl/ *noun*
the part of you that many people think does not die when your body dies

sound¹ /saʊnd/ *noun*
something you hear ▶ *the sound of birds singing*

> **Sound** is the general word for anything that you hear: *the sound of music* ▶ *the sound of a baby crying.* A **noise** is usually something which is loud and not nice: *Stop making that terrible noise!*

sound² *verb*
1 to seem ▶ *That sounds like a good idea.* ▶ *It sounds as if you like your new job.*
2 to make a sound ▶ *When the bell sounds, come in.*

sound³ *adjective*
1 sensible; likely to produce good results ▶ *sound advice* ▶ *a sound investment*
2 in good condition; healthy or strong ▶ *The floors are sound but the roof leaks.*

sound⁴ *adverb*
sound asleep completely asleep ▶ *The baby is sound asleep.*

sound effects /ˈsaʊnd ɪˌfekts/ *plural noun*
the sounds produced artificially for a film, radio programme, etc.

soundly /ˈsaʊndli/ *adverb*
sleep soundly to sleep deeply and well

soundproof /ˈsaʊndpruːf/ *adjective*
not allowing sound to go through
▶ *soundproof walls*

soundtrack /ˈsaʊndtræk/ *noun*
the recorded music from a film

soup /suːp/ *noun*
liquid food made from meat, fish, or
vegetables ▶ *a bowl of chicken soup*

sour /saʊəʳ/ *adjective*
1 tasting sharp, like a LEMON
2 (used about milk) bad because it is
too old

source /sɔːs/ *noun*
where something comes from ▶ *The
river is the source of all our water.*
▶ *That book is a good source of
information.*

south /saʊθ/ *noun, adjective, adverb*
the direction that is on the right when
you look at the sun at the start of the
morning. ▶ *London is in the south of
England.* ▶ *the south side of the city*
▶ *Birds fly south in winter.* ▶ *living
south of Oxford*

southbound /ˈsaʊθbaʊnd/ *adjective*
travelling or leading towards the
south ▶ *southbound traffic*

southeast /ˌsaʊθˈiːst/ *noun, adjective,
adverb*
the direction that is between south
and east ▶ *in the southeast of a
country* ▶ *the southeast part of a city*
▶ *to travel southeast* ▶ *living
southeast of Oxford*

southerly /ˈsʌðəlɪ/ *adjective*
1 towards the south ▶ *a ship on a
southerly course*
2 (used about the wind) blowing from
the south

southern /ˈsʌðən/
adjective
in or of the south ▶ *a southern town*
▶ *southern cooking*

southerner /ˈsʌðənəʳ/ *noun*
someone who comes from the south
of a country

South Pole /ˌsaʊθ ˈpəʊl/ *noun*
the most southern point of the Earth

southward /ˈsaʊθwəd/ *adjective*
towards the south ▶ *They headed in a
southward direction.*

southwards /ˈsaʊθwədz/ *adverb*
towards the south ▶ *We travelled
southwards for three days.*

southwest /ˌsaʊθˈwest/ *noun,
adjective, adverb*
the direction that is between south
and west ▶ *in the southwest of a
country* ▶ *the southwest part of a city*
▶ *to travel southwest* ▶ *living
southwest of Oxford*

souvenir /ˌsuːvəˈnɪəʳ/ *noun*
something that you buy or keep to
help you remember a place or an
event ▶ *holiday souvenirs*

sovereign /ˈsɒvrɪn/ *noun*
a king or queen

sow /səʊ/ *verb (past participle **sown**
/səʊn/)*
to put seeds in the ground so that
they will grow into plants

soya bean /ˈsɔɪə biːn/ *(also **soybean**
/ˈsɔɪbiːn/) noun*
a bean that you can cook and eat,
often used instead of meat to make
other foods

space /speɪs/ *noun*
1 (no plural) the empty area that
surrounds the sun, the Earth, etc.
2 an empty space ▶ *Is there a space
for me at your table?* ▶ *There isn't
enough space for any more furniture.*

spaceship /ˈspeɪsʃɪp/ *noun*
a vehicle that can carry people
through space ▶ *They travelled to the
moon in a spaceship.*

space shuttle /ˈspeɪs ˌʃʌtl/ *noun*
a type of spaceship that can leave the
Earth to travel in space and then
return to the Earth again

spacious /ˈspeɪʃəs/ *adjective*
having a lot of space in which you

S

can move around ▶ *a spacious kitchen*

spade /speɪd/ *noun*
a tool that you use for making holes in the earth or turning the earth over before growing plants

spaghetti /spə'getɪ/ *noun (no plural)*
a kind of Italian food made from flour and water, which looks like long, thin pieces of string

span¹ /spæn/ *noun*
1 the amount of time during which something exists or happens ▶ *Most children have a short attention span.* ▶ *The mayfly has a two-day life span.*
2 wing span the distance from one side of a plane's or bird's wing to the other ▶ *The plane has a wing span of 40 feet.*

span² *verb (present participle spanning, past spanned)*
to include all of a period of time ▶ *His career spanned 40 years.*

spaniel /'spænjəl/ *noun*
a type of dog with long, soft ears and big eyes

spank /spæŋk/ *verb*
to hit a child on the bottom with an open hand as a punishment

spanner /'spænər/ *noun*
a tool that you use for turning things that are tight

spare¹ /speər/ *adjective*
1 kept in addition to what you usually have or need ▶ *If you have a spare bed, may I stay tonight?*
2 spare time time when you are not working or busy ▶ *He paints pictures in his spare time.*

spare² *verb (present participle sparing, past spared)*
to be able to give or lend something ▶ *Can you spare me some money?*

spark /spɑːk/ *noun*
a very small piece of burning material that jumps from a fire

sparkle /'spɑːkəl/ *verb (present participle sparkling, past sparkled)*
to shine with bright points of light, like a diamond ▶ *sparkling eyes*

sparrow /'spærəʊ/ *noun*
a small, brown bird that is very common in many parts of the world

sparse /spɑːs/ *adjective*
existing only in small amounts ▶ *a rocky area with sparse vegetation* (adverb: **sparsely**)

spasm /'spæzəm/ *noun*
an uncontrollable movement in which your muscles suddenly become tight ▶ *back spasms*

spat /spæt/
the PAST TENSE and PAST PARTICIPLE of the verb **spit**

spate /speɪt/ *noun*
a large number of similar, especially bad, events that happen within a short period of time ▶ *a spate of burglaries*

speak /spiːk/ *verb (past tense spoke* /spəʊk/, *past participle spoken* /'spəʊkən/)
1 to say words aloud ▶ *Children learn to speak when they are very small.* ▶ *Can I speak to you about something?*
2 to be able to talk in a particular language ▶ *She speaks English and German.*

speaker /'spiːkər/ *noun*
1 a person who is talking to a large group of people about something ▶ *Our next speaker has come all the way from New York: Professor Gill.*
2 the part of a radio, CD player, television, etc. where the sound comes out

spear /spɪər/ *noun*
a long, thin weapon with a pointed end that is thrown at a person or an animal

spearhead /'spɪəhed/ *verb*
to lead an attack or an organized action ► *British soldiers spearheaded the attack.*

special /'speʃəl/ *adjective*
1 not usual or ordinary; important for a reason ► *This is a special day in the history of our country.*
2 only for a particular person, group, or thing ► *a special school for deaf children*

special effects /ˌspeʃəl ɪˈfekts/ *plural noun*
images and sounds produced for a film or television programme that make something that does not really happen or exist seem real

specialist /'speʃəlɪst/ *noun*
a person who knows a lot about a particular thing

speciality /ˌspeʃɪˈælɪtɪ/ *noun (plural specialities)*
1 a subject that you know a lot about ► *My speciality is European history.*
2 food that is cooked in a particular restaurant or area in a special way and is always good ► *Fish is the speciality of the restaurant.*

specialize /'speʃəlaɪz/ *verb (present participle specializing, past specialized)*
to study or know about one particular thing ► *That doctor specializes in children's illnesses.*

specially /'speʃəlɪ/ *adverb*
1 for one purpose ► *I came here specially to meet you.*
2 more than usual ► *He is not specially clever, but he works hard.*

species /'spiːʃiːz/ *noun (plural species)*
a group of plants or animals of the same type ► *a rare species of bird*

specific /spəˈsɪfɪk/ *adjective*
clear and exact ► *Can you be specific about your reasons for leaving?*

specifically /spəˈsɪfɪklɪ/ *adverb*
clearly and exactly ► *I specifically told you not to do that.*

specify /'spesɪfaɪ/ *verb (past specified)*
to give exact details about something ► *Did he specify which route he would take?*

specimen /'spesɪmən/ *noun*
a small amount of something which is used as an example of what the whole thing is like ► *The doctor took a specimen of blood from his arm.*

speck /spek/ *noun*
a small piece of something ► *a speck of dust*

spectacle /'spektəkəl/ *noun*
an unusual or a strange thing to see ► *the bizarre spectacle of Tom dressed as a woman*

spectacles /'spektəkəlz/ *plural noun*
glasses for your eyes, set in a frame which rests on your nose and ears
SAME MEANING: **glasses**

spectacular /spekˈtækjʊləʳ/ *adjective*
very special; causing admiration ► *a spectacular view from the top of the mountain*

spectator /spekˈteɪtəʳ/ *noun*
a person who goes to watch a sport being played

speculate /'spekjʊleɪt/ *verb (present participle speculating, past speculated)*
to guess the reason for something ► *Everyone speculated about why he left.*

sped /sped/
a PAST TENSE and PAST PARTICIPLE of the verb **speed**

speech /spiːtʃ/ *noun*
1 (no plural) the ability to speak ► *Speech is learnt in the first years of life.*
2 (plural **speeches**) a long set of words spoken for people to listen to

▶ *The President made a speech about the economy.*

speechless /'spiːtʃləs/ *adjective*
unable to speak because you are too angry, shocked, upset, etc. ▶ *She was speechless when I told her the news.*

speech marks /'spiːtʃ mɑːks/ *plural noun*
the signs (" ") or (' '), used in writing to show what somebody says
SAME MEANING: **inverted commas**

speed¹ /spiːd/ *noun*
how fast something moves ▶ *a speed of 80 miles an hour* ▶ *to increase the speed of something* ▶ *to travel at high speed*

speed² *verb (past **speeded** or **sped** /sped/)*
1 to move quickly ▶ *The car sped off into the distance.* ▶ *The holidays sped by (=passed very quickly).*
2 speed up to start to go faster ▶ *You work too slowly; try to speed up a bit.*
OPPOSITE (**2**): **slow down**

speedboat /'spiːdbəʊt/ *noun*
a small, fast boat with a powerful engine

speeding /'spiːdɪŋ/ *noun (no plural)*
the crime of driving too fast ▶ *The police stopped me for speeding.*

speed limit /'spiːd ˌlɪmɪt/ *noun*
a law which says how fast you can travel on certain roads ▶ *to break the speed limit*

spell¹ /spel/ *verb (past **spelled** or **spelt** /spelt/)*
to say the letters that make up a word ▶ *You spell dog D-O-G.*

spell² *noun*
a set of magic words used to make something happen

spelling /'spelɪŋ/ *noun (no plural)*
the act of saying the letters that make up words ▶ *to be good at spelling*

spelt /spelt/
a PAST TENSE and PAST PARTICIPLE of the verb **spell**

spend /spend/ *verb (past **spent** /spent/)*
1 to pay out money to buy things ▶ *How much money do you spend each week?*
2 to pass or use time ▶ *I spent an hour reading.*

sperm /spɜːm/ *noun (no plural)*
a liquid produced inside a man's sex organs, containing cells that join with an egg in a woman to produce new life

sphere /sfɪə/ *noun*
a solid, round shape, like a ball

spherical /'sferɪkəl/ *adjective*
having a round shape like a ball

spice /spaɪs/ *noun*
a seed, root, or other part of a plant, used to give a strong or hot taste to food ▶ *Pepper is a spice.*

spicy /'spaɪsɪ/ *adjective (**spicier, spiciest**)*
having a strong, hot taste ▶ *spicy food*

spider /'spaɪdər/ *noun*
a creature with eight legs, which uses threads from its body to catch insects

spied /spaɪd/
the PAST TENSE and PAST PARTICIPLE of the verb **spy**

spies /spaɪz/
the plural of **spy**

spike /spaɪk/ *noun*
a long, thin object with a sharp point, especially a piece of metal

spiky /'spaɪkɪ/ *adjective (**spikier, spikiest**)*
having a lot of sharp points ▶ *She had short, spiky hair.*

spill /spɪl/ *verb (past **spilled** or **spilt** /spɪlt/)*
1 to let a liquid fall and pour out ▶ *I spilt coffee on the table.*

2 (used about a liquid) to pour out by mistake ▶ *The coffee spilt all over the table.*

spin /spɪn/ *verb (present participle **spinning**, past **spun** /spʌn/)*
1 to go round and round fast ▶ *The wheels of the car were spinning round.*
2 to make thread by twisting cotton, wool, etc. round

spinach /'spɪnɪdʒ/ *noun (no plural)*
a vegetable with big, dark green leaves

spinal /'spaɪnl/ *adjective*
of or affecting the SPINE ▶ *a spinal injury*

spin doctor /'spɪn ˌdɒktəʳ/ *noun*
a person whose job is to give information to the public in a way that makes a politician or an organization seem very good

spin-dryer /ˌspɪn 'draɪəʳ/ *noun*
a machine which removes the water from wet clothes by moving them round and round very fast

spine /spaɪn/ *noun*
the long row of bones in your back
SAME MEANING: **backbone**

spineless /'spaɪnləs/ *adjective*
lacking courage and determination ▶ *He's too spineless to speak for himself.*

spinning wheel /'spɪnɪŋ ˌwiːl/ *noun*
a wheel used in the past to make thread from wool

spin-off /'spɪn ɒf/ *noun*
a product that a person or company develops from something else ▶ *The film's spin-offs include toys, clothes, and a magazine.*

spinster /'spɪnstəʳ/ *noun*
a woman who has never married and is not likely to marry in the future
COMPARE: **bachelor**

spiral /'spaɪrəl/ *noun, adjective*
a shape that goes round and round as it goes up or down

spire /'spaɪəʳ/ *noun*
a tall tower with a point at the top, which is part of a church

spirit /'spɪrɪt/ *noun*
1 the part of you that many people think does not die when your body dies
2 spirits *plural noun* strong alcoholic drink such as RUM or BRANDY ▶ *He never drinks spirits.*

spiritual /'spɪrɪtʃʊəl/ *adjective*
1 relating to someone's mind and their deepest thoughts and feelings, rather than things such as money, possessions, etc. ▶ *spiritual health and wellbeing*
2 relating to religion ▶ *spiritual songs*

spit /spɪt/ *verb (present participle **spitting**, past **spat** /spæt/)*
to throw liquid with your mouth; to throw something out of your mouth ▶ *He spat on the floor.* ▶ *The child spat out its food.*

spite /spaɪt/ *noun (no plural)*
1 the feeling of wanting to hurt or annoy another person ▶ *to do something out of spite*
2 in spite of even though something else happens or is true ▶ *I went out in spite of the rain.* ▶ *In spite of being the youngest, she was the cleverest child in the class.*

spiteful /'spaɪtfəl/ *adjective*
unkind and nasty ▶ *a spiteful remark (adverb: **spitefully**)*

splash¹ /splæʃ/ *noun (plural **splashes**)*
the sound made by something falling into a liquid ▶ *She jumped into the river with a splash.*

splash² *verb*
to move liquid in a noisy way and make someone or something wet ▶ *The children splashed about in the pool.*

splatter /'splætəʳ/ *verb*
(used about liquids) to hit loudly

S

against a surface ▶ *Rain splattered against the window.*

splendid /'splendɪd/ *adjective*
very great or fine ▶ *You've done a splendid job.*

splint /splɪnt/ *noun*
a flat piece of wood or plastic that stops a broken bone from moving ▶ *I have to wear a splint until my leg gets better.*

splinter /'splɪntə'/ *noun*
a thin, sharp piece of wood or metal ▶ *I have got a splinter in my finger.*

split¹ /splɪt/ *verb (present participle* **splitting***, past* **split***)*
1 to break, especially from one end to the other ▶ *We split the wood into long, thin pieces.* ▶ *My trousers split when I sat down.*
2 to share something ▶ *We split the work between us.*

split² *noun*
a break ▶ *a split in my trousers*

split second /ˌsplɪt 'sekənd/ *noun*
a split second a very short period of time ▶ *For a split second, I thought I'd won.*

spoil /spɔɪl/ *verb (past* **spoilt** /spɔɪlt/ *or* **spoiled***)*
1 to ruin something good so that it becomes useless, less enjoyable, etc. ▶ *Don't let his bad mood spoil your evening.*
2 to be too kind to a child and give them too much attention so that they start to behave badly ▶ *Some parents really spoil their children.*

spoilsport /'spɔɪlspɔːt/ *noun*
a person who spoils other people's fun ▶ *Don't be such a spoilsport.*

spoilt¹ /spɔɪlt/
a PAST TENSE and PAST PARTICIPLE of the verb **spoil**

spoilt² *adjective*
bad and selfish as a result of being given too much money, attention, etc. ▶ *a spoilt child*

spoke¹ /spəʊk/
the PAST TENSE of the verb **speak**

spoke² *noun*
one of the bars joining the outer ring of a wheel to the centre

spoken /'spəʊkən/
the PAST PARTICIPLE of the verb **speak**

spokesman /'spəʊksmən/ *noun (plural* **spokesmen** /-mən/*)*
a person who has been chosen to speak officially for a group

spokesperson /'spəʊks,pɜːsən/ *noun (plural* **spokespeople** /-ˌpiːpəl/*)*
a person who has been chosen to speak officially for a group

spokeswoman /'spəʊks,wʊmən/ *noun (plural* **spokeswomen** /-ˌwɪmɪn/*)*
a woman who has been chosen to speak officially for a group

sponge /spʌndʒ/ *noun*
a soft sea creature like a piece of rubber with many holes, or a substance like it, used for washing your body

spongy /'spʌndʒi/ *adjective (***spongier***, ***spongiest***)*
soft and full of air or liquid, like a sponge ▶ *spongy, wet earth*

sponsor¹ /'spɒnsə'/ *verb*
1 to provide some of the money for an event, a television programme, etc. so that you can advertise something at the event or on the programme ▶ *The tournament is sponsored by a tobacco company.*
2 to agree to give someone money for a CHARITY if they walk, swim, etc. a particular distance ▶ *I'm doing a walk for charity – will you sponsor me?* ▶ *a sponsored swim*

sponsor² *noun*
a person or company that provides some of the money for an event, a television programme, etc.

sponsorship /'spɒnsəʃɪp/ *noun (no plural)*
the act of sponsoring an event or a person, or the money given by a sponsor ▶ *We are still trying to get sponsorship for the competition.*

spontaneity /'spɒntə'niːətɪ/ *noun (no plural)*
the quality of deciding to do things suddenly, without planning them ▶ *He brings enthusiasm and spontaneity to our work.*

spontaneous /spɒn'teɪnɪəs/ *adjective*
done suddenly without being planned ▶ *The audience gave a spontaneous cheer.* (adverb: **spontaneously**)

spooky /'spuːkɪ/ *adjective* (**spookier, spookiest**)
strange and frightening ▶ *a spooky old house*

spool /spuːl/ *noun*
a round thing for winding thread, wire, etc. round

spoon /spuːn/ *noun*
an instrument with a round part, used for eating liquids, mixing things in cooking, etc.

spoonful /'spuːnfʊl/ *noun (plural* **spoonsful** *or* **spoonfuls**)
the amount a spoon holds ▶ *a spoonful of sugar*

sport /spɔːt/ *noun*
a game or competition where you use your body, such as tennis or football ▶ *to practise a sport* ▶ *Do you like sport?* ▶ *He's good at sport.*

sports car /'spɔːts kɑːʳ/ *noun*
a fast car, usually for two people, with a roof that opens

sports centre /'spɔːts ˌsentəʳ/ *noun*
a building where you can go to do different sports for pleasure

sportsman /'spɔːtsmən/ *noun (plural* **sportsmen** /-mən/)
a man who plays sports

sportswoman /'spɔːts,wʊmən/ *noun (plural* **sportswomen** /-ˌwɪmɪn/)
a woman who plays sports

sporty /'spɔːtɪ/ *adjective* (**sportier, sportiest**)
good at or liking sport ▶ *I'm not very sporty.*

spot¹ /spɒt/ *noun*
1 a small mark on your skin ▶ *She had spots on her face when she was ill.*
2 a small circle of colour ▶ *a white dress with red spots on it*
3 a place ▶ *It's a very pretty spot.*

spot² *verb (present participle* **spotting**, *past* **spotted**)
to see or notice someone or something ▶ *I spotted you at the party.*

spot check /ˌspɒt 'tʃek/ *noun*
a check that is done without warning ▶ *Police are making spot checks on cars.*

spotless /'spɒtləs/ *adjective*
completely clean ▶ *The kitchen was spotless.*

spotlight /'spɒtlaɪt/ *noun*
1 a very powerful light that you can point at different things
2 in the spotlight receiving a lot of attention from newspapers or television

spotted /'spɒtɪd/ *adjective*
covered with small circles of colour ▶ *a spotted dress*

spotty /'spɒtɪ/ *adjective* (**spottier, spottiest**)
1 with skin that is covered with small marks ▶ *a spotty face*
2 spotted

spouse /spaʊs/ *noun*
a person's husband or wife

spout /spaʊt/ *noun*
the long, thin part of a container through which liquid is poured

sprain /spreɪn/ *verb*
to damage a part of your body by

S

turning it suddenly ► *He sprained his ankle when he fell.*

sprang /spræŋ/
the PAST TENSE of the verb **spring**

sprawl /sprɔːl/ *verb*
to lie or sit with your arms and legs stretched out ► *Jo lay sprawled on the sofa.*

spray¹ /spreɪ/ *verb*
to make something wet with small drops ► *He sprayed water over the flowers.* ► *He sprayed the flowers with water.*

spray² *noun*
a container for liquid, used for making things wet with small drops of the liquid ► *a perfume spray*

spread /spred/ *verb (past **spread**)*
1 to cover something thinly ► *She spread the bread with butter.* ► *She spread the butter on the bread.*
2 to open wide ► *The bird spread its wings.*
3 to move over an area ► *The illness spread quickly through the village.* ► *The news spread quickly.*

spreadsheet /'spredʃiːt/ *noun*
a computer PROGRAM that you use for showing and calculating lists of numbers

spree /spriː/ *noun*
a short period of time when you do a lot of something you enjoy ► *a shopping spree*

spring¹ /sprɪŋ/ *noun*
1 the season after winter, in cool countries, when plants start to grow again ► *in the spring* ► *spring flowers*
2 a river coming up from the ground
3 a twisted, round piece of metal wire which you can find inside a bed, etc.

spring² *verb (past tense **sprang** /spræŋ/, past participle **sprung** /sprʌŋ/)*
to jump ► *She sprang out of her chair.*

spring-clean /ˌsprɪŋ 'kliːn/ *verb*

to clean a place thoroughly ► *I'm going to spring-clean the bedrooms today.*

spring onion /ˌsprɪŋ 'ʌnjən/ *noun*
a small, white onion with a long, green stem

springtime /'sprɪŋtaɪm/ *noun (no plural)*
the time of year when it is spring

sprinkle /'sprɪŋkəl/ *verb (present participle **sprinkling**, past **sprinkled**)*
to let small drops or pieces fall on the surface of something ► *She sprinkled cheese on the potatoes.*

sprint /sprɪnt/ *verb*
to run very fast for a short distance ► *He sprinted after the bus.*

sprout¹ /spraʊt/ *verb*
to start to grow ► *These seeds have sprouted quickly.*

sprout² *noun*
a small, round, green vegetable with leaves pressed tightly together

sprung /sprʌŋ/
the PAST PARTICIPLE of the verb **spring**

spun /spʌn/
the PAST TENSE and PAST PARTICIPLE of the verb **spin**

spur¹ /spɜːr/ *noun*
do something on the spur of the moment to do something suddenly, without planning it ► *On the spur of the moment, she decided to take a holiday.*

spur² *verb (present participle **spurring**, past **spurred**)*
spur someone on to encourage someone to try harder ► *The fear of failure spurred him on.*

spurt¹ /spɜːt/ *verb*
to flow out suddenly with a lot of force ► *Juice spurted out over her fingers.*

spurt² *noun*
1 a sudden, short increase in effort, speed, etc. ► *With one final spurt, she reached the top of the hill.*

2 a stream of liquid that comes out suddenly ▶ *Water was coming out in spurts.*

spy¹ /spaɪ/ *noun (plural spies)*
a person whose job is to discover secret information, usually about another country
SAME MEANING: **secret agent**

spy² *verb (past spied)*
to watch people secretly in order to discover facts or information about them

squabble¹ /'skwɒbəl/ *verb (present participle squabbling, past squabbled)*
to quarrel about small things ▶ *The children were squabbling about who had won the game.*

squabble² *noun*
a small quarrel

squad /skwɒd/ *noun*
1 a group of soldiers or police officers who work together ▶ *the anti-terrorist squad*
2 the group of players that a sports team is chosen from

squadron /'skwɒdrən/ *noun*
a military group consisting of planes or ships

squalor /'skwɒlə'/ *noun (no plural)*
extremely dirty and unhealthy conditions ▶ *people living in squalor*

squander /'skwɒndə'/ *verb*
to waste time or money ▶ *He had squandered all his money on clothes.*

square¹ /skweə'/ *noun*
1 a shape with four straight sides of equal length
2 an open place in a town, with buildings all around it

square² *adjective*
having four straight sides of equal length ▶ *The window was square.*

squash¹ /skwɒʃ/ *noun (no plural)*
1 a fruit drink ▶ *a glass of orange squash*

2 a game for two people played indoors with a ball and RACKETS ▶ *a game of squash*

squash² *verb*
to hurt or damage something by pressing it ▶ *The fruit at the bottom of the box had been squashed.*

squat¹ /skwɒt/ *verb (present participle squatting, past squatted)*
1 to balance on your feet with your knees bent ▶ *He squatted down next to the child.*
2 to live somewhere without permission and without paying rent

squat² *noun*
a home that people are living in without permission and without paying rent

squeak¹ /skwiːk/ *verb*
to make a short, high, thin sound ▶ *Is that your chair squeaking?*

squeak² *noun*
a short, high, thin sound ▶ *the squeak of a mouse*

squeaky /'skwiːkɪ/ *adjective (squeakier, squeakiest)*
making a short, high, thin sound ▶ *a squeaky voice*

squeal¹ /skwiːl/ *verb*
to make a loud, high cry or sound ▶ *children squealing with delight*

squeal² *noun*
a loud, high cry ▶ *a squeal of pain*

squeamish /'skwiːmɪʃ/ *adjective*
easily upset by seeing unpleasant things ▶ *I couldn't be a nurse – I'm too squeamish.*

squeeze /skwiːz/ *verb (present participle squeezing, past squeezed)*
to press something ▶ *Squeeze some lemon juice on to the salad.*

squid /skwɪd/ *noun*
a sea creature with a long body and ten arms, which is eaten as food

S

squint¹ /skwɪnt/ *verb*
1 to look at something with your eyes partly closed in order to see better ► *He looked at me, squinting in the sun.*
2 to have a condition in which each of your eyes looks in a different direction

squint² *noun*
a condition in which each of your eyes looks in a different direction

squirm /skwɜːm/ *verb*
to twist your body from side to side because you are uncomfortable or nervous ► *Stop squirming so I can comb your hair!*

squirrel /'skwɪrəl/ *noun*
a small animal that has a brown or grey, hairy coat and a thick tail and lives in trees

squirt /skwɜːt/ *verb*
to force a liquid out of a narrow hole in a thin, fast stream, or to be forced out of a narrow hole in this way ► *He squirted mustard on his burger.*

St
1 a short way of writing the word **saint** in a name ► *St John*
2 a short way of writing the word **street** in an address ► *Bond St*

stab /stæb/ *verb (present participle* **stabbing***, past* **stabbed***)*
to wound someone with a pointed weapon ► *to stab someone with a knife*

stabbing¹ /'stæbɪŋ/ *noun*
a crime in which someone is stabbed

stabbing² *adjective*
(used about pains) very sudden and strong

stability /stə'bɪlətɪ/ *noun (no plural)*
the state of not moving or changing

stabilize /'steɪbɪlaɪz/ *verb (present participle* **stabilizing***, past* **stabilized***)*
to stop changing and to become

steady, or to make something do this ► *The financial markets are finally stabilizing.*

stable¹ /'steɪbəl/ *noun*
a building in which a horse lives

stable² *adjective*
1 not likely to change suddenly and cause problems ► *a stable government*
2 firmly in place, and not likely to move or change ► *Is that ladder stable?*
OPPOSITE (**1** and **2**): **unstable**

stack¹ /stæk/ *noun*
a large, tidy pile ► *a stack of books*

stack² *verb*
to put things into a tidy pile ► *Will you stack the dirty plates?*

stadium /'steɪdɪəm/ *noun*
a large, outdoor sports field with seats all round it ► *a football stadium*

staff /stɑːf/ *noun (no plural)*
a group of people working together for the same organization ► *the school staff* (=all the teachers) ► *the staff in our London office*

stag /stæg/ *noun*
an adult male DEER

stage /steɪdʒ/ *noun*
1 a time or step in a long event ► *Children go through various stages of development.*
2 the part of a theatre where the actors stand and perform

stagger /'stæɡəʳ/ *verb*
to walk in an unsteady way, as if you are soon going to fall ► *The wounded man staggered along.*

staggered /'stæɡəd/ *adjective*
very shocked or surprised ► *I was staggered to hear you're leaving.*

staggering /'stæɡərɪŋ/ *adjective*
very surprising or shocking ► *a staggering amount of money*

stag night /'stæg naɪt/ *noun*
a social occasion when a man goes

out with his male friends just before his wedding

stain¹ /steɪn/ *verb*
to make a dirty mark that cannot be taken away ▶ *The coffee stained his shirt.*

stain² *noun*
a dirty mark ▶ *a coffee stain*

stair /steə^r/ *noun*
one of the steps in a set of stairs ▶ *Jane sat on the bottom stair.*

staircase /'steəkeɪs/ *noun*
a set of steps inside a building ▶ *at the top of the staircase*

stairs /steəz/ *plural noun*
a set of steps leading up and down inside a building ▶ *to climb some stairs* ▶ *at the top of the stairs*

stairway /'steəweɪ/ *noun*
a STAIRCASE, especially a large or an impressive one

stake /steɪk/ *noun*
1 be at stake to be likely to be lost if a plan or an action is not successful ▶ *There's a lot at stake in this game.*
2 stakes *plural noun* money that you risk losing as the result of a game, race, etc. ▶ *Gamblers in Las Vegas often play for high stakes.*
3 a long, sharp piece of wood, metal, etc. that you push into the ground to mark something or to support a plant

stale /steɪl/ *adjective*
tasting old and dry; not fresh ▶ *stale bread*

stalk /stɔːk/ *noun*
the tall, main part of a plant

stalker /'stɔːkə^r/ *noun*
a person who follows and watches someone for a long time in a way that annoys or frightens them

stall /stɔːl/ *noun*
a small, open shop, especially one in a market ▶ *a fruit stall*

stallion /'stæljən/ *noun*
an adult male horse

stamina /'stæmɪnə/ *noun (no plural)*
physical or mental strength that lets you continue doing something for a long time

stammer /'stæmə^r/ *verb*
to speak with difficulty, repeating the same sounds ▶ *"Th-th-thank you," he stammered.*
SAME MEANING: **stutter**

stamp¹ /stæmp/ *noun*
1 a small piece of special paper that you stick on letters and parcels to show how much you have paid to send them
2 an instrument that you press onto ink and then press onto paper to make a mark

stamp² *verb*
1 to mark a word or sign on something using a special instrument
2 to walk with noisy, heavy steps; to bring your foot down hard on something ▶ *He stamped on the insect.*

stampede /stæm'piːd/ *noun*
a situation in which a large number of animals or people suddenly run somewhere ▶ *There was a stampede for the door.*

stance /stɑːns/ *noun*
someone's public attitude to something ▶ *The church will not change its stance on divorce.*

stand¹ /stænd/ *verb (past **stood** /stʊd/)*
1 to support yourself upright on your legs and feet ▶ *I had to stand all the way home on the bus.*
2 to be in a certain place ▶ *The house stands at the top of the hill.*
3 to move in a particular direction when you are standing ▶ *She stood back to let me pass.*
4 can't stand to dislike something strongly ▶ *I can't stand getting up early.*
5 stand by (a) to do nothing while

something unpleasant is happening
▶ *How can you stand by and watch those men attack him?*
(b) to be ready to help if someone needs you ▶ *Doctors are standing by.*
6 stand for to be a short form or the first letter of a word ▶ *What does PTO stand for?*
7 stand up to be on your feet ▶ *I've been standing up all day.* ▶ *Stand up, children.*
8 stand up for someone or something to say that someone or something is right ▶ *He always stands up for his wife.*

stand² *noun*
a place where people can stand or sit to watch sports

standard¹ /'stændəd/ *noun*
1 a level of quality which is considered acceptable ▶ *Your work is not up to the necessary standard.*
2 an accepted level used to make comparisons ▶ *By European standards, this is a low salary.*

standard² *adjective*
usual ▶ *It's standard practice to check luggage at airports.*

standardize /'stændədaɪz/ *verb (present participle **standardizing**, past **standardized**)*
to make all the things of one type the same as each other

standby /'stændbaɪ/ *noun*
on standby ready to do something if needed ▶ *There are medical staff on standby at the stadium.*

standing¹ /'stændɪŋ/ *noun (no plural)*
the opinion that people have about someone, and how good and important they are ▶ *The President's standing has never been higher.*

standing² *adjective*
1 a standing invitation an invitation to visit someone whenever you want
2 give somebody a standing ovation

to stand and clap after a performance, to show that you think it is very good

standpoint /'stændpɔɪnt/ *noun*
a particular way of thinking about something ▶ *Obviously, from my standpoint it's a brilliant idea.*
SAME MEANING: **point of view**

standstill /'stænd,stɪl/ *noun (no plural)*
a situation in which things are not moving, or no one is doing anything ▶ *The whole city came to a complete standstill on the day of the funeral.*
▶ *Work on the new bridge is at a standstill.*

stank /stæŋk/
the PAST TENSE of the verb **stink**

staple¹ /'steɪpəl/ *noun*
a small, U-shaped piece of metal wire that you push through pieces of paper to fasten them together

staple² *verb (present participle **stapling**, past **stapled**)*
to fasten pieces of paper together with staples ▶ *She stapled the pages together.*

stapler /'steɪplər/ *noun*
a machine for putting staples through paper

star¹ /stɑːr/ *noun*
1 a small point of light that can be seen in the sky at night
2 a shape with five or six points sticking out of it
3 a famous actor, singer, sportsperson, etc. ▶ *a film star*

star² *verb (present participle **starring**, past **starred**)*
to have a person as the most important actor ▶ *an old film starring Charlie Chaplin*

starch /stɑːtʃ/ *noun (no plural)*
1 a substance in foods such as bread, rice, and potatoes
2 a substance used for making cloth stiff

stardom /'stɑːdəm/ *noun (no plural)*
the state of being very famous as an actor, a singer, a sports player, etc.

stare /steəʳ/ *verb (present participle staring, past stared)*
to look steadily at something for a long time ▶ *He stared at the word, trying to remember what it meant.*

stark¹ /stɑːk/ *adjective*
1 very simple and plain-looking ▶ *the stark beauty of the desert*
2 unpleasantly clear and impossible to avoid ▶ *the stark realities of drug addiction*

stark² *adverb*
stark naked not wearing any clothes

star sign /'stɑː saɪn/ *noun*
one of the 12 signs based on the time of the year when you were born, which some people believe show what kind of person you are ▶ *"What star sign are you?" "I'm a Leo."*

start¹ /stɑːt/ *verb*
to begin ▶ *If you are ready, you may start your work.* ▶ *The children started singing.*
OPPOSITE: **finish, stop**

start² *noun*
1 the beginning of an activity or of a state of affairs ▶ *We made an early start that morning.*
2 the first part of something ▶ *The start of the film was boring.*
OPPOSITE (2): **end, finish**

starter /'stɑːtəʳ/ *noun*
the first part of a meal

startle /'stɑːtl/ *verb (present participle startling, past startled)*
to surprise someone or give them a shock ▶ *You startled me when you came in.*

starvation /stɑːˈveɪʃən/ *noun (no plural)*
dying or feeling very weak because you do not have enough to eat

starve /stɑːv/ *verb (present participle starving, past starved)*
to die of hunger
COMPARE: **fast**

starving /'stɑːvɪŋ/ *adjective*
1 dying of hunger ▶ *starving children*
2 very hungry ▶ *I'm starving – is dinner ready yet?*

stash /stæʃ/ *verb*
to keep something in a secret place ▶ *The money is stashed away in a Swiss bank.*

state¹ /steɪt/ *verb (present participle stating, past stated)*
to say something in a formal way or on a formal occasion ▶ *He stated that he had never seen the accused man before.*

state² *noun*
1 the condition of something; how good, bad, etc., something is ▶ *The economy is in a very bad state.* ▶ *He's in a state of shock.*
2 a country, or a part of a country, which governs itself ▶ *the state of Mississippi*
3 the government of a country ▶ *In Britain, the health service is mostly run by the state.*

statement /'steɪtmənt/ *noun*
something that is said in a formal way or on a formal occasion ▶ *The man made a statement to the police.*

state-of-the-art /ˌsteɪt əv ðiː ˈɑːt/ *adjective*
using the newest methods, materials, or knowledge ▶ *state-of-the-art technology*

States /steɪts/ *noun*
the States the United States

state school /'steɪt skuːl/ *noun*
a school which provides free education and is paid for by the government

statesman /'steɪtsmən/ *noun (plural statesmen /-mən/)*
an important person in a government

static¹ /ˈstætɪk/ *adjective*
not changing or moving ▶ *Prices have been fairly static.*

static² (also **static electricity** /ˌstætɪk ɪlekˈtrɪsəti/) *noun (no plural)*
electricity produced when two surfaces rub together

station /ˈsteɪʃən/ *noun*
1 a place where buses or trains stop ▶ *a railway station* ▶ *a bus station*
2 a building for some special work ▶ *a police station*

stationary /ˈsteɪʃənəri/ *adjective*
not moving; still ▶ *The car was stationary when the accident happened.*

stationery /ˈsteɪʃənəri/ *noun (no plural)*
paper, pens, pencils, notebooks, and other things used for writing

statistics /stəˈtɪstɪks/ *plural noun*
a set of numbers that give information about something ▶ *the latest crime statistics*

statue /ˈstætʃuː/ *noun*
a figure of a person or an animal, made of stone, metal, or wood

stature /ˈstætʃər/ *noun (no plural)*
the importance that someone has because of their work or achievements ▶ *a musician of great stature*

status /ˈsteɪtəs/ *noun (no plural)*
1 the position that someone has in a country or in an organization ▶ *She fought to improve the status of women in society.* ▶ *marital status*
2 special importance that someone has because of their job, achievements, or social position ▶ *He wanted a job with status.*

staunch /stɔːntʃ/ *adjective*
very loyal ▶ *a staunch supporter*

stave /steɪv/ *verb (present participle **staving**, past **staved**)*
stave off something to prevent something unpleasant from

happening ▶ *The team did their best to stave off defeat.*

stay /steɪ/ *verb*
1 to continue to be in a particular place, state, job, etc. ▶ *Stay in your classroom until it is time to go home.* ▶ *I tried to stay calm.*
2 to live somewhere as a guest for a short time ▶ *They're staying at a hotel.*

steadfast /ˈstedfɑːst/ *adjective*
refusing to change your beliefs ▶ *his steadfast loyalty to his country*

steadily /ˈstedɪli/ *adverb*
not changing very much ▶ *We drove steadily at 30 miles an hour.*

steady /ˈstedi/ *adjective, adverb (steadier, steadiest)*
1 firm; not moving ▶ *Hold the chair steady while I stand on it.*
OPPOSITE: **unsteady**
2 regular; not changing very much ▶ *a steady job* ▶ *a steady speed*

steak /steɪk/ *noun*
a thick, flat piece of meat or fish

steal /stiːl/ *verb (past tense **stole** /stəʊl/, past participle **stolen** /ˈstəʊlən/)*
to take something that does not belong to you, without asking for it ▶ *Someone's stolen my bag!*
LOOK AT: **rob**

steam¹ /stiːm/ *noun (no plural)*
the gas that water becomes when it boils ▶ *There was steam coming from the washing machine.*

steam² *verb*
1 to produce steam
2 to cook something by putting it in steam

steamed-up /ˌstiːmd ˈʌp/ *adjective*
covered with steam ▶ *My glasses were all steamed-up.*

steel /stiːl/ *noun (no plural)*
a hard metal made of specially treated iron, used for knives, machines, etc.

steep /stiːp/ *adjective*
having a slope which is at a large angle and difficult to go up ▶ *a steep hill* (adverb: **steeply**)

steeple /'stiːpəl/ *noun*
a tall, pointed church tower

steer /stɪəʳ/ *verb*
to direct or guide a vehicle ▶ *He steered the ship carefully between the rocks.*

steering wheel /'stɪərɪŋ ˌwiːl/ *noun*
the wheel that you turn to make a car move to the left or right

stem /stem/ *noun*
the central part of a plant from which the leaves or flowers grow

stench /stentʃ/ *noun (plural* **stenches***)*
a very strong, unpleasant smell ▶ *the stench of rotting meat*

stencil /'stensəl/ *noun*
a piece of paper, plastic, etc. that has holes in the shape of letters or patterns in it, which you use for painting letters or patterns onto a surface

step¹ /step/ *verb (present participle* **stepping***, past* **stepped***)*
to move one foot up and put it down in front of the other ▶ *He stepped over the dog.* ▶ *We all stepped back to let the doctor through.*

step² *noun*
1 one movement forwards or backwards with your foot ▶ *He took a step towards the door.*
2 the sound made when you take a step ▶ *I heard steps outside.*
3 one part of a set of stairs ▶ *There are two steps up onto the bus.*
4 an event in a set of events ▶ *The first step in changing a car tyre is to loosen the wheel.*

stepbrother /'step.brʌðəʳ/ *noun*
a boy or man who is not your brother but is the son of someone who is married to one of your parents

step-by-step /ˌstep baɪ 'step/ *adjective*
dealing with things carefully and in a fixed order ▶ *step-by-step instructions* ▶ *a step-by-step recipe*

stepchild /'steptʃaɪld/ *noun (plural* **stepchildren** /-ˌtʃɪldrən/*)*
a child that your husband or wife has from a previous relationship

stepdaughter /'step.dɔːtəʳ/ *noun*
a daughter that your husband or wife has from a previous relationship

stepfather /'step.fɑːðəʳ/ *noun*
a man who marries your mother but is not your father

stepladder /'step.lædəʳ/ *noun*
a LADDER with two sloping parts joined at the top

stepmother /'step.mʌðəʳ/ *noun*
a woman who marries your father but is not your mother

stepsister /'step.sɪstəʳ/ *noun*
a girl or woman who is not your sister but is the daughter of someone who is married to one of your parents

stepson /'stepsʌn/ *noun*
a son that your husband or wife has from a previous relationship

stereo /'steriəʊ/ *noun*
a machine for playing TAPES, CDS, etc. that produces sound from two SPEAKERS

stereotype /'steriətaɪp/ *noun*
an idea that many people have of what a type of person is like, especially an idea which is wrong or unfair ▶ *The characters in the film are just stereotypes.*

sterile /'steraɪl/ *adjective*
1 completely clean and not containing any BACTERIA ▶ *a sterile bandage*
2 unable to have children

sterilize /'sterɪlaɪz/ *verb (present participle* **sterilizing***, past* **sterilized***)*
1 to make something completely

S

clean so that it contains no BACTERIA
▶ *a sterilized needle*
2 to perform a medical operation on
someone so that they cannot have
any children

sterling /'stɜːlɪŋ/ *noun (no plural)*
the type of money used in Britain

stern /stɜːn/ *adjective*
firm and serious ▶ *a stern teacher*

stew¹ /stjuː/ *noun*
meat or fish, and vegetables, cooked
slowly together in liquid

stew² *verb*
to cook food slowly in liquid

steward /'stjuːəd/ *noun*
a man who looks after passengers on
a boat or plane

stewardess /'stjuːədes/ *noun (plural
stewardesses)*
a woman who looks after passengers
on a boat or plane

stick¹ /stɪk/ *noun*
1 a long, thin piece of wood
2 a thin piece of wood or metal which
some people use to help them to
walk ▶ *Gran has to walk with a stick
now.*

stick² *verb (past stuck /stʌk/)*
1 to fix something with a special
substance like GLUE ▶ *I stuck a stamp
on the letter.*
2 to put something pointed into
something else ▶ *She stuck her fork
into the meat.*
3 to become or stay fixed ▶ *The door
had stuck and we could not get out.*
4 stick something out to make
something come out from inside
▶ *She stuck her hand out of the car
and took the ticket.*

sticker /'stɪkə*/ *noun*
a small piece of paper or plastic, with
a picture or writing on it, that you can
stick on something

sticky /'stɪkɪ/ *adjective (stickier,
stickiest)*

covered with or containing something
which fixes itself to anything it
touches ▶ *sticky hands*

sties /staɪz/
the plural of **sty**

stiff /stɪf/ *adjective*
not able to move or bend easily ▶ *The
cards were made of stiff paper.*

stifle /'staɪfəl/ *verb (present
participle stifling, past stifled)*
to stop something from happening or
developing ▶ *He tried to stifle a
yawn.* ▶ *Annette felt college was
stifling her creativity.*

stifling /'staɪflɪŋ/ *adjective*
very hot, so that you feel
uncomfortable ▶ *the stifling heat*

stiletto /stɪ'letəʊ/ *noun*
a woman's shoe with a high, thin heel

still¹ /stɪl/ *adverb*
1 up to this or that time ▶ *My father
still remembers his first day at
school.*
2 even ▶ *The first question was
difficult, but the second was harder
still.*
3 even so ▶ *It was raining, but she
still went out.*

still² *adjective*
not moving; quiet ▶ *The sea was calm
and still.* ▶ *Keep still while I comb
your hair.*

stillborn /'stɪlbɔːn/ *adjective*
born dead ▶ *a stillborn calf*

stimulate /'stɪmjʊleɪt/ *verb (present
participle stimulating, past
stimulated)*
1 to encourage something to grow
and develop, or happen more ▶ *The
drug stimulates the flow of blood to
the brain.*
2 to make someone interested and
excited ▶ *toys that stimulate children*

stimulating /'stɪmjʊleɪtɪŋ/ *adjective*
interesting and giving you new ideas
▶ *a stimulating conversation*

stimulus /'stɪmjʊləs/ *noun (plural* **stimuli** /-laɪ/)
1 something that encourages another thing to grow and develop, or happen more ▶ *a stimulus to industrial development*
2 something that makes you feel interested or excited ▶ *Children need the visual stimulus of pictures in a book.*

sting¹ /stɪŋ/ *verb (past* **stung** /stʌŋ/)
to hurt someone by pricking their skin ▶ *The bee stung her leg.*

sting² *noun*
1 the part of an insect, or of a plant, that can hurt you by pricking your skin
2 a pain or wound caused by a sting

stingy /'stɪndʒɪ/ *adjective* (**stingier, stingiest**)
not generous with your money

stink¹ /stɪŋk/ *verb (past tense* **stank** /stæŋk/, *past participle* **stunk** /stʌŋk/)
to smell very unpleasant

stink² *noun*
a very unpleasant smell

stir /stɜːʳ/ *verb (present participle* **stirring**, *past* **stirred**)
1 to mix a liquid round with a spoon ▶ *He put sugar in his tea and stirred it.*
2 to move a little ▶ *The leaves stirred in the wind.*

stir-fry /'stɜː fraɪ/ *verb (past* **stir-fried**)
to cook vegetables or meat quickly in a little hot oil

stirring /'stɜːrɪŋ/ *adjective*
making people feel very excited, proud, or eager to do something ▶ *a stirring speech*

stirrup /'stɪrəp/ *noun*
one of the two metal things that you put your feet in when you are riding a horse

stitch¹ /stɪtʃ/ *noun (plural* **stitches**)
1 a piece of thread left in cloth after being pulled through the cloth in a needle ▶ *a white tablecloth with blue stitches round the edge*
2 a turn of wool round a needle in KNITTING

stitch² *verb*
to sew something ▶ *to stitch a button onto a shirt*

stock¹ /stɒk/ *noun*
1 a store of goods in a shop ▶ *We have a large stock of exotic fruit.*
2 in stock ready for sale in a shop ▶ *I'm sorry, but we've only got black boots in stock.*
3 out of stock not there in the shop or ready for sale ▶ *Brown boots are out of stock.*

stock² *verb*
to have something for sale in a shop ▶ *Do you stock camping equipment?*

stockbroker /'stɒk,brəʊkəʳ/ *noun*
a person whose job is to buy and sell company SHARES for other people

stock exchange /'stɒk ɪks,tʃeɪndʒ/ *noun*
1 a place where people buy and sell the SHARES of many different companies
2 the stock exchange the business of buying and selling SHARES ▶ *He made a lot of money on the stock exchange.*

stocking /'stɒkɪŋ/ *noun*
one of a pair of very thin coverings that women wear on their legs and feet
COMPARE: **tights**

stock market /'stɒk ,mɑːkɪt/ *noun*
a STOCK EXCHANGE

stockpile /'stɒkpaɪl/ *verb (present participle* **stockpiling**, *past* **stockpiled**)
to collect a large supply of something because you think that it may not be

available later ▶ *People have been stockpiling food in case there is a strike.*

stocky /'stɒkɪ/ *adjective* (**stockier, stockiest**)
having a short, heavy, strong-looking body ▶ *a stocky man*

stole /stəʊl/
the PAST TENSE of the verb **steal**

stolen /'stəʊlən/
the PAST PARTICIPLE of the verb **steal**

stomach /'stʌmək/ *noun*
the part of your body where food goes when you swallow it

stomachache /'stʌmək,eɪk/ *noun*
a pain in your stomach ▶ *I've got a stomachache.*

stone /stəʊn/ *noun*
1 a small piece of rock
2 (no plural) rock ▶ *The walls are made of stone.*
3 the hard, inside part of some fruits
4 a piece of coloured rock of great value, such as a diamond, that is used in a ring or other piece of jewellery

stoned /stəʊnd/ *adjective*
1 very relaxed or excited because of taking an illegal drug ▶ *His friends just sit around and get stoned all day.*
2 very drunk

stony /'stəʊnɪ/ *adjective* (**stonier, stoniest**)
1 covered with stones or containing stones ▶ *a stony path*
2 unfriendly, especially because you feel angry ▶ *a stony silence*

stood /stʊd/
the PAST TENSE and PAST PARTICIPLE of the verb **stand**

stool /stuːl/ *noun*
a chair without a back or sides

stoop /stuːp/ *verb*
to bend your body over forwards and down ▶ *He had to stoop to get through the doorway.*

stop¹ /stɒp/ *verb* (*present participle* **stopping**, *past* **stopped**)
1 to end something; to finish doing something ▶ *We stopped talking as she came into the room.*
OPPOSITE: **start**
2 to prevent something happening ▶ *They stopped me leaving.* ▶ *You must stop Joe* **from** *telling them.*
3 to finish moving ▶ *The bus stopped and I got off.*

stop² *noun*
a place where a bus or train stops ▶ *We waited at the bus stop.*

stopper /'stɒpəʳ/ *noun*
something which closes an opening, especially of a bottle

stopwatch /'stɒpwɒtʃ/ *noun* (*plural* **stopwatches**)
a watch for measuring the exact time it takes to do something

storage /'stɔːrɪdʒ/ *noun* (no plural)
the act of keeping things somewhere until you need them ▶ *All our furniture is in storage.*

store¹ /stɔːʳ/ *verb* (*present participle* **storing**, *past* **stored**)
to put something away or keep it for use later ▶ *I stored all the potatoes from the garden.*

store² *noun*
1 things kept for future use ▶ *a store of apples*
2 a large shop
3 a place for keeping things ▶ *a weapon store*

storeroom /'stɔːrʊm/ *noun*
a room where you store things ▶ *We use this bedroom as a storeroom.*

storey /'stɔːrɪ/ *noun*
one level in a building ▶ *Our house has three storeys.*

storm /stɔːm/ *noun*
bad weather in which there are high winds and sometimes thunder and rain

stormy /'stɔːmɪ/ *adjective* (**stormier, stormiest**)
very rainy and windy ► *stormy weather*

story /'stɔːrɪ/ *noun* (plural **stories**)
a description of a set of events that can be real or imaginary ► *Please read us a story!*

stout /staʊt/ *adjective*
rather fat ► *a stout, 40-year-old man*

stove /stəʊv/ *noun*
a machine that you use for cooking on, or for heating a room ► *a gas stove*

straddle /'strædl/ *verb* (present participle **straddling**, past **straddled**)
to sit or stand with your legs on either side of something ► *He sat straddling the gate.*

straggly /'strægəlɪ/ *adjective* (**stragglier, straggliest**)
growing or spreading out in an untidy way ► *straggly hair*

straight¹ /streɪt/ *adjective*
1 not bending or curved ► *straight hair*
2 level ► *Is this picture straight?*
3 in order ► *I want to get the house straight before the others arrive.*

straight² *adverb*
1 in a line which does not bend ► *The car was coming straight towards me.*
2 directly; without going anywhere else or doing anything else ► *He went straight to his friend to ask for help.*
3 straight away now ► *I must see you straight away.*
4 straight on in the same direction ► *Go straight on until you get to the crossroads.*

straighten /'streɪtn/ *verb*
to make or become level, tidy, or not curved ► *She straightened the picture on the wall.*

straightforward /ˌstreɪt'fɔːwəd/ *adjective*
easy to do or understand ► *It's a straightforward question.*

straightjacket /'streɪtˌdʒækɪt/ *noun*
another word for **straitjacket**

strain /streɪn/ *verb*
1 to do something with great effort ► *She had to strain to hear me.*
2 to damage a part of your body by using it wrongly or too much ► *I strained my back when I lifted the box.*
3 to take the lumps out of a food or liquid by putting it through an instrument with small holes in it ► *to strain the tea*

strainer /'streɪnər/ *noun*
a kitchen tool used for separating solid food from a liquid

strait /streɪt/ *noun*
a narrow piece of water between two pieces of land

straitjacket (also **straightjacket**) /'streɪtˌdʒækɪt/ *noun*
a very tight piece of clothing that is sometimes put on a violent or mentally ill person to stop them from moving their arms

strand /strænd/ *noun*
a long, thin piece of something, usually thread or hair

stranded /'strændɪd/ *adjective*
in a difficult place or state with no help ► *I was stranded in a foreign country with no money.*

strange /streɪndʒ/ *adjective*
1 unusual, surprising, and difficult to understand ► *a strange sound*
2 not what you are used to ► *a strange city* (adverb: **strangely**)

stranger /'streɪndʒər/ *noun*
a person you do not know

strangle /'stræŋgəl/ *verb* (present participle **strangling**, past **strangled**)
to kill or try to kill someone by holding their throat tightly, stopping them from breathing
SAME MEANING: **throttle**

S

strap¹ /stræp/ *noun*
a narrow piece of leather, plastic, cloth, etc. used for fastening something or carrying something

strap² *verb (present participle* **strapping**, *past* **strapped**)
to fasten something with a strap ▶ He strapped the bag onto his bicycle.

strategic /strə'ti:dʒɪk/ *adjective*
1 done as part of a military, business, or political plan ▶ The President made an important strategic decision.
2 a strategic position or place is very effective or useful for doing something ▶ He placed himself in a strategic position next to the door. *(adverb:* **strategically***)*

strategy /'strætədʒɪ/ *noun (plural* **strategies***)*
a set of plans used to achieve something or to help you be successful ▶ What's your strategy going to be for winning the election?

straw /strɔː/ *noun*
1 *(no plural)* dry stems of grain plants, such as wheat ▶ a bag made of straw
2 a dry stem of a grain plant, such as wheat
3 a thin tube for drinking through ▶ He drank the milk through a straw.

strawberry /'strɔːbərɪ/ *noun (plural* **strawberries***)*
a small, soft, red fruit

stray¹ /streɪ/ *adjective*
(used about animals) lost from home ▶ a stray dog

stray² *verb*
to wander away from home or from the right way ▶ She strayed **from** the road and got lost.

streak /striːk/ *noun*
a long, thin line ▶ a streak **of** paint on the wall

stream /striːm/ *noun*
1 a small river

2 a long line of something moving ▶ a stream **of** cars

streamline /'striːmlaɪn/ *verb (present participle* **streamlining**, *past* **streamlined***)*
1 to make something such as a business or process become simpler and more effective ▶ The hospital has streamlined the paperwork for doctors.
2 to give something such as a vehicle a smooth shape so that it moves easily through the air or water

street /striːt/ *noun*
a road in a town ▶ Across the street from the school is the library. ▶ Robert lives in Bridge Street.
COMPARE: **avenue**

streetlight /'striːtlaɪt/ *noun*
a tall post in a street, with a light at the top

strength /streŋθ/ *noun (no plural)*
the ability to move or lift heavy things ▶ I haven't the strength to move this table by myself.

strengthen /'streŋθən/ *verb*
to make someone or something stronger ▶ exercises to strengthen your arms

strenuous /'strenjʊəs/ *adjective*
using a lot of effort or strength ▶ strenuous exercise ▶ He made strenuous efforts to persuade them to change their minds.

stress¹ /stres/ *noun*
1 *(no plural)* the feeling of being worried and tense because of difficulties in your life ▶ The stress of working for the examinations made him ill.
2 *(plural* **stresses***)* special force that is put onto a word or part of a word ▶ In the word "chemistry", the stress is on the first part of the word.

stress² *verb*
1 to say a word or part of a word with special force ▶ We stress the first part of the word "chemistry".

2 to make it very clear that a particular fact is important ▶ *I must stress that we haven't much time.* SAME MEANING (**2**): **emphasize**

stressed /strest/ *(also **stressed out** /ˌstrest ˈaʊt/) adjective*
worried and unable to relax ▶ *You look really stressed out. What's the matter?*

stressful /ˈstresfəl/ *adjective*
making you worried and unable to relax ▶ *Pilots have a stressful job.*

stretch /stretʃ/ *verb*
1 to make or become larger or longer by pulling ▶ *She stretched the rope between the two poles.* ▶ *This jumper's stretched in the wash* (=when it was being washed).
2 to straighten your arms, legs, and body to their full length ▶ *He stretched his legs out in front of him.*
3 to reach, spread out, or cover ▶ *The forest stretched for miles.*

stretcher /ˈstretʃər/ *noun*
a frame on which a person who is ill or wounded can be carried

strewn /struːn/ *adjective*
strewn on, across, etc. something
thrown or dropped somewhere in an untidy way ▶ *Toys were strewn all over the floor.*

strict /strɪkt/ *adjective*
severe, and very firm, especially about behaviour ▶ *They are very strict with their children.*

strictly /ˈstrɪktli/ *adverb*
1 severely
2 exactly ▶ *What he says is not strictly true.*

stride¹ /straɪd/ *verb (present participle **striding**, past tense **strode** /strəʊd/, past participle **stridden** /ˈstrɪdn/)*
to walk with large steps ▶ *He strode angrily into the classroom.*

stride² *noun*
a large step ▶ *With two strides, he crossed the room.*

strike¹ /straɪk/ *verb (present participle **striking**, past **struck** /strʌk/)*
1 to hit someone or something ▶ *He was struck on the head by a falling rock.*
2 to stop working, usually because you want more money
3 to give you a particular feeling or idea ▶ *He struck me **as** being a very clever man.*
4 (used about a clock) to make a sound to show what time it is ▶ *The clock struck three.*

strike² *noun*
1 a time when people do not work because they want more money or better conditions ▶ *There is a strike at the factory.*
2 on strike refusing to work ▶ *The workers are on strike.*

striker /ˈstraɪkər/ *noun*
1 a person who has stopped working in order to get better pay or working conditions ▶ *Strikers stopped cars entering the factory.*
2 a football player whose main job is to try to get GOALS ▶ *Shearer was the team's best striker.*

striking /ˈstraɪkɪŋ/ *adjective*
1 unusual and noticeable ▶ *There's a striking similarity between them.*
2 very attractive, often in an unusual way ▶ *She's a very striking woman.*

string /strɪŋ/ *noun*
1 (no plural) thin rope used for fastening things ▶ *The parcel was tied with string.*
2 a fine piece of wire used in some musical instruments, such as a VIOLIN

strip¹ /strɪp/ *noun*
a long, narrow piece of something ▶ *a strip **of** paper*

strip² *verb (present participle **stripping**, past **stripped**)*
1 to pull off an outer covering ▶ *He stripped the paper off the wall.*

2 to take off your clothes ► *John stripped off his shirt.*

stripe /straɪp/ *noun*
a long, thin line ► *A tiger has stripes.*

striped /straɪpt/ *adjective*
having long, thin lines of colour
► *a striped shirt*

strive /straɪv/ *verb (present participle **striving**, past tense **strove** /strəʊv/, past participle **striven** /'strɪvən/)*
to try very hard to do something ► *He always strives to do his best.* ► *Ross is constantly striving for perfection.*

strode /strəʊd/
the PAST TENSE of the verb **stride**

stroke¹ /strəʊk/ *noun*
1 a movement of your arms when you are swimming ► *With a few strong strokes, he reached the child.*
2 the sound of the bell in a clock
3 a sudden illness in your brain ► *She couldn't walk very well after her stroke.*
4 a soft, gentle movement of your hand across something ► *Give the cat a stroke.*

stroke² *verb (present participle **stroking**, past **stroked**)*
to move your hand over something gently ► *He stroked the baby's head.*

stroll¹ /strəʊl/ *verb*
to walk slowly ► *We strolled through the park.*

stroll² *noun*
a slow walk for pleasure ► *Let's go for a stroll.*

strong /strɒŋ/ *adjective*
1 having power or force ► *He is a very strong man.* ► *She is a strong swimmer.*
OPPOSITE: **weak**
2 firm; that will not break or change easily ► *a strong fence* ► *strong belief*
3 having a powerful effect on you
► *strong liquor* ► *a strong smell*

strongly /'strɒŋlɪ/ *adverb*
1 used to emphasize that someone has a firm opinion about something that they think is important ► *I believe strongly in the importance of education.* ► *I strongly advise you to get more facts before deciding.*
2 tasting or smelling a lot of something ► *The house smelt strongly of gas.*

strove /strəʊv/
the PAST TENSE of the verb **strive**

struck /strʌk/
the PAST TENSE and PAST PARTICIPLE of the verb **strike**

structural /'strʌktʃərəl/ *adjective*
relating to the structure of something
► *structural damage to the aircraft*

structure /'strʌktʃə^r/ *noun*
1 a building or framework ► *The new hospital will be a huge structure.*
2 the way in which something is arranged ► *the structure of the company*

struggle¹ /'strʌgəl/ *verb (present participle **struggling**, past **struggled**)*
to fight ► *I struggled to get free.*

struggle² *noun*
a fight ► *We had a struggle to stop the robber.*

strut /strʌt/ *verb (present participle **strutting**, past **strutted**)*
to walk in a very proud and annoying way ► *He struts around the club as if he owns it.*

stub¹ /stʌb/ *noun*
the part of a cigarette or pencil that is left after the rest has been used

stub² *verb (present participle **stubbing**, past **stubbed**)*
stub your toe to hurt your toe by hitting it against something

stubble /'stʌbəl/ *noun (no plural)*
the very short hairs on a man's face when he has not SHAVED

stubborn /'stʌbən/ *adjective*
having a strong will and not willing to change your ideas easily ▶ *She won't do what I ask – she can be very stubborn.* (adverb: **stubbornly**)
SAME MEANING: **obstinate**

stuck /stʌk/
the PAST TENSE and PAST PARTICIPLE of the verb **stick**

stud /stʌd/ *noun*
1 a small, round piece of metal stuck into the surface of something as a decoration, or onto the bottom of a shoe to stop you from sliding ▶ *a leather jacket with silver studs*
2 a small, round EARRING

student /'stju:dənt/ *noun*
a person who is learning, especially at a college or university ▶ *He is a student of Irish history.*

studio /'stju:dɪəʊ/ *noun*
1 a room for working in, especially at painting or photography ▶ *a painter's studio*
2 a room in which films or radio or television shows are made

studious /'stju:dɪəs/ *adjective*
spending a lot of time reading and studying

study¹ /'stʌdɪ/ *verb (past **studied**)*
1 to learn about something ▶ *I am studying art.*
2 to look at something carefully ▶ *Before we go, we'll have to study the map.*

study² *noun (plural **studies**)*
1 learning ▶ *He will finish his studies next year.*
2 a room for working in

stuff¹ /stʌf/ *noun (no plural)*
1 any substance or material ▶ *There's some white stuff on this plate.*
2 several different things, which you are talking about in general ▶ *I've got a lot of stuff to do today.*

stuff² *verb*
1 to fill something with a substance ▶ *a pillow stuffed **with** feathers*
2 to push something into something else quickly and untidily ▶ *She stuffed the letter into her pocket.*

stuffing /'stʌfɪŋ/ *noun (no plural)*
a substance that is put inside something

stuffy /'stʌfɪ/ *adjective (**stuffier, stuffiest**)*
with no clean air ▶ *It's very stuffy in here; let's open a window.*

stumble /'stʌmbəl/ *verb (present participle **stumbling**, past **stumbled**)*
to nearly fall when you are walking ▶ *She stumbled over the cat in the dark.*

stump /stʌmp/ *noun*
a part that is left when something is cut down ▶ *He sat on a tree stump.*

stun /stʌn/ *verb (present participle **stunning**, past **stunned**)*
to surprise or shock someone so much that they do not react ▶ *Everyone was stunned by Betty's answer.*

stung /stʌŋ/
the PAST TENSE and PAST PARTICIPLE of the verb **sting**

stunk /stʌŋk/
the PAST PARTICIPLE of the verb **stink**

stunning /'stʌnɪŋ/ *adjective*
1 very beautiful ▶ *You look absolutely stunning!*
2 very surprising or shocking ▶ *stunning news*

stunt¹ /stʌnt/ *noun*
1 a dangerous thing that someone does to entertain people, especially in a film ▶ *There's a great stunt in which his car has to jump across a 15-metre gap.*
2 something that people do to get attention ▶ *The photograph was just a publicity stunt.*

S

stunt² *verb*
to stop something from growing or developing properly ▶ *The plant's growth has been stunted by lack of light.*

stupid /'stjuːpɪd/ *adjective*
not clever; not sensible ▶ *a stupid question* ▶ *a stupid person* (adverb: **stupidly**)

stupidity /stjuː'pɪdətɪ/ *noun (no plural)*
behaviour that is not clever or sensible

stupor /'stjuːpəʳ/ *noun*
a state in which you are almost unconscious ▶ *He was lying on the bed in a drunken stupor.*

sturdy /'stɜːdɪ/ *adjective* (**sturdier, sturdiest**)
strong and firm ▶ *sturdy shoes*

stutter /'stʌtəʳ/ *verb*
to speak with difficulty, repeating the same sounds ▶ *"I c-c-can't help it,"* she stuttered.
SAME MEANING: **stammer**

sty /staɪ/ *noun (plural* **sties***)*
a place for pigs to live in

style /staɪl/ *noun*
1 a way of doing something ▶ *his style of writing*
2 the fashion or design of something ▶ *Shoes are available in several interesting styles.* ▶ *His hair was cut in a very strange style.*
3 a sort or type ▶ *a new style of car*

stylish /'staɪlɪʃ/ *adjective*
attractive and fashionable ▶ *Joe always wears very stylish clothes.* (adverb: **stylishly**)

sub /sʌb/ *noun*
1 a SUBMARINE
2 a SUBSTITUTE

subconscious¹ /sʌb'kɒnʃəs/ *adjective*
(used about feelings) affecting your behaviour although hidden in your mind (adverb: **subconsciously**)

subconscious² *noun*
the part of your mind that has thoughts and feelings that you do not realize exist, but which influence your behaviour

subdue /səb'djuː/ *verb (present participle* **subduing***, past* **subdued***)*
to stop someone from behaving violently ▶ *Police were sent in to subdue the crowd.*

subdued /səb'djuːd/ *adjective*
1 quiet, especially because you are sad or worried ▶ *You seem a bit subdued.*
2 not as bright or loud as usual ▶ *subdued lighting*

subject /'sʌbdʒɪkt/ *noun*
1 something that you study ▶ *English is my favourite subject.*
2 something that you talk or write about ▶ *She has written several books on the subject.*
3 a person who belongs to a country ▶ *She is a British subject.*
4 the person or thing that does the action of a verb; the noun that usually goes in front of the verb. In the sentence "Jane bought some bread", Jane is the subject
COMPARE (**4**): **object**

subjective /səb'dʒektɪv/ *adjective*
influenced by your own opinions and feelings rather than facts
COMPARE: **objective**

subjunctive /səb'dʒʌŋktɪv/ *noun*
a verb form used to express a doubt, wish or possibility. In the sentence "He suggested we leave early", "leave" is the subjunctive

submarine /ˌsʌbmə'riːn/ *noun*
a ship that can travel under the water

submerge /səb'mɜːdʒ/ *verb (present participle* **submerging***, past* **submerged***)*
to put something below the surface of water ▶ *The town was completely submerged by the floods.*

submission /səb'mɪʃən/ *noun* (no plural)
the act of agreeing to do what someone tells you to ➤ *The soldiers beat them into submission.*

submit /səb'mɪt/ *verb* (present participle **submitting**, past **submitted**)
1 to write something formal and give it to someone to look at or consider ➤ *I've been asked to submit a report to the committee.* ➤ *Have you submitted your job application yet?*
2 to agree to do something because someone is forcing you to do it ➤ *He was losing the fight, but he wouldn't submit.*

subordinate¹ /sə'bɔːdɪnət/ *noun*
a person who has a less important job than another person in an organization ➤ *It's important to get on well with both your colleagues and your subordinates.*

subordinate² *adjective*
less important than something else, or having a lower rank or less authority ➤ *a subordinate position*

subscribe /səb'skraɪb/ *verb* (present participle **subscribing**, past **subscribed**)
to pay money so that you receive a newspaper or magazine regularly ➤ *I've always subscribed to "National Geographic" magazine.*

subscription /səb'skrɪpʃən/ *noun*
an amount of money that you pay to get a newspaper or magazine regularly, or to belong to an organization

subsequent /'sʌbsɪkwənt/ *adjective*
coming after something else ➤ *His illness and subsequent death were a terrible shock to us all.* (adverb: **subsequently**)

subside /səb'saɪd/ *verb* (present participle **subsiding**, past **subsided**)
to become less strong ➤ *The storm subsided around dawn.*

subsidiary¹ /səb'sɪdɪəri/ *noun* (plural **subsidiaries**)
a company that another company owns or controls ➤ *Ford has subsidiaries all over the world.*

subsidiary² *adjective*
less important than something else ➤ *We have to study two subsidiary subjects as well as our main subject.*

subsidize /'sʌbsɪdaɪz/ *verb* (present participle **subsidizing**, past **subsidized**)
to pay part of the cost of something ➤ *The government subsidizes school meals.*

subsidy /'sʌbsɪdi/ *noun* (plural **subsidies**)
money that a government or an organization pays to help with the cost of something ➤ *government subsidies to farmers*

substance /'sʌbstəns/ *noun*
something you can touch like a liquid, a solid, or a powder ➤ *The bag was covered with a sticky substance.* ➤ *poisonous substances*

substantial /səb'stænʃəl/ *adjective*
large in amount or size ➤ *A substantial amount of money is missing.* ➤ *We ate a substantial breakfast before setting off.* (adverb: **substantially**)

substitute¹ /'sʌbstɪtjuːt/ *noun*
a person who takes the place of someone else ➤ *a substitute goalkeeper*

substitute² *verb* (present participle **substituting**, past **substituted**)
to use something new or different instead of something else ➤ *You can substitute olive oil for butter.*

subtitles /'sʌbˌtaɪtlz/ *plural noun*
words on a film or television SCREEN that translate what the actors are saying ➤ *a French film with English subtitles*

S

subtle /'sʌtl/ *adjective*
not very noticeable, strong, or bright ➤ *a subtle change* ➤ *a subtle smell of roses (adverb: subtly)*

subtract /səb'trækt/ *verb*
to take away one number from another ➤ *If you subtract 3 from 5, you get 2.*
COMPARE: **add**

subtraction /səb'trækʃən/ *noun*
the taking away of one number from another
COMPARE: **addition**

suburb /'sʌbɜ:b/ *noun*
an outer part of a town ➤ *a suburb of London*

suburban /sə'bɜ:bən/ *adjective*
of or from an outer part of a town ➤ *suburban districts of London*

subway /'sʌbweɪ/ *noun*
a path that goes under a road or railway ➤ *If you need to cross the road, use the subway.*

succeed /sək'si:d/ *verb*
1 to do well; to get what you wanted ➤ *If you try hard, you'll succeed.*
OPPOSITE: **fail**
2 succeed in doing something to be able to do something ➤ *He succeeded in passing his driving test.*

success /sək'ses/ *noun*
1 *(no plural)* the act of doing or getting what you hoped for ➤ *his success in the examination*
2 *(plural successes)* something that pleases people, or someone who does well ➤ *Her party was a great success.*
OPPOSITE: **(1 and 2): failure**

successful /sək'sesfəl/ *adjective*
having done well or pleased people ➤ *a successful actor (adverb: successfully)*
OPPOSITE: **unsuccessful**

succession /sək'seʃən/ *noun (no plural)*

a number of things that happen one after the other ➤ *They finally managed to win a game after a succession of failures.* ➤ *United have won four championships in succession.*

successive /sək'sesɪv/ *adjective*
happening one after the other ➤ *I had to go to London on three successive days.*

successor /sək'sesəʳ/ *noun*
the person who has someone's job after they leave ➤ *Who will be his successor?*

succinct /sək'sɪŋkt/ *adjective*
clear and not containing many words ➤ *a succinct answer to the question (adverb: succinctly)*

succulent /'sʌkjʊlənt/ *adjective*
(used about food) having a lot of juice and tasting very good ➤ *a succulent steak*

succumb /sə'kʌm/ *verb*
to be unable to stop yourself from being influenced by someone or from wanting something ➤ *Eventually, she succumbed to his charms.*

such /sʌtʃ/ *adjective, adverb*
1 like the thing just mentioned ➤ *He shouted "Go away", or some such remark.*
2 used to make what you are saying stronger or greater ➤ *It's such a lovely day.*
3 such as for example ➤ *I like sports, such as tennis.*

suck /sʌk/ *verb*
to hold something in your mouth and pull on it with your tongue and lips ➤ *Don't suck your thumb, Katie.*

sudden /'sʌdn/ *adjective*
1 happening quickly or without being expected ➤ *Her illness was very sudden.*
2 all of a sudden unexpectedly and quickly ➤ *All of a sudden, the lights went out.*

suddenly /'sʌdnlɪ/ adverb
quickly and unexpectedly ➤ *I suddenly remembered that it was Jim's birthday.*

suds /sʌdz/ plural noun
the BUBBLES you get when you mix soap and water ➤ *soap suds*

sue /sju:/ verb (present participle **suing**, past **sued**)
to start a legal process to get money from someone who has harmed you ➤ *They're suing us for £10,000.*

suede /sweɪd/ noun (no plural)
a material with a slightly rough surface, made from animal skin

suffer /'sʌfə'/ verb
to be in pain or trouble ➤ *She was suffering from some sort of mental illness.*

suffering /'sʌfərɪŋ/ noun
great pain or difficulty which you experience ➤ *There was a lot of suffering during the war.*

sufficient /sə'fɪʃənt/ adjective
enough ➤ *The police have sufficient proof to arrest him.*
OPPOSITE: **insufficient**

suffix /'sʌfɪks/ noun (plural **suffixes**)
letters that you add to the end of a word to change the meaning; for example, if you add the suffix -ness to kind, you get the word kindness.
COMPARE: **prefix**

suffocate /'sʌfəkeɪt/ verb (present participle **suffocating**, past **suffocated**)
to die because there is not enough air, or to kill someone by preventing them from breathing ➤ *He suffocated her with a pillow.*

sugar /'ʃʊgə'/ noun (no plural)
a substance made from some plants, used to make food sweet

suggest /sə'dʒest/ verb
to say to someone that something is a good idea ➤ *I suggested that it would be quicker to travel by train.*

suggestion /sə'dʒestʃən/ noun
an idea of what you might do in a particular set of conditions ➤ *Can I make a suggestion?*

suicidal /ˌsuːɪ'saɪdl/ adjective
feeling so unhappy that you want to kill yourself ➤ *I felt almost suicidal when my mother died.*

suicide /'suːɪsaɪd/ noun
the act of deliberately killing yourself ➤ *More and more young men are committing suicide.*

suit¹ /suːt/ verb
1 to be right or convenient for someone ➤ *It's a small house, but it suits our needs.*
2 to make someone look good ➤ *That dress suits you.*
LOOK AT: **fit**

suit² noun
a set of clothes made from the same material, including a short coat with trousers or skirt ➤ *a dark suit*

suitable /'suːtəbəl/ adjective
right or acceptable for a particular set of conditions or purpose ➤ *This toy is not suitable for young children.*
OPPOSITE: **unsuitable**

suitcase /'suːtkeɪs/ noun
a large bag for carrying clothes in, for example on holiday
COMPARE: **briefcase**

suite /swiːt/ noun
1 a set of expensive rooms in a hotel ➤ *the honeymoon suite*
2 a set of furniture for a room that is all made of similar material ➤ *a dining room suite*

sulk /sʌlk/ verb
to feel angry for a time, usually silently ➤ *When we told her she couldn't come with us, she went and sulked in her room.*

sulky /'sʌlkɪ/ adjective (**sulkier**, **sulkiest**)
often sulking ➤ *a sulky child*

S

sullen /'sʌlən/ *adjective*
in a bad temper but not saying anything ▶ *Simon sat in the corner, looking sullen.*

sulphur /'sʌlfə^r/ *noun (no plural)*
a yellow, chemical powder that smells unpleasant

sultan /'sʌltən/ *noun*
a Muslim leader, especially in the past

sultana /sʌl'tɑːnə/ *noun*
a dried, white GRAPE

sum /sʌm/ *noun*
1 a simple calculation using numbers ▶ *Children learn to do sums at school.*
2 an amount of money ▶ *I've had to spend a large sum **of** money on my car.*

summarize /'sʌməraɪz/ *verb (present participle **summarizing**, past **summarized**)*
to give only the main information about something without all the details ▶ *I'll summarize the main points of his speech.*

summary /'sʌməri/ *noun (plural **summaries**)*
a short statement that gives the main information about something without all the details ▶ *Write a summary of the article.*

summer /'sʌmə^r/ *noun, adjective*
the season, in cool countries, when it is warmest ▶ *a summer holiday*
COMPARE: **winter**

summertime /'sʌmətaɪm/ *noun (no plural)*
the time of year when it is summer ▶ *It gets very hot in summertime.*

summit /'sʌmɪt/ *noun*
the top ▶ *a mountain summit*

summon /'sʌmən/ *verb*
to call for someone to come to you ▶ *The teacher summoned all the children to the room.*

sun /sʌn/ *noun*
1 the large ball of fire in the sky which gives light and heat
COMPARE: **moon**
2 the light and heat from the sun ▶ *Sit in the sun and get warm.*

sunbathe /'sʌnbeɪð/ *verb (present participle **sunbathing**, past **sunbathed**)*
to lie in the sun to make your body brown

sunburn /'sʌnbɜːn/ *noun (no plural)*
sore, red skin from spending too much time in strong sunlight
COMPARE: **suntan**

sunburnt /'sʌnbɜːnt/ *(also **sunburned** /'sʌnbɜːnd/) adjective*
having skin that is red and painful because you have stayed too long in the sun ▶ *Be careful not to get sunburnt.*

sun cream /'sʌn kriːm/ *noun (no plural)*
SUNSCREEN

Sunday /'sʌndeɪ, -dɪ/ *noun*
the first day of the week; the day on which Christians go to church

sunflower /'sʌnflaʊə^r/ *noun*
a tall plant with a large, yellow flower, and seeds that you can eat

sung /sʌŋ/
the PAST PARTICIPLE of the verb **sing**

sunglasses /'sʌn,ɡlɑːsɪz/ *plural noun*
glasses with dark glass in them, which you wear when it is very sunny or bright

sunk /sʌŋk/
the PAST PARTICIPLE of the verb **sink**

sunlight /'sʌnlaɪt/ *noun (no plural)*
natural light from the sun ▶ *He stepped out into the strong sunlight.*

sunny /'sʌnɪ/ *adjective (**sunnier**, **sunniest**)*
full of bright sunlight ▶ *The day was bright and sunny.*

S

sunrise /ˈsʌnraɪz/ *noun*
the time in the morning when the sun first appears

sunscreen /ˈsʌnskriːn/ *noun*
a cream that you put on your skin to stop the sun from burning you

sunset /ˈsʌnset/ *noun*
the time when the sun disappears and night begins

sunshine /ˈsʌnʃaɪn/ *noun (no plural)*
light and heat from the sun ▶ *The children played in the sunshine.*

suntan /ˈsʌntæn/ *noun*
the brown colour of your skin after you have been out in the hot sun ▶ *She's got a great suntan.*
COMPARE: **sunburn**

super /ˈsuːpə/ *adjective*
very nice or exciting ▶ *We had a super day at the seaside.*

superb /suːˈpɜːb/ *adjective*
very fine ▶ *Her dancing is superb.*

superficial /ˌsuːpəˈfɪʃəl/ *adjective*
1 done quickly, and not in a thorough or careful way ▶ *The police carried out only a superficial examination of the body.* ▶ *a superficial knowledge of the subject*
2 not very deep or serious ▶ *Our car escaped with only superficial damage.* ▶ *superficial injuries*
3 not thinking about serious or important things ▶ *He's not as superficial as he seems.*

superintendent /ˌsuːpərɪnˈtendənt/ *noun*
1 a person who is officially responsible for looking after a building
2 a British police officer

superior /suːˈpɪərɪəʳ/ *adjective*
better than someone or something else ▶ *Our products are far superior to theirs.*
OPPOSITE: **inferior**

superlative /suːˈpɜːlətɪv/ *noun, adjective*
a word or a form of a word that shows that something is the best, worst, biggest, smallest, etc. of its kind. The superlative of *good* is *best*.
COMPARE: **comparative**

supermarket /ˈsuːpəˌmɑːkɪt/ *noun*
a big food shop in which you choose the things that you want, and pay as you go out

supermodel /ˈsuːpəˌmɒdl/ *noun*
a very famous fashion model

supernatural¹ /ˌsuːpəˈnætʃərəl/ *adjective*
relating to events, creatures, etc. that cannot be explained by science or natural causes ▶ *They believed that cats had supernatural powers.*

supernatural² *noun*
the supernatural strange events that cannot be explained by science or natural causes ▶ *Do you believe in the supernatural?*

supersonic /ˌsuːpəˈsɒnɪk/ *adjective*
faster than the speed of sound ▶ *a supersonic plane*

superstar /ˈsuːpəˌstɑːʳ/ *noun*
a person who is extremely famous and popular

superstition /ˌsuːpəˈstɪʃən/ *noun*
something that people believe that cannot be proved, and is probably not true ▶ *Some people think that the number 13 is unlucky, but that is just a superstition.*

superstitious /ˌsuːpəˈstɪʃəs/ *adjective*
believing that some objects or actions are lucky and others are unlucky ▶ *Are you superstitious?*

superstore /ˈsuːpəstɔːʳ/ *noun*
a very large shop ▶ *a computer superstore*

supervise /ˈsuːpəvaɪz/ *verb (present participle **supervising**, past **supervised**)*
to watch over people while they work, to see that they are doing the

S

right thing ▶ *The teacher supervised our examination.*

supervision /ˌsuːpəˈvɪʒən/ *noun (no plural)*
watching over people while they work to make sure that they are doing the right thing ▶ *We worked under the teacher's supervision.*

supervisor /ˈsuːpəvaɪzəʳ/ *noun*
a person whose job is to watch over people while they work, to see that they are doing the right thing

supper /ˈsʌpəʳ/ *noun*
an evening meal
COMPARE: **dinner**

supple /ˈsʌpəl/ *adjective*
able to bend and move easily ▶ *supple leather* ▶ *Yoga makes you very supple.*

supplement /ˈsʌplɪmənt/ *noun*
1 an additional part of a newspaper or magazine ▶ *This week's magazine contains a free fashion supplement.*
2 a special food or drink that contains substances that are good for your body ▶ *He takes vitamin supplements every morning.*

supplier /səˈplaɪəʳ/ *noun*
a company that provides goods for shops and businesses ▶ *an office equipment supplier*

supplies /səˈplaɪz/ *plural noun*
things that you need for daily life ▶ *We cannot get supplies to the village because of the snow.*

supply¹ /səˈplaɪ/ *noun (plural **supplies**)*
an amount of something that you keep and that can be used when it is needed ▶ *We keep a large supply of food in the house.*

supply² /səˈplaɪ/ *verb (past **supplied**)*
to give or sell something that someone needs ▶ *That company supplies paper **to** schools.*

support¹ /səˈpɔːt/ *verb*
1 to hold or keep something up ▶ *These posts support the roof.*

2 to give help, money, or food to someone ▶ *She supports her husband on the money she earns from teaching.*
3 to be on the side of someone, or want them to succeed ▶ *Which football team do you support?*

support² *noun*
1 something that holds something else up ▶ *There are two large, wooden supports that hold up the roof.*
2 *(no plural)* encouragement and help ▶ *Thank you for your support.*

supporter /səˈpɔːtəʳ/ *noun*
a person who supports a particular person, team, or plan ▶ *loyal supporters of the President* ▶ *a crowd of football supporters*

supportive /səˈpɔːtɪv/ *adjective*
giving help and encouragement ▶ *My parents are usually very supportive.*

suppose /səˈpəʊz/ *verb (present participle **supposing**, past **supposed**)*
1 to think that something is probably true or that something will probably happen ▶ *I suppose he's gone home.* ▶ *He'll come with us, I suppose.*
2 used to ask what might happen ▶ *Suppose Mum found out? She'd go crazy!*

supposed /səˈpəʊzd/ *(past participle of the verb **suppose**)*
be supposed to (a) to be expected to do something ▶ *You're not supposed to smoke in here.*
(b) to be considered to be ▶ *It's supposed to be a good film.*

supposedly /səˈpəʊzɪdlɪ/ *adverb*
used to say that you do not believe what you are saying, even though other people think it is true ▶ *These chemicals are supposedly harmless.*

supposing /səˈpəʊzɪŋ/ *conjunction*
if ▶ *Supposing you catch the next bus, you'll be home before 10 o'clock.*

suppress /səˈpres/ *verb*
1 to stop people from opposing the

S

government, especially by using force ➤ *The army was called in to suppress the revolt.*

2 to control a feeling, so that you do not show it or it does not affect you ➤ *Andy could barely suppress his anger.*

supreme /suːˈpriːm/ *adjective*
highest; best ➤ *The most important law court is called the Supreme Court.*

sure /ʃʊəʳ/ *adjective*
1 certain ➤ *I am sure that I put the money in the box.*
OPPOSITE: **unsure**
2 make sure (a) to find out for certain ➤ *I'll just make sure the car's locked.* **(b)** to arrange that something will certainly happen ➤ *Make sure you get here before 3 o'clock.*

surely /ˈʃʊəlɪ/ *adverb*
1 certainly ➤ *This will surely mean that more people will lose their jobs.*
2 a word used when you think something must be true ➤ *Surely you remember him?*

surf¹ /sɜːf/ *noun (no plural)*
white waves when they come into the land

surf² *verb*
to ride on a special narrow board over waves as they come into the land

surface /ˈsɜːfɪs/ *noun*
the outside, flat part or top of something ➤ *Don't scratch the surface of the table.*

surfboard /ˈsɜːfbɔːd/ *noun*
a special narrow piece of wood or plastic which people lie or stand on when going over big waves as they come into the land

surfing /ˈsɜːfɪŋ/ *noun (no plural)*
the sport of riding on a special narrow board over waves as they come into the land

surge¹ /sɜːdʒ/ *verb (present participle surging, past surged)*

(used about crowds of people) to move forward suddenly ➤ *The crowd surged through the gates.*

surge² *noun*
a sudden large increase in something ➤ *He felt a sudden surge of anger.* ➤ *a surge in oil prices*

surgeon /ˈsɜːdʒən/ *noun*
a doctor who cuts into people's bodies to mend parts inside them

surgery /ˈsɜːdʒərɪ/ *noun*
1 *(no plural)* the cutting open of a person's body to mend parts inside them
2 *(plural surgeries)* a place where you can go to see a doctor or DENTIST

surgical /ˈsɜːdʒɪkəl/ *adjective*
of or used for medical operations ➤ *surgical instruments*

surname /ˈsɜːneɪm/ *noun*
a name used by a family, usually written last – for example, in the name Peter White, White is the surname
COMPARE: **first name**
SAME MEANING: **last name**

surplus¹ /ˈsɜːpləs/ *noun (plural surpluses)*
more of something than you need ➤ *The country produces a huge surplus of grain.*

surplus² *adjective*
more than what is needed ➤ *surplus land*

surprise¹ /səˈpraɪz/ *noun*
1 an unexpected event ➤ *Don't tell him about the present – it's a surprise.*
2 the feeling that you have when something unexpected happens ➤ *I looked at him in surprise – I hadn't expected to see him again.*
3 give someone a surprise to do something or give someone something which they do not expect ➤ *I didn't tell her we were going on holiday because I wanted to give her a surprise.*

4 take someone by surprise to happen unexpectedly ▶ *When he offered me the job, it took me completely by surprise.*

surprise² *verb (present participle* **surprising**, *past* **surprised**)
to do something which someone does not expect ▶ *His anger surprised me – I didn't think he would mind.*

surprised /sə'praɪzd/ *adjective*
not expecting something ▶ *I'm surprised you haven't been there before.* ▶ *He seemed surprised at my question.* ▶ *She was surprised to find Sally waiting for her.*

surprising /sə'praɪzɪŋ/ *adjective*
unusual or unexpected and making you feel surprised ▶ *surprising news* ▶ *It's surprising how little a computer costs now.* ▶ *It's hardly surprising that they lost the game.* (adverb: **surprisingly**)

surrender /sə'rendə'/ *verb*
to stop fighting because you know that you cannot win

surround /sə'raʊnd/ *verb*
to be or go all round something ▶ *The fence surrounds the school.*

surroundings /sə'raʊndɪŋz/ *plural noun*
the area around something ▶ *The house is in beautiful surroundings.*

surveillance /sə'veɪləns/ *noun (no plural)*
(used about the police, army, etc.) the art of carefully watching a person or place ▶ *The police kept the group under surveillance.*

survey /'sɜːveɪ/ *noun*
a set of questions that you ask a lot of people in order to find out about their opinions ▶ *a survey of people's eating habits*

surveyor /sə'veɪə'/ *noun*
a person whose job is to examine and measure land or buildings

survival /sə'vaɪvəl/ *noun (no plural)*
continuing to live after a difficult or dangerous time ▶ *We had little hope of survival.*

survive /sə'vaɪv/ *verb (present participle* **surviving**, *past* **survived**)
to continue to live after an accident or illness ▶ *The man was very ill, but he survived.*

survivor /sə'vaɪvə'/ *noun*
a person who continues to live after an accident or illness ▶ *The survivors of the crash are in hospital.*

susceptible /sə'septəbəl/ *adjective*
likely to be affected by an illness or a problem ▶ *Young children are susceptible to colds.*

suspect¹ /sə'spekt/ *verb*
to think that something is true, though you do not know ▶ *I suspect that he's lying.*

suspect² /'sʌspekt/ *noun*
a person who you think has done something wrong ▶ *The police have taken the suspect to the police station.*

suspend /sə'spend/ *verb*
1 to hang something from above ▶ *The lamp was suspended from a hook.*
2 to delay or stop something ▶ *We suspended the building work during the rain.*

suspense /sə'spens/ *noun (no plural)*
a delay which excites people or makes them afraid ▶ *Please tell us what happened; we can't stand the suspense.*

suspension /sə'spenʃən/ *noun*
1 the act of not allowing someone to work or go to school for a fixed time because they have broken the rules ▶ *The players received a three-match suspension for fighting.*
2 *(no plural)* the part of a vehicle that makes it move up and down more gently when the surface of the road is uneven, so that it is more comfortable to ride in

suspicion /sə'spɪʃən/ *noun*
1 a feeling that something may be true
2 a feeling that something may be wrong ▶ *I have a suspicion that he's not telling the truth.*

suspicious /sə'spɪʃəs/ *adjective*
1 feeling that something is wrong ▶ *I am suspicious of that woman – I think she may have stolen something from our shop.*
2 making you feel that something is wrong ▶ *His behaviour was very suspicious.*

sustain /sə'steɪn/ *verb*
1 to make something continue to exist ▶ *Can the team sustain their lead in the competition?*
2 sustain an injury, sustain damage to be injured or damaged ▶ *Mr Turner sustained serious head injuries in the attack.*

swagger /'swægəʳ/ *verb*
to walk with a swinging movement, in a way that seems too proud and confident

swallow¹ /'swɒləʊ/ *verb*
to take food or drink down your throat and into your stomach ▶ *She swallowed some milk.*

swallow² *noun*
a small bird with a tail divided into two parts

swam /swæm/
the PAST TENSE of the verb **swim**

swamp /swɒmp/ *noun*
land which is always soft and wet

swan /swɒn/ *noun*
a large, white water bird with a long, curved neck

swap (also **swop**) /swɒp/ *verb* (present participle **swapping**, past **swapped**)
to exchange something you have for something that someone else has ▶ *He swapped his torch for a CD.*

▶ *We swapped places so that I could look out of the window.*

swarm¹ /swɔːm/ *noun*
a large group, especially of insects ▶ *a swarm of bees*

swarm² *verb*
to move in a large group

swat /swɒt/ *verb* (present participle **swatting**, past **swatted**)
to hit an insect to try to kill it

sway /sweɪ/ *verb*
to move slowly from side to side ▶ *The trees swayed in the wind.*

swear /sweəʳ/ *verb* (past tense **swore** /swɔːʳ/, past participle **sworn** /swɔːn/)
1 to use very bad words ▶ *He was so angry that he swore at his mother.*
2 to promise ▶ *I swear I won't tell anyone your secret.*

swearword /'sweəˌwɜːd/ *noun*
a word that is considered to be rude or shocking by most people

sweat¹ /swet/ *noun (no plural)*
water which comes out of your skin when you are hot or afraid ▶ *Sweat poured down his face as he ran.*

sweat² *verb*
to produce water through your skin because you are hot or afraid ▶ *She was sweating as she reached the top of the hill.*

sweatband /'swetbænd/ *noun*
a narrow piece of material that you wear round your wrist or forehead to stop sweat running down

sweater /'swetəʳ/ *noun*
a piece of clothing, usually made of wool, that covers the top part of your body
SAME MEANING: **jersey, jumper, pullover**

sweatshirt /'swet-ʃɜːt/ *noun*
a thick, soft, cotton shirt without buttons

sweaty /'swetɪ/ *adjective* (**sweatier, sweatiest**)

S

covered with sweat ► *I was hot and sweaty from working in the sun.*

sweep /swiːp/ *verb (past **swept** /swept/)*
1 to clean something with a brush ► *I swept the floor.*
2 to move quickly ► *The crowd swept through the gates.*

sweet[1] /swiːt/ *adjective*
1 containing or tasting of sugar ► *I don't like sweet things.*
2 pleasant and loving ► *What a sweet smile she has!*

sweet[2] *noun*
1 a small, sugary thing to eat
2 sweet food served at the end of a meal
SAME MEANING (**2**): **pudding, dessert**

sweetcorn /'swiːtkɔːn/ *noun (no plural)*
the yellow seeds of a tall plant, eaten as food

sweeten /'swiːtn/ *verb*
to make a food or drink taste sweeter ► *The cake is sweetened with honey.*

sweetener /'swiːtnə^r/ *noun*
a substance used instead of sugar to make food or drink taste sweeter

sweetheart /'swiːthɑːt/ *noun*
a person that you are in love with

swell /swel/ *verb (past participle **swollen** /'swəʊlən/)*
to become larger ► *A bee has stung my hand and it is swelling up like a balloon.*

swelling /'swelɪŋ/ *noun*
a place on your body that has become larger than usual ► *I've got a nasty swelling on my foot.*

swept /swept/
the PAST TENSE and PAST PARTICIPLE of the verb **sweep**

swerve /swɜːv/ *verb (present participle **swerving**, past **swerved**)*
to move suddenly to one side when you are moving along ► *The car swerved to avoid the dog.*

swift /swɪft/ *adjective*
fast ► *a swift runner*

swim[1] /swɪm/ *verb (present participle **swimming**, past tense **swam** /swæm/, past participle **swum** /swʌm/)*
to move through water by using your legs and arms ► *He swam across the river.*

swim[2] *noun*
a time when you swim ► *to go for a swim*

swimmer /'swɪmə^r/ *noun*
someone who swims

swimming /'swɪmɪŋ/ *noun (no plural)*
the act of moving through the water using your arms and legs ► *I'm going to have swimming lessons.*

swimming costume /'swɪmɪŋ ˌkɒstjuːm/ *noun*
a piece of clothing that a girl or woman wears for swimming
SAME MEANING: **swimsuit**

swimming pool /'swɪmɪŋ ˌpuːl/ *noun*
a place where people can go to swim

swimming trunks /'swɪmɪŋ ˌtrʌŋks/ *plural noun*
a piece of clothing that a man or boy wears for swimming

swimsuit /'swɪmsuːt/ *noun*
a piece of clothing that a girl or woman wears for swimming
SAME MEANING: **swimming costume**

swindle /'swɪndl/ *verb (present participle **swindling**, past **swindled**)*
to get money from someone by tricking them ► *Sherman had swindled the woman **out of** thousands of pounds.*

swing[1] /swɪŋ/ *verb (past **swung** /swʌŋ/)*
to move freely from a fixed point ► *The boy swung over the river on a rope.* ► *The sign was swinging in the wind.*

swing² noun
a seat hanging on ropes or chains for children to play on

swipe /swaɪp/ verb (present participle **swiping**, past **swiped**)
1 to steal something ▶ Who's swiped my pencil?
2 (also **swipe at**) to hit or try to hit someone or something by swinging your arm at them ▶ She swiped at him, but he quickly moved out of the way.

swirl /swɜːl/ verb
to turn around and around ▶ Leaves swirled to the ground.

switch¹ /swɪtʃ/ noun (plural **switches**)
something that you press, turn, or pull to put something such as a light on or off

switch² verb
1 to change ▶ I used to cook on electricity, but I've switched to gas.
2 switch something off to put off something like a light by pushing a button ▶ Could you switch the television off?
3 switch something on to put on something like a light by pushing a button ▶ Could you switch on the television?

switchboard /'swɪtʃbɔːd/ noun
the place in a large organization where telephone calls are answered and connected to the people who work there ▶ Hello, you're through to the switchboard.

swivel /'swɪvəl/ verb (present participle **swivelling**, past **swivelled**)
to turn around while staying in the same place, or to make something do this ▶ a chair that swivels

swollen /'swəʊlən/
the PAST PARTICIPLE of the verb **swell**

swoop /swuːp/ verb
to fly down very quickly ▶ The bird swooped down to the lake.

swop /swɒp/ verb (present participle **swopping**, past **swopped**)
another word for **swap**

sword /sɔːd/ noun
a sharp, pointed weapon like a long knife that you hold in your hand and fight with
COMPARE: **dagger**

swore /swɔːr/
the PAST TENSE of the verb **swear**

sworn /swɔːn/
the PAST PARTICIPLE of the verb **swear**

swot¹ /swɒt/ noun
a person who studies too hard ▶ "I got 89% in my French test." "What a swot!"

swot² (also **swot up**) verb (present participle **swotting**, past **swotted**)
to study hard ▶ I need to swot up on my maths before the exam.

swum /swʌm/
the PAST PARTICIPLE of the verb **swim**

swung /swʌŋ/
the PAST TENSE and PAST PARTICIPLE of the verb **swing**

syllable /'sɪləbəl/ noun
a part of a word which contains one vowel sound. There are two syllables in "window": "win" and "dow"

syllabus /'sɪləbəs/ noun (plural **syllabuses**)
a list of all the things that students will study on a course

symbol /'sɪmbəl/ noun
a sign that means or shows something else ▶ the five-ring symbol of the Olympic Games

symbolic /sɪm'bɒlɪk/ adjective
be symbolic of something to mean or represent something ▶ The new bridge is symbolic of the link between the two countries.

symbolize /'sɪmbəlaɪz/ verb (present participle **symbolizing**, past **symbolized**)

S

to be a symbol that means or represents something ▶ *A wedding ring symbolizes a couple's vows to each other.*

symmetrical /sɪˈmetrɪkəl/ *(also* **symmetric** /sɪˈmetrɪk/*) adjective* having halves or sides that are exactly the same size and shape

symmetry /ˈsɪmɪtri/ *noun (no plural)* the state of having two halves or sides that are exactly the same size and shape

sympathetic /ˌsɪmpəˈθetɪk/ *adjective* kind and understanding about someone else's unhappiness ▶ *When I told her why I was worried, she was very sympathetic.*
OPPOSITE: **unsympathetic**

sympathize /ˈsɪmpəθaɪz/ *verb (present participle* **sympathizing,** *past* **sympathized)**
1 to be kind to someone who is sad by showing that you understand their problems
2 to support someone's ideas or actions ▶ *On the whole, I sympathize with their aims.*

sympathy /ˈsɪmpəθi/ *noun (plural* **sympathies)**
a feeling of kind understanding and sharing another person's unhappiness ▶ *I have been a prisoner myself, so I have a lot of sympathy with other people in prison.*

symphony /ˈsɪmfəni/ *noun (plural* **symphonies)**
a long piece of music that is written for an ORCHESTRA

symptom /ˈsɪmptəm/ *noun* a sign of something, especially an illness ▶ *Fever is a symptom of many illnesses.*

synagogue /ˈsɪnəgɒg/ *noun* a building where Jewish people meet for religious services

sync /sɪŋk/ *noun*
1 in sync happening at the same time ▶ *The band wasn't in sync with the drummer.*
2 out of sync not happening at the same time ▶ *The sound was out of sync with the pictures.*

syndicate /ˈsɪndɪkət/ *noun* a group of people or companies that have joined together for business reasons

syndrome /ˈsɪndrəʊm/ *noun* a medical condition that produces a particular set of problems

synonym /ˈsɪnənɪm/ *noun* a word with the same meaning as another word in the same language ▶ *"Enormous" is a synonym of "huge".*

syntax /ˈsɪntæks/ *noun (no plural)*
the way words are arranged to form sentences or phrases

synthesizer /ˈsɪnθəsaɪzəʳ/ *noun* an electronic musical instrument that can sound like many different musical instruments

synthetic /sɪnˈθetɪk/ *adjective* made from artificial substances, not natural ones ▶ *synthetic fabrics like acrylic*

syphon /ˈsaɪfən/ *noun, verb* another word for **siphon**

syringe /səˈrɪndʒ/ *noun* an instrument with a needle at one end for giving people medicine through their skin

syrup /ˈsɪrəp/ *noun (no plural)* a thick liquid made by boiling sugar in water or fruit juice

system /ˈsɪstəm/ *noun* a group of things or ideas working together in one arrangement ▶ *the public transport system* ▶ *What system of government do you have in your country?*

systematic /ˌsɪstɪˈmætɪk/ *adjective*
using a planned and organized method ➤ *a systematic search of the building* (adverb: **systematically**)

Tt

tab /tæb/ *noun*
1 pick up the tab to pay for something, especially a meal in a restaurant
2 keep tabs on someone to carefully watch what someone is doing ➤ *The police are keeping close tabs on her.*

table /ˈteɪbəl/ *noun*
a piece of furniture with a flat top and three or four legs ➤ *The family was sitting at the kitchen table.*

tablecloth /ˈteɪbəlˌklɒθ/ *noun*
a cloth which you put over a table

tablespoon /ˈteɪbəlˌspuːn/ *noun*
a large spoon that you use for serving food

tablet /ˈtæblɪt/ *noun*
a small, hard ball of medicine that you swallow when you are not well
SAME MEANING: **pill**

table tennis /ˈteɪbəl ˌtenɪs/ *noun (no plural)*
a game in which two or four players hit a small ball over a net across a table
SAME MEANING: **ping-pong**

tabloid /ˈtæblɔɪd/ *noun*
a newspaper that has small pages, short, simple reports, and usually not much serious news ➤ *Don't believe everything you read in the tabloids.*

taboo /təˈbuː/ *noun*
something that you must not do or talk about because it offends or embarrasses people

tack¹ /tæk/ *verb*
tack something on to add something to another thing ➤ *Joan tacked a few words on the end of my letter.*

tack² *noun*
a small nail with a sharp point and a flat top ➤ *carpet tacks*

tackle /ˈtækəl/ *verb (present participle **tackling**, past **tackled**)*
1 to begin work on something ➤ *I must tackle that report this evening.*
2 to try to stop someone in a game and take the ball away from them ➤ *He tackled the other player and kicked the ball across the field.*

tact /tækt/ *noun (no plural)*
the ability to say or do things without hurting or offending people

tactful /ˈtæktfəl/ *adjective*
careful not to say or do things that hurt or offend people
OPPOSITE: **tactless**

tactic /ˈtæktɪk/ *noun*
an action that you plan carefully in order to achieve what you want ➤ *The team have prepared their tactics for the game.*

tactless /ˈtæktləs/ *adjective*
not careful about hurting or offending people ➤ *His tactless remarks upset her very much.*
OPPOSITE: **tactful**

tadpole /ˈtædpəʊl/ *noun*
a small, black water creature that becomes a FROG or a TOAD

tag /tæg/ *noun*
a small piece of paper or material fixed to something to give information about it ➤ *Look for a name tag on the coat to see who it belongs to.* ➤ *a price tag*

tail /teɪl/ *noun*
the part of an animal that sticks out at the end of its back ➤ *The dog was happy to see her and wagged its tail.*

tail light /ˈteɪl laɪt/ *noun*
one of the two red lights at the back of a car or plane

tailor /ˈteɪləʳ/ *noun*
a person who makes suits, coats, etc.
COMPARE: **dressmaker**

tailor-made /ˌteɪlə ˈmeɪd/
adjective
very suitable for someone or
something ▶ *The job seems tailor-made for him.*

take /teɪk/ *verb (present participle*
***taking**, past tense **took** /tʊk/,
past participle **taken** /ˈteɪkən/)*
1 to get hold of something ▶ *The
mother took her child by the hand.*
▶ *Shall I take your coat?*
2 to carry something to another place
▶ *Can you take this shopping home
for me, please?*
COMPARE (**2**): **bring**
3 to go with somebody to another
place ▶ *I'll take you to the station.*
4 to remove something from a place
or to steal it ▶ *Who has taken the last
piece of cake?* ▶ *The thief took all the
jewellery.*
5 to swallow medicine ▶ *I've taken
some medicine for my cough.*
6 to travel in a vehicle ▶ *We took a
taxi as we were late.*
7 to need a particular amount of time
▶ *The journey to London takes three
hours.*
8 take after someone to look or
behave like a relative who is older
than you ▶ *He takes after his father.*
9 take care of someone to look after
someone ▶ *Who will take care of me
when I am old?*
10 take it for granted that ... to
believe something without having
any doubts about it ▶ *I took it for
granted that I would be invited to my
brother's wedding.*
11 take off (used about a plane) to
leave the ground
OPPOSITE: **land**
12 take something off to remove a
piece of clothing ▶ *He took his coat
off.*

13 take place to happen ▶ *The
accident took place on Saturday
night.*
LOOK AT: **happen**
14 Take a seat something you say
when you are inviting someone to sit
down

takeaway /ˈteɪkəweɪ/ *noun*
1 a cooked meal that you buy to eat
at home or outside ▶ *We had a
takeaway for our supper last night.*
2 a place that sells cooked meals for
you to eat somewhere else

taken /ˈteɪkən/
the PAST PARTICIPLE of the verb **take**

take-off *(also **takeoff**)* /ˈteɪkɒf/ *noun*
the moment when a plane leaves the
ground and flies into the air

tale /teɪl/ *noun*
a story

talent /ˈtælənt/ *noun*
the ability to do a particular thing
well ▶ *My sister has great musical
talent.*

talented /ˈtæləntɪd/ *adjective*
able to do a particular thing very well
▶ *a talented actress*

talk¹ /tɔːk/ *verb*
to speak ▶ *They were talking **about**
the weather.* ▶ *Their baby is just
learning to talk.*

talk² *noun*
1 a conversation ▶ *We had a long
talk.*
2 an informal speech ▶ *The singer
came to our school to give a talk on
music.*

talkative /ˈtɔːkətɪv/ *adjective*
liking to talk a lot

tall /tɔːl/ *adjective*
1 higher than other people or other
things ▶ *James is taller than Paul, but
Richard is the tallest.* ▶ *a tall building*
2 having a particular height ▶ *He is 1
metre 80 centimetres tall.* ▶ *How tall
are you?*

talon /'tælən/ *noun*
one of the sharp, curved nails on the feet of some birds that hunt other animals

tame¹ /teɪm/ *adjective*
(used about an animal) trained to live with people ▶ *a tame monkey*
OPPOSITE: **wild**

tame² *verb (present participle taming, past tamed)*
to train a wild animal to live with people

tamper /'tæmpəʳ/ *verb*
tamper with something to change something without permission, especially in order to damage it
▶ *Someone had tampered with the car's brakes.*

tan /tæn/ *noun*
a SUNTAN

tangerine /ˌtændʒəˈriːn/ *noun*
a fruit like a small, sweet orange

tangle /'tæŋgəl/ *noun*
a knotted mass of string, hair, or thread ▶ *The string was in a tangle.*

tangled /'tæŋgəld/ *adjective*
twisted into knots ▶ *tangled hair*
▶ *tangled wool*

tank /tæŋk/ *noun*
1 a container to hold liquids or gas
▶ *The petrol tank is empty.*
2 a heavy vehicle with guns on it, used in battle

tanker /'tæŋkəʳ/ *noun*
a ship or lorry that carries large amounts of oil or other liquids ▶ *an oil tanker*

Tannoy /'tænɔɪ/ *noun trademark*
a system of LOUDSPEAKERS that people use to announce things in public places ▶ *I heard my name called over the Tannoy.*

tantrum /'tæntrəm/ *noun*
a short period of time when someone, especially a child, suddenly becomes very angry ▶ *She had a*
tantrum when I refused to buy her any sweets.

tap¹ /tæp/ *verb (present participle tapping, past tapped)*
to strike something lightly ▶ *Lucy's mother tapped on her bedroom door to see if she was awake.*

tap² *noun*
an instrument on the end of a pipe, which can be turned to let liquid or gas out

tap dancing /'tæp ˌdɑːnsɪŋ/ *noun (no plural)*
a type of dancing in which dancers wear special shoes to make a sound when they move their feet to the music

tape¹ /teɪp/ *noun*
1 a long, thin band of plastic inside a small case, on which you can record sound or pictures ▶ *Which tape (=of music) shall we listen to next?*
2 a long, thin band of sticky material used for fastening things
3 a long, thin band of cloth or paper

tape² *verb (present participle taping, past taped)*
1 to record music or a film, etc.
▶ *Shall we tape the film and watch it tomorrow?*
2 to fasten something with tape that sticks ▶ *She closed the box and taped it up.*

tape deck /'teɪp dek/ *noun*
the part of a STEREO which you use to play and record music on tapes

tape measure /'teɪp ˌmeʒəʳ/ *noun*
a narrow band of cloth or plastic used for measuring

tape recorder /'teɪp rɪˌkɔːdəʳ/ *noun*
a machine which records and plays music and other sounds

tapestry /'tæpəstrɪ/ *noun (plural tapestries)*
a piece of heavy cloth that is covered with a picture made of coloured threads

tar /tɑːʳ/ *noun (no plural)*
a thick, black substance which is used in making roads

target /'tɑːgɪt/ *noun*
an object that you try to hit with a gun or an arrow

tarmac /'tɑːmæk/ *noun (no plural)*
a mixture of TAR and very small stones, used to make the surface of roads

tart /tɑːt/ *noun*
a piece of pastry with fruit or JAM cooked on top of it
COMPARE: **pie**

tartan /'tɑːtn/ *noun*
a cloth with a special pattern of squares on it

task /tɑːsk/ *noun*
a piece of work which must be done ▶ *Washing the dishes is a task I do not enjoy.*
SAME MEANING: **job**

taste¹ /teɪst/ *noun*
1 *(no plural)* the special sense by which we know one food from another ▶ *My sense of taste isn't very good.*
2 *(no plural)* the feeling that a particular food gives you when it is in your mouth ▶ *a sweet taste*
3 someone's particular choice ▶ *She has good taste in clothes.*

taste² *verb (present participle tasting, past tasted)*
1 to try food or drink by taking a little into your mouth ▶ *Can I taste your drink?*
2 to have a particular feeling in your mouth ▶ *This wine tastes odd.*

tasteful /'teɪstfəl/ *adjective*
attractive and of good quality ▶ *a tasteful birthday card (adverb : tastefully)*

tasteless /'teɪstləs/ *adjective*
1 not attractive and not of good quality ▶ *Some of her clothes are really tasteless!*

2 likely to offend people ▶ *tasteless jokes*
3 *(used about food)* not having any taste ▶ *This soup's completely tasteless.*

tasty /'teɪsti/ *adjective (tastier, tastiest)*
having a very nice taste ▶ *a tasty meal*

tattered /'tætəd/ *adjective*
old and torn ▶ *tattered curtains*

tattoo¹ /tæ'tuː/ *verb*
to draw a picture or write words on someone's skin by pricking it and putting colouring substances on it

tattoo² *noun*
a picture or word put on someone's skin by pricking it and putting colouring substances on it

taught /tɔːt/
the PAST TENSE and PAST PARTICIPLE of the verb **teach**

taunt /tɔːnt/ *verb*
to say unkind things to someone in order to upset them ▶ *The other kids taunted each other about their clothes.*

taut /tɔːt/ *adjective*
stretched tight ▶ *They pulled the rope until it was taut.*

tax¹ /tæks/ *noun (plural taxes)*
money which must be paid to the government from the money you earn

tax² *verb*
to make people pay a certain amount of money to the government

tax-free /ˌtæks 'friː/ *adjective*
that you do not have to pay tax on ▶ *a tax-free savings account*

taxi /'tæksi/ *noun*
a car with a driver who will take you somewhere if you pay him or her ▶ *I'll take a taxi to the station.*
SAME MEANING: **cab**

tea /tiː/ *noun*
1 *(no plural)* a hot drink made by pouring boiling water onto special dry leaves ▶ *a pot of tea*

T

2 a cup of tea ► *Two teas, please.*
3 an evening meal ► *What are we having for tea tonight?*
4 a small meal in the afternoon, in which people usually eat bread and cakes and drink tea
COMPARE (**3** and **4**): **dinner, lunch**

teabag /ˈtiːbæg/ *noun*
a small paper bag containing dried tealeaves on which you pour hot water to make a cup of tea

teach /tiːtʃ/ *verb (past taught /tɔːt/)*
1 to give people lessons in a particular subject, especially in a school ► *Miss Jones teaches history.*
2 to show someone how to do something ► *Who taught you to ride a bicycle?*
LOOK AT: **know**

teacher /ˈtiːtʃəʳ/ *noun*
a person who gives lessons, especially in a school

teaching /ˈtiːtʃɪŋ/ *noun (no plural)*
the work of being a teacher ► *I'd like to go into teaching when I finish college.*

team /tiːm/ *noun*
1 a group of people who play games against other groups ► *a football team*
2 a group of people who work together on something ► *a team of writers*

teammate /ˈtiːm-meɪt/ *noun*
a person who is in the same team as you ► *His teammates cheered as he scored.*

teapot /ˈtiːpɒt/ *noun*
a pot used for making tea

tear¹ /tɪəʳ/ *noun*
1 a drop of water from your eye
2 in tears crying ► *She was in tears all morning.*

tear² /teəʳ/ *noun*
a split in something where it has torn ► *a tear in his trousers*

tear³ /teəʳ/ *verb (past tense tore /tɔːʳ/, past participle torn /tɔːn/)*
1 to make a split or a hole in something ► *He tore his trousers.* ► *She tore the piece of paper in half.*
2 to pull something roughly from a place ► *You can tear a page out of my notebook.*
3 tear something up to destroy something made of paper by pulling it into little pieces ► *She tore up the letter.*

tearful /ˈtɪəfəl/ *adjective*
crying or almost crying ► *She looked very tearful.*

tease /tiːz/ *verb (present participle teasing, past teased)*
to make fun of a person playfully or unkindly ► *You must not tease your little sister.*

teaspoon /ˈtiːspuːn/ *noun*
a small spoon used to mix sugar or milk in tea, coffee, etc.

teat /tiːt/ *noun*
1 the part of a female animal that baby animals suck to get milk
2 the soft, rubber part of a baby's bottle that a baby sucks

tea towel /ˈtiː ˌtaʊəl/ *noun*
a piece of cloth that you use for drying cups, plates, etc. after washing them

technical /ˈteknɪkəl/ *adjective*
having or needing special knowledge about a particular science or machine

technician /tekˈnɪʃən/ *noun*
a person who has special knowledge about certain machines or instruments ► *Anne is training to be a technician.*

technique /tekˈniːk/ *noun*
a way of doing something ► *new teaching techniques*

technological /ˌteknəˈlɒdʒɪkəl/ *adjective*
relating to technology ► *the latest technological developments*

technology /tek'nɒlədʒɪ/ *noun (no plural)*
knowledge about science, and about the making of machines, instruments, etc. ▶ *Modern technology has made many jobs easier.*

teddy bear /'tedɪ beəʳ/ *noun*
a soft toy which looks like a bear

tedious /'tiːdɪəs/ *adjective*
long and uninteresting ▶ *a tedious book*
SAME MEANING: **boring**

teem /tiːm/ *verb*
teem with to be full of people or animals that are moving around ▶ *The ground was teeming with ants.*

teenage /'tiːneɪdʒ/ *adjective*
aged between 13 and 19, or suitable for people of this age ▶ *She teaches teenage girls.* ▶ *a teenage magazine*

teenager /'tiːneɪdʒəʳ/ *noun*
a person who is between 13 and 19 years old

teens /tiːnz/ *plural noun*
the time in your life when you are aged between 13 and 19 ▶ *She got married when she was still in her teens.* ▶ *She was in her late teens (=17, 18, or 19).*

tee shirt /'tiː ʃɜːt/ *noun*
a T-SHIRT

teeth /tiːθ/
the plural of **tooth**

teetotal /tiː'təʊtl/ *adjective*
never drinking alcohol ▶ *He's been teetotal for years.*

telecommunications /ˌtelɪkəmjuːnɪ-'keɪʃənz/ *plural noun*
the process or business of sending and receiving messages by telephone, radio, SATELLITE, etc.

telegram /'telɪɡræm/ *noun*
a message sent by telegraph

telegraph /'telɪɡrɑːf/ *noun (no plural)*
a way of sending messages quickly by electric wire or radio signals

telephone¹ /'telɪfəʊn/ *(also phone) noun*
a machine you use to speak to someone who is in another place ▶ *Can I use your telephone, please?* ▶ *Will you answer the telephone?*

telephone² *(also phone) verb (present participle telephoning, past telephoned)*
to speak to someone by telephone ▶ *I telephoned the office, but there was no reply.* ▶ *I telephoned the restaurant and spoke to the manager.*

telephone box /'telɪfəʊn ˌbɒks/ *noun (plural telephone boxes)*
a small shelter in the street where there is a public telephone

telephone number /'telɪfəʊn ˌnʌmbəʳ/ *noun*
the number which you need to ring when you want to talk to someone on the telephone ▶ *Do you have John's telephone number?*

telescope /'telɪskəʊp/ *noun*
an instrument that you look through to see objects which are very small or far away from you
COMPARE: **binoculars**

teletext /'telɪtekst/ *noun (no plural)*
a system for providing written information on television

televise /'telɪvaɪz/ *verb (present participle televising, past televised)*
to broadcast something on television ▶ *The concert will be televised in the autumn.*

television /'telɪvɪʒən/ *(also TV) noun*
1 a machine that receives electrical signals and sends out pictures and sound ▶ *Turn the television on.*
2 *(no plural)* the system of sending and receiving pictures and sounds by electrical signals ▶ *They were watching television.*

3 on television shown on the television ► *What's on television tonight?*

teleworker /ˈtelɪwɜːʳkəʳ/ *noun*
someone who works from home using a computer and e-mail

tell /tel/ *verb (past told /təʊld/)*
1 to speak to someone or inform them about something ► *Tell me what happened.*
LOOK AT: **say**
2 to advise or instruct someone ► *I told him to see a doctor about his chest pains.* ► *Dad told me to be home by 10.*
3 tell someone off to scold someone ► *My mother told me off for swearing.*
4 tell tales to lie or be unkind about someone, because you want them to be punished ► *Charlie is always telling tales about Susie.*
5 I told you so something you say when something happens that you had already warned someone about

telly /ˈtelɪ/ *noun (plural **tellies**)*
a television

temp¹ /temp/ *noun*
a person who works for different companies for short periods of time ► *We will need a temp while our usual secretary is away.*

temp² *verb*
to work as a temp ► *Anne's temping until she can find another job.*

temper /ˈtempəʳ/ *noun*
1 the way you feel, especially when you are angry ► *He was in a bad temper all day.*
2 lose your temper to become angry suddenly

temperament /ˈtempərəmənt/ *noun*
your basic character, which controls whether you are usually happy, sad, friendly, etc. ► *a baby with a sweet temperament*

temperamental /ˌtempərəˈmentl/ *adjective*
becoming angry, excited, etc. very easily and in a way that does not seem reasonable ► *She's so temperamental that I never know how she's going to react.*

temperate /ˈtempərət/ *adjective*
having neither very hot nor very cold weather ► *Britain has a temperate climate.*

temperature /ˈtemprətʃəʳ/ *noun*
1 the amount of heat or cold ► *In summer, the temperature can reach 40°C.*
2 have a temperature to have a higher body temperature than usual, especially because you are ill

template /ˈtempleɪt/ *noun*
1 a piece of paper, plastic, etc. that you use to help you cut other materials in the same shape
2 a computer FILE that you use as a model for producing many similar documents ► *a template for writing business letters*

temple /ˈtempəl/ *noun*
1 a holy building
2 the part of your head above and in front of your ear

temporarily /ˈtempərərəlɪ, ˈtempərəlɪ/ *adverb*
for a short time only ► *temporarily closed*

temporary /ˈtempərərɪ, ˈtempərɪ/ *adjective*
lasting or meant to last for a short time ► *a temporary job*
COMPARE: **permanent**

tempt /tempt/ *verb*
1 to try to make someone do something wrong
2 to make someone want to do something ► *Can I tempt you to another piece of this cake?*

temptation /tempˈteɪʃən/ *noun*
a strong feeling of wanting something

that you should not have ▶ *I resisted the temptation to have another cake.*

tempting /'temptɪŋ/ *adjective*
something that is tempting seems attractive because you would like to have it ▶ *a tempting job offer*

ten /ten/ *adjective, noun*
the number 10

tenant /'tenənt/ *noun*
a person who pays money to use a house or land

tend /tend/ *verb*
tend to to happen often or usually ▶ *I tend to get tired in the evening.*

tendency /'tendənsɪ/ *noun (plural tendencies)*
something that happens regularly ▶ *She has a tendency to shout when she gets angry.*

tender /'tendə'/ *adjective*
1 soft, and easy to eat ▶ *tender meat* OPPOSITE: **tough**
2 kind and gentle ▶ *a tender expression on her face*

tenner /'tenə'/ *noun*
£10 or a ten-pound note

tennis /'tenɪs/ *noun (no plural)*
a game played by two or four people in which you hit a ball over a net

tenor /'tenə'/ *noun*
a male singer with quite a high voice

tense¹ /tens/ *adjective*
1 nervous and worried ▶ *The players were tense at the start of the game.*
2 tightly stretched ▶ *tense muscles* OPPOSITE (**1** and **2**): **relaxed**

tense² *noun*
the form of a verb that shows when the action of the verb happens. "I look" and "I am looking" are present tenses; "I looked", "I was looking", and "I have looked" are past tenses; "I will look" and "I am going to look" are future tenses

tension /'tenʃən/ *noun*
1 (*no plural*) a nervous feeling that you have when you do not know what is going to happen ▶ *The tension as we waited for some news was unbearable.*
2 the feeling that exists when people do not trust each other and may suddenly attack each other ▶ *efforts to calm racial tensions*

tent /tent/ *noun*
a shelter made of thick cloth spread over poles

tentacle /'tentəkəl/ *noun*
one of the long, soft arms of a sea creature such as an OCTOPUS

tentative /'tentətɪv/ *adjective*
1 not definite or certain ▶ *tentative plans*
2 done as though you are not sure what you are doing ▶ *a tentative smile*
(*adverb:* **tentatively**)

tenth /tenθ/ *adjective, noun*
1 10th
2 one of ten equal parts

tepid /'tepɪd/ *adjective*
slightly warm ▶ *All we got was a cup of tepid tea.*

term /tɜːm/ *noun*
1 a fixed length of time ▶ *He was made manager of the football team for a term of one year.*
2 a part of the school year ▶ *There are three terms in a school year.*

terminal /'tɜːmɪnəl/ *noun*
a place where buses, planes, etc. begin or end their journey

terminology /,tɜːmɪ'nɒlədʒɪ/ *noun*
the technical words that are used in a subject ▶ *a dictionary of medical terminology*

terminus /'tɜːmɪnəs/ *noun (plural terminuses)*
the place at the end of a railway line or bus service where the trains and buses end their journey

terms /tɜːmz/ *plural noun*
the things that you must agree to do or accept, especially in a contract

terrace /'terɪs/ *noun*
1 a level area cut out from the side of a hill
2 a flat area outside a house, where you can sit and have a drink, etc.
3 a row of houses joined together

terraced house /ˌterɪst 'haʊs/ *noun*
(*plural* **terraced houses** /-'haʊzɪz/)
a house which is part of a row of houses all joined together

terrible /'terəbəl/ *adjective*
1 very serious; causing you to be afraid ▶ *a terrible accident* ▶ *a terrible noise*
2 very bad ▶ *Your writing is terrible.*
SAME MEANING (**1** and **2**): **awful**

terribly /'terəblɪ/ *adverb*
1 very ▶ *We're terribly sorry.*
SAME MEANING: **awfully**
2 very badly ▶ *She behaved terribly.*

terrier /'terɪə'/ *noun*
a type of small dog

terrific /tə'rɪfɪk/ *adjective*
very good; enjoyable ▶ *a terrific holiday*

terrified /'terɪfaɪd/ *adjective*
very frightened ▶ *I'm terrified of flying.*

terrify /'terɪfaɪ/ *verb* (*past* **terrified**)
to fill someone with fear ▶ *I was terrified by the storm.*

territory /'terɪtərɪ/ *noun* (*plural* **territories**)
1 land ruled by one government ▶ *This island is British territory.*
2 an area belonging to one person or animal ▶ *Male tigers will not allow other males to enter their territory.*

terror /'terə'/ *noun (no plural)*
great fear ▶ *a feeling of terror*

terrorism /'terərɪzəm/ *noun (no plural)*
the use of violence to try to force a government to do something ▶ *The*

government said the bombing was an evil act of terrorism.

terrorist /'terərɪst/ *noun*
a person who uses violence to try to force a government to do something

test¹ /test/ *verb*
1 to look at something to see if it is correct or will work properly ▶ *Could you test the brakes for me, please?*
2 to ask someone questions to see if they know the answers ▶ *The teacher tested the children on their homework.*

test² *noun*
an examination ▶ *I passed my driving test today.* ▶ *a history test*

testify /'testɪfaɪ/ *verb* (*past* **testified**)
to formally say in a law court what you know about something ▶ *She testified that she had seen the man leaving the bank.*

testimony /'testɪmənɪ/ *noun* (*plural* **testimonies**)
a formal statement that someone makes in a law court

test tube /'test tjuːb/ *noun*
a small, thin, glass container used in scientific tests

tetanus /'tetənəs/ *noun (no plural)*
a serious disease that makes your muscles stiff and is caused by an infection in a wound

text /tekst/ *noun*
the writing in a book

textbook /'tekstbʊk/ *noun*
a book with facts about a particular subject that is used by people studying that subject

textile /'tekstaɪl/ *noun*
any material or cloth that is made by weaving

texture /'tekstʃə'/ *noun*
the way that a surface, material, food, etc. feels when you touch it or taste it ▶ *The fats in chocolate are what give it its smooth texture.*

than /ðən; *strong* ðæn/ *preposition, conjunction*
used when you are comparing things
▶ *My brother is older than me.*
▶ *Mary earns more than I do.*

thank /θæŋk/ *verb*
to tell someone that you are grateful
▶ *I thanked her for the present.*

thankful /'θæŋkfəl/ *adjective*
very glad ▶ *I was thankful that the exams were over.*

thanks /θæŋks/ *plural noun*
1 the things you say to show you are grateful ▶ *a letter of thanks*
2 thanks to because of ▶ *Thanks to Peter, we won the game.* ▶ *We've missed the train, thanks to you.*

thankyou /'θæŋkju:/ *noun*
1 something that you say or do to thank someone for something ▶ *a special thankyou for all your help*
2 Thank you (*also* **thanks**) something you say to someone to show you are grateful ▶ *Thank you for the present.*
▶ *"Do you want another piece of cake?" "No, thank you."*

that[1] /ðæt/ *adjective, pronoun*
1 (*plural* **those** /ðəʊz/) the one over there; the one further away than this one ▶ *They don't live here; they live in that house over there.*
2 (*plural* **those**) used to mean the one mentioned already ▶ *Did you bring that photograph?* ▶ *We played football, and after that (=next) we went home.*
3 (/ðət/) used instead of **who, whom, which** ▶ *He's the man that sold me the bicycle.*
4 That's it something you say when you have finished something

that[2] /ðət/ *conjunction*
used to join two parts of a sentence
▶ *I think that it might rain tomorrow.*

that[3] /ðæt/ *adverb*
so ▶ *I don't like it that much!* ▶ *Slow down – I can't walk that fast.*

thatch /θætʃ/ *noun* (*no plural*)
a roof covering made of dry grass

thatched /θætʃt/ *adjective*
(used about a roof) made of dry grass ▶ *a thatched roof*

thaw /θɔ:/ *verb*
to become soft or liquid, after having been frozen ▶ *The ice slowly started to thaw.*

the /ðə, ði; *strong* ði:/ *definite article*
1 a word used before a NOUN, when it is clear who or what is meant
▶ *There's someone outside; it's the boy from the house across the road.*
2 used in front of the names of seas, rivers, deserts, etc. ▶ *the Mediterranean Sea*
3 used to talk about a class or group of people or things ▶ *The rich* (=rich people) *should pay higher taxes.*
4 used when saying the date ▶ *Friday the 4th of May*

theatre /'θɪətə*r*/ *noun*
a building in which people can go and see plays being acted

theatrical /θɪ'ætrɪkəl/ *adjective*
relating to the theatre ▶ *a theatrical production*

theft /θeft/ *noun*
1 (*no plural*) the crime of stealing
▶ *He was put in prison for car theft.*
2 an act of stealing something
▶ *When she discovered the theft of her bag, she went to the police.*

their /ðə*r*; *strong* ðeə*r*/ *adjective*
belonging to them ▶ *The children carried their bags to school.*

theirs /ðeəz/ *pronoun*
something belonging to them ▶ *When our computer broke, Tom and Sue let us use theirs.*

them /ðəm; *strong* ðem/ *pronoun*
the people or things that have already been mentioned ▶ *We gave them some food.* ▶ *We gave it to them.* ▶ *I can't find my shoes; have you seen them?*

theme /θiːm/ *noun*
the general idea or subject that a talk or a piece of writing is about

theme park /'θiːm paːk/ *noun*
an AMUSEMENT PARK that is based on one subject, such as water or space travel

themselves /ðəm'selvz/ *pronoun*
1 the same people, animals, or things as the sentence is about; the same people as **they** in a sentence ➤ *The travellers washed themselves in the river.* ➤ *They bought themselves a new car.*
2 used to give **they** a stronger meaning ➤ *They decorated the house themselves.*
3 by themselves (a) without help from anyone else ➤ *The children did the drawing by themselves.*
(b) alone ➤ *They spent the afternoon by themselves.*

then /ðen/ *adverb*
1 at another time; not now ➤ *She lived in a village then, but now she lives in Glasgow.*
2 afterwards; next ➤ *We saw a film and then went for a meal.*
3 if that is true ➤ *"I've lost my ticket." "Then you'll have to pay again."*

theological /ˌθiːə'lɒdʒɪkəl/ *adjective*
relating to the study of religion

theology /θɪ'ɒlədʒɪ/ *noun (no plural)*
the study of religion

theory /'θɪərɪ/ *noun (plural theories)*
an idea that tries to explain something

therapy /'θerəpɪ/ *noun (plural therapies)*
the treatment of mental or physical illness, especially without using drugs or operations ➤ *He's having therapy to help with alcohol addiction.*

there¹ /ðeəʳ/ *adverb*
in or near that place ➤ *Don't sit there*

on your own; come and sit with us. ➤ *Look at that man over there.* ➤ *"Have you been to that new restaurant?" "Yes, we went there last night."*
COMPARE: **here**

there² *pronoun*
there is used to show that someone or something exists or that something happens ➤ *There is a letter for you.* ➤ *There was a policeman outside the house yesterday.* ➤ *Is there anything I can do to help?*

thereabouts /ˌðeərə'bauts/ *adverb*
near the number, amount, time, etc. that you have just mentioned ➤ *We should arrive at 9 o'clock or thereabouts.*

therefore /'ðeəfɔːʳ/ *adverb*
for that reason ➤ *The car is smaller and therefore cheaper to run.*

thermal /'θɜːməl/ *adjective*
1 relating to or caused by heat ➤ *thermal energy*
2 (used about clothes) designed to keep you warm ➤ *a thermal vest*

thermometer /θə'mɒmɪtəʳ/ *noun*
an instrument that measures heat and cold ➤ *The doctor put a thermometer in my mouth to see if I had a temperature.*

thermostat /'θɜːməstæt/ *noun*
a piece of equipment that controls the temperature of a room, machine, etc.

thesaurus /θɪ'sɔːrəs/ *noun (plural thesauruses)*
a book containing lists of words that have similar meanings

these /ðiːz/ *adjective, pronoun*
the ones here; the ones nearer than that one or those ones ➤ *I don't like these sweets; those are nicer.*

they /ðeɪ/ *pronoun*
the people, animals, or things already mentioned ➤ *My friends are playing football and they want us to play too.*

they'd /ðeɪd/
1 they had ➤ *They'd already left the house.*
2 they would ➤ *They said they'd help.*

they'll /ðeɪl/
they will ➤ *They'll probably arrive tomorrow.*

they're /ðeəʳ, ðeɪəʳ/
they are ➤ *They're playing football.*

they've /ðeɪv/
they have ➤ *They've gone shopping.*

thick /θɪk/ *adjective*
1 having a large distance between one side and the other ➤ *thick walls*
2 with a lot of something grouped closely together ➤ *thick, black hair*
OPPOSITE (**1** and **2**): **thin**
3 difficult to see through ➤ *thick smoke* ➤ *thick clouds*
4 not flowing easily ➤ *This soup is too thick.*
OPPOSITE (**4**): **runny**
5 stupid ➤ *Her brother's really thick.*

thickness /'θɪknəs/ *noun (no plural)*
how thick something is ➤ *Look at the thickness of that wall!*

thief /θiːf/ *noun (plural* **thieves** /θiːvz/)
a person who steals ➤ *a car thief*
COMPARE: **burglar, robber**

thigh /θaɪ/ *noun*
the part of your leg above your knee

thimble /'θɪmbəl/ *noun*
a hard covering for the top of your finger which you use when sewing

thin /θɪn/ *adjective (* **thinner, thinnest** *)*
1 narrow; not thick ➤ *This string is too thin; I need something stronger.*
2 not having much fat on your body ➤ *You should eat more; you're too thin.*
OPPOSITE (**2**): **fat**
3 flowing easily ➤ *thin oil*

thing /θɪŋ/ *noun*
1 an object ➤ *What is that thing on the table?*

2 an act or event ➤ *That was a silly thing to do.*
3 **things** *plural noun* your belongings ➤ *They packed all their things for the journey.*

think /θɪŋk/ *verb (past* **thought** /θɔːt/)
1 to use your mind to have ideas ➤ *Think carefully before you decide.* ➤ *What are you thinking about?*
2 to have an opinion; to believe something ➤ *What do you think of my singing?* ➤ *"Do you think it will rain tomorrow?" "Yes I think so."* ➤ *"Is Emma coming to the party?" "I don't think so."*

thinking /'θɪŋkɪŋ/ *noun (no plural)*
someone's opinions and ideas about something ➤ *modern scientific thinking on the origins of the universe*

thinly /'θɪnlɪ/ *adverb*
without using or having much ➤ *Spread the butter thinly.*

third /θɜːd/ *adjective, noun*
1 3rd
2 one of three equal parts

third person /,θɜːd 'pɜːsən/ *noun*
the third person the form of a verb that you use with "he", "she", "it", or "they" in English

thirst /θɜːst/ *noun (no plural)*
the feeling of wanting or needing to drink something
COMPARE: **hunger**

thirsty /'θɜːstɪ/ *adjective (* **thirstier, thirstiest** *)*
wanting or needing to drink something ➤ *Can I have some water? I'm really thirsty.*
COMPARE: **hunger**

thirteen /,θɜː'tiːn/ *adjective, noun*
the number 13

thirteenth /,θɜː'tiːnθ/ *adjective*
13th

thirtieth /'θɜːtɪ-əθ/ *adjective*
30th

thirty /'θɜːtɪ/ *adjective, noun*
the number 30

this /ðɪs/ *adjective, pronoun*
1 (*plural* **these** /ðiːz/) the one here; the one nearer than that one ▶ *This is my nephew.*
2 nearest to the present time ▶ *Shall we go out this afternoon?*

thistle /'θɪsəl/ *noun*
a plant with sharp, pointed leaves

thorn /θɔːn/ *noun*
a sharp or pointed part of a plant

thorough /'θʌrə/ *adjective*
complete and careful, with nothing missed out ▶ *The police made a thorough search of the house.*

thoroughly /'θʌrəlɪ/ *adverb*
1 very much ▶ *He thoroughly enjoyed the meal.*
2 completely and carefully ▶ *Check your work thoroughly.*

those /ðəʊz/ *adjective, pronoun*
the ones over there; the ones further away than this or these ones ▶ *I don't like these sweets; those are nicer.*

though /ðəʊ/ *conjunction*
1 even if; in spite of the fact that ▶ *Though he was poor, he was happy.*
2 **as though** as if ▶ *She looked as though she had been crying.*

thought¹ /θɔːt/
the PAST TENSE and PAST PARTICIPLE of the verb **think**

thought² *noun*
1 (*no plural*) the act of thinking ▶ *After much thought, he decided not to buy the car.*
2 an idea or opinion that you have in your mind ▶ *She's a quiet girl and doesn't share her thoughts.*

thoughtful /'θɔːtfəl/ *adjective*
1 serious and quiet because you are thinking ▶ *She looked thoughtful.*
2 kind and always thinking of things you can do to make other people

happy ▶ *It was thoughtful of you to remember my birthday.*
(*adverb:* **thoughtfully**)

thoughtless /'θɔːtləs/ *adjective*
not thinking about other people or how your actions or words will affect them ▶ *a thoughtless remark*
(*adverb:* **thoughtlessly**)

thousand /'θaʊzənd/ *adjective, noun*
the number 1,000 ▶ *a thousand years ago* ▶ *thousands of miles away*

thousandth /'θaʊzəndθ/ *adjective*
1,000th

thrash /θræʃ/ *verb*
1 to easily beat someone in a game ▶ *We thrashed them 10–0.*
2 to hit someone violently, usually as a punishment

thread¹ /θred/ *noun*
a long, single piece of cotton, silk, or other material used in weaving or sewing

thread² *verb*
to put a thread through something ▶ *I can't thread this needle.*

threat /θret/ *noun*
a warning that someone will hurt you if you do not do what they want

threaten /'θretn/ *verb*
to say that you will hurt another person if they do not do what you want

three /θriː/ *adjective, noun*
the number 3

three-dimensional /ˌθriː dɑɪˈmenʃənəl/ (*also* **3-D** /ˌθriː ˈdiː/) *adjective*
having or seeming to have length, depth, and height ▶ *a three-dimensional model*

three-quarters /ˌθriː ˈkwɔːtəz/ *noun, adverb*
three out of four equal parts of something ▶ *The box was three-quarters full.*

threw /θruː/
the PAST TENSE of the verb **throw**

thrill¹ /θrɪl/ *verb*
to fill somebody with excitement
➤ *The traveller thrilled us with his stories.*

thrill² *noun*
an excited feeling

thrilled /θrɪld/ *adjective*
very excited, pleased, or happy
➤ *She'll be thrilled when she hears the news.*

thriller /'θrɪləʳ/ *noun*
an exciting film or book about murder or crime

thrilling /'θrɪlɪŋ/ *adjective*
very exciting ➤ *a thrilling end to the game*

throat /θrəʊt/ *noun*
1 the part at the back of your mouth, where you swallow ➤ *He couldn't speak because he had a sore throat.*
2 the front part of your neck

throb /θrɒb/ *verb*
*(present participle **throbbing**, past **throbbed**)*
to hurt with a strong, regular pain
➤ *My finger was throbbing.*

throne /θrəʊn/ *noun*
a special chair on which a king or queen sits during ceremonies

throttle¹ /'θrɒtl/ *verb (present participle **throttling**, past **throttled**)*
to kill or try to kill someone by holding their throat tightly, stopping them from breathing
SAME MEANING: **strangle**

throttle² *noun*
a part of a vehicle that controls the speed of the engine by controlling the amount of FUEL going into it

through /θruː/ *preposition, adverb*
1 from one side or end of something to the other ➤ *We walked through the market to the car park.* ➤ *She looked through the book until she found the*
page she wanted. ➤ *I hammered the nail into the wood and it went right through.*
2 by way of ➤ *The thief got in through the window.*

throughout /θruː'aʊt/ *preposition*
1 in every part of something ➤ *He is famous throughout the world.*
2 from the beginning to the end of something ➤ *It rained throughout the night.*

throw¹ /θrəʊ/ *verb (past tense **threw** /θruː/, past participle **thrown** /θrəʊn/)*
1 to send something through the air by moving your arm and pushing the thing out of your hand ➤ *He threw the ball to me, and I caught it.*
2 throw something away, throw something out to get rid of something you do not want
3 throw someone out to force someone to leave a place ➤ *He was thrown out of the restaurant because he was drunk.*

throw² *noun*
an act of throwing

thrown /θrəʊn/
the PAST PARTICIPLE of the verb **throw**

thrust /θrʌst/ *verb (past **thrust**)*
to push suddenly and hard ➤ *We thrust our way through the crowd.*

thud /θʌd/ *noun*
a sound made by something heavy and soft falling ➤ *He fell out of the tree and landed on the ground with a thud.*

thug /θʌg/ *noun*
a violent person

thumb /θʌm/ *noun*
the short, thick finger on your hand which is separate from your other fingers

thump /θʌmp/ *verb*
to hit someone with your hand tightly closed

thunder /'θʌndəʳ/ *noun (no plural)*
the loud sound heard in the sky during a storm

thunderous /'θʌndərəs/ *adjective*
very loud ➤ *thunderous applause*

thunderstorm /'θʌndə,stɔːm/ *noun*
a storm with heavy rain, thunder, and lightning

Thursday /'θɜːzdeɪ, -dɪ/ *noun*
the fifth day of the week

tick¹ /tɪk/ *noun*
1 the sound made by a watch or clock
2 a mark (✔) which shows that something is correct or done

tick² *verb*
1 to make the sound a watch or clock makes
2 to make a mark (✔) to show that something is correct or has been done

ticket /'tɪkɪt/ *noun*
a small piece of paper or card which shows you have paid to do something, e.g. to travel on a bus, to watch a film at the cinema, etc. ➤ *a bus ticket*

tickle /'tɪkəl/ *verb (present participle tickling, past tickled)*
to touch a person lightly and make them laugh ➤ *I tickled her under her arms.*

tide /taɪd/ *noun*
the rise and fall of the sea that happens twice every day

tidy¹ /'taɪdɪ/ *adjective (tidier, tidiest)*
in good order, with things neatly arranged ➤ *a tidy room*
OPPOSITE: **untidy**

tidy² *verb (past tidied)*
to make something neat ➤ *Tidy your room, please.*

tie¹ /taɪ/ *noun*
a narrow band of cloth worn around the neck, especially by a man

tie² *verb (present participle tying, past tied)*
1 to fasten something with string or rope ➤ *She tied the dog to the lamppost.*
OPPOSITE: **untie**
2 tie something up to fasten something with string or rope ➤ *Tie the parcel up with some string.*

tier /tɪəʳ/ *noun*
1 a row of seats that has other rows above or below it ➤ *We were in the first tier of seats.*
2 one of several levels in a system or an organization ➤ *a company with four tiers of management*

tiger /'taɪgəʳ/ *noun*
a large, fierce, wild cat that has yellow fur with black bands

tight /taɪt/ *adjective*
1 pulled or drawn closely together ➤ *a very tight knot*
OPPOSITE: **slack**
2 fitting part of your body closely ➤ *These shoes are too tight.*
OPPOSITE: **loose**

tighten /'taɪtn/ *verb*
to make or become tight ➤ *I need to tighten this screw; it's very loose.*
OPPOSITE: **loosen**

tightly /'taɪtlɪ/ *adverb*
firmly ➤ *Tie the string tightly*

tightrope /'taɪt-rəʊp/ *noun*
a wire high above the ground that a performer walks along in a CIRCUS

tights /taɪts/ *plural noun*
a very tight piece of clothing, made of thin material, which women wear to cover their feet, legs, and the lower part of their body ➤ *a pair of tights*
COMPARE: **stockings**

tile /taɪl/ *noun*
a flat piece of baked clay used for covering roofs, floors, or walls

till¹ /tɪl/ *noun*
a container or drawer for money in a shop

T

till² *preposition, conjunction*
until ➤ *Let's wait till tomorrow.* ➤ *I'll keep it till you come back.*

tilt /tɪlt/ *verb*
to move or cause something to move by lifting one end

timber /'tɪmbəʳ/ *noun (no plural)*
wood prepared for building; trees to be used for building

time¹ /taɪm/ *noun*
1 *(no plural)* minutes, hours, days, weeks, months, years ➤ *How do you spend your time at home?*
2 *(no plural)* a number of minutes, hours, etc. ➤ *It takes a long time to learn a new language.*
3 a certain occasion ➤ *We'll go by car next time.*
4 a particular minute or hour of the day ➤ *What time is it?*
5 times (a) used to show how often something happens ➤ *I go swimming three times a week.* ➤ *How many times have you seen that film?*
(b) used when you compare things to say how much bigger, smaller, etc. one thing is than the other ➤ *This school is three times bigger than my old one.*
(c) multiplied by ➤ *Five times four is twenty.*
6 about time something you say when you think something should be done now ➤ *It's about time you got a job.*
7 all the time continuously ➤ *It rained all the time on holiday.*
8 at a time in one group; together ➤ *She can only have two visitors at a time.*
9 at times sometimes ➤ *I hated my job at times.*
10 for the time being for now; for a little while ➤ *You can live with us for the time being.*
11 from time to time sometimes, but not very often ➤ *We go to the theatre from time to time.*

12 have a good time to enjoy yourself ➤ *Have a good time at the cinema.* ➤ *Did you have a good time last night?*
13 just in time at the last moment, just before it was too late ➤ *The police arrived just in time.*
14 on time at the right time; not early, not late ➤ *The train arrived on time.*
15 take your time to use all the time you need to do something ➤ *There's no hurry – take your time.*
16 tell the time to read a clock or watch correctly ➤ *She can't tell the time yet; she's only two!*

> Remember to use **'s** in the expressions *in a week's time* (=in a week from now), *in a month's time*, *in a year's time*, etc.

time² *verb (present participle **timing**, past **timed**)*
to measure how long it takes to do something

timeless /'taɪmləs/ *adjective*
not affected by changes over time ➤ *the timeless beauty of the sea*

time off /,taɪm 'ɒf/ *noun (no plural)*
time when you do not have to be at work or school ➤ *I'd like some time off this week.*

time out /,taɪm 'aʊt/ *noun*
1 a short break during a sports game to let the players rest or plan how they will play the rest of the game
2 take time out to rest or do something different from your usual job or activities

timer /'taɪməʳ/ *noun*
a part of a machine or system that you use to make it stop or start at a particular time ➤ *You can set the timer to switch the cooker off.*

timetable /'taɪm,teɪbəl/ *noun*
a list of times when things will happen ➤ *a train timetable* ➤ *a school timetable*

timid /'tɪmɪd/ *adjective*
shy and nervous ► *a timid girl who never spoke* (adverb: **timidly**)

tin /tɪn/ *noun*
1 (*no plural*) a soft, white metal
2 a container made of this metal
► *a tin of beans*
SAME MEANING (**2**): **can**

tingle /'tɪŋgəl/ *verb* (*present participle* **tingling**, *past* **tingled**)
(used about skin, hands, etc.) feeling uncomfortable and giving you slight stinging pains ► *My fingers tingled with the cold.*

tinker /'tɪŋkəʳ/ *verb*
to make small changes to something to improve it or make it work better, often in a way that causes problems ► *He spends Sundays tinkering with his bike.*

tinkle /'tɪŋkəl/ *verb* (*present participle* **tinkling**, *past* **tinkled**)
to make a sound like small bells ► *The glasses tinkled as he carried them.*

tinned /tɪnd/ *adjective*
preserved in a tin ► *tinned fruit*
SAME MEANING: **canned**

tin opener /'tɪn ˌəʊpənəʳ/ *noun*
a tool for opening tins of food

tinsel /'tɪnsəl/ *noun* (*no plural*)
Christmas decorations made of thin pieces of shiny paper joined together in rows ► *They hung tinsel on the Christmas tree.*

tint /tɪnt/ *noun*
a small amount of a colour ► *His eyes had a yellow tint.*

tinted /'tɪntɪd/ *adjective*
(used about glass) slightly coloured so that less light can pass through it

tiny /'taɪnɪ/ *adjective* (**tinier, tiniest**)
very small
SAME MEANING: **minute**

tip¹ /tɪp/ *verb* (*present participle* **tipping**, *past* **tipped**)

1 to lean or cause to lean at an angle ► *I tipped the table and the glasses fell off it.*
2 to give a small amount of money to a waiter, a taxi driver, etc.
3 tip over to turn over or cause something to turn over ► *I tipped the box over and the chocolates fell out.*

tip² *noun*
1 the pointed end of something ► *the tip of a finger*
2 a small amount of money given to someone who has done something for you ► *Shall we leave the waiter a tip?*
3 a useful piece of advice ► *Have you got any tips on making cakes?*
SAME MEANING (**3**): **pointer**

tiptoe¹ /'tɪptəʊ/ *verb* (*past* **tiptoed**)
to walk on your toes, especially when you are trying not to make any noise ► *I tiptoed past the sleeping child.*

tiptoe² *noun*
on tiptoe walking on your toes, especially when you are trying not to make any noise

tire /taɪəʳ/ *verb* (*present participle* **tiring**, *past* **tired**)
to make someone feel that they need rest

tired /taɪəd/ *adjective*
1 needing rest or sleep ► *I felt tired after work.*
2 be tired of something to become disinterested in something because you have done it many times before ► *She was tired of cooking for her family.*
3 be tired out to be completely tired

tiresome /'taɪəsəm/ *adjective*
annoying or boring ► *I'm sick of hearing your tiresome excuses.*

tissue /'tɪʃuː/ *noun*
a thin, soft piece of paper used as a handkerchief

title /'taɪtl/ *noun*
1 the name of a story, a book, a film, etc.

2 a word such as Mrs., Sir, etc., used in front of a person's name

T-junction /'ti: ˌdʒʌŋkʃən/ *noun*
a place where two roads meet and form the shape of the letter T

to /tə, tʊ; *strong* tu:/ *preposition*
1 in the direction of ➤ *He ran to the door to see who was there.* ➤ *He sent a letter to his parents.* ➤ *It took 20 minutes to drive to town.*
2 as far as ➤ *When we got to the river, we sat down.*
3 until ➤ *She works from 2 o'clock to 10 o'clock.*
4 used to show how many minutes there are until the next hour ➤ *It's ten to nine.*
5 used to show why you do something ➤ *She worked hard to earn some extra money.*
6 used with a verb to show the INFINITIVE ➤ *to go* ➤ *to stop*

toad /təʊd/ *noun*
a small, jumping animal like a large FROG

to and fro /ˌtu: ən 'frəʊ/ *adverb*
in one direction and then another ➤ *The washing swung to and fro in the breeze.*

toast /təʊst/ *noun (no plural)*
bread which you make brown and harder by cooking it in small, flat pieces ➤ *I had toast for breakfast.*

toaster /'təʊstəʳ/ *noun*
an electric machine that is used for making toast

tobacco /tə'bækəʊ/ *noun (no plural)*
the dried leaves of a plant used for smoking in pipes and cigarettes

toboggan /tə'bɒgən/ *noun*
a wooden or plastic board that curves up at the front, used for going down a hill over snow

tobogganing /tə'bɒgənɪŋ/ *noun (no plural)*
the activity or sport of going down

hills that are covered in snow on a toboggan ➤ *We went tobogganing in the park.*

today /tə'deɪ/ *noun, adverb*
1 this day ➤ *Today is Monday.*
2 modern times ➤ *Many people use computers today.*

toddler /'tɒdləʳ/ *noun*
a young child who has just learnt to walk

toe /təʊ/ *noun*
one of the five parts on the end of your foot

toenail /'təʊneɪl/ *noun*
the nail on a toe

toffee /'tɒfi:/ *noun*
a hard, brown sweet

together /tə'geðəʳ/ *adverb*
1 one with another; in a group ➤ *The children played together in the street.* ➤ *I stuck the two pieces of paper together.*
2 at the same time ➤ *The two letters arrived together.*

toilet /'tɔɪlɪt/ *noun*
1 a container joined to a waste pipe, used for getting rid of body waste
2 a room with this in it ➤ *Where is the toilet, please?*
SAME MEANING (**1** and **2**): **lavatory, loo**

toilet paper /'tɔɪlɪt ˌpeɪpəʳ/ *noun (no plural)*
thin, soft paper which you use to clean yourself after getting rid of body waste

toiletries /'tɔɪlɪtrɪz/ *plural noun*
things such as soap that you use when you wash yourself

toilet roll /'tɔɪlɪt ˌrəʊl/ *noun*
a roll of toilet paper

token /'təʊkən/ *noun*
a sign ➤ *We shook hands as a token of our friendship.*

told /təʊld/
the PAST TENSE and PAST PARTICIPLE of the verb **tell**

tolerant /'tɒlərənt/ *adjective*
letting other people do or say what
they want, even if you do not approve
of it ▶ *We should be tolerant of other
people's beliefs.*
OPPOSITE: **intolerant**

tolerate /'tɒləreɪt/ *verb (present
participle **tolerating**, past **tolerated**)*
to accept behaviour or a situation
that you do not like or approve of ▶ *I
will not tolerate this sort of behaviour.*

toll /təʊl/ *noun*
1 the number of people that have
been killed by something ▶ *The death
toll from the crash has risen to 20.*
2 take its toll to have a bad effect on
someone or something over a long
period of time ▶ *Years of smoking
have taken their toll on his health.*
3 money that you pay so that you can
use a road, bridge, etc. ▶ *a toll bridge*

tomato /tə'mɑːtəʊ/ *noun (plural
tomatoes)*
a red, juicy fruit that you eat raw or
cooked

tomb /tuːm/ *noun*
a hole in the ground into which a
dead person is put

tomboy /'tɒmbɔɪ/ *noun*
a young girl who likes to play rough
games like a boy

tombstone /'tuːmstəʊn/ *noun*
a piece of stone put over a tomb,
often with the name of the dead
person on it

tomorrow /tə'mɒrəʊ/ *noun, adverb*
the day after this day ▶ *It's too late to
do it now; let's do it tomorrow.*
COMPARE: **yesterday**

ton /tʌn/ *noun*
1 a measure of weight equal to 2,240
pounds
2 a measure of weight equal to 1,000
kilos

tone /təʊn/ *noun*
the sound of a voice or of a musical

instrument, etc. ▶ *Her voice has a
pleasant tone.*

tongs /tɒŋz/ *plural noun*
an instrument made of two narrow
pieces of metal joined at one end,
used for picking things up ▶ *He
picked up the hot coal with a pair of
tongs.*
COMPARE: **tweezers**

tongue /tʌŋ/ *noun*
1 the part inside your mouth that
moves when you speak
2 hold your tongue not to speak ▶ *I
wanted to tell the teacher she was
stupid, but I held my tongue.*

tongue-tied /'tʌŋ taɪd/ *adjective*
unable to speak because you are
nervous

tonight /tə'naɪt/ *noun, adverb*
the night at the end of today ▶ *We
are going to a party tonight.*

tonne /tʌn/ *noun*
a measure of weight equal to 1,000
kilos

too /tuː/ *adverb*
1 also ▶ *"I'm really hungry." "Me too."*
2 more than is needed or wanted
▶ *He drives too fast.* ▶ *She drinks too
much.*

took /tʊk/
the PAST TENSE of the verb **take**

tool /tuːl/ *noun*
an instrument which helps you to do
special jobs, e.g. build or repair
something

tooth /tuːθ/ *noun (plural **teeth**
/tiːθ/)*
1 one of the white, bony objects that
grow in your mouth ▶ *You should
brush your teeth after every meal.*
2 something which is shaped like
this, e.g. each of the sharp parts on a
comb or SAW

toothache /'tuːθeɪk/ *noun (no plural)*
a pain in a tooth ▶ *I've had toothache
all day.*

toothbrush /'tuːθbrʌʃ/ *noun (plural* **toothbrushes**)
a small brush for cleaning your teeth

toothpaste /'tuːθpeɪst/ *noun (no plural)*
a substance used for cleaning your teeth

top¹ /tɒp/ *noun*
1 the highest part of something ➤ *He climbed to the top **of** the hill.*
2 the lid or cover of something ➤ *He took the top off the box.*
OPPOSITE (**1** and **2**): **bottom**
3 a piece of clothing that you wear on the top part of your body ➤ *I need a top to wear with these trousers.*

top² *adjective*
1 highest ➤ *Put it in the top drawer.*
2 be top of the class to have the highest marks in the class

topic /'tɒpɪk/ *noun*
something to talk or write about

topical /'tɒpɪkəl/ *adjective*
relating to something that is important at the present time ➤ *a new TV show dealing with topical issues*

topless /'tɒpləs/ *adjective*
not wearing any clothes on the upper part of the body ➤ *topless sunbathing*

topping /'tɒpɪŋ/ *noun*
food that you put on top of other food ➤ *cake with a chocolate topping*

topple /'tɒpəl/ *verb (present participle* **toppling**, *past* **toppled**)
to become unsteady and fall down ➤ *The pile of books toppled onto the floor.*

top-secret /ˌtɒp 'siːkrət/ *adjective*
that must be kept completely secret ➤ *top-secret information*

torch /tɔːtʃ/ *noun (plural* **torches**)
an electric light that you can carry around with you ➤ *He shone his torch into the dark cupboard.*

tore /tɔːʳ/
the PAST TENSE of the verb **tear**

torment /tɔː'ment/ *verb*
to deliberately hurt, upset, or annoy someone ➤ *Stop tormenting your sister!*

torn /tɔːn/
the PAST PARTICIPLE of the verb **tear**

tornado /tɔː'neɪdəʊ/ *noun (plural* **tornadoes** *or* **tornados**)
a storm with a strong wind which spins very fast

torpedo /tɔː'piːdəʊ/ *noun (plural* **torpedoes**)
a weapon which is fired through the water from a ship to destroy another ship

torrent /'tɒrənt/ *noun*
a fast flow of water ➤ *The river was a torrent after the storm.*

torrential /tə'renʃəl/ *adjective*
(used about rain) very rapid and strong ➤ *torrential rain*

torso /'tɔːsəʊ/ *noun*
the main part of your body, not including your arms, legs, or head ➤ *He had injuries to his head and torso.*

tortoise /'tɔːtəs/ *noun*
a land animal that has a body covered by a round, hard shell and moves very slowly

torture¹ /'tɔːtʃəʳ/ *verb (present participle* **torturing**, *past* **tortured**)
to cause great pain to someone on purpose, especially so that they give you information

torture² *noun (no plural)*
a way of causing great pain to someone, especially so that they give you information

toss /tɒs/ *verb*
1 to throw ➤ *They tossed the ball to each other.*
2 to move about or up and down ➤ *The horse tossed its head in the air.*

total¹ /'təʊtl/ *noun*
everything added together ➤ *The city*

spent a total of half a million pounds on the library.

total² adjective
complete ▶ total silence

totally /'təʊtl-ɪ/ adverb
completely ▶ I totally agree.

totter /'tɒtə'/ verb
to walk in an unsteady way ▶ a woman tottering around in high heels

touch¹ /tʌtʃ/ verb
1 to put your hand or another part of your body on or against something ▶ Don't touch that pot; it's very hot.
2 to bring, put, or be on or against something ▶ Make sure the wires are not touching.

touch² noun
1 (plural **touches**) an act of putting part of your body on or against something ▶ I felt the touch of his hand.
2 (no plural) the sense with which you feel the hardness, softness, etc. of something
3 get in touch to write to someone or telephone them ▶ I must get in touch with my old schoolfriends to see what they are doing now.
4 keep in touch to speak or write to someone regularly ▶ Do you still keep in touch with John?

touchdown /'tʌtʃdaʊn/ noun
1 the moment when a plane lands on the ground
2 (used about RUGBY or American football) an act of scoring points by taking the ball over the other team's line

touching /'tʌtʃɪŋ/ adjective
making you feel sad, or sorry for someone ▶ a touching story

touchy /'tʌtʃɪ/ adjective (**touchier, touchiest**)
easily annoyed or upset ▶ Are you always so touchy about your work?

tough /tʌf/ adjective
1 strong and brave

2 hard, and not easy to bite ▶ This meat is very tough.
OPPOSITE (**2**): **tender**
3 difficult ▶ a tough exam

toughen /'tʌfən/ (also **toughen up** /ˌtʌfən 'ʌp/) verb
to become stronger, or to make someone or something stronger ▶ The government wants to toughen up the law on drugs.

tour¹ /tʊə'/ noun
1 a journey during which several places are visited ▶ They have gone on a tour of the States.
2 a trip to or through a place ▶ We went on a tour **of** the city.

tour² verb
to visit many different parts of a country or an area

tourism /'tʊərɪzəm/ noun (no plural)
travelling to a place for pleasure on holiday ▶ The town depends on tourism for most of its income.

tourist /'tʊərɪst/ noun
a person who travels for pleasure

tourist office /'tʊərɪst ˌɒfɪs/ noun
a place where tourists can go to get information

tournament /'tʊənəmənt/ noun
a sports competition ▶ a tennis tournament

tow /təʊ/ verb
to pull a vehicle along by a rope or chain ▶ We towed the car to the garage.

towards /tə'wɔːdz/ preposition
1 in the direction of ▶ She walked towards the door. ▶ He stood with his back towards us.
2 near in time ▶ Towards evening, the day became cooler.

towel /'taʊəl/ noun
a piece of cloth used for drying things

tower /'taʊə'/ noun
a tall, narrow building or part of a building ▶ a church tower

T

town /taʊn/ *noun*
a place with many houses and other buildings where people live and work
COMPARE: **city**

town hall /ˌtaʊn ˈhɔːl/ *noun*
a building which is used as offices for local government and as a place for public meetings

toxic /ˈtɒksɪk/ *adjective*
poisonous ➤ *The children live within 4 miles of a toxic waste site.*

toy /tɔɪ/ *noun*
a special object made for children to play with

trace¹ /treɪs/ *noun*
a mark or sign that shows that someone or something has been in a place ➤ *They searched the building but did not find any trace of the criminal.*

trace² *verb (present participle* **tracing**, *past* **traced**)
1 to copy a picture, plan, etc. by drawing on a thin piece of paper put over it
2 to try to find someone or something by looking for signs they have left behind ➤ *They traced the criminal to a house in the city.*

track¹ /træk/ *noun*
1 a rough path
2 a set of marks on the ground left by an animal or a person ➤ *The hunter followed the animal's tracks.*
3 a special path for races

track² *verb*
to follow an animal's track

tracksuit /ˈtræksuːt/ *noun*
a warm, loose suit which you wear for sport or around the house

tractor /ˈtræktər/ *noun*
a machine used for pulling heavy carts and farm machinery

trade¹ /treɪd/ *noun*
1 *(no plural)* the buying and selling of goods ➤ *Trade with other countries increased by 15% last year.*

2 a kind of business ➤ *the clothes trade*
3 a job that needs special training to do ➤ *She's a dressmaker by trade.*

trade² *verb (present participle* **trading**, *past* **traded**)
to buy and sell goods ➤ *We trade with many other European countries.*

trademark /ˈtreɪdmɑːk/ *noun*
a special name, mark, or word on a product that shows it is made by a particular company

trader /ˈtreɪdər/ *noun*
a person who buys and sells goods

tradesman /ˈtreɪdzmən/ *noun (plural* **tradesmen** /-mən/)
a person who buys and sells goods, especially a person who runs a shop

tradition /trəˈdɪʃən/ *noun*
an old custom passed on from parents to their children ➤ *an old family tradition*

traditional /trəˈdɪʃənəl/ *adjective*
that has been done in the same way for a long time ➤ *a traditional family Christmas*

traffic /ˈtræfɪk/ *noun (no plural)*
the movement of cars and other vehicles in the streets, or of ships or planes ➤ *The traffic's awful tonight!*

traffic jam /ˈtræfɪk ˌdʒæm/ *noun*
a long line of vehicles that cannot move forward because the road is blocked

traffic lights /ˈtræfɪk ˌlaɪts/ *plural noun*
lights that change colour to direct the traffic on roads

traffic warden /ˈtræfɪk ˌwɔːdn/ *noun*
an official whose job is to check that cars and other vehicles are parked where they are allowed to park

tragedy /ˈtrædʒədi/ *noun (plural* **tragedies**)
1 something terrible that happens ➤ *Her son's death was a tragedy.*

2 a serious play with a sad ending
COMPARE (**2**): **comedy**

tragic /'trædʒɪk/ *adjective*
very sad ▶ *a tragic accident*
(*adverb:* **tragically**)

trail /treɪl/ *noun*
1 a set of marks on the ground that
show where someone or something
has been ▶ *a trail of blood*
2 a path across rough country

trailer /'treɪlə/ *noun*
a two-wheeled cart pulled by a car, etc.

train¹ /treɪn/ *noun*
1 a number of railway carriages for
people or goods, pulled along by an
engine
2 by train on a train ▶ *We went by
train.*

train² *verb*
to make yourself, or someone else,
ready to do something difficult
▶ *I am training for the race.* ▶ *She is
training to become a nurse.*

trainee /ˌtreɪ'niː/ *noun*
a person who is being trained for a
job ▶ *a trainee nurse*

trainer /'treɪnə/ *noun*
a person who teaches you a sport or
helps you to exercise

trainers /'treɪnəz/ *plural noun*
special shoes for playing sport

training /'treɪnɪŋ/ *noun (no plural)*
special activities in which you learn
how to do a particular job or play a
sport

trait /treɪ/ *noun*
a quality that is part of someone's
character ▶ *Jealousy is one of his
worst traits.*

traitor /'treɪtə/ *noun*
a person who helps people who are
not friends of his or her country

tram /træm/ *noun*
an electric vehicle for carrying
passengers, which moves along the
street on metal tracks

tramp /træmp/ *noun*
a person with no home or job who
wanders from place to place begging
for food or money

trample /'træmpəl/ *verb (present
participle* **trampling***, past* **trampled***)*
to walk heavily on something ▶ *He
trampled on my flowers when he was
getting his football.*

trampoline /'træmpəliːn/ *noun*
a piece of sports equipment that you
jump up and down on, made of a
sheet of material tightly stretched
across a large frame

trance /trɑːns/ *noun*
in a trance seeming to be asleep, but
still able to hear and understand
things ▶ *The children watched TV as
if they were in a trance.*

tranquil /'træŋkwɪl/ *adjective*
calm and peaceful ▶ *the tranquil
waters of the lake*

tranquillizer /'træŋkwɪlaɪzə/ *noun*
a medicine that makes someone calm
or sleepy ▶ *Since his mother's death,
he has been taking tranquillizers.*

transatlantic /ˌtrænzət'læntɪk/
adjective
crossing the Atlantic Ocean, or
involving people on both sides of the
Atlantic ▶ *a transatlantic flight*

transfer¹ /træns'fɜː/ *verb (present
participle* **transferring***, past*
transferred*)*
to move people or things from one
place to another ▶ *His employer
transferred him to another office.*

transfer² /'trænsfɜː/ *noun*
the act of transferring a person ▶ *Can
I have a transfer to a new office?*

transform /træns'fɔːm/ *verb*
to change something or someone
completely in appearance or nature
▶ *She transformed the room
completely with some paint and new
curtains.*

T

transfusion /træns'fjuːʒən/ *noun*
the act of putting blood into
someone's body, for example after an
accident ▶ *She needed to have a
blood transfusion.*

transistor /træn'zɪstər/ *(also
transistor radio* /træn,zɪstə 'reɪdɪəʊ/)
noun
a small radio

transitive /'trænzətɪv/ *adjective*
(used about verbs) needing an object.
In the sentence **"I gave the book to
Jane"**, **"gave"** is a transitive verb
COMPARE: **intransitive**

translate /træns'leɪt/ *verb (present
participle translating, past
translated)*
to give the meaning of words of one
language in another language ▶ *He
translated the speech from Spanish
into English.*
COMPARE: **interpret**

translation /træns'leɪʃən/ *noun*
1 something that has been translated
2 *(no plural)* the act or job of
translating

translator /træns'leɪtər/ *noun*
a person whose job is to translate
things from one language into
another ▶ *She works as a translator
at the UN.*

transmission /trænz'mɪʃən/ *noun
(no plural)*
the process of sending out radio or
television signals ▶ *The announcer
apologized for the break in
transmission.*

transmit /trænz'mɪt/ *verb (present
participle transmitting, past
transmitted)*
to send out radio or television signals
▶ *We will be transmitting live from
the cricket ground.*

transmitter /trænz'mɪtər/ *noun*
a piece of equipment that sends out
radio or television signals ▶ *a radio
transmitter*

transparent /træn'spærənt/ *adjective*
that you can see through ▶ *Glass is
transparent.*

transplant /'trænsplɑːnt/ *noun*
a medical operation in which doctors
remove a part of someone's body and
replace it with a part from another
person's body ▶ *a heart and lung
transplant*

transport¹ /træn'spɔːt/ *verb*
to carry goods or people from one
place to another ▶ *The goods were
transported by train.*

transport² /'trænspɔːt/ *noun (no plural)*
1 the moving of goods or people from
one place to another
2 cars, buses, trains, etc. ▶ *public
transport*

trap¹ /træp/ *noun*
1 an instrument for catching an
animal ▶ *a mouse caught in a trap*
2 a plan to catch a person ▶ *The
police set a trap for the thieves.*

trap² *verb (present participle
trapping, past trapped)*
1 to catch a person or an animal in a
trap ▶ *The police trapped the thieves.*
2 **be trapped** to be unable to escape
from a dangerous or unpleasant
place or set of conditions ▶ *She was
trapped in the burning house.*

trauma /'trɔːmə/ *noun (no plural)*
the shock caused by an unpleasant
and upsetting experience, or an
experience that causes this feeling
▶ *Children often have trouble coping
with the trauma of divorce.*

traumatic /trɔː'mætɪk/ *adjective*
very shocking and upsetting ▶ *a
traumatic experience*

travel¹ /'trævəl/ *verb (present
participle travelling, past travelled)*
1 to go from place to place ▶ *to travel
round the world*
2 to move along ▶ *We were travelling
at 60 miles an hour when the accident
happened.*

travel² *noun (no plural)*
going from place to place ➤ *Heavy rain is making road travel difficult.*

travel agency /'trævəl ˌeɪdʒənsɪ/ *noun (plural **travel agencies**)*
a business which arranges people's journeys and holidays

travel agent /'trævəl ˌeɪdʒənt/ *noun*
a person who owns or works in a travel agency

traveller /'trævələʳ/ *noun*
a person who is on a journey

traveller's cheque /'trævələz ˌtʃek/ *noun*
a special cheque that you take to another country and can use to get money in that country

trawler /'trɔːləʳ/ *noun*
a boat for fishing

tray /treɪ/ *noun*
a flat piece of wood, metal, etc. on which things can be carried

treacle /'triːkəl/ *noun (no plural)*
a dark, sweet, sticky liquid made from sugar plants, used in cooking

tread /tred/ *verb (past tense **trod** /trɒd/, past participle **trodden** /'trɒdn/)*
1 to stand on something ➤ *I trod on his foot by accident.*
2 to remain upright in deep water by moving your legs

treason /'triːzən/ *noun (no plural)*
an action which harms the ruler, leader, or government of a country

treasure /'treʒəʳ/ *noun (no plural)*
a collection of gold, silver, etc. ➤ *They found the treasure buried under a tree.*

treat¹ /triːt/ *noun*
something special which gives you pleasure ➤ *Her birthday treat was a visit to the theatre.*

treat² *verb*
1 to behave towards a person or an

animal in a particular way ➤ *He treats his dog very badly.*
2 to handle something in a particular way ➤ *Glass must be treated carefully.*
3 to try to cure an illness ➤ *Doctors cannot treat this illness successfully.*
4 to give someone something special ➤ *I'm going to treat myself **to** a new coat.*

treatment /'triːtmənt/ *noun*
1 a way of making a sick person better ➤ *The treatment cured him completely.*
2 *(no plural)* the way you behave towards a person or an animal ➤ *complaints about the treatment of political prisoners*

treaty /'triːtɪ/ *noun (plural **treaties**)*
an agreement between two or more countries ➤ *a peace treaty*

treble /'trebəl/ *verb (present participle **trebling**, past **trebled**)*
to become three times as big or three times as much as before ➤ *Prices have trebled in the last year.*
SAME MEANING: **triple**

tree /triː/ *noun*
a large plant with branches, leaves, and a thick trunk

trek /trek/ *verb (present participle **trekking**, past **trekked**)*
to make a long and difficult journey on foot ➤ *We're planning to go trekking in Nepal.*

tremble /'trembəl/ *verb (present participle **trembling**, past **trembled**)*
to shake because you are very afraid or very angry ➤ *to tremble with fear*

tremendous /trə'mendəs/ *adjective*
1 very large or very great in amount
2 wonderful ➤ *We went to a tremendous party.*

tremendously /trə'mendəslɪ/ *adverb*
very ➤ *tremendously difficult*

trench /trentʃ/ *noun (plural **trenches**)*
a long, narrow hole dug in the earth

T

trend /trend/ *noun*
the way a situation is generally developing or changing ➤ *Tourist numbers are lower this year – a trend which is worrying the tourism industry.*

trendy /'trendɪ/ *adjective (**trendier, trendiest**)*
modern and fashionable ➤ *We ate in a trendy Italian restaurant.*

trespass /'trespəs/ *verb*
to go onto someone else's land without permission ➤ *The farmer said we were trespassing.*

trespasser /'trespəsəʳ/ *noun*
a person who goes onto someone else's land without permission

trial /'traɪəl/ *noun*
1 the time when people in a court of law decide whether a person is guilty of a crime ➤ *The murder trial lasted a month.*
2 a test to see if something is good or bad
3 **on trial** accused of a crime, and having a court of law decide whether you are guilty or not ➤ *She was on trial for murder.*

triangle /'traɪæŋgəl/ *noun*
a flat shape with three straight sides and three angles

triangular /traɪ'æŋgjʊləʳ/ *adjective*
shaped like a triangle

tribal /'traɪbəl/ *adjective*
belonging to a tribe ➤ *tribal music*

tribe /traɪb/ *noun*
a group of people of the same race, who share the same language, customs, etc.

tribunal /traɪ'bjuːnl/ *noun*
a type of law court that has official authority to deal with a particular situation or problem ➤ *a war crimes tribunal*

tributary /'trɪbjʊtərɪ/ *noun (plural **tributaries**)*
a small stream or river that joins a larger river

tribute /'trɪbjuːt/ *noun*
something done, said, or given to show respect or admiration for someone ➤ *The doctor paid tribute to the nurses by praising their work.*

trick¹ /trɪk/ *noun*
1 an action meant to deceive someone ➤ *The phone call was a trick to get me out of the office.*
2 a clever act done to amuse people ➤ *I can do magic tricks.*
3 **play a trick on someone** to deceive someone or make them look stupid, especially to amuse others ➤ *The children played a trick on their teacher.*

trick² *verb*
to deceive or cheat someone ➤ *He tricked me into giving him the money.*

trickle¹ /'trɪkl/ *verb (present participle **trickling**, past **trickled**)*
(used about a liquid) to flow in a few drops or a thin stream ➤ *Blood trickled from the wound.*

trickle² *noun*
a thin line or a few drops of liquid

tricky /'trɪkɪ/ *adjective (**trickier, trickiest**)*
difficult and complicated to do or to deal with ➤ *I had this really tricky maths problem to solve.*

tricycle /'traɪsɪkəl/ *noun*
a bicycle with three wheels, which is usually for children

tried /traɪd/
the PAST TENSE and PAST PARTICIPLE of the verb **try**

trigger /'trɪgəʳ/ *noun*
a small part of a gun which you pull with your finger to fire it

trilogy /'trɪlədʒɪ/ *noun (plural **trilogies**)*
a set of three books, plays, films, etc., which all have the same subject or characters

trim /trɪm/ *verb (present participle **trimming**, past **trimmed**)*
to make something neat by cutting it ▶ *She trimmed his hair.*

trinket /'trɪŋkɪt/ *noun*
a piece of jewellery or a small, pretty object that is not worth much money

trio /'triːəʊ/ *noun*
a group of three people, especially musicians

trip¹ /trɪp/ *noun*
a short journey ▶ *a trip to town*

trip² *verb (present participle **tripping**, past **tripped**)*
to hit your foot against something and fall or nearly fall ▶ *Be careful! Don't trip over that box.*

triple¹ /'trɪpəl/ *adjective*
consisting of three parts ▶ *The prison has a triple barrier around it.*

triple² *verb (present participle **tripling**, past **tripled**)*
to become three times as big or three times as much as before ▶ *The population may triple in 20 years.*
SAME MEANING: **treble**

triplet /'trɪplɪt/ *noun*
one of three children who are born at the same time and have the same mother ▶ *Di gave birth to triplets last year.*

tripod /'traɪpɒd/ *noun*
a piece of equipment with three legs that you use to support something such as a camera

triumph /'traɪʌmf/ *noun*
a victory ▶ *I'll never forget Celtic's triumph over Rangers.*

triumphant /traɪˈʌmfənt/ *adjective*
feeling very pleased because you have succeeded or won ▶ *a triumphant army*

trivial /'trɪvɪəl/ *adjective*
not important or serious ▶ *He told me all the trivial details of his daily life.*

trod /trɒd/
the PAST TENSE of the verb **tread**

trodden /'trɒdn/
the PAST PARTICIPLE of the verb **tread**

trolley /'trɒlɪ/ *noun*
a small, light cart which you push by hand and use to carry heavy things. You find trolleys in SUPERMARKETS and in railway stations and AIRPORTS

trombone /trɒmˈbəʊn/ *noun*
a metal musical instrument that you play by blowing into it and moving a long tube backwards and forwards

troop /truːp/ *verb*
to walk somewhere in a group ▶ *The children all trooped into the dining room and sat down.*

troops /truːps/ *plural noun*
soldiers

trophy /'trəʊfɪ/ *noun (plural **trophies**)*
a prize given to a person who has won a game or race

tropical /'trɒpɪkəl/ *adjective*
1 of or from the tropics ▶ *a tropical plant*
2 very hot ▶ *tropical weather*

tropics /'trɒpɪks/ *plural noun*
the tropics the hottest parts of the world

trot /trɒt/ *verb (present participle **trotting**, past **trotted**)*
to run with short steps ▶ *The horse trotted along the road.* ▶ *The little girl trotted behind her father.*

trouble¹ /'trʌbəl/ *noun*
1 *(no plural)* difficulty ▶ *Did you have any trouble finding the restaurant?*
2 *(no plural)* something which causes a lot of problems ▶ *He hasn't got a job; that's the trouble.*
3 **be in trouble** to have a difficult problem, usually because you have done something wrong ▶ *He's in trouble **with** the police.*
4 **get into trouble** to give yourself a difficult problem

T

5 get someone into trouble to get someone else into a difficult situation

6 no trouble not inconvenient; not an effort ► *I'll drive you to the station; it's no trouble.*

7 troubles *plural noun* problems ► *Tell me all your troubles.*

trouble² *verb (present participle **troubling**, past **troubled**)*
1 to cause someone unhappiness, anxiety, or pain ► *Her child's behaviour troubled her.*
2 to cause additional work for someone ► *I'm sorry to trouble you, but could you help me with this letter?*

troubled /'trʌbəld/ *adjective*
having a lot of problems or difficulties ► *one of the most troubled areas of the world*

troublemaker /'trʌbəl,meɪkə'/ *noun*
a person who deliberately causes trouble

troublesome /'trʌbəlsəm/ *adjective*
causing a lot of trouble ► *a troublesome employee*

trough /trɒf/ *noun*
a long, narrow wooden or metal container used to hold food or water for animals

trousers /'traʊzəz/ *plural noun*
a piece of clothing that covers the lower part of your body, with a covering for each of your legs ► *a pair of trousers*

trout /traʊt/ *noun (plural **trout**)*
a brown or silvery fish that lives in rivers

trowel /'traʊəl/ *noun*
a small tool used for digging small holes, taking plants out of the ground, etc.

truant /'truːənt/ *noun*
1 a child who stays away from school without a good reason
2 play truant to stay away from school without a good reason ► *The teacher*

punished David for playing truant.

truce /truːs/ *noun*
an agreement between two enemies to stop fighting or arguing for a short time ► *The two countries have called a truce.*

truck /trʌk/ *noun*
1 a lorry
2 an open cart used on a railway for carrying heavy goods

trudge /trʌdʒ/ *verb (present participle **trudging**, past **trudged**)*
to walk with slow, heavy steps because you are tired ► *An old man was trudging up the hill.*

true /truː/ *adjective*
1 correct; real ► *Is it true that you've resigned?* ► *a true story*
OPPOSITE: **untrue**
2 come true (used about dreams and wishes) to happen ► *His wish came true.*

truly /'truːlɪ/ *adverb*
really ► *I am truly grateful for all your help.*

trumpet /'trʌmpɪt/ *noun*
a musical instrument made of brass that you play by blowing through it

truncheon /'trʌnʃən/ *noun*
a short, thick stick used by the police

trunk /trʌŋk/ *noun*
1 the main stem of a tree
2 the human body without the head and limbs
3 a large box to carry clothes in when you travel
4 the long nose of an elephant
5 trunks *plural noun* a piece of clothing like very short trousers, which men wear for swimming

trust¹ /trʌst/ *verb*
1 to believe that someone is honest or good ► *Don't trust him – he never tells the truth.*
2 to be sure that someone will do something ► *Can I trust you to behave properly?*

trust² *noun (no plural)*
the belief that someone is good or honest; the belief that something will happen ▶ *the lack of trust between local people and the police*

trustworthy /'trʌst,wɜːðɪ/ *adjective*
able to be trusted ▶ *Let Paul look after the money; he's trustworthy.*

truth /truːθ/ *noun (no plural)*
what is true; the correct facts ▶ *You should always tell the truth.*

truthful /'truːθfəl/ *adjective*
1 telling the truth ▶ *Paul is very truthful.*
2 correct ▶ *a truthful statement*

try¹ /traɪ/ *verb (past tried)*
1 to attempt to do something ▶ *He tried to climb the tree, but couldn't.* ▶ *Please try not to be late.*
2 to test something to see if you like it ▶ *Have you tried this chocolate?*
3 try something on to put on a piece of clothing to see if it fits you

try² *noun (plural tries)*
an attempt ▶ *If you can't open the box, let me have a try.*

tsar (also **tzar, czar**) /zɑːʳ/ *noun*
a ruler of Russia before 1917

T-shirt /'tiː ʃɜːt/ *noun*
a piece of clothing with a round neck and short sleeves, which you usually wear in summer

tub /tʌb/ *noun*
a round container for holding things ▶ *a tub of margarine* ▶ *a flower tub*

tuba /'tjuːbə/ *noun*
a large, metal musical instrument that you play by blowing into it, and that has a wide opening that points upwards

tube /tjuːb/ *noun*
1 a hollow pipe made of metal, plastic, glass, or rubber
2 a soft metal or plastic container with a cap ▶ *a tube of toothpaste*
3 the Tube the London Underground railway

tuck /tʌk/ *verb*
1 to push or put something into or under something else ▶ *Tuck your shirt into your trousers.*
2 tuck someone in to make someone comfortable in bed by pulling the covers over them

Tuesday /'tjuːzdeɪ, -dɪ/ *noun*
the third day of the week

tuft /tʌft/ *noun*
a group of hairs, blades of grass, etc. growing together

tug¹ /tʌg/ *verb (present participle tugging, past tugged)*
to pull hard ▶ *The child tugged at my hand to make me go with her.*

tug² *noun*
1 a sudden, strong pull
2 a small, powerful boat used for guiding large ships into and out of a port

tuition /tjuːˈɪʃən/ *noun (no plural)*
the teaching of a subject to one student or a small group of students ▶ *private tuition*

tumble /'tʌmbəl/ *verb (present participle tumbling, past tumbled)*
to fall suddenly ▶ *She tumbled down the stairs.*

tumbler /'tʌmbləʳ/ *noun*
a drinking glass with a flat bottom and straight sides

tummy /'tʌmɪ/ *noun (plural tummies)*
your stomach ▶ *I've got a tummy ache.*

tumour /'tjuːməʳ/ *noun*
a group of cells in the body that grow more quickly than normal and that can cause serious illness or death ▶ *a brain tumour*

tuna /'tjuːnə/ *noun*
a large fish that lives in the sea, or the meat from this fish

tune¹ /tjuːn/ *noun*
a number of musical notes put together to make a pleasant sound

T

➤ *That song has a happy tune.*
COMPARE: **song**

tune² *verb (present participle **tuning**, past **tuned**)*
to set the strings of a musical instrument so that they give the right sound ➤ *to tune a piano*

tunnel¹ /ˈtʌnl/ *noun*
a passage through a hill or under a river, etc. for cars or trains to pass

tunnel² *verb (present participle **tunnelling**, past **tunnelled**)*
to make a passage through a hill or under a river, etc.

turban /ˈtɜːbən/ *noun*
a long piece of cloth which you wind tightly round your head to cover it

turf /tɜːf/ *noun (no plural)*
short grass and the soil under it

turkey /ˈtɜːkɪ/ *noun*
a large farm bird that is used for food

turn¹ /tɜːn/ *verb*
1 to go round and round, or make something go round and round ➤ *The wheels slowly began to turn.* ➤ *Turn the wheel to the right.*
2 to change direction, or make something change direction ➤ *She turned left at the end of the road.* ➤ *He turned the box upside down.* ➤ *He was turning the pages of the book with great interest.*
3 to move so that your body is facing another way ➤ *She turned round to look behind her.* ➤ *He turned and waved.*
4 turn a corner to go round a corner
5 turn something down (a) to reduce the sound of a radio, etc., or the heat of a heater ➤ *Turn the television down; it's too loud.*
(b) to say no to an offer ➤ *He turned down the job.*
6 turn something into something to change something into something else ➤ *She turned her bedroom into an office.*

7 turn something off to make something stop working ➤ *Turn the radio off.*
8 turn something on to make something start working ➤ *Turn the heating on.*
9 turn something out to make a light stop shining ➤ *She turned out the light.*
10 turn over to move so that you are lying in a different position ➤ *He turned over and went to sleep.*
11 turn up to arrive at a place ➤ *He turned up with his brother.*

turn² *noun*
1 a turning movement ➤ *the turn of a wheel*
2 a change of direction ➤ *a turn to the left*
3 your time to do something ➤ *It's my turn to pay.*
4 take it in turns if people take it in turns to do something, first one person does it, then another ➤ *We took it in turns to drive.*

turning /ˈtɜːnɪŋ/ *noun*
a road that branches from another one

turning point /ˈtɜːnɪŋ pɔɪnt/ *noun*
the time when an important change starts to happen ➤ *The film marks a turning point in Kubrick's career.*

turnip /ˈtɜːnɪp/ *noun*
a round, white vegetable that grows under the ground

turnout /ˈtɜːnaʊt/ *noun*
the number of people who go to an event such as a party, a meeting, or an election ➤ *There was an excellent turnout at the meeting.*

turquoise /ˈtɜːkwɔɪz/ *adjective, noun*
a bright blue-green colour

turtle /ˈtɜːtl/ *noun*
an animal which has a hard, round shell over its body, and lives mainly in the sea

tusk /tʌsk/ *noun*
a long, pointed tooth which grows

outside the mouths of some animals,
e.g. elephants

tutor¹ /'tjuːtəʳ/ *noun*
a person who teaches one student or
a small group of students ➤ *Her tutor
teaches her at home.*

tutor² *verb*
to teach someone ➤ *He tutored me **in**
English.*

tutorial /tjuːˈtɔːrɪəl/ *noun*
a class in which a small group of
students discuss a subject with their
tutor ➤ *Most of the teaching is done
in small tutorials.*

TV /ˌtiː ˈviː/ *noun*
1 a television ➤ *Turn on the TV.*
2 (*no plural*) the system of sending
and receiving pictures and sounds by
electrical signals ➤ *We're watching TV.*
3 on TV shown on the television
➤ *There's a film on TV tonight.*

tweed /twiːd/ *noun* (*no plural*)
a thick, wool cloth that is used
especially for making clothes such as
coats and suits

tweezers /'twiːzəz/ *plural noun*
a small instrument made of two
narrow pieces of metal joined at one
end, used for picking up very small
objects ➤ *a pair of tweezers*
COMPARE: **tongs**

twelfth /twelfθ/ *adjective*
12th

twelve /twelv/ *adjective, noun*
the number 12

twentieth /'twentɪ-əθ/ *adjective*
20th

twenty /'twentɪ/ *adjective, noun*
the number 20

twice /twaɪs/ *adverb*
two times ➤ *You've asked me that
question twice.*

twig /twɪg/ *noun*
a small branch on a tree

twin /twɪn/ *noun*
one of two children born to the same

mother at the same time

twinge /twɪndʒ/ *noun*
a sudden, slight pain

twinkle /'twɪŋkəl/ *verb* (*present
participle **twinkling**, past **twinkled**)
to shine with an unsteady light ➤ *The
stars twinkled in the sky.*

twist¹ /twɪst/ *verb*
1 to wind things together or around
something else ➤ *She twisted her hair
round her fingers.*
2 to turn something ➤ *Twist the lid to
open it.*
3 to turn in several directions ➤ *The
path twisted up the hill.*

twist² *noun*
1 something made by twisting ➤ *a
twist in the branch*
2 a movement which turns something
round ➤ *He gave the lid a twist to
open it.*
3 a bend ➤ *a road full of twists and
turns*

twitch¹ /twɪtʃ/ *verb*
to move suddenly and quickly
without control ➤ *The horse twitched
its ears.*

twitch² *noun* (*plural **twitches***)
a sudden movement of a muscle
which you cannot control

two /tuː/ *adjective, noun*
the number 2

two-way /ˌtuː ˈweɪ/ *adjective*
moving in two opposite directions
➤ *two-way traffic*

tycoon /taɪˈkuːn/ *noun*
a person who is very successful in
business and has a lot of money ➤ *an
oil tycoon*

tying /'taɪ-ɪŋ/
the PRESENT PARTICIPLE of the verb **tie**

type¹ /taɪp/ *noun*
a particular kind ➤ *A rose is a type **of**
flower.*
SAME MEANING: **kind, sort**
LOOK AT: **kind**

T

type² *verb (present participle* **typing,** *past* **typed)**
to write something using a TYPEWRITER ➤ *to type a letter*

typewriter /'taɪpˌraɪtəʳ/ *noun*
a machine used to type letters

typhoon /ˌtaɪ'fuːn/ *noun*
a tropical storm with very strong winds

typical /'tɪpɪkəl/ *adjective*
the same as other people or things belonging to that group or kind ➤ *a typical little boy who enjoys being naughty*

typically /'tɪpɪklɪ/ *adverb*
1 used to say that something is typical ➤ *a typically Japanese dish*
2 used to say that something usually happens in a particular way ➤ *Prices typically start at around £600.*

typing /'taɪpɪŋ/ *noun (no plural)*
the activity of writing something using a TYPEWRITER ➤ *Are you any good at typing?*

typist /'taɪpɪst/ *noun*
a person whose job is to type

tyrant /'taɪərənt/ *noun*
a person with complete power who uses it cruelly

tyre /taɪəʳ/ *noun*
a thick rubber part, often filled with air, which fits round the outside edge of a wheel ➤ *a bicycle tyre*

Uu

UFO /'juːfəʊ, ˌjuː ef 'əʊ/ *noun*
an UNIDENTIFIED FLYING OBJECT; a moving object in the sky, that some people believe could be carrying creatures from another world

ugly /'ʌglɪ/ *adjective (**uglier, ugliest**)*
unpleasant to look at ➤ *an ugly face*

ulcer /'ʌlsəʳ/ *noun*
a painful area on your skin or inside your body, that may BLEED ➤ *a mouth ulcer*

ultimate /'ʌltɪmət/ *adjective*
1 used to say that something is the most important final result in a series of things ➤ *Our ultimate aim is to be the best women's football team in the country.*
2 used to say that something is the best, greatest, or worst of its kind ➤ *It has been described as the ultimate pop video.*

ultimately /'ʌltɪmətlɪ/ *adverb*
1 finally, after many other things have happened ➤ *Their efforts ultimately resulted in his release from prison.*
2 used to emphasize the most important or basic part of a situation ➤ *Ultimately, it's your decision.*

ultraviolet /ˌʌltrə'vaɪələt/ *adjective*
(used about light) making your skin darker ➤ *the risks of exposure to ultraviolet light*

umbrella /ʌm'brelə/ *noun*
a piece of cloth or plastic stretched over a frame, which you can hold over yourself to keep off the rain

umpire /'ʌmpaɪəʳ/ *noun*
a person who decides about the points won in a game, especially in cricket

UN /ˌjuː 'en/ *noun*
the UN the UNITED NATIONS

unable /ʌn'eɪbəl/ *adjective*
unable to do something not having enough power, skill, knowledge, time, or money to do something ➤ *Owing to illness, she was unable to attend the meeting.*
OPPOSITE: **able**

unacceptable /ˌʌnək'septəbəl/ *adjective*
wrong or bad in a way that should not be allowed to continue ➤ *The amount of traffic on these roads is completely unacceptable.* ➤ *The*

standard of your work is unacceptable.
OPPOSITE: **acceptable**

unanimous /juˈnænɪməs/ adjective
agreed by everyone ▶ a unanimous
decision

unarmed /ʌnˈɑːmd/ adjective
not carrying a gun or other weapon
OPPOSITE: **armed**

unattended /ˌʌnəˈtendɪd/ adjective
left alone without being watched or
looked after ▶ Passengers should not
leave their bags unattended.

unattractive /ˌʌnəˈtræktɪv/ adjective
not causing pleasure; not beautiful;
not attractive ▶ an unattractive
industrial area of the city

unavailable /ˌʌnəˈveɪləbəl/ adjective
1 not able to meet someone or do
something, especially because you
are too busy ▶ I'm afraid she's
unavailable at the moment.
2 not able to be bought or obtained
▶ an album previously unavailable on
CD
OPPOSITE: (**1** and **2**): **available**

unaware /ˌʌnəˈweəʳ/ adjective
not noticing or knowing about
something ▶ She seemed completely
unaware **of** what was happening.
OPPOSITE: **aware**

unbearable /ʌnˈbeərəbəl/ adjective
too bad to be accepted; not bearable
▶ The noise was unbearable and we
hurried out of the room.

unbeatable /ʌnˈbiːtəbəl/ adjective
much better than other things ▶ Their
prices are unbeatable!

unbelievable /ˌʌnbɪˈliːvəbəl/
adjective
very surprising; not believable ▶ It
was unbelievable how quickly she did
it. (adverb: **unbelievably**)

uncertain /ʌnˈsɜːtn/ adjective
not sure or certain ▶ He was
uncertain what to do. ▶ Our holiday
plans are still uncertain.

uncertainty /ʌnˈsɜːtnti/ noun (plural
uncertainties)
the state of not being sure or certain
▶ There is uncertainty over the future
of the project.

uncle /ˈʌŋkəl/ noun
the brother of one of your parents, or
the husband of the sister of one of
your parents ▶ Hello, Uncle John.
COMPARE: **aunt**

unclear /ʌnˈklɪəʳ/ adjective
1 difficult to understand or be sure
about ▶ The law is unclear on this
issue.
2 not sure about something or not
able to understand it ▶ I'm a little
unclear about what they mean.
OPPOSITE: (**1** and **2**): **clear**

uncomfortable /ʌnˈkʌmftəbəl/
adjective
1 not pleasant to sit on, lie on, or
wear; not comfortable ▶ an
uncomfortable chair ▶ an
uncomfortable bed ▶ an
uncomfortable shirt that was too
tight round the neck
2 not relaxed ▶ She felt hot and
uncomfortable in her heavy suit. ▶ an
uncomfortable situation
(adverb: **uncomfortably**)

uncommon /ʌnˈkɒmən/ adjective
not usual or common
SAME MEANING: **rare**

unconscious /ʌnˈkɒnʃəs/ adjective
not knowing what is happening or
feeling anything; not conscious
▶ After she hit her head, she was
unconscious for several minutes.

uncontrollable /ˌʌnkənˈtrəʊləbəl/
adjective
impossible to stop; not controllable
▶ uncontrollable laughter

uncooked /ʌnˈkʊkt/ adjective
(used about meat and other food) not
cooked
SAME MEANING: **raw**

U

uncooperative /ˌʌnkəʊˈɒpərətɪv/ *adjective*
unwilling to work with other people, or help them, or do what they want when they ask
OPPOSITE: **cooperative**

uncountable /ʌnˈkaʊntəbəl/ *adjective*
in grammar, an uncountable noun has no plural. "Water", "gold", and "furniture" are examples of uncountable nouns
OPPOSITE: **countable**

uncover /ʌnˈkʌvəʳ/ *verb*
1 to take something from on top of something else ▶ *He uncovered the dish and showed us the food.*
2 to find out a crime or something like a crime ▶ *The police uncovered a plan to steal some money.*

undecided /ˌʌndɪˈsaɪdɪd/ *adjective*
not having made a decision about something ▶ *Many people are still undecided about how they will vote.*

under /ˈʌndəʳ/ *preposition, adverb*
1 in or to a lower place; below ▶ *She sat out of the sun under a tree.* ▶ *The shoes were under the bed.*
2 less than ▶ *You can buy a good computer for under £700.* ▶ *All the children are under 12 years old.* ▶ *children of nine and under*
3 working for or obeying someone ▶ *She's got three secretaries working under her.*

underage /ˌʌndəˈreɪdʒ/ *adjective*
too young to legally buy alcohol, drive a car, etc. ▶ *underage drinking*

underclothes /ˈʌndəˌkləʊðz/ *plural noun*
clothes that you wear next to your body and under other clothes ▶ *There are some clean underclothes in the drawer.*
SAME MEANING: **underwear**

undergo /ˌʌndəˈɡəʊ/ *verb (past tense **underwent** /-ˈwent/, past participle **undergone** /-ˈɡɒn/)*
to experience something that is unpleasant but necessary ▶ *He underwent five operations on his foot.*

undergraduate /ˌʌndəˈɡrædjʊət/ *noun*
a student at a university

underground[1] /ˈʌndəɡraʊnd/ *adjective,* /ˌʌndəˈɡraʊnd/ *adverb*
under the ground ▶ *There is an underground passage from the cliff to the castle.* ▶ *They put the telephone line underground.*

underground[2] /ˈʌndəɡraʊnd/ *noun*
a railway system in which the trains run in passages below the ground, especially the system in London ▶ *We went there by underground.*

undergrowth /ˈʌndəɡrəʊθ/ *noun (no plural)*
thickly growing plants underneath trees ▶ *They pushed their way through the undergrowth.*

underline /ˌʌndəˈlaɪn/ *verb (present participle **underlining**, past **underlined**)*
to put a line under a word or words ▶ *This sentence is underlined.*

underneath /ˌʌndəˈniːθ/ *preposition, adverb*
under ▶ *She sat underneath the tree out of the sun.* ▶ *He got out of the car and looked underneath.*

underpants /ˈʌndəpænts/ *plural noun*
a short piece of clothing that men or boys wear under their other clothes on the lower part of their body ▶ *a pair of underpants*

underpass /ˈʌndəpɑːs/ *noun (plural **underpasses**)*
a road or path that goes under another road or a railway

understand /ˌʌndəˈstænd/ *verb (past **understood** /-ˈstʊd/)*
to know the meaning of words or

ideas, or why people behave as they do ▶ *Do you understand every word on this page?* ▶ *I don't understand why he hasn't got any money.*

understandable /ˌʌndəˈstændəbəl/ *adjective*
(used about behaviour or feelings) reasonable because of the situation ▶ *Of course she's upset. It's a perfectly understandable reaction.*

understanding¹ /ˌʌndəˈstændɪŋ/ *noun (no plural)*
knowledge of the meaning of words or ideas, or why people behave as they do ▶ *His understanding of English is very good.*

understanding² *adjective*
kind and sympathetic ▶ *She was very understanding when I told her my problem.*

understood /ˌʌndəˈstʊd/
the PAST TENSE and PAST PARTICIPLE of the verb **understand**

undertake /ˌʌndəˈteɪk/ *verb (present participle **undertaking**, past tense **undertook** /-ˈtʊk/, past participle **undertaken** /-ˈteɪkən/)*
undertake to do something to promise or agree to do something ▶ *She undertook to pay the money back before July.*

undertaker /ˈʌndəteɪkəʳ/ *noun*
a person whose job is to arrange funerals

undertook /ˌʌndəˈtʊk/
the PAST TENSE of the verb **undertake**

underwater /ˈʌndəwɔːtəʳ/ *adjective*, /ˌʌndəˈwɔːtəʳ/ *adverb*
used or done below the surface of the water ▶ *an underwater camera* ▶ *They swam out to the boat underwater.*

under way /ˌʌndə ˈweɪ/ *adjective*
1 to be under way to have started
2 to get under way to start

underwear /ˈʌndəweəʳ/ *noun (no plural)*
clothes that you wear next to your body under other clothes ▶ *She changes her underwear (=puts on clean underwear) every day.*
SAME MEANING: **underclothes**

underwent /ˌʌndəˈwent/
the PAST TENSE of the verb **undergo**

undeveloped /ˌʌndɪˈveləpt/ *adjective*
(used about land) that has not been built on or used for anything ▶ *undeveloped areas of the city*

undo /ʌnˈduː/ *verb (past tense **undid** /ʌnˈdɪd/, past participle **undone** /ʌnˈdʌn/)*
to untie or unfasten something ▶ *He undid the string round the parcel.*

undone /ˌʌnˈdʌn/ *adjective*
(used about items of clothing) not having been fastened ▶ *Your skirt's undone.*

undoubtedly /ʌnˈdaʊtɪdli/ *adverb*
certainly ▶ *He is undoubtedly one of the best writers of his generation.*

undress /ʌnˈdres/ *verb*
1 to take your clothes off ▶ *The doctor asked me to undress.* ▶ *She undressed the baby.*
OPPOSITE: **dress**
2 get undressed to take your clothes off ▶ *I got undressed and went to bed.*

uneasily /ʌnˈiːzɪli/ *adverb*
in a way that shows that you are slightly afraid ▶ *He looked at me uneasily.*

uneasy /ʌnˈiːzi/ *adjective (**uneasier**, **uneasiest**)*
a little afraid ▶ *I had an uneasy feeling that someone was watching me.*

unemployed /ˌʌnɪmˈplɔɪd/ *adjective*
having no paid work; not employed ▶ *He was unemployed for two years after leaving college.*

unemployment /ˌʌnɪmˈplɔɪmənt/ *noun (no plural)*

U

not having a job ▶ *Unemployment in this town has been very high (=many people without work) since the factory closed.*
OPPOSITE: **employment**

uneven /ʌnˈiːvən/ *adjective*
not level or flat ▶ *an uneven road*
OPPOSITE: **even**

unexpected /ˌʌnɪkˈspektɪd/ *adjective*
not what you think will happen; not expected ▶ *an unexpected visitor (adverb: **unexpectedly**)*

unfair /ʌnˈfeəʳ/ *adjective*
not treating people equally ▶ *It's unfair to punish Peter and not James – they were both behaving badly. (adverb: **unfairly**)*
OPPOSITE: **fair**

unfaithful /ʌnˈfeɪθfəl/ *adjective*
having a sexual relationship with someone else when you are already married or have a partner; not faithful

unfamiliar /ˌʌnfəˈmɪliəʳ/ *adjective*
not what you are used to; strange; not familiar ▶ *unfamiliar ideas*

unfashionable /ʌnˈfæʃənəbəl/ *adjective*
not popular at the present time
OPPOSITE: **fashionable**

unfasten /ʌnˈfɑːsən/ *verb*
to open the two sides of a piece of clothing, bag, belt, etc. ▶ *He unfastened his jacket and sat down.*
OPPOSITE: **fasten**

unfavourable /ʌnˈfeɪvərəbəl/ *adjective*
not good for something; not favourable ▶ *unfavourable weather for the show*

unfinished /ʌnˈfɪnɪʃt/ *adjective*
not complete yet; not finished ▶ *an unfinished building*

unfit /ʌnˈfɪt/ *adjective*
1 not healthy because you have not been taking enough exercise
2 unsuitable or not good enough for

something ▶ *animal food unfit for humans* ▶ *unfit to be the captain*
OPPOSITE (**1** and **2**): **fit**

unfold /ʌnˈfəʊld/ *verb*
to open out something from a folded position ▶ *She took the letter out of the envelope and unfolded it carefully.*
OPPOSITE: **fold**

unfortunate /ʌnˈfɔːtʃənət/ *adjective*
having bad luck; unlucky
OPPOSITE: **fortunate**

unfortunately /ʌnˈfɔːtʃənətlɪ/ *adverb*
a word used to say that you are sorry or disappointed about something ▶ *Unfortunately, I can't come to your party.*
OPPOSITE: **fortunately**

unfriendly /ʌnˈfrendlɪ/ *adjective* (**unfriendlier, unfriendliest**)
not kind and pleasant
OPPOSITE: **friendly**

ungrateful /ʌnˈɡreɪtfəl/ *adjective*
not showing any thanks when someone is kind and generous ▶ *Don't think I'm ungrateful, but I can't accept your offer.*
OPPOSITE: **grateful**

unhappily /ʌnˈhæpɪlɪ/ *adverb*
1 in a sad or worried way ▶ *"I can't," she said unhappily.*
2 unfortunately ▶ *Unhappily, he didn't get a place at university.*
OPPOSITE (**1** and **2**): **happily**

unhappy /ʌnˈhæpɪ/ *adjective* (**unhappier, unhappiest**)
sad or worried; not happy ▶ *an unhappy marriage* ▶ *She was unhappy about the children going out alone.*

unhealthy /ʌnˈhelθɪ/ *adjective* (**unhealthier, unhealthiest**)
1 not in good health; not healthy ▶ *He looks thin and unhealthy.*
2 causing bad health ▶ *It's very unhealthy to eat so much fat.*
OPPOSITE (**1** and **2**): **healthy**

U

unhelpful /ʌn'helpfəl/ *adjective*
not helping someone else; not helpful

uniform /'juːnɪfɔːm/ *noun*
clothes worn for a special job or for
school ▶ *The British police wear dark
blue uniforms.*

unimportant /ˌʌnɪm'pɔːtənt/ *adjective*
not worth worrying about; not
important ▶ *All these small details
are quite unimportant.*

uninhabited /ˌʌnɪn'hæbɪtɪd/
adjective
where nobody lives ▶ *an uninhabited
island*

uninterested /ʌn'ɪntrəstɪd/ *adjective*
not interested ▶ *The whole class
seemed completely uninterested **in**
the lesson.*

uninteresting /ʌn'ɪntrəstɪŋ/
adjective
not catching or keeping your
attention; not interesting
SAME MEANING: **dull, boring**

union /'juːnjən/ *noun*
1 *(no plural)* the coming or joining
together of two people or groups
▶ *the union of East and West Germany*
2 a group of workers who have joined
together to protect their pay and
working conditions

unique /juː'niːk/ *adjective*
the only one of its type ▶ *a unique
chance to see inside the palace*

unisex /'juːnɪseks/ *adjective*
for both men and women ▶ *a unisex
hairdresser's*

unit /'juːnɪt/ *noun*
1 one complete thing or set ▶ *This
lesson is divided into four units –
speaking practice, writing practice,
new words, and a word game.*
2 an amount or a quantity used as a
standard of measurement ▶ *The
pound is the unit of money in Britain.*

unite /juː'naɪt/ *verb (present
participle **uniting**, past **united**)*

to join together into one and act
together ▶ *The threat of a foreign
attack united the government and its
opponents.*

united /juː'naɪtɪd/ *adjective*
1 agreeing with all the other people in
a group about something ▶ *The
people in the town were united in
their opposition to the plans.*
2 (used about countries) consisting
of two or more countries or states
that have joined together ▶ *hopes for
a united Ireland*

United Nations /juːˌnaɪtɪd 'neɪʃənz/
noun
the United Nations an organization of
countries which tries to solve the
world's problems

universal /juːnɪ'vɜːsəl/ *adjective*
for all the people in the world or in a
particular group ▶ *Love and death are
universal themes in art.*

universe /'juːnɪvɜːs/ *noun*
all the stars, space, etc. that exist

university /juːnɪ'vɜːsətɪ/ *noun (plural
universities)*
a place of education at the highest
level, where degrees are given ▶ *"Has
he got a job?" "No, he's still at
university." ▶ She went to Leeds
University. ▶ She went to the
University of Leeds.*
COMPARE: **college**

unjust /ˌʌn'dʒʌst/ *adjective*
not fair or reasonable ▶ *an unjust
ruler ▶ unjust laws*
OPPOSITE: **just**

unkind /ˌʌn'kaɪnd/ *adjective*
rather cruel ▶ *unkind **to** animals*
OPPOSITE: **kind**

unknown /ˌʌn'nəʊn/ *adjective*
not known ▶ *The cause of the disease
is unknown.*

unleaded /ʌn'ledɪd/ *adjective*
(used about petrol) containing no
LEAD

U

unless /ən'les/ *conjunction*
1 if not ➤ *He won't go to sleep unless you tell him a story.*
2 except when ➤ *My baby sister never cries unless she is hungry.*

unlike /ʌn'laɪk/ *preposition*
different from; not like ➤ *She's quite unlike her mother; she's tall, and her mother's very short.*

unlikely /ʌn'laɪklɪ/ *adjective*
(**unlikelier, unlikeliest**)
not expected ➤ *They are unlikely to come, with this awful weather.*
OPPOSITE: **likely**

unlimited /ʌn'lɪmɪtɪd/ *adjective*
as much as you want ➤ *The rail ticket allows students to have unlimited travel for a month.*
OPPOSITE: **limited**

unlit /ʌn'lɪt/ *adjective*
dark because there are no lights on ➤ *a small, unlit road*

unload /ʌn'ləʊd/ *verb*
to take goods off a vehicle ➤ *Two men unloaded the lorry*
OPPOSITE: **load**

unlock /ʌn'lɒk/ *verb*
to open something with a key ➤ *She unlocked the door and went in.*
OPPOSITE: **lock**

unlucky /ʌn'lʌkɪ/ *adjective* (**unluckier, unluckiest**)
not having or giving good luck; not lucky ➤ *Some people think that 13 is an unlucky number.* ➤ *I was unlucky – I missed the bus by just one minute.*

unmarried /ʌn'mærɪd/ *adjective*
not married ➤ *an unmarried man*
SAME MEANING: **single**

unmistakable /ʌnmɪ'steɪkəbəl/ *adjective*
easy to recognize ➤ *the unmistakable smell of gas*

unnatural /ʌn'nætʃərəl/ *adjective*
not what is usual, expected, or normal; not natural ➤ *It's unnatural for a child to be so quiet.*

unnecessary /ʌn'nesəsərɪ/ *adjective*
not needed ➤ *Don't bring any unnecessary luggage.*
OPPOSITE: **necessary**

unoccupied /ʌn'ɒkjʊpaɪd/ *adjective*
not having anyone in it or using it ➤ *The top floor of the house was completely unoccupied.*
OPPOSITE: **occupied**

unofficial /ʌnə'fɪʃəl/ *adjective*
not accepted or approved by anyone in authority ➤ *There were unofficial reports that the president was seriously ill. (adverb: **unofficially**)*
OPPOSITE: **official**

unpack /ʌn'pæk/ *verb*
to take things out of a case or box ➤ *I'm just going to unpack my case.* ➤ *He unpacked and had a bath.*
OPPOSITE: **pack**

unpaid /ʌn'peɪd/ *adjective*
1 working without receiving any money ➤ *We have several unpaid helpers at the school.*
2 (used about bills or debts) not paid

unpleasant /ʌn'plezənt/ *adjective*
not nice or enjoyable ➤ *an unpleasant smell (adverb: **unpleasantly**)*
OPPOSITE: **pleasant**

unplug /ʌn'plʌg/ *verb* (*present participle **unplugging**, past **unplugged**)*
to take the PLUG on a piece of electrical equipment out of the SOCKET ➤ *Don't forget to unplug the TV before you come to bed.*

unpopular /ʌn'pɒpjʊləʳ/ *adjective*
not liked by many people
OPPOSITE: **popular**

unrealistic /ʌnrɪə'lɪstɪk/ *adjective*
not basing your ideas on what is really likely to happen or what someone is really able to do ➤ *A lot of young people have unrealistic expectations about marriage.*
OPPOSITE: **realistic**

unreasonable /ʌn'riːzənəbəl/
adjective
not fair or not acceptable ▶ *Do you think I'm being unreasonable?*
▶ *unreasonable demands*
OPPOSITE: **reasonable**

unreliable /ˌʌnrɪ'laɪəbəl/ *adjective*
that you cannot trust or depend on
▶ *I wouldn't ask him to help – he's very unreliable.*
OPPOSITE: **reliable**

unruly /ʌn'ruːlɪ/ *adjective*
behaving in an uncontrolled or violent way ▶ *an unruly crowd*

unsafe /ʌn'seɪf/ *adjective*
dangerous; not safe

unsatisfactory /ˌʌnsætɪs'fæktərɪ/
adjective
not good enough ▶ *unsatisfactory work*
OPPOSITE: **satisfactory**

unscrew /ʌn'skruː/ *verb*
to open or undo something by twisting it ▶ *I unscrewed the top of the jar.*

unselfish /ʌn'selfɪʃ/ *adjective*
not caring about your own advantage but thinking about other people's needs
OPPOSITE: **selfish**

unsettled /ʌn'setld/ *adjective*
1 (used about the weather) wet and changing often ▶ *The forecast is for more unsettled weather.*
OPPOSITE: **settled**
2 feeling worried, nervous, or unsure ▶ *Children often feel unsettled by divorce.*

unsettling /ʌn'setlɪŋ/ *adjective*
making you feel nervous, worried, or unsure ▶ *an unsettling experience*

unsophisticated /ˌʌnsə'fɪstɪkeɪtɪd/
adjective
1 simple and not modern ▶ *Farmers were still using unsophisticated methods.*

2 knowing little about modern ideas and fashions ▶ *unsophisticated audiences*

unstable /ʌn'steɪbəl/ *adjective*
1 likely to change suddenly and cause problems ▶ *The country is unstable and tourists have been warned not to go there.*
2 likely to fall over ▶ *an unstable wall*
OPPOSITE: (**1** and **2**): **stable**

unsteady /ʌn'stedɪ/ *adjective*
(**unsteadier, unsteadiest**)
shaking and moving, and not staying in place; not steady ▶ *This chair's very unsteady; will you hold it while I stand on it? (adverb: **unsteadily**)*

unsuccessful /ˌʌnsək'sesfəl/ *adjective*
not having the result you aimed for ▶ *an unsuccessful attempt to rescue a cat*
OPPOSITE: **successful**

unsuitable /ʌn'suːtəbəl/ *adjective*
not good for a particular purpose
▶ *The film is quite unsuitable for children.*
OPPOSITE: **suitable**

unsure /ʌn'ʃʊəʳ/ *adjective*
not certain or confident about something ▶ *At first, he was unsure **about** accepting the job.*
OPPOSITE: **sure**

unsympathetic /ˌʌnsɪmpə'θetɪk/
adjective
not feeling sorry for someone when something bad happens to them
OPPOSITE: **sympathetic**

untidy /ʌn'taɪdɪ/ *adjective* (**untidier, untidiest**)
in disorder; not neat ▶ *Her room was ever so untidy – there were clothes all over the floor.*
OPPOSITE: **tidy**

untie /ʌn'taɪ/ *verb* (present participle **untying**, past **untied**)
to undo a piece of string, a knot, etc.
▶ *She untied the parcel and looked inside.*
OPPOSITE: **tie**

U

until /ən'tɪl/ *(also till) preposition, conjunction*
up to the time when something happens ▶ *We can't go until Monday.* ▶ *I couldn't sew until I was twelve.*

untrue /ʌn'truː/ *adjective*
not correct or real
OPPOSITE: **true**

unused /ʌn'juːzd/ *adjective*
not used ▶ *The unused bottles were returned to the shop.*

unusual /ʌn'juːʒʊəl/ *adjective*
not usual; strange ▶ *an unusual hat* (adverb: **unusually**)

unveil /ʌn'veɪl/ *verb*
to officially let people know about something that was a secret ▶ *BMW will unveil their latest car at the Motor Show.*

unwell /ʌn'wel/ *adjective*
not well; ill ▶ *He has been unwell since Sunday.*

unwilling /ʌn'wɪlɪŋ/ *adjective*
not willing ▶ *He seemed unwilling to come with us.* (adverb: **unwillingly**)

unwind /ʌn'waɪnd/ *verb (past unwound* /ʌn'waʊnd/)
1 to become calm, not anxious or busy ▶ *A hot bath helps you to unwind at the end of the day.*
2 to undo something that has been wound ▶ *She unwound the wool from the ball.*

unwise /ʌn'waɪz/ *adjective*
not reasonable or wise ▶ *It's unwise to go out in this cold weather.*

unwound /ʌn'waʊnd/
the PAST TENSE and PAST PARTICIPLE of the verb **unwind**

unwrap /ʌn'ræp/ *verb (present participle **unwrapping**, past **unwrapped**)*
to take the covering off a parcel ▶ *She unwrapped her present in great excitement.*
OPPOSITE: **wrap**

up¹ /ʌp/ *adverb, preposition, adjective*
1 to or in a higher place away from the ground ▶ *She climbed up the tree.* ▶ *The village is high up in the hills.*
2 showing increase ▶ *Spending on holidays is up* (=people are spending more on holidays).
OPPOSITE: (1 and 2): **down**
3 out of bed ▶ *Are you up yet?*
4 near or towards a person or thing ▶ *He came up to me and asked my name.*
5 completely finished, or so as to be completely finished ▶ *Eat up your potatoes.*
6 up and down in one direction and then in the opposite direction ▶ *She walked up and down while she was waiting.*
7 up the road along the road ▶ *He ran up the road.* ▶ *They live just up the road.*
8 up to as much or as many as ▶ *You can earn up to £25,000 a year.* ▶ *The room can hold up to 200 people.*
9 up to, up until until ▶ *I've never thought about it up to now.* ▶ *She lived at home right up until she got married.*
10 be up to something (a) to be secretly busy doing something bad ▶ *I think he's up to something.* (b) to be strong enough or good enough to do something ▶ *Are you up to a walk along the beach?*
11 What's up? What's the matter?

up² *verb (present participle **upping**, past **upped**)*
to increase an amount or a level ▶ *They've just upped her pay.*

upbringing /'ʌp,brɪŋɪŋ/ *noun*
the way your parents treated you when you were a child, and the things they taught you ▶ *I had a strict, religious upbringing.*

update¹ /ʌp'deɪt/ *verb (present participle **updating**, past **updated**)* to add new parts or the most recent information to something so that it stays modern ▶ *We need to update our computers every 12 months.*

update² /'ʌpdeɪt/ *noun*
the most recent news about something ▶ *a news update from the BBC*

upfront /ʌp'frʌnt/ *adjective*
speaking honestly about something and not trying to keep anything secret ▶ *He's very ambitious, but at least he's upfront about it.*

upgrade /ʌp'greɪd/ *verb (present participle **upgrading**, past **upgraded**)*
to change something so that it is better or more modern ▶ *We need to upgrade our computer system.*

upheaval /ʌp'hiːvəl/ *noun*
a very big change that causes problems ▶ *the upheaval of moving house*

upheld /ʌp'held/
the PAST TENSE and PAST PARTICIPLE of the verb **uphold**

uphill /ʌp'hɪl/ *adverb*
going towards the top of a hill ▶ *walking uphill*
OPPOSITE: **downhill**

uphold /ʌp'həʊld/ *verb (past **uphold** /-'held/)*
to support a law or decision and make sure it continues to exist ▶ *We must uphold the rights of all people.*

uplifting /ʌp'lɪftɪŋ/ *adjective*
making you feel happy ▶ *an uplifting piece of music*

upon /ə'pɒn/ *preposition*
on ▶ *The village stands upon a hill.*

upper /'ʌpə/ *adjective*
higher ▶ *the upper part of the body*

upper class /ʌpə 'klɑːs/ *noun*
the upper class the group of people who belong to the highest social class

upright /'ʌpraɪt/ *adjective*
straight up ▶ *Put the bottle upright, not on its side.*

uprising /'ʌpˌraɪzɪŋ/ *noun*
a situation in which a large group of people fight against the people who have power in their country, especially in order to try to change the government ▶ *the Hungarian uprising of 1956*

uproar /'ʌp-rɔː/ *noun*
1 *(no plural)* a lot of shouting and noise ▶ *The school was in uproar.*
2 angry protest about something that has just been announced ▶ *The decision is likely to cause an uproar.*

uproot /ʌp'ruːt/ *verb*
1 to make someone leave their home and move to a new place ▶ *The war has uprooted whole families.*
2 to pull a plant and its roots out of the ground

upset¹ /ʌp'set/ *adjective*
feeling unhappy or anxious about something ▶ *She was upset because he wouldn't talk to her.*

upset² *verb (present participle **upsetting**, past **upset**)*
1 to knock something over ▶ *I upset the soup all over the table.*
2 to make someone unhappy or anxious ▶ *It upset me when he told me how ill she was.* ▶ *He upset me when he laughed at my idea.*
3 to spoil something that was planned ▶ *The rain upset our plans for a barbecue.*

upside down /ʌpsaɪd 'daʊn/ *adverb*
in a position with the top facing down and the bottom facing up

upstairs /ʌp'steəz/ *adjective, adverb*
on an upper floor in a building, or going towards the upper floor ▶ *We could hear a party in the flat upstairs.* ▶ *"Where is she?" "Upstairs."* ▶ *The children watched from an upstairs window.*
OPPOSITE: **downstairs**

U

up-to-date /ˌʌp tə ˈdeɪt/ *adjective*
modern and new

upwards /ˈʌpwədz/ *adverb*
going, looking, or facing up ➤ *The
feather floated gently upwards.* ➤ *I
pointed upwards towards his window.*
OPPOSITE: **downwards**

uranium /jʊˈreɪniəm/ *noun (no
plural)*
a RADIOACTIVE metal used to produce
NUCLEAR power and weapons

urban /ˈɜːbən/ *adjective*
of a town or city ➤ *Most people live in
urban areas.*

urge¹ /ɜːdʒ/ *verb (present participle
urging, past **urged**)*
to try very hard to persuade someone
to do something ➤ *He urged her to
rest.*

urge² *noun*
a strong wish ➤ *She suddenly had an
urge to go back to New York.*

urgency /ˈɜːdʒənsɪ/ *noun (no plural)*
the state of being urgent ➤ *The
minister stressed the urgency of the
situation.*

urgent /ˈɜːdʒənt/ *adjective*
needing to be done without delay;
very important ➤ *I must post this
letter; it's very urgent.* (adverb:
urgently)

us /əs; *strong* ʌs/ *pronoun*
the person who is speaking and some
other person or people, used in
sentences like this: *The teacher told
us (=me and the other students) to
be quiet.* ➤ *Please give the book back
to us.*

usable /ˈjuːzəbəl/ *adjective*
available or in a good enough
condition for you to use ➤ *The PC
comes with 128KB of usable memory.*

usage /ˈjuːsɪdʒ/ *noun (no plural)*
1 the way that words are used in a
language ➤ *modern English usage*
2 the amount of something that is

used, or the way it is used ➤ *Drug
usage is increasing.*

use¹ /juːz/ *verb (present participle
using, past **used**)*
1 to do something with something or
put it into action for a purpose ➤ *Do
you know how to use a computer?*
➤ *What do you use this thing **for**?*
2 **use something up** to use
something until it has all gone ➤ *Have
you used all the toothpaste up?*

use² /juːs/ *noun*
a purpose; being used; using ➤ *What's
the use of waiting for her?* ➤ *It's no
use waiting for her.* ➤ *Do you approve
of the use of guns by the police?*
➤ *The machine is ready for use.* ➤ *I
was given the use **of** their swimming
pool.*

used /juːzd/ *adjective*
(used about cars and machines) not
new ➤ *used cars*

used to¹ /ˈjuːst tuː/ *adjective*
knowing what something or someone
is like, so that it does not seem
strange, unusual, or difficult ➤ *He's
used to traffic because he often
drives in town.* ➤ *He's used to driving
in town.* ➤ *I didn't like the new school
at first, but I got used to it.*

used to² *verb*
used with another verb to show that
something was done often in the
past, but is not done now ➤ *He used
to play football every Saturday when
he was young.* ➤ *My father didn't use
to smoke, but now he does.*

> The NEGATIVE of **used to** is **used
> not to** or **didn't use to**: *I used not
> to like fish.* ➤ *I didn't use to like
> fish.* The question form of **used to**
> is **Did you/he/she use to ...?**:
> *Did you use to go there often?*

useful /ˈjuːsfəl/ *adjective*
having a good purpose; helpful
➤ *That's a useful knife.* (adverb:
usefully)

useless /'juːsləs/ *adjective*
having no good purpose ➤ *This knife is useless – the handle's broken!* (adverb: **uselessly**)

user /'juːzəʳ/ *noun*
a person who uses something, especially a product or service ➤ *telephone users*

user-friendly /juːzə 'frendlɪ/ *adjective*
designed to be easy for people to use ➤ *Manufacturers should make their equipment more user-friendly.*

usual /'juːʒʊəl/ *adjective*
1 done or happening most often, or as expected ➤ *We had lunch at our usual table by the window.*
2 as usual as is common or has happened many times before ➤ *As usual, he arrived late.*

usually /'juːʒʊəlɪ/ *adverb*
generally ➤ *I'm usually at school early, but today I was late.*

utensil /juːˈtensəl/ *noun*
a tool or an object used in the kitchen ➤ *cooking utensils*

utmost /'ʌtməʊst/ *adjective, noun*
1 the most possible ➤ *with her utmost strength*
2 do your utmost to make the greatest possible effort ➤ *They did their utmost to prevent the disease spreading.*

utter¹ /'ʌtəʳ/ *verb*
to say ➤ *He looked at me without uttering a word.*

utter² *adjective*
complete ➤ *We watched in utter amazement.* (adverb: **utterly**)

U-turn /'juː tɜːn/ *noun*
1 the action of turning your car around in the road and going back in the direction you came from ➤ *You can't do a U-turn on the motorway!*
2 the act of changing a previous decision and doing something

completely different ➤ *The government has done a complete U-turn on economic policy.*

Vv

v. /viː, ˈvɜːsəs/ *preposition*
a short way of writing and saying the word **versus**

vacancy /'veɪkənsɪ/ *noun (plural **vacancies**)*
1 a room in a hotel or guesthouse that is not being used ➤ *No vacancies.*
2 an unfilled job ➤ *a vacancy for a driver*

vacant /'veɪkənt/ *adjective*
1 (used about a seat, room, or house) not being used or lived in ➤ *We looked all over town for a vacant room.* ➤ *The toilet is vacant now.*
2 (used about a job) not filled

vacation /vəˈkeɪʃən/ *noun*
a holiday from school or university ➤ *She worked in France during the long vacation.*

vaccinate /'væksɪneɪt/ *verb (present participle **vaccinating**, past **vaccinated**)*
to put a substance into someone's body as a protection against a disease

vaccination /ˌvæksɪˈneɪʃən/ *noun*
a substance put into someone's body as a protection against a disease

vaccine /'væksiːn/ *noun*
a substance given to people to stop them getting a disease, which contains a very small amount of the GERM that causes the disease ➤ *the measles vaccine*

vacuum¹ /'vækjʊm/ *noun*
a space with no air in it

V

vacuum² *verb*
to clean a floor with a VACUUM CLEANER
➤ *Have you vacuumed the sitting room yet?*
SAME MEANING: **hoover**

vacuum cleaner /'vækjʊm ˌkliːnəʳ/ *noun*
a machine which cleans the floor by sucking up dirt
SAME MEANING: **Hoover**

vacuum flask /'vækjʊm ˌflɑːsk/ (also **flask**) *noun*
a container used to keep drinks either hot or cold

vague /veɪg/ *adjective*
not clear in your mind ➤ *I have a vague idea where the house is.*
(adverb: **vaguely**)

vain /veɪn/ *adjective*
too proud of yourself, especially of what you look like ➤ *She's very vain – she's always looking at herself in the mirror.*

valid /'vælɪd/ *adjective*
1 able to be used and officially correct ➤ *a valid passport*
2 reasonable and likely to be right ➤ *I can think of many valid reasons not to talk to her again.*

valley /'vælɪ/ *noun*
the land lying between two lines of hills or mountains, often with a river running through it

valuable /'væljʊəbəl/ *adjective*
1 worth a lot of money ➤ *a valuable diamond*
2 very useful ➤ *valuable advice*

valuables /'væljʊəbəlz/ *plural noun*
things that you own that are worth a lot of money, such as jewellery or cameras

value¹ /'væljuː/ *noun*
the amount that something is worth
➤ *What is the value of your house?*
➤ *Your advice has been of great value.*

value² *verb (present participle* **valuing**, *past* **valued**)
1 to think that something is worth a lot ➤ *I really value your advice.*
2 to say how much something is worth ➤ *He valued the ring at £350.*

valve /vælv/ *noun*
part of a pipe which opens and shuts in order to control the flow of liquid, air, or gas passing through it ➤ *a new valve for my bicycle tyre*

vampire /'væmpaɪəʳ/ *noun*
a person in stories who bites people's necks and sucks their blood

van /væn/ *noun*
a road vehicle smaller than a lorry, used for carrying goods

vandal /'vændl/ *noun*
a person who intentionally damages or destroys public property

vandalism /'vændəlɪzəm/ *noun (no plural)*
intentional damage to and destruction of public property

vandalize /'vændəlaɪz/ *verb (present participle* **vandalizing**, *past* **vandalized**)
to damage or destroy a piece of public property intentionally ➤ *All the public telephones round here have been vandalized.*

vanilla /və'nɪlə/ *noun (no plural)*
a special taste added to some sweet foods ➤ *vanilla ice cream*

vanish /'vænɪʃ/ *verb*
to go away and not be seen any more
➤ *When I looked again, he'd vanished.*

vanity /'vænətɪ/ *noun (no plural)*
being too proud of your appearance or your abilities

vapour /'veɪpəʳ/ *noun (no plural)*
a lot of small drops of liquid in the air, for example in the form of clouds, mist, or steam

variable /'veərɪəbəl/ *adjective*
likely to change often ➤ *The weather is quite variable at this time of year.*

variant /'veəriənt/ *noun*
something that is slightly different from the usual form ▶ *a spelling variant*

variation /,veəri'eiʃən/ *noun*
a change or difference ▶ *We noticed huge price variations between different shops.* ▶ *The variation in results might be due to a fault in the experiment.*

varied /'veərid/ *adjective*
consisting of many different types of thing, person, etc. ▶ *Try to eat a varied diet.*

variety /və'raiəti/ *noun*
1 (no plural) difference ▶ *You need variety in your life.*
2 a variety of a group containing different sorts of the same thing ▶ *These shirts come in a variety of colours.*
3 (plural **varieties**) a type which is different from others in the same group ▶ *different varieties of banana*
4 (no plural) theatre or television amusement which includes singing, dancing, jokes, and acts of skill ▶ *a variety show*

various /'veəriəs/ *adjective*
different ▶ *There are various colours to choose from; which do you like best?*

varnish¹ /'vɑːniʃ/ *noun* (plural **varnishes**)
a liquid that is put onto wood to give it a hard, shining surface

varnish² *verb*
to put a special liquid on wood to give it a hard, shining surface

vary /'veəri/ *verb* (past **varied**)
to change ▶ *The weather varies from day to day.*

vase /vɑːz/ *noun*
a pot for putting cut flowers in

vast /vɑːst/ *adjective*
very big ▶ *a vast difference between temperatures in the north and in the south*
SAME MEANING: **huge, enormous**

vat /væt/ *noun*
a very large container for holding liquids ▶ *a vat of wine*

vault /vɔːlt/ *noun*
an underground room in which the bodies of the dead are placed, or in which valuable things are stored

VCR /,viː siː 'ɑːʳ/ *(also videorecorder) noun*
a VIDEO CASSETTE RECORDER; a machine that you use to record television broadcasts and play them back later. You can also use it to play VIDEOS which you have bought or hired

VDU /,viː diː 'juː/ *noun*
a VISUAL DISPLAY UNIT; a machine that looks like a television, and shows information from a computer or a WORD PROCESSOR

've /v, əv/ *verb*
have ▶ *I've got a letter for you.* ▶ *We've finished.*

veal /viːl/ *noun* (no plural)
meat from a very young cow

veer /viəʳ/ *verb*
to change direction suddenly ▶ *The car veered off the road and crashed.*

vegan /'viːgən/ *noun*
someone who does not eat anything that is produced from animals, including milk, cheese, or eggs, usually because they believe that it is wrong to kill animals for food

vegetable /'vedʒtəbəl/ *noun*
a plant such as a carrot, cabbage, or potato, which is grown in order to be eaten

vegetarian /,vedʒi'teəriən/ *noun, adjective*
a person who does not eat meat or fish, usually because they believe that it is wrong to kill animals for food

V

vegetation /ˌvedʒɪˈteɪʃən/ noun (no plural)
the plants, flowers, trees, etc. that grow in a particular area ➤ dense vegetation

vehicle /ˈviːəkəl/ noun
something such as a bicycle, car, or bus, which carries people or goods

veil /veɪl/ noun
a covering for a woman's head and face ➤ In many Muslim countries, the women wear veils.

vein /veɪn/ noun
one of the tubes in your body that carry blood to your heart

Velcro /ˈvelkrəʊ/ noun trademark (no plural)
a material used for fastening shoes, clothes, etc., made from two special pieces of cloth that stick to each other

velvet /ˈvelvɪt/ noun (no plural)
a type of cloth with a soft surface

vendetta /venˈdetə/ noun
a serious argument between people, which continues for a long time and often involves them trying to harm each other ➤ They were involved in a spiteful vendetta against their neighbours.

vengeance /ˈvendʒəns/ noun (no plural)
punishment given to someone for harm they have done to you or your family

venison /ˈvenɪzən/ noun (no plural)
the meat of a DEER

venom /ˈvenəm/ noun (no plural)
1 poison produced by some snakes, insects, etc.
2 great anger or hatred ➤ a speech full of venom

venomous /ˈvenəməs/ adjective
1 (used about snakes, insects, etc.) producing poison ➤ a venomous spider
2 full of anger or hatred ➤ a venomous look

vent¹ /vent/ noun
a hole in something that lets air in and lets smoke out

vent² verb
(used about people who want to get rid of their anger, FRUSTRATION, etc.) to do something that shows how angry, FRUSTRATED, etc. you feel

ventilate /ˈventɪleɪt/ verb
(present participle **ventilating**, past **ventilated**)
to allow fresh air into a room or building

venture¹ /ˈventʃəʳ/ noun
a new business activity that might earn money but involves taking risks ➤ an exciting new business venture

venture² verb
(present participle **venturing**, past **ventured**)
to go somewhere or do something that may involve risks because you are not sure what will happen ➤ He was the first member of his family to venture **into** politics.

venue /ˈvenjuː/ noun
a place where a concert, sports game, etc. takes place ➤ a popular jazz venue

verandah /vəˈrændə/ noun
a roofed area built onto a house, with no outside wall

verb /vɜːb/ noun
a word that tells you what someone or something does or is. In the sentence "She wrote a letter", "wrote" is a verb

verbal /ˈvɜːbəl/ adjective
spoken rather than written ➤ He received a verbal warning.

verdict /ˈvɜːdɪkt/ noun
a decision made by a law court ➤ What's the verdict? Is he guilty or not guilty?

verge /vɜ:dʒ/ noun
the piece of land along the side of a road in a country area, usually covered with grass

versatile /'vɜ:sətaɪl/ adjective
having many different skills or uses
▶ a versatile tool ▶ a versatile actor

verse /vɜ:s/ noun
1 (no plural) lines of writing which have a RHYTHM (=musical beat) and often a RHYME (=the words at the end of the lines sound alike)
2 a set of lines which forms one part of a poem or song

version /'vɜːʃən/ noun
a story told by one person compared with the same story told by another
▶ I have heard two different versions of the accident.

versus /'vɜːsəs/ preposition
against a person or team in a sports match ▶ Are you going to watch the football match? It's England versus Germany.

vertical /'vɜ:tɪkəl/ adjective
standing straight up; upright ▶ a vertical line
COMPARE: **horizontal**

vertigo /'vɜ:tɪgəʊ/ noun (no plural)
the DIZZY feeling that is caused by looking down from a very high place
▶ Do you suffer from vertigo?

very /'verɪ/ adverb
1 used to make another word stronger ▶ It's very hot in this room.
▶ I'm very well, thank you. ▶ very carefully
COMPARE: **quite**
2 not very used to make another word very weak. For example, if you say that someone is "not very big", you mean that they are rather small ▶ They didn't stay very long (=they only stayed a short time).

vessel /'vesəl/ noun
1 a ship or large boat
2 a container for keeping liquids in

vest /vest/ noun
a piece of clothing that you wear next to your skin and under other clothes on the upper part of your body

vet /vet/ noun
a doctor for animals

veteran /'vetərən/ noun
1 a person who was a soldier, sailor, etc. in a war
2 a person who has had a lot of experience of doing something
▶ veteran Hollywood entertainer Bob Hope

veto¹ /'vi:təʊ/ verb (present participle **vetoing**, past **vetoed**)
to officially refuse to allow something to happen, especially something that other people or organizations have agreed ▶ Britain and the US vetoed the proposal.

veto² noun (plural **vetoes**)
the act of officially refusing to allow something to happen ▶ France has threatened to use its veto.

via /'vaɪə/ preposition
travelling through a place ▶ I travelled from London to Birmingham via Oxford.

viaduct /'vaɪədʌkt/ noun
a long, high bridge across a valley

vibrant /'vaɪbrənt/ adjective
1 full of excitement and energy ▶ New York is a very vibrant city.
2 (used about colours) very bright and attractive ▶ vibrant reds and yellows

vibrate /vaɪ'breɪt/ verb (present participle **vibrating**, past **vibrated**)
to shake quickly and many times
▶ The music was so loud, the whole house was vibrating.

vibration /vaɪ'breɪʃən/ noun
a continuous, slight, shaky movement
▶ If you touch the machine, you'll feel the vibration.

V

vicar /'vɪkəʳ/ *noun*
a Christian priest who looks after one church
COMPARE: **bishop**

vice /vaɪs/ *noun*
a bad habit or something bad about someone's character ► *Smoking is my only vice.*

vice- /vaɪs/
a word used with a title, to mean that the person is next below the person with the title. For example, the **vice-president** is the next person in importance below the president ► *the American vice-president*

vice versa /ˌvaɪs 'vɜːsə/ *adverb*
used to talk about the opposite of a situation you have just described ► *The boys like films that don't appeal to the girls, and vice versa.*

vicinity /vɪ'sɪnəti/ *noun (no plural)*
the area surrounding a place ► *The market is in the vicinity of (=near) the school.*

vicious /'vɪʃəs/ *adjective*
cruel and showing the desire to hurt people ► *He gave the dog a vicious kick.*

victim /'vɪktɪm/ *noun*
a person who suffers from an illness or action ► *She was the victim of a road accident.*

victorious /vɪk'tɔːriəs/ *adjective*
winning ► *the victorious team*

victory /'vɪktəri/ *noun (plural victories)*
an act of winning a war, a fight, or a game ► *The party is hoping for victory in the next election.*
OPPOSITE: **defeat**

video¹ /'vɪdiəʊ/ *noun*
1 a film which you can show at home, on a television ► *Can I have a video for my birthday?* ► *Where's the video of the wedding?* ► *We've got the royal wedding on video.*

2 (*also* **videorecorder**) a machine that you use to record television broadcasts and play them back later. You can also use it to play videos which you have bought or hired.
► *Set the video to go on at 8 o'clock.*

video² (*also* **videotape**) *verb (present participle* **videoing**, *past* **videoed**)
to record a television programme or a real event on a special film that you can see later on your television set
► *I haven't got time to watch the film tonight, but I'm going to video it.*

video cassette /'vɪdiəʊ kə'set/ *noun*
a special film in a plastic case, which you can watch at home on your VIDEO

video game /'vɪdiəʊ ɡeɪm/ *noun*
a game which you play by pushing buttons that move parts of the special pictures on your television

videorecorder /'vɪdiəʊrɪˌkɔːdəʳ/ (*also* **video, VCR**) *noun*
a machine that you use to record television broadcasts and play them back later. You can also use it to play VIDEOS which you have bought or hired.

video shop /'vɪdiəʊ ʃɒp/ *noun*
a shop where you can hire VIDEOS

videotape¹ /'vɪdiəʊˌteɪp/ *noun*
a long, narrow band of material on which television pictures and sound can be recorded

videotape² (*also* **video**) *verb (present participle* **videotaping**, *past* **videotaped**)
to record a television broadcast or a real event on a special film that you can see later on your television set

view /vjuː/ *noun*
1 the ability to see something from a particular place ► *The factory spoilt my view of the mountain.*
2 the things that you can see from a particular place ► *The view from the top of the hill was lovely.*

3 an opinion ▶ *What's your view on school punishments?*

viewer /'vjuːəʳ/ *noun*
a person who watches television

vigil /'vɪdʒɪl/ *noun*
a situation in which people stand or sit quietly somewhere, especially in order to protest about something or to stay with someone who is ill ▶ *A crowd of people held a vigil outside the embassy.*

vigilant /'vɪdʒɪlənt/ *adjective*
watching carefully what happens, so that you notice anything dangerous or illegal ▶ *People should remain vigilant at all times and report any suspicious packages to the police.*

vigorous /'vɪɡərəs/ *adjective*
very active or strong ▶ *The vigorous, young plants grew fast.*

vile /vaɪl/ *adjective*
very unpleasant ▶ *That's a vile colour!*

villa /'vɪlə/ *noun*
a pleasant house in Spain, France, Italy, etc., where people go for a holiday

village /'vɪlɪdʒ/ *noun*
a small place in a country area, where people live, not so large as a town

villager /'vɪlɪdʒəʳ/ *noun*
a person who lives in a village

villain /'vɪlən/ *noun*
1 the chief bad character in a play or film
2 a bad person; a criminal

vindictive /vɪn'dɪktɪv/ *adjective*
deliberately cruel and unfair ▶ *Sometimes, she can be very vindictive.*

vine /vaɪn/ *noun*
a plant with climbing stems, especially one that produces the fruit from which wine is made

vinegar /'vɪnɪɡəʳ/ *noun (no plural)*
a very sour liquid used in preparing food

vineyard /'vɪnjɑːd/ *noun*
a piece of land where vines are grown for producing wine

vintage¹ /'vɪntɪdʒ/ *adjective*
1 (used about wine) of good quality and made in a particular year
2 (used about cars) made in the early part of the 20th century
3 used to emphasize that something is one of the best of its kind ▶ *vintage recordings*

vintage² *noun*
a particular year in which a wine is made

vinyl /'vaɪnəl/ *noun (no plural)*
a type of strong plastic

viola /vɪ'əʊlə/ *noun*
a wooden musical instrument, shaped like a VIOLIN but larger, and with a lower sound

violence /'vaɪələns/ *noun (no plural)*
1 the use of force to hurt someone ▶ *There is a lot of violence on television these days.*
2 very great force ▶ *the violence of the storm* ▶ *the violence of her feelings*

violent /'vaɪələnt/ *adjective*
1 using force to hurt someone ▶ *a violent man who attacked his next-door neighbour*
2 having great force ▶ *a violent storm*

violet¹ /'vaɪələt/ *noun*
1 a small flower with a sweet smell
2 *(no plural)* the colour of the violet, which is a mixture of blue and red

violet² *adjective*
having a colour which is a mixture of blue and red

violin /ˌvaɪə'lɪn/ *noun*
a musical instrument with four strings, played with a BOW (=threads tightly stretched on a long, thin piece of wood which are drawn across the strings to make a sound)

violinist /ˌvaɪə'lɪnɪst/ *noun*
a person who plays the violin

VIP /ˌviː aɪ ˈpiː/ *noun*
a Very Important Person; a person who receives special treatment because they are famous or powerful

viper /ˈvaɪpər/ *noun*
a small, poisonous snake

virgin[1] /ˈvɜːdʒɪn/ *noun*
a person who has never had sex

virgin[2] *adjective*
(used about land, forests, etc.) still in a natural condition and not used or spoiled by people ➤ *300 acres of virgin forest*

virile /ˈvɪraɪl/ *adjective*
(used about men) strong in a sexually attractive way

virtual /ˈvɜːtʃuəl/ *adjective*
1 very close to being something ➤ *Even a virtual beginner can use this computer.*
2 using virtual reality ➤ *a virtual library*

virtually /ˈvɜːtʃuəli/ *adverb*
almost completely ➤ *The town was virtually empty.*

virtual reality /ˌvɜːtʃuəl riˈæləti/ *noun (no plural)*
pictures and sounds created by a computer that make you feel as though you are in a real situation or place

virtue /ˈvɜːtjuː/ *noun*
a good quality of someone's character ➤ *Honesty is a great virtue.*

virtuoso /ˌvɜːtʃuˈəʊsəʊ/ *noun*
a person who is extremely skilful at doing something, especially at playing a musical instrument ➤ *a piano virtuoso*

virtuous /ˈvɜːtʃuəs/ *adjective*
behaving in a way that is morally good or kind ➤ *a decent, virtuous man*

virus /ˈvaɪrəs/ *noun (plural* **viruses***)*
a living thing, even smaller than bacteria, which causes infectious disease

visa /ˈviːzə/ *noun*
an official mark put into a PASSPORT, giving a person permission to enter, pass through, or leave a particular country ➤ *Do Americans need visas to visit Britain?*

visibility /ˌvɪzəˈbɪləti/ *noun (no plural)*
the distance that you can see, especially when this is affected by the weather conditions ➤ *There is poor visibility on many roads due to heavy fog.*

visible /ˈvɪzəbəl/ *adjective*
able to be seen ➤ *The smoke from the fire was visible from the road.*
OPPOSITE: **invisible**

vision /ˈvɪʒən/ *noun*
1 (no plural) sight ➤ *She has extremely good vision.*
2 something that you imagine might happen one day ➤ *He had a vision of himself as a rich businessman.*

visit[1] /ˈvɪzɪt/ *verb*
to go and see a person or place ➤ *We visited our friends in town.*

visit[2] *noun*
an act of visiting a person or place ➤ *We had a visit from your teacher.* ➤ *She paid us a visit.* ➤ *a visit to the doctor*

visitor /ˈvɪzɪtər/ *noun*
someone who visits a person or place

visor /ˈvaɪzər/ *noun*
the front part of a HELMET (=hard hat) that comes down in front of your eyes to protect them

visual /ˈvɪʒuəl/ *adjective*
1 relating to seeing or your ability to see ➤ *The movie has a strong visual impact.*
2 the visual arts arts such as painting, not music or literature (adverb: **visually**)

visual aid /ˌvɪʒuəl ˈeɪd/ *noun*
something such as a picture, film, etc. that is used to help people learn

visualize /ˈvɪʒuəlaɪz/ *verb (present participle* **visualizing**, *past* **visualized***)*
to imagine something ▶ *I tried to visualize myself winning the race.*

vital /ˈvaɪtl/ *adjective*
necessary for life; very important ▶ *a vital piece of information*

vitamin /ˈvɪtəmɪn/ *noun*
a chemical substance in certain foods, which is important for growth and good health ▶ *Oranges contain vitamin C.*

vivacious /vɪˈveɪʃəs/ *adjective*
having a lot of energy and enjoying life ▶ *a vivacious young woman*

vivid /ˈvɪvɪd/ *adjective*
1 bright or strong in colour ▶ *vivid red hair*
2 producing clear pictures in your mind ▶ *a vivid description of the accident*

vocabulary /vəˈkæbjʊləri/ *noun*
1 *(no plural)* words ▶ *After we'd done the grammar exercise, we learnt some new vocabulary.*
2 *(plural* **vocabularies***)* all the words you know in a language ▶ *He has a very large vocabulary (=he knows a lot of words).*

vocal /ˈvəʊkəl/ *adjective*
speaking publicly about your opinions in a way that makes a lot of people notice you ▶ *Environmental groups have become increasingly vocal.*

vocalist /ˈvəʊkəlɪst/ *noun*
a person who sings with a group playing POP music ▶ *She was a vocalist in a successful band.*

vocals /ˈvəʊkəlz/ *plural noun*
the part of a piece of music that is sung rather than played on an instrument ▶ *The song features Elton John on vocals.*

vocation /vəʊˈkeɪʃən/ *noun*
the feeling that the purpose of your life is to do a particular kind of work, especially work that involves helping people ▶ *He discovered his vocation as a nurse in a large hospital.*

vocational /vəʊˈkeɪʃənəl/ *adjective*
concerned with teaching or learning the skills needed to do a job ▶ *vocational training*

vodka /ˈvɒdkə/ *noun*
1 *(no plural)* a strong alcoholic drink from Russia that has no colour
2 a glass of this drink ▶ *Can I have two vodkas, please?*

vogue /vəʊg/ *noun*
be in vogue to be fashionable and popular ▶ *Japanese food is very much in vogue these days.*

voice /vɔɪs/ *noun*
the sound that you make when you speak or sing ▶ *We could hear the children's voices in the garden.* ▶ *She spoke in a loud voice.*

voice mail /ˈvɔɪs meɪl/ *noun (no plural)*
a system that records telephone calls so that you can listen to them later ▶ *If I'm not there, leave a message on my voice mail.*

void¹ /vɔɪd/ *adjective*
not legally or officially acceptable ▶ *The result of the race was declared void.*

void² *noun*
1 a feeling that you no longer have something you need that is important to you ▶ *Their son's death left a void in their lives.*
2 an empty space where nothing exists ▶ *He plunged headlong into the void.*

volatile /ˈvɒlətaɪl/ *adjective*
1 (used about people) often changing suddenly from being happy to being angry or upset
2 (used about situations) likely to change suddenly and become worse

volcano /vɒlˈkeɪnəʊ/ *noun (plural volcanoes)*
a mountain from which burning and melted rock sometimes comes

volley /ˈvɒlɪ/ *noun*
a large number of bullets, rocks, etc. fired or thrown at the same time ▶ *a volley of shots*

volleyball /ˈvɒlɪbɔːl/ *noun (no plural)*
a game in which a large ball is knocked backwards and forwards across a net by hand

volt /vəʊlt/ *noun*
a measure of electricity

volume /ˈvɒljʊm/ *noun*
1 *(no plural)* the space that something contains or fills
2 the amount of sound that something makes ▶ *She turned down the volume on the radio.*
3 a book, especially one of a set

voluntarily /ˈvɒləntərəlɪ/ *adverb*
done of your free will and not because you are forced

voluntary /ˈvɒləntərɪ/ *adjective*
acting or done willingly, without payment ▶ *She's a voluntary worker at the hospital.*

volunteer¹ /ˌvɒlənˈtɪəʳ/ *noun*
a person who offers to do something ▶ *We want some volunteers to deliver the food to the old people.*

volunteer² *verb*
to offer to do something ▶ *We all volunteered to deliver the food to the old people.*

vomit /ˈvɒmɪt/ *verb*
to bring food up from your stomach

vote¹ /vəʊt/ *verb (present participle voting, past voted)*
1 with other people, to choose someone for an official position by, for example, secretly marking a paper with a cross, or by putting up your hand in a meeting ▶ *I voted for the socialist candidate.*
2 with other people, to choose one of several possibilities by, for example, marking a paper in secret or putting up your hand ▶ *Most people voted for a football club.*

vote² *noun*
a choice of one of several possibilities made officially by, for example, marking a paper in secret or putting up your hand to be counted ▶ *There were seven votes for the plan and three votes against it.*

voter /ˈvəʊtəʳ/ *noun*
a person who votes or who has the right to vote

voting /ˈvəʊtɪŋ/ *noun (no plural)*
the act of choosing someone for an official position in an election, or choosing one of several possibilities in a vote ▶ *Voting ends at 10.00 pm tonight.*

vouch /vaʊtʃ/ *verb*
vouch for to say that something is definitely true or good, or that someone is honest and will behave properly ▶ *I can vouch for the accuracy of the report* (=I know it is correct).

voucher /ˈvaʊtʃəʳ/ *noun*
a ticket that you can use instead of money to pay for things ▶ *free cinema vouchers*

vow¹ /vaʊ/ *verb*
to make a serious promise that you will definitely do something ▶ *I vowed that I would never drink again.*

vow² *noun*
a serious promise ▶ *marriage vows* ▶ *She made a vow to herself that she would never go back.*

vowel /ˈvaʊəl/ *noun*
1 one of the written letters **a, e, i, o,** or **u**
COMPARE: **consonant**
2 a speech sound in which you let your breath out without any stopping or closing of the air passage

voyage /ˈvɔɪ-ɪdʒ/ *noun*
a long journey by sea or in space

vs
a short way of writing the word **versus**

vulgar /ˈvʌlgəʳ/ *adjective*
very rude, low, or having very bad manners and going against the accepted standards of polite society

vulnerable /ˈvʌlnərəbəl/ *adjective*
not protected, and therefore easily harmed, hurt, or attacked ▶ *Elderly people living alone are very vulnerable.* ▶ *The town is very vulnerable to attack.*

vulture /ˈvʌltʃəʳ/ *noun*
a large, wild bird that eats dead animals

Ww

W
a short way of writing the words **west** or **western**

wade /weɪd/ *verb (present participle wading, past waded)*
to walk through water which is quite deep ▶ *We had to wade across the river.*
COMPARE: **paddle**

waft /wɒft/ *verb*
to move gently through the air ▶ *Smoke wafted in through the open window.*

wag /wæg/ *verb (present participle wagging, past wagged)*
to move something from side to side ▶ *The dog wagged its tail.*

wage /weɪdʒ/ *noun (also wages plural noun)*
a fixed amount of money paid to someone every week or every month for the job they do, especially

someone who works in a factory or a shop ▶ *Wages keep going up.* ▶ *wage demands* ▶ *the average weekly wage*

wagon /ˈwægən/ *noun*
1 a cart with four wheels, usually pulled by horses or oxen
2 an open container with four wheels, pulled by a train

wail /weɪl/ *verb*
to cry with a long, loud sound showing sadness or pain ▶ *The child was wailing unhappily.*

waist /weɪst/ *noun*
the narrow part round the middle of your body ▶ *Ann wore a tight belt around her waist.*

waistcoat /ˈweɪskəʊt/ *noun*
a piece of clothing that you wear on the upper part of your body over a shirt. It has buttons down the front and no arms

wait[1] /weɪt/ *verb*
to stay somewhere until someone comes or something happens
▶ *Please wait here until I come back.*
▶ *I was waiting for the bus.*

wait[2] *noun*
a time of doing nothing until something happens ▶ *He had a long wait for the train, as it was an hour late.*

waiter /ˈweɪtəʳ/ *noun*
a man who brings food to people in a restaurant

waiting list /ˈweɪtɪŋ lɪst/ *noun*
a list of people who are waiting to have something that is not available for them now ▶ *There's a long waiting list for eye operations.*

waiting room /ˈweɪtɪŋ rʊm/ *noun*
a room for people who are waiting, for example to see a doctor

waitress /ˈweɪtrəs/ *noun (plural waitresses)*
a woman who brings food to people in a restaurant

W

wake /weɪk/ *verb (present participle* **waking**, *past tense* **woke** /wəʊk/ *or* **waked**, *past participle* **woken** /'wəʊkən/)
1 to stop sleeping ➤ *I woke early this morning.*
2 to make someone stop sleeping ➤ *Be quiet, or you will wake the baby.*
3 wake up to stop sleeping ➤ *Please wake me up at 8 o'clock.*

walk¹ /wɔːk/ *verb*
to move forward by putting one foot in front of the other ➤ *We walk **to** school every day.*

walk² *noun*
a journey on foot ➤ *Shall we go for a walk this afternoon?* ➤ *It is a long walk **to** the town.*

walkie-talkie /ˌwɔːkɪ ˈtɔːkɪ/ *noun*
a two-way radio which a person carries so that they can talk to another person and listen to messages

walking stick /ˈwɔːkɪŋ stɪk/ *noun*
a long stick that people who are old or ill use to help them walk

Walkman /ˈwɔːkmən/ *noun* **trademark**
a small machine for playing music, which has EARPHONES and which you can carry with you

wall /wɔːl/ *noun*
1 something built, especially of bricks or stone, which goes round a house, town, field, etc. ➤ *There was a wall around the park.*
2 one of the sides of a building or room ➤ *We have painted all the walls white.*

wallet /ˈwɒlɪt/ *noun*
a small, flat case for cards or paper money, usually carried in a pocket by a man

wallpaper /ˈwɔːlˌpeɪpəʳ/ *noun (no plural)*
special paper used to cover the walls of a room

walnut /ˈwɔːlnʌt/ *noun*
a nut that looks like a brain, which has a large, light brown shell

waltz¹ /wɔːls/ *noun (plural* **waltzes**)
a dance in which two people hold each other and move slowly around a room

waltz² *verb*
to dance round the room together doing a waltz

wan /wɒn/ *adjective (* **wanner**, **wannest**)
looking pale, weak, or tired ➤ *a wan smile*

wand /wɒnd/ *noun*
a long, thin stick that you hold in your hand when you are doing magic tricks ➤ *He waved his wand, and a rabbit appeared.*

wander /ˈwɒndəʳ/ *verb*
to walk slowly without purpose ➤ *The children wandered about in the woods.*

wane /weɪn/ *verb (present participle* **waning**, *past* **waned**)
to gradually become weaker or less ➤ *After a while, his enthusiasm for the sport began to wane.*

wannabe /ˈwɒnəbiː/ *noun*
a person who tries to look or behave like a famous or popular person ➤ *Tom Cruise wannabes*

want¹ /wɒnt/ *verb*
1 to wish to have something ➤ *I want a bicycle for my birthday.*
2 to need something ➤ *I want to go home.*
3 should or ought ➤ *You want to leave early to avoid the traffic.*

want² *noun (no plural)*
need; lack; not having something necessary ➤ *The children were in want of food.* ➤ *The corn was dying from want of rain.*

wanted /ˈwɒntɪd/ *adjective*
(used about a criminal) being looked for by the police, because they may

W

have done something against the law ► *He is wanted for murder.*

war /wɔːʳ/ *noun*
1 a time of fighting between countries ► *a prisoner of war*
COMPARE: **battle**
2 at war fighting ► *The two countries were at war for two years.*
3 declare war to start a war ► *One country declared war on another.*
4 go to war to be fighting ► *The country is preparing to go to war.*

ward /wɔːd/ *noun*
a room in a hospital where sick people stay

warden /wɔːdn/ *noun*
a person who looks after a large building where people live, a public place, etc. ► *the warden of an old people's home*

warder /wɔːʳdəʳ/ *noun*
a person whose job is to guard people in prison

wardrobe /wɔːdrəʊb/ *noun*
a cupboard in which you hang your clothes

warehouse /weəhaʊs/ *noun (plural warehouses* /-ˌhaʊzɪz/)
a large building for storing things

wares /weəʳ/ *plural noun*
things that you can buy ► *The man spread his wares on the table.*

warfare /wɔːfeəʳ/ *noun (no plural)*
the fighting which happens in a war

warlike /wɔːlaɪk/ *adjective*
eager to fight wars, or often fighting wars ► *a warlike race*

warm¹ /wɔːm/ *adjective*
1 not cold but not hot ► *warm water*
2 able to keep out the cold and make you warm ► *warm clothes*
3 friendly ► *a warm welcome*

warm² *verb*
1 to make or become hotter ► *The hot drink warmed him through.*
2 warm something up to make

something become hotter ► *I'll just warm the soup up.*

warm-hearted /ˌwɔːm ˈhɑːtɪd/ *adjective*
friendly and kind ► *a warm-hearted old lady*

warmly /wɔːmlɪ/ *adverb*
1 in a way that will stop you from feeling cold ► *You need to dress warmly.*
2 in a friendly way ► *She greeted them warmly.*

warmth /wɔːmθ/ *noun (no plural)*
1 heat; the feeling of being hot ► *the warmth of the fire*
2 friendliness ► *the warmth of her welcome*

warm-up /wɔːm ʌp/ *noun*
a set of gentle exercises that you do to prepare for a sport ► *We always do a ten-minute warm-up before a game.*

warn /wɔːn/ *verb*
to tell someone of something bad which might happen ► *Police are warning drivers not to go out unless they have to.* ► *I warned her that I might be late.*

warning /wɔːnɪŋ/ *noun*
something which tells someone about a possible problem or danger ► *The planes attacked without warning.*

warp /wɔːp/ *verb*
(used about wood or metal) to become bent or twisted, especially because of the effect of heat or water

warrant /wɒrənt/ *noun*
a paper saying that someone may do something ► *The police must have a search warrant to search a house.*

warren /wɒrən/ *noun*
a group of holes underground where wild rabbits live

warrior /wɒrɪəʳ/ *noun*
a very brave person who fought in battles in the past

W

warship /'wɔːʃɪp/ *noun*
a large ship used for war

wart /wɔːt/ *noun*
a small, hard, raised spot that grows on your skin

wary /'weərɪ/ *adjective* (**warier, wariest**)
careful because you think that someone or something may harm you ➤ *Children should be wary of strangers.*

was /wəz; *strong* wɒz/ *verb*
the PAST TENSE of the verb **be** that we use with "I", "he", "she", and "it" ➤ *I was angry.*

wash¹ /wɒʃ/ *verb*
1 to make something clean with water and soap ➤ *Have you washed your hands?*
2 to flow over or against something ➤ *The waves washed against the shore.*
3 wash up to clean the dishes, knives, forks, etc. after a meal ➤ *Who's going to wash up tonight?*

wash² *noun*
1 have a wash to wash yourself, especially your hands and face ➤ *She had a quick wash.*
2 give someone or something a wash to wash someone or something ➤ *Could you give the car a wash?*
3 in the wash being washed ➤ *Your shirt is in the wash.*

washbasin /'wɒʃbeɪsən/ *noun*
a large bowl or basin fixed to a wall for washing your hands and face

washing /'wɒʃɪŋ/ *noun (no plural)*
clothes which need to be washed or have just been washed

washing machine /'wɒʃɪŋ məʃiːn/ *noun*
a machine for washing clothes

washing-up /ˌwɒʃɪŋ ˈʌp/ *noun*
do the washing-up to clean the dishes, knives, forks, etc. after a meal ➤ *It's your turn to do the washing-up.*

wasn't /'wɒzənt/
was not ➤ *I wasn't at school yesterday.*

wasp /wɒsp/ *noun*
a flying insect like a bee, which stings

waste¹ /weɪst/ *verb (present participle* **wasting***, past* **wasted***)*
to use something wrongly or use too much of something ➤ *Don't waste your money on rubbish like that.*

waste² *noun (no plural)*
1 a wrong or bad use of something ➤ *The meeting was a waste of time.*
2 used, damaged, or unwanted things ➤ *The waste from the factory was taken away in lorries.*

wasteful /'weɪstfəl/ *adjective*
using much more of something than you should ➤ *a wasteful use of water*

wasteland /'weɪstlænd/ *noun*
an area of unattractive land that is not being used for anything

wastepaper basket /ˌweɪst'peɪpə ˌbɑːskɪt/ *noun*
a container into which you put paper and other small things that you do not need and want to get rid of

watch¹ /wɒtʃ/ *noun (plural* **watches***)*
1 a small clock that you wear on your wrist
2 keep watch to look out for danger ➤ *You keep watch while we're asleep.*
3 keep a close watch on something to keep looking at something carefully ➤ *You'll have to keep a close watch on the children.*

watch² *verb*
1 to look at something for a period of time and pay attention to it ➤ *Do you watch much television?*

Compare **watch, see,** and **look at.**
See is the general word for what you do with your eyes: *I can't see – it's too dark.* ➤ *We saw them standing outside the station.* If you **look at** something, you move your eyes towards it because

W

you want to see it: *Look at me!*
▶ *They were looking at the
pictures.* If you **watch** something,
you move your eyes towards it
and pay attention to it for a long
time. Use **watch** when you are
talking about something such as
a television programme or a
sports event where things are
changing or moving: *We watched
a film on television.* ▶ *He goes to
watch the football every Saturday.*

2 to look after someone or something
▶ *Will you watch the baby?*

3 watch out to be careful to avoid
something dangerous or unpleasant
▶ *You can ride your bike here, but
watch out for the cars.*

watchman /ˈwɒtʃmən/ *noun (plural
watchmen /-mən/)*
a guard, especially of a building

water¹ /ˈwɔːtər/ *noun (no plural)*
the liquid in rivers, lakes, and seas

water² *verb*
to put water onto land or plants

waterfall /ˈwɔːtəfɔːl/ *noun*
a place where water falls over rocks
from a high place to a lower place

watering can /ˈwɔːtərɪŋ kæn/ *noun*
a container that you use for pouring
water on plants

waterlogged /ˈwɔːtəlɒɡd/ *adjective*
(used about land) very wet or covered
with water ▶ *The pitch was
waterlogged.*

watermelon /ˈwɔːtəˌmelən/ *noun*
a large, round, green fruit which is
red inside with black seeds

waterproof /ˈwɔːtəpruːf/ *adjective*
not allowing water to go through
▶ *a waterproof coat*

water skiing /ˈwɔːtə ˌskiːɪŋ/ *noun
(no plural)*
a sport in which someone wearing
SKIS on their feet is pulled behind a
boat over water

watertight /ˈwɔːtətaɪt/ *adjective*
not allowing any water to get in or
out ▶ *a watertight container*

watt /wɒt/ *noun*
a measure of electrical power ▶ *a 60-
watt light bulb*

wave¹ /weɪv/ *noun*
1 one of the raised lines of water on the
surface of the sea which rise and fall
2 a movement of your hand from side
to side ▶ *She gave a wave as she left
the house.*

wave² *verb (present participle
waving, past **waved**)*
1 to hold your arm up in the air and
move your hand from side to side
▶ *We waved goodbye to them.*
2 to move or cause to move from side
to side or up and down ▶ *The
branches waved in the wind.*

wavelength /ˈweɪvleŋθ/ *noun*
1 the size of radio wave that a radio
company uses to broadcast its
programmes ▶ *What wavelength is
Radio 1 on?*
2 be on the same wavelength to
think in the same way about
something as someone else does
▶ *We've never been on the same
wavelength about music.*

waver /ˈweɪvər/ *verb*
to be uncertain about a decision for a
short time ▶ *Paul wavered for a few
moments before accepting the offer.*

wavy /ˈweɪvi/ *adjective (**wavier,
waviest**)*
1 (used about hair) having gentle
curves rather than straight or curly
▶ *wavy, grey hair*
2 (used about lines) having a series
of curves

wax /wæks/ *noun (no plural)*
the hard substance which candles are
made of

way /weɪ/ *noun*
1 direction ▶ *Look both ways before
you cross the road.*

2 distance ➤ *We have to go a long way to school.*
LOOK AT: **far**

3 a road or path ➤ *Can you tell me the way **to** the station?*

4 how a thing is done or works ➤ *The best way to learn a language is to live in the country where it is spoken.*

5 by the way a phrase you use when you want to talk about something different from what you have just been talking about

6 find your way to find where you want to go

7 lose your way to become lost and not know how to find the place you are looking for

8 in the way in a position that stops you from going somewhere ➤ *We tried to turn left but a bus was in the way.*

9 out of the way not in a position that stops you going somewhere ➤ *Could you move that chair out of the way?*

10 on the way while going somewhere ➤ *We'll stop and have lunch on the way.*

11 the right way round facing in the right direction ➤ *Have I got this skirt on the right way round?*

12 the wrong way round not facing in the right direction ➤ *You've got that skirt on the wrong way round.*

way of life /ˌweɪ əv 'laɪf/ *noun (plural **ways of life**)*
the way someone lives, especially the people in a particular area or country ➤ *the American way of life*

way out /ˌweɪ 'aʊt/ *noun (plural **ways out**)*
the way out a door through which you can leave a place
SAME MEANING: **exit**

WC /ˌdʌbəlju: 'si:/ *noun*
a TOILET

we /wɪ; *strong* wi:/ *pronoun*
the person who is speaking and some other person or people ➤ *When my friend comes to see me, we play football.*

weak /wi:k/ *adjective*
1 not strong in body or character ➤ *She was very weak after her illness.*
2 containing a lot of water or having not much taste ➤ *weak tea*
OPPOSITE (**1** and **2**): **strong**

weaken /'wi:kən/ *verb*
to make or become less strong

weakness /'wi:knəs/ *noun*
1 *(plural **weaknesses**)* a fault ➤ *What are your strengths and weaknesses?*
2 *(no plural)* a lack of strength in a person's body or character

wealth /welθ/ *noun (no plural)*
a large amount of money, land, etc. that a person owns ➤ *a woman of immense wealth*

wealthy /'welθɪ/ *adjective (**wealthier, wealthiest**)*
rich; having a lot of money ➤ *a wealthy family*
OPPOSITE: **poor**

weapon /'wepən/ *noun*
a thing with which you fight ➤ *Hand over your weapon.*

wear /weəʳ/ *verb (past tense **wore** /wɔ:ʳ/, past participle **worn** /wɔ:n/)*
1 to have or carry something on your body, especially as clothing ➤ *She was wearing a very pretty dress.*
2 to weaken or damage something because of continual use ➤ *You've worn a hole in your sock.*
3 wear well to remain in good condition ➤ *That suit has worn well; it is three years old and still looks new.*
4 wear off to become less ➤ *The pain is wearing off a bit.*
5 wear out to become old and weak, and no longer good enough to use ➤ *My running shoes are wearing out.*

wearily /'wɪərɪlɪ/ *adverb*
in a tired way ➤ *"I can't help you any more," she said wearily.*

weary /'wɪərɪ/ adjective (**wearier, weariest**)
tired ► *a weary smile*

weasel /'wiːzəl/ noun
a small, wild animal that looks like a long rat

weather /'weðəʳ/ noun (no plural)
the state of the wind, rain, sunshine, etc. ► *I don't like cold weather.* ► *The weather has been lovely this week.*

weather-beaten /'weðə ˌbiːtn/ adjective
made rough by the wind and the sun ► *a weather-beaten face*

weather forecast /'weðə ˌfɔːkɑːst/ noun
a report on the television or radio, or in a newspaper, that says what the weather is expected to be like ► *The weather forecast for tomorrow isn't very good.*

weather forecaster /'weðə ˌfɔːkɑːstəʳ/ noun
a person whose job is to read the weather forecast on the television or radio

weave /wiːv/ verb (present participle **weaving**, past tense **wove** /wəʊv/, past participle **woven** /'wəʊvən/)
1 to make threads into cloth, by moving one thread over and under a set of longer threads on a LOOM
2 to make something in this way ► *I wove a mat.*

weaving /'wiːvɪŋ/ noun (no plural)
making cloth ► *She is very good at basket-weaving.*

web /web/ noun
a net of thin threads made by a SPIDER

Web /web/ noun
the WORLD WIDE WEB

webbed /webd/ adjective
(used about feet) having skin between the toes ► *Ducks have webbed feet.*

webcam /'webkæm/ noun
a camera that films something and then sends the images immediately from your computer to other computers

website /'websaɪt/ noun
a place on the INTERNET where you can find information about something ► *The club has a very good website.*

we'd /wɪd; strong wiːd/
1 we would ► *The hill was so steep I thought we'd never get to the top.*
2 we had ► *My sister and I didn't go to the film because we'd seen it before.*

wedding /'wedɪŋ/ noun
the ceremony in which a man and a woman get married ► *I'm going to my brother's wedding tomorrow.*
COMPARE: **marriage**

wedding ring /'wedɪŋ rɪŋ/ noun
a ring that you wear to show that you are married

wedge¹ /wedʒ/ noun
a piece of something that is thick at one end, and thin and pointed at the other end ► *a wedge of chocolate cake*

wedge² verb (present participle **wedging**, past tense **wedged**)
1 to force something into a small space ► *I wedged the book in at the end of the shelf.*
2 **wedge something open, wedge something shut** to put something under a door, window, etc. to make it stay open or shut

Wednesday /'wenzdeɪ, -dɪ/ noun
the fourth day of the week

weed¹ /wiːd/ noun
a wild plant which grows where you do not want it

weed² verb
to remove unwanted wild plants from the ground ► *I spent the afternoon weeding the garden.*

W

week /wiːk/ *noun*
a period of seven days, especially from Sunday to Saturday ➤ *I play tennis twice a week.* ➤ *Will you come and see us next week?*
LOOK AT: **time**

weekday /'wiːkdeɪ/ *noun*
any day except Saturday or Sunday

weekend /wiːkˈend/ *noun*
Saturday and Sunday ➤ *I don't work at the weekend.*

weekly /'wiːklɪ/ *adjective, adverb*
happening once a week ➤ *a weekly paper* ➤ *It comes out weekly.*

weep /wiːp/ *verb (past* **wept** */wept/)*
to cry ➤ *She wept when she heard the awful news.*

weigh /weɪ/ *verb*
1 to measure how heavy a thing is ➤ *He weighed the fish.*
2 to have a particular weight ➤ *The fish weighed 2 kilos.*

weight /weɪt/ *noun (no plural)*
the heaviness of something ➤ *The baby's weight was 4 kilos.*

weightlifting /'weɪtˌlɪftɪŋ/ *noun (no plural)*
the sport of lifting heavy weights

weir /wɪəʳ/ *noun*
a wall that is built across a river to control the flow of water

weird /wɪəd/ *adjective*
strange; unusual ➤ *weird clothes*
SAME MEANING: **odd**

welcome¹ /'welkəm/ *adjective*
1 wanted; happily accepted ➤ *You are always welcome in my home.* ➤ *A change in the law would be very welcome.*
2 make someone welcome to behave in a friendly way towards someone

welcome² *verb (present participle* **welcoming**, *past* **welcomed**)
to meet or greet someone or something with pleasure ➤ *My aunt welcomed me at the door.*

welcome³ *noun*
a greeting when someone arrives ➤ *We were given a warm welcome.*

weld /weld/ *verb*
to join metal objects together by heating them and pressing them together

welfare /'welfeəʳ/ *noun (no plural)*
a person's health, comfort, and happiness ➤ *The teachers were concerned about the child's welfare.*

well¹ /wel/ *adjective*
in good health ➤ *I don't feel very well.*
OPPOSITE: **unwell**

well² *adverb (* **better** /'betəʳ/, **best** /best/)
1 in a good or satisfactory way ➤ *Mary can read very well.* ➤ *Well done!* ➤ *Did you sleep well?*
OPPOSITE: **badly**
2 completely; thoroughly ➤ *Shake well before opening.*
3 as well also ➤ *I'd like a cup of tea, and an apple as well.*
4 as well as and also ➤ *I'm learning French as well as German.*

well³ *interjection*
a word you often say when you start speaking ➤ *"Where are you going on holiday?" "Well, we may go to France."*

well⁴ *noun*
a deep hole in the ground, from which water or oil is taken

we'll /wɪl; *strong* wiːl/
we will ➤ *We'll see Jane tomorrow.*

well-balanced /ˌwel ˈbælənst/ *adjective*
1 sensible and not easily upset ➤ *a happy, well-balanced child*
2 (used about meals or DIETS) containing all the things you need to stay healthy

well-behaved /ˌwel bɪˈheɪvd/ *adjective*
polite and behaving well ➤ *His children are so well-behaved.*

W

wellbeing /ˌwel'biːɪŋ/ *noun (no plural)*
a feeling of being comfortable, healthy, and happy

well-built /ˌwel 'bɪlt/ *adjective*
big and strong ▶ *a well-built man*

well-dressed /ˌwel 'drest/ *adjective*
wearing good clothes ▶ *a well-dressed TV presenter*

well-fed /ˌwel 'fed/ *adjective*
getting plenty of good food ▶ *The local cats look well-fed and healthy.*

wellingtons /ˈwelɪŋtənz/ *(also **wellington boots** /ˈwelɪŋtən ˌbuːts/) plural noun*
long, rubber boots that you wear to keep your feet dry

well-kept /ˌwel 'kept/ *adjective*
neat and tidy ▶ *a well-kept garden*

well-known /ˌwel 'nəʊn/ *adjective*
known by many people ▶ *a well-known writer*

well-off /ˌwel 'ɒf/ *adjective*
having a lot of money
SAME MEANING: **rich**

well-paid /ˌwel 'peɪd/ *adjective*
getting a lot of money for a job ▶ *Work in advertising is very well-paid indeed.* ▶ *a well-paid lawyer*

well-read /ˌwel 'red/ *adjective*
having read a lot and knowing a lot about many subjects

well-timed /ˌwel 'taɪmd/ *adjective*
said or done at a very suitable moment ▶ *My arrival wasn't very well-timed.*

well-wisher /ˈwel ˌwɪʃəʳ/ *noun*
a person who shows that they want you to succeed or be happy and healthy ▶ *Hundreds of well-wishers have left flowers at the hospital.*

went /went/
the PAST TENSE of the verb **go**

wept /wept/
the PAST TENSE and PAST PARTICIPLE of the verb **weep**

were /wəʳ; *strong* wɜːʳ/ *verb*
the PAST TENSE of the verb **be** that is used with "you", "we", and "they" ▶ *You were born in Ireland, weren't you?*

we're /wɪəʳ; *strong* 'wiːəʳ/
we are ▶ *We're in the same class at school.*

weren't /wɜːnt/
were not ▶ *You weren't here yesterday, were you?*

west /west/ *noun, adjective, adverb*
1 the direction in which the sun goes down ▶ *Glasgow is in the west of Scotland.* ▶ *the west coast* ▶ *living west of Cardiff* ▶ *We travelled west for two days.*
2 a west wind a wind that comes from the west

westbound /ˈwestbaʊnd/ *adjective*
travelling or leading towards the west ▶ *an accident in the westbound lane*

westerly /ˈwestəlɪ/ *adjective*
1 towards the west ▶ *They travelled in a westerly direction.*
2 (used about wind) blowing from the west

western /ˈwestən/ *adjective*
in or of the west

westward /ˈwestwəd/ *adjective*
towards the west ▶ *Walk in a westward direction for 3 miles.*

westwards /ˈwestwədz/ *adverb*
towards the west ▶ *to travel westwards*

wet¹ /wet/ *adjective (**wetter, wettest**)*
1 covered with or containing liquid ▶ *My hair is wet.* ▶ *Don't touch the wet paint.*
2 rainy ▶ *a wet day*
OPPOSITE (**1** and **2**): **dry**

wet² *verb (present participle **wetting**, past **wet** or **wetted**)*
to make something wet
OPPOSITE: **dry**

we've /wɪv; *strong* wiːv/
we have ▶ *We've missed the train!*

W

whale /weɪl/ *noun*
a very large animal that looks like a very large fish and lives in the sea

wharf /wɔːf/ *noun (plural **wharfs** or **wharves** /wɔːvz/)*
a place built on the edge of water where you can take things on and off a ship

what /wɒt/ *adjective, pronoun*
1 which thing or things ➤ *What is your name?* ➤ *What did you say?*
2 which ➤ *What time is it?* ➤ *What tools do I need for this job?*
3 the thing or things that ➤ *She told me what to do.* ➤ *I didn't know what had happened.*
4 used to show surprise or other strong feelings ➤ *What a silly thing to do!*
5 what for why ➤ *What are you using those scissors for?*
6 What about ...? words you use when you suggest something ➤ *"Where shall we go?" "What about the park?"*

whatever /wɒt'evər/ *pronoun*
anything at all that; no matter what ➤ *You may do whatever you want.* ➤ *Whatever I say, she always disagrees.*

wheat /wiːt/ *noun (no plural)*
a grass plant with grain seeds that are made into flour

wheel /wiːl/ *noun*
an object like a large circle which turns round and round

wheelbarrow /'wiːl,bærəʊ/ *noun*
a cart with a wheel at the front and two handles at the back

wheelchair /'wiːl,tʃeər/ *noun*
a special chair with big wheels, which is used to move people who cannot walk

wheeze /wiːz/ *verb (present participle **wheezing**, past **wheezed**)*
to breathe with difficulty and make a whistling sound in your chest ➤ *The old man coughed and wheezed.*

when /wen/ *adverb, conjunction*
1 at what time ➤ *When does the bus leave?*
2 at a particular time ➤ *I lived in this village when I was a boy.*

whenever /wen'evər/ *adverb, conjunction*
1 at any time; every time ➤ *Please come to see me whenever you can.* ➤ *Whenever I see him, I ask how he is.*
2 used to make the word **when** stronger ➤ *Whenever did you have time to do all that work?*

where /weər/ *adverb, conjunction*
1 in or to what place ➤ *Where is that train going?* ➤ *He doesn't know where his friends are.*
2 in which; at which ➤ *The house where I live has a green door.*

whereabouts[1] /,weərə'baʊts/ *adverb*
used to ask where something or someone is ➤ *Whereabouts do you live?*

whereabouts[2] /'weərəbaʊts/ *noun (no plural)*
the place where someone or something is ➤ *His whereabouts are a mystery.*

wherever /weər'evər/ *adverb*
1 at or to any place ➤ *I will drive you wherever you want to go.*
2 used to make the word **where** stronger ➤ *You are very late; wherever have you been?*

whet /wet/ *verb (present participle **whetting**, past **whetted**)*
whet someone's appetite to make someone want more of something by letting them try it or see what it is like ➤ *This book has really whetted my appetite for science fiction.*

whether /'weðər/ *conjunction*
if ➤ *I don't know whether he'll come or not.*

W

which /wɪtʃ/ *adjective, pronoun*
1 what person or thing ▶ *Which of you is the oldest?* ▶ *Which shoes shall I wear?*
2 that ▶ *Did you see the letter which came today?*
3 used to add more information to a sentence ▶ *We went to Ely, which is a town near Cambridge.*

whichever /wɪtʃ'evə'/ *adjective, pronoun*
1 any of a group of things or people ▶ *You can choose whichever one you like.* ▶ *Take whichever you want.*
2 used to say that it is not important how you do something because the result will be the same in every case ▶ *Whichever way you look at it, he's guilty.*

whiff /wɪf/ *noun*
a slight smell ▶ *a whiff of cigarette smoke*

while¹ /waɪl/ *conjunction*
all the time that; during the time that ▶ *I met her while I was at school.* ▶ *While the child played, her mother worked.*

while² *noun*
a length of time ▶ *After a while, she fell asleep.* ▶ *We had to wait a little while.*

whilst /waɪlst/ *conjunction*
WHILE

whim /wɪm/ *noun*
a sudden feeling that you want to do something, without any particular reason ▶ *I went to see the film on a whim.*

whimper /'wɪmpə'/ *verb*
to make small, weak cries of fear or pain ▶ *The dog whimpered in the corner.*

whine¹ /waɪn/ *verb (present participle **whining**, past **whined**)*
to make a high, sad sound ▶ *The dog whined at the door.*

whine² *noun*
a high, sad cry or sound ▶ *the whine of an aircraft engine*

whinge /wɪndʒ/ *verb (present participle **whingeing**, past **whinged**)*
to complain in an annoying way about something unimportant ▶ *She's been whingeing to him about the amount of work she has to do.*

whip¹ /wɪp/ *noun*
a long piece of leather or rope, fastened to a handle, used for hitting animals or people

whip² *verb (present participle **whipping**, past **whipped**)*
1 to hit a person or an animal with a whip ▶ *He whipped the horse to make it run faster.*
2 to beat cream or eggs until they are stiff ▶ *whipped cream*

whirl /wɜːl/ *verb*
to move or make something move round and round very fast ▶ *The wind whirled the leaves into the air.*

whirlpool /'wɜːlpuːl/ *noun*
water that turns around and around very quickly, pulling things towards it and then down into it

whirlwind¹ /'wɜːlˌwɪnd/ *noun*
a strong wind that turns around and around very quickly and causes a lot of damage

whirlwind² *adjective*
exciting and happening very quickly ▶ *After a whirlwind romance, they got married.*

whirr /wɜː'/ *verb*
to make a continuous, low sound ▶ *A helicopter whirred overhead.*

whisk¹ /wɪsk/ *verb*
1 to mix eggs, cream, etc. in a bowl very quickly so that air is mixed in ▶ *Whisk the cream until it is thick.*
2 to take someone somewhere very quickly ▶ *They whisked her to hospital.*

whisk² *noun*
a small kitchen tool made of curved pieces of wire, used for whisking eggs, cream, etc.

whisker /ˈwɪskə^r/ *noun*
one of the long, stiff hairs that grow near the mouth of dogs, cats, rats, etc.

whisky /ˈwɪskɪ/ *noun*
1 *(no plural)* a strong alcoholic drink made especially in Scotland
2 *(plural **whiskies**)* a glass of this drink ➤ *Can I have two whiskies, please?*
SAME MEANING: **Scotch**

whisper¹ /ˈwɪspə^r/ *noun*
words which you speak very quietly ➤ *She spoke in a whisper.*

whisper² *verb*
to speak very quietly

whistle¹ /ˈwɪsəl/ *noun*
1 an instrument which makes a high sound when you blow through it ➤ *The teacher blew a whistle to start the race.*
2 a thin, high sound made by putting your lips together and blowing through them ➤ *When he gave a whistle, his dog ran to him.*

whistle² *verb (present participle **whistling**, past **whistled**)*
1 to make a high sound by putting your lips together and blowing through them ➤ *He whistled to his dog.*
2 to make music by doing this ➤ *He whistled the song.*

white¹ /waɪt/ *adjective*
1 of the colour of the paper in this book ➤ *a white dress*
2 with light-coloured skin ➤ *Some of the children were white; the others were black.*

white² *noun*
1 *(no plural)* white colour ➤ *She was dressed in white.*
2 a person with light-coloured skin
3 the white part of your eye, or of an egg

whiteboard /ˈwaɪtbɔːd/ *noun*
a large, white board used for writing on in classrooms

white-collar /ˌwaɪt ˈkɒlə^r/ *adjective*
working in offices, banks, etc.
➤ *white-collar workers*
COMPARE: **blue-collar**

whittle /ˈwɪtl/ *verb (present participle **whittling**, past **whittled**)*
whittle something down to gradually reduce a number or an amount ➤ *I've whittled the list down to just four people now.*

whizz¹ /wɪz/ *verb*
to move very quickly ➤ *A bullet whizzed past his ear.*

whizz² *noun (plural **whizzes**)*
be a whizz at something to be very good at something ➤ *Peter is a whizz at maths.*

who /huː/ *pronoun*
1 what person or people ➤ *Who gave you that book?* ➤ *Who are those people?*
2 that ➤ *The man who lives in that house is my uncle.*

who'd /huːd/
1 who had ➤ *She asked who'd seen the film.*
2 who would ➤ *He wanted to know who'd be able to help him.*

whoever /huːˈevə^r/ *pronoun*
1 any person that; no matter who ➤ *Whoever those people are, I don't want to see them.*
2 used to make the word **who** stronger ➤ *Whoever told you that silly story?*

whole¹ /həʊl/ *adjective*
complete; total ➤ *They told me the whole story.*

whole² *noun (no plural)*
1 the complete amount or thing ➤ *Two halves make a whole.*
2 the whole of all of ➤ *He put the whole of his money into the bank.*

W

3 on the whole in general ▶ *On the whole, I agree with you.*

wholehearted /ˌhəʊlˈhɑːtɪd/ *adjective*
complete and without any doubts ▶ *You have my wholehearted support.* (adverb: **wholeheartedly**)

wholemeal /ˈhəʊlmiːl/ *adjective*
made using all the parts of the grains of wheat ▶ *wholemeal bread*

wholesale /ˈhəʊlseɪl/ *adjective*
1 connected with the sale of goods in large quantities, usually at low prices ▶ *wholesale prices*
2 very great, and affecting large areas, numbers of people, etc., and usually having a very bad effect ▶ *the wholesale destruction of the rainforest*

wholesaler /ˈhəʊlˌseɪləʳ/ *noun*
a person or company that buys goods in large quantities and sells them to shops, usually at low prices

wholesome /ˈhəʊlsəm/ *adjective*
good for your health ▶ *We eat only wholesome, natural foods.*

who'll /huːl/
who will ▶ *Who'll be here tomorrow?*

wholly /ˈhəʊl-lɪ/ *adverb*
completely ▶ *This is wholly unacceptable.*

whom /huːm/ *pronoun*
1 what person or people (used when it is the object of the verb or after a preposition) ▶ *Whom did you see?*
2 that ▶ *a man whom she met on holiday*

who're /ˈhuːəʳ/
who are ▶ *Who're you going to vote for?*

who's /huːz/
1 who is ▶ *Who's coming to the party?*
2 who has ▶ *Who's eaten my apple?*

whose /huːz/ *adjective, pronoun*
of who or whom; belonging to who or whom ▶ *Whose coat is that?* ▶ *Whose*

is this? ▶ *This is the woman whose little boy was ill.*

who've /huːv/
who have ▶ *people who've got problems*

why /waɪ/ *adverb, conjunction*
for what reason ▶ *Why is she crying?*
▶ *I can't tell you why she is crying.*
▶ *No one knows why.*

wicked /ˈwɪkɪd/ *adjective*
very bad; evil ▶ *a wicked person* (adverb: **wickedly**)

wicket /ˈwɪkɪt/ *noun*
one of the sets of sticks that the BOWLER tries to hit with the ball in a game of CRICKET

wide¹ /waɪd/ *adjective*
1 large from side to side; broad ▶ *a wide road* ▶ *2 metres wide*
OPPOSITE: **narrow**
2 fully or completely open ▶ *wide eyes*

wide² *adverb*
1 completely ▶ *The door was wide open.*
2 a great distance from side to side ▶ *He stood with his legs wide apart.*

wide-eyed /ˌwaɪd ˈaɪd/ *adjective, adverb*
with your eyes wide open because you are very surprised or interested ▶ *The children stared wide-eyed at the magician.*

widely /ˈwaɪdlɪ/ *adverb*
1 in a lot of different places or by a lot of people ▶ *products that are widely available* ▶ *a widely read newspaper*
2 to a large degree; a lot ▶ *Prices vary widely from shop to shop.*

widen /ˈwaɪdn/ *verb*
to become wider, or to make something wider ▶ *They're widening the road.*

widespread /ˈwaɪdspred/ *adjective*
happening in many places, among many people, or in many situations ▶ *the widespread use of illegal drugs*

W

widow /ˈwɪdəʊ/ *noun*
a woman whose husband is dead

widowed /ˈwɪdəʊd/ *adjective*
if someone is widowed, their
husband or wife is dead

widower /ˈwɪdəʊəʳ/ *noun*
a man whose wife is dead

width /wɪdθ/ *noun*
the distance from one side of
something to the other; how wide
something is ➤ *What is the width of
this material?*

wield /wiːld/ *verb*
1 to have and use power and
influence ➤ *The United States wields
enormous political influence.*
2 to hold or use a weapon ➤ *a gang
of young men wielding knives*

wife /waɪf/ *noun (plural **wives**
/waɪvz/)*
the woman to whom a man is married
COMPARE: **husband**

wig /wɪg/ *noun*
a covering for your head, made of hair
from other people or of artificial hair,
and meant to look like your own hair

wiggle /ˈwɪgəl/ *verb (present
participle **wiggling**, past **wiggled**)*
to move part of your body from side
to side or up and down ➤ *She
wiggled her bottom as she danced.*

wild /waɪld/ *adjective*
1 not trained to live with people
➤ *wild animals*
OPPOSITE: **tame**
2 living in the natural state ➤ *We
picked wild flowers in the woods.*
3 violent ➤ *a wild look in her eyes*
4 not easily controlled ➤ *The children
went wild with delight.*

wilderness /ˈwɪldənəs/ *noun*
a large, natural area of land with no
buildings ➤ *Fifty years ago, this area
was just a wilderness.*

wildlife /ˈwaɪldlaɪf/ *noun (no plural)*
animals that live in natural conditions

wildly /ˈwaɪldli/ *adverb*
in a way that is careless and not
controlled ➤ *He drives rather wildly.*
➤ *I'm not wildly excited about it.*

wilful /ˈwɪlfəl/ *adjective*
1 doing what you want, even though
people tell you not to ➤ *His daughter
became a wilful teenager.*
2 done deliberately and without
caring about the possible harmful
results ➤ *This act of wilful damage
could have caused an accident.*

will¹ /wɪl/ *verb*
1 used with other verbs to show that
something is going to happen ➤ *It will
probably rain tomorrow.*
COMPARE: **shall, should, would**
2 used in questions when asking to
do something, or used when offering
to do something ➤ *Will you help me,
please?* ➤ *I'll do whatever you say.*

will² *noun*
1 *(no plural)* power in the mind or
character to do exactly what you want
➤ *He no longer has the will to live.*
2 a piece of paper that says who will
have a person's belongings after he
or she is dead ➤ *The man left his farm
to his son in his will.*

willing /ˈwɪlɪŋ/ *adjective*
1 ready ➤ *Are you willing to help?*
2 eager and wanting to do something
very much ➤ *willing helpers (adverb:
willingly)*
OPPOSITE: **unwilling**

willow /ˈwɪləʊ/ *noun*
a tree often found near water, with
very long, thin branches that hang
down

willpower /ˈwɪlˌpaʊəʳ/ *noun (no
plural)*
the ability to make yourself do
something even if it is difficult or
unpleasant ➤ *Losing weight takes a
lot of willpower.*

wilt /wɪlt/ *verb*
(used about plants or flowers) to

W

bend and become weak because of
age, a lack of water, etc.

wily /'waɪlɪ/ *adjective (wilier, wiliest)*
clever at getting what you want,
especially by tricking people

wimp /wɪmp/ *noun*
a person who is too afraid to do
something because they think it is
difficult or unpleasant ▶ *Don't be
such a wimp!*

win¹ /wɪn/ *verb (present participle
winning, past won /wʌn/)*
1 to be first or do best in a
competition, race, or fight ▶ *Who won
the race?*
OPPOSITE: **lose**
2 to be given something because you
have done well in a race or
competition ▶ *He won first prize in
the competition.*

win² *noun*
a success in a competition, race, or
fight ▶ *They've had several wins this
season.*

wince /wɪns/ *verb (present participle
wincing, past winced)*
to suddenly change the expression
on your face when you see or
remember something painful or
embarrassing ▶ *He winced as he
remembered their first meeting.*

wind¹ /waɪnd/ *verb (past wound
/waʊnd/)*
1 to turn something round and round
in order to make it work ▶ *Can you
wind that clock for me?*
2 to make something into a ball or
twist it round something else ▶ *She
wound the rope around her arm.*
3 to move something by turning a
handle or pushing a button ▶ *She
wound down the car window.*
4 to bend and turn ▶ *The path wound
along the side of the river.*

wind² /wɪnd/ *noun*
air which moves quickly ▶ *The wind
blew the leaves off the trees.*

windfall /'wɪndfɔːl/ *noun*
an amount of money that you get
when you do not expect it

windmill /'wɪndmɪl/ *noun*
a tall building with large sails which
are turned round by the wind and
used to power a machine that
crushes grain or pumps water

window /'wɪndəʊ/ *noun*
an opening with glass across it in the
wall of a building or side of a car, etc.
to allow light and air to enter
▶ *Please shut the window.*

window shopping /'wɪndəʊ ʃɒpɪŋ/
noun (no plural)
the activity of looking at goods in
shops, without intending to buy them

window sill /'wɪndəʊ ˌsɪl/ *noun*
a flat shelf below a window

windscreen /'wɪndskriːn/ *noun*
the piece of glass across the front of
a car

windscreen wiper /'wɪndskriːn
ˌwaɪpə/ *noun*
a long object that moves across a
windscreen to remove rain

windsurfer /'wɪndˌsɜːfə/ *noun*
a person who goes windsurfing

windsurfing /'wɪndˌsɜːfɪŋ/ *noun (no
plural)*
the sport of sailing across water by
standing on a special board and
holding on to a large sail ▶ *I go
windsurfing most weekends.*

windswept /'wɪndswept/ *adjective*
very windy and offering no
protection from the wind ▶ *a
windswept beach*

wind turbine /'wɪnd ˌtɜːbaɪn/ *noun*
a tall structure with parts that are
turned by the wind, used for making
electricity

windy /'wɪndɪ/ *adjective (windier,
windiest)*
with a lot of wind ▶ *windy weather*

W

wine /waɪn/ *noun*
1 *(no plural)* an alcoholic drink made from a small, round, juicy fruit (GRAPE)
2 a glass of this drink ▶ *Can I have two white wines, please?*

wing /wɪŋ/ *noun*
1 a movable part of the body of a bird or an insect which it uses for flying
2 one of the two flat parts that stick out of a plane's sides and help it to stay in the air

wingspan /ˈwɪŋspæn/ *noun*
the distance from the end of one wing to the end of the other

wink¹ /wɪŋk/ *verb*
to close and open one eye quickly ▶ *He winked at me.*
COMPARE: **blink**

wink² *noun*
an act of closing and opening one eye quickly

winner /ˈwɪnəʳ/ *noun*
a person who comes first or does best in a competition, race, or fight

winnings /ˈwɪnɪŋz/ *plural noun*
money that you win in a game or competition ▶ *She went to collect her winnings.*

winter /ˈwɪntəʳ/ *noun, adjective*
the season in cool countries when it is cold and plants do not grow
COMPARE: **summer**

wintry /ˈwɪntrɪ/ *adjective (**wintrier, wintriest**)*
typical of winter, especially because it is cold or snowing ▶ *wintry weather*

wipe¹ /waɪp/ *verb (present participle **wiping**, past **wiped**)*
to make something dry or clean with a cloth ▶ *Will you wipe the table?* ▶ *She wiped the marks off the table.*

wipe² *noun*
a cleaning or drying movement with a cloth ▶ *She gave her face a wipe.*

wiper /ˈwaɪpəʳ/ *noun*
a WINDSCREEN WIPER

wire /waɪəʳ/ *noun*
1 *(no plural)* thin, metal thread ▶ *a wire fence*
2 a piece of thin metal used for carrying electricity from one place to another

wireless /ˈwaɪələs/ *noun (plural **wirelesses**)*
a radio

wiry /ˈwaɪərɪ/ *adjective (**wirier, wiriest**)*
1 (used about people) thin but strong ▶ *his wiry, athletic body*
2 (used about hair) stiff and curly

wisdom /ˈwɪzdəm/ *noun (no plural)*
good sense and judgement

wise /waɪz/ *adjective*
having or showing good sense and cleverness; able to understand things and make the right decision ▶ *a wise old man (adverb: **wisely**)*

wisecrack /ˈwaɪzkræk/ *noun*
something funny that someone says, especially when they should be more serious ▶ *She's always making wisecracks in meetings with clients.*

wish¹ /wɪʃ/ *verb*
1 to want something that is not possible ▶ *I wish I was rich.*
2 to want something ▶ *I wish to see you in my office immediately!*
3 wish someone something to hope that someone has something ▶ *We wish you success in your new job.*

wish² *noun (plural **wishes**)*
1 a feeling of wanting something, especially something that is not possible ▶ *She had a secret wish to be a singer.*
2 a thing that you hope for or want ▶ *It was my mother's wish that I should go.*

wishful thinking /ˌwɪʃfəl ˈθɪŋkɪŋ/ *noun (no plural)*
the hope that something good might happen, even though it is impossible

W

► *Their hopes of a peace settlement are just wishful thinking.*

wisp /wɪsp/ *noun*
1 a small, thin piece of hair ► *Wisps of hair kept falling into her eyes.*
2 a small, thin line of smoke or cloud ► *They could see a wisp of smoke in the distance.*

wistful /'wɪstfl/ *adjective*
a little sad because you know you cannot have something you want ► *a wistful expression* (adverb: **wistfully**)

wit /wɪt/ *noun (no plural)*
the ability to talk in a clever and amusing way

witch /wɪtʃ/ *noun (plural* **witches***)*
a woman who is believed to have magic powers

witchcraft /'wɪtʃkrɑːft/ *noun (no plural)*
the use of magic, usually to do bad things

with /wɪð/ *preposition*
1 in the company of ► *She comes to school with her sister.*
2 using ► *He opened the door with his key.* ► *Simon filled the bucket with water.*
3 having ► *a white dress with red spots*
4 because of ► *They smiled with pleasure.*
5 by or next to something, or among or included in something ► *Mix the flour with some milk.*
6 showing a particular way of behaving ► *He fought with great courage.*

withdraw /wɪð'drɔː/ *verb (past tense* **withdrew** /-'druː/, *past participle* **withdrawn** /-'drɔːn/)
1 to take something away ► *She withdrew all her money from the bank.*
2 to move or make something move away ► *The soldiers withdrew from the village.*

withdrawal /wɪð'drɔːəl/ *noun*
1 the act of taking some of your money out of a bank ► *You have made three withdrawals this month.*
2 the act of moving soldiers out of an area ► *the withdrawal of NATO forces from Bosnia*
3 *(no plural)* the set of unpleasant physical and mental feelings that someone who has regularly been taking a drug gets when they stop taking it ► *withdrawal symptoms*

withdrawn[1] /wɪð'drɔːn/ *adjective*
quiet and not wanting to talk to people ► *He became very withdrawn after his father died.*

withdrawn[2]
the PAST PARTICIPLE of the verb **withdraw**

withdrew /wɪð'druː/
the PAST TENSE of the verb **withdraw**

wither /'wɪðə/ *verb*
to become dry and then die ► *The plants withered in the dry weather.*

withhold /wɪð'həʊld/ *verb (past* **withheld** /-'held/)
to refuse to give information, money, etc. to someone ► *His name has been withheld for legal reasons.*

within /wɪð'ɪn/ *preposition, adverb*
1 in less than a particular period of time ► *Within a year he was dead.*
2 in; inside ► *Within these old walls, there was once a town.*

without /wɪð'aʊt/ *preposition*
1 not having something ► *You can't see the film without a ticket.*
2 **without doing something** not doing something ► *He left without saying goodbye.*

withstand /wɪð'stænd/ *verb (past* **withstood** /-'stʊd/)
to be strong enough not to be harmed by something ► *material that can withstand high temperatures*

witness[1] /'wɪtnəs/ *noun (plural* **witnesses***)*

a person who sees something happen ▶ *Police are looking for witnesses after the accident.*

witness² *verb*
to see something happen ▶ *Did you witness the accident?*

witness box /ˈwɪtnəs ˌbɒks/ *noun* (plural **witness boxes**)
the place where someone stands to give information in a law court

witty /ˈwɪti/ *adjective* (**wittier, wittiest**)
clever and amusing ▶ *a witty person* (adverb: **wittily**)

wives /waɪvz/
the plural of **wife**

wizard /ˈwɪzəd/ *noun*
1 a man who is believed to have magic powers
2 a person who is very good at doing something ▶ *a chess wizard*

wobble /ˈwɒbəl/ *verb* (present participle **wobbling**, past **wobbled**)
to move from side to side in an unsteady way ▶ *The table is wobbling.*

wobbly /ˈwɒbli/ *adjective* (**wobblier, wobbliest**)
moving from side to side in an unsteady way ▶ *a wobbly chair*

wok /wɒk/ *noun*
a large, round pan for cooking Chinese food

woke /wəʊk/
the PAST TENSE of the verb **wake**

woken /ˈwəʊkən/
the PAST PARTICIPLE of the verb **wake**

wolf /wʊlf/ *noun* (plural **wolves** /wʊlvz/)
a wild animal that is like a large dog

woman /ˈwʊmən/ *noun* (plural **women** /ˈwɪmɪn/)
a fully-grown human female
COMPARE: **man**

womb /wuːm/ *noun*

the part of a woman's body where a baby grows before it is born

women /ˈwɪmɪn/
the plural of **woman**

won /wʌn/
the PAST TENSE and PAST PARTICIPLE of the verb **win**

wonder¹ /ˈwʌndəʳ/ *verb*
1 to want to know something ▶ *I wonder why James is always late for school.*
2 to be surprised ▶ *We all wondered at our luck.*

wonder² *noun*
1 (no plural) a feeling of surprise and admiration ▶ *They were filled with wonder when they saw the spaceship.*
2 **no wonder** it is no surprise ▶ *No wonder he is not hungry; he has been eating sweets all day.*
3 a person or thing that makes you feel great admiration

wonderful /ˈwʌndəfəl/ *adjective*
very good ▶ *wonderful news* (adverb: **wonderfully**)

won't /wəʊnt/
will not ▶ *We won't be late home.*

wood /wʊd/ *noun*
1 (no plural) the material of which the trunks and branches of trees are made
2 a small forest ▶ *He was lost in the wood.*

wooded /ˈwʊdɪd/ *adjective*
covered with trees ▶ *They walked through a wooded valley.*

wooden /ˈwʊdn/ *adjective*
made of wood ▶ *wooden furniture*

woodland /ˈwʊdlənd/ *noun*
an area of land that is covered with trees

woodwind /ˈwʊdˌwɪnd/ *noun* (no plural)
musical instruments shaped like straight tubes, which you blow into

W

woodwork /ˈwʊdwɜːk/ *noun (no plural)*
1 the parts of a building that are made of wood ➤ *A lot of the woodwork was rotten and had to be replaced.*
2 the activity of making wooden objects ➤ *Her hobbies are painting, cookery, and woodwork.*

woodworm /ˈwʊdwɜːm/ *noun*
an insect that makes holes in wood

wool /wʊl/ *noun (no plural)*
1 the soft, thick hair of sheep
2 the thread or material made from the hair of sheep ➤ *The dress was made of wool.*

woollen /ˈwʊlən/ *adjective*
made of wool ➤ *a woollen dress*

woolly /ˈwʊlɪ/ *adjective*
made of wool ➤ *a woolly hat*

word /wɜːd/ *noun*
1 a letter or letters, which together make something we can understand ➤ *What's the French word for "mouse"?*
2 *(no plural)* a promise ➤ *I give you my word that I will return.*
3 give the word to tell someone to start doing something ➤ *When I give the word, you may start the exam.*
4 have a word with someone to talk to someone in private ➤ *Peter, could I have a word with you after class?*
5 in other words a phrase you use before you repeat the same thing using different words
6 in your own words not repeating what someone else has said ➤ *Tell me what happened in your own words.*
7 send word to send a message ➤ *Send me word as soon as you get home.*
8 take someone's word for it to believe what someone says about something

word processor /ˈwɜːd ˌprəʊsesəʳ/ *noun*

a machine used for writing letters and reports and for storing information

wore /wɔːʳ/
the PAST TENSE of the verb **wear**

work¹ /wɜːk/ *verb*
1 to be busy doing an activity ➤ *I've been working in the garden all afternoon.*
2 to have a job ➤ *He works in a factory.*
3 to move or go properly ➤ *Does this light work?*
4 to make someone or something do something ➤ *Can you work this machine?*
5 work out to end well ➤ *The marriage didn't work out.*
6 work something out to find an answer to something ➤ *She worked out the total in her head.*

work² *noun (no plural)*
1 an activity that keeps you busy and is usually not for pleasure ➤ *Dad's doing some work on the car.*
2 a job or business ➤ *to go to work*
3 what you produce while doing your job ➤ *He sells his work at the market.*
4 at work doing some work
5 in work with a job ➤ *the number of people in work*
6 out of work with no job, but wanting a job ➤ *I've been out of work for six months.*
7 get to work, set to work to start doing something ➤ *They set to work on the garden.*

Compare **work** and **job**. **Job** is a noun which has a plural (=jobs). **Work** has the same meaning but has no plural: *He's trying to find **a** job.* ➤ *He's trying to find **some** work.* **Work** can also be used as a general word when you are talking about several different jobs. If you say "I've got a lot of work to do", it could mean that you have either one big job to do, or lots of different jobs.

W

workable /'wɜːkəbəl/ *adjective*
that will work effectively and be
successful ▶ *a workable solution*

workaholic /ˌwɜːkə'hɒlɪk/ *noun*
a person who spends all their time
working

worked up /ˌwɜːkt 'ʌp/ *adjective*
very upset or angry ▶ *I don't see why
you're getting so worked up about it.*

worker /'wɜːkər/ *noun*
a person who does a particular job
▶ *office workers*
COMPARE: **labourer**

workforce /'wɜːkfɔːs/ *noun*
all the people who work in a country
or company ▶ *A quarter of the
workforce will lose their jobs.*

working /'wɜːkɪŋ/ *adjective*
1 having a job ▶ *working parents*
2 relating to work ▶ *bad working
conditions*
3 be in (good) working order to be
working well and not broken ▶ *My
father's watch is still in good working
order.*

working class /ˌwɜːkɪŋ 'klɑːs/ *noun*
**the working class, the working
classes** people who do not have
much money or power, and who
usually do physical work

working-class /ˌwɜːkɪŋ ˌklɑːs/
adjective
of or about the working class ▶ *He
came from a working-class
background.*

workings /'wɜːkɪŋz/ *plural noun*
the way in which something works
▶ *They didn't understand the
workings of the heating system.*

workload /'wɜːkləʊd/ *noun*
the amount of work that a person has
to do ▶ *My workload keeps
increasing.*

workman /'wɜːkmən/ *noun (plural
workmen /-mən/)*
a man who works with his hands,
especially in a trade

workmanship /'wɜːkmənʃɪp/ *noun
(no plural)*
the skill with which something has
been made ▶ *a high standard of
workmanship*

workout /'wɜːkaʊt/ *noun*
a series of physical exercises that you
do to keep your body strong and
healthy

works /wɜːks/ *plural noun*
a factory ▶ *the steel works*

worksheet /'wɜːkʃiːt/ *noun*
a piece of paper with questions,
exercises, etc. for students to
practise what they have learned

workshop /'wɜːkʃɒp/ *noun*
1 a room or building where people
make or repair things
2 a meeting at which people try to
improve their skills by discussing
their experiences and doing practical
exercises

workstation /'wɜːkˌsteɪʃən/ *noun*
the part of an office where you work,
including your desk, computer, etc.

worktop /'wɜːktɒp/ *(also work
surface* /'wɜːk ˌsɜːfɪs/) *noun*
a flat surface in a kitchen, on which
you can prepare food

world /wɜːld/ *noun*
1 the Earth on which we live ▶ *This
car sells well all over the world.*
2 all people thought of together ▶ *I
don't want the whole world to see us.*

world-class /ˌwɜːld 'klɑːs/ *adjective*
among the best in the world
▶ *a world-class tennis player*

world-famous /ˌwɜːld 'feɪməs/
adjective
famous all over the world ▶ *a world-
famous writer*

worldwide /ˌwɜːld'waɪd/ *adjective,
adverb*
in every part of the world ▶ *The
company employs 2,000 people
worldwide.*

W

World Wide Web /ˌwɜːld waɪd
'web/ *noun*
the World Wide Web a system that
connects together information and
pictures from computers in many
parts of the world, so that people can
find them on the INTERNET

worm /wɜːm/ *noun*
a long, thin creature with a soft body
and no bones or legs that lives in the
ground

worn /wɔːn/
the PAST PARTICIPLE of the verb **wear**

worn-out /ˌwɔːn 'aʊt/ *adjective*
1 very tired, especially because you
have been working hard ➤ *I'm worn-
out – I need a holiday.*
2 too old or damaged to use any
more ➤ *worn-out shoes*

worried /'wʌrɪd/ *adjective*
anxious ➤ *He seems worried **about**
something.* ➤ *a worried look on her
face*

worry¹ /'wʌrɪ/ *verb (past **worried**)*
to feel or make someone feel anxious
➤ *My parents worry **about** me if I
come home late.* ➤ *The news of the
fighting worried us.*

worry² *noun*
1 *(no plural)* a feeling of fear and
uncertainty about something ➤ *The
worry showed on her face.*
2 *(plural **worries**)* someone or
something that makes you feel
anxious ➤ *My father has a lot of
worries.*

worrying /'wʌrɪ-ɪŋ/ *adjective*
making you feel anxious ➤ *a worrying
piece of news*

worse /wɜːs/ *adjective, adverb*
1 less good; more bad ➤ *My writing is
bad, but yours is worse.*
2 more ill ➤ *I'm afraid she's worse
today.*
3 more badly ➤ *You're behaving even
worse than your brother!*
OPPOSITE (**1, 2,** and **3**): **better**

worsen /'wɜːsən/ *verb*
to become worse ➤ *The hospital says
his condition is worsening.*

worse off /ˌwɜːs 'ɒf/ *adjective*
poorer, or in a worse situation than
before ➤ *Cheer up – we could be
worse off.*
OPPOSITE: **better off**

worship¹ /'wɜːʃɪp/ *verb*
*(present participle **worshipping**,
past **worshipped**)*
to pray to and show great respect to
God

worship² *noun (no plural)*
a strong feeling of love, respect,
and admiration for someone, usually
God

worst /wɜːst/ *adjective, adverb, noun*
1 most bad ➤ *Your spelling is the
worst I've seen.*
2 most badly ➤ *They were all very
bad, but you behaved worst of all.*
OPPOSITE (**1** and **2**): **best**

worth¹ /wɜːθ/ *preposition*
1 with a value of ➤ *How much is this
bicycle worth?* ➤ *It's worth £50.*
2 good enough or useful enough for
something ➤ *That film is really worth
seeing.*

worth² *noun (no plural)*
value ➤ *The thieves took £1,000
worth of clothing.*

worthless /'wɜːθləs/ *adjective*
with no value; useless

worthwhile /ˌwɜːθ'waɪl/ *adjective*
deserving the effort needed or the
time and money you spend

worthy /'wɜːðɪ/ *adjective (**worthier,
worthiest**)*
deserving; good enough for ➤ *He is
worthy **of** our trust.*

would /wəd; *strong* wʊd/ *verb*
1 the word for **will** in the past tense
➤ *They said they would play football
on Saturday.*
2 used when you are talking about

W

something that is probable ▶ *I would be surprised if he came now.*
3 used as a polite way of asking someone something ▶ *Would you like a cup of tea?*

wouldn't /'wʊdnt/
would not ▶ *I knew she wouldn't come.*

would've /'wʊdəv/
would have ▶ *I would've come if I'd had time.*

wound¹ /waʊnd/
the PAST TENSE and PAST PARTICIPLE of the verb **wind**

wound² /wu:nd/ *verb*
to damage or hurt someone ▶ *Was he badly wounded?*

wound³ /wu:nd/ *noun*
a part of your body that has been cut or damaged

wound-up /ˌwaʊnd 'ʌp/ *adjective*
very angry, nervous, or excited ▶ *He gets really wound-up when the other children tease him.*

wove /wəʊv/
the PAST TENSE of the verb **weave**

woven /'wəʊvən/
the PAST PARTICIPLE of the verb **weave**

wrangle /'ræŋɡəl/ *verb (present participle **wrangling**, past **wrangled**)*
to argue with someone angrily for a long time

wrap /ræp/ *verb (present participle **wrapping**, past **wrapped**)*
to put something all round an object ▶ *I wrapped the book in strong paper and posted it.*
OPPOSITE: **unwrap**

wrapper /'ræpəʳ/ *noun*
the paper or plastic that covers something you buy, especially food ▶ *The ground was covered in sweet wrappers.*

wrapping /'ræpɪŋ/ *noun*
paper, cloth, etc. that is wrapped around something to protect it

wrapping paper /'ræpɪŋ ˌpeɪpəʳ/ *noun (no plural)*
coloured paper that you use to wrap presents

wreath /ri:θ/ *noun (plural **wreaths** /ri:ðz/)*
a ring of flowers and leaves

wreck¹ /rek/ *noun*
a ship, car, building, etc. that has been partly destroyed

wreck² *verb*
to destroy something ▶ *The ship was wrecked on the rocks.*

wreckage /'rekɪdʒ/ *noun (no plural)*
the broken parts of something ▶ *the wreckage of the plane after the crash*

wrench /rentʃ/ *verb*
to pull or turn something suddenly and with force ▶ *He wrenched the door open.*

wrestle /'resəl/ *verb (present participle **wrestling**, past **wrestled**)*
to fight a person and try to throw them to the ground

wrestler /'resləʳ/ *noun*
a person who wrestles as a sport

wrestling /'reslɪŋ/ *noun (no plural)*
a sport in which two people fight and try to throw each other to the ground

wretched /'retʃɪd/ *adjective*
1 very unhappy or unlucky ▶ *He led a wretched life with his first wife.*
2 used when you feel angry with someone or something ▶ *The wretched thing's broken again!*

wriggle /'rɪɡəl/ *verb (present participle **wriggling**, past **wriggled**)*
to twist from side to side ▶ *The snake wriggled through the grass.*

wring /rɪŋ/ *verb (past **wrung** /rʌŋ/)*
to twist something, especially in order to remove water from it

wrinkle /'rɪŋkəl/ *noun*
1 a line in an old person's skin
2 a line or fold in cloth

wrinkled /'rɪŋkəld/ *adjective*

W

1 (used about a person's skin) having a lot of lines because of age
2 (used about cloth) having a lot of lines or folds

wrist /rɪst/ noun
the joint between your hand and the lower part of your arm

wrist watch /'rɪst wɒtʃ/ noun (plural **wrist watches**)
a watch which you can fasten around your wrist

write /raɪt/ verb (present participle **writing**, past tense **wrote** /rəʊt/, past participle **written** /'rɪtn/)
1 to make letters or words on paper, using a pen or pencil ► The children are learning to write.
2 to produce and send a letter ► He writes **to** me every day.
3 to make something, such as a book or play, by writing ► She's written several books.

write-off /'raɪt ɒf/ noun
(used about vehicles) so badly damaged in an accident that it is not worth repairing ► The car's a write-off.

writer /'raɪtəʳ/ noun
a person who writes books, especially as their job

writhe /raɪð/ verb (present participle **writhing**, past writhed)
to twist your body, especially because you have a lot of pain ► writhing in agony

writing /'raɪtɪŋ/ noun (no plural)
1 the activity of writing ► creative writing
2 the way or style in which someone writes ► What beautiful writing!
SAME MEANING (**2**): **handwriting**

written /'rɪtn/
the PAST PARTICIPLE of the verb **write**

wrong[1] /rɒŋ/ adjective
1 not good ► Telling lies is wrong.
2 not correct ► I gave the wrong answer.

3 not suitable ► This is the wrong time to visit her.
OPPOSITE (**1**, **2**, and **3**): **right**

wrong[2] adverb
1 incorrectly ► You've spelt the word wrong.
OPPOSITE: **right**
2 get something wrong to make a mistake or not get the correct answer
3 go wrong (**a**) to not happen as you wanted
(**b**) to stop working properly
► Something's wrong with the car.

wrong[3] noun (no plural)
something bad, incorrect, or unacceptable ► Small children do not know right from wrong.
OPPOSITE: **right**

wrongdoing /'rɒŋ,du:ɪŋ/ noun
something wrong or against the law
► They found no evidence of wrongdoing.

wrongly /'rɒŋli/ adverb
because of a mistake or wrong belief
► He was wrongly accused of stealing.

wrote /rəʊt/
the PAST TENSE of the verb **write**

wrung /rʌŋ/
the PAST TENSE and PAST PARTICIPLE of the verb **wring**

wry /raɪ/ adjective (**wrier**, **wriest**)
showing a mixture of amusement and disappointment ► a wry smile

WWW /,dʌbəlju: dʌbəlju: 'dʌbəlju:/
a short way of writing and saying the words **World Wide Web**

XxYyZz

Xerox /'zɪərɒks/ noun trademark
(plural **Xeroxes**)
a copy of a piece of paper that is made by using a special machine

Xmas /'krɪsməs, 'eksməs/ noun (no plural)
a short way of writing the word **Christmas**

x-ray /'eks reɪ/ noun
a photograph of the inside of your body, taken with a special light which cannot normally be seen, and used by a doctor ▶ The x-ray showed that the boy's leg was broken.

xylophone /'zaɪləfəʊn/ noun
a musical instrument with flat, wooden or metal bars that you hit with a stick

yacht /jɒt/ noun
1 a boat with sails
2 a big motorboat that people can live and travel in on holiday, or race in

yachtsman /'jɒtsmən/ noun (plural **yachtsmen** /-mən/)
a man who sails a yacht

yachtswoman /'jɒts,wʊmən/ noun (plural **yachtswomen** /-,wɪmɪn/)
a woman who sails a yacht

yank /jæŋk/ verb
to suddenly pull something hard ▶ The boy yanked at his mother's coat.

yap /jæp/ verb (present participle **yapping**, past **yapped**)
(used about dogs) to BARK a lot in an excited way

yard /jɑːd/ noun
1 a piece of ground next to a building, with a wall or fence round it ▶ the school yard
2 a measure of length, the same as 3 feet; nearly a metre ▶ 5 yards (=5 yd) of material

yarn /jɑːn/ noun (no plural)
thick thread that you use for KNITTING

yawn¹ /jɔːn/ verb
to open your mouth wide and breathe deeply because you are tired or do not find something interesting ▶ I felt so sleepy I couldn't stop yawning.

yawn² noun
an act of opening your mouth wide and breathing deeply because you are tired or do not find something interesting

yd
a short way of writing the word **yard** or **yards** when they are used for measuring things

yeah /jeə/ adverb
yes

year /jɪəʳ/ noun
a measure of time, 365 days ▶ She is seven years old. ▶ in the year 1267
LOOK AT: **time**

yearly /'jɪəlɪ/ adjective, adverb
every year; once a year

yeast /jiːst/ noun (no plural)
a living substance which makes bread rise and is used in making beer, wine, etc.

yell /jel/ verb
to shout or cry very loudly

yellow /'jeləʊ/ adjective, noun
the colour of the sun, or the middle part of an egg ▶ a yellow flower ▶ dressed in yellow

yelp /jelp/ verb
(used about dogs) to make a short, high sound because of pain or excitement

yes /jes/ adverb
a word you use to answer a question, to show that something is true, or that you agree with something ▶ "Can you read this?" "Yes, I can."

yesterday /'jestədeɪ, -dɪ/ noun, adverb
the day before this day ▶ It was very hot yesterday.
COMPARE: **tomorrow**

yet /jet/ adverb
1 used in questions to ask if something you are expecting to happen has already happened ▶ Has he arrived yet?

2 not yet used when you are saying that something you are expecting to happen has not happened until now, but will happen soon ▶ *He hasn't arrived yet.* ▶ *"Are they here?" "No, not yet."*

LOOK AT: **just**

Use **yet** in questions and in NEGATIVE sentences: *Have you finished yet?* ▶ *I'm not ready yet.* In other types of sentences, use **already**: *I have already finished.*

yield /jiːld/ *verb*
1 to give fruit, etc. ▶ *The trees yielded a large crop of apples.*
2 to accept defeat or give someone else control of something ▶ *The government yielded **to** public demands for lower taxes.* ▶ *The politicians yielded power to the army.*

yob /jɒb/ *noun*
a young man who is rude and often violent ▶ *A gang of yobs damaged all the seats on the train.*

yoga /ˈjəʊɡə/ *noun (no plural)*
a system of exercises which helps you to relax your body and mind

yoghurt /ˈjɒɡət/ *noun (no plural)*
a food made with milk that has been treated in a special way to make it thick and a bit sour

yoke /jəʊk/ *noun*
a piece of wood put across the necks of cattle when they pull carts

yolk /jəʊk/ *noun*
the yellow part inside an egg
COMPARE: **white**

you /juː/ *pronoun (plural **you**)*
1 the person or people that the speaker is talking to ▶ *You can swim fast.* ▶ *Shall I get you a drink, John?*
2 people in general ▶ *It's not good for you to eat too much meat.* ▶ *You can't believe what politicians say.*

you'd /juːd/
1 you had ▶ *I called at your house, but you'd already left.*

2 you would ▶ *If you brushed your hair, you'd look tidier.*

you'll /juːl/
you will ▶ *You'll get it tomorrow.*

young¹ /jʌŋ/ *adjective*
not having lived very long ▶ *a young child* ▶ *a young woman*
OPPOSITE: **old**

young² *plural noun*
young people or animals ▶ *a turtle and her young*

youngster /ˈjʌŋstəʳ/ *noun*
a young person

your /jəʳ; strong jɔːʳ/ *adjective*
belonging to you ▶ *Put your books on your desks.*

you're /jəʳ; strong jɔːʳ/
you are ▶ *You're late again!*

yours /jɔːz/ *pronoun*
1 something belonging to you ▶ *Are all these pencils yours?*
2 Yours faithfully words used at the end of a formal or business letter that begins **Dear Sir** or **Dear Madam**
3 Yours sincerely words used at the end of a formal or business letter that begins **Dear Mrs Smith, Dear Mr Jones**, etc.

When you are ending a formal letter or a business letter (not a letter to a friend), put **Yours sincerely** if you began the letter with the name of the person: *Dear Mrs Jones ... Yours sincerely, Mary Smith*. If you are writing to an organization and do not know the name of the person who will read your letter, begin your letter **Dear Sir/Madam** and end **Yours faithfully**: *Dear Sir/Madam ... Yours faithfully, Mary Smith*.

yourself /jɔːˈself/ *pronoun (plural **yourselves** /jɔːˈselvz/)*
1 the same person as the one that the speaker is talking to ▶ *Did you hurt yourself?* ▶ *You can't lift that by yourself* (=without help). ▶ *Why are*

you playing by yourself (=alone)?
2 used to give the word **you** a stronger meaning ► *You told me the story yourself.*

youth /juːθ/ *noun*
1 *(no plural)* the time when a person is young ► *In his youth, he was a soldier.*
2 *(plural* **youths** /juːðz/) a young man
3 *(no plural)* young people ► *The youth of this country have fought hard for greater freedom.*

youth club /ˈjuːθ klʌb/ *noun*
an organization that arranges meetings and activities in which young people in an area can be together and enjoy themselves

youthful /ˈjuːθfəl/ *adjective*
seeming younger than you really are ► *He has kept his youthful good looks.*

youth hostel /ˈjuːθ ˌhɒstl/ *noun*
a building in which young people on holiday can stay cheaply for the night

you've /jəv; *strong* juːv/
you have ► *You've forgotten your coat.*

yo-yo /ˈjəʊ jəʊ/ *noun*
a toy made of a round piece of plastic or wood that moves up and down a string

zany /ˈzeɪni/ *adjective* (**zanier**, **zaniest**)
unusual and funny ► *a zany new TV comedy*

zeal /ziːl/ *noun* *(no plural)*
great interest in something and eagerness to do it ► *political zeal*

zebra /ˈzebrə, ˈziːbrə/ *noun*
an African wild animal like a horse, which has black or dark brown and white lines all over its body

zebra crossing /ˌzebrə ˈkrɒsɪŋ, ˌziːbrə-/ *noun*
a set of black and white lines painted across a road to show that people who are walking can cross there when the traffic stops

zero /ˈzɪərəʊ/ *noun* (*plural* **zeros** or **zeroes**)
the number 0
SAME MEANING: **nought**
LOOK AT: **0**

zigzag /ˈzɪgzæg/ *noun*
a pattern like a long line of Zs all joined together

zillion /ˈzɪljən/ *noun*
an extremely large number or amount

zip¹ /zɪp/ *noun*
a fastener often used on clothes, that has two sets of metal or plastic teeth and a sliding piece that draws them together

zip² *verb* (*present participle* **zipping**, *past* **zipped**)
to fasten something with a zip ► *She zipped up her dress.*

zone /zəʊn/ *noun*
an area where a particular thing happens or where there are particular rules ► *a no-parking zone* ► *a war zone*

zoo /zuː/ *noun*
a place where different animals are kept for people to look at and study

zoology /zuːˈɒlədʒi/ *noun* *(no plural)*
the scientific study of animals and their behaviour

zoom /zuːm/ *verb*
to travel somewhere very quickly ► *Cars zoomed past us.*

Z